D1525538

MARK
8–16

VOLUME 27A

THE ANCHOR YALE BIBLE is a project of international and interfaith scope in which Protestant, Catholic, and Jewish scholars from many countries contribute individual volumes. The project is not sponsored by any ecclesiastical organization and is not intended to reflect any particular theological doctrine.

THE ANCHOR YALE BIBLE is committed to producing commentaries in the tradition established half a century ago by the founders of the series, William Foxwell Albright and David Noel Freedman. It aims to present the best contemporary scholarship in a way that is accessible not only to scholars but also to the educated nonspecialist. Its approach is grounded in exact translation of the ancient languages and an appreciation of the historical and cultural context in which the biblical books were written, supplemented by insights from modern methods, such as sociological and literary criticism.

John J. Collins
GENERAL EDITOR

THE ANCHOR YALE BIBLE

MARK
8–16

◆

A New Translation
with Introduction and Commentary

JOEL MARCUS

YALE

THE ANCHOR YALE BIBLE

Yale University Press
New Haven & London

Set in Electra type by dix!

Printed in the United States of America by Vail-Ballou, Binghamton, N.Y.

The Library of Congress has catalogued volume 27, Mark 1–8, as follows:

LIBRARY OF CONGRESS CATALOGING-IN-PUBLICATION DATA
Bible. N.T. Mark I–VIII. English. Marcus. 1999.
   Mark 1–8: a new translation with introduction and commentary / Joel Marcus.
   p. cm. — (The Anchor Bible ; v. 27)
   Includes bibliographical references and indexes.
   1. Bible. N.T. Mark—Commentaries. I. Marcus, Joel, 1951– .
   II. Title. III. Series: Bible. English. Anchor Bible.
   1964; v. 27.
   BS192.2.A1   1964.G3 vol. 27
   [BS2583]
   220. 7'7 s—dc21
   [226. 3'077]   98-8741
                                           CIP

Mark 8–16 is Volume 27A of the Anchor Yale Bible.
ISBN: 978-0-300-14116-0

The paper in this book meets the requirements of ANSI/NISO Z39.48-1992
(Permanence of Paper). It contains 30 percent postconsumer waste (PCW) and
is certified by the Forest Stewardship Council (FSC).

A catalogue record for this book is available from the British Library.

10 9 8 7 6 5 4 3 2 1

TO DALE ALLISON

from whose writings I have gained much
from whose friendship I have gained more

CONTENTS

◆

APPENDICES

PREFACE

◆

I began the first volume of this commentary shortly after the birth of my daughter Rachel; I finish this second and last volume a few weeks shy of her sixteenth birthday and her driving test. In that time our family has lived on two continents and in four cities. Librarians in Princeton, Glasgow, Boston, and now Durham, North Carolina, have helped secure the sometimes odd materials I asked to see. In completing the present volume, I have been particularly thankful for the superb collection of the Duke Divinity School Library and for the unstinting help of its librarians, Roger Loyd, Roberta Schaafsma, and Andy Keck.

Even more than to the librarians, however, my deepest gratitude is to my readers and editors. The former Series Editor of the Anchor Yale Bible, the late David Noel Freedman, over the past sixteen years offered encouragement and critique in equal measure. But he also let me go my own way, even when he passionately disagreed, for example, on the designation for Jesus' brother, whom I have followed English tradition in calling James (see vol. 1, pp. 180–81). "It is long since time," Freedman wrote to me, "that some brave New Testament scholar decided to use the name that is spelled correctly whether in the original Hebrew, or Greek transcription: Iakob." I regret that I am not that scholar. I also regret, and more deeply, that he did not live to see this volume in print.

In addition to Noel Freedman, four scholar friends read through the manuscript from start to finish. When, as sometimes happened, two or three of them objected to the same assertion or argument, I knew I was in trouble. Aside from such convergences, each gave me something different. Mike Winger brought his sharp, lawyerly mind to bear on my syntax and logic. He also penned the single most brilliant criticism I have ever had the pleasure of receiving. In my original draft of the COMMENT on 12:35–37, I wrote, "Joy breaks forth when the Markan Jesus alludes to the new creation, as joy broke forth when God brought forth the old." Mike's marginal notation to this purple prose was: "A 3rd 4th is 1 2 many."

Like Mike, Bart Ehrman slashed away at my logic. I also suspected that he knew more than I did about textual criticism, so I tended to listen to him on that issue. Of all the readers, Dave Adams was the most consistently and critically engaged on those occasions when I ventured out from the familiar shores of exegesis into the (for me) relatively uncharted waters of theology.

And as for Dale Allison—what can I say about the countless ways in which he has generously enriched this commentary? He frequently adduced relevant parallels from ancient Judaism, but just as frequently pointed me to parallels closer to hand, from the New Testament itself. He drew on his deep knowledge of the history of interpretation to give my ideas a pedigree—or, on occasion, to query why they lacked one. ("Has anyone, in all the two thousand years of interpreting this text, ever come up with this idea before? Because if not, it's probably wrong.") Yet he occasionally said things like, "There's a lot of new stuff here that is not crazy"— and that seemed to be a compliment. In any event, Dale has been a constant support, and helper, and friend, as well as an inspiration—not least because he had actually finished a multivolume Gospel commentary, and a great one. In fact, my debt to him is double, since "Davies and Allison" first pointed me in so many fruitful directions, and then the principal author of that commentary helped in so many ways to hone the thoughts it had inspired.

When this Gang of Four had done their work, and after I had spent over a year incorporating their revisions, the commentary went up for one final review, before the piercing editorial eye of Carol Shoun, the Faculty Editorial Associate at Duke Divinity School. Like many of my Duke colleagues, I thought of myself as a good writer until I met Carol. Her editing has strengthened the work in innumerable ways, not just in terms of style but also in terms of coherence of thought and internal consistency. I am deeply grateful for Carol's painstaking, supremely intelligent labors and cheerful support and handholding.

In addition to my debt to these patient readers, I would like to acknowledge gratefully the support I have received from Dean Gregory Jones of Duke Divinity School and the Henry Luce Foundation. The former granted me a Dean's leave, and the latter a Luce Senior Fellowship, both of which enabled me to spend a year finishing this commentary at the National Humanities Center. I am very thankful for the staff of that wonderful institution. I am also grateful for the help of Jill Hicks, Scott Ryan, Ben McCoy, Brian Gamel, Zack Phillips, and Tucker Ferda— all of whom have done a heroic job under extreme pressure on the modern author and ancient literature indexes. And many thanks to Leslie Phillips, the proofreader of this volume, for her meticulous care and patience with an exacting author.

I am sure that I have not said the last word on this cryptic and intriguing Gospel. I am grateful that I have never gotten bored—though I have sometimes gotten tired—in the sixteen years I have been working on the commentary. I look forward to meeting the author someday and finally discovering what the numbers in 8:19–21 are all about, among other mysteries.

A long note on translations: throughout the volume, I have noted the places in which I have altered the text in the interests of accuracy, style, inclusive language, etc. from the default translations listed below.

All translations of Markan texts are my own, while translations of other biblical texts are, unless otherwise noted, from the New Revised Standard Version. In the figures, however, I have used my own, superliteral translations.

Unless otherwise noted, translations of the Pseudepigrapha are from Charlesworth, ed., *Old Testament Pseudepigrapha*. Unless otherwise noted, translations of Philo, Josephus, and other classical writers are from the Loeb Classical Library. For citation of Septuagint passages, I have generally used, but sometimes altered, Brenton's translation, but the verse numbers follow the Rahlfs edition rather than Brenton.

As for the Dead Sea Scrolls: passages are usually cited according to the enumeration and translation of García Martínez and Tigchelaar, *The Dead Sea Scrolls Study Edition*. Where there is a different enumeration in Emmanuel Tov, ed., *The Dead Sea Scrolls Electronic Library* (revised ed., 2006), I have recorded it in parentheses. Passages from the Thanksgiving Scroll are cited according to the rearrangement of columns that has now been generally accepted and is used in Tov, the translation of García Martínez and Tigchelaar, and the latest edition of Vermes, among others. The earlier column numbers, however, are given in parentheses. Thus, for example, "1QH 14(6):17–18." Passages not found in García Martínez/Tigchelaar are cited according to the enumeration in Tov. Enumeration of Scrolls passages is generally by column and line number. When there are several fragments, enumeration is by fragment, column, and line number (thus, 4Q270 7 1:17–18 = fragment 7, column 1, lines 17–18) or, if there is only one column in a fragment, by fragment and line number (thus, 4Q266 11:3–5 = fragment 11, lines 3–5). Where there is a difference in enumeration between García Martínez/Tigchelaar and Tov, I have given the latter in brackets.

With regard to rabbinic citations: passages from the Mishnah are, unless otherwise noted, cited according to Danby's enumeration and translation. Passages from *Midrash Rabbah* are, unless otherwise noted, cited according to enumeration and translation in the Soncino edition edited by Freedman and Simon. Passages from the Babylonian Talmud are, unless otherwise noted, cited from the Soncino edition edited by Epstein and translated by Simon. Passages from the Jerusalem Talmud are cited by mishnah; in parentheses I have given the page and sector from the standard enumeration in the Scaliger manuscript edited by Sussmann and the volume and page in Neusner's *Talmud of the Land of Israel*, for example, "*y. Qidd.* 1:1 (58c; Neusner, 26.12)." Passages from the Mekilta are cited by tractate and number, and have the volume and page number from Lauterbach's translation in parentheses. Passages from *Sipra, Sipre,* and the *Tosefta* follow the enumeration in Neusner's translations.

In working with the *Gospel of Thomas*, I have made use of, but have sometimes altered, the translations of Guillaumont et al., and of H.-G. Bethge in the fifteenth edition of Aland, *Synopsis Quattuor Evangeliorum*. For Nag Hammadi texts, I have cited according to the enumeration of manuscript page and line number in Robinson et al., *Nag Hammadi Library*.

Like most authors of long works, I suspect, I have sometimes wondered if I would live to see its end. Friends will testify to the somewhat neurotic provisions I made for its completion if something unforeseen should happen. I am especially thankful to my friend and former doctoral student, Suzanne Henderson, who graciously agreed several years ago to finish the manuscript if I should be prevented from doing so. Suzanne, you are hereby released from your promise.

LIST OF FIGURES

◆

Principal Abbreviations

◆

AASF	Annales Academiae scientiarum fennicae
AYB	Anchor Yale Bible
AYBD	D. N. Freedman, ed., *The Anchor Yale Bible Dictionary*
AYBRL	Anchor Yale Bible Reference Library
AGJU	Arbeiten zur Geschichte des antiken Judentums und des Urchristentums
AnBib	Analecta Biblica
ANRW	H. Temporini and W. Haase, eds. *Aufstieg und Niedergang der römischen Welt*
ANTC	Abingdon New Testament Commentary
ArBib	The Aramaic Bible
ATANT	Abhandlungen zur Theologie des Alten und Neuen Testaments
b.	Babylonian Talmud
BAR	*Biblical Archaeology Review*
BBB	Bonner biblische Beiträge
BDAG	W. Bauer et al., *A Greek-English Lexicon of the New Testament and Other Early Christian Literature*, Third Edition.
BDF	F. Blass, A. Debrunner, and R. W. Funk, *A Greek Grammar of the New Testament*
BETL	Bibliotheca ephemeridum theologicarum lovaniensium
BevT	Beiträge zur evangelischen Theologie
BGBE	Beiträge zur Geschichte der biblischen Exegese
Bib	*Biblica*
BibOr	Biblica et orientalia
BJRL	*Bulletin of the John Rylands University Library of Manchester*
BJS	Brown Judaic Studies
BN	*Biblische Notizen*
BRev	*Bible Review*
BT	*The Bible Translator*
BZ	*Biblische Zeitschrift*
BZAW	Beiheft zur Zeitschrift für die alttestamentliche Wissenschaft
BZNW	Beiheft zur Zeitschrift für die neutestamentliche Wissenschaft
CahRB	Cahiers de la Revue biblique
CBQ	*Catholic Biblical Quarterly*
CBET	Contributions to Biblical Exegesis and Theology
CBQMS	Catholic Biblical Quarterly—Monograph Series
CEJL	Commentaries on Early Jewish Literature
ConBNT	Coniectanea biblica, New Testament
DOP	*Dumbarton Oaks Papers*
DSD	*Dead Sea Discoveries*
EBib	Etudes bibliques
EDNT	H. Balz and G. Schneider, eds., *Exegetical Dictionary of the New Testament.*
EKKNT	Evangelisch-katholischer Kommentar zum Neuen Testament
EncJud	*Encyclopaedia Judaica*

ETL	*Ephemerides theologicae lovanienses*
EvT	*Evangelische Theologie*
ExpT	*Expository Times*
FB	Forschung zur Bibel
FRLANT	Forschungen zur Religion und Literatur des Alten und Neuen Testaments
Gesenius	E. Kautzsch and A. E. Cowley, *Gesenius' Hebrew Grammar*
Gk	Greek
HBD	P. J. Achtemeier, ed. *Harper's Bible Dictionary*
HDR	Harvard Dissertations in Religion
Heb	Hebrew
HNT	Handbuch zum Neuen Testament
HTKNT	Herders theologischer Kommentar zum Neuen Testament
HTR	*Harvard Theological Review*
HTS	Harvard Theological Studies
HUCA	*Hebrew Union College Annual*
HUT	Hermeneutische Untersuchungen zur Theologie
IDB	G. A. Buttrick, ed., *The Interpreter's Dictionary of the Bible*
IEJ	*Israel Exploration Journal*
Int	*Interpretation*
JAAR	*Journal of the American Academy of Religion*
JBL	*Journal of Biblical Literature*
JdI	*Jahrbuch des deutschen archäologischen Instituts*
JE	*The Jewish Encyclopedia*
JETS	*Journal of the Evangelical Theological Society*
JJS	*Journal of Jewish Studies*
JQR	*Jewish Quarterly Review*
JRS	*Journal of Roman Studies*
JSJ	*Journal for the Study of Judaism*
JSNT	*Journal for the Study of the New Testament*
JSNTSup	Journal for the Study of the New Testament: Supplement Series
JSOT	*Journal for the Study of the Old Testament*
JSOTSup	Journal for the Study of the Old Testament: Supplement Series
JTS	*Journal of Theological Studies*
JTSA	*Journal of Theology for South Africa*
KJV	King James Version
LCL	Loeb Classical Library
LD	Lectio divina
LSJ	H. D. Liddell et al., *A Greek-English Lexicon with a Supplement*
LUÅ	Lunds universitets årsskrift
LXX	Septuagint
m.	Mishnah
MHT	J. H. Moulton, et al., *A Grammar of New Testament Greek*
M-M	J. H. Moulton and G. Milligan, *The Vocabulary of the Greek Testament*
MT	Masoretic Text [Hebew Bible]
NEAEHL	E. Stern, ed., *The New Encyclopedia of Archaeological Excavations in the Holy Land*
NewDocs	*New Documents Illustrating Early Christianity*
NICINT	New International Commentary on the New Testament
NIGTC	New International Greek Testament Commentary
NJPS	New Jewish Publication Society Translation
NovT	*Novum Testamentum*
NovTSup	Novum Testamentum, Supplements
NRSV	New Revised Standard Version
NT	New Testament

NTAbh	Neutestamentliche Abhandlungen
NTOA	Novum Testamentum et Orbis Antiquus
NTS	*New Testament Studies*
NTTS	New Testament Tools and Studies
OCD	S. Hornblower and A. Spawforth, eds., *The Oxford Classical Dictionary*, 3rd ed.
OT	Old Testament
OTL	Old Testament Library
OTP	J. H. Charlesworth, ed., *The Old Testament Pseudepigrapha*
PDM	*Papyri demoticae magicae*
PEQ	*Palestine Exploration Quarterly*
PGM	*Papyri graecae magicae*
PTMS	Pittsburgh Theological Monograph Series
QD	Quaestiones disputatae
RAr	*Revue archéologique*
RB	*Revue biblique*
RevQ	*Revue de Qumran*
RSV	Revised Standard Version
SANT	Studien zum Alten und Neuen Testament
SBAB	Stuttgarter biblische Aufsatzbände
SBLDS	Society of Biblical Literature—Dissertation Series
SBLEJL	Society of Biblical Literature Early Judaism and Its Literature
SBLSBS	Society of Biblical Literature Sources for Biblical Study
SBLSP	*Society of Biblical Literature Seminar Papers*
SBLSS	Society of Biblical Literature—Semeia Studies
SBM	Stuttgarter biblische Monographien
SBS	Stuttgarter Bibelstudien
SBT	Studies in Biblical Theology
SEÅ	*Svensk exegetisk årsbok*
SJLA	Studies in Judaism in Late Antiquity
SJT	*Scottish Journal of Theology*
SNTSMS	Society for New Testament Studies Monograph Series
SNTW	Studies in the New Testament and Its World
SSEJC	Studies in Scripture in Early Judaism and Christianity
JSPSup	Journal for the Study of the Pseudepigrapha: Supplement Series
ST	*Studia theologica*
SUNT	Studien zur Umwelt des Neuen Testaments
SVTP	Studia in Veteris Testamenti pseudepigrapha
t.	Tosefta
Tbei	*Theologische Beiträge*
TDNT	G. Kittel and G. Friedrich, eds., *Theological Dictionary of the New Testament*
Tg.	Targum
ThViat	*Theologia viatorum*
TTZ	*Trierer theologische Zeitschrift*
TynBul	*Tyndale Bulletin*
TZ	*Theologische Zeitschrift*
VTS	Vetus Testamentum Supplements
WBC	Word Biblical Commentary
WMANT	Wissenschaftliche Monographien zum Alten und Neuen Testament
WUNT	Wissenschaftliche Untersuchungen zum Neuen Testament
y.	Yerushalmi = Jerusalem [Palestinian] Talmud
ZAW	*Zeitschrift für die alttestamentliche Wissenschaft*
ZNW	*Zeitschrift für die neutestamentlichen Wissenschaft und die Kunde der älteren Kirche*
ZTK	*Zeitschrift für Theologie und Kirche*

BIBLIOGRAPHY

◆

Works are cited in the text according to the word or words printed below in boldface.

Abbott, E. A. *The Fourfold Gospel. Section V: The **Founding** of the New Kingdom or Life Reached Through Death*. Cambridge: At the University Press, 1917.

Abegg, M. "**Messianic Hope** and 4Q285 : A Reassessment." *JBL* 113 (1994): 81–91.

Achtemeier, P. J., ed. *Harper's Bible Dictionary*. San Francisco: Harper & Row, 1985. [Cited as **HBD**]

Aland, K. *Did the Early Church Baptize Infants?* London: SCM, 1962.

———. "Der wiedergefundene **Markusschluss**? Eine methodologische Bemerkung zur textkritischen Arbeit." *ZTK* 67 (1970): 3–13.

———. *Synopsis quattuor evangeliorum. Locis parallelis evangeliorum apocryphorum et patrum adhibits*. 15th rev. ed. Stuttgart: Deutsche Bibelgesellschaft, 1995.

Alexander, P. S. "**3 Enoch** and the Talmud." *JSJ* 18 (1987): 40–68.

———. "The **Family** of Caesar and the Family of God: The Image of the Emperor in the Heikhalot Literature." Pp. 276–97 in *Images of Empire*, ed. L. Alexander. JSOTSup 122. Sheffield: Sheffield Academic Press, 1991.

Alford, H. *The Greek Testament with a Critically Revised Text, a Digest of Various Readings, Marginal References to Verbal and Idiomatic Usage, Prolegomena, and a Critical and Exegetical Commentary*. Chicago: Moody Press, 1958 (orig. 1849–60). [Cited as **Alford**]

Allen, W. C. "The **Aramaic Element** in St. Mark." *ExpT* 13 (1901–2): 328–30.

Allison, D. C. " '**Elijah** Must Come First.' " *JBL* 103 (1984): 256–58.

———. "**Anticipating** the Passion: The Literary Reach of Matthew 26:47–27:56." *CBQ* 56 (1994): 701–14.

———. *The **End** of the Ages Has Come: An Early Interpretation of the Passion and Resurrection of Jesus*. Philadelphia: Fortress, 1985.

———. *The **Intertextual Jesus**: Scripture in Q*. Valley Forge, Pa.: Trinity Press International, 2000.

———. ***Jesus** of Nazareth: Millenarian Prophet*. Minneapolis: Fortress, 1998.

———. *The **Jesus Tradition** in Q*. Valley Forge, Pa.: Trinity Press International, 1997.

———. "**Mark 12.28–31** and the Decalogue." Pp. 270–78 in *The Gospels and the Scriptures of Israel*, ed. C. A. Evans and W. Stegner. JSNTSup 104/SSEJC 3. Sheffield: Sheffield Academic Press, 1994.

———. *The **New Moses**: A Matthean Typology*. Edinburgh: T & T Clark, 1993.

———. "**Q 12:51–53** and Mark 9:11–13 and the Messianic Woes." Pp. 289–310 in *Authenticating the Words of Jesus*, ed. B. D. Chilton and C. A. Evans. NTTS 38.2. Leiden/Boston/Köln: Brill, 1999.

———. ***Resurrecting Jesus**: The Earliest Christian Tradition and Its Interpreters*. New York/London: T & T Clark, 2005.

――――. *Studies in Matthew: Interpretation Past and Present.* Grand Rapids: Baker Academic Press, 2005.

――――. *Testament of Abraham.* CEJL. Berlin/New York: Walter De Gruyter, 2003.

――――. "**What Was** the Star That Guided the Magi?" *BRev* 9.6 (1993): 20–24, 63.

Alt, A. "Das **Verbot** des Diebstahls im Dekalog." Pp. 330–40 in *Kleine Schriften zür Geschichte des Volkes Israel.* München: Beck, 1953.

Alter, R. *Genesis: Translation and Commentary.* New York/London: W. W. Norton, 1996.

Ambrozic, A. M. *The **Hidden Kingdom**: A Redaction-Critical Study of the References to the Kingdom of God in Mark's Gospel,* CBQMS 2. Washington, D.C.: Catholic Biblical Association, 1972.

――――. "**New Teaching** with Power (Mk 1:27)." Pp. 113–49 in *Word and Spirit: Essays in Honor of David Michael Stanley, S.J. on His 60th Birthday,* ed. J. Plevnik. Willowdale, Ont.: Regis College, 1975.

Amiram, D. H. K., E. Arieh, and T. Turcotte. "**Earthquakes** in Israel and Adjacent Areas: Macroseismic Observations Since 100 B.C.E." *IEJ* 44 (1994): 260–305.

Anderson, G. A. "The **Exaltation** of Adam and the Fall of Satan." Pp. 83–110 in *Literature on Adam and Eve: Collected Essays,* ed. G. Anderson, M. Stone, and J. Tromp. SVTP 15. Leiden/Boston/Köln: Brill, 1997.

――――. "**Garments** of Skin, Garments of Glory." Unpublished paper.

Anderson, J. K. "**Horses**." P. 728 in *OCD.*

Anon. "**Adamites**." In *Catholic Encyclopedia, Online Edition,* 1999 (orig. 1907).

Anon. "**Blessing of Children**." In *EncJud,* CD-ROM Edition.

Anon. *Wonders and Miracles: Stories of the Lubavitcher Rebbe.* Kfar Chabad, Israel: Maareches Ufaratzta, 1993.

Apuleius. *The **Golden Ass**.* Trans. P. G. Walsh. World's Classics. Oxford and New York: Oxford University Press, 1995.

Argyle, A. W. "The **Meaning** of *kath'hēmeran* in Mark XIV. 49." *ExpT* 63 (1951–52): 354.

――――. "O. Cullmann's **Theory** Concerning *kōlyein*." *ExpT* 67 (1955): 17.

Athanassakis, A. N. *The **Homeric Hymns**.* Baltimore and London: Johns Hopkins, 1976.

Atkinson, K. "On the **Herodian Origin** of Militant Davidic Messianism at Qumran: New Light from *Psalm of Solomon* 17." *JBL* 118 (1999): 435–60.

Attridge, H. W. *The Epistle to the **Hebrews**.* Hermeneia. Philadelphia: Fortress, 1989.

Auerbach, E. *Mimesis: The Representation of Reality in Western Literature.* Princeton University Press, 1953.

Aufhauser, J. B. *Buddha und Jesus in ihren Paralleltexten.* Bonn: A. Marcus & E. Weber, 1926.

Aune, D. E. *Prophecy in Early Christianity and the Ancient Mediterranean World.* Grand Rapids: Eerdmans, 1983.

――――. *Revelation.* 3 vols. WBC 52. Nashville: Thomas Nelson, 1997–98.

Avigad, N., and H. Geva. "**Jerusalem**, the Second Temple Period." Pp. 2.717–57 in *NEAEHL,* 1993.

Bacchiocchi, S. *The **Time** of the Crucifixion and the Resurrection with Other Essays.* Biblical Perspectives 4. Berrien Springs, Mich.: Biblical Perspectives, 1985.

Badian, E. "**Iulius Caesar**, Gaius (1)." Pp. 780–82 in *OCD.*

Bainton, R. L. *Here I Stand: A Life of Martin Luther.* New York: Times Mirror, 1960.

Balabanski, V. *Eschatology in the Making: Mark, Matthew and the Didache.* SNTSMS 97. Cambridge: Cambridge University Press, 1997.

Balch, D. L. "**Household Codes**." Pp. 3.318–20 in *AYBD*.
————. *Let Wives be Submissive: The Domestic Code in 1 Peter*. SBLMS. Chico: Scholars Press, 1981.
Balz, H. "*Gazophylakion*." P. 1.232 in *EDNT*.
————, and G. Schneider. *Exegetical Dictionary of the New Testament*. 3 vols. Grand Rapids: Eerdmans, 1990–93. [Cited as **EDNT**]
Bar-Ilan, M. "**Tiqun** Lel Shevuot: Emergence and Precedents [Hebrew]." *Mehqarei Hag* 8 (1996): 28–48.
Barnett, P. W. "The Jewish **Sign Prophets**—A.D. 40–70: Their Intentions and Origin." *NTS* 27 (1980–81): 679–97.
Barr, J. " '**Abbā** Isn't 'Daddy.' " *JTS* N.S. 39 (1988): 28–47.
Barrett, C. K. "The **Allegory** of Abraham, Sarah, and Hagar in the Argument of Galatians." Pp. 1–16 in *Rechtfertigung. Festschrift für Ernst Käsemann*, ed. J. Friedrich et al. Tübingen: Mohr (Siebeck), 1976.
————. "The **Background** of Mark 10:45." Pp. 1–18 in *New Testament Essays: Studies in Memory of Thomas Walter Manson 1893–1958*. Manchester: Manchester University Press, 1959.
————. *A Critical and Exegetical Commentary on the **Acts** of the Apostles*. Edinburgh: T & T Clark, 1994–98.
————. "I Am **Not Ashamed** of the Gospel." In *Foi et salut selon S. Paul (Épître aux Romains 1,16). Colloque œcuménique à l'abbaye de S. Paul hors les murs, 16–21 avril 1968*. AnBib 42. Rome: Pontifical Biblical Institute, 1970.
Barth, K. *The Epistle to the **Romans***. London/Oxford/New York: Oxford University Press, 1977 (orig. 1918).
Bartlett, D. L. *Fact and Faith: Coming to Grips with Miracles in the New Testament*. Valley Forge: Judson Press, 1975.
Bassler, J. M. *God and Mammon: Asking for Money in the New Testament*. Nashville: Abingdon, 1991.
Bastien, P. *Le buste mónetaire des empereurs romains*. Wetteren, Belgium: Éditions Numismatique Romaine, 1992–94.
Bauckham, R. *The **Climax** of Prophecy: Studies on The Book of Revelation*. Edinburgh: T & T Clark, 1993.
————. *Jude and the Relatives of Jesus in the Early Church*. Edinburgh: T & T Clark, 1990.
————. "The **Martyrdom** of Enoch and Elijah: Jewish or Christian?" *JBL* 95 (1976): 447–58.
————. "The **Parting** of the Ways: What Happened and Why." *ST* 47 (1993): 135–51.
Bauer, W. *Orthodoxy and Heresy in Earliest Christianity*. Philadelphia: Fortress, 1971 (orig. 1934).
Bauer, W., et al. *A Greek-English Lexicon of the New Testament and Other Early Christian Literature*. 3rd ed. Chicago/London: University of Chicago Press, 2000. [Cited as **BDAG**]
Baumgarten, J. M. "A 'Scriptural' **Citation** in 4Q Fragments of the Damascus Document." *JJS* 43 (1992): 95–98.
Beardslee, W. A. "**Saving** One's Life by Losing It." *JAAR* 47 (1979): 57–72.
Beasley-Murray, G. R. *Jesus and the Last Days: The Interpretation of the Olivet Discourse*. Peabody, Mass.: Hendrickson, 1993. [Cited as **Beasley-Murray**]
Beckwith, R. *The Old Testament **Canon** of the New Testament Church and Its Background in Early Judaism*. Grand Rapids: Eermans, 1985.

Beentjes, P. C. *The Book of Ben Sira in Hebrew: A Text Edition of All Extant Hebrew Manu-scripts and a Synopsis of All Parallel Hebrew Ben Sira Texts*. VTS 68. Leiden/New York/Köln: E. J. Brill, 1997.

Begg, C. " 'Josephus's Portrayal of the Disappearance of Enoch, Elijah, and Moses': Some Observations." *JBL* 109 (1990): 691–93.

Behm, J. "*Geuomai*." Pp. 1.675–77 in *TDNT* (1964; orig. 1933).

———. *Die Handauflegung im Urchristentum nach Verwendung, Herkunft und Bedeutung in religionsgeschichtlichem Zusammenhang untersucht*. Leipzig: A. Deichert, 1911.

Belleville, L. L. *Reflections of Glory: Paul's Polemical Use of the Moses-Doxa Tradition in 2 Corinthians 3.1–18*. JSNTSup 52. Sheffield: JSOT Press, 1991.

Ben-Amos, D., and J. R. Mintz. *In Praise of the Baal Shem Tov [Shivhei Ha-Besht]: The Earliest Collection of Legends About the Founder of Hasidism*. Northvale, N.J./London: Jason Aronson Inc., 1993.

Bengel, J. A. *Gnomon of the New Testament*. 3 vols. Edinburgh: T & T Clark, 1873.

Bennett, E. N. "St. John xii. 3.—The Word *pistikēs*." *Classical Review* 4 (1890): 319.

Bensly, R. L., and W. E. Barnes. *The Fourth Book of Maccabees and Kindred Documents in Syriac*. Cambridge: At the University Press, 1895.

Berger, K. *Die Gesetzauslegung Jesu. Ihr historischer Hintergrund im Judentum und im Alten Testament. Teil I: Markus und Parallelen*. WMANT 40. Neukirchen: Neu-kirchener Verlag, 1972.

Bernard, A. *Le paneion d'El-Kanaïs: les inscriptions grecques*. Leiden: Brill, 1972.

Bernhard, A. "Papyrus Oxyrhnchus 1224." http://www.gospels.net/translations/poxy1224 translation.html

Bernstein, A. E. *The Formation of Hell: Death and Retribution in the Ancient and Early Christian Worlds*. Ithaca/London: Cornell University Press, 1993.

Bertram, G. "*Stereos, ktl.*" Pp. 7.609–14 in *TDNT* (1971).

Best, E. *Following Jesus: Discipleship in the Gospel of Mark*. JSNTSup 4. Sheffield: JSOT Press, 1981.

———. "Mark's Use of the Twelve." *ZNW* 69 (1977): 11–35.

———. "Peter in the Gospel According to Mark." *CBQ* 40 (1978): 547–58.

———. "The Role of the Disciples in Mark." *NTS* 23 (1977): 377–401.

Betz, O. *What Do we Know About Jesus?* Philadelphia: Westminster Press, 1968.

Beyer, H. W. "*Diakoneō, ktl.*" Pp. 2.81–93 in *TDNT* (1964; orig. 1935).

Beyer, K. *The Aramaic Language: Its Distribution and Subdivisions*. Göttingen: Vanden-hoeck & Ruprecht, 1986.

———. *Semitische Syntax im Neuen Testament. Teil 1: Satzlehre*. SUNT. Göttingen: Vandenhoeck & Ruprecht, 1962.

Bieler, L. *THEIOS ANĒR. Das Bild des "göttlichen Menschen" in Spätantike und Frühchristentum*. Damstadt: Wissenschaftliche Buchgesellschaft, 1967 (orig. 1935–36).

Bietenhard, H. "*Onoma, ktl.*" Pp. 5.242–83 in *TDNT* (1967; orig. 1954).

Birdsall, J. N. "Review of W. R. Farmer, *The Last Twelve Verses of Mark*." *JTS* 26 (1975): 151–60.

Black, M. *An Aramaic Approach to the Gospels and Acts*. 3rd ed. Oxford: Clarendon Press, 1967.

———. *The Book of Enoch or I Enoch: A New English Edition*. SVTP 7. Leiden: E. J. Brill, 1985.

———. "The Theological Appropriation of the Old Testament by the New Testament." *SJT* 39 (1986): 1–17.

Blass, F. "On **Mark xii. 42** and xv. 16." *ExpT* 10 (1898/99): 185–87.

———, A. Debrunner, and R. W. Funk. *A Greek Grammar of the New Testament and Other Early Christian Literature.* Chicago/London: University of Chicago, 1961. [Cited as **BDF**]

Blenkinsopp, J. "The **Oracle** of Judah and the Messianic Entry." *JBL* 80 (1961): 55–64.

Blinzler, J. *The **Trial** of Jesus: The Jewish and Roman Proceedings Against Jesus Christ Described and Assessed from the Oldest Accounts.* Westminster, Md.: Newman Press, 1959.

Blood-Patterson, P. ***Rise Up** Singing: The Group-Singing Song Book.* Bethlehem, Pa.: Sing Out Corporation, 1988.

Blumenfeld, B. *The Political **Paul**: Justice, Democracy and Kingship in a Hellenistic Framework.* JSNTSup 210. London/New York: Sheffield Academic Press, 2001.

Bock, D. L. ***Blasphemy** and Exaltation in Judaism and the Final Examination of Jesus: A Philological-Historical Study of the Key Jewish Themes Impacting Mark 14:61–64.* WUNT 2. Reihe 106. Tübingen: Mohr Siebeck, 1998.

Bode, E. L. *The **First Easter** Morning: The Gospel Accounts of the Women's Visit to the Tomb of Jesus.* AnBib 45. Rome: Biblical Institute Press, 1970.

Bokser, B. *The **Origins** of the Seder: The Passover Rite and Early Rabbinic Judaism.* Berkeley: University of California Press, 1984.

Bolte, J., and G. Polívka. ***Anmerkungen** zu der Kinder u. Hausmärchen der Brüder Grimm.* Hildesheim: Georg Olms Verlagsbuchhandlung, 1963 (orig. 1914).

Bonsirven, J. "**Hoc est** corpus meum. Recherches sur l'original araméen." *Bib* 29 (1948): 205–19.

Booth, W. C. *The **Rhetoric** of Fiction.* Chicago: University of Chicago Press, 1966.

Boomershine, T. E. "**Peter's Denial** as Polemic or Confession: The Implications of Media Criticism for Biblical Hermeneutics." *Semeia* 39 (1987): 47–68.

———. "**Mark 16:8** and the Apostolic Commission." *JBL* 100 (1981): 225–39.

Borg, M. *Conflict, **Holiness** and Politics in the Teaching of Jesus.* New York: Mellen, 1998. Rev. ed.

Boring, M. E. ***Sayings** of the Risen Jesus: Christian Prophecy in the Synoptic Tradition.* SNTSMS. Cambridge: University Press, 1982.

———. ***Truly Human**/Truly Divine: Christological Language and the Gospel Form.* St. Louis: CBP Press, 1984.

Bornkamm, G. ***Jesus** of Nazareth.* New York, Hagerstown, San Francisco, London: Harper & Row, 1960.

Boswell, J. *The **Kindness** of Strangers: The Abandonment of Children in Western Europe from Late Antiquity to the Renaissance.* New York: Pantheon, 1988.

Bovon, F. *Das Evangelium nach **Lukas** (Lk 1,1–9,50).* EKKNT 3.1. Zürich/Neukirchen-Vluyn: Benziger/Neukirchener, 1989.

Brandenburger, E. ***Markus 13** und die Apokalyptik.* FRLANT 13. Göttingen: Vandenhoeck & Ruprecht, 1984.

Brandon, S. G. F. ***Jesus** and the Zealots: A Study of the Political Factor in Primitive Christianity.* New York: Charles Scribner's Sons, 1967.

Braude, W. G. ***Pesikta Rabbati**: Discourses for Feasts, Fasts, and Special Sabbaths.* Yale Judaica Series 18. New Haven/London: Yale University Press, 1968.

Braun, H. "***Planaō**, ktl.*" Pp. 6.228–53 in *TDNT* (1968).

Brenton, L. C. L. *The **Septuagint** with Apocrypha: Greek and English.* Grand Rapids: Zondervan, 1982 (orig. 1851).

Breuer, M. "**Pilpul.**" In *EncJud, CD-ROM Edition.*

Brewer, D. I. "Jewish **Women** Divorcing Their Husbands in Early Judaism: The Background to Papyrus Ṣe'elim 13." *HTR* 92 (1999): 349–57.

Brin, G. "**Divorce** at Qumran." Pp. 231–44 in *Legal Texts and Legal Issues: Proceedings of the Second Meeting of the International Organization for Qumran Studies, Cambridge 1995. Published in Honour of Joseph M. Baumgarten,* ed. M. Bernstein et al. Leiden/New York/Köln: Brill, 1997.

Broadhead, E. K. "**Which Mountain** Is 'This Mountain'? A Critical Note on Mark 11:22–25." *Paradigms* 2 (1986): 33–38.

———. *Teaching with Authority: Miracles and Christology in the Gospel of Mark.* JSNTSup 74. Sheffield: JSOT, 1992.

Brock, S. *The Luminous Eye: The Spiritual World Vision of Saint Ephrem.* Cisterian Studies Series 124. Kalamazoo, Mich.: Cisterian Publications, 1985.

Brockelmann, K. *Lexicon Syriacum.* Hildesheim/Zürich/New York: Georg Olms Verlag, 1995 (orig. 1928). [Cited as **Brockelmann**]

Brooke, G. J. "**4Q500 1** and the Use of Scripture in the Parable of the Vineyard." *DSD* 2 (1995): 268–94.

Brooten, B. J. "**Konnten** Frauen im alten Judentum die Scheidung betreiben? Überlegungen zu Mk 10, 11–12 und 1 Kor 7,10–11." *EvT* 42 (1982): 65–80.

———. "Zur **Debatte** über das Scheidungsrecht der jüdischen Frau." *EvT* 43 (1983): 466–78.

Brown, R. E. *The **Birth** of the Messiah: A Commentary on the Infancy Narratives in Matthew and Luke.* AYBRL. New York: Doubleday, 1993 (orig. 1979); reprint, New Haven: Yale University Press.

———. *The **Death** of the Messiah: From Gethsemane to the Grave. A Commentary on the Passion Narratives in the Four Gospels.* AYBRL. New York: Doubleday, 1994; reprint, New Haven: Yale University Press.

———. *The **Epistles** of John.* AYB 30. Garden City, N.Y.: Doubleday, 1982; reprint, New Haven: Yale University Press.

———. *The Gospel According to John.* AYB 29 & 29A. Garden City, N.Y.: Doubleday, 1966–70; reprint, New Haven: Yale University Press. [Cited as **Brown**]

———. "The ***Gospel of Peter*** and Canonical Gospel Priority." *NTS* 33 (1987): 321–43.

———. *An Introduction to New Testament **Christology**.* New York/Mahwah: Paulist Press, 1994.

———. *The **Virginal Conception** and Bodily Resurrection of Jesus.* New York/Paramus/Toronto: Paulist Press, 1973.

Bruce, F. F. "**Render** Unto Caesar." Pp. 249–64 in *Jesus and the Politics of His Day,* ed. E. Bammel and C. F. D. Moule. Cambridge: Cambridge University Press, 1984.

Buchanan, G. W. *Jesus: The King and His Kingdom.* Macon, Ga.: Mercer University Press, 1984.

Bultmann, R. "***Aischynō, ktl.***" Pp. 1.189–90 in *TDNT* (1964; orig. 1933).

———. *The Gospel of **John**: A Commentary.* Philadelphia: Westminster Press, 1971 (orig. 1964).

———. *History of the Synoptic Tradition.* New York: Harper & Row, 1963. [Cited as **Bultmann**]

———. *Theology of the New Testament.* 2 vols. in 1. New York: Scribners, 1951–55.

Bünker, M. " '**Gebt** dem Kaiser, was des Kaisers ist!' Aber: Was ist des Kaisers?" *Kairos* 29 (1987): 85–98.

Burchard, C. "**Markus 15,34.**" *ZNW* 74 (1983): 1–11.

Burger, C. *Jesus als Davidssohn. Eine traditionsgeschichtliche Untersuchung.* FRLANT 98. Göttingen: Vandenhoeck & Ruprecht, 1970.

Burkert, W. *Ancient Mystery Cults.* Cambridge, Mass./London: Harvard University Press, 1987.

Burkitt, F. C. *Evangelion da-Mepharreshe. The Curetonian Version of the Four Gospels, with the Readings of the Sinai Palimpest and the Early Syriac Patristic Evidence.* 2 vols. Cambridge: Cambridge University Press, 1904.

Burton, E. D. W. *Syntax of the Moods and Tenses in New Testament Greek.* Grand Rapids: Kregel, 1976 (orig. 1900). [Cited as **Burton**]

Buttrick, G. A., ed. *The Interpreter's Dictionary of the Bible: An Illustrated Encyclopedia.* 4 vols. Abingdon: Nashville, 1962. [Cited as **IDB**]

Cahill, M. *The First Commentary on Mark: An Annotated Translation.* New York/Oxford: Oxford University Press, 1998. [Cited as **Cahill**]

Calvin, J. *Commentary on a **Harmony** of the Evangelists, Matthew, Mark, and Luke.* Grand Rapids, Mich.: Christian Classics Ethereal Library, 1999 (orig. 1555). http://www .ccel.org/ccel/calvin/calcom32.html

Camery-Hoggatt, J. *Irony in Mark's Gospel: Text and Subtext.* SNTSMS 72. Cambridge: Cambridge University Press, 1992.

Campbell, R. A. *The **Elders**: Seniority within Earliest Christianity.* SNTW. Edinburgh: T & T Clark, 1994.

Capps, D. *Reframing: A New Method in Pastoral Care.* Minneapolis: Fortress, 1990.

Carlson, S. C. *The **Gospel Hoax**: Morton Smith's Invention of Secret Mark.* Waco, Tex.: Baylor University Press, 2005.

Carroll, J. T. *Response to the End of History: Eschatology and Situation in Luke–Acts.* SBLDS 92. Atlanta: Scholars Press, 1988.

Carroll, L. *The Annotated **Alice**: The Definitive Edition.* New York: Norton, 1999.

Carroll, S. "**Bethphage**." P. 1.715 in *AYBD.*

Carter, W. *Households and Discipleship: A Study of Matthew 19–20.* JSNTSup 103. Sheffield: Sheffield Academic Press, 1994.

Casey, M. *Aramaic Sources of Mark's Gospel.* SNTSMS 102. Cambridge/New York/ Melbourne: Cambridge University Press, 1998.

Catchpole, D. "The Fearful **Silence** of the Women at the Tomb: A Study in Markan Theology." *JTSA* 18 (1977): 3–10.

Catchpole, D. R. "The 'Triumphal' **Entry**." Pp. 319–34 in *Jesus and the Politics of His Day,* ed. E. Bammel and C. F. D. Moule. Cambridge: Cambridge University Press, 1984.

———. "The **Answer** of Jesus to Caiaphas (Matt. XXVI. 64)." *NTS* 17 (1971): 213–26.

Cathcart, K. J., and R. P. Gordon. *The **Targum** of the Minor Prophets.* ArBib 14. Wilmington, Del.: Michael Glazier, Inc., 1989.

Charlesworth, J. H., ed. *The Old Testament Pseudepigrapha.* 2 vols. Garden City, N.Y.: Doubleday, 1983. [Cited as **OTP**]

———. *Rule of the Community and Related Documents.* The Dead Sea Scrolls: Hebrew, Aramaic, and Greek Texts with English Translations. Tübingen/Louisville: Mohr (Siebeck)/Westminster John Knox, 1994.

Chávez, E. G. *The Theological **Significance** of Jesus' Temple Action in Mark's Gospel.* Toronto Studies in Theology 87. Lewiston/Queenston/Lampeter: Edwin Mellen Press, 2002.

Chester, A. "The **Sibyl** and the Temple." Pp. 37–69 in *Templum Amicitiae: Essays on the Second Temple Presented to Ernst Bammel.* Edited by W. Horbury. JSNTSup 48. Sheffield: JSOT Press, 1991.

Chilton, B. D. *God in Strength*: *Jesus' Announcement of the Kingdom*. Studien Zum Neuen Testament und Seiner Umwelt. Serie B, Teil 1. Freistadt: Plöch, 1970.

———. *The Isaiah Targum: Introduction, Translation, Apparatus and Notes*. ArBib 11. Wilmington, Del.: Glazier, 1987.

———. "**Jesus** Ben David: Reflections on the Davidssohnfrage." *JSNT* 14 (1982): 88–112.

Clark, E. A. "**Constraining** the Body, Expanding the Text: The Exegesis of Divorce in the Later Latin Fathers." Pp. 153–71 in *The Limits of Ancient Christianity: Essays on Late Antique Thought and Culture in Honor of R. A. Markus*, ed. W. E. Klingshirn and M. Vessey. Ann Arbor: University of Michigan Press, 1999.

Clark, K. W. "**Golgotha**." P. 2.439 in *IDB*.

———. "The **Meaning** of [KATA]KYPIEYEIN." Pp. 207–12 in *The Gentile Bias and Other Essays*. NovTSup 54. Leiden: Brill, 1980.

Clarke, G. W. "**Religio Licita**." Pp. 5.665–67 in *AYBD*.

Clines, D., ed. *The* **Dictionary** *of Classical Hebrew*. Sheffield: Sheffield Academic Press, 1993– .

Cohen, S. J. D. "Epigraphical **Rabbis**." *JQR* N.S. 72 (1981–82): 1–17.

Cohn, N. *The* **Pursuit** *of the Millennium: Revolutionary Millenarians and Mystical Anarchists of the Middle Ages*. Rev. ed. New York: Oxford University Press, 1970.

Colani, T. *Jésus Christ et les croyances messianiques de son temps*. Strasbourg: Treuttel et Wurtz, 1864.

Collins, A. Y. "The **Appropriation** of the Psalms of Individual Lament by Mark." Pp. 223–41 in *The Scriptures in the Gospels*, ed. C. M. Tuckett. BETL 131, 1997.

———. "The **Charge** of Blasphemy in Mark 14.64." *JSNT* 26 (2004): 379–401.

———. "Mark and His Readers: The **Son of God Among Greeks** and Romans." *HTR* 93 (2000): 85–100.

———. "Mark and His Readers: The **Son of God Among Jews**." *HTR* 92 (1999): 393–408.

———. "The **Worship** of Jesus and the Imperial Cult," 1998. Conference Paper, International Conference on the Historical Origins of the Worship of Jesus, 13–17 May 1998, St. Mary's College, University of St. Andrews.

Collins, J. J. *Daniel*: *A Commentary on the Book of Daniel*. Hermeneia. Minneapolis: Fortress, 1993.

———. "**Marriage**, Divorce, and Family in Second Temple Judaism." Pp. 104–62 in *Families in Ancient Israel*, ed. L. G. Perdue et al. Louisville: Westminster John Knox, 1997.

———. *The* **Scepter** *and the Star: The Messiahs of the Dead Sea Scrolls and Other Ancient Literature*. AYBRL. New York: Doubleday, 1995; reprint, New Haven: Yale University Press.

Collins, R. F. *Divorce in the New Testament*. Good News Studies 28. Collegeville, Minn.: Liturgical Press, 1992.

Colpe, C. "*Ho huios tou anthrōpou*." Pp. 8.400–77 in *TDNT* (1972).

Colwell, E. C. "A **Definite Rule** for the Use of the Article in the Greek New Testament." *JBL* 52 (1933): 12–21.

Condit, I. J. *The* **Fig**. A New Series of Plant Science Books 19. Waltham, Mass.: Chronica Botanica Co., 1947.

Connolly, A. L. "**Frankincense** and Myrrh." *NewDocs* 4 (1979): 129–31.

Constantelos, D. J. *Byzantine* **Philanthropy** *and Social Welfare*. New Brunswick, N.J.: Rutgers University Press, 1968.

Conybeare, F. C., and St. George Stock. *A Grammar of Septuagint Greek*. Grand Rapids: Zondervan, 1980 (orig. 1905).

Corbett, P. E. *The Roman Law of Marriage*. Oxford: Clarendon Press, 1930.

Corbo, V. C. "**Golgotha**." Pp. 2.1071–73 in *AYBD*.

Corley, K. E. *Private Women, Public Meals: Social Conflict in the Synoptic Tradition*. Peabody, Mass.: Hendrickson, 1993.

Cotton, H. M., and E. Qimron. "**XḤev/Se ar 13** of 134 or 135 C.E.: A Wife's Renunciation of Claims." *JJS* 49 (1998): 108–18.

Cowley, A. E. *The Samaritan Liturgy*. Oxford: Clarendon Press, 1909.

Craig, K. M. *A Poetics of Jonah: Art in the Service of Ideology*. Columbia: University of South Carolina Press, 1993.

Craig, W. L. "Was Jesus Buried in Shame? **Reflections** on B. McCane's Proposal." *ExpT* 115 (2004): 404–9.

Cranfield, C. E. B. *The Gospel According to Saint Mark*. CGTC. Cambridge: Cambridge University Press, 1974 (orig. 1959). [Cited as **Cranfield**]

———. "St. **Mark, 9.14–29**." *SJT* 3 (1950): 57–67.

Crawford, B. S. "**Near Expectation** in the Sayings of Jesus." *JBL* 101 (1982): 225–44.

Crossan, J. D. *The Cross That Spoke: The Origins of the Passion Narrative*. San Francisco: Harper & Row, 1988.

———. "**Empty Tomb** and Absent Lord (Mark 16:1–8)." Pp. 135–52 in *The Passion in Mark: Studies on Mark 14–16*, ed. W. H. Kelber. Philadelphia: Fortress, 1976.

———. *In Parables: The Challenge of the Historical Jesus*. New York: Harper & Row, 1973.

———. "Mark and the **Relatives** of Jesus." *NovT* 15 (1973): 81–113.

———. *Who Killed Jesus? Exposing the Roots of Anti-Semitism in the Gospel Story of the Death of Jesus*. San Francisco: HarperCollins, 1991.

Croy, N. C. *The Mutilation of Mark's Gospel*. Nashville: Abingdon, 2003.

Cullmann, O. *Baptism in the New Testament*. Philadelphia: Westminster Press, 1950.

———. *Peter: Disciple, Apostle, Martyr. A Historical and Theological Study*. 2nd ed. London: SCM, 1962.

Dahl, N. A. "**Contradictions** in Scripture." Pp. 159–77 in *Studies in Paul*. 1969. Minneapolis: Augsburg, 1977.

———. "The **Crucified Messiah**." Pp. 10–36 in *The Crucified Messiah*. Minneapolis: Augsburg, 1974 (orig. 1960).

———. "**Messianic Ideas** and the Crucifixion of Jesus." Pp. 382–403 in *The Messiah: Developments in Earliest Judaism and Christianity. Princeton Symposium on Judaism and Christian Origins*. Minneapolis: Fortress, 1992.

———. "The **Purpose** of Luke–Acts." Pp. 87–98 in *Jesus in the Memory of the Early Church*. Minneapolis: Augsburg, 1976.

Dahood, M. *Psalms*. AYB 16, 17, 17A. New York: Doubleday, 1965–70; reprint, New Haven: Yale University Press.

Danby, H. *The Mishnah: Translated from the Hebrew with Introduction and Brief Explanatory Notes*. Oxford: Oxford University Press, 1933. [Cited as **Danby**]

Danker, F. W. "The **Demonic Secret** in Mark: A Reexamination of the Cry of Dereliction (15 34)." *ZNW* 61 (1970): 48–69.

Danson, J. M. "The **Fall** of St. Peter." *ExpT* 19 (1907): 307–8.

Daube, D. "**Concessions** to Sinfulness in Jewish Law." *JJS* 10 (1959): 1–13.

———. *The New Testament and Rabbinic Judaism*. New York: Arno, 1973 (orig. 1956).

———. "On **Acts 23**: Sadducees and Angels." *JBL* 109 (1990): 493–97.

Dautzenberg, G. *Sein Leben bewahren*. Psychē *in den Herrenworten der Evangelien*. SANT. München: Kösel-Verlag, 1966.

———. *Studien zur Theologie der Jesustradition*. SBAB 19. Stuttgart: Verlag Katholisches Bibelwerk GmbH, 1995.

Davies, W. D. *Paul and Rabbinic Judaism: Some Rabbinic Elements in Pauline Theology*. New York/Evanston: Harper & Row, 1948.

———, and Dale C. Allison. *A Critical and Exegetical Commentary on the Gospel According to Saint Matthew*. 3 vols. ICC. Edinburgh: T & T Clark, 1988–97. [Cited as **Davies and Allison**]

Davis, P. G. "Mark's Christological **Paradox**." *JSNT* 35 (1989): 3–18.

Dayagi-Mendeles, M. *Perfumes and Cosmetics in the Ancient World*. Jerusalem: Israel Museum, 1989.

de Boer, M. C. *The **Defeat** of Death: Apocalyptic Eschatology in 1 Corinthians 15 and Romans 5*. JSNTSup, 22. Sheffield: Sheffield Academic Press, 1988.

———. *Johannine Perspectives on the Death of Jesus*. Contributions to Biblical Exegesis and Theology 17. Kampen: Kok Pharos, 1996.

Deissmann, A. *Light from the Ancient East: The New Testament Illustrated by Recently Discovered Texts of the Graeco-Roman World*. Grand Rapids: Baker Book House, 1978 (orig. 1922).

de Jonge, M. "**Jesus, Son of David** and Son of God." Pp. 95–104 in *Intertextuality in Biblical Writings: Essays in Honour of Bas Van Iersel*, ed. S. Draisma. Kampen: Kok, 1989.

———. "The **Use** of the Word 'Anointed' in the Time of Jesus." *NovT* 8 (1966): 132–48.

Deming, W. "Mark 9.42–10.12, Matthew 5.27–32, and *b*. Nid. 13b: A First Century **Discussion** of Male Sexuality." *NTS* 36 (1990): 130–41.

de Moor, J. C. "The Targumic **Background** of Mark 12:1–12: The Parable of the Wicked Tenants." *JSJ* 29 (1998): 63–80.

Denniston, J. D. *The **Greek Particles***. Oxford: Clarendon Press, 1934.

Dentzer, J.-M. "Aux **origines** de l'iconographie du banquet couché." *RAr* (1971), 215–58.

Denyer, N. "**Mark 16:8** and Plato, *Protagoras* 328D." *TynBul* 57 (2006): 149–50.

Derrett, J. D. M. " '**Eating up** the Houses of Widows': Jesus' Comment on Lawyers?" *NovT* 14 (1972): 1–9.

———. *Law in the New Testament*. London: Darton, Longman & Todd, 1970.

———. "Law in the New Testament: The Palm Sunday **Colt**." *NovT* 13 (1971): 241–58.

———. "**Why Jesus** Blessed the Children (Mk 10:13–16 Par.)." *NovT* 25 (1983): 1–18.

deSilva, D. A. *Introducing the **Apocrypha***. Grand Rapids: Baker Academic, 2002.

De Vaux, R. *Ancient Israel*. New York: McGraw-Hill, 1965.

Dewey, K. E. "**Peter's Curse** and Cursed Peter (Mark 14:53–54, 66–72)." Pp. 96–114 in *The Passion in Mark: Studies on Mark 14–16*, ed. W. Kelber. Philadelphia: Fortress, 1976.

Dibelius, M. *From Tradition to Gospel*. Cambridge: James Clarke, 1971 (orig. 1933). [Cited as **Dibelius**]

———. "**Gethsemane**." *Crozer Quarterly* 12 (1935): 254–65.

Dimant, D. "*4QFlorilegium and the Idea of the Community as Temple*." Pp. 165–89 in *Hellenica et Judaica. Hommage à Valentin Nikiprowetzky* ‫ל״ז‬, ed. A. Caquot, M. Hadas-Lebel, and J. Riaud. Leuven/Paris: Éditions Peeters, 1986.

———. *Qumran Cave 4. XXI. Parabiblical Texts, Part 4: Pseudo-Prophetic Texts*. Discoveries in the Judaean Desert 30. Oxford: Clarendon Press, 2001.

Dittenberger, W. *Sylloge Inscriptionum Graecarum*. 3rd. ed. Leipzig: S. Hirzel, 1915–24.

Dodd, C. H. *According* to the Scriptures: The Sub-Structure of New Testament Theology. London: Nisbet, 1952.

———. *Historical Tradition* in the Fourth Gospel. Cambridge: Cambridge University Press, 1963.

———. *The Parables* of the Kingdom. Glasgow: Collins, 1961 (orig. 1935).

Donahue, J. R. *Are You the Christ?* SBLDS 10. Missoula: Society of Biblical Literature, 1973.

Dormeyer, D. *Die Passion Jesu als Verhaltensmodell: literarische und theologische Analyse der Traditions- und Redaktionsgeschichte der Markuspassion.* NTAbh 11. Münster: Verlag Aschendorff, 1974.

Dostoyevsky, F. *The Brothers Karamazov.* New York: Penguin Books, 1958.

Douglas, L. *The Memory of Judgment: Making Law and History in the Trials of the Holocaust.* New Haven: Yale University Press, 2001.

Dowd, S. E. *Prayer, Power, and the Problem of Suffering.* SBLDS 105. Atlanta: Scholars Press, 1988.

Drury, J. "Luke." Pp. 418–39 in *The Literary Guide to the Bible,* ed. R. Alter and F. Kermode. Cambridge, Mass.: Belknap Press of Harvard University Press, 1987.

Dubis, M. *Messianic Woes in First Peter: Suffering and Eschatology in 1 Peter 4:12–19.* Studies in Biblical Literature 33. New York: Peter Lang, 2002.

Duling, D. C. "Solomon, Exorcism, and the Son of David." HTR 68 (1975): 235–52.

Dunn, J. D. G. *Baptism* in the Holy Spirit. London: SCM, 1970.

———. "The Messianic Secret in Mark." Pp. 116–31 in *The Messianic Secret,* ed. C. M. Tuckett. Philadelphia: Fortress, 1983 (orig. 1974).

Ebeling, G. *Dogmatik des christlichen Glaubens. Zweiter Teil: Der Glaube an Gott den Versöhner der Welt.* Tübingen: Mohr (Siebeck), 1979.

Eckstein, H.-J. "Markus 10,46–52 als Schlüsseltext des Markusevangeliums." ZNW 87 (1996): 33–50.

Edwards, D. "Dress and Ornamentation." Pp. 2.232–38 in *AYBD.*

Edwards, W. D., W. J. Gabel, and F. E. Hosmer. "On the Physical Death of Jesus Christ." *Journal of the American Medical Association* 255 (1986): 1455–63.

Ehrlich, U. *The Nonverbal Language* of Prayer: A New Approach to Jewish Liturgy. TSAJ 105. Tübingen: Mohr (Siebeck), 2004.

Ehrman, B. D. *Lost Christianities: The Battle for Scripture and the Faiths We Never Knew.* New York/Oxford: Oxford University Press, 2003.

———. *The Orthodox Corruption of Scripture: The Effect of Early Christological Controversies on the Text of the New Testament.* New York/Oxford: Oxford University Press, 1993.

———. *Truth* and Fiction in The Da Vinci Code: A Historian Reveals What We Really Know About Jesus, Mary Magdalene, and Constantine. New York/Oxford: Oxford University Press, 2004.

———, and Mark A. Plunkett. "The Angel and the Agony: The Textual Problem of Luke 22:43–44." CBQ 45 (1983): 401–16.

Ekblad, E. R. *Isaiah's Servant Poems* According to the Septuagint: An Exegetical and Theological Study. CBET 23. Louvain: Peeters, 1999.

Elbogen, I. *Jewish Liturgy: A Comprehensive History.* Philadelphia/New York/Jerusalm: Jewish Publication Society/Jewish Theological Seminary, 1993.

Eliach, Y. *Hasidic Tales* of the Holocaust. New York: Random House, 1982.

Elias, J. *The Haggadah: Passover Haggadah.* ArtScroll Mesorah Series. New York: Mesorah Publications, 1977.

Elliott, J. H. *1 Peter: A New Translation with Introduction and Commentary.* AYB 37B. New York: Doubleday, 2000; reprint, New Haven: Yale University Press.

Elliott, J. K. *The Apocryphal New Testament: A Collection of Apocryphal Christian Literature in an English Translation.* Oxford/New York: Clarendon Press/Oxford University Press, 1993. [Cited as **Elliott**]

———. "The **Text** and Language of the Endings to Mark's Gospel." *TZ* 27 (1971): 254–62.

Elon, M. *Jewish Law: History, Sources, Principles.* 4 vols. Philadelphia/Jerusalem: Jewish Publication Society, 1994.

Emerton, J. A. "The **Origin** of the Son of Man Imagery." *JTS* 9 (1958): 225–42.

Encyclopaedia Judaica. CD-ROM edition. Jerusalem: Keter, 1997 (orig. 1971–72). [Cited as **EncJud**]

Epp, E. J. *The Theological **Tendency** of Codex Bezae Cantabrigiensis in Acts.* SNTSMS 3. Cambridge University Press, 1966.

Epstein, I., ed. *Hebrew-English Edition of the **Babylonian Talmud**.* London: Soncino Press, 1988.

Ernst, J. *Das Evangelium nach Markus.* Regensburger Neues Testament. Regensburg: Friedrich Pustet, 1981.

Evans, C. A. *Jesus and His Contemporaries: Comparative Studies.* Boston/Leiden: Brill, 2001.

———. "**Jesus' Action** in the Temple: Cleansing or Portent of Destruction?" *CBQ* 51 (1989): 237–70.

———. *Jesus and the **Ossuaries**.* Waco, Tex.: Baylor University Press, 2003.

———. *Mark 8:27–16:20.* WBC. Nashville: Thomas Nelson, 2001. [Cited as **Evans**]

———. "On the **Vineyard Parables** of Isaiah 5 and Mark 12." *BZ* 28 (1984): 82–86.

Evans, C. F. *Saint Luke.* New Testament Commentaries. London/Philadelphia: SCM/Trinity Press International, 1990.

Fadiman, A. *The **Spirit** Catches You and You Fall Down: A Hmong Child, Her American Doctors, and the Collision of Two Cultures.* New York: Farrar, Straus and Giroux, 1998.

Faierstein, M. M. "**Why** Do the Scribes Say That Elijah Must Come First?" *JBL* 100 (1981): 75–86.

Fanning, B. M. *Verbal **Aspect** in New Testament Greek.* Oxford: Clarendon Press, 1990.

Farmer, W. R. *The Last Twelve **Verses** of Mark.* SNTSMS 25. London/New York: Cambridge University Press, 1974.

Feldmeier, R. *Die **Krisis** des Gottessohnes. Die Gethsemaneerzählung als Schlüssel der Markuspassion.* WUNT N.S. 21. Tübingen: Mohr (Siebeck), 1987.

Fine, S. "A **Note** on Ossuary Burial and the Resurrection of the Dead in First-Century Jerusalem." *JJS* 51 (2000): 69–76.

Finegan, J. *The **Archeology** of the New Testament: The Life of Jesus and the Beginning of the Early Church.* Princeton: Princeton University Press, 1969.

Firmage, E. "**Zoology** (Fauna)." Pp. 6.1109–67 in *AYBD*.

Fischel, H. A. "The **Uses** of Sorites (*Climax, Gradatio*) in the Tannaitic Period." *HUCA* 44 (1973): 119–51.

Fitzmyer, J. A. "**Abba** and Jesus' Relation to God." Pp. 15–38 in *A cause de l'Evangile: études sur les Synoptiques et les Actes: offertes au P. Jacques Dupont, O.S.B. à l'occasion de son 70e anniversaire.* LD 123. Paris: Cerf, 1985.

———. *The Gospel According to **Luke**.* AYB 28 & 28A. New York: Doubleday, 1981–85; reprint, New Haven: Yale University Press.

———. "The Matthean **Divorce Texts** and Some New Palestinian Evidence." Pp. 79–111 in *To Advance the Gospel: New Testament Studies*. Crossroad: New York, 1981.

———. "**More** About Elijah Coming First." *JBL* 104 (1985): 295–96.

———. ***Romans**: A New Translation with Introduction and Commentary*. AYB 33. New York: Doubleday, 1993; reprint, New Haven: Yale University Press.

———. *Tobit*. CEJL. Berlin/New York, 2003.

Fleddermann, H. "The Discipleship **Discourse** (Mark 9:33–50)." *CBQ* 43 (1981): 57–75.

———. "The **Flight** of a Naked Young Man (Mark 14:51–52)." *CBQ* 41 (1979): 412–18.

Fletcher-Louis, C. H. T. ***Luke–Acts**: Angels, Christology and Soteriology*. WUNT 94. Tübingen: Mohr (Siebeck), 1997.

Flückiger-Guggenheim, D. ***Göttliche Gäste**: Die Einkehr von Göttern und Heroen in der griechischen Mythologie*. Bern: Peter Lang, 1984.

Flusser, D. " 'At the **Right Hand** of Power'." *Immanuel* (1982): 41–46.

———. " '**Do Not** Commit Adultery', 'Do Not Murder.'" *Textus* 4 (1964): 220–24.

———. "**Two Notes** on the Midrash on 2 Sam vii." *IEJ* 9 (1959): 99–109.

———, and S. Safrai. "A **Fragment** of the Songs of David and Qumran." Pp. 83–105 in *Bible Studies Y.M. Grintz in Memoriam*, ed. B. Uffenheimer. Tel Aviv: Tel Aviv University/Hakibbutz Hameuchad Publishing, 1982.

Foerster, W. "***Klēros**, ktl.*" Pp. 3.758–85 in *TDNT* (1965; orig. 1938).

Forsyth, N. *The **Old Enemy**: Satan and the Combat Myth*. Princeton: Princeton University Press, 1987.

Fortna, R. T. "**Jesus and Peter** at the High Priest's House: A Test Case for the Question of the Relation Between Mark's and John's Gospels." *NTS* 24 (1977–78): 371–83.

Fossum, J. E. "**Ascensio**, Metamorphosis: The 'Transfiguration' of Jesus in the Synoptic Gospels." Pp. 71–97 in *The Image of the Invisible God: Essays on the Influence of Jewish Mysticism on Early Christology*. NTOA 30. Freiburg and Göttingen: Universitätsverlag and Vandenhoeck & Ruprecht, 1995.

Foster, P. "**Why** Did Matthew Get the *Shema* Wrong? A Study of Matthew 22:37." *JBL* 122 (2003): 309–33.

France, R. T. *The Gospel of **Mark***. NIGTC. Grand Rapids/Cambridge/Carlisle: Eerdmans/Paternoster, 2002.

Freedman, D. N., ed. *The Anchor Yale Bible Dictionary*. 6 vols. New York: Doubleday, 1992; reprint, New Haven: Yale University Press. [Cited as ***AYBD***]

Freedman, H., and M. Simon, eds. *The **Midrash Rabbah***. 5 vols. London/Jerusalem/New York: Soncino Press, 1977 (orig. 1938).

Frenschkowski, M. ***Offenbarung** und Epiphanie*. WUNT 2. Reihe 79. 2 vols. Tübingen: Mohr (Siebeck), 1995–97.

Friedlander, G. ***Pirkê** de Rabbi Eliezer*. New York: Hermon Press, 1965.

Fulda, H. *Das **Kreuz** und die Kreuzigung : eine antiquarische Untersuchung nebst Nachweis der vielen seit Lipsius verbreiteten Irrthümer : zugleich vier Excurse über verwandte Gegenstände*. Breslau: Wilhelm Koebner, 1878.

Funk, R. W., and R. W. Hoover. *The **Five Gospels**: The Search for the Authentic Words of Jesus*. New York: Polebridge Press/Macmillan, 1993.

Furnish, V. ***Theology** and Ethics in Paul*. Nashville: Abingdon, 1968.

Fusco, V. ***Parola** e regno: la sezione delle parabole (Mc. 4, 1–34) nella prospettiva marciana*. Alosiana 13. Brescia: Morcelliana, 1980.

———. ***Povertà** e Sequela. Le Pericope Sinottica Della Chiamata del Ricco (Mc. 10,17–31 Parr.)*. Brescia: Paideia Editrice, 1991.

García Martínez, F., and E. J. C. Tigchelaar. *The Dead Sea Scrolls Study Edition*. 2 vols. Leiden/New York/Köln: Brill, 1997.

———. "**Man and Woman**: Halakhah Based Upon Eden in the Dead Sea Scrolls." Pp. 95–115 in *Paradise Interpreted: Representations of Biblical Paradise in Judaism and Christianity*, ed. G. P. Luttikhuizen. Leiden/Boston/Köln: Brill, 1999.

Garnsey, P., and R. Saller. *The Roman Empire: Economy, Society and Culture*. Berkeley/ Los Angeles: University of California Press, 1987.

Garrett, S. R. *The Demise of the Devil: Magic and the Demonic in Luke's Writings*. Minneapolis: Fortress, 1989.

———. *The Temptations of Jesus in Mark's Gospel*. Grand Rapids/Cambridge: William B. Eerdmans, 1998.

Gärtner, B. *The Temple and the Community in Qumran and the New Testament*. SNTSMS 1. Cambridge: University Press, 1965.

Gasque, W. "**Cyrene**." Pp. 1.1230–31 in *AYBD*.

Gaston, L. **No Stone** *on Another: Studies in the Significance of the Fall of Jerusalem in the Synoptic Gospels*. NovTSup 23. Leiden: Brill, 1970.

Gaventa, B. R. "The **Maternity** of Paul: An Exegetical Study of Galatians 4:19." Pp. 189– 201 in *The Conversation Continues: Studies in Paul and John in Honor of J. Louis Martyn*, ed. R. T. Fortna and B. R. Gaventa. Nashville: Abingdon, 1990.

Gealy, F. D. "**Centurion**." Pp. 1.547–48 in *IDB*.

Georgi, D. *The Opponents of Paul in Second Corinthians*. Philadelphia: Fortress, 1986.

Gese, H. "**Psalm 22** und das Neue Testament: Der älteste Bericht vom Tode Jesu und die Entstehung des Herrenmahles." Pp. 180–201 in *Vom Sinai zum Zion. Alttestamentliche Beiträge zum biblischen Theologie*. BEvT 64. München: Kaiser, 1974.

Geva, H. "**Jerusalem**, the Second Temple Period." Pp. 717–57 in *NEAEHL*, 1993.

Gevirtz, S. "**Curse**." Pp. 1.749–50 in *IDB*, 1962.

Gibson, J. "The **Function** of the Charge of Blasphemy in Mark 14:64." Paper. Society of Biblical Literature Conference. Atlanta, 2003.

Giesen, H. "**Hōra**." Pp. 506–8 in *EKKNT*, 1993.

Ginzberg, L. *The Legends of the Jews*. 7 vols. Philadelphia: Jewish Publication Society, 1909–38.

Glatzer, N. H., ed. *The Passover Haggadah with English Translation Introduction and Commentary*. New York: Schocken, 1979.

Gnilka, J. *Das Evangelium nach Markus*. 2 vols. EKKNT 2. Zürich/Neukirchen: Benziger/Neukirchener, 1978–79. [Cited as **Gnilka**]

Goguel, M. *The Life of Jesus*. 1932. New York: Macmillan, 1948.

Goldberg, A. M. "**Sitzend** zur Rechten der Kraft." *BZ* N.S. 8 (1964): 284–93.

Goldin, J. *The Fathers According to Rabbi Nathan*. Yale Judaica Series 10. New Haven/ London: Yale University Press, 1955.

Goldschmidt, D. *The Passover Haggadah: Its Sources and History* [Hebrew]. Jerusalem: Bialik Institute, 1960.

Good, D. J. *Jesus the Meek King*. Harrisburg, Pa.: Trinity Press International, 1999.

Goodacre, M. *The Case Against Q: Studies in Markan Priority and the Synoptic Problem*. Harrisburg, Pa.: Trinity Press International, 2002.

———. "**Prophecy** Historicized or History Scripturized? Reflections on the Origin of the Crucifixion Narrative." Paper presented at the Society of Biblical Literature Annual Meeting. Denver, 2001.

Goodman, M. *The Ruling Class of Judaea: The Origins of the Jewish Revolt Against Rome A.D. 66–70*. Cambridge/New York/Melbourne: Cambridge University Press, 1987.

Goodwin, W. W. *A Greek Grammar.* London: Macmillan, 1894.

Goor, A. "The **History** of the Fig in the Holy Land from Ancient Times to the Present Day." *Economic Botany* 19 (1965): 124–35.

Gornatowski, A. *Rechts und links im antiken Aberglauben.* Klassische Philologie. Breslau: R. Nischkowsky, 1936.

Gould, E. P. *A Critical and Exegetical Commentary on the Gospel According to St. Mark.* ICC. New York: Charles Scribner's Sons, 1896.

Grant, R. M. "**Augustus.**" Pp. 1.317–19 in *IDB.*

———. "The **Coming** of the Kingdom." *JBL* 67 (1948): 297–303.

———. *The Earliest Lives of Jesus.* New York: Harper & Brothers, 1961.

———. *Miracle and Natural Law in Graeco-Roman and Early Christian Thought.* Amsterdam: North-Holland, 1952.

Gray, R. *Prophetic Figures in Late Second Temple Jewish Palestine: The Evidence from Josephus.* New York/Oxford: Oxford University Press, 1993.

Gray, S. W. *The Least of My Brothers: Matthew 25:31–46, a History of Interpretation.* SBLDS 114. Atlanta: Scholars Press, 1989.

Greenberg, M. "The **Decalogue Tradition** Critically Examined." In *The Ten Commandments in History and Tradition*, ed. B.-Z. Segal and G. Levi. Jerusalem: Magnes Press, 1990.

Greenblatt, S. *Will in the World: How Shakespeare Became Shakespeare.* New York/London: W. W. Norton, 2004.

Greeven, H., and E. Güting, eds. *Textkritik des Markusevangeliums.* Theologie, Forschung und Wissenschaft 11. Münster: Lit Verlag, 2005.

Gregory, C. R. *Das Freer-Logion.* Leipzig: Hinrichs, 1908.

Grenfell, B. P., and A. S. Hunt. *The Oxyrhynchus Papyri. Part III.* London: Egypt Exploration Fund, 1903.

Grotius, H. *Annotationes in Novum Testamentum.* Erlangen/Leipzig: Tetzschner, 1755–57.

Grubbs, J. E. *Women and the Law in the Roman Empire: A Sourcebook on Marriage, Divorce, and Widowhood.* London/New York: Routledge, 2002.

Gruber, M. I. *Aspects of Nonverbal Communication in the Ancient Near East.* Studia Pohl: Dissertationes scientificae de rebus Orientis Antiqui 12/I. Rome: Biblical Institute Press, 1980.

Gruen, E. S. *Heritage and Hellenism: The Reinvention of Jewish Tradition.* Berkeley: University of California Press, 1998.

Grundmann, W. "*Dexios.*" Pp. 2.37–40 in *TDNT* (1964; orig. 1935).

Guillaumont, H.-Ch., et al. *The Gospel According to Thomas.* San Francisco: Harper & Row, 1959.

Gundel, W., ed. *Neue astrologische Texte des Hermes Trismegistos. Funde und Forschungen auf dem Gebiet der antiken Astronomie und Astrologie.* Abhandlungen der Bayerischen Akademie der Wissenschaften. Philosophisch-Historische Abteilung. Neue Folge, Heft 12. München: Verlag der Bayerischen Akademie der Wissenschaften, 1936.

Gundry, R. H. *Mark: A Commentary on His Apology for the Cross.* Grand Rapids: Eerdmans, 1993. [Cited as **Gundry**]

———. *Matthew: A Commentary on His Literary and Theological Art.* Grand Rapids: Eerdmans, 1982.

Gunkel, H. *Genesis.* Mercer Library of Biblical Studies. Macon, Ga.: Mercer University Press, 1997 (orig. 1901).

———. "Das **vierte Buch Esra**." Pp. 2.331–402 in _Die Apokryphen und Pseudepigraphen des alten Testaments_, ed. E. Kautzsch. Tübingen: Mohr, 1900.

Hagner, D. A. "James." Pp. 3.616–18 in _AYBD_.

Hahn, F. _The Titles of Jesus in Christology: Their History in Early Christianity._ Lutterworth Library. New York/Cleveland: World Publishing, 1969.

Halbertal, M. "**Coexisting** with the Enemy: Jews and Pagans in the Mishnah." Pp. 159–72 in _Tolerance and Intolerance in Early Judaism and Christianity_, ed. G. N. Stanton and G. G. Stroumsa. Cambridge: Cambridge University Press, 1998.

Hammer, P. L. "The _Understanding_ of Inheritance _(Klēronomia)_ in the New Testament." Ph.D. dissertation. Theological Faculty: University of Heidelberg, 1958.

Harder, G. "Das eschatologische **Geschichtsbild** der sogenannten kleinen Apokalypse." _ThViat_ 9 (1953): 70–87.

Hare, D. R. A. _The Theme of **Jewish Persecution** of Christians in the Gospel According to St. Matthew._ SNTSMS 6. Cambridge: Cambridge University Press, 1967.

———. _Matthew._ Interpretation. Louisville: John Knox Press, 1993.

Harnack, A. von. "**Probleme** im Texte der Leidensgeschichte Jesu." Pp. 1.86–104 in _Studien zur Geschichte des Neuen Testaments und der alten Kirche._ Berlin: De Gruyter, 1931 (orig. 1901).

Harner, P. B. "Qualitative Anarthrous **Predicate Nouns**: Mark 15:39 and John 1:1." _JBL_ 92 (2004): 75–87.

Harrill, J. A. _The **Manumission** of Slaves in Early Christianity._ HUT 32. Tübingen: Mohr (Siebeck), 1995.

Harrington, D. J. "The **Ideology** of Rule in Daniel 7–12." _SBLSP_ 38 (1999): 540–51.

Harris, W. V. "**Demography**, Geography and the Sources of Roman Slaves." _JRS_ 89 (1999): 62–75.

Hart, H. St J. "The **Coin** of 'Render Unto Caesar (a Note on Some Aspects of Mark 12:13–17; Matt. 22:15–22; Luke 20:20–26)." Pp. 241–48 in _Jesus and the Politics of His Day_, ed. E. Bammel and C. F. D. Moule. Cambridge: Cambridge University Press, 1984.

Hartman, L. **Prophecy Interpreted**: _The Formation of Some Jewish Apocalyptic Texts of the Eschatological Discourse Mark 13 Par._ ConBNT 1. Lund: Gleerup, 1966.

Harvey, A. E. "**Genesis** Versus Deuteronomy? Jesus on Marriage and Divorce." Pp. 55–65 in _The Gospels and the Scriptures of Israel_, ed. C. A. Evans and W. Stegner. JSNTSup 104/SSEJC 3. Sheffield: Sheffield Academic Press, 1994.

———. _Jesus and the Constraints of History._ Philadelphia: Westminster Press, 1982.

Hauck, F. "_**Halas**._" Pp. 1.228–9 in _TDNT_ (1964; orig. 1933).

Hauck, F., and W. Kasch. "_**Ploutos, ktl.**_" Pp. 6.318–32 in _TDNT_ (1968; orig. 1959).

Hauck, F., and S. Schulz. "_**Poreuomai, ktl.**_" Pp. 6.566–79 in _TDNT_ (1968; orig. 1959).

Hays, R. B. _The **Faith** of Jesus Christ: An Investigation of the Narrative Substructure of Galatians 3:1–4:11._ SBLDS. Chico: Scholars Press, 2001 (orig. 1983).

Heaney, S. **Beowulf**: _A New Verse Translation._ New York/London: Norton, 2000.

Heil, J. P. "A **Note** on 'Elijah with Moses' in Mark 9,4." _Bib_ 80 (1999): 115.

Henderson, S. _**Christology** and Discipleship in the Gospel of Mark._ SNTSMS 135. Cambridge: Cambridge University Press, 2006.

Hengel, M. _The **Charismatic Leader** and His Followers._ SNTW. New York: Crossroad, 1981 (orig. 1968).

———. _**Crucifixion** in the Ancient World and the Folly of the Message of the Cross._ Philadelphia: Fortress, 1977.

———. "Das **Gleichnis** von den Weingärtnern Mc 12 1–12 im Lichte der Zenonpapyri und der rabbinischen Gleichnisse." *ZNW* 59 (1968): 1–39.

———. *Judaism and Hellenism: Studies in Their Encounter in Palestine During the Early Hellenistic Period.* Philadelphia: Fortress, 1974.

———. *Studies in Early **Christology**.* Edinburgh: T & T Clark, 1995.

———. ***Studies** in the Gospel of Mark.* Philadelphia: Fortress, 1985.

———. *Was Jesus a **Revolutionist**?* Facet Books. Biblical Series 28. Philadelphia: Fortress, 1971.

———. *The **Zealots**: Investigations Into the Jewish Freedom Movement in the Period from Herod I Until 70 A.D.* Edinburgh: T & T Clark, 1989 (orig. 1961).

Hepper, F. N. *Baker **Encyclopedia** of Bible Plants.* Grand Rapids: Baker Book House, 1992.

Hermann, J. G. J. ***Opuscula**.* Leipzig: Gerhard Fleischer, 1827.

Herr, M. D. "**Aggadah**." In *EncJ CD-ROM Edition.*

Heschel, A. J. *The **Prophets**.* New York: Harper & Row, 1975 (orig. 1962).

———. *The **Sabbath**: Its Meaning for Modern Man.* New York: Farar, Straus and Giroux, 1951.

Hester, J. D. "Socio-Rhetorical **Criticism** and the Parable of the Tenants." *JSNT* 45 (1992): 27–57.

Himmelfarb, M. ***Tours** of Hell: An Apocalyptic Form in Jewish and Christian Literature.* Philadelphia: University of Pennsylvania Press, 1983.

Hirsch, E. *Das **vierte Evangelium** in seiner ursprünglichen Gestalt, verdeutscht und erklärt.* Tübingen: Mohr, 1936.

Hirsch, E. G., and J. D. Eisenstein. "**Wine**." In *Jewish Enyclopedia, Online Edition.* http://www.jewishencyclopedia.com/.

Hirschfeld, Y. *The Palestinian **Dwelling** in the Roman-Byzantine Period.* Studium Biblicum Franciscanum, Collectio Minor 34. Jerusalem: Franciscan Printing Press/Israel Exploration Society, 1995.

Hirshman, M. C. *A **Rivalry** of Genius : Jewish and Christian Biblical Interpretation in Late Antiquity.* SUNY Series in Judaica. Albany: State University of New York Press, 1996.

Hoffman, L. A. "A **Symbol** of Salvation in the Passover Seder." Pp. 109–31 in *Passover and Easter: The Symbolic Structuring of Sacred Seasons,* ed. P. F. Bradshaw and L. A. Hoffman. Two Liturgical Traditions 6. South Bend, Ind.: University of Notre Dame Press, 1999.

Hoffmann, D. ***Mechilta** de-Rabbi Simon b. Jochai: Ein Halachischer und Haggadischer Midrasch zu Exodus.* Frankfurt: J. Kaufmann, 1905.

Hofius, O. "The **Lord's Supper** and the Lord's Supper Tradition: Reflections on 1 Corinthians 11:23b–25." Pp. 75–115 in *One Loaf, One Cup. Ecumenical Studies of 1 Cor 11 and Other Eucharistic Texts,* ed. B. Meyer. New Gospel Studies 6. Macon, Ga.: Mercer University Press, 1993.

Holland, T. A., and E. Netzer. "**Jericho**." Pp. 3.723–39 in *AYBD.*

Hollander, H. W., and M. de Jonge. *The **Testaments** of the Twelve Patriarchs: A Commentary.* SVTP 8. Leiden: Brill, 1985.

Holleman, J. ***Resurrection** and Parousia: A Traditio-Historical Study of Paul's Eschatology in 1 Corinthians 15.* NovTSup 84. Leiden/New York/Köln: Brill, 1996.

Homan, M. M., and M. A. Gstohl. "**Jesus the Teetotaler**: How Dr. Welch Put the Lord on the Wagon." *BRev* 18 (2002): 28–29.

Hooker, M. D. *A Commentary on the Gospel According to St Mark.* Black's New Testament Commentaries. London: A & C Black, 1991. [Cited as **Hooker**]

————. *The Signs of a Prophet: The Prophetic Actions of Jesus.* Harrisburg, Pa.: Trinity Press International, 1997.

————. *The Son of Man in Mark. A Study of the Background of the Term "Son of Man" and Its Use in St. Mark's Gospel.* London: SPCK, 1967.

————. "**Trial** and Tribulation in Mark XIII." *BJRL* 65 (1982): 78–99.

Horbury, W. "The **Cult** of Christ and the Cult of the Saints." *NTS* 44 (1998): 444–69.

————. *Jewish **Messianism** and the Cult of Christ.* London: SCM, 1998.

Horsley, R. A. *Hearing the Whole Story: The Politics of Plot in Mark's Gospel.* Louisville: Westminster John Knox, 2001.

————. *Jesus and the Spiral of Violence: Popular Jewish Resistance in Roman Palestine.* San Francisco: Harper & Row, 1987.

Horsley, R. A., and J. S. Hanson. *Bandits, Prophets, and Messiahs: Popular Movements at the Time of Jesus.* New Voices in Biblical Studies. San Francisco: Harper & Row, 1985.

Hornblower, S., and A. Spawforth. *The Oxford Classical Dictionary.* 3rd ed. Oxford/New York: Oxford University Press, 1996. [Cited as **OCD**]

Howard, G. "**Faith of Christ**." Pp. 2.758–60 in *AYBD.*

Hubaut, M. *La **parabole** des vignerons homicides.* CahRB. Louvain: Gabalda, 1976.

Hudson, J. T. "**Irony** in Gethsemane? (Mark Xiv. 41.)." *ExpT* 46 (1934–35): 382.

Huizenga, L. A. "Der **Jesus** des Matthäusevangeliums und der Isaak der antiken jüdischen Enzyklopädie. Akedah-Überlieferungen und das Matthäusevangelium." Pp. 71–92 in *Die Bibel im Dialog der Schriften: Konzepte intertextueller Bibellektüre,* ed. S. Alkier and R. B. Hays. Tübingen: Francke Verlag, 2005.

Hultgren, A. J. *The **Parables** of Jesus: A Commentary.* Grand Rapids: Eerdmans, 2000.

Hünemörder, C. "**Lorbeer**." Pp. 7.440–42 in *Der Neue Pauly: Enzklopädie der Antike,* ed. H. Cancik. Stuttgart, 1999.

Hunt, A. S., and C. C. Edgar. *Select **Papryi** II: Non-Literary Papyri. Public Documents.* Cambridge, Mass./London: Harvard University Press/Heinemann, 1977.

Ilan, T. *Jewish **Women** in Greco-Roman Palestine.* Peabody, Mass.: Hendrickson, 1996.

————. "Notes and Observations on a Newly Published **Divorce Bill** from the Judaean Desert." *HTR* 89 (1996): 195–202.

————. "**Notes** on the Distribution of Jewish Women's Names in Palestine in the Second Temple and Mishnaic Periods." *JJS* 40 (1989): 186–200.

————. "The Provocative **Approach** Once Again: A Response to Adiel Schremer." *HTR* 91 (1998): 203–4.

Isaac, B. "**Judaea** After AD 70." *JJS* 35 (1984): 44–50.

Isho'dad of Merv. *Commentaries on the New Testament.* Piscataway NJ: Gorgias Press, 2005 (orig. 1911–16).

Jackson, H. M. "Why the **Youth** Shed His Cloak and Fled Naked: The Meaning and Purpose of Mark 14:51–52." *JBL* 116 (1997): 273–89.

————. "The **Death** of Jesus in Mark and the Miracle from the Cross." *NTS* 33 (1987): 16–37.

Jacobson, H. *A **Commentary** on Pseudo-Philo's Liber Antiquitatum Biblicarum with Latin Text and English Translation.* 2 vols. AGJU 31. Leiden/New York/Köln: Brill, 1996.

Jannaris, A. N. "**NARDOS PISTIKĒ** or 'Spikenard.'" *Classical Review* 16 (1902): 459–60.

Jastrow, M. *A Dictionary of the Targumim, the Talmud Babli and Yerushalmi, and the Midrashic Literature*. New York: Judaica, 1982 (orig. 1886–1903). [Cited as **Jastrow**]

Jellinek, A. **Bet Ha-Midrash**. 2 vols. Wien: Brothers Winter, 1873.

Jenni, E. "**Messiah, Jewish**." Pp. 3.360–65 in *IDB*.

Jensen, R. M. "**How Pilate** Became a Saint." *BRev* 19.6 (2003): 22–31, 47.

———. "**Living Water**: Images, Settings, and Symbols of Early Christian Baptism in the West." Doctoral dissertation. Columbia University, 1991.

———. *Understanding Early Christian Art*. New York/London: Routledge, 2000.

Jeremias, J. "**Der Eckstein**." *Angelos* 1 (1925): 65–70.

———. *The Eucharistic Words of Jesus*. Philadelphia: Fortress, 1966.

———. *Infant Baptism in the First Four Centuries*. London: SCM, 1960 (orig. 1938).

———. *Jerusalem in the Time of Jesus: An Investigation into Economic and Social Conditions During the Time of Jesus*. Philadelphia: Fortress, 1969.

———. "**Kephalē Gōnias**—'Akrogōniaios." ZNW 29 (1930): 264–80.

———. "**Mc 14,9**." ZNW 44 (1952): 103–7.

———. *New Testament Theology*. Part 1, *The Proclamation of Jesus*. London: SCM, 1971.

———. *The Origins of Infant Baptism: A Further Study in Reply to Kurt Aland*. London: SCM, 1963.

———. *The Parables of Jesus*. 2d rev. ed. New York: Scribners, 1972 (orig. 1954).

———. "**Pascha**." Pp. 5.896–904 in *TDNT* (1967; orig. 1954).

———. "**Polloi**." Pp. 6.536–45 in *TDNT* (1968; orig. 1959).

———. *The Prayers of Jesus*. SBT 2nd Series 6. London: SCM, 1967.

———. "Die **Salbungsgeschichte** Mc 14 3–9." ZNW 35 (1936): 75–82.

Jervell, J. *Imago Dei: Gen. 1,26f. im Spätjudentum, in der Gnosis und in den paulinischen Briefen*. FRLANT 76. Göttingen: Vandenhoeck & Ruprecht, 1960.

The Jewish Encyclopedia: A Descriptive Record of the History, Religion, Literature, and Customs of the Jewish People from the Earliest Times to the Present Day. Online edition (orig. 1881). [Cited as **JE**]

Johnson, E. S. "**Mark 10:46–52**: Blind Bartimaeus." *CBQ* 40 (1978): 191–204.

———. "Mark 8.22–26: The **Blind Man** from Bethsaida." *NTS* 25 (1979): 370–83.

Johnson, M. *The Rites of Christian Initiation: Their Evolution and Interpretation*. Collegeville, Minn.: Liturgical Press, 1999.

Jonas, H. *The Gnostic Religion: The Message of the Alien God and the Beginnings of Christianity*. 2nd ed. Boston: Beacon Press, 1963.

Jones, B. W. "**Caesar**." Pp. 1.797–98 in *AYBD*.

Juel, D. H. *Mark*. Augsburg Commentary on the New Testament. Minneapolis: Augsburg, 1990.

———. *Messiah and Temple: The Trial of Jesus in the Gospel of Mark*. SBLDS. Missoula: Scholars, 1977.

———. *Messianic Exegesis: Christological Interpretation of the Old Testament in Early Christianity*. Philadelphia: Fortress, 1988.

Just, F. "Was **Blind Bartimaeus** a 'Son of Impurity'?" Society of Biblical Literature—Synoptic Gospels Section. San Francisco, 1998.

Kähler, H. *Alberti Rubeni Dissertatio de Gemma Augustea*. Monumenta Artis Romanae 9. Berlin: Gebr. Mann, 1968.

Kähler, M. *The So-Called Historical Jesus and the Historic Biblical Christ*. Philadelphia: Fortress, 1964 (orig. 1892).

Käsemann, E. "The **Righteousness** of God in Paul." Pp. 168–82 in *New Testament Questions of Today*. Philadelphia: Fortress, 1969.

———. "**Sentences** of Holy Law in the New Testament." Pp. 66–81 in *New Testament Questions of Today*. Philadelphia: Fortress, 1969 (orig. 1954).

Kaminski, G. "**Thesauros**. Untersuchungen zum antiken Opferstock." *JdI* 106 (1991): 63–181.

Kannaday, W. C. *Apologetic Discourse and the Scribal Tradition: Evidence of the Influence of Apologetic Interests on the Text of the Canonical Gospels*. Society of Biblical Literature Text-Critical Studies 5. Atlanta: Society of Biblical Literature, 2004.

Kautzsch, E., and A. E. Cowley. *Gesenius' Hebrew Grammar*. 2nd ed. Oxford: At the Clarendon Press, 1910. [Cited as **Gesenius**]

Kazmierski, C. R. *Jesus, the Son of God: A Study of the Markan Tradition and Its Redaction by the Evangelist*. FB 33. Würzburg: Echter, 1979.

Keel, O. *The **Symbolism** of the Biblical World. Ancient Near Eastern Iconography and the Book of Psalms*. New York: Seabury, 1978.

Kelber, W. *The **Kingdom** in Mark: A New Place and a New Time*. Philadelphia: Fortress, 1974.

Kelber, W., A. Kolenkow, and R. Scroggs. "**Reflections** on the Question: Was There a Pre-Markan Passion Narrative?" Pp. 505–85 in *SBLSP 1971*.

Kelhoffer, J. A. *Miracle and Mission: The Authentication of Missionaries and Their Message in the Longer Ending of Mark*. WUNT. Tübingen: Mohr (Siebeck), 2000.

———. "The **Witness** of Eusebius' *Ad Marinum* and Other Christian Writings to Text-Critical Debates Concerning the Original Conclusion to Mark's Gospel." *ZNW* 92 (2001): 78–112.

Kempthorne, R. "The **Marcan Text** of Jesus' Answer to the High Priest (Mark XIV 62)." *NovT* 19 (1977): 197–208.

Kertelge, K. "Das **Doppelgebot** der Liebe im Markusevangelium." *TTZ* 103 (1994): 38–55.

———. "**Lytron**." Pp. 2.364–66 in *EDNT*, 1981.

Kiilunen, J. *Das **Doppelgebot** der Liebe in synoptischer Sicht. Ein redaktionskritischer Versuch über Mk 12,28–34 und die Parallelen*. AASF Series B, Vol. 250. Helsinki: Suomalainen Tiedeakatemia, 1989.

Kimelman, R. "The **Messiah** of the Amidah: A Study in Comparative Messianism." *JBL* 116 (1997): 313–20.

———. "The **Shema** and Its Blessings: The Realization of God's Kingship." Pp. 73–86 in *The Synagogue in Late Antiquity*, ed. L. Levine. Philadelphia: ASOR, 1987.

King, P. J., and L. E. Stager. *Life in Biblical Israel*. Louisville/London: Westminster John Knox Press, 2001.

Kingsburgy, J. D. *The **Christology** of Mark's Gospel*. Philadelphia: Fortress, 1983.

Kirby, P. "The **Case** Against the Empty Tomb." *Journal of Higher Criticism* 9 (2002): 175–202.

Kirsch, J. P. "**Peter**, Saint." In *Catholic Encyclopedia, Online edition*. Http://www.newadvent.org/cathen/.

Kittel, G. "*Erēmos*." Pp. 2.657–60 in *TDNT* (1964; orig. 1935).

———, and G. Friedrich, eds. *Theological Dictionary of the New Testament*. 10 vols. Grand Rapids: Eerdmans, 1964–76. [Cited as **TDNT**]

Kitzinger, E. "A Marble **Relief** of the Theodosian Period." *DOP* 14 (1960): 17–42.

Klassen, W. "**Kiss** (NT)." Pp. 4.89–92 in *AYBD*.

Klauck, H. J. *Allegorie und Allegorese in synoptischen Gleichnistexten*. NTAbh 13. Münster: Aschendorff, 1978.

———. *The Religious Context of Early Christianity.* SNTW. Edinburgh: T & T Clark, 2000.

Klausner, J. *Jesus of Nazareth: His Life, Times, and Teaching.* New York: Macmillan, 1929.

———. *The Messianic Idea in Israel: From Its Beginning to the Completion of the Mishnah.* New York: Macmillan, 1955.

Klijn, A. F. J. "The Question of the Rich Young Man in a Jewish-Christian Gospel." *NovT* 8 (1966): 149–55.

Kloner, A. "Did a Rolling Stone Close Jesus' Tomb?" *BAR* 25 (September–October 1999): 22–29, 76.

Kloppenborg, J. S. "Self-Help or *Deus Ex Machina* in Mark 12.9?" *NTS* 50 (2004): 495–518.

Klostermann, E. *Das Markusevangelium.* HNT 3. Tübingen: Mohr (Siebeck), 1950. [Cited as Klostermann]

Knabenbauer, J. *Commentarius in quatuor S. Evangelia Domini No. Jesu Christi. Vol. 2. Evangelium Secundum S. Marcum.* Paris: Sumptibus P. Lethielleux, 1894.

Knobloch, F. W. "Adoption." Pp. 1.76–79 in *AYBD.*

Knox, W. L. "The Ending of St. Mark's Gospel." *HTR* 35 (1942): 13–23.

Kobelski, P. J. *Melchizedek and Melchireša'.* CBQMS 10. Washington, D.C.: Catholic Biblical Association, 1981.

Koehler, L., and W. Baumgartner. *The Hebrew and Aramaic Lexicon of the Old Testament. Study Edition.* Leiden/Boston/Köln: Brill, 2001. [Cited as Koehler-Baumgartner]

Koester, H. "History and Development of Mark's Gospel (from Mark to Secret Mark and 'Canonical' Mark)." Pp. 35–57 in *Colloquy on New Testament Studies: A Time for Reappraisal and Fresh Approaches,* ed. B. Corley. Macon, Ga.: Mercer University Press, 1983.

Kohler, K. "Adoption." Pp. 1.206–8 in *JE.*

Kollmann, B. *Jesus und die Christen als Wundertäter. Studien zu Magie, Medizin und Schamanismus in Antike und Christentum.* FRLANT 170. Göttingen: Vandenhoeck & Ruprecht, 1996.

Kraeling, C. H. *The Synagogue.* The Execavations at Dura-Europos Conducted by Yale University and the French Academy of Inscriptions and Letters. Final Report VIII, Part I. New Haven: Yale University Press, 1956.

Kraft, R. A. "Was There a 'Messiah-Joshua' Tradition at the Turn of the Era?" 1992. Http://ccat.sas.upenn.edu/gopher/other/journals/kraftpub/Christianity/Joshua.

Kramer, D. *The Meanings of Death in Rabbinic Judaism.* London/New York: Routledge, 2000.

Kraus, H.-J. *Psalms: A Commentary.* Minneapolis: Augsburg, 1988–89.

Krause, D. "The One Who Comes Unbinding the Blessing of Judah: Mark 11.1–10 as a Midrash on Genesis 49.11, Zechariah 9.9, and Psalm 118.25–26." Pp. 141–53 in *Early Christian Interpretation of the Scriptures of Israel: Investigations and Proposals,* ed. C. A. Evans and J. A. Sanders. JSNTSup 148/Studies in Scripture in Early Judaism and Christianity 5. Sheffield: Sheffield Academic Press, 1996.

Kreitzer, L. J. *Striking New Images: Roman Imperial Coinage and the New Testament World.* JSNTSup 134. Sheffield: Sheffield Academic Press, 1996.

Kretschmar, G. "Die Geschichte des Taufgottesdienstes in der alten Kirche." Pp. 1–348 in *Der Taufgottesdienst.* Leiturgia 5. Kassel: Johannes Stauda-Verlag, 1970.

Kugel, J. L. *Traditions of the Bible: A Guide to the Bible as It Was at the Start of the Common Era.* Cambridge, Mass./London: Harvard University Press, 1998.

Kuhn, H.-W. "Der Gekreuzigte von Givʿat ha-Mivtar." Pp. 303–34 in *Theologia Crucis—*

Signum Crucis. Festschrift für Erich Dinkler zum 70. Geburtstag, ed. C. Andresen and G. Klein. Tübingen: Mohr (Siebeck), 1979.

———. "Die **Kreuzesstrafe** während der frühen Kaiserzeit. Ihre Wirklichkeit und Wertung in der Umwelt des Urchristentums." Pp. 2.25.1.648–793 in ANRW, 1982.

———. "Zum **Problem** des Verhältnisses der markinischen Redaktion zur israelitisch-jüdischen Tradition." Pp. 299–309 in *Tradition und Glaube: das frühe Christentum in seiner Umwelt. Festgabe für Karl Georg Kuhn zum 65. Geburtstag*, ed. G. Jeremias et al. Göttingen: Vandenhoeck & Ruprecht, 1971.

———. "Das **Reittier** Jesu in der Einzugsgeschichte des Markusevangeliums." ZNW 50 (1959): 82–91.

Kuhn, K. G. "**Jesus** in Gethsemane." Pp. 81–111 in *Redaktion und Theologie des Passionsberichtes nach den Synoptikern*. Wege der Forschung 481. Darmstadt: Wissenschaftliche Buchgesellschaft, 1981 (orig. 1952/53).

———. "New Light on **Temptation**, Sin, and Flesh in the New Testament." Pp. 94–113 in *The Scrolls and the New Testament*, ed. K. Stendahl. New York: Harper, 1957.

Kümmel, W. G. *Promise and Fulfillment: The Eschatological Message of Jesus*. London: SCM, 1957.

Künzi, M. *Das **Naherwartungslogion** Markus 9,1 par: Geschichte seiner Auslegung*. BGBE. Tübingen: Mohr (Siebeck), 1977.

Kurz, W. S. *Farewell Addresses in the New Testament*. Zaccheus Studies: New Testament. Collegeville, Minn.: Liturgical Press, 1990.

Kutsko, J. "**Caesarea Philippi**." P. 1.803 in *AYBD*.

Kvalvaag, R. W. "The **Spirit** in Human Beings in Some Qumran Non-Biblical Texts." Pp. 159–80 in *Qumran Between the Old and New Testaments*, ed. F. H. Cryer and T. L. Thompson. JSOTSup 290/Copenhagen International Seminar 6. Sheffield: Sheffield Academic Press, 1998.

Lagrange, M. J. *Évangile selon Saint Marc*. 2nd ed. Études Bibliques. Paris: Lecoffre, 1920 (orig. 1910). [Cited as **Lagrange**]

Lamarche, P. *Évangile de Marc*. EB. Paris: Editions J. Gabalda et Cie, 1996. [Cited as **Lamarche**]

Lampe, G. W. H. *A Patristic Greek Lexicon*. Oxford: Clarendon Press, 1961.

———. "St. Peter's **Denial**." BJRL 55 (1972–73): 346–68.

Lane, W. L. *The Gospel of Mark*. NICNT. Grand Rapids: Eerdmans, 1974. [Cited as **Lane**]

Lapin, H. "**Rabbi**." Pp. 5.600–2 in *AYBD*.

Latham, J. E. *The Religious **Symbolism** of Salt*. Théologie Historique 64. Paris: Éditions Beauchesne, 1982.

Laufen, R. *Die **Doppelüberlieferungen** der Logienquelle und des Markusevangeliums*. BBB 54. Bonn: Peter Hanstein Verlag, 1980.

Lauterbach, J. Z. *Mekilta de-Rabbi Ishmael*. Philadelphia: Jewish Publication Society, 1961 (orig. 1933–35). [Cited as **Lauterbach**]

Le Déaut, R. *La **nuit** pascale. Essai sur la signification de la Pâque juive à partir du Targum d'Exode XII 42*. AnBib 22. Rome: Biblical Institute Press, 1963.

Lee, G. M. "**Mark 14,72**: *epibalōn eklaien*." Bib 53 (1972): 411–12.

———. "**St. Mark Xiv. 72**: *epibalōn eklaien*." ExpT 61 (1949–50): 160.

Lehmann, K. *Auferweckt am dritten Tag nach der Schrift. Früheste Christologie, Bekenntnisbildung und Schriftauslegung im Lichte von 1 Kor. 15, 3–5*. QD 38. Freiburg/Basel/Wien: Herder, 1968.

Levenson, J. D. *The **Death** and Resurrection of the Beloved Son: The Transformation of Child Sacrifice in Judaism and Christianity*. New Haven/London: Yale, 1993.

Levine, L. I. *The Ancient Synagogue: The First Thousand Years.* New Haven/London: Yale University Press, 2000.

Lewis, C. T., and C. Short. *A Latin Dictionary Founded on Andrews' Edition of Freund's Latin Dictionary.* Oxford: Clarendon, 1879. [Cited as **Lewis and Short**].

Lewis, N. *Life in Egypt Under Roman Rule.* Oxford: Clarendon Press, 1983.

Leyerle, B. "**Meal Customs** in the Greco-Roman World." Pp. 29–61 in *Passover and Easter: Origin and History to Modern Times*, ed. P. F. Bradshaw. L. A. Hoffman. South Bend, Ind.: University of Notre Dame Press, 1999.

Liddell, H. G., R. Scott, and S. Jones. *A Greek-English Lexicon with a Supplement.* Oxford: Clarendon Press, 1968. [Cited as **LSJ**]

Liebers, R. *"Wie **geschrieben** steht": Studien zu einer besonderen Art frühchristlichen Schriftbezuges.* Berlin/New York: De Gruyter, 1993.

Lightfoot, J. B. *The Apostolic Fathers: Clement, Ignatius, and Polycarp.* Grand Rapids: Baker Book House, 1981 (orig. 1889–90).

———. *St. Paul's Epistles to the **Colossians** and Philemon.* Lynn, Mass.: Hendrickson Publishers, 1981 (orig. 1875).

Lightfoot, R. H. *The **Gospel Message** of St. Mark.* Oxford: Clarendon, 1950.

———. *History and Interpretation in the Gospels.* London: Hodder & Stoughton, 1935.

Lincoln, A. T. "The **Promise** and the Failure: Mark 16:7, 8." *JBL* 108 (1989): 283–300.

Lindars, B. *New Testament **Apologetic**: The Doctrinal Significance of the Old Testament Quotations.* Philadelphia: Westminster Press, 1961.

Linnemann, E. *Studien zur Passionsgeschichte.* FRLANT 102. Göttingen: Vandenhoeck & Ruprecht, 1970.

Loader, W. R. G. *Jesus' **Attitude** Towards the Law: A Study of the Gospels.* Tübingen: Mohr (Siebeck), 1997.

Lohmeyer, E. *Das Evangelium des Markus.* 11th ed. MeyerK. Göttingen: Vandenhoeck & Ruprecht, 1951 (orig. 1937). [Cited as **Lohmeyer**]

———. *Galiläa und Jerusalem.* FRLANT. Göttingen: Vandenhoeck & Ruprecht, 1936.

Lohse, E. "*Cheir, ktl.*" Pp. 9.424–37 in *TDNT* (1974).

Longenecker, R. N. *Paul: Apostle of Liberty.* New York/Evanston/London: Harper & Row, 1964.

Lövestam, E. "Die **Davidssohnfrage**." *SEÅ* 27 (1962): 72–82.

———. *Jesus and "**This Generation**": A New Testament Study.* ConBNT 25. Stockholm: Almqvist & Wiksell International, 1995.

———. *Spiritual **Wakefulness** in the New Testament.* LUÅ N.F. 1.55.3. Lund: CWK Gleerup, 1963.

Ludolphy, I. "Zur **Geschichte** der Auslegung des Evangelium infantium." Pp. 71–86 in *Taufe und neue Existenz*, ed. E. Schott. Berlin: Evangelische Verlagsanstalt, 1973.

Lührmann, D. *Das Markusevangelium.* HNT 3. Tübingen: Mohr (Siebeck), 1987. [Cited as **Lührmann**]

Lull, J., ed. *King **Richard III**.* The New Cambridge Shakespeare. Cambridge: Cambridge University Press, 1999.

Lust, J., et al. *A Greek-English **Lexicon** of the Septuagint.* 2 vols. Stuttgart: Deutsche Bibelgesellschaft, 1992–96.

Luz, U. *Matthew 21–28: A Commentary.* Hermeneia. Minneapolis: Fortress, 2005.

Ma'oz, Z. U. "Banias." In *NEAEHL* 1.136–43.

MacDonald, D. R. *The **Homeric Epics** and the Gospel of Mark.* New Haven/London: Yale University Press, 2000.

Mack, B. A *Myth of Innocence: Mark and Christian Origins.* Philadelphia: Fortress, 1988.

Madigan, K. "*Christus Nesciens*? Was Christ Ignorant of the Day of Judgment? Arian and Orthodox Interpretations of Mark 13:32 in the Ancient Latin West." *HTR* 96 (2003): 255–78.

Magness, J. "Ossuaries and the Burials of Jesus and James." *JBL* 124 (2005): 121–54.

Magness, J. L. *Sense and Absence: Structure and Suspension in the Ending of Mark's Gospel.* SBLSS. Atlanta: Scholars Press, 1986.

Mailer, N. *The Prisoner of Sex.* Boston/Toronto: Little, Brown, 1971.

Malbon, E. S. "Fallible Followers: Women and Men in the Gospel of Mark." *Semeia* 28 (1983): 29–48.

———. "The Poor Widow in Mark and Her Poor Rich Readers." *CBQ* 53 (1991): 589–604.

Malherbe, A. J. *The Cynic Epistles: A Study Edition.* SBLSBS. Missoula: Scholars Press, 1977.

Malina, B., and R. L. Rohrbaugh. *Social Science Commentary on the Synoptic Gospels.* Minneapolis: Fortress, 1992.

Maloney, E. C. *Semitic Interference in Marcan Syntax.* SBLDS 51. Chico: Scholars Press, 1981.

Malul, M. "Adoption of Foundlings in the Bible and Mesopotamian Documents: A Study of Some Legal Metaphors in Ezekiel 16.1–7." *JSOT* 46 (1990): 97–126.

Manson, T. W. "The Cleansing of the Temple." *BJRL* 33 (1951): 271–82.

Mantel, H. *Studies in the History of the Sanhedrin.* Cambridge, Mass.: Harvard University Press, 1961.

Marcus, J. "Authority to Forgive Sins Upon the Earth: The Shema in the Gospel of Mark." Pp. 196–211 in *The Gospels and the Scriptures of Israel,* ed. C. A. Evans and W. Stegner. JSNTSup 104/SSEJC 3. Sheffield: Sheffield Academic Press, 1994.

———. "The Beelzebul Controversy and the Eschatologies of Jesus." Pp. 247–77 in *Authenticating the Activities of Jesus,* ed. B. Chilton and C. A. Evans. Leiden/Boston/Köln: Brill, 1999.

———. "Crucifixion as Parodic Exaltation." *JBL* 125 (2006): 111–25.

———. "Entering Into the Kingly Power of God." *JBL* 107 (1986): 663–75.

———. "Idolatry in the New Testament." *Int* 60 (2006): 134–46.

———. "The Intertextual Polemic of the Markan Vineyard Parable." Pp. 211–27 in *Tolerance and Intolerance in Early Judaism and Christianity,* ed. G. N. Stanton and G. G. Stroumsa. Cambridge: Cambridge University Press, 1998.

———. "The Jewish War and the *Sitz im Leben* of Mark." *JBL* 111 (1992): 441–62.

———. "John the Baptist and Jesus." Pp. 1.179–97 in *When Judaism and Christianity Began: Essays in Memory of Anthony J. Saldarini,* ed. A. J. Avery-Peck, D. Harrington, and J. Neusner. Supplements to the Journal for the Study of Judaism. Leiden/Boston: Brill, 2004.

———. "Mark 14:61: Are You the Messiah-Son-of-God?" *NovT* 31 (1988): 125–41.

———. "Mark 4:10–12 and Marcan Epistemology." *JBL* 103 (1984): 557–74.

———. "Mark—Interpreter of Paul." *NTS* 46 (2000): 1–15.

———. *The Mystery of the Kingdom of God.* SBLDS 90. Atlanta: Scholars Press, 1986.

———. "A Note on Markan Optics." *NTS* 45 (1999): 250–56.

———. "Rivers of Living Water from Jesus' Belly (John 7:38)." *JBL* 117 (1998): 328–30.

———. "The Role of Scripture in the Gospel Passion Narratives." Pp. 205–33 in *The Death of Jesus in Early Christianity,* ed. J. T. Carroll and J. B. Green. Peabody, Mass.: Hendrickson, 1995.

———. "**Son of Man** as Son of Adam." *RB* 110 (2003): 1–24, 370–86.

———. *The* **Way** *of the Lord: Christological Exegesis of the Old Testament in the Gospel of Mark.* Louisville/Edinburgh: Westminster John Knox/T & T Clark, 1992.

Margulies, M. *Midrash* **Wayyikra Rabbah***: A Critical Edition Based on Manuscripts and Genizah Fragments with Variants and Notes.* Jerusalem: Wahrmann Books, 1972.

Marshall, C. D. **Faith** *as a Theme in Mark's Narrative.* SNTSMS 64. Cambridge: Cambridge University Press, 1989.

Marshall, I. H. *The Gospel of* **Luke***: A Commentary on the Greek Text.* NIGTC. Exeter/Grand Rapids: Paternoster/Eerdmans, 1978.

Martin, D. B. **Slavery** *as Salvation: The Metaphor of Slavery in Pauline Christianity.* New Haven/London: Yale University Press, 1990.

Martin, E. L. **Secrets** *of Golgotha: The Forgotten History of Christ's Crucifixion.* Alhambra, Calif.: Ask Publications, 1988.

Martin, L. "**Date Setters**." *Guardian of Truth* (1994). Http://www.bible.ca/pre-date -setters.htm.

Martin, T. W. "**Watch** During the Watches (Mark 13:35)." *JBL* 120 (2001): 685–701.

Martola, N. "**Eating** the Passover Lamb in House-Temples in Alexandria." *Jewish Studies in a New Europe: Proceedings of the Fifth Congress of Jewish Studies in Copenhagen 1994 Under the Auspices of the European Association for Jewish Studies* (1994), 521–31.

Martyn, J. L. **Galatians***: A New Translation with Introduction and Commentary.* AYB 33A. New York: Doubleday, 1997; reprint, New Haven: Yale University Press.

———. *The* **Gospel** *of John in Christian History: Essays for Interpreters.* Theological Inquiries. New York: Paulist, 1978.

———. **History** *and Theology in the Fourth Gospel.* 3rd ed. Louisville/London: Westminster John Knox, 2003.

———. "A Law-Observant **Mission** to Gentiles." Pp. 7–24 in *Theological Issues in the Letters of Paul.* SNTW. Edinburgh/Nashville: T & T Clark/Abingdon, 1997.

Maslen, M. W., and P. D. Mitchell. "**Medical Theories** on the Cause of Death in Crucifixion." *Journal of the Royal Society of Medicine* 99 (2006): 185–88.

Matera, F. J. *The* **Kingship** *of Jesus: Composition and Theology in Mark 15.* SBLDS 66. Chico: Scholars Press, 1982.

Maurer, C. "**Hypnos***, ktl.*" Pp. 8.545–58 in *TDNT* (1972).

McArthur, H. K. "On the **Third Day**." *NTS* 18 (1971): 81–86.

McCane, B. R. "**Jews, Christians, and Burial** in Roman Palestine." Ph.D. diss. Duke, 1992.

———. *Roll Back the* **Stone***: Death and Burial in the World of Jesus.* Harrisburg, Pa./London/New York: Trinity Press International, 2003.

McDowell, J. **Evidence** *That Demands a Verdict: Historical Evidences for the Christian Faith.* San Bernardino, Calif.: Campus Crusade for Christ International, 1972.

McKelvey, R. J. "Christ the **Cornerstone**." *NTS* 8 (1961–62): 352–59.

———. *The* **New Temple***: The Church in the New Testament.* Oxford Theological Monographs. London: Oxford University Press, 1969.

McLaren, J. S. **Power and Politics** *in Palestine: The Jews and the Governing of Their Land 100 BC–AD 70.* JSNTSup 63. Sheffield: JSOT Press, 1991.

McNamara, M. *The* **New Testament** *and the Palestinian Targum to the Pentateuch.* AnBib 27. Rome: Pontifical Biblical Institute, 1966.

McVey, K. E. **Ephrem** *the Syrian: Hymns.* CWS. New York/Mahwah: Paulist Press, 1989.

Meeks, W. A. *The First Urban Christians: The Social World of the Apostle Paul.* New Haven/London: Yale University Press, 1983.

———. "The Image of the Androgyne: Some Uses of a Symbol in Earliest Christianity." *Journal of the History of Religions* 13 (1973): 165–208.

———. "Moses as God and King." Pp. 354–71 in *Religions in Antiquity: Essays in Memory of Erwin Ramsdell Goodenough*, ed. J. Neusner. Studies in the History of Religions 14. Leiden: Brill, 1968.

———. *The Prophet-King: Moses Traditions and the Johannine Christology.* NovTSup 14. Leiden: Brill, 1967.

Meggitt, J. J. *Paul, Poverty and Survival.* SNTW. Edinburgh: T & T Clark, 1998.

Meier, J. P. "From Elijah-Like Prophet to Royal Davidic Messiah." Pp. 45–83 in *Jesus: A Colloquium in the Holy Land*, ed. D. Donnelly. New York/London: Continuum, 2001.

———. "The Historical Jesus and the Historical Herodians." *JBL* 119 (2000): 740–46.

———. *A Marginal Jew: Rethinking the Historical Jesus.* AYBRL. New York: Doubleday, 1991– ; reprint, New Haven: Yale University Press.

Mendels, D. *The Rise and Fall of Jewish Nationalism: Jewish and Christian Ethnicity in Ancient Palestine.* AYBRL. New York: Doubleday, 1992; reprint, New Haven: Yale University Press.

Merkel, H. "Peter's Curse." Pp. 66–71 in *The Trial of Jesus: Cambridge Studies in Honour of C. F. D. Moule*, ed. E. Bammel. SBT Second Series 14. London: SCM, 1970.

Meshorer, Y. *Ancient Jewish Coinage.* Dix Hills, N.Y.: Amphora Books, 1982.

Metzger, B. M. "Names for the Nameless in the New Testament: A Study in the Growth of Christian Tradition." Pp. 79–99 in *Kyriakon. Festschrift Johannes Quasten*, ed. Patrick Granfield and Josef A. Jungmann. Münster: Aschendorff, 1970.

———. *A Textual Commentary on the Greek New Testament.* London/New York: United Bible Societies, 1971. [Cited as Metzger]

Meye, R. P. *Jesus and the Twelve: Discipleship and Revelation in Mark's Gospel.* Grand Rapids: Eerdmans, 1968.

Meyer, E. *Forschungen zur alten Geschichte.* Halle: Max Niemeyer, 1892.

Meyer, L. V. "Remnant." Pp. 5.669–71 in *AYBD*.

Meyer, M. W. "Mystery Religions." Pp. 4.941–45 in *AYBD*.

Meyers, C. L., and E. Meyers. *Zechariah 9–14: A New Translation with Introduction and Commentary.* AYB 25C. New York: Doubleday, 1993; reprint, New Haven: Yale University Press.

Meyers, E. M. *Jewish Ossuaries: Reburial and Rebirth. Secondary Burials in Their Ancient Near Eastern Setting.* BibOr 24. Rome: Biblical Institutes Press, 1971.

Michaelis, W. "Myron, Myrizō." Pp. 4.800–1 in *TDNT* (1967; orig. 1942).

Michel, O. *Mikros, ktl.* Pp. 4.648–59 in *TDNT* (1967; orig. 1942).

———. "Eine philologische Frage zur Einzugsgeschichte." *NTS* 6 (1959): 81–82.

Mihailov, G. *Inscriptiones Graecae in Bulgaria Repertae.* Vol. 2: *Inscriptiones Inter Danubium et Haemum Repertae.* Series Epigraphica 5. Sofia: Academia Litterarum Bulgarica. Institutum Archaeologicum, 1958.

Milgrom, J. *Leviticus: A New Translation with Introduction and Commentary.* 3 vols. AYB 3A, 3B, and 3C. New York: Doubleday, 1991–2001; reprint, New Haven: Yale University Press.

Milikowsky, C. "Elijah and the Messiah [Hebrew]." *Jerusalem Studies in Jewish Thought* 2 (1982–83): 491–96.

Millar, F. *The Roman Near East* 31 BC–AD 337. Cambridge, Mass./London: Harvard University Press, 1993.

Miller, S. *Women in Mark's Gospel*. JSNTSup 259. London/New York: T & T Clark International, 2004.

Minear, P. "The **Needles's Eye**." *JBL* 61 (1942): 157–69.

Moloney, F. J. *The Gospel of Mark: A Commentary*. Peabody, Mass.: Hendrickson, 2002. [Cited as **Moloney**]

———. "The **Johannine Paraclete** and Jesus." Pp. 213–28 in *Dummodo Christus annuntietur: studi in onore del Prof. Jozef Heriban*, ed. A. Strus and R. Blatnicky. Rome: LAS, 1998.

Moo, D. J. *The Old Testament in the Gospel Passion Narratives*. Sheffield: Almond, 1983.

Moore, C. A. *Tobit: A New Translation with Introduction and Commentary*. AYB 40A. New York: Doubleday, 1996; reprint, New Haven: Yale University Press.

Moore, G. F. *Judaism in the First Centuries of the Christian Era*. New York: Schocken, 1971 (orig. 1927–30). [Cited as **Moore**]

Morgan, M. A. *Sepher Ha-Razim*. Texts and Translations 25. Pseudepigrapha Series 11. Chico: Scholars Press, 1983.

Morray-Jones, C. R. A. "Transformational **Mysticism** in the Apocalyptic-Merkabah Tradition." *JJS* 43 (1992): 1–31.

Motyer, S. "The **Rending** of the Veil: A Markan Pentecost?" *NTS* 33 (1987): 155–57.

Moule, C. F. D. *An Idiom Book of New Testament Greek*. 2nd ed. Cambridge: Cambridge University Press, 1959.

Moulton, J. H. "*Skandalon*." *ExpT* 26 (1914–15): 331–32.

———, et al. *A Grammar of New Testament Greek*. 4 vols. Edinburgh: T & T Clark, 1908–65. [Cited as **MHT**]

———, and G. Milligan. *The Vocabulary of the Greek Testament*. Grand Rapids: Eerdmans, 1930. [Cited as **M-M**]

Mowinckel, S. *He That Cometh*. Nashville: Abingdon, 1954.

Mudiso Mbâ Mundla, J.-G. *Jesus und die Führer Israels. Studien zu den sog. Jerusalemer Streitgesprächen*. NTAbh N.F. 17. Münster: Aschendorff, 1984.

Müller, P. *Anfänge der Paulusschule. Dargestellt am zweiten Thessalonicherbrief und am Kolosserbrief*. Zürich: Theologischer Verlag, 1988.

———. *In der Mitte der Gemeinde. Kinder im Neuen Testament*. Neukirchen-Vluyn: Neukirchener Verlag, 1992.

———. *'Wer ist dieser?' Jesus im Markusevangelium. Markus als Erzähler, Verkündiger und Lehrer*. Biblisch-Theologische Studien 27. Neukirchen-Vluyn: Neukirchener, 1995.

Murphy-O'Connor, J. *The Holy Land: An Oxford Archaeological Guide from Earliest Times to 1700*. 4th ed. Oxford Archaeological Guides. Oxford/New York: Oxford University Press, 1998.

Mussies, G. "The **Use** of Hebrew and Aramaic in the Greek New Testament." *NTS* 30 (1984): 416–32.

Mussner, F. *Der Galaterbrief*. HTKNT 9. Freiburg/Basel/Wien: Herder, 1981.

Myers, C. *Binding the Strong Man: A Political Reading of Mark's Story of Jesus*. Maryknoll, N.Y.: Orbis, 1988.

Myers, J. M. *I and II Esdras: Introduction, Translation and Commentary*. Garden City, N.Y.: Doubleday, 1974.

Myllykoski, M. *Die letzten Tage Jesus. Markus und Johannes, ihre Traditionen und die his-*

torische Frage. AASF Series B, Vol. 256. Helsinki: Suomalainen Tiedeakatemia, 1991.

Nardoni, E. "A **Redactional Interpretation** of Mark 9:1." *CBQ* 43 (1981): 365–84.

Naveh, J., and S. Shaked. ***Magic Spells*** *and Formulae: Aramaic Incantations of Late Antiquity.* Jerusalem: Magnes Press, 1993.

Neirynck, F. ***Duality*** *in Mark: Contributions to the Study of the Markan Redaction.* BETL 31. Leuven: Leuven University Press, 1972.

———. "La **fuite** du jeune homme en Mc 14,51–52." *ETL* 55 (1979): 43–66.

———. "Marc 16,1–8: Tradition et rédaction. **Tombeau** vide et angélophanie." Pp. 239–72 in *Evangelica.* Leuven: Leuven University Press, 1982.

———. "*TIS ESTIN HO PAISAS SE.*" Mt 26,68/Lk 22,64 (Diff. Mk 14,65)." *ETL* 63 (1987): 5–17.

Nestle, E. "Die unverfälschte köstliche **Narde.**" *ZNW* 3 (1902): 169–71.

Neusner, J. ***Sifra***: *An Analytical Translation.* BJS 138–40. Providence, R.I.: Brown University Press, 1988.

———. ***Sifre*** *to Deuteronomy: An Analytical Translation.* 2 vols. BJS 98, 101. Atlanta: Scholars Press, 1987.

———. *The* ***Talmud*** *of the Land of Israel: A Preliminary Translation and Explanation.* 35 vols. Chicago/London: University of Chicago Press, 1982–95.

———. *The* ***Tosefta***. *Translated from the Hebrew with a New Introduction.* 2 vols. Peabody, Mass.: Hendrickson, 2002.

Newsom, C. ***Songs*** *of the Sabbath Sacrifice: A Critical Edition.* HSS. Atlanta: Scholars Press, 1985.

Nickelsburg, G. W. E. *1* ***Enoch*** *1.* Hermeneia. Minneapolis: Fortress, 2001.

———. "**Enoch, Levi, and Peter**: Recipients of Revelation in Upper Galilee." *JBL* 100 (1981): 575–600.

———. ***Resurrection***, *Immortality, and Eternal Life in Intertestamental Judaism.* HTS 26. Cambridge, Mass.: Harvard University, 1972.

Niebuhr, K.-W. "4Q 521,2 II—ein eschatologischer **Psalm.**" Pp. 151–68 in *Mogilany 1995: Papers on the Dead Sea Scrolls Offered in Memory of Aleksy Klawek,* ed. Z. J. Kapera. Qumranica Mogilanensia. Kraków, 1996.

Niederwimmer, K. *The* ***Didache***: *A Commentary.* Hermeneia. Minneapolis: Fortress, 1998.

Nielsen, E. *The* ***Ten Commandments*** *in New Perspective: A Traditio-Historical Approach.* SBT. London: SCM, 1968.

Nineham, D. E. *Saint Mark.* Pelican New Testament Commentaries. Middlesex: Penguin, 1963. [Cited as **Nineham**]

Noack, W. "**Salt** as a Metaphor in Instructions for Discipleship." *ST* 6 (1952): 165–78.

Nolland, John. "**Sib. Or. III.265–94.**" *JTS* 30 (1979): 158–66.

Nützel, J. M. *Die* ***Verklärungserzählung*** *im Markusevangelium.* FB 6. Würzburg: Echter, 1973.

O'Connor, F. "**Everything** That Rises Must Converge." Pp. 405–20 in *The Complete Stories.* New York: Farrar, Straus and Giroux, 1979.

O'Connor, M. "Biblical Hebrew **Lexicography**: *Tp* 'Children, Dependents' in Biblical and Qumranic Hebrew." *Journal of Northwest Semitic Languages* 25 (1999): 25–40.

Oden, T. C., and C. A. Hall, eds. *Mark.* Ancient Christian Commentary on Scripture. New Testament 2. Downers Grove, Ill.: InterVarsity Press, 1998. [Cited as **Oden and Hall**]

Oepke, A. "***Baptō, ktl.***" Pp. 1.529–46 in *TDNT* (1964; orig. 1933).

Öhler, M. "Die **Verklärung** (Mk 9:1–8): die Ankunft der Herrschaft Gottes auf der Erde." *NovT* 38 (1996): 197–217.

Olson, K. A. "**Eusebius** and the Testimonium Flavianum." *CBQ* 61 (1999): 305–22.

Orlov, A. A. "**Vested** with Adam's Glory: Moses as the Luminous Counterpart of Adam in the Dead Sea Scrolls and in the Macarian Homilies." *Xristianskij Vostok* 4 (2002): 740–55.

Osborne, B. A. E. "**Peter**: Stumbling-Block and Satan." *NovT* 15 (1973): 187–90.

Otto, R. *The* **Idea** *of the Holy: An Inquiry Into the Non-Rational Factor in the Idea of the Divine and Its Relation to the Rational.* London: Oxford University Press, 1929.

Overman, J. A. **Matthew's Gospel** *and Formative Judaism: The Social World of the Matthean Community.* Minneapolis: Fortress, 1990.

Owen, O. T. "**One Hundred and Fifty Three Fishes**." *ExpT* 100 (1988–89): 52–54.

Paesler, K. *Das* **Tempelwort** *Jesu. Die Traditionen von Tempelzerstörung und Tempeler-neuerung im Neuen Testament.* FRLANT 184. Göttingen: Vandenhoeck & Ruprecht, 1999.

Partington, A. *The Oxford* **Dictionary** *of Quotations.* Oxford/New York: Oxford University Press, 1992.

Patsch, H. "**Potērion**." Pp. 3.141–42 in *EDNT*, 1993.

Pattengale, J. A. "**Arimathea**." P. 1.378 in *AYBD*.

Patterson, O. **Slavery** *and Social Death: A Comparative Study.* Cambridge, Mass./London: Harvard University Press, 1982.

Payne Smith, R. A *Compendious Syriac Dictionary.* Winona Lake, Ind.: Eisenbrauns, 1998 (orig. 1903). [Cited as **Payne Smith**]

Penn, M. P. " 'With a Chaste and Closed **Mouth**': Kissing, Social Boundaries, and Early Christian Communities." Ph.D. dissertation. Duke University, Graduate Program in Religion, 1999.

Perella, N. J. *The* **Kiss** *Sacred and Profane: An Interpretative History of Kiss Symbolism and Related Religio-Erotic Themes.* Berkeley/Los Angeles: University of California Press, 1969.

Perrin, N. "The **Christology** of Mark: A Study in Methodology." Pp. 125–40 in *The Interpretation of Mark*, 2nd ed., ed. W. Telford. Studies in New Testament Interpretation. Philadelphia: Fortress, 1985 (orig. 1971).

———. **Rediscovering** *the Teaching of Jesus.* New York: Harper & Row, 1976 (orig. 1967).

———. "Towards an **Interpretation** of the Gospel of Mark." Pp. 1–78 in *Christology and a Modern Pilgrimage: A Discussion with Norman Perrin.* Ed. H. D. Betz. Claremont: The New Testament Colloquium, 1971.

———, and D. C. Duling. *The New Testament: An* **Introduction**. *Proclamation and Parenesis, Myth and History.* 2d ed. New York: Harcourt Brace Jovanovich, 1982.

Pesch, R. *Das Markusevangelium.* HTKNT 2. Freiburg: Herder, 1976. [Cited as **Pesch**]

———. **Naherwartungen**. *Tradition und Redaktion in Mk 13.* Kommentare und Beiträge zum Alten und Neuen Testament. Düsseldorf: Patmos, 1968.

Pfeiderer, O. "Über die **Composition** der eschatologischer Rede, Mt. 24.4ff." *Jahrbuch für deutsche Theologie* 13 (1868): 134–49.

Philipson, D. "**Blessing of Children**." P. 243 in *JE*, 1902.

Phillips, L. Edward. *The* **Ritual Kiss** *in Early Christian Worship.* Joint Liturgical Studies 36. Cambridge: Grove Books, 1996.

Pitre, B. **Jesus**, *the Tribulation, and the End of the Exile.* WUNT 2.Reihe 204. Tübingen/Grand Rapids: Mohr (Siebeck)/Baker, 2005.

Pommier, J. "Société **Ernest Renan**. Seance Du 27 Mars 1920." *Revue de l'histoire des religions* 81 (1920): 203–11.

Pope, M. H. "Bible, **Euphemism** and Dysphemism in the." Pp. 1.720–25 in *AYBD*.

Pope-Hennessy, J. *Raphael: The Wrightsman Lectures*. London: Phaidon, 1970.

Popkes, W. *Christus Traditus. Eine Untersuchung zum Begriff der Dahingabe im Neuen Testament*. ATANT 49. Zürich/Stuttgart: Zwingli Verlag, 1967.

Price, J. *Jerusalem Under Siege: The Collapse of the Jewish State 66–70 C.E.* Brill's Series in Jewish Studies 4. Leiden/New York/Köln: Brill, 1992.

Price, S. R. F. *Rituals and Power: The Roman Imperial Cult in Asia Minor*. Cambridge: Cambridge University Press, 1984.

Puech, É. "Une **apocalypse** messianique (4Q521)." *RevQ* 15 (1992): 475–522.

———. "Some **Remarks** on 4Q246 and 4Q521 and Qumran Messianism." Pp. 545–65 in *The Provo International Conference on the Dead Sea Scrolls: Technological Innovations, New Texts, and Reformulated Issues*, ed. D. W. Parry and E. Ulrich. Studies on the Texts of the Desert of Judah 30. Leiden/Boston/Köln: Brill, 1999.

Rahlfs, A. *Septuaginta id est Vetus Testamentum graece iuxta LXX interpretes*. Stuttgart: Deutsche Bibelgesellschaft, 1935.

Rahmani, L. Y. A *Catalogue* of Jewish Ossuaries in the Collections of the State of Israel. Jerusalem: Israel Antiquities Authority/Israel Academy of Sciences and Humanities, 1994.

Räisänen, H. *The "Messianic Secret" in Mark's Gospel*. SNTW. Edinburgh: T & T Clark, 1990. [Cited as **Räisänen**]

Ramsay, W. M. *Cities and Bishoprics of Phrygia*. Oxford: At the Clarendon Press, 1895.

Reardon, B. P., ed. *Collected Ancient Greek Novels*. Berkeley/Los Angeles/London: University of California Press, 1989.

Reich, R. "**Caiaphas Name** Inscribed on Bone Boxes." *BAR* 18 (1992): 40–44, 76.

Reif, S. C. *Judaism and Hebrew Prayer: New Perspectives on Jewish Liturgical History*. Cambridge: Cambridge University Press, 1993.

Reimarus, H. S. *Fragments*. Scholars Press Reprints and Translations Series. Chico: Scholars Press, 1985 (orig. 1779).

Reinbold, W. *Der älteste* **Bericht** *über den Tod Jesu*. BZAW 69. Berlin/New York: De Gruyter, 1994.

Reinhold, M. "**History** of Purple as a Status Symbol in Antiquity." *Latomus* 116 (1970): 5–73.

Reiser, M. *Jesus and Judgment: The Eschatological Proclamation in Its Jewish Context*. Minneapolis: Fortress, 1997.

Reitzenstein, R. *Hellenistic* **Mystery-Religions**: *Their Basic Ideas and Significance*. PTMS 15. Pittsburgh: Pickwick Press, 1978 (orig. 1926).

Rengstorf, K. H. *The Complete* **Concordance** *to Flavius Josephus. Study Edition*. 2 vols. Leiden: Brill, 2002.

———. "**Doulos, ktl.**" Pp. 2.261–83 in *TDNT* (1964; orig. 1935).

———. "**Hamartōlos, ktl.**" Pp. 1.317–35 in *TDNT* (1964; orig. 1933).

———. "Die **stolai** der Schriftgelehrten." Pp. 383–404 *in Abraham unser Vater: Juden und Christen im Gespräch über die Bibel. Festschrift für Otto Michel zum 60. Geburtstag*, ed. O. Betz, M. Hengel, and P. Schmidt. Leiden/Köln: Brill, 1963.

Reploh, K. G. *Markus,* **Lehrer** *der Gemeinde*. SBM 9. Stuttgart: Katholisches Bibelwerk, 1969.

Richard, S. L. "**Fuller**." P. 323 in *HBD*.

Riesenfeld, H. *Jésus transfiguré*. Acta Seminarii Neotestamentici Upsaliensis 17. Copenhagen: Munksgaard, 1947.

Robbins, V. K. "The Healing of Blind **Bartimaeus** (10:46–52) in the Markan Theology." Pp. 37–58 in *New Boundaries in Old Territory: Form and Social Rhetoric in Mark*, ed. D. B. Gowler. Emory Studies in Early Christianity 3. New York: Peter Lang, 1994 (orig. 1973).

Robertson, A. T. *A Grammar of the Greek New Testament in the Light of Historical Research*. Nashville: Broadman Press, 1934 (orig. 1914). [Cited as **Robertson**]

Robinson, J. M. "**Jesus**: From Easter to Valentinus (or to the Apostle's Creed)." *JBL* 101 (1982): 5–37.

Robinson, R. *Plato's Earlier **Dialectic***. New York & London: Garland, 1980.

Rochais, G. *Les **récits** de résurrection des morts dans le Nouveau Testament*. SNTSMS 40. Cambridge: Cambridge University Press, 1981.

Roh, T. *Die **familia dei** in den synoptischen Evangelien*. NTOA 37. Freiburg/Göttingen: Universitätsverlag Freiburg/Vandenhoeck & Ruprecht, 2001.

Rordorf, W. "La **vigne** et le vin dans la tradition juive et chrétienne." Pp. 493–508 in *Liturgie, foi et vie des premiers chrétiens. Études patristiques*. Théologie historique 75. Paris: Beauchesne, 1986 (orig. 1971).

Ross, J. F. "**Wine**." Pp. 4.849–52 in *IDB*, 1962.

Rossé, G. *The **Cry** of Jesus on the Cross: A Biblical and Theological Study*. Mahwah, N.J.: Paulist Press, 1987.

Rostovtzeff, M. *The Social and Economic **History** of the Roman Empire*. Oxford: Clarendon Press, 1926.

Roth, C. "Messianic **Symbols** in Palestinian Archaeology." *PEQ* (1955), 151–64.

Routledge, R. "**Passover** and Last Supper." *TynBul* 53 (2002): 203–21.

Rubenstein, J. L. *The History of **Sukkot** in the Second Temple and Rabbinic Periods*. BJS 302. Atlanta: Scholars Press, 1995.

———. "The **Symbolism** of the *Sukkah*." *Judaism* 43 (1994): 371–87.

Rubin, N., and A. Kosman. "The **Clothing** of the Primordial Adam as a Symbol of Apocalyptic Time in the Midrashic Sources." *HTR* 90 (1997): 155–74.

Rudolph, W. "**Zu Mal 2.10–16**." *ZAW* 93 (1981): 85–90.

Runnalls, D. "The **King** as Temple Builder: A Messianic Typology." Pp. 15–37 in *Spirit Within Structure: Essays in Honor of George Johnston on the Occasion of His Seventieth Birthday*, ed. E. J. Furcha. Allison Park, Pa.: Pickwick Publications, 1983.

Ruzer, S. "The Double **Love** Precept in the New Testament and in the Rule of the Congregation [Heb]." *Tarbiz* 71 (2002): 353–70.

Saldarini, A. J. "**Sanhedrin**." Pp. 5.975–80 in *AYBD*.

Sanders, E. P. *Jesus and Judaism*. Philadelphia: Fortress, 1985.

———. *Judaism: Practice and Belief 63 BCE–66 CE*. London/Philadelphia: SCM/Trinity Press International, 1992.

———. *Paul and Palestinian Judaism: A Comparison of Patterns of Religion*. Philadelphia: Fortress, 1977.

Sanders, J. T. *The Jews in Luke–Acts*. Philadelphia: Fortress, 1987.

Sandnes, Karl Olav. "**Imitatio Homeri**? An Appraisal of Dennis R. MacDonald's 'Mimesis Criticism'." *JBL* 124 (2005): 715–32.

Sariola, H. *Markus und das **Gesetz**. Eine redaktionskritische Untersuchung*. Annales Academiae Scientiarum Feunicae Dissertationes Humanarum Litteratum 56. Helsinki: Suomalainen Tiedeakatemia, 1990.

Sasson, J. M. *Jonah: A New Translation with Introduction, Commentary, and Interpreta-*

tion. AYB 24B. New York: Doubleday, 1990; reprint, New Haven: Yale University Press.

Schaberg, J. "**Daniel 7–12** and the New Testament Passion-Resurrection Predictions." *NTS* (1985), 208–22.

Schaeffer, S. E. "The '*Gospel of Peter*,' the Canonical Gospels, and Oral Tradition." Ph.D. dissertation. Union Theological Seminary, 1991.

Schäfer, P. *Die **Vorstellung** vom heiligen Geist in der rabbinischen Literatur.* SANT 28. München: Kösel, 1972.

Schenke, L. *Auferstehungsverkündigung und leeres Grab. Eine traditionsgeschichtliche Untersuchung von Mk 16,1–8.* SBS 33. Stuttgart: Verlag Katholisches Bibelwerk, 1968.

———. *Studien zur Passionsgeschichte des Markus. Tradition und Redaktion in Markus 14,1–42.* FB 4. Würzburg: Echter Verlag, 1971.

Schereschewsky, B. "**Bigamy** and Polygamy." In *EncJud*, CD-ROM Edition.

Schlatter, A. *Die Evangelien nach Markus und Lukas.* Stuttgart: Calwer, 1947.

Schlosser, J. *Le règne de Dieu dans les dits de Jesus.* EBib. Paris: J. Gabalda, 1980.

Schmidt, D. "The LXX **Gattung** 'Prophetic Correlative'." *JBL* 96 (1977): 517–22.

Schmidt, K. L. "**Kollaō**, *proskollaō*." Pp. 3.822–23 in *TDNT* (1965; orig. 1938).

Schmidt, T. E. *Hostility to Wealth in the Synoptic Gospels.* JSNTSup. Sheffield: Sheffield Academic Press, 1987.

———. "**Mark 15.16–32**: The Crucifixion Narrative and the Roman Triumphal Procession." *NTS* 41 (1995): 1–18.

Schmithals, W. *Das Evangelium nach Markus.* Ökumenischer Taschenbuchkommentar Zum Neuen Testament. Gütersloh/Würzburg: Mohn/Echter, 1979. [Cited as **Schmithals**]

———. "Der **Markusschluss**, die Verklärungsgeschichte und die Aussendung der Zwölf." *ZTK* 69 (1972): 379–411.

Schnackenburg, R. *The Gospel According to St. John.* New York: Crossroad, 1968–82. [Cited as **Schnackenburg**]

Schneck, R. *Isaiah in the Gospel of Mark, I–VIII.* Bibal Dissertation Series 1. Vallejo, Calif.: Bibal, 1994.

Schneider, Carl. "**Katapetasma**." Pp. 3.628–70 in *TDNT* (1965; orig. 1938).

———. "**Kathēmai**, *ktl.*" Pp. 3.440–4 in *TDNT* (1965; orig. 1938).

Schneider, G. "**Episkiazō**." Pp. 2.34–35 in *EDNT*.

Schoeps, H. J. *Paul: The Theology of the Apostle in the Light of Jewish Religious History.* Philadelphia: Westminster Press, 1961.

Schonfield, H. J. *The Passover Plot.* New York: Bantam, 1965.

Schrage, W. "**Typhlos**, *ktl.*" Pp. 8.270–94 in *TDNT* (1972).

Schremer, A. "**Divorce** in Papyrus Ṣe'elim 13 Once Again: A Reply to Tal Ilan." *HTR* 91 (1998): 193–202.

Schrenk, G. "**Leimma**, *ktl.*" Pp. 4.194–214 in *TDNT* (1967; orig. 1942).

———. "**Thelō**, *ktl.*" Pp. 3.44–62 in *TDNT* (1965; orig. 1938).

Schröger, F. "**Kathizō**." Pp. 2.24–25 in *EDNT*, 1991.

Schürer, E. *The History of the Jewish People in the Age of Jesus Christ (175 B.C.–A.D. 135),* ed. G. Vermes, F. Millar, and M. Goodman. Edinburgh: T & T Clark, 1973–87. [Cited as **Schürer**]

Schwankl, O. *Die **Sadduzäerfrage** (Mk 12, 18–27 parr.). Eine exegetisch-theologische Studie zur Auferstehungserwartung.* BBB 66. Frankfurt am Main: Athenäum, 1987.

Schwartz, D. R. "Did the Jews Practice **Infant Exposure** and Infanticide in Antiquity?" *Studia Philonica Annual* 16 (2004): 61–95.

———. "**Law** and Truth: On Qumran-Sadducean and Rabbinic Views of Law." Pp. 229–40 in *The Dead Sea Scrolls: Forty Years of Research*, ed. D. Dimant and U. Rappaport. Leiden: Brill, 1992.

———. "Pontius **Pilate**." Pp. 5.395–401 in *AYBD*.

———. "**Temple** and Desert: On Religion and State in Second Temple Period Judaea." Pp. 29–43 in *Studies in the Jewish Background of Christianity*. WUNT 60. Tübingen: Mohr (Siebeck), 1992 (orig. 1987).

———. "The **Three Temples** of 4QFlorilegium." *RevQ* 10 (1979): 83–91.

———. "**Whence** the Voice? A Response to Bruce W. Longenecker." *JSJ* 31 (2000): 42–46.

Schwartz, S. *Josephus and Judaean Politics*. Columbia Studies in the Classical Tradition 18. Leiden: Brill, 1990.

Schwarz, G. " 'Und er **begann** zu weinen'? (Markus 14, 72)." *BN* 78 (1995): 18–20.

Schweitzer, A. *The **Quest** of the Historical Jesus: First Complete Edition*. Minneapolis: Fortress, 2001 (orig. 1901).

Schweizer, E. *The Good News According to Mark*. Atlanta: John Knox, 1970. [Cited as **Schweizer**]

———. "**Scheidungsrecht** der jüdischen Frau? Weibliche Jünger Jesu." *EvT* 42 (1982): 294–300.

———, et al. "**Huois**, *huiothesia*." Pp. 8.363–92 in *TDNT* (1972).

———, et al. "**Psychē**, *ktl.*" Pp. 9.608–66 in *TDNT* (1974).

Schwemer, A. M. "**Antijudaismus** in der Markuspassion?" *TBei* 32 (2001): 6–25.

Schwier, H. *Tempel und Tempelzerstörung. Untersuchungen zu den theologischen und ideologischen Faktoren im ersten jüdisch-römischen Krieg (66–74 n. Chr.)*. NTOA 11. Göttingen: Vandehoeck & Ruprecht, 1989.

Scott, J. C. *Domination and the Arts of Resistance: Hidden Transcripts*. New Haven/London: Yale University Press, 1990.

Scroggs, R. *The **Last Adam**: A Study in Pauline Anthropology*. Oxford: Blackwell, 1966.

———, and K. I. Groff. "**Baptism** in Mark: Dying and Rising with Christ." *JBL* 92 (1973): 531–48.

Seal, W. O. "The **Parousia** in Mark: A Debate with Norman Perrin and His 'School.' " Doctoral dissertation. Union Theological Seminary in the City of New York, 1983.

Segal, A. F. *Two Powers in the Heaven: Early Rabbinic Reports about Christianity and Gnosticism*. SJLA 25. Leiden: Brill, 1977.

Segal, J. P. *The **Hebrew Passover**: From the Earliest Times to A.D. 70*. London Oriental Series 12. London/New York/Toronto: Oxford University Press, 1963.

Segal, M. Z. *The Complete Book of **Ben Sira** [Hebrew]*. Jerusalem: Keter, 1972.

Senior, D. *The **Passion** of Jesus in the Gospel of Mark*. Passion Series 2. Wilmington, Del.: Glazier, 1984.

Shae, G. S. "The **Question** of the Authority of Jesus." *NovT* 16 (1974): 1–29.

Shemesh, A. "4Q271.3: A **Key** to Sectarian Matrimonial Law." *JJS* 49 (1998): 244–63.

Sider, Ronald J. *Andreas Bodenstein von **Karlstadt***. Studies in Medieval and Reformation Thought 11. Leiden: Brill, 1974.

Sigal, P. *The **Halakah** of Jesus of Nazareth According to the Gospel of Matthew*. Lanham, Md./New York/London: University Press of America, 1986.

Skehan, P. W., and A. A. Di Lella. *The Wisdom of **Ben Sira**: A New Translation with Notes*

Introduction and Commentary. AYB 39. New York: Doubleday, 1987; reprint, New Haven: Yale University Press.

Smallwood, E. M. *The Jews Under Roman Rule: From Pompey to Diocletian.* SJLA 20. Leiden: Brill, 1976.

Smith, C. W. F. "No Time for Figs." *JBL* 79 (1960): 315–27.

Smith, D. M. *John.* ANTC. Nashville: Abingdon, 1999.

———. *John Among the Gospels.* 2nd ed. Minneapolis: Fortress, 2001.

Smith, H. *Ante-Nicene Exegesis of the Gospels.* London: SPCK, 1925–29.

Smith, M. *Clement of Alexandria and a Secret Gospel of Mark.* Cambridge, Mass.: Harvard University Press, 1973.

———. "Clement of Alexandria and Secret Mark: The Score at the End of the First Decade." *HTR* 75 (1982): 449–61.

———. *Jesus the Magician.* New York: Harper & Row, 1978.

———. "What Is Implied by the Variety of Messianic Figures?" *JBL* 78 (1959): 66–72.

Smith, R. H. *Pella of the Decapolis.* Wooster, Mass.: The College of Wooster, 1973–89.

Smith, S. H. "The Function of the Son of David Tradition in Mark's Gospel." *NTS* 42 (1996): 523–39.

Smith, T. V. *Petrine Controversies in Early Christianity.* WUNT 2.15. Tübingen: Mohr (Siebeck), 1985.

Smyth, H. W. *Greek Grammar.* Cambridge, Mass.: Harvard University, 1956 (orig. 1920).

Snodgrass, K. *The Parable of the Wicked Tenants: An Inquiry Into Parable Interpretation.* WUNT 27. Tübingen: Mohr (Siebeck), 1983.

Soards, M. L. "The Question of a Pre-Marcan Passion Narrative." Pp. 1492–1524 in *The Death of the Messiah: A Commentary on the Passion Narratives in the Four Gospels,* by R. E. Brown. AYBRL. New York: Doubleday, 1994; reprint, New Haven: Yale University Press.

Sokoloff, M. *A Dictionary of Jewish Babylonian Aramaic of the Talmudic and Geonic Periods.* Dictionaries of Talmud, Midrash and Targum III/Publications of the Comprehensive Aramaic Lexicon Project. Ramat-Gan/Baltimore/London: Bar Ilan University Press/Johns Hopkins University Press, 2002.

———. *A Dictionary of Jewish Palestinian Aramaic of the Talmudic and Geonic Periods.* 2nd ed. Dictionaries of Talmud, Midrash and Targum II/Publications of the Comprehensive Aramaic Lexicon Project. Ramat-Gan/Baltimore/London: Bar Ilan University Press/Johns Hopkins University Press, 2002.

Solzhenitsyn, A. *The Gulag Archipelago 1918–1956.* Glasgow: Collins/Fontana, 1974.

Sommer, B. D. *A Prophet Reads Scripture: Allusion in Isaiah 40–66.* Contraversions. Stanford: Stanford University Press, 1998.

Sowers, S. "The Circumstances and Recollection of the Pella Flight." *TZ* 5 (1970): 305–20.

Spiegel, S. *The Last Trial: On the Legends and Lore of the Command to Abraham to Offer Isaac as a Sacrifice: The Akedah.* Woodstock, Vt.: Jewish Lights, 1993 (orig. 1950).

Stählin, G. "Phileō, ktl." Pp. 9.113–71 in *TDNT* (1974).

———. "Xenos, ktl." Pp. 5.1–36 in *TDNT* (1967; orig. 1954).

Standaert, B. H. M. G. M. *L'Évangile selon Marc. Composition et genre littéraire.* Nijmegen: Stichting Studentenpers, 1978.

Stauffer, E. "Messias oder Menschensohn?" *NovT* 1 (1956): 81–102.

———. *New Testament Theology.* London: SCM, 1955 (orig. 1941).

Steck, O. H. *Israel und das gewaltsame Geschick der Propheten. Untersuchungen zur Über-*

*lieferung des deuteronomistischen Geschichtsbildes im Alten Testament, Spätju-
dentum und Urchristentum.* WMANT. Neukirchen-Vluyn: Neukirchener, 1967.

Stegemann, H. *The Library of Qumran: On the Essenes, Qumran, John the Baptist, and
Jesus.* Leiden/Grand Rapids: Brill/Eerdmans, 1998.

Stegemann, W. "Gab es eine jüdische **Beteiligung** an der Kreuzigung Jesu?" *Kirche und
Israel* 13 (1998): 3–24.

———. "Lasset die **Kinder** zu mir kommen. Sozialgeschichtliche Aspekte der Kinder-
evangeliums." Pp. 114–44 in *Traditionen der Befreiung. Sozialgeschichtliche
Bibelauslegungen. Band 1. Methodische Zugänge,* ed. W. Schottroff and W. Stegemann. München: Kaiser/Burckhardthaus-Laetare, 1980.

Steier, A. "**Lorbeer.**" Pp. 13.1431–42 in *Paulys Real-Encyclopädie der classischen Altertum-
swissenschaft.* Stuttgart: J. B. Metzler, 1927.

Stein, R. H. "Is the **Transfiguration Account** (Mark 9:2–8) a Misplaced Resurrection-
Account?" *JBL* 95 (1976): 79–96.

Stendahl, K. "**Prayer** and Forgiveness." *SEÅ* 22–23 (1957–58): 75–86.

Sterling, G. E. "**Jesus** as Exorcist: An Analysis of Matthew 17:24–30; Mark 9:14–29; Luke
9:37–43a." *CBQ* 55 (1993): 467–93.

Stern, D. "**Jesus' Parables** from the Perspective of Rabbinic Literature: The Example of
the Wicked Husbandmen." Pp. 42–80 in *Parable and Story in Judaism and Christianity,* ed. C. Thoma and M. Wyschogrod. Studies in Judaism and Christianity.
New York/Mahwah: Paulist Press, 1989.

———. *Parables in Midrash: Narrative and Exegesis in Rabbinic Literature.* Cambridge,
Mass./London: Harvard University Press, 1991.

Stern, E., ed. The *New Encyclopedia of Archaeological Excavations in the Holy Land.*
4 vols. Jerusalem: Israel Exploration Society/Carta, 1993. [Cited as **NEAEHL**]

Stock, K. *Boten aus dem Mit-Ihm-Sein. Das Verhältnis zwischen Jesus und den Zwölf nach
Markus.* AnBib 70. Rome: Biblical Institute, 1975.

Stone, M. E. *Fourth Ezra: A Commentary on the Book of Fourth Ezra.* Hermeneia. Minneapolis: Fortress, 1990.

———. *Signs of the Judgment, Onomastica Sacra, and the Generations from Adam.* University of Pennsylvania Armenian Texts and Studies 3. Chico: Scholars Press,
1981.

Strack, H. L., and P. Billerbeck. *Kommentar zum Neuen Testament aus Talmud und Midrasch.* 6 vols. München: Beck, 1924–61. [Cited as **Strack-Billerbeck**]

Strauss, D. F. *The Life of Jesus Critically Examined.* 1840. Philadelphia: Fortress, 1972.

———. *A New Life of Jesus.* 2nd ed. London/Edinburgh: Williams and Norgate, 1879.

Streeter, B. H. *The Four Gospels: A Study of Origins.* London: Macmillan, 1924.

Strelan, R. "**Recognizing** the Gods (Acts 14.8–10)." *NTS* 46 (2000): 488–503.

Strobel, A. *Kerygma und Apokalyptik. Ein religionsgeschichtlicher und theologischer Beitrag zur Christusfrage.* Göttingen: Vandenhoeck & Ruprehct, 1967.

Stuckenbruck, L. T. "The **Throne-Theophany** of the Book of Giants: Some New Light on
the Background of Daniel 7." Pp. 211–20 in *The Scrolls and the Scriptures: Qumran Fifty Years Later,* ed. S. E. Porter and C. A. Evans. JSPSup 26. Roehampton
Institute London Papers 3. Sheffield: Sheffield Academic Press, 1997.

Sugirtharajah, R. S. "**Men,** Trees and Walking: A Conjectural Solution to Mk 8:24." *ExpT*
103 (1992): 172–74.

———. "The **Widow's Mites** Revalued." *ExpT* 103 (1991): 42–43.

Sussmann, Y. *Talmud Yerushalmi. According to Ms. Or. 4720 (Scal. 3) of the Leiden Uni-*

versity Library. With Restorations and Corrections. Jerusalem: Academy of the Hebrew Language, 2005.

Swanson, R. J. *Mark.* New Testament Greek Manuscripts: Variant Readings Arranged in
Horizontal Lines Against Codex Vaticanus. Sheffield, England/Pasadena, Calif.:
Sheffield Academic Press/William Carey International University Press, 1995.

Swete, H. B. *The Gospel According to St Mark.* London/New York: Macmillan, 1898.
[Cited as **Swete**]

Syrén, R. *The **Blessings** in the Targums: A Study on the Targumic Interpretations of Genesis
49 and Deuteronomy 33.* Acta Academiae Aboensis, Ser. A, Humaniora 64.1. Åbo:
Åbo Akademi, 1986.

Tabory, J. *The **Passover Ritual** Throughout the Generations* [Hebrew]. Tel Aviv: Hakibbutz
Hameuchad, 1996.

Tagawa, K. *Miracles et évangile. La pensée personnelle de l'évangéliste Marc.* Études
d'Histoire et de Philosophie Religieuses 62. Paris: Presses Universitaires de
France, 1966.

Talbert, C. H. *What Is a Gospel? The Genre of the Canonical Gospels.* Philadelphia: Fortress, 1977.

Talmon, S. "The **Concepts** of Māšîaḥ and Messianism in Early Judaism." Pp. 79–115 in
The Messiah: Developments in Earliest Judaism and Christianity, ed. J. H. Charlesworth. The First Princeton Symposium on Judaism and Christian Origins. Minneapolis: Fortress, 1992.

Taylor, J. "The **Coming** of Elijah, Mt 17,10–13 and Mk 9,11–13: The Development of the
Texts." *RB* 98 (1991): 107–19.

Taylor, N. H. "Palestinian Christianity and the **Caligula Crisis.**" *JSNT* 61–62 (1996):
101–24, 13–41.

Taylor, V. *The Gospel According to Saint Mark.* 2nd ed. 1950. Grand Rapids: Baker, 1981.
[Cited as **Taylor**]

Telford, W. R. *The **Barren Temple** and the Withered Fig Tree: A Redaction-Critical Analysis of the Cursing of the Fig-Tree Pericope in Mark's Gospel and Its Relation to the
Cleansing of the Temple Tradition.* JSNTSup. Sheffield: JSOT Press, 1980.

Temkin, O. *The **Falling Sickness**: A History of Epilepsy from the Greeks to the Beginnings
of Modern Neurology.* 2nd ed. Baltimore and London: Johns Hopkins Press, 1971
(orig. 1945).

Temporini, H., and W. Haase, eds. *Aufstieg und Niedergang der römischen Welt. Geschichte und Kultur Roms im Spiegel der neueren Forschung.* Berlin/New York:
De Gruyter, 1972– .

Theissen, G. *The **Gospels** in Context: Social and Political History in the Synoptic Tradition.* Minneapolis: Fortress, 1991.

———. *The Miracle Stories of the Early Christian Tradition.* SNTW. Edinburgh: T & T
Clark, 1983. [Cited as **Theissen**]

———, and A. Merz. *The **Historical Jesus.*** London: SCM, 1998.

Theophylact. *The **Explanation** by Blessed Theophylact Archbishop of Ochrid and Bulgaria
of the Holy Gospel According to St. Mark.* Bl. Theophylact's Explanation of the
New Testament 2. House Springs, Mo.: Chrysostom Press, 1993.

Thomas Aquinas. *Catena **Aurea**: Commentary on the Four Gospels Collected Out of the
Works of the Fathers.* Oxford: Parker, 1842.

Thomas, J. C. "A **Reconsideration** of the Ending of Mark." *JETS* 26 (1983): 407–19.

Thomas, K. *Religion and the Decline of Magic: Studies in Popular Beliefs in Sixteenth-*

and Seventeenth-Century England. Harmondsworth/New York: Penguin Books, 1971.

Thomas, K. J. "Liturgical **Citations** in the Synoptics." *NTS* 22 (1976): 205–14.

Tiller, P. A. *A **Commentary** on the Animal Apocalypse of* 1 Enoch. SBLEJL. Atlanta: Scholars Press, 1993.

Tolbert, Mary Ann. ***Sowing** the Gospel: Mark's World in Literary-Historical Perspective.* Philadelphia: Fortress, 1989. [Cited as **Tolbert**]

Toomer, G. J. "**Clocks**." P. 350 in *OCD.*

Torrey, C. C. *The **Second Isaiah**; a New Interpretation.* New York: C. Scribner's Sons, 1928.

Tov, E., ed. *The Dead Sea Scrolls **Electronic Library**.* Provo: Brigham Young University, 2006.

Townsend, J. T. *Midrash **Tanhuma**.* 3 vols. Hoboken, N.J.: Ktav Publishing, 1989–2003.

Trudinger, L. P. " '**Eli**, Eli, Lama Sabachthani?' A Cry of Dereliction? or Victory?" *JETS* 17 (1974): 235–38.

Turner, N. "The Translation of *Moichatai ep' Autēn.*" *BT* 7 (1956): 151–52.

Ulansey, D. "The **Heavenly Veil** Torn: Mark's Cosmic *Inclusio.*" *JBL* 110 (1991): 123–25.

Urbach, E. E. *The **Sages**: Their Concepts and Beliefs.* Publications of the Perry Foundation. Jerusalem: Magnes Press, Hebrew University, 1979.

van der Horst, P. W. "*Ancient Jewish **Epitaths**: An Introductory Survey of a Millennium of Jewish Funerary Epigraphy (300 BCE–700 CE).* Kampen: Kok Pharos, 1991.

———. "**Can** a Book End with *gar*? A Note on Mark xvi. 8." *JTS* 23 (1972): 121–24.

———. "A **New Altar** of a Godfearer?" *JJS* 43 (1992): 32–37.

VanderKam, J. C. *From **Joshua to Caiaphas**: High Priests After the Exile.* Minneapolis/Assen: Fortress/Van Gorcum, 2004.

van der Toorn, K. "**Mill**, Millstone." Pp. 4.831–83 in *AYBD.*

Van Eijk, T. H. C. "**Marriage** and Virginity, Death and Immortality." Pp. 209–35 in *Epektasis: Mélanges patristiques offerts au Cardinal Jean Daniélou,* ed. Jacques Fontaine and Charles Kannengiesser. Paris: Beauchesne, 1972.

van Hasselt, F. J. F. "De **vijgeboom**, waaran Jezus 'niets dan bladeren vond'." *Nieuwe Theologische Studiën* 8 (1925): 225–27.

van Henten, J. W. *The Maccabean **Martyrs** as Saviours of the Jewish People: A Study of 2 and 4 Maccabees.* JSJSup 57. Leiden/New York/Köln: Brill, 1997.

Vanhoye, A. "La **fuite** du jeune homme nu (Mc 14,51–52)." *Bib* 52 (1971): 401–6.

van Iersel, B. M. F. "The Gospel According to St. Mark—Written for a **Persecuted** Community?" *Nederlands Theologisch Tijdschrift* 34 (1980): 15–36.

———. ***Mark**: A Reader-Response Commentary.* JSNTSup 164. Sheffield: Sheffield Academic Press, 1998.

Van Rompay, L. "**Griekse Woorden** in de Syrische en Sahidische Evangeliën." Masters thesis. Faculty of Arts: Catholic University of Louvain, 1971.

———. "Oh That I Had **Wings** Like a Dove! Some Remarks on Exclamatory Clauses in Syriac." Pp. 91–105 in *Studies in Semitic and General Linguistics in Honor of Gideon Goldenberg,* ed. T. Bar and E. Cohen. Münster: Alter Orient und Altes Testament, 2007.

———. "The Rendering of *prosōpon lambanein* and Related Expressions in the Early Oriental Versions of the New Testament." *Orientalia lovaniensia periodica* 6–7 (1975–76): 569–75.

van Unnik, W. C. " '**Alles** ist dir möglich' [Mk 14, 36]." Pp. 27–36 in *Verborum Veritas.*

Festschrift für Gustav Stählin zum 70. Geburtstag, ed. O Böcher and K. Haacker. Wuppertal: Theologischer Verlag Rolf Brockhaus, 1970.

Van Voorst, R. E. *Jesus Outside the New Testament: An Introduction to the Ancient Evidence.* Grand Rapids/Cambridge: Eerdmans, 2000.

Veldhuizen, A. "De alabasten flesch." *Theologische Studiën* 24 (1906): 170–72.

Vermes, G. *The Complete Dead Sea Scrolls in English.* 4th ed. London: Penguin Books, 1997.

———. *Jesus the Jew: A Historian's Reading of the Gospels.* Philadelphia: Fortress, 1981.

Vieillefond, J.-R. *Les "Cestes" de Julius Africanus. Étude sur l'ensemble des fragments avec édition, traduction et commentaires.* Firenze/Paris: Edizioni Sansoni Antiquariato/ Librairie Marcel Dider, 1970.

Voelz, J. W. "The Language of the New Testament." Pp. 893–977 in *ANRW* II.25.2. Berlin/New York: De Gruyter, 1984.

Volz, P. *Die Eschatologie der jüdischen Gemeinde im neutestamentlichen Zeitalter nach den Quellen der rabbinischen, apokalytpischen und apokryphen Literatur.* 2nd ed. Tübingen: Mohr (Siebeck), 1934.

von Rad, G. *Genesis: A Commentary.* OTL. Philadelphia: Westminster Press, 1976.

von Wahlde, U. C. "Mark 9:33–50: Discipleship: The Authority That Serves." *BZ* N.S. 29 (1985): 49–67.

Vos, J. S. "Die hermeneutische Antinomie bei Paulus." *NTS* 38 (1992): 254–70.

Waetjen, H. "The Ending of Mark and the Gospel's Shift in Eschatology." *Annual of the Swedish Theological Institute* 4 (1965): 114–31.

Wagner, J. R. "Psalm 118 in Luke–Acts: Tracing a Narrative Thread." Pp. 154–78 in *Early Christian Interpretation of the Scriptures of Israel: Investigations and Proposals,* ed. C. A. Evans and J. A. Sanders. JSNTSup 148/Studies in Scripture in Early Judaism and Christianity 5. Sheffield: Sheffield Academic Press, 1996.

Walker, W. O. "The Lord's Prayer in Matthew and John." *NTS* 28 (1982): 237–56.

Wallace, D. B. *Greek Grammar Beyond the Basics: An Exegetical Syntax of the New Testament.* Grand Rapids: Zondervan, 1996. [Cited as Wallace]

Watson, D. F. "Gehenna." Pp. 2.926–28 in *AYBD.*

Watts, R. E. *Isaiah's New Exodus and Mark.* WUNT. Tübingen: Mohr (Siebeck), 1997.

———. "Jesus' Death, Isaiah 53, and Mark 10:45: A Crux Revisited." Pp. 125–51 in *Jesus and the Suffering Servant: Isaiah 53 and Christian Origins,* ed. W. H. Bellinger and W. R. Farmer. Harrisburg, Pa.: Trinity Press International, 1998.

Weder, H. "Perspektive der Frauen?" *EvT* 43 (1983): 175–8.

Weeden, T. J. "The Heresy That Necessitated Mark's Gospel." Pp. 89–104 in *The Interpretation of Mark,* ed. W. Telford. Studies in New Testament Interpretation. Philadelphia: Fortress, 1995 (orig. 1968).

———. *Mark: Traditions in Conflict.* Philadelphia: Fortress, 1971.

Wegner, J. R. *Chattel or Person? The Status of Women in the Mishnah.* New York/Oxford: Oxford University Press, 1988.

Weiser, A. "*Diakonos, ktl.*" Pp. 1.302–4 in *EDNT,* 1990.

Weiss, K. "*Pous.*" Pp. 6.624–31 in *TDNT* (1968; orig. 1959).

Weisse, C. H. *Die evangelische Geschichte kritisch und philosophisch bearbeitet.* Leipzig: Breitkopf & Härtel, 1838.

Wellhausen, J. *Das Evangelium Marci übersetzt und erklärt.* 2nd ed. Berlin: Georg Reimer, 1909. [Cited as Wellhausen]

Werner, E. " 'Hosanna' in the Gospels." *JBL* 65 (1946): 97–122.

Westcott, B. F., and F. J. A. Hort. *Introduction to the New Testament in the Original Greek with Notes on Selected Readings.* Peabody, Mass.: Hendrickson, 1988 (orig. 1882).

Wildberger, H. *Isaiah 1–12: A Commentary.* Continental Commentaries. Minneapolis: Fortress, 1991 (orig. 1980).

Wilfand, D. "The **End** of Mark." Term paper, Greek exegesis of Mark. Duke University Graduate Program in Religion, 2006.

Williams, C. H. *I Am He: The Interpretation of 'Anî Hû' in Jewish and Early Christian Literature.* WUNT 2.113. Tübingen: Mohr (Siebeck), 2000.

Williams, P. J. "The Linguistic **Background** to Jesus' Dereliction Cry (Matthew 27:46; Mark 15:34)." Pp. 1–12 in *The New Testament in Its First Century Setting: Essays on Context and Background in Honour of B. W. Winter on His 65th Birthday,* ed. P. J. Williams et al. Grand Rapids/Cambridge: Eerdmans, 2004.

Williams, S. K. *Jesus' Death as Saving Event: The Background and Origin of a Concept.* HDR 2. Missoula: Scholars Press, 1975.

Wilson, S. G. *Related Strangers: Jews and Christians 70–170 C.E.* Minneapolis: Fortress, 1995.

Windisch, H. "Die **Sprüche** vom Eingehen in das Reich Gottes." ZNW 27 (1928): 163–92.

Winston, D. *The Wisdom of Solomon. A New Translation with Introduction and Commentary.* AYB 43. New York: Doubleday, 1979; reprint, New Haven: Yale University Press.

Wohlers, M. *Heilige Krankheit. Epilepsie in antiker Medizin, Astrologie und Religion.* Marburger Theologische Studien 57. Marburg: N. G. Elwert Verlag, 1999.

Wolohojian, A. M. *The Romance of Alexander the Great by Pseudo-Calllisthenes.* New York/London: Columbia University Press, 1969.

Wrede, William. *The Messianic Secret.* Cambridge: James Clarke & Co., 1971 (orig. 1901). [Cited as **Wrede**]

Wright, A. G. "The **Widow's Mites**: Praise or Lament?" *CBQ* 44 (1982): 256–65.

Wright, D. F. "**Out**, In, Out: Jesus' Blessing of the Children and Infant Baptism." Pp. 188–206 in *Dimensions of Baptism: Biblical and Theological Studies,* ed. S. E. Porter and A. R. Cross. JSNTSup 234. Sheffield Academic Press, 2002.

Yadin, Y. "The **Scroll** of the War of the Sons of Light Against the Sons of Darkness." Oxford: Oxford University Press, 1962.

———. "The **Temple Scroll**." Pp. 156–66 in *New Directions in Biblical Archaeology,* ed. D. N. Freedman and J. C. Greenfield. New York: Doubleday, 1971 (orig. 1969).

Yarnold, E. *The Awe-Inspiring Rites of Initiation: Baptismal Homilies of the Fourth Century.* Middlegreen, Slough: St Paul Publications, 1972.

Yavetz, Z. *Plebs and Princeps.* Oxford: At the Clarendon Press, 1969.

Zager, W. *Gottesherrschaft und Endgericht in der Verkündigung Jesus. Eine Untersuchung zur Markinischen Jesusüberlieferung einschliesslich der Q-Parallelen.* BZNW 82. Berlin/New York: De Gruyter, 1996.

Zahn, T. *Einleitung in das Neue Testament.* 2nd ed. Leipzig: Deichert, 1900.

Zanker, P. *The Power of Images in the Age of Augustus.* Jerome Lectures 16. Ann Arbor: University of Michigan Press, 1988.

Zeller, D. "**Bedeutung** und religionsgeschichtlicher Hintergrund der Verwandlung Jesu (Markus 9:2–8)." Pp. 303–22 in *Authenticating the Activities of Jesus,* ed. B. Chilton and C. A. Evans. NTTS 28.2. Leiden/Boston/Köln: Brill, 1999.

————. "La **métamorphose** de Jésus comme épiphanie (Mc 9, 2–8)." Pp. 167–86 in *L'Évangile exploré: Mélanges offerts à Simon Légasse à l'occasion de ses soixante-dix ans*, ed. A. Marchadour. LD 166. Paris: Editions du Cerf, 1996.

Zerwick, M. *Biblical Greek Illustrated by Examples*. Rome: Pontifical Biblical Institute, 1963. [Cited as **Zerwick**]

————. *Untersuchungen zum **Markus-Stil**. Ein Beitrag zur stilistischen Durcharbeitung des Neuen Testaments*. Scripta Pontificii Instituti Biblici. Rome: Pontifical Biblical Institute, 1937.

Zias, J. "Crucifixion in Antiquity: The Evidence," 1998. Http://www.centuryone.org/crucifixion2.html.

————, and E. Sekeles. "The **Crucified Man** from Givʿat Ha-Mivtar: A Reappraisal." *IEJ* 35 (1985). 22–27.

Zimmermann, F. *The **Aramaic Origin** of the Four Gospels*. New York: Ktav, 1979.

Zugibe, F. T. *The **Crucifixion** of Jesus: A Forensic Enquiry*. New York: M. Evans, 2005.

MARK 8:22–16:8:
A TRANSLATION

◆

Fourth Major Section (8:22–10:52)
On the Way: Blindness and Sight

8 ²²And they came to Bethsaida. And people brought a blind man to him and pleaded with him to touch him. ²³And taking the blind man by the hand, he led him out of the village and spat on his eyes and laid his hands on him and asked him, "Do you see anything?" ²⁴And he, looking up and beginning to see again, said, "I see people . . . because . . . I see people like walking trees." ²⁵Then Jesus laid his hands on his eyes again, and his sight broke through, and he was restored, and he saw all things clearly from that moment on. ²⁶And he sent him home, saying, "Do not even go into the village."

²⁷And Jesus and his disciples went out into the villages of Caesarea Philippi. And on the way he was asking his disciples and saying to them, "Who do people say that I am?" ²⁸And they said to him, "Some say John the Baptist, and others Elijah, and others that you are one of the prophets." ²⁹And he asked them, "But you, who do *you* say that I am?" And Peter answered and said to him, "You are the Christ." ³⁰And he vehemently ordered them to speak to nobody about him.

³¹And he began to teach them that it was necessary that the Son of Man should suffer many things and be rejected by the elders and the chief priests and the scribes, and be killed, and after three days arise. ³²And he was making this statement frankly. And Peter took him aside and began to rebuke him. ³³But he, turning and looking at his disciples, rebuked Peter and said, "Get behind me, Satan! For you are fixing your thoughts not on the things of God but on those of human beings."

³⁴And summoning the crowd with his disciples, he said to them, "If anyone wants to follow after me, let him renounce himself and take up his cross, and let him follow me. ³⁵For whoever wants to save his life will destroy it; but whoever will destroy his life for me and the good news will save it. ³⁶For what use would it be for a human being to gain the whole world and to forfeit his life? ³⁷For what could a human give in exchange for his life? ³⁸For whoever is ashamed of me and of my words in this adulterous and sinful generation, the Son of Man also will be ashamed of him when he comes in the glory of his Father with the holy angels."
9 ¹And he said to them, "Amen, I say to you, there are some of those who are standing here who surely will not taste death before they see the dominion of God fully come in power."

²And after six days Jesus took Peter and James and John and led them up to a high mountain privately, by themselves, and was transformed before them, ³and his clothes became so dazzlingly white that no launderer on earth could whiten them so. ⁴And there appeared to them Elijah with Moses, and they were talking with Jesus. ⁵And Peter answered and said to Jesus, "Rabbi, it is good for us to be here; and let us make three tents, one for you and one for Moses and one for Elijah." ⁶(For he did not know what to answer; for they had become afraid.) ⁷And there came a cloud, overshadowing them; and there came a voice out of the cloud: "This is my beloved Son; listen to him." ⁸And suddenly, when they looked around, they no longer saw anyone except Jesus alone with them.

⁹And as they were coming down from the mountain, he commanded them not to describe to anyone what they had seen until the Son of Man had been raised from among the dead. ¹⁰And they latched onto this saying, arguing among themselves about what this "rising from among the dead" was.

¹¹And they asked him, saying, "Why then do the scribes say that Elijah must come first?" ¹²And he said to them, "Is it really the case that Elijah, when he comes first, restores all things? How then has it been written concerning the Son of Man that he is to suffer many things and be treated with contempt? ¹³But I say to you that Elijah also has come, and they have done to him whatever they wanted—as it has been written concerning him."

¹⁴And as they came to the disciples, they saw a great crowd around them and scribes arguing with them. ¹⁵And all the crowd, when they saw him, were immediately awestruck, and they ran forward and hailed him. ¹⁶And he asked them, "What were you arguing about with them?"

¹⁷And one from the crowd answered him, "Teacher, I brought my son to you because he has a mute spirit. ¹⁸And wherever he is when it grabs him, it tears him, and he foams at the mouth and grinds his teeth and becomes rigid. And I asked your disciples to cast it out, but they didn't have the strength." ¹⁹And he answered and said to them, "O faithless generation, how long will I be with you? How long will I put up with you? Bring him to me." ²⁰And they brought him to him. And seeing him, the spirit immediately convulsed the boy, and he fell on the ground and was rolling around foaming at the mouth. ²¹And Jesus asked his father, "How long has he been like this?" And he said, "From childhood. ²²And many times it has thrown him into the fire and into waters in order to destroy him. But if you can do anything, have pity on us and help us!" ²³But Jesus said to him, " 'If you can'? All things are possible to the one who believes!" ²⁴The father of the child immediately cried out and said, "I believe; help my unbelief!"

²⁵And Jesus, seeing that a crowd was gathering together rapidly, rebuked the unclean spirit and said to it, "Mute and deaf spirit, I command you, come out of him and don't ever enter him again!" ²⁶And shouting and convulsing him greatly, it came out; and he became like a corpse, so that many people were saying that he had died. ²⁷But Jesus seized his hand and raised him, and he arose.

²⁸And when Jesus had gone into a house, his disciples asked him privately, "Why weren't we able to cast it out?" ²⁹And he said to them, "This sort of spirit can't be gotten out in any way except by prayer."

³⁰And going out from there, they went through Galilee, and he did not want anybody to know it, ³¹for he was teaching his disciples and saying to them, "The Son of Man will be turned over to the hands of human beings, and they will kill him, and when he has been killed, after three days he will arise." ³²But they did not understand the saying, and they were afraid to ask him.

³³And they came to Capernaum. And when he was in the house, he asked them, "What were you discussing on the way?" ³⁴But they were silent, for they had been discussing with each other on the way who was the greatest. ³⁵And sitting down, he called the Twelve and said to them, "If anyone wants to be first, he shall be the last of all and the servant of all." ³⁶And taking a child, he set him in their midst,

and embracing him, he said to them, [37]"Whoever receives one such child in my name receives me, and whoever receives me does not receive me but the one who sent me."

[38]John said to him, "Teacher, we saw someone casting out demons in your name and we forbade him, because he did not follow us." [39]But Jesus said, "Don't forbid him, for there is no one who will do a work of power in my name and will be able to malign me soon. [40]For the one who is not against us is for us.

[41]"For whoever gives you a cup of water to drink in the name, because you belong to Christ, amen, I say to you, that one will by no means lose his reward. [42]And whoever offends one of these little ones who believe, it would be better for him to have a millstone hung around his neck and for him to be cast into the sea. [43]And if your hand offends you, cut it off—it is better to enter life maimed than to have two hands and go away to Gehenna, to the fire that cannot be put out. [45]And if your foot offends you, cut it off—it is better to enter life lame than to have two feet and be cast into Gehenna. [47]And if your eye offends you, cast it out—it is better to enter the dominion of God one-eyed than to have two eyes and be cast into Gehenna, [48]where their worm does not die and the fire is not put out. [49]For everyone will be salted with fire. [50]Salt is good; but if the salt becomes unsalty, what will you salt it with? Have salt in yourselves and be at peace with each other."

10 [1]And rising from there, he went into the region of Judaea and Transjordan, and crowds again came together to him, and as was his custom, he again began teaching them. [2]And coming forward, Pharisees were asking him if it was permissible for a man to divorce a woman, testing him. [3]But he answered and said to them, "What did Moses command you?" [4]They said, "Moses gave permission to write a bill of relinquishment and to divorce." [5]Jesus said, "He wrote you this commandment with a view toward your hard-heartedness; [6]but from the beginning of the creation 'male and female he made them'; [7]'on account of this a man shall leave his father and mother and shall be joined to his wife, [8]and the two shall become one flesh.' So they are no longer two people, but one flesh. [9]What therefore God has yoked together, let not a human being separate."

[10]And when they were again in the house, the disciples asked him concerning this. [11]And he said to them, "Whoever divorces his wife and marries another commits adultery against her. [12]And she, if she divorces her husband and marries another, commits adultery."

[13]And people were bringing him children, in order that he might touch them; but the disciples rebuked them. [14]But when he saw this, Jesus became annoyed and said to them, "Let the children come to me! Don't forbid them!—for to such ones belongs the dominion of God. [15]Amen, I say to you, whoever does not receive the dominion of God like a child will never enter it." [16]And he embraced them and blessed them, laying his hands on them.

[17]And as he was setting out on the way, a man came running up, and falling down on his knees before him, he asked him, "Good teacher, what shall I do to inherit eternal life?" [18]But Jesus said to him, "Why do you call me good? There is nobody good except One, that is, God. [19]You know the commandments: 'Do not murder, do not commit adultery, do not steal, do not bear false witness, do

not defraud, honor your father and mother.' " ²⁰He said to him, "Teacher, I have
observed all these things from my youth up." ²¹And Jesus, looking at him, was
moved with love for him and said to him, "You are missing one thing: go, sell
whatever you have and give to the poor, and you will have treasure in heaven; and
come on, follow me!" ²²But he, indignant at Jesus' word, went away grieving, for
he had great estates.

²³And Jesus, looking around, said to his disciples, "How hard it will be for the
rich to enter the dominion of God!" ²⁴And the disciples were astonished at his
words. But Jesus again answered and said to them, "Children, how hard it is to
enter the dominion of God! ²⁵It is easier for a camel to pass through the eye of
a needle than for a rich person to enter the dominion of God." ²⁶And they were
even more amazed, saying among themselves, "And who then can be saved?"
²⁷Looking at them, Jesus said, "With human beings it is impossible, but not with
God; for all things are possible with God."

²⁸Peter began to say to him, "Look, *we* have left everything and have followed
you." ²⁹Jesus said, "Amen, I say to you, there is no one who has left house or brothers or sisters or mother or father or children or fields for my sake and for the sake of
the good news ³⁰who will not receive a hundredfold now, in this time, houses and
brothers and sisters and mothers and children and fields—with persecutions—
and in the coming age, eternal life. ³¹But many first ones will be last, and last ones
first."

³²And they were on the way, going up to Jerusalem, and Jesus was going be-
fore them, and they were astonished; and those following were afraid. And taking
the Twelve again, he began to tell them the things that would happen to him:
³³"Look, we are going up to Jerusalem; and the Son of Man will be turned over
to the chief priests and the scribes, and they will condemn him to death and turn
him over to the Gentiles; ³⁴and they will mock him and spit on him and scourge
him and kill him; and after three days he will arise."

³⁵And James and John, the sons of Zebedee, came up to him, saying to him,
"Teacher, we want you to do for us whatever we ask of you." ³⁶He said to them,
"*What* do you want me to do for you?" ³⁷They said to him, "Grant us that one of us
should sit on your right and one on your left, in your glory." ³⁸Jesus said to them,
"You don't know what you are asking. Can you drink the cup I drink or be baptized with the baptism I am baptized with?" ³⁹They said to him, "We can." Jesus
said to them, "The cup I drink you *will* drink, and the baptism I am baptized with
you *will* be baptized with—⁴⁰but to sit at my right or my left is not mine to give but
is for those for whom it has been prepared."

⁴¹And when they heard it, the other ten began to be annoyed with James and
John. ⁴²And calling them, Jesus said to them, "You know that those who are
thought to rule over the Gentiles lord it over them, and their great ones oppress
them. ⁴³But it is not so among you; but whoever among you wants to be great shall
be your servant, ⁴⁴and whoever among you wants to be the first shall be the slave
of all. ⁴⁵For even the Son of Man did not come to be served but to serve, and to
give his life as a ransom for many."

⁴⁶And they came to Jericho. And as he was going out of Jericho along with

his disciples and a large crowd, a blind beggar named Bartimaeus (the son of Timaeus) was sitting beside the way. [47]And when he heard that it was Jesus of Nazareth, he began to shout and say, "Son of David! Jesus! Have mercy on me!" [48]And many people began rebuking him, telling him to be quiet. But he shouted all the more, "Son of David! Have mercy on me!" [49]And Jesus stood still and said, "Call him." And they called the blind man, saying to him, "Be brave! Get up! He's calling you!" [50]And throwing off his garment, he leaped up and came to Jesus. [51]And Jesus answered him and said, "What do you want me to do for you?" And the blind man said to him, "Rabbouni, let me see again." [52]And Jesus said to him, "Go! Your faith has saved you." And immediately he began to see again, and he followed him in the way.

Fifth Major Section (11:1–13:37)
Teaching : The Vestibule to the Passion Narrative

11 [1]And when they drew near to Jerusalem, to Bethphage and Bethany, toward the Mount of Olives, he sent out two of his disciples [2]and said to them, "Go into the village opposite you, and when you go into it, you will immediately find a colt tied up, upon which no human being has ever yet sat. Untie and bring it. [3]And if anyone says to you, 'Why are you doing that?' say to him, 'The master has need of it, and he will immediately send it back here again.' " [4]And they went out and found a colt tied up at a door outside, in the street, and untied it. [5]And some of the people who were standing around there said to them, "What are you doing, untying that colt?" [6]And they spoke to them as Jesus had told them to, and they let them go.

[7]And they brought the colt to Jesus and put their clothes on it, and he sat on it. [8]And many spread their clothes in the way, and others spread leafy branches, cutting them from the fields. [9]And those who went ahead and those who followed cried out, "Hosanna! Blessed is he who comes in the name of the Lord! [10]Blessed is the coming dominion of our father David! Hosanna in the highest places!"

[11]And he went into Jerusalem, into the Temple, and looked around at everything; but since the hour was already late, he went out to Bethany with the Twelve.

[12]And the next day as they were going out of Bethany, he became hungry. [13]And seeing from far away a fig tree that had leaves on it, he came, wondering if he would find anything on it. And coming up to it, he did not find anything on it except leaves; for it was not the time for figs. [14]And he answered and said to it, "Let no one ever eat fruit from you again." And his disciples heard him.

[15]And they came to Jerusalem; and going into the Temple, he began to throw out those who were selling and buying in the Temple; and he overturned the tables of the money changers and the seats of those who were selling doves; [16]and he did not allow anyone to carry a container through the Temple. [17]And he was teaching and saying to them, "Has it not been written, 'My house shall be called a house of prayer for all the nations'? But you have made it a den of brigands." [18]And the chief priests and the scribes heard it; and they were looking for a way to destroy

him. For they were afraid of him, for the whole crowd was overwhelmed by his teaching. ¹⁹And when evening came, they went out of the city.

²⁰And passing by early in the morning, they saw the fig tree withered from the roots. ²¹And Peter, remembering, said to him, "Rabbi, look—the fig tree you cursed has withered!" ²²And Jesus answered and said to them, "Have faith in God. ²³Amen, I say to you that whoever says to this mountain, 'Be lifted up and cast into the sea' and does not doubt in his heart but believes that what he says will happen, it will be his. ²⁴Therefore I say to you, everything you pray and ask for, believe that you have received it, and it will be yours. ²⁵And when you stand praying, forgive, if you have anything against anyone, so that your Father in heaven may also forgive you your transgressions."

²⁷And they came to Jerusalem again. And as he was walking about in the Temple, the chief priests and the scribes and the elders came up to him, ²⁸and they said to him, "By what authority are you doing these things? Or who has given you this authority, so that you do these things?" ²⁹But Jesus said to them, "*I* will ask *you* one thing, and you answer me, and then I will tell you by what authority I do these things. ³⁰The baptism of John—from heaven or from human beings? Answer me!" ³¹And they debated among themselves, saying, "If we say, 'From heaven,' he will say, 'Why then did you not believe him?' ³²But do we dare to say, 'From human beings'?" (They feared the crowd, for all considered John really to be a prophet.) ³³And they answered and said to Jesus, "We do not know." And Jesus said to them, "Neither will I tell you by what authority I do these things."

12 ¹And he began to speak to them in parables: "A man planted a vineyard and put a fence around it, and dug out a wine vat, and built a tower, and let it out to tenant farmers, and went abroad. ²And at the proper time he sent a servant to the tenant farmers, that he might receive from the tenant farmers some of the fruits of the vineyard. ³And they took him and beat him and sent him away empty. ⁴And again, he sent to them another servant; him also they wounded in the head and dishonored. ⁵And he sent another; him also they killed, and many others, beating some, killing others. ⁶He still had one, his beloved son. He sent him last of all to them, saying, 'They will respect my son.' ⁷But those tenant farmers said among themselves, 'This is the heir. Come on, let's kill him, and the inheritance will be ours!' ⁸And they seized and killed him and threw him out of the vineyard. ⁹What then will the lord of the vineyard do? He will come and destroy the tenant farmers and give the vineyard to others. ¹⁰And have you not read this scripture: 'The stone that the builders rejected—it has become the head of the corner; ¹¹this has come from the Lord, and it is amazing in our eyes'?"

¹²And they wanted to arrest him, and yet they feared the crowd; for they knew that he had spoken the parable against them. And they left him and went away.

¹³And they sent to him some of the Pharisees and some of the Herodians, that they might trap him in his speech. ¹⁴And they came and said to him, "Teacher, we know that you are truthful and that you don't care what anyone thinks. For you don't look at the face of human beings, but you teach the way of God truthfully. Is it permissible to give tribute money to Caesar or not? Shall we give, or shall we not give?" ¹⁵But he, seeing their pretense, said to them, "Why are you testing me?

Bring me a denarius, so that I may see it." [16]And they brought one. And he said to them, "Whose image is this, and whose inscription?" And they said to him, "Caesar's." [17]And Jesus said to them, "Pay to Caesar the things of Caesar, and the things of God to God." And they were amazed at him.

[18]And Sadducees came to him, who say that there is no resurrection, and they were asking him, saying, [19]"Teacher, Moses wrote to us, 'If someone's brother dies and he leaves a wife and he does not leave a child, his brother should take his wife and raise up offspring for his brother.' [20]There were seven brothers. And the first took a wife, and when he died he didn't leave offspring. [21]And the second took her and died and didn't leave behind offspring, and the third similarly. [22]And the seven of them didn't leave offspring. Last of all the woman also died. [23]In the resurrection, when they rise, whose wife will she be? For all seven of them had her as a wife."

[24]And Jesus said to them, "Aren't you deceived, in that you don't know the scriptures or the power of God? [25]For when they rise from among the dead, they neither marry nor are taken in marriage but are like the angels who are in heaven. [26]And concerning the dead, that they are raised—haven't you read in the book of Moses, how God spoke to him at the bush, saying, 'I am the God of Abraham and the God of Isaac and the God of Jacob'? [27]He is not a God of the dead but of the living. You are greatly deceived."

[28]And one of the scribes, coming forward and hearing them debate, and seeing that he answered them well, asked him, "What is the first of all the commandments?" [29]Jesus answered, "The first is, 'Hear, Israel, the Lord our God is one Lord, [30]and you shall love the Lord your God out of your whole heart and out of your whole soul and out of your whole mind and out of your whole strength.' [31]And the second is this, 'And you shall love your neighbor as yourself.' There is no other commandment greater than these."

[32]And the scribe said to him, "Well said, teacher; you have truthfully said that he is one, and there is no other besides him; [33]and to love him out of one's whole heart and out of one's whole understanding and out of one's whole strength, and to love one's neighbor as oneself, is greater than all burnt offerings and sacrifices."

[34]And Jesus, seeing that he answered intelligently, said to him, "You are not far from the dominion of God." And no one dared ask him anything anymore.

[35]And Jesus answered and said, teaching in the Temple, "How do the scribes say that the Christ is the Son of David? [36]David himself said in the Holy Spirit, 'The Lord said to my lord, "Sit on my right until I put your enemies under your feet." ' [37]David himself calls him 'lord'; and how is he his son?" And the large crowd heard him gladly.

[38]And in his teaching he said, "Watch out for those scribes who like to go around in long robes, and like greetings in the marketplaces [39]and the first seats in the synagogues and the first couches at feasts; [40]who devour the houses of widows and make long prayers as a pretext. These men will receive greater condemnation."

[41]And sitting opposite the treasury, he was watching how the crowd was throwing money into the treasury. And many rich people were throwing in a large amount. [42]And one poor widow came and threw in two *lepta*, that is, a *quadrans*. [43]And calling his disciples, he said to them, "Amen, I say to you, this poor widow

has thrown in more than all of those who have been throwing into the treasury. ⁴⁴For they all threw in out of their abundance, but she has thrown in out of her scarcity everything she had, even her whole living."

13 ¹And as he was coming out of the Temple, one of his disciples said to him, "Teacher, look! Such stones and such buildings!" ²And Jesus said to him, "Do you see these great buildings? There surely won't be left a stone upon a stone here that won't surely be thrown down."

³And as he was sitting on the Mount of Olives, opposite the Temple, Peter and James and John and Andrew asked him privately, ⁴"Tell us, when will these things be? And what is the sign, when all these things will be accomplished?"

⁵And Jesus began to say to them, "Look out, lest someone lead you astray. ⁶Many people will come in my name, saying, 'I am he,' and they will lead many people astray. ⁷But when you hear about wars and rumors of wars, don't be disturbed— they have to happen, but it is not yet the end. ⁸For nation will be raised against nation and dominion against dominion; there will be earthquakes in place after place; there will be famines. These things are the beginning of the labor pains.

⁹But you, look to yourselves—they will turn you over to councils, and in synagogues you will be beaten, and you will be arraigned before rulers and kings for my sake, as a witness to them. ¹⁰And first the good news must be preached to all the nations. ¹¹And when they arrest you and turn you over, don't think beforehand about what you are to say, but whatever is given you in that hour, say that; for it is not you who are speaking, but the Holy Spirit. ¹²And brother will turn brother over to death, and a father his child, and children will rise up against their parents and have them put to death. ¹³And you will be hated by all for the sake of my name. But the one who endures to the end, he will be saved.

¹⁴But when you see the "abomination of desolation" standing where he should not—let the reader understand—then let those in Judaea flee to the mountains, ¹⁵and let not the person on the roof come down or go in to get anything out of his house, ¹⁶and let not the person in the field turn back to pick up his garment. ¹⁷And alas for pregnant women and for nursing mothers in those days! ¹⁸And pray that it may not happen during a storm. ¹⁹For those days will be such tribulation, that there has not been such from the beginning of the creation, which God created, until now, and never will be. ²⁰And if the Lord had not shortened the days, no flesh would be saved. But on account of the chosen ones, whom he chose, he shortened the days.

²¹"And then if anyone says to you, 'Look, here is the Christ!' or 'Look, there!' do not believe it. ²²For false Christs and false prophets will be raised up and will give signs and wonders in order to lead astray—if possible—the chosen ones. ²³You then, look out. See, I have foretold all things to you.

²⁴"But in those days, after that tribulation, the sun will be darkened, and the moon will not give its light, ²⁵and the stars will be falling from heaven, and the powers in the heavens will be shaken. ²⁶And then they will see the Son of Man coming in clouds with great power and glory. ²⁷And then he will send out the angels and he will gather his chosen ones from the four winds, from the end of the earth to the end of heaven.

[28]"From the fig tree, learn the parable. When its branch is already becoming tender and putting forth leaves, you know that the harvest is near. [29]So you also, when you see these things happening, you know that he is near, at the doors. [30]Amen, I say to you, this generation will not pass away before all these things come to pass. [31]Heaven and earth will pass away, but my words will never pass away. [32]But concerning that day or hour no one knows—neither the angels in heaven nor the Son—except the Father.

[33]"Look out, don't fall asleep!—for you don't know when the time is. [34]It is like a man away from home, who has left his house and has given his slaves authority, to each his work, and the doorkeeper he has commanded to keep awake. [35]So keep awake!—for you don't know when the lord of the house is coming, whether at evening or midnight or cockcrow or early in the morning, [36]in case he comes suddenly and finds you sleeping. [37]And what I say to you I say to all: Keep awake!"

Sixth Major Section (14:1–15:47)
Dying : The Passion Narrative

14 [1]And the Passover and the Feast of Unleavened Bread was to come after two days, and the chief priests and the scribes were seeking how they might stealthily seize and kill him. [2]For they were saying, "Not during the feast, lest there be a disturbance among the people."

[3]And while he was in Bethany in the house of Simon, the man with scale-disease, as he was reclining there, a woman came, having an alabaster jar of perfume of pure, precious nard; and breaking the alabaster jar, she poured the perfume over his head. [4]But there were some who were expressing their indignation to each other: "Why has this waste of perfume occurred? [5]For this perfume could have been sold for more than three hundred denarii and given to the poor!" And they were outraged at her. [6]But Jesus said, "Leave her alone! Why are you bothering her? She's done a good deed to me. [7]For the poor you always have with you, and whenever you want to you can do them good; but me you won't always have. [8]She has done what she could; she has come beforehand to anoint my body for burial. [9]Amen, I say to you, wherever the good news is proclaimed in all the world, what she has done will also be spoken of, as a memorial for her."

[10]And Judas Iscariot, one of the Twelve, went away to the chief priests in order to turn him over to them. [11]And when they heard, they were glad, and they promised to give him money. And he was seeking how he might find the right time to turn him over.

[12]And on the first day of the Feast of Unleavened Bread, when they sacrificed the Passover, his disciples said to him, "Where do you want us to go out and prepare, so that you may eat the Passover?" [13]And he sent out two of his disciples and said to them, "Go into the city, and a man will meet you carrying a ceramic water jar. Follow him, [14]and wherever he goes in, say to the master of the house, 'The teacher says, "Where is my lodging, where I may eat the Passover with my disciples?"' [15]And he will show you a large upper room, furnished and prepared;

and there prepare for us." [16]And the disciples went out and went into the city and found it just as he had told them, and they prepared the Passover.

[17]And when it was evening, he came with the Twelve. [18]And as they were reclining and eating, Jesus said, "Amen, I say to you, one of you will turn me over, the one eating with me." [19]They began to grieve and to say to him one after the other, "It's not me, is it?" [20]But he said to them, "One of the Twelve, the one dipping with me in the one bowl. [21]For the Son of Man is going away, as it has been written concerning him, but alas for that man through whom the Son of Man is being turned over. It would have been better for that man if he had never been born."

[22]And as they were eating, he took bread, blessed, broke, and gave it to them, and said, "Take, this is my body." [23]And taking a cup and giving thanks, he gave it to them, and they all drank from it. [24]And he said to them, "This is my blood of the covenant, which is poured out on behalf of many. [25]Amen, I say to you, I will never again drink from the fruit of the vine until that day when I drink it anew in the dominion of God."

[26]And after singing a hymn, they went out to the Mount of Olives. [27]And Jesus said to them, "You will all be tripped up, for it has been written, 'I will strike the shepherd, and the sheep will be scattered.' [28]But after I have been raised up, I will go before you into Galilee." [29]Peter said to him, "Even if all will be tripped up, I won't." [30]And Jesus said to him, "Amen, I say to you: Today, in this night, before the rooster crows twice, you will deny me three times." [31]But he kept speaking vehemently: "If I have to die with you, I will never deny you." And they all also said likewise.

[32]And they came to a place named Gethsemane, and he said to his disciples, "Sit here while I pray." [33]And he took Peter and James and John with him, and he began to be overwhelmed and anxious, [34]and he said to them, "My soul is very sad, to the point of death. Stay here and keep awake." [35]And going forward a bit, he fell on the ground and began to pray that, if it were possible, the hour might pass from him; [36]and he said, "*Abba* (Father), all things are possible for you—take this cup from me! But not what I want, but what you want." [37]And he came and found them sleeping, and he said to Peter, "Simon, are you sleeping? Didn't you have the strength to keep awake one hour? [38]Keep awake and pray, so that you may not enter into testing; the spirit is willing, but the flesh is weak." [39]And again he went away and prayed, saying the same thing. [40]And again he came and found them sleeping, for their eyes were weighed down; and they didn't know what to answer him. [41]And he came a third time and said to them, "Do you intend to sleep away the rest of the night, and take your rest? Is the hour far away? It has come; look, the Son of Man is being turned over to the hands of the sinners. [42]Get up, let's go! Look, the one who will turn me over has come near."

[43]And immediately, as he was still speaking, Judas, one of the Twelve, arrived; and with him a crowd with swords and clubs from the chief priests and the scribes and the elders. [44]The one who was turning him over had given them a signal, saying, "Whoever I kiss, he's the one; seize him and lead him away securely." [45]And when he arrived, he immediately went up to Jesus and said to him, "Rabbi!" and kissed him. [46]And they laid hands on him and took him into custody. [47]But a cer-

tain one of those who were present drew a sword and struck the high priest's slave and cut off his ear.

⁴⁸And Jesus answered and said to them, "Have you come out as against a brigand to apprehend me? ⁴⁹During the daytime I have been with you, teaching in the Temple, and you did not seize me. But in order that the scriptures may be fulfilled . . ."

⁵⁰And abandoning him, they all ran away. ⁵¹And a certain youth was following along with him, clothed with a linen cloth over his nakedness; and they seized him. ⁵²But he, abandoning the linen cloth, ran away naked.

⁵³And they led Jesus away to the high priest, and all the chief priests and the elders and the scribes gathered together. ⁵⁴And Peter was following from a distance into the inside, into the courtyard of the high priest, and he was sitting with the attendants and warming himself at the light.

⁵⁵And the chief priests and the whole Sanhedrin were seeking testimony against Jesus, in order to kill him, and they weren't finding it. ⁵⁶For many people were bearing false witness against him, and their testimonies were not agreeing. ⁵⁷And some people were rising up and bearing false witness against him, saying, ⁵⁸"We heard him saying, '*I* will destroy this Temple made by hands, and within three days I will build another that is not made by hands.' " ⁵⁹And even then their witness did not agree. ⁶⁰And the high priest rose up into the middle and asked Jesus, saying, "You make no reply? Why are these people testifying against you?" ⁶¹But he was silent, and he did not answer anything.

And again the high priest asked him and said to him, "You are the Christ the Son of the Blessed One!?" ⁶²And Jesus said, "*You* have said that I am; and you will see the Son of Man sitting on the right hand of the Power and coming with the clouds of heaven!" ⁶³But the high priest tore his garments and said, "Why do we need additional witnesses? ⁶⁴You have heard the blasphemy. What does it seem to you?" And they all condemned him as deserving death. ⁶⁵And some began to spit on him and to cover his face and to hit him and to say to him, "Prophesy!" And the attendants received him with slaps.

⁶⁶And as Peter was in the courtyard below, one of the slave girls of the high priest came ⁶⁷and saw Peter warming himself, and looking intently at him, she said, "You too were with the Nazarene, Jesus." ⁶⁸But he denied it, saying, "I don't know or understand what you're saying." And he went outside into the forecourt. ⁶⁹And the slave girl, seeing him, began to say again to the bystanders, "This man is one of them." ⁷⁰But he denied it again.

And a little later the bystanders again said to Peter, "You really are one of them, because you're a Galilean." ⁷¹But he began to call down curses and to swear, "I don't know this man that you're talking about!" ⁷²And immediately the rooster crowed for the second time. And Peter remembered the word that Jesus had said to him, "Before the rooster crows twice, you will deny me three times." And rushing outside, he wept.

15 ¹And immediately, early in the morning, the chief priests, having taken counsel with the elders and the scribes and the whole Sanhedrin, bound Jesus and led him away and turned him over to Pilate. ²And Pilate asked him, "*You* are the king of the Jews?" But he answered him, saying, "*You* are saying it." [3]And the chief priests accused him of many things. [4]And Pilate asked him again, saying, "You make no reply? See what great things they are charging you with!" [5]But Jesus did not answer anything anymore, so that Pilate was amazed.

[6]But during the feast he used to release to them one prisoner whom they had requested. [7]Now there was a man called Barabbas who was bound together with the insurrectionists who had committed murder in the insurrection. [8]And the crowd went up and began to ask him to act as he was accustomed to do for them. [9]But Pilate answered them, saying, "Do you want me to release to you the king of the Jews?" [10]For he knew that the chief priests had turned him over out of envy. [11]But the chief priests stirred up the crowd to ask that he might release Barabbas to them instead. [12]But Pilate again answered them, saying, "What then shall I do with the one whom you call the king of the Jews?" [13]They cried out again, "Crucify him!" [14]But Pilate said to them, "What has he done wrong?" But they cried out even more, "Crucify him!" [15]And Pilate, wishing to satisfy the crowd, released Barabbas to them and turned Jesus over, after flogging him, in order that he might be crucified.

[16]Then the soldiers led him away, into the courtyard—that is, of the praetorium—and they called together the whole cohort. [17]And they put purple clothes on him and wove and placed on him a crown of thorns. [18]And they began to salute him: "Hail, king of the Jews!" [19]And they were beating his head with a cane, and they were spitting on him and bending the knee and bowing down to him. [20]And when they had mocked him, they took the purple clothes off him and put his own clothes on him.

And they led him out in order to crucify him. [21]And they pressed into service a certain passerby, Simon of Cyrene, who was coming in from the country, the father of Alexander and Rufus, in order that he might carry his cross. [22]And they bore him away to the place called "Golgotha," which is translated "The Place of the Skull." [23]And they were trying to give him myrrhed wine, but he would not accept it. [24]And they crucified him, and they divided his clothes, casting lots for them, to see who would get what. [25]It was the third hour, and they crucified him. [26]And the inscription of the charge against him was inscribed, "The King of the Jews." [27]And with him they crucified two brigands, one on his right and one on his left.

[29]And the passersby were blaspheming him, shaking their heads and saying, "Ha! You who destroy the Temple and build it in three days, [30]save yourself by coming down from the cross!" [31]Likewise the chief priests were mocking him to each other, along with the scribes, saying, "He saved others; himself he cannot save. [32]The Christ, the king of Israel? Let him now come down from the cross, in order that we might see and believe!" And those who were crucified along with him were railing against him.

[33]And when the sixth hour arrived, there was darkness over the whole earth until the ninth hour. [34]And at the ninth hour Jesus cried out with a loud voice, "*Elōi, Elōi, lama sabachthani*," which is translated, "My God, my God, why have you abandoned me?"

[35]And some of those who were standing about, hearing it, said, "Look, he is calling Elijah!" [36]And one of them ran and filled a sponge with vinegar and put it around a reed and tried to give it to him to drink, saying, "Let me be! Let's see if Elijah is going to come to take him down!" [37]But Jesus, having given a loud cry, expired.

[38]And the veil of the sanctuary was ripped in two from top to bottom. [39]And the centurion who was standing opposite him, seeing that he expired in this manner, said, "Truly this man was God's son!"

[40]And there were also women watching from far away, among whom were Mary the Magdalene, and Mary the mother of James the Small and of Joses, and Salome, [41]who used to follow him when he was in Galilee and used to serve him, and many others who had come up with him to Jerusalem.

[42]And when it was already evening, since it was the Preparation Day (that is, the day before the Sabbath), [43]there came Joseph from Arimathaea, a prominent member of the council, who was also himself expecting the dominion of God. Plucking up his courage, he went in to Pilate and requested the body of Jesus. [44]But Pilate wondered whether he could already have died and, summoning the centurion, asked him whether he had already died. [45]And having found out from the centurion, he granted the corpse to Joseph. [46]And having bought a linen cloth, he took him down and wrapped him in the linen cloth and placed him in a tomb that had been hewed out of a rock, and he rolled a stone against the door of the tomb. [47]And Mary the Magdalene and Mary of Joses beheld where he had been laid.

Epilogue (16:1–8)
The Empty Tomb

16 [1]And when the Sabbath had passed, Mary the Magdalene and Mary of James and Salome bought spices in order that they might come and anoint him. [2]And very early in the morning, on the first day of the week, they came to the tomb after the sun had risen. [3]And they said to each other, "Who will roll the stone away from the door of the tomb for us?" [4]And looking up, they beheld that the stone had already been rolled away (for it was very large).

[5]And going into the tomb, they saw a young man sitting on the right, dressed in a white robe, and they were astounded. [6]But he said to them, "Do not be astounded. You seek Jesus the Nazarene, the crucified one. He has been raised; he is not here. See the place where they laid him! [7]But go, say to his disciples (and to Peter), 'He is going before you into Galilee. There you will see him, just as he said to you.' " [8]But they went out and fled from the tomb, for trembling and astonishment had taken hold of them. And they did not say anything to anyone, for they were afraid.

TRANSLATION,
NOTES,
AND
COMMENTS

◆

FOURTH MAJOR SECTION
(MARK 8:22–10:52)

◆

INTRODUCTION
ON THE WAY: BLINDNESS AND SIGHT

The first half of Mark has been dominated by Jesus' healing miracles, in the form of both individual narratives and summary passages. But in the present section, which begins the Gospel's second half, there are only three healing narratives, and in the remainder of the Gospel there are none—until the resurrection, which in a way is the biggest healing miracle of all. Perhaps Mark would have invoked the principle of 6:5–6 to explain this diminution: in the "mystery of the dominion of God" (cf. 4:11), the opposition to God increases as the time of eschatological tribulation draws near, and even Jesus' miraculous healing power is affected. As another Gospel puts it, the night is coming, when no one can work (John 9:4).

But the three miracles that *are* present in 8:22–10:52 are significant, and they somewhat offset this gloomy prospect. This section contains the only Markan stories of the healing of blind people (8:22–26; 10:46–52), and these two narratives frame the entire section, which is otherwise dominated by Jesus' teaching of the disciples. This is not a haphazard arrangement. Throughout the section, the Markan disciples show themselves to be "blind"—terribly imperceptive and in need of the illumination of Jesus' teaching. They ask inane questions (9:10–11; 10:10), make stupid remarks (9:5–6), grasp for personal power (9:33–34; 10:35–40), mistake the merciful nature of Jesus' mission (9:38), and otherwise show themselves deficient in appreciating the unique way in which God's dominion is manifesting itself through Jesus (8:31–33; 9:32; 10:13–14, 24, 26, 32). Yet they also, through their representative Peter, display an insight about Jesus that transcends human knowledge (8:28–29)—although Peter immediately, and almost predictably, falls into a Satanic delusion about it (8:33). Despite such stumbles, however, the Markan disciples are on the road to clear vision (cf. 16:7). In many ways they are like the blind man in the first story who, after Jesus' initial touch, sees indistinctly and must await Jesus' second touch in order to receive perfect sight (cf. Johnson, "Blind Man," and the COMMENT on 8:22–26).

Besides these two healings of blind men, which frame the section, there is one other miracle, the exorcism of an epileptic boy in 9:14–29. This is a dramatic tale that is intimately linked with the vital subject of faith and disbelief (see 9:19, 23–24, 28–29), and it has an important structural role in the overall outline of the

Gospel (see the introduction to the COMMENT on 9:14–29). The importance of all three healing miracles, moreover, is reinforced by the fact that they are linked with two other structurally significant devices in our section, the three passion predictions and the references to "the way," which fall into three clusters (see figure 21 for the interrelation of these structural devices). These juxtapositions are, again, probably no accident: the "way" of Jesus and the disciples, which ultimately leads to death in Jerusalem, is the journey on which human blindness is healed, human subjection to demonic forces terminated, and the royal power of God experienced (cf. the section's frequent references to the dominion of God).

Figure 21: Structural Devices in Mark 8:22–10:52

Passage	Healings	"The Way"	Passion Predictions
8:22–26	blind man		
8:27–33		8:27 *en tę hodǭ* = "in/on the way"	8:31–33: first prediction
8:34–9:1			
9:2–8			
9:9–13			
9:14–29	epileptic boy		
9:30–32			9:30–32: second prediction
9:33–37		9:33–34 *en tę hodǭ* = "in/on the way"	
9:38–40			
9:41–50			
10:1–12			
10:13–16			
10:17–22		10:17 *eis hodon* = "on the way"	
10:23–31			
10:32–34		10:32 *en tę hodǭ* = "in/on the way"	10:32–34: third prediction
10:35–45			
10:46–52	blind man	10:46 *para tēn hodon* = "beside the way"	
		10:52 *en tę hodǭ* = "in/on the way"	

There is significant scriptural background to this theme of the royal way of Jesus, especially in Deutero-Isaiah (see Marcus, *Way*, 31–37, and Watts, *New Exodus*, 221–94). As pointed out in the COMMENT on 1:2–3, the opening of the Gospel has already established a strong connection between the "way" of Jesus and "the way of the Lord," which is spoken of in Isa 40:3 and other Deutero-Isaian passages (Isa 35:8–10; 43:16–21; 51:9–10; 52:1–12; 62:10–12). This dual "way" now becomes the dominant motif of the Gospel, and the Deutero-Isaian context remains in view. It is not accidental, for example, that various Isaian passages link the Lord's way both with the healing of the blind (Isa 35:1–7; 42:16) and with the revelation of the dominion of God (40:1–11, esp. in the Targum, and 52:1–12). Influencing the whole section, then, is the Deutero-Isaian conception of God's "way," his triumphal progress up to Jerusalem in a saving act of holy war that will liberate and enlighten his elect people and demonstrate his gracious sovereignty over the world.

But as I have pointed out elsewhere:

> An ironic twist . . . has inverted the normal way of painting the Deutero-Isaian picture of victorious holy war. Jesus announces to his companions that he is going up to Jerusalem not in order to triumph over his enemies in a conventional way but in order to be killed by them. Nothing could be more antithetical to conventional notions of victory than Jesus' long prophecy of his own betrayal, condemnation, mockery, physical abuse, and execution (10:33–34). Yet, it must be forcefully added, this prophecy is not a *denial* of the Deutero-Isaian hope for a holy war victory; it is, rather, a radical, cross-centered *adaptation* of it. For those with eyes to see (see 4:9, 23), the fearful trek of the befuddled, bedraggled little band of disciples *is* the return of Israel to Zion, and Jesus' suffering and death there *are* the prophesied apocalyptic victory of the divine warrior. The same spirit that will later shape the Markan passion narrative infuses Mark 8:22–10:52, a unitary redefinition of apocalyptic eschatology that paradoxically hears in Jesus' cry of dereliction the triumph song of Yahweh's return to Zion, that paradoxically sees in his anguished, solitary death the long-awaited advent of the kingdom of God. (*Way*, 36)

I would now add a point made by Watts (*New Exodus*, 115 n. 135): this Markan redefinition of apocalyptic triumph is prefigured in Deutero-Isaiah itself. The famous "Suffering Servant" song (Isa 52:13–53:12) is located between two depictions of the glorious new exodus that will manifest God's cosmic sovereignty (52:1–12; 54:1–17), and this context perhaps suggests that for Deutero-Isaiah, as later for Mark, the Servant's suffering is the divinely appointed means for the realization of the dominion of God.

Like Deutero-Isaiah, Mark ties together the themes of suffering and divine power. Indeed, with the exception of 10:1–12, all the passages in our section have to do either explicitly or implicitly with these two themes, which for the most part alternate throughout the section (see figure 22). Thus, Mark's audience is continually reminded not only of Jesus' suffering but also of the necessity that

Figure 22: The Themes of Suffering and Power in Mark 8:22–10:52

8:22–26   Healing of blind man in two stages: manifestation of Jesus' POWER
8:27–30   Peter's confession of Jesus as Messiah: title of POWER
8:31–33   First passion prediction: necessity of SUFFERING
8:34–9:1   Teaching about following the Messiah: necessity of SUFFERING
9:2–8   The transfiguration: manifestation of Jesus' POWER
9:9–13   Discussion about Elijah's coming: necessity of SUFFERING
9:14–29   Exorcism of epileptic boy: manifestation of Jesus' POWER
9:30–32   Second passion prediction: necessity of SUFFERING
9:33–37   Teaching about greatness: necessity of SUFFERING (becoming last
           of all)
9:38–40   Teaching about alien exorcist: reference to works of POWER
9:41–50   Teaching about reward and punishment: necessity of SUFFERING
           (cutting off hand, etc.)
10:1–12   Discussion of divorce
10:13–16   Becoming like a child in order to enter the dominion of God
           (= God's royal POWER)
10:17–22   Discussion with rich man about attaining eternal life: necessity of
           SUFFERING (loss of riches)
10:23–31   Discussion with disciples about wealth: promise of POWER (they will
           receive one hundredfold when they abandon things in this age)
10:32–34   Third passion prediction: necessity of SUFFERING
10:35–45   Rejection of James and John's request for privileged places: necessity
           of SUFFERING, becoming servant of all
10:46–52   Healing of blind Bartimaeus: manifestation of Jesus' POWER

they should participate in it, picking up their crosses and following him to the death (cf. 8:34). But this suffering is not to be embraced for its own sake. Losing one's life also means saving it (8:35), not only as an individual but also as a member of the community that "follows the Lamb wherever he goes" (Rev 14:4) and whose members find support and empowerment within that fellowship on the move—new houses and brothers and sisters and mothers and children and lands, along with all their persecutions (Mark 10:29–30). If, then, those who are healed of their blindness set out with Jesus on a journey that moves toward suffering and death in Jerusalem (cf. 10:52), they also join him on the way that leads to the resurrection (8:31; 9:31; 10:34).

JESUS HEALS A BLIND MAN IN TWO STAGES (8:22–26)

8 ²²And they came to Bethsaida. And people brought a blind man to him and pleaded with him to touch him. ²³And taking the blind man by the hand, he led him out of the village and spat on his eyes and laid his hands on him and asked him, "Do you see anything?" ²⁴And he, looking up and beginning to see again,

said, "I see people . . . because . . . I see people like walking trees." ²⁵Then Jesus laid his hands on his eyes again, and his sight broke through, and he was restored, and he saw all things clearly from that moment on. ²⁶And he sent him home, saying, "Do not even go into the village."

NOTES

8 22. *Bethsaida.* Gk *Bēthsaidan.* On this locality, see the NOTE on "toward Bethsaida" in 6:45. In 8:23, 26 Mark calls it a *kōmē,* or village, though elsewhere in the NT (Luke 9:10; John 1:44) and in Josephus (*War* 3.515) it is referred to as a *polis,* or city (cf. Johnson, "Blind Man," 371). The latter designation reflects the work of Herod Philip, who according to Josephus (*Ant.* 18.28) increased the population of the *kōmē,* built up its fortifications, and advanced its status to that of a *polis,* which he called "Julias" after the Emperor Augustus's daughter Julia. But calling Bethsaida a *kōmē* is not necessarily an error or a sign of a redactional seam (against, e.g., Bultmann, 213; Johnson, ibid.; with Theissen, 127). Elsewhere (*Against Apion* 1.197) Josephus himself quotes without demurral the comment of Hecataeus of Abdera, "The Jews have many fortresses and villages in different parts of the country, but only one fortified city," that is, Jerusalem.

people brought. Gk *pherousin,* lit. "they brought," another instance of the impersonal use of the third person plural (see the NOTE on "the people were amazed" in 1:22).

23. *spat on his eyes.* Gk *ptysas eis ta ommata,* lit. "having spat on his eyes." On the use of spittle in ancient healings, see the NOTE on "spat" in 7:33; for its use as an eye salve in particular, see the stories about Vespasian cited in the COMMENT on 8:22–23, as well as Pliny, *Natural History* 28.37.86 and Jewish Sabbath ordinances such as *b. Šabb.* 108b ("[To put] tasteless saliva, even on the eye, is forbidden [on the Sabbath]"; cf. Kollmann, *Jesus,* 235).

As noted in the introduction to the COMMENT, *ommata* is a more poetic term than the more usual *ophthalmoi,* which is used in 8:25. It is frequently employed in philosophical contexts in which physical sight becomes an image for spiritual insight; see, for example, Plato's allegory of the cave and the three texts from Philo that are referred to in the COMMENT on 8:24.

laid his hands on him. Gk *epitheis tas cheiras autǭ,* lit. "having laid his hands on him"; from the context (8:25) it is clear that this means laying hands on his *eyes.* The phrase about laying on of hands also occurs in healing contexts in 5:23; 6:5; 7:32; 8:25; and elsewhere in the NT. Ancient healers frequently cured by means of a magical touch of the hand, which is often portrayed both in pictorial representations and in literature (see Lohse, *"Cheir,"* 425; Theissen, 92–93). In an Egyptian magical spell for curing a child, for example, the magician says, "My hands lie on this child, and the hands of Isis lie on him, as she lays her hands on her son Horus" (Papyrus 3027 from the Berlin Museum, cited by Behm, *Handauflegung,* 104). Especially close to our story is the account in an inscription in which a blind man turns toward the statue of the healing god Asclepius, lays (*epitheinai*) his hand (singular) on his own eyes, and begins to see again (*aneblepse*; on this word see the

NOTE on "looking up and beginning to see again" in 8:24; Dittenberger, *Sylloge* 3.1173; cf. Kollmann, *Jesus*, 235). Although the gesture of laying on of hands for healing is absent from the OT and rabbinic literature (see Davies and Allison, 2.126 n. 15), it is present in the exorcism described in 1QapGen 20:29 ("I . . . laid my hands upon his [hea]d").

↓ Note that Tobit 11:11 (S) describes a combination of magical actions in the healing of a blind man that are similar to those in our story: Tobias first *breathes* on his father's eyes, an action similar to *spitting* on them. He then *smears* medicine on them, presumably with his fingers, an action similar to *laying hands* on them.

Do you see anything? Gk *ei ti blepeis*, lit. "If you see anything?" As Taylor (370–71) notes, this usage of *ei* with a direct question is unclassical. Some important manuscripts (e.g., ℵ, A, *f*[1, 13], the Latin and most Syriac witnesses) consequently transform it into an indirect question by changing *blepeis* ("you see") to *blepei* ("he sees"). *Ei* is, however, used frequently with direct questions in the LXX (e.g., Gen 17:17; 43:7, 27; 1 Sam 15:32; cf. Conybeare and Stock, *Grammar* §100), where it usually translates the Hebrew interrogative particle *hă* (see Lagrange, 212). It is also sometimes used for *'im* (which, like *ei*, usually means "if") as the introduction to a direct question (see, e.g., 1 Kgs 1:27 and cf. Gesenius, 473–75). The phonological similarity of *'im* to *ei* may help explain the frequency of the translation with *ei*. In dependence on the LXX, *ei* also introduces direct questions frequently in the NT (see *MHT* 4.54).

24. *looking up and beginning to see again.* Gk *anablepsas* can have either of these meanings, since the prefix *ana-* can signify either "up" or "again" (this ambiguity is the basis for the play on words between "born from above" and "born again" in John 3:1–9). Mark uses both nuances elsewhere ("look up" in 6:41; 7:34; 16:4; "see again" in 10:51–52), so context must be used in determining the sense here. Johnson ("Blind Man," 376–77) argues that, both in the NT and in nonbiblical Greek, *anablepein* always means "to regain sight" when it is used in the context of blindness. But the other nuance cannot be excluded from our passage; it corresponds to Mark's graphic method of storytelling, and what the man sees—namely, people with the appearance of *trees*—is presumably something that one would look upward to see. Moreover, given the symbolic dimension of the verse (see the COMMENT on 8:24), it is germane that, as Johnson himself notes, *anablepein* frequently means "to look up to God or to heaven," as earlier in Mark at 6:41 (see also Gen 15:5; Isa 40:26; Josephus, *Ant.* 11.64). Mark, then, may intend both nuances of *anablepein*, hence the translation "looking up and beginning to see again."

I see people . . . because . . . I see people like walking trees. Gk *blepō tous anthrōpous hoti hōs dendra horō peripatountas*, lit. "I see people because as trees I see walking-around-ones." *Blepō* and *horō* are synonyms; the fact that two synonymous verbs are used is part of the passage's extraordinary richness of epistemological vocabulary (see the COMMENT on 8:25–26). The sentence, however, is awkward, and this awkwardness has caused manuscripts such as D to omit both *hoti* and *horō*, leaving "I see people as walking trees"; but on the principle that the more difficult text is usually original, this smoother reading is probably secondary.

Scholars have sometimes explained the awkwardness as the mistranslation of an

Aramaic original. Allen ("Aramaic Element," 330), for example, thinks that *hoti* = "because" is a mistranslation of the Aramaic *dĕ*, which can also mean "who"; the original, then, read "I see people whom I see as walking trees." Black (*Aramaic Approach*, 53–54) opines that the underlying Aramaic employed a construction in which the subject or object of a subordinate clause is displaced to become the subject or object of a main clause, thus giving it special emphasis; the Aramaic original read "I see people that like trees they are walking" and meant simply "I see that people are walking like trees" (cf. the similar constructions in Mark 7:2; 11:32; and 12:34). But both of these reconstructions leave unexplained the Markan repetition of verbs for seeing, and Allen's is implausible because almost any translator would know that Aramaic *dĕ* can mean "who." While mistranslation of an Aramaic original may be a partial explanation for the disjointed Markan syntax, it is also possible that the grammar is meant to mirror the fractured perception being described.

The blind man's cryptic words about walking trees recall other passages from the history of religions, though it is difficult to know what to make of some of the parallels. Taylor (371), for example, cites the "striking Hellenistic parallel" of an inscription in which a blind man is healed by a vision of the healing god Asclepius going over his eyes with his fingers, and his first post-healing sight is of the trees in the Temple (Dittenberger, *Sylloge* 3.1168). Sugirtharajah ("Men") refers to Judg 9:7–15, in which a fable about walking (and talking) trees is used to criticize kingship; Mark, therefore, is using tree imagery to show "that kingship is useless and that [Mark's readers] should look for a different model." This is overstated. While there is Markan precedent for using a tree as a symbol of kingship (see the COMMENT on 4:30–32), our passage is actually supporting the idea that Jesus is the messianic king (see the COMMENT on 8:22–23), although the nature of his kingship will need to be carefully defined (8:27–33).

25. *his sight broke through.* Gk *dieblepsen*, lit. "he saw through." As Johnson ("Blind Man," 377) points out, this word can mean either "stare" (e.g., Plato, *Phaedo* 86D) or "see clearly." The latter is the meaning in the only other NT usage, Matt 7:5//Luke 6:42, and probably in our passage as well, but *dieblepsen* is not exactly synonymous with *eneblepen*, which occurs a few words later, so that the description is not tautologous (against Taylor, 372). Rather, in line with the extramission theory of vision (see the NOTE on "clearly" below), the distinction between these two verbs is probably that the beam of light within the man's eye breaks through the internal barrier that has been blocking it and is therefore free to travel out into the external world (*dieblepsen*) and begin striking objects there (*eneblepen*), thereby restoring his sight (cf. again Matt 7:5//Luke 6:42 and *diorōsin* in Philo, *On Dreams* 1.248).

he was restored. Gk *apekatestē.* This implies that the man was once able to see but subsequently lost his sight; cf. the LXX of Exod 4:7 and Lev 13:16, both of which use the same Greek verb to speak of the restoration of a previous condition of health. In contrast, the Johannine story of the healing of a blind man by Jesus' spittle emphasizes that the man has been blind *from birth* (John 9:1–2); this feature may represent a Johannine radicalization of a story like ours.

he saw . . . from that moment on. Gk *eneblepen.* The nuance of "from that moment on" is conveyed by the switch from the aorist verbs *dieblepsen* ("his sight
broke through") and *apekatestē* ("was restored") to the imperfect verb *eneblepen*
(cf. Johnson, "Blind Man," 378–79). On the inceptive use of the imperfect, see the
NOTE on "and the fever left her, and she began serving them" in 1:31.

all things. Gk *hapanta.* Since the passage is symbolic of a growth in spiritual
vision (see the COMMENT on 8:24), it is possible that the concluding Markan
reference to the blind man seeing *all things* (*hapanta*) has a symbolic dimension
as well; the enlightenment that Christ brings grants knowledge of all mysteries
(cf. 1 Cor 13:2). Philo's *On Abraham* 70–71, which, like our passage, uses gradual
growth in vision as a symbol for progression in spiritual understanding (see the
discussion of this passage in the COMMENT on 8:24), concludes with Abraham
discerning God, "the overseer of *the All* (*tou pantos*)."

clearly. Gk *tēlaugōs,* lit. "in a far-shining way"; the word is a compound of *tēle* =
"at a distance, far off" and *augē* "light/beam," and it is used most often in poetic
descriptions of the radiance of the sun or of gods, people, and things that are like
it in brightness or splendor (see LSJ 1787). Its usage here reflects the most common ancient theory of vision, according to which sighted creatures see by means
of light beams that come *out* of their eyes rather than into them (see the significantly titled chapter "The Eye as a Lamp" in Allison, *Jesus Tradition,* 133–67). In
the case of a blind person, however, the beam is trapped and unable to make its
way to external objects, so vision cannot ensue (cf. Plato, *Timaeus* 45d–e: "The
eyelids . . . when they are shut tight, curb the power of the inner fire"; LCL trans.
alt.). When such a person's vision becomes "far-shining," the beam is freed to
travel the necessary distance to objects in the outside world, and the person sees
clearly (cf. the NOTE on "his sight broke through" above). Philo frequently uses
tēlaugōs and the cognate adjective in this sense in passages that, like our story,
compare physical sight to spiritual sight (e.g., *Unchangeableness of God* 29; *Noah's
Work as a Planter* 22; see Marcus, "Optics").

26. *And he sent him home.* Gk *kai apesteilen auton eis oikon.* In the original
story taken up by Mark, the *oikos* was probably the place where the miracle would
be confirmed by family and neighbors, as in the narrative underlying John 9:1–9
(cf. Martyn, *History,* 35–36). The Markan addition of 8:26b, however, has turned
the *oikos* into a place of concealment, as it typically is in Mark (cf. 5:19–20; 7:17,
24; 9:28; 10:10; cf. Theissen, 146–48).

Do not even go into the village. Gk *mēde eis tēn kōmēn eiselthēs.* As noted in the
introduction to the COMMENT, this is probably a redactional addition: it corresponds to Mark's messianic secret motif, creates a parallel with the redactional
command to silence that ends the following story (8:30), and causes a logical problem similar to that precipitated by the addition of 5:43a: how can the healing ultimately remain secret (cf. the introduction to the COMMENT on 5:21–43)?

Some manuscripts read *mēdeni eipēs eis tēn kōmēn* ("do not speak to anyone
in the village") or something similar, and Räisänen (163–64) argues that this is
the original reading, since it is even more difficult than the command not to re-
enter the village. The text chosen, however, is supported by all the major textual

families, and it is actually harder to imagine that the man would never return to his native village (as in the reading chosen) than to suppose that he would just keep mum about the way in which he was healed. The alternate reading may be designed to conform our passage even more closely to 8:30 (cf. Metzger, 99).

COMMENT

Introduction. The scene in which Jesus' disciples are rebuked for their lack of spiritual vision ("Having eyes, do you not see?" 8:18) is immediately followed by a symbolic tale in which a man is cured of his blindness after first passing through an intermediate state of indistinct vision. The impression that this juxtaposition is deliberate is reinforced by the succeeding narrative, in which Peter also displays genuine but faulty perception: he recognizes Jesus' messianic identity (8:29), but fails to attain a clear insight into what that identity betokens (8:32–33).

As noted in the introduction to the COMMENT on the healing of the deaf-mute in 7:31–37, the numerous similarities between that narrative and the present one suggest that the two pericopes (see the GLOSSARY) originally belonged together in some sort of pre-Markan collection. This theory is more likely than the proposal of Hooker (197) that the similarities are the result of Markan editing; they neither reflect typical Markan theological interests nor are laden with redactional vocabulary, and Mark seems more interested in linking our passage with the other healing-of-the-blind miracle (10:46–52) than in associating it with the healing of the deaf-mute (see the introduction to 8:22–10:52). Besides splitting our passage off from the deaf-mute story in 7:31–37, Mark is probably also responsible for the ending in 8:26b ("Do not even go into the village"), which corresponds to his messianic secret motif (cf. the NOTE on these words). The very beginning of the pericope, 8:22a, may also reflect Markan redaction (cf. Johnson, "Blind Man," 370–72), but it is possible that the localization in Bethsaida is traditional; 6:45 suggests that there was a pre-Markan story in which Jesus landed in Bethsaida (see the NOTE on "toward Bethsaida" in 6:45).

One of the most striking features of the passage is its extraordinary profusion of words having to do with eyes and seeing. In these five short verses, the verb *blepein* ("to see," twice in 8:23–24) and three different compounds (*anablepein, diablepein,* and *emblepein,* 8:24–25) are mobilized five times, and the related verb *horan* (also translated "see," 8:24) is used once. The adjective *typhlos* ("blind," twice in 8:22–23) and the rare, poetic adverb *tēlaugōs* ("clearly," lit. "in a far-shining way" 8:25) also appear, as do two different words for "eyes," the common noun *ophthalmoi* (8:25) and the poetic term *ommata* (8:23). Also impressive is the emphasis on the physicality of Jesus' actions: people plead with him to *touch* the blind man, he *takes* this sufferer *by the hand*, he *spits* on his eyes, and he *lays hands* on him twice.

The passage falls into five parts, which revolve around the cryptic statement in 8:24:

8:22   INTRODUCTION: Blind man brought to Jesus with request for healing
        (*erchontai . . . eis*)
8:23   FIRST HEALING TOUCH (*cheiras . . . eis ta ommata autou . . . blepeis*)
8:24   BLIND MAN'S RESPONSE: "People like walking trees"
8:25   SECOND HEALING TOUCH (*cheiras . . . epi tous ophthalmous
                autou . . . dieblepen*)
8:26   CONCLUSION: Blind man sent home healed (*eis . . . eiselthēs*)

The passage is chiastically structured, with matching language in the introduction and conclusion and in the two healing touches. The unmatched part is the central one, the blind man's response in 8:24, which receives a great deal of emphasis from the fact that it is the only place in the whole story where he speaks; the cryptic nature of his words, moreover, itself grabs the reader's attention.

8:22–23: introduction and first healing touch. After the troubling shipboard conversation about forgotten bread, dangerous leaven, and distorted perception (8:14–21), Jesus and his disciples dock at Bethsaida (8:22a), the intended goal of an earlier boat journey (cf. 6:45, 53). For hearers who remember the earlier tale, this delayed arrival might suggest that a new epoch in Jesus' ministry is opening up. From now on his travel will be exclusively on foot, except for his triumphal entry into Jerusalem astride a donkey (11:1–10). Walking is a slower and generally more arduous method of travel than navigation, and the change in the mode of transport corresponds to the increasing difficulty of Jesus' mission, which is indicated as well by the decline in the frequency of miracles in this section of the Gospel (see the introduction to 8:22–10:52). But walking is also a motif loaded with OT symbolism, which Mark will exploit to the full (see the NOTE on "foot" in 9:45).

A blind man is brought to Jesus, presumably by his friends or relatives, who request that the wonder-worker might heal him by means of his charismatic touch (8:22b). Jesus signals his willingness to do so by taking the man by the hand and leading him out of town (8:23a). As in the related story of the healing of a deaf-mute (7:33), this seclusion from the sight of the crowd is a traditional motif suggesting that a mysterious action too sacred for public display is about to take place. But in the Markan context it also has deeper reverberations supplied by the OT (see Schneck, *Isaiah*, 233–36). In the past, God *took* Israel *by the hand* and *led them out* of Egypt (Jer 31:32; the Greek [38:32] is very close to that in our verse). In the eschatological future, similarly, he will *grasp their hand, lead them out* of bondage, and *open their blind eyes* (Isa 42:6–7). Through its OT background, our story is linked with the theme of the new exodus along the Lord's triumphal way, a theme that plays a prominent role throughout this section of the Gospel (see again the introduction to 8:22–10:52 and cf. the COMMENT on 8:24 below).

Having led the blind man out of town, Jesus sets the healing in motion by performing the sort of dramatic gestures that are known from other ancient stories of miraculous healing: he spits on the man's eyes and lays his hands on them (8:23b; see the NOTES on "spat" in 7:33, "spat on his eyes" in 8:23, and "laid his hands on him" in 8:23). Again, however, these traditional gestures take on a deeper meaning in the context of Mark's Gospel and his world. In ancient literature, healing of physical sight is often conflated with repair of spiritual vision; the Mithras liturgy in the great magical papyrus of Paris, for example, recommends application of a magical eye salve in order to increase the spiritual acuity of the recipient (*PGM* 4.770–80). The use of such magical means also reflects on the status of their bestower. Suetonius, for example, tells a story, in many ways parallel to ours, about the emperor-to-be Vespasian healing a blind man by means of his spittle (*Vespasian* 7.2–3; cf. Tacitus, *Histories* 4.81.1), introducing it with the words

> Vespasian, who against all expectation had *mounted the throne* as a wholly new prince, still lacked *presence* (*auctoritas*) and *divinely confirmed majesty* (*maiestas*). But this was granted to him [when he healed the blind man]. (Schrage trans., "*Typhlos*," 274 n. 23)

In this case, the healing of the blind man points toward the royal authority of the healer. This sort of belief continued in the West until recently; Thomas (*Religion*, 227–37), for example, chronicles the medieval and early modern conviction that the English king's touch had the power to cure diseases (cf. Shakespeare, *Macbeth* 4.3.140–59, and Tolkien, *The Return of the King*, ch. 8: "The hands of the king are the hands of a healer"). In ancient Judaism the royal charisma expected of the messianic king apparently included the ability to cure blindness; 4Q521 speaks of the Lord "giving sight to the blind," and the context suggests that this miracle will occur through the instrumentality of "his [God's] Messiah" (cf. *T. Isa* 42:1–7 and Chilton, *Isaiah Targum*, 81n). And the Q pericope (see GLOSSARY under "Q") Matt 11:2–6//Luke 7:18–23 assumes that there was a common expectation that the Messiah would, among his other healing miracles, give sight to the blind. Thus, the Markan juxtaposition of our story of the healing of a blind man with Peter's acclamation of Jesus as Messiah (8:27–30) is natural, and it is probably not a coincidence that the other story of the healing of a blind man (10:46–52) is framed by passages that also allude to Jesus' royal power (see the reference to Jesus' kingly glory in 10:37 and the royal, triumphal entry in 11:1–10).

8:24: the blind man's response. But despite this royal touch, an obstacle to the blind man's complete healing remains. In response to Jesus' question whether he sees anything, the man replies in a disjointed manner that reflects his fractured perception: "I see people . . . because . . . I see people like walking trees" (see the NOTE on these words in 8:24). The healing, then, has not yet been totally effective; the man is not blind anymore, but neither does he yet see with fully functional eyes (cf. Swete, 164). In contrast to all the other healings recorded in the Jesus tradition, this one is not instantaneous; it will require a second contact with Jesus' hand before it can be complete (8:25). What might be the meaning of this strange and anomalous therapy?

As has already been suggested in the introduction to this COMMENT, for Mark the intermediate state of the man's vision after Jesus' first healing touch is probably symbolic. It corresponds to the intermediate state of the disciples' spiritual perception at this point and indeed throughout the Gospel; like the disciples in the immediately preceding passage (8:18), the man has eyes but does not yet see clearly, though he will eventually do so (cf. 8:21: "Do you *not yet* understand?"). This sort of comparison between physical and spiritual vision was a commonplace in the ancient world, and it often went along with the view that the natural human state was one of spiritual blindness. Thus, in *Gen. Rab.* 53.14, R. Benjamin b. Levi and R. Jonathan b. Amram say that "all may be presumed to be blind, until the Holy One, blessed be He, enlightens their eyes."

As this tradition in *Genesis Rabbah* suggests, however, the pessimistic view of the natural human ability to see truth often goes hand in hand with an optimistic assessment of what is possible when divine grace appears on the scene. But since the distance from human blindness to divine illumination is so huge, it is frequently emphasized that the latter must be approached in stages. In Plato's famous cave allegory in *Republic* 7.515c–17a, for example, the man who is released from the cave and dragged into the light is at first dazzled and unable to see anything, but his eyes gradually adjust until he can discern shadows and reflections of terrestrial objects, then the objects themselves, and finally the moon, stars, and sun. A growth in vision is thus described, as in Mark, and Plato, like Mark, uses this growth as an image for deepening spiritual insight. The image of progressively improving vision is also found in Diaspora Jewish circles, sometimes in ways remarkably similar to our passage; Philo's *On Abraham* 70–71, for example, describes spiritual growth as a gradual opening of the soul's eye (*omma*), and *On Sobriety* 3 asserts that divine revelation can happen only if that eye "is nowhere suffused as by rheum or closed, but is able to open itself fully and completely" (see also *On Mating* 135 and cf. Johnson, "Blind Man," 375 n. 35; Martyn, *Galatians*, 398–400). Similarly, in the case of the Markan blind man, complete recovery of sight is contingent on the removal of the impediment to vision that still remains after Jesus' first healing touch.

In OT and Jewish contexts this theme of healing of visual impairment is often wedded to a dynamic view of world history, in which clear vision is a gift of God reserved for the age to come (for a good discussion of the blindness motif in paganism, the OT, and Judaism, see Klauck, *Allegorie*, 348–51). Already the idea of an eschatological cure for blindness is found in passages from the OT prophet Isaiah (Isa 29:18; 35:5; 42:6–7, 16; 61:1 LXX), and given the Isaian background of the present section of the Gospel, these passages are especially important parallels to our story (see the introduction to 8:22–10:52). In later Jewish interpretation, moreover, these Isaian passages are sometimes understood figuratively, as prophecies of the healing of spiritual blindness, again as in our passage (see, e.g., *Tg. Isa* 42:6–7 and *Pesiq. Rab. Kah.* 4.7).

Furthermore, some Jewish and Christian apocalyptic sources adapt the motif of a progression in vision to the idea of a sequence of world epochs. Within the NT itself, for example, Paul asserts that Christians possess at present only a partial vision, as "in a mirror, dimly," but that "when the complete comes, the partial will come to an end" (1 Cor 13:9–12). The *Damascus Document* from Qumran comes even closer to our story, since in one passage it designates the epochs before the end as periods of blindness (CD 16:2–6). Significantly, these eras are associated with the hostile activity of Mastema, a Qumran term for Satan, and the latter is linked with blindness elsewhere in Jewish and Christian traditions as well (see the introduction to the COMMENT on 8:27–33). Another *Damascus Document* passage, CD 1:5–12, describes a progression in these periods of perception, from an initial revelation that nevertheless leaves God's elect groping for the way like blind people, to a second enlightenment, in which God heals their residual blindness by "rais[ing] up for them a Teacher of Righteousness to guide them in the way of His heart" (Vermes trans. alt.). This passage is particularly close to the Markan healing-of-blind-men stories in that blindness and its progressive cure are associated with the motif of "the way." In Mark, healing of blindness is linked with the way motif both in the context of the present narrative (see "on the way" in 8:27) and in the story of Bartimaeus (see 10:46, 52).

8:25–26: second healing touch and conclusion. Like the Qumran sectarians before the coming of the Teacher of Righteousness, the blind man in our story still "gropes for the way," even though he has already received a measure of divine healing power. The darkness has begun to give way to the light (cf. John 1:5; 1 John 2:8), but there is still demonic resistance from the side of the darkness (for demonic resistance in other healing stories, including our passage's twin, 7:31–37, see the NOTES on "sighed" in 7:34 and 8:12 and "testing" in 8:11, and the COMMENT on 7:31–34). Another contact with Jesus is necessary, and this happens at the climax of the story, in a climactic verse that displays an extraordinary concentration of epistemological language: Jesus again lays his hands on the man's *eyes*, the man's *sight breaks through* and *is restored*, and he *sees* all things *clearly* (8:25; on the ancient optical theory implicit here, see the NOTES on "his sight broke through," "he saw . . . from that moment on," and "clearly" in 8:25).

If, as argued above, the blind man's intermediate state of seeing-yet-not-seeing corresponds to the disciples' position throughout the Gospel, to what does his final state of clear vision correspond? Lightfoot (*History*, 90–91) thinks that the disciples' partial blindness is healed immediately at Peter's confession in 8:29. Verses 8:32–33, however, imply that Peter's spiritual vision is still seriously defective (cf. Hooker, 198). The conclusion of our passage, rather, points toward the resurrection as the point of clear vision, since here Jesus sends the man home, implicitly forbidding him to make his healing known ("Do not even go into the village," 8:26b). This veto on publicity, which is a Markan redactional touch, conforms our passage to the Gospel's messianic secret motif, and the next instance of such a veto, a scant twenty verses further on, alludes to Jesus' resurrection as the point at which secrecy will give way to publicity (9:9). This allusion is given an epistemological correlate at the end of the Gospel when the proclamation of Jesus' resurrection is linked with the promise that the disciples will *see* him in Galilee (16:6–7). As in the Jewish literature discussed above in the COMMENT on 8:24, the "present evil age" is one of hiddenness and imperfect vision, but the age to come, the aeon of the resurrection, will be an epoch of openness and insight (see Marcus, "Epistemology"). Jesus forbids publicity about his healings and

his identity because those things can truly be understood only in the light of his
resurrection—which is also the light that dispels human blindness (see the AP-
PENDIX "The Messianic Secret Motif" in vol. 1).

At the present point in Mark's story, to be sure, the reason for the vetoes on
publicity is still a literary gap in the narrative (see the discussion of "gaps" in the
COMMENT on 4:3–8). Indeed, it is probably a gap that has been growing more
and more puzzling for Markan readers in their first hearing of the Gospel, as the
vetoes have been piling up since the beginning of Jesus' ministry (1:34, 44; 3:12;
5:43), and in the last couple of chapters have become especially frequent (7:24,
36; 8:26; cf. 8:30 in the next passage). The explicit linkage made in 9:9 between
the resurrection and an end to silence, then, will likely come as a long-hoped-for
revelation, the beginning of the solution to a readerly frustration that has become
increasingly pressing.

But before that revelation can happen, other matters must be brought to the attention of Mark's readers. They must be reminded of who Jesus is and of what his
identity implies for the fate of his disciples and of the world in general, both in this
age and in the next. It is to these crucial matters that the following passages in the
Gospel address themselves.

JESUS IS RECOGNIZED AS MESSIAH AND
PROPHESIES HIS DEATH AND RESURRECTION (8:27–33)

8 27And Jesus and his disciples went out into the villages of Caesarea Philippi.
And on the way he was asking his disciples and saying to them, "Who do people
say that I am?" 28And they said to him, "Some say John the Baptist, and others
Elijah, and others that you are one of the prophets." 29And he asked them, "But
you, who do *you* say that I am?" And Peter answered and said to him, "You are the
Christ." 30And he vehemently ordered them to speak to nobody about him.

31And he began to teach them that it was necessary that the Son of Man should
suffer many things and be rejected by the elders and the chief priests and the
scribes, and be killed, and after three days arise. 32And he was making this statement frankly. And Peter took him aside and began to rebuke him. 33But he, turning and looking at his disciples, rebuked Peter and said, "Get behind me, Satan!
For you are fixing your thoughts not on the things of God but on those of human
beings."

NOTES

8 27. *Caesarea Philippi.* Gk *Kaisareias tēs Philippou.* A predominantly Gentile
town in the Golan Heights region, about twenty-five miles north of the Sea of
Galilee. Upper Galilee is linked in ancient Jewish sources with visionary activity
and ascent to the heavenly Temple (see *1 Enoch* 12–16 and *T. Levi* 2–7), so it is
an appropriate place for revelation of an important aspect of Jesus' identity (see
Nickelsburg, "Enoch, Levi, and Peter"). The older name of Caesarea Philippi was

Panias (cf. its modern name, Banias), after the Greek god Pan, who had a sacred grotto there. The town was renamed Caesarea in honor of Augustus Caesar by Herod the Great's son Philip (see Josephus, *War* 2.168; *Ant.* 18.28); the appellation "Philippi" was added to distinguish it from the big city of the same name on the coast. Even before this renaming, the inland city was associated with imperial power. Herod the Great built and dedicated to Augustus a white marble temple there, and in this temple Augustus received divine honors (Josephus, *War* 1.404–6; *Ant.* 15.363–64; cf. Collins, "Worship"). Perhaps in reaction to this perceived act of hubris, a later Jewish tradition speaks of the miraculous fall of a gate in Panias as a sign of the coming of the Messiah (*b. Sanh.* 98a). During the Great Revolt of the Jews against the Romans, much of the Jewish population of the city was massacred (Josephus, *Life* 54); later the Roman general Vespasian was feted there by his troops for his success in suppressing the rebellion (Josephus, *War* 3.443–44). The city was thus associated with imperial rule, messianic hopes, and violent death—all of which make it a fitting backdrop for our story (see further Ma'oz, "Banias," and Kutsko, "Caesarea Philippi").

he was asking his disciples and saying to them. Gk *epērōta tous mathētas autou legōn autois.* This is a Semitic form of redundancy, similar to "answered and said," which occurs in 8:29 and elsewhere in the Gospel (cf. the NOTE on "he answered and said" in 3:33).

28. *John the Baptist . . . Elijah . . . one of the prophets.* Gk *Iōannēn ton baptistēn . . . Ēlian . . . heis tōn prophētōn.* It is not surprising that Jesus should be identified as a great figure of the past returned from the dead, given the widespread ancient Jewish belief that the OT saints and other worthies of bygone eras are alive (for Jewish parallels, see the COMMENT on 12:24–27 and cf. Mark 9:4; Luke 16:22–31; Heb 12:1). Because of their aliveness, they can be invoked for aid in present distress (cf. 15:35 and see Horbury, "Cult").

29. *But you, who do you say that I am?* Gk *hymeis de tina me legete einai.* The personal pronoun *hymeis* is superfluous in Greek, and its presence here is probably emphatic (cf. the NOTE on "Give . . . yourselves" in 6:37).

answered and said. Gk *apokritheis . . . legei.* See the NOTE on this idiom in 3:33.

You are the Christ. Gk *sy ei ho Christos.* For Mark's readers these words would probably echo a familiar Christian confession, *Iēsous estin ho Christos* ("Jesus is the Christ" or "the Christ is Jesus"; cf. John 20:31; Acts 5:42; 9:22; 17:3; 18:5, 28; 1 John 2:22; 5:1; and see Schnackenburg, 3.338; de Boer, *Johannine Perspectives*, 89–90, 251–52).

30. *vehemently ordered.* Gk *epetimēsen.* This is the same word that is translated "rebuked" in 8:33; on its nuances, see the COMMENT on 1:23–26.

31. *he began to teach them that.* Gk *ērxato didaskein autous.* This is the introduction to the first of the three passion predictions that form the backbone of this section of the Gospel (8:31; 9:31; 10:33–34); "began to" thus suggests the beginning of a series. Here, as at other points in the Gospel, Jesus' "teaching" (*didaskein*) causes offense (cf. 6:2–3; 11:17–18)—even, worryingly enough, to his own disciples.

it was necessary that, etc. To study the similarities and differences of the three passion predictions, see figure 23. All have a similar structure: (a) a reference to the Son of Man, (b) a reference to those who will be responsible for his death, (c) a prophecy of his death, and (d) a prophecy of his resurrection "after three days." There are individual variations; the second and third, for example, speak of the Son of Man being "turned over" to his enemies, whereas the first speaks of the necessity of his suffering and rejection by them; the second speaks of these opponents in a very general way, as "human beings," whereas the first and third spell them out as the chief priests and the scribes. Most strikingly, the third gives a detailed description, unparalleled in the other two, of the specific sufferings that the Son of Man will endure.

While many scholars, such as Bultmann (*Theology*, 1.29), have argued that the passion predictions are prophecies-after-the-fact because of their detailed correspondence to what actually happened, others, such as Jeremias (*New Testament Theology*, 281–86) and Allison (*End*, 137–40), have contended that they contain a historical core; an apocalyptic prophet could well have expected his martyrdom as part of the end-time sufferings of the people of God and his resurrection after a short period as part of the general resurrection.

Figure 23: The Passion Predictions

Mark 8:31	*Mark 9:31*	*Mark 10:33–34*
it was necessary that		
the Son of Man	the Son of Man	the Son of Man
should suffer many things and be rejected	will be turned over	will be turned over
by the elders and the chief priests and the scribes	to the hands of human beings	to the chief priests and the scribes
		and they will condemn him to death
		and turn him over to the Gentiles
		and they will beat him
		and spit on him
		and scourge him
and be killed	and they will kill him	and kill him
and after three days arise	and . . . after three days he will arise	and after three days he will arise

it was necessary that. Gk *dei*, which introduces an impersonal construction. But *why* was it necessary that Christ should suffer, according to Mark? Presumably because God willed it (cf. "the things of God" in 8:33); like the "divine passive" (1:41; 2:5; 3:5; etc.), the impersonal *dei* can be a subtle way of speaking of God's agency. The necessity of Jesus' death is closely linked with its being foretold in scripture; cf. 9:12, which reproduces the wording of our passage but substitutes "it has been written" for "it was necessary." But these observations still beg the question why God willed Jesus' scripturally foretold death. The closest that Mark comes to an answer is the "ransom" saying in 10:45 (see the COMMENT on 10:41–45) and the imagery of the death scene in 15:33–41 (see the COMMENT on that section).

the Son of Man. Gk *ton huion tou anthrōpou*. Since part of the background for the Son of Man figure in Mark seems to be biblical and Jewish traditions about Adam (see Marcus, "Son of Man"), it may be relevant that when Adam and Eve sinned, they were cursed with various sufferings by God (Gen 3:16–19). See also the COMMENT on 8:31–33, where it is noted that in Daniel 7 the "one like a son of man" is associated with the suffering saints.

many things. Gk *polla*. This adverbial construction of which Mark is extremely fond (cf. 3:12; 5:10, 23, 38, 43; 6:20; 9:26; 15:3) could be translated "greatly." But "many things" also makes a great deal of sense, and it corresponds to the detailed description of sufferings in the third passion prediction (10:33–34).

be rejected by the elders and the chief priests and the scribes. Gk *apodokimasthēnai hypo tōn presbyterōn kai tōn archiereōn kai tōn grammateōn*. On the scribes, see the APPENDIX "The Scribes and the Pharisees" in vol. 1. On the elders and the chief priests, see the APPENDIX "The Jewish Leaders in Mark" at the end of this volume. It is highly unusual for the elders to appear at the *start* of a list of Jesus' opponents, and it is just possible that the first *kai* ("and") here is epexegetical, that is, that our phrase should be translated "be rejected by the elders, *that is*, by the chief priests and the scribes" (cf. Luke 22:66, where the council of elders includes chief priests and scribes). In the other Markan instances, however, the elders seem to be a lay group distinct from the chief priests and the scribes, which are both priestly collectives, so this interpretation is unlikely.

and be killed. Gk *kai apoktanthēnai*. The passion prediction does not say who will do the killing, and by putting "and be killed" *after* "by the elders and the chief priests and the scribes," it distances these Jewish leaders from the execution itself. To be sure, a later passion prediction (10:33–34), as well as the passion narrative itself, portray the same leaders condemning Jesus and delivering him to the Romans for execution. But Mark, unlike later anti-Jewish polemic (e.g., John 19:16; Gos. Pet. 4:10; perhaps Luke 23:13, 25–26, 33), does not make them *directly* responsible for Jesus' death.

after three days. Gk *meta treis hēmeras*. As pointed out in the NOTE on "for three days" in 8:2, in biblical and Jewish traditions this expression is sometimes a general term for a short period of unspecified duration. Such inexact usage increases the chances that Jesus may actually have used the phrase in a prophecy of his suffering and subsequent vindication (cf. Jeremias, *New Testament Theology*, 285). But even if, contrary to this idiom, "three days" is taken literally—as it probably was by Mark's readers—there is not necessarily a discrepancy between "*after* three days" in our passage and Jesus' resurrection "*on* the third day" in the Gospel story and the pre-Pauline formula in 1 Cor 15:4. There are several OT passages in which an activity goes on "for three days" and then ends "on the third day" (see Gen 42:17–18; Exod 19:11–16 LXX; Esth 4:16–5:1); "after three days" and "on the third day," therefore, can be equivalent phrases (see Lehmann, *Auferweckt*, 165–66; Bode, *First Easter*, 109–10). This interchangeability continues in later Jewish texts; in *Esth. Rab.* 9.2, for example, which comments on Esth 5:1 ("And it came to pass *on the third day*"), we read: "Israel are never left in dire distress *more than three days* . . . Of Jonah it says, 'And Jonah was in the belly of the fish *three days and three nights*' (Jonah 2:1). The dead also will come to life only *after three days*, as it says, '*On the third day* he will raise us up, that we may live in his presence' (Hos 6:2)." This and other rabbinic traditions (e.g., *Gen. Rab.* 56.1; *Midr. Psalms* 22:5; *Yal. Šim.* Joshua 12 [on Josh 2:16]) interpret Hos 6:2 as a prophecy of eschatological resurrection "on the third day" and thus suggest that that OT verse may provide part of the scriptural basis for the *dei* ("it was necessary that") in our passion prediction (cf. McArthur, "Third Day").

This scriptural background, however, does not necessarily mean that Mark or a Christian predecessor has created 8:31 out of Hos 6:2; if they had done so, they would probably have had Jesus say "on the third day" rather than "after three days." The use of the latter formulation is another indication that some form of the saying probably goes back to Jesus.

arise. Gk *anastēnai. Stēnai* means "to rise," and *ana* can mean either "up" or "again"; both senses of *ana* are played on in John 3:3–34, where Jesus speaks of being born *anōthen* ("from above"), which Nicodemus interprets as "born again." Similarly, *anastēnai* in our passage is probably a double entendre: Jesus will rise *up* from the realm of the dead, but he will also rise *again* (i.e., come back to life) after being driven to death (cf. 1 Thess 4:14: "Jesus died and rose again").

32. *And he was making this statement frankly.* Gk *kai parrēsią ton logon elalei. Parrēsią* can mean either "openly and boldly" or "in public." The latter nuance might be suggested by the implied contrast with 8:29–30, where Jesus commands that Peter's insight into his messiahship be kept under wraps: his coming death and resurrection he announces publicly. Against this interpretation, however, 8:31 says that the passion prophecy was addressed to "*them*," that is, the disciples, and the two other passion predictions are delivered only to Jesus' followers (cf. 9:30 and 10:32). The implication of 8:32a, then, may be that Jesus is now speaking *clearly* to his disciples about his coming death rather than referring to it *allusively* as in 2:20.

took him aside. Gk *proslabomenos . . . auton,* lit. "taking him"; the same middle-voice verb is used in Acts 18:26 for Priscilla and Aquila taking Apollos aside to teach him undisturbed (BDAG 883[3]). There is thus, as Cranfield (279) remarks, "a suggestion of patronizing about it," as if Peter were qualified to instruct Jesus.

began to rebuke him. Gk *ērxato epitiman autǭ.* For other misguided rebukes in Mark, see 10:13, where the disciples rebuke those bringing little children to Jesus, and 10:48, where the crowd rebukes blind Bartimaeus (cf. Robbins, "Bartimaeus," 49).

33. *turning and looking at his disciples, rebuked Peter.* Gk *epistrapheis kai idōn tous mathētas autou epetimēsen Petrǭ.* This awkward stage direction is probably meant to suggest that the misunderstanding of the divine purpose voiced by Peter is one that is potentially or actually shared by the other disciples (cf. Best, "Peter," 549); Jesus, therefore, after rebuking Peter, instructs all of the disciples (along with the crowd) in the necessity of sharing his sufferings (8:34–38). After the other two passion predictions, moreover, there are similar instances of misunderstanding from members of the Twelve (see 9:32–34, 38; 10:35). Peter, then, is not unique in his obtuseness.

ᴸ This inclusion of the other disciples in the rebuke may be meant to suggest that some in Mark's audience share Peter's opposition to the proclamation of Jesus' suffering; if so, the effect is similar to "let the reader understand" (13:14) or "what I say to you I say to all" (13:37). But the clause may also be an ironic comment on Peter's imperfect discipleship; if a *mathētēs* (disciple) is, literally, a "learner," then Peter, despite the insight of 8:29, has not yet learned his lesson very well. Cf. the similar irony in 16:7, "Say to his disciples (and to Peter). . . ."

A close parallel to Jesus rebuking Peter as "Satan" for trying to divert him from the path of suffering and death is offered by *Gen. Rab.* 56.4, where Samael = Satan tries unsuccessfully to dissuade Abraham from carrying out the sacrifice of his son Isaac and to dissuade Isaac from submitting to it. Here Gen 22:8 is paraphrased, "God will take care of the person who rebukes Satan" (cf. Strack-Billerbeck 1.747).

Get behind me. Gk *hypage opisō mou.* This command has been interpreted in three main senses (cf. Smith, *Petrine,* 167): (1) as an order for Peter to be off and get out of Jesus' sight; (2) as an injunction for Peter to get out of Jesus' way, that is, to cease being an obstruction to him; and (3) as a command to Peter to resume the path of discipleship rather than trying to *lead* Jesus.

In favor of #1, Black (218) cites 2 Kgs 9:19, *epistrephou eis ta opisō mou* = "turn behind me," which he paraphrases, "[Get] away from me that I no longer see thee." This interpretation of 2 Kgs 9:19, however, is not certain; the NRSV, for example, translates the Hebrew here as "fall in behind me," which is also a possible rendering of the Greek and would support interpretation #3. Also, a command for Peter to depart makes little sense in the narrative context; by 9:2 he is not only back among the Twelve but in its inner circle. Jesus might, however, be addressing Satan in Peter rather than Peter himself; the story, then, would be similar to Jesus' commands to demons to depart in Markan exorcism stories (1:25; 5:8; 9:25; cf. Osborne, "Peter," 188).

In favor of #2 is the added clause "for you are a hindrance to me" (my trans.) in Matt 16:23. While the interpretation found in the Matthean text cannot be decisive for the exegesis of the Markan one, this reading has in its favor that Peter is trying to prevent Jesus from embracing the destiny that God has laid out for him.

But if this is the meaning, it is not clear why Jesus says "Get behind me" rather than "Get out of my way."

Interpretation #3 has been preferred by ecclesiastical interpreters down through the ages, partly because it holds out the prospect of Peter's restoration to Jesus' good graces; these interpreters sometimes contrast the longer phrase here, *hyage opisō mou Satana*, with the curt dismissal of Satan in Matt 4:10, *hyage Satana* ("Go, Satan!"—see, e.g., Origen, *Commentary on Matthew* 12.22, and cf. Pseudo-Ignatius, *Philippians* 12; Augustine, *Commentary on Psalm* 70, par. 4). Apologetic though this reading may be, it is also the most viable interpretation of the command in its present context, since the next Markan verse uses *opisō mou* to speak of following Jesus as a disciple (8:34; cf. 1:17, 20). There is, then, a certain analogy to John 21:20–22 in Mark 8:32–33: Peter makes a stupid remark and Jesus rebukes him for it, then calls him to resume a life of discipleship. (The parallels do not stop here; both Mark 8:34–9:1 and John 21:18–23 refer to disciples who follow Jesus in the way of the cross and to others who will not die before the parousia comes.) Both the Markan passage and the Johannine one may be drawing on a preexistent sequence of sayings (cf. the COMMENTS on 8:27–33 and 8:34–9:1).

Satan. Gk *Satana.* The word here preserves some of its original sense of "adversary" (see the NOTE on "by Satan" in 1:13); Peter has, at least temporarily, become a "Satan" because he is opposing the revealed will of God (cf. Origen, *Commentary on Matthew* 12.21, and Forsyth, *Old Enemy*, 288). Davies and Allison (2.663) compare *T. Job* 41–42, in which Elihu is "filled with Satan" so that the one speaking in him is "not a human but a beast." Elihu's fate is eschatological destruction (*T. Job* 43), as Peter's will be if he does not heed the warning to get back in step behind Jesus.

For some exegetes, the Markan Jesus' harsh language against Peter here, and Peter's abandonment of Jesus at the end of the Gospel, suggest that he and the Twelve with whom he is associated are incorrigible (see, e.g., Weeden, "Heresy," *Traditions*; Dewey, "Peter's Curse"; and Tolbert, *Sowing*). But the parallelism with the preceding story of the cure of a blind man in two stages (8:22–26) is against this extreme position, since the healing narrative suggests that Peter and the other disciples must pass through an intermediate stage of partial sight, partial blindness before arriving at the full insight symbolized by the cured blind man's final condition (cf. Best, "Peter," 549–50). Smith (*Petrine*, 170) argues against this defense of Peter, asserting that 8:22–26 is juxtaposed with 10:46–52 rather than 8:27–33; this argument, however, relies on a false dichotomy, since it is perfectly possible for 8:22–26 to be closely connected with both later stories. If, moreover, 8:33 were a definitive rejection of Peter, his continuing role in the story would make little sense.

There is little doubt, however, that some later Christians found Mark's portrayal of Peter here overly harsh. Luke's parallel to our passage, for example, omits Peter's rebuke of Jesus and Jesus' counterrebuke of Peter as "Satan" (Luke 9:18–22). In his passion narrative, to be sure, Luke transmits a saying of Jesus that is similar to Mark 8:33 in associating Peter with the other disciples and with Satan and in using the verb *epistrephein* ("to turn"), but the context makes the criticism much less severe (Luke 22:31–32). These Lukan verses most likely represent an independent pre-Lukan tradition (cf. Marshall, *Luke*, 819), but they are probably in some way related to Mark 8:33.

[the things] of human beings. Gk *ta tōn anthrōpōn*. To be on the side of humans qua humans is to be on the side of Satan and at enmity with God (see 7:8 and cf. Jas 4:4); only divine grace permits escape from this condition of Satanic blindness and bondage.

COMMENT

Introduction. The symbolic story of the healing of the blind man is significantly followed by a two-part narrative, in the first section of which Jesus solicits opinions about himself, hears from Peter the declaration that he is the Messiah, and tells (lit. "rebukes") the disciples not to divulge this news (8:27–30). When, however, Jesus goes on to specify the sort of Messiah he is—one who will suffer, die, and rise again—Peter responds by rebuking *him*, and Jesus in turn reprimands Peter as a "Satan" whose thoughts are operating on the human level rather than the divine one (8:31–33). Peter's half-percipient, half-insensible condition is similar to that of the half-seeing, half-blind sufferer in the previous narrative, and the pervasive exorcistic language of "rebuking" suggests that this condition is the result of a struggle between divine revelation and demonic resistance. This connection with the story of the blind man is strengthened by the fact that, in Jewish traditions and the NT, Satan and the demons are frequently portrayed as blinders of human beings (see, e.g., *T. Sim.* 2:7; *T. Jud.* 19:4; Acts 26:18; 2 Cor 4:4; cf. Schrage, "*Typhlos*," 285).

Mark seems to have shaped the present passage not only by this significant juxtaposition with 8:22–26 but also by redactional touches such as "on the way" in 8:27, the injunction to silence in 8:30, "began to," "many things," and "and the scribes" in 8:31, and the awkward note about Jesus looking at the disciples in 8:33. But he has not created the passage out of thin air; as noted in the introduction to 8:1–21, the basic events described in Mark 8:1–33 are matched in John 6:1–71, and direct dependence of John on Mark is unlikely (cf. Dodd, *Historical Tradition*, 218–22; Räisänen, 175). The present passage in particular is parallel to John 6:66–71, although the latter contains no injunction to silence or passion prediction, which are probably Markan additions. The passion prediction does have roots in the tradition, since it contains elements similar to the independent saying in Luke 22:31–32 (see the NOTE on "Satan" in 8:33). Mark, however, has probably inserted it at this point in the narrative, introduced the motif of Peter objecting to it, and changed the form of the saying about Satan.

As the previous passage was dominated by verbs of seeing, this one is dominated by verbs of speaking ("ask," "answer," "rebuke," "teach," and three different verbs for "say"; cf. Gnilka, 2.13). This preponderance of speaking verbs reflects the passage's character as a dramatic dialogue of ideas, which appears to be carefully constructed to express two closely related themes: Jesus' messiahship (8:27–30) and his approaching passion, death, and resurrection (8:31–33). The two parts of the passage follow a similar pattern: (1) question or statement of Jesus (8:27 + 29a, 31–32a); (2) response of Peter (8:29b, 32b); and (3) counterresponse of Jesus, introduced by *epitimēsen* ("rebuked": 8:30, 33). Jesus thus has the first and last word, but Peter and the other disciples are also significant characters in the dialogue, and the word *mathētai* ("disciples") appears at the beginning and end of the pericope (8:27, 33), signaling the increasing concentration of this section of the Gospel on discipleship (Gnilka, ibid.). The ambiguous position of the disciples here is highlighted by the two juxtapositions of *mathētai* with *anthrōpoi* in the passage: at the beginning Peter, as the representative of the disciples, displays a wisdom transcending that of other humans (8:27–30), but at the end he is ranged on the side of demonized humanity against the revelation of God (8:33).

But the central focus of the passage, as indeed of the Gospel as a whole, is on the identity and fate of the Messiah rather than the nature of his followers—though of course the two things are interrelated (see Henderson, *Christology*). If the uses of *anthrōpoi* in 8:27 and 8:33 frame the whole dialogue with references to humanity in its ignorance of and estrangement from God, it is also significant that the singular form of the word recurs at the dialogue's center in a reference to the Son of Man (*ton huion tou anthrōpou*), whose path to suffering and death is the fulfillment of a divine imperative (8:31; for similarly loaded usages of *anthrōpos* see the COMMENTS on 7:14–15 and 7:20–23). Nothing, then, seems capable of ending the alienation and blindness of humanity to God's will except the faithful death of the Son of Man (cf. Davis, "Paradox").

8:27–30: who is Jesus? Our passage begins with the exit of Jesus and the disciples from Bethsaida (8:22) and their movement to the extreme northern portion of the Golan Heights region, to the villages surrounding the Hellenistic city of Caesarea Philippi (8:27a; see the NOTE on "Caesarea Philippi" in 8:27). The association of this city with Caesar (i.e., the Roman emperor) is probably significant in view of the continuation of the pericope; the ground is being laid for Peter's confession of Jesus as the Christ, the Messiah, the Jewish leader whose advent was expected to terminate the oppressive rule of Rome—an expectation that was probably well known to Mark's audience because of the messianic dimension of the Jewish revolt of 66–73 C.E. (see the APPENDIX "The Meaning of Christ = Messiah" and Marcus, "Jewish War," 456–60). This militant atmosphere is reinforced by the specification that the following conversation takes place "on the way" (8:27b), a phrase that invokes the Isaian picture of a divine victory march culminating in the redemption of Zion (see the introduction to 8:22–10:52).

But despite the revolutionary associations of the setting, Jesus takes his time in revealing his great secret; if he is the Messiah, that implies not only that he is God's holy warrior but also that he is a consummate teacher who knows how to lead his followers step by step from one insight to another (see Isa 11:2 and again the APPENDIX "The Meaning of Christ = Messiah"). The drawn-out nature of this pedagogical process is emphasized by the pervasive use of imperfect verbs of speaking (*epērōta* = "he was asking" in 8:27 and 8:29; *elalei* = "he was saying" in 8:32), by the phrase "began to teach" in 8:31, and by the implication that the revelation is gradually unfolding as Jesus and his disciples are passing through the villages (plural) of the Caesarea Philippi area. "Who do people say that I am?" he asks them leadingly (8:27c), in what Räisänen (174) rightly terms a Socratic question. The disciples, getting into the linear flow of things, respond by listing a series of interpretative options: John the Baptist, Elijah, or one of the prophets of old returned from the realm of death (8:28).

These are the same popular opinions that were canvassed in 6:14–15, and they are mentioned in the same order. This repetition is probably deliberate and suggests that while Mark considers the first two opinions to be wrong and the third to be only partly right, they nevertheless point to important aspects of Jesus' mission. All three possibilities link Jesus with the prophetic office (on John the Baptist as a prophet, see 11:32), and elsewhere in the Gospel we learn that the Markan Jesus does regard himself as a prophet (see 6:4). In our own passage, indeed, he goes on to prophesy, making a detailed and accurate prediction of his rejection, execution, and resurrection (8:31). Jesus, then, although more than a prophet, is one nevertheless (cf. Matt 11:9//Luke 7:26), and to that extent the popular opinion is correct. Furthermore, the crowd's belief that Jesus is a figure returned from the dead may suggest that it rightly considers the eschatological events to be in progress, since resurrection was expected to take place at the end (cf. Matt 27:51–53). The eschatological resonance is all the more obvious in that the first figure mentioned, John the Baptist, is pictured in the Gospel tradition as preparing people for the eschaton (see 1:4–8; Matt 3:7–10//Luke 3:7–9) and the second, Elijah, was commonly expected to return to usher it in (Mal 4:5–6). All of the popular opinions, moreover, liken Jesus to people who were persecuted, sometimes to the point of death (cf. 6:14–29 and 9:13 for John the Baptist and 1 Kings 19 for Elijah; Matt 16:14 extends the analogy by adding to the list Jeremiah, another suffering prophet). In this particular, too, the crowd demonstrates a theologically reliable intuition about Jesus.

But while the opinions reported by the disciples contain some elements of truth, they are not, from Mark's point of view, the whole truth. The Markan Jesus, therefore, now switches gears, leaving behind the realms of popular opinion and abstract discussion to confront the disciples directly with the crucial question, "But you, who do *you* say that I am?" (8:29a). Enough disclosure has already occurred in the narrative to point toward the right answer, and our passage is linked with these earlier revelations by the form of the inquiry. As Müller (*Wer Ist*, 80–81) points out, it caps a series of rhetorical questions about Jesus' identity that has extended from the Gospel's first chapter:

1:27 "What is this? A new teaching with authority!"
4:41 "Who then is this?—for even the wind and sea obey him!"
6:2 "Where does this man get these things from?"

All of these questions, like the one in our passage, followed Jesus' performance of a miracle and broached the issue of his identity.

In the present case, the preceding miracle was one that suggested kingly power (see the COMMENT on 8:22–23). Peter's answer, then, seems logical enough:

"You are the Christ" (8:29b)—that is, the Messiah, the coming eschatological king of Jewish expectation (although not all Jews expected the Messiah to work wonders; see again the APPENDIX "The Meaning of Christ = Messiah"). In making this insightful reply, Peter for the first time in the narrative emerges as an individual distinct from the rest of the Twelve, a distinctiveness that will continue throughout the second half of the Gospel (see 9:5–6; 10:28; 14:29–31, 37, 54, 66–72; 16:7; cf. Smith, *Petrine*, 164). This distinctiveness, however, has been anticipated in the first half of the Gospel, where Peter has always been listed first among the followers of Jesus (1:16, 29, 36; 3:16; 5:37) and where he and his brother Andrew were the first people to be called by Jesus to a life of discipleship (1:16–18). Now, at the start of the narrative's second half, he is the first person to recognize Jesus' messiahship.

Some exegetes, to be sure, have disputed this positive evaluation of Peter's confession. Cullmann (*Peter,* 178–80) and Dunn ("Messianic Secret," 126–28), for example, have argued that the Markan report of the incident is historically accurate and that Jesus forbade the disciples to publicize Peter's confession because it was based on a nationalistic misunderstanding of "Messiah." Other interpreters, such as Weeden (*Traditions,* 64–69), think that the interdict on publicizing Peter's opinion reveals not that the historical Jesus had reservations about the title "Messiah" but that Mark does. But these negative interpretations of Peter's confession itself (as opposed to his rejection of the idea of suffering messiahship in 8:32) are unlikely to be correct. The Markan Jesus' prohibitions of publicity, such as that addressed to the disciples in 8:30, are directed at *correct* evaluations of Jesus, not at incorrect ones (see 1:24–25; 3:11–12; cf. 1:11; 9:7). The prohibition, indeed, actually serves to heighten the importance of the suppressed secret (cf. Dan 8:26; 12:4; 4 *Ezra* 14:26, 45–46). Peter's confession, moreover, is introduced by the weighty biblical formula "answered and said," which implies its correctness (cf. Gnilka, 2.14), and it contrasts with the implicitly mistaken view of the populace; and elsewhere in the Gospel, "Christ" is an acceptable title for Jesus (see 1:1; 9:41; 14:61). The juxtaposition with the healing story in 8:22–26 points in the same direction, since it suggests that Peter's insight is a result of revelation; the eyes of the blind have been opened, or at least half-opened, by an act of divine grace (cf. Matt 16:17 and see Wrede, 78). "You are the Christ," then, is a correct statement—as the last two words of 8:30 imply—*peri autou* ("about him"; cf. Catchpole, "Entry," 326; Gundry, 445).

Peter's confession may very well echo a primitive Christian confession that was known to Mark's readers from their own worship services (see the NOTE on "You are the Christ" in 8:29). Jesus is the Messiah because he is the expected king of Israel who will teach his people the righteous ways of the God of Israel and establish God's dominion over the earth by defeating His enemies (see again the APPENDIX "The Meaning of Christ = Messiah"). For Markan hearers aware of the catalytic role played by messianic claimants in the Jewish War against the Romans, and perhaps even being persecuted because of their refusal to accept these claims (cf. 13:6–9, 21–22), the assurance that Jesus and no other is the Messiah would come as a powerful encouragement to maintain fidelity to him alone. The ban on publicity that Jesus issues immediately after Peter's pronouncement (8:30) implies not that it is mistaken but that its disclosure now would be premature: only at Jesus' death and resurrection will the true shape of his kingship emerge (see the APPENDIX "The Messianic Secret Motif" in vol. 1).

8:31–33: but what sort of Messiah? These climactic events, and the messianic suffering that will lead up to them, are now explicitly prophesied by Jesus in the first of three similarly structured passion predictions (8:31; 9:31; 10:33–34), which form the backbone of the middle section of the Gospel. At the beginning of the present prediction, in contrast to the other two, stands the weighty word *dei*, "it was necessary"; it is vital for the Markan Jesus to stress, in this first open prophecy of his death and resurrection, that those unexpected occurrences reflect the divine will (cf. Gnilka, 2.12). This sort of emphasis is common in apocalyptic prophecies of end-time events. As *Sib. Or.* 14.357 puts it: "A strong necessity insists that all these things be accomplished" (cf. 3.572).

In the Markan case, the *dei* also implies that Jesus' death and resurrection have been prophesied in the scriptures, and OT texts such as the Suffering Servant passages from Isaiah, the psalms of the Righteous Sufferer, and the prophecy of resurrection "on the third day" in Hos 6:2 probably lie in the background (see the NOTES on "it was necessary that" and "after three days" in 8:31 and on "how then has it been written concerning" in 9:12). But since Jesus' prophecy specifically concerns the suffering, death, and resurrection of *the Son of Man*, it is also likely that Daniel 7 is in view. There "one like a son of man" is exalted to heavenly glory, and this exaltation is linked with the vindication of the people of God after they have suffered for "a time, two times, and half a time" (see Hooker, *Son of Man*, 189–98; Schaberg, "Daniel 7–12"; Allison, *End*, 140). This note of vindication is also present in the three passion predictions, all of which end with a reference to resurrection.

The point, however, seems to be lost on Jesus' chief disciple, the master's prophecy of suffering and death having absorbed all his attention. Though just a few moments before, Peter had attained a pinnacle of insight into Jesus' messiahship, he now plunges to a nadir of obtuseness by taking Jesus aside, as though to instruct him (see the NOTE on "took him aside" in 8:32), and "rebuking" him for his prophecy of doom (8:32b). He thus sets himself up against the revealed will of God (*dei* = "it was necessary"); no wonder Jesus responds by calling him by the name of Satan, the adversary to the divine purpose (8:33).

We shall never understand this passage rightly, however, if we do not realize how natural Peter's reaction is. Modern Christians, cushioned by two thousand years of church teaching, find the idea of a suffering Messiah unremarkable, but "from the beginning it was not so" (cf. Matt 19:8). Intrinsic to the OT/Jewish idea of the Messiah was the notion of triumph, not suffering and death (see the APPENDIX "The Meaning of Christ = Messiah"). Since the master's fate has direct consequences for his followers, the notion of a suffering Messiah also confounds the disciples' natural desire to share in the earthly Jesus' messianic glory; instead they will soon be bidden to participate in his crucifixion (8:34–35; cf. 10:35–45).

Another possibly scandalous aspect of Jesus' prophecy is the schism that it describes between the Messiah and the other leaders of Israel, including the chief priests. As opposed to this scenario, many Jews cherished scripturally rooted hopes for an eschatological alliance of the Messiah *with* the high priest (see again the APPENDIX "The Meaning of Christ = Messiah").

Peter would have good reasons, therefore, for rejecting the idea of a Messiah at loggerheads with Israel's leadership and delivered to death. Indeed, for one accustomed to seeing the world as a battleground between good and evil supernatural powers, an outlandish idea of this sort might appear to be the work of the devil himself (cf. the NOTE on "He has gone out of his mind" in 3:21). Peter therefore "rebukes" Jesus for his prophecy, and this verb probably has something of the same deep, exorcistic sense that it gathers to itself elsewhere in the Gospel (see the COMMENT on 1:23–26): Peter attributes Jesus' foreboding about death to a Satanic assault, and he tries to cast it out of Jesus' mind.

Jesus, however, quickly rounds on Peter and rebukes *him* in turn as a "Satan" whose thoughts have placed him in opposition to the plans of God (8:33). For Jesus it is the avoidance of messianic suffering, not resignation to it, that constitutes the devilish temptation that must be exorcised (cf. 14:35–38; Matt 4:8–10//Luke 4:5–8). Both parties to this exchange, it should be noted, have accepted the idea that Jesus is the Messiah (8:29–30); the point at issue is exactly how his messianic victory over the forces of evil will be accomplished. For Peter, steeped in traditional versions of Davidic messiahship, the struggle anticipated is one in which victory will be accomplished through a military assault on flesh-and-blood enemies (cf. the Qumran War Scroll). According to such a scenario, the premature death of Jesus, the Messiah and therefore the captain of the armies of God, would be a devastating blow to God's forces and a spectacular coup for the opposition. For Jesus, however, the messianic victory will in the first instance be a cosmic one over supernatural foes (cf. 1:24; 3:23–27), and it will be achieved not by a conventional battle but by death and resurrection. Any effort to divert him from this extraordinary work is a Satanic temptation, an attempt to substitute the narrow, unimaginative schemes of human beings (*ta tōn anthrōpōn*) for the majestic, world-transforming plans of the God of the new creation (*ta tou theou*). "For my thoughts are not your thoughts, nor are your ways my ways" (Isa 55:8). Such attempts to whittle God down to human size must be fiercely and even violently resisted, because the battle hangs in the balance: "Get behind me, Satan!"

From Mark's point of view, Peter's objection to Jesus' prophecy, natural though it may be, represents a fall from grace into the realm of demonic delusion. The scene comes perilously close to the terrifying picture presented in 1QS 2–3, in which the blindness spread by the Angel of Darkness in the time of eschatological testing penetrates even into the elect community, and some of that community's members turn aside and are cast out of the covenant forever (cf. Marcus, "Epistemology"). The first of the disciples, similarly, seems to be teetering on the verge of apostasy.

Teetering on the verge—but not falling over it. For Jesus, even in this moment of supreme danger, does not command the disciple who has become Satan's mouthpiece to go away from him (contrast Matt 7:23; 25:41) but rather to go *behind* him, that is, to resume the path of following that he has momentarily forsaken (see the NOTE on "Get behind me" in 8:33). Peter is a man in the middle, a disciple in whose heart the forces of God and Satan contend fiercely with each other, a person who, like the half-healed blind man in 8:24, sees but does not see. He may, therefore, fall into the clutches of Satanic delusion from time to time, but he will subsequently be pulled back to the path of following. Precisely for this reason, Mark's readers, who also are being tempted to forsake the path of suffering discipleship (13:13, 19–22), will be able to identify with Peter. There is still hope for Peter, then; he can yet return to the fold. The juxtaposition with 8:22–26, indeed, suggests that he will in the end be enlightened (see the NOTE on "Satan" in 8:33)—as Mark's readers would have known that he had been.

In the next passage the Markan Jesus will make clear that this apostolic journey toward the light will involve following him in the path of suffering and death—and thereby finding true life.

JESUS PROCLAIMS THE GAINS AND LOSSES IN FOLLOWING HIM (8:34–9:1)

8 ³⁴And summoning the crowd with his disciples, he said to them,"If anyone wants to follow after me, let him renounce himself and take up his cross, and let him follow me. ³⁵For whoever wants to save his life will destroy it; but whoever will destroy his life for me and the good news will save it. ³⁶For what use would it be for a human being to gain the whole world and to forfeit his life? ³⁷For what could a human give in exchange for his life? ³⁸For whoever is ashamed of me and of my words in this adulterous and sinful generation, the Son of Man also will be ashamed of him when he comes in the glory of his Father with the holy angels." 9 ¹And he said to them, "Amen, I say to you, there are some of those who are standing here who surely will not taste death before they see the dominion of God fully come in power."

NOTES

8 34. *summoning.* Gk *proskalesamenos.* This is principally a legal term (see LSJ 1515 and cf. Mark 3:23), but it can also have a military nuance (= muster, e.g., Xenophon, *Anabasis* 7.7.2; 2 Macc 8:1; cf. Mark 15:44 and 2 Macc 14:12), and this would be in accordance with the military atmosphere of our passage. Since the OT exodus traditions provide important background for Mark's Gospel, and since those traditions regard the Israelites in the wilderness as an armed camp, it is also relevant that Exod 3:18 and 5:3 LXX use *proskaleisthai* for God's calling the Israelites to follow Moses into the wilderness.

wants to. Gk *thelei.* This may be a Markan addition to the pericope; note its absence from the parallels in Q and John (see figures 24 and 25) and cf. its presence in Mark 9:35 and 10:44, where two out of the three Synoptic parallels (see the GLOSSARY under "Synoptic Gospels") again lack it (Matt 23:11; Luke 22:26; contrast Matt 20:26).

after me. Gk *opisō mou.* This phrase can be used in military contexts for following someone into battle (see, e.g., Judg 3:28; 4:14; 6:34–35; 1 Kgdms 11:7), an implication already present in Mark 1:17 (see the COMMENT on 1:16–18).

let him renounce himself. Gk *aparnēsasthō heauton.* Greek masculine pronouns can refer to both sexes, and this is undoubtedly the case here, since the sentence begins, "If *anyone* wants to follow after me." But to translate with "let him or her renounce himself or herself," etc. would be awkward. The NRSV attempts to get around the problem by changing the singulars to plurals: "If any want to become my followers, let them deny themselves and take up their cross and follow me," etc. This revision, however, loses the original's sense of existential immediacy, of Jesus confronting the individual with a stark personal decision between following and not following.

Figure 24: Markan and Q Versions of the Sayings about Taking Up the Cross and Losing One's Life

Mark 8:34 (par. Matt 16:24/ Luke 9:23)	Matthew 10:37–38 = Q	Luke 14:26–27 = Q
if anyone wants to follow		if someone comes to me
	the one who loves father or mother more than me	and does not hate father and mother, etc.
		and his own life also
	is not worthy of me . . .	he cannot be my disciple
let him renounce (aparnēsasthō) himself		
and take up (aratō) his cross	and he who does not take (lambanei) his cross	he who does not bear (bastazei) his own cross
and let him follow me	and follow after me	and come after me
	is not worthy of me	cannot be my disciple

Mark 8:35 (par. Matt 16:25/ Luke 9:24)	Matthew 10:39 = Q	Luke 17:33 = Q
for whoever wants to save his life	the one who finds his life	whoever seeks to hold onto his life
will destroy it	will destroy it	will destroy it
but whoever will destroy his life for me and the good news	and the one who destroys his life for my sake	and whoever will destroy it
will save it	will find it	will keep it alive

Figure 25: Mark 8:31–38 and John 12:23–26

Mark 8	*John 12*
31: It was necessary that the Son of Man should suffer . . . and be rejected . . . and be killed, and . . . rise.	23: The hour has come for the Son of Man to be glorified [= crucified and resurrected].
34: If anyone wants to follow after me, let him renounce himself and take up his cross, and let him follow me.	25: The one who loves his life destroys it, but the one who hates his life in this world will keep it for eternal life.
35: Whoever wants to save his life will destroy it; but whoever will destroy his life for me and the good news will save it.	26a: If anyone serves me, let him follow me . . .
38: Whoever is ashamed of me . . . the Son of Man also will be ashamed of him when he comes in the glory of his Father . . .	26c: If anyone serves me, the Father will honor him.

take up his cross. Gk *aratō ton stauron autou.* Perhaps already in Jesus' day the image of taking up one's cross had become a proverbial one for giving oneself up to death; as Taylor (381) puts it, citing passages from Josephus (*War* 2.241, 306; 5.449–51; *Ant.* 17.295): "Death by crucifixion under the Romans was a sufficiently familiar sight in Palestine to be the basis of the saying." Cf. the admittedly later *Gen. Rab.* 56.3, in which Isaac shoulders the wood intended for his own sacrifice (cf. Gen 22:6) "as one who carries his cross on his shoulder" (my trans.; cf. the continuation of this *Genesis Rabbah* passage in the NOTE on "turning and looking at his disciples, rebuked Peter" in 8:33). This parallel is particularly interesting because in some ancient Jewish texts, including *Genesis Rabbah* (64.3), atoning power is ascribed to Isaac's self-sacrifice, as it is to Jesus' death in Mark (10:45; 14:24) and other early Christian writings (see Schoeps, *Paul*, 141–49; Spiegel, *Last Trial*, passim; for other possible influences of Jewish traditions about the "binding of Isaac" on Mark, see the NOTES on "beloved" in 1:11 and "Jesus' sojourn in the wilderness" in 1:12–13).

let him follow me. Gk *akoloutheitō moi.* While in the Q form of the saying (Matt 10:37–38//Luke 14:26–27) the image of following Jesus is used only once, in the Markan form it is used twice, here and in the first clause, "If anyone wants to follow after me" (see figure 24). Laufen (305) suggests that the phrase may have a different nuance in each part (see the COMMENT on 8:34–35).

Davies and Allison (2.671) note that the verb here is a third person *present* imperative, whereas *aparnēsasthō* ("let him renounce himself") and *aratō* ("let him take up") are third person *aorist* imperatives. The grammar thus reinforces what is obvious from the context, that "let him renounce himself and take up his cross" refers to the beginning of the journey, whereas "and follow me" refers to a continuing determination to stick to the chosen path.

35. *life.* Gk *psychēn*, a word that reflects the Hebrew *nepeš*, both of which originally referred to the breath of life, and both of which can be translated as "soul," "self," or "life." The reference in the OT is always to the life of the individual rather than life in general, for which other terms are used (*ḥayyîm, zōē*; cf. Dautzenberg, *Leben*; Schweizer, "*Psychē*").

38. *whoever is ashamed of me and of my words.* Gk *hos gar ean epaischynthē me kai tous emous logous.* The Q parallel (Matt 10:32–33//Luke 12:8–9) speaks of renouncing Jesus rather than being ashamed of him, and it lacks the reference to Jesus' words (see figure 26). Colpe ("*Ho huios tou anthrōpou*," 447 n. 331) suggests that the alternation between "renounce" and "is ashamed" may reflect the closeness between the Aramaic words *kpr* ("renounce") and *ḥpr* ("be ashamed"). It is also possible, however, that Mark's "shame" language and allusion to Jesus' words represent his own redaction, since they mirror early Christian attitudes toward Jesus' words or the good news (cf. 10:29 and Rom 1:16; 2 Tim 1:8; Fitzmyer, *Romans*, 255).

Figure 26: Markan and Q Versions of the Saying about Being Ashamed of/Renouncing Jesus

Mark 8:38 (par. Matt 16:27/Luke 9:26)	Matthew 10:32–33 = Q	Luke 12:8–9 = Q
	everyone then who will acknowledge me before human beings	everyone who acknowledges me before human beings
	I also will acknowledge him before my Father in heaven	the Son of Man will acknowledge him before the angels of God
for whoever is ashamed of me and of my words in this adulterous and sinful generation	and whoever renounces (*arnēsētai*) me before human beings	and the one who renounces (*arnēsamenos*) me before human beings
the Son of Man also will be ashamed of him	I also will renounce (*arnēsomai*) him	he will be renounced (*aparnēthēsetai*)
when he comes in the glory of his Father with the holy angels	before my Father in heaven	before the angels of God

in this adulterous and sinful generation. Gk *en tē geneą tautę tē moichalidi kai hamartōlǭ*. See the NOTE on "this generation" in 8:12 for the background of this phrase in Jewish traditions about the wicked generations of the flood and the exodus. The flood traditions are particularly important in the present context, since

Noah's contemporaries, whose sins included both literal adultery and the spiritual adultery of idolatry (see, e.g., *1 Enoch* 8, and cf. Black, *1 Enoch*, 127), ignored his preaching of righteousness (cf. "is ashamed of me and of my words") and were consequently carried away in the judgment of the flood (see 2 Pet 2:5). Our passage, then, illustrates the principle enunciated in Matt 24:37//Luke 17:26: "As it was in the days of Noah, so too it will be in the days of the Son of Man," and the implication is that "this adulterous and sinful generation" will be the final one.

the Son of Man. Gk *ho huios tou anthrōpou.* Matthew, in his version of the Q parallel (Matt 10:33), changes this to "I also will deny him," so it is obvious that he understood the Markan Jesus' "Son of Man" as a self-reference. For Bultmann (*Theology*, 1.29), however, the more original "Son of Man" language indicates that the historical Jesus distinguished himself from the expected future Son of Man figure, though he saw the two as connected: one's standing before the Son of Man at the eschatological judgment would be determined by one's present attitude toward Jesus. Others (e.g., Vermes, *Jesus*, 168) have argued that in ancient Aramaic "Son of Man" can be a modest or reserved circumlocution for "I," so that Jesus may have been using the phrase to speak about himself in a roundabout way. In any case, the early church, including Mark, understood Jesus' allusions to "the Son of Man" as self-references. Here it is possible that Mark appreciates and is exploiting the ambiguity inherent in the "Son of Man" terminology in the interest of his messianic secret motif: for the disciples, who have heard Jesus acclaimed as Messiah/Son of Man in 8:27–33, "Son of Man" in 8:38 is a self-reference, but for the crowd, who have been excluded from that conversation, it is a reference to another figure.

will be ashamed of him. Gk *epaischynthēsetai auton.* In the LXX, as Bultmann ("*Aischynō*," 189–91) points out, God is usually the subject of *aischynein*, and the "shame" he brings is his judgment (e.g., Pss 44:9 [43:8 LXX]; 119:31, 116 [118:31, 116 LXX]). The Markan Jesus as Son of Man, therefore, takes over part of the judging role of the OT God, just as he shares in his "Father's" glory (see the NOTE on "in the glory of his Father" below). There is a similar picture of the eschatological disgrace of the wicked before the Son of Man in *1 Enoch*: their faces will change color and will be covered with *shame* (46:6), and they will be downcast because they have "*denied* the Lord of Spirits and his Anointed One" (Black trans., emphasis added), who is the *Son of Man* (48:8–10; cf. 48:2), and have persecuted the faithful, who depend upon the name of the Lord of Spirits (46:7–8).

The Markan passage, however, differs from the *1 Enoch* texts in speaking of the Son of Man *being ashamed* (passive voice) of the members of the wicked generation, not of his *bringing them to shame* (active or middle voice). Although, as Bultmann notes, in the LXX the three voices of the verb are very close in meaning to each other and it is often difficult to distinguish the middle from the passive, there still may be a subjective nuance in our passage's reference to the Son of Man's shame, especially given the background in the OT flood story (see the NOTE on "in this adulterous and sinful generation" above), where God *regrets* having made humanity (Gen 6:6–7). This nuance makes the scene, as Barrett ("Not Ashamed," 36) puts it, "not an entirely victorious one for the Son of Man. . . .He is called upon as witness to answer the question: Are these men, who profess to be so, truly yours? And must answer in confusion: No, indeed; I am ashamed that they should take my name on their lips."

when he comes. Gk *hotan elthę.* This description and that in 14:62 are based on Daniel 7, where the "one like a son of man" *comes* to the Ancient of Days (= God) in heaven and is given *glory* by him in a celestial enthronement scene, which is later connected with *judgment* (Dan 7:13–14, 22, 26; see the COMMENT on 8:38–9:1). The Markan passages, however, have transformed the Danielic imagery so that the Son of Man comes *from* heaven rather than *to* it (see Perrin, *Rediscovering*, 173–85).

in the glory of his Father. Gk *en tę doxę tou patros autou.* The Son of Man thus shares his "Father's" divine attribute of glory, which reflects the frequent OT references to "the glory of the Lord"; cf. *Pss. Sol.* 17:31–32, which significantly changes Isa 66:18–20, "they . . . shall see my [God's] glory," into an allusion to seeing the glory both of the coming Messiah and of the Lord (see Horbury, *Messianism*, 103). The potential Christological implications of this parallel between the glory of Christ and that of God are brought out by Chrysostom (*Homily* on Matt 16:24): "Do you see how the glory of the Father and of the Son is all one? But if the glory be one, it is quite evident that the substance also is one." See also Dan 7:14, where glory is one of the attributes that the "one like a son of man" receives from the Ancient of Days.

with the holy angels. Gk *meta tōn angelōn tōn hagiōn.* Like the previous phrases, this one probably reflects Daniel 7, which features millions of angels worshiping God (7:10), and in which the "one like a son of man" is associated with "the people of the holy ones of the Most High" (7:25–27), who may be angels (see Collins, *Daniel*, 313–19). However, it is also possible, and perhaps more natural, to interpret "the people of the holy ones of the Most High" in Dan 7:27 as human saints, and this sort of interpretation of Daniel 7 may be in the background of the description in 1 Thess 4:14 of Jesus coming with the saints, as well as the connection that Mark draws between Jesus' fate and that of his disciples (see the introduction to the COMMENT). In Zech 14:5, similarly, we are told that the Lord will come (*hēxei*), "and all the holy ones with him" (*kai pantes hoi hagioi met' autou*), at the eschaton.

9 1. *there are some of those who are standing here,* etc. Gk *eisin tines hōde tōn hestēkontōn,* etc. This is one of the most troubling verses in the NT for those who hold that Jesus was infallible, since it seems at face value, and especially in connection with the previous verse, to forecast the complete establishment of the dominion of God through Jesus' return in glory within a generation of this utterance. Not surprisingly, many Christian exegetes down through the centuries have found other referents for "the dominion of God fully come in power," such as the transfiguration of Jesus, his resurrection and/or ascension, his gift of the Holy Spirit, the miraculous growth of the church, and the destruction of Jerusalem (see Künzi, *Näherwartungslogion*). Some of the modern exegetes who have argued that the saying does *not* go back to the historical Jesus but is a product of early Christian eschatology have been motivated by a similar desire to rescue Jesus from error.

But even apart from such apologetics, the authenticity of the saying is still debatable. In favor of it, it is certainly plausible that an apocalyptic thinker such as Jesus might have believed that the end would come within a generation or so of his own lifetime, as the parallels from ancient Jewish literature attest. In 4 *Ezra* 4:26, for example, the seer is promised that if he lives long enough he will marvel, "because the age is hastening swiftly to its end," and in CD 20:13–15 it is implied that there will be a gap of forty years between the death of the Teacher of Righteousness and the end of the "age of wrath." The Kaddish prayer, which is still recited in synagogues today, asks for the establishment of the dominion of God "in your lifetime and during your days, and within the life of the entire house of Israel."

Against authenticity, a saying promising that *some* of Jesus' followers would survive until his return is plausible as the church's response to the disturbing fact that some of their number had recently died (cf. 1 Cor 15:51; 1 Thess 4:13–15; John 21:21–23). (Chilton [*God in Strength*, 260–62] and Davies and Allison [2.189], who think that Mark 9:1 comes from the historical Jesus, also think that *tines* ["some"] represents Markan redaction.) These deaths refuted the primitive Christian expectation that because Jesus had conquered death, dying was now a thing of the past, at least for Christians (cf. John 8:51–52 and see Boring, *Sayings*, 186). Mark 9:1, then, could possibly be a saying of ecclesiastical origin, a prophetic word of comfort imparted by the Spirit to console those who had waited for a long time and were on the brink of giving up, like the structurally similar Luke 2:26 (cf. Gnilka, 2.26; Crawford, "Near Expectation").

These arguments are fairly evenly balanced, but the criterion of dissimilarity suggests that it is more likely that Mark 9:1 is an authentic saying of Jesus, since its nonfulfillment reflects poorly on Jesus' predictive powers. The other theory requires us to believe that a church concerned about the delay of the parousia (see the GLOSSARY) put a saying into Jesus' mouth that offered assurance that the end was coming soon, then preserved this fictive saying (in several versions) long after its relevance had passed. This is possible, but it seems more likely that the saying was preserved, despite its nonfulfillment, because it was remembered as a word of the earthly Jesus.

will . . . taste death. Gk *geusōntai thanatou*. This is a Semitic idiom that occurs in the NT (John 8:52; Heb 2:9), a late-first-century Jewish apocalypse (4 *Ezra* 6:26), and rabbinic traditions (cf. Strack-Billerbeck, 1.751–52), but not in the OT, though the latter does speak of "the bitterness of death" (1 Sam 15:32; cf. Sir 41:1 and Behm, "*Geuomai*," 676–77). This "bitterness" language and Heb 2:9 might support Behm's contention that "to taste death" is "a graphic expression of the hard and painful reality of dying" experienced by all human beings. But John 8:52, 4 *Ezra* 6:26, and some of the rabbinic traditions suggest another and not incompatible nuance, which fits very well with the context in our passage: the people referred to will not have even the slightest experience, the tiniest "taste," of death.

before they see the dominion of God fully come in power. Gk *eōs an idōsin tēn basileian tou theou elēlythuian en dynamei.* Dodd (*Parables*, 43) famously argued that this meant "before they see that the dominion of God has *already* come [in my ministry]," an interpretation in line with his theory that Jesus' eschatology was "realized," that is, that he expected no catastrophic future eschatological events. This interpretation assumes that the perfect participle *elēlythuian* ("having come") refers to an action anterior to that of the introductory verb *idōsin* ("they see"). This exegesis is grammatically possible, but it is also possible that *elēlythuian* implies a simultaneous action, since the tense of Greek participles does not have to do primarily with time but with kind of action, and the perfect implies only that the action indicated by the participle is completed at the time that the main verb takes place. As Schlosser (*Règne*, 1.332–35) points out, in OT and NT instances that use "to see" + a participle, some (e.g., Exod 14:30; Num 24:2; Acts 16:27) imply a previous action, whereas others (e.g., Exod 23:5; Deut 22:1; 1 Macc 15.20; Rev 9:1) imply a simultaneous one; the question, therefore, cannot be settled on grammatical grounds alone. A reference to the parousia is supported both by the saying in 13:30, which is parallel in structure to 9:1 ("Amen, I say to you" + "surely will not" + "before"), and by the present Markan context, in which the reference to the dominion of God "fully come in power" (9:1) immediately follows the reference to the Son of Man "com[ing] in glory" with an angelic retinue at the parousia (8:38; cf. 13:24–27 and see Schlosser, *Règne*, 1.324–27).

The Markan placement of 9:1, however, also connects the coming of the dominion of God in power with the transfiguration (9:2–8), which 9:9 seems to understand as a foreshadowing of the resurrection—a natural interpretation, since Jesus is portrayed in the transfiguration narrative as speaking with two people who are no longer on earth (Elijah and Moses). A resurrectional interpretation of 9:1 is also supported by the fact that *en dynamei* ("in power") is used in Rom 1:4 to designate the condition of the resurrected Jesus (cf. 1 Cor 6:14; 15:43; and see Schlosser, *Règne*, 1.338). By the time they reached 9:9, therefore, Mark's audience would probably understand "the dominion of God fully come in power" telescopically, as a reference to the resurrectional glory of Jesus prefigured in the transfiguration and soon to be publicly displayed at the parousia (cf. Nardoni, "Redactional Interpretation").

COMMENT

Introduction. Having prophesied his own suffering, death, and resurrection (8:31–32), Jesus now proclaims a similar fate for his faithful followers. The connection between the destiny of the master and that of his disciples is not only logical but also scriptural, since according to Daniel 7 the story of the "one like a son of man," with whom Jesus identified himself in 8:31, is intimately tied up with the suffering and vindication of "the people of the holy ones of the Most High" (see Schaberg, "Daniel 7–12"; Allison, *End*, 140; Marcus, *Way*, 167–71).

Our passage is made up of individual sayings or couplets, some of which probably did not originally belong together. Verse 9:1, for example, deals with a question not raised in the context (when will the dominion of God fully come?) and is prefaced by a formula ("Amen, I say to you") that Mark often uses to introduce his own insertions (cf. 3:28; 10:15; 13:30; 14:9; 14:25). There is nothing corresponding to it, moreover, in John 12:23–26, which otherwise parallels Mark 8:31–9:1 in many ways (see figure 25), and the sayings in 8:34–35 and 8:38 are found in Q in contexts different from their Markan ones (see figures 24 and 26). Besides adding the traditional saying 9:1, Mark has also put his stamp on the passage through other redactional touches, some of which are evident through their repetition of Markan themes and vocabulary and/or their divergences from Q: "summoning the crowd with his disciples" in 8:34a, "wants to" in 8:34b and 8:35a, "and the good news" in 8:35, "and of my words" in 8:38, and the language of shaming in 8:38, which is similar to language used in the Pauline correspondence (see the NOTE on "whoever is ashamed of me and of my words" in 8:38).

In its present form, our passage is arranged in couplets; it moves from a double exhortation to follow Jesus to the death (8:34–35) to a double saying about the supreme importance of preserving one's "life" (8:36–37) to a double eschatological prediction (8:38–9:1). Grammatically, the middle verses, 8:35–38, which consist of four *gar* ("for") clauses, are set off from the bookends in 8:34 and 9:1, which have a distinctive introductory formula ("and he said to them"). The whole passage is chiastically arranged:

8:34   *kai . . . eipen autois* ("and . . . he said to them"), *ei tis* ("if anyone")
8:35   *hos gar* ("for whoever")
8:36   *ti gar* ("for what") + *anthrōpos* ("human being")
8:37   *ti gar* ("for what") + *anthrōpos* ("human being")
8:38   *hos gar* ("for whoever")
9:1   *kai elegen autois* ("and he said to them"), *eisin tines* ("there are some")

The larger context is also chiastic in terms of its themes, since it moves from the revelation of Jesus' *messiahship* (8:27–30) to a prophecy of his *suffering* (8:31–33) to an exhortation for the disciples to participate in that *suffering* (8:34–37) to a prophecy of his return in *messianic glory* (8:38–9:1). If, then, as commentators often rightly emphasize, the Markan theme of Jesus' messiahship is qualified by that of his suffering, the converse is also true: Jesus' passion is placed in the apocalyptic context of his vindication at the imminent eschaton, when his messiahship will be publicly demonstrated (cf. 14:61–62).

✓ *8:34–35: the exhortation to follow.* After his fierce denunciation of Peter's demonic blindness to the necessity of his messianic suffering (8:33), Jesus summons the crowd along with his disciples to instruct them further in this necessity (8:34a). The use here of the verb *proskalesamenos* ("summoning") tempers the severity of the previous rebuke and holds out the prospect of renewed discipleship, since it recalls happier relations between Jesus and the Twelve: his initial calling of them as a group (3:13), his dispatch of them on their first missionary journey (6:7), and his commissioning of them to meet the needs of the crowd in the wilderness (8:1)—all events that involved their participation in his work. This reassuring note is reinforced by the reminder that, despite all their stumbling, the Twelve are still "his disciples." It is also relevant to the overall context that *proskaleisthai* can have a military nuance (see the NOTE on "summoning" in 8:34), since the dominant image in our passage is that of Jesus leading his troops into battle.

⤹ But it is not only the disciples who are mustered by Jesus in 8:34; the crowd, too, is summoned to join in the march. What Jesus has to say here has the widest possible significance for every human being on earth, so it does not remain a private teaching for the ears of the Twelve only. It is proclaimed, rather, to a large audience symbolizing "the vague amorphous mass of men which is the object of evangelization" (Best, "Role," 92; cf. Lohmeyer, 170–71). Correspondingly, the first words of the teaching itself are "If *anyone* wants to follow after me . . ." The Markan Jesus' call to follow him in the hard way of discipleship, then, is not a "counsel of perfection" addressed to a spiritual elite but the apocalyptically realistic advice that, for *everyone*, life is *only* to be found by treading the pathway of death.

\ Jesus' instruction begins with an exhortation to take up one's cross and move forward in his wake "if anyone wants to" do so (8:34b). "Wants to" may be a Markan addition (see the NOTE on "wants to" in 8:34), and it is certainly consonant with Markan anthropology. It is not a given that one *will* want to follow Jesus; indeed, the hearts of many are hardened against him, either temporarily or permanently (cf. 3:5; 4:10–12; 8:17). And if one does find oneself moved to follow, that is a sign that one has been the recipient of a special, lifesaving grace not vouchsafed to most.

The question is whether one will have the will, courage, and endurance to "follow after" Jesus (*opisō mou akolouthein*, 8:34b), and this redundant locution expresses a typically Markan double entendre, since it conjures up both the image of a pupil following his teacher at a respectful distance and that of a soldier following a military leader into battle (see the NOTE on "Come on after me" in 1:17 and the COMMENT on 1:16–18). The teaching nuance goes along with the pedagogical terms in the context ("teach" in 8:31, "disciples" = "learners" in 8:34), the military nuance with the fact that the discussion since 8:29 has been about Jesus' messiahship, and one of the predominant images of the Messiah in contemporary Judaism was that of a military leader (see the APPENDIX "The Meaning of Christ = Messiah"). Mark's audience would have been especially aware of this image from their contact with the Jewish Revolt, which seems to have been catalyzed by messianic claimants who would have had to reckon with the possibility that they would end up carrying and hanging on crosses (see the NOTE on "take up his cross" in 8:34 and Hengel, *Zealots*, 260). The question of Jesus' messiahship, then, has not been left behind, but has merely shifted gears as the conversation has turned to a discussion of suffering and death.

Specifically, those who wish to follow the Messiah Jesus into the eschatological battle are given fair warning that such a course will require renouncing oneself (*aparnēsasthō heauton*) and taking up one's cross (8:34c). To renounce oneself is, as John Chrysostom comments, to treat oneself as if one were another person:

> He that is denying another . . . should he see him either beaten, or bound, or led to execution, or whatever he may suffer, does not stand by him, does not help him, is not moved, feels nothing for him, as being once for all alienated from him . . . [In the same way, the disciple of Jesus should] have nothing to do

with himself, but give himself up to all dangers and conflicts; and let him so
feel, as though another were suffering it all. (*Homily* 55.2 on Matt 16:24)

Although these vivid words from Chrysostom need to be balanced against the
Markan account of Jesus in Gethsemane, who is *not* indifferent to the approach
of death (14:35–36), they do capture the radical nature of the renunciation that
Jesus enjoins. Chrysostom's paraphrase of *aparnēsasthō* is supported by forms
of the same verb in the later scene of Peter's denial of Jesus (14:30–31, 68–72);
(*ap*)*arneisthai* thus means to disclaim any connection with another person (see
Davies and Allison, 2.670). As will be argued in the COMMENT on 14:66–72,
this denial narrative has been framed against the backdrop of the interrogation
of later Christians, when they were pressed by government officials to deny Jesus
and thereby save their lives; this same situation of judicial persecution is in view
a little later in our own passage when the Markan Jesus speaks of those who are
"ashamed of me . . . in this adulterous and sinful generation" (8:38). The alternative for the Markan community, then, is either to renounce Jesus or to renounce
oneself; as van Iersel ("Persecuted," 25) puts it, self-denial is opposed not so much
to self-love as to denial of Jesus.

Just how far this self-denial is expected to go is indicated by the second part of
the exhortation in 8:34, which employs the perhaps traditional image of taking up
one's cross (see the NOTE on "take up his cross" in 8:34). The reference is to one
of the cruel and shameful aspects of the dishonorable punishment of crucifixion:
the condemned prisoner was forced to carry part of his own instrument of death,
the horizontal crossbeam, or *patibulum*, which itself could be called a "cross," to the
execution site (see the NOTE on "in order that he might carry his cross" in 15:21).
The requirement of carrying the cross added to the humiliation of the prisoner by
forcing him to assist vigorously in his own punishment and providing his tormentors with an extended opportunity for abuse. "Let him take up his cross," then, is
an exhortation to surrender life with the same utter seriousness as the condemned
and maltreated prisoner on his way to execution. To use the modern idiom, popularized by a film about a man on death row, one is to consider oneself a "dead man
walking" and let every aspect of one's existence be governed by that knowledge.

Although originally the saying in 8:34 may not have had Jesus' own crucifixion
in view—it is striking that it speaks of Jesus' *followers* taking up their crosses, not
of *him* doing so—in the Markan context it would be understood as an allusion to
Jesus' own impending fate. This is especially because the image of following Jesus
appears both at the beginning and at the end of the verse, so that its two otherwise
redundant instances might be paraphrased, "If anyone wants to follow after me
[into the eschatological battle] . . . let him take up his cross and follow me [in the
way of the cross]." Thus understood, the saying manifests a characteristic Markan
fusion of the notions of victory and suffering death.

But why should one accept the dreadful burden of the cross? Why should one
want to follow Jesus (cf. 8:34b), if discipleship means entry into a living death? The
Markan Jesus adds to the exhortation in 8:34 four *gar* ("for") clauses (8:35–38) that
attempt to justify it. The theme of the first three of these clauses (8:35–37) is life:

against the disturbing and counterintuitive exhortation in 8:34 to embrace death, he now sets the assertion, emphasized by repetition, that those who suffer death "for me and the good news" will paradoxically find life (8:35).

This saying probably draws on pep talks from ancient generals, who were in the habit of exhorting their troops to stand fast and fight by warning them that flight in battle frequently leads to soldiers' deaths, whereas boldness can preserve them (see, e.g., Homer, *Iliad* 5.529–32; 15.561–64; Dionysius of Halicarnassus, *Roman Antiquities* 9.9.9; Sallust, *War with Cataline* 58.15–17; Cicero, *Tuscan Disputations* 2.54; cf. Beardslee, "Saving," and Gundry, 455). The parallels in Xenophon are especially striking, since they are similar to Jesus' saying not only in thought but also in form and vocabulary:

> Therefore, as you desire victory, stand and fight; for (*gar*) it would be folly for men who desire to win a battle to turn their backs and offer to the enemy the side of their body that is without eyes or hands or weapons; any one who wishes to live (*tis zēn boulomenos*) would be a fool if he tried to run away, when he knows that it is the victors who save their lives (*hoi men nikōntes sōzontai*), while those who try to run away are more likely to meet their death than those who stand their ground. (*Cyropaedia* 3.3.45)

> Whoever is desirous of saving his life (*hostis te zēn epithymei*), let him strive for victory; for (*gar*) it is the victors that slay and the defeated that are slain. (*Anabasis* 3.2.39)

> Courage is more likely to save lives (*sōzei tas psychas*) than running away. (*Cyropaedia* 4.1.5; LCL trans. alt.)

In these passages, as in Mark, a leader addresses "whoever wishes to save his life," using vocabulary similar to Mark's (*sōzein* = "to save," *psychē* = "life") and employing *gar* ("for") clauses to back up his exhortation to self-sacrifice. And the message is the same paradoxical one as that of the Markan Jesus: if you wish to save your life, throw it away! Our passage, then, is probably an eschatological overhaul of a common trope, a revision informed by the apocalyptic conviction that in view of God's imminent reversal of earthly conditions, all worldly goods, including one's own life, are dispensable.

Mark's understanding of this self-sacrifice is illuminated by comparison with 10:29–30, which is the other Markan passage that speaks of renunciation "for me and the good news." Here the primary sacrifices in view are separation from family and property, the things that are at the center of one's daily existence and therefore of one's "life." But there is also a reference to an existence "with persecutions," which presumably includes, in some cases, persecution unto death—a situation that the Markan community was apparently having to face (see 13:9–13). The meaning of "destroying one's life" in 8:35a, then, is probably both literal and metaphorical, and the case is probably the same with "saving one's life" in 8:35b. On the one hand, it refers to outcroppings of the age to come in the present evil one: the discovery of a new family in the Christian community, the communion of new "brothers and sisters and mothers and children" in shared houses and fields. On the other hand, it refers to a strictly eschatological hope, the certainty of eternal life "in the coming age" if and when the prop of mutual support is kicked away and the believer is called upon to make the ultimate sacrifice (cf. again 10:29–30)—an idea commonly found in Jewish martyrologies (see, e.g., 2 Macc 7:36–37; 4 Macc 5:6; 6:15, 27; Josephus, *War* 1.650; 2.153; van Iersel, "Persecuted," 25).

Counterintuitive as it is, the truth of Jesus' words about finding life on the pathway of death has not lacked witnesses. In our century, for example, Alexander Solzhenitsyn has described the mindset that enabled him and other political prisoners to overcome their interrogators in the Soviet gulags in terms that echo our passage:

> From the moment you go to prison you must put your cozy past firmly behind you. At the very threshold, you must say to yourself, "My life is over, a little early to be sure, but there's nothing to be done about it. I shall never return to freedom. I am condemned to die—now or a little later . . . I no longer have any property whatsoever. For me those I love have died, and for them I have died. From today on, my body is useless and alien to me. Only my spirit and my conscience remain precious and important to me."
>
> Confronted by such a prisoner, the interrogator will tremble.
>
> Only the man who has renounced everything can win that victory. (*Gulag*, 130)

8:36–37: nothing is more precious than (eschatological) life. The preciousness of this victory-through-renunciation is underscored by the double saying that follows. The implicit answer to the question of why one should "want to" follow Jesus continues in the assertion that nothing is more valuable or tailored to the individual's needs than the "life" that discipleship brings. Here the focus becomes intensely personal. The subject is no longer a vaguely defined "someone" or "anyone," as it was in 8:34–35 and will be again in 8:38; it is now "a human being," the hearer himself/herself in confrontation with a dramatic choice between death and life —"the world" and his or her soul—and the sense of personal involvement is increased by the use of rhetorical questions. The alternative posed in the first of these sayings between "the world" and "life" is thoroughly apocalyptic; some Greco-Roman philosophers, by contrast, saw "the world" as the highest good, the marvelous order (the original meaning of *kosmos*) that embraces everything, including the human lives that find their proper place within that harmony. For the apocalypticist, however, as later for the Gnostic, "the world" and the true self were not friends but bitter enemies (cf. Jonas, *Gnostic Religion*, 241–54).

As had happened previously in 8:35, here in 8:36–37 secular wisdom has been taken up and transformed. The basic idea behind 8:36–37 is the commonplace that "you can't take it with you" when you die (see, e.g., *Iliad* 9.401–9; Sir 11:18–19; Luke 12:16–20; Jas 4:13–16). Nothing is more precious than life, so one should not endanger one's existence for trifles; as Davies and Allison (2.672) put it: "What good is even the greatest possession if there is no possessor to enjoy it?" But here this counsel of self-interest has been both deepened and apocalypticized. Now the emphasis is not merely on physical life but on the true life of the self (for Mark's "rudimentary theology of the self," see the NOTE on "root in themselves" in 4:17). The *psychē*, the "life" or "self," is the "one thing needful" (cf. Luke 10:42), the prerequisite for the enjoyment of everything else; if one loses this indispensable subject, one will not be able to delight in anything. The profit and loss, moreover, are no longer limited to this life, as the linkage with the apocalyptic sayings in 8:38–9:1 makes clear: the forfeiture of *psychē* referred to is not just physical death at the termination of one's allotted lifespan but also postmortem judgment at the world's fast-approaching end. As the close parallel in 2 *Apoc. Bar.* 51:15 puts it: "For what then have people lost their life, and for what have those who were on the earth exchanged their soul?"

A similar process of eschatologizing the hope for "life" can be glimpsed in the history of the interpretation of an OT passage that may undergird 8:36–37. Psalm 49:7–9 provides a notable parallel to the thought of these two verses:

> Truly no one can ransom himself, or give to God the price of his life, for the ransom of his life is costly, and can never suffice, that he should continue to live on for ever, and never see the Pit. (RSV alt.)

Here we have both the idea that nothing is more precious than life (cf. Mark 8:36) and the thought that there is no substitute for it (cf. Mark 8:37; see Davies and Allison, 2.674). The parallel becomes even more striking when the Targum's rendering of these verses is compared, for there "life," which in the original psalm is ordinary human existence that ends in death, becomes eternal life beyond the grave, which involves escape from the terrors of the last judgment: "And he will live again with eternal life; he will not see the judgment of Gehenna" (Targum on Ps 49:9).

8:38–9:1: *a forecast of ultimate victory for God, Jesus, and his followers.* This eschatological horizon becomes explicit in the last couplet of the passage, which sketches the final victory of God and Jesus.

The first verse of the couplet, Mark 8:38, takes up the thought of loss from 8:36–37 and develops it into a vivid vignette of the future judgment, focusing on the negative side of the event, the eschatological "shaming" of those whose standards have been dictated by "this adulterous and sinful generation" and who therefore have become "ashamed" of Jesus. There is bitter irony in this description of people who have been embarrassed, not by their complicity with a sinful "generation," but by Jesus and his life-giving words. By depicting their future discomfiture, our verse continues to answer the implicit question of why one should "want to" follow Jesus (cf. 8:34) by refuting the impression that those who do so will suffer loss. The reverse turns out to be true: it is those who have *refused* to follow, who have been ashamed of Jesus and his words, who will be penalized.

Formally this saying is a "sentence of holy law," a structure identified by Käsemann ("Sentences") on the basis of several NT examples (e.g., Rom 2:12; 1 Cor

3:17; 2 Cor 9:6; Rev 22:18–19), although Käsemann wrongly asserts that this form is an exclusively post-Easter phenomenon (see Schmidt, *"Gattung"* for LXX parallels, and Aune, *Prophecy*, 237–40). These "sentences" apocalypticize the *lex talionis*, the OT rule of "eye for eye, tooth for tooth" (Exod 21:24), in such a way that the protasis (the "if" clause or its relative conditional correlate) comes to refer to human action in the present, while the apodosis (result clause) comes to refer to a divine action of punishment or reward in the eschatological future. The Markan version of the saying presents only the negative side of this pattern, not mentioning at all, as the Q form does (see figure 26), Jesus' eschatological acknowledgment of those who have confessed him in the present evil age. Mark, however, probably understands 9:1, which he has added to the present context, as the completion of the thought in 8:38: those who resist the powerful temptation to be "ashamed" of Jesus and his words will receive their reward not so much through a celestial pat on the back as through their experience of the all-embracing "dominion of God fully come in power."

But what does it mean to be "ashamed" of Jesus and his words? As we have already seen, Mark's hearers would probably interpret this as an allusion to the situation of interrogation before magistrates, in which Christians were called upon to curse or deny Jesus or else be martyred. But given the larger context, in which Peter has just been scandalized at Jesus' prophecy of his rejection, suffering, and death (8:31–32), and given the revulsion with which the "utterly vile death on the cross" (Origen, *Commentary on* Matthew 27:22–26) was regarded in antiquity (see the APPENDIX "Crucifixion"), 8:38 probably also contains a reference to a tendency both within and outside the Christian community to gloss over, downplay, or take offense at Jesus' crucifixion. This suggestion is strengthened by an OT echo, since Isaiah 52–53 alludes repeatedly to the onlookers' *shame* at the humiliating suffering and death of the Lord's righteous Servant (52:14; 53:3, 8) but also, like our Markan verse, implies that this shamed and humiliated Servant will subsequently be exalted and will discomfit those who have been ashamed of him (52:12–15; 53:10–12).

The second half of the "sentence of holy law" in 8:38 portrays this eschatological reversal—the dramatic turning point at which "this adulterous and sinful generation" will give way to God's new world of holiness and divine glory. The description of the Son of Man coming with the angels in his Father's glory, apparently as a judge, is redolent with OT associations, especially from Daniel 7 (see the NOTES on "when he comes," "in the glory of his Father," and "with the holy angels" in 8:38). The Markan Son of Man's implied role as judge is reminiscent of the same OT passage, since the "one like a son of man" in Daniel 7 is depicted in almost identical terms as "the people of the holy ones of the Most High," to whom judgment is given; naturally enough, the later author of the Jewish pseudepigraphon *1 Enoch* pictures the Son of Man himself as a judge (see the APPENDIX "The Son of Man" in vol. 1), a role that seems to be presupposed in several NT Son of Man passages (e.g., Mark 14:62; Matt 25:31–46; John 5:27).

But the Son of Man's "coming" at the eschaton will not only show him as the eschatological judge but will also establish with certainty that he is, and always has been, God's triumphant Messiah, thus confirming the basic correctness of Peter's insight in 8:29 and binding our whole passage together as a testimony to Jesus' kingship. For the Son of Man's coming "in the glory of his Father with the holy angels" in 8:38 is parallel to the coming of the dominion of God in power in 9:1. As in Psalm 2 and later messianic texts such as *Pss. Sol.* 17, therefore, a militant royal figure, the establishment of whose dominion will simultaneously be the establishment of the dominion of God, is coming into view. In our passage, moreover, the advent of the Son of Man is accompanied by an overwhelming demonstration of angelic might ("with the holy angels"); in the Qumran War Scroll, similarly, the Davidic Messiah will fight God's battles in the final eschatological war and will be aided by hosts of angels fighting on his side to establish the dominion of God (see 1QM 6:6; 4Q285 1 9 [8 10]).

But when will this eschatological consummation take place? It is one thing to be asked to make the supreme sacrifice in order to win a climactic battle but quite another to be called upon to do so time after time with no end in sight. The final saying in our section is meant to assure Mark's community that the latter is *not* the case; Jesus' call to self-sacrifice is saved from becoming an invitation to masochism because it is coupled with the belief that the sacrifices demanded are part of a divine movement that is already secretly at work to transform the world ("the dominion of God") and will soon become publicly visible everywhere ("in power"). This establishment of "the dominion of God . . . in power" will take place within the lifetime of some of Jesus' original hearers: before they all die, he will return in glory (cf. John 21:22). For a Markan audience living a generation or so after Jesus' ministry, these words would point with a wonderful precision to their own time as the era in which "this adulterous and sinful generation" would give way to God's new world.

Is Mark 9:1, then, a false prophecy? In a sense, yes, since Mark, like Jesus before him, apparently expected the end to come within a few years. But as we have just seen, Mark also, like Jesus before him, saw the eschatological epoch as already dawning, a point driven home by the transfiguration narrative that immediately follows (9:2–8). "The dominion of God . . . come in power," then, is not only a future to be hoped for but also a presence to be experienced now, and this combination of present advent and hope for the future is more important than the question of the exact timing of the end. The latter is a secret that no human being, not even Jesus, can claim to know—as he himself will acknowledge later in the Gospel (see 13:32).

But how is that dominion's presence to be experienced? Where is one to look to see it revealed? And how does this new revelation relate to the old, old story of God's dealings with Israel? These are among the questions that the following narrative will address.

THE TRANSFIGURATION (9:2–8)

9 ²And after six days Jesus took Peter and James and John and led them up to a high mountain privately, by themselves, and was transformed before them, ³and his clothes became so dazzlingly white that no launderer on earth could whiten them so. ⁴And there appeared to them Elijah with Moses, and they were talking with Jesus. ⁵And Peter answered and said to Jesus, "Rabbi, it is good for us to be here; and let us make three tents, one for you and one for Moses and one for Elijah." ⁶(For he did not know what to answer; for they had become afraid.) ⁷And there came a cloud, overshadowing them; and there came a voice out of the cloud: "This is my beloved Son; listen to him." ⁸And suddenly, when they looked around, they no longer saw anyone except Jesus alone with them.

NOTES

9 2. *after six days.* Gk *meta hēmeras hex.* Time indications in Mark are rare, and when they do occur they tend to be vague (e.g., "in those days" in 1:9; 8:1; etc.; "that day" in 4:35; or "several days later" in 2:1). "After six days," then, is unusual, and it probably has some sort of symbolic resonance. Philo (*Allegorical Interpretation* 1.2.4) says that six is an appropriate number for mortal things, seven for immortals ones. Origen (*Commentary on Matthew* 12:36) links our phrase with the Genesis account of the creation of the world in six days, culminating with the Sabbath on the seventh. Certainly the rhapsodic way in which Peter responds to the whole experience ("it is good for us to be here," 9:5) would fit in with Jewish feelings about the Sabbath as a "sanctuary in time" and a foretaste of the world to come (see Heschel, *Sabbath*, passim). But the most important biblical background is that of Moses' ascent of Sinai after six days (Exod 24:16), since Mosaic symbolism runs all through our passage (see the section on Moses in the APPENDIX "History-of-Religions Backgrounds to the Transfiguration"). Cf. *T. Ps.-J.* Exod 24:1, which inserts an additional reference to the seventh day when speaking of Moses' ascent of Sinai.

and was transformed before them. Gk *kai metemorphōthē emprosthen autōn.* On the background of *metemorphōthē* ("he was transformed"), see the section on epiphanies of gods, goddesses, or angels in human form in the APPENDIX "History-of-Religions Backgrounds to the Transfiguration."

3. *his clothes became so dazzlingly white.* Gk *ta himatia autou egeneto stilbonta leuka lian,* lit. "his clothes became dazzling, extremely white," a typically Markan double expression (see Neirynck, *Duality*). In Matt 17:2 and Luke 9:29 it is Jesus' *face,* in addition to his *clothes,* that become radiant, and this is one of several "minor agreements" of Matthew and Luke over against Mark in this narrative. The terminology, however, is different in the two evangelists, and it is probable that each of them, realizing the Mosaic background of the story (see again the section on Moses in the APPENDIX "History-of-Religions Backgrounds to the Transfiguration"), has independently conformed his narrative to the description of Moses' radiant face in Exod 34:29.

launderer. Gk *gnapheus.* Older translations use "fuller," one who thickens (fulls), cleans, bleaches, shrinks, or dyes wool or woolen cloth. The Greek term comes from *knēn*, to scrape or use a carding comb (*knaphos*). But it is the cleaning and bleaching functions that are in view in our passage; these were carried out in OT and Greco-Roman times by washing with lye, cleansing with pressure, and setting out in the sun to bleach (cf. Mal 3:2; 2 Sam 19:24). Old Testament texts such as Ps 51:7; Jer 2:22; 4:14; and Mal 3:2–3 use this bleaching process as a metaphor for spiritual purification (see Richard, "Fuller"). The Psalms and Malachi passages, moreover, stress that this cleansing is accomplished by God or a heavenly messenger, and this is similar to our passage's implication that the source of the radiance is divine.

4. *And there appeared to them Elijah with Moses.* Gk *kai ōphthē autois Ēlias syn Mōusēs.* The order Elijah-Moses is unexpected, since Moses was the more prominent figure, but Mark seems to wish to subordinate Moses to Elijah (see the COMMENT on 9:2–4). Heil ("Note"), however, argues against this exegesis, claiming that in the Markan instances of "X with Y," Y is always the more prominent figure. He points especially to 4:10 and 8:34 ("those around him with the Twelve"; "the crowd with his disciples"), in both of which the group indicated by "with" consists of Jesus' inner circle (cf. 2:26; 15:27, 32 for other Markan usages of *syn*). But given the frequently harsh Markan picture of the Twelve (see, e.g., 6:52; 8:17–21, 30–33; 14:50–52, 66–72), it may be that the *syn* terminology is actually intended as a disparagement of the latter and that the inclusion of others is meant to counter a tendency toward exclusivism within the Markan community (see the introduction to the COMMENT on 4:10–12.).

The most frequent interpretation of Moses and Elijah (attested already by Origen, *Commentary on Matthew* 12.38) is that the former represents the biblical books of the Law and the latter the books of the Prophets; the narrative is thus implying that the scriptures bear witness to Jesus, since "the Law and the Prophets" can stand for the scriptures in general (see, e.g., Matt 5:17; Luke 16:16; John 1:45; Rom 3:21). It is a problem for this interpretation, however, that Moses too was a prophet (see, e.g., Deut 34:10), and indeed he is frequently referred to by Philo and Josephus as "*the* Prophet" (see Meeks, *Prophet-King*, 125–26, 137–38), so it is hard to see him as a representative of the Law as distinct from the Prophets. A further problem is that Jewish texts fail to link Elijah with the books of the Prophets, and in fact he would be a strange choice to represent them, since he was not a writing prophet (cf. Öhler, "Verklärung," 205 n. 25).

Rather, the key to the symbolism of the appearance of "Elijah with Moses" on the mountain probably lies in their common association with Mt. Sinai = Horeb, where they both encountered God (Exodus 19–24, 34; 1 Kgs 19), and with eschatological expectations. On the basis of biblical prophecy (Mal 4:5–6), and partly because he had been translated to heaven rather than dying in the normal way (2 Kgs 2:11), Elijah was expected to return in the end-time and herald the advent of the Messiah and the end of the age (see the COMMENT on 9:11–13 below). Moses was also sometimes related to the eschaton, either by being the *model* for the eschatological redeemer, as in the "prophet like Moses" passage cited at the climax of our narrative (Deut 18:15, 18; see the NOTE on "This is my beloved Son; listen to him" in 9:7), or by himself being identified as an eschatological figure. In *Deut. Rab.* 3.17, for example, God promises: "Moses, I swear to you . . . in the time to come when I bring Elijah, the prophet, unto them, the two of you shall come together" (cf. Allison, *New Moses*, 75). Note that here, as in our Markan passage, Moses is subordinated to Elijah.

5. *Rabbi*. Gk *Rabbi*, the transliteration of a Hebrew word that literally means "my great one." As Lapin ("Rabbi") points out, all four Markan instances reflect this etymology in that they convey a sense of Jesus' greatness: three are associated with astounding miracles (9:5; 10:51; 11:21), and the fourth is Judas' acclamation of his renowned master (14:45). It is striking that Mark does not translate *Rabbi* or the related Aramaic term *Rabbouni* (10:51); he evidently expects his hearers to be familiar with these terms.

In Jewish sources, "Rabbi" and "Rab" ("great one") eventually became technical terms for ordained teachers and/or jurists and are still used so today. Scholars of Judaism, however, debate how far the development toward "Rabbi" as a technical term had gone in NT times. Some think that it was not yet a title but only a vague honorific, roughly equivalent to "sir." In support of this interpretation are Matt 20:33, which translates *rabbouni* from Mark 10:51 with *kyrie* ("sir"), and early inscriptions from Palestine and the Diaspora that use *rab*, *rabbî*, and related words as general terms of respect for influential men who were not necessarily teachers (see the catalog in Cohen, "Rabbis"). In addition, neither of the two great Pharisaic teachers of the pre-70 period, Hillel and Shammai, is referred to as *rabbî* in ancient sources, and all of the NT passages, as well as most of the early rabbinic attestations (e.g., *m. Ned.* 9:5; *m. Roš Haš.* 2:9), employ the term in direct address, which would be compatible with the nontitular interpretation. At the same time, several NT texts (Matt 23:7–8; John 1:38; 3:2) already suggest a special connection between the term *rabbi* and the teaching office. As Cohen ("Rabbis," 9) sums up the situation, in the first several centuries of the Christian era the term was "a popular designation for anyone of high position, notably—but not exclusively—a teacher" (cf. Overman, *Matthew's Gospel*, 44–48). Although Mark himself associates *rabbi* more with miracles than with teaching, these two kinds of activity of Jesus are intimately linked in the evangelist's mind (see esp. 1:27).

6. *For he did not know what to answer*. Gk *ou gar ēdei ti apokrithē*. The Gethsemane scene (14:40) contains almost identical wording; the disciples are befuddled both by Jesus' transfiguration, which prefigures his resurrection (see the COMMENT on 9:2–4), and by his suffering in Gethsemane, which prefigures his death.

for they had become afraid. Gk *ekphoboi gar egenonto*. As elsewhere in Mark, Peter's characteristics, including his faults, are shared with the other disciples (cf. 1:36; 8:32–33; 14:29–31, 37; 16:7). Of these Markan parallels, the most striking is 16:7, since both passages employ a short *gar* ("for") clause about fear and link Peter with others of the Twelve. Verse 16:7, moreover, occurs in the empty tomb narrative, which demonstrates Jesus' resurrection, and the transfiguration is a proleptic resurrection appearance (see again the COMMENT on 9:2–4).

7. *cloud.* Gk *nephelē.* In the OT, the divine presence frequently resides in a cloud, and this sort of cloud is often linked with Moses on his ascents of Sinai (Exod 19:9–13; 24:15–18; 34:1–5) and in his association with the Tabernacle (see, e.g., Exod 33:9–10; 40:34–38; Num 9:15–23; 11:24–25; Deut 31:14–15). Eschatologically minded Jews sometimes expected this cloud to return in the end-time, as is shown, for example, by 2 Macc 2:8: "Then the Lord will disclose these things, and the glory of the Lord and the cloud will appear, as they were shown in the case of Moses."

overshadowing them. Gk *episkiazousa autois. Episkiazein* can mean either to cast a shadow (see, e.g., Acts 5:15) or to cover (e.g., Exod 40:34; Luke 1:35), sometimes in a gesture of protection (e.g., Ps 91:4 [90:4 LXX]), sometimes in such a way that what lies beneath is hidden (e.g., Sophocles, *Trachiniai* 914). In the present context, the nuances of covering and concealment are probably present, since the passage seems to echo Exod 40:34–35 (*episkiazein* + cloud + tent + Moses typology), in which the cloud covers the Tabernacle, and since in the next verse Moses and Elijah disappear (cf. Schneider, "*Episkiazō*").

But who are "they" whom the cloud overshadows? Verse 9:6, which ends with a description of the disciples' fear, is probably a Markan insertion (see the introduction to the COMMENT). In the pre-Markan story, which probably lacked that verse, "them" probably alluded to Jesus, Moses, and Elijah, who were mentioned immediately beforehand in 9:4–5; the cloud overshadows the three supernatural beings, and when it disappears, two of them vanish along with it, as often happens in stories of translation to heaven (see, e.g., *Iliad* 3.380–81; *1 Enoch* 14:8; Acts 1:9; 1 Thess 4:17; Rev 11:12; cf. Öhler, "Verklärung," 210–11). Zeller ("Bedeutung," 308–9) thinks that for Mark the disciples must at least be included in the "them," since they are the subject in 9:6b and 9:8 and the object of the divine address in 9:7cd. But Mark may not have realized that his insertion of 9:6 had changed the grammatical emphasis. In support of this reading, the voice in 9:7 comes *out of* the cloud, and this implies that the disciples whom it addresses are external to it.

This is my beloved Son; listen to him. Gk *Houtos estin ho huios mou ho agapētos, akouete autou.* "Listen to him" (*akouete autou*) is probably an allusion to Deut 18:15, 18, where Moses tells the Israelites that after his death God will raise up for them a prophet like him: "To him you shall listen" (*autou akousesthe,* my trans.); this is especially likely in view of the many other Mosaic features in the narrative (see again the section on Moses in the APPENDIX "History-of-Religions Backgrounds to the Transfiguration"). By the first century the image of this Mosaic prophet had probably merged in some circles with that of the Messiah (see the NOTE on "sign" in 8:11) and in others with that of Elijah; see, for example, John 6:14, which fuses a reference to "the prophet" (like Moses?) with one to "the one who is coming" (= Elijah? cf. Mal 3:1; Matt 11:3–14; and Martyn, *Gospel,* 26–27; Allison, *New Moses,* 91–95).

In a private communication, Dale Allison points out that there is an interesting parallel to this and other features of the transfiguration narrative in 1QH 12[4]:5–6, 24, 27: "I give you thanks, Lord, because you have lightened my face for your covenant . . . Like perfect dawn you have revealed yourself to me with per[fect] light . . . Those who walk on the path of your heart have listened to me . . . Through me you have enlightened the face of the Many . . . for you have shown me your wondrous mysteries." This passage, like ours, speaks of a chosen teacher whom God enlightens, to whom he reveals his mysteries, and to whom God's adherents must listen.

8. *no longer saw anyone.* Gk *ouketi oudena eidon.* A typically Markan double negative (for another double expression, see the NOTE on "his clothes became so dazzlingly white" in 9:3 above).

COMMENT

Introduction. Jesus' prophecy to some of his followers of a revelation of "the dominion of God fully come in power" within a short time (9:1) is immediately followed by his glorious transfiguration before three of them, and the juxtaposition implies that this visionary experience is at least a partial fulfillment of that prophecy.

This juxtaposition is probably the work of Mark himself. It is it in line not only with Markan theology but also with the overall structure of the Gospel. The transfiguration story, with its acclamation of Jesus as Son of God by a voice from heaven, forms a centerpiece between the beginning and the end of the narrative, where we find similarly worded acclamations (1:11; 15:39). This placement, too, is likely the work of the author.

Not that Mark has concocted the transfiguration story out of whole cloth. The comment in 9:6 about Peter not knowing what to say, for example, devalues his previous suggestion that the disciples build booths for Jesus—a suggestion that otherwise seems fully in accord with the imagery of the story (see below in the COMMENT on 9:5–6); the reference to his fright, moreover, fits uneasily with the joyful tone of 9:5a, "Rabbi, it is good for us to be here" (cf. Nützel, *Verklärungserzählung,* 125). Mark 9:6, then, is probably the evangelist's editorial insertion into a preexistent narrative in order to highlight the obtuseness of the disciples and the fallacy of Peter's suggestion. Besides this qualifying insertion, other Markan redactional features may include "privately" (*kat' idian*) in 9:2, which is typical Markan vocabulary, the order "Elijah with Moses" in 9:4, which is consonant with Mark's eschatological interpretation of the event (see below), and the double negative in 9:8 (see the NOTE on "no longer saw anyone" in 9:8).

The passage is a symmetrical composition with a chiastic structure:

A   Jesus alone with the disciples (9:2a)
B   Transfiguration (9:2b–3)
C   Appearance of Elijah and Moses with Jesus (9:4)
C′   Peter's suggestion of booths for Jesus, Moses, and Elijah (9:5–6)
B′   Voice from heaven, interpreting transfiguration (9:7)
A′   Jesus alone with the disciples (9:8)

As in 8:27–33, a Christological revelation is accompanied by a Markan emphasis on apostolic obtuseness. But also as in 8:27–33, followed by 8:34–9:1, the disciples are not left totally in the dark, since their misunderstanding is followed by further enlightenment; our passage moves from a visionary event (9:2–4) to a mistaken estimation of its meaning (9:5–6) to a correct interpretation (9:7).

9:2–4: *scene setting and vision.* The narrative begins with Jesus singling out three of his disciples, Peter and James and John, for a special revelation, and leading them up a high mountain (9:2a). Mark discloses that this mountaintop experience occurred "after six days," and it is likely that this detail is symbolically important, suggesting, among other things, a similarity between Jesus and Moses, who was famous for ascending Mount Sinai after six days of waiting (Exod 24:16; *b. Yoma* 4b; cf. the NOTE on "after six days" in 9:2). This is just the first of a number of parallels between our passage and traditions about Moses (see the section on Moses in the APPENDIX "History-of-Religions Backgrounds to the Transfiguration").

This Mosaic typology continues in the next step of the narrative, the description of the transfiguration proper (9:2b–3), since Moses, too, was "transfigured" on a mountain: when he came down from Sinai after his second sojourn there, his face shone so brilliantly that he covered it with a veil to shield the people (Exod 34:29–35). Paul's treatment of this episode in 2 Cor 3:7–18, which itself probably draws on a preexistent exegetical tradition, reveals how alive the story was in Jewish and early Christian circles (see Georgi, *Opponents,* 254–71; Belleville, *Reflections*).

But the parallel with Moses in this part of the transfiguration narrative is only partial, since Mark, unlike Matthew and Luke, does not describe Jesus' *face* but only his *clothing* as radiant. This celestially bright clothing is less evocative of Moses than it is of Adam, whose likeness the Markan Jesus frequently bears (see the subject index in vols. 1 and 2 under "Adam"). Adam's "garments of glory" (mentioned, e.g., in the Targums on Gen 3:21) were the subject of immense interest among Jews and Christians in this period; among those speculations was the belief that the Messiah would recover the glorious Adamic raiment at the eschaton. Jesus' "flashy" clothing is also reminiscent of the dress of kings on important occasions, including enthronements (see the sections on Adam and on royal epiphanies in the APPENDIX "History-of-Religions Backgrounds to the Transfiguration"). Jesus' dazzling apparel, then, is a pictorial code suggesting his status as the new Adam and King Messiah on the way to enthronement.

The submergence of the Mosaic likeness under other images continues in the following verse, in which Elijah and Moses suddenly appear and are seen by the astonished disciples to converse with Jesus (9:4). Mark does not tell us what the three discussed, though Luke 9:31 attempts to fill this gap in the Markan narrative. For Mark, however, the point of fascination seems to be not what they said to each other but simply Jesus' ability to carry on a conversation with these two long-dead biblical heroes. As Öhler ("Verklärung," 207) points out, a similar theme comes to the fore in *Apoc. Zeph.* 8:4, where the seer expresses wonderment at being able to understand the language of angels (cf. 1 Cor 13:1). The whole atmosphere, then, is numinous, even dreamlike. Jesus, Moses, and Elijah seem to exist on a plane of their own, separate from that of the three mortals who look on as though from afar, thunderstruck.

But what is the significance of the way in which Mark describes Jesus' conversation partners? Both the order and the grammatical subordination of Moses to Elijah ("Elijah *with* Moses") are unexpected, since Moses lived long before Elijah and was generally the more prominent figure; if anything, Elijah was considered to be a throwback to Moses (see Allison, *New Moses*, 39–45). The reverse order, Moses-Elijah, then, would be expected, and indeed is what is found in the following Markan verse (9:5) and in the Matthean and Lukan retellings of the present one.

The unusual order Elijah-Moses, which may result from Markan redaction, probably reflects the greater prominence of Elijah in eschatological contexts. According to the OT, Elijah was taken up alive to heaven (2 Kgs 2:11), and similar rumors sometimes attached themselves to Moses, despite the explicit statement of Deut 34:5–6 that he died and was buried (see again the section on Moses in the APPENDIX "History-of-Religions Backgrounds to the Transfiguration"). But if Elijah (definitely) and Moses (possibly) had not really died, they could easily return to visible life, and they were expected to do so just before the eschaton as a sign that the whole universe was about to enter that deathless state in which they themselves already existed (cf. 9:11). Hence the sudden appearance of "Elijah with Moses" in the Markan narrative suggests that the transfiguration is an anticipation of the wave of divine glory that is about to flood the earth.

But it also anticipates the first breaker of that eschatological tsunami, Jesus' resurrection. The fact that Elijah and sometimes Moses were believed to have eluded death is an obvious point of similarity with Jesus' resurrection. Many exegetes, therefore, have interpreted the transfiguration as an anticipation of Jesus' resurrection (see already Bede, *Homilies on the Gospels* 1.24, and cf. Jensen, *Understanding*, 159–60 for the link between transfiguration and resurrection in early Christian art). This theory is related to, but logically distinct from, the assertion that the story *originated* as a resurrection appearance (see the section on resurrection appearances in the APPENDIX "History-of-Religions Backgrounds to the Transfiguration"). A resurrectional interpretation of the transfiguration is strengthened by the fact that at the beginning of the next pericope (9:9) Jesus forbids publicity about what has just happened until after "the Son of Man ha[s] been raised from among the dead."

9:5–6: *Peter's suggestion.* What the three chosen disciples are experiencing, therefore, is a foretaste of Jesus' resurrection glory; and Jesus' return to life, similarly, points forward to the general resurrection of the dead (see the linkage between the two events in 9:9–10). It was expected among Jews that when the latter event occurred, when the dominion of God came in power (cf. 9:1), not only the Messiah but the whole of redeemed humanity represented by Adam would regain the splendor that had been lost through the fall (see the section on Adam in the APPENDIX "History-of-Religions Backgrounds to the Transfiguration")—a detail that, as we have already seen, hooks up with Jesus' brilliant vesture. Perhaps not coincidentally, several early Jewish and Christian traditions locate paradise itself on a mountain (see ibid.); the mountaintop location of our passage, therefore, also suggests a return to Eden. Understandably enough, Peter wants to prolong his sojourn in this re-creation of paradise; he therefore breaks into the three-way parley of the supernatural figures with the rapturous comment, "Rabbi, it is good for us to be here" (9:5a).

⤙ Peter follows up this exclamation with the suggestion that he and his fellow disciples should erect three tents, one for Jesus, one for Moses, and one for Elijah (9:5b)—reversing the order in which the two OT figures were mentioned in the previous verse and thus perhaps revealing that he misses the Markan point about subordinating the Mosaic image to the Elijan one. Although the Markan editorial comment in the next verse brands Peter's intervention here an instance of apostolic misunderstanding, it is likely that in the pre-Markan narrative, which lacked 9:6, it was regarded as appropriate. As we have seen, much of the narrative is stamped with Mosaic symbolism, and the imagery of tents is compatible with this symbolism, since Moses was associated with a tent, the Tabernacle (see the NOTE on "cloud" in 9:7), and he and his followers sojourned in tents, or booths, during their wilderness wanderings. This mode of living was recalled in the Festival of Tabernacles (Sûkkôt), many features of which also seem to be echoed in the Markan transfiguration. The experience of living in booths during that holiday, for example, was frequently regarded as a foretaste of eschatological existence and of the bliss of the righteous dead, and this dimension coheres with the eschatological and resurrectional nuances of our story (see Riesenfeld, *Jésus transfiguré*, and the section on Tabernacles in the APPENDIX "History-of-Religions Backgrounds to the Transfiguration"). Peter's initial reaction to the vision, therefore, is understandable. It is also very similar to the reaction of Enoch to his heavenly vision in the beautiful passage in *1 Enoch* 39:4–8:

> And there I saw another vision of *the dwellings of the righteous* and the
>   *resting-places of the holy*,
> And there my eyes saw their dwellings with the angels
> And their *resting-places with the holy ones* . . .
> And I saw their *abode beneath the wings* of the Lord of spirits,
> And all the righteous and elect were *radiant like the brightness of fire*
>   before him . . .
> There I *desired to dwell* and *my spirit longed for that abode*. (Black trans.)

Here Enoch, like Peter in our passage, longs to stay in the heavenly place in which he finds himself, which he links with the habitations of the saints (cf. the three Markan tents), divine protection (cf. "overshadowing them"), and celestial radiance (cf. Jesus' garments and Öhler, "Verklärung," 209).

Despite the apparent logic of Peter's suggestion, however, Mark seems to consider it a serious error, as the editorial comment in 9:6 makes clear. This mistakenness probably resides not so much in the idea of tents and the associated eschatological imagery as it does in one or both of the following factors, which relate to the beginning and end of Peter's statement in Mark 9:5:

(1) "Rabbi, it is good for us to be here. . . ." If Mark wants his hearers to believe that Peter is sincere (and this is debatable, since Peter's words are in tension with the redactional comment that he and the others were afraid), his exclamation might suggest a reprehensible desire to linger on the Edenic mountain with Jesus. Such a desire might be construed as conflicting with the divine command, "Listen to him" (9:7). Listening to Jesus means hearkening to his exhortation to take up one's cross and follow (8:34), and that means descending with Jesus from the Mount of Transfiguration into the valley of human weakness, need, and pain (cf. 9:14–29)—the valley in which Jesus himself will soon lose his life (cf. 9:11–13 and Chrysostom, *Homilies on Matthew* 56.3).

(2) ". . . one for you and one for Moses and one for Elijah." We have already mentioned the possibility that Peter's order, Moses-Elijah, may reveal a failure to grasp the subordination of the Mosaic image to the Elijan one. A related shortcoming is that it implies a parity between Jesus on the one hand and Moses and Elijah on the other (see Jerome, *Homily 80*, cited in Oden and Hall, 119–20). Although both Moses and Elijah are, in a way, forerunners of Jesus, his status transcends theirs. And although the Markan Jesus is in some ways like Elijah (see the COMMENT on 8:27–30), Mark has already twice rejected the Elijah role as an adequate description of Jesus (6:15; 8:27–30), and in the very next passage Jesus will assign the role of Elijah to John the Baptist rather than himself. Nor is the Mosaic image big enough to encompass the Markan Jesus, despite the Moses-like features of the transfiguration. Moses wrote in and for the age of humanity's hardness of heart, but that age is now passing away (cf. 10:3–6). Later renditions of the transfiguration narrative go further along this same Christocentric road by omitting all reference to Moses and Elijah (2 Pet 1:16–18; *Acts of Peter* 20; *Acts of Thomas* 143; *Acts of John* 90; cf. Zeller, "Métamorphose," 185).

9:7–8: heavenly voice and conclusion. In the Markan version, Peter's ill-advised suggestion is immediately swept aside by two climactic divine acts, the appearance of a cloud that overshadows Jesus, Moses, and Elijah, and the sounding forth from that cloud of a voice identifying Jesus as God's beloved Son.

The appearance of the cloud (9:7a) negates Peter's suggestion that he and his fellow disciples pitch tents on the mountain to shelter Jesus, Moses, and Elijah; God requires no human partners to see to the well-being of his holy ones but himself sends his overshadowing, protective cloud (cf. the similar use of *episkiazein* = "to overshadow" in Luke 1:35 and see Origen, *Commentary on Matthew* 12:42). The cloud that covers and momentarily obscures Jesus, Moses, and Elijah, then, is not only an awe-inspiring cloud of glory filled with the divine presence, like that which Moses encountered on Sinai and in the Tabernacle (see the NOTE on "cloud" in 9:7), but also a cloud of protection demonstrating that Jesus, like Moses and Elijah, is God's servant, whose ultimate rescue from the realm of death lies in God's hands alone. This would be an important image for the persecuted Markan Christians to see, since they are followers of a Messiah who was put to death in a horrible and unexpected manner; it would assure them not only of God's countervailing and death-defying concern for Jesus' fate but also, implicitly, of his care for their own: "With his pinions he will overshadow you, and under his wings you will hope" (Ps 91:4 [90:4 LXX]).

But Jesus is not only *similar to* Moses and Elijah; he is also *more than* them, as the divine voice from the cloud immediately makes clear (9:7b). "*This* is my beloved Son," it says: "listen to *him!*" (emphasis added). On the one hand, this divine acclamation implies Jesus' continuity with Moses and Elijah, since "listen to him" echoes Moses' own words about the arising of a prophet like himself (Deut 18:15, 18), an oracle that by the first century was being read eschatologically and interpreted as a reference to Elijah or the Messiah (see the NOTE on "This is my beloved Son; listen to him" in 9:7). On the other hand, however, the voice designates only *one* of the three personages, Jesus, as God's Son, and this is a title that hints at an identity greater than that of Moses or Elijah (cf. Heb 3:1–6; on the Son of God title, see the NOTE on "You are my . . . son" in 1:11).

This superiority to Moses and Elijah is confirmed by the conclusion of the pericope; suddenly the disciples look around and see no one "except Jesus alone with them" (9:8). Jesus' two OT forerunners have vanished, presumably taken back to heaven by the cloud that moments before had engulfed them along with Jesus; and Jesus alone, again in a dreamlike motif, suddenly appears again at the disciples' side. The concluding phrase, "with them," would reverberate loudly for the hard-pressed members of the Markan community: unlike Moses and Elijah, Jesus does not belong only to the past and future but is presently "with them." And just as their status as disciples means that they have been chosen by Jesus "in order that *they* might be with *him*" (3:14), so their election includes the privilege of having *him* with *them*, even in the midst of their suffering.

In the transfiguration, then, the Markan audience has been shown a vision of Jesus in his Adamic, messianic glory, a vision that counterbalances the strong emphasis in the preceding pericopes on the necessity of joining in Jesus' march to extinction (8:31–37) and thus "remov[ing] the offence of the cross from the disciples' heart" (Leo the Great, *Sermon 51*). The Markan community may be called on to follow Jesus to death, but even as they do so, he will be with them, and the glory that he once displayed on the mountain will break forth for them time and again—even at moments when they are so frightened that they do not know what to say (cf. 9:6; 13:11).

The main emphasis of the passage, however, is not on the nature of discipleship but on the person of Jesus, and to explore this complex subject Mark sets his transfiguration narrative against the background not only of tales found in his larger religious world (see again the APPENDIX "History-of-Religions Backgrounds to the Transfiguration") but also of earlier and later stories in his Gospel, especially in the prologue and passion narrative—that is, the beginning and end of the Gospel. Our passage, for example, parallels the first verse of the Gospel proper (1:2), which links Jesus with both Moses (through the citation of Exod 23:20) and Elijah (through the citation of Mal 3:1), and the latter typology is developed in the immediately subsequent pericope, which portrays John the Baptist wearing Elijah-like clothes (1:6) and preaching an Elijah-like message (that a stronger one is coming, 1:7–8; cf. 2 Kgs 2:6–14). In the baptism scene, moreover, as in ours, Jesus goes up (out of the water) and is proclaimed "my beloved Son" by a voice from heaven (1:10–11).

But the strongest linkages are between our passage and the Gospel's conclusion. In both, for example, Peter is linked with others of the Twelve (9:6; 16:7), and Jesus is identified as the Son of God in a revelatory moment (9:7; 15:39). Both also emphasize the fear of the human witnesses and their incapacity to convey the message, in sentences that are startlingly similar in structure and vocabulary ("For he did not know what to answer; for they had become afraid" [9:6]; "And they did not say anything to anyone, for they were afraid" [16:8]; cf. the NOTE on "for they had become afraid" in 9:6). The passages are held together, therefore, by the motifs of divine revelation and human trepidation.

The contrasts between the two sections, however, are even more striking (see Davies and Allison, 2.706–7). Here we read of an unearthly light (9:2–3); there we find a supernatural darkness (15:33). Here Jesus' clothes become gloriously luminous, in a transformation betokening messianic power (9:2–3); there his clothes are stripped off, in an action mocking his claim to be "the king of the Jews" (15:24, 26). Here two OT saints, one of whom is Elijah, speak intimately with Jesus, thus demonstrating their identification with him (9:4); there two criminals rail against him, thus demonstrating their alienation from him, and other mockers refer sarcastically to an Elijan intervention that fails to occur (15:32, 35–36). Here Peter says, "It is good for us [disciples] to be here" and proposes building tents to memorialize the event (9:5); there the other disciples flee (14:50), and Peter, after following from a distance, ends up denying Jesus and going out (14:54, 66–72), thus showing that in his eyes it is no longer a good thing to be with Jesus. Here God's voice booms out his commitment to his "beloved Son" (9:7); there God is silent, and his Son pierces the air with the anguished question, "Why have you abandoned me?" (15:34).

Yet these sharp contrasts point to a deeper unity: transfiguration and crucifixion are two sides of the complex, divine-but-human identity of the Son. As Davies and Allison (2.706) put it:

> As God's Son, it is Jesus' lot to participate in the polarities, indeed the whole gamut, of human experience. This is because the Son of God is the Messiah . . . and that means the eschatological man, in whom the eschatological pattern of suffering-vindication, tribulation-salvation must play itself out. Therefore in fulfilling the prophets and their ancient oracles of doom and consolation, Jesus is humiliated and exalted, surrounded by saints and ringed by sinners, clothed with light and yet wrapped in a garment of darkness.

The transfiguration story emphasizes strongly the bright side of this polarity. At the present point in the Markan narrative, to be sure, this heartening revelation of Christological glory is restricted to the innermost circle of disciples, but it will soon become part of their joyful proclamation to the world. That will happen, as the next passage makes clear, when "the Son of Man ha[s] been raised from among the dead" (9:9).

JESUS SPEAKS OF ELIJAH AND THE SON OF MAN (9:9–13)

9 ⁹And as they were coming down from the mountain, he commanded them not to describe to anyone what they had seen until the Son of Man had been raised from among the dead. ¹⁰And they latched onto this saying, arguing among themselves about what this "rising from among the dead" was.

¹¹And they asked him, saying, "Why then do the scribes say that Elijah must come first?" ¹²And he said to them, "Is it really the case that Elijah, when he comes first, restores all things? How then has it been written concerning the Son of Man that he is to suffer many things and be treated with contempt? ¹³But I say to you that Elijah also has come, and they have done to him whatever they wanted—as it has been written concerning him."

NOTES

9 9. *And as they were coming down from the mountain.* Gk *kai katabainontōn autōn ek tou orous.* This phrase is part of the Mosaic typology of Mark 9:2–15. In the LXX, Exod 34:29 uses almost identical phrasing with respect to Moses (*katabainontos de autou ek tou orous,* "and as he was coming down from the mountain"), and other forms of *katabainein + ek tou orous* are frequently employed with respect to him (Exod 19:14; 32:1; 34:29; Num 20:28; Deut 9:15; 10:5), but only twice with respect to other people (Num 20:28; Josh 2:23).

until. Gk *ei mē hotan,* lit. "except when." This awkward use of an exceptive clause to indicate a temporal limit may be a Semitism; see Beyer, *Semitische Syntax,* 132–34.

had been raised from among the dead. Gk *ek nekrōn anastę̄.* Cf. the NOTE on "from among the dead" in 6:14. Even without the definite article, as here, *nekroi* can mean "*the* dead"; see already Thucydides, *History* 4.14.5; 5.10.12. In the present context the nuance is probably "all the dead, all those who are in the underworld" (BDAG 668 [B1]); the Sinaiticus Syriac manuscript renders "from the house of the dead." In early Christian thought, Jesus rises from among the mass of dead people as "the first fruits of those who have fallen asleep" (1 Cor 15:20 RSV).

The phrase "to be raised from among the dead" or "to rise from among the dead" occurs throughout the NT but never in the LXX, though Sir 48:5 does speak of Elijah raising a dead person from death and from Hades (the realm of the dead; cf. de Boer, *Defeat,* 107). There is one occurrence outside Christian literature, but this is from the mid-second century C.E. (Phlegon of Tralles, cited in BDAG, 83 [7]), and so the possibility of Christian influence cannot be excluded.

The absence of references to *anastasis ek nekrōn* in Jewish literature points to the singularity of what the Christians proclaimed: the resurrection, not of the dead in general, but of *one* from among their number (cf. the NOTE on "what this 'rising from among the dead' was" in 9:10).

10. *they latched onto this saying, arguing among themselves.* Gk *ton logon ekratēsan pros heautous syzētountes. Kratein* means "to hold, seize, retain"; for literal usages in Mark, see 3:21; 6:17; 12:12, etc., and for a different figurative usage, see 7:3, 4, 8. *Pros heautous* ("among themselves") could go either with *ekratēsan*, which immediately precedes it, or with *syzētountes* ("arguing"), which immediately follows it. The latter is more likely, since "they latched onto the saying among themselves" is awkward, while "they disputed among themselves" is attested in Luke 22:23, and there is something similar in Mark 9:34.

Although the disciples' confusion here is part of the general Markan theme of their incomprehension, their fervent occupation with Jesus' word is laudable (cf. Luke 2:19, 51).

what this "rising from among the dead" was. Gk *ti estin to ek nekrōn anastēnai.* The *to* is anaphoric (see the GLOSSARY), hence the translation "this" (cf. Robertson, 1065).

The disciples are not confused about the concept of the general resurrection, "the rising *of* the dead" (*anastasis [tōn] nekrōn*; cf. Matt 22:31; 1 Cor 15:12–13, 21, 42; etc.), but about Jesus' prophecy of his resurrection from *among* the dead (*to ek nekrōn anastēnai*), apparently apart from the general resurrection; the perplexing point is how this one resurrection can occur in isolation from the resurrection of all (see Collins, "Appropriation," 233 n. 49). As Davies and Allison (2.714 n. 19) point out, such a confusion could have arisen in a post-Easter setting if the earthly Jesus had not distinguished his own resurrection from the general one. It has been suggested, however, that some pre-Christian Jews believed in the possibility of a righteous individual's resurrection before the eschaton; van Henten (*Martyrs*, 175) and Holleman (*Resurrection*, 146–47), for example, have found this concept in 2 Maccabees 7. The case, however, is debatable. Much depends on the exact translation of 2 Macc 7:36, which Holleman renders, "My brothers have now fallen in loyalty to God's covenant, after a brief pain leading to eternal life" and takes to imply that the martyrs' suffering will immediately be followed by eternal life, which 2 Macc 7:14 calls "resurrection." In the 2 Maccabees passage, however, the brevity of the pain is being contrasted to the eternity of the reward, and the latter holds true whether or not the reward begins immediately after death; this text, then, does not prove Holleman's case.

In our passage, in any event, resurrection is being discussed in an eschatological framework. The object of resurrection is an end-time figure, the Son of Man, and Jesus' allusion to his resurrection immediately turns his disciples' minds to the scriptural expectation of the coming of Elijah before "the great and terrible day of the Lord" (Mal 4:5–6). In such a framework it is the general resurrection that is expected, not just that of an individual.

11. *Why then do the scribes say that Elijah must come first?* Gk *Hoti legousin hoi grammateis hoti Ēlian dei elthein prōton.* On the usage of *hoti* ("why") in a direct

question, see the NOTE on "Why does he eat with tax collectors and sinners?" in 2:16. Sinaiticus, L, and a few Latin manuscripts read "the Pharisees and the scribes" (hoi Pharisaioi kai hoi grammateis) rather than "the scribes," and Freedman suggests that "the Pharisees" may have been omitted because of the repeated oi syllable. Despite Sinaiticus, however, the attestation for the longer reading is weak, and it may be an assimilation to 7:1, 5.

Bultmann (260), J. Taylor ("Coming"), and others have suggested that 9:11 originally followed 9:1, picking up the prophecy of eschatological advent and raising a question about its timing. This sequence, however, seems unlikely. Mark 9:1 prophesies the full revelation of God's dominion within a generation or so (only some in Jesus' audience will live to see it). The question in 9:11, by contrast, presupposes that the general resurrection is either imminent or already manifesting itself; the problem is why Elijah, who was supposed to prepare the way for it, has not yet come. This question would make more sense in response to a saying of Jesus identifying his advent with the already accomplished inbreaking of the dominion of God, such as Matt 12:28//Luke 11:20.

According to the disciples, the scribes say that "Elijah must come first." Most exegetes regard this as a reference to a Jewish expectation that Elijah would precede the Messiah; they cite passages such as Justin Martyr, Dialogue with Trypho 49:1, in which the Jew Trypho says, "We all expect that Christ will be a human born of humans, and that Elijah when he comes will anoint him . . . But from the circumstance that Elijah has not yet come, I infer that this man [Jesus] is not he" (ANF trans. alt.; cf. 8:4). Recently, however, Faierstein ("Why") and Fitzmyer ("More") have pointed out that OT and early Jewish texts such as Mal 4:5–6 (Heb 3:23–24) and Sir 48:10 speak only of Elijah coming before the end, not of him coming before the Messiah. Clear Jewish attestations of the idea of Elijah preceding the Messiah are later than NT times (b. 'Erub. 43ab; Tg. Ps.-J. on Deut 30:4; etc.), and Faierstein and Fitzmyer think that Jewish tradents may have gotten the idea from the Christians rather than the other way around. But Mark 9:9–11// Matt 17:9–10 attribute to the scribes the idea that Elijah will come before the Son of Man, and Mark at least regards "Son of Man" as synonymous with "Messiah" (cf. 8:29–31; 14:61–62); this passage, then, seems to imply a Jewish expectation that Elijah will come before the Messiah (see Milikowsky, "Elijah"; Allison, "Elijah"; Marcus, Way, 110). Probably Allison is right about the way in which this expectation developed from its scriptural source: Malachi says that Elijah will come before the end, and later Jews believed that the Messiah would come at the end; they therefore concluded that Elijah would come before the Messiah.

12. Is it really the case that Elijah, when he comes first, restores all things? Gk Ēlias men elthōn prōton apokathistanei panta. Codex Bezae (D) reads, "If Elijah when he comes restores all things, then how has it been written . . . ?" Although this is not the original reading, it probably conveys the intended sense: the Markan Jesus is not affirming that Elijah restores all things, as in the usual interpretation ("Elijah is indeed coming first to restore all things" NRSV), but questioning it. Denniston (Greek Particles, 366–68), to be sure, implies that men invariably expects a positive answer, but as Weisse (Geschichte, 1.545) already noted in 1838,

men can be used for questions that presuppose an affirmative answer on the part of the addressee but a negative one on the part of the questioner (see, e.g., Aristophanes, *Birds* 1214, and Euripides, *Ion* 520). When 9:12a is taken as a question, the verse as a whole makes better sense, since the continuation, which speaks of the suffering of the Son of Man, does not *confirm* the reference to Elijah's restoration of the world but *contradicts* it. If Elijah had already restored everything before the Messiah came, if the breach in human relations had already been healed, as promised in Mal 4:5–6, what need would there be for the Son of Man's suffering (cf. Wellhausen, 76; Marcus, *Way*, 99)?

How then has it been written concerning. Gk *kai pōs gegraptai epi.* The perfect passive verb *gegraptai* ("it has been written") always refers to OT scripture in the NT; in the present instance the point is that Jesus' death fulfills the divine will laid out in the scriptures (cf. 14:49). There is, however, no discrete OT passage that describes the suffering and rejection of the Son of Man. The psalms of the Righteous Sufferer (e.g., Ps 22, 41, 69) and the Deutero-Isaian passages about the Lord's Suffering Servant (Isa 50:4–9; 52:13–53:12) recount the afflictions of an innocent victim, but do not mention the Son of Man. Daniel 7 speaks of "one like a son of man," but he does not suffer (though he is linked with "the people of the holy ones of the Most High," who do: Dan 7:13–14, 18, 21–22, 25–27). Psalm 80:14–17 calls on God to look down from heaven on Israel, his plundered vine, and to lay his hand on "the son of man whom you have made strong for yourself" (RSV alt.), who is probably the king (see Dahood, *Psalms*, 2.260), but again, this figure does not himself suffer.

In Jewish sources and the NT, however, "it has been written" and similar formulas can sometimes refer to a conflation of scriptural passages or an exegetical conclusion rather than a scriptural citation in the strict sense (see Marcus, *Way*, 94–97). For example, in the very first instance of "as it has been written" in Mark (1:2–3), the passage quoted is a fusion of three OT texts (Exod 23:20; Mal 3:1; Isa 40:3). In Gal 4:22, similarly, Paul uses "it has been written" to "summarize a quantity of OT material spread over a number of chapters in Genesis" (Barrett, "Allegory," 9), and John 7:38 applies "as the scripture has said" to an exegetical conclusion drawn from different scriptural passages (Isa 12:3; Zech 14:8; and perhaps others; see Marcus, "Rivers"). This NT procedure has Jewish precedents; Baumgarten ("Citation"), for example, points to two fragments of the *Damascus Document* (4Q266 11:3–5 and 4Q270 7 1:17–18) that apply exactly the phrase used in our passage, "it has been written concerning . . . ," to a text that is "not a quotation in the literal sense, but the product of the interpretation applied by Qumran exegetes to a combination of scriptural passages" (Deut 30:4 and Lev 26:31; cf. CD 9:9; 11:20–21; 20:15–17).

13. *Elijah also has come.* Gk *kai Ēlias elēlythen.* The implication is that not only the suffering of the Son of Man but also that of Elijah is prophesied in the scriptures. On the interpretation of the *kai* as "also," see Liebers, *Geschrieben*, 94.

they have done to him whatever they wanted. Gk *epoiēsan autǭ hosa ēthelon.* On the one hand, John the Baptist's death is ascribed to the malice of human beings, but on the other hand, as the next clause makes clear, it comes about according to the will of God expressed in the scriptures. There is a similar ambiguity in many of the sayings about the "turning over" of John the Baptist and Jesus (1:14; 3:19; 10:33; 14:21, 41).

as it has been written concerning him. Gk *kathōs gegraptai ep' auton.* Some interpreters (e.g., Liebers, *Geschrieben*, 369–76; Collins, "Appropriation," 234–35) take this as a general reference to the rejection of prophets, but the wording is not "as it has been written concerning *them*" but "as it has been written concerning *him.*" There is a problem, however, with taking the referent as Elijah: no OT passage prophesies that the eschatological Elijah will suffer violence (cf. the NOTE on "How then has it been written concerning" in 9:12 for the similar problem about the prophecy of the Son of Man's suffering). First Kings 19:1–2, 10, 14 describes the persecution of Elijah by King Ahab and his wife, Jezebel, but this is the historical Elijah, not the eschatological one, and he is not murdered; indeed, the evil monarchs rather than Elijah end up being killed (1 Kgs 21–22). And the two OT texts from Malachi that speak of the eschatological Elijah (3:1–4; 4:5–6) imply a successful ministry in a context of holy-war triumph and societal reconciliation. To be sure, the two slain eschatological "witnesses" in Rev 11:1–13 are modeled on Elijah and Moses, since the miracles they perform are similar to those accomplished by the OT figures, but this does not mean that there was a preexistent Jewish tradition about the martyrdom of the returning Moses and Elijah (see Bauckham, *Climax*, 273–83); the stories about the latter, rather, are "a Christian innovation deriving . . . from the Christian innovation of the martyrdom of the Messiah" (Bauckham, "Martyrdom," 458).

Similarly, in the present instance "as it has been written concerning him," like the corresponding expression in 9:12 (see the NOTE on "How then has it been written concerning" in 9:12), refers to an exegetical conclusion that draws on several OT passages and has as its presupposition the Christian dogma of the Messiah's suffering. Specifically, perhaps, it designates the way in which the "scriptural" expectation that Elijah will be the Messiah's predecessor is reconciled with the "scriptural" expectation that the Son of Man will be a suffering Messiah (see the COMMENT on 9:11–13 and Marcus, *Way*, 105–7).

COMMENT

Introduction. The stupendous vision of the transfiguration, in which Jesus is viewed by three disciples in an anticipation of his resurrectional glory, is immediately and logically followed by a comment linking the transfiguration with the resurrection (9:9–10) and a question-and-answer session on another eschatological subject, the timing of Elijah's advent (9:11–13).

This little dialogue is not all of a piece. The first couple of verses, which deal with Jesus' resurrection (9:9–10), probably come from the evangelist's hand. The transitional 9:9, Jesus' command to silence, is full of Markan vocabulary ("coming down," "commanded," "anyone," "seen"), employs a favorite Markan grammatical form (the genitive absolute), expresses a typical Markan theme (the messianic secret), and refers baldly to the post-Easter period. If this verse is redactional, how-

ever, then 9:10, which describes the disciples' bewilderment at Jesus' reference
to his resurrection, is probably so also, since it depends on 9:9. This possibility is
strengthened by the presence, again, of typical Markan vocabulary and themes
("the word" [see 1:45; 2:2; 10:24], "latched onto" [*kratein*; see 7:3 7:4 9:9 12:12 14:1
14:49], "arguing among themselves" [see 8:11; 9:14, 16; 12:28; cf. 9:34]) and a common Markan construction (the articular infinitive).

As for 9:11–13, the substance of this discussion on Elijah's advent probably pre-
dates the evangelist's work, since it fits uneasily into its Markan context; although
the disciples have just seen Elijah appearing with Moses, they illogically raise an
objection having to do with the necessity of Elijah coming first. But within this
pre-Markan pericope, many scholars have detected a foreign body in 9:12b, where
a question about the Son of Man briefly interposes itself into the discussion of
Elijah, and this part of the verse has been viewed as so disruptive that it has been
identified either as clumsy Markan redaction (e.g., Liebers, *Geschrieben*, 73–83)
or a post-Markan gloss (e.g., Bultmann, 125).

Mark 9:12b, however, is disruptive only if 9:12a is taken as a statement (see, e.g.,
NRSV: "Elijah is indeed coming first to restore all things"). If it is taken as a question, as in the present translation, the passage flows more smoothly and is similar
to other Synoptic texts in which Jesus plays scripture off against scripture (see
below in the COMMENT on 9:11–13). Allison ("Q 12:51–53," 306–10), accordingly, argues that 9:11–13 is a unity and goes back to the historical Jesus, though
he asserts that in its original context "Son of Man" had a collective referent rather
than an individual one. This may be, but it is also possible that the passage represents an early Christian attempt to define the relation between Jesus and John
the Baptist, and between the Messiah and Elijah. In any case, even if 9:11–13 rests
on tradition, it has been retold with much Markan redactional vocabulary ("the
scribes," "first," "all," "it has been written" [2x], "suffer many things," consecutive
hina = "that" [see the NOTE on "in order that" in 4:12], and *kai pōs* = "how then"
[cf. 4:13b]).

The passage thus falls into two sections, 9:9–10, which deals with Jesus' resurrection, and 9:11–13, which deals with his relation to Elijah. There is an implicit
connection between these two subjects, since Elijah is described in a famous OT
passage as having been taken up to heaven while still alive (2 Kgs 2:11). But the
end of the pericope links Elijah and Jesus more with suffering than with glorious
resurrection. Indeed, in the overall passage there is a progression from Jesus' resurrection (9:9–10) to Elijah's advent (9:11–12a) to the suffering of both Jesus and
his "Elijah," John the Baptist (9:12b–13).

9:9–10: the disciples' puzzlement about Jesus' resurrection. The passage begins
by identifying the setting as the path down from the Mount of Transfiguration
(9:9a); the prospect of a return to the public sphere induces Jesus to lay on his
three accompanying disciples a strict prohibition against telling anyone what they
have seen until the Son of Man rises from among the dead (9:9b). This is, as
Gnilka (2.40–41) notes, the last of the "messianic secret" commands in the Gospel and the only one to which a time restriction is attached; its climactic position

suggests that it has programmatic significance and that the earlier injunctions may fall under the same limit. Secrecy until the resurrection makes sense because the transfiguration is an anticipation of the resurrection, and the healings about which Jesus has previously forbidden publicity foreshadow the power that will become operative in the world through that event (cf. the COMMENT on 5:35-43).

The resurrection of Jesus is such a crucial turning point because, in line with OT and Jewish conceptions about the general resurrection, it is associated with the new age in which God's glorious, life-giving power will be fully disclosed (see, e.g., Dan 12:1-3, 13; *1 Enoch* 91:10; 92:3; 4Q521; cf. Marcus, "Epistemology," 567-70). Indeed, the OT book of Daniel, which has influenced Mark extensively, repeatedly uses language similar to that found in Mark 9:9 in order to speak of the necessity of secrecy until the new age comes: "Go your way, Daniel, for the words are to remain secret and sealed until the time of the end" (Dan 12:9; cf. 8:26; 12:4). Mark 9:9, then, serves to link Jesus' resurrection with the eschatological turning point.

Jesus' command to silence, however, baffles the disciples. What, they ask each other, does this "rising from among the dead" mean (9:10)? The really baffling thing, however, is why they are so baffled! It is hard to believe that many first-century Jews would have been ignorant of the idea of resurrection, even if some were skeptical about it; the idea is already attested in the OT (Dan 12:2), and it was a major source of controversy between the Jewish sects of the first century according to the Gospels (Mark 12:18-27 pars.), Acts (23:6-8), and Josephus (*Ant.* 18.14, 16, 18). The editorial statement about the disciples' puzzlement, however, has to be taken in the context of Jesus' preceding reference to his own resurrection, apparently apart from the general one; the disciples' problem may be figuring out the way in which the two events are related to each other (see the NOTE on "what this 'rising from among the dead' was" in 9:10). It is evident from 1 Cor 15:20-28 that this was an issue that exercised early Christians, for here Paul is concerned to establish the correct order of resurrections: first Christ's, as a kind of "first fruits"; then, at his "coming," that of the people who belong to him (i.e., Christians); finally, perhaps, everyone's (cf. 1 Thess 4:13-17).

9:11-13: the question about Elijah. A concern with this problem of the eschatological timetable helps explain the next turn in the conversation. Unexpectedly, the disciples do not ask the question that Mark told us was on their minds, namely, the exact nuance of "the resurrection from among the dead," but "Why then do the scribes say that Elijah must come first?" (9:11). The two issues are related, in that the separation of the resurrection of an eschatological figure, the Son of Man, from the general resurrection might suggest the need to revise other elements in the eschatological schedule, such as the coming of Elijah before the Messiah (see the NOTE on "Why then do the scribes say that Elijah must come first?" in 9:11). The Markan Jesus, moreover, with his reference to his forthcoming resurrection, seems to be implying that he will be exiting from the scene in short order; but if he is the Messiah, and if Elijah is to come before the Messiah, it is logical to wonder how he can make his exit before Elijah puts in an appearance.

The scribal expectation to which the disciples refer is based on a passage from Malachi that speaks of Elijah coming "before the great and terrible day of the Lord" on a mission that includes healing the rupture in human relations, which threatens to devastate the whole planet: "He will turn the hearts of parents to their children and the hearts of children to their parents, so that I will not come and strike the earth with a curse" (Mal 4:5–6 NRSV alt.; cf. Sir 48:10; Luke 1:16–17). In *Mishnah 'Eduyot* 8:7 the sages draw the logical conclusion from this passage that "Elijah will come . . . to make peace in the world." But the Markan Jesus, with typical exegetical boldness, challenges this scripturally based expectation of familial and cosmic reconciliation: *"Is it really the case that* Elijah, when he comes first [= before the Messiah], restores all things?" (9:12a; see the NOTE on this clause in 9:12).

The reason for this reservation immediately becomes plain: if it were Elijah's role to fix human society, bring peace, and even repair the universe ("all things"), there would be no need for his successor, the Messiah, to suffer and be rejected, as is also prophesied in the scriptures—"How then has it been written concerning the Son of Man that he is to suffer many things and be treated with contempt?" (9:12b). The two scriptural expectations, in other words, contradict each other, and only one of them can be unequivocally affirmed. Our passage thus falls into a group of ancient Jewish and Christian exegeses that attempt to mediate between apparently conflicting scriptural texts, and of which there are several examples elsewhere in the Synoptic tradition (Mark 10:2–9; 12:35–37; Matt 10:34–36//Luke 12:51–53 = Q; see the NOTE on "Is it really the case that Elijah, when he comes first, restores all things?" in 9:12 and Allison, "Q 12:51–53," 303–4). The basic method of dealing with these conflicts is to establish one text as the authoritative one and then to show that the other can be reconciled with it, sometimes by means of a third passage that mediates between the two (see Dahl, "Contradictions"; Marcus, *Way*, 94–110). This is exactly what happens in Mark 9:12–13: the scriptural expectation that Elijah will play the forerunner role by restoring all things is played off against the biblical expectation that the Son of Man will suffer, and the resolution is to affirm that Elijah *will* go before the Messiah, but in the way of death rather than in a mode of conventional triumph, "as it has been written concerning him" (see the NOTES on "How then has it been written concerning" in 9:12 and "as it has been written concerning him" in 9:13.)

At stake here is not a simple clash of proof texts, but the very nature of the Messiah's mission. Is it to be a mere "mopping-up operation" after Elijah has done the hard work? Or is the Messiah's contribution so crucial, and the evil that he must engage so radical, that there is no room for a lesser figure such as Elijah to play a restorative role? The issue is similar to that outlined by a later Talmudic tradition declaring that the Messiah will come either to a generation that is completely righteous or to one that is completely wicked (R. Johanan in *b. Sanh.* 98a). The scribal opinion cited by the Markan disciples seems to take the first tack: Elijah will come before the Messiah, restore all things—in part perhaps by showing Israel the solution to knotty issues of Jewish law (see *m. Bab. Meṣ* 1:8; 3:4; etc.)—and thus make Israel and the world fit to receive their king; only then will the Messiah come. Jesus, however, takes the opposite line: the Messiah will come to an "adulterous and sinful" generation (cf. 8:38; 9:19) that will demonstrate its total unworthiness by killing him. But nothing short of this death on the cross, whereby Jesus gives his life as a "ransom for many" (10:45), will be able to strike the bloody and decisive blow against the powers of evil that rule the present age.

The Messiah's mission of suffering also has consequences for the mission of Elijah, as Jesus divulges at the conclusion of the discussion (9:13). If the Son of Man is to be a suffering Messiah, and Elijah is to be the Messiah's forerunner, then it stands to reason that Elijah himself must be a suffering figure: the servant is not above his master, but shares his fate (cf. Matt 10:24–25//Luke 6:40//John 13:16). Therefore Jesus, in the concluding line of the pericope, affirms both that Elijah has come and that he has suffered violence from human beings.

Mark's readers would doubtless understand this suffering Elijah figure as John the Baptist. The opening lines of the Gospel (1:2–4) already ascribed to the Baptist a passage from Malachi (3:1) that was commonly linked, on the basis of the catchword "messenger," with Mal 4:5–6, which speaks of the returning Elijah. Mark's readers subsequently were treated to a long and detailed account of the Baptist's imprisonment and execution by Herod Antipas (6:14–29). So when they heard the Markan Jesus say that "Elijah *has* come, and they have done to him whatever they wanted," they would be almost certain to identify this Elijah with the murdered Baptist.

The chain of suffering witnesses, however, does not reach merely from the Baptist to Jesus but also extends into Mark's time. In the eschatological timeline of the Gospel, first John proclaims the good news, is turned over to the authorities, and is killed (1:4, 7, 14; 6:17–28); then Jesus proclaims the good news, is turned over, and is killed (1:14, etc.; 9:31, etc.); and finally the Christians proclaim the good news, are turned over, and are killed (13:9–11; cf. Perrin and Duling, *Introduction*, 110, 238). The members of the Markan community, then, would hear the exegetical argument in 9:9–13 not just as an academic lesson about the past but also as a crucial message concerning their own time: those who conform to the pattern shown forth by the Son of Man, either before he comes or after he goes, will find themselves embarking on the same death-march as he has (cf. 8:34–35). The suffering of the Markan community is no accident; like that of Jesus and John the Baptist before him, it comes to pass "as it has been written" (cf. the NOTE on "as it has been written concerning him" in 9:13). For a persecuted Markan community located in the bewildering context of the Jewish War, in which triumphant, wonder-working prophets and "Messiahs" have arisen and are performing miracles that can deceive the very elect (13:21–22), this Markan emphasis on the suffering of Elijah and the Messiah would provide an epistemological criterion for distinguishing God's true servants from their Satanic counterfeits (cf. Revelation 13).

Not that suffering and wonder working are necessarily contradictory realities, any more than are death and resurrection. The juxtaposition of our passage with the next one suggests that the divine healing power breaks forth even in the midst of the evil and faithless generation that drives to their deaths its bearers of good news.

JESUS HEALS AN EPILEPTIC BOY (9:14–29)

9 ¹⁴And as they came to the disciples, they saw a great crowd around them and scribes arguing with them. ¹⁵And all the crowd, when they saw him, were immediately awestruck, and they ran forward and hailed him. ¹⁶And he asked them, "What were you arguing about with them?"

¹⁷And one from the crowd answered him, "Teacher, I brought my son to you because he has a mute spirit. ¹⁸And wherever he is when it grabs him, it tears him, and he foams at the mouth and grinds his teeth and becomes rigid. And I asked your disciples to cast it out, but they didn't have the strength." ¹⁹And he answered and said to them, "O faithless generation, how long will I be with you? How long will I put up with you? Bring him to me." ²⁰And they brought him to him. And seeing him, the spirit immediately convulsed the boy, and he fell on the ground and was rolling around foaming at the mouth. ²¹And Jesus asked his father, "How long has he been like this?" And he said, "From childhood. ²²And many times it has thrown him into the fire and into waters in order to destroy him. But if you can do anything, have pity on us and help us!" ²³But Jesus said to him, " 'If you can'? All things are possible to the one who believes!" ²⁴The father of the child immediately cried out and said, "I believe; help my unbelief!"

²⁵And Jesus, seeing that a crowd was gathering together rapidly, rebuked the unclean spirit and said to it, "Mute and deaf spirit, I command you, come out of him and don't ever enter him again!" ²⁶And shouting and convulsing him greatly, it came out; and he became like a corpse, so that many people were saying that he had died. ²⁷But Jesus seized his hand and raised him, and he arose.

²⁸And when Jesus had gone into a house, his disciples asked him privately, "Why weren't we able to cast it out?" ²⁹And he said to them, "This sort of spirit can't be gotten out in any way except by prayer."

NOTES

9 15. *were . . . awestruck.* Gk *exethambēthēsan.* On the possible background of this element in the account in Exod 34:29–35 of the people's awe at Moses' radiance when he descends from Sinai, see Nineham (245–46). The LXX does not use *ekthambeisthai*, but speaks of the people's fear (*ephobēthēsan*). Tagawa (*Miracles,* 106) sees a further difference that for him disqualifies the Exodus passage from being the background here: in Exodus the people are afraid to approach Moses, whereas in Mark they run to Jesus and greet him. But in the Exodus passage, too, the people eventually overcome their fear and come to Moses. It may be that our story intends a comparison as well as a contrast: Moses' radiance is terrifying, but Jesus' is both awe inspiring and attractive (on this paradoxical combination, see

Otto, *Idea*, passim). See also 2 Cor 3:12–18, which compares and contrasts the radiance of Christ with that of Moses.

17. *my son*. Gk *ton huion mou*. Each of the first four major sections of the Gospel according to our outline (see vol. 1, p. 64) contains a prominent exorcism: the demoniac in the Capernaum synagogue in Section 1 (1:21–28), the Gerasene demoniac in Section 2 (5:1–20), the daughter of the Syrophoenician woman in Section 3 (7:24–30), and the boy here in Section 4. The first two of these exorcisms concern adult demoniacs, the first a Jew and the second a Gentile. The second two concern child demoniacs, the first a Gentile and the second a Jew; in the first of these the possessed girl's mother intercedes for her, while in the second the possessed boy's father intercedes for him. In both of these cases the healing is preceded by a discussion with the scribes (7:1–15; 9:14). In both cases Jesus delays the healing, and this delay is linked with the situation of the present generation (7:27; 9:19, 21a). In both cases, however, the parent persists in supplication, and the healing is linked with the faith the parent demonstrates (7:29; 9:23–24).

a mute spirit. Gk *pneuma alalon*, that is, a spirit that prevents him from speaking. The boy appears to be an epileptic, as is shown by Matthew's diagnosis (17:15) and by the correspondence between the boy's symptoms and other ancient descriptions of epilepsy (see Kollmann, *Jesus*, 211–13; Wohlers, *Heilige Krankheit*, 21–23); on the epileptic's inability to speak during a seizure, for example, see Pseudo-Hippocrates, *On the Sacred Disease* 7:1; 10:6. According to Mark 9:25, the spirit is also deaf, a reflection of the epileptic's insensibility when undergoing a seizure.

In ancient paganism, epilepsy was often referred to as "the sacred disease," though there was no unanimity about the reason for this nomenclature; some thought it was because the malady was sent by a god, others because it attacked those who had sinned against a divinity, and still others because it could be healed only by divine intervention (see Aretaeus of Cappadocia, *Chronic Diseases* 1.4). Jews and Christians, however, avoided this terminology, not wanting to associate the deity too closely with such a terrible affliction; instead epilepsy was often attributed to demons (for an odd example, see *b. Git.* 70a, in which the epilepsy of a child is blamed on "the demon of the privy" that adhered to the child's father when he had sex too soon after relieving himself). Indeed, so close was the disease's linkage with possession in the popular mind that in later, Byzantine times Christians simply referred to it as "the demon" (see Temkin, *Falling Sickness*, 86). Wohlers (*Heilige Krankheit*, 128–30) thinks that the demonological explanation of epilepsy first arose in Christian circles, but this thesis requires him to ascribe the first-century C.E. passage in Aretaeus to Christian influence without proof (cf. also *T. Sol.* 18:21[88]).

The demonological interpretation of epilepsy was doubtless influenced by sufferers' loss of control over themselves, the sense they conveyed of being victims of an attack from the outside—an impression still preserved in the modern English term "seizure" (see the NOTE on "wherever he is when it grabs him" in 9:18). Physicians, however, tended to reject such demonological explanations and to attribute epilepsy to a variety of physiological causes such as a superfluity of phlegm in the brain, disturbances in sexual function, climatic factors, and diet. The etiology of epilepsy, therefore, became a crucial battleground between the scientific and magical views of illness (see Temkin, *Falling Sickness*, 4). Nor has this conflict ended in modern times; for a sad case study of mutual misunderstanding in California in the 1980s, see Anne Fadiman's book *The Spirit Catches You and You Fall Down: A Hmong Child, Her American Doctors, and the Collision of Two Cultures.*

18. *wherever he is when it grabs him.* Gk *hopou ean auton katalabē*, lit. "wherever it grabs him"; the meaning is that the spirit attacks and convulses the boy wherever he happens to be, as subsequently happens in 9:20. The verb used here, *katalambanein*, has the same root as the verb from which "epilepsy" comes, *epilambanein*, which literally means "to seize." "In Greek, just as in modern speech, one would say of any disease that it has 'seized' a man, and this terminology perhaps goes back to a very old magic conception according to which all diseases were believed 'attacks' and seizures by gods and demons, as documented in Babylonian medicine. Since epilepsy was the demoniac disease par excellence, the term gradually acquired a more particular meaning and came to signify epileptic seizure" (Temkin, *Falling Sickness*, 21).

they didn't have the strength. Gk *ouk ischysan*. A fundamental theme of our passage is that Jesus has the strength or power to accomplish what no mere human being can do; cf. 3:27, where a cognate word, *ischyros* ("strong"), is used to express the same point. Cf. also the NOTE on "a mute spirit" in 9:17, where it is pointed out that some ancient pagans called epilepsy the "sacred disease" because they believed that only a god could heal it. Davies and Allison (2.723) compare 2 Kgs 4:18–37, in which Elisha's disciple Gehazi is unable to resuscitate a dead child, but Elisha can and does.

19. *O faithless generation, how long will I be with you? How long will I put up with you?* Gk *Ō genea apistos, heōs pote pros hymas esomai; heōs pote anexomai hymōn.* On the echoes of Num 14:11 and Deut 32:20 here, see the COMMENT on 9:17–19. In these Pentateuchal passages it is *God* who is exasperated with his people's faithlessness and who threatens to hide his face from a perverse, faithless generation. As elsewhere in his use of OT traditions, Mark implicitly likens Jesus not only to Moses but also to God (cf. the COMMENTS on 6:48–50 and 8:10–13; Nineham, 243; Lövestam, *This Generation*, 55).

Who is included in the "faithless generation" berated by Jesus? The scribes doubtless belong to it (cf. 8:10–13, where their allies the Pharisees test Jesus in a skeptical manner and are referred to as "this generation" that seeks a sign), but they are not the center of attention here. The disciples, rather, are the primary referent, since it is their failure that has just been described. But Marshall (*Faith*, 117–18) may be right in his assertion that the rebuke also includes the crowd and the father of the possessed boy. The term "generation" is all-embracing, so a linkage with the crowd is natural, and the wording of the father's appeal in 9:24, "help my unbelief," suggests that he sees himself as belonging, at least with one aspect of his being, to the "faithless/unbelieving generation" that Jesus has just mentioned.

Bring him to me. Gk *pherete auton pros me.* Jesus is not just addressing the father; *pherete* is a second person *plural.* Since this second person plural repeats those in 9:19ab ("... how long will I be with you? How long will I put up with you?"), the reference may be both to the crowd and to the disciples (see the previous NOTE).

20. *the boy.* Gk *auton,* lit. "him," but the specification is necessary to keep the dramatis personae straight; similarly interpretative is "Jesus" in 9:21. The tendency to omit subjects is characteristic of Mark's popular style of narration (see the NOTE on "people came" in 5:14).

21. *How long has he been like this?* Gk *Posos chronos estin hōs touto gegonen autǭ,* lit. "How long a time has it been like this to him?" that is, "How long has he been in this condition?" Miracle stories often stress the length of the illness to show that it was incurable by natural means (cf., e.g., 5:25–26; Luke 13:11; Philostratus, *Life of Apollonius* 3.38; 6.43; Bultmann, 221; Theissen, 51–52). The sufferers in Acts 3:2 and John 9:1 trump the epileptic boy in our story, since they have been ill not just from childhood but from birth. For other aspects of Jesus' question, including its relation to the Markan idea of salvation history, see the COMMENT on 9:20–24.

from childhood. Gk *ek paidiothen. Paidiothen* by itself means "from childhood," so the present phrase is a typically Markan redundancy that is part of the popular style of the Gospel. As Kollmann (*Jesus,* 212) notes, the father's reply emphasizes the gravity of the disease, a typical element in healing stories (see the previous NOTE), but it also corresponds to ancient medicine, which identified epilepsy as an ailment that appeared in childhood. Epilepsy was even sometimes called "the child's disease" (*paidion,* given as a synonym for epilepsy from Galen on; see Temkin, *Falling Sickness,* 115–16, and cf. LSJ 1287 [III]).

22. *it has thrown him into the fire and into waters.* Gk *kai eis pyr auton ebalen kai eis hydata.* Cf. Caelius Aurelianus, *Chronic Diseases* 1.4.68: epileptics sometimes fall into rivers or the sea. Water, along with fire, is frequently associated with demons in magical texts (see, e.g., *PGM* 4.1460–65 and *PDM* 14.490–95). In Mark 5:10 and Luke 8:31, however, the demons may be afraid of the water (see the NOTE on "out of the land" in 5:10).

23. *'If you can ...'?* Gk *To Ei dynē,* lit. "The 'If you can ...'" As in classical Greek, the neuter article *to* is used before quoted words, sentences, and sentence fragments (see BDF §267 [1]). As Metzger (100) notes, the awkwardness of the construction gave rise to numerous textual variants.

All things are possible to the one who believes. Gk *panta dynata tǭ pisteuonti.* See the COMMENT on 9:20–24 for the ambiguity about whether "the one who believes," whose belief makes all things possible, is Jesus or the petitioner. Paul captures a similar ambiguity in Phil 4:13, where all-sufficiency is ascribed both to the Christian ("I can do all things") and to Christ ("through him who strengthens me").

25. *a crowd.* Gk *ochlos.* One of the Latin terms for epilepsy is *morbus comitialis* ("the social disease"), and some later interpreters such as Johann Agricola and Erasmus attributed this name to the tendency of epileptics to suffer attacks in

crowded places (see Temkin, *Falling Sickness*, 8 n. 33). If such an idea existed in antiquity, it might help explain why the Markan Jesus heals the boy at the moment that a crowd is gathering: he is concerned that the presence of a throng might trigger another seizure.

the unclean spirit. Gk *tǭ pneumati tǭ akathartǭ.* Epilepsy was popularly regarded as a contaminating and contagious disease; see, for example, Apuleius (*Apology* 44:11), who says that fellow slaves spat when they saw an epileptic slave, that nobody dared to eat from the same dish or drink from the same cup as him, and that he was eventually sent away "lest he contaminate the family" (cf. Theophrastus, *Characters* 16; Pliny, *Natural History* 28, 35; see Temkin, *Falling Sickness*, 8, and cf. 114–17).

don't ever enter him again. Gk *mēketi eiselthēs eis auton*; the last three words are a deliberate inversion of *exelthe ex autou* ("come out of him") in the previous clause. Anxiety about repossession is prevalent in ancient exorcism-stories (see, e.g., Matt 12:43–45//Luke 11:24–26; Tob 6:8, 17–18; Josephus, *Ant.* 8.46–47; *Acts of Thomas* 77; Marcus, "Beelzebul," 273–74).

26. *he became like a corpse.* Gk *egeneto hōsei nekros.* As Theissen (66–67) points out, in exorcism stories the reality of the cure is often demonstrated through an act of violence by the departing demon, like the stampede of pigs in Mark 5:13. Non-biblical examples are even clearer; see, for example, Josephus, *Ant.* 8.48: "Then, wishing to convince the bystanders and prove to them that he had this power, Eleazar placed a cup or footbasin full of water a little way off and commanded the demon, as it went out of the man, to overturn it and make known to the spectators that he had left the man." Similarly, Philostratus, *Life of Apollonius* 4.20: "But Apollonius addressed [the demon] with anger, as a master might a shifty, rascally, and shameless slave and so on, and he ordered him to quit the young man and show by a visible sign that he had done so"; the demon complies by knocking over a statue (the motif of exorcistic anger here is reminiscent of Mark's use of "to rebuke" in exorcistic contexts [1:25; 3:12; 9:25] and of the indignation of Jesus in 1:41).

28. *Why.* Gk *hoti.* Some texts, including Alexandrinus and Bezae, change the wording to *dia ti* ("on account of what"), which is a more usual way of expressing "why" than *hoti.* On Mark's fondness for the interrogative use of *hoti,* see the NOTE on "Why does he eat with tax collectors and sinners?" in 2:16.

29. *This sort of spirit can't be gotten out in any way.* Gk *touto to genos en oudeni dynatai exelthein,* lit. "this sort cannot go out by any means." The reference could be either to "this sort" of spirit being exorcised or to "this sort" of miracle "going out," that is, occurring (see Marshall, *Faith,* 222). The use of *exelthein* to refer to exorcism in 9:25–26 and elsewhere in the Gospel (1:25–26; 5:8, 13; 7:29–30) makes the former meaning more likely.

except by prayer. Gk *ei mē en proseuchē.* On healing through prayer see 1 Kgs 17:21; *b. Hag.* 3a; *b. Ber.* 34b (cf. Theissen, 65). Most texts add "and fasting," an accretion that is resisted in good early manuscripts and that probably reflects a later ecclesiastical emphasis on fasting (see the NOTE on "on that day" in 2:20 and the introduction to the COMMENT on 2:18–22; cf. Metzger, 101). Cranfield

("Mark 9.14–29," 62 n. 1) cites Byzantine manuscripts of Acts 10:30 and 1 Cor 7:5 that have similar additions.

COMMENT

Introduction. After the magnificent mountaintop experience of the transfiguration (9:2–8) and the discussion about eschatological matters on the way down from the mountain (9:9–13), Jesus and his closest disciples return to the world below to confront the misery, disease, and hardheartedness of humanity—but also its desperate hopes.

Most exegetes agree that this passage was originally an independent pericope, which Mark himself is responsible for placing at this point in the Gospel. He would do so in part because it presupposes Jesus' having been separated from at least some of his disciples (see 9:18 and cf. Davies and Allison, 2.720–21; Kollmann, *Jesus*, 210). The account includes several repetitions and awkwardnesses, and this has caused some scholars to see it as the conflation of two sources. For example, there are two descriptions of the illness (9:17–18, 21–22), the boy is brought forward twice for healing (9:17, 20), there are two identifications of the demon (9:17, 25), the demon reacts twice to Jesus' presence (9:20, 26), and there is the difficulty that the crowd, which is already on the scene in 9:14, seems to be arriving for the first time in 9:25. Theissen (136) responds that these repetitions are intensifications rather than evidence of different sources, but the two rapidly assembling crowds in 9:15 and 9:25 certainly appear to be a doublet. Whether or not *Mark* is the one who has combined the two narratives, however, remains uncertain.

Two of the evangelist's contributions to the pericope are fairly plain: he has expanded a simple introduction that described Jesus' return to his disciples into the elaborate scene setting in 9:14–16, and he has penned the concluding scene in 9:28–29. Markan redaction is often visible at the beginning and end of a pericope, which indeed is the case here. Both sections are full of Markan vocabulary, and private instruction (9:28) is a special Markan theme. The scribes who appear in 9:14–16, moreover, play no subsequent role in the story, but they do serve to link our passage with the previous one (cf. 9:11). Mark may also be responsible for the use of the verb *dynasthai* ("can, be able") and the cognate adjective *dynatos* ("possible"), which are so prominent throughout the passage (five times in 9:22–23, 28–29, versus only twice in Matthew's account and once in Luke's) and which express such an important Markan theme (cf. also *ischyein* in 9:18 and see the introduction to the COMMENT on 3:20–35, where it is suggested that the prominence of *dynasthai* in that passage is due to Markan redaction). If so, it is possible that the exchange about faith in 9:22b–24, of which the instances of *dynasthai* form a crucial part, is also a Markan creation (cf. Theissen, 136).

The passage in its present form has four parts: (1) Jesus' return to the public sphere (9:14–16), (2) his conversation with the father of the possessed boy (9:17–24), (3) the exorcism itself (9:25–27), and (4) the concluding account of Jesus' private conversation with the disciples (9:28–29). Of these elements, the second, the conversation with the boy's father, is especially prominent, dwarfing the exorcism and taking up half of the narrative's sixteen verses with a discussion of the relation between spiritual power, faith, and unbelief. The didactic elements, however, do not overwhelm the narratives ones; the whole scene, rather, is coherent and dynamic. There are, for example, rapid shifts in point of view from one character to the other, which are illustrated by the alternating subjects of *idein* ("to see"): Jesus and the inner circle of disciples (9:14), the crowd (9:15), the demon (9:20), and Jesus (9:25). The "seeing" in each case is linked to a disturbance, and the whole dramatic narrative is unified by the narrator's desire to demonstrate the dominance of Jesus' point of view over that of the other characters.

Because of the length of the discussion between Jesus and the father, our treatment of it will be subdivided into two sections: the description of the demonized boy's condition (9:17–19) and the conversation about healing, faith, and unbelief (9:20–24).

9:14–16: Jesus' return to public life. Following the transfiguration (9:2–8) and the discussion on the way down from the mountain about Elijah's eschatological role (9:9–13), Jesus returns to "the world of guilt and sorrow" (O'Connor, "Everything," 420), only to find that world in an uproar. The uproar is caused by a dispute between the scribes and the disciples who remained below while the other three climbed the Mount of Transfiguration with Jesus (9:14). Although the disciples do not play a major role in the rest of the passage, the references to them at the beginning and the end are important, since the pericope is set within a section of the Gospel that has fundamentally to do with following Jesus (8:22–10:52). Seen in this context, the portrayal of the possessed boy's father, who both has and does not have faith, is probably meant to be understood as paradigmatic of the faithful-yet-faithless disciples, just as the description of the blind man who sees yet does not see (8:22–26) mirrors their imperfect spiritual vision.

Mark does not inform his readers about the subject of the dispute between the disciples and the scribes, but from the continuation of the story it may be inferred that it is the disciples' inability to perform an exorcism, which in the scribes' opinion discredits them and their master. The hostile attitude of the scribes is somewhat similar to that demonstrated in 3:22, where they acknowledged Jesus' exorcistic power but ascribed it to a demon. The Markan scribes, then, damn Jesus and his disciples if they exorcise but also damn them if they don't, and Mark would probably attribute the unremitting hostility itself to a demonic source (see the COMMENT on 3:28–30). This opposition provides a link with the previous Markan exorcism (7:24–30), which was also preceded by a dispute with the scribes (7:1–23), and with the Gospel's first exorcism, where they were already making their presence known (1:22). In all three instances, the scribes are probably meant to be understood as an embodiment of the anti-God force that is about to become directly and terrifyingly visible in a demonic manifestation.

Unsurprisingly, after the Mosaic features of the transfiguration (see the APPENDIX "History-of-Religions Backgrounds to the Transfiguration"), the subsequent passage is in some ways similar to the return of Moses from Sinai (Exodus 32). In both cases the leader, on his descent, sees a terrible spectacle that is stamped by the continuing presence of sin and hardheartedness in a world that is on the road to redemption. Some Jewish legends, moreover, attribute the sin of the golden calf, with which Moses is confronted on his descent of Sinai, to the instigation of Satan (e.g., *Tg. Ps.-J.* Exod 32:1; *Pirqe R. El.* 45), in a manner not unlike the Markan portrayal of demonic resistance to Jesus. The scribes' complaint about Jesus' disciples is also reminiscent of the OT exodus traditions, where the recalcitrant Israelites murmur against Moses (cf. the COMMENT on 8:8–9 and the NOTE on "testing" in 8:11). Finally, since nothing else in the story suggests a motive for the awestruck reaction of the crowd to Jesus in 9:15, we may be meant to see this feature as an allusion to Exod 34:29–30, where the descending Moses inspires awe by his radiance (see the NOTE on "were . . . awestruck" in 9:15).

9:17–19: *the description of the boy's condition.* In response to Jesus' question as to the cause of the commotion (9:16), a man steps forward from the crowd and describes bringing his demon-possessed son to be exorcised by Jesus' disciples (9:17–18). The terminology in which the man recalls this encounter is significant: "Teacher, I brought my son *to you*" (9:17a). The prosaic meaning of this statement is that the man set out to bring the boy to Jesus, but found him away at the time and turned to his adherents. But Mark's readers might see a deeper implication: bringing a demoniac to the disciples is equivalent to bringing him to Jesus himself, since Jesus has commissioned the Twelve to "be with him" and "to have authority to cast out demons" (3:14–15; cf. Matt 10:40//Luke 10:16). Through their union with Jesus, the disciples possess exorcistic power, which they have demonstrated in action earlier in the Gospel (6:7, 13). Now, however, a second attempt to utilize this power has failed, and at the end of the passage the disciples will return to the question why (9:28–29).

The father of the boy goes on to provide a detailed description of the symptoms of the demon's attack, which include muteness, convulsions, foaming at the mouth, teeth-grinding, and rigidity (9:17b–18). It is clear from this description, from the subsequent account of the boy's seizure (9:20), and from the father's further narrative (9:21–22) that the boy is an epileptic, and he would have been recognized as such by ancient readers (see the NOTES on "a mute spirit" in 9:17, "wherever he is when it grabs him" in 9:18, "from childhood" in 9:21, and "it has thrown him into the fire and into waters" in 9:22). Our passage unambiguously attributes this illness to a demon, a fact that may disturb Christians who want to reconcile the biblical worldview with the modern scientific one. It is important to observe, however, that our passage is not primarily about Mark's belief in the power of demons; it is primarily about his belief that through Jesus this terribly powerful hostile force has been overcome. Thus, the theme of the passage is similar to that of the Beelzebul controversy in 3:20–30. Both passages give special prominence to the roots *dyn-* ("to be able") and *isch-* ("strong") in a context having to do with exorcism: Jesus vanquishes supernatural foes that were powerful enough to defeat everyone else. As Marshall (*Faith,* 115–16) points out, the magnificence of this achievement is driven home by the narrative's stress on the inability of the disciples to help the boy (9:18), on the long duration of the illness

(9:21), on the ferocity of the demonic resistance (9:20, 26), on the self-destructive nature of the demoniac's behavior (9:17–18, 20–22, 26), and on the difficulty of exorcising "this sort" of demon (9:29).

✓ Jesus' initial reaction to the man's description of the disciples' failure to heal his son is extraordinarily passionate: "O faithless generation, how long will I be with you? How long will I put up with you?" (9:19a). Since a shortcoming of the disciples has just been recounted, these words probably apply in the first instance to them (see the NOTE on "O faithless generation," etc. in 9:19), especially since the time element in "how long will I be with you?" echoes that in Jesus' recent words to his disciples, "Do you not yet understand?" (8:21). As Marshall (*Faith*, 220) remarks, the disciples' failure is made all the more serious by this reference to Jesus' approaching departure from the world, which is accentuated by the flanking references to his passion (9:9–13, 30–32). Time is running out for the disciples to get on board.

Jesus' words also allude to the exodus and wilderness traditions that have played such an important role in this section of the Gospel and that we have already seen to be echoed in the account of Jesus' descent from the mountain and reentry into public life. As is observed in the NOTE on "this generation" in 8:12, the wilderness traditions are usually in the background in the NT references to "this generation." Jesus' complaint here, moreover, is similar to God's complaint to Moses in Numbers 14 after the Israelite spies' evil report about the promised land and the people's assertion that it would be better to return to Egypt: "*How long* will this people despise me? And *how long* will they *refuse to believe* in me, in spite of all the signs that I have done among them?" (Num 14:11; cf. Lövestam, *This Generation*, 54–55). Language similar to that of Mark 9:19 is also present in Deuteronomy 32, where the exodus group is excoriated as a "perverse *generation*, children in whom there is *no faithfulness*" (Deut 32:20; cf. 32:5); probably catching the allusion to this passage, Matthew and Luke have added the word "perverse" to the dominical denunciation (cf. Lövestam, *This Generation*, 47; for this and the other "minor agreements" in the passage, see Sterling, "Jesus"; Kollmann, *Jesus*, 210–11; Davies and Allison, 2.719).

If the exodus and wilderness traditions are in the background, however, they imply not only God's frustration with the faithlessness and idolatry of the new Israel but also his enduring care for them despite their failings. As the continuation of the passage from Deuteronomy 32 makes clear, the Lord is not only a deity who wounds and kills but also one who heals and makes alive (32:39). Although he will punish Israel for its idolatry, in the end he "will vindicate his people, have compassion on his servants, *when he sees that their power is gone*" (32:36). The larger context of the Deuteronomy passage, then, dovetails with our passage's theme of divine power overruling human impotence. Moreover, if the Mount of Transfiguration is in some ways comparable to Mount Sinai, it is significant that Jewish legends portray the Israelites being miraculously healed of their diseases at the foot of the latter (*Mekilta* Baḥodesh 9 [Lauterbach 2.266–67]; *Num. Rab.* 7.1; etc.; see Ginzberg, *Legends*, 2.374; 3.78, 213; 6.176; Lövestam, *This Generation*, 47). It may be part of the Mosaic typology, then, that the Markan Jesus concludes

his address to the "faithless generation" not with a rebuke but with a renewed commission; still addressing the disciples, perhaps along with the crowd, he says of the
demon-possessed boy, "Bring him to me" (see the NOTE on these words in 9:19).
Even at their lowest ebb, the disciples are not barred from participating in Jesus'
communication of the liberative power of God into a demon-possessed world.

9:20–24: *the conversation about healing, faith, and unbelief.* The ushering of
the demonized boy into Jesus' presence sets off an abrupt and violent reaction:
the possessing demon, seeing the healer, immediately attacks its host with one of
those epileptic seizures that has just been described, convulsing the boy, striking
him down, and causing him to foam at the mouth and roll about on the ground
(9:20). This attack is probably a challenge to Jesus by the self-confident demon
that has defeated all previous attempts to oust it, and the spirit's antagonistic, con-
temptuous attitude mirrors that of the scribes who have presumably reproached
the disciples for their failure to defeat the demon (9:14).

To some readers it may seem incongruous, even callous, that with the boy rolling about in convulsions at his feet, the Markan Jesus calmly asks the boy's father, "How long has he been like this?" (9:21a). This question, however, serves at
least three purposes. First, in narrative terms it elicits from the father a statement
that stresses the duration of his son's condition, thus increasing the magnitude of
the eventual healing. Second, in terms of exorcistic technique, it represents an
intelligence-gathering operation; Jesus is culling information about the nature of
the demon, which according to ancient ideas will be vital for the job of expelling
it. Third, in terms of Markan salvation history, the question links the termination of the demon's rule over the boy with God's eschatological action in history
through the death of Jesus, since it recalls Jesus' question, "*how long* will I be with
you?" (9:19).

The father replies that his son has been suffering such seizures since childhood
(9:21b) and adds a detail that stresses the destructive nature of the spirit: sometimes it throws him into fire or water "in order to destroy him" (9:22a; cf. 5:13). In
the overall Markan narrative, these words echo the complaint of another demon:
"Have you come to destroy us?" (1:24). They are a reminder of the deadly enmity
between Jesus, the liberator and healer of human beings, and the demon world
that is intent on oppressing and destroying them. This mutual enmity will have
fateful consequences for Jesus himself, as the placement of our passage between
two prophecies of his death suggests (9:12, 30–32).

The father's recollection of the frequency with which the spirit has driven his
son to the brink of death moves him to conclude by beseeching Jesus passionately
for his aid: "But if you can do anything, have pity on us and help us!" (9:22b). As
Marshall (*Faith*, 122) points out, the father's identification with his son's fate is
affectingly portrayed here by the use of the first person plural pronoun: "have pity
on *us* and help *us*." But there may be more to this plea than a sense of identification, since it also seems to echo liturgical formulas from the OT and later Jewish
literature, which often call on God to have mercy on "us" (e.g., Ps 123:2–3; Sir
36:1; Pr Azar 1:12) or to help "us" (e.g., 2 Chron 14:11; Ps 79:9; Add Esth 14:14).

These liturgical intercessions, moreover, frequently invoke God's love as a motive for such assistance and contrast divine sufficiency with human powerlessness. In Ps 44:26, for example, the petitioner pleads with God to "rise up, come to our help; deliver us for the sake of your steadfast love" [RSV alt.], and in Pss 60:11 and 108:12 he calls on the deity to "grant us help against the foe, for human help is worthless"—a conclusion with which the epileptic's father, disillusioned by the disciples' failure, might well concur. It seems plausible, then, that Mark's audience would see in the father's plea an echo of a prayer formula current in their community and that the Markan narrative is placing Jesus in a position analogous to God's (cf. the NOTE on "O faithless generation," etc. in 9:19).

These liturgical echoes do not vitiate the pathos of the father's request; yet Jesus in his response seems to ignore this emotional dimension, focusing instead on the question of trust in God. This does not, however, mean that the Markan Jesus is callous; sometimes compassion can be expressed not by weeping with sufferers but by opening their eyes to a larger perspective in which suffering is not the last word (see Capps, *Reframing*). In any case, as in his initial response to the Syrophoenician woman (7:27), Jesus at first appears to duck the request for a healing or at least to delay it (see the NOTE on "my son" in 9:17). The situation is also close to that in the healing of Jairus' daughter (5:35–43); as Marshall (*Faith*, 122) puts it, both stories feature "a scenic structure in which unexpected developments in the plot lead to the temporary postponement of the cure in order to bring to the surface the fundamental importance and essential character of faith." This is only one of several similarities between the two healing stories (see figure 27).

In the present instance the delaying moment comes through Jesus' rejection of the father's conditional clause, "if you can do anything"; he confronts the lack of confidence implicit in this phrasing with the assurance that all things are possible to "the one who believes" (9:23). Exegetes are divided about the import of this response: is it that *the father's* faith could make all things possible, including the cure of his son, or that all things, including this exorcism, are possible for *Jesus*, the man of perfect faith? (This exegetical dispute is similar to that among Pauline interpreters about whether the *pistis Iēsou* that justifies human beings is faith *in* Jesus or the faith/faithfulness *of* Jesus; cf. Howard, " 'Faith of Christ' ").

The Markan evidence about the meaning of the phrase "the one who believes" is equivocal. On the one hand, the man seems to take it as a reference to himself, since he responds by assuring Jesus that he does indeed believe, albeit imperfectly. Elsewhere in the Gospel, moreover, the faith of Jesus' petitioners is linked with miraculous healing (5:34; 10:52), whereas faith is never directly attributed to Jesus himself. On the other hand, the two other Markan instances of the expression *panta dynata* ("all things are possible": 10:27; 14:36) ascribe omnipotence to God rather than a human capacity, and we have just seen that our narrative may place Jesus in a position analogous to that of God. The implicit question that has precipitated Jesus' declaration about the all-sufficiency of faith, moreover, is whether *Jesus* can heal the petitioner's son ("If *you* can . . ."); it would make sense, then, that his response refers to his own faith rather than that of the petitioner. With such conflicting signals in the text, it may be best to go with Marshall's conclusion

Figure 27: The Healings of Jairus' Daughter and an Epileptic Boy

	Jairus' Daughter: Mark 5:21–24, 35–43	Epileptic Boy: Mark 9:14–29
Father intercedes for child with life-threatening illness	"My little daughter is about to die; come and lay your hands on her" (5:23)	"And many times it has thrown him into the fire and into waters in order to destroy him. But if you can do anything, have pity on us and help us!" (9:22)
Delay of healing leads to discussion of faith	Jesus stops to heal woman with flow of blood and Jairus' daughter dies; Jesus tells Jairus, "Don't be afraid, just keep on believing" (5:25–36)	Jesus stops to address father's expression of doubt, saying, "All things are possible to the one who believes!" Father replies, "I believe; help my unbelief!" (9:23–24)
Child appears to be dead	"Your daughter has died" (apethanen, 5:35; cf. 5:39–40)	He became like a corpse, so that many people were saying that he had died (apethanen, 9:26)
Jesus takes child's hand	Taking the child's hand (kratēsas tēs cheiros tou paidiou, 5:41)	Taking his hand (kratēsas tēs cheiros autou, 9:27; cf. paidiou, 9:24)
Jesus raises child	Jesus says, "Girl, I say to you: Rise!" (egeire). And immediately she arose (anestē, 5:41–42)	[Jesus] raised him (ēgeiren auton), and he arose (anestē, 9:27)

(Faith, 120) that Jesus' statement is deliberately ambiguous and is meant to leave room for both interpretations: the father is being asked to turn his attention from his own seemingly hopeless situation to the Faithful One who holds all power in his hand, and that act of reorientation is itself called "faith."

But where is such faith to come from? In a "haunting cry" (Nineham, 244) of great honesty, which will be of immense comfort to Christians who find themselves similarly placed on the uncertain border between faith and doubt, the father exclaims, "I believe; help my unbelief!" (9:24). The emphatic identification of the petitioner as "the father of the child" again stresses the close relation between him and his son. No designation of the actor is actually necessary, and, even if it were, "of the child" would be superfluous; the whole phrase, moreover, is highlighted by asyndeton (see the GLOSSARY).

In the logic of the present Markan story, however, the relation between the father and the son is not the center of attention but merely the pretext for the crucial discussion about faith and unbelief. Because of the interior conflict in the child who is so dear to him, the father is forced to confront his own internal division, his condition as simultaneously a believer and a doubter. "I believe," he declares, and much of the narrative up to this point supports this assertion: he has brought his sick child to Jesus and has persisted in trying to get treatment for him even after the disciples have turned out to be incompetent and Jesus himself has responded in a seemingly indifferent manner. But, he adds, "help my unbelief." In contrast to the scale-diseased man in 1:40, who believes that Jesus *can* heal if only he *will*, the epileptic's father still has some residual doubt about whether Jesus is actually *capable* of succoring him. He does not want to give way to this doubt, but he feels himself unable to escape it on his own—another example of the theme of human incapacity that pervades the passage. As Marshall (*Faith*, 118) comments, the last part of his plea is both an acknowledgment that he belongs to the faithless generation that has rejected Jesus' claims and a recognition that if he is to attain faith, it must come as a gift from above. He is, then, in Luther's great phrase, *simil justus et peccator*, at once righteous and a sinner; a citizen both of the old age with its miasma of skepticism and despair, and of the new age that is lit up by the hope that "if you believe, you will see the power of God" (John 11:40; my trans.).

The father of the epileptic boy is therefore, in this double-mindedness, a perfect symbol for the Christian disciple. Whereas logically faith and unbelief are opposites, in Christian experience they are simultaneous realities; the one who believes is always concurrently involved in a battle against disbelief. It is significant, therefore, as Marshall (*Faith*, 120–21) points out, that in the transition from the plea of 9:22 to that of 9:24, the father moves from an aorist imperative verb (*boēthēson hēmin*, "help us") to a present imperative, which implies ongoing action (*boēthei mou tē apistia*, "help my unbelief"). This view of faith as constantly under attack, and the consequent necessity of seeking divine succor at all times, dovetails with Jesus' later exhortation of the disciples to continual prayer in view of their divided condition of willing spirit/weak flesh (14:38). It also accords with the overall Markan portrayal of the disciples as people of faith, who leave all to follow Jesus and work miracles in his name, but who also show themselves to be miserably "faithless" at crucial junctures in the narrative.

Dividedness, however, does not necessarily mean stalemate. The boy's father, like the Markan disciples, may fall back into the disbelief of "this generation," but that is not where he really belongs anymore, as shown by the fact that he both recognizes his unbelief and prays to be delivered from it. As Marshall concludes his treatment of the colloquy between Jesus and the father:

> It is this clear perception of unbelief as a problem, and his prayer for on-going deliverance from it, that distinguishes the father's *apistia* from the *apistia* of Nazareth (6:6) or the unbelieving generation (9:19). There, unbelief is concealed and recalcitrant; here it is repentant. (*Faith*, 122)

9:25–27: the exorcism itself. The repentant, believing-yet-fearing-to-believe exclamation of the agonized father is followed by an augmentation of the crowd, which presumably has been attracted by the spectacle provided by the boy's fit and the father's cry. Jesus, seeing the commotion, and perhaps fearing that it will set off another seizure (see the NOTE on "a crowd" in 9:25), immediately goes into action and orders the demon to depart from the boy (9:25). The terms of this command are borrowed from contemporary magical practice; not only does Jesus use an adjuration formula that is common in the magical papyri ("I command you"; cf. *PGM* 1.254; 7.331; etc.), but he also orders the demon never to return, a frequent motif in pagan and Jewish as well as Christian exorcisms (see the NOTE on "don't ever enter him again" in 9:25).

Jesus' word of command, however, is not just a piece of magic, but a weapon in God's cosmic, eschatological war against Satan, which is rapidly approaching its decisive battle. This eschatological framework is suggested by the narrator's use of *epetimēsen* ("rebuked") to characterize the adjuration; as shown in the COMMENT on 1:23–26, this term is redolent of creation myths and dreams of eschatological victory. In this sort of apocalyptic context, the command to the demon never to return gains an added eschatological resonance: the exorcism is permanent because it is part of God's definitive victory over the forces of evil.

Within the Markan Gospel, this apocalyptic victory is tied up with Jesus' death and resurrection, and the conclusion of the exorcism itself suggests this connection. The demon, in a dramatic demonstration of Jesus' power (see the NOTE on "he became like a corpse" in 9:26), but also perhaps in a last paroxysm of hatred for Jesus and its erstwhile host, comes out of the boy with such violence that it seems to have killed him (9:26); Jesus, however, seizing the boy's hand, pulls him up out of the grasp of death (9:27). Although the boy may seem to have expired, death will not be allowed to have the final word—a lesson that Mark's readers might apply to departed fellow Christians (cf. Nineham, 244). But the more direct association is with Jesus himself, since the terminology in our story ("had died . . . raised . . . arose"), which is similar to that in the healing of Jairus' daughter (see again figure 27), is also reminiscent of that applied to Jesus' own death and resurrection (see the COMMENT on 5:35–43), and the curious redundancy "raised him and he arose" supports the view that the description is symbolic. Mark seems to be saying that the power by which Jesus raises the seemingly dead boy to life is the same power by which God will raise Jesus himself (see Nineham, 244; Rochais, *Récits*, 60; Marshall, *Faith*, 123).

This resurrectional power of Jesus has just been glimpsed in the transfiguration (9:2–8; see the COMMENT on 9:2–4). The juxtaposition between the transfiguration and our passage, then, is not simply fortuitous, an insight brilliantly captured in Raphael's 1520 painting *Transfiguration* (Vatican Pinacoteca), in which the two scenes are merged. As Goethe describes the painting, Raphael depicts the disciples, the possessed boy, and his family in the lower part of the canvas, capturing their defeated mood after the failure of the disciples' exorcistic efforts. "At this moment he alone who has power appears, transfigured in glory, and all are looking up at him and pointing to the vision as the only source of salvation"

(*Italienische Reise*, cited in Pope-Hennessy, *Raphael*, 73–74). Jesus descends from the Mount of Transfiguration still blazing with resurrectional splendor, and it is this radiance that overwhelms the stubborn and seemingly invincible demon that has driven the helpless epileptic nearly to death.

9:28–29: *the concluding discussion with the disciples.* But why were the disciples, who had previously seemed to share in Jesus' power to cast out demons (3:15; 6:7, 13), unable to exorcise this particular spirit? This is the question they put to Jesus after they have withdrawn with him privately to a house (9:28)—a Markan device for raising issues that are of concern to the Markan community (see 7:17–23 and cf. 4:10–20, 33–34; 13:3–37). Jesus' response is that "this sort" of demon can be dislodged only by prayer (9:29); the problem thus has partly to do with the trouble-some kind of spirit that had inhabited the boy. This reply is in accord with ancient conceptions that saw epilepsy as a disease that could be healed only by a god or someone with divine power (see the NOTE on "a mute spirit" in 9:17).

But Jesus' answer raises as many questions as it answers, since Jesus himself, despite his prescription of prayer as the antidote for an epileptic spirit, is not de-scribed as praying before he expels the demon. It may be that his prayer is implied or that Mark has already identified him sufficiently as a man of prayer that he need not do so here (see 1:35; 6:46; cf. 14:32–42). It is still striking, however, that in 9:29 he lays down a rule for exorcism that he himself is not described as fulfilling. And why does the account of the exorcism identify *faith* as the crucial factor in miracle working, when Jesus' private instruction to the disciples singles out *prayer*?

These are the sorts of aporias, or narrative difficulties, that Martyn (*History*) links with the two-level nature of Gospel narratives: on one level the evangelist is telling a story about what happened "way back when" in Jesus' time, but on another level he is telling a story about what is happening *now* to his own Christian community, and the merging of these two narrative planes contributes to literary incongruities. Thus, in the post-Easter period, physical contact with Jesus is no longer possible, but prayer is—hence Jesus' answer to the disciples in 9:29. Moreover, as we have seen, in our passage Jesus is, in some sense, the object rather than the subject of prayer.

But there *is* a character in the story who prays, and that is the boy's father (cf. Mar-shall, *Faith*, 223). As has been shown above, his very language in addressing Jesus is reminiscent of liturgical intercession, and his believing-yet-disbelieving posture is meant by Mark to be an image of the way in which Christians stand before God and Jesus in prayer. The gap between the two levels of the Markan narrative, then, is bridged both by seeing the church's prayers as an expression of faith and by see-ing the father's supplication before Jesus, which is faithful in its very confession of faithlessness, as a kind of prayer.

As noted above, what happens "in the house" is often a reflection of what is going on in the house-churches that make up the Markan and other Christian communities, and the disciples' complaint, "Why weren't *we* able to cast it out?" probably echoes something that people within the Markan Christian community are saying. This question from within the community, moreover, apparently corresponds to, and is exacerbated by, one that is being raised from outside by hostile voices (cf. 9:14): if the Christians' master is, as they claim, the all-powerful one whom God has vindicated by resurrection, why do his followers not retain the miracle-working force that he possessed during his lifetime? This issue would be particularly pressing for a Markan community situated in proximity to the Jewish War, in which other messianic claimants were performing signs and wonders that elicited faith in their supernatural status and were thus constituting a powerful temptation to the Markan Christians (cf. 13:21–22).

Mark's response to this temptation is twofold. On the one hand, the evangelist implies that miracle-working power is still available to Christians through the grace of Jesus and God; mountains may still be uprooted and cast into the sea (11:23). The frequency of healing stories and exorcisms within the Gospel, as well as the accounts of apostolic success in healing, suggest that such extraordinary happenings are still recognizable in Mark's time. On the other hand, the Gospel also shows, especially in its second half, that at times the divine power of Jesus seems to be in eclipse. While the omnipotent God may still inspire effective intercessions for miracle-working power, he may also choose to inspire prayers like that of Jesus himself in Gethsemane: "Not what I want, but what you want" (14:36).

In the case of Jesus, that prayer of supreme faithfulness will eventually lead to a final, incomparable release of divine power into the world; but, as the next passage shows, that release can occur only when the one who utters the prayer is turned over to the hostile will of an unbelieving generation and "they have done to him whatever they wanted" (9:13).

JESUS AGAIN PROPHESIES HIS DEATH AND RESURRECTION (9:30–32)

9 ³⁰And going out from there, they went through Galilee, and he did not want anybody to know it, ³¹for he was teaching his disciples and saying to them, "The Son of Man will be turned over to the hands of human beings, and they will kill him, and when he has been killed, after three days he will arise." ³²But they did not understand the saying, and they were afraid to ask him.

NOTES

9 31. *was teaching.* Gk *edidasken.* The imperfect tense here probably refers to repeated occasions of teaching, since Jesus' desire to instruct his disciples privately explains the secretiveness of his trip through Galilee, which presumably lasts several days.

and saying to them. Gk *kai elegen autois hoti.* On the redundant formulation "teaching . . . and saying to them," cf. the NOTE on "he answered and said" in 3:33. On *hoti* functioning to introduce a quotation, see the NOTE on "and saying" in 1:15.

The Son of Man will be turned over. Gk *Ho huios tou anthrōpou paradidotai.* On the translation of *paradidotai,* see the NOTES on "handed over" in 1:14 and "betrayed" in 3:19. Part of the background to the prophecy lies in Isa 53:6, 12 LXX, where *paradidonai* is used to speak of God's delivery of his Suffering Servant to death (cf. Marcus, *Way,* 162, 188–89, 193–94). But the verb also appears in Dan 7:25–27 LXX, in which "the holy ones of the Most High," who are linked with the "one like a son of man," are "turned over to the hands" of their enemy until the moment of eschatological vindication, which elsewhere in Daniel is associated with resurrection (Dan 12:1–3; cf. Davies and Allison, 2.733, and the introduction to the COMMENT on 8:34–9:1).

In our passage a present passive form of *paradidonai* is used, but it has a futuristic sense; the parallels in Matt 17:22 and Luke 9:44, as well as the passion prediction in Mark 10:33, all employ the future passive of the same verb. On this futuristic usage of the present, see Burton (9), who cites our verse, and Fanning (*Verbal Aspect,* 225), who says that the tense is employed "in prophetic or oracular pronouncements, giving a vision of a future occurrence as if it were occurring already." It thus conveys much the same sense as *dei* ("it is necessary") in the passion prediction in 8:31.

to the hands of human beings. Gk *eis cheiras anthrōpōn.* Since the hand is the "tool of tools" for human activity (Aristotle, *On the Soul* 3.8), "hand" is often used, in both Jewish and non-Jewish sources, in a transferred sense for the active power of a person (see Lohse, "*Cheir*"). To fall into the hands of someone, therefore, means to be delivered to his or her control, and this can be a terrifying thing if the controller is hostile; see, for example, Josh 2:24: "The Lord has given all the land into our hands; moreover all the inhabitants of the land melt in fear before us" (cf. Heb 10:31). In the present instance, however, the phrase may retain a literal nuance as well, since at Jesus' arrest the members of the apprehending party "laid hands on him and took him into custody" (14:46).

The LXX contains many instances in which God threatens to turn Israel over to the hands (*paradōsō . . . eis cheiras*) of their enemies. The locution is especially common in the great prophets of judgment, Jeremiah (21:10; 22:25; 46:24 [26:24 LXX]; etc.) and Ezekiel (7:21; 11:9; 16:39; etc.). It can also be used to threaten Israel's enemies; in Isa 19:4, for example, God promises that he will turn Egypt over to the hands of human beings (*paradōsō tēn Aigypton eis cheiras anthrōpōn*), a close parallel to our pericope. In such passages, human beings are assumed to be hostile; in Jer 38:16 [45:16 LXX] turning the prophet over *eis cheiras anthrōpōn toutōn* ("to the hands of these human beings") is tantamount to killing him (cf. 39:17 [46:17 LXX]). It is therefore better to fall into the hands of God than into those of humans (see 2 Sam 24:14//1 Chron 21:13; Sir 2:18), since God is merciful, whereas human beings customarily are not.

COMMENT

Introduction. After vanquishing a stubborn demon that even his disciples were unable to conquer and raising an apparently dead boy to life (9:14–29), Jesus continues on his journey with those same disciples, instructing them further in the mystery of his own approaching death and resurrection.

This passage is substantially a Markan composition. It is full of typically Markan vocabulary ("going out," "Galilee," "know," "teaching," "disciples," "and saying to them," "ask"), and both the introductory verse (9:30) and the concluding one (9:32) reflect the Markan messianic secret theme and make little sense on a historical level (see below). The one part of the passage that may have a traditional core is the pronouncement itself, which is the simplest of all the detailed passion predictions and displays certain features that could reflect Aramaic idiom (e.g., "turned over to the hands" and the play of words on "Son of Man" and "human beings"); "after three days," moreover, is in tension with Markan chronology (see the NOTE on "after three days" in 8:31 and Davies and Allison, 2.732). Yet the verse also mirrors an important Markan theme in its juxtaposition of "the Son of Man" with "to the hands of human beings" (see below). As Brown (*Death*, 2.1482) points out, moreover, "turned over to the hands" also occurs in the Greek of the LXX, and the play of words on "Son of Man"/"human beings" works in Greek as well. Even detection of an Aramaic substratum, moreover, would not necessarily prove that the saying is dominical or vitiate the idea of Markan composition, since not only Jesus but also members of the early church, including perhaps Mark himself, spoke Aramaic. It is impossible, then, to say with any certainty whether 9:31 is traditional or a Markan composition.

The pericope consists of three sentences. The first and third (9:30, 32) are short and emphasize limitations on revelation; the second (9:31) is long and teaches the central message of the passage, the divine necessity of Jesus' death and resurrection. As is typical in Mark's Gospel, the truth of God revealed in Jesus' teaching is framed by the ignorance of human beings.

9:30–32: Jesus' prediction of his death and resurrection, and the disciples' response. The passage begins with an account of Jesus departing from the scene of the exorcism of the epileptic boy and going throughout Galilee incognito (9:30). The reason for this low-publicity tour is that he is teaching the disciples about his approaching death and resurrection (9:31).

Looked at logically, this motivation is puzzling: why should Jesus try to prevent knowledge of his presence in Galilee, just because he is teaching his disciples about his death and resurrection? If he needed to teach them something not meant for the ears of all, it would be easier and more straightforward simply to isolate himself with them for a short period, as he does elsewhere in the Gospel, most recently in 9:28–29. It does not seem credible that Jesus would *repeatedly* hold forth in clear terms on the subject of his forthcoming death and resurrection (see the NOTE on "was teaching" in 9:31), that his disciples would *repeatedly* misunderstand these references, and yet that they would *repeatedly* refrain from asking him about them (cf. Wrede, 82–100).

Our passage, then, is probably not a historical reminiscence but a piece of Markan theology reflecting the idea that the necessity of Jesus' death and resurrection became clear only in the post-Easter period; before that epoch, even Jesus' disciples could not and did not understand it (see the APPENDIX "The Messianic Secret Motif" in vol. 1). This theological construction overlaps with Jewish ideas about the necessity of the Messiah or Son of Man remaining hidden until the time for his revelation. As *Midr. Psalms* 21:1 puts it: "This is the Messiah, the Son of David, who is hidden until the time of the end" (my trans.; cf. *1 Enoch* 62:7; *4 Ezra* 13:52; Justin, *Dialogue* 8:4; 110:1; Matt 24:26–27; John 7:27; Mowinckel, *He That Cometh*, 304–8). For Mark's Christian readers, this revelatory restriction would have a positive side, for they would know that *now*, since Easter, they live in an era in which the constraint illustrated in 9:30 is shattered and in which Jesus' messiahship, and the paradoxical way in which it has manifested itself, is being proclaimed to all (cf. 1:1; 13:10; 14:9).

The "teaching" that follows the itinerary in 9:30 is the simplest of all the developed passion predictions, consisting solely of a prophecy of (1) the Son of Man's delivery into the hands of his enemies, (2) his death at their hands, and (3) his resurrection (9:31). Yet this apparently simple prophecy reflects a deeper Markan preoccupation through its repetition of the word *anthrōpos* ("man, human being"): "The Son of Man (*ho huios tou* **anthrōpou**) will be turned over to the hands of human beings (*eis cheiras* **anthrōpōn**)." This repetition enshrines a terrible inversion. It would be natural to expect that the Son of Man, the inclusive representative of humanity (see the APPENDIX "The Son of Man" in vol. 1), would be received by his fellow human beings with joy. Instead he is turned over to their most violent impulses (cf. "they have done to him whatever they wanted" in 9:13); *anthrōpoi* have become the enemies of their own "Son" (cf. Gnilka, 2.54). It is consonant with this pessimistic interpretation of "to the hands of human beings" that in 2 Sam 24:14//1 Chron 21:13 falling into human hands is considered a terrible fate because of the ruthlessness of humankind (cf. Sir 2:18 and Lagrange, 213).

A clue to the mystery of this awful reversal of "the way it ought to be" may lie in the juxtaposition of our passage with the exorcism in 9:14–29: the same demonic power that warped the epileptic's life is responsible for the eerie, unnatural hostility of human beings to the Son of Man who came to save them (10:45). A similar juxtaposition of the evil of demons with that of humans is visible in 7:1–30, where negative references to the perversity of *anthrōpoi* (7:7, 15, 20–21, 23) are immediately followed by the exorcism of an unclean spirit (7:24–30).

Jesus' disciples react to his prophecy of death and resurrection with silent bewilderment, but are afraid to ask about it (9:32); a similar incomprehension had greeted Jesus' allusion to his resurrection in 9:9. On a narrative level, the disciples' reserve may partly be a response to what had occurred in 8:31–33, where Peter protested Jesus' first clear passion prediction, only to find himself, and by implication the rest of the Twelve, roundly rebuked by Jesus. The Markan disciples may not have become more enlightened since then, but they do seem to have become more gun-shy.

Their fear of asking Jesus about his passion prediction, however, does not bode well for them. As we have seen in the COMMENT on 4:10, earlier in the narrative it was a sign of the disciples' privileged, elect position that they, in contrast to the "outsiders," came forward to make inquiries of Jesus. The important place ascribed to questioning here would ring a bell for ancient readers from a wide variety of backgrounds, since Plato had ascribed a central place to the method of question-and-answer in the discovery of truth (see Robinson, *Dialectic*, 75–84). The Jewish tradition similarly valorized inquiry; in *m. 'Abot* 6:6, for example, question-and-answer is one of the virtues of Torah study (cf. Breuer, "Pilpul"). It is a serious matter, then, that on the present occasion the Markan disciples do *not* inquire about Jesus' prophecy of death and resurrection, especially since this prophecy goes to the heart of the Christian mystery. In the Markan context the disciples' reluctance to ask is a sign of spiritual malady, as is suggested not only by its coupling with the theme of ignorance but also by a comparison with previous passages in which their misunderstandings were mentioned:

6:52	For they did not understand about the loaves, but their heart was hardened.
8:17	Do you not yet perceive or understand? Has your heart been hardened?
8:33	Get behind me, Satan! For you are fixing your thoughts not on the things of God but on those of human beings.
9:32	But they did not understand the saying, and they were afraid to ask him.

This comparison suggests that the disciples' present psychological state, what we might call their "question anxiety," is part of a deeper disorder of the soul ("hardness of heart") that ultimately can be traced back to Satan.

Our passage thus ends on a note of apostolic silence and incomprehension. But all is not darkness and Satanic disorder. At the beginning of the next pericope, Jesus will ask a question himself and thereby take the initiative lost by the disciples' reticence. Good teacher that he is, the Markan Jesus does not allow his pupils' inhibition and confusion to destroy the lesson; rather, by his own inquiry he reframes the subject in an existentially involving manner. The next passage will progress logically, then, from the death and resurrection of Jesus to the way in which his stumbling followers may, despite their missteps, share in his exaltation by participating in his humiliation.

A COLLECTION OF SAYINGS ON CHRISTIAN LIVING (MARK 9:33–50)

◆

INTRODUCTION

The next section of the Gospel takes place in Capernaum, the Galilean village from which Peter, Andrew, James, and John came (see 1:16–21, 29–30) and in which Jesus had last taught and ministered in 2:1–3:6. Then he was arguing with his overt enemies, the scribes and Pharisees; now he is engaged in a much more difficult struggle with the misunderstanding of his own disciples and the sorts of problems that will bedevil their heirs, the members of the early Christian church.

As many scholars have noted, the material that falls between the entrance into Capernaum in 9:33 and the departure for Judaea and the Transjordan in 10:1 is catechetical in nature (see the GLOSSARY) and sometimes linked principally by catchword (see figure 28). For example, the opening pericope, 9:33–37, concerns the issue of greatness and ends with Jesus hugging a child and saying, "Whoever receives one such child in my name receives me." The next pericope, 9:38–40, picks up the catch phrase "in my name" but uses it to explore a completely different theme, exorcism in Jesus' name by those outside the circle of disciples. Even the linking feature, "in my name," means something rather different in the two sections; in 9:33–37 it signifies accepting someone *for the sake of* Jesus, but in 9:38–40 it designates someone who acts *in the power of* Jesus. The linkages between the other sections of 9:33–50 are similarly artificial.

It is probable that the catchword composition reflects the catechetical origin of the material in this section. Catchword composition is a mnemonic device admirably suited to catechesis, and its special prominence throughout the section suggests employment of a source. At one point, however, Mark himself seems to be responsible for a catchword connection, since he probably inserted 9:38–40 or 41; 9:37 forms a smoother linkage with either 9:41 or 9:42 than it does with 9:38, and the story about the alien exorcist in 9:38–40 seems to reflect a post-Easter setting (see the COMMENT on 9:38–40) and a particular Markan concern with the meaning of Jesus' exorcisms (see 1:21–28; 3:20–30; 9:28–29; cf. Fleddermann, "Discourse," 64–65).

Other editorial activity is noticeable, as is frequently the case, at the beginning and the end of the passage. At the beginning, the motifs of private instruction in a house and being "on the way," the verbs "to ask" (*eperōtan*) and "to discuss" (*dialogizesthai*), and the *gar* ("for") clause are all typical Markan characteristics (see Fleddermann, "Discourse," 59). It is jarring, moreover, that Jesus addresses the disciples in 9:33–34, but then "calls the Twelve" to him in 9:35 (see Gnilka, 2.55). It is likely, then, that the evangelist himself is responsible for much of 9:33–34. It is also probable that Mark has added the concluding saying in 9:50b, "Have salt in yourselves and be at peace with each other," which forms an inclusion (see the GLOSSARY) with the theme of intracommunity strife in 9:33–34 (cf. Lane, 339).

Figure 28: Catchword Associations in Mark 9:33–50

9:34	they had been discussing *with each other* . . . who was the *greatest*
9:35	if anyone wants to be *first*, he shall be the *last* of all and the servant of all
9:36	and taking a *child*, he set him in their midst
9:37	whoever receives one such *child in my name*
9:38	we saw someone *casting out* demons *in your name*
9:39	there is no one who will do a work of power *in my name*
9:41	whoever gives you a cup of water to drink *in the name*
9:42	whoever *offends* one of these little ones who believe, *it would be better (kalon estin)* for him . . . to *be cast* into the sea
9:43	if your hand *offends* you, *cut it off*—it is better *(kalon estin)* to *enter life* maimed than to have two hands and go away *to Gehenna*, to the *fire that cannot be put out*
9:45	if your foot *offends* you, *cut it off*—it is better *(kalon estin)* to *enter life* lame than to have two feet and *be cast into Gehenna*
9:47–48	if your eye *offends* you, *cast it out*—it is better *(kalon estin)* to enter *the dominion of God* one-eyed than to have two eyes and *be cast into Gehenna*, where . . . the *fire is not put out*
9:49	everyone will be *salted* with *fire*
9:50a	*salt is good (kalon)*; but if the *salt* becomes *unsalty*, what will you *salt* it with?
9:50b	have *salt* in yourselves and be at peace *with each other*

with each other	34				50b
greatest/first/last	34 35				
child		36 37			
in my/your/the name		37 38 39 41			
cast(ing) (it) out/be cast		38	42	45 47–48	
offends			42	45 47–48	
it would be/is better/good			42 43 45 47–48		50a
cut it off			43 45		
enter life/the dominion of God			43 45	47–48	
fire			43	47–48 49	
that cannot be/is not put out			43	47–48	
(in)to Gehenna			43 45 47–48		
salt(ed)/unsalty					49 50a 50b

Although most of the material in the section comes from a pre-Markan collection of instructional sayings, this does not mean that it is alien to Markan interests. The Gospel has stressed the necessity of following Jesus even to the point of death in order to find one's life (8:34–37); the exhortation to become the last in order to become first (9:33–37) falls on prepared ground. We have already noted how the story of the alien exorcist (9:38–40) fits with Markan themes. And the eschatological sayings in 9:41–50 echo the theme of passages such as 8:38–9:1 and look forward to the detailed end-time prophecy in chapter 13. The catchword arrangement of the material, moreover, does not mean that Mark and his hearers would prescind from finding logical connections between the component parts. Indeed, the inclusion of the section within the Markan story would necessitate an effort to interpret it as part of that narrative, and that is what we will attempt to do in what follows.

JESUS TALKS ABOUT GREATNESS (9:33–37)

9 ³³And they came to Capernaum. And when he was in the house, he asked them, "What were you discussing on the way?" ³⁴But they were silent, for they had been discussing with each other on the way who was the greatest. ³⁵And sitting down, he called the Twelve and said to them, "If anyone wants to be first, he shall be the last of all and the servant of all." ³⁶And taking a child, he set him in their midst, and embracing him, he said to them, ³⁷"Whoever receives one such child in my name receives me, and whoever receives me does not receive me but the one who sent me."

NOTES

9 34. *on the way.* Gk *en tē hodō*. The repetition of this phrase, after its occurrence in 9:33, is awkward, which is doubtless why it has been deleted by some later scribes (A, D, Δ, etc.). The repetition, however, is probably deliberate (see the COMMENT on 9:33–35).

who was the greatest. Gk *tis meizōn*, lit. "who the greater"; there is no verb, and in koine Greek the comparative often replaces the superlative (see Robertson, 667–69, and Moule, *Idiom Book*, 97–98). The Syriac versions render *meizōn* with *rab*, and our passage may be related in some way to the emerging institution of the rabbinate, on which see the NOTE on "Rabbi" in 9:5. Matthew 23:1–12, which warns against being called "rabbi," contains a version of our saying.

Origen (*Commentary on Matthew* 13.14) links the disciples' query ingeniously with the Gospel context by suggesting that it sprang from the recent experience of the transfiguration, where Jesus segregated himself with three disciples, indicating their precedence over the other members of the Twelve (Mark 9:2 pars.); it was natural that the question should subsequently arise as to which individual in this inner circle was the greatest.

35. *sitting down.* Gk *kathisas*. In the Gospels, including Mark, Jesus often sits

to teach (cf. 4:1; 12:41; 13:3; Matt 5:1; 26:55; Luke 4:20–21; 5:3; John 8:2; cf. Matt 23:2). This was the characteristic posture of teachers in antiquity, as ancient depictions show (cf. C. Schneider, "*Kathēmai*," 443), and the common rabbinic idiom "sits and interprets" suggests that the same custom prevailed among Jews (*Exod. Rab.* 8.3; *b. Ber.* 27b; *b. Bes.* 15b; etc.). Pupils also sat (see Mark 3:32; *m. 'Abot* 1:4; etc.), but usually in a humbler position than the teacher (e.g., on the ground; see *'Abot R. Nat.* [A] 6). The association of the sitting posture with teaching and learning eventually led to *yĕšîbâh* (lit. "sitting") becoming a technical term for a Jewish religious school; this usage may already be reflected in the Hebrew original of Sir 51:28–29, as attested by the reading of Manuscript B: "Many heard my instruction in my youth . . . may my soul [perhaps a mistake for "your soul"] rejoice *byšybty* [in my sitting]" (my trans.; cf. Hengel, *Judaism*, 1.79; 2.54 n. 165; M. Segal, *Ben Sira*, 358, 363; Beentjes, *Ben Sira*, 94). The sitting posture may also imply judgment on the disciples, as Knabenbauer (*Evangelium*, 247–48) suggests; for the association of sitting with judgment see Dan 7:26; Matt 19:28; 25:31; Mark 13:3; John 19:13; Acts 23:3; 25:6, 17. Also, in view of the extensive comparison of Jesus to Moses in this section of the Gospel (see the subject index under "Moses"), it may be significant that Moses is often presented as "sitting" on Mount Sinai (see Deut 9:9 MT; Ezekiel the Tragedian, *Exagogē* 75; *b. Meg.* 21a; cf. Matt 23:2 and Allison, *New Moses*, 175–79).

If anyone wants to be first, he shall be the last of all and the servant of all. Gk *ei tis thelei prōtos einai estai pantōn eschatos kai pantōn diakonos.* This logion (see the GLOSSARY) is related conceptually to the one found in Matt 23:12//Luke 14:11//Luke 18:14 (cf. Matt 18:4): "Whoever exalts himself shall be humbled, and whoever humbles himself shall be exalted." The latter saying has many parallels in the history of religions (e.g., Prov 29:23; Ezek 21:26; Diogenes Laertius, *Lives of Eminent Philosophers* 1:69; Luke 1:52; *b. Erub.* 13b) and is rooted in secular wisdom (cf. its association with table manners in Luke 14:7–11 and *Lev. Rab.* 1.5): humility is the best policy, whereas self-aggrandizement eventually leads to humiliation. In the present context, however, the thought takes on a more eschatological coloring (see the COMMENT on 9:33–35), and with this feature is linked the idiosyncratic Markan reference to service ("and the servant of all"): those who not only accept their lowly status but actively serve others do not expect to be rewarded in this world but only by the manifestation of the eschatological power of God. Like other sayings of Jesus in Mark (cf., e.g., the COMMENTS on 2:21–22 and 4:21–23), ours represents an eschatologizing of secular wisdom.

he shall be. Gk *estai.* On the use of the future in an imperatival sense, which is found in both biblical and secular Greek, see Robertson, 874–75 and Zerwick, 94. Most of the examples are in the second person, as in the Ten Commandments (Exod 20:3–17), but there are occasional instances in the third person, as here (see, e.g., Mark 10:43–44//Matt 20:26–27; Luke 1:32; 10:6).

servant. Gk *diakonos.* This noun, from which the English word "deacon" comes, is cognate with the verb *diakonein,* "to serve" (see the NOTES on "were serving" in 1:13; "and the fever left her, and she began serving them" in 1:31; and the COMMENT on 1:29–34). The term is frequently used in Greek literature to indicate a menial worker such as a waiter at table, who is usually a slave (see Xenophon, *Memorabilia* 1.5.2; Josephus, *Ant.* 6.52; etc.), and in the Gospels its cognates maintain the nuance of humble service (see, e.g., Matt 25:42–44; Luke 12:37; 17:8; John 12:2). Correspondingly, in Acts and the Pauline literature, diaconal "service" and the office of the deacon are often associated with support for the needy (see, e.g., Acts 6:2–3; Rom 15:25, 31; 16:1–2; 2 Cor 8:4, 19–20; 9:1, 12; cf. Beyer, "*Diakoneō*"; A. Weiser, "*Diakonos*").

36. *taking a child.* Gk *labōn paidion.* The same verb is used in a context having to do with adoption in Exod 2:9; for other features suggestive of adoption, see the NOTE on "embracing him" in 9:36 and the COMMENT on 9:36–37.

Black (221–22) thinks that the Markan combination of the image of the servant with that of the child reflects the Aramaic *ṭalyâ'*, which can have both meanings; he acknowledges, however, that the Greek *pais* and *paidion* are susceptible to the same double entendre. As Stegemann ("Kinder," 123) points out, the fact that such terms denote both slaves and children speaks volumes about the status of children in antiquity.

Paidion can refer to a newborn infant (e.g., Matt 2:8, 9, 11, etc.; John 16:21; *Barn.* 6:17), as well as to an older child (e.g., Matt 11:16//Luke 7:32; Mark 7:28, 30; see BDAG 749). The Greek word is neuter in gender and can be used either for a boy or for a girl. The *Scholars Bible*, however, goes too far in using the feminine pronoun here; if a girl were meant, the child's gender would probably be specified as worthy of note. The Syrophoenician woman's daughter, for example, is referred to as a *paidion* (7:30) only after her gender has been well established by three instances of *thygatrion* ("daughter"), a gender-specific term (7:25, 26, 29). Lacking such a specification, one would assume that the child in our passage is a boy, and that is how the Syriac versions take it.

Later interpreters try to fill in the features of the anonymous child who is embraced by Jesus. Swete (193) offers the novelistic remark that "a child is playing near" and ingeniously suggests that perhaps the child is Peter's son or daughter—a proposal combining the location in Capernaum, which according to 1:21, 29 was Peter's home, with the implication drawn from 1:30 and 1 Cor 9:5 that Peter was married and, presumably, a father. Similarly, a widespread church tradition, which first appears in the ninth century (Anastasius Bibliothecarius in Migne, *Opera* 3.42), identifies the child as Ignatius of Antioch, drawing on a literal interpretation of Ignatius' epithet "the God-borne one" (cf. Lightfoot, *Apostolic Fathers*, 1.27).

embracing him. Gk *enankalisamenos.* Jesus' embrace of the child may be a symbolic act of adoption, since ancient adoptions sometimes included gestures of picking the child up, embracing it, or otherwise bringing it into contact with the adoptive parent's body. In Babylonian legal documents, for example, a standard part of the procedure for adopting an exposed infant is "to raise it up" (see, e.g., *Codex Hammurabi* 185 and cf. Malul, "Adoption"), and Plautus (*Casket Comedy* 124) has a woman use *sustuli* ("I raised up") to refer to rescuing an abandoned baby from an alley and rearing it as her own. Genesis 30:3, similarly, may reflect a rite of putting an adopted child on the parent's knees (see Knobloch, "Adoption," 77). According to Diodorus Siculus (*Library of History* 4.39.2), Hera adopted Herakles by taking him to her body; Diodorus notes that the "barbarians" continue this rite "to this day." The Vulgate likewise interprets Naomi's placement of Ruth's baby on her own breast (Ruth 4:16) as an act of adoption (see Kohler, "Adoption," 208).

37. *receives me.* Gk *eme dechetai.* The idea that the person who receives a humble child is actually receiving Jesus is reminiscent of the common ancient motif of the incognito hero or god, in which gods visit the earth in disguise and receive good or poor treatment before finally revealing themselves and requiting their erstwhile hosts with rewards or chastisements (see, e.g., Homer, *Odyssey* 17.485–87, and the story of Philemon and Baucis in Ovid, *Metamorphoses* 8.613–715; cf. Stählin, "*Xenos*," 22; Flückiger-Guggenheim, *Göttliche Gäste*). The Jewish counterpart is biblical tales about angels being welcomed or mistreated by figures such as Abraham and Sarah (Gen 18:2–15), Lot and the men of Sodom (Gen 19:1–14), Manoah (Judg 13:15–23) or Tobit (Tob 12:1–20; see Attridge, *Hebrews*, 386); such stories stress the duty of hospitality to strangers, whereby, as Heb 13:2 puts it, some have entertained angels unawares (cf. Tertullian, *On Prayer* 26, who quotes the Hebrews passage in interpreting our text).

This motif appears in the Christian sphere in Matt 25:31–46, which is closely related to our pericope (see the COMMENT on 9:36–37, and for the history of interpretation of Matt 25:31–46, see Gray, *Least*). Particularly relevant for comparison with Mark 9:37 are passages in which reception of strangers is encouraged by the principle of Matt 25:40, 45 that actions done to needy strangers are done to Christ (see, e.g., *Rule of St. Benedict* 53). Sometimes this motif assumes a graphic form in which Christ, in the guise of a poor person, stands at the door and knocks (cf. Rev 3:20) or wanders the earth disguised as a stranger to test people's reactions to him (cf. Bolte and Polívka, *Anmerkungen*, 210–29). Such ideas have persisted into recent times; Eliach (*Tales*, 53–55), for example, relates the true story of a Jewish boy who saved his life during the Holocaust by convincing a superstitious Lithuanian peasant woman that he was the Lord Jesus Christ come down to earth, wounded and bleeding, and that she should therefore take him in. The American folk song "Tramp on the Street" (words in Blood-Patterson, *Rise Up Singing*, 186), employs the same motif when it asks its hearers whether they would take Jesus in if he knocked on their door, or "Would you leave him to die like a tramp on the street?"

does not receive me but the one who sent me. Gk *ouk eme dechetai alla ton aposteilanta me.* In line with the Semitic idiom of "dialectical negation," this probably means "does not *so much* receive me as receive the one who sent me"; for this idiom, see the COMMENT on 7:14–15.

COMMENT

Introduction. Jesus' second detailed passion prediction (9:31), like the first (8:31) and the third (10:33–34), is followed by an incident that illustrates the disciples' misunderstanding of the strange logic of the dominion of God (8:32–33; 9:32–34; 10:35–37); in each case, this demonstration of apostolic misunderstanding is in turn followed by renewed instruction of the disciples (8:34–9:1; 9:35–37; 10:38–

45). This repeated pattern probably reflects Markan composition, and it high-lights two important Markan themes: the fallibility of the disciples, and Jesus' continued commitment to them (cf. Fusco, *Parola*, 138).

As for the editing of the passage, it has been suggested in the introduction to 9:33–50 that Mark is largely responsible for the first two verses, though some sort of tradition may underlie 9:34, which is partially paralleled in *Gospel of Thomas* 12. As in 9:35–36, a commendation of children occurs in *Gospel of Thomas* logion 4 in con-junction with a saying about the first and the last, but without the sort of exhortation to receive little children that occurs in 9:37. All of this adds force to the idea that our passage was not an original unity. Moreover, doublets and partial doublets to 9:34 and 9:35–37 occur in 10:14–16, 10:35–37, and 10:43–44 (see figure 29), and some of these suggest that our pericope is secondary. For example, Jesus' act of embracing a child fits better in 10:16, where it is coupled with a blessing, than it does in our pas-sage, where the staging is awkward: Jesus first sets the child in the midst of the circle of disciples, then picks him up and embraces him. As Taylor (406) points out, more-over, the saying in 9:37, which speaks of *receiving* children, would be more appropri-ate in 10:13–16, where children are blessed (and hence received), than it is in the present context, where no comparable act takes place. And the saying in 10:15, which is about receiving God's dominion with the humility of a child, would fit better in the present context, where the discussion revolves around the notion of precedence. (See figure 30 for a possible rearrangement of the elements of the two pericopes.) Hooker (228) suggests that these two sayings may have gotten reversed during the oral stage of the tradition, but she admits that it is also possible that the disruption is Mark's work, since the sayings fit what Mark is doing in the two passages.

Structurally, the passage in its present form has two subsections, the discussion of greatness in 9:33–35 and the exhortation to receive children in 9:36–37. After the scene-setting 9:33–34, each subsection consists of an action of Jesus followed by a pronouncement. Although the second pronouncement, 9:37, is considerably longer than the first, 9:35b, the first is more important. Indeed, the identification of humility as the path to greatness is the theme of much of the rest of 9:33–50, so that Fleddermann ("Discourse," 61) is exaggerating only slightly when he calls 9:35b "the topic sentence of the discourse."

9:33–35: the discussion of greatness. Following the tour of Galilee in which Jesus issues a second warning about his approaching death and resurrection (9:30–32), He returns with the disciples to Capernaum (9:33a), the home village of the first quartet of them (1:16–20) and the place where he performed his initial, programmatic healings (1:21–34). Given these earlier passages, "the house" that Jesus and the disciples enter (9:33b) is probably the Capernaum abode of Peter, where Jesus went right after commissioning him and the three others, and where he healed Peter's mother-in-law, who immediately got up and began serving them (*diēkonoun autois*, 1:29–31). This selfless act of *diakonia* offers an ironic and un-flattering counterpoint to the self-aggrandizing tendencies of Peter and the other disciples, which will be countered by Jesus' call to become a *diakonos* ("servant"; on this term, see the NOTE on "servant" in 9:35).

678

Figure 29: Parallels to Mark 9:33–37

Mark 9:33–34	Matthew 18:1	Luke 9:46	Gospel of Thomas 12
Jesus to disciples:	disciples to Jesus:	an argument arose among them	disciples to Jesus:
"What were you discussing on the way?"			
but they were silent			
			"We know that you will go away from us.
for they had been discussing with each other . . . who was the greatest	"Who is the greatest in the dominion of heaven?"	as to who was the greatest of them	Who is it that will then be great over us?"
			Jesus: "James the Just, for whose sake heaven and earth came into being"

Mark 9:35	Mark 10:43–44//Matthew 20:26–27	Luke 22:26	Matthew 23:11	Luke 9:48c
if anyone wants to be first	whoever wants to be great among you	the greater among you	the greater among you	
he shall be the last of all		let him become as the younger one		
and the servant of all	shall be your servant		shall be your servant	
	and whoever among you wants to be the first	and the ruler		the one who is lesser among all of you
	shall be the slave of all	as the one serving		this one is great

Mark 9:36	Mark 10:16
and taking a child	and embracing them

<h2 style="text-align:center">Figure 29: Parallels to Mark 9:33–37 (continued)</h2>

Mark 9:36	Mark 10:16
he set him in their midst	he blessed them
and embracing him, he said to them	laying his hands on them

Mark 9:37a	Mark 10:14–15	Matthew 18:5	Luke 9:48a
whoever receives one such child	let the children come to me . . . to such ones belongs the dominion of God	whoever receives one such child	whoever receives this child
	whoever does not receive the dominion of God like a child . . .		
in my name		in my name	in my name
receives me		receives me	receives me

Mark 9:37b	Luke 9:48b	Matthew 10:40	Luke 10:16
and whoever receives me	and whoever receives me	the one who receives me	the one who rejects me
does not receive me but the one who sent me	receives the one who sent me	receives the one who sent me	rejects the one who sent me

<h2 style="text-align:center">Figure 30: Rearrangement of Mark 9:33–37 and 10:13–16</h2>

9:34	10:14
they had been discussing with each other . . . who was the greatest	Jesus: "Let the children come to me! Don't forbid them!"
9:35	**10:16**
Jesus: "If anyone wants to be first, he shall be the last."	and he embraced them and blessed them
10:15	**9:37**
"Whoever does not receive the dominion of God like a child will never enter it."	"Whoever receives one such child in my name receives me."

Once they are in the house together, Jesus asks the Twelve what they have been discussing "on the way" (*en tę hodǭ*, 9:33c). This phrase is immediately repeated for effect in 9:34, where the narrator informs his readers that "on the way" the disciples had been discussing who among them was the greatest. This repetition of "on the way" is another instance of Markan irony; God's way, "the way of the Lord," which has been the Gospel's subject from its opening verses (1:1–3), and which is a particularly prominent theme in the present section of the Gospel (see the introduction to 8:22–10:52), is, as we shall immediately learn (9:35; cf. 10:41–45), a way of selfless service, of putting oneself last, in order that others may be benefited and God's triumph may be announced. The disciples, however, have chosen another way, a path of self-promotion, which is not the way of the Lord; their ways, then, are not God's ways, and their thoughts are distant from his (cf. 8:33; Isa 55:8–9).

The phrase "who was the greatest" is delayed, and it thereby comes to occupy the place of emphasis at the end of the chiastically-shaped pair of sentences in 9:33–34:

A   what (*ti*)
B   in the way
. C   were you discussing?
D   they were silent
C′   for among themselves they had been discussing
B′   in the way
A′   who (*tis*) was the greatest

This delay of the crucial clause underlines the irony that after Jesus' hard-hitting instruction about the necessity of following in the way of self-denial (8:34–38), the disciples have fallen into a senseless argument about their relative greatness. The theme of apostolic incomprehension, so prominent in this section of the Gospel (see 8:31–33; 9:6, 10, and cf. 8:14–21), continues. In the previous passage, the disciples misunderstood the necessity of Jesus' arrest, suffering, and resurrection (9:32), and here they mistake the way in which power is to be attained and exercised in the dominion of God (9:33–34). These two levels of confusion are related (cf. Phil 2:1–11): the failure to understand that glory comes through the type of service demonstrated in Jesus' selfless death for humanity (cf. 10:35–45) leads to grasping for the sort of domination that prevails in the world, where the central question always remains, "Who is the greatest?"

As Gnilka (2.56) points out, it is initially unclear what the temporal horizon of this question is, especially since there is no verb (see the NOTE on "who was the greatest" in 9:34): does it refer to relative greatness now, or to ranking in the eschatological future, as in the Matthean parallel (Matt 18:1) and the partial parallel later in Mark (10:35–37)? The future interpretation is supported by numerous Jewish passages in which those who suffer or abase themselves for God's sake in this life will be exalted in the next. In the Babylonian Talmud, for example, *b. B. Meṣ.* 85b uses imagery similar to ours (the great, the small, the servant) to speak of the eschatological rank of the faithful person, and in *b. B. Bat.* 10b Joseph, the son of R. Joshua, describes the world to come, which he has glimpsed in a near-death experience, as "an upside-down world—the high were low and the lowly were high" (my trans.).

But since the temporal horizon is not specified in our passage, the question may be not only who *will be* but also who *is* the greatest, and the passage may have been taken by Mark's readers as reflecting leadership problems within the contemporary world, including their own community. This sort of post-Easter perspective becomes even clearer in the *Gospel of Thomas* version of the discussion (logion 12), where the issue explicitly becomes who will rule the community after Jesus has departed. In Mark's mind, to be sure, this postresurrectional context is linked with the eschaton, since for him the post-Easter period is one in which the powers of the new age are already breaking in.

Although Mark does not explicitly say so, he implies that Jesus, by means of the supernatural insight he has so often displayed (2:5, 8; 3:4–5; 5:30; etc.), knows the topic of the disciples' covert discussion; confronted with their shamefaced silence (9:34b), he sits down, thus assuming the characteristic posture of the ancient teacher (see the NOTE on "sitting down" in 9:35), and launches into a discourse that engages precisely the issue they have been debating (9:35). Jesus does not condemn the disciples' desire to be preeminent, but takes it for granted; the issue is not so much whether one should want to be great as the manner in which true greatness is to be achieved. The answer Jesus proffers is that, in the upside-down logic of the dominion of God, the person who wants to become first must make him- or herself last of all and servant of all.

9:36–37: the Parable of the Child. Jesus follows this pronouncement with an enacted parable involving a child, who happens to be conveniently nearby (see the NOTE on "taking a child" in 9:36). This sort of symbolic action performed on a human subject is common in the OT, especially the Prophets, and in later Jewish literature; the most extreme example comes from the prophet Hosea, who turned his stormy relationship with his wife into a parable of the ups and downs of God's liaison with Israel. As in some OT parallels (e.g., Jer 1:11–12; Amos 8:2), the enacted parable in Mark turns on a paronomasia (see the GLOSSARY) or double entendre (*paidion* can mean either "slave" or "child") and transforms an object into a kind of narrative text (see Black, 221). In our specific case, Jesus' actions of taking the child into the middle of the circle of the disciples, picking him up, and hugging him (9:36) illustrate the servant-like attitude that he wishes to inculcate: anyone who receives a child "in my name" receives Jesus himself, and the one who receives Jesus receives the one who sent him (i.e., God). The Markan Jesus thereby applies both to his representatives and to himself a legal axiom that would later become well known among the rabbis: "A man's messenger is as the man himself" (see, e.g., *m. Ber.* 5:5 and *b. Qid.* 41b; Müller [*Anfänge*, 220–23] argues convincingly that the principle goes back to NT times).

But what exactly is meant by receiving "one such child" in Jesus' name? In the history of interpretation, two basic answers have been proffered: (1) the child is to be understood literally, and the disciples are being exhorted to receive children; and (2) he is to be understood symbolically, as a representative of Jesus' childlike followers, whom outsiders are exhorted to receive (see Müller, *Mitte*, 212–14). Of these two opinions, the second, "Christian" interpretation has been the more popular because it is supported by the doublet in 10:13–16 and the Matthean parallel in Matt 18:1–5. Five verses after ours, moreover, Jesus will speak of the "little ones who believe," and this will immediately follow a reference to his disciples (9:41–42). Strong as these cues are, however, the literal dimension is also suggested by the immediate context. The focus in our pericope is primarily on the child himself, as shown by Jesus' emphatic actions of picking him up, hugging him, and leading him into the circle of the disciples. In contrast to the doublet, Jesus does not speak here of the child as a model (contrast Matt 18:4: "whoever abases himself *like* this child"; my trans.) but as a concrete object of mercy ("whoever receives one such child"). It may be, then, that Mark has a combination of referents in mind; the child in the parable is meant to stand for other children who are to be "received," including Christian children.

But what sort of reception does Mark have in mind? As Müller (*Mitte*, 215–16) has shown, the verb used here, *dechesthai* ("to receive"), is often employed in early Christian contexts to speak of the extension of hospitality and support (see, e.g., Acts 18:27–28; 21:17; Gal 4:14; 2 Cor 7:15; Col 4:10; *Did.* 11:1–2; 12:1). But why would children need such hospitality? One possible answer is that infants were often exposed at birth (see Boswell, *Kindness*), and this practice was not limited to pagans, though it was probably rarer among Jews than among Gentiles (see Schwartz, "Infant Exposure"). Since *paidion* can designate an infant (see the NOTE on "taking a child" in 9:36), it is conceivable that part of the message of 9:36–37 is to take abandoned infants into one's family. It is also plausible that, in situations of persecution contemplated by Jesus or realized in early Christian communities, some children were deprived of their parents (cf. Pesch 2.107 and W. Stegemann, "Kinder," 129–30) or that parents who became wandering missionaries had to give up their children, at least temporarily (cf. 10:29). Certainly later Christians were known for their care and support for orphans, and there are many early Christian texts that exhort kindness to them, calling them "children of the church" and urging adults to "act the part of parents," that is, adopt them (see *Clementine Homilies* 3.71; *Epistle of Clement to James* 8; *Apostolic Constitutions* 4.1.1; Tertullian, *Apology* 39; J. Lightfoot, *Apostolic Fathers*, 2.2.304–5). These interpretations are in line with the overall flow of thought in our passage, since care of abandoned children is an example of the sort of humble, everyday service to others that Jesus has just called for (9:35) and that is the antithesis of the self-serving attitude that the disciples have just displayed (9:34).

This suggestion also makes sense of the transition to the final verse in the pericope, the equation of receiving children with receiving Jesus (9:37a). As in the Matthean Parable of the Sheep and the Goats, the person who fulfills the needs of one of his poor, helpless fellow creatures discovers that he has actually been serving Jesus. As Jesus puts it in that parable: "As you did it to one of the least of these brothers or sisters of mine, you did it to me" (Matt 25:40, 45; my trans.). Verse 9:37 thus continues the old motif, found in both pagan and Jewish literature, of the incognito hero or god. In some later Christian developments of this motif, Jesus wanders the earth disguised as a homeless vagabond, and people are judged by the compassion or indifference they show to him (see the NOTE on "receives me" in 9:37). Our verse may be meant in a similarly realistic manner: Jesus really *is* present, in some mysterious way, in the needy child who lands on the Christian's doorstep. The child in our passage, then, is not, as in 10:14–15, an example to be emulated, but a needy person to be served in concrete, nitty-gritty ways.

The conclusion of the passage extends the principle that receiving a child is receiving Jesus by adding that receiving Jesus is receiving the one who sent him, God (9:37b). This assertion may originally have functioned as an encouragement to practical hospitality, as in the *Mekilta* Amalek 3 (Lauterbach 2.178): "The person who receives his fellow, it is as if he had received the divine presence" (my trans.; cf. *y. Erub.* 5:1 [22b; Neusner 12.147] and Jeremias, *New Testament Theology*, 254). In view of Jesus' complaint in the Q saying Matt 8:20//Luke 9:58 that "foxes have holes, and the birds of the air have nests; but the Son of Man has nowhere to lay his head," it is even possible that the second part of 9:37 originally functioned as the itinerant Jesus' own plea for lodging and support: it is God himself knocking on the door when Jesus solicits a bed for the night.

In the context of Mark's Christology, however, the saying in 9:37b takes on larger dimensions. The one who receives Jesus receives not Jesus alone but God as well, a statement in line with the strong connection between these two figures from the very beginning of the Gospel. The way of Jesus the Messiah is the way of the Lord (1:1–3), and some of the healing stories have implied that where Jesus is acting, there God is powerfully present (2:7, 10; 5:19–20). The two stories of Jesus demonstrating his sovereignty over the unruly sea, moreover, have portrayed him in ways similar to the depiction of the God of the OT (see the COMMENTS on 4:37–39 and 6:48–50). A question may arise, however, as to how feeble humans can overcome their fear and come into personal contact with, or "receive," such an awesome figure (cf. John 6:21, "then *they were willing* to take him into the boat"; my trans.). Our passage provides the paradoxical answer: the godlike Jesus is received every time a Christian takes an abandoned child into his or her house, or performs a similar act of charity.

The observation in 9:37, then, supplies the definitive response to the small-minded striving after greatness that was the original catalyst for the passage (9:34). No greater distinction can be imagined than hosting God himself; in comparison with such a privilege, questions of relative superiority or inferiority in human society become laughably inconsequential. But the way to achieve this greatest of all honors is to serve the needy, those who cannot take care of themselves, in whom Christ and God himself lie mysteriously hidden.

In the next passage this principle of hidden divine action will be extended even further: God will be seen to act, not only through the most negligible members of the Christian community, but also through outsiders.

JESUS REJECTS THE EXCLUSION OF AN ALIEN EXORCIST (9:38–40)

9 ³⁸John said to him, "Teacher, we saw someone casting out demons in your name and we forbade him, because he did not follow us." ³⁹But Jesus said, "Don't forbid him, for there is no one who will do a work of power in my name and will be able to malign me soon. ⁴⁰For the one who is not against us is for us."

NOTES

9 38. *in your name.* Gk *en tǭ onomati sou.* Because of the ancient association of the name of a person or thing with its presence or power, "in the name of" can mean "in the power of" (see, e.g., 11:9; 13:13; cf. Ps 54:1; Acts 4:7) or "for the sake of" (see, e.g., 9:37, 41; cf. Bietenhard, "*Onoma*"). But in the present instance the reference is first and foremost to magical manipulation of the name in a literal sense: the would-be exorcist pronounces Jesus' name in order to bring his spiritual force to bear on demons.

because he did not follow us. Gk *hoti ouk ēkolouthei hēmin.* Does "did not follow us" imply that this exorcist is a non-Christian, or does it imply that he is a follower of Jesus outside the official circles represented by John, who later became one of the "pillars" of the Jerusalem church (cf. Gal 2:9), and by the Twelve? In favor of the former interpretation, the name of Jesus is frequently invoked in later pagan magical texts (see, e.g., *PGM* 3.420; 4.1233; 4.3020; 12.192; cf. Smith, *Jesus*, 63), and in Acts 19:13–17 it is used by the seven sons of Sceva, itinerant Jewish exorcists who are not believers. In favor of the latter interpretation, Matt 7:22–23 reveals that within Christian circles there could be doubts about certain Christian exorcists (see Kollmann, *Jesus*, 336). But the Markan Jesus says that the exorcist who has performed miracles in his name will not "be able to malign me soon," which suggests that he might otherwise be tempted to do so; he therefore does not seem to be a Christian but an outsider.

39. *Don't forbid him.* Gk *mē kōlyete auton.* Although the question has been raised by John, he seems to be acting as a spokesman for the Twelve, since Jesus replies with a second person plural (*kōlyete*).

In Num 11:24–30, Joshua, Moses' "elect" disciple, calls on Moses to forbid (*kōlyson*) Eldad and Medad, who were not present at the impartation of the Spirit to the seventy elders, from prophesying. These elders, like the Markan band of Twelve, are a commissioned group who have been granted particular spiritual power (cf. Mark 3:13–14), and Moses rebuffs his disciple's elitist suggestion with words that could easily be put into the Markan Jesus' mouth: "Are you jealous on my account?" As Garrett (*Demise*, 134 n. 44) points out, Luke seems to recognize that the Eldad and Medad story underlies Mark 9:38–40, since his parallel, Luke 9:49–50, is almost immediately followed by the account of the mission of the *seventy* (Luke 10:1).

a work of power in my name and will be able. Gk *dynamin epi tǭ onomati mou kai dynēsetai.* There is a Greek pun here that is difficult to reproduce in English, since the noun "work of power," *dynamis,* and the verb "to be able," *dynasthai,* are cognates.

40. *For the one who is not against us is for us.* Gk *hos gar ouk estin kath' hēmōn, hyper hēmōn estin.* Some manuscripts, including Alexandrinus, Bezae, some Latin witnesses, and some Syriac and Bohairic texts, read *hymōn* ("you" [pl.]) rather than *hēmōn.* Wellhausen (76) prefers this reading as more consonant with the rest of the passage, which concerns the man's alienation from the disciples rather than from Jesus. For this very reason, however, "against us . . . for us" is the more difficult reading, and its attestation is so strong (‫א‬, B, C, W, etc., *f*[1 13], sy[s], co, etc.) that it is probably original; "against you . . . for you" is probably a scribal amelioration.

COMMENT

Introduction. After responding to his disciples' dispute about greatness by calling on them to receive children and thus to follow along his path of humility, Jesus takes up another apostolic question that flows from a similar spiritual malady, the desire to restrict the exorcistic use of Jesus' name to an in-group that follows "us."

With respect to redactional features, Mark, as noted in the introduction to 9:33–50, is probably responsible for the insertion of the pericope into its present position. Aside from this, it is hard to identify Markan editorial activity. "Teacher" (*didaskalos*), along with the cognate verb "to teach" (*didaskein*), is one of the evangelist's preferred terms for Jesus, but it also fits the story well, so it may be original. A better candidate for redactional intervention is the verb *dynasthai* ("to be able") in 9:39, since this is one of Mark's favorite verbs (33 usages in Mark, as opposed to 27 in Mathew and 26 in Luke) and is often redactional. In 3:22–27, moreover, this verb seems to have been introduced redactionally into a passage that, like ours, deals with exorcism (see the introduction to the COMMENT on 3:20–35).

The pericope falls into three sections: (1) John's report to Jesus about the way in which he and the other disciples have dealt with the alien exorcist (9:38), (2) Jesus' rejection of this approach (9:39), and (3) Jesus' enunciation of a general principle with respect to treatment of outsiders (9:40). The alternation of personal pronouns to refer to Jesus on the one hand and the disciples on the other is revealing. The disciples begin by associating themselves with Jesus, recounting to him their assumption of the authority to prevent an outsider from using his name ("because he did not follow *us*"). Jesus seems at first to distance himself from their presumption of a linkage with him, addressing them in the second person plural and implying that he disapproves of what they have done ("Don't [*you*] forbid them"). At the end, however, he reforges the link with them through a renewed use of the first person plural ("For the one who is not against *us* is for *us*").

9:38–40: the case of the alien exorcist. The pericope begins with John the son of Zebedee, a member of the inner circle of three disciples (see the NOTE on "James the son of Zebedee and his brother John" in 1:19), bringing up a problem, the actions of a healer who is not one of "us" but nevertheless uses Jesus' name to perform exorcisms. It is uncertain whether this story reflects an episode in the life of the historical Jesus or is a product of the theology of the early church. In favor of the latter, the formula "because he did not follow *us*" (rather than "because he did not follow *you*," which might be more appropriate in Jesus' lifetime) may reflect the post-Easter period, in which Jesus' authority was being mediated by the representatives he had left behind on earth (cf. Hooker, 229). In favor of the former, the pericope's openness to outsiders, including non-Christian exorcists, contrasts with the restrictive attitude of the later church (see, e.g., Acts 19:13–17; Justin, *1 Apol.* 54–58; Augustine, *City of God* 10.16; 22.10) but coheres with the probably authentic saying in Matt 12:27//Luke 11:19 (cf. Marcus, "Beelzebul," 270–71).

In any case, whether the question first arose in the lifetime of Jesus or in the early church, the Markan Jesus rejects the exclusionary attitude propounded by John, observing that people such as the alien exorcist who work wonders in Jesus' name will not subsequently find it easy to malign him (9:39b). This remark seems to make the apocalyptic assumption that the normal situation in "the present evil age" (cf. Gal 1:4) is that humanity opposes God's will and disparages its agents (cf. Mark 13:13; Acts 28:22). But Jesus' response also implies that a force has been released into the world that will ultimately prove to be more potent than the age's inbuilt inclination to slander—the power of Jesus' name itself (on the linkage between name and power, see the NOTE on "in your name" in 9:38). Because of this power, even those who start out manipulating Jesus' name for their own purposes may unexpectedly find themselves being drawn into its sphere of influence; the same eschatological *dynamis* that was manifested in the exorcism through speaking the name will tame the tongue that uttered it.

Such exceptions to the general disparagement of Jesus and the Christians are to be welcomed and encouraged because, as Jesus says in the proverb that concludes the passage, "The one who is not against us is for us" (9:40). A late-third- or early-fourth-century papyrus, *P.Oxy.* 1224, which may be a fragment of an apocryphal Gospel, adds the explanation that "the one who is far away today, tomorrow will be close to you" (trans. A. Bernhard, "Papyrus"). According to this interpretation, Mark 9:40 is not so much a statement about the present as a prophecy of the future (cf. Bovon, *Lukas*, 1.315). Yet, as we saw in the treatment of the proverb in 9:35, there is also a sense in which the hoped-for eschatological reversal has already become a part of the community's experience (see the COMMENT on 9:33–35). Mark, then, not only dreams that those who are neutral about the Christian mission will one day join it; he also discerns in their departure from the prevailing hostility a sign that God is already at work in them.

In saying that "the one who is not against us is for us," the Markan Jesus makes use of a proverbial saying that can be expressed either positively, as here, or negatively, as in the Q logion Matt 12:30//Luke 11:23, "The one who is not with me is against me" (NRSV alt.). Both forms are paralleled in Cicero, *Ligario* 33: "We hold all those to be enemies who are not with us, whereas you view all those who are not against you as belonging to your side." It is somewhat surprising that Mark chooses the positive form, since elsewhere in his Gospel he expresses a sectarian "us-against-them" attitude that would seem to be more compatible with the negative formulation; in 4:11–12, for example, the disciples are designated recipients of a mystery that is deliberately withheld from outsiders (cf. Hooker, 229). But the outsiders in 4:11 are linked with the scribes of 3:22–30, since the scribes are associated with Jesus' family (3:21–22), and the latter are described as "standing outside" (3:31–32). These scribes blaspheme against the Holy Spirit by attributing Jesus' exorcisms to Beelzebul. By contrast, the alien exorcist in 9:38–40 is incapable of maligning Jesus and presumably has a positive attitude toward exorcisms worked in his name. For Mark, then, Christian exorcism seems to be a make-or-break issue, and one's attitude toward it comes close to defining whether one is inside or outside the dominion of God.

That dominion (*basileia*) has both "already" and "not yet" elements (see the subject index in vols. 1 & 2 under "Dominion of God"), and this paradoxical combination also contributes to the seemingly contradictory Markan attitude toward outsiders. The full public manifestation of the *basileia* has not yet come, and until it does, blind hostility toward Jesus and his disciples will prevail among "those outside." Yet the *basileia* is already secretly and powerfully at work in the world, as can be seen in the miracle that some people are departing from the general animus. The same mixture of apocalyptic pessimism and apocalyptic optimism will later lead the Markan Jesus both to prophesy that near-universal hatred will be directed against his followers (13:9, 11–13) and to call them, in a redactional insertion, to extend their mission to the whole world (13:10).

Despite the optimistic tone of our pericope's conclusion, the Markan hearers are constantly reminded that adherence to Jesus may lead to suffering, betrayal, and death. As Jesus will emphasize in the next passage, however, an even more terrible fate awaits those who turn their backs on the divine redemption of the world.

JESUS TALKS ABOUT REWARD AND PUNISHMENT IN THE AFTERLIFE (9:41–50)

9 [41]"For whoever gives you a cup of water to drink in the name, because you belong to Christ, amen, I say to you, that one will by no means lose his reward. [42]And whoever offends one of these little ones who believe, it would be better for him to have a millstone hung around his neck and for him to be cast into the sea. [43]And if your hand offends you, cut it off—it is better to enter life maimed than to have two hands and go away to Gehenna, to the fire that cannot be put out. [45]And if your foot offends you, cut it off—it is better to enter life lame than to have two feet and be cast into Gehenna. [47]And if your eye offends you, cast it out—it is better to enter the dominion of God one-eyed than to have two eyes and be cast into Gehenna, [48]where their worm does not die and the fire is not put out. [49]For everyone will be salted with fire. [50]Salt is good; but if the salt becomes unsalty, what will you salt it with? Have salt in yourselves and be at peace with each other."

NOTES

9 41. *For whoever gives you a cup of water to drink,* etc. Gk *hos gar an potisę̄ hymas potērion hydatos,* etc. The word for "cup," *potērion,* and the word for "to drink," *potisę̄,* are cognates.

Many exegetes include this verse in the previous passage (9:38–40), since the saying about giving a cup of water to disciples seems to extend the thought of 9:40 that "the one who is not against us is for us." There are good reasons, however, for thinking that 9:41 begins a new unit rather than ending an old one. It is easy to interpret "the one who is not against us is for us" as a response to the problem posed by the alien exorcist (9:38), whereas the saying about giving a cup of water to a disciple seems to have little relevance to that problem. The saying about the cup of water, moreover, introduces the theme of eschatological reward and loss, which dominates the following subsection (9:41–50).

in the name, because you belong to Christ. Gk *en onomati hoti Christou este.* Because of the context, *onomati* ("in the name") is definite despite the lack of a definite article, which is not required when the noun is the object of a preposition (see, e.g., *ap᾽ agoras* ["from the marketplace"] in 7:4 and *en archę̄* ["in the beginning"] in John 1:1; cf. BDF §255). The awkward "in the name, because you belong to Christ" might be the result of a dittography (see the GLOSSARY) in an Aramaic original that meant simply "in the name of Christ"; the Peshitta for "because . . . belong to Christ" is *dĕdamĕšîḥâ᾽,* which begins with two dalaths. But more likely "because you belong to Christ" is a gloss by Mark or a later scribe to explain the ambiguous phrase "in the name," which might be a reference either to the name of the disciple (cf. Matt 10:42) or to the name of Christ (cf. Acts 5:41; 3 John 7; Ignatius, *Ephesians* 3:1).

reward. Gk *misthon.* This term literally means a financial recompense for services rendered and can be translated "wages" (see, e.g., Jas 5:4; Matt 20:8; John 4:36). In several NT passages it is understood metaphorically as the reward of eschatological blessing that the objects of God's grace will receive for their labors and sufferings in this life (see, e.g., Matt 5:12//Luke 6:23; Luke 6:35; 1 Cor 3:14; 2 John 8; Rev 11:18; 22:12), and this eschatological usage reflects a Jewish prototype (see Wis 5:15; 4 *Ezra* 7:83; 13:56; *m. Abot* 2:1–2, 14–16; 5:1). In some of these NT "reward" passages, as in Mark 9:41–42, a statement about God's future reward for the righteous is immediately followed by one about his future punishment of the wicked (see Luke 6:23–26; Col 3:23–25; Rev 11:18; the last, like Mark 9:41, links the concept of reward with that of the name of God or Christ). Wisdom of Solomon 5:15–23 suggests that this eschatological reward/punishment pattern, which is a form of the Two Ways motif (see the COMMENT on 9:41–42), also goes back to a Jewish prototype.

42. *offends.* Gk *skandalisę̄.* On this verb, see the NOTE on "fall away" in 4:17. Deming ("Discussion," 134) notes that prior to the NT it occurs only in translations of Semitic texts.

little ones. Gk *mikrōn.* Does this refer to literal children, as Bultmann (144–45) thinks, or to Christians as God's "little ones"? Jesus makes a child the subject of a symbolic action in 9:35–37, and this action may be meant as an exhortation to adopt literal children (see the COMMENT on 9:36–37), so one might be inclined to think that "little ones" in 9:42 is also a reference to children. But verses 9:38–41 intervene, and the immediately preceding verse, 9:41, concerns outsiders' treatment of the Twelve ("whoever gives *you* a cup of water"), who are adult Christians; for Mark, then, "little ones" is probably a term for the Christian community (cf. Matt 10:40–42; 18:6–14; Luke 9:48; 17:2; cf. Müller, *Mitte*, 261–69). This interpretation is supported by the fact that in the OT/Jewish tradition, "little ones" can be a term for the people of God in their weakness, apparent insignificance, and subjection to suffering and abuse (see, e.g., Zech 13:7; *2 Apoc. Bar.* 48:19; cf. 1 Sam 9:21; Isa 60:22). The usage of *mikroi* in Zech 13:7 is particularly relevant, since the Markan Jesus cites this verse in 14:27 to refer to his followers' fate, and elsewhere in the Synoptic tradition he alludes to it in calling them a "little flock" (Luke 12:32; see Marshall, *Luke*, 530). There is an analogy in the Qumran (see the GLOSSARY) community's designation of itself as "the poor ones" (1QpHab 12:3, 6, 10; 4QpPs37 2:10; 1QM 11:9).

who believe. Gk *tōn pisteuontōn.* These words are probably a Markan addition (see the introduction to the COMMENT). Good ancient manuscripts (e.g., A, B, L, W) add *eis eme* ("in me"), but this phrase is missing from ℵ, C*, D, Δ, and it is easier to explain scribal insertion (as an assimilation to Matt 18:6 and a clarification that believers *in Christ* are meant) than it is to explain scribal deletion.

better. Gk *kalon*, lit. "good." This is probably a Semitism; Semitic languages lack the comparative form and therefore use the positive for the comparative (see BDF §245 and MHT, 31–32).

millstone. Gk *mylos onikos*, lit. "millstone of a donkey," that is, not the stone from a small hand-mill worked by a human being ("the millstone of a man") but a large, heavy one turned by donkey power (see BDAG 661[2] and van der Toorn, "Mill"). A millstone around the neck was a proverbial symbol for suffering or difficulty then as now (see, e.g., *b. Qid.* 29b and cf. *b. Sanh.* 93b), and Rev 18:21 uses the image of plunging a millstone into the sea as a symbol for irrevocable loss. The Jesus tradition, however, seems to be the first place where the symbol of the millstone around the neck is fused with that of one cast into the sea (see Davies and Allison, 2.763).

43. *hand.* Gk *cheir.* The hand is associated with sexuality and sexual sin (see, e.g., Isa 57:8; Song 5:4; *m. Nid.* 2:1; *b. Nid.* 13b) and can be a euphemism for the penis (Isa 57:8; Song 5:4?; 1QS 7:13; cf. Pope, "Euphemism," 720–21; Charlesworth, *Rule*, 33); *m. Nid.* 2:1, moreover, suggests that amputation of the hand is an appropriate penalty for masturbation (cf. Gundry, 524). But, to paraphrase Freud, sometimes a hand is just a hand, and in the Bible the term is usually taken literally. The hand is the basic corporeal instrument for accomplishing one's purposes (Exod 19:13; Deut 28:12; Eccl 2:11; 9:10; Pss 28:4; 90:17, etc.), and *1 Enoch* 100:9 links the works of evildoers' hands in this sense with the threat that they will burn in fire: "Woe to all you, sinners . . . on account of the works of your hands . . . You shall burn in a blazing fire" (Black trans.).

cut it off. Gk *apokopson autēn.* How literally are hearers meant to take these injunctions to amputate the offending hand or foot and to pluck out the offending eye? In favor of a literal interpretation, Zager (*Gottesherrschaft*, 214–15) points out that the OT calls for the amputation of the hand of a woman who grabs a man's testicles (Deut 25:11–12) and that it implies the amputation of hand and foot and the plucking out of eyes in the three "eye for eye" passages (Exod 21:23–25; Lev 24:20; Deut 19:21). *Mishnah Niddah* 2:1 also speaks of amputating an offending hand, and in *b. Nid.* 13b a rabbi justifies this penalty with a formula strikingly close to the one in Mark: "It is preferable [that his hand should be cut off and] that his belly should be split than that that he should go down into the pit of destruction" (Soncino trans. alt.). In a similarly literal vein, Philo commends people who bite off their tongues rather than divulge secrets to their torturers (*The Worse Attacks the Better* 176).

Elsewhere in the Jewish tradition, however, the OT amputation penalties are often interpreted as symbols rather than literal commands. In *Special Laws* 3.179, for example, Philo offers a symbolic interpretation of the hand amputation penalty in Deut 25:11–12, and most rabbis evince a similar tendency to interpret "eye for eye, tooth for tooth, hand for hand, foot for foot" in an allegorical manner, specifically as a reference to financial compensation (see, e.g., *b. B. Qam.* 83b–84a). Similarly, while R. Tarfon takes "let it be cut off" in *m. Nid.* 2:1 literally, other rabbis affirm that it should be treated as an execration rather than a law (*b. Nid.* 13b). As Zager (217–18) observes, moreover, the rhetoric of Mark 9:43–47 itself suggests that the injunctions to self-amputation are not meant literally; only one of each paired member, for example, is to be amputated, although both were probably involved in the sin. All in all, it seems probable that most of Mark's readers would have interpreted the imperatives in 9:43–47 in a nonliteral manner.

⁴*to enter life maimed.* Gk *kyllon eiselthein eis tēn zōēn.* The presupposition seems to be that the dead will be resurrected with the same sort of bodily defects, such as lameness or blindness, that afflicted them during their lifetime; see 2 *Apoc. Bar.* 50:2; *b. Sanh.* 91b; *Tanḥuma* (Buber) Wayyigash 11.9 (Townsend, 1.279); and *Eccl. Rab.* 1.6 [1.4.2], which bases this theory on Eccl 1:4: "As a generation goes [= dies], so it comes [= is resurrected]" (cf. Moore, 2.380–81; Davies and Allison, 1.525). These rabbinic traditions go on to affirm that immediately after their resurrection, the disabled will be healed of their disabilities, and the same assumption may underlie our passage: the lame or blind will *enter* eternal life maimed, but they will not *remain* in that condition (cf. Allison, *Jesus,* 140).

Gehenna. Gk *tēn Geennan.* This, the most common name for the place of eternal punishment in ancient Judaism and early Christianity, comes from the Hebrew *gê-ḥinnōm* and the Aramaic *gêhinnām,* both of which mean "the Valley of Hinnom," a depression running south-southwest of the Old City of Jerusalem. Here the Israelites, according to the OT, engaged in idolatrous worship of the Canaanite God Molech, sacrificing their children to him by fire (2 Kgs 23:10; Jer 7:31; 32:35; cf. 2 Kgs 16:3; 21:6). Because of these sacrifices, the valley may have been viewed as the gate of the underworld. The prophet Jeremiah denounces the sacrifices but continues to associate the valley with death and judgment, saying that the dead bodies of the wicked killed by the Babylonians will be cast into it (Jer 7:30–34; 19:6–9), and Isa 30:33 threatens Molech himself with fiery judgment in it. These associations with death, judgment, and fire contributed to the later Jewish conception of Gehenna as a place of eternal postmortem punishment in fire (see, e.g., *Sib. Or.* 1.100–103; 2.283–312; *4 Ezra* 7:36; *b. Roš Haš.* 16b–17a). The term eventually became independent of its localization in the Hinnom Valley; *4 Ezra* 7:36, for example, places it opposite the Garden of Eden (see further Bernstein, *Formation*, passim, and Watson, "Gehenna").

44. Many manuscripts add "where their worm does not die and the fire is not put out" here and in 9:46, but the clause is omitted in important early texts (‭א‬, B, C, W, and various versions) and is probably a scribal assimilation to 9:48 designed to increase the rhetorical power of the passage. If, on the contrary, the clause had been original and had been omitted by accident, this mishap would have had to happen, improbably, twice. It is equally hard to postulate a theological motive for excision, since a scribe opposed to the idea of hellfire would presumably have deleted 9:48 as well.

45. *foot.* Gk *pous.* Deming ("Discussion"), followed by Gundry (524) and Allison (*Jesus*, 178–82), argues that "foot" is a euphemism for the penis. The plural form "feet" may denote male genitalia in some OT passages (e.g., Exod 4:25; Judg 3:24; Ruth 3:7; 1 Sam 24:3; 2 Sam 11:8; Isa 6:2; cf. Pope, "Euphemism," 721), and it is possible that the singular "foot" has the same nuance in Tob 6:3 (see C. Moore, *Tobit*, 199). A double entendre may also be present in Job 31:1–12, where Job protests that he has neither let his *eyes* wander after a virgin nor turned his *foot* to deceit. This passage is similar to Mark 9:45–48 not only in linking sins of the foot with sins of the eye (cf. 1QS 1:6, which speaks of *walking* after *eyes* of fornication) but also in describing the consequence of these sins as "a *fire* consuming down to *Abaddon*" (a synonym for Gehenna). These nuances were sometimes picked up by later commentators; see, for example, the interpretation of Exod 4:25 in *y. Ned.* 3:9 (38b; Neusner, 23.70), where the opinion that Zipporah touched the feet of the child is interpreted as meaning that she touched his body (i.e., his penis). See also the reuse of Isa 6:2 in Ezek 1:11 and the Targum on both passages. But as both Job 31 and 1QS 1 illustrate, the more usual and direct connection of "foot" is with the biblical metaphor of walking; the feet are the means of transport to the place where sins are committed (cf. Weiss, "*Pous*," 628).

be cast into Gehenna. Gk *blēthēnai eis tēn Geennan.* On the image of being cast into Gehenna, cf. *1 Enoch* 54:1–6; 90:25; 91:9; 98:3 v.l.; *2 Enoch* 63:4; Luke 3:9 = Matt 3:10 (attributed to John the Baptist); Rev 19:20; 20:3, 10, 14–15. As these citations reveal, this violent image is rooted in apocalyptic ideas. Many manuscripts (e.g., *l*[70], A, D, K) add "of fire" or "into the fire that cannot be put out," but the shorter reading is decisively supported by an impressive range of texts (‭א‬, B, C, L, W, etc.; see Metzger, 102). Some texts also add a repetition of 9:48 here; cf. the NOTE on 9:44.

47. *eye.* Gk *ophthalmos.* The eye is especially associated with sexual sins (e.g., Gen 39:7; Sir 9:5, 8; 1QS 1:6; Matt 5:28), but it can also be linked with pride, envy, avarice, and other transgressions that, like lust, have more to do with attitude and

proclivity than with overt action (see, e.g., Isa 5:15; Eccl 4:8; Matt 20:15; Brown, Epistles, 311).

48. *where their worm does not die and the fire is not put out*. Gk *hopou ho skōlēx autōn ou teleutą kai to pyr ou sbennytai*, a formulation close to that in Isa 66:24. The worms, presumably, are eating the bodies of their victims. Dale Allison points out the similarity of this picture of eternal torment to that in the Greek myth about Prometheus, who was chained to a rock and had his liver devoured by an eagle. At night the liver would be restored, and the next day the eagle would devour it all over again. It is probably just coincidental, however, that Prometheus was being punished for giving humanity the gift of *fire*.

49. *For everyone will be salted with fire*. Gk *pas gar pyri halisthēsetai*. Leviticus 2:13 ("and every sacrifice will be salted with salt," my trans.) is probably in the background here, a fact recognized by scribes who have either added the quotation to the words under discussion (D and various Old Latin mss.) or substituted it for them (A, K, Π, etc.; cf. Metzger, 102–3). It is natural to associate the salted sacrifices of Lev 2:13 with fire, since the context of the OT passage speaks of an offering that is engulfed in flames (Lev 2:9–10; cf. Ezek 43:24). The redundancy of the phrase "salted with salt" in Lev 2:13 apparently bothered some ancient Jewish exegetes (see, e.g., *b. Men.* 21a), and one method of eliminating this redundancy was to distinguish a salting with salt from a salting with fire. It is also perhaps relevant that in *b. Men.* 21a, Lev 2:13 is interpreted as a reference to "the salt of Sodom," a term for salt from the Dead Sea, near the site of the biblical Sodom. This salt was probably associated in the popular mind with the OT scene of judgment on Sodom, in which *fire* rained down from heaven and Lot's wife was turned into a pillar of *salt* (Gen 19:24–26; cf. Deut 29:23, in which cursed land becomes like Sodom and Gomorrah, with "all its soil *burned* out by sulfur and *salt*"). Salt of Sodom, then, may have been thought of as a particularly "fiery" salt. In *t. Men.* 9:15 this salt is termed "salt of conflict," an epithet that contrasts strikingly with Mark 9:50c, where salt is a symbol for peace (see the NOTES on "Have salt in yourselves" and "be at peace with each other" in 9:50).

50. *Salt is good*, etc. Gk *kalon to halas*, etc. Latham (*Symbolism*, 131–32, 163, 237) points to an ingenious ancient exegesis that connects this affirmation with the previous context: since salt kills worms, the salt referred to in our verse is the antidote to the undying worm of 9:48 (Methodius, *Banquet of the Ten Virgins*, Oration 1)!

but if the salt becomes unsalty, what will you salt it with? Gk *ean de to halas analon genētai en tini auto artysete*. The same saying occurs in *b. Bek.* 8b, and some scholars (e.g., Hauck, "*Halas*") have seen this Talmudic passage as a mockery of Jesus' teaching. Nothing in the context, however, suggests a polemical reading, and the Jesus tradition and the Talmud passage may both be recycling a common proverb (cf. Job 6:6 and see Noack, "Salt," 174; Davies and Allison, 1.474 n. 7). Diogenes Laertius (*Lives of Eminent Philosophers* 4.67) reports that Timon, a third-century B.C.E. Skeptical philosopher, derided the speech of the Academics as *analistos* = "without salt," that is, foolish; on salt as a symbol for wisdom, see the next NOTE.

Salt cannot actually lose its salinity, and some exegetes have therefore suggested that the reference is to a Dead Sea admixture containing substances such as carnallite that leave a stale taste once the pure salt had been dissolved away (see Jeremias, *Parables*, 168–69; Marshall, *Luke*, 596; and on Dead Sea salt, cf. the NOTE on "For everyone will be salted with fire" in 9:49). But the scientific facts are beside the point; "unsalty salt" is a striking figure for worthlessness.

Have salt in yourselves. Gk *echete en heautois hala.* As MHT (3.43–44) points out, our verse preserves the classical distinction between *heautoi* and *allēloi*: the former refers to oneself, the latter to others.

Salt here seems to represent an internal quality, and it is therefore relevant that salt is often associated with wisdom in ancient texts. The plural Greek form *hales*, like the Latin plural form *sales*, can denote wit (see, e.g., Plutarch, *Moralia* 514EF), and the singular occasionally has the same significance (see, e.g., Cicero, *On the Orator* 1.34.159; cf. LSJ 73 [IV] and Lightfoot, *Colossians*, 232–33). Correspondingly, "salty" in Jewish texts can mean wise or bright, as in *b. Qidd.* 29b: "If his son is eager to learn and bright" (*mĕmûllah*, lit. "salted" [trans. from Jastrow, 788]; cf. the comparison of the Torah to salt in *Soperim* 15:8). On the other side, *tāpel* and *sĕrê*, which mean "unseasoned" or "tasteless" and correspond to Mark's *analon* ("unsalty"), can be synonyms for "foolish" or "dull," like the English "insipid" (see, e.g., Lam 2:14 and *Tg. Qoh.* 10:1; cf. Noack, "Salt," 175–76; Jeremias, *Parables*, 168). This sapiential interpretation of salt is confirmed by the Q form of our passage (Matt 5:13//Luke 14:34), which uses the awkward locution "if the salt becomes foolish" (*ean to halas mōranthē*). A similar nuance is apparent in Col 4:5–6, where "Let your speech always be . . . seasoned with salt" is equivalent to "Conduct yourselves wisely toward outsiders" (see Evans, *Luke*, 580). Later church tradition continues the sapiential trajectory of exegesis (see, e.g., Ephrem, *Hymns on the Nativity* 15:10, and cf. Latham, *Symbolism*, 106–7, 136).

be at peace with each other. Gk *eirēneuete en allēlois.* Cf. 1 Thess 5:13, "Be at peace among yourselves" (*en heautois*), which Furnish (*Theology*, 54) terms "impressively close" to Mark 9:50 and sees as a Pauline allusion to Jesus' saying. From its tie with meals in general and with sacrifices in particular (see the NOTE on "For everyone will be salted with fire" in 9:49), salt became associated with conviviality and fellowship; a "covenant of salt," for example, is a pledge of perpetual goodwill between God and humans (see Num 18:19 and 2 Chron 13:5), and Philo speaks of "the board and salt which people have devised as the symbols of true friendship" (*On Joseph* 210 [Loeb. trans. alt.]; cf. *Special Laws* 3.96; *On Rewards and Punishments* 154; Ezra 4:14; Latham, *Symbolism*, 50–63). In Acts 1:4 the word for Jesus' sharing a meal with the disciples is *synalizomenos*, which literally means "taking salt together."

COMMENT

Introduction. After the passage about the alien exorcist (9:38–40), which ends with a warning against *premature* judgment, the Markan Jesus moves on to a series of sayings on the *final* judgment—the most extended Markan discourse on that theme. Judgment is an emotional subject, and it seems to have agitated later Christian scribes, who frequently augmented and intensified the already-passionate language of the text (see the NOTES on 9:44 and "be cast into Gehenna" in 9:45).

Although judgment is the overriding theme of the section, that generalization does not apply to the final saying about having salt in oneself and peace with one's neighbors (9:50c), which may have been tacked on to the end of the pre-Markan unit in 9:33–50 by the evangelist himself (see the introduction to 9:33–50). It is difficult to know whether 9:41 belonged to this pre-Markan unit, which seems at least to have lacked the intrusive 9:38–40 (see again the introduction to 9:33–50); 9:41 connects smoothly with 9:37, but so does 9:42. Perhaps 9:41 is secondary, but was already introduced at a pre-Markan stage of development. Another possibly redactional feature is the *hoti* clause in 9:41a ("because you belong to Christ"), which appears to be an attempt to explain the unclear preceding phrase about giving disciples a cup of water "in the name" (see the NOTE on "in the name, because you belong to Christ" in 9:41). In the following verse, the qualification of "these little ones" as those "who believe," like the *hoti* clause in 9:41, makes the Christian referent unmistakable and is also possibly Markan; it is missing in the Q form preserved in Luke 17:2 and reflects the Gospel's stress on faith (cf. 2:5; 4:40; 5:34; 9:23–24; 10:52; 11:22–23; 15:32, most of which are probably redactional).

Despite the fact that the material here is basically organized by catchword, it is possible to discern a loose structure. Each of the two sayings in 9:41–42 is introduced by "whoever" (*hos an*), and the two present contrasting ways of treating Christians, along with their corresponding eschatological rewards. Each of the three sayings in 9:43–48 is introduced by "and if" and describes an offense of a body part and the amputation this offense necessitates. Finally, 9:49–50 is introduced by "everyone" and presents three sayings about salt.

9:41–42: two ways of responding to Christians. The principle that "the one who is not against us is for us" (9:40) is now trumped by the case of a person who is not only not hostile to Christians but actively supports them, albeit with a simple cup of water (9:41); a missionary situation like that described in 6:7–10, in which wandering Christians are dependent on the kindness of strangers, is probably in view. This example of support is followed by a portrayal of the opposite sort of treatment, the case of the person who offends one of the "little ones" (9:42). The beginning of our passage, then, is an instance of the widespread ancient motif of the Two Ways, which is found in the OT (e.g., Deut 30:19; Ps 1:1–6), early Judaism (e.g., 1QS 3:18–4:26; *1 Enoch* 94:1–11; *T. Asher* 1:3–5), and nascent Christianity (e.g., Matt 7:13–14//Luke 13:23–24; *Did.* 1–5; *Barn.* 18–20), as well as in the larger Greco-Roman world (e.g., Xenophon, *Memorabilia* 2.1.21–34; cf. Niederwimmer, *Didache*, 59–63). As is usual in appearances of this motif, the "way of life" is set forth first, with its eschatological reward held out as an enticement (9:41), followed by a description of the "way of death" and its eschatological punishment as a warning (9:42; cf. the NOTE on "reward" in 9:41).

In our passage both "ways" have to do with the manner in which outsiders respond to members of the Christian community. The good way, the way of life, is to succor the members of that community; those who do so will not fail to obtain an eschatological reward (cf. the NOTE on "reward" in 9:41). This pledge is a testimony to the beleaguered position of some early Christians: for an outsider to act charitably toward them is apparently such a rare event that it merits special mention and the promise of end-time recompense. This sort of attitude would make most sense in a life setting in which Christians were persecuted and therefore small acts of human kindness toward them required courage (cf. Brown, *Death*, 1.289–90, for later situations in which Christians were proscribed and harboring them was a crime).

◁Tiny actions in the present age, then, will have momentous consequences when the mustard seed of God's dominion has burst into bloom (cf. 4:30–32), and this is good news for those who have followed the hard and narrow pathway that leads to life (cf. Matt 7:14) by showing compassion to Christ's ambassadors on earth. It is bad news, however, for those who have pursued the broad highway that leads to death (cf. Matt 7:13) by offending "these little ones who believe" (9:42), which in context seems to be a reference to Christians, perhaps again Christian missionaries. Offenses against such "little ones" will meet with a recompense so terrible that a horrifying death would be preferable. Later in the Gospel, the Markan Jesus will render against Judas a similarly structured verdict ("it would be better" + reference to nonexistence or death: 14:21), and this example may illuminate the life setting of the threat against offenders in 9:42, since the scenario of Judas-like betrayal to death is probably familiar to the persecuted Markan community (see 13:12–13). Van Iersel ("Persecuted," 26–27) aptly compares the reward/punishment scheme in our passage to that in the martyr stories in 4 Maccabees 9, where one of the martyrs denounces his torturer in these terms:

> For we, through this severe suffering and endurance, shall have the prize of virtue and shall be with God, on whose account we suffer; but you, because of your bloodthirstiness toward us, will deservedly undergo from the divine justice eternal torment by fire. (4 Macc 9:8–9; cf. 2 Macc 7)

Here, as in our passage, a description of the reward of the righteous is followed by a reference to the terrible fate of the wicked, and the continuation of both passages describes the latter fate as eternal punishment by fire. The violent imagery of Mark 9:42, then, may reflect the extremity of the situation in which the members of the Markan community and their Christian forebears have found themselves. It is even possible that the "millstone around the neck" punishment with which persecutors are threatened is an eschatological *lex talionis* (see the GLOSSARY) for the similar treatment meted out to Christians (see Suetonius, *Augustus* 67 for this method of execution, and *1 Enoch* 100:7–9, in which the burning of the wicked in Gehenna is a retaliation in kind for incinerating the righteous; cf. Himmelfarb, *Tours*, index under "Measure-for-measure punishments" for other examples of eschatological *lex talionis*).

9:43–48: the cost of discipleship. The focus now shifts from offenses against the Markan Christians to offenses potentially committed by them. The church, then, is not an island of sanctity in a sea of sin but an arena in which Satan remains active (cf. Marcus, "Epistemology," 568–70). To speak of offenses committed by the Markan Christians, however, is not entirely true to the syntax of the passage, which personifies parts of the body and refers to their potential to "offend" the addressees (cf. *T. Reuben* 3:3–4, which locates evil spirits in various parts of the body, and *b. Shabb.* 105b, which describes the Evil Inclination as the strange god in the human body). To be caught up in these sins, then, is not to be a totally free agent but to be swayed by corporeal factors that seem to take on a life of their own and end up destroying one's existence. This point is reinforced by the fact that while 9:43 speaks of sinners *going* to Gehenna, 9:45 and 9:47b alter this to "*being cast into* it" (*blēthēnai eis*), a divine passive (see the GLOSSARY) that echoes the language of exorcism (*ekballein* = "to cast out"; cf. the usage of this verb in 9:47a).

⌐ In three formally parallel statements, Jesus warns against actions of hand, foot, and eye that "offend" one's own best interests, averring that it is better to amputate the body part in question than to carry one's whole body into Gehenna, the place of eternal, fiery punishment (see the NOTE on "Gehenna" in 9:43). Because of the absence of a relevant context, it is not immediately clear what sorts of offenses Mark has in mind here; Matthew, in his Sermon on the Mount, interprets the sins of hand and eye as references to adultery and the lust that causes it (Matt 5:27–30), but in his parallel to our passage he links them with communal discord (Matt 18:6–35).

Deming ("Discussion"), followed by Gundry (524–25) and Allison (*Jesus*, 178–82), asserts that Matthew got it right the first time: Mark 9:43–47 is about sexual sin. These scholars argue that in the OT "foot" can be a euphemism for the penis and that hand, foot, and eyes are linked with sexual sins in the OT and/or post-biblical Jewish texts (see the NOTES on "hand" in 9:43, "foot" in 9:45, and "eye" in 9:47). Deming lays great stress on the correspondence between our passage and *b. Nid.* 13b, which in his view discusses masturbation ("adultery with the hand"), adultery proper ("adultery with the foot"), and pederasty. The passage goes on to warn that such sins will cause their perpetrators to "go down to the pit of destruction"—a striking parallel to the threat in our passage that sins of hand, foot, and eye will lead to the fires of Gehenna. Deming might have strengthened this point by reference to *Mek. R. Shim.* Yitro 20:14 on Exod 20:13 (Hoffmann, *Mechilta*, 111), which forbids adultery "by hand or foot or eye or heart." Deming finds that the Markan context, too, is in favor of this sexual interpretation, since 9:42 speaks of "offending against one of these little ones," which in his interpretation means pederasty, and 10:1–12 is a discussion of divorce, which Jesus defines as adultery.

Striking as the parallel with *b. Niddah* 13b is, however, Deming's proposal is unconvincing as an exegesis of the present Markan passage for several reasons. (1) As Deming admits, the juxtaposition with 9:41 suggests that Mark himself views the "little ones" in 9:42 as disciples rather than literal children; for Mark, then, it is unlikely that pederasty is in view. (2) The order "hand . . . foot . . . eye" is difficult to reconcile with the proposed interpretation, since according to the latter it is the offense perpetrated by the "foot" = penis that is the most serious of the three. With this term coming in the middle of the sequence rather than at one of its extremes, it is impossible to see "hand . . . foot . . . eye" as either a descending series or an ascending one (on these two sorts of series, see Fischel, "Uses"). (3) If "foot" can mean penis in the OT, so can "hand" (see the NOTE on "hand" in 9:43), yet Deming interprets the latter term literally. (4) As for the crucial *b. Niddah* 13b, to interpret "adultery by hand/foot" as masturbation/penile intercourse is difficult, since male masturbation involves the penis just as much as intercourse does. In glossing this passage, moreover, neither Rashi nor the Tosaphot interpret "foot" as penis, and the Tosaphot decipher the phrase as a reference to rubbing the organ with the (literal) hand or (literal) foot. In the related passage in *Mek. R. Shim.* on Exod 20:13, similarly, "hand," "foot," and "eye" are understood literally. (5) While hand and foot in *b. Niddah* 13b and hand, foot, and eye in *Mek. R. Shim.* are linked with sexual sins, this exegesis depends on the context (i.e., the reference to adultery) rather than the words themselves. In a different context the same words would have a different meaning; Jellinek, *Bet ha-Midrasch* 6.45, for example, associates sins of hand and foot with murder, and 1QS 10:13 uses hand and foot as a hendiadys (see the GLOSSARY) for human action in general: "When I first stretch out my hand and my foot, I will praise his [God's] name" (Charlesworth trans. alt.). (6) Most problematic for the X-rated interpretation, Mark 9:43 does not say that the person who amputates his foot will enter eternal life as a eunuch but as a lame person, and it implies that if he abstains from offenses of the foot, he will be able to enter it with both feet—an interesting picture to contemplate if "foot" means penis (cf. Gundry, 524).

The tripartite division into offenses of hand, foot, and eye, then, probably does not indicate a particular kind of offense such as sexual sin. As in many biblical contexts, rather, the *hand* is the instrument for the commission of sin, the *foot* is the means of transport to the place of its commission, and the *eye* is the means by which the temptation to commit it enters in (see the NOTES on "hand" in 9:43, "foot" in 9:45, and "eye" in 9:47). If this is true, "cut it off" and "pluck it out" are not to be taken literally (see the NOTE on "cut it off" in 9:43) but as injunctions of increasing inwardness against sin in general:

"If your *hand* offends you . . .": Don't *commit* sins! (9:43)
"If your *foot* offends you . . .": Don't *go anywhere* where you may commit
    sins! (9:45)
"If your *eye* offends you . . .": Don't even *think* about committing sins! (9:47)

The consequences of ignoring these warnings are driven home at the end of the subsection by the description of Gehenna as the place "where their worm does not die and the fire is not put out" (9:48), an allusion to Isa 66:24. This scriptural text, which was well known (see, e.g., Jdt 16:17; Sir 7:17) and was probably more memorable for being from the last verse in Isaiah (see Allison, *Intertextual Jesus*, 227), did not originally refer to hellfire but to a this-worldly judgment on the enemies of Israel (cf. Isa 66:15–16). In later Judaism, however, it was applied to the eternal punishment of the wicked (see, e.g., *LAB* 63:4; *t. Ber.* 5:31; *b. Roš. Haš.* 17a), and Jesus' predecessor John the Baptist used it in this sense (see Matt 3:12//Luke 3:17).

In the church it became the classic text for establishing the everlastingness of their torment (see, e.g., Augustine, *City of God* 21.9, and cf. Bernstein, *Formation*, passim). The image is a particularly horrific one, conjoining torture from within (the worm that devours one's insides) with torment from without (fire), but it is difficult to know how literally it is meant to be taken in the present passage, since the entire context is hyperbolic (see again the NOTE on "cut it off" in 9:43). It is impossible to exclude the notion of future punishment from the teaching of Jesus (see Reiser, *Jesus*), though in a canonical context this concept is partially offset by Pauline statements that imply ultimate salvation for all (Rom 5:18; 11:32; 1 Cor 15:22) even while Paul reckons with a postmortem judgment for sin (Rom 2:6–9; cf. the NOTE on "many" in 10:45).

9:49–50: *three sayings about salt.* The section closes with three sayings about salt (9:49, 50a, and 50b); the first two conclude the theme of judgment, and the third wraps the whole section up by returning to the theme of communal discord/concord found at the beginning (9:33–34).

The first of these sayings, "Everyone will be salted with fire," is perhaps the most enigmatic logion of Jesus in the NT. From the preceding context, in which fire has functioned as a symbol of punishment (9:43–48), the "salting with fire" would appear to be negative and destructive; perhaps the underlying thought is that *everyone*, not just the wicked, will have to pass through a searing judgment (cf. Allison, *End*, 19–22). From the following context, however, in which salt is explicitly said to be a good thing (9:50), salting with fire might be thought to be positive. Perhaps the image is of a fire that can be either destructive or purgative, depending on the previous actions (9:41–48) and disposition (9:50) of the person being judged (cf. *T. Ab.* 13:11–13; 1 Cor 3:13–15). In the OT and early Christian texts, fire can have both aspects, sometimes in the same text and in close proximity to one another (see, e.g., Mal 3:2–3; 4:1). Some exegetes, correspondingly, have concluded that "baptism with . . . fire" in Matt 3:11–12//Luke 3:16–17 is a double entendre (see Dunn, *Baptism*, 8–14), and the same ambiguity might apply to the fire symbol in our saying; the eschatological fire will punish the wicked but refine the righteous (cf. Isa 43:2; *Pss. Sol.* 15:4–5; *Sib. Or.* 2.252–54; 1QH 14[6]:17–18).

If this interpretation is correct, the following saying, about the goodness of salt and the necessity of preserving its savor (9:50ab), emphasizes the juncture at which Jesus' addressees stand: *now* is the moment when the critical decision will be made that will determine whether the eschatological fire will purify or punish them. The present moment, then, calls for the exercise of apocalyptic discernment, and it is this faculty that is now implied by the salt metaphor, since salt often appears as a symbol for wisdom (see the NOTE on "Have salt in yourselves" in 9:50). The rhetorical question about unsalty salt and the statement about the inability of any external thing to restore its savor is thus a way of restating the point of 8:36–37, that to trade eternal life for anything, even the most precious object in the world, is to make a fool's bargain.

It is also to give up the wellspring of communal peace, as the Markan Jesus suggests with his concluding exhortation to "have salt in yourselves and be at peace with each other" (9:50c). He thus implies a profound connection between internal substance (what the Bible calls "wisdom") and external harmony (see the NOTE on "be at peace with each other" for the connection between salt and peace). The concluding exhortation in 9:50, then, returns to the point of departure in the whole of 9:33–50, the human selfishness and conceit that give rise to disunity and intolerance, wreaking havoc in the church as well as in other arenas (9:33–37, 38–40). In the course of our subsection, a horrific picture has been painted of the fate to which such selfish impulses, if unchecked, ultimately lead human beings: a place of torment, in which the only companions portrayed are devouring worms and consuming fire (9:48). Now, however, an image of communal harmony ("be at peace with each other") is counterposed to the portrait of lonely horror, and this eschatological reality of communal peace is implied to be available through the wisdom that is already streaming forth from the giver of all good gifts (cf. Jas 1:17).

In the next passage, it will become apparent that this incursion into the earthly sphere of the peace of the end-time, which is also the peace of the beginning, has startling consequences for the marriage relationship, a union that has been divinely ordained but humanly troubled "from the beginning of the creation" (10:6).

JESUS ARGUES THE PERMANENCE OF MARRIAGE (10:1–12)

10 ¹And rising from there, he went into the region of Judaea and Transjordan, and crowds again came together to him, and as was his custom, he again began teaching them. ²And coming forward, Pharisees were asking him if it was permissible for a man to divorce a woman, testing him. ³But he answered and said to them, "What did Moses command you?" ⁴They said, "Moses gave permission to write a bill of relinquishment and to divorce." ⁵Jesus said, "He wrote you this commandment with a view toward your hard-heartedness; ⁶but from the beginning of the creation 'male and female he made them'; ⁷'on account of this a man shall leave his father and mother and shall be joined to his wife, ⁸and the two shall become one flesh.' So they are no longer two people, but one flesh. ⁹What therefore God has yoked together, let not a human being separate."

¹⁰And when they were again in the house, the disciples asked him concerning this. ¹¹And he said to them, "Whoever divorces his wife and marries another commits adultery against her. ¹²And she, if she divorces her husband and marries another, commits adultery."

NOTES

10 1. *the region of Judaea and Transjordan.* Gk *ta horia tēs Ioudaias kai peran tou Iordanou.* This is the best-attested reading (א, B, C*, L, etc.), but many texts leave out the *kai*, yielding "the region of Judaea beyond the Jordan" (C², D, W, Δ, Θ, etc.), which is also the reading of Matt 19:1. This text is grammatically smooth but

geographically incorrect, since Judaea extended only to the Jordan, not beyond it. Lührmann (169) opts for the shorter reading, thinking that it testifies to Mark's ignorance of the geography of Palestine, but it is unlikely that an author who clearly distinguished between Judaea and Transjordan in 3:7–8 would conflate them seven chapters later. It is more likely, rather, that the shorter reading is a grammatical amelioration and/or an assimilation to Matt 19:1, where "beyond the Jordan" may reflect the point of view of an evangelist living in Coele Syria (cf. Davies and Allison, 3.7).

2. *if it was permissible for a man to divorce a woman.* Gk *ei exestin andri gynaika apolysai.* The word for "divorce," *apolysai,* literally means "let go, send away, dismiss"; in ancient divorce laws, one party (usually the man) sends the other away, that is, evicts her or him from the house.

As pointed out in the COMMENT on 10:1–4, the question asked by the Pharisees is strange, given that all first-century Jewish groups known to us permitted divorce; Matt 19:3, therefore, changes the wording to "is it permissible to divorce one's wife *for every cause*," reflecting a controversy between the Pharisaic houses of Hillel and Shammai about the legitimate grounds for marital termination (see *m. Giṭ.* 9:10; *b. Giṭ.* 90a).

There was, however, some hostility to divorce within the OT/Jewish tradition. In the OT prophetic book of Malachi, for example, God says that he hates divorce, and the passage is interestingly similar to ours in that it takes Genesis 1–2 as a scriptural justification for this anti-divorce stand (see Rudolph, "Zu Mal 2.10–16"). On the basis of CD 4:20–5:1, which prohibits men from "taking two wives during their lifetime," it has also sometimes been claimed that the Qumran sectarians prohibited divorce (see, e.g., Fitzmyer, "Divorce Texts"). As Shemesh ("Key," 245–46) and Brin ("Divorce") point out, however, another Qumran passage, which was published after Fitzmyer wrote his article, specifically recognizes divorce (11QTemple 54:4–5; cf. also perhaps CD 13:15–17), and probably CD 4:20–5:1 merely prohibits bigamy and/or the remarriage of a divorcé while his former wife lives (cf. Collins, "Marriage," 129; on CD 4:20–5:1, see further the NOTE on "male and female he made them" in 10:6). It is perhaps significant, however, that 11QTemple 57:16–19 forbids the Israelite *king* from divorcing; it may be, then, that the Qumran sect regarded divorce as a concession to human sinfulness (cf. the COMMENT on 10:5–9) and expected a higher standard of behavior from its monarch. Fitzmyer ("Divorce Texts," 101–2) also points out that the OT forbids priests from marrying divorced women (Lev 21:7; cf. Ezek 44:22) and speculates that Jesus' veto on divorce may have something to do with his extension of priestly rules to non-priests (for Pharisaic extension of priestly rules to laypersons, see the NOTE on "nor, when they come from the marketplace, etc." in 7:4 and the APPENDIX "The Scribes and the Pharisees" in vol. 1).

3. *answered and said.* Gk *apokritheis eipen.* On this biblical idiom, see the NOTE on the phrase in 3:33.

What did Moses command you? Gk *ti hymin eneteilato Mōusēs.* Some early Christian commentators interpret this question as Jesus' way of playing *Moses'* commandment (Deut 24:1) off against *God's* (Gen 1:27; 2:24): Moses and not God commanded divorce (see, e.g., Ptolemaeus, *Epistle to Flora* 4; Ambrose, *Exposition of Luke* 8.7–9; cf. *b. Sanh.* 99a; Davies and Allison, 3.14; Clark, "Constraining," 157, 163–64). But Mark 7:8–13 has clearly identified Moses' commandments with God's, and in a few verses Jesus will affirm the binding character of the Decalogue (see the GLOSSARY), which is a central part of the Mosaic Torah (10:19). While the editorial comment in 7:19 does imply that the food laws of the Pentateuch are no longer binding on Jesus' followers, it does so without highlighting the contradiction to the Mosaic regulations. Mark, moreover, knows and apparently accepts the Jewish tradition that not just the Law proper but also the narratives of the Pentateuch were written by Moses (see 12:26 and cf. *Midr. Psalms* 1:2; cf. also the phrase "the Law and the Prophets" in Jewish literature and the NT, e.g., Sirach prologue; 2 Macc 15:9; Matt 5:17; etc.). The Genesis narratives that the Markan Jesus quotes with approval in 10:6–8, then, are for him part of what "Moses wrote" (cf. 10:5 and see Chrysostom, *Homily on Matthew* 62).

4. *Moses gave permission.* Gk *epetrepsen Mōusēs.* Some exegetes (e.g., Lane, 354–55; Schweizer, 203; Sanders, *Jesus,* 256–57) have found a key to the passage in the contrast between Jesus' question, which asks about what Moses *commanded,* and the Pharisees' reply, which talks only about what he *allowed*; in Jesus' opinion, then, God *permitted* divorce as a concession, but never *commanded* it. This exegesis, however, is unsustainable; the Pharisees are merely using common terminology for what may or may not be done (cf. the frequent rabbinic contrast between what is forbidden, *'asûr,* and what is permitted, *mûtār*), and the Markan Jesus himself will immediately go on to refer to the passage from Deuteronomy 24 as "this *commandment*" (cf. Gundry, 538; Davies and Allison, 3.13).

to write a bill of relinquishment and to divorce. Gk *biblion apostasiou grapsai kai apolysai.* This clipped judicial terminology approximates that of Deut 24:1, 3 (cf. Jer 3:8), though Deuteronomy has *exapostelei* ("send away") rather than *apolysai* ("divorce"; cf. the NOTE on "if it was permissible for a man to divorce a woman" in 10:2). *Apostasion* is a legal term signifying a relinquishment of that which one has previously claimed or owned, and it is cognate with *apostasia,* from which we get "apostasy" (renunciation of one's former religious convictions; see BDAG 120).

5. *with a view toward your hard-heartedness.* Gk *pros tēn sklērokardian hymōn,* lit. "toward the hard-heartedness of you." In strictly grammatical terms, *pros tēn sklērokardian hymōn* might mean "in order to bring about the hardness of your hearts" (on *pros* + accusative to indicate purpose, see BDAG 874[3c]). Gundry (538) argues for this intentional interpretation of the *pros*: Moses made provision for divorce *in order to induce* hard-heartedness. This interpretation would draw Mark 10:5 close to 13:22, which uses *pros* + articular infinitive to speak of an intention to deceive; to 4:11–12, which alludes to a divinely willed spiritual blindness; to Ezek 20:25, in which God gives Israel statutes that are not good in order to punish them for previous sins; and to Pauline texts such as Gal 3:19 and Rom 5:20; 7:13, which imply that the Law was given in order to provoke transgression (cf. Berger, *Gesetzauslegung,* 268–69).

But despite considerable evidence for Pauline influence on Mark in general (see the INTRODUCTION in vol. 1, pp. 73–75, and Marcus, "Interpreter"), in this particular case it is probably an error to read Mark through Pauline lenses. The negative presentation of the purpose of the Law in Galatians and Romans is at odds with the usual OT and Jewish view, in which the Torah is the antidote to transgression (see Martyn, *Galatians*, 355). Even Ezek 20:25 does not speak of statutes given in order to harden hearts; from the previous context in Ezekiel, an obdurate and rebellious heart would seem to be the *cause* of God's wrath rather than its result (see Ezek 20:8, 13, 16, 21; cf. CD 2:17–19; 3:5–7; 8:18–19; 19:32–33). If Mark had really wanted to convey the radical idea that God intended the OT divorce laws to induce Israelite sin, he would have expressed that concept more clearly, as he does in 4:12 and as Paul himself does in the texts cited in the previous paragraph.

It is likelier that *pros tēn sklērokardian hymōn* means "with reference to . . ." or "on account of your hard-heartedness" (cf. Justin, *Dialogue* 18.2) and that the Markan Jesus is saying that the Mosaic provision for divorce was a concession to human sinfulness (on this meaning of *pros*, see BDAG 875 [3e] and Zerwick §98; cf. Mark 12:12; Matt 27:14; Acts 24:16; Rom 10:21a). This concessive interpretation of *pros tēn sklērokardian* is in keeping with the wording of 10:4, "Moses *gave permission*. . . ." There are plentiful Jewish parallels for the idea that particular passages in the Torah are a compromise with human weakness. Daube, for example, discusses in this light the attitude toward the monarchy in 1 Sam 8:4–22 and the posture toward slavery, polygamy, and sabbatical-year debts in later Jewish thought ("Concessions"). Some Jewish Christian and Jewish texts, similarly (e.g., *Clementine Recognitions* 1.35–36; Maimonides, *Guide of the Perplexed* 3.32), regard sacrifice as a concession to the sin of the Israelites (cf. Berger, *Gesetzauslegung*, 269).

Biblical interpreters have sometimes adopted fanciful explanations of the hard-heartedness referred to here; several Antiochene exegetes, for example, suggest that Moses was afraid that bad-tempered husbands would kill their wives if they were forced to keep them and that therefore he allowed divorce as a lesser evil (E. Clark, "Constraining," 158 n. 16, citing Chrysostom, Theodore of Mopsuestia, Theodoret of Cyrrhus, and Jerome).

6. *but from the beginning of the creation.* Gk *apo de archēs ktiseōs.* Schoeps (*Paul*, 180–81) notes the parallel with the line of argument in Gal 3:15–20, in which the older ordinance (in Paul's case, the promise to Abraham) has priority over the newer one (in Paul's case, the Mosaic Law). Davies and Allison (3.15) argue that rabbinic parallels to this logic are lacking; on the contrary, *b. Pesah.* 6b asserts that "there is no before and after in the Scripture." *Jubilees* (e.g., 6:17–19; 16:20–23) and various rabbinic traditions (e.g., *m. Qidd.* 4:14; *Gen. Rab.* 64.4) do retroject Mosaic ordinances into earlier periods (see Kugel, *Traditions*, 705–9), but these anachronisms are based not on a desire to affirm the superiority of the earlier epochs but on a wish to assert the consistency and eternal validity of the Law.

For the Markan Jesus, however, the situation that prevailed "from the beginning of the creation" is the standard to which everything, including the Torah, must conform (cf. the COMMENT on 10:5–9). A similar belief has been invoked, in Jewish and Christian history, to justify practices as diverse as vegetarianism (see Gen 1:29), nudism (see Gen 2:25), and social and sexual equality (see Gen 2:18; 3:16). Some rabbinic traditions, for example, acknowledge that until the time of the flood (cf. Gen 9:3), humanity was vegetarian (see, e.g., *b. Sanh.* 59*b*), and it may be that the Jewish ascetics who abstained from meat and wine in the wake of the Second Temple's destruction (see *t. Soṭah* 15:11) and the vegetarian and water-drinking Jewish Christians (see Irenaeus, *Against Heresies* 5.1.3; Epiphanius, *Panarion* 30.3.7; 30.14.3) were partly inspired by apocalyptic hopes for a return to paradise (wine was not cultivated until after the Fall according to Gen 9:20–21). In the patristic period, similarly, Christian sectarians known as Adamites called their church Paradise, condemned marriage as foreign to Eden, and worshiped in the nude (see Epiphanius, *Panarion* 52; Augustine, *Heresies* 31; cf. "Adamites"). The revolutionary potential of the return-to-paradise idea was illustrated at the outbreak of the English Peasants' Revolt in 1381, when John Ball preached a fiery sermon on the text "When Adam delved and Eve span, who was then the gentleman?" in which he denounced all postlapsarian divisions based on rank (Partington, *Dictionary*, 545:10). In our own time, Joni Mitchell has recycled the idea of a return to paradise in her song "Woodstock," which calls on her hearers to join her in "get[ting] ourselves back to the garden [of Eden]."

√Meeks ("Image") has argued in an influential article that the use of Gen 1:27 + 2:18–24 in later Jewish and Christian literature, including Gal 3:28, reflects a widespread ancient myth of primal androgyny: the original human had both sets of sexual organs but was subsequently split in two, and the separated halves have been seeking reunification ever since (see, e.g., Plato, *Symposium* 189c–191d; *Gen. Rab.* 8.1). As Martyn (*Galatians*, 379–81) points out, however, our text presents the original situation as one of sexual differentiation rather than one of unity; humanity has been "male and female" from the beginning of creation, not as the result of a primal fall from bisexuality.

male and female he made them. Gk *arsen kai thēly epoiēsen autous.* These words correspond to the LXX of Gen 1:27. The same OT text, in its Hebrew version, is cited in CD 4:20–21 to make the related point that bigamy and/or the remarriage of a divorcé are prohibited (cf. Mark 10:11–12); the author denounces those who "are caught twice in fornication by taking two wives in their lives, even though the principle of creation is 'male and female he created them.'" The citations of Gen 1:27 in the Qumran and Gospel texts are similar not only in function but also in introductory formula ("the principle of creation"/"from the beginning of the creation"; on CD 4:20–21, see further the NOTE on "if it was permissible for a man to divorce a woman" in 10:2).

7. on account of this. Gk *heneken toutou.* According to Davies and Allison (3.11), this part of the quotation of Gen 2:24 presumes knowledge of the OT context; the reference is not to the citation of Gen 1:27 in 10:6 but to the story of Eve coming from Adam's rib in Gen 2:21–23. But while Gen 2:21–23 may very well be in the background, Mark 10:6 and 10:7–8 are more closely linked than Davies and Allison recognize: the complementary sexual equipment of the first couple (10:6), which is intertwined with their reciprocal sexual urge (10:7–8), shows that they were designed for each other by God (10:9).

shall leave. Gk *kataleipsei.* In the Peshitta, as in *Tg.Onq.* Gen 2:24, the verb used here is *šbq*, which has the root meaning "abandon" or "forsake" (a form of this verb is transliterated *sabachthani* in Jesus' cry of dereliction in 15:34); the same root can mean "to divorce" and is used in the Syriac versions of 10:2, 4, 11–12 (cf. Jastrow, 1516–17). Although the wordplay is no longer present in Greek, it may be that part of the original rhetoric of the passage was that one should "leave" one's parents but not one's mate.

and shall be joined to his wife. Gk *kai proskollēthēsetai pros tēn gynaika autou.* This clause, which is part of the citation of Gen 2:24, appears in most manuscripts, but a few, including some weighty witnesses (ℵ, B, Ψ), omit it. As Gundry (530–31) points out, if the latter witnesses were right and the original manuscripts of Mark lacked 10:7b, Mark's procedure here would be similar to that in 10:4, where he skips the middle part of the OT text he quotes (Deut 24:1). Gundry rightly concludes, however, that it is more likely that Mark 10:7b is original, since the clause is necessary for the sense of the sentence. It could have been left out by accident (haplography), especially since the next Markan clause also begins with *kai* ("*and* the two shall become one flesh"), or it could have been intentionally omitted because of its graphic sexual connotation (cf. 1 Cor 6:16–17 and Schmidt, "*Kollaō*"; on patristic embarrassment with this aspect of Gen 2:24, see Clark, "Constraining," 155).

8. *and the two shall become one flesh.* Gk *kai esontai hoi dyo eis sarka mian.* This is the end of the quotation of Gen 2:24 that begins in 10:7. In the Genesis account itself, "one flesh" refers either to the mechanics of sex or to the child that results from sexual union, or to both (cf. Gunkel, *Genesis,* 13; von Rad, *Genesis,* 85). The idea of sexual merging is accentuated in the LXX, where "the two shall become one flesh" replaces the MT's "they shall become one flesh." E. Clark ("Constraining," 167, citing Basil of Ancyra, Theodore of Mopsuestia, and Zeno of Verona) observes that in the early church the sexual connotations of the "two in one flesh" phrasing "ensured that arguments about marriage and divorce would be framed in ways that rested heavily on sexual conduct." The LXX translators, however, may have added "the two" in order to discourage polygamy or second marriages (cf. Brewer, "Women," 355), thus making this version a particularly convenient point of departure for our Markan pericope (Tertullian gives a similar stress to "the two" in Gen 2:24 OL; see also the introduction to the COMMENT).

But Gen 2:24 entered into discussions of divorce independently of the LXX as well. Already Mal 2:10–16 MT opposes divorce with a reference to God's will in creation (cf. Mark 10:6a) and an apparent allusion to Gen 2:24, "Did he [God] not make one?" (see J. Collins, "Marriage," 126, and Davies and Allison, 3.12). Genesis 2:24 MT is also invoked in the discussions of matrimonial law in *Gen. Rab.* 18.5 and *y. Qidd.* 1:1 (58c; Neusner, 26.12; see Shemesh, "Key," 250 n. 21). Although *Gen. Rab.* 17.3 does not cite Gen 2:24 directly, it alludes to it in a way that is similar to that in our Markan text, implying that a rabbi and his former wife remain "one flesh" despite their divorce and remarriage to different partners (cf. Harvey, "Genesis," 58). To be sure, this rabbinic tradition does not imply that either the rabbi or his former wife have sinned in remarrying, but it may be a remnant of an exegetical tradition that concerned itself with the implications of Gen 2:24 for the question of divorce.

9. *What therefore God has yoked together, let not a human being separate.* Gk *ho oun ho theos synezeuxen anthrōpos mē chōrizetō.* For the idea that God brings man and wife together, see Gen 24:44; Tob 8:6; *T. Reub.* 4:1; the last passage designates the wife a *syzygon* ("yoke-mate"; cf. Phil 4:3), a noun that is cognate with Mark's verb *synezeuxen* (cf. J. Collins, *Divorce*, 98–99). Tobit 6:18 and *b. Moʿed. Qat.* 18b display the related idea of mates predestined for each other from the beginning of the world (cf. "from the beginning of the creation" in 10:6 and see C. Moore, *Tobit*, 207–8).

Ambrose (*Exposition of Luke* 8.9) paraphrases our verse in a pointedly anti-Mosaic and anti-Jewish manner: "What God has united, the Jew [i.e., Moses] does not separate" (cited by Clark, "Constraining," 164). This is probably *not* what Mark means; the *anthrōpos* in question is not Moses but the Pharisee who misuses Moses' writings through misunderstanding their true purpose (see the NOTE on "What did Moses command you" in 10:3 and the COMMENT on 10:5–9). Cf. 7:8–13, where "the commandment of God" is *connected* with Moses and *contrasted* to the Pharisaic "tradition of human beings." In the logic of Mark's narrative, however, pronouncements such as 10:9 and 7:19 might suggest that Jesus was setting his authority above that of Moses and might therefore contribute to the question the Jewish leaders will ask him in 11:28: "By what authority are you doing these things?"

11. *and he said to them.* Gk *kai legei autois.* Matthew (19:9) omits Mark 10:10, and thus in Matthew's Gospel Jesus' statement about adulterous remarriages is no longer private instruction to the disciples but a continuation of the answer to the Pharisees. Yet the Matthean Jesus still prefaces this declaration with "And I say to you," which is a remnant of the Markan tradition. This is one of several instances in which Matthean redaction of Mark is easier to explain than Markan redaction of Matthew (cf. the INTRODUCTION in vol. 1, p. 42 [item 4]).

commits adultery against her. Gk *moichatai epʼ autēn.* The construction *moichasthai epi* is unusual, and it is unclear what *epi* means in the context and whether *autēn* refers to the first wife or the second. In *Pss. Sol.* 8:10 *moichasthai* + accusative means "to commit adultery with" (cf. the related verb *moicheuesthai* + accusative in Lev 20:10), and Turner ("Translation") argues that our phrase should be interpreted similarly, as a reference to adultery *with* the second wife. In favor of this interpretation, the second woman (*allēn* = "another") is the nearer antecedent of *autēn* ("her"). But if Mark had meant "commit adultery with," why did he not use the usual idiom *moichasthai* + accusative or a straightforward preposition such as *syn* or *meta* (both = "with")? It is probably best, then, to go with the common translation "commits adultery against her," which corresponds to a frequent sense of *epi* (see LSJ 623 [C4]; BDAG 366[12]; J. Collins, *Divorce*, 101). This translation is supported by the related saying in Matt 5:32, which says that the divorcing man commits an offense against his first wife.

12. *And she, if she divorces her husband and marries another.* Gk *kai ean autē*

apolysasa ton andra autēs gamēsȩ allon. Many exegetes (recently Schweizer, "Scheidungsrecht," and Weder, "Perspektive") see the Markan Jesus' reference to the case of the woman divorcing her husband, which is *not* mentioned in the previous discussion between Jesus and the Pharisees, as a nod to Roman law, which permitted women as well as men to initiate divorce proceedings (see, e.g., Cicero, *Letters to His Friends* 8.7.2 [Loeb: 92]; Gaius, *Institutes* 7.137a; Justinian, *Digest* 23.2.45.5; 24.2.4,8; cf. Corbett, *Roman Law*, 242–43; Grubbs, *Women*, 187–218). Jewish law, according to this view, restricted the right of divorce to males; the private discussion with the disciples, then, reflects the situation of the Markan community in the larger Hellenistic world rather than that of the historical Jesus in early-first-century Palestine, and Matthew's omission of the Markan reference to the woman divorcing her husband flows out of his more Jewish perspective. In favor of this interpretation, the OT mentions only the husband's right to divorce (see the fountainhead passage in Deut 24:1, which is quoted in 10:4), and this pattern continues in rabbinic legislation (see the explicit emphasis on the one-sidedness of divorce laws in *m. Yeb.* 14:1). According to the Mishnah (see the GLOSSARY), to be sure, women have the right to be divorced from their husbands under certain circumstances (*m. Ketub.* 7:5, 9–10; *m. Ned.* 11:12), but even in these cases the woman does not divorce the man directly; he is compelled by the court to divorce her (see J. Collins, "Marriage," 120).

In the last twenty years, however, other scholars, some of whom relate their historical reconstructions to modern feminist concerns, have claimed that in significant Jewish circles women *did* have the right to initiate divorce (see, e.g., Brooten, "Konnten" and "Debatte"; Ilan, "Divorce Bill" and "Approach"; Cotton and Qimron, "XHev/Se ar 13"; Brewer, "Women"). Marriage contracts from the fifth-century B.C.E. Jewish colony in Elephantine, Egypt, make reference to women divorcing men, and Josephus reports that Herod the Great's sister Salome and Agrippa's daughter Herodias divorced their husbands (*Ant.* 15.259–60; 18.136). It has been asserted, moreover, that Papyrus Ṣe'elim 13, a fragmentary text found in Wadi Muraba'at in the Judaean desert and originating in the time of the Bar Kochba Revolt (134–35 C.E.), is a writ of divorce sent by a Palestinian Jewish woman to her husband (see also *y. Ket.* 5:8 [30b], cited in Brewer, "Women," 356). Later Samaritan and Karaite sources show that this trajectory of women divorcing men continued into the Middle Ages in Jewish and quasi-Jewish circles.

Skeptics have countered that the Samaritan and Karaite documents are late, that the Elephantine community was widely separated from first-century Palestine in space and time, that Josephus explicitly labels the actions of Salome and Herodias as contrary to Jewish law, and that the Muraba'at document either is not a writ of divorce or represents the halakah (see the GLOSSARY) of a fringe group (see Schweizer, "Scheidungsrecht," 296; Schremer, "Divorce"). Cotton and Qimron ("XHev/Se ar 13") support the skeptics on a minor point, arguing that the Muraba'at text is not a writ of divorce but a waiver of claims by the wife, but they undermine them on the major one, since the waiver assumes that the woman has previously divorced her husband.

It may be too early to declare a winner in this debate, but if the conclusions of

Cotton and Qimron prevail, one will at least have to say that *some* early-second-century Palestinian Jewish circles countenanced wives divorcing their husbands. The crucial question is how typical these circles were; as Cotton and Qimron (13) put it: "Either these Jews went against the Halakha [that restricted the initiation of divorce to men] or the Halakha had not yet become normative." Cotton and Qimron themselves lean toward the latter explanation, pointing out that the Muraba'at document does not seem to come from a fringe group but from one closely associated with the leader of the Jewish Revolt, Simon bar Kosibah (Bar Kochba), who is invoked in the first line. To be sure, the categorical nature of Josephus' assertion that Salome and Herodias, in divorcing their husbands, were not following their country's law, is weighty. The *Temple Scroll* passage that mentions divorce, moreover (see the NOTE on "if it was permissible for a man to divorce a woman" in 10:2), does not consider the case of a woman divorcing her husband. And in view of the formulation in Deut 24:1, 3, which considers only the case of a man divorcing his wife, it is hard to imagine that the Sadducees, who emphasized the letter of the written Law, would have gone along with female-initiated divorce. It may be, however, that sects such as the Pharisees (to whom Josephus belonged), the Sadducees, and the Qumran group were stricter about limiting divorce to males than were some other Jewish factions (cf. Brooten, "Konnten," 79; J. Collins, "Marriage," 121).

COMMENT

Introduction. After the private instruction to the disciples in 9:33–50, Jesus broadens his audience in 10:1–9 to include the crowds and his opponents, and the latter throw him what they hope will be a curve ball, a question about the controversial subject of divorce. Jesus responds by declaring marital termination to be contrary to God's original will as expressed in creation, then clarifies this declaration by private instruction to the Twelve, in which he speaks of people who divorce and remarry as adulterers (10:10–12). This progression in the dialogue from crowds to opponents to disciples probably reflects the fact that marriage and divorce were of concern both outside and inside the church, as is confirmed by the well-known arguments between the proto-rabbinical houses of Hillel and Shammai (see the NOTE on "if it was permissible for a man to divorce a woman" in 10:2) and by Paul's discussion in 1 Cor 7:10–16.

Markan redaction is most prominent, as usual, at the beginning and end of the passage. At the beginning, 10:1 is thick with typical Markan vocabulary ("from there," "region," "crowds," "again" [2x], "teaching") and contains geographical references (Judaea and Transjordan) that echo an earlier redactional notice (3:7–8) and allude to the Markan Jesus' habit of teaching ("as was his custom"). At the end, 10:10–12 contains the characteristic Markan motif of Jesus secluding himself in a house with the disciples, where they ask him a question about the teaching he has just given and he clears up their confusion (cf. 4:10–20; 7:17–23; 9:28–29); the introduction to this private scene, moreover, displays typical Markan vocabulary ("again," "house," "disciples," "asked"). The issue discussed here, moreover, is slightly different from that debated in 10:1–9: not whether one is permitted to *divorce* but whether divorced people are permitted to *remarry*. It is not clear whether most Jewish women in Palestine possessed the right to initiate divorce, but women did possess this right under Roman law (see the NOTE on "And she, if she divorces her husband and marries another" in 10:12); Jesus' response in 10:12, therefore, may expand the horizon to include the practice in the greater Greco-Roman world. The house scene in 10:10–12, then, may very well represent Markan redaction, though it is probable that it has developed a pre-Markan core saying (cf. the Q saying Matt 5:32//Luke 16:18 and J. Collins, *Divorce*, 100–3).

⤷The material between 10:1 and 10:10, however, seems to be substantially pre-Markan and may have a complicated tradition history behind it. Genesis 1:27 (cited in Mark 10:6) and 2:24 (cited in Mark 10:7–8a) are frequently combined in early Christian literature (Gal 3:28; 1 Cor 11:8–12; *Gospel of Thomas* 22), and this combination may have Jewish antecedents (see *b. 'Erub.* 18a and cf. Jervell, *Imago Dei*, 108). The line of thought in 10:6–9, moreover, is not entirely clear; why, for example, does Jesus cite Gen 1:27 (10:6), when it does not seem to contribute to his point that divorce is forbidden? One of the Qumran texts, the *Damascus Document* (CD 4:20–21), quotes the same OT passage to make a similar argument against remarrying while one's original spouse lives, and the Qumran text appears to base this conclusion on a literalistic reading of Gen 1:27, which speaks of a male and a *female*, singular, not of a male and *females*, plural (cf. *Tg. Neof.* and *Frg. Tg.* Gen 1:27 and see Sigal, *Halakah*, 112; J. Collins, *Divorce*, 97). It may be, then, that a previous version of the exegetical argument in Mark 10:6–9 worked more literally with the Genesis texts.

The pericope in its present form divides naturally into four sections: the stage-setting notice about the crowds (10:1), the initial dialogue between the Pharisees and Jesus (10:2–4), Jesus' response about the original will of God (10:5–9), and his further explanation of this response to the disciples (10:10–12).

10:1–4: stage-setting and initial dialogue. After finishing his long private discourse to the Twelve in Peter's house in Capernaum (9:33), Jesus departs for Judaea and the Transjordan region, where a familiar pattern repeats itself: crowds gather to him and he teaches them (cf. 2:13; 4:1–2; 6:34). The audience, however, includes not only receptive hearers but also some Pharisees, who are described as "testing" (*peirazontes*) Jesus with a hostile inquiry (10:2a). The same verb was applied to the Pharisees in 8:11 and will be employed for them again in 12:13–15, when they will try to entrap him in talk; here, as in those other instances, the word hints at a demonic influence behind Pharisaic hostility to Jesus (cf. its usage in 1:13 with Satan as its subject and see the NOTE on "testing" in 8:11). If, then, the Markan Jesus will go on in our passage to accuse his Pharisaic interlocutors of hard-heartedness (10:5), the evangelist would view this condition as a result not simply of human malice but also of supernatural interference (cf. Gundry, 536). To add to the picture of supernaturally influenced hostility, the badgering Pharisees are described as "coming forward" (*proselthontes*), a verb that can have a nuance of attack (see LSJ 1511 [2] and cf. the COMMENT on a similar compound verb, *exēlthon*, in 1:35–39). Thus, as happens throughout the Gospel, Mark pictures the reaction to Jesus as a divided one: for some, such as the crowd, Jesus' teaching conveys "the mystery of the dominion of God," while for others it provokes hostile incitement, perhaps partly because of their jealousy at the enthusiastic reaction of the multitudes (cf. 2:6–8, 12; 4:10–12; 12:12, 35–37; Bede, *Exposition of Mark* 10:1b–10:2a).

◁ The particular form that the attack takes is a question from the Pharisees about whether it is permissible for a man to divorce his wife (10:2b). It is odd that this question should be raised at all, since, as the Pharisees will immediately remind Jesus, the Law of Moses makes explicit provision for divorce (see 10:4) and therefore all of the major Jewish sects in the first century seem to have permitted it (see the NOTE on "if it was permissible for a man to divorce a woman" in 10:2). It may be, therefore, that we should assume that Jesus' reputation for opposing divorce has preceded him and that the Pharisees want to get him into trouble by forcing him to acknowledge this (cf. J. Collins, *Divorce*, 94).

In good Jewish fashion (cf. Bultmann, 42–44), Jesus responds to the Pharisees' question with a counterquestion: "What did Moses command you?"(10:3). In asking what Moses commanded, Jesus is invoking a mutually agreed on authority that is acceptable alike to the Pharisees, to the crowd, to himself, and to his disciples. Similarly, in an earlier argument with the Pharisees, Jesus invoked Moses as a witness against the Pharisaic position on ritual purity (7:10–13). The question, then, is not whether the Mosaic Law is authoritative but how it should be interpreted (cf. the NOTE on "What did Moses command you?" in 10:3). At the same time, however, a certain relativizing and limiting of the Torah is implied in the formulation "What did Moses command *you*?" (see Pesch, 2.122, and J. Collins, *Divorce*, 94); as Gundry (529–30) points out, in a Jewish context one would more likely expect, "What did Moses command *us*?" The distancing language here prepares for 10:5, in which "you" will be used twice to indicate the Pharisees and their spiritual ancestors as the addressees of the Mosaic provision for divorce.

The Pharisees respond to Jesus' question with the obvious answer by echoing the language of the Pentateuch: "Moses gave permission to write a bill of relinquishment and to divorce" (10:4; cf. Deut 24:1, 3). It is perhaps significant, given what was just said about the pointed emphasis on the pronoun "you" in Jesus' utterances in 10:3 and 10:5, that the Pharisees' intervening response omits any pronoun at all ("Moses gave permission," not "Moses gave *us* permission"). The Pharisees, in other words, reject Jesus' implication that the Mosaic divorce law was directed particularly at *them*; they see it, rather, as having general applicability. And, indeed, there is nothing in Deut 24:1 itself to suggest any sort of limitation, aside from the implicit restriction of all Israelite law to the chosen people. The verse is a classic example of the OT's casuistic, or case, law (see the GLOSSARY). It states a condition, which it assumes will arise often enough ("if then she finds no favor in his eyes . . ." [RSV]), and includes in the statement a provision for the dissatisfied husband's drafting a writ of divorce. No denunciation of this act is implied; what is disallowed, in fact, is not divorce but taking a divorced wife back after she has subsequently married and divorced another man.

10:5–9: Jesus' response. The Pharisees, then, have thrown down the gauntlet by citing authoritative scripture in support of the Jewish male's right to divorce. Jesus responds by giving his own interpretation of Deut 24:1: Moses, he says, gave "you" the commandment permitting divorce "with a view toward your hard-heartedness" (10:5). He thus does what any scriptural exegete worth his salt must do when confronted by a passage that seems to refute his position, namely, show how it may be understood within his own frame of reference (see Dahl, "Contradictions," 162–65). He then goes on to cite the biblical passages that he considers to be most directly applicable, Gen 1:27 and 2:24 (10:6–8a), texts that in his view prohibit divorce. Our pericope, then, is one of several within Mark's Gospel that try to reconcile seemingly contradictory OT passages (cf. the COMMENTS on 9:11–13 and 12:35–37).

In this particular case, the Markan Jesus relativizes the Deuteronomy text by limiting it in two respects: in terms of the group it addresses and in terms of duration. With regard to the former, he suggests that Moses' words are not directed to everyone but only to the Pharisees and their spiritual ancestors, the "hard-hearted" Israelites who have, from the beginning of the people's existence, repudiated the will of God (cf. Acts 7:51–53). With regard to the latter, the continuation of the passage in 10:6a ("but from the beginning of the creation . . .") implies that this Mosaic provision was meant to prevail only for a limited time, until the dawning of the eschatological era that would restore the conditions of Eden (on the removal of hard-heartedness in the new age, see the COMMENT on 8:17–21, and cf. Ezek 11:19). These two limitations, of audience and of aeon, are interrelated: the Pharisees are, in the view of the Markan Jesus, people who take their cues from the dying old age, whereas Jesus and the Markan Christians are people who rejoice in the dawning light of the new age—which is also the recaptured radiance of Eden.

The Markan Jesus thus resurrects the original version of the Law, which had become corrupted, as Moses himself does in *Jub.* 6:18–19. *Jubilees* and the Qumran literature, moreover, occasionally use Genesis as a source for halakah, as Jesus does here (see, e.g., CD 4:21–5:1; *Jub.* 2:17–22, 25–33; 3:8–14, 26–31; 4:1–6; cf. Shemesh, "Key," 251). But, despite these precedents, it is still a radical step for the Markan Jesus to imply that "halakah based upon Eden" (cf. García Martínez, "Man and Woman") might *supersede* the halakah of Sinai. Indeed, the Mishnah and later commentators in the Pharisaic-rabbinic stream of Jewish tradition specifically reject such a move, asserting that the pre-Mosaic divine statutes were valid only because they were confirmed at Sinai (see *m. Ḥul.* 7:6 and Maimonides' commentary on it, cited in Elon, *Jewish Law*, 1.233–34).

Jesus' daring affirmation of the contrary, the halakic priority of Eden, is accomplished through the citation of the two Genesis texts, 1:27 and 2:24, which were probably already combined in pre-Markan tradition (10:6–8a; see the introduction to the COMMENT). These passages speak of Adam and Eve as beings whose complementary sexual equipment proves that they were designed for each other (10:6, citing Gen 1:27) and whose resultant sexual union (10:7–8, citing Gen 2:24) is part of an indelible marital bond created by God (10:9). The presupposition of this argument seems to be that sexual union creates a permanent ontological fusion of the individuals involved. Shemesh ("Key") has discerned a similar presupposition in 4Q271 3:12, which bans marriage to a woman who has previously had sexual experience; in CD 4:20–5:1, which invokes Gen 1:27 to forbid second marriages (see the NOTE on "if it was permissible for a man to divorce a woman" in 10:2); and in *Gen. Rab.* 18.5, which asserts on the basis of Gen 2:24 that Gentiles acquire a wife through sexual intercourse, even with a prostitute. In the Christian sphere, 1 Cor 6:16 similarly uses Gen 2:24 to argue for the permanence of the union created by sexual intercourse, even with prostitutes (for an interestingly parallel modern theory about the merging of essences in sex, see Mailer, *Prisoner*, 188–92).

Jesus concludes his scriptural argument for the permanence of the marriage bond by saying, "What therefore God has yoked together, let not a human being separate" (10:9). The antithesis here between *theos* and *anthrōpos*, between divine and human actions, corresponds to the apocalyptic antimony sketched out in earlier Markan passages such as 7:7–23 and 8:33. It is *God's* will that human beings should be permanently joined in marriage; it is only the *human* perversity characteristic of the old aeon that has separated what the deity has so obviously fused. This conclusion interprets the divine will not only from the mechanics of sexual intercourse, in which one body merges into another ("and the two shall become one flesh"), but also from the attraction of male to female ("a man shall leave his father and mother and shall be joined to his wife"). In the view of the Markan Jesus, then, both the sexual act and the desire that gives rise to it are reflections of the divine will ("what . . . God has yoked together").

10:10–12: private clarification of Jesus' teaching on divorce. As frequently happens in Mark (2:17, 22, 28; etc.), the response of Jesus' opponents to his pronouncement is not recorded; it may be that Mark wishes to leave the impression that they are thunderstruck and silenced by his retort, as happens in 12:17 (cf. 12:34). The scene immediately shifts to "the house" in which Jesus is staying, and, as also frequently happens (cf. 4:10; 7:17; 9:28), this domicile becomes the place where the disciples ask Jesus privately for clarification of what he has just said (10:10). Their puzzlement underlines the radicality of Jesus' position, which troubled not only outsiders but also Christians. Indeed, the Markan scenes that take place in houses typically transcend the horizon of the historical Jesus to treat the concerns of early Christian communities, which usually met in houses; and in the present instance this setting is especially appropriate, since the issue of marriage, as well as that of treatment of children (see 10:13–16), came under the general rubric of household management in the Hellenistic world (cf. Balch, *Wives* and "Household Codes").

Jesus responds to the disciples' apparent bemusement by asserting that a man who divorces his wife and marries another woman commits adultery (10:11), as does a woman who divorces her husband and marries another man (10:12; cf. the NOTE on "And she, if she divorces her husband and marries another" in 10:12). This reference to remarriage as adultery extends the logic of 10:6–9: since the first marriage remains in effect, to enter into a second union is to commit adultery. It might at first seem more logical to assert that the divorcing person, who is "really" still married to the former partner, commits bigamy if he or she remarries. Bigamy, however, is not defined as a sin in the OT, at least for men, and in fact polygamy was practiced by OT worthies such as Abraham and Jacob. Although many later Jews frowned on the practice, it was not formally outlawed in rabbinic circles until the thirteenth century of our era (see Schereschewsky, "Bigamy and Polygamy"). Adultery, by contrast, was always regarded as a serious transgression; the taboo against it is one of the Ten Commandments (Exod 20:14; Deut 5:18), and it was punishable by death (see Lev 20:10; Deut 22:22; *b. Sanh.* 52b). Jesus, then, compares remarriage to adultery rather than bigamy partly because the former was a sin under Jewish law, whereas the latter was not.

This designation of remarriage as adultery connects 10:11–12 with the previous subsection of our pericope, in which indissoluble marriage was linked with a "realistic" and almost magical view of the permanent fusion of persons created by sexual congress (on "realistic" vs. "nominalistic" conceptions of law, see Schwartz, "Law"). The fact that the pericope now ends with an expression of concern about sexual defilement (*moichatai* = "commits adultery" is the final word) underlines the extent to which a preoccupation with sexuality has pervaded the whole passage.

The saying of Jesus forbidding divorce was well known throughout the early church; in 1 Corinthians, for example, Paul refers approvingly to a word of the Lord that affirmed that a wife should not leave her husband and that a husband should not divorce his wife (7:10–11). Yet Paul introduces several qualifiers into his exegesis of this saying. He adds, for example, that if the woman *does* divorce her husband, she should remain single—thus implicitly recognizing that divorce will happen and not condemning it out of hand. And he goes on to restrict Jesus' ruling further by saying that it applies only to instances in which both partners are believers; otherwise, "if the unbelieving partner separates, let it be so; in such a case the brother or sister is not bound." In this case, Paul is willing to set aside his genuine concern for purity in marriage (cf. 1 Cor 6:16; 7:14) in favor of something that he apparently considers more important: "For God has called us to peace" (7:15b RSV).

The church, either in its wisdom or in its confusion, chose to canonize *both* Paul's more relaxed attitude toward divorce, which comes closer to the late Roman idea that marriage is based on consent (cf. E. Clark, "Constraining," 155), *and* Jesus' uncompromising opposition to it—although this opposition is mitigated in the most influential Gospel by an exception clause that regards fornication as a legitimate ground for divorce (Matt 5:32; 19:9). To many, the Pauline position, with its exaltation of familial and communal harmony over purity considerations and its recognition that in some cases peace is best served by divorce, may seem more attractive than strict adherence to the Markan Jesus' verdict, which may appear to be based on an excessive anxiety about sexual defilement. And, indeed, it is hermeneutically revealing, as David Adams points out in private correspondence, that "already in earliest Christianity the church saw fit to modify even dominical teaching on important subjects, a responsible freedom that, as precedent, is probably more significant than any one of the teachings as such." Adams cites, in addition to the instances mentioned above, the example of 1 Cor 9:14–15, "where Paul transforms a dominical *mandate* [cf. Luke 10:7] into an apostolic *option*."

This important insight, however, does not mean that Christians are free simply to ignore Jesus' commandment about divorce; they need to ask, rather, what it is trying to get at. When this is done, it becomes clear that the concern it expresses about defilement is only the reverse side of a "high" view of marriage and of the sexual act, one that ascribes transformative significance to that act and the relation it creates. When one body enters or is entered by another, a transaction of eternal significance has taken place—one that, in its merging of opposites and resolution of contradictions, mirrors the oneness of God with the world in the new age inaugurated by Jesus' advent (on "God is one" as an eschatological hope, see Zech 14:9 and cf. Marcus, "Authority," 210). And in a culture in which sex is often trivialized and used merely for private gratification or for asserting domination over others, we need to listen attentively to Jesus' word. At the same time, we need also to be aware of the absurdities to which it might lead if applied in isolation from Paul's concern for "peace"; is a child who has been sexually abused by an adult, for example, to be regarded as permanently "wedded" to his or her abuser?

For ancient thinkers, including biblical ones, marriage and heterosexual sex were inextricably linked with the divine gift of children; indeed, in Gen 1:28 God's first blessing of humanity after he has created them male and female is "Be fruitful and multiply." It is no accident, therefore, that our passage, in which Jesus traces the institution of marriage back to "the beginning of the creation," is immediately followed by his blessing of children.

JESUS BLESSES CHILDREN (10:13–16)

10 ¹³And people were bringing him children, in order that he might touch them; but the disciples rebuked them. ¹⁴But when he saw this, Jesus became annoyed and said to them, "Let the children come to me! Don't forbid them!—for to such ones belongs the dominion of God. ¹⁵Amen, I say to you, whoever does not receive the dominion of God like a child will never enter it." ¹⁶And he embraced them and blessed them, laying his hands on them.

NOTES

10 13. *people were bringing him children.* Gk *prosepheron autǭ paidia*, lit. "they were bringing children to him." On the impersonal use of third person plural verbs, which is especially characteristic of Semitic prose, see the NOTES on "the people were amazed" in 1:22 and "people came" in 5:14. Matthew, sensing the nuance, changes the wording to "children were being brought to him" (*prosēnechthēsan autǭ paidia*, 19:13).

Prospherein can mean either "carry to" (e.g., Gen 27:25; 43:26; Judg 5:25) or "lead to" (e.g., Matt 18:24; Luke 23:14), and *paidia*, correspondingly, can designate either newborn babies (Gen 17:12; Matt 2:8, 9, 11, etc.), older, semi-independent children (Matt 11:16//Luke 7:32), or even adolescents (Mark 5:39–42; cf. Davies and Allison, 3.33). Both Luke 18:15 and *Gospel of Thomas* 22 have taken the *paidia* here as infants, and John 3:3, 5 places in the context of birth a saying related to Mark 10:15. In the LXX, moreover, *prospherein* almost always means "carry to" rather than "lead to." The infant interpretation also comports with our passage's emphasis on their passivity (10:15: "Whoever does not *receive* the dominion of God like a child") and overall seems slightly more likely than the alternatives.

rebuked them. Gk *epetimēsan autois.* The disciples rebuke those who bring the children to Jesus. It is theoretically possible, to be sure, that the disciples chastise the children themselves, since Jesus immediately says that the children should be allowed to come (cf. Gundry, 384). The bringers of the children, however, are the subject of the previous clause, and the children may be infants (see the previous NOTE), in which case a rebuke to them would be illogical. Some Markan witnesses (e.g., A, D, W, etc.) make it unambiguous that the disciples are rebuking the children's guardians by changing "them" to "those bringing them" (*tois prospherousin auta*).

14. *Let the children come to me! Don't forbid them!* Gk *aphete ta paidia erchesthai pros me, mē kōlyete auta.* As Lane (359–60) points out, the impression of Jesus' irritation is increased by the "sharp staccato effect" of the asyndeton (see the GLOSSARY). One important explanation for his vehemence is the theory, championed especially by Jeremias (*Infant Baptism*, 48–55) and Cullmann (*Baptism*, 25–26, 76–79), that the passage reflects an early church debate about the baptism of children. According to this explanation, the disciples here, as in 9:38–40, represent a conservative, insular ecclesiology, in this case one that rejects infant baptism, whereas Jesus' "don't forbid them" (cf. 9:39) reflects the more relaxed attitude of Christians who, "in the name of Jesus," baptize children.

All of the evidence for this baptismal interpretation, however, is of a circumstantial nature; there is no "smoking gun." Infant baptism is not mentioned explicitly in Christian texts until the late second century, when Hippolytus (*Apostolic Tradition* 19–21) prescribes it and Tertullian (*On Baptism* 18) opposes it (for a detailed look at the history of interpretation, see D. Wright, "Out"). The advocates of the baptismal interpretation of our text, however, respond that it is hard to believe that the practice arose suddenly at this time, especially in view of the texts in Acts that speak of a person being baptized along with his or her household or family (10:2, 47–48; 11:14; 16:15, 33; cf. 1 Cor 1:16 and Jeremias, *Origins*, 64–75; Kretschmar, *Geschichte*, 81–86). Infant baptism *may* have already existed, then, in NT times, and could therefore have provided the backdrop for our passage.

But what is the evidence that it *did*? Advocates of the baptismal interpretation point especially to the pericope's use of the language of "forbidding," which forms a regular part of early baptismal texts (Matt 3:14; Acts 8:36; 10:47; 11:17; Epiphanius, *Panarion* 30.13), and of "Let . . . !," which can also appear in them (Epiphanius, *Panarion* 30.13). Baptism, moreover, typically involved laying on of hands

(Acts 19:5–6; Heb 6:2; Tertullian, *On Baptism* 8; Hippolytus, *Apostolic Tradition* 19), and the theme of the dominion of God can also have baptismal resonances (1 Cor 6:9–11; Col 1:13; Mark 1:14–15; *Secret Gospel of Mark* 3:8–10; cf. the introduction to the COMMENT on 1:14–15). Furthermore, the Fourth Gospel places its parallel to Mark 10:15 (John 3:3, 5) in a context evocative of baptism. And, as we have noted, it is likely that the children in our passage are infants.

These are interesting correspondences, and they help explain why our passage was eventually adduced in favor of infant baptism, but they do not add up to convincing proof that the pericope itself reflects the practice (see Aland, *Did*). The fulcrum of the baptismal theory, the verb *keleuein*, is not a technical term for a part of the baptismal rite but the most common verb for preventing anything (see Argyle, "Theory"), and it is perfectly understandable in the flow of the narrative: the disciples are to encourage access to Jesus, not to stand in its way. The vehemence of the disciples in preventing approach to Jesus and of Jesus in rebuking them, moreover, fits into a frequent Markan pattern of apostolic misunderstanding and dominical rebuke (see the COMMENT on 10:13–16). We cannot afford to be dogmatic; it is *possible* that infant baptism was already being practiced in the first century, despite the lack of direct evidence, and that our passage is meant to defend the practice. But nothing in the pericope demands such an explanation.

such ones. Gk *toioutōn.* This word featured prominently in the debates about infant baptism that followed the Reformation; the Anabaptists, who opposed infant baptism, stressed that the text does not say "*these* ones" but "*such* ones," thus distancing the referent from the children themselves. Zwingli, however, responded that if the kingdom of heaven belonged to those who were *like* children, it appertained all the more to the children themselves (see Ludolphy, "Geschichte," 75). The Markan meaning of "such ones" is probably "these children and others like them," but the word also paves the way for 10:15, in which children become a metaphor for believers.

15. *whoever does not receive the dominion of God like a child will never enter it.* Gk *hos an mē dexētai tēn basileian tou theou hōs paidion ou mē eiselthȩ̄ eis autēn.* The COMMENT on 10:13–16 points out that the main OT background to the Gospel sayings about "entering the dominion of God" is the image of the Israelites poised to enter the promised land. It therefore may be significant that Deut 1:35–39 warns that the evil wilderness generation will not enter the land, but only "your children, who today do not yet know right from wrong, they shall enter there" (cf. Buchanan, *Jesus*, 29–30).

COMMENT

Introduction. Having proclaimed the permanence of marriage (10:1–12), Jesus now turns to the related theme of children—a natural progression, and one that is mirrored in other ancient Jewish and Christian literature (see Eph 5:21–6:4; Col 3:18–21; Josephus, *Against Apion* 2.199–204; cf. Davies and Allison, 3.31 n. 5). Ancient household codes customarily treat, along with the subject of acquiring wealth, three relationships: husband-wife, father-children, and master-slave.

The first two of these relationships are discussed in the first two pericopes of Mark 10 (10:1–12, 13–16) and the last in the chapter's penultimate passage (10:43–44). Wealth, moreover, is the subject of the following two pericopes (10:17–22, 23–31). Mark, then, may have modeled chapter 10, especially its initial triptych, on Hellenistic household codes (cf. Carter, *Households*, 20–21).

As noted in the introduction to the COMMENT on 9:33–37, our passage is in several ways a doublet of the earlier pericope; both texts, for example, deal with Jesus' acceptance of a child or children, whom he embraces, and in both the child functions as a metaphor for the disciple. It is likely, then, that our text and 9:33–37 are elaborations of the same basic tradition—a hypothesis borne out by the fact that in our pericope the disciples display no awareness of Jesus' recent endorsement of children (cf. Davies and Allison, 3.32–33). In the development of these doublets, the saying about receiving the dominion of God like a child (10:15) and the one about receiving a child in Jesus' name (9:37) may have been swapped, either in the pre-Markan stage of the tradition or by Mark himself (cf. the apparently independent forms of this wandering logion in John 3:3, 5; *Gospel of Thomas* 22; and perhaps Matt 18:3; see Davies and Allison, 2.756–57; P. Müller, *Mitte*, 54).

Aside from the possibly redactional introduction of 10:15, which prepares for the teaching on self-abnegation in 10:29 and 10:42–45, Markan editorial activity may also be visible at the end of 10:16. The phrase "laying his hands on them" there, in combination with "and he embraced them" (lit. "embracing them") at the beginning of the verse, creates a typically Markan double expression (cf. Gundry, 551), but it also produces an awkwardness: how exactly does Jesus lay hands on a child he is already embracing? The doublet in 9:36, moreover, contains the participle "embracing" but not the phrase about the laying on of hands. Mark himself, then, may be responsible for the latter, which does produce an awkwardness, but may reflect Mark's desire to liken Jesus' action to a rite of parental blessing (see below).

In terms of structure, the beginning of the passage, in which children are brought to Jesus in order to be touched by him (10:13a), is recapitulated but trumped by the ending, in which he not only touches them but also takes them up in his arms and blesses them (10:16); as Bengel (*Gnomon* on Mark 10:16) comments, therefore, he does even more than was asked. Between the request and its fulfillment, the disciples object to the approach of the children (10:13b), and Jesus rebuts their objection. His response occupies the center of the passage and consists of a specific answer to the disciples' complaint (10:14) and a general instruction that transforms children into models of discipleship (10:15). The importance of this latter instruction, as well as its possible origin outside the present pericope (see the previous paragraph), is suggested by its introductory formula, "Amen, I say to you. . . ."

10:13–16: Jesus rebukes the disciples and blesses the children. An unspecified group ("they," transcribed here as "people") bring children to Jesus, in order that he might touch and bless them (10:13a); it is probable that the conveyers are the children's parents, that the children are infants, and that they are borne in rather than being self-propelled (see the NOTE on "people were bringing him children" in 10:13). In any case, the children's passivity is emphasized by "people were bringing."

There is not much evidence that rabbis or other ancient holy men habitually blessed children, although Jeremias (*Infant Baptism*, 49) points to a tradition in late Talmudic work, *b. Soṭ.* 18:5, that tells of scribes performing this office on the Day of Atonement. Jeremias himself, along with others, thinks that our passage reflects controversies in the early church about infant baptism, but the evidence in favor of this theory is scanty (see the NOTE on "Let the children come to me! Don't forbid them!" in 10:14).

Probably the more relevant background is parental blessing of children, which is frequent in the OT (Gen 9:26–27; 27:1–40; 28:1–4; etc.) and attested in intertestamental Judaism (Sir 3:9). The most important example of this practice, in terms of the later history of tradition, is Jacob's blessing of Joseph's sons, Ephraim and Manasseh, in Genesis 48 (cf. H. Grotius, *Annotationes*, on Matt 19:13). This blessing includes an embrace (48:10) and an imposition of hands (48:14), which makes it similar to the conclusion of our passage (10:16; cf. Derrett, "Why Jesus"). The connection between the OT model and the early Christian practice of imposing hands was already noticed by Tertullian (*On Baptism* 8), who derives the latter from "the old sacramental rite in which Jacob blessed his grandsons" (see Jensen, *Living Water*, 263–64). The linkage is also suggested by early Christian art, which frequently depicts this OT benediction, probably because it was the model for a Christian ritual practice (see Jensen, *Understanding*, 123). First-century Judaism may have been an intermediary between the OT and early Christianity in this regard; one of the mid-third-century paintings from the Dura Europos synagogue prominently displays the blessing of Ephraim and Manasseh by Joseph, including a curiously elongated right hand (lower center panel; see Kraeling, *Synagogue*, 221–23), and at least from the Middle Ages on we have evidence for a widespread Jewish custom of paternal benediction (see Philipson, "Blessing of Children," the *EncJud* article of the same name, and Derrett, "Why Jesus," 13).

To be sure, the theory that a Jewish rite of parental blessing undergirds our pericope faces the same basic problem as the theory of a background in infant baptism: there is no direct first-century evidence for such a rite. But positing such a Jewish rite, which at least has a direct biblical model, makes a lot of sense of our passage in its context. The parents' request for Jesus to bless their children becomes a plea for him to become a kind of godfather to them, and Jesus goes on to associate these godchildren with his followers. In the colloquy just a few verses later, correspondingly, Jesus calls his disciples "children" (10:24) and conspicuously omits "fathers" from the list of surrogate relatives that believers will discover in their new Christian "family" (10:29–30). This may be because God himself, acting through Jesus, has assumed the paternal role (cf. Matt 23:9–10 and the use of "father" as an honorific in early Judaism; see Levine, *Synagogue*, 404).

Whatever the background to the parents' request, the disciples are "agin' it," as they show by rebuking the parents (10:13b). Similar efforts of disciples to restrict

access to their masters are found in the OT (2 Kgs 4:27) and in rabbinic traditions (b. Ketub. 63a; b. Ned. 50a; cf. Davies and Allison, 3.33), but the particular
vehemence of the disciples' objection and of Jesus' reaction ("rebuked them . . .
became annoyed") demands further explanation. Commentators' attempts to do
so have ranged from the plausible to the risible and have included the disciples'
conviction that Jesus' touch should be reserved for healing, their anxiety lest
the children exhaust him, and even their desire for a bribe (see Derrett, "Why
Jesus," 11)!

It is more helpful to eschew such rationalistic, psychologizing explanations and
to see the disciples' misguided attempt to limit access to Jesus as part of a larger
Markan motif of misunderstanding. As Moloney (197) points out, the disciples'
obtuseness in our passage is especially pronounced because Jesus has recently instructed them about the necessity of receiving children (9:35–37); the case, then,
is parallel to that in 8:1–9, where they failed to recognize Jesus' ability to supply
bread after just having had it demonstrated magnificently in 6:30–44. The apostolic density thus fits into a pattern of incomprehension that elsewhere in Mark,
as here, provokes irritated rejoinders from Jesus (see 4:13; 8:16–21, 32–33); our
passage is particularly reminiscent of 8:32–33, where the chief of the disciples rebukes Jesus, and finds himself rebuked in turn, for failing to see that God can work
through what is weak, low, and despised in the world—in that case, the dishonor
and suffering of the cross (cf. 1 Cor 1:27–28).

The Markan Jesus' exaltation of the child as the model for the disciple, however,
probably would have struck ancient hearers as unusual. In antiquity in general, the
dominant features of the image of the child were its vulnerability, dependence,
and social marginality (see Müller, Mitte, 161–62); it is revealing that one of the
main terms for "children," ṭap, can also denote dependent persons in general in
biblical and Qumranic Hebrew (see M. O'Connor, "Lexicography"). In ancient
Jewish texts, tenderness toward children is often displayed, but they usually do not
function as religious models (although see the NOTE on "little ones" in 9:42).
The reverse, rather, is often true; as R. Dosa b. Harkinas puts it in m. Abot 3:11:
"Morning sleep and midday wine and children's talk and sitting in the meeting-
houses of the people of the land put a person out of the world" (Danby trans. alt.).
Children, then, while not evil, can be a distraction from the serious adult business
of Torah study and the practice of good deeds, for which they are unqualified.
To make the transition from the status of a child who is incapable of full participation in the world of the Torah to the status of a bar mitzvah (lit. "son of the
commandment") who is competent to "take the yoke of the dominion of heaven
upon himself" is a consummation devoutly to be wished (cf. Marcus, "Entering,"
672–73).

The centerpiece of our passage uses this common image of children, but
reverses it: precisely these deficient ones, who have no intrinsic right to claim
membership in the dominion of God, constitute its leading citizens (10:14c). This
reversal, in which Jesus favors the disprized over the prized, echoes his teaching
earlier in Mark: he comes to call sinners rather than the righteous, the sick rather

than the well, the last rather than the first (cf. 2:17; 9:35). He does so, not because the children, the sick, and the unrighteous possess hidden virtues, but because of the peculiar dynamic associated with God's action in the world, which is epitomized by the mind-boggling conundrum that one cannot enter the dominion of God unless one first receives it (10:15). This paradox renders questionable the common assumption that in the sayings about "entering the dominion of God," of which this is the second in the Gospel (cf. 9:47; 10:23, 25), *basileia* abandons its usual nuance of "royal power" (cf. the NOTE on "the dominion of God" in 1:15) and becomes instead a place ("kingdom"). In the Bible, people frequently "enter into" an action; in John 4:38, for example, we read that "others have labored, and you have entered into their labor" (cf. Matt 25:21, 23), and the OT is full of idioms such as entering into judgment, into the might of God, and into the righteousness of God (see Marcus, "Entering"). It may be, then, that the Synoptic idiom of "entering (into) the dominion of God" signifies entering into (i.e., participating in) God's demonstration of his sovereignty over the earth.

This interpretation would be in line with the main OT background for the phrase, which lies in the images of the wilderness generation invading Canaan and of later Israelites bursting through the Temple gates at festival times ("*tôrôt* of entry"; cf. Windisch, "Sprüche"). In these Israelite examples, entering parties do so not under their own power but as they are incorporated into the victory procession of the triumphant divine king and holy warrior (see, e.g., Pss 24; 68:24–25; Isa 52:8–12). Thus, the resolution to the paradox between receiving the *basileia* on the one hand and entering it on the other does not lie in a distinction between present acceptance and future admission (against Gundry, 551) but in an image that combines passivity (being carried) with activity (moving in)—but activity that is contingent on the action of Another.

The divine mercy that is the central concern of our passage is beautifully demonstrated at its end, where Jesus confirms by a gesture the attitude of acceptance he has just proclaimed, taking the children into his embrace (presumably one by one), blessing them, and laying hands on them (10:16). This gesture, beyond its possible paternal resonance, caps the sense of apocalyptic advent that has permeated the narrative since the references to the dominion of God in 10:14–15. If those references began in a context of wrath and counterwrath hinting at apocalyptic judgment ("rebuked them . . . became annoyed"), they now give way to a conclusion that points toward the ultimate restoration of the world through the all-embracing mercy of God. As Victor of Antioch (cited in Aquinas, *Catena Aurea* on Mark 10:16) puts it: "Fitly does he take them up into his arms to bless them, as it were, lifting into his own bosom, and reconciling himself to his creation, which in the beginning fell from him, and was separated from him."

But there is a price to be paid by those who would "enter the dominion of God," who would become the human instruments for the extension of the divine embrace that recovers the world for God. The Gospel's next two, closely related passages will stress that price, along with the hundredfold blessing of those who are willing to pay it.

JESUS CALLS A RICH MAN (10:17–22)

10 [17]And as he was setting out on the way, a man came running up, and falling down on his knees before him, he asked him, "Good teacher, what shall I do to inherit eternal life?" [18]But Jesus said to him, "Why do you call me good? There is nobody good except One, that is, God. [19]You know the commandments: 'Do not murder, do not commit adultery, do not steal, do not bear false witness, do not defraud, honor your father and mother.' " [20]He said to him, "Teacher, I have observed all these things from my youth up." [21]And Jesus, looking at him, was moved with love for him and said to him, "You are missing one thing: go, sell whatever you have and give to the poor, and you will have treasure in heaven; and come on, follow me!" [22]But he, indignant at Jesus' word, went away grieving, for he had great estates.

NOTES

10 17. *as he was setting out.* Gk *ekporeuomenou autou.* The participle and pronoun are singular, designating Jesus alone; no mention is made of the disciples until 10:23, and 10:17–22 reads like a self-contained unit. It is probable that the original narrative concerned only Jesus and the rich man and that the discussion between Jesus and the disciples in 10:23–31 reflects a later development of the tradition (cf. Gnilka, 2.84).

a man. Gk *heis,* lit. "one" (masculine). Matthew 19:20 makes this figure into a young man (*neaniskos*), whereas Luke 18:18 calls him a ruler (*archōn*); by a process of harmonization, therefore, Christian tradition has designated him "the rich young ruler." In Mark, however, the man does not seem to be young (see the NOTE on "from my youth up" in 10:20), and there is no indication that he is a ruler.

to inherit eternal life. Gk *hina zōēn aiōnion klēronomēsō,* lit. "in order that I might inherit eternal life." This image is related to OT and Jewish texts in which Abraham and his descendants are promised the land of Canaan as an inheritance (Gen 15:7; Exod 32:13; Josh 13:7; *Jub.* 22:27; etc.). In some later traditions, this promise is broadened into one of inheriting the whole earth (e.g., Sir 44:21; *Jub.* 22:14; Rom 4:13), partly because of the ambiguity in Hebrew *'ereṣ* and Greek *gē,* which can mean either "land" or "earth." But the disappointment of such hopes on the worldly level led to their transposition into an eschatological key (see, e.g., Isa 60:21; *1 En.* 5:7; Matt 5:5) and the frequent substitution of "eternal life" and related phrases for an earthly inheritance (see, e.g., *1 En.* 40:9; *Pss. Sol.* 14:6; *m. 'Abot* 5:19; *b. Qidd.* 40b; cf. Volz, *Eschatologie,* 341–42; Foerster, "*Klēros,*" 779–80). For many apocalypticists, it is the poor who will eventually receive the divine inheritance; Jas 2:5, for example, says that God has "chosen the poor in the world to be . . . heirs of the dominion that he has promised to those who love him" (NRSV alt.; cf. Luke 6:21).

18. *There is nobody good except One, that is, God.* Gk *oudeis agathos ei mē heis* *ho theos.* God is associated with good in Gen 1:1–2:3, but the most important biblical background for the awkward phrase *ei mē heis ho theos,* which is found also in 2:7, is the Shema in Deut 6:4 (*kyrios ho theos hēmōn kyrios heis estin,* "the Lord our God, the Lord is one" [my trans.]). Gundry (561) doubts the allusion, since the emphasis in the Markan text is that God alone is good, while that in the Shema is that he alone is God. But a scriptural echo need not express exactly the same thought as the source text, and if Mark had not desired to allude to the Shema, his thought could have been more smoothly expressed ("no one is good except God"). In Jewish interpretations, moreover, the Shema implies the uniqueness of divine attributes as well as of the divine existence; in *Deut. Rab.* 2.31, for example, it is used to prove the singularity of God's glory.

19. *Do not murder,* etc. Gk *mē phoneusēs,* etc. Here Jesus quotes the second table of the Decalogue, which governs relations among human beings (commandments 6–10, according to the usual count; on the different methods of enumerating the Decalogue, see Nielsen, *Ten Commandments,* 10–13). He then tacks on a reference to the fifth commandment, so that the order of the commandments cited in our passage is 6, 7, 8, 9, 10, 5. The sequence of the Decalogue was flexible; the LXX (B), the Nash papyrus, Philo, and a copy of Deuteronomy from Qumran, for example, reverse the sixth and seventh commandments, putting "Do not commit adultery" before "Do not murder," perhaps in order to join the familial commandments honoring parents and prohibiting adultery (see K. J. Thomas, "Citations"; Flusser, "Do Not"). The alteration of the usual order in our passage may also be thematically significant (see the COMMENT on 10:17–20).

The verbs in Mark's rendering of the Decalogue basically follow the LXX of Exod 20:12–17//Deut 5:16–21, though the grammatical form differs (*mē* + aorist subjunctive rather than *ou* + future indicative), and the order is that of the MT rather than that of the majority of LXX manuscripts (cf. K. J. Thomas, "Citations"). The one striking exception to the LXX verbiage is the tenth commandment, where Mark has *mē aposterēsēs* ("Do not defraud") rather than *ouk epithymēseis* ("You shall not covet"). This paraphrase is in line with the interpretation of the tenth commandment in certain Jewish traditions, in which it forbids not only craving for others' possessions but also usurping them (see, e.g., *Mekilta* Baḥodesh 8 [Lauterbach 2.266] and *Mekilta R. Šim.* Yitro 17 [Hoffmann, 112]; cf. Greenberg, "Decalogue Tradition," 106–9). This makes the tenth commandment similar in meaning to the eighth, "You shall not steal," but the latter may have originally referred to kidnapping rather than robbery in general (see Alt, "Verbot," and cf. *b. Sanh.* 86a). Matthew and Luke, however, as well as some Markan scribes (B, K, W, Δ, and several versions), omit *mē aposterēsēs* from their parallel to our passage, apparently not recognizing it as a paraphrase of the tenth commandment (cf. Taylor, 428; Metzger, 105).

Why does Mark rephrase this commandment rather than rendering it literally? The basic meaning of *aposterein* is "to take away illegitimately"; the word is often used in contexts suggestive of social oppression, especially keeping back a hireling's wages (see, e.g., Deut 24:14 [Alexandrinus]; Mal 3:5; Sir 4:1; Jas 5:4). This and similar types of exploitation frequently characterized the landed aristocracy in first-century Palestine (see Goodman, *Ruling Class*, 51–68), and our passage may wish to link the wealthy man in the narrative with this group and their practices (see the NOTES on "You are missing" and "sell whatever you have and give to the poor" in 10:21 and "he had great estates" in 10:22).

20. *from my youth up.* Gk *ek neotētos mou.* This phrase implies that the man is no longer young; Matthew, who makes him into a *neaniskos* ("young man"), omits it.

21. *looking at him.* Gk *emblepsas autǭ.* The fact that this gaze is followed by a spiritual diagnosis ("You are missing one thing") suggests that it is the sort of instantaneous, supernatural character analysis that is frequently attributed to holy people (cf. Bieler, *THEIOS ANĒR*, 87–94; for other NT instances, see John 1:42, 47–48; 4:16–19; Acts 5:1–11; and cf. 1 Cor 14:25: "the secrets of his heart are disclosed" [RSV]). A particularly striking parallel is provided by Porphyry, *Life of Pythagoras* 54, in which the rich Cylon approaches Pythagoras and asks to partake in his philosophical life; Pythagoras, however, divines Cylon's worthless character from his physical features and sends him away in an aggrieved state (*elypēsen*; cf. *lypoumenos* = "grieving" in Mark 10:22). Similar gifts of charismatic insight are attested in the Jewish world; the Instructor (*maskil*) at Qumran, for example, is also called the Examiner (*mĕbaqqer*) because of his role of spiritually scrutinizing each community member and new recruit "concerning his insight and his deeds in connection with the law" (1QS 5:23–24; 6:13–21). This is comparable to the way in which Jesus in our story supernaturally weighs and finds wanting the rich man's claim to have observed the Torah perfectly (see the COMMENT on 10:21–22). Even in modern times, stories of Hasidic masters, including the Baal Shem Tov and the Lubavitcher Rebbe, often stress the holy man's penetrating eyes, supernatural ability to uncover secrets, and extraordinary power to make accurate and effective spiritual diagnoses and prescriptions (see, e.g., Ben-Amos and Mintz, *Praise*, 37–38, 71–72, 75–76; anon., *Wonders*, 1.12, 20–21, 35, 39, 52).

moved with love for him. Gk *ēgapēsen auton.* This verb is frequently used for a father's love for his son in Genesis (22:2; 25:28; 37:3; 44:20), and that association fits in with other indications of Jesus' fatherly relation to the rich man in the passage (see the COMMENTS on 10:17–20 and 10:21–22). As the first of the Genesis passages cited above reminds us, however, a father's love may involve the son in a sacrifice.

You are missing. Gk *hysterei.* This verb is phonologically but not etymologically connected with the word for "defraud" (*aposterēsēs*) in 10:19; Mark may wish to suggest that the man's spiritual lack is related to a violation of the tenth commandment.

sell whatever you have and give to the poor. Gk *hosa echeis pōlēson kai dos tois ptōchois.* In Luke 19:8 and *y. Hor.* 3:4 (48a; Neusner 34.114–15) it is considered to be a sign of extraordinary piety when a rich man repents and gives away *half* of his goods (cf. Philostratus, *Life of Apollonius* 1.13); Jesus' call to the man in our story to give away *everything*, then, goes beyond what is elsewhere expected of penitents. This more radical demand may have something to do with the man's prior mistreatment of or apathy toward the poor; see the COMMENT on 10:21–22 and cf. the *Gospel of the Hebrews*, in which Jesus declares that the rich man's indifference to his starving, ill-clad neighbors invalidates his claim to have fulfilled the Law and the Prophets (cf. Klijn, "Question," 150).

treasure in heaven. Gk *thēsauron en ouranō̦.* This is a standard expression, and it and related concepts appear in Jewish texts (e.g., Tob 4:8–9; Philo, *On Rewards and Punishments* 104; *4 Ezra* 7:77; *t. Pe'ah* 4:18) as well as elsewhere in the Synoptic tradition (Matt 6:19–21//Luke 12:33–34) and the larger NT canon (1 Tim 6:17–19; Heb 11:26). In several of these passages, as in ours, an implicit contrast is set up between the treasures of earth, which are not worth having, and the treasures of heaven, which are; the former, therefore, may be cheerfully sacrificed in favor of the latter. The idea is often framed in eschatological terms; in *t. Pe'ah* 4:18, for example, King Monobazus of Adiabene gives away his earthly wealth in order to have "imperishable treasure for the age to come," and even the normally uneschatological Philo uses the "treasure in heaven" image in an eschatological context (*On Rewards and Punishments* 104–6).

22. *indignant . . . went away grieving.* Gk *stygnasas . . . apēlthen lypoumenos. Stygnazein* and cognate words come from a root meaning "to hate" and can have an implication not only of sorrow (cf. RSV: "his countenance fell") but also of resentment (see, e.g., Dan 2:12; cf. LSJ 1657; Lagrange, 267; Taylor, 430). The latter nuance is appropriate in the present context, since it reverses the reverence implied by the man's kneeling before Jesus in 10:17, just as "went away grieving" reverses "came running up."

for he had great estates. Gk *ēn gar echōn ktēmata polla. Ktēmata* can mean possessions in general, but it often connotes landed property in particular (see, e.g., Acts 5:1, 3, and cf. M-M 362; Lane, 362 n. 33). The latter nuance would be appropriate in the present passage: Jesus asks a landowner to stop exploiting his workers (cf. the NOTE on "Do not murder, etc." in 10:19) and instead to become their benefactor.

Chrysostom (*Homily on Matthew* 63.2) cleverly relates "grieving" to "for he had great estates" rather than "went away": the man is unhappy because wealth increases sorrow.

COMMENT

Introduction. Having exalted children as a paradigm for discipleship within the dominion of God, the Markan Jesus now confronts a radically different representative of humanity, a wealthy man who approaches him to ask a question concerning attainment of eternal life. The question that arises with regard to his wealth, however, fits into the "household code" pattern that began in 10:1 (see the introduction to the COMMENT on 10:13–16). In contrast to children, whose weakness, dependence, and disqualification from the realm of the Law were proverbial (see the COMMENT on 10:13–16), this man is not only well-off materially but also "rich" in terms of Torah observance (cf. Phil 3:6–8). Jesus, however, discerns in the man's wealth an obstruction to his participation in the dominion of God and calls him, for his own good, to abandon it and follow him. Contrary to what Shakespeare's Richard II alleges (5.5.13–17), this emphasis on the arduous sacrifice necessary to enter the dominion of God is not really contradictory to 10:13–16, which treats the dominion of God as a gift: the man's trust in the delusive security afforded by his wealth prevents him from becoming a "child" who relies exclusively on the largesse of the heavenly Father.

This passage is probably dependent on pre-Markan tradition, but it also shows features of Markan redaction. The introductory phrase "and as he was setting out on the way" in 10:17, for example, matches the Markan predilection for the genitive absolute construction and the "way" theme in this section of the Gospel (see Gnilka, 2.84); the original version may have run something like "As Jesus was passing by . . ." (cf. 1:16; 2:14). In the next verse, "Why do you call me good?" (10:18a) is probably a historical memory, since it has proved troublesome for Christians to explain over the years (cf. already Matt 19:17 and see Taylor, 426–27). But the following part of Jesus' reply, the allusion to the Shema in 10:18b ("There is nobody good except One, that is, God") may be editorial, since the final phrase is matched word for word in 2:7, which is part of a Markan insertion (see the NOTE on "There is nobody good except One, that is, God" in 10:18). Also perhaps redactional are the reference to Jesus looking at the man in 10:21, which corresponds to a frequent Markan motif (see, e.g., the introductions to the COMMENTS on 1:16–20 and 3:20–35 and the COMMENT on 6:30–34), and the parenthetical *gar* ("for") clause at the conclusion of the pericope (10:22b).

Jesus' encounter with the rich man (10:17–22) will be treated separately from his discussion of riches with the disciples (10:23–31), even though the two are part of one long unit. The present subsection has its own well-defined structure. The eager and reverent approach of the man at the beginning (10:17a) is matched by his sad and sullen departure at the end (10:22). In between, Jesus responds to the first part of the man's query ("Good teacher," 10:17b) with a counterquestion ("Why do you call me good?" 10:18a) and a reference to the central creed in the Torah, the Shema (10:18b). He then answers the second part of the query ("what shall I do to inherit eternal life?" 10:17c) with a reference to another crucial Torah passage that was traditionally linked with the Shema, the Decalogue (10:19; see, e.g., the Nash papyrus; *m. Tam.* 5:1; *b. Ber.* 12a; *Did.* 1:1–2:2; cf. Allison, "Mark 12.28–31," 274–77). But the man's reply that he is already observing these commandments (10:20), countered by Jesus' call to abandon everything and follow him (10:21), transfers the discussion from the realm of the Torah to that of the dominion of God (cf. 10:23)—an arena into which the man is unable to follow Jesus. Dramatically, then, the big break comes between 10:20 and 10:21.

10:17–20: the man's approach and the initial conversation. After the private conversation with the disciples concerning divorce (10:10–12) and the blessing of children (10:13–16), both of which take place in a house, Jesus sets out on a journey (10:17a), apparently with his disciples in tow (10:23–31), and probably already heading toward Jerusalem (cf. 10:32). The trip is interrupted, however, even before it properly begins, by a man who runs up and throws himself on the ground before Jesus (10:17b), his speed reflecting the urgency of his question and his kneeling posture his reverence before the one who, he believes, can answer it (for prostration before gods, holy people, and kings, see 1 Kgs 19:18; 2 Kgs 1:13; 1 Chr 29:20; Mark 15:19). The man immediately gives verbal expression to the reverence he has just displayed, calling Jesus a "good teacher" and bringing forth the problem that has compelled him to come: "What shall I do to inherit eternal life?" (10:17c). This question uses imagery that goes back to the OT's patriarchal narratives, in which Abraham, Isaac, and Jacob were promised that their offspring would ultimately possess the land in which they themselves sojourned; in later Judaism the promise was transposed into an eschatological key and became a metaphor for participation in the life of the world to come (see the NOTE on "to inherit eternal life" in 10:17). The import of the man's question, then, is, "What can I do now in order to ensure that in the eschatological future I may receive the inheritance that God has promised to his favored ones?"

Jesus' preliminary response (10:18–19) is firmly embedded in the realm of the Law, and specifically the Decalogue (Exod 20:1–17; Deut 5:6–21). Its initial part alludes to the Shema in Deut 6:4–5, viewed by many early Jews and Christians as the functional equivalent of the first table of the Decalogue, which deals with relations between humans and God (see, e.g., Philo, *On the Decalogue* 108–10, and cf. Allison, "Mark 12.28–34"). The second part of the answer (10:19) quotes from the second table of the Decalogue, which refers to relations between human beings. These observations suggest a closeness between our pericope and the discussion about the heart of the Law in 12:28–34: in both cases Jesus is addressed as "teacher," is asked a question related to the central requirements of the Torah, and responds in terms that summarize the two tables of the Decalogue; in neither, however, does observance of these commandments suffice for entry into God's dominion ("missing one thing"/"not far from the dominion of God"; cf. Sariola, *Gesetz*, 204). Such summaries of the Law were frequent in Jewish contexts (see the NOTE on "second" in 12:31), and an appeal to the Decalogue in response to a question about the attainment of eternal life would have been perfectly predictable; it was a basic principle of the OT and Judaism that the pathway to life was observance of the statutes of the Torah (see, e.g., Deut 30:15–16; Lev 18:5; *Pss. Sol.* 14:2; *m. 'Abot* 2:7), and these in turn were epitomized by the Decalogue, which was considered to be a summary of the whole Law (see Philo, *On the Decalogue* 19–20; 154; *Special Laws* 1.1; *Targ. Ps.-J.* Exod 24:12). Matthew, then, is only bringing out Mark's meaning when he has Jesus say, "If you wish to enter into life, keep the commandments" (Matt 19:17).

The specific way in which the Markan Jesus alludes to the Shema, however, has proved troubling to Christians down through the centuries: "Why do you call me good? There is nobody good except One, that is, God" (10:18). There could be no more dramatic illustration of what Karl Barth, echoing Kierkegaard, has called "the infinite qualitative distinction" between God and humanity (*Romans*, 10); Jesus seems to range himself with sinful humanity in its alienation from the only good being, God. On the level of the historical Jesus, this solidarity with sinful humanity is of a piece with Jesus' participation in John's "baptism of repentance leading to the forgiveness of sins" (1:4; cf. the COMMNENT on 1:9). But the statement is more than a fossil left over from an early, pre-Markan stage in tradition history, since Mark himself seems to be deeply influenced by an apocalyptic pessimism, which he would probably call apocalyptic *realism*, that places all of humanity on the opposite side of the ledger sheet from God (see 8:33). Gundry (561), to be sure, is right to point out that elsewhere in the Synoptic tradition Jesus *does* describe some human beings as good (Matt 12:35//Luke 6:45; Matt 25:21// Luke 19:17; Matt 5:45; 7:15–19; 22:10; 25:23; Luke 8:15), but it is surely significant that *none* of these passages is from Mark.

This apocalyptic pessimism about human possibility, however, stands in a dialectical relation with an optimism engendered by Mark's belief in the irruption of a new divine reality into the human sphere—an irruption that, in his view, has occurred through the advent of Jesus. If, then, the Markan Jesus asks, "Why do you call me good?" and ascribes goodness to the One God alone, in the next breath he demonstrates a godlike power and mercy by supernaturally divining the secret obstacle that is troubling his interlocutor and lovingly holding out the solution to him (10:21). It is relevant, moreover, in view of the concatenation of references to Jesus' mercy and status as a teacher, on the one hand, and of allusions to the Shema, the Decalogue, and attainment of life, on the other, that the second benediction of the Shema, which probably goes back to Second Temple times, is a panegyric to the love that God has shown to Israel by "teaching them statutes of life" in the Torah (cf. Elbogen, *Liturgy,* 23). In addition, several features in our text seem to echo a Deuteronomic passage that in Mark 12:32 will be associated with the Shema:

> To you it was shown so that you would acknowledge that the LORD is God; *there is no other besides him* . . . And because he *loved* your ancestors, he chose their descendants after them. He brought you out of Egypt with his own presence, by his great power, driving out before you nations greater and mightier than yourselves, to bring you in, giving you their land for a *possession,* as it is still today. So acknowledge today and take to heart that the LORD is God in heaven above and on the earth beneath; *there is no other.* Keep his statutes and his commandments, which I am commanding you today *for your own well-being* and that of your descendants after you, so that you may long remain in the land that the LORD your God is giving you for all time. (Deut 4:35–40)

There is thus an intimate connection between the idea of a divine inheritance, the affirmation of God's unique oneness, and the assertion of his incomparable goodness and mercy to Israel, and all of this suggests that the merciful Jesus cannot be radically separated from the One God to whom he refers in 10:18.

The allusion to the Shema, however, is only implicit, while that to the Ten Commandments is explicit: in response to the man's question about the way to inherit eternal life, the Markan Jesus points to the second table of the Decalogue (10:19). The first two-thirds of this list is more or less standard, but there are two surprises at its end, and these reveal something of the special emphasis of our passage:

(1) The penultimate commandment in the series is rendered "Do not defraud" rather than the expected "Do not covet." This emphasis on the unjust actions to which craving may lead is consonant with Jewish interpretations of the tenth commandment, but it is possible that the passage is also highlighting the sort of exploitation of the peasantry that was common among great landowners in first-century Palestine, in whose number the rich man in our story apparently belongs. Indeed, in view of some of the other exegetical clues in the passage, the Markan Jesus may mean to suggest that the man himself is guilty of such oppression (see the NOTES on "Do not murder, etc." in 10:19, "You are missing" and "sell whatever you have and give to the poor" in 10:21, and "for he had great estates" in 10:22).

(2) At the very end of the list the Markan Jesus tacks on a reference to the injunction to honor parents, which is from the end of the *first* table of the Decalogue. This unusual order, which by end-stress (see the GLOSSARY) seems to assign special prominence to the commandment about honoring parents, may relate to the setting of our passage in a section of the Gospel that highlights the position of Jesus as the father, in association with God, of a new Christian family (see the COMMENTS on 10:13–16 and 10:28–31). Just as the Markan Jesus has symbolically displayed his love for his followers by bestowing a parental benediction on children who came to him (10:15–16), so now he demonstrates his fatherly affection for a potential disciple by trying to lead him to the path in which true blessedness is found.

The man replies to Jesus' citation of the Decalogue, "Teacher, I have observed all these things from my youth up" (10:20). There is no reason to doubt his sincerity (contrast Taylor, 425; Myers, *Binding*, 272); as Origen (*Commentary on Matthew* 15.14) and Chrysostom (*Homily on Matthew* 63.1) point out, the narrative itself seems to affirm it in the next verse when it describes Jesus' positive counter-response ("looking at him, was moved with love for him and said . . ."). At the same time, however, Jesus' striking reformulation of the tenth commandment to refer to misappropriation may already hint that the man's observance of the Torah is less perfect than he believes.

10:21–22: the call rejected. Jesus' gaze burrows into the rich man's soul ("looking at him") and with an intuition guided by fatherly affection ("moved with love for him") brings the obstacle to light: "You are missing one thing" (10:21a). Ironically, then, this "man who has everything" still lacks the one necessary thing (cf. Luke 10:42)—the gift of being free enough from his possessions to follow Jesus' call wholeheartedly. As pointed out in the NOTE on "looking at him" in 10:21, Jesus' discernment of a spiritual lack in the man demonstrates the sort of supernatural insight that is often ascribed to holy people. But it also helps answer the implicit question that was raised by 10:18 about the relation between Jesus and the good God, who in the biblical and Jewish traditions shows his goodness not only by being good in himself but also by doing good to others (see the common rabbinic formula "who is good and does good," *m. Ber.* 9:2; etc.) and whose oneness is inseparable from this overflowing kindness (see above on the second benediction of the Shema). If now, a few short verses after the reference to God's unique goodness, *Jesus* is portrayed in a way that combines benevolence with an extraordinary spiritual capability, the implication must be that Jesus' outreach to the rich man is a manifestation of the divine power and mercy. Another way of understanding the Shema's affirmation of the unique goodness of God thus begins to emerge: No one but God is good, and so when Jesus demonstrates a godlike beneficence, he is not acting through a human capacity but through the eschatological power of God (cf. the COMMENT on 5:18–20). In its canonical context, then, our passage does not deny Jesus' goodness but ascribes it to its divine origin, so that the question in 10:18a comes to mean, "Do you realize that I am good only because God is?" (cf. again the COMMENT on 5:18–20; Gundry, 561; Marcus, "Authority," 208–11).

Along with his charismatic insight into the man's condition, Jesus offers a prescription for its cure: "Go, sell whatever you have and give to the poor" (10:21b). If the Markan Jesus' statement about human goodness has caused problems for subsequent Christians, so, too, has his command to give away all one's wealth— largely because Christians have been reluctant to do so. As Fusco (*Povertà*, 18–37) shows in a helpful survey, many exegetes have followed the lead of Clement of Alexandria, who insists that the instruction is not to be interpreted literally but allegorically; the command to sell everything, then, signifies that the man should rid himself of his anxieties and passions about his wealth, not the wealth itself (*Who Is the Rich Man That Shall Be Saved?* 11). Those who, contrary to such evasions, take the command literally have usually based their arguments on the Matthean parallel, in which it is preceded by the condition "If you wish to be perfect . . ." (Matt 19:21); this qualifier led many medieval Roman Catholic theologians to distinguish between "counsels of salvation" appropriate for everyone and "counsels of perfection" appropriate only for the clergy, placing the command to sell all in the latter category. Luther, while rejecting the scholastic distinction, also limits the application of Jesus' injunction, teaching that it was aimed only at this particular man, in whom Jesus detected a soul-destroying addiction to Mammon (WA 47, 348.26–40; 350.13–40).

There is some merit in Luther's general line of approach, since the Jesus of the Gospels never makes radical poverty a universal condition of discipleship, and indeed from earliest times there has been a wide diversity of Christian teaching on wealth (see Bassler, *God and Mammon*). In Mark itself, although Jesus instructs his apostles not to take anything on their missionary journey, he can do so only because he is confident that others will supply their needs (6:8–11); there must, therefore, be people who have *not* given everything away, and the command to do so is aimed at a small group rather than the Markan community as a whole or people in general. In the present case, moreover, we have seen that the man may be a landowner, who like most members of his class would have been more concerned with the creation of wealth than with the welfare of the peasants who worked his estate; in this case, Jesus' command to "sell whatever you have and give to the poor" would be aimed both at correcting a spiritual distortion ("You are missing one thing") and at filling the physical void in the bellies of those whom the man has exploited ("and give to the poor").

This call to abandon possessions for the sake of the dominion of God may not have struck all of Mark's readers as novel. In one of the Cynic Epistles, for example, Diogenes describes how he converted a young man to philosophy, with the happy result that "from the next day, after he *distributed his property* to his relatives, he took up the provision bag, doubled his coarse cloak, and *followed me*" (Epistle 38; Malherbe trans. alt.; on Cynic gear, see the NOTES on "staff" and "provision bag" in 6:8 and "two tunics" in 6:9). Even more germane is the parallel in 1 Macc 2:27–28, in which pious Jews at the beginning of the Maccabean Revolt are called to prove their *zeal for the Law* by *abandoning all their possessions* and *following* a charismatic leader into holy war (see the COMMENT on 1:16–18). The correspondence, then, embraces not only leaving possessions and following a leader but also fulfillment of the Torah (cf. Mark 10:19) and participation in God's climactic demonstration of his royal power over the world (cf. 10:25).

Such single-minded commitment may involve losing not only one's possessions but also one's life; for the members of the Markan community it implies an existence filled "with persecutions" (10:30) and even with death (13:12). But Jesus has already announced that those who lose their lives through following him will find them (8:34–35), and a later parable will make clear that violent death is the mark of God's "heir" (12:7). The ultimate answer, then, to the question, "What shall I do to inherit eternal life?" is "Take up your cross, and follow me" (cf. 8:34). This call to follow is not simply an invitation to self-denial, since Jesus forthrightly promises the man "treasure in heaven" if he will embrace it. As Chrysostom (*Homily on Matthew* 63.2) astutely notes, the fact that Jesus uses the treasure image here, rather than repeating "eternal life" from 10:17, implies that any sacrifice the man is called on to make will be more than compensated (cf. "a hundredfold" in 10:30 and the NOTE on "treasure in heaven" in 10:21).

The man, however, is unable to trust God in the way that Jesus suggests; at Jesus' word he becomes resentfully depressed (*stygnasas*) and goes away grief stricken (10:22). This rapid movement from enthusiasm and ardent quest to sadness and resentment is a marvel of biblical narrative art: Mark's quickly sketched portrait of the ups and downs of the rich man in confrontation with Jesus is reminiscent of his description of the manic-depressive Herod in confrontation with John the Baptist (6:14–29) and anticipates Shakespearean characters such as Claudius in *Hamlet* and Antonio in *Measure for Measure*, who career between aspirations for a new life and the downward pull of their passions and addiction to power. Or, to return to the imagery of our Gospel, the antihero in the narrative calls to mind the bad soil in the Parable of the Sower, which stands for people in whom "the cares of the age and the deceitfulness of wealth and desires for other things . . . strangle the word" or who receive the word with joy but immediately fall away when the going gets rough (4:16–19). Indeed, it is paradoxical that the only individual in the Gospel whom Jesus is explicitly said to love ends up rejecting his call; as Best (*Following*, 169) puts it, contrasting the end of our passage with the positive response of disciples in 1:16–20 and 2:14: "Acceptance of the call arises out of its compelling nature . . . and needs no explanation; rejection however must be explained." But, if that is so, there will be more and more that needs to be explained as the Gospel progresses and the "mystery of the dominion of God" deepens (cf. 4:11)—as God's supposedly all-powerful and glorious Messiah encounters increasing opposition, slander, and hate, until finally he meets an agonizing and lonely death under a darkened sky (15:33–37).

In the next passage we will see how this mystery extends even beyond Jesus' death and resurrection into the lives of his followers, who will find themselves immeasurably enriched with new houses, families, and fields—but will also discover that these blessings come "with persecutions" (10:30).

JESUS DISCUSSES WEALTH (10:23–31)

10 ²³And Jesus, looking around, said to his disciples, "How hard it will be for the rich to enter the dominion of God!" ²⁴And the disciples were astonished at his words. But Jesus again answered and said to them, "Children, how hard it is to enter the dominion of God! ²⁵It is easier for a camel to pass through the eye of a needle than for a rich person to enter the dominion of God." ²⁶And they were even more amazed, saying among themselves, "And who then can be saved?" ²⁷Looking at them, Jesus said, "With human beings it is impossible, but not with God; for all things are possible with God."

²⁸Peter began to say to him, "Look, *we* have left everything and have followed you." ²⁹Jesus said, "Amen, I say to you, there is no one who has left house or brothers or sisters or mother or father or children or fields for my sake and for the sake of the good news ³⁰who will not receive a hundredfold now, in this time, houses and brothers and sisters and mothers and children and fields—with persecutions—and in the coming age, eternal life. ³¹But many first ones will be last, and last ones first."

NOTES

10 24. *answered and said.* Gk *apokritheis legei,* lit. "answering says." The OT idiom (see the NOTES on "[he] answered and said" in 3:33 and 7:28 and the COMMENT on 7:27–28) is not reproduced mechanically here but is used to indicate a response to the disciples' amazement (see Gundry, 556).

how hard it is to enter the dominion of God! Gk *pōs dyskolon estin eis tēn basileian tou theou eiselthein.* Some important texts (A, C, D, Θ, etc.) have instead "how hard it is *for those who trust in riches* (*tous pepoithotas epi chrēmasin*) to enter . . . ," and Freedman suggests that this may be the original text; the italicized words may have dropped out because of homoeoteleuton (*estin* . . . *chrēmasin*; on homoeoteleuton, see the GLOSSARY). It seems more likely, however, that the shorter text is original and that the italicized words have been added to soften the rigor of Jesus' saying: it is not a crime to *be* rich but only to *trust* in one's riches (cf. 1 Tim 6:17 and Lane, 363 n. 35).

25. *it is easier for a camel to pass through the eye of a needle than.* Gk *eukopōteron estin kamēlon dia trymalias raphidos dielthein ē.* As Grant (*Miracle*, 133 n. 1) points out, the formula "it is easier for . . . than . . ." occurs also in Luke 16:17 to designate an impossible event (heaven and earth passing away), to which an even more impossible event (the Law changing) is compared. The unexpected conclusion in our passage that the second impossible event, the entry of a rich person into God's dominion, is actually possible (10:27) may reflect a later development of the tradition (see the introduction to the COMMENT on 10:23–31). A similar ameliorating tendency may be responsible for the scribal substitution of *kamilon* ("rope," as in 13 28 Arm Geo, etc.) for *kamēlon* ("camel") and for the fantasy that Jerusalem had a small gate called "The Needle's Eye," through which camels might pass (already ascribed to Anselm in Aquinas, *Catena Aurea* on Matt 19:23–26); as Minear ("Needle's Eye," 169) puts it, such interpretations "dwarf the camel and expand the needle's eye." In one later apocryphal work, *The Acts of Andrew and Peter* (17), a needle's eye actually grows miraculously until a camel is able to pass through it, thus signifying that rich people can indeed be saved. Bede (*Exposition of Mark* 10:24), by contrast, offers an allegorical interpretation: Christ himself is the camel, and the eye of the needle represents the pangs of his passion. As Grant (*Miracle*, 133) puts it, such explanations reflect a wish to make the impossible appear a bit more possible and thus to salvage the rich for the dominion of God.

The camel was proverbial for its size (see, e.g., Lucian, *Saturnalian Epistles* 1.19), but the elephant, which is larger than the camel, is employed in preference to the camel in rabbinic traditions that speak of a large beast passing through a needle's eye (*b. Ber.* 55b and *b. B. Meṣ.* 38). It may be, then, that the camel's reputation as a beast of burden and the idea of riches as an encumbrance are as important to our passage as the camel's size; the already impossible task of a large animal getting through the eye of a needle is made even more absurd when the animal is loaded down with possessions (cf. Jerome, *Commentary on Matthew* on 19:24–26, and Gundry, 565).

26. *even more.* Gk *perissos.* On the comparative nuance of this adverb, see "*Perissos*," BDAG 805 (3), and "*Perissōs*," BDAG 806.

among themselves. Gk *pros heautous.* This could mean either "within themselves" or "among themselves," but the latter is more likely in view of parallels such as 8:16 and 9:10 (cf. 9:34).

27. *With human beings it is impossible, but not with God; for all things are possible with God.* Gk *para anthrōpois adynaton, all' ou para theǭ · panta gar dynata para tǭ theǭ.* An emphasis on God's ability to do the seemingly impossible is common in Greco-Roman religious and philosophical thought; Grant (*Miracle*, 127), for example, cites an undated inscription from Phrygia: "I give thanks to Mother Leto because out of impossibilities she makes possibilities" (cf. Ramsay, *Cities*, 1.153). This idea is also found in the OT (see, e.g., Job 42:2) and is greatly expanded and sharpened in postbiblical Judaism and early Christianity, where the motif of the "impossible divine possibility" is often connected with creation *ex nihilo* and the resurrection of the dead (see, e.g., Galen, *On the Use of the Bodily Parts* 11.14, and Origen, *Against Celsus* 5.14). As van Unnik ("Alles") points out,

moreover, the LXX has introduced the concept into several OT texts in which it is not explicit in the Hebrew original (see Gen 18:14; Job 10:13; Zech 8:6). In one of these passages, Gen 18:14, Sarah laughs in disbelief at the angelic announcement that she will bear a son in her old age, and the angel responds by asking, "Shall anything be impossible with God?" This LXX text is particularly close to ours because of its use of the unusual construction *para tǭ theǭ* for "with God" (cf. Gundry, 38–39). Philo (*On Abraham* 112), in commenting on it, says that afterward Sarah was ashamed of her skeptical laughter, "for she knew that all things were possible with God" (*panta gar ēdei theǭ dynata*). An allusion to the Genesis 18 prophecy of a miraculous birth makes sense in the Markan context, since in 10:24 Jesus has referred to the disciples as his "children" and in 10:29–30 he will go on to speak of the divine creation of a new family.

Of the three Markan references to divine possibility, one (9:23) deals with a persistent demon, a second (10:27) concerns the power of possessions, and a third (14:36) has to do with the threat of apostasy. Schmidt (*Hostility*, 206 n. 89) points out that this series corresponds to the three seed-destroyers in the explanation of the Parable of the Sower (4:14–19).

28. *we have left everything.* Gk *hēmeis aphēkamen panta.* The *hēmeis* ("we") is not technically necessary, and in the context is emphatic, contrasting with the recalcitrance of the rich man. Later commentators think that Peter's remark reveals an unbecoming pride, and such an evaluation has some cogency, given Peter's subsequent history and the ambiguity of 10:31 (see the end of the COMMENT on 10:28–31). The negative evaluation of Peter is clearer in Matthew, where Peter adds, "What then will we have?" (Matt 19:27). Neither in Mark nor in Matthew, however, does Jesus rebuke Peter for his remark; instead, he proceeds straightforwardly to outline the rewards for the sort of renunciation that Peter has described.

29. *who has left house or brothers or sisters or mother or father or children.* Gk *hos aphēken oikian ē adelphous ē adelphas ē mētera ē patera ē tekna.* As Gundry (557) notes, the list of abandoned relations is chiastic with respect to gender. Contrary to Pesch (2.149) and Schmidt (*Hostility*, 115), the order is not one of rising importance, since in a patriarchal society brothers are more important than sisters and fathers than children. The order is different in the Q text Luke 14:25–27 (cf. Matt 10:37–39), where we have father/mother/brothers/sisters, and this sequence is supported by *Gospel of Thomas* 55 (cf. *Gospel of Thomas* 101). It may be that Mark, aware of the tension between the fifth commandment and Jesus' command to leave parents (see the COMMENT on 10:28–31), has preferred a form of the text that shifts the reference to abandonment of parents to a less prominent place near the end.

or fields. Gk *ē agrous.* The reference to fields (cf. 10:30) is awkwardly late, and it may have been added by Mark to link our passage with the previous one, in which the rich man seems to be conceived as a landowner (see the NOTES on "Do not murder, etc." in 10:19 and "for he had great estates" in 10:22)

30. *who will not receive a hundredfold now, etc.* Gk *ean mē labē hekatontaplasiona nyn en tǭ kairǭ toutǭ,* etc. Clement of Alexandria (*Who Is the Rich Man* 4.10)

provides an alternate version of this saying: "He shall receive in return a hundred-fold. To what end [does he expect] to have now in this time fields and riches and houses and brothers with persecutions? But in the coming age there is eternal life" (Taylor trans., 435). Clement thus denigrates the rewards "in this time" as unworthy of comparison to eternal life. By contrast, however, our version of the saying treats *both* sorts of rewards as worthwhile.

with persecutions. Gk *meta diōgmōn*. As Schmidt (*Hostility*, 115–16) points out, interpreters have been uncomfortable with the dissonance of this phrase in a list of rewards. On the basis of a putative Aramaic original from the root *rdp*, which can connote either friendly pursuit or persecution, Zimmermann (*Aramaic Origin*, 90–91) reinterprets *diōgmōn* as "other things that people strive for." In Mark, however, *diōgmos* means "persecution" (cf. 4:17), and it is more likely that the phrase is a Markan insertion to remind the community that its participation in the dominion of God does not remove it from the arena of earthly suffering (cf. Myers, *Binding*, 276).

in this time . . . in the coming age. Gk *en tǭ kairǭ toutǭ . . . en tǭ aiōni tǭ erchomenǭ.* In the NT period the dualism between "this age" or "this world" of eschatological tribulation (cf. 4:19: "the cares of the age") and "the coming age" or "the coming world" becomes common. *First Enoch*, for example, contrasts "this world of unrighteousness" (48:7) with "the coming world" (71:15), and Matt 12:32 says that the blasphemer against the Holy Spirit will not be forgiven "either in this age or in the coming age" (NRSV alt.). Paul, too, often speaks of "this age" (Rom 12:2; 1 Cor 2:6, 8; Gal 1:4; etc.), and his use of the expression "the present time" (*ho nyn kairos*), which he employs in eschatological contexts elsewhere (Rom 3:26; 8:18), shows that "time" can be synonymous with "age." Later in the first century, *4 Ezra* 7:50 says explicitly that God has made not one age but two (for other examples of the concept in *4 Ezra*, see Stone, *Fourth Ezra*, 92–93). Similarly, *2 Apoc. Bar.* 83:8 threatens sinners with exclusion from "both ages" (*utrumque saeculum*). In rabbinic literature, to be sure, "this world" (*'ôlām hazzeh*) and "the coming world" (*'ôlām habbā'*) are used by preference to "this age" and "the coming age," but these two ways of talking are close, since the age to come is already present in the heavenly world (cf. *1 En.* 71:15 and Volz, *Eschatologie*, 64–66).

31. *But many first ones will be last.* Gk *polloi de esontai prōtoi eschatoi.* "Many," which is missing in the Q parallel (Matt 20:16//Luke 13:30), is one of Mark's favorite words. Here it may be designed to hint at the "impossible possibility" that some rich people will be saved (cf. the COMMENT on 10:23–27): not *all* of those who are "first" in the world, but only *many* of them, will find themselves "last" in the eschatological judgment (cf. 1 Cor 1:26–29).

COMMENT

Introduction. The rich man, unable to meet Jesus' challenge to begin a new life of discipleship, goes away disconsolate. Somewhat sadly himself, one may suppose (cf. "moved with love for him" in 10:21), Jesus now turns to his followers to salvage some lessons for them from the unhappy encounter.

This colloquy is neither unitary nor an original part of the narrative, as is indicated by the sudden appearance of the disciples in 10:23 and the tension between the assertion in 10:25 that entry into the dominion of God is impossible for the rich and the qualification in 10:27 that God can make this impossibility happen. Mark seems to have constructed the conversation out of preexistent sayings: the proverb about the needle's eye in 10:25, the promise of rewards for sacrifice in 10:29–30, and the saying about the first and the last in 10:31 (cf. Matt 20:16//Luke 13:30). Markan editorial activity is evident in the framing verses (10:23–24, 26–27, 28), which are full of redactional vocabulary and Markan themes ("looking around," "astonished," "again," "answered and said," "amazed," "saying among themselves," "all," "began to say," "followed," the impossible divine possibility, and the self-exaltation of the disciples). The evangelist may also be responsible for individual touches in other verses, such as "fields," "and for the sake of the good news," "now, in this time," and "with persecutions," in 10:29–30, the order brothers/sisters/mother/father in 10:29–30, and "many" in 10:31, all of which are awkward and correspond to Markan themes (see the NOTES on "who has left houses or brothers or sisters or mother or father or children" and "or fields" in 10:29 and "with persecutions" in 10:30).

In its present form the colloquy between Jesus and the disciples falls into two parts, 10:23–27 and 10:28–31, each of which ends with a proverb (10:27c; 10:31). In the first of these subsections, Jesus' statements about the danger of wealth alternate with expressions of apostolic astonishment, and the subsection is framed by verses in which Jesus looks at the disciples and makes a statement about the difficulty of entering the dominion of God. In the second subsection, Peter's assertion that the disciples have done what Jesus is calling for is followed by a long promise from Jesus about the rewards of such self-sacrifice. Thus, while the first section emphasizes the cost of discipleship, the second highlights its rewards.

10:23–27: the dangers of wealth. As the rich man is departing (10:22), Jesus wheels to confront his disciples (10:23a), a gesture that suggests the relevance for them of the issue that has provoked the man's departure. Given Jesus' loving reaction to the man's initial query (10:21), his exclamation, "How hard it will be for the rich to enter the dominion of God!" (10:23b) is probably meant to convey not only a negative verdict on his withdrawal but also disappointed surprise that anyone would resist the offer of treasure in heaven for the sake of earthly rewards (for another example of dominical surprise, see 6:6a). This exclamation is another recognition within the narrative of "the mystery of the dominion of God" (4:11), the disconcerting providence that causes God's supposedly all-powerful word to encounter a mysterious resistance from negative forces such as "the cares of the age and the deceitfulness of wealth" (cf. 4:19 and Best, *Following*, 169).

If Jesus' initial statement in our passage contains an element of surprise, the disciples' surprise in response is even greater (10:24). Indeed, this whole first subsection of our passage alternates between dominical references to obstacles to entering the *basileia* (10:23, 24b–25, 27) and editorial descriptions of apostolic shock (10:24a, 26):

10:23   Jesus: Hard for the rich to enter dominion of God
10:24a   disciples' astonishment (*ethambounto*)
10:24b   Jesus: Hard (for all) to enter dominion of God
10:25   Jesus: Impossible for the rich to enter dominion of God
10:26   disciples' great amazement (*perissōs exeplēssonto*)
10:27   Jesus: Impossible for human beings, but not for God

A progression is discernible here from difficulty to impossibility, from the rich to all human beings, and toward increasingly acute levels of apostolic bewilderment (cf. Dowd, *Prayer*, 76–77); in the end, however, the omnipotence of God trumps the disconcerting incapacity of human beings (cf. Schweizer, 215; Gnilka, 2.84).

The narrative does not state the reason for the disciples' surprise at Jesus' initial exclamation, but it presumably concerns Jesus' negative attitude toward wealth. The surprise is consonant with certain OT teachings, especially in the Deuteronomic and wisdom traditions, which suggest that those who obey God's commandments will be rewarded with prosperity (e.g., Deut 28:1–6; Prov 10:22; Sir 11:17). There is a correspondingly positive evaluation of wealth in much Greco-Roman literature from Homer on (see Hauck and Kasch, "Ploutos," 319–23; Dowd, *Prayer*, 76). Yet even the OT wisdom tradition is not unequivocally positive about wealth (see, e.g., Prov 11:28; 16:8; 19:1, 10; 22:1; 28:11), and there are harsh critiques of it and exaltations of poverty elsewhere within the OT, especially in the Prophets (e.g., Isa 10:1–4; 53:9; Amos 2:6–8; Mic 2:1–5). The Psalms, too, frequently praise the poor whose only hope is God and criticize the rich who exploit and persecute them (e.g., Pss 10:2–11; 12:5; 37:12–22). This pattern is continued within later Judaism, for example, in Philo (see Schmidt, *Hostility*, 76–84) and in apocalyptic circles such as those represented in *1 Enoch* 94–98. Non-Jewish thinkers, too, frequently adopt a critical attitude toward wealth; Plato, for example, distinguishes the true riches that come with a good and prudent life from the counterfeit treasures of gold (*Republic* 7.521a), and the Cynics are especially fierce in their disdain for material possessions (see, e.g., Malherbe, *Cynic Epistles*, index under "*Plouteō*," "*Ploutizō*," and "*Ploutos*").

It is thus not immediately apparent why the Markan disciples should be caught off guard by Jesus' denunciation of riches, especially when they themselves have already subordinated pursuit of wealth to the call of the dominion of God (1:16–20; cf. 2:14)—a fact that Peter will mention shortly (10:28; cf. 6:8–9). The discrepancy has not gone unnoticed by commentators, who have adopted various expedients for explaining it, such as overemphasizing the positive aspects of the ancient attitude toward wealth (see, e.g., Dowd, *Prayer*, 76) or suggesting that the disciples are altruistically concerned for others (see, e.g., Chrysostom, *Homilies on Matthew* 63 [on 19:16]). It is plausible, however, that the Markan community itself contains wealthy people (cf. 14:1–9; 15:40–41) and that the disciples' shocked reaction to Jesus' words reflects those members' dismay (cf. Minear, "Needle's Eye," 166; Reploh, *Lehrer*, 196). Indeed, a community such as Mark's would have *needed* wealthy patrons if some of its members followed the urging in 10:29 and cut themselves off from the primary unit of economic subsistence in the ancient world, the family. It probably came as a relief to some in the Markan community, therefore, to hear Jesus end up declaring that the humanly impossible salvation of the rich becomes a possibility through the power of God (10:27).

Before this encouraging conclusion can be reached, however, Jesus first increases the disciples' astonishment by declaring that entry into the dominion of God is difficult, not only for the rich, but for all (10:24b–25). This warning is reminiscent of the famous Q saying about the narrow gate that leads to life (Matt 7:13–14//Luke 13:23–24), and, like that saying, it expresses a typically apocalyptic sense that salvation is restricted to the few who are ready for arduous self-sacrifice (see, e.g., 4 Ezra 7:59–61; T. Abr. A 11:11; cf. Mark 13:13b). At the same time, however, "dominion of God" retains, even in the "entering" sayings, the sense of a divine action into which human beings can be incorporated (see the COMMENT on 10:13–16), and in our particular case Jesus' pronouncement is introduced by the word "Children," which implies that the disciples already stand in a filial relation to Jesus. Even this strict warning about "entrance requirements," therefore, is far from being an exhortation to lift oneself by one's bootstraps into the kingdom of God.

This observation, however, does not lessen the seriousness of the warning about the obstacle that riches pose for participation in God's triumphal march into the world, which Jesus repeats in 10:25. Whereas human beings generally think of wealth as an unmitigated good that provides access to abundant life, Jesus paradoxically describes it as an impediment to the attainment of that which is truly important: "It is easier for a camel to pass through the eye of a needle than for a rich person to enter the dominion of God" (10:25). This deliberately grotesque image draws on traditional understandings. The camel, which was the largest animal native to Palestine, was proverbial for its size, while the needle's eye was proverbial for its smallness (see the NOTE on "it is easier for a camel to pass through the eye of a needle than" in 10:25). The obvious implication of this pointed saying, taken in isolation, is that it is impossible for the rich to enter the dominion of God (cf. Dowd, *Prayer*, 76)—an implication, however, that has been strenuously resisted in the history of interpretation (see again the NOTE on "it is easier for a camel to pass through the eye of a needle than" in 10:25). Even more worryingly, the saying's linkage with Jesus' assertion about the general difficulty of entering the *basileia* implies that the number of people who will finally squeeze into God's dominion is limited indeed. The disciples' response is thus justified: "Who . . . can be saved?' " (10:26). The Peshitta translates this last verb with "live," thus driving home the thematic connection with the rich man's question about attaining life in 10:17.

The logical answer to the disciples' query would seem to be that it is *the poor* who will be delivered at the eschaton, and this indeed is the answer that Jesus himself gives elsewhere in the tradition (Luke 6:20; cf. Pss. Sol. 10:6; Test. Jud. 25:4; Jas 2:5). In the present passage, however, Jesus shifts the subject of the conversation from the group that will be saved to the agent of salvation, combining his conclusion with the sort of loving gaze that he had turned on the rich man in the preceding story (*emblepsas*, 10:21): "Looking at them, Jesus said, 'With human beings it is impossible, but not with God; for all things are possible with God' " (10:27). Because of this linkage with the previous passage, the verb is probably meant to be associated with the divine grace that transforms the impossible into the possible by creating a new people of God out of hopeless human material—an interpretation supported by the word "children" in 10:24 and the echo in 10:27 of the angelic announcement in Genesis 18 about a miraculous birth that will bring Israel into being (see the NOTE on "With human beings it is impossible, etc." in 10:27).

10:28–31: the rewards of discipleship. But the assertion that salvation comes through a miraculous action of God rather than through the striving of humanity (cf. Rom 9:16) does not imply that all human actions carry the same weight in the divine scales, a point hammered home in the second subsection of our passage, 10:28–31. This segment takes its point of departure from the emphatic assertion of Peter (see the NOTE on "*we* have left everything" in 10:28) that he and his fellow disciples have done what the rich man could not bring himself to do, namely, leave everything to follow Jesus (10:28). Jesus responds with two long clauses that are largely symmetrical (10:29–30):

Amen, I say to you, there is no one who has left
  house
    or brothers
      or sisters
        or mother
          or father
            or children
              or fields
                for my sake and for the sake of the good news
who will not receive a hundredfold now, in this time
  houses
    and brothers
      and sisters
        and mothers
          and children
            and fields
              with persecutions
and in the coming age, eternal life.

This symmetry highlights the claim that nothing of consequence will be lost through discipleship; indeed, the abandoned elements will be replaced a hundredfold. But there is also a striking contrast between the plethora of benefits promised for "this time" and the single reward guaranteed for the coming age, which implies that the latter, eternal life, is more valuable than all the advantages of the present age. It is also noteworthy that "with persecutions" occupies a place parallel to "for my sake and for the sake of the good news": sharing with Jesus in

his power-laden proclamation of the good news also means sharing in his sufferings (cf. Phil 3:10).

These verses emphasize that following Jesus may involve a painful separation
from family members (cf. 1:18–20; 13:12–13), but they promise that Christians
will discover a new family in the church, as well as new "houses" (or "households") and "fields." The reference to fields is interesting, since it is reminiscent of
Acts 4:32–37, where a rich man sells a field and lays the proceeds at the apostles'
feet; this whole passage, along with Acts 2:44–45, gives a graphic picture of the
Christian "family" in Jerusalem sharing everything and supporting the needy
among themselves through the largesse of the rich. Although this picture is ideal-
ized, there is no doubt that early Christians were famous for their mutual support
of each other, which was sometimes regarded as excessive by outsiders; Tertullian,
for example, says that the Christians' enemies *charge* them with loving each other
(*Apology* 39; cf. Lucian, *Death of Peregrinus* 12–13; Constantelos, *Byzantine Philanthropy*, 11–16).

Such philanthropy flowed out of the Christians' sense that they were members of the eschatological family that had been created by God's action in Christ.
This family consciousness, seen throughout the NT (cf. 3:34–35; John 19:26; Rom
16:13; 1 Tim 5:1–2, as well as the ubiquitous "brothers"), has deep roots in the OT
and Second Temple Judaism. In the OT and intertestamental Jewish texts, for
example, fellow Jews are frequently called "brothers" (see, e.g., Deut 3:18; 24:7;
2 Macc 1:1, although "gender-inclusive" translations such as the NRSV obscure
this), and God is conceived as the patriarch of the extended clan of Israel (see,
e.g., Exod 4:22; Hos 11:1). Sometimes, moreover, Jewish literature recognizes that
the family of God may find itself in competition with the natural one. In a long
and deeply emotive description of conversion to Judaism, for example, Aseneth
describes her abandonment by her mother and father, who have come to hate
her, and her orphan-like flight to a surrogate father, the God of Israel (*Joseph and
Aseneth* 11–12). By becoming a Jew and marrying Joseph, she joins a new family, the people of Israel, who are all "the sons of the Most High" (16:14; cf. 1QH
17[9]:34–35).

In one way, however, our passage is more radical than these precedents, since
it speaks of *abandoning* relatives rather than of *being abandoned* by them. This
more aggressive approach, which is also manifest elsewhere in the Jesus tradition
(cf. Mark 1:18–20; Matt 8:21–22//Luke 9:59–60; Matt 10:34–36//Luke 12:51–53),
creates some tension with the fifth commandment, the imperative to honor parents (Exod 20:12//Deut 5:16), which the Markan Jesus has just quoted approvingly in 10:19 (cf. 7:10). The comparison and contrast are especially pronounced
because this commandment promises blessings to those who honor their parents,
and later Jewish traditions interpret those blessings as applying not only to the
present world but also to the world to come (see, e.g., *Deut. Rab.* 1.15; *Sipre Deut.*
336). There is discord, therefore, between the fifth commandment, which in the
OT and Jewish tradition promises blessings in this life and the next to those who
honor their parents, and the Jesus tradition, which promises similar blessings to
those who *abandon* them.

The idea of rejecting parents for the sake of the dominion of God, however, also has an OT precedent in the Deuteronomic description of Levi, "who said of his father and mother, 'I regard them not'; he ignored his kin, and did not acknowledge his children" (Deut 33:9). The continuing importance of this OT text for later Judaism is attested by its citation in Philo (e.g., *Allegorical Interpretation* 1.52; *On Drunkenness* 72) and the Dead Sea Scrolls (4QTest 14–20; cf. Josephus, *War* 2.134), and Hengel (*Zealots*, 148) thinks that it influenced the revolutionaries of the Jewish War (see *Ant.* 18.23), whose activities probably form the background to the composition of Mark's Gospel (see the INTRODUCTION in vol. 1, pp. 33–37). Apart from the influence of Deut 33:9, several passages in 4 Maccabees emphasize that love of God and his Law trumps family relationships (2:10–12; 13:23–14:1; 15:1, 8, 14, 24), and outsiders picked up this Jewish emphasis; Tacitus, for example, describes converts to Judaism as people who have been taught "to despise the gods, to disown their country, and to regard their parents, children, and brothers as of little account" (*Histories* 5.5). It is significant that this passage, as well as the *Joseph and Aseneth* section described above, deals with *converts* to Judaism; converts to Christianity, such as the members of the Markan community, doubtless experienced a similar alienation from their natal families.

Aside from its tension with the fifth commandment, the most striking thing about the list of lost-and-found family members in 10:29–30 is its two omissions. First, there is no reference to abandonment of husband or wife, and this accords with Jesus' teaching about indissoluble marriage in 10:1–12; it is logical that Luke, whose Jesus *does* talk about leaving one's wife (18:29; cf. 14:26), also omits the teaching about permanent marriage (cf. Clark, "Constraining," 160). Second, there is no reference to fathers in the list of new relatives in 10:30, even though they are mentioned in the list of abandoned family members in 10:29 (3:34 also omits mention of fathers; see the NOTE on "my . . . mother" in 3:35). It is probable that God takes the earthly father's place, as in Ps 27:10; 1QH 17[9]:34–35; and *Joseph and Aseneth* 11–12 (cf. Matt 23:9–10; Gundry, 558; Roh, *Familia dei*, 136–39). But in view of the fact that Jesus has just referred to the disciples as his *own* children (10:24) and the possible paternal imagery of his lifting the child in 9:36, his blessing of children in 10:16, and his loving glance in 10:21 (see the COMMENTS on 9:36–37, 10:13–16, and 10:21–22), it is also conceivable that Jesus himself functions as a father figure for the "orphaned" Markan Christians. Perhaps Mark thinks of both God and Jesus as surrogate fathers to the disciples; in early Christianity the idea of the paternity of God does not necessarily exclude the presence of other spiritual fathers (see, e.g., 1 Cor 4:15; Gal 4:19; Phlm 10; and the use of "father" language among rabbis and in Christian monasticism).

The Markan Jesus promises that all of these new familial relationships, as well as "houses" and "fields," will be multiplied a hundredfold to faithful disciples (10:30), and this "hundredfold" terminology, along with the reference to the good news in 10:29 and the phrases "in this time" and "with persecutions" in 10:30, recalls the Parable of the Sower, which uses "a hundredfold" to speak of the eschatological blessing engendered by "the word" in an age otherwise dominated by weakness, loss, suffering, and death (see the NOTE on "thirtyfold and sixtyfold and a hundredfold" in 4:8 and the COMMENT on 4:3–8). Thus, the terminology of 10:29–30 points not only to a futuristic eschatology ("and in the coming age, eternal life") but also to a partially realized one; the new age is already breaking in, but in order to see it one must have eyes opened to discern the power that breaks forth in the midst of weakness ("with persecutions").

This eschatological context carries over into the final verse of the pericope, the well-known statement about the first becoming last and the last first (10:31; cf. 9:35). The flow of thought in the passage suggests that many of those such as the rich man, who have tried to make themselves "first" by holding onto their property and stable familial relations "in this time," will find themselves last at the eschaton. Conversely, those such as the disciples, who have given up everything and thus have made themselves "last," will be first—a position of privilege anticipated by the bountiful "family life" already being experienced within the Christian community. But it is also possible to interpret 10:31 as a warning against apostolic arrogance that qualifies the promise directed to the disciples in 10:30: in spite of the privileges you now enjoy, you could still find yourselves coming up short. This interpretation would be in line with the overall portrayal of the disciples in our pericope and in the Gospel as a whole. The subsection begins with Peter calling attention to the disciples' seeming ability to escape the verdict that Jesus has just rendered against the rich ("Look, *we* have left everything and have followed you"). It thus anticipates 14:27–29, where Peter will go one step further and identify *himself* as the sole exception to Jesus' prophecy of general apostasy—a claim that his subsequent denial of Jesus will prove to be misguided (14:37, 50, 66–72). Thus, the disciples, who think of themselves as "first," could eventually find themselves disqualified by the same principle of eschatological reversal upon which they have relied (cf. 1 Cor 10:12 and see Taylor, 435; Schmidt, *Hostility*, 116). This is not the main point of 10:31 (see the NOTE on "*we* have left everything" in 10:28), but it gives the passage's end a disturbing undertone.

The juxtaposition of 10:31 with the passion prediction in 10:32–34 suggests an even more ominous exegetical possibility: if the first will become last, then Jesus, who by rights is "the first" (cf. Col 1:15), must become the last of all and the servant of all through the suffering and brutality of the shameful death of the cross (see 10:45 and cf. Phil 2:6–8). But if the last will become first, there is also the hope that he, along with those who follow him "on the way" of suffering and death, will experience the eschatological power of the resurrection even as they tread that path (cf. Phil 2:9–11). Mark's Gospel thus points toward a double reversal: the first becomes last in order ultimately to become first again.

In the next passage, this double reversal will be given its most explicit Markan expression as Jesus alludes to his fulfillment of messianic hopes (the Son of Man going up to Jerusalem), his descent to the valley of death, and his emergence from that valley after three days.

JESUS PROPHESIES HIS DEATH AND RESURRECTION A THIRD TIME (10:32–34)

10 ³²And they were on the way, going up to Jerusalem, and Jesus was going before them, and they were astonished; and those following were afraid. And taking the Twelve again, he began to tell them the things that would happen to him: ³³"Look, we are going up to Jerusalem; and the Son of Man will be turned over to the chief priests and the scribes, and they will condemn him to death and turn him over to the Gentiles; ³⁴and they will mock him and spit on him and scourge him and kill him; and after three days he will arise."

NOTES

10 32. *and Jesus was going before them, and they were astonished; and those following were afraid. And taking the Twelve again* . . . Gk *kai ēn proagōn autous ho Iēsous, kai ethambounto, hoi de akolouthountes ephobounto. Kai paralabōn palin tous dōdeka.* . . . The disciples' fear and astonishment would be more logical coming *after* Jesus' prophecy of suffering and death (10:33–34) rather than before it. Bede (*Exposition of Mark* 10:32), aware of this problem, takes it as a reaction to the two previous prophecies of the same event (8:31; 9:31). Mark's readers, too, can easily fill this "blank" (see the GLOSSARY), since they know that Jesus' death occurred in Jerusalem, and "on the way" will remind them of the previous predictions (see Best, *Following,* 120).

The grammar seems to distinguish the "they" who are astonished from "those following" who are afraid, and to differentiate both from the Twelve whom Jesus takes aside privately. Certain manuscripts, however, simplify matters either through omission of "and those following were afraid" (D, K, 28, etc.) or through identification of the first two groups as one, for example, by replacing *hoi de akolouthountes* ("and those following") with *kai akolouthountes* ("and following"; e.g., A and Byzantine witnesses). Some scholars follow the lead of these texts by arguing that 10:32 refers only to two groups, the Twelve and a larger body of disciples (see, e.g., Wrede, 276–78), or only to one, the Twelve (e.g., Meye, *Jesus,* 159–65; Best, "Use," 21–24). Their arguments include the following: (1) Astonishment and fear are close to each other, and throughout the Gospel both have been ascribed to the disciples (see 4:41; 6:49–51; 9:6; 10:24, 26; cf. 16:8), who sometimes appear to be synonymous with the Twelve (see, e.g., 6:7 in conjunction with 6:30, 35; and 14:10, 17, 20 in conjunction with 14:12–14, 16, 32). (2) If Jesus goes before the group that is astonished, he is followed by the group that is afraid. (3) *Akolouthountes* may be a circumstantial participle, so that *hoi de akolouthountes ephobounto* means "and they as they followed were afraid" (cf. the similar constructions in 6:49 and 14:11 and cf. Cranfield, 335; Best, "Use," 24).

These arguments, however, are not convincing. Just because groups are engaged in similar activities and have similar reactions, that does not mean they are the same group, and the Twelve are the object of *paralabōn* ("taking"), which elsewhere in Mark always implies leaving one group behind in favor of another (cf. 4:36; 5:40; 9:2; 14:33). Elsewhere in Mark, moreover, the *ho de/hoi de* construction always indicates a change of subject, and in 11:9 *hoi akolouthountes* is substantive ("those who followed") rather than circumstantial (cf. Gundry, 570).

It is more likely, then, that Mark intends to distinguish three concentric circles of adherents in 10:32: the Twelve, "those following," and a more loosely defined set of sympathizers similar to the "many" who prepare Jesus' way in 11:8. The idea of concentric circles of followers turns up elsewhere in the Gospel: in 3:13–14, for example, the appointment of the Twelve is preceded by the calling of a larger body of disciples; in 4:10 "those around him with the Twelve" implies the same two groups; and in 8:34 Jesus calls not just the disciples but also the crowd to follow him.

33. *Look, we are going up to Jerusalem*, etc. Gk *Idou anabainomen eis Hierosolyma*, etc. On the detailed correspondence between this prophecy and its fulfillment in chapters 14–15, see the introduction to the COMMENT. Best ("Use," 22–23) points out that the prediction omits some prominent features of the Markan passion narrative (the elders, the false witnesses, and ill-treatment by the Jewish authorities), and he uses these absences to argue for the prophecy's origin in a pre-Markan Jewish Christian community interested in exculpating the Jews and incriminating the Romans. The prediction, however, also omits the Roman but not the Jewish trial, which seems odd if Mark is trying to incriminate the Romans; it may be that the omissions in the prediction are simply in the interest of shortening a long passage.

the Son of Man will be turned over, etc. Gk *ho huios tou anthrōpou paradothēsetai*, etc. The prediction is strongly colored by the language and thought of the Deutero-Isaian songs of the Suffering Servant (Isa 50:4–9 and 52:13–53:12; see Marcus, *Way*, 188–90, and Watts, "Jesus' Death," 134–36). Isaiah 53:6, 12 LXX speaks of the Servant being "turned over" (*paredōken, paredothē*) by God to suffering and death, but this death results more directly from a "judgment" rendered by human beings, just as in the Markan prophecy the Son of Man will be "turned over" (*paradothēsetai*) by both God and Judas (see the COMMENT on 10:33–34) to opponents who will condemn him and sentence him to death. In Isa 50:4–6, moreover, the Lord's Servant endures spitting (*emptysmatōn*) and beating (*mastigas*), terms that are cognate with *emptysousin* ("they will spit on") and *mastigōsousin* ("they will scourge") in Mark 10:34 (the Isaian text is echoed elsewhere in the Jesus tradition, not only in the passion narrative but also in Matt 5:39//Luke 6:29; cf. Allison, *Intertextual Jesus*, 107–9, 120–22). The Servant is "exalted" by God (Isa 52:13), and Isa 53:10–12 seems to imply his triumph over death, so that there are also points of contact with the Markan Jesus' prophecy of the resurrection. Moreover, the astonishment of the disciples in 10:32 (*ethambounto*) is similar to that of the nations in Isa 52:15 (*thaumasontai*). Another scriptural influence is probably Daniel 7; see the COMMENT on 8:31–33.

COMMENT

Introduction. After confronting the rich man (10:17–22) and discoursing with the disciples about the dangers of wealth (10:23–31), Jesus, with his followers, resumes his way up to Jerusalem from the Judaean and Transjordanian regions (cf. 10:1); along the way he speaks once more of the fate that awaits him in the holy city. This is the most detailed of the three passion predictions that punctuate the central section of the Gospel (8:31–33; 9:30–32; 10:32–34); it reads, as Nineham (278) puts it, "like a printed programme of a Passion Play," and the events prophesied are fulfilled to a T within the subsequent narrative: Jesus is turned over to a crowd led by the chief priests and the scribes (14:43–50); he is condemned to death by them (14:53–64) and delivered to the Gentile authorities (15:1); the latter expose him to mockery and torture (15:15–20a); he is executed (15:20b–37); and after three days he rises from the dead (16:1–8).

One suspects, on the basis of these correspondences, that this most detailed passion prediction is largely the work of Mark, especially when one compares it to the vaguer formulations in 8:31 and 9:31 (see the NOTE on "it was necessary that, etc." in 8:31 and cf. Lamarche, 233; Brown, *Death*, 2.1477). But one also suspects that were he writing freely, Mark would have composed a sentence smoother than 10:32, which many later scribes felt obliged to alter (see the NOTE on "and Jesus was going before them, etc." in 10:32). Perhaps in Mark's source the reference to Jesus going before the astonished disciples introduced 10:35, in which James and John bridge the implied distance to lay before him a request to share in the imminent public manifestation of his messianic glory (cf. Schmithals, 2.461). The rest of 10:32 (from "and those following were afraid"), which contains several Markan terms ("the Twelve," "again," "began to"), is probably Markan redaction, as is "on the way" at its start.

In terms of structure, the pericope is divided into the narrative introduction (10:32) and the prophecy itself (10:33–34), both of which are characterized by quick, almost cinematic shifts in focus between Jesus, the groups following him, and the groups opposed to him (see the COMMENT on 4:1–2 for the similar technique there). These quick cuts correspond rhetorically to the pericope's dramatic sense of movement ("going up to Jerusalem . . . going before them . . . those following"), which hints at the divine power that is propelling Jesus inexorably toward his fate (cf. Best, *Following*, 121).

10:32: narrative introduction. The substantial truth of Peter's assertion, "Look, *we* have left everything and have followed you" (10:28) is now confirmed by the detailed description of the group that escorts Jesus up to Jerusalem and thus resists the temptation, to which the rich man had succumbed, to fall away (cf. John 6:66–69). The Markan grammar seems to distinguish three subsets within this accompanying group: those "going up" with Jesus, who are astonished; "those following," who are afraid; and the Twelve, whom Jesus instructs privately (see the NOTE on "and Jesus was going before them, etc." in 10:32).

The language of "going up," which is applied to the first group here, but also to Jesus and the Twelve in 10:33, is a natural one to use for a trip to Jerusalem, which is "a city built on a hill" (Matt 5:14), twenty-five hundred feet above sea level. Precisely because of this association with the holy city, however, "going up" in the OT has associations of spiritual pilgrimage (see, e.g., Ps 122:1, 4; Isa 2:2–3) that in Deutero-Isaiah (40:1–11) are fused with the notion of God's liberative "way," by which he leads his exiled people back to the holy land in a saving act of holy war (see Marcus, *Way*, 12–37; Watts, *New Exodus*, passim). Mark probably has this passage and the Deutero-Isaian "way" theme in general in mind throughout the central section of his Gospel (see the introduction to 8:22–10:52), and the description of Jesus going before his disciples "on the way" up to Jerusalem may also awaken memories of other assaults on the city that were partly inspired by the Deutero-Isaian vision of redemptive holy war. In 2 Macc 10:1, for example, we read that in the climactic event of the Maccabean Revolt, "[Judas] Maccabaeus and his men, with the Lord leading them (*tou kyriou proagontos autous*), recovered the sanctuary and the city." This passage not only talks about a momentous conquest of Jerusalem under divine guidance but also uses the same verb for "going before" or "leading," *proagein*, that Mark does for Jesus in 10:32 (and 14:28 and 16:7). This verb reappears in Josephus' descriptions of the militant activities of first-century C.E. charismatic Jewish revolutionary figures, whose goals were similar to those of the Maccabees (see, e.g., *War* 2.259; 7.438; cf. Hengel, *Charismatic Leader*, 21 n. 20). The great Jewish revolt of 66–73 C.E., which forms the background to the composition of Mark's Gospel (see the INTRODUCTION in vol. 1, pp. 33–37), was led by like-minded figures, and it is probable that Mark's readers would be reminded by 10:32 of these warrior Messiahs and their holy war against Rome, which culminated in a battle over Jerusalem.

Thus, the Markan description of Jesus' ascent to Jerusalem, with bands of followers trailing in his wake, is redolent of other scenes of ascent and divine triumph that were alive in the hopes, living memories, and hallowed traditions of Israel. This triumphant nuance will be reinforced later in the Gospel when Mark employs *proagein* for the post-Easter Jesus' remobilization of his band of disciples for mission in Galilee (14:28; 16:7). The astonishment and fear experienced by the accompanying groups in 10:32, therefore, may imply not only trepidation but also wonder that God's victory is beginning and that they are being swept up into its forward momentum (see the COMMENT on 10:13–16).

But the fear is also fear, reflecting the same old resistance that had caused Peter to protest when he first heard Jesus prophesy his death (8:31–32; cf. 9:31). And while it arises partly out of the disciples' devotion to Jesus, it contains also an admixture of self-concern: if they are accompanying Jesus up to Jerusalem, they may also share in his ruin if he should fall into enemy hands (cf. John 11:16), as frequently happened when revolutionary movements foundered (cf. Acts 5:36–37). The fear of "those following" (*hoi . . . akolouthountes*) probably relates also to the fearful Markan present, especially since the phrase can be used in early Christian texts for people who follow the *risen* Jesus to the death (see Rev 14:4; Eusebius, *Ecclesiastical History* 5.1.10; John 12:26; etc.; cf. Aune, *Revelation*, 2.812–14). Thus, as in 4:36, the wideness of the description of Jesus' accompanying group allows the members of the Markan community to read themselves into a depiction of apostolic dread (see the COMMENT on 4:35–36).

10:33–34: the passion prediction. The Markan Jesus has an odd way of allaying that fear: taking the Twelve aside, he prophesies in explicit terms the horrors that will befall him when they reach their destination. This is the most detailed of the three passion predictions, probably because it is the last, almost immediately preceding Jesus' entry into Jerusalem (11:1–11), where the prophesied events will occur. Its importance is highlighted not only by its length and its introduction with the solemn formula "he began to tell them the things that would happen to him" (10:32 end) but also by the fact that it is the only one of the three predictions to begin with the significant word *idou* ("Look"). This word connects our passage with Peter's declaration in 10:28: "Look, *we* have left everything and have followed you"; abandoning everything to follow Jesus, then, means going with him all the way to the cross (cf. 8:34–35).

Like Peter in 10:28, Jesus follows his *idou* with a first person plural verb ("We are going up," 10:33a), but the subject does not remain "we" for long, since in the coming passion the disciples will abandon Jesus. The subject, therefore, quickly switches to Jesus himself, who is described as a passive victim through the use of a future passive verb ("will be turned over," 10:33b; cf. Gnilka, 2.97). This passivity is grammatically reinforced by a further change in subject, from Jesus to his enemies, whose acts of condemnation, torture, and execution occupy the greater part of the prophecy and occur in two stages and an ascending order: two actions by the Jewish opponents (condemnation and turning over to the Gentiles, 10:33c) and four by the non-Jewish ones (mocking, spitting, scourging, and killing, 10:34a). Finally, at the conclusion of the prophecy (10:34b), Jesus reemerges as the subject, signifying that at the end of three days he will emerge from the passivity that characterized him during his torture and death into the living and powerful activity that still sustains the Markan community.

For most of the prophecy, however, Jesus' enemies and their mistreatment of him hold center stage. It is particularly significant that the first part of the prophecy, the description of the actions of the Jewish opponents (10:33), is framed by two uses of the verb *paradidonai* ("to turn over"), which appears in the passive voice at the beginning, with Jesus as its subject (*"will be turned over* to the chief priests and the scribes"), and in the active voice at the end, with the Jewish opponents as its subject (*"they will . . . turn him over* to the Gentiles"). The implied agent of the first giving over is not specified, but the same verb is used with reference to Judas elsewhere in the Gospel (3:19; 14:10, 18, 21, 42, 44), so he at least must be included. But because of the many links of our pericope with the Suffering Servant passages in Deutero-Isaiah, the second of which uses *paradidonai* for God's delivery of his chosen agent to suffering and death (Isa 53:6, 12 LXX; see the NOTE on "the Son of Man will be turned over" in 10:33), the divine will also is probably in view when the Markan Jesus speaks of the Son of Man being turned over to his enemies. Thus, the reverberations of Isaiah 50 and 53 here function in a similar way to the use of *dei* in the first passion prediction, namely, to emphasize that "it was necessary," because God willed it, "that the Son of Man should suffer many things" (see 8:31). And the different voices of *paradidonai* within 10:33 suggest the same mysterious intersection of the divine and human wills as the usages of the verb in 14:18, 21 do: the Son of Man goes as it has been written that he must, yet the immediate agents of his murder are responsible human subjects.

But how is Jesus' prophecy of his suffering and death in 10:33–34 an effective response to the terror that the disciples have displayed in 10:32? First, suffering and death does not have the last word; that place, rather, is filled by *anastēnai* ("to arise") in all three passion predictions. The resurrection is the ultimate and determinative reality, even if its significance seems to be dwarfed by the massiveness of the suffering that precedes it. Second, if the background of our passage is in Deutero-Isaiah, and if that OT witness is viewed as a unity, it is telling that the Suffering Servant passages are integrated into a section whose overarching theme is the triumph of God over his foreign enemies and even over the recalcitrance of Israel (Isaiah 40–66). The suffering and death of the Servant, therefore, cannot be separated from the victory of the Divine Warrior; it is, rather, the costly means by which that victory will be achieved (see the introduction to 8:22–10:52). The suffering and death of the Markan Jesus, similarly, is not just a trial to be borne but the means by which God's dominion will be established and the "many" ransomed from the forces that have held them in bondage (cf. 10:45).

In the next passage, the Markan Jesus will call on his disciples to share in this victory by being "baptized" into the messianic suffering that brings it to pass.

JESUS DISCUSSES SERVING AND BEING SERVED (10:35–45)

10 ³⁵And James and John, the sons of Zebedee, came up to him, saying to him, "Teacher, we want you to do for us whatever we ask of you." ³⁶He said to them, "*What* do you want me to do for you?" ³⁷They said to him, "Grant us that one of us should sit on your right and one on your left, in your glory." ³⁸Jesus said to them, "You don't know what you are asking. Can you drink the cup I drink or be baptized with the baptism I am baptized with?" ³⁹They said to him, "We can." Jesus said to them, "The cup I drink you *will* drink, and the baptism I am baptized with you *will* be baptized with—⁴⁰but to sit at my right or my left is not mine to give but is for those for whom it has been prepared."

⁴¹And when they heard it, the other ten began to be annoyed with James and John. ⁴²And calling them, Jesus said to them, "You know that those who are thought to rule over the Gentiles lord it over them, and their great ones oppress them. ⁴³But it is not so among you; but whoever among you wants to be great shall be your servant, ⁴⁴and whoever among you wants to be the first shall be the slave of all. ⁴⁵For even the Son of Man did not come to be served but to serve, and to give his life as a ransom for many."

NOTES

10 35. *James and John.* Gk *Iakōbos kai Iōannēs.* Matthew 20:20 softens the unattractive Markan portrayal of the sons of Zebedee in 10:35 by making their mother rather than the sons themselves request preferential treatment and by reporting their request indirectly ("asked a favor of him") rather than quoting their words, which in the Markan version sound manipulative ("do for us whatever we ask").

36. **What** *do you want.* Gk *ti thelete.* The emphasis in the translation conveys that Jesus is resisting the demand that he give the brothers *whatever* they ask.

37. *Grant us,* etc. Gk *dos hēmin,* etc. James and John's request for positions of honor is perhaps unsurprising in view of Jesus' promise, a few lines before our pericope, that at the eschaton the last will become first (10:31)—an assurance that could be taken as implying a hierarchy within the dominion of God. A similar conclusion seems to flow from the passages in Matthew and Luke that allude to the person who is "least in the dominion of heaven/God" (Matt 5:19; Matt 11:11//Luke 7:28), which might suggest that others are great in it. Such hierarchical conceptions are common in certain strains of Jewish apocalypticism; in 1QSa 2:11–13, for example, each member of the eschatological community sits "according to his glory" in the assembly of the last days (cf. Müller, *Mitte,* 211–12, and, for rabbinic examples, Strack-Billerbeck, 1.249–50; 4.1138–39).

left. Gk *aristerōn.* Both this word and *euōnymōn,* the word for "left" in 10:40, are euphemisms (cf. LSJ 740); the former literally means "on the best side" and the latter "on the well-favored side." Both reflect the common view that the left hand is unlucky and that direct mention of it should be avoided; the switch from the one term to the other may reflect a desire to present a moving target to the evil eye.

38. *the cup.* Gk *to potērion.* The cup is a metaphor for one's portion in life, what one has been given to "drink," whether of good or ill. It can sometimes symbolize a happy fate, for example, the overflowing cup of Ps 23:5 and the "cup of salvation" in Ps 116:13; in the OT and related literature, however, the cup is usually the poisoned chalice of the Lord's wrath, the affliction that he pours out upon those who richly deserve divine punishment (see, e.g., Ps 75:8; Isa 51:17, 22; Jer 25:15–18, 27–28; cf. 1QpHab 11:14; Rev 16:19). In one OT passage it is implied that the innocent may have to drink a cup of suffering that they do not deserve (Jer 49:12), and in later texts the cup can be associated with death or martyrdom, with no implication of punishment (see, e.g., "cup of death" in *T. Ab.* 1:3; *Tg. Neof.* Gen 40:23 and Deut 32:1; *Martyrdom of Polycarp* 14:2; *Martyrdom of Isaiah* 5:13; cf. Brown, *Death,* 1.169; Allison, *Testament of Abraham,* 72–73).

be baptized with the baptism I am baptized with. Gk *to baptisma ho egō baptizomai baptisthēnai.* In nonbiblical Greek, words of the *bapt-* group are used figuratively for the immersion of people in various sorts of evils (see, e.g., Josephus, *War* 4.137; Libanius, *Orations* 18.286; cf. Oepke, "*Baptō,*" 530, 545), and in the OT and Jewish texts water and flood imagery are deployed in a similar way (see, e.g., Ps 42:7; Isa 43:2; 1QH 11[3]:28–36). Sometimes, as in 1QH 11(3):28–36, the overflowing evil is eschatological in nature, and this eschatological sense carries over to the figurative uses of *baptisma* and *baptisthēnai* in Luke 12:50, as the highly apocalyptic context of that saying shows (cf. Allison, *End*, 124–28).

40. *is not mine to give.* Gk *ouk estin emon dounai.* This saying, like Jesus' admission that even he does not know the hour of the end (13:32), caused much embarrassment for later Christian theologians, since it seemed to drive a wedge between Jesus and God; see, for example, the tortuous explanations of Chrysostom, *Homilies on Matthew* 65.3; Calvin, *Harmony* 2.422; Bengel, *Gnomon* on Matt 20:23.

but is for those for whom it has been prepared. Gk *alla hois hētoimastai.* This is a good example of a divine passive (see the GLOSSARY); even though God is not explicitly named, the clear implication is that he rather than Jesus is responsible for the disposition of the seats at Jesus' side.

42. *lord it over . . . oppress.* Gk *katakyrieuousin . . . katexousiazousin.* Both of these terms consist of the prefix *kata-*, which often has negative connotations, plus a verb signifying rule. Clark ("Meaning") argues against a negative implication here, asserting that there is no place in all of Greek literature where *katakyrieuein* means "to lord it over." But while *katakyrieuein* can be used without the implication of oppression (see, e.g., Gen 1:28; Ps 72:8 [71:8 LXX]; Jer 3:14), most of the instances in the LXX have to do with violent conquest (see, e.g., Num 21:24; 32:22, 29; Pss 10:5, 10 [9:26, 31 LXX]; 110:2 [109:2 LXX]; 1 Macc 15:30) or other situations in which one entity aggressively usurps another (e.g., sin's domination in Ps 19:13 [18:14 LXX] and 119:133 [118:133 LXX]; cf. *katadynasteuousin* in Jas 2:6). As Gundry (579) points out, moreover, when Luke tones down the meaning of 10:42, changing the oppressive kings of the Gentiles into the Gentiles' *benefactors*, he also eliminates the *kata-* prefix from *kyrieuein* and *exousiazein* (see Luke 22:25).

43. *But it is not so.* Gk *ouch houtōs de estin.* Many manuscripts (A, C³, K, X, etc.) change the *estin* ("is") to *estai* ("will be") because of a logical difficulty: it is obviously not *yet* true that the disciples have adopted the way of service.

43–44. *your servant . . . slave of all.* Gk *hymōn diakonos . . . pantōn doulos.* Both *diakonos* and *doulos* generally belong to the vocabulary of slavery, though a *diakonos* might occasionally be a freedman or other free servant. *Doulos* emphasizes the involuntary aspect of slavery and is a legal term, whereas *diakonos* stresses the services rendered to the master (see Beyer, "*Diakoneō*," 81). The closest ancient parallel to our passage is 1 Cor 9:19, where Paul paradoxically juxtaposes his freedom from all people with his slavery to all.

Outside the Christian sphere, there are few approximations to the idea that a leader ought to be his people's slave. The idea of the meek and magnanimous king is common in Hellenistic literature (see Good, *Jesus*, 47–49 and passim), to be sure. This is not the same thing, however, as associating kingship with the degradation of slavery, and when the "servant king" idea appears in Greco-Roman sources, it is customarily used in a negative sense to denounce demagogues who pander to the crowd and thus acts as "slaves" to the lower classes (see, e.g., Plato, *Republic* 569b; Cicero, *On the Paradoxes of the Stoics* 41; Philo, *On Joseph* 35; Martin, *Slavery*, 86–116). The abhorrence with which such role reversals were viewed is illustrated by Appian, *Civil Wars* 4.13, which describes "a shocking change" among the nobility of Rome: they "threw themselves with lamentations at the feet of their slaves, giving to the servant the character of savior and master" (cited in Garnsey and Saller, *Roman Empire*, 107).

The few significant extra-Christian instances of a positive use of the servant-king image include Claudianus Aelianus (*Historical Miscellany* 2.20), who describes the "honorable slavery" of King Antigonus, and 1 Kgs 12:7, where elders advise King Rehoboam to become an *'ebed/doulos* to his oppressed people, that is, to serve their needs (cf. Rengstorf, "*Doulos*," 267). This biblical tale is recalled in the Talmud, along with the cautionary words of R. Gamaliel II to disciples appointed to governmental posts: "Do you imagine that I offer you rulership? It is servitude I offer you" (*b. Hor.* 10a–b). Servitude and sovereignty, then, are logical opposites, whereas our passage claims that the former is the pathway to the latter.

45. *the Son of Man did not come to be served but to serve.* Gk *ho huios tou anthrōpou ouk ēlthen diakonēthēnai alla diakonēsai.* This clause invokes the Greek versions of Dan 7:13–14, which refer to all peoples *serving* (*latreuousa/douleusousin*) the "one like a *son of man*" (*hōs huios anthrōpou*). Although Mark uses *diakonein* rather than *latreuein* or *douleuein* in 10:45, *doulos*, a noun cognate to *douleuein*, has just appeared in 10:44, and both Mark 10:45 and Dan 7:13–14 have the idea of a "Son of Man" figure being served, which can scarcely be a coincidence (see Hooker, *Son of Man*, 141). The Markan Jesus, to be sure, says that the Son of Man came to serve rather than be served, which is the opposite of the impression that one gets from Daniel 7, but Mark's *ouk . . . alla* ("not . . . but") construction may reflect an awareness that Jesus is reversing a scriptural expectation, as is expressed in Barrett's paraphrase: "not, *as you might think* . . . to be served, but to serve" ("Background," 8).

ransom. Gk *lytron.* This word comes from *lyein*, "to release," and is used, often in the plural, for sums paid to secure the freedom of prisoners of war, slaves, and debtors (see Kertelge, "*Lytron*," 365). Of these contexts, that of the slave is most relevant, because of the slave imagery in 10:43–45 ("servant . . . slave . . . to serve"). Slave ransom could sometimes take the form of one person substituting for another in servitude, as in *1 Clem.* 55:2, which uses language similar to that in Mark 10:45: "We know that many among ourselves have given themselves to bondage that they might ransom (*lytrōsontai*) others" (cf. Harrill, *Manumission*, 30–31; Harris, "Demography," 73).

The use of ransom terminology for expiation has precedents within the Jewish sphere. Ransom is already connected with atonement in certain OT texts (e.g., Exod 21:30; 30:10–12; Num 35:31), and the Talmud punningly concludes from such passages that a ransom (*kûpĕrā'*) is an atonement (*kĕpārāh*; see *b. B. Qam.* 40a; *b. Mak.* 2b). In some Diaspora Jewish texts, moreover, a righteous individual or group can function as a ransom for the foolishness or sins of the larger group. Philo (*Sacrifices of Abel and Cain* 121), for example, says that the wise person is a ransom (*lytron*) for the fool, and 4 Maccabees, which was probably written in the first half of the first century C.E., describes the sacrificed life (*psychē*) or blood of a righteous individual as a recompense for the sins of the nation (4 Macc 6:28–29; 17:21–22; on the dating and relevance of 4 Maccabees, see Williams, *Jesus' Death*, 165–202; deSilva, *Apocrypha*, 355–56).

Given our passage's proximity to the discussions of wealth and eternal life in 10:17–31, it is interesting to note the association of riches, ransom, and eternal life in Ps 49:7–9:

> Truly, no ransom avails for one's life,
>   there is no price one can give to God for it.
> For the ransom of life is costly,
>   and can never suffice,
> that one should live on forever
>   and never see the grave.

many. Gk *pollōn*. As Bengel (*Gnomon* on Matt 20:28) notes, the implied contrast is not between "many" and "all" but between the many saved and the one life given up for them (cf. Rom 5:12, 15). Jeremias ("*Polloi*"), in fact, argues that in Semitic texts "many" (*rabbîm* and related terms) often has the inclusive sense of "all" and that one of these texts is Isa 52:13–53:12, which underlies the present verse (see the parallel between "he bore the sin of *many*" in 53:12 and "the LORD has laid on him the iniquity of us *all*" in 53:6). In Isaiah, moreover, the "many" delivered by the Lord's Suffering Servant seem to include not only Israelites (53:12) but also hostile pagans (52:14–15). Jeremias concludes, therefore, that "many" in Mark 10:45 indicates the sum total of humanity (cf. "slave of *all*" in 10:44), and he cites the parallel in 1 Tim 2:6 ("who gave himself a ransom for *all*") as confirmation.

This universalistic interpretation, however, goes beyond the evidence. "Many" has an inclusive sense only in certain contexts, and such a context is lacking in the present case. As for Isa 52:13–53:12, which is crucial to Jeremias' case, it is unclear that the "many" of 52:14–15 is identical with the "many" of 53:11–12. In the Dead Sea Scrolls (1QS 6:1, 15–16, 18, 21, etc.) and rabbinic literature, moreover, *(ha)rabbîm* is a term for the totality of the elect community or of Israel, not of humanity in general (cf. Lane, 384). Similarly, the *polloi* of Mark 10:45 are probably the elect community rather than humanity as a whole. This interpretation is supported by the observation that in a recent verse, 10:31, the "many . . . last" who will become "first" seem, because of the juxtaposition with 10:28–30, to be the persecuted Christian community. Even more important, the verses immediately preceding ours (10:43–44) indicate that our passage is dealing with the situation that obtains "among *you*," that is, in the church, and the "all" to whom one is to become a slave in 10:44 seem to be the same as the "you" to whom one is to become a servant in 10:43—that is, again, the members of the Christian community.

COMMENT

Introduction. The disciples now show a sort of misunderstanding opposite to that which they have recently manifested: whereas before they were overcome with fear about what would befall their master in Jerusalem (see 10:32), now two of them are so intoxicated with the prospect of his resurrection that they need to be reminded of the cross.

There are a number of tensions in the passage as it presently stands. Jesus, for example, responds twice to James and John's misguided power grab, first by saying that the privileges they are requesting are not his to give (10:38–40), second by asserting that the path to glory is service (10:42–45). While these two answers do not necessarily contradict each other, 10:42–45 makes more sense as a reaction to James and John's request (10:37) than as a response to the indignation of the ten other disciples (10:41). Even the first scene in the passage, moreover, does not appear to be all of a piece, since 10:38 seems to imply that those who share in Jesus' cup and baptism of suffering will gain places on his right hand and his left, whereas 10:39–40 asserts that even though James and John *will* share his suffering, that does *not* guarantee them the spots they covet (cf. Nineham, 279). Perhaps at an earlier stage the pericope consisted of the request of James and John (10:35–37), Jesus' rejection of that request (10:40), and his exaltation of service over being served (10:42b–45). The intervening pieces (10:38–39 and 10:41–42a) may be redactional; they contain typical Markan vocabulary ("know," "can," "heard," "began to," "calling") and embody common redactional themes: the incomprehension of the disciples (10:38a; cf. 4:13; 6:52; 8:17–18, 21; etc.), the necessity of suffering (10:38b–39; cf. 8:31–33, 34–37; 9:12–13, 31; 10:33–34; 13:9–13), and dissension within the apostolic ranks (10:41; cf. 9:10, 33–34; 14:29–31).

Despite its possible growth over time, the passage holds together as a redactional unity. Both sections begin with descriptions that put disciples in a bad light: James and John's ambition in the first part (10:35–37), the indignation of the other disciples in the second (10:41). The desire of James and John for places of honor in the first section (10:37), moreover, is comparable to the pagan rulers' ambition to be great in the second (10:42a). And both subdivisions end up relating the fate of the disciples to the destiny of Jesus himself, in the first case by linking their "cup" and "baptism" with his (10:39), in the second by associating apostolic self-abnegation with Jesus' sacrifice of his life as "a ransom for many" (10:42b–45).

10:35–40: sharing in Jesus' cup and baptism. Jesus and the disciples resume their way up to Jerusalem, presumably with Jesus again in the vanguard (cf. 10:32a). Two of the Twelve, the sons of Zebedee, James and John, now break away from the others to approach him with a request for a special favor. Rather than laying their bid right on the table, however, James and John begin with an attempt at manipulation that is breathtaking in its audacity, in effect asking Jesus to sign a blank check: "Teacher, we want you to do for us whatever we ask . . ." (10:35b; cf. Gundry, 577).

Jesus parries this manipulation by insisting that the brothers state their request

(10:36), to which they respond by asking that they be allowed to sit on his right and left hand "in your glory" (10:37). The association of "glory" with a sitting posture, and especially with a throne, is common in biblical and Jewish texts (cf. Davies and Allison, 3.55). Usually, however, only one throne is envisaged, on which sits either a human king (e.g., Isa 22:23; Zech 6:13; Sir 47:11) or God (e.g., Jer 14:21; Wis 9:10; *1 En.* 9:4) or some godlike being, such as the Son of Man in *1 Enoch* (e.g., *1 En.* 45:3; 51:3; 55:4).

Occasionally, however, the enthronement of others alongside such exalted beings, and a plurality of thrones, can be implied (see, e.g., 1 Sam 2:8; Ps 113:7–8). The two most famous instances of co-enthronement are Psalm 110 and Daniel 7, both of which are key texts elsewhere in Mark (cf. Mark 8:38; 12:35–37; 14:62). Daniel 7 is particularly relevant to the present context because it speaks of the *glory* of the "one like a son of man" (Dan 7:14 MT LXX; cf. "in your glory" in Mark 10:37) and pictures "the people of the holy ones of the Most High" sharing in the enthronement and judicial prerogative that earlier were ascribed to him and to God (cf. Dan 7:9, 13–14, 27; for a synopsis of the allusions to Daniel within our passage, see figure 31). Later Jewish and Christian texts, moreover, use Daniel 7 in a way that approximates the request of James and John. *First Enoch* 108:12–15, for example, merges the picture of enthronement and judgment from Daniel 7 with the portrayal of resurrectional glory in Dan 12:1–3: "And I will bring forth in shining light those who have loved my holy Name, and I will seat each on the throne of his honor . . ." (Black trans.); the passage goes on to speak of the righteous observing the punishment of the wicked. Similarly, Matt 19:28//Luke 22:30 and Rev 3:21; 4:4 employ the imagery of Daniel 7 to make the point that in the eschatological future Jesus' disciples will sit on thrones and judge their fellow human beings (cf. Allison, *Intertextual Jesus*, 137–40).

Daniel 7, however, also speaks of "the beast" making war on the saints, prevailing over them, and wearing them out in the period of intense suffering that must precede the final consummation (Dan 7:21, 25). Correspondingly, Jesus responds to his disciples' enthusiasm for positions of power by asking whether they can drink the same cup or be baptized with the same baptism as he (10:38). In the OT the basic idea in the cup image is that of bitter suffering, often with a connotation of punishment and disgrace (see the NOTE on "the cup" in 10:38); in one passage, as a matter of fact, "cup" is a synonym for shame and an antonym for glory (Hab 2:16). The transition from the brothers' request to share in Jesus' glory to his question about sharing in his cup, therefore, is logical. The baptismal image has a similar nuance of subjection to suffering and even to eschatological tribulation (see the NOTE on "be baptized with the baptism I am baptized with" in 10:38). Jesus' eschatological reservation, then, is nicely paraphrased by Chrysostom: "You speak of honors, but I am discoursing of wrestlings and toil; for this is not a time of rewards, but of blood, of battles, and dangers" (*Homilies on Matthew* 65.2). We note, therefore, a significant shift within the Markan narrative: whereas in earlier chapters the waters of the eschatological storm were depicted as being unable to touch Jesus' followers, much less Jesus himself (cf. 4:35–41; 6:45–52), Jesus now speaks of being overwhelmed by the flood of death and of his disciples going down

Figure 31: Allusions to Daniel and Isaiah in Mark 10:35–45

Mark 10:35–45	*Daniel and Isaiah*
37: Grant us that one of us should sit on your right and one on your left	Dan 7:9, 13–14, 27: the "people of the holy ones of the Most High" share in the dominion of the "one like a son of man"
in your glory	Dan 7:14: "to him [the 'one like a son of man'] was given . . . glory"
38: Can you drink the cup I drink or be baptized with the baptism I am baptized with?	Dan 7:21, 25: the beast will make war on the "holy ones," prevail against them, and wear them out
40: to sit at my right or my left is not mine to give but is for those for whom it has been prepared [by God]	Dan 4:17: the Most High rules the kingdom of human beings and "gives it to whom he will" (cf. 4:22; 2:21)
42: those who are thought to rule over the Gentiles	Daniel 7–12: pagan leaders' authority is a sham; behind them stand angels/demons and ultimately God
lord it over them, and their great ones oppress them	Dan 7:5: "Arise, devour many bodies!"
	Dan 7:7: "terrifying and dreadful and exceedingly strong . . . devouring, breaking in pieces, and stamping what was left with its feet"
	Dan 7:23: "shall devour the whole earth, and trample it down, and break it to pieces"
43–44: whoever wants to be great/first shall be servant/slave of all	Dan 4:17: God gives power to "the lowliest of human beings"
45: Son of Man did not come to be served	Dan 7:13–14: all people will serve the "one like a son of man"
but to serve	Isa 53:11: God's "righteous one" serves many well
and to give his life (*psychē*)	Isa 53:12: because his life (*psychē*) was delivered to death
as a ransom for many	"he bore the sin of many"
	"and was delivered on account of their sins"
	Isa 53:11: God's righteous servant will "make many righteous"
	"and he shall bear their iniquities"
	Cf. Dan 12:2: and "many of those who sleep in the dust of the earth shall awake"

with him. For frequent hearers of Mark's Gospel, this shift toward suffering and death would be reinforced by the fact that the request of James and John to be seated on Jesus' right and left hand ironically foreshadows the crucifixion scene, in which Jesus will be "enthroned" between two malefactors (see 15:27 and cf. Allison, "Anticipating," 710–11).

For the Markan community, however, the figurative and eschatological sense of the cup and baptism metaphors, as referring to imminent suffering, would probably be overlaid by a sacramental one; as Smith (*Clement*, 187) points out, these two interpretations are not mutually exclusive. Mark's Christian readers drink the Lord's cup at communion and thus proclaim his death until he comes (cf. 1 Cor 11:26); they also share in that death in a deep sacramental sense through baptism (cf. Rom 6:3). They would therefore hear as addressed to *themselves* the question that Jesus asks James and John in 10:38, and they would thus be reminded that the sacraments mirror the tribulation that they are experiencing and that Jesus endured before them.

Despite this somber warning of imminent tribulation, James and John, like Peter in 14:29–31, respond positively to Jesus' question about their willingness to share it (10:39a), and Jesus in turn prophesies that they will indeed do so (10:39b). There is a well-attested tradition about James' early martyrdom, which occurred sometime between 42 and 44 C.E. (see Acts 12:2) and therefore probably would have been known to the Markan community. But there is no such tradition about John's martyrdom, and indeed Irenaeus records that he lived to a ripe old age, dying under the emperor Trajan, who reigned from 98 to 117 C.E. (*Against Heresies* 2.22.5; 3.3.4)—about a generation after Mark was written. Perhaps Mark would have thought that Jesus' prophecy implied suffering and rejection, but not necessarily death.

The main point of this first part of the passage, however, is not the reference to the future tribulation of James and John but the separation of this anticipated suffering from the notion of places of honor in the new age (10:40). The Markan Jesus does not deny that there will *be* such places, only that there is a simple formula for calculating who will occupy them. Even he does not know who will be seated at his right and left hand when he comes in his glory, any more than he knows the hour of the end (cf. 13:32); both are up to and known by God alone (cf. the NOTE on "but is for those for whom it has been prepared" in 10:40). Unlike the Overseer at Qumran (cf. CD 13:11–12), then, Jesus prescinds from ranking his disciples' spiritual attainments and future positions in the eschatological epoch, instead deferring to God. This theme is similar to that in a number of OT passages that ascribe to God the power to set leaders up and to pull them down (see, e.g., Job 12:18–19 LXX; Ps 75:7; Dan 2:21; 4:17, 25). Three of these passages are from Daniel, a book that, as we have seen, is invoked throughout our pericope (see again figure 31), and one of these Danielic texts anticipates the next part of Jesus' teaching (10:43–44) when it says that God's control over kings is "to the end that the living may know that the Most High rules the kingdom of human beings, and *gives it to whom he will*, and *sets over it the lowliest of human beings*" (Dan 4:17 RSV alt.).

10:41–45: *the path of service*. The impetus for this second stage of the conversation is provided by the annoyance of the ten remaining disciples at the attempt by James and John to steal the show (10:41). Jesus, either overhearing or, more likely, divining this irritation (cf. 2:6–8; 3:5; 8:14–15; 9:33–35), calls the others over and reprises themes that he has expressed recently in the narrative: the last shall be first, and the way to become great is to become the humblest of all (cf. 9:35; 10:31). This response, as we have already noted, may have been a way of correcting the ambition of James and John at an earlier stage of tradition history. In the present form of the passage the point may be that those who are most appalled at the self-aggrandizement of others often secretly long to aggrandize themselves. But the Markan Jesus may also be implying that if the others are angry at James and John for trying to get ahead of them, they need to realize that precedence in the domin-ion of God entails self-abnegation rather than dominance.

In any event, Jesus responds to the indignation of these disciples by counterpos-ing the way in which greatness is measured in the world with the way it is reckoned within the dominion of God (10:42b–43); the operative phrase is "not so among you" (10:43a). It seems odd at first that in 10:42b *Gentile* kings and rulers, but not *Jewish* ones, are identified as oppressive—in defiance of the fact that Jewish rulers in the first couple of centuries B.C. and the first century C.E. frequently were as exploitative and corrupt as their pagan counterparts. This distinction, however, corresponds to the viewpoint expressed in Daniel 7, in which the four Gentile world empires are portrayed as exercising cruel and oppressive power. Daniel may also help explain the strange phrase in 10:42, "those who *are thought* to rule over the Gentiles" (*hoi dokountes archein tōn ethnōn*); in the apocalyptic way of think-ing classically represented by Daniel 7–12, earthly rulers are not really sovereign but only seem to be so, since behind them stand angelic and demonic forces, and ultimately God (cf. 4 Macc 13:14, "Let us not fear him who thinks he is killing us" [*ton dokounta apoktennein*]; see Marcus, "Epistemology," 557–58; Harrington, "Ideology," 545).

Jesus' revelation of the impotence of worldly rulers is followed by a description of the topsy-turvy nature of *true* greatness, which is experienced by those who have given up all claims to conventional power and instead have turned them-selves into servants of their fellow human beings (10:43–44). This idea has been presented within the Markan narrative recently (see 9:35; 10:31), but it is now radicalized by being depicted with the vocabulary of slavery (see the NOTE on "your servant . . . slave of all" in 10:43–44). For free people in the Greco-Roman world there were few greater horrors than being enslaved, a status reduction that is not incidentally associated with death both in our passage (10:45b) and in Phil 2:7–8 (cf. Patterson, *Slavery*, 38–45). In our passage, Jesus calls on his followers to take upon themselves a condition that would have been viewed as the nadir of degradation, yet he paradoxically proclaims it to be the path to glory.

The justification for this extraordinary assertion comes in 10:45: "For even the Son of Man did not come to be served but to serve, and to give his life as a ran-som for many." The "for" (*gar*) here suggests that the depiction of Jesus' service-unto-death (10:45) somehow grounds the assertion that the way to be exalted is to become the slave of all (10:43–44). But how? The answer usually given is that the disciples are being called to model themselves on Jesus' example of servitude; as he has become a slave, so should they (see, e.g., Nineham, 280; Pesch, 2.162; Gundry, 581). While there is an element of truth in this exemplarist interpretation, it does not explain how slavery leads to *exaltation*, as 10:43–44 implies. The OT passages alluded to in Mark 10:45, namely, Daniel 7–12 and Isaiah 52:13–53:12, are helpful in this regard. In the former, the "people of the holy ones," who are strongly linked with the "one like a son of man," endure eschatological tribulation but also turn "many" to righteousness and eventually are enthroned along with the many in the splendor of eternal life (Dan 7:18, 25–27; 12:1–3). In the latter, the Lord's Suffering Servant, having borne the sin of "many" and died an atoning death on their behalf, is exalted and glorified (*doxasthēsetai*, Isa 52:13; cf. 53:12 and the NOTES on "ransom" and "many" in 10:45). Thus, the larger contexts of the OT passages illuminate the unspoken logic of Mark 10:42–45: those who participate in the Son of Man's descent into the abyss will also share in his exaltation (cf. Phil 2:5–11; on the parallels between these two passages, which may reflect their common background in Isa 52:13–53:12, see figure 32). This merger of the Danielic Son of Man figure with the Suffering Servant from Isaiah 52–53 is partly paralleled in the *Similitudes of Enoch* (*1 Enoch* 36–71), which may be pre-Christian (see Davies, *Paul*, 279–80).

Although both Daniel 7 and Isaiah 52–53 are thus invoked in the concluding verse of our passage, they function in different ways. Daniel 7 is alluded to in an almost polemical manner: the Son of Man did *not* come to be served, as he does in Dan 7:14, but to serve, and to give his life as a ransom, as he does in Isaiah 53 (see the NOTE on "the Son of Man did not come to be served but to serve" in 10:45). To be sure, the contrast with Daniel 7 is not absolute, since later in the chapter "the people of the holy ones of the Most High," with whom the "one like a son of man" is associated, are fiercely persecuted by the beast (Dan 7:25). The "one like a son of man" himself, however, does not suffer in Daniel. But for an author with as deep a view of sin as Mark, the Savior cannot simply be the glorious, domineering

Figure 32: Parallels between Philippians 2:5–11 and Mark 10:43–45, with Common Allusions to Isaiah 52:13–53:12

Philippians 2:5–11	Mark 10:43–45
taking the form of a slave (cf. Isa 52:13: "my servant")	will be your servant . . . will be the slave of all
	the Son of Man did not come to be served but to serve (cf. Isa 52:13: "my servant")
obedient to the point of death (cf. Isa 53:7, 12)	and to give his life as a ransom for many (cf. Isa 53:4–8, 10, 12)
therefore God . . . highly exalted him (cf. Isa 52:13; 53:12) and gave him the name that is above every name	slavery is the path to exaltation and to being "first" (cf. Isa 52:13; 53:12)

judge of Daniel 7 who rewards the saints according to their deserts; he must also be the sacrificial lamb who *makes* many righteous by donating his life as a ransom for their sins, as in Isaiah 53.

This ransom saying, with which the passage concludes (10:45b), is of central importance in Mark's narrative because it is the clearest Markan reflection on the saving purpose of Jesus' death (cf. 14:24). That death is to be a "ransom," a payment of the price that the "many" are unable to pay themselves. The servitude imagery of the previous verses and the use of *diakonein* in the present context favor the view that this ransom is conceived as a slave price: Jesus sells himself into slavery in order to liberate his brothers and sisters from bondage (see the NOTES on "ransom" and "many" in 10:45 and cf. Phil 2:7–8). It is not specified to whom this ransom is paid, and in church history interpreters have split over whether the recipient is God (e.g., Gregory Nazanianzus, *Orations* 45.22; John Damascene, *Concerning the Orthodox Faith* 3.27) or the devil (e.g., Origen, *Commentary on Matthew* 16:8; Gregory of Nyssa, *Great Catechism* 21–23). In favor of the latter interpretation, ransoms are usually paid to hostile powers, and it is easy to imagine Satan as a slave master, especially in view of the "binding and loosing" terminology in the Strong Man parable in 3:27. But the apparent background of our passage in Isaiah 53 leaves room for doubt, since in Isaiah it pleases *the Lord* to bruise his righteous Servant, laying the iniquity of the nation upon him and thus exacting from him the price for their sin.

In any event, our passage ends with an allusion to Isaiah 52–53, which speaks of the Lord's righteous Servant, who pours out his soul unto death to atone for the iniquity of "many." Service to others is thus implicitly correlated with service of God. In the canonical context of Isaiah, significantly, the suffering of the Lord's Servant fits into a larger framework of joyful redemption. Within Isaiah 52–53 itself, the sufferer is an enlightened one who illuminates others and thus reverses the sentence of blindness pronounced on the people in Isa 6:9–10—a passage prominently quoted in Mark 4:12 (see Isa 52:13, 15; 53:11 LXX; cf. Ekblad, *Servant Poems*, 179–80, 250–52). And within the larger framework of Isaiah, the servant's sacrifice becomes the means by which the divine warrior wins his amazing victory over death and its allies—a triumph that includes miraculous events such as valleys being elevated, the desert blooming, and the blind joyfully receiving their sight (see Isa 29:18; 35:1–7; 40:1–11; 42:1–17). It is not surprising, then, that our passage about the slave-like death of the Son of Man is immediately followed by one in which the Son of David miraculously opens the eyes of the blind.

JESUS HEALS ANOTHER BLIND MAN (10:46–52)

10 [46]And they came to Jericho. And as he was going out of Jericho along with his disciples and a large crowd, a blind beggar named Bartimaeus (the son of Timaeus) was sitting beside the way. [47]And when he heard that it was Jesus of Nazareth, he began to shout and say, "Son of David! Jesus! Have mercy on me!" [48]And many people began rebuking him, telling him to be quiet. But he shouted

all the more, "Son of David! Have mercy on me!" ⁴⁹And Jesus stood still and said, "Call him." And they called the blind man, saying to him, "Be brave! Get up! He's calling you!" ⁵⁰And throwing off his garment, he leaped up and came to Jesus. ⁵¹And Jesus answered him and said, "What do you want me to do for you?" And the blind man said to him, "Rabbouni, let me see again." ⁵²And Jesus said to him, "Go! Your faith has saved you." And immediately he began to see again, and he followed him in the way.

NOTES

10 46. *Jericho.* Gk *Ierichō*. This ancient town (its earliest surviving buildings have been dated to 9000 B.C.E.) is located 825 feet below sea level, on the eastern flank of ancient Judaea, ten miles northwest of the north shore of the Dead Sea and only twelve miles east of Jerusalem. The old settlement was abandoned after the Babylonian invasions in the sixth century B.C.E.; the new one, which features in our story, developed in the irrigated oasis about a mile to the southwest. Because of its proximity to Jerusalem and its mild winter climate, Jericho was used as a winter resort by the Hasmonaean kings and Herod the Great. Biblically, however, its greatest importance flows from the fact that it was the first city captured by the invading Israelites and the staging ground for the conquest of the rest of Canaan under Joshua (Joshua 2; 5:13–6:26; etc.; see Holland and Netzer, "Jericho"). Jesus, the new Joshua, likewise begins his climactic "invasion" of Judaea by passing through Jericho on his way up to Jerusalem (on the importance of the image of Joshua in postbiblical Jewish messianism, see Sir 46:1; *Sib. Or.* 5.256–59; Josephus, *Ant.* 20.97–99; Kraft, "Messiah-Joshua"; Schwartz, "Whence," 43).

And as he was going out of Jericho. Gk *kai ekporeuomenou autou apo Ierichō.* It is strange that Jesus' entrance into and exit from Jericho are noted, but not what he did in between. Koester ("History," 41–42) observes that in the *Secret Gospel of Mark* a short incident intervenes, and he argues that the awkwardness of the Markan version results from the elimination of this incident. It is more likely, however, that 10:46ab is the sort of gap that a later editor or forger such as the *Secret Gospel* author would have exploited (for a critique of Koester's theory of the relationship between canonical Mark and *Secret Mark*, see the INTRODUCTION in vol. 1, pp. 47–51, and for new evidence that the latter is a modern forgery, see Carlson, *Gospel Hoax*). Other scholars (e.g., Gnilka, 2.108; Lamarche, 263) theorize that the Bartimaeus narrative originally occurred on the road *to* Jericho (as in Luke 18:35) but that Mark displaced it to the road *out* in the interest of his conception that discipleship means following Jesus "up to Jerusalem," the city of suffering and death. It is more likely, however, that the story originally began with Jesus' exit (alone) from Jericho (10:46b) and that "And they came to Jericho" (10:46a) is a Markan connective designed to bring the disciples into view and to get Jesus to the location where the pre-Markan narrative occurred (see Smith, "Function," 525).

a blind beggar named Bartimaeus (the son of Timaeus). Gk *ho huios Timaiou Bartimaios typhlos prosaitēs,* lit. "the son of Timaeus, Bartimaeus, a blind beggar." Here, as in 10:47 ("Son of David! Jesus"), there is an unusual reversal of the normal word order, which is name + patronymic (see the GLOSSARY). "Bartimaeus" itself, however, means "son of Timaeus," since the Aramaic word *bar* denotes "son of" (cf. *bar mitzvah* = "son of the commandment"); "the son of Timaeus, Bartimaeus," therefore, is an Aramaic patronymic preceded by its Greek translation. Timaeus = *Timaios* is a common Greek name (cf. the title character in one of Plato's dialogues) derived from the word for "valuable, honored." It is ironic that the beggar is the son of a man whose name in Greek means "honored"; Augustine remarks that the man has fallen from prosperity to "the most notorious and remarkable wretchedness" (*Harmony of the Gospels* 2.65).

It is unusual but not unprecedented for a Palestinian Jew to be identified by *bar* + a Greek name; rabbinic literature, in fact, knows of a R. Joshua bar Ṭimai or bar Ṭimi (*Qoh. Rab.* 9.9.1). Aramaic etymologies for the name, however, have also been proposed. Lagrange (285), for example, suggests a derivation from *bar sāmē* ("the son of a blind man"), and others have derived it from *bar ṭĕmē'* ("son of the unclean"). Some of the Dead Sea Scrolls consider blindness to be a defilement that excludes one from membership in the eschatological community (see 11QTemple 45:12–14; 4QMMTᶜ 1–2; 1QSa 2:3–10; cf. Just, "Blind Bartimaeus"), and 11QTemple 2:1–3; 45:12–13, basing itself on Lev 21:18 and 22:22, prohibits blind people from entering Jerusalem, the city in which God dwells, lest they defile it (*yṭm'w*). In Mark, by contrast, Bartimaeus is healed of his (defiling?) blindness and follows Jesus on the way up to the holy city (10:52). These connections with Aramaic terms are intriguing, but Mark is writing in Greek and underlines the Greek connotation of the name.

47. *Son of David! Gk huie Dauid.* On the Markan usages of this title and its history-of-religions background, including its association with David's son Solomon as healer, see the APPENDIX "The 'Son of David' Title."

Some exegetes have argued that the blind man, in using the nationalistic term "Son of David" for Jesus, betrays a spiritual blindness that matches his physical condition (see already Origen, *Commentary on Matthew* 16.9, and cf. Kelber, *Kingdom*, 95; Johnson, "Mark 10:46–52," 197). But nothing in the narrative indicates that Bartimaeus' understanding of Jesus' identity is defective, and in fact Jesus himself praises his faith (10:52). The rhetoric of the passage, moreover, emphasizes the "Son of David" title, which Bartimaeus persists in shouting out (see Marshall, *Faith*, 127); it precedes Jesus' proper name in 10:47, which is unusual for a patronymic, and totally displaces it in 10:48. Furthermore, the crowd's attempt to silence Bartimaeus (10:48) has a rhetorical boomerang effect, emphasizing the acclamation that the unsympathetic bystanders take pains to suppress.

50. *throwing off his garment. Gk apobalōn to himation autou.* The garment Bartimaeus casts off is his *himation*, or outer tunic, but he is probably still wearing his *chitōn*, or inner tunic (see BDAG 475 and cf. the NOTE on "two tunics" in 6:9). Nevertheless, some scribes seem to have been concerned by the possible implication of nakedness; the minuscule manuscript 565 (cf. also syrˢⁱⁿ) substitutes *epibalōn* ("putting on") for *apobalōn* (cf. Swete, 230).

Why, though, does Bartimaeus divest himself of his *himation* as he comes to Jesus? Some think he has spread his cloak on the ground to collect alms, a technique still used in the Middle East (Gundry [596] cites Judg 8:25 as a distant comparison). The blind man's action of throwing away his garment would then be analogous to that of people who abandon their goods to follow Jesus (e.g., in 1:18, 20; 10:21, 28–29) or people who cast away the accoutrements of former illness and dependence, such as the crutches on display at the healing waters of Lourdes. Without further specification, however, most readers would think of a garment worn rather than one spread on the ground. Another possibility is that the beggar disencumbers himself of the cloak that hinders his quick approach to Jesus—cf. Homer, *Iliad* 2.182–84; 2 Kgs 7:15; Heb 12:1—but this seems unlikely because Jesus is close by, in contrast to the situation in these parallels, which envisage a long run. Jesus, moreover, is surrounded by a crowd, which is a more serious impediment to Bartimaeus' approach than the latter's garment. Gundry (602) mentions other explanations that seem even less likely, such as that the man is wearing his cloak over his shoulders or that he is sitting on it as he begs.

Since other features of the narrative are reminiscent of baptism (see the COMMENT on 10:49–52), it may be that the man's divestiture is meant to remind readers of pre-baptismal disrobing (on this disrobing see Hippolytus, *Apostolic Tradition* 21:3; Chrysostom, *Baptismal Homily* 2.11; Cyril of Jerusalem, *Mystagogical Catechesis* 2.2; Meeks, "Image," 183–84 n. 82; M. Johnson, *Rites*, 122 and passim). The earliest commentary on Mark supports this hypothesis by echoing the baptismal language in Eph 4:22; Col 3:9: "He is said to jump nude out of the old man" (Pseudo-Jerome, *Exposition of* Mark 10:50 [Cahill, 81]; for another Markan disrobing that may have baptismal connections, see the APPENDIX "The Youth Who Ran Away Naked [Mark 14:51–52]"). Old Testament passages may also contribute to the symbolism of the cast-off garment. In Zech 3:1–10, for example, the regeneration of the high priest is symbolized by the removal of his filthy clothes and linked with the coming of "the Branch" of David—a term close to "Son of David" in our passage.

51. *Rabbouni.* Gk *Rabbouni.* This Hebrew/Aramaic term is vocalized as *ribbôni* in *Tg. Onq.* Gen 33:11, and older commentaries (e.g., Wellhausen, 85) judge the Markan form to be an error. The Cairo Genizah fragments, however, have confirmed that *rabbûni* is indeed an early Palestinian Aramaic word (it is found twice in the Genizah manuscripts D and Z of the Targum on Gen 44:18; cf. Black, *Aramaic Approach*, 23–24). Etymologically, *rabbouni* is related to *rabbi* (see the NOTE on "Rabbi" in 9:5); both words can be translated "my master," and Matthew renders both of them with *kyrie*, "lord" (Matt 17:4; 20:33; cf. Luke 18:41). *Rabbouni*, however, may have a more exalted nuance than *rabbi*; in rabbinic traditions *ribbon* and related words are more often used of God than of human beings (see Gundry, 602–3), and in Mark itself the character who calls Jesus *rabbouni* is praised for his faith (10:51–52), whereas those who call him *rabbi* are either ignorant (9:5–6) or treacherous (14:45). Unlike Matthew (23:7) and John (1:38; 3:2), Mark does not translate or paraphrase either term, perhaps because both are familiar to his readers (on the bilingual character of the first-century Decapolis

region, see Millar, *Near East*, 413, and on the tendency to leave religious terms untranslated, see Mussies, "Use," 429–30).

let me see again. Gk *hina anablepsō*, lit. "in order that I might see again"; on the imperative use of *hina*, see the NOTE on "come and lay your hands on her" in 5:23. *Anablepein* is a compound of the prefix *ana* = "up" or "again" and *blepein* = "to see"; cf. 8:24, where *anablepsas* conveys both meanings. In NT times the prefix sometimes lost its force, so that *anablepein* could mean simply "to see"; compare, for example, John 9:11, 15, 18, where it is used with reference to a man born blind (cf. BDAG 59). It is theoretically possible that the man in our story, too, has been blind from birth and that *hina anablepsō* should be translated simply "in order that I might see." As Gundry (603) points out, however, if this were the case, the man's blindness from birth ought to be mentioned, as it would enhance the miracle (cf. John 9:1–2).

52. *Go!* Gk *Hypage*. This injunction occurs at the end of several Markan miracle stories (1:44; 2:11; 5:19, 34; 7:29), where it is usually a command to go home. Bartimaeus, however, chooses instead to follow Jesus "in the way."

followed him in the way. Gk *ēkolouthei autō en tē hodō*. Kingsbury (*Christology*, 104–5 n. 159) argues that "followed" here is used not in the metaphorical sense of becoming a disciple, as in 1:18; 2:14; 8:34; 10:21, 28, but in the literal sense of walking after, as in 3:7; 5:24; 11:9; 14:13, 54. Bartimaeus, then, does not become a disciple but a part of the enthusiastic crowd that accompanies Jesus (part of the way?) from Jericho to Jerusalem. But the placement of the two healing-of-blindness stories at the beginning and end of a section primarily concerned with instruction of the uncomprehending disciples (8:22–10:52) suggests that these stories are more closely related to discipleship than Kingsbury allows (see the introduction to 8:22–10:52 and the COMMENT on 8:22–26). Bartimaeus, moreover, does not just follow Jesus but follows him *in the way, en tē hodō*, and that combination of terms has most recently been used of the Twelve in 10:32 (cf. 10:17, 21, though contrast 11:8–9).

COMMENT

Introduction. In the previous passage Jesus has called his disciples to participate in his pattern of humbling himself, even to the point of death, for the sake of the "many." The present pericope, then, comes as a welcome reminder that this life of shared suffering is also a life in which one's eyes are opened and one sees things as they are—and what one sees with this corrected vision is Jesus treading a path that converts death into victory.

Our pericope seems to be a traditional tale that Mark has touched up especially at the beginning and the end, as is his wont. Probably 10:46a ("And they came to Jericho") is an editorial addition to bring the disciples into a story that originally began with Jesus (alone) *leaving* Jericho. The awkwardly belated phrase in 10:46b, "along with his disciples and a large crowd," is a redactional phrase that is also designed to widen the audience; as Smith ("Function," 525) points out, Mark likes to portray Jesus accompanied by both a smaller and a larger entourage (cf. 3:7;

4:10; 8:34; 10:32). At the end of the passage, "and he followed him in the way" is also probably redactional; it fits into the larger Markan "way" theme and may have replaced an original ending describing the crowd's astonishment.

In terms of structure, the passage, like 5:24b–34, appears at first as an interruption: Jesus is on his way out of Jericho, beginning the last leg of his journey to Jerusalem (cf. 10:32), when his progress is halted by the importunity of Bartimaeus. Unsurprisingly in a story about a man who is dependent on his sense of hearing, verbs of speaking dominate; forms of "to say" are used six times, "to call" three times, "to shout" twice, and "to rebuke" and "to answer" once each (see Eckstein, "Markus 10,46–52," 38–39). The passage is bracketed by an introduction that sets the stage and introduces the characters (10:46) and a conclusion that resolves the tensions and forms a transition to the next pericope (10:52b). In between, there are three little scenes, the first involving Bartimaeus and the crowd (10:47–48), the second involving Jesus, the crowd, and Bartimaeus (10:49–50), and the third involving Jesus and Bartimaeus (10:51–52a), each with the same pattern of action, reaction, and result (cf. Eckstein, ibid.).

10:46–48: *the blind man's plea.* The passage begins with an odd juxtaposition of references to the ancient city of Jericho: "And they came to Jericho. And as he was going out of Jericho" (10:46a). Jesus' arrival at the ancient portal to Palestine, then, is described, as well as his departure from it, but not what he did while there. Although this awkwardness probably reflects the editorial history of our passage (see the introduction to the COMMENT and the NOTE on "And as he was going out of Jericho" in 10:46), in its present form it also serves to heighten the desperation of Bartimaeus' plight. Not only is he a blind, helpless beggar who is dependent on the alms thrown him by passersby, but his one chance for salvation is about to vanish, since Jesus has no sooner arrived in his town than he has hurried off with his face set toward Jerusalem (cf. 10:32–34; Luke 12:50). The danger that Bartimaeus will miss his opportunity is underscored by the fact that the phrase "beside the way" (*para tēn hodon*) and the theme of hearing ("when he heard that it was Jesus of Nazareth") have previously occurred in a parabolic description of seed cast where it cannot bear fruit, since it is immediately devoured by Satan's minions (4:4, 15).

Bartimaeus, however, is unwilling to let his chance for deliverance slip away so easily. Informed that it is Jesus who is passing by (10:47a), he lets loose a volley of cries: "Son of David! Jesus! Have mercy on me!" (10:47b). As Eckstein ("Markus 10,46–52," 41–42) points out, this linkage of the cry for help with the name of the founding king of the Israelite dynasty makes our pericope similar to passages in both Jewish and pagan literature in which a petitioner entreats a king for a boon, which can include miraculous healing (see, e.g., the passages about Vespasian discussed in the COMMENT on 8:22–23 and 2 Sam 14:4; 2 Kgs 6:26). Correspondingly, one of the nuances of "Son of David" is royal and, by extension, messianic. This implication is supplemented by a second dimension of the title, which associates Jesus with David's son Solomon, who becomes a great exorcist and healer in Jewish legends (see the APPENDIX "The 'Son of David' Title").

Bartimaeus' invocation of Jesus as the "Son of David," therefore, exactly fits the remedy he seeks.

The exorcistic, Solomonic dimension to the "Son of David" title in 10:47–48 also helps explain the next development in the story, the crowd's futile attempt to silence Bartimaeus (10:48). The description of this attempt employs the loaded term "rebuked," which Mark frequently associates with the struggle against demons (see 1:25; 3:12; 9:25; cf. 4:39); the crowd's reproof of Bartimaeus' importunity, then, may in the Markan context represent a satanically instigated attempt to steal the word of hope that has been sown in the beggar sitting "beside the way" (cf. again the Parable of the Sower in Mark 4:4, 15). This exegesis is supported by the earliest extant commentary on Mark, which paraphrases 10:48a: "Sins and demons suppress the cry of the poor man, which the Lord heard" (Pseudo-Jerome, *Exposition of Mark* 10:48 [Cahill, 81]). As in the narrative of Peter's confession, the proclamation of Jesus' messianic identity (cf. 8:29) is followed by a demonic "rebuke" (cf. 8:32b).

This attempt to silence him, however, makes Bartimaeus cry out more loudly than ever, "Have mercy on me!" (*eleēson me*, 10:48b). The blind man's persistence is exemplary; when people tell God's elect that their cause is hopeless, they turn to him all the more resolutely and thus demonstrate their faith (cf. "your faith has saved you" in 10:52). As in 9:14–27, the focus of attention in our story is as much on the struggle to believe as it is on the miracle itself, and it is not surprising that the passage has links with the context of worship, in which faith is expressed communally. In particular, the blind man's repeated shout has entered the Christian liturgy in its Matthean form *kyrie eleēson* ("Lord, have mercy," Matt 20:30–31), and *eleēson me* may already have been a liturgical formula for Mark and his community, since it occurs frequently in the psalms as an address to God (see Pss 6:2; 9:13; 41:4, 10 [40:5, 11 LXX]; cf. Marshall, *Faith*, 128). The prosaic, this-worldly surface of 10:47–48, therefore, masks a titanic struggle between the royal ensign of God's liberation, roaring through Jericho like a new Joshua on his way up to "conquer" Jerusalem (see the NOTE on "Jericho" in 10:46), and the forces of sickness and demonic oppression that oppose him. On the margin of the battle, by the side of the road, sits a blind man, who has lived in the realm of darkness but now hears a rumor of a liberator on the march, and who cries out desperately for succor before hope disappears over the horizon. Like the Greek seer Tiresias, this blind man, ironically, sees more clearly than the sighted people around him, who try to squelch his insight (cf. MacDonald, *Homeric Epics*, 97–101). The uncanny effect of this sort of blind sight is evoked by Douglas' description of a Holocaust survivor who wore dark glasses during her testimony at Adolf Eichmann's trial in Jerusalem: "She appeared, then, to be blind (though she was not), an impression made all the more striking as the dramatic force of her testimony found focus in the words, 'I saw everything' " (*Memory*, 104).

10:49–52: miracle and discipleship. The blind man in our story "sees" with a strangely piercing vision, and the sharpness of his insight ("Son of David!"), together with the urgency of his request ("Have mercy on me!"), induces Jesus to stop and call for the petitioner to be brought forward (10:49a). Jesus himself, then, overrules the resistance of his supporters in order to confront the needs of the person who has accosted him. He thereby transforms the rebuking crowd into a supportive one; instead of trying to shush Bartimaeus, they now encourage him by telling him of Jesus' summons (10:49b). This sudden change of heart is a comic but realistic touch; charity, like hatred, can be contagious, and an authoritative figure's concern for the down-and-out can quickly convert popular hostility into benevolence. But there is also a deeper issue at stake: if earlier in the Gospel a close adherent of Jesus suddenly became a mouthpiece for Satan (8:32–33), and if later a sympathetic Jerusalem crowd (11:1–10) will abruptly transmute into a hostile one (15:11–15), our passage shows that the reverse can occur as well. In Mark the battle line between the warring apocalyptic camps is more porous than it is, for example, at Qumran (cf. 1QS 3:15–4:26).

In response to Jesus' call, which is mediated by the crowd, Bartimaeus leaps up, throws off his garment (see the NOTE on "throwing off his garment" in 10:50), and comes to Jesus (10:50). Jesus in turn responds by asking Bartimaeus what he wants him to do for him. The answer should be obvious—to heal his eyes!—but the request for healing is a standard part of ancient miracle stories (see Theissen, 53–55). There is, moreover, a theological point to Jesus' straightforward question: he is always eager to receive the petitions of the desperate. To be sure, Jesus has just refused the request of James and John, which he likewise had elicited with the question, "What do you want me to do for you?" (10:36; cf. Robbins, "Healing," 239). James and John, however, were requesting the choice seats in the dominion of God, perhaps partly out of a desire to dominate their fellows (cf. 10:42), whereas Bartimaeus asks simply to *see*—a request that Jesus is eager to fulfill.

Bartimaeus asks more precisely to see *again* (see the NOTE on "let me see again" in 10:51), and this detail may imply a ray of hope for the members of the Twelve, including James and John, as well. For the Twelve are people who *have seen*, who have been given the mystery of the dominion of God (4:11), who have discerned the majesty and authority of Jesus and therefore have followed him in the way (see 1:16–20; 3:13–19; 6:7–13). If recently they have seemed to sink into mental blindness, that does not necessarily mean that incomprehension will be their final condition; as philosophers and mystics down through the centuries have known, loss of vision may be a step in the path of spiritual growth (cf. Plato, *Republic* 7.515c–516b; Dante, *Paradiso* 25–26; John of the Cross, *Dark Night of the Soul* 1.8). The Twelve, then, like the blind man at the beginning of this section of the Gospel (8:22–26), may pass from their present state of mingled sight and blindness into one in which they see clearly; having once lost their vision, they, like Bartimaeus, may begin to see again.

In response to Bartimaeus' request for renewed vision, Jesus says, "Go! Your faith has saved you" (10:52a), and the wonder immediately transpires: Bartimaeus' sight is restored, and he follows Jesus "in the way" (10:52b). The conclusion of the story, which is probably a Markan addition, enables it to transcend the miracle-story genre; without decreasing the supernatural element, the emphasis on following introduces a likeness to the call narratives in 1:16–20; 2:13–14; and 3:13–19 (see the NOTE on "followed him in the way" in 10:52). Jesus, to be sure, does not say "Follow me" but "Go" (cf. Kingsbury, *Christology*, 104 n. 159). But the careful reader of Mark's Gospel has already learned that Jesus' words can sometimes imply more than, or even the opposite of, what they seem at first glance to mean (cf. 7:24–30); like some later rabbis confronted with prospective proselytes, Jesus pushes away with the left hand but pulls forward with the right and stronger one (see *b. Sanh.* 107b; *Mekilta* Amalek 3 [Lauterbach 2.173]). Bartimaeus, sensing this hidden dimension in Jesus' parting words, uses the freedom that Jesus has given him ("Go") to choose the life of discipleship that, with his restored vision, he perceives to be the logical consequence of the saving faith that has liberated him from darkness.

The paradigmatic function of Bartimaeus as a symbol of the new disciple of Jesus is consonant with the observation that certain features of the narrative are reminiscent of early Christian baptism, and they may very well have reminded Mark's readers of that rite. Baptism is described in many ancient sources as an "illumination" (see, e.g., Justin Martyr, *First Apology* 1.61; Clement of Alexandria, *Pedagogue* 1.6; *Exhortation to the Gentiles* 12; Gregory Nazianzus, *Orations* 39–40), and ancient Christian art frequently depicts biblical stories of the healing of blind people, especially that of the man born blind in John 9, in baptismal settings (see Kitzinger, "Relief," and Jensen, *Understanding*, index under "blind man, healing of"). Other features of the Bartimaeus narrative that are reminiscent of baptism include the removal of clothing (see the NOTE on "throwing off his garment" in 10:50), the command to rise (cf. Rom 6:4), the formula "your faith has saved you" (see the NOTE on this formula in 5:34), and even the "way" language (cf. Acts 9:17–18; 18:25; the former passage links Paul's baptism with the restoration of his sight). It is possible, indeed, to imagine an early Christian baptismal service structured around the basic elements of our story.

> Baptizand: "Have mercy on me!"
> Deacon, in role of Jesus (to congregation): "Call him."
> Congregation: "Be brave, get up, he's calling you."
> Baptizand removes clothes and approaches deacon.
> Deacon to baptizand: "What do you want me to do?"
> Baptizand: "I want to be illuminated."
> Deacon, baptizing him: "Your faith has saved you."

These baptismal elements cohere with the new exodus typology that is so prominent throughout this section of the Gospel, since baptism is interpreted along exodus lines already in the NT (see 1 Cor 10:1–5). As pointed out in the introduction to 8:22–10:52, the most important biblical background to the new exodus idea is Isaiah's proclamation that now, as once under Moses and Joshua, God is creating a "way" through the wilderness as he leads his people back to Zion in a saving act of holy war. This "way" theme is especially prominent in the second half of Isaiah (Deutero-Isaiah) and occurs also in Isaiah 35, which may have originally belonged with Deutero-Isaiah (cf. Torrey, *Second Isaiah*, 279–301) and was already used by Mark in 7:31–37 (see the COMMENT on 7:35–37):

> The wilderness and the dry land shall be glad, the desert shall rejoice and blossom . . . Strengthen the weak hands, and make firm the feeble knees. Say to those who are of a fearful heart, "Be strong, do not fear! Here is your God . . . he will come and save you." Then the eyes of the blind shall be opened, and the ears of the deaf unstopped; then the lame shall leap like a deer, and the tongue of the speechless sing for joy. . . . A highway shall be there, and it shall be called the Holy Way. . . . And the ransomed of the LORD shall return, and come to Zion with singing; everlasting joy shall be upon their heads. (Isa 35:1–10)

Here we have not only a depiction of blind eyes miraculously opened (cf. Isa 29:18; 42:16–18) but also an exhortation to be courageous (cf. "Be brave" in Mark 10:49), a portrait of healed people leaping for joy (cf. "leaped up" in Mark 10:50), the promise to the faithful that God will save them (cf. "Your faith has saved you" in Mark 10:52), and the motif of God's ransomed people proceeding along the holy way that leads back to Zion (cf. the "ransom" saying in Mark 10:45 and "he followed him in the way [up to Jerusalem]" in 10:52). Even the location of our pericope in the oasis town of Jericho, on the margin between the Jordan Valley and the Judaean desert, corresponds to the wilderness setting of the Isaian oracle and its picture of the desert blooming (the LXX of Isa 35:2 explicitly mentions "the desert places of Jordan"). Our passage, then, appears to illustrate Mark's conviction that the good news about Jesus unfolded "as it ha[d] been written in Isaiah the prophet" (1:2; cf. the echoes of Isaiah 35 in Matt 11:5//Luke 7:22, as pointed out by Allison, *Intertextual Jesus*, 109–14).

The Jewish War, which forms the backdrop to the composition of Mark's Gospel, was catalyzed by Isaian and other biblical hopes for the redemption of Zion (see Josephus, *War* 6.313, and cf. Hengel, *Zealots*, 249–55; Schwartz, "Temple"; Marcus, "Jewish War," 457; *Way*, 22–23). According to some forms of those hopes, the human agent of apocalyptic deliverance would be the Messiah, a "son of David" who would purge Jerusalem, its Temple, and the world as a whole of pagan rule through the might of the Lord of Hosts (see the APPENDIX "The 'Son of David' Title"). The acclamation in 10:47, which juxtaposes the title "Son of David" with the name "Jesus of Nazareth," would probably, therefore, be heard by Mark's audience against the competing claims of messianic figures who had, in Mark's own time, led the bloody revolt against Rome that culminated in their desperate stand in the Jerusalem Temple (cf. 13:6, 21–22). For the Markan community, however, it is Jesus rather than Menachem son of Judas or Simon bar Giora who is the true "Son of David"—a status that he confirms in our pericope by his miraculous, Solomon-like healing of blind Bartimaeus.

In the next few passages of the Gospel, the truth of Jesus' Davidic sonship will be recognized even by the inhabitants of the capital city itself, as Jesus enters Jerusalem like a royal conqueror and single-handedly occupies and purifies his own "house," the Temple.

FIFTH MAJOR SECTION
(MARK 11:1–13:37)

◆

INTRODUCTION
TEACHING: THE VESTIBULE TO THE
PASSION NARRATIVE

Mark 11:1–11 represents a significant turning point in the Markan narrative: here Jesus for the first time enters Jerusalem, the city in which he is fated to suffer and die. The passion narrative proper, however, does not begin until 14:1–2, when the chief priests and the scribes gather to plot Jesus' death; from that point on, events move swiftly and inexorably toward their dramatic climax (the crucifixion) and their amazing denouement (the resurrection). Chapters 11–13, therefore, may be designated the vestibule to the passion narrative.

The material from 11:1 through the end of the Gospel is mostly teaching, and is linked both geographically, by its location in Jerusalem, and chronologically. As Bultmann (341) notes, the pericopes in chapters 11–16 have been fashioned into a chronological framework of seven days; Mark, then, seems already to have an idea of Holy Week (see figure 33). This seven-day scheme, however, is historically dubious; the separation of the day of the entry into Jerusalem from that of the cleansing of the Temple, for example, is contradicted by Matthew and Luke, and it is implausible (see the introduction to the COMMENT on 11:1–11). Indeed, Jesus may actually have entered Jerusalem months before his death rather than a week previous to it (see the NOTES on "leafy branches" in 11:8, "Hosanna" and "Blessed is he who comes in the name of the Lord" in 11:9, and "for it was not the time for figs" in 11:13).

Beyond its setting within the Holy Week framework, the material in chapters 11–13, which deals with the first three days, has its own internal coherence, including several framing devices. As Telford (*Barren Temple*, 216–17) has pointed out, the references to the Mount of Olives at the beginning of chapter 11 and the beginning of chapter 13 (11:1; 13:3) frame the intervening section, as do the description of Jesus' triumphal entry, which ends somewhat anticlimactically (11:1–11), and the prophecy of his victorious return, which will be anything but anticlimactic (13:24–37). In the passage after his entry, Jesus curses a fig tree in his disciples' presence and it withers as a sign of eschatological judgment (11:12–14, 20), whereas at the end of chapter 13 he strengthens his followers' eschatological hope by telling a parable about a blossoming fig tree (13:28–29). Similarly, in

768

Figure 33: "Holy Week" in Mark 11–16

DAY	Sunday	Monday	Tuesday	Wednesday	Thursday	Friday	Saturday	Sunday
SECTION	11:1–11	11:12–19	11:20–13:37	14:1–11	14:12–72	15:1–47		16:1–8
EVENTS	Triumphal entry	Cursing of fig tree + cleansing of Temple	Debates with authorities + eschatological discourse	Plot to kill Jesus + anointing at Bethany	Preparations, supper, Gethsemane, arrest, "Jewish trial"	"Roman trial," crucifixion, death, burial		Empty tomb narrative
TIME REFS.		11:12: "the next day"		14:1: two days before the Passover	14:12: "on the first day of . . . unleavened bread"			16:1: "when the Sabbath had passed"
			11:20: "in the morning"			15:1: "immediately, early in the morning"		16:2: "very early in the morning, on the first day of the week . . . after the sun had risen"

Thursday (cont.)	*Friday* (cont.)
	15:25: third hour: crucifixion
	15:33: sixth hour: darkness
	15:34: ninth hour: loud cries and death
14:17: "when it was evening"	15:42: "when it was . . . evening . . . the day before the Sabbath"
14:30: "Today, in this night, before the rooster crows twice"	
14:72: second cockcrow	

chapter 11 Jesus' opponents call his authority into question (11:27–33), whereas in chapter 13 he prophesies that at the parousia even they will be forced to acknowledge his "great power and glory" (13:24–27). The most important framing devices have to do with the Temple: "In 11:11, [Jesus] visits the Temple for the first time; in 13:1, he leaves it for the last time. In 11:17, he utters his rebuke against it; in 13:2, he pronounces its destruction" (Telford, *Barren Temple*, 217). Nowhere else in the narrative is the Temple theme so prominent; almost all of the Markan usages of *hieron* ("Temple") occur here (11:11, 15 [2x], 16, 27; 12:35; 13:1, 3), and the exception (14:49) is a flashback to this section.

Despite the overall coherence of chapters 11–13 through the Temple setting, the Holy Week scheme, and the theme of conflict with the Jewish leaders, Mark does not seem to have formed the section entirely on his own but to have "felt his way through . . . inherited material," as Seamus Heaney describes the procedure of the author of Beowulf (*Beowulf*, xi). This inherited material may have included sources such as the triumphal entry + cleansing of the Temple (11:1–11, 15–19), a triad of controversy stories in which Jesus defends himself against the hostile questions his audacity has elicited (11:27–33; 12:13–27), another triad about his relations with scribes (12:28–40), and the eschatological discourse (chapter 13). Some of the inherited material may have come from an expanded pre-Markan passion narrative (see the introduction to chapters 14–15).

Whatever the precise origin of their various components, chapters 11–13 serve Mark's purpose well, since their theme of mutual hostility between Jesus and the religious leaders lays the groundwork for the passion narrative. This theme pervades nearly every pericope, which is dominated by Jesus' "teaching with authority" (cf. 1:22). Near the beginning of the section, he antagonizes the chief priests and the scribes by his violent demonstration in the Temple (11:15–19), which causes them, together with the elders, to question by what authority he acts—an inquiry that he pointedly refuses to answer (11:27–33). He then tells a parable that they realize is directed against them (12:1–12), to which they and their agents respond by asking him two trick questions (12:13–17 and 12:18–27). The sympathetic scribe who approaches Jesus next is an exception to this pattern of mutual hostility, and he is pronounced "not far from the dominion of God" (12:28–34), but immediately afterward Jesus goes on the offensive again, refuting a scribal opinion about the ancestry of the Messiah (12:35–37) and denouncing the scribes for their rapacious hypocrisy (12:38–40). This charge is apparently meant to be linked with the contrast between the poor widow who gives to the Temple out of her want and the rich who give out of their excess (12:41–44).

The conclusion of this story praises the widow's willingness to contribute everything she has, "even her whole living." This phrase forms a natural transition to the passion narrative, but the eschatological discourse of chapter 13, which takes its nominal point of departure from the Temple setting, intervenes. Here, in a manner typical of Jewish and Christian patriarchs and martyr figures, Jesus, sensing the approach of death, peers into the future and prophesies the tribulation and testing that await his followers and indeed the whole world—testing that will result at least in part from hostility of the sort that his opponents have displayed toward him in chapters 11 and 12. But just as certain as these trials is the promise that Jesus makes to those who will have to undergo them: "The one who endures to the end . . . will be saved" (13:13). This is a lesson that the ending of Mark's Gospel will, in a typically mysterious manner, confirm with regard to Jesus himself (16:1–8).

JESUS ENTERS JERUSALEM (11:1–11)

11 ¹And when they drew near to Jerusalem, to Bethphage and Bethany, toward the Mount of Olives, he sent out two of his disciples ²and said to them, "Go into the village opposite you, and when you go into it, you will immediately find a colt tied up, upon which no human being has ever yet sat. Untie and bring it. ³And if anyone says to you, 'Why are you doing that?' say to him, 'The master has need of it, and he will immediately send it back here again.' " ⁴And they went out and found a colt tied up at a door outside, in the street, and untied it. ⁵And some of the people who were standing around there said to them, "What are you doing, untying that colt?" ⁶And they spoke to them as Jesus had told them to, and they let them go.

⁷And they brought the colt to Jesus and put their clothes on it, and he sat on it. ⁸And many spread their clothes in the way, and others spread leafy branches, cutting them from the fields. ⁹And those who went ahead and those who followed cried out, "Hosanna! Blessed is he who comes in the name of the Lord! ¹⁰Blessed is the coming dominion of our father David! Hosanna in the highest places!"

¹¹And he went into Jerusalem, into the Temple, and looked around at everything; but since the hour was already late, he went out to Bethany with the Twelve.

NOTES

11 1. *Bethphage*. Gk *Bēthphagē*. This name probably derives from the Aramaic *bêt paggē'* = "house of unripe figs" (cf. BDAG 175); the reference to this village is placed either intentionally or by chance at the beginning of a section of the Gospel in which Jesus curses a fig tree (11:12–14). Rabbinic sources mention a village with a similar name whose outer wall was the official limit of the city of Jerusalem (see, e.g., *b. Men.* 78b). The Crusaders associated Bethphage with a location west of Bethany, on the eastern slopes of the Mount of Olives, the site of a present-day Franciscan chapel. But Mark's terminology seems to imply that travelers from the east came to Bethphage before reaching Bethany (cf. Jerome, *Letter* 108.12); the site, therefore, might be the Arab village of Abu Dis, just east of Bethany (see Finegan, *Archeology*, 90–91; Carroll, "Bethphage").

Bethany. Gk *Bēthanian*. Nehemiah 11:32 mentions a place called *'Ănānyāh*, apparently on the Mount of Olives; this could also have been called *bêt 'Ănānyāh* = "the house of Ananiah," that is, Bethany. The site of Bethany is usually identified with the Arab village of El 'Azariyeh, which is on the east slope of the Mount of Olives, some two miles from the Old City of Jerusalem (cf. John 11:18 and see Finegan, *Archeology*, 91–92).

the Mount of Olives. Gk *to oros tōn elaiōn*. This low ridge of three hills, the highest of which is about 2700 feet above sea level, faces the Old City of Jerusalem across the Kidron Valley to the east. The two OT passages that mention this site associate it with the eschatological manifestation of God's kingship through military triumph (Zech 14:1–5, 9; cf. Josephus, *War* 2.262; *Ant.* 20.169–70) and with David's weeping flight from Jerusalem after his sovereignty is rejected by the Israelites (2 Sam 15:30). These associations carry over to the Markan references to the Mount, with our passage and 13:1–4 13:3 emphasizing eschatological battle and triumph, and 14:26–31 stressing suffering and rejection.

2. *and when you go into it, you will immediately find.* Gk *kai euthys eisporeuomenoi eis autēn heurēsete*, lit. "and immediately going into it you will find." This is another example of a premature *euthys*, on which see the NOTE on "And as he was coming up out of the water, he immediately" in 1:10.

colt. Gk *pōlon*. In classical Greek, this term indicates the foal of a horse and then, by extension, of any animal (see LSJ 1560–61). BDAG (900) argues that when, as in our passage, *pōlos* stands alone, unmodified by another animal name (e.g., "colt of a donkey"), it indicates a horse, but Kuhn ("Reittier") and Michel ("Frage") have shown that the word can denote a donkey in such circumstances (see, e.g., Judg 10:4; 12:14; Justin, *Dialogue* 32.1, 5–6; 54.5–7). Donkeys were much more apt to be left unattended in village squares than were horses, which were rare, expensive, and generally reserved for military or elite use (see Firmage, "Zoology," 1136; Anderson, "Horses"). *Pōlos*, moreover, is used for the young donkey on which the king enters Jerusalem in Zech 9:9, a passage that seems to undergird our account (cf. Matt 21:5 and the COMMENT on 11:1–6). This Zecharian passage presupposes an ancient Near Eastern understanding of the donkey or mule as a royal animal (see 1 Kgs 1:33, 38 and cf. Davies and Allison, 3.116–17) and was frequently interpreted in rabbinic Judaism as a messianic oracle (see, e.g., *b. Sanh.* 98a and *Gen. Rab.* 75.6); indeed, so influential was this oracle that *b. Ber.* 56b says that a person who dreams of a donkey hopes for eschatological salvation.

tied up. Gk *dedemenon*. See the NOTE on "a colt tied up . . . in the street" in 11:4.

upon which no human being has ever yet sat. Gk *eph' hon oudeis oupō anthrōpōn ekathisen*, lit. "upon which no one not yet of human beings has sat." This is another of Mark's characteristic double negatives (see the subject index in vols. 1 and 2 under "Double expressions" and "Double negatives"). Strauss (*Life*, 555) appositely compares Luke 23:53 and John 19:41, in which Jesus is honored by being laid in a grave that has not previously been occupied. The motif of the unridden colt, moreover, may be part of the royal imagery of our passage; cf. *m. Sanh.* 2:5, which stipulates that no one may subsequently mount an animal that has been ridden by a king (see Derrett, "Colt," 248–49). More specifically, our passage draws on Zech 9:9 (cf. the NOTE on "colt" above), which pictures the Davidic king riding into Jerusalem on a "new colt." Later exegetes of this passage may have wondered how a grown man could mount a new(-born) colt without the animal collapsing under his weight; our text may be responding that the colt is "new," not in the sense of being newborn, but in the sense of never having been ridden.

3. *The master has need of it.* Gk *ho kyrios autou chreian echei.* The meaning of

kyrios here is ambiguous; it could be construed as the owner of the donkey or as God ("the Lord") or as Jesus, who elsewhere in Mark is called or associated with *ho kyrios* (see 11:9–10 and cf. the COMMENT on 1:2–3 and the NOTE on "Lord" in 7:28). If the *kyrios* here is Jesus, he may be exercising a right of impressment, as other influential and powerful people, including teachers, did in the Greco-Roman world (see *b. Yoma* 35b and cf. Mark 15:21; Matt 5:40–41; Stauffer, "Messias," 85; Derrett, "Colt"). For an example of impressment of donkeys in anticipation of a royal visit, see Hunt and Edgar, *Papyri*, #211, and cf. #414, which describes the preparations for the arrival of the finance minister: "We have borrowed five riding donkeys . . . and have got ready the forty baggage donkeys; and we have begun to make the road." In Mark, similarly, Jesus' adherents not only "borrow" a donkey for his visit but also symbolically make a road on which he may travel (11:8; cf. 1:2–3).

4. *a colt tied up . . . in the street.* Gk *pōlon dedemenon . . . epi tou amphodou.* *Amphodon* originally meant a city quarter crossed by streets; by synecdoche (see the GLOSSARY) it then came to mean a street as well (cf. BDAG 55). But it is not the most common term for "street," and its mention here may derive from Gen 49:10–12, which was usually interpreted as a messianic oracle (see already the LXX, targumim, and 4QCommGenA [4Q252] 5:1–5; cf. Blenkinsopp, "Oracle," 57). Genesis 49:11 describes Judah, the ancestor and prototype of the Messiah, tying his colt to an *ampelon* (vine), a word that bears a resemblance to *amphodon.*

5. *some of the people who were standing around there.* Gk *tines tōn ekei hestēkotōn.* Luke makes the objectors into the *kyrioi* ("owners") of the donkey, thus creating a stark contrast between Jesus' claim as *kyrios* (Mark 11:3//Luke 19:31) and the property rights of the donkey's ostensible owners.

6. *and they let them go.* Gk *kai aphēkan autous.* The seeming implausibility of the disciples' being allowed to go off with someone else's donkey can be explained in different ways, depending partly on the meaning of *kyrios* in 11:3 (see the NOTE on "The master has need of it" in 11:3): (1) If the *kyrios* is meant to be the owner of the donkey, the bystanders may be being duped into thinking that the disciples are this man's agent (cf. Hooker, 258). (2) If the *kyrios* is meant to be Jesus, the bystanders may be acquiescing to the requisition of the donkey by one who possesses sovereign authority (cf. Derrett, "Colt"). (3) If the *kyrios* is meant to be God, the response may reflect the semimagical power of the divine name (cf. Strauss, *Life*, 555). On the historical level, a combination of #1 and #2 is probable, whereas on the level of Markan interpretation, a mixture of #2 and #3 is likely.

8. *many . . . others.* Gk *polloi . . . alloi.* In Matthew (21:8) and John (12:12) those who hail Jesus are not disciples but the Jerusalem crowd; Luke (19:37), however, makes them the crowd *of disciples*, and this may be close to Mark's meaning, since there is no change of subject between 11:6–7 and 11:8; cf. also "those who followed" (*hoi akolouthountes*) in 11:9. But if so, a bigger group than the Twelve may be envisaged; cf. "those around him with the Twelve" in 4:10 and the NOTE on "the disciples' question" in 4:10.

leafy branches. Gk *stibadas.* In its classical usages this term means "a kind of bed or mattress made of straw, rushes, reeds, leaves, etc." (BDAG 945). It does not occur elsewhere in the LXX or early Christian literature, and the present translation is reached from the context and the Matthean parallel, which changes *stibadas* to *kladous* ("branches"); in any event, the term is poetically appropriate, since the *stibadas* are strewn on the ground.

The Peshitta renders *stibadas* with *sawkē'* = "branches," a term etymologically related to Sukkot, the Feast of Tabernacles. Some scholars (e.g., Smith, "No Time," 319) have argued that Jesus' triumphal entry actually occurred during Sukkot, partly because of the prominent role played in that holiday by the *lûlāb*, a bouquet of interwoven branches of palm, myrtle, and willow that is waved in festal processions (see *m. Suk.* 3:4 and cf. John 12:13, which specifies that the Jerusalem crowds greeted Jesus with palm fronds—hence the designation "Palm Sunday"). Other Tabernacles associations of our passage and its surrounding context include the use of Psalm 118 (see the next two NOTES) and Jesus' expectation that he would find ripe figs on the tree in 11:13 (Tabernacles is a harvest festival).

9. *Hosanna!* Gk *hōsanna*. This is a transliteration of *hôšî'ānnā'* ("Save, please!") from Ps 118:25, which is often rendered in rabbinic texts (e.g., *b. Suk.* 37ab) in the shorter form *hôša'nā'* (cf. Jastrow, 341). In the psalm the context is liturgical, and later Jewish texts associate the term especially with the Feast of Tabernacles (Sukkot), applying it to the woven branches (*lûlābîm*) that were waved at that holiday's solemn processions (see *b. Suk.* 37ab). In the psalm and later Jewish usages, "Hosanna" is a supplication to God to save his beleaguered people, whereas in most early Christian texts it becomes, under the influence of our scene, an acclamation addressed to Christ or God (see Matt 21:9, 15; *Did.* 10:6; Eusebius, *Ecclesiastical History* 2.23.14). But in our passage the term may retain some of its supplicatory sense; see the NOTE on "Hosanna in the highest places!" in 11:10.

Blessed is he who comes in the name of the Lord! Gk *eulogēmenos ho erchomenos en onomati kyriou*. This is a citation of Psalm 118:26a [117:26a LXX], which comes near the conclusion of the Hallel (Psalms 113–18), a group of psalms that was recited at the Jewish holidays of Tabernacles, Hanukkah, Passover, and Weeks (see Wagner, "Psalm 118," 160–61); Psalm 118, however, seems to have been particularly associated with Tabernacles (see Smith, "No Time," 319, and the previous NOTE). In the original psalm, the benediction was not messianic but liturgical, reflecting the way in which those already in the Temple precincts welcomed arriving pilgrims in God's name (see the parallelism with "we bless you from the house of the LORD," 118:26b). All of the later Gospel writers, however, take the verse to be an allusion to Jesus himself; Matthew inserts a reference to "the Son of David," and both Luke and John have the crowd calling him a king (see figure 34). Although Mark is not as explicit as the other three, his interpretation may be messianic too, since 11:9–10 parallels the acclamation of "he who comes in the name of the Lord" with a blessing on "the coming dominion of our father David" (cf. the use of the "Son of David" title in 10:47–48). Even if so, however, the "messianic secret" motif may not be compromised, since those who hail Jesus may be disciples rather than outsiders (see the NOTE on "many . . . others" in 11:8).

Strack and Billerbeck (1.849, 876; 2.256) and Jeremias (*Eucharistic Words*, 256–60) assert that a messianic understanding of Ps 118:26 was already present in the Judaism of Jesus' time. This is possible, since the NT passages that use Ps 118:26

Figure 34: The Acclamation of the Crowd at the Triumphal Entry

Mark 11:9	*Matthew 21:9*	*Luke 19:38*	*John 12:13*
Hosanna	Hosanna		Hosanna
	to the Son of David		
blessed is he who comes	blessed is he who comes	blessed is he who comes	blessed is he who comes
		the king	
in the name of the Lord	in the name of the Lord	in the name of the Lord	in the name of the Lord
			the king of Israel
blessed is the coming dominion of our father David			
		peace in heaven	
Hosanna in the highest places	Hosanna in the highest places	and glory in the highest places	

(the present passage and Matt 23:39 = Luke 13:35) assume rather than argue for a messianic interpretation, and other NT and early Christian passages (Mark 12:10; Acts 4:11; 1 Pet 2:7; *Barn.* 6:4; *Acts of Peter* 24) reveal a tendency to read Psalm 118 Christologically. Nevertheless, the Jewish texts cited by Jeremias et al. (*b. Pesaḥ.* 118a; *Pes. Rab.* 31:6; *Midrash Psalms*; etc.) are later than the NT period and prove only that the Hallel psalms were read *eschatologically*, not *messianically*.

10. *Blessed is the coming dominion of our father David!* Gk *eulogēmenē hē erchomenē basileia tou patros hēmōn Dauid.* This part of the acclamation seems to echo the famous oracle in 2 Samuel 7, which mentions a son of David who will establish his father's dominion by building God a "house." In the original oracle, this son is Solomon, but later the passage was understood as a testimony to David's eschatological scion, the Messiah (see *Pss. Sol.* 17:4; 4QFlor; Luke 1:32–33; Heb 1:5; cf. Juel, *Messianic Exegesis*, 59–88). The import of the whole oracle is the divine blessing on the Davidic dynasty (see the repeated use of "blessing" terminology in 2 Sam 7:29), which corresponds to "Blessed is . . ." in our passage. The oracle, moreover, refers to Solomon not only as David's son but also as God's (2 Sam 7:14), which parallels the frequent Markan references to Jesus as the Son of God (1:11; 3:11; 5:7; etc.), as well as the way in which the verse previous to ours speaks of him as the one who comes "in the name of the Lord." In addition, 2 Samuel 7 conjoins the Son of God title with the expectation that the Messiah will build a new Temple, and this expectation seems to be reflected in Mark 14:57–62 (see the COMMENT on 14:55–59).

Hosanna in the highest places! Gk *hōsanna en tois hypsistois.* Jerusalem itself is a "high place" situated on a limestone plateau 2600 feet above sea level, and pilgrims are ubiquitously described as "going up" to it in the OT, so that the crowd's acclamation fits with the scene of a pilgrim's arrival in the high-altitude holy city. But the main referent here is to heaven as the dwelling place of God, who is perhaps being invited to send his salvific power down now that his designated agent has finally arrived at the place that is the center of the divine purposes on earth (see the COMMENT on 11:7–11). As Werner ("Hosanna," 119) points out, our clause seems to be paraphrased in *Acts of Pilate* 1:4: "Save us, you who are in the highest places!"

11. *went into Jerusalem, into the Temple, and looked around at everything.* Gk *eiselthen eis Hierosolyma eis ton hieron kai periblepsamenos panta.* The Markan narrative describes only one visit of Jesus to Jerusalem, and "looked around at everything" is compatible with the view that this is his first excursion to the Temple; cf. 13:1, in which one of the disciples reacts to the splendor of the Temple with the awe of a country bumpkin on his first trip to the big city. But the Gospel of John details several visits of Jesus to Jerusalem before the climactic one in which he loses his life (see John 2:13–25; 5:1–47; 7:10–10:39), and Brown (1.117–18) argues convincingly that this is more likely to be historical than the schematic Markan picture in which Jesus comes up to Jerusalem just once for a climactic confrontation with the Jewish and imperial authorities.

COMMENT

Introduction. A turning point in the narrative now arrives: after ten chapters in which Jesus has been active in Galilee in northern Palestine and the Transjordan area to the east, he enters the capital city, Jerusalem, and rides in state up to that city's holiest site and the central institution of the Judaism of his time, the Temple. This entry into Jerusalem is a significant transition in Jesus' itinerary, not only because of the intrinsic importance of Jerusalem and its Temple, but also because of their close association with the Davidic Messiah, who was expected to purge them of ungodliness and thereby inaugurate God's dominion on earth (see *Pss. Sol.* 17:22–31; Fourteenth Benediction).

As befits such an important passage, it is carefully constructed. The notice about *approaching* Jerusalem at the beginning of the pericope (11:1) is matched by the notice about *entering* it at the end (11:11), and each of these reports features a double place-name of the form *eis* ["to"] + "Jerusalem," *eis* + second place. The story of the finding of the colt (11:1–6) will be strikingly paralleled by the story of the finding of the room for the Passover celebration (14:12–16; see figure 35). Whereas in Matthew and Luke Jesus' triumphal entry into Jerusalem is immediately followed by his disruption of the Temple trade, in Mark Jesus merely surveys the Temple and goes away, returning only on the morrow to attack. This survey, however, fits into Mark's theme of the "possessive gaze" of Jesus (see Ambrozic, "New Teaching," 143 n. 53), and the Markan staging allows the attack on the Temple to be intercalated between the two parts of the cursing of the fig

Figure 35: Parallels between Mark 11:1–6 and 14:12–16

Mark 11:1–6	*Mark 14:12–16*
and he sent out two of his disciples	and he sent out two of his disciples
and he said to them	and he said to them
"Go into the village . . ."	"Go into the city . . ."
Instructions about finding a colt and what to do if challenged	Instructions about meeting a man carrying a water jug and following him to a place in which to prepare Passover
and they spoke to them *as Jesus had told them* to, and they let them go	and they went into the city and found it just *as he had told them*, and they prepared the Passover

tree, a typically Markan sandwich structure that illuminates both tales. Moreover, the repetition of the substance of 11:11a ("And he went into Jerusalem, into the Temple") in 11:15a ("And they came to Jerusalem; and going into the Temple") is a telltale sign that the intervening material is an intrusion (cf. 2:5, 10; 3:7–8; 3:14, 16; 4:31–32). It is likely, then, that in the pre-Markan story Jesus entered Jerusalem on a colt to the hosannas of his adherents and then immediately cleansed the Temple. Besides the withdrawal in 11:11b, Markan redactional touches may include the superfluous and awkward references to Jerusalem, Bethany, and the Mount of Olives in 11:1a and 11:11a.

In its present Markan structure, the passage tells a double story of entry and withdrawal: first the disciples go into the village, find the colt, and come back to Bethany (11:1–6), then Jesus goes into Jerusalem on the colt, looks around, and comes back to Bethany (11:7–11). The disciples thus fulfill John the Baptist's injunction to "prepare the way of the Lord" (1:3).

11:1–6: a colt to ride on. "The way" of Jesus (cf. 10:52) at last leads up to Jerusalem. The capital city, however, is approached in stages, as befits its monumental significance in the history of Israel in general and its involvement with Jesus' destiny in particular. First Jesus and his disciples draw near to Bethphage and Bethany, outlying villages on the Mount of Olives that marked the city limits (11:1a; see the NOTES on "Bethphage" and "Bethany" in 11:1); later Jesus will enter the walled city proper, and finally the Temple itself (11:11a).

At the approach to Bethphage and Bethany, Jesus makes some preliminary arrangements, dispatching two unnamed followers to prepare for his advent (11:1–6)—in the same way that, later, he will dispatch two disciples to make preparations for the Last Supper (14:12–16). In both instances, Jesus foretells the way in which the mission will turn out, and on both occasions things occur exactly as he has predicted. To Mark's readers, these correspondences would be a clear indication of Jesus' prophetic insight. In fact, however, neither narrative specifically mentions clairvoyance, and it is possible that, if historical memory undergirds our account, they relate to prearranged signals necessitated by official hostility.

The disciples are dispatched to get a young animal (probably a donkey; see the NOTE on "colt" in 11:2) on which Jesus will complete his journey up to Jerusalem—a noteworthy departure from his previous pattern, since he has walked all over Palestine up to this point (cf. Aquinas, *Catena Aurea* on 11:7; Hooker, 257). The acquisition of the mount is therefore a hint that something momentous is about to occur. Specifically, the disciples are to go into the neighboring village, find a colt tied up in the street, loosen it, and bring it back to Jesus (11:2). Jesus' detailed instructions extend to what they are to say if challenged: "The master has need of it" (11:3). Even those not familiar with OT messianic prophecies would probably interpret these instructions as implying something like kingly authority, since Jesus' assertion of a claim that supersedes that of the colt's nominal owner is an act of impressment—the sort of act frequently associated with royal officials or kings (see the NOTE on "The master has need of it" in 11:3). Moreover, as Harvey (*Jesus*, 120–29) argues, the mere fact that Jesus *rides* into the holy city, rather than *walks* into it, as may have been customary, may imply a claim to unprecedented authority (cf. *m. Ḥag.* 1:1).

The royal implications of Jesus' entrance on a donkey would be deepened for those familiar with the scriptures, since the Markan description seems to echo two OT passages, Gen 49:11 and Zech 9:9:

> *Genesis 49:10–11 LXX*: A ruler will not depart from Judah and a leader from between his loins until there comes that which is laid up for him (MT: "until Shiloh comes"); and he is the expectation of the nations, tying (*desmeuōn*) his colt (*ton pōlon autou*) to a vine (*pros ampelon*) and to a tendril the colt of his donkey (*ton pōlon tēs onou autou*).

> *Zechariah 9:9 LXX*: Rejoice greatly, daughter of Zion; proclaim, daughter of Jerusalem: Look, your king is coming to you, righteous and a savior is he; humble, and riding on a donkey (*hypozygion*) and a new colt (*pōlon neon*; MT: "humble and riding on a donkey and on a colt the foal of donkeys").

These passages were both understood as messianic oracles in ancient Judaism (see the NOTES on "colt" in 11:2 and "a colt tied up . . . in the street" in 11:4), and the one from Zechariah has the same essential elements as Mark 11:1–11: the entry of the king, the messianic animal, and the jubilation of the people (cf. Kuhn, "Reittier," 90). This passage, moreover, goes on to speak of the eschatological lordship of the Israelite king (Zech 9:10), thus corresponding to the Jerusalem crowd's acclamation of "the coming dominion of our father David" (Mark 11:10). The Genesis text is reflected in the otherwise superfluous note that the colt is *tied* (11:2, 4). The two OT passages were traditionally related (see, e.g., their juxtaposition in *Gen. Rab.* 98.9), and it is likely that the Zecharian oracle was exegetically derived from the Genesis one (cf. Krause, "One," 143–47).

Following Jesus' detailed instructions, the disciples go into "the village" (presumably Bethphage, the first one mentioned), find the colt, and untie it (11:4). Challenged by the bystanders (11:5), they reply in the words Jesus has instructed them to use. They are then themselves released, just as he has prophesied (11:6). All is going according to plan; the stage is now set for Jesus' procession into the holy city.

11:7–11: the triumphal entry. That entrance begins with the disciples bringing the colt to Jesus and putting their garments on it; Jesus is then seated on this improvised saddle (11:7). Although the disciples' action has the practical purpose of making the rider more comfortable and less likely to slip from his perch (cf. Marshall, *Luke*, 714), the detail with which this seating is described suggests that it also has symbolic dimensions. For one thing, the disciples are performing an act of obeisance; since a person is identified with his clothes, the disciples' seating of Jesus on their garments is equivalent to prostrating themselves before him (cf. 11:8a and Davies and Allison, 3.123).

The seating may also underline the impression of Jesus' royal status. The first commentary on Mark glosses "he sat on it" as "he began to reign on it" (Pseudo-Jerome, *Exposition of Mark* 11:7 [Cahill, 84]), and this interpretation is supported by the observation that in 1 Kgs 1:38, 44, David's representatives seat his son Solomon on David's donkey as a preparation for anointing him king in his father's place. This echo is appropriate in a passage in which the crowds will shortly hail Jesus as the vanguard of "the coming dominion of *our father David*" (11:10; on other Solomonic dimensions of Jesus' identity, see the APPENDIX "The 'Son of David' Title"). In the next verse, moreover, some members of the crowd strew their clothes in Jesus' way (11:8a), and this action too may have a royal nuance (cf. 2 Kgs 9:13 and *Acts of Pilate* 1:2 [Elliott trans.]: "For as soon as he saw him the messenger worshipped him, and spread his scarf on the ground, and made him walk on it like a king"). The strewing of leafy branches cut from the neighboring fields (11:8b) may have a similar import; an important parallel is offered by 1 Macc 13:51, where Simon Maccabaeus enters Jerusalem triumphantly, accompanied by "praise and palm branches . . . and with hymns and songs," an act that is later (14:7) termed an establishment of lordship. Significantly, Simon's triumphal entry is conjoined with his act of cleansing Jerusalem from pollution (1 Macc 13:49–50; cf. Mark 11:15–19). As Catchpole ("Entry," 319–21) shows, this passage is just one of a series of ancient Jewish texts that conjoin triumphal entry into Jerusalem, popular acclaim, and cultic activity in the Temple, often with some sort of royal nuance (cf. Josephus, *Ant.* 11.325–39; 12.348–49; 13.304–6; 16.12–15; 17.194–239, 324–28).

The messianic significance of Jesus' entry into Jerusalem is further underlined by the following, climactic verses. In 11:9a the crowds greet Jesus with a cry of "Hosanna," the transliteration of a Hebrew word that means "Save, please!" and is addressed to God in its OT source (see the NOTE on "Hosanna!" in 11:9). In 11:9b–10a, moreover, they pair a blessing on the one "who comes in the name of the Lord" with a benediction on "the coming dominion of our father David." For the reader of Mark the clear implication is that Jesus is "the coming one" (cf. Matt 11:3//Luke 7:19), the scion of David who will reestablish his ancestor's earthly dominion through the mighty power of the God who dwells "in the highest places" (see the NOTE on "Hosanna in the highest places!" in 11:10). The concluding cry, "Hosanna in the highest places!" (11:10b), then, becomes similar in import to the final invocation of the Jewish Kaddish prayer: "He who makes peace in his high places, may he make peace upon us and on all Israel."

"Hosanna" and "Blessed is he who comes in the name of the Lord" are both drawn from Psalm 118, which was probably already interpreted eschatologically, and perhaps messianically, in first-century Judaism (see the NOTES on these expressions in 11:9) and which will be quoted again in Mark 12:10–11. This psalm pictures Jerusalem surrounded by its pagan enemies but saved by the exalted right hand of the Lord (Ps 118:10–16). The image seems ideally suited to ignite the sort of apocalyptic fervor that characterized the Jewish revolt against the Romans— the defining historical event behind the composition of Mark (see the INTRODUCTION in vol. 1, pp. 33–37). Another OT passage echoed by the crowd's acclamation of Jesus, the famous oracle about the dominion of the house of David in 2 Samuel 7, links the coming rule of David's son with the military defeat of Israel's enemies and the building of God's Temple—which a later midrash (4QFlor) interprets as purifying it from Gentile contamination. It seems reasonable to assume, therefore, that both Psalm 118 and 2 Samuel 7 may have been known and exploited by revolutionaries such as Menachem son of Judas the Galilean, who may have been a Davidide (see Hengel, *Zealots*, 299–300), and who entered Jerusalem "as a king" surrounded by armed followers at the start of the revolt, later appearing in the Temple dressed in royal robes (Josephus, *War* 2.433–34, 444).

Seen against this putative background in triumphant messianism, or even against the expectations raised by its first ten verses, our passage's ending seems curiously anticlimactic: Jesus enters the city, presumably still riding on his "borrowed" donkey, and goes into the Temple, presumably having dismounted (11:11a). After the unprecedented step of riding into Jerusalem; after the royally symbolic action of mounting an animal that no one has yet ridden; after the fulfillment of the messianic oracle from Zech 9:9; after the way Jesus' followers respond to these implicit royal claims by hailing him as "he who comes in the name of the Lord," the one to restore the dominion of his "father" David; after striding into the holy Temple, the center of God's purposes on earth—after all this buildup, Jesus merely looks around and retires to Bethany to spend the night there with his disciples (11:11b)! How much more consonant with what precedes, how much more conventionally messianic, is the conclusion of the passage in Matthew and Luke, where Jesus immediately purges the Temple of its defilements. *That* is the way a Messiah is supposed to act.

But this is not to be the last of the Markan Jesus' departures from the expected pattern. In the next passage he *does* cleanse the Temple, but he uses the occasion to proclaim judgment, not on the pagan oppressors of Israel, but on that nation's own leaders.

JESUS CURSES THE FIG TREE AND CLEANSES
THE TEMPLE (11:12–25)

11 ¹²And the next day as they were going out of Bethany, he became hungry. ¹³And seeing from far away a fig tree that had leaves on it, he came, wondering if he would find anything on it. And coming up to it, he did not find anything on it except leaves; for it was not the time for figs. ¹⁴And he answered and said to it, "Let no one ever eat fruit from you again." And his disciples heard him.

¹⁵And they came to Jerusalem; and going into the Temple, he began to throw out those who were selling and buying in the Temple; and he overturned the tables of the money changers and the seats of those who were selling doves; ¹⁶and he did not allow anyone to carry a container through the Temple. ¹⁷And he was teaching and saying to them, "Has it not been written, 'My house shall be called a house of prayer for all the nations'? But you have made it a den of brigands." ¹⁸And the chief priests and the scribes heard it; and they were looking for a way to destroy him. For they were afraid of him, for the whole crowd was overwhelmed by his teaching. ¹⁹And when evening came, they went out of the city.

²⁰And passing by early in the morning, they saw the fig tree withered from the roots. ²¹And Peter, remembering, said to him, "Rabbi, look—the fig tree you cursed has withered!" ²²And Jesus answered and said to them, "Have faith in God. ²³Amen, I say to you that whoever says to this mountain, 'Be lifted up and cast into the sea' and does not doubt in his heart but believes that what he says will happen, it will be his. ²⁴Therefore I say to you, everything you pray and ask for, believe that you have received it, and it will be yours. ²⁵And when you stand praying, forgive, if you have anything against anyone, so that your Father in heaven may also forgive you your transgressions."

NOTES

11 12. *he became hungry.* Gk *epeinasen.* As Telford (*Barren Temple*, 198 n. 31) notes, in the only other passage in which Mark employs *epeinasen*, 2:25–26, the context is also cultic; both, moreover, use the verb *eiselthein* ("to go into") and speak of "the house of God." Perhaps the parallel is intentional; in 2:25–26, sovereignty over "the house of God" is ascribed to King David, and in 11:12–19 Jesus, the new David, makes a similar claim to lordship over the Temple. But, if so, the differences are also striking: David's hunger is assuaged by a friendly high priest, but Jesus goes hungry and curses the fig tree that is linked with the Temple and its functionaries.

13. *wondering if he would find anything on it.* Gk *ei ara ti heurēsei en autę̄.* The word "wondering" is not present in the Greek, but the sentence is probably an example of "virtual questions expressing an uncertain expectation associated with an effort to attain something" (Zerwick §403; cf. Phil 3:12; Rom 1:10).

for it was not the time for figs. Gk *ho gar kairos ouk ēn sykōn.* As Manson ("Cleansing," 277–78) points out, fig trees in Palestine have ripe fruit between May and

October but not in early April, the probable time of Jesus' crucifixion (on the
chronology of Jesus' death, see Brown, *Death*, 2.1350–78). The Markan *gar* ("for")
clause acknowledges this difficulty but does not really resolve it: why does Jesus
expect figs out of season? For Manson, this discrepancy, along with some details
of the triumphal entry narrative, suggests that these two stories were originally set
during the Feast of Tabernacles, which occurs in the autumn (see the NOTE on
"leafy branches" in 11:8).

14. *fruit.* Gk *karpon.* The use of this word, rather than "figs," invokes the biblical motif of fruitfulness or fruitlessness as a symbol of spiritual health or disease
(Ps 92:12–15; Hos 10:1, 13; Sir 27:6; Matt 7:16–20; John 15:1–11; Gal 5:22–24; etc.;
see Telford, *Barren Temple*, 261).

his disciples heard . . . Gk *ēkouon hoi mathētai autou.* This clause could also
be translated "the disciples heard him," if *autou* is taken as going with *ēkouon*
("heard") rather than *hoi mathētai* ("the disciples"). But the latter is the more
natural way of construing the Greek, and it reinforces the Markan theme of the
secret instruction of the disciples (cf. "to his own disciples" in 4:34).

15. *going into the Temple, he began to throw out those who were selling and buying in the Temple,* etc. Gk *eiselthōn eis to hieron ērxato ekballein tous pōlountas kai
tous agorazontas en tǭ hierǭ,* etc. "To throw (or cast) out" (*ekballein*) is the term
used elsewhere in Mark for exorcism (1:34, 39; 3:15, 22–23; etc.), and its employment here may be a hint that the buyers and sellers who profane the Temple are
Satan's tools (cf. Broadhead, *Teaching*, 171; Chávez, *Significance*, 137–38). The
"sellers" may include not only those providing doves for sacrifice but also money
changers, who sell the Tyrian coinage acceptable at the Temple in exchange for
the other currencies brought by pilgrims.

Sanders (*Jesus*, 61–76) argues that such trading was not an abuse but a necessary
part of the functioning of the sacrificial system. The profits of the animal sellers
and money changers were not inordinate, and these merchants performed necessary services, since pilgrims had to be able to convert their money into Tyrian
coinage and to buy unblemished animals in the vicinity of the Temple, it being
impractical to bring their own animals from homes far away, only perhaps to have
them judged unfit for sacrifice. For Sanders, then, Jesus was bent not on ridding
the Temple of abuses but on prophesying its destruction, which he accomplished
through the sort of parabolic action typical of prophets, stopping sacrificial activity temporarily to point toward its permanent cessation, and overturning the tables
of the money changers to symbolize the imminent demise of the sanctuary.

Whatever the pros or cons of this interpretation of the historical Jesus' purpose
(see the criticism of Evans, "Jesus' Action"), it remains a question whether Mark
thinks Jesus' Temple action symbolized the destruction of the Temple or simply
pointed to abuses that cried out for rectification. The strongest argument in favor
of the destruction interpretation is the link with the words of Jesus' curse in 11:14,
"Let no one ever eat fruit from you again," which seems to imply the cessation
of the Temple system. Elsewhere, moreover, the Markan Jesus prophesies the
Temple's destruction openly (13:1–2; cf. 14:58 and Telford, *Barren Temple*, 261).

But other Markan wording suggests that the evangelist thinks the Temple was being abused: (1) The otherwise superfluous repetition of "into/in the Temple" in 11:15 (cf. also "through the Temple" in 11:16) may hint that the activity described is inappropriate in a holy place. Even granting Sanders' point that money changing and the selling of animals were necessary, these activities did not have to take place within the Temple precincts. (2) Although *spēlaion lēstōn* in 11:17 should probably be translated "den of brigands" rather than "den of thieves" (see the NOTE on "den of brigands" in 11:17), a brigand is still someone who earns his living by stealing other people's money and goods, and those hostile to the money changers and merchants might view them in this light (cf. modern disparagement of financiers as "robber barons" or "corporate raiders"). (3) If the interdict on the conveyance of containers through the Temple in 11:16 is meant to recall Zech 14:21 (see the NOTE on "and he did not allow anyone to carry a container through the Temple" in 11:16), Mark would seem to be implying that trade in the Temple was a sacrilege (cf. John 2:16).

At least as far as Mark's view goes, then, the either/or of reformation or destruction is a false dichotomy. For Mark, perhaps, trading in the Temple was an abuse that Jesus tried to correct while already knowing that this attempt would fail. His Temple demonstration, therefore, symbolized both the reform attempt and the judgment of destruction that would follow its failure.

16. *and he did not allow anyone to carry a container through the Temple.* Gk *kai ouk ēphien hina tis dienenkē skeuos dia tou hierou.* *Skeuos* can simply mean an "object" or "thing," but through the addition of a qualifier or by context it can become an object of a particular kind, such as a cultic one (cf. *Par. Jer.* 3:7; Philo, *Life of Moses* 2.94; Josephus, *War* 6.389; Heb 9:21; BDAG 927). In the present connection it probably refers to a container used for transporting animal blood and other sacrificial elements. If so, there may be an allusion to Zech 14:21—"And there shall no longer be traders in the house of the LORD of hosts on that day"—a passage that speaks of the eschatological exclusion from the Temple of the merchants who supplied ritually pure containers for sacrifices. They will no longer be necessary, because all the pots in Jerusalem will be holy. But a *skeuos* can also be a weapon (see, e.g., Gen 27:3; Deut 1:41), and this meaning fits the violent connotation of the word "brigand" in the next verse, which would probably remind the Markan community of the recent intrusion of armed revolutionaries into the Temple precincts (see the NOTE on "den of brigands" 11:17).

17. *My house shall be called a house of prayer for all the nations.* Gk *ho oikos mou oikos proseuchēs klēthēsetai pasin tois ethnesin.* This is a citation of Isa 56:7 in a form virtually identical with that of the LXX. Mark is not the first postbiblical writer to echo this passage; 1 Macc 7:37, for example, says, "You, O Lord, chose this house to be called by your name, and to be a house of prayer and petition for your people" (Brenton trans. alt.). In 1 Maccabees, however, the universalistic nuance of the Isaian passage ("for all the nations"), which is so important for Mark, is deliberately restricted to Israel ("for your people"; cf. Watts, *New Exodus*, 323). Other ancient Jews such as Josephus (e.g., *War* 4.182; 5.17, 563) and the author of the Letter of Aristeas (e.g., 99), however, took pride in the popularity of the Jewish Temple among Gentiles (cf. S. Schwartz, *Josephus*, 26–28).

den of brigands. Gk *spēlaion lēstōn.* This part of Jesus' denunciation echoes Jer 7:11: "Has this house, which is called by my name, become a den of brigands in your sight?" (NRSV alt.). It may have been combined with Isa 56:7 partly on the basis of *gĕzērāh šāwāh* (analogy; see the GLOSSARY), since both passages speak of the Temple as God's house and use the verb "to call." The context of the expression in Jeremiah is significant, since it is part of a judgment on those who trust overmuch in the Temple (Jer 7:4); instead of preserving "the house of the Lord" that has become a den of brigands, God will pour out his anger on it, burn it with fire, and cast its adherents out of his sight (7:14–20). Not only is this scenario of judgment and exile from Israel similar to that in Mark 12:9, but the prophecy of the Temple's destruction may reverberate in the Markan context of the Jewish War, in which some revolutionaries seem to have trusted in the inviolability of the Temple (see Hengel, *Zealots,* 221–24).

Lēstēs, like the Hebrew term it translates, *pārîṣ,* refers not so much to a thief as to one who robs by violence, that is, a brigand, highwayman, or bandit. It is also the word commonly used by Josephus to refer to the Jewish revolutionaries of the Great Revolt against Rome (see Marcus, "Jewish War," 449–51), and in the Markan context it may be a two-level term. On the level of Jesus it probably refers to the merchants in the Temple and their high-priestly supporters (cf. the denunciation of the violence and extortion of the high-priestly house of Annas and Caiaphas in *t. Men.* 13:21–22 and *b. Pes.* 57a). For the Markan community, however, it would also echo the situation in their own day, in which revolutionary activism had penetrated even the ruling elite of Judaea (see Goodman, *Ruling Class,* 167–75; Schwier, *Tempel,* 128, 139, 162, 176–77, 190–201) and militantly anti-Gentile "brigands," led by messianic pretenders, had set up their headquarters within the sanctuary itself.

18. *were looking for a way to destroy him.* Gk *ezētoun pōs auton apolesōsin,* lit. "they were seeking how they might destroy him." The language here repeats that in 3:6, where the Pharisees took counsel with the Herodians, "in order that they might destroy him" (*hopōs auton apolesōsin*). The plot, which has lain curiously dormant since then, is now revived; in 12:12 the chief priests, scribes, and elders will try to arrest Jesus, and in the next verse they will send the Pharisees and the Herodians to entrap him verbally (thus uniting the disparate groups of enemies mentioned in 3:6 and 11:18). The successful execution of the conspiracy, however, must await the treachery of one of Jesus' own followers (cf. 14:1–2, 10–11).

was overwhelmed. Gk *exeplēsseto.* Elsewhere this verb has been translated "was amazed" or "was astonished" (see 1:22; 6:2; 7:37; 10:26), but the emphasis here is not so much on befuddlement as on intensity of impact: Jesus makes so great an impression on the crowd that the leaders fear that their authority is jeopardized (cf. 1:22).

11 20. *they saw the fig tree withered from the roots.* Gk *eidon tēn sykēn exērammenēn ek rizōn.* In Luke 13:6–9 Jesus tells a parable about a fig tree, which in the context seems to symbolize Jerusalem or Israel, that is threatened with destruction if it does not bear fruit. It is possible that our miracle story, in which a fig tree symbolizing the Jerusalem Temple is cursed with fruitlessness, has developed

from this parable. For another possible source, see the NOTE on "this mountain" in 11:23.

21. *the fig tree you cursed.* Gk *hē sykē hēn katērasō.* In his response to this observation, Jesus speaks of praying rather than cursing, and Dowd (*Prayer*, 58, 119–20) concludes that Mark thinks of Jesus' words in 11:14 as a prayer. The point, however, is analogy rather than identity; Jesus' curse is like a prayer in invoking divine power, but unlike it in addressing the affected object rather than God (cf. Gevirtz, "Curse").

22. *Have faith in God.* Gk *echete pistin theou*, lit. "have (or hold onto) faith (or faithfulness) of God." As Taylor (466) notes, the variant "*If* you have faith in God . . ." (*ei echete*) is well supported by ℵ, D, Θ, *f*[13], etc., and scribal inattention could easily transform EIEXETE into EXETE; it would be possible, therefore, to see "If you have faith in God . . ." as the original text. But as Metzger (109) points out, elsewhere the solemn expression "Amen, I say to you" is always introductory and never preceded by a protasis (see the GLOSSARY), and the reading of ℵ, etc. could well be an assimilation to Luke 17:6.

The context suggests that trusting in God's power ("faith in God") enables seemingly impossible things to happen (for history-of-religious parallels, see Dowd, *Prayer*, 96–117). But the implication may also be that such miracles reveal God's power, which enables him to fulfill his promises and thus to establish his trustworthiness ("the faithfulness of God"). For the similar ambiguity in the Pauline phrase *pistis Iēsou Christou* ("faith of/in Jesus Christ"), see Hays, *Faith*.

23. *this mountain.* Gk *tǭ orei toutǭ.* In Luke 17:6 = Q it is not a mountain that is uprooted but a *sykaminos* = "mulberry tree," a word that has the same initial letters as *sykē* = "fig tree." Dodd (*Parables*, 49 n. 33) suggests that this saying about the theoretical ability of the faithful person to destroy a *sykaminos* is the origin of our story about Jesus' magical destruction of a *sykē*. Telford (*Barren Temple*, 102), however, notes that all other forms of the saying speak of the uprooting of a mountain (see figure 36), and he judges the Lukan form to be secondary.

If the saying has a specific mountain in mind, it is probably either the Mount of Olives or the Temple Mount. From 11:12–15, the fig tree appears to lie between Bethany and Jerusalem, hence on the Mount of Olives. Zechariah 14:4 speaks of an eschatological fissure of this mountain running from east to west (*yāmmāh*), a term that literally means "to the sea," and Grant ("Coming," 298–301; *Miracle*, 167) concludes that "this mountain" is the Mount of Olives (for other echoes of Zechariah 9–14 in chapter 11, see the NOTES on "the Mount of Olives" in 11:1, "colt" and "upon which no human being has ever yet sat" in 11:2, and "and he did not allow anyone to carry a container through the Temple" in 11:16). As Dowd (*Prayer*, 74) points out, however, in the Zecharian passage the mountain actually moves north and south rather than east and west, so a supposed mistranslation of *yāmmāh* is irrelevant.

The more likely candidate for "this mountain" is the Temple Mount, which faces travelers as they approach Jerusalem from Bethany. Some rabbinic traditions (e.g., *b. Pesaḥ* 87b; *b. Giṭ.* 56b) refer to the Temple Mount as "this mountain" (see Telford, *Barren Temple*, 170 n. 65), and a biblical oracle (Zech 4:7) addresses

Figure 36: The Saying about the Uprooted Mountain/Tree

Mark 11:23	Matthew 21:21	Matthew 17:20 = Q	Luke 17:6 = Q	Gospel of Thomas 106	Gospel of Thomas 48	1 Corinthians 13:2
Amen, I say to you that	Amen, I say to you	For amen, I say to you				If I have all faith
	if you have faith and do not doubt	if you have faith like a mustard grain	If you had faith like a mustard grain			
	not only will you do what concerns the fig tree (sykē)					
whoever says to this mountain	but even if you say to this mountain	you will say to this mountain	you would say to the mulberry tree (sykaminos)	And when you say	they shall say to the mountain	
"Be lifted up and cast into the sea"	"Be lifted up and cast into the sea"	"Move from here to there"	"Be uprooted and planted in the sea"	"Mountain, be moved"	"Be moved"	so as to remove mountains . . .
and does not doubt in his heart						
but believes that what he says will happen						
it will be for him	it will happen	and it will move	and it would obey you	it will be moved	and it will be moved	

the Temple as a "great mountain" that will become a plain before Zerubbabel, the Davidic king (see Abbott, *Founding*, 208). Another OT passage (Isa 2:2//Mic 4:1) speaks of "the mountain of the LORD's house" being "raised above the hills" in the last days. Dowd (*Prayer*, 72) objects that the mountain in this oracle is established rather than removed, but it is possible that Jesus is twisting the oracle as he echoes it (on this sort of reversal of a well-known biblical passage, see Marcus, "Intertextual Polemic," 214–16; Sommer, *Prophet*, 36–46). As Dodd (*Parables*, 50 n. 33) puts it: "The hope of Israel had been that the temple should, on 'the Day of the Lord' (when the Kingdom of God should be revealed), stand upon its lofty hill as the religious center of the whole world. Jesus says, on the contrary, that, now that the Kingdom of God has come, the temple has no further place; it will be sunk, hill and all, into the sea."

Be lifted up and cast into the sea. Gk *arthēti kai blēthēti eis tēn thalassan.* In Homer, *Odyssey* 9.644–50, the Cyclops tears off the top of a mountain and casts it into the sea in a vain attempt to destroy the ship of Odysseus and his companions. It is difficult to know what, if anything, to make of this parallel, but it does at least illustrate the obvious point that a godlike power is necessary to pull up a mountain and heave it into the sea (the Cyclops is the son of the sea god Poseidon).

24. *have received.* Gk *elabete.* Although the aorist tense is well supported, many scribes apparently considered it overly bold and changed it to a present (e.g., A, K, X, Π) or a future (e.g., D, Θ, Latin versions; cf. Matt 21:22; see Metzger, 110). The aorist, however, is a significant indication of the eschatological perspective that undergirds our passage: one is to act "as if" one's request had already been received, since "the present form of this world is passing away" and the age of fulfillment is about to arrive (cf. 1 Cor 7:29–31). Fanning (*Verbal Aspect*, 273) lists our passage as one of a number in the NT in which "the Greek aorist indicative [is] used to some degree under Hebrew influence to portray a future occurrence as if already done" (cf. Mark 13:20; Luke 1:51–54; John 13:31; Rom 8:30; Jude 14; 1 Thess 2:16?).

25. *And when you stand praying, forgive, if you have anything against anyone.* Gk *kai hotan stēkete proseuchomenoi, aphiete ei ti echete kata tinos.* As Bultmann (132) points out, this seems to be a variant of Matt 5:23–24; the latter may be more primitive than the Markan form, since it presupposes the existence and validity of the sacrificial system in Jerusalem (cf. the possibly independent *Did.* 14:2 and Davies and Allison, 1.516). If so, Mark's anti-Temple bias may help account for the present abbreviated form. On other parallels with Matthew's Sermon on the Mount, see the next NOTE.

so that your Father in heaven may also forgive you your transgressions. Gk *hina kai ho patēr hymōn ho en tois ouranois aphȩ̄ hymin ta paraptōmata hymōn.* This sounds like a condensation of parts of the Lord's Prayer, especially in its Matthean version ("Our Father in heaven . . . forgive us our debts, as we also have forgiven our debtors," Matt 6:9, 12; for another Markan echo of the Matthean version of the Lord's Prayer, see the NOTE on "not what I want, but what you want" in 14:36). Some texts (A, D, K, X, etc.) follow it with 11:26, "But if you do not forgive, neither will your Father in heaven forgive you your transgressions" (my trans.), which echoes the conclusion of the Lord's Prayer in Matthew (Matt 6:15). The verse might have dropped out by haplography (see the GLOSSARY), since its concluding words are the same as the final words of 11:25, but "its absence from early witnesses that represent all text-types makes its highly probable that the words were inserted by copyists in imitation of Matt 6:15" (Metzger, 110).

On the principle that one must forgive in order to be forgiven, see Sir 28:1–5; Matt 18:21–35; t. B. Qam. 9:30; b. Šabb. 151b; Dowd, Prayer, 126 n. 18.

COMMENT

Introduction. After his triumphal entrance into Jerusalem (11:1–11a) and subsequent withdrawal to the outlying suburbs (11:11b), Jesus now returns to the capital city and the Temple. On the way, he curses a fig tree (11:12–14) and then enters the Temple, violently halting the trade that is going on there and explaining this action in terms borrowed from the OT (11:15–19). On the way back to Bethany, the disciples observe that the cursed fig tree has suddenly withered, and Jesus uses this miracle as the point of departure for lessons about faith and prayer (11:20–25).

As noted in the introduction to the COMMENT on 11:1–11, Mark himself is probably responsible for splitting the fig tree narrative into two halves and placing them around the cleansing of the Temple in a sort of interpretative envelope. In the resultant story, the tree's withering is observed only on the day after Jesus curses it; in the pre-Markan story, as in Matt 21:18–19, the tree probably shriveled immediately upon receiving Jesus' curse ("withered from the roots" makes more sense in this context). Mark himself, then, probably penned the introductory verse (11:12), which situates the fig tree story within his larger narrative, as well as verses 11:20–22, which resume the tale after the Temple action (cf. the correspondence between Peter's remembering in 11:21 and 14:72). It is possible that he is also responsible for the scriptural citation and allusion in the account of the Temple action (11:17); a more appropriate scripture is cited at the corresponding point in John (2:17), and the Markan references fit the Markan life setting suspiciously well (see the NOTES on "and he did not allow anyone to carry a container through the Temple" in 11:16 and "den of brigands" in 11:17 and the COMMENT on 11:15–19). In 11:20–25, Mark has probably incorporated a preexistent catechetical tradition (11:23–25), which he connects loosely with the previous context by means of the redactional 11:20–22. Besides these major redactional interventions, other probable Markan features in the section include the note about the disciples *hearing* in 11:14b; the explanatory qualification "except leaves" and the typically Markan *gar* clause ("for it was not the time for figs") in 11:13; the entrance into Jerusalem in 11:15a and the exit from it in 11:19; "began to" in 11:15b; "and he was teaching and saying to them" in 11:17; the description of the reaction of the chief priests and the scribes in 11:18; "does not doubt in his heart but believes that what he says will happen" in 11:23; and "everything" in 11:24.

Using material of diverse origin, then, Mark has composed one of his most original and revealing compositions. The center of the composition is Jesus' action in the Temple, which the surrounding fig tree story interprets, not only by casting the sanctuary in the role of the fruitless tree, barren and cursed, but also by presenting an alternative: faith and prayer that bypass the sacrificial system of the "den of brigands" and appeal directly to the heavenly Father for mercy.

11:12–14: Jesus curses a fig tree. After spending the night in Bethany, Jesus and his disciples head back toward Jerusalem (11:12). On the way Jesus becomes hungry and approaches a fig tree to see if it has any fruit on it (11:13a). Finding no figs there (11:13b), he curses the tree with the threatening prophecy that it will never bear fruit again (11:14).

From earliest times, exegetes have been bothered by the seeming harshness and unfairness of Jesus' wrath against an insentient object, especially when Mark himself tells us that "it was not the time for figs." Rationalizing explanations and retellings have jumped into this narrative breach. Matthew, for example, already omits the clause about it not being the time for figs (Matt 21:19), and van Hasselt ("Vijgeboom") hypothesizes that the owner of the tree, not wanting others to enjoy his produce, had picked it clean before harvest time; Jesus' curse, therefore, was a justified punishment for his greediness!

If we do not want to go down such speculative exegetical routes, we should start by inquiring how trees, and especially fig trees, were regarded in the biblical world. As Telford shows in an enlightening monograph (*Barren Temple*, 187–89), in the context of Jewish legends there is nothing unusual about a charismatic teacher addressing a tree and the tree responding, as is illustrated by rabbinic anecdotes about a carob tree uprooting itself at R. Eliezer's command (*b. B. Meṣi'a* 59ab; cf. Mark 11:23) or a fig tree bearing fruit before its time at a word from R. Jose (*b. Ta'an.* 24a).

Old Testament, Jewish, and NT texts, moreover, show that the fig and other plants often symbolize good and bad people, the leaders of Israel, or the nation as a whole (see, e.g., Jer 24:1–10; Matt 15:13; Luke 13:6–9; *Esth. Rabb.* 9.2); that these symbols are often used in eschatological contexts, to speak either of judgment on Israel (Isa 34:4; Amos 8:1–3; Matt 15:13; Luke 13:6–9; 23:31; Rev. 6:13–14) or the manifestation of God's end-time grace toward it (see, e.g., Mark 13:28–32; *Cant. Rab.* 2.13.4; *Pes. Rab.* 41.2); and that there is an especially close connection between this tree imagery on the one hand and Jerusalem and its Temple on the other (see, e.g., Ezek 47:1–12; 1 Cor 3:5–17; *Pes. Rab.* 41.2). Telford particularly highlights five OT passages (Isa 28:3–4; Jer 8:13; Hos 9:10, 16; Joel 1:7, 12; Mic 7:1), all of which, like Mark 11:12–14, 20, use the withering of the fig tree as a symbol for eschatological judgment on Israel, and all of which occur in scriptural contexts that were regularly mined by early Christians. These passages in their contexts also exhibit, according to Telford (*Barren Temple*, 155), several themes linking them with each other and the Markan context:

the corruption and consequent condemnation of the nation, her leaders, her Temple and its cultus [cf. Mark 12:1–12—JM]; the appearance of Yahweh in wrath to curse the land and blast the trees [cf. Mark 11:20]; the moving of the mountains [cf. Mark 11:23]; the destruction of Jerusalem and its Temple [cf. Mark 13:1–2]; the blossoming of Israel, God's tree, in the New Age [cf. Mark 13:28–32]; the abundant fertility of this period [cf. Mark 4:1–20]; the elevation of the Temple Mount and its future exalted status [cf. again Mark 11:23?].

Seen against this biblical background, we might be tempted to interpret the fig tree in our story as a symbol for the nation as a whole, but the conclusion of the next scene reveals that at this point in the Gospel a large portion of the people ("the whole crowd") is still responsive to Jesus; only the chief priests and the scribes oppose his action and message (11:18; cf. 12:12; 14:1–2; cf. also, however, 15:11–15). Especially in view of the Temple setting of our narrative, the most immediate culprits seem to be the Temple and its functionaries (cf. the parallel between "seeing . . . a fig tree" in 11:13 and "looked around at everything" in the Temple in 11:11). Jesus' inability to find fruit on the tree, and his consequent curse against it, stands for the conclusion that the Temple leadership is hopelessly corrupt; in the larger Markan story, the barrenness of the fig tree anticipates the "abomination of *desolation*" that is prophesied of the Temple in 13:14. For Mark, indeed, the Temple seems to be firmly entrenched in the sphere of the sterile old age that is headed for destruction (cf. "for it was not the time for figs" in 11:13c and see Broadhead, *Teaching*, 177).

For the Markan community, which either knows that the Temple has been razed or can see that its destruction is imminent (see the INTRODUCTION in vol. 1, pp. 37–39), this cataclysmic event, which Jesus prophesies by means of his curse on the fig tree, will prove the absolute trustworthiness of his word. Therefore the final editorial remark in this subsection of our passage, "And his disciples heard him" (11:14b), is not superfluous but a nudge to the audience parallel to 13:14 ("let the reader understand"); both call attention to an event in the Temple that has recently happened or is presently occurring in the audience's world.

11:15–19: Jesus' Temple demonstration. In 11:14, then, Jesus has predicted the Temple's destruction in symbolic words, which his disciples have duly noted; he will now act it out before their eyes, in a parabolic demonstration like the strange symbolic "signs" of the OT prophets (see Hooker, *Signs*, 6, 44–48). This demonstration begins with the laconic introduction "And they came to Jerusalem" (11:15a). While this clause repeats the substance of 11:11a ("And he went into Jerusalem"), the change to the plural includes the disciples—whose hearing of Jesus' curse on the fig tree has just been underlined—in Jesus' entry, thus making them witnesses of the action that will begin to realize the curse. Readers familiar with the scriptures and the history of the Temple might be reminded of the story of Nehemiah, who like Jesus comes into the holy city astride a beast of burden (Neh 2:12; cf. Mark 11:4–7) and whose words, "And I came to Jerusalem" (Neh 2:11, my trans.), were the preamble to an account of rebuilding the walls and restoring the gates of the city with the active support of the chief priests and other leaders (cf. Neh 2:16–18; 3:1–2). The Markan Jesus, on the other hand, comes to threaten the destruction of the Temple and thus to earn the deadly enmity of the chief priests and their allies (cf. 11:18).

He does so by launching an all-out attack on the trade that is going on in the Temple precincts, probably in the Court of the Gentiles (see Sanders, *Jesus*, 365 n. 6), expelling buyers and sellers (11:15b), overturning the tables of money changers and dove merchants (11:15c), and stopping anyone from carrying a sacred vessel through the area (11:16). In reality, the effect of Jesus' demonstration on Temple business was probably more symbolic than economic; as Sanders (*Jesus*, 69–70) points out, it is doubtful that one person acting alone (the disciples are not described as helping) could have made much of a dent in the vast amount of trade going on in the huge court.

But if the purpose of the attack is symbolic, what does it symbolize? Sanders himself (*Jesus*, 61–76) argues that Jesus intended to point toward the imminent destruction of the Temple as part of the catastrophic end-time events, not to "cleanse" or reform it; his action, then, was similar to that of another Jesus, the son of Ananias, who prophesied the Temple's imminent end and thus earned the enmity of the chief priests and other leaders in the years immediately preceding its demise (see Josephus, *War* 6.300–9). This interpretation fits the Markan portrayal to a certain extent, since in its context Jesus' curse on the fig tree ("Let no one ever eat fruit from you again") seems to imply that the Temple will soon cease functioning. Sanders, moreover, is right to emphasize the eschatological dimension of Jesus' action, since the turn of the ages is frequently associated with catastrophes in or replacement of the Temple (see, e.g., Dan 9:24–27; 11:31; 12:11; Tob 14:5; *1 En.* 89:73; 90:28–29; Rev 11:2). But Jesus' demonstration, in Mark's telling, also seems to look forward to an eschatological elimination of the perceived abuse of trade in the Temple, in line with the prophecy in Zech 14:21: "And there shall no longer be traders in the house of the LORD of hosts on that day" (see the NOTE on "going into the Temple, he began to throw out those who were selling and buying in the Temple, etc." in 11:15).

The idea of the Messiah restoring the Temple has deep roots in Jewish tradition, and the Markan Jesus appears to be following this tradition, though in a distinctive way. In the ancient Near East generally there was a strong connection between kings and temples, and monarchs frequently built, restored, and/or officiated at sanctuaries (see Runnalls, "King"). In the Israelite sphere, this connection is visible preeminently in 2 Samuel 7, a passage that, as we have seen, is echoed in Mark 11:1–11 and 14:57–62 (see the NOTE on "Blessed is the coming dominion of our father David!" in 11:10 and the COMMENT on 11:7–11). In later years this oracle was interpreted messianically; 4QFlor, for example, makes the Temple the focus of a messianic prophecy based largely on 2 Samuel 7. Similarly, Zech 6:12–13 speaks of David's "branch" building the Second Temple, and the Targum on this passage interprets it as a reference to the Messiah (cf. Sir 51:12.vii–viii [Heb B; see Skehan and Di Lella, *Ben Sira*, 568–69]; *Sib. Or.* 5.414–33; the Eighteen Benedictions; *Tg. Is.* 52:13; 53:5; *Lev. Rab.* 9.6; *Num. Rab.* 18.21; Juel, *Messiah and Temple*, 169–209). This traditional linkage between Messiah and Temple helps explain Josephus' report that one of the leaders in the Jewish War, Menachem son of Judas, followed his triumphal entry into Jerusalem with an appearance in the Temple in royal robes (*Ant.* 2.433–34, 444) and that even after it had been destroyed, another possible messianic claimant, Simon bar Giora, "popped up out of the ground at the very place where the Temple had once stood" clad in similar garments (*War* 7.29–31).

In such traditions, however, Messiah and Temple often go together in ways that are opposed to the Markan emphasis on the Gentile mission and the dream that God's house will become "a house of prayer for all the nations" (11:17, citing Isa 56:7; see the NOTE on "My house shall be called a house of prayer for all the nations" in 11:17). The messianic image, indeed, is often militantly anti-Gentile, harking back to its roots in a Davidic dynasty whose main foreign-policy objective was maintaining the independence of Israel, by military force if necessary, against the imperialistic designs of surrounding countries. Already in Psalm 2, therefore, the anointed king fights God's battles against the hostile nations that have arisen against him, and in later passages such as *Psalms of Solomon* 17 and *Sib. Or.* 5.414–43, this and similar oracles are reinterpreted as references to the Messiah's defeat of the massed might of the pagan world in a climactic apocalyptic battle (cf. Atkinson, "Herodian Origin").

Such expectations of eschatological victory over the nations are sometimes coupled with the hope that God or the Messiah will cleanse the Temple of the defiling presence of Gentiles. This attitude is already foreshadowed in 1 Macc 13:49–53, where Simon Maccabaeus (who, though not a Davidide, became the sovereign of Judaea) rids Jerusalem of impurity by driving out Gentiles (cf. 1 Macc 14:36), and in 2 Macc 10:5, where Judas Maccabaeus purifies the Temple from pollution by foreigners. Similarly, in *1 En.* 89:73, Temple offerings are polluted because the Israelites who present them have intermarried with Gentiles (see Black, *1 Enoch*, 273), but this pollution will be removed in the new Temple that "the Lord of the sheep" will erect in the age to come (90:28–29). In *Pss. Sol.* 17:22, 30, moreover, God's anointed one cleanses Jerusalem (including, by implication, the Temple) by ridding it of Gentile contamination (cf. 17:28). The contrast with the inclusiveness of Mark 11:17 is especially striking in 4QFlor, where, a few lines before an allusion to the Davidic Messiah (1:10–12), 2 Sam 7:10 is reinterpreted as a reference to

the house into which shall not enter . . . ever an Ammonite, or a Moabite, or a bastard, or a foreigner, or a proselyte, never, because his holy ones are there . . . Foreigners shall not again lay it waste as they laid waste, in the past, the tem[ple of I]srael on account of their sins. (4QFlor 1 1:3–6)

For the author of 4QFlor, who here follows the lead of Ezek 44:5–9, Gentiles will "desolate" the present Temple but will be excluded from the eschatological one (cf. the Temple Scroll, in which the Court of the Gentiles is eliminated). Indeed, because of the proximity of the reference to the Davidic Messiah, it is possible that the author of the *Florilegium* sees the latter as the agent of this "cleansing." A similarly messianic, anti-Gentile "cleansing" theology may well have motivated the revolutionary leaders of later first-century Judaea to suspend the customary sacrifices on behalf of the emperor and hence to trigger the Great Revolt (see Josephus, *War* 2.409; cf. 2.414, 562–64 and Hengel, *Zealots*, 217–21; Schwier, *Tempel*, 55–74, 119–20; Marcus, *Jewish War*, 450 n. 47).

Thus, while the Markan Jesus in some ways fulfills the traditional expectations for the Messiah, combining his triumphal entry into Jerusalem with a dramatic action laying claim to and purging the Temple, in other ways he defies the messianic image prevalent in Mark's world. While other eschatologically minded Jews, caught up in the horror and excitement of the war against Rome, dream of a Messiah who will purge the Temple by ridding it of foreign influences, Mark's Messiah cleanses it by expelling the (Jewish) traders who defile the Court of the Gentiles and thereby thwart the Temple's divinely intended purpose of becoming a "house of prayer for all peoples." And while other Jews view the Davidic Messiah as the Temple's *restorer*, the Markan Jesus' demonstration points toward its *destruction* (see Telford, *Barren Temple*, 261–62).

The chief priests and the scribes, naturally enough, respond to Jesus' assault on the Temple with deadly animosity: they plot to destroy him, because they see that the crowd is overwhelmed by his teaching (11:18). The leaders' hostile response here recalls the reaction to Jesus' first miracle, the exorcism in the Capernaum synagogue in 1:21–28; there, too, the crowd was overwhelmed by his teaching (1:22, 27), and the scribes were implicitly criticized for lacking authority (see 1:22: "as one who had authority, and not in the way the scribes did"). There, too, moreover, there was talk of destruction, with the demons asking fearfully, "Have you come to destroy us?" (1:24). Now, however, the chief priests and the scribes, whom Mark thinks belong to the demonic side of the eschatological war, respond to Jesus' attempt to "exorcise" their dependents, the traders, by attempting to destroy him in turn (cf. 3:6 and see the NOTE on "going into the Temple, he began to throw out those who were selling and buying in the Temple, etc." in 11:15).

This subsection ends with Jesus' exit from the city at sunset (11:19). That he has apparently stayed the whole day, despite the hostility of the chief priests and the scribes, is testimony to the charismatic authority and popular support that worry these leaders. But the conclusion of the passage will describe something even more ominous: the withering of the fig tree with which the narrative has associated these officials.

11:20–25: the lesson from the withered fig tree. The next morning, on the way back into the city, Jesus and his disciples see the cursed fig tree, which has shriveled in the interval (11:20), and Peter recalls the curse of the previous day (11:21). Readers who have followed the narrative carefully up to this point would be predisposed to infer that Jesus' effective curse on the tree has negative implications for the Temple with which the tree has been linked by the Markan sandwich structure. This intuition is confirmed later in the Gospel when Jesus prophesies that not one of the Temple's stones will remain standing upon another (13:2); the implied picture of a building razed to its foundations coheres with our description of a fig tree withered "from the roots" (11:20). As Myers (*Binding*, 304) points out, moreover, the two passages are linked by the disciples' use of "Rabbi/Teacher, look!" (*ide*) with reference both to the fig tree (11:21) and to the Temple (13:1).

Jesus' initial reply to Peter's observation, "Have faith in God" (11:22), could also be interpreted as "hold onto the faithfulness of God" (see the NOTE on "Have faith in God" in 11:22) and might at first be construed as an exhortation not to give up on the Temple. The Temple is still, after all, God's house (cf. 11:17), and in the OT (e.g., Psalm 46), intertestamental literature (e.g., 2 Macc 3:22–39; 8:2), and even the NT (e.g., Rom 9:4–5), the faithfulness of God is manifested by his continuing commitment to it (see esp. 2 Macc 3:22, which twice uses the verb *pisteuein* ["have faith" or "entrust"] in a prayer for divine protection of the Temple). It is probable, moreover, that in the Markan context the Jewish revolutionaries, who established the headquarters for their last-ditch battle against the Romans in the Temple itself, stressed God's eternal loyalty to the sacred edifice (cf. Josephus, *War* 5.459; 6.285–86; Hengel, *Zealots*, 240–44).

But if the narrative briefly allows hope for the Temple's continued protection by God, it dashes it in the very next verse, where we read of a prayer not that "this mountain" may be preserved but that it may be uprooted and cast into the ocean (11:23). Although the primary purpose of this assurance is to emphasize the power of faith, there may be a sidelong glance here at the destruction of the sanctuary, since "this mountain" can be a term for the Temple Mount (see the NOTE on "this mountain" in 11:23). The Markan Jesus, indeed, may be polemically reversing biblical oracles that stress divine protection of the Temple and its coming eschatological exaltation. In Psalm 46, for example, Israel is exhorted to trust in the God who will deliver Zion from the raging waters, and the splendid eschatological vision in Isaiah 2/Micah 4 portrays the Temple Mount as exalted over all other mountains. The Markan Jesus, however, converts the positive Isaian image (exaltation) into a symbol for destruction (lifted up and cast into the sea) and transforms what the Psalm avers to be impossible (subjugation by the waters of chaos) into the Temple's certain fate (cf. the NOTE on "this mountain" in 11:23).

Yet although the Markan Jesus prophesies the end of the Temple, the site above all sites where Jews hoped their prayers would be heard, he also affirms the power of prayer in a series of sayings that begin with the formula "Amen, I say to you . . ." (11:23a; on this unusual formula, see the NOTE on "Amen" in 3:28 and the COMMENT on 3:28–30). Thus, as Dowd (*Prayer*, 45, 53) suggests, there is coherence in the progression from 11:12–19 to 11:20–25: Jesus first attacks the old locus of prayer, then assures his followers that prayer is nevertheless more efficacious than ever. The guarantor for its effectiveness, however, is no longer the "Temple made by hands" (cf. 14:58) but the eschatological authority of Jesus ("Amen, I say to you . . ."). As Dowd points out, similar moves away from a Temple-centered piety were forced on other Jews by the destruction of the Temple in 70 C.E., and some of them, such as the Pharisees and the Dead Sea Sect, already anticipated the shift before that date (see *Prayer*, 47–51).

Specifically, Jesus promises that those who banish doubt and believe that their requests will be granted will see them fulfilled (11:23b). This point is then reiterated emphatically in 11:24: *everything* that you ask for, believe that you have *already* received it, and so you shall (see the NOTE on "have received" in 11:24). These categorical promises of answered prayer are paralleled elsewhere in the Synoptic tradition (see Matt 7:7–11//Luke 11:5–13), but later they were qualified when Christians began to notice that not all their requests were in fact fulfilled (see, e.g., John 14:13, "Whatever you ask *in my name*," and John 15:7, "*If* you abide in me, and my words abide in you"). These "realistic" amendments, however, only underline the extraordinary absoluteness of the promise in our passage, which is a testimony to the sense of advent that pervaded the ministry of Jesus and the earliest post-Easter church: God's new-age power has broken into the world, and therefore the age of eschatological wish fulfillment has arrived.

To be sure, there are a few hints of qualification in the concluding verses of the Markan pericope. In 11:24, "pray and ask for" may not be a hendiadys (see the GLOSSARY) but a significant progression; the requests that are answered are not just the first thing that pops into the supplicant's head but petitions that emerge from a state of meditation. And the implication of 11:25 may be that certain spiritual states, such as resentment, can stymie God's desire to grant his people's petitions; forgiveness of others, therefore, is a condition for answered prayer (cf. Matt 6:14–15; 18:15–35; Luke 17:3–6; Davies and Allison, 1.616–17). Stendahl ("Prayer") interprets this verse against the backdrop of the apocalyptic belief that the powers of the new age, including omnipotent prayer, can be manifested within the elect community only if its members maintain unbroken, well-ordered relations with one another (cf. 1QS 5:1–7; 8:4–10; 1 Cor 5:1–5; Matt 18:15–20; Luke 17:3–6). Yet the Markan Jesus does not limit forgiveness to the elect group; rather, he takes up the situation that arises "if you have anything against *anyone*" (emphasis added). The logic seems to be that forgiveness is a prerequisite for miracle working, both in the sense that the petitioners' sins must be forgiven (cf. 2:5–12), and in the sense that they, too, must learn to forgive. In the larger NT context, however, this forgiveness of others is not merely a prerequisite for God's forgiveness but also a product of that forgiveness (cf. Eph 4:32; Col 3:13); the new-age power that moves mountains can also perform the miracle of removing resentment from the heart.

In the Markan situation, 11:23–25 would probably be heard as a counterbalance to the doubt, despair, and bitterness prevailing within a community racked by war and persecution, in which family members are betraying each other to death and Christians are being hated by "all" (cf. 13:12–13). The hearers, then, are people in a desperate situation that seems to negate any hope that God hears their prayers. The instruction on faith and prayer in 11:23–25 would assure them that, all appearances to the contrary, their prayers *were* being answered, that they had *not* been abandoned by God, and that even now, in the midst of persecution and death, God was employing them to pluck up and break down the powers of this world and to build up and plant the structures of his dominion (cf. Jer 1:10). Thus, the exhortation not to doubt but to keep on believing, and the promise of answered prayer, have much the same valence as the assurance in 13:13: "The one who endures to the end . . . will be saved." Our verses, indeed, put extraordinary emphasis on the necessity of perseverance in belief; as figure 36 shows, the Markan form of the "mountain" saying stresses the temptation to doubt, and the corresponding necessity to keep on believing, more than any other version of the logion. The exhortation in 11:23–24, moreover, contains a series of four verbs in the present tense, a grammatical structure that strongly accentuates the need for continuous prayer (believe . . . pray . . . ask for . . . believe"), and the verbs are chiastically arranged to begin and end with the word "believe." Our passage, then, is not an example of magical thinking; it emphasizes sharply the necessity of perseverance in the face of a seemingly contradictory reality. Far from being a fantasy of revenge, moreover, it concludes with an appeal for forgiveness: God's foot soldiers must realize that bitterness is a luxury they can no longer afford, since it cuts them off from the fatherly, empowering, forgiving presence that alone can win the battle against the overwhelming power of the Enemy (11:25).

In 11:12–25 Jesus has implicitly challenged priestly authority by symbolically enacting the destruction of the Temple, and he has concluded by proclaiming that forgiveness is available without the Temple on the basis of his own word ("Amen, I say to you"). It is no wonder, then, that in the next passage the offended representatives of that system challenge him to specify the authority by which he presumes to act.

JESUS DEFLECTS A CHALLENGE TO HIS AUTHORITY (11:27–33)

11 ²⁷And they came to Jerusalem again. And as he was walking about in the Temple, the chief priests and the scribes and the elders came up to him, ²⁸and they said to him, "By what authority are you doing these things? Or who has given you this authority, so that you do these things?" ²⁹But Jesus said to them, "I will ask *you* one thing, and you answer me, and then I will tell you by what authority I do these things. ³⁰The baptism of John—from heaven or from human beings? Answer me!" ³¹And they debated among themselves, saying, "If we say, 'From heaven,' he will say, 'Why then did you not believe him?' ³²But do we dare to say, 'From human beings'?" (They feared the crowd, for all considered John really to be a prophet.) ³³And they answered and said to Jesus, "We do not know." And Jesus said to them, "Neither will I tell you by what authority I do these things."

NOTES

11 29. *and you answer me.* Gk *kai apokrithēte moi*. This imperative is equivalent to a conditional clause ("and if you answer me"; cf. Matt 21:24). Beyer (*Semitische Syntax*, 238–55, esp. 252) identifies this conditional use of the imperative as particularly characteristic of Semitic syntax, although he acknowledges that it is found occasionally in Greek as well. Apparently both Matthew and Luke found the imperative awkward, since both altered the Markan wording.

30. *from heaven.* Gk *ex ouranou.* "Heaven" is a frequent circumlocution for "God" in Jewish texts; see, for example, Dan 4:26 [4:23 THEOD.]; 1 Macc 4:10,

24; and rabbinic phrases such as "for the sake of heaven" and "the dominion of heaven" (cf. Moore, 1.430). The same circumlocution is attested in an epigram concerning the pagan wonder-worker Apollonius of Tyana: "The land of Tyana nursed him, but it was really heaven who bore him so that he might expel the sufferings of mortals" (*NewDocs* 3.49). The idiom is also common in the NT; besides our passage, see Luke 15:18, 21 ("I have sinned against heaven and before you") and the frequent Matthean phrase "the dominion of heaven" (*hē basileia tōn ouranōn*: Matt 3:2; 4:17; 5:3, 10, etc.), which is Matthew's version of "the dominion of God" (cf. BDAG 739 [3]).

31. *Why then did you not believe him?* Gk *dia ti oun ouk episteusate autǭ*. In some manuscripts the *oun* ("then") is missing, but it may have dropped out by homoeoarcton (see the GLOSSARY). For Bultmann (20), the force of Jesus' counterquestion about John the Baptist's credentials (11:30) is that Jesus, like John, derives his authority from heaven. Bultmann has to admit, however, that this reading does not cohere with Jesus' anticipated retort, "Why then did you not believe him?" which seems to imply a direct relationship between John and Jesus rather than a parallel one to God. For Meier (*Marginal Jew*, 2.163–67), the linkage between the two men is that Jesus continues John's practice of baptizing (cf. John 3:22; 4:1); therefore accepting John's baptism means accepting Jesus'. But our passage makes no specific reference to Jesus' baptismal practices, and "the baptism of John" in 11:30 may be a shorthand way of referring to the Baptist's whole ministry (cf. Acts 1:22 and Taylor, 470). Meier's reconstruction, moreover, succeeds no better than Bultmann's as an exegesis of the exact Markan wording, "Why then did you not believe him?" which refers to John's message rather than his ritual practice.

It seems more likely that 11:31 is a reference to a general belief that John had acknowledged Jesus as his successor. It is unlikely that this feature of the narrative is a total Markan or early Christian fiction, since John's acknowledgment of Jesus is not the main point of the story but an assumption on which it is based, and the story would not have much persuasive power unless this assumption were known to be indisputable by the narrative's audience. If so, however, it is puzzling that the Q pericope Matt 11:2–6//Luke 7:18–23 depicts John, in prison toward the end of his life, apparently in doubt as to whether Jesus is "the coming one" (see the NOTE on "stronger" in 1:7 and the COMMENT on 1:7–8). For an attempt to reconcile these two passages, see Marcus, "John the Baptist," where it is suggested that John acknowledged Jesus as his successor, the Elisha to his Elijah, but not as the Messiah.

32. *"But do we dare to say, 'From human beings'?"* (*They feared the crowd . . .*). Gk *alla eipōmen ex anthrōpōn;—ephobounto ton ochlon*. This translation construes *eipōmen* as a deliberative subjunctive, that is, one that considers a potential course of action (cf. the Vulgate and the NJB). Some translations, however, construe the subjunctive with the *ean* of the previous verse and translate, "But if we say, 'From human beings . . .' " (e.g., Syr[S], KJV, NIV). But if this translation, which produces a jarring anacoluthon (see the GLOSSARY), had been Mark's intended meaning, he probably would have repeated the *ean*.

COMMENT

Introduction. The provocation implicit in Jesus' triumphal entry into Jerusalem (11:1–11) and especially in his militant action in the Temple (11:15–19) has not gone unheeded. The religious leaders now strike back, challenging his credentials to act with such audacity.

The apparent reference to the Temple cleansing at the beginning of our pericope ("By what authority are you doing these things?") has helped convince many scholars that the two passages were originally sequential, a conclusion supported by John 2:14–18 and the observation that the intervening Markan pericope, 11:20–25, is part of a typically Markan sandwich structure (see the introduction to the COMMENT on 11:1–11 and Telford, *Barren Temple*, 47–48). Our passage is also strongly linked with two of the narratives that follow, the debate about taxes in 12:13–17 and the dispute about the resurrection in 12:18–27. All three are controversy stories, and all three begin with a group of Jewish leaders coming to challenge Jesus. They form, moreover, a logical progression with a concentric structure, since the chief priests were Sadducees:

11:27   chief priests (and scribes and elders) come to Jesus (*erchontai . . . pros auton*)
12:13   they send Pharisees and Herodians to Jesus
12:18   Sadducees come to Jesus (*erchontai pros auton*)

It is plausible, therefore, that our passage was the midpoint of a pre-Markan source that consisted of the triumphal entry, the cleansing of the Temple, our text, and the debates about taxes and the resurrection. Appropriately enough, this central section expresses the essential issue of the whole collection, namely, the authority of Jesus. Mark's editorial work further underlines the importance of this issue by placing the passage between two parables of judgment (the withered fig tree and the vineyard) and by making a double question out of 11:28. Mark reminds his readers of the setting in Jerusalem and the popularity of Jesus by means of the introductory 11:27a and the parenthetical sentence in 11:32, which includes a characteristically Markan *gar* ("for") clause. Mark may also have added the scribes and the elders to the list of opponents in 11:27b (the same three groups appear in 14:43 and 15:1).

The passage is arranged in a series of short scenes: (1) the Jewish leaders approach Jesus with a challenging question (11:27–28), (2) Jesus poses a counterquestion (11:29–30), (3) the leaders debate the counterquestion among themselves and return an inconclusive answer (11:31–33a), and (4) Jesus refuses to answer their original question (11:33b; on the form here, which is an adaptation of a Hellenistic convention, see Daube, *New Testament*, 151–57). As Davies and Allison (3.156) point out, the wording of this refusal (". . . by what authority I do these things") reproduces that of the leaders' original question ("By what authority are you doing these things?"), thus forming an inclusion around the passage. The macrostructure of this section of the Gospel is equally artful; as Dowd (*Prayer*, 38) points out, in its present form 11:12–33 forms a double intercalation:

Episode 1: fig tree is cursed (11:12–14)
Episode 2: Temple is cleansed (11:15–19)
Response 1: fig tree is observed to be withered (11:20–25)
Response 2: Temple action is challenged (11:27–33)

11:27–30: question and counterquestion. Jesus and his disciples now return to the "scene of the crime," the Jerusalem Temple that, on the previous day, he had cleared of traders. In so doing, he aroused the enmity of the chief priests and the scribes, who have consequently decided to kill him (11:27a; cf. 11:15–18). Ignoring the danger, however, Jesus begins walking about in his enemies' stronghold, the Temple, and is immediately accosted by a group of them, who ask him by what authority he has acted (11:28)—a reference first and foremost to the violent demonstration of the day before. The question contains implicit menace; those who presumed to act in God's name could, if their claims were invalidated, be executed as false prophets (see Deut 13:1–5; 18:20). Even short of capital punishment, an attack on the Temple could be dangerous to the perpetrator, as the example of Jesus son of Ananias shows (for this other Jesus, see Josephus, *War* 6.300–9, cited in the COMMENT on 13:1–2). The sovereign unconcern with which Jesus walks about in the Temple, therefore, is already a demonstration of the *exousia* ("authority") about which his enemies question him.

His initial reply to their challenge is also a demonstration of *exousia*, in that he refuses to answer directly but instead poses a counterquestion, adding that he will answer their inquiry only after his own has earned a response (11:29). Evans (204) rightly calls this reply a role reversal, and we may wonder whether it is historically plausible that the authorities would have acceded to it. Shae ("Question," 13–14) points out that the posing of a counterquestion is a standard feature of rabbinic debates (see, e.g., *b. Sanh.* 65b; *Gen. Rab.* 27.4), and Evans (203) notes that the same pattern occurs in Mark 12:13–17. But in these parallels, the counterquestion is something that both parties agree on, whereas in the present case, as we shall see, it is not.

The counterquestion is whether John's baptism was "from heaven" (i.e., from God; see the NOTE on "from heaven" in 11:30) or merely from human beings (on the Markan antithesis between the human and the divine, see the COMMENTS on 7:14–15 and 7:20–23 and the NOTE on "[the things] of human beings" in 8:33). This question places the Jewish leaders in a quandary, and their confusion and indecision are already suggested by Jesus' immediate reiteration of his demand, "Answer me!" (11:30; cf. 11:29b). In biblical dialogue, a character's repetition of a phrase, without intervening response, sometimes implies that his interlocutors have been rendered speechless (see, e.g., Gen 16:10–11; 20:9–10; 41:39–41; 42:1–2; cf. Alter, *Genesis*, 70, 94, 240, 244). Jesus' repetition of "Answer me!" also underlines his *exousia* again; as in the Johannine trial scene, he sounds more like a prosecuting attorney or a judge than like someone who is himself being interrogated (cf. John 18:19–24, 28–38; 19:1–11; Schnackenburg, 3.238–39, 259–67).

11:31–33: the leaders' response, and Jesus'. The Jewish leaders face a dilemma as they ponder their reply to Jesus' counterquestion about the validity and significance of Johannine baptism (11:31–32). They know how popular John's mission was, and how widespread the response to his call for repentance and cleansing baptism; indeed, according to Matt 3:7, even Pharisees and Sadducees joined in the Baptist movement. Denial of the divine authority of John's mission, then, does not seem to be a viable option, as it might turn popular opinion against the deniers. But neither is admitting its authority, since John's eschatological baptism was interwoven with his eschatological preaching about the coming one (see 1:4–8), and John seems to have identified Jesus with the latter (see the NOTE on "Why then did you not believe him?" in 11:31). Finding themselves unable either to affirm or to deny John's divine authorization, the leaders declare themselves agnostic ("We do not know," 11:33).

This is a damning admission: the highest religious authorities in the land claim not to know whether John, whose reputation for piety had been sealed by his martyrdom, had been sent by God. To be sure, the claim of agnosticism seems on the surface to be disingenuous; as the internal dialogue in 11:31–32 reveals, the leaders are more interested in the political ramifications of their response than they are in its truth (cf. Gnilka, 2.139). But Mark would probably say that such disinterest is itself a sign of an inability to discern the truth, so there is a sense in which the authorities' "We do not know" is accurate. Jesus, significantly, does not respond in kind, with a confession of ignorance, since in the Markan portrayal he is fully conscious of the source of his authority (cf. 3:22–27). He says, rather, "Neither *will I tell you* by what authority I do these things" (11:33). With this bold, even insolent refusal to answer the authorities' question, a response that is a final demonstration of *exousia*, the pericope concludes.

The question about authority would have been a pressing one for the members of the persecuted, marginal Markan community. By what authority did *they* presume to act? And who had bestowed this authority on *them*? Lacking recognition as followers of an authorized religion (cf. Clarke, "Religio Licita"), and finding themselves in conflict with the authorities of the religion that they *professed* to belong to, Judaism, they would have been in a weak position to meet such challenges. The obvious answer, that God had given them their authority, could not in itself convince either their enemies or members of "the crowd" who might be attracted to Christianity but had not yet committed themselves to it. Many people claim to receive messages from God; not many of them can verify their claims, and not a few of them turn out to be mad.

In this context, the way in which our passage alludes to John's support for Jesus is important. The Markan community believes in a Messiah who did not proclaim himself, who hid his identity in a cloak of indirection, but whose transcendent status was proclaimed by his famous and powerful forerunner. The "Jesus movement," therefore, did not come out of nowhere; these things were not "done in a corner" (Acts 26:26). There *was* a predecessor, and he proclaimed that Jesus' status would eventually trump his—as even the enemies of the Christians indirectly conceded by refusing to acknowledge the forerunner's divine commission.

By implication, Jesus possesses even greater *exousia* than John (cf. Matt 11:11//

Luke 7:28). The reader of this Gospel, however, knows that their divine commissions did not prevent either man from being rejected and murdered by his contemporaries (cf. 9:12–13)—a scenario that now is being repeated in the Markan community itself (cf. 13:9–13). This point will be confirmed in the immediately ensuing parable, in which a vineyard owner (God) sends a series of slaves (the prophets) to his recalcitrant tenants, including one whom they behead (John). He then sends his beloved son (Jesus), whom the tenants murder and cast out of the vineyard (12: 1–8). A divine commission, therefore, does not preclude a martyr's death; it may even demand it. But this passage will also demonstrate to Mark's readers that death is not the end, because there is another kind of *exousia* abroad in the world than the *katexousia* ("tyranny") of those who destroy, murder, and impose their violent wills upon their fellows (cf. 10:42–45). In the death of the innocent, which ransoms "many," the God who holds all *exousia* in his hand is secretly at work, transforming the rubble of destruction into the cornerstone of a new and living Temple in a way that confounds human reckoning: "This has come from the Lord, and it is amazing in our eyes" (12:10–11).

THE PARABLE OF THE VINEYARD (12:1–12)

12 ¹And he began to speak to them in parables: "A man planted a vineyard and put a fence around it, and dug out a wine vat, and built a tower, and let it out to tenant farmers, and went abroad. ²And at the proper time he sent a servant to the tenant farmers, that he might receive from the tenant farmers some of the fruits of the vineyard. ³And they took him and beat him and sent him away empty. ⁴And again, he sent to them another servant; him also they wounded in the head and dishonored. ⁵And he sent another; him also they killed, and many others, beating some, killing others. ⁶He still had one, his beloved son. He sent him last of all to them, saying, 'They will respect my son.' ⁷But those tenant farmers said among themselves, 'This is the heir. Come on, let's kill him, and the inheritance will be ours!' ⁸And they seized and killed him and threw him out of the vineyard. ⁹What then will the lord of the vineyard do? He will come and destroy the tenant farmers and give the vineyard to others. ¹⁰And have you not read this scripture: 'The stone that the builders rejected—it has become the head of the corner; ¹¹this has come from the Lord, and it is amazing in our eyes'?"

¹²And they wanted to arrest him, and yet they feared the crowd; for they knew that he had spoken the parable against them. And they left him and went away.

NOTES

12 1.*in parables. Gk en parabolais.* Although Mark uses the plural, there is only a single obvious parable here, that of the vineyard (12:1–9; cf. 3:23; 4:2, 10–11). The implication may be that Mark is presenting one of a larger number of parables that Jesus spoke at the time, or *parabolai* may designate the individual comparisons

within the larger story (cf. Schlatter, *Evangelien*, 96–99). It is also possible, however, that Mark regards the scriptural citation in 12:10–11 as a parable.

A man planted a vineyard. Gk *ampelōna anthrōpos ephyteusen*. This imagery and many other details in 12:1 come from Isaiah 5, where the vineyard stands for Israel and the man for God (see the COMMENT on 12:1–5). Such use of agricultural images for salvation-historical realities is common in the OT and postbiblical Judaism (cf. the COMMENTS on 4:3–8; 4:30–32; 11:12–14). Several rabbinic parables, for example, compare God to the owner of a planted field, and in *Sipre Deut.* 312 the owner takes the field away from tenant farmers who have plundered it (= the Gentiles) and gives it to his son (= Israel; cf. Stern, "Jesus' Parables," 60–61). It is possible that this is a rabbinic riposte to our text, in which the wicked tenants are Israel and the "others" to whom the vineyard is given are the church.

put a fence around it. Gk *periethēken phragmon.* In contrast to the other elements in 12:1 (vineyard, wine vat, tower), the fence is not present in Isa 5:1–2 MT, but it is in the LXX, which may preserve the original better than the MT; cf. Isa 5:5 MT, in which the angry owner removes the vineyard's fence.

dug out a wine vat, and built a tower. Gk *ōryxen hypolēnion kai ōkodomēsen pyrgon.* Ancient Jewish and Christian texts interpret the tower and wine vat in Isaiah 5 as the Temple and its altar (4Q500; *1 En.* 89:56, 66–67; *Barn.* 16:1–5; *Tg. Isa.* 5:1–2; *t. Suk.* 3:15; cf. Evans, "Vineyard Parables," and Brooke, "4Q500 1"). These identifications may carry over to the Markan passage, in which case the fence might stand for the walls of Jerusalem.

went abroad. Gk *apedēmēsen*, lit. "went away from home." Absentee landlords were a fact of life in first-century Palestine (see Jeremias, *Parables*, 75; Hengel, "Gleichnis," 21–23). As Hultgren (*Parables*, 264, 361) points out, the motif of a king or wealthy man leaving his servants in charge while he goes away is popular both in the parables of Jesus (cf. Mark 13:34//Luke 12:36; Matt 24:45–46// Luke 12:42–43; Matt 25:14–15//Luke 19:12–13) and in their rabbinic counterparts (*'Abot R. Nat.* 14 [Neusner, 107]; *Mekilta* Baḥodesh 5 [Lauterbach 2.236]; *Cant. Rab.* 7.14.1)

2. *at the proper time.* Gk *tǭ kairǭ*, lit. "at the time," but *kairos* often has the sense of the appropriate moment for doing something (cf. Matt 24:45//Luke 12:42; John 7:6, 8; BDAG 497).

some of the fruits of the vineyard. Gk *apo tōn karpōn tou ampelōnos*, lit. "from the fruits of the vineyard." The use of the partitive genitive (see Robertson, 519; MHT 3.209) emphasizes the kindness of the vineyard owner: he does not take all of the fruits, or even most of them, but only some.

4. *wounded in the head.* Gk *ekephaliōsan*. Unfortunately, this meaning is otherwise unattested for *kephalioun*, which elsewhere means "to sum up" (see Taylor, 474). But since the word for "head," *kephalē*, is included in the verb, "wounded in the head" is a good guess, although "head-butted" is also a possible meaning. Mark's readers might have thought of John the Baptist, who was beheaded (cf. 6:24–28), though the reference is out of place within the sequence of the parable; John would fit better among the "many others" of 12:5, who immediately precede the "beloved son." Still, it would be consonant with Markan theology

that the wound to the head of God's servant John is balanced by the exaltation of Jesus, the rejected stone, to "the head of the corner" (12:10; cf. the COMMENT on 6:29).

6. *He still had one, his beloved son.* Gk *eti hena eichen huion agapēton*, lit. "still one he had, a beloved son." The grammatically awkward phrase "beloved son" echoes the *ʿĀqēdāh*, the story of Abraham's near-sacrifice of his son Isaac (cf. Gen 22:2, 12, 16); in both cases "beloved son" occurs in a context of death (see Kazmierski, *Jesus*, 53–56, and the NOTE on "beloved" in 1:11).

Stern ("Jesus' Parables") suggests that, contrary to later Christian interpretations, for Jesus himself the "beloved son" was John the Baptist, who was murdered by Herod Antipas (see 6:14–29). The murder of the son, however, is presented as a collective decision by the tenant farmers, who are further identified as the "builders" (= religious leaders of the nation) in 12:10. These details fit Jesus, who persistently clashed with his nation's leadership, better than they do John, about whom such conflicts are not reported.

last of all. Gk *eschaton*. In Christian biblical theology, this neuter adjective (here used adverbially) has become a technical term for the end of days, and already in the LXX expressions such as *ep' eschatou tōn hēmerōn* ("at the end of days") are often used in "eschatological" contexts (see, e.g., Num 24:14; Deut 4:30; 32:20; Isa 2:2; Jer 30:24 [37:24 LXX]; Dan 10:14). This usage carries over to intertestamental Judaism (see, e.g., 1QSa 1:1; 1QpHab 2:5–6; 9:6; 4QFlor 1 1:15, 19) and the NT (see, e.g., 2 Tim 3:1; Heb 1:2; Jas 5:3; 2 Pet 3:3; cf. 1 Cor 15:26, 45, 52; 1 Pet 1:5, 20; 1 John 2:18; Jude 18).

will respect. Gk *entrapēsontai*. This verb can also mean "feel shame on account of" (LSJ 577 III 3b), and this may be a secondary meaning here (see the COMMENT on 12:6–9).

7. *Come on, let's kill him.* Gk *deute apokteinōmen auton*. This exhortation is probably an echo of the biblical story of Joseph and his brothers, since the tenants' words are identical with those of Joseph's evil brothers in Gen 37:20. The exhortation was memorable enough to be reapplied to the attempted murder of Joseph's wife in *Jos. Asen.* 27:8. Joseph's brothers, moreover, resolve to *throw* him into a pit, a further verbal connection with our parable (cf. "threw him out of the vineyard," Mark 12:8). Several of the references to the Joseph story in the *Testaments of the Twelve Patriarchs* emphasize Jacob/Israel's love for his son Joseph as the motivation for the other sons' attempt to kill him (*T. Sim.* 2:6–7; *T. Dan* 1:5–7; *T. Jos.* 1:2–3; cf. *T. Gad* 1:5 and Pesch, 2.219), and Joseph calls himself "the beloved of Israel" in *T. Jos.* 1:2–4, creating links with the "beloved son" of Mark 12:6. Perhaps because they recognize the Joseph typology, Matthew and Luke add a reference to the tenants seeing the vineyard owner's son as he approached them (Matt 21:38//Luke 20:14; cf. Gen 37:18). For another usage of the Joseph typology in the Jesus tradition, see Matt 24:45–51// Luke 12:42–46, and for later Christian examples, see Acts 7:9–16; *1 Clem* 4:9, Hubaut, *Parabole*, 46–50; Allison, *Intertextual Jesus*, 87–92.

and the inheritance will be ours. Gk *kai hēmōn estai hē klēronomia*. According to Jeremias (*Parables*, 74–76), the tenant farmers' hopes are rational, because (1) the owner is far away, probably abroad, and the indigenous peasants are rising up in revolt against him and the other foreign landlords; and (2) the son's arrival implies to the tenants that the owner is dead, and if they kill the son they can claim his land on the legal principle that ownerless property goes to the first person on the spot who can establish a claim by occupation (Jeremias here cites *y. B. Bat.* 3:3 [14a; Neusner, 30.59–62] and *b. B. Bat.* 54a). Jeremias' two scenarios, however, contradict each other: the first presupposes an anarchic wartime situation, the second a peacetime setting in which the rule of law prevails. Moreover, there is nothing in our story to indicate either that the tenants' action is part of a general revolt or that the tenants think the original owner dead, and neither Roman nor Jewish courts would have acknowledged the legal claim of tenants who had killed the previous owner. Although tenants who illegally occupied farms were sometimes difficult to dislodge (see Kloppenborg, "Self-Help," 516), it is hard to believe that usurping tenants could have reasonably expected to get away with murder. The tenants, rather, act irrationally, as God charges Israel with doing in Isa 1:2–3; 5:21 (on the relation of Isaiah 5 to our parable, see the COMMENT on 12:1–5).

The tenants' attempt to usurp the inheritance that rightfully belongs to the son may, for Mark's readers, echo debates between Christians and non-Christian Jews about the heirs of God's promises to Abraham (cf. Levenson, *Death*, 229). The Targum equates the vineyard in Isa 5:1 with the inheritance from Abraham (see de Moor, "Background," 77), and Jewish exegetes asserted, on the basis of OT passages such as Genesis 15, 17, and 21, that the Jews were Abraham's heirs (see, e.g., *Jub.* 1:19, 21; 22:9–10, 15, 29; *Pss. Sol.* 14:15). In 1QH 14[6]:8, however, the divine mercies do not extend to all Jews but only to the elect, who are called "the remnant in your inheritance," that is, in Israel (see Hammer, "Understanding," 42). Going further in the same direction, some first-century Christians claimed that they rather than the Jews were Abraham's heirs, an argument that was probably a response to the Jewish claim that becoming a child of Abraham was dependent on observance of the Torah (see Gal 3:6–29; Rom 4:13–25; Martyn, "Mission"; *Galatians*, 302–6). The inheritance dispute between Jews and Christians continued in the late first and early second centuries, as illustrated by *Barn.* 13:1: "Now let us see whether this people [the Christians] or the former people [the Jews] is the heir, and whether the covenant is for us or for them" (cf. *Barn.* 14:4 and Justin, *Dialogue* 25–27; cf. Hubaut, *Parabole*, 48–49).

8. *killed him and threw him out of the vineyard.* Gk *apekteinan auton kai exebalon auton exō tou ampelōnos.* Matthew 21:39 and Luke 20:15 change the order to "threw him out of the vineyard and killed him," reflecting both OT law (the blasphemer is to be put to death "outside the camp," Lev 24:14, 23) and the Christian memory that Jesus had suffered outside the walls of Jerusalem (Heb 13:12–13; cf. John 19:17, 20).

9. *the lord of the vineyard.* Gk *ho kyrios tou ampelōnos.* On a prosaic level, this phrase means "the master of the vineyard"; but since *Kyrios* is the translation for God's personal name YHWH in the LXX, and since the vineyard owner here stands for God, "lord of the vineyard" is probably a double entendre (cf. the

NOTES on "of the Lord" in 1:3 and "Lord" in 7:28 and the COMMENTS on 1:2–3 and 12:6–9).

He will come and destroy the tenant farmers and give the vineyard to others. Gk *eleusetai kai apolesei tous geōrgous kai dōsei ton ampelōna allois.* The element of retributive justice against the tenant farmers is not present in the *Gospel of Thomas* version of the parable (see the introduction to the COMMENT and figure 37), but it was probably part of the original rendering, which otherwise lacks closure; cf. John 15:1–8, which seems to be a Johannine mutation of the parable and contains this element. The vineyard owner's vengeance is not, however, a realistic feature, since neither Greco-Roman nor Jewish law would have permitted him to take the law into his own hands (see Kloppenborg, "Self-Help"). It probably, rather, reflects the parable's background in Isaiah 5 (see Isa 5:5–6 and the COMMENT on 12:1–5) and the persistent note of warning about judgment in the message of Jesus (see Reiser, *Jesus and Judgment*).

The immediate context of our text encourages readers to see the tenants as a symbol for the Jewish leaders; as recently as 11:18 the chief priests and the scribes have taken counsel to destroy Jesus (cf. 12:7), and since 11:27 these two groups, along with the elders, have been engaged in a hostile dialogue with him. When Jesus has finished the parable, moreover, the leaders perceive that it is directed against them, and they consequently want to arrest him. They are prevented from doing so only by their fear of the crowd, which at this stage in the narrative supports Jesus (12:12). If we follow the allegory strictly, then, the removal of the vineyard from the tenants and its transfer to "others" should refer to the deposition of the Jewish leadership from jurisdiction over Israel and the transfer of that authority to others, perhaps the leaders of the church, as in Acts 4:5–6, 11 (cf. Dahl, "Purpose," 91).

For Mark, however, both the tenant farmers and the "others" probably have a broader significance. By the end of the Gospel it is not just the leaders but also the Jerusalem crowd who reject Jesus (15:6–15). Mark 12:3–5, moreover, speaks allegorically of the murder of the prophets (see the COMMENT on 12:1–5), and in the OT, Jewish traditions, and the NT, these murders are laid at the door not only of Israel's leaders but also of the people as a whole (see Marcus, "Intertextual Polemic," 224 n. 14; cf. *1 En.* 89:52–53, cited in the COMMENT on 12:1–5). Readers, moreover, who knew (or could foresee) the climactic events of the Jewish War of 66–73 C.E.—the demolition of Jerusalem, the slaughter or deportation into slavery of its inhabitants and of masses of other Jews, and the confiscation and/or selling of at least some of the Jewish land in Judaea (see Josephus, *War,* 7.1–4, 216)—would have been reminded by the parable's conclusion of such wider consequences (cf. Smallwood, *Jews,* 339–51, and Isaac, "Judaea"). Therefore they would probably be inclined to link the banished tenants with a larger group than the Jewish leadership, and the favored "others" with a larger group as well—perhaps the increasingly Gentile church that was beginning to see itself as the true Israel (cf. Justin, *Dialogue* 52). Later Christians (see, e.g., Matt 23:37–39; Luke 21:20–24; *Gos. Pet.* 7:25; Justin, *Dialogue* 16; Tertullian, *Answer to the Jews* 13) and at least one pagan (see *Letter of Mara bar Sarapion*) saw the

Figure 37: The Parable of the Vineyard in the Synoptic Gospels and the Gospel of Thomas

Mark 12:1–12	Matthew 21:33–46	Luke 20:9–19	Gospel of Thomas 65–66
And he began to speak to them in parables:	Hear another parable:	And he began to say this parable to the people:	He said:
A man planted a vineyard	There was a man, a landowner, who planted a vineyard	A man planted a vineyard	A good man had a vineyard.
and put a fence around it	and put a fence around it		
and dug out a wine vat	and dug out a wine press in it		
and built a tower	and built a tower		
and let it out to tenant farmers	and let it out to tenant farmers	and let it out to tenant farmers	He gave it to tenant farmers so that they would work in it and he would receive its fruit from them.
and went away.	and went away.	and went away for a long time.	
And at the proper time	And when the time for the fruits drew near	And at the proper time	
he sent a servant to the tenant farmers	he sent his servants to the tenant farmers	he sent a servant to the tenant farmers	He sent his servant
that he might receive from the tenant farmers of the fruits of the vineyard.	to receive his fruits.	that they might give him from the fruit of the vineyard.	so that the tenant farmers would give him the fruit of the vineyard.
And seizing him,	And the tenant farmers, seizing his servants,	But the tenant farmers sent him back empty	Seizing his servant,
they beat him	beat one,	after beating him.	they beat him
and sent him away empty.	killed one,		and almost killed him.
	and stoned one.		
			The servant came and told it to his master.
			His master said, Perhaps they did not know him.
And again, he sent to them another servant;	Again he sent other servants, more than the first ones,	And he proceeded to send another servant.	He sent another servant;
him also they wounded in the head and dishonored.	and they did to them likewise.	But they also sent this one back empty after having beaten and dishonored him.	the tenant farmers beat the other one too.
And he sent another;		And he proceeded to send a third;	
him also they killed		but they severely wounded this one and threw him out.	

others.

He still had one, his beloved son.
He sent him last of all to them, saying,
They will respect my son.
But those tenant farmers said among
themselves, This is the heir.
Come on, let's kill him, and the
inheritance will be ours!
And they seized
and killed him
and threw him out of the vineyard.

What then will the owner of the
vineyard do?
He will come and destroy the tenant
farmers
and he will give the vineyard to others.

And have you not read this scripture:
The stone that the builders rejected

it has become the cornerstone;
this has come from the Lord
and it is amazing in our eyes?

Finally he sent to them his son,
saying, They will respect my son.
But the tenant farmers, seeing the son, This is the
heir.
said among themselves,
Come on, let's kill him, and we shall
have his inheritance!
And seizing him
they threw him out of the vineyard
and killed [him].

When therefore the owner of the
vineyard comes, what will he
do to those tenants?
They said to him, He will destroy the
evildoers evilly
and he will give away the vineyard to
other tenant farmers
who will render back to him the fruits in
their proper times.

Jesus said to them,
Have you never read in the scriptures:
The stone that the builders rejected

it has become the cornerstone;
this has come from the Lord
and it is amazing in our eyes?

The master of the vineyard said, What
shall I do?
I will send my beloved son;
perhaps they will respect him.
But the tenant farmers, seeing him,
discussed among themselves, saying,
This is the heir.
Let's kill him, that the inheritance
might be ours!
And throwing him out of the vineyard
they killed [him].
What then will the owner of the
vineyard do to them?
He will come and destroy these tenant
farmers
and he will give the vineyard to others.

Hearing it they said, May it not be!
But he, looking at them, said,
What then is this that has been written:
The stone that the builders rejected

it has become the cornerstone?

And everyone who falls upon that stone
will be crushed,
and him upon whom it falls, it will
pulverize him.

Then the owner sent his son,
saying, Perhaps they will respect my
son.
Those tenant farmers, knowing that he
was the heir of the vineyard

seized
and killed him.

Whoever has ears, let him hear!

Jesus said,

Show me the stone that the builders
rejected;
it is the cornerstone.

destruction of the Temple and the associated sufferings of the Jews as punishment for their murder of the prophets, Jesus, and the Christians. The possibility of a wider referent for the Markan tenants is enhanced by the wording of *Tg. Isa.* 5:6: "And I will make them [to be] banished; they will not be helped and they will not be supported, and they will be cast out and forsaken" (Chilton trans.). Here the OT passage that undergirds our parable (see the COMMENT on 12:1–5) is reinterpreted as an allusion to the exile of the Jews from their land. Similarly, *Pss. Sol.* 9:1, a pre-Christian text, speaks of the exile of the Jews from their "inheritance" as punishment for their sins: "When Israel was taken into exile to a foreign country, when they neglected the Lord, who had redeemed them, they were expelled from the inheritance which the Lord had given them."

Mark, then, seems to be moving in the direction of Matthew's supersessionist (see the GLOSSARY) interpretation of the parable (see Matt 21:43), although he is less explicit than Matthew. On the hermeneutical problems posed by supersessionist texts, see the COMMENT on 12:6–9.

10. *The stone that the builders rejected.* Gk *lithon hon apedokimasan hoi oikodomountes.* It is possible that in the original form of the parable there was a play on words between the Hebrew terms for "son" (*ben*), "stone" (*'eben*), and "builders" (*bônîm*; see Black, "Theological Appropriation," 12). While Jesus spoke Aramaic rather than Hebrew, Snodgrass (*Parable*, 113–18) points out that *'eben* and *ben* are sometimes retained in the Aramaic Targums; *bônîm*, moreover, has an Aramaic cognate.

Mark 12:10–11 is a quotation from Ps 118:22–23 [117:22–23 LXX]; verses 25–26 of the same psalm were recited by the ecstatic crowd at Jesus' triumphal entry into Jerusalem in 11:9–10 (see the NOTE on "Blessed is he who comes in the name of the Lord!" in 11:9 and the COMMENT on 11:7–11). In its original context the psalm speaks of Israel besieged by the hostile nations that surround it yet triumphant over them through the power of God; Israel itself, therefore, or its Davidic king, may originally have been the stone despised by "the builders" (of empires?) but exalted to the central position in God's Temple (see the next NOTE). A Cairo Genizah text, the "Fragment of the Songs of David," which is dated by Flusser and Safrai ("Fragment") to the first century, reinterprets the rejected stone as the Davidic Messiah, whose exaltation is his military triumph over "all the nations" that have scorned him (the Targum and the *Midrash Psalms* also apply these verses to David). The Jewish revolutionaries whose struggle forms the backdrop to our Gospel, and who may have been led by putative "Messiahs," probably interpreted the psalm in a similar way (see Marcus, *Way*, 115–18). The Markan Jesus' use of the psalm to rebuke the leaders of Israel and threaten that their "vineyard" will be turned over to "others" may therefore be an inversion of a popular scriptural interpretation.

the head of the corner. Gk *kephalēn gōnias.* Jeremias ("*Kephalē gōnias*" and "Eckstein") argues that this is not a foundation stone but an elevated cornerstone or keystone (the "corner" could be the point of an arch). His chief evidence for this view is *Test. Sol.* 22:7–9; 23:1–4, in which King Solomon says, "And there was a great cornerstone (*lithos akrogōniaios*) that I wished to put at the head of the corner (*eis kephalēn gōnias*) crowning the Temple of God. And all the tradesmen and all the spirits who labored on it came together to bring the stone and set it on the pinnacle of the Temple" (*eis to pterygion tou naou*; J. H. Elliott trans., *1 Peter*, 429). They are unable to budge the stone, but Solomon constrains a powerful demon to lift it, carry it up a flight of stairs, and insert it into the keystone position; he then exults in the words of Ps 118:22. Other scholars, however, suggest that in our passage a foundational cornerstone is meant, arguing that the later legend in *Testament of Solomon* does not demonstrate the original meaning of Psalm 118, that *kephalē* can indicate horizontal rather than vertical extension, and that 1 Pet 2:6–8 implies that the *kephalē gōnias* of Psalm 118 is equivalent to the *lithos akrogōniaios* ("cornerstone") of Isa 28:16 (see, e.g., McKelvey, "Cornerstone"; J. H. Elliott, *1 Peter*, 429–30; BDAG 542 [2b]).

Despite these objections, Jeremias' interpretation seems more likely. The word *kephalē* usually suggests vertical extension, and that is especially likely when an allusion is being made to Jesus' resurrection (cf. 12:36, where the latter is described as an exaltation to God's right hand). The issue, moreover, is not the original meaning of "head of the corner" in Psalm 118 but the meaning of the phrase in NT times, and *Test. Sol.* 22:7–9 is strong evidence for a vertical interpretation of the latter and for a distinction rather than an identity between *kephalē gōnias* and *lithos akrogōniaios*. As for 1 Pet 2:6–8, this passage brings together, by the principle of *gĕzērāh šāwāh* (see the GLOSSARY), three OT passages that speak of stones, interpreting all three as references to Jesus, but the cornerstone from Isa 28:16 and the stone of stumbling from Isa 8:14 clearly differ from each other, and the *kephalē gōnias* from Ps 118:22 [117:22 LXX] is not necessarily identical with either. It is best, then, to think of the *kephalē gōnias* in Mark as an elevated stone, and Stern (*Parables*, 195) may capture Mark's thought when he writes that such a stone "must be irregularly shaped in order to fit its strategic position at the apex of the arch. In other words: the stone that the builders initially rejected because it seemed misshapen proved in the end to be the perfect shape for the capstone."

11. *amazing.* Gk *thaumastē*. This word recalls the Markan miracle stories, which often end on a note of amazement (1:27; 2:12; 5:20; etc.; see the subject index in vols. 1 and 2 under "Amazement"). Several Markan passages imply that Jesus healed people through the same power that God would later use to raise him from the dead (see the NOTE on "Rise!" in 5:41 and the COMMENTS on 1:29–31; 2:10b–12; 8:1–4; 9:25–27). It is no surprise, then, to see amazement associated here with Jesus' resurrection.

12. *and yet they feared the crowd.* Gk *kai ephobēthēsan ton ochlon.* The "yet" is not present in the Greek, but it is implied by the contrast with the previous clause: the leaders want to arrest Jesus but are unable to do so because of the crowd's support for him, which they are afraid to oppose.

for they knew that he had spoken the parable against them. Gk *egnōsan gar hoti pros autous tēn parabolēn eipen.* This is an example of Mark's tendency to displace words or clauses (cf. the NOTES on "[. . .]immediately[. . .]" in 1:10; 1:21; 1:29; 6:25). The *gar* ("for") clause explains why the authorities wished to arrest Jesus, not why they were afraid of the crowd.

COMMENT

Introduction. After parrying the religious leaders' hostile challenge to his authority, Jesus tells a parable that suggests their spiritual sterility, unmasks their murderous intentions, and prophesies that they will be destroyed when "the lord of
the vineyard" comes in power and judgment. This parable, moreover, hints at the
answer to the question he had previously evaded (11:28): he has the authority to do
"these things" because he is God's beloved son (12:6).

In terms of redaction history, the structure of parable (12:1–9) + scriptural interpretation (12:10–11) is probably original; it corresponds to the common rabbinic
combination of *māšāl* (parable) + *nimšāl* (interpretation), the latter of which often
consists simply of a proof text (see Stern, *Parables*, 18), and the combination of the
two is supported by the *Gospel of Thomas* parallel (65–66). The Qumran text 1QS
8:4–10, moreover, combines the image of the elect community as an everlasting
plant (cf. the vineyard in our parable) with that of a precious cornerstone that does
not shake (cf. the cornerstone in 12:10–11; see Brooke, "4Q500"), and 1QS 11:7–8
merges it with the themes of election (cf. the beloved son in 12:6), inheritance
(cf. 12:7), and a holy building (cf. again 12:10–11 and see Hammer, "Understanding," 44).

The *Gospel of Thomas* parallel features three embassies rather than four and
lacks the detailed description of construction work found in Mark 12:1 and the
account of retributive justice in Mark 12:9 (see figure 37). Many scholars (e.g.,
Jeremias, *Parables*, 70–77; Crossan, *Parables*, 86–99) think this simpler Thoma-
sine form original, but it is possible that these differences reflect Thomas' lack of
interest in the OT echoes in 12:1 and his offense at the judgment theme in 12:9,
and Thomas may have introduced the gnostic motif of the tenants not recognizing the servant. Some of the other variations of Mark from the *Gospel of Thomas*,
however, may represent Markan editing, since they reflect prominent Markan
themes or vocabulary: "the proper time" (*tǭ kairǭ*) in 12:2 (cf. 1:15; 14:11), "many
others" in 12:5 (*polloi* is one of Mark's favorite words), and the turning of the vineyard over to "others" 12:9 (see the subject index in vols. 1 and 2 under "Gentiles").
Also probably Markan are the introductory 12:1a and the coda in 12:12.

The passage falls into two major parts: the parable itself (12:1b–9) and its scriptural interpretation (12:10–11); these major portions are framed by matching references to Jesus' interaction with the hostile Jewish leaders (12:1a, 12). The parable
proper may be subdivided into the preliminary 12:1–5, which is characterized by
parataxis, and the climactic 12:6–9, which is characterized by hypotaxis (on these
terms, see the GLOSSARY).

12:1–5: the construction of the vineyard and the mistreatment of the servants. Following his verbal coup against the leaders' challenge to his authority (11:27–33),
Jesus goes on the offensive against them "in parables" (on parables as verbal weapons, see Marcus, *Mystery*, 108). The particular parable chosen by Jesus deals with
a man, his vineyard, and the tenant farmers to whom he lets it. He begins by describing in elaborate detail the man's construction of a vineyard, which he plants

and fences in, then augments with a wine vat and tower (12:1b). This description is reminiscent of the most famous "vineyard" passage in scripture, Isa 5:1–2, and Mark's vocabulary echoes the LXX of this passage ("vineyard," "plant," "put around," "fence," "dig," "wine vat," "build," and "tower"; cf. Evans, 224–25). In Isaiah 5 itself, the vineyard is Israel (see Isa 5:7), and this identification fits in with the general context of Jesus' polemic against the Jewish leaders (cf. 12:1a, 12) and his recent attack on their central institution, the Temple (11:15–18). Beyond this foundational vineyard image, and the identification of the man as God (see below), some of the other features of 12:1 may also have an allegorical significance (see the NOTE on "dug out a wine vat, and built a tower"), but the main purpose of 12:1 is not to present an elaborate allegory but to emphasize, with scripturally resonant language, the loving care of the owner in creating and protecting his vineyard. In contrast to the long and detailed description of the construction work, the owner's subsequent actions are summarized tersely: he lets the vineyard out to tenants and goes away (12:1c).

The absentee landlord, however, has not forgotten his vineyard; "at the proper time," that is, the time of the harvest, he commissions a servant to collect some of its fruits from the tenants (12:2). This servant meets with a bad reception; the tenants beat him and send him away empty-handed (12:3), keeping the fruits for themselves. In biblical narrative, "fruits" is often a loaded term, designating the reward God gives to the just or the form of human life that should grow out of a proper relationship with him (see, e.g., Ps 1:3; Isa 3:10; Matt 3:8–10//Luke 3:8–9; Gal 5:22; and cf. Isa 5:2, 4). The denial of fruits to the vineyard owner and the mistreatment of his servant (12:3), therefore, are ominous developments that already place the tenants in a bad light, especially since the servant is dispatched "at the proper time" (*tǭ kairǭ*; cf. the NOTE on "at the proper time" in 12:2). Class-conscious interpretations of the parable that call for identification with the landless, impoverished tenants and a negative judgment on the rapacious absentee landlord, therefore, are questionable, especially since the parable gives no indication either that the tenants are destitute or that the landlord is excessive in his demands (against Malina and Rohrbaugh, *Commentary*, 255; Hester, "Criticism")—indeed, quite the contrary (see the NOTE on "some of the fruits of the vineyard" in 12:2 and de Moor, "Background," 65). The landowner, rather, is a cipher for God, as in the scriptural base-text of Isaiah 5 and many rabbinic parables (see the NOTE on "A man planted a vineyard" in 12:1).

Undeterred by the mistreatment of his first messenger, the owner dispatches a second on the same mission (12:4); like his predecessor, however, this messenger is abused, suffering a wound to the head (see the NOTE on "wounded in the head" in 12:4). Still not daunted, the owner sends a third servant, then many others, all of whom are either beaten or killed (12:5). This series of mistreated messengers would probably remind Mark's hearers of the prophets, who in the OT and later Jewish literature were called God's servants and often suffered ill-treatment from their fellow Israelites and the people's leaders (see, e.g., 1 Kgs 18:4, 13; 19:10; 2 Chron 16:10; 24:21; Jer 2:30; 20:2; *Jub.* 1:12; *Asc. Isa.* 2:16; 5:1–14; *Liv. Pro.* passim; Josephus, *Ant.* 10.38; cf. Steck, *Israel*). The prophets' mistreatment, moreover, is cited frequently in the NT as an anticipation of the persecution suffered by Jesus and his followers (1 Thess 2:15; Matt 5:12//Luke 6:23; Matt 23:31, 34, 37; Luke 11:47–49; 13:33–34; Acts 7:52). An especially striking intertestamental Jewish parallel, *1 En.* 89:52–53, uses allegorical language similar to ours to speak of the prophets' persecution and murder:

> And the Lord of the sheep [= the Israelites] summoned some [= the prophets] from among the sheep and sent them to the sheep, and the sheep began to kill them, but one of them [= Elijah] escaped safely and was not killed. It sprang away and cried out over the sheep, and they wished to kill it; but the Lord of the sheep saved it from the hands of the sheep and brought it up to me and made it dwell (there). And many other sheep he sent to those sheep to testify and lament over them. (Nickelsburg trans.)

Not only the embassy from "the lord of the sheep" (cf. "the lord of the vineyard" in Mark 12:9) but also the murder of those sent, who include "many other[s]," are reminiscent of our passage. One of these ambassadors, moreover, escapes the common fate by exaltation to a superterrestrial abode within sight of the heavenly Temple (cf. *1 En.* 87:3; see Tiller, *Commentary,* 248–50). This is similar to the implication of Mark 12:10 that Jesus will be exalted to become the keystone of a new Temple (see the COMMENT on 12:10–12). Furthermore, in the continuation of the *1 Enoch* passage, the lord of the sheep abandons his house (= Jerusalem) and its tower (= the earthly Temple; cf. the NOTE on "dug out a wine vat, and built a tower" in 12:1), allowing them to be destroyed, as punishment for the murder of his messengers (*1 En.* 89:54–56). Similarly, in Mark, the lord of the vineyard punishes the wicked tenants by destroying them and transferring the vineyard to others—an allusion, perhaps, to the destruction of Jewish sovereignty in Palestine in the war that demolished the Temple (cf. the NOTE on "He will come and destroy the tenant farmers and give the vineyard to others" in 12:9).

12:6–9: the murder of the son. In a difference from the course of events in *1 Enoch* 89, however, the figure in Mark who is exalted to heaven is first subjected to ignominious murder. This dramatic development in the narrative is signaled by the asyndeton of 12:6a (see the GLOSSARY), which has an ominous ring: *eti hena eichen,* "He still had one." Not for very long, however, once he sends this last messenger into the killing fields, saying in a stage whisper, "They will respect my son" (12:6b). The repetition of the last word ("beloved *son* . . . they will respect my *son*") highlights the pathos of the father's dispatch of his offspring, while the word for "last of all," *eschaton,* would remind Mark's hearers of the salvation-historical horizon of the parable, which echoes the gracious way in which the God of the OT kept sending messengers to Israel despite their recalcitrance (see the NOTE on "last of all" in 12:6 and Gnilka, 2.146). Although at first glance the father's prophecy, "They will respect my son," seems astoundingly naive given the tenants' abuse and murder of the previous messengers, in the Markan context it probably contains a grim irony: in the end the tenants *will* "respect" the son, when they pay for his murder with their lives (12:9) and see him returning "in the glory of his Father with the holy angels" (8:38; cf. 13:26 and the NOTE on "will respect" in 12:6).

At first, the tenant farmers' response to the father's final embassy appears encouraging: "This is the heir. Come on . . ." (12:7a). Readers might momentarily imagine that the tenants have recognized the son as his father's surrogate and therefore have decided, rationally enough, to leave him alone; perhaps "Come on" will be followed by "let's get out of here!" But if 12:7a raises such hopes, 12:7b immediately dashes them; instead of adopting the prudent course of respecting the son, the tenants adopt the insane one of murdering him and trying to appropriate his inheritance for themselves (see the NOTE on "and the inheritance will be ours" in 12:7). Their recognition of the son, then, turns out to be analogous to that of the demons, who realize that Jesus is God's son, but for that very reason oppose him with might and main and thereby seal their own destruction (see 1:24; 3:11).

The words in which the tenants express their resolve, "let's kill him," are probably an intentional echo of the speech of Joseph's evil brothers in Gen 37:20 (see the NOTE on "Come on, let's kill him" in 12:7). There are also, however, significant differences from the story invoked, which Mark might expect biblically literate readers to recognize (on the rhetorical strategy of discontinuity-within-continuity, see Sandnes, *"Imitatio Homeri?"*). Unlike the wicked tenants in Mark, the brothers in Genesis do *not* succeed in carrying out their plan to kill "the beloved son," who in fact prospers, becoming the lord of Egypt. Joseph consequently ends up forgiving his brothers and discerning the hand of God in their actions against him (Gen 45:4–8); in *T. Benj.* 3:6–8 he even begs his father, Jacob, who is otherwise inclined, to join him in forgiving them. In Mark, by contrast, the father does *not* forgive the persecutors of his son, who has *not* been saved, but executes merciless judgment upon them. That judgment seems to follow the principle of *lex talionis* (see the GLOSSARY): the tenants have *killed* the son and *cast him out of the vineyard* (12:8); in retaliation, the "lord of the vineyard" will *destroy* them and *give the vineyard to others* (12:9).

How are we to decode the parable's concluding note of harsh retributive justice? As the NOTE on "He will come and destroy the tenant farmers and give the vineyard to others" in 12:9 shows, the immediate context (11:27; 12:1, 12) suggests that the tenants stand for the Jewish leaders who oppose Jesus and who, in the Gospel's narrative, will be primarily responsible for his death (on the question of the historicity of this ascription, see the introduction to 14:1–15:47). The "others," then, would be the leaders of the church, who will assume jurisdiction over "Israel" when its own leadership disqualifies itself through rejection of Jesus (cf. Matt 19:28; Luke 22:29–30). But the Christian readers of the Markan parable probably knew of or could foresee the effects of the Jewish War of 66–73 C.E., in which not only the leaders but also the people suffered, and in which Jerusalem was leveled, its inhabitants slaughtered or deported to slavery, and the land of at least some Judaean Jews confiscated (see the NOTE on "He will come and destroy the tenant farmers and give the vineyard to others" in 12:9). It seems likely, then, that they would read the parable's conclusion through the lens of these events and therefore ascribe a wider significance to the parable: Israel has lost its status as the people of God—as symbolized by its catastrophic defeat in the war—and has been replaced by the church.

Our parable thus moves in the direction of supersessionism (see the GLOSSARY and cf. Levenson, *Death*, 227–29), but that does not mean that present-day Christian readers are required to follow it there. The parable is almost a parody of Isaiah 5; the people of Israel are no longer symbolized by the vineyard, which in Isaiah remains God's treasured possession despite his anger at its misuse (cf. Marcus, "Intertextual Polemic," 214–16, on the tendency of Jewish exegesis to find a hint of continuing divine commitment in the reference to Israel as the Lord's vineyard in Isa 5:7a). They are represented, rather, by workers who have contracted to tend the vineyard and who can easily be replaced if they prove unsuitable for the job. A large part of the reason for this deformation of the original Isaian image lies in the tense historical situation of Jesus and the early Christians, which culminated in the persecution and revolutionary violence directed against the Markan community during the Jewish War. This deformation, however, cannot simply be accepted as "gospel" by modern-day Christians after seventeen centuries of a *different* sort of outrage, namely, Christian persecution of Jews. Perhaps, rather, modern-day Christians need to take a step backward from Mark to Isaiah, which after all is part of their canon, too, "to follow the roots of Mark's rented and forfeited vineyard backward into Isaiah's tenderly nurtured vineyard that has sprung Eden-like from God's hand, and to which he remains committed in spite of all the wild growth that has sprung up there and that grieves his heart—as he also remains committed to us in spite of all the wildness and murder that have sprung up in ours" (Marcus, "Intertextual Polemic," 223).

12:10–12: the interpretation of the parable. The Markan Jesus concludes his discourse by shifting the scriptural referent from Isaiah 5 to Psalm 118:22–23 [117:22–23 LXX]. Although this psalm quotation may originally have been linked with the parable by means of a Hebrew pun (see the NOTE on "the stone that the builders rejected" in 12:10), the wordplay is absent in Mark's Greek. The Markan connection between parable and interpretation is of a subtler and more significant kind. The only note of vindication in the parable is communal; the vineyard is taken away from Israel and its leaders and given to "others," the members of the new Israel, the Christian church. The interpretation in 12:10–12, however, adds the note of personal vindication lacking in the parable itself: the rejected stone, which readers would naturally link with the murdered son, is exalted to the head of the corner. Christians would immediately recognize this exaltation as a cipher for Jesus' resurrection (cf. the use of the same scripture for the same purpose in Acts 4:11–12 and 1 Pet 2:4–10). But the communal emphasis of the parable is not entirely lost in this scene of personal vindication, because the rejected stone becomes the capstone of a new Temple, and this scenario was interpreted in early Christianity as a reference to Christ's foundation, through his death and resurrection, of a sanctuary of "living stones," that is, the Christian community (cf. again 1 Pet 2:4–10; on Jewish parallels to the idea of the community as a Temple, see McKelvey, *New Temple*, 46–53).

The foundation of this new Temple through the vindication of the rejected "stone" is described, in the conclusion of the psalm quotation, as a work of God: "this has come from the Lord" (12:11a). This emphasis again indirectly answers the scribes' hostile question in 11:28 (see the introduction to the COMMENT): Jesus' authority comes not from human beings but "from the Lord," from heaven (cf. 11:30–31), to which he will soon be exalted. The psalm goes on to describes this exaltation as "amazing in our eyes" (12:11b), a phrase that anticipates the positive reaction to Jesus' message both by Mark's readers and by the crowd, whose presence seems to be implied by12:12b. But a response of amazement can also have a negative connotation (cf. the COMMENTS on 6:1–3 and 12:15–17), and that nuance may also be present here, since Jesus' primary audience is the religious leadership with which he has just locked horns (12:12c). *Their* amazement is their stupefaction at his effrontery in predicting their demise (cf. 12:9), and they therefore renew their efforts to arrest him, with the object of destroying *him* (12:12a; cf. 11:18a). Thwarted by the presence of the crowd (12:12b), however, they "left him and went away"—a redundant phrase that probably emphasizes not only their physical removal from Jesus but also their alienation from him and the God he represents (cf. John 13:30).

Their withdrawal does not signal surrender but merely the adoption of a subtler approach. From now on they will not confront Jesus directly but will act through surrogates—even as they themselves, in Mark's view, are surrogates for Jesus' *real* enemies, the demons (see the subject index in vols. 1 and 2 under "Enemies of Jesus, human and demonic"). In the next passage, they will dispatch Pharisees and Herodians to try to trip Jesus up in the political minefield of first-century Jewish relationships with Rome.

JESUS IS QUESTIONED ABOUT PAYING TAXES TO THE EMPEROR (12:13–17)

12 ¹³And they sent to him some of the Pharisees and some of the Herodians, that they might trap him in his speech. ¹⁴And they came and said to him, "Teacher, we know that you are truthful and that you don't care what anyone thinks. For you don't look at the face of human beings, but you teach the way of God truthfully. Is it permissible to give tribute money to Caesar or not? Shall we give, or shall we not give?" ¹⁵But he, seeing their pretense, said to them, "Why are you testing me? Bring me a denarius, so that I may see it." ¹⁶And they brought one. And he said to them, "Whose image is this, and whose inscription?" And they said to him, "Caesar's." ¹⁷And Jesus said to them, "Pay to Caesar the things of Caesar, and the things of God to God." And they were amazed at him.

NOTES

12 13. *the Herodians.* Gk *tōn Hērǫdianōn.* On the identity of the Herodians, see Meier (*Marginal Jew*, 3.560–65, and "Herodians"), who considers the fourteen(!)

major options for interpreting this term—which appears only in our passage, its Matthean parallel (22:16), and Mark 3:6. Meier concludes that "Herodians" means "the household servants or slaves of Herod, his officials or courtiers . . . and more generally all the supporters of Herod's regime, whether or not they belonged to an organized group or party." Since the Herodian dynasty was supported by the Romans, the Herodians would probably have insisted on payment of taxes to Caesar. As late as 66 C.E., Agrippa II, a Herodian ruler, tried to persuade his fellow Jews to pay their taxes and thus avert the Great Revolt (*War* 2.404). When he failed, and the Jews withheld their taxes, the war ensued (cf. *War*, 5.405–6; Hengel, *Zealots*, 137–38).

Despite such speculations, the truth is that we know nothing for certain about the Herodians, since the few NT texts that mention them tell us nothing about them.

trap. Gk *agreusōsin*. The verb means "to take by hunting or fishing, to catch" (LSJ 14); for other hunting metaphors in Mark, see 1:17, 36.

14. *we know.* Gk *oidamen*. A few lines earlier, Jesus' chief opponents said *ouk oidamen*, "We do not know," in answer to the question whether John the Baptist's authority, and hence Jesus', was human or divine (11:33). Now, however, their agents say "we know" that Jesus is truthful and teaches the way of God. Although this statement is insincere (see "seeing their pretense" in 12:15), the reader would regard it as an unwitting witness to the truth (cf. Evans, 245).

and that you don't care what anyone thinks. Gk *kai ou melei soi peri oudenos*, lit. "and you don't care about no one," a typically Markan double negative, a form more acceptable in ancient Greek than in modern English. "And that you don't care about anything" is also a possible translation, but the context suggests that the Pharisees and Herodians are trying to get Jesus into trouble by making him offend the dignity of the emperor, so a personal interpretation of *peri oudenos* is more likely.

For you don't look at the face of human beings. Gk *ou gar blepeis eis prosōpon anthrōpōn.* In Semitic contexts "face" is a synonym for a person's appearance, dignity, or identity, and "receiving the face" means showing partiality (see Koehler-Baumgartner, 2.940; Lust, *Lexicon*, 2.406–7; BDAG 888 [2–4]). The Markan phrase "look at the face" is a variation on this idiom; Van Rompay ("Rendering," 570) considers it "an attempt to translate the idiomatic Hebrew expression in a way more understandable to Greek readers." Elsewhere, however, Mark uses Semitisms freely (see the subject index in vols. 1 and 2 under "Semitisms"), and other NT writers do not seem to worry about the intelligibility of "receiving the face" (see Luke 20:21; Gal 2:6; Jas 2:9; etc.). Mark's "look at the face," rather, may consciously echo 1 Sam 16:7: "For God does not see (*opsetai*) as a human being looks (*emblepsetai*); for a human being looks (*opsetai*) at the face (*prosōpon*), but God looks at the heart." On this passage, see further the COMMENT on 12:13–14.

Is it permissible. Gk *exestin.* In Matt 17:24 a similar question arises about paying the didrachma Temple tax, but it is not worded in terms of the *permissibility* of such payments, as the present question is. Payment of the Temple tax, unlike payment of tribute to Caesar, was not problematic from the point of view of Jewish law, since it did not involve acknowledging foreign overlordship of the Holy Land and using a coin that might be considered idolatrous (see the COMMENTS on 12:13–14 and 12:15–17).

tribute money. Gk *kēnson.* This is a Latin loanword ("census") that originally meant a registration of property for the purposes of taxation (cf. Lewis and Short, 315). In Greek, however, the word came to mean the tax itself, specifically the "head tax" (*tributum capitis*), that is, the poll tax (D and some ancient versions substitute *epikephalaion* ["head tax"] and its synonyms for *kēnson*; cf. Hart, "Coin," 241). As Hengel (*Zealots*, 135–36) points out, it is a measure of the hatred the *kēnsos* aroused that it came into Hebrew and Aramaic as a loanword meaning "fine" or "penalty" (*qĕnās, qĕnāsāʾ*; see Jastrow, 1393–94). The Jews were not the only imperial subjects who bitterly resented the Roman head tax as a symbol of subservience; cf. Shakespeare's *Cymbeline* (3.1), in which a character from the newly conquered British Isles defiantly asserts that "Britain is / A world by itself; and we will nothing pay / For wearing our own noses."

to Caesar. Gk *Kaisari.* After Julius Caesar's assassination in 44 B.C.E., his family name was taken over by his adopted son, Octavian, who became the emperor Augustus; Augustus subsequently transmitted the cognomen Caesar to those whom he adopted and their direct descendants, including the emperors Tiberius and Caligula. The later emperors Claudius and Nero also called themselves Caesar, though they were not in the line of descent from Julius Caesar and Augustus; at least by their time, "Caesar" had become synonymous with "emperor." The title proved remarkably durable; both the German "Kaiser" and the Russian "Tsar" are versions of it (cf. Badian, "Iulius Caesar"; Jones, "Caesar").

15. *seeing.* Gk *idōn.* Most texts have "knowing" (*eidōs*), but the evidence for *idōn* includes important early manuscripts and Alexandrian, Western, and Caesarean text-types (א*, D, *f*[13], 28, 565, *pc*, it). *Idōn*, moreover, is the more difficult reading (how can one *see* hypocrisy?), but it is in accord with Markan usage elsewhere (see "seeing their faith" in 2:5 and cf. 12:28, where there is the same sort of variation between *idōn* and *eidōs* in the manuscripts).

pretense. Gk *hypokrisin*, from which the English "hypocrisy" comes. The word derives from the verb *hypokrinesthai* = "to answer" (cf. *apokrinesthai*, the normal NT term for "to answer"), which then becomes a term for taking part in a dialogue and hence for playing a role on stage (see LSJ 1885). If there was an Aramaic underlay to our story, however, the base conception was probably different. The Ḥarklean Syriac version renders "their pretense" with *messab ʾappêhun* = "their taking a face," a phrase that can, in other Aramaic dialects, mean "showing partiality" (see Jastrow, 915; Sokoloff, *Palestinian Aramaic*, 70) and is in fact almost identical with the phrase that the Sinaiticus codex of the Syriac uses in 12:14 to speak about partiality (*nĕsab . . . bʾappēʾ*; cf. the NOTE on "for you don't look at the face of human beings" in 12:14). It is possible, therefore, that an early Aramaic version of our narrative punned on two senses of "taking a face," that is, showing partiality (12:14) and acting deceitfully (12:15; cf. the pun on two senses of "lift up the head" in Genesis 40).

Why are you testing me? Gk *ti me peirazete.* An impressive series of manuscripts, including P⁴⁵, read *hypokritai* = "hypocrites" after *peirazete*. Taylor (479) thinks this reading may be original, since *hypokrisin . . . hypokritai* accords with Markan style elsewhere (see, e.g., 7:13). But how are we to explain the term's omission in most manuscripts? It is more likely that "hypocrites" is an early scribal addition influenced by the parallel in Matt 22:18.

so that I may see it. Gk *hina idō*. In his willingness to look at the coin, Jesus differs from R. Nahum bar Simai and other Jewish holy men, whose piety was such that they never looked at the image on a coin in their lives (see *y. ʿAbod. Zar.* 3:1 [42c; Neusner 33.112]; *b. Pesaḥ.* 104a; Hippolytus, *Refutation of All Heresies* 9.26; etc.; cf. Hart, "Coin," 241–42, and Levine, *Synagogue*, 453 n. 55).

17. *and the things of God to God.* Gk *kai ta tou theou tō theō*. The *Gospel of Thomas* version (100) adds: "And what is mine give me" (cf. figure 38), a secondary, Christological expansion.

Ancient interpreters beginning with Tertullian (*Against Marcion* 4.38; *On Idolatry* 15) and modern exegetes such as Bornkamm interpret "the things of God" as a reference to human beings: "The coin which bears the image of Caesar, we owe to Caesar. We, however, as men who bear the image of God [cf. Gen 1:26], owe ourselves to God" (Bornkamm, *Jesus*, 123). But since there are no vocabulary overlaps with Gen 1:26, an allusion to that verse is doubtful (cf. Davies and Allison, 3.217).

COMMENT

Introduction. After telling a parable that would, for Mark's first readers, reverberate with echoes of the tragic Jewish revolt against the Romans (12:1–12), Jesus fields a question about one of the flash points of that revolt, the divisive issue of paying taxes to the emperor. This question is also indirectly related to the previous passage: the conception of the land of Israel as an "inheritance" from God (cf. 12:7) implied to some Palestinian Jews that no foreigner should have the right to tax them (see 4Q542 and cf. *Pss. Sol.* 17:21–24; Evans, *Jesus*, 144; Hengel, *Zealots*, 131–33). In our passage, Jesus' interlocutors try to manipulate him into making a similar sort of revolutionary, anti-Roman declaration.

The passage probably comes from a pre-Markan source that included the questions about authority (11:27–33) and the resurrection (12:18–27; see the introduction to 11:1–13:37). The Synoptic version is considerably more complicated than the forms found in early-second-century documents, *Gos. Thom.* 100; *P.Egerton* 2; and Justin, *1 Apology* 1.17 (see figure 38); the preamble of the Markan form (12:13–14) in particular is, as Bruce ("Render," 257) notes, lengthy, but this is not necessarily a sign of secondary development, since it fits the context: the interlocutors are trying their hand at manipulation. In some particulars the second-century forms may have abbreviated the Synoptic ones (cf. Evans, 243), but certain other features of the Markan version are characteristic of the evangelist, including the language about perception ("know," "look at," "seeing," "see"); the use of double expressions, including a double negative; and the themes of teaching (cf. 1:21–22; 2:13; etc.), "the way of God/the Lord" (cf. 1:2–3; 8:27; 9:33–34; etc.), and the "test-

Figure 38: The Saying about Paying Tribute to Caesar

Mark 12:13–17	Matthew 22:16–22	Luke 20:20–26	Justin, 1 Apology 1.17.2	P.Egerton 2.2r.11–14	Gospel of Thomas 100
And they [the chief priests, the scribes, and the elders; see 11:28] sent to him some of the Pharisees and some of the Herodians	And they [the Pharisees; see 22:15] sent to him their disciples with the Herodians,	And watching him closely, they [the scribes and the chief priests; see 20:19] sent spies who pretended to be righteous,	And at that time some people came up to him	. . . coming to him	
that they might trap him by means of a word.		that they might catch him out by a word,			
		so as to turn him over to the rule and authority of the governor.			
And they came and said to him,	saying,	And they asked him, saying,	and asked him	they began to test him by examination, saying,	
"Teacher, we know that you are truthful and that you don't care what anyone thinks.	"Teacher, we know that you are truthful and that you teach the way of God in truth and that you don't care what anyone thinks.	"Teacher, we know that you speak and teach rightly		"Teacher Jesus, we know that you have come from God.	

Figure 38: The Saying about Paying Tribute to Caesar (continued)

Mark 12:13–17	Matthew 22:16–22	Luke 20:20–26	Justin, 1 Apology 1.17.2	P.Egerton 2.2r.11–14	Gospel of Thomas 100
For you don't look at people's appearance,		and that you don't accept appearance,			
but you teach the way of God truthfully.		but you truthfully teach the way of God.		For what you do bears witness beyond all the prophets.	
	Tell us, then, how it seems to you:			Tell us, then:	They [Jesus' disciples; see 99] showed Jesus a gold coin and said to him,
Is it permissible to give tribute money to Caesar or not?	Is it permissible to give tribute money to Caesar or not?	Is it permissible for us to give tax to Caesar or not?"	if it was necessary to pay taxes to Caesar.	Is it permissible [to p]ay to kings the things that are fitting for their rule?	"Those who are of Caesar demand taxes from us."
Shall we give, or shall we not give?"				Sha[ll we p]ay to them or not?"	
But he, seeing their pretense, said to them,	But Jesus, knowing their wickedness, said to them,	But he, knowing their trickery, said to them,	And he answered,	But Jesus, seeing their plan and becoming indignant, said to them,	
"Why are you testing me?	"Why are you testing me, you hypocrites?			"Well did Isaiah prophesy concerning you, saying . . . " + citation of Isa 29:13	

		He said to them,			
					"Pay the things of Caesar to Caesar.
					Pay the things of God to God.
					And my things pay to me."
	"Tell me, whose image does the coin bear?"				
	And they said, "Caesar's."	And again he answered in return,	"Pay therefore the things of Caesar to Caesar	and the things of God to God."	
"Show me a denarius.					
	Whose image and inscription does it bear?"	And he said to them,	"Then pay the things of Caesar to Caesar	and the things of God to God."	And they were not able to pounce on his word before the people,
	And they said, "Caesar's."				and amazed at his answer, they were silent.
"Show me the coin of the tribute money."					
And they brought a denarius to him.	"Whose image and inscription is this?"				
And he said to them,	And they said to him, "Caesar's."	Then he said to them,	"Pay the things of Caesar to Caesar	and the things of God to God."	
"Bring me a denarius, so that I may see it."					
And they brought one.	"Whose image is this, and whose inscription?"				
And he said to them,	And they said to him, "Caesar's."	And Jesus said to them,	"Pay to Caesar the things of Caesar,	and the things of God to God."	
And they were amazed at him.					

ing of Jesus" by the Pharisees (cf. 8:11). These features may represent Markan editing, which is also evident at the beginning of the passage, where the evangelist has
probably added the Herodians to the interlocutors to form an inclusion with 3:6
(see Meier, *Marginal Jew*, 4.563–64), and at its end, where the amazement evoked
by Jesus' response fits into a typical Markan pattern (cf. 1:22; 6:2; 10:26).

The passage falls into two parts. In the first, which is characterized by parataxis
(see the GLOSSARY), the initiative lies with Jesus' opponents (12:13–14); in the
second, which is characterized by hypotaxis (see again the GLOSSARY), the initiative lies with Jesus (12:15–17).

12:13–14: the Pharisees and the Herodians lay a trap for Jesus. The passage begins with some Pharisees and Herodians being "sent"—presumably by the Jewish
leaders described in 11:27, who have just been parabolically assaulted by Jesus—to
lay a verbal trap for him (12:13). This is a somewhat unrealistic picture; it is hard
to imagine members of the elite Herodian circle being "sent" by anyone, including the religious leaders described in 11:27 (cf. Meier, *Marginal Jew*, 3.563–64). At
the same time, it is not implausible that these two groups would have raised the
question that they do here. Jesus came from the realm ruled by Herod Antipas,
spoke of the coming dominion of God, and was commonly believed to be descended from David, all of which would have made him politically threatening to
the Herodians (see Meier, *Marginal Jew*, 3.562). It is plausible, therefore, that the
Herodians would have wanted to feel him out on the "hot-button" issue of Roman
taxation, which would have been particularly sensitive because the Herodian dynasty was dependent on imperial patronage.

Unlike the accommodationist Herodians, some Pharisees were of a revolutionary bent and objected to paying taxes to the Roman government. A Pharisee
named Zadok, for example, joined Judas the Galilean's early-first-century revolt
against Rome, which seems to have been sparked by the imperial attempt to lay
Judaea under tribute (see Josephus, *War* 2.118). The majority of Pharisees in Jesus'
time, however, probably treated the pagan government as a necessary evil, with
which one should cooperate but not fraternize (cf. *m. 'Abot* 1:10; 2:3; 3:2); thirty
years later a leading Pharisee, Yohanan ben Zakkai, advocated submission to
the Romans rather than revolution (see *b. Giṭ.* 56b; *'Abot R. Nat.* [A] 4 [Goldin,
35–37]; cf. Bruce, "Render," 250–51). It is presumably Pharisees of this latter, accommodationist stripe whom Mark portrays as colluding with the Herodians and
trying to get Jesus into trouble with the Romans (cf. 3:6; 12:12; against Evans,
244, who supposes that Mark is picturing two groups with opposing views—an
interpretation that goes all the way back to Jerome [see Aquinas, *Catena Aurea*
1.749]).

These cooperating groups, Mark tells us, come to Jesus with the intention of
trapping him verbally (12:13b). They lay their trap carefully, beginning with thick
flattery about Jesus' candor and his refusal to "look at the face of" (i.e., show favoritism toward) any human being (see the NOTE on "for you don't look at the face
of human beings" in 12:14). They then spring their trap: "Is it permissible to give
tribute money to Caesar or not?" (12:14c).

The trap has been artfully laid, because already the flattering remark that Jesus does not regard people's "faces" might imply an incriminating "no" answer. The remark echoes the statement in 1 Sam 16:7 that God looks at the heart rather than the face of people (see the NOTE on "for you don't look at the face of human beings" in 12:14); the context in the OT passage, significantly, has to do with the replacement of one king (Saul) by another (David), an issue similar to that in our passage (Caesar vs. Christ). The 1 Samuel passage, moreover, is especially relevant because David was the ancestor of the Messiah. And the Messiah, according to Isa 11:3, will imitate God in that he will ignore appearances in making judgments (see Wildberger, *Isaiah 1–12*, 475, and cf. *1 En.* 49:4). Thus, if Jesus is the Messiah, as his recent actions have seemed to suggest (cf. 11:1–11, 15–19), he should ignore human appearance and dignity—even the false dignity, the "face," of the pagan ruler Caesar (cf. 10:42: "those who are *thought* to rule over the Gentiles").

The Isaian context, moreover, suggests that this appearance-ignoring Messiah will also be a militant warrior against God's foes (see Isa 11:4), and 4QpIsa^a (4Q161) 8–10 3:1–25 [1–29] interprets these foes as the Kittim—that is, the Romans. Thus, a first-century Jewish text identifies the Messiah of Isaiah 11, who ignores appearance, as the scourge of the Romans—a combination of themes strikingly similar to that found in the leading question of Mark 12:14. Instead of submitting to the Roman yoke by paying the tribute money, therefore, Jesus, if he is really the Messiah, should subject the Romans to *his* yoke (cf. *Pss. Sol.* 17:30, "He will have gentile nations serving under his yoke"). The upshot is that being the Messiah would in the view of many Jews imply rejecting the payment of tribute to Caesar (cf. Luke 23:2, in which the charge that Jesus makes himself a king is linked with the charge that he forbids the payment of tribute to Caesar).

The word "face" (*prosōpon*), moreover, can refer to a bust or portrait (see LSJ 1533 III), and Mark's audience would have known that the portrait of the emperor was engraved on the tribute coin even before being reminded of that fact in 12:16. They would also have known, as will be discussed in the COMMENT on 12:15–17, that this image and the accompanying inscription implied the emperor's divinity. Paying the tribute money, therefore, involved acknowledging not only Roman sovereignty over the Holy Land (in contradiction to the biblical idea of the land as the heritage and property of God; cf. Hengel, *Zealots*, 133) but also the emperor's divine status (in contradiction to the first commandment). In this context, the interlocutors' insinuation that Jesus does not respect the "face" of people appears to be a deliberate provocation to commit *lèse majesté* by denigrating the idolatrous picture of the emperor engraved on the coin of tribute. The gravity of such an act is illustrated by the notice of Philostratus (*Life of Apollonius* 1.15) that, in Tiberius' time, statues of the emperor were more inviolable than those of Zeus: "A master is said to have been guilty of impiety, merely because he struck his own slave when the latter had on his person a silver drachma coined with the image of Tiberius" (LCL trans. alt.).

12:15–17: Jesus' response. The Pharisees and Herodians, then, are egging Jesus on to perform an act of impiety and political revolt against the emperor. Jesus, however, eludes their trap and regains the initiative, as signaled by the switch from parataxis to hypotaxis in 12:15. He is able to do so because of a quality of spiritual vision that cuts through the duplicity of his interlocutors' question ("seeing their pretense," 12:15a). Indeed, the Pharisees and Herodians in the narrative do not really believe—as their question might seem to imply—that paying tribute to the emperor is contrary to the Torah; such an implication runs counter to their practice of cooperating with Rome. The question, then, has been advanced solely to get Jesus into trouble. Jesus not only discerns this stratagem but also unmasks it ("Why are you testing me?" 12:15b), thus ironically demonstrating the very candor for which they have just insincerely praised him. But there is also a deeper dimension to his complaint, "Why are you testing me?" For the allusion to testing recalls the programmatic Satanic assault that he experienced at the beginning of the Gospel (1:12–13), which in the present context has become a temptation to seize earthly power from Caesar (cf. Matt 4:8–9//Luke 4:5–7).

Rejecting this demonic temptation, however, Jesus calls for a denarius to be brought, "so that I may see it" (12:15c). The Matthean parallel, "Show me the coin of the tribute money" (Matt 22:19, my trans.), brings out part of the logic of this command; Roman taxes were paid in Roman currency, such as the denarius, so Jesus is asking to be shown the sort of coin in which the tax would customarily be remitted (cf. Bruce, "Render," 258). But the Markan *hina* clause, "so that I may see it," which is lacking in Matthew and Luke, is not superfluous. The same spiritual acuity that has unmasked the attempt of the Pharisees and the Herodians to trap him will now enable Jesus to expose the true nature of the Roman coin, and with it of the tribute to which it is devoted.

And what does Jesus "see"? The denarius was a valuable Roman coin, equivalent to sixteen *asses* (in Matt 20:2 it represents a day's wages). According to Hart ("Coin," 243), the denarius in use in our story can be identified with considerable certainty, since only two denarii were produced during Tiberius' reign, and the first passed out of circulation quickly, while the second was minted "in quite extraordinary numbers." On the obverse of this coin, Tiberius' laurel-crowned head is portrayed surrounded by the inscription *TI[BERIVS] CAESAR DIVI AVG[VSTI] F[ILIUS] AVGVSTVS* ("Tiberius Caesar, son of the deified Augustus, [himself] Augustus"). This inscription continues on the reverse side of the coin, where it reads *Pontif[ex] Maxim[us]* = "High Priest" and is accompanied by a picture of a seated lady who probably represents Pax, the embodiment of the peace of the Empire (for photographs, see Hart, "Coin," 246).

There would be good reasons for Jews to be outraged at the requirement that they pay their taxes in this sort of coin. Not only does it portray the emperor as the highest official of the Roman religion (the *Pontifex Maximus*), but it also makes him an *object* of that religion; he is the son of the deified Augustus, and himself Augustus, a term meaning "the one to be served with religious awe" and carrying its own implication of divinity (see Florus, *Epitome* 2.34, and cf. Grant, "Augustus"; Klauck, *Context*, 29; Zanker, *Power*, 98). The laurel crown on his head, moreover, associates him with the gods Apollo and Zeus (see, e.g., Ovid, *Tristia* 3.1.35–48, 77–78, and Pliny, *Natural History* 15.136; cf. Steier, "Lorbeer";

Hünemörder, "Lorbeer"; Bastien, *Buste*, 1.61–66). The coin, then, is not only an economic instrument and a symbol of the Jews' political subjection to Rome but also a part of the developing ruler cult of the first century (see Kreitzer, *Striking*, 69–98; on Tiberius' participation in the ruler cult, see Klauck, *Context*, 302–3).

With this background in mind, however, Jesus' response to the presentation of the coin at first seems puzzling. When the denarius is fetched, he asks whose inscription and image are engraved upon it and is told that they belong to Caesar (12:16). Then, runs Jesus' inference, "Pay to Caesar the things of Caesar, and the things of God to God" (12:17a)—a response that amazes and silences his opponents (12:17b). But *why* are they amazed? What does Jesus' reply actually mean? Its import would be unambiguous if, in the religious world of the first century, the sphere of God and that of the emperor were clearly demarcated from each other. But such was not the case, as we have just seen; the very coin in which the tribute money was paid melded those two realms in a way that was intolerable for many Jews, since it portrayed the emperor as a god. In this context, Jesus' reply seems to beg the central question of the whole discussion: What exactly belongs to Caesar, and what to God? (cf. Bünker, "Gebt").

The answers to this question have been legion, and have often depended on the political leanings of the commentator. Horsley (*Hearing*, 43), an exegete sympathetic to Marxism, suggests that Jesus, while "cleverly avoiding a direct answer," is in fact forbidding the payment of tribute, "since according to Israelite tradition everything belongs to God and nothing to Caesar." The main line of interpretation, however, sees Jesus as approving the payment of tribute. According to some, he does so enthusiastically, on the presumption that Caesar is the servant of God (cf. Rom 13:1–7); therefore giving Caesar what is Caesar's *is* giving God what is God's (cf. Derrett, *Law*, 335–36). According to others, Jesus is recognizing a limited governmental claim that is distinct from the claim of God (cf. Justin, *1 Apology* 17.2), and this interpretation seems more in line with the distinction implied in 12:16: the image and inscription relate to Caesar rather than God. In any case, the interpretation that sees Jesus as advocating payment seems exegetically sounder than the "tax revolt" position, since Jesus has been asked about tribute to Caesar, has elicited the statement that the portrait and inscription on the tribute coin are Caesar's, and has concluded that one should pay Caesar with that which is his—that is, it would seem, the coin. He appears to deliberately ignore the fact that the inscription and portrait also link Caesar with God—a strategy comparable to Paul's denial of the existence of idols in 1 Cor 8:4–6 and Rabban Gamaliel's demythologizing interpretation of the pagan symbolism of the bathhouse in *m. 'Abod. Zar.* 3:4 (cf. Halbertal, "Coexisting").

In the end, though, Jesus' concluding statement, "Pay to Caesar the things of Caesar, and the things of God to God," remains somewhat ambiguous; one *could* interpret it in a militant rather than a quietistic sense (cf. Evans, 247). The clever ambiguity of the reply is probably the reason for his interlocutors' amazement, with which the passage concludes (12:17b). Jesus has succeeded in saying something that neither gives a pretext for reporting him to the Romans nor undermines his popularity by endorsing foreign rule unequivocally. The Markan Jesus, then, does not lay down a hard-and-fast rule for Christians' relation to ruling authorities; as Gnilka (2.153–54) points out, his concluding pronouncement instead leaves room for the discernment of his hearers as to when the claims of Caesar and God conflict and when they do not. Clearly early Christians knew of instances when they did, and when that happened the choice was obvious (cf. Acts 5:29: "We must obey God rather than human beings" [my trans.]). Our passage itself, by the order of its clauses, implies that the demands of God transcend those of Caesar. But the demands of these two "rulers" do not *always* clash, and when they do not, it is possible to remain loyal to both.

The Markan community lives in the wake of the Jewish revolt against Rome—a revolt that, as we have seen, was set off by the Palestinian Jews' refusal to pay their imperial taxes. The question about tribute, therefore, is not of mere antiquarian interest to them but is literally a matter of life and death, and it is possible that some Christians known to them, or even members of their own community, have been carried away by revolutionary enthusiasm, have refused to pay, and have suffered the consequences (cf. 13:22). An insurrectionary refusal to pay the tribute is a real temptation to Mark's audience—as, in our passage, it is to Jesus himself (cf. again 12:15). In this context, the Markan Jesus' reminder that the claims of God and those of the emperor sometimes overlap, and that there may be a middle path between idolatry of Caesar and revolt against him, would be a word on target to people pressured to choose one side or the other.

Our passage, then, deals with the believer's relationship to the ultimate earthly authority, who holds in his hands the power of life and death. The next passage will deal with the believer's relationship to the power of death itself.

JESUS IS QUESTIONED ABOUT THE RESURRECTION (12:18–27)

12 [18]And Sadducees came to him, who say that there is no resurrection, and they were asking him, saying, [19]"Teacher, Moses wrote to us, 'If someone's brother dies and he leaves a wife and he does not leave a child, his brother should take his wife and raise up offspring for his brother.' [20]There were seven brothers. And the first took a wife, and when he died he didn't leave offspring. [21]And the second took her and died and didn't leave behind offspring, and the third similarly. [22]And the seven of them didn't leave offspring. Last of all the woman also died. [23]In the resurrection, when they rise, whose wife will she be? For all seven of them had her as a wife."

[24]And Jesus said to them, "Aren't you deceived, in that you don't know the scriptures or the power of God? [25]For when they rise from among the dead, they neither marry nor are taken in marriage but are like the angels who are in heaven. [26]And concerning the dead, that they are raised—haven't you read in the book of Moses, how God spoke to him at the bush, saying, 'I am the God of Abraham and the God of Isaac and the God of Jacob'? [27]He is not a God of the dead but of the living. You are greatly deceived.

NOTES

12 18. *Sadducees.* Gk *Saddoukaioi.* On this Jewish sect, see the APPENDIX "The Sadducees" at the end of this volume.

19. *offspring.* Gk *sperma,* lit. "seed." The term is transferred from the male sperm to its product, the resultant child or children. Even more broadly, it can become a collective term for the sum total of a person's descendants; see , for example, the discussion of the "seed of Abraham" in Romans 4.

20. *seven brothers.* Gk *hepta adelphoi.* Tobit 3:7–17 tells the story of a demonized girl young woman who has had seven husbands, each of whom died on their wedding night. Perhaps the Sadducees' question somehow reflects this story, or else both it and our passage reflect a common folk tale or motif (see Davies and Allison 3.225 and n. 27).

21. *leave behind.* Gk *katalipōn,* lit. "leaving behind." This is synonymous with *aphēken/aphēkan,* which is used in the surrounding verses (12:20, 22); the alternation seems to be for purely stylistic reasons.

23. *when they rise.* Gk *hotan anastōsin.* These words are omitted in many texts, including some very good and early manuscripts (א, B, C, L, Δ, Ψ, 33, etc., plus some Latin manuscripts, the Peshitta, and Coptic versions), whereas the manuscript evidence for their attestation is not as impressive (A, Θ, $f^{1,\,13}$, as well as the Majority Text, most Latin manuscripts, sy[s.h.], and Bohairic). But the omission of these awkward, superfluous words is much easier to explain than their addition, and as Metzger (110–11) points out, the pleonasm (see the GLOSSARY) corresponds to Markan style (cf. 13:19: "from the beginning of the *creation,* which God *created,* until now"). "When they rise," then, is probably original.

The Sadducees' question seems to assume that they know without asking that Jesus believes in the resurrection of the dead; their question, assuming this belief, tries to ridicule him by a *reductio ad absurdum.* This may be an indication that most of the Jewish populace of Palestine believed in resurrection. The Pharisees certainly did, and they were, according to Josephus, the most influential Jewish sect (see *War* 2.162; *Ant.* 18.15). The Essenes probably did as well (Josephus, *War* 2.154; cf. 4Q521). The Sadducees, who disagreed, were a sect whose members were mostly limited to the socioeconomic elite.

Though ours is the only passage in the Gospels in which the resurrection becomes a matter of debate, elsewhere in the tradition Jesus makes statements that assume belief in the resurrection or at least in a postmortem existence (see, e.g., the passion predictions in 8:31, etc.; 9:42–50; Matt 12:41–42//Luke 11:31–32 = Q; Luke 14:14; 16:19–31).

25. *neither marry nor are taken in marriage.* Gk *oute gamousin oute gamizontai.* This phrase reflects the patriarchal nature of Jewish marriage law, in which men are active agents and women are passive; as was generally the case in the ancient world, the Jewish wife was legally a piece of property sold by her father to her husband (cf. Wegner, *Chattel,* 42–45; Ilan, *Jewish Women,* 88–89). It is grammatically unclear whether the implied subject of *gamizontai* is fathers, who give their daughters in marriage, or husbands, who acquire them. Jewish legal terminology,

however, suggests the latter; see, for example, *m. Qidd.* 1:1: "By three means is the woman acquired . . . by money or by writ or by intercourse" (cf. BDAG 118). This also seems to be the way in which the Peshitta takes our verse: "For when they rise from among the dead, they won't take wives, neither will the women belong to men" (i.e., be married to them).

The Markan Jesus provides no biblical justification for his assertion that the resurrected saints will not marry because they will become like angels. He does go on to cite Exod 3:6, in which the Lord identifies himself as "the God of Abraham and the God of Isaac and the God of Jacob." This citation, however, is used to support only the idea of resurrection in general, not the point about angelic celibacy. It is possible that at an earlier stage of the tradition, the citation of Exod 3:6 *did* support the latter point, the implication being that the Lord is the God of Abraham, Isaac, and Jacob—*not* of Sarah, Rebecca, and Rachel. This hypothesis is rendered more plausible by the observations in the COMMENT on 12:24–27 about ancient Jewish conceptions of angels as male (cf. *Gos. Thom.* 114, which speaks of women being saved by becoming men).

are like the angels who are in heaven. Gk *eisin hōs angeloi hoi en tois ouranois,* lit. "are like angels, the ones in heaven." Most manuscripts, including ℵ, C, D, K, L, Δ, *f*¹, and most minuscules, omit the definite article before *en tois ouranois* ("like angels in heaven"), while a few (B, Θ, 2427) insert it not only there but also before *angeloi,* giving a reading whose sense is pretty much identical to that given here. The reading chosen, however, which is attested with minor variants by A, Γ, Ψ, *f*¹³, 33, 565, etc., l vgˢ boᵐˢ, is the most difficult and the one that best explains the existence of the others; scribes would tend either to drop the definite article or add an extra one in order to create greater smoothness. The omission of this article could also have arisen by haplography (ΑΓΓΕΛΟΙΟΙ; on haplography see the GLOSSARY).

On the idea that the resurrected dead will be like angels, see *Eschatological light, stars, and angels* in the APPENDIX "History-of-Religions Backgrounds to the Transfiguration." One of the texts mentioned there is 2 *Apoc. Bar.* 51:5, 10, which speaks of this angelic existence in the future tense ("they will be like angels and be equal to the stars," 51:10). Does Jesus' contrasting use of the present tense imply that, for him, the blessed dead are *already* raised and living like angels? This is apparently the way in which the Lukan parallel takes Jesus' response, since it says that already in this life, before they die, the righteous are "children of the resurrection" and cannot die anymore, being equal to angels (Luke 20:34–36); presumably their physical death does not alter this angelic, resurrected status. This Lukan pericope became determinative for monastic exegesis, which regularly describes the celibate state as a foretaste of the resurrection life (see, e.g., *Acts of Paul and Thecla* 5, 12; Clement of Alexandria, *Stromateis* 3.48.1; cf. Van Eijk, "Marriage"; Fletcher-Louis, *Luke-Acts,* 81–86). The alternative is to say that in our passage Jesus is using the present tense futuristically, to point to a coming event that is so certain that it can be spoken of as if it has already occurred. The next couple of verses, however, point toward a more literal interpretation of the tense: the Lord is *presently* the God of Abraham, Isaac, and Jacob, who are therefore still alive. On the Jewish and early Christian idea that the righteous, upon their death, immediately enter eternal life, a concept that is often linked with belief in an interim state of blessedness before the final resurrection, see, among other passages, Wis 3:1–4; 2 Macc 7:36; 4 Macc 16:25; 17:18–19; *1 En.* 9:10; 39:6–8; Josephus, *War* 3.374; 7.344; Luke 16:22–31; 23:42–43; 2 Cor 5:1–4; Phil 1:20–24; Rev 6:9–11.

26. *in the book of Moses, how God spoke to him at the bush.* Gk *en tē biblō Mōuseōs epi tou batou pōs eipen autō ho theos,* lit. "in the book of Moses at the bush how God said to him." It is possible that *epi tou batou* means "in the passage of scripture concerning the bush"; cf. the formula *en Ēlią* = "in [the section about] Elijah" in Rom 11:2, to which Evans (255) compares *m. 'Abot* 3:7, "in [the section about] David." But our passage uses not *en* ("in") but *epi* ("at"), and this preposition is connected not with a human character but with a piece of foliage. It is likely, then, that we are dealing simply with a displaced phrase rather than with a citation formula (on formula-driven displacements in Mark, see the NOTE on "And as he was coming up out of the water, he immediately" in 1:10).

As Schwankl (*Sadduzäerfrage,* 319) points out, here as in 10:6–8 Jesus invokes a Torah passage that comes earlier in the biblical narrative than the passage cited by his opponents, and in 10:6 he emphasizes the temporal priority ("but from the beginning of the creation"; cf. Matt 19:8). Paul adopts a similar exegetical strategy in Gal 3:17, where he claims that the promise to Abraham supersedes the Law, which came in 430 years later. These NT passages probably reflect the Greco-Roman principle that older laws trump more recent ones (see Vos, "Antinomie," 261), which was probably influencing Jewish thinkers by Jesus' time (cf. the rabbinic principle that "everything that precedes in scripture precedes in importance" [my trans.], e.g., *Mekilta* Baḥodesh 8 [Lauterbach 2.259; cf. *b. Qidd.* 40b; Longenecker, *Paul,* 123 n. 63; Mussner, *Galaterbrief,* 241).

I am the God of Abraham and the God of Isaac and the God of Jacob. Gk *egō ho theos Abraam kai theos Isaak kai theos Iakōb.* This is almost identical with the LXX of Exod 3:6 (cf. also 3:15–16). In the COMMENT on 12:24–27 it is pointed out that this formula in its original context implies only that God's succor, which he has showed in the past to the patriarchs, will now be extended to their descendants; the "I am" clause, therefore, means, "I am the same deity who spoke to and delivered Abraham, Isaac, and Jacob." The Markan Jesus, however, treats the phrase in question literally, as was commonly done in Jewish homiletical exegesis (see Marcus, "Role," 230–31): "I *am* [presently] the God of Abraham, Isaac, and Jacob [and therefore they must be alive]." Cf. Isho'dad of Merv, *Commentary on Matthew* 17 [on Matt 22:32]: "For God would not have called himself the God of these people, if he had not known that their souls were alive, and was also intending to raise their bodies again and give them to their souls."

Jesus' linkage of the formula from Exodus with the idea of resurrection may have had Jewish precedents. The first of the Eighteen Benedictions, which was becoming the standard Jewish prayer by the end of the first century, invokes the God of Abraham, Isaac, and Jacob, and the second describes him as the God who gives life to the dead (cf. Schwankl, *Sadduzäerfrage,* 289–90). Moreover, in a Tannaitic midrash (*Tanḥuma* [Buber] Shemot 1.16 [Townsend 2.15]), Moses mistakenly thinks that his father Amram is alive when he hears God say, "I am the God of your father" (Exod 3:6a). In a medieval compilation, *Sekel Tov*, he takes the same declaration as a promise that Amram is destined for the world to come.

COMMENT

Introduction. Having answered a question that took him into the worldly realms of coinage, taxation, and politics (12:13–17), Jesus now responds to one that takes him into the otherworldly domain of the resurrection via a discussion about marriage and its postmortem consequences.

Jesus had engaged a topic related to marriage (divorce) in the earlier controversy story in 10:2–9, and there are striking similarities between the structure and content of the two passages (cf. Schwankl, *Sadduzäerfrage*, 319–20). In both,

(1) The point of departure is the marriage laws of the Torah.
(2) Moses is invoked by both Jesus and his opponents.
(3) Jesus' opponents appeal to Deuteronomy.
(4) Jesus appeals to a passage from earlier in the Torah than Deuteronomy (Gen 1:27; 2:24 in the first case, Exod 3:6 in the second).
(5) Jesus' opponents emphasize the authority of *Moses*, whereas Jesus emphasizes what *God* has done or will do, although he implies that the latter is consistent with Moses' writings rightly understood.
(6) Jesus diagnoses his opponents' problem as a perceptual defect (hard-heartedness in the one case, ignorance in the other). This defect prevents them from interpreting scripture correctly.
(7) Jesus relativizes the proof text of his opponents, in the one case by appealing to the beginning of the world (10:6), in the other by appealing to the eschaton ("in the resurrection, when they rise," 12:23). Beginning and end are related in the apocalyptic worldview, since the end recapitulates and perfects the beginning (see the COMMENT on 10:5–9).

These similarities could reflect later Christian editorial activity (cf. the parallel to Paul's hermeneutical strategy in Gal 3:17, on which see the NOTE on "in the book of Moses, how God spoke to him at the bush" in 12:26). But there is nothing in either passage that is implausible in the setting of the historical Jesus. Indeed, the ambivalent stance toward the authority of Moses and the unusual, creative exegesis that reaches back *ad fontes* in the name of an apocalyptic revelation are characteristic of him (cf. e.g. Matt 5:21–48, on the substantial historicity of which see Davies and Allison, 1.504–5). Our passage, moreover, makes no reference to Jesus' own resurrection, which is the usual way in which the early church argued for the general doctrine (cf. Gnilka, 2.160–61). It is probably, therefore, substantially historical.

Internally, the passage is carefully structured. It is divided into two parts, the Sadducees' question (12:18–23), which is characterized by parataxis, and Jesus' response (12:24–27), which is hypotactic throughout (on these syntactical terms, see the GLOSSARY). Despite this disjunction, the two parts are closely linked in structure. Near the beginning of the first part, the Sadducees cite what "Moses wrote" in the Law to provide a context for their skeptical question about the resurrection (12:19); near the end of his response, Jesus refers to what is written "in the book of Moses" as a proof text for the resurrection (12:26). As Meier (*Marginal Jew*, 3.417) points out, the introduction to the Sadducees' question (12:18) concerns the *fact* of the resurrection, whereas their question itself (12:19–23) concerns its *mode*. Jesus then deals with these issues in reverse order: first the mode of resurrection existence (12:24–25), then its reality (12:26–27). As Meier further notes, the two parts of Jesus' answer are each introduced by a censorious rhetorical question ("Aren't you deceived . . . ?" and "haven't you read . . . ?"), and this response has a chiastic structure that mirrors that of the pericope as a whole:

A   Aren't you deceived, not knowing
B   the scriptures
C   or the power of God
C′   in heaven people don't marry (but live an existence transformed
               by God's power)
B′   scriptural citation
A′   You are greatly deceived

This evidence renders questionable the assertion of Bultmann (26) that the discussion of scripture in 12:26–27 is a later addition to the passage; it seems, rather, to be an integral and probably original part of the story. Mark's redactional contributions to the passage, indeed, seem to be minor, perhaps being limited to the *gar* ("for") clause in 12:23b and the concluding "You are greatly deceived" in 12:27b.

12:18–23: the Sadducees' question. Like the Pharisees and Herodians in the previous passage, the Sadducees now approach Jesus with a trick question. Although they are not directly accused of hypocrisy and of "testing" Jesus, as the Pharisees and the Herodians were (12:15), it is apparent that they are guilty of both, since in order to trip him up they ask a question whose presupposition, the reality of the resurrection, contradicts their own beliefs. Mark underlines this disjunction by reminding his readers that Sadducees do not believe in the resurrection of the dead (12:18; see the APPENDIX "The Sadducees"). Since the negated belief, unlike the common Hellenistic notion of the immortality of the soul, involves the postmortem recovery of a body, questions naturally arise about those with whom corporeal links were established in this life, especially spouses. Do conjugal relations continue, and, if so, in what way?

It is a natural question, but the Sadducees broach it in a most unnatural manner: posing a hypothetical case that is designed to ridicule belief in the resurrection of the dead and those such as Jesus who embrace the doctrine. The case takes its point of departure from an institution that scholars have dubbed "levirate" marriage (from the Latin *levir* = "husband's brother"). According to this ancient

Israelite custom, a man whose married brother had died without leaving children would marry his deceased brother's wife and "raise up offspring for [his] brother" (see Gen 38:8; Deut 25:5). This practice seems already to be opposed within the OT itself by Lev 18:16; 20:21 (see Milgrom, *Leviticus*, 2.1545), but it appears to have become common in the Second Temple period (see Ilan, *Jewish Women*, 152–55). Only later, in the Tannaitic era (see the GLOSSARY), was it more or less completely replaced by another OT rite, *ḥalîṣāh*, whereby the man renounces his right to marry his deceased brother's wife and ceremonially frees her to wed someone else (see Deut 25:7–10; Ruth 4). The institution of levirate marriage appears to have been an invitation to both male fantasy and male anxiety; in the apocryphal-sounding story in *y. Yeb.* 4:12 (6b; Neusner, 4.168), for example, R. Judah the Patriarch convinces a man with twelve deceased brothers to marry all twelve widows, despite the man's protest that he lacks the "power" to do so (cf. Ilan, *Jewish Women*, 155). Another concern is more evident in our passage: if 10:1–12 has emphasized the reality and durability of the bond established by sexual union, what will happen in the next life in cases in which several men have slept with the same woman?

12:24–27: *Jesus' response.* Like the Pharisees and the Herodians before them (see the COMMENT on 12:13–14), the Sadducees have laid their trap carefully; indeed, the narrative devotes a third more space to their question than it does to Jesus' reply. But when Jesus' turn comes, he deftly retakes the initiative, signaled grammatically by the switch from parataxis to hypotaxis and the otherwise superfluous invocation of his name in 12:24a (cf. Gnilka, 2.157). His tone is aggressive: "Aren't you deceived (*ou . . . planasthe*), in that you don't know . . . ?" This tone matches the intention of the Sadducees' question, which as we have seen is an attempt to ensnare Jesus (cf. 12:13, 15).

The beginning of Jesus' response, however, is not just a reproof but also a diagnosis: the underlying ground of the Sadducees' error is that they have been misled ("Aren't you deceived . . . ?"; cf. the use of the same verb in 12:27; 13:5–6). Similarly, in Paul's writings the warning *mē planasthe* ("do not be deceived") occurs in contexts linking ethics with eschatology, especially through the idea of punishments and rewards after death (1 Cor 6:9; 15:32–33; Gal 6:7–8). The latter is precisely what the Sadducees denied (see Josephus, *War* 2.165; *Ant.* 18.16). The Markan narrative shows them to have been deceived about a matter of supreme importance ("You are greatly deceived," 12:27b), as is also said about the judgment-denying reprobates in Wis 2:21–24 (cf. Schwankl, *Sadduzäerfrage*, 358):

Thus they reasoned, but they were deceived (*eplanēthēsan*), for their wickedness blinded them, and they did not know the secret purposes of God, nor hope for the wages of holiness, nor discern the prize for blameless souls; for God created man for incorruption, and made him in the image of his own eternity, but through the devil's envy death entered the world, and those who belong to his party experience it. (RSV alt.)

Here the ultimate source of error about life after death turns out to be the devil. Similarly, an earlier Markan passage depicted a divine intention to blind "those outside" (4:11–12) working itself out through God's opponent, Satan (4:15). This intra-Markan connection is substantiated by early Christian and Jewish texts in which Satan is referred to by epithets such as "the deceiver," "the prince of deceit," and "the spirit of deceit," or in which he is otherwise linked with deception (see Rev 12:9; 20:3, 8, 10; 1QS 4:9; *T. Sim.* 2:7; *T. Jud.* 19:4; cf. 2 Thess 2:8–12).

According to the Markan Jesus, the result of such demonic interference in the thought processes of Jesus' Sadducean interrogators is that they have forfeited knowledge both of the scriptures and of the power of God (12:24b). Jesus then explains this charge in reverse order, starting with a description of the postmortem state as one in which people, through the divine power active in their postresurrection bodies, live an existence similar to that of the angels—that is, it would seem, a celibate life (12:25). As Davies and Allison (3.229) point out, this does not mean that the angels or resurrected humans were considered to be sexless. The angels described in the OT and Jewish literature, rather, are sexed beings, usually conceived of as male (according to *Jub.* 15:27, they were even created circumcised), and they are perfectly capable of having sex with humans, as Gen 6:1–4 demonstrates. This miscegenation across the angelic/human divide was, according to a widely attested intertestamental interpretation of the Genesis passage, the primal sin (see, e.g., *Jub.* 4:22; 5:1–11; 1QapGen 2:1; 2 *Apoc. Bar.* 56:12); those who engaged in it were punished by being imprisoned in chains beneath the earth, upon which their offspring, the demons, have wreaked havoc ever since. In a classic expression of this theme, *1 En.* 15:3–10, God rebukes the fallen angels in ways that provide an enlightening parallel to Mark 12:25:

> Why have you forsaken the high heaven, the eternal sanctuary; and lain with women, and defiled yourselves with the daughters of men; and taken for yourselves wives, and done as the sons of earth . . . ? You were holy ones and spirits, living forever. With the blood of women you have defiled yourselves, and with the blood of flesh you have begotten; and with the blood of men you have lusted, and you have done as they do—flesh and blood, who die and perish. Therefore I gave them women, that they might cast seed into them, and thus beget children by them, that nothing fail them upon the earth. But you originally existed as spirits, living forever, and not dying for all the generations of eternity. Therefore I did not make women among you . . . The spirits of heaven, in heaven is their dwelling; but the spirits begotten on earth, on earth is their dwelling. (Nickelsburg trans., punctuation alt.)

Being deathless, heavenly beings, angels do not need and therefore should avoid sexual intercourse, which is a special gift bestowed on humans for the purpose of propagating their species. In this context, the concluding words in Mark 12:25, "are like the angels *who are in heaven*" (see the NOTE on the text there), may not be superfluous; when people are raised from the dead, they will resemble those members of the divine court who remained in their heavenly dwelling place and did not forsake it for the fleshpots of earth (cf. Jude 6).

Our Gospel passage will trouble many modern Christians—not least because of its implied endorsement of the opinion that sex exists solely for the purpose of procreation. Redeemed existence in the next life is portrayed as bodily but asexual; with such a heaven, some might argue, there will be no further need for hell. Such skeptics may sympathize with Milton's Satan, a former angel who is moved to jealous fury when he observes the innocent coupling of the first humans in Eden (*Paradise Lost* 4.492–511; 9.263–64). Milton himself portrays the unfallen angels engaging in a purified and spiritual form of sex (*Paradise Lost* 8.612–629), and some rabbis and other Jewish thinkers, similarly, believed that sexual intercourse would be a part of life in the age to come (cf. *1 En.* 10:17; *b. Šabb.* 30b; *Midr. Psalms* 73:4). Jesus, however, seems in our passage to dispute such opinions, as did other rabbis; in *b. Ber.* 17a, for example, Rav implies that the beatific vision will replace and transcend earthly pleasures, including those associated with procreation.

The Markan Jesus, similarly, implies that those who imagine that marital relations will continue in the future world have not yet sufficiently grasped (or been grasped by) "the power of God." We can only conclude that, for Jesus, the divine creativity has something better than sex in store for the redeemed. And those who have read the rapturous last canto of Dante's *Divine Comedy*, or the description in Job 38:7 of the morning stars singing together, the divine beings shouting for joy; or have gazed at William Blake's radiant engraving of the latter text; or have listened to the movingly human yet intensely mystical ending of Mahler's *Resurrection Symphony*—such audiences may experience a similar intimation that the future life will be characterized by exaltation and even by ecstasy, and that this ecstasy will somehow be reflected not only in purified souls but also in glorified and mutually glorifying bodies. This intuition of the corporeal nature of redemption is confirmed by the linkage that our passage forges between redeemed humans and the angels *in heaven*, since elsewhere in Mark heaven is the origin of the miraculous divine power that creates food in the wilderness (6:41), sweeps away physical deficiencies (7:34), and fills Jesus' own body with wonder-working power (1:10–11).

Having shown that the scriptural institution of levirate marriage does not, as the Sadducees imply, contradict the idea of resurrection, Jesus concludes by showing that that idea is, as a matter of fact, supported by scripture (12:26–27). He does not, however, invoke one of the late OT passages that proclaim resurrection more or less clearly, such as Dan 12:2–3 (see also Isa 26:19 and Ezek 37:1–14). Instead he appeals to one of the constitutive events in the life of the people of Israel—God's self-revelation to Moses at the burning bush in Exod 3:6 (Mark 12:26). In that passage, and in similar formulas elsewhere in the OT, the deity refers to himself as "the God of Abraham, and the God of Isaac, and the God of Jacob" (cf. Exod 3:15–16), despite the fact that Abraham, Isaac, and Jacob are long dead; knowledge of the larger context of the Exodus passage, then, is necessary for understanding the argument. Jesus' conclusion is that Abraham, Isaac, and Jacob must still be alive, since the scriptural formula shows the Lord to be the God not of the dead but of the living (12:27a).

This is hardly the sense that the formula "the God of Abraham, of Isaac, and of Jacob" had in the original. When he says in Exod 3:6 that he is the God of Abraham, Isaac, and Jacob, the OT God means that just as he delivered those patriarchs from their distresses, so will he now liberate and succor their enslaved descendants. The formula thus speaks of God's faithfulness to those with whom he has entered into covenant relationship (cf. Gen 28:13–15; 32:9–12; 35:3; 48:15–16). It is a logical extrapolation, however, that this divine faithfulness to the patriarchs, which frequently resulted in their deliverance from fear, suffering, and the danger of death, will ultimately be crowned by their liberation from the power of death itself; and, indeed, intertestamental Jewish literature and the NT frequently suggest that the patriarchs are or will be with God in the age to come (see *T. Jud.* 25:1; *T. Benj.* 10:6; 4 Macc 7:19; 16:25; Hebrews 11). In particular, the notion of Abraham's postmortem existence was so firmly planted in the popular imagination that Luke 16:22–23 uses "the bosom of Abraham" as a transparent image for the blessed afterlife (cf. 4 Macc 13:17 v.l.; *T. Ab.* A 20:14; Allison, *Testament of Abraham*, 407–8). But this idea is a *development* of the biblical portrait of the patriarchs, not a simple exegesis of it or of the triadic formula linking the patriarchs with God (cf. Schwankl, *Sadduzäerfrage*, 388–403).

Why does the Markan Jesus avoid the more obvious OT passages and use this roundabout method of scriptural proof for his point about resurrection? Part of the answer probably lies in the historical Jesus' predilection for subtle exegesis—not just to be difficult, but in order to stretch the minds of his hearers, as his parables also do. Part of it probably relates to the centrality of the burning bush passage in Judaism, as opposed to the marginality of texts such as Daniel 12 (cf. *m. Sanh.* 9:1 on the necessity of proving the resurrection of the dead from the Torah). But it probably also has to do with the conclusion toward which the argument is driving, namely, that the God whom Jesus proclaims is a God of the currently living and not a God of the currently dead (12:27a; cf. the NOTE on "are like the angels who are in heaven" in 12:25). Passages such as Dan 12:2–3; Isa 26:19; and Ezek 37:1–14 speak of a resurrection that *will* occur at the conclusion of history, at the eschaton. The Markan Jesus, however, seems to want to speak of a resurrection life that has already in some sense begun (see the NOTE on "are like the angels who are in heaven" in 12:25). He clinches this point by turning against the Sadducees what may have been a Sadducean slogan: "He is not a God of the dead but of the living" (oral suggestion from Stephen Chester). For the Sadducees, this slogan would have been a denial of the importance of life after death; for Jesus it becomes a refutation of the idea that the dead are really dead.

It would be vital for the persecuted Christians of the Markan community to hear this message, and they would know that it had been confirmed by Jesus' own resurrection. Those among them, therefore, who have been turned over to a martyr's death (cf. 13:12) have not been lost but are hidden from the living by the thinnest and most permeable of membranes. They are in this sense, too, "like the angels who are in heaven," who can see what is taking place on earth and even in some sense participate in it. The Markan Christians' own situation of persecution and distress, which probably made them feel that they themselves had one foot in the grave, would have made this reminder that their God was a lord of *living* beings even more necessary. In this sense, the end of Jesus' reply, with its stress on the aliveness of those who are in God's hand, matches the beginning, with its stress on the divine power manifested in resurrection life. The Markan Christians, like Paul's Philippian addressees, are invited to experience and acknowledge not only their fellowship in Jesus' sufferings and death but also, in the midst of those deathly realities, the power of his resurrection (Phil 3:10–11).

In this and the previous pericope, the Markan Jesus has faced challenges about whether his teaching coheres with or contradicts the Torah. In the next passage these challenges will be boiled down to their essence, as he finds himself questioned about the central teaching of the Torah and relates this teaching to his own proclamation of the dominion of God.

JESUS IS QUESTIONED ABOUT THE HEART OF THE LAW (12:28–34)

12 ²⁸And one of the scribes, coming forward and hearing them debate, and seeing that he answered them well, asked him, "What is the first of all the commandments?" ²⁹Jesus answered, "The first is, 'Hear, Israel, the Lord our God is one Lord, ³⁰and you shall love the Lord your God out of your whole heart and out of your whole soul and out of your whole mind and out of your whole strength.' ³¹And the second is this, 'And you shall love your neighbor as yourself.' There is no other commandment greater than these."

³²And the scribe said to him, "Well said, teacher; you have truthfully said that he is one, and there is no other besides him; ³³and to love him out of one's whole heart and out of one's whole understanding and out of one's whole strength, and to love one's neighbor as oneself, is greater than all burnt offerings and sacrifices."

³⁴And Jesus, seeing that he answered intelligently, said to him, "You are not far from the dominion of God." And no one dared ask him anything anymore.

NOTES

12 28. *seeing that he answered them well.* Gk *idōn hoti kalōs apekrithē autois.* As pointed out in the introduction to the COMMENT, Mark portrays the scribe as sympathetic to Jesus and "not far from the dominion of God," whereas Matthew and Luke portray him as "testing" Jesus in a hostile manner. Augustine ingeniously reconciles these two characterizations: "It may be that though he came as a tempter, he was corrected by the answer of the Lord" (*Harmony of the Gospels* 2.73).

first of all the commandments. Gk *entolē prōtē pantōn.* This is not a reference to what is usually called "the first commandment," that is, the first of the ten, the demand to worship Yahweh only (Exod 20:3; on the enumeration of the Ten Commandments, see Nielsen, *Ten Commandments*, 10–13). *Prōtē* can connote priority in importance as well as in time and space (see BDAG 893–94 [2]). It is interesting, nevertheless, that the Shema, which Jesus cites in reply (Mark 12:29–30; see Deut 6:4–5), is essentially equivalent to the first commandment—both call for exclusive and wholehearted allegiance to the God of Israel.

29. *Hear, Israel.* Gk *akoue Israēl.* This is the beginning of the Shema (so-called from its first word, *šĕma'* = "Hear!"), the famous declaration of faith from Deuteronomy (6:4–9; 11:13–21) and Numbers (15:37–41), whose opening lines are quoted in the rest of this verse and the next one. According to *m. Tam.* 5:1, the Shema was recited daily in the Temple, and, if this is so, the Temple setting of our passage is especially appropriate for an allusion to the Shema. Foster ("Why," 326), however, questions the historicity of this Mishnaic information, asserting that it is "an attempt to legitimize rabbinic prayer practice by retrojecting it into a Second Temple setting." But the Mishnaic passage refers to several other prayers that it claims were recited in the Temple, and not all of them seem like rabbinic retrojections; one, for example, is a benediction on the outgoing course of priests. It is likely that the reference to Shema recital is an authentic memory as well, as is shown by its connection with the traditional Temple response "blessed be the name of his glorious kingdom for ever and ever" (cf. Reif, 83). Many of the prayer practices of the rabbinic era probably grew out of the Temple worship (see Reif, index under "Temple and sacrifice"); the correspondences between the two, therefore, are not necessarily retrojections.

30. *and you shall love the Lord your God out of your whole heart and out of your whole soul and out of your whole mind and out of your whole strength.* Gk *kai agapēseis kyrion ton theon sou ex holēs kardias sou kai ex holēs psychēs sou kai ex holēs dianoias sou kai ex holēs tēs ischyos sou.* On the meaning of "love" here, see the NOTE on "And you shall love your neighbor as yourself" in 12:31. In Deut 6:5 LXX a different word is used for "strength" (*dynameōs*), and there are only three phrases beginning with "out of your whole . . ." (see figure 39 and Davies and Allison, 3.242). The additional phrase in our passage is *ex holēs dianoias sou* ("out of your whole mind"), which could be an alternate translation of the Hebrew for the first phrase, since *dianoia* can be used to render the Hebrew *lĕbāb* ("heart"; see, e.g., Deut 6:5 LXX B, and Berger, *Gesetzauslegung*, 69). It is more likely, however, as Ruzer ("Love Precept," 8–10) suggests, that "out of your whole mind" and "out of your whole strength" are alternate renderings of *bkl m'dk*, the third and final object of love in Deut 6:5 MT; he cites as a parallel 1QS 1:11–12, where *d't* ("knowledge") and *kwḥ* ("strength") seem to paraphrase *m'd* from Deut 6:5. In any case, "heart," "soul," "mind," and "strength" are all roughly equivalent; they do not designate four different kinds of human capacity but the human mind and will, viewed from slightly different angles. The word *ex* is usually translated "with" (e.g., "with your whole heart"), but the Greek conveys the idea of thoughts and actions that issue from the interior of the human being (cf. Mark 7:21–23 and Berger, *Gesetzauslegung*, 68).

31. *second.* Gk *deutera.* The earliest commentary on Mark explicates this dou-

Figure 39: Versions of Deuteronomy 6:5

Deuteronomy 6:5 MT	Deuteronomy 6:5 LXX A	Deuteronomy 6:5 LXX B	Mark 12:30	Mark 12:33
ואהבת את יהוה אלהיך	καὶ ἀγαπήσεις κύριον τὸν θεόν σου	καὶ ἀγαπήσεις κύριον τὸν θεόν σου	καὶ ἀγαπήσεις κύριον τὸν θεόν σου	καὶ τὸ ἀγαπᾶν αὐτὸν
בכל לבבך	ἐξ ὅλης τῆς καρδίας σου	ἐξ ὅλης τῆς διανοίας σου	ἐξ ὅλης καρδίας σου	ἐξ ὅλης τῆς καρδίας
ובכל נפשך	καὶ ἐξ ὅλης τῆς ψυχῆς σου	καὶ ἐξ ὅλης τῆς ψυχῆς σου	καὶ ἐξ ὅλης τῆς ψυχῆς σου	
			καὶ ἐξ ὅλης διανοίας σου	καὶ ἐξ ὅλης τῆς συνέσεως
ובכל מאדך	καὶ ἐξ ὅλης τῆς δυνάμεως σου	καὶ ἐξ ὅλης τῆς δυνάμεως σου	καὶ ἐξ ὅλης τῆς ἰσχύος σου	καὶ ἐξ ὅλης τῆς ἰσχύος
and you shall love the Lord your God	and you shall love the Lord Your God	and you shall love the Lord your God	and you shall love the Lord your God	and to love him
with your whole heart	out of your whole heart	out of your whole mind	out of your whole heart	out of the whole heart
and with your whole soul	and out of your whole soul	and out of your whole soul	and out of your whole soul	
			and out of your whole mind	and out of the whole understanding
and with your whole might	and out of your whole power	and out of your whole power	and out of your whole strength	and out of the whole strength

ble commandment with an allegorical interpretation of Cant 8:1: "Our infancy is nourished from these two breasts raised above the heart of the bride" (Pseudo-Jerome, *Exposition of Mark* 12:28 [Cahill, 91]). Many ancient Jews, when called upon to summarize the Law, immediately thought of the Decalogue (cf., e.g., Philo, *On the Decalogue* 19–20, 154; *Special Laws* 1.1; *Tg. Ps.-J.* Exod 24:12; *Cant. Rab.* 1.2 §2). The latter has traditionally been divided into two "tables," consisting of the first four or five commandments, which enjoin a proper relation to God, and the second five or six, which enjoin a proper relation to other human beings. The first table could easily be reduced to the Shema, which was fused with the Decalogue in the Nash papyrus (second–first centuries B.C.E.), phylacteries from Qumran, and the liturgy of the Second Temple (*m. Tam.* 5:1; *b. Ber.* 12a)—not to mention their proximity to each other already in Deuteronomy 5–6 (see Levine, *Ancient Synagogue*, 520–22). The second table could easily be reduced to Lev 19:18 (see, e.g., Rom 13:9 and Jas 2:8, and cf. the other passages cited in the next NOTE). The Markan Jesus' response, therefore, which combines the Shema with Lev 19:18, could be viewed as an epitome of the whole Law because it is an epitome of the two tables of the Decalogue, and this would help explain the "first . . . second" terminology (cf. Allison, *Resurrecting Jesus*, 152–60).

And you shall love your neighbor as yourself. Gk *agapēseis ton plēsion sou hōs seauton.* This is a quotation of Lev 19:18; on this verse as a summary of the Law, see Gal 5:14; Rom 13:8–10; Jas 2:8–12; *b. Šabb.* 31a; *Sipra Qodašim* 4.11; and the COMMENT on 12:28–31. As with the command to love God, "love" here refers as much to deeds as it does to emotions, to the accomplishment of good for the other, which is why it can be commanded (see Davies and Allison, 3.241; Milgrom, *Leviticus*, 2.1653). This interpretation is supported by passages that explicate or allude to Lev 19:18 by means of the Golden Rule, since the latter speaks of what one *does* for the neighbor (Matt 7:12//Luke 6:31; Rom 13:8–10; *Did.* 1:2; *Tg. Ps.-J.* Lev 19:18). Contrary to a popular modern interpretation (surprisingly seconded by Milgrom, *Leviticus*, 2.1656), the commandment is not intended to encourage people to love themselves as a precondition for loving others. Self-love is assumed; Jesus calls his addressees to act toward others with the same degree of goodwill that they naturally accord to themselves (cf. *Jub.* 30:24).

In Mark, unlike in Luke, the scribe does not ask the follow-up question, "And who is my neighbor?" (Luke 10:29). In the original OT context of Lev 19:18, the neighbor is the fellow Israelite, but both the Dead Sea Scrolls (e.g., CD 6:20–21) and the Johannine literature (e.g., John 13:34–35; 1 John 2:9–11; 4:20) narrow this to the fellow member of the elect community. Some Jewish thinkers, however, like Jesus in the Parable of the Good Samaritan (Luke 10:25–37), give the commandment a universalistic interpretation: the neighbor is anyone encountered who is in need (see, e.g., *T. Iss.* 5:2; 7:6; and cf. Milgrom, *Leviticus*, 2.1654). The immediate Markan context provides no clue as to the meaning of "neighbor," though in view of the Markan Jesus' openness to Gentiles it certainly transcends the boundaries of Israel. But does it include outsiders to the church, or even enemies, as in Matt 5:43–48//Luke 6:27–36? Such an interpretation might be supported by Markan passages such as 9:40 ("the one who is not against us is for us") and 10:45; 14:24 (Jesus' death for "many"). At the same time, the Markan Jesus' threats against his betrayer (14:21) and other heinous sinners (e.g., 9:42–48) suggest that there are some limits to the divine compassion.

32. *and there is no other besides him.* Gk *kai ouk estin allos plēn autou.* This is, as Allison (*Testament of Abraham,* 192–93) points out, a biblical topos; nearly identical clauses appear in several OT passages (Exod 8:10; Deut 4:35, 39; 32:39; 2 Sam 7:22; Isa 44:6; 45:5–6, 21–22; 46:9; Joel 2:27) and in pseudepigraphical Jewish works (*T. Abr.* 8:7; *2 En.* 36:1). The Markan phrase is especially close to the formulations in Isa 45:21–22 (*kai ouk estin allos plēn emou,* "and there is no other besides me").

33. *is greater than all burnt offerings and sacrifices.* Gk *perissoteron estin pantōn tōn holokautōmatōn kai thysiōn. Holokautōmata* are literally "whole burnt offerings," that is, sacrifices completely consumed by fire. The phrase "burnt offerings and [other] sacrifices," therefore, is comparable to "tax collectors and [other] sinners" in 2:15 (see the NOTE on "and sinners" in 2:15): the first group is a subset of the second.

In its context, the present phrase recalls 1 Kgdms 15:22 ("Does the Lord take as much pleasure in burnt offerings and sacrifices as in hearing the voice of the Lord?") and Hos 6:6 ("For I want mercy rather than sacrifice, and knowledge of God rather than burnt offerings"). Both of these OT passages have further intertextual connections with our Markan pericope; the 1 Kingdoms text speaks of hearing the Lord's voice (cf. "Hear, Israel" in Mark 12:29), and the Hosea text stresses devotion to God, mercy toward fellow humans, and knowledge (cf. in our passage "out of your whole *mind* . . . out of one's whole *understanding* . . . answered *intelligently*").

34. *seeing that he answered intelligently.* Gk *idōn auton hoti nounechōs apekrithē,* lit. "seeing him, that he answered intelligently." Several early and/or reliable manuscripts, including ℵ, D, L, W, Δ, Θ, *f*[1, 13], 28, 33, etc., lat sy[s], omit *auton* ("him"). But other good manuscripts, including A, B, Ψ, 087, 2427, Majority Text, a sy[p, h], include the word, and the omission may from the smoothing out of an awkward text that reflects Semitic syntax (on the proleptic pronoun as an Aramaism, see Black, 96–100).

And no one dared ask him anything anymore. Gk *kai oudeis ouketi etolma auton eperōtēsai,* lit. "and no one no longer dared ask him," a typically Markan double negative. Both the hostile questioners of the previous passages (11:27–33; 12:13–17, 18–27) and the sympathetic interlocutor of the present one now fall silent—a common way of showing the superior wisdom and/or charismatic power of the speaker (cf. 3:4; 4:39; 9:34; and *b. Sanh.* 98a: "At this R. Eliezer remained silent"). Silence can also connote religious awe (cf. Donahue, *Are You,* 86), and it is interesting that *Gen. Rab.* 65.21 links such silence with recitation of the Shema (cf. Mark 12:29–30): "When Israel says, 'Hear, O Israel,' the angels are silent and drop their wings."

COMMENT

Introduction. In recent passages, the Markan Jesus has debated with representatives of the leading Jewish groups in first-century Palestine: the chief priests,
the scribes, and the elders (11:27), the Pharisees and the Herodians (12:13), and
the Sadducees (12:18). Now, at the conclusion of this series of controversy stories, his interlocutor is again a scribe. But while antagonistic scribes have been
Jesus' most persistent opponents since the beginning of the Gospel (1:22; 2:6–7,
16; 3:22; 7:1–13; 11:18, 27), and he will attack them in the immediately following
passages (12:35, 38–40), *this* scribe, uniquely in the Markan narrative, turns out to
be sympathetic toward Jesus and his cause (cf. Kuhn, "Problem," 301–5; Kertelge,
"Doppelgebot," 47). The scribe's departure from the general hostility of his class
is perhaps a sign that no human being can safely be judged an outsider once God
has begun to establish his dominion in the earthly sphere (cf. 12:34, "You are not
far from the dominion of God").

Strikingly, however, the scribe in the parallel passages in Matthew (22:34–40)
and Luke (10:25–28) is hostile; in both cases he is described as "testing" Jesus. Nor
is this the only agreement between Matthew and Luke over against Mark; both
call Jesus' questioner a lawyer (*nomikos*), both have him address Jesus as "teacher"
in his initial approach, and both substitute "in the Law" for "of all" in the parallels
to Mark 12:28. Both also share a number of omissions, including the first sentence
of the Shema (Mark 12:29; cf. Deut 6:4), the scribe's approbatory repetition of
the answer (12:32–33), and Jesus' encomium of him (12:34). These agreements
of Matthew and Luke against Mark can scarcely be accidental, or coincidences
in their editing of the Markan text (against Kiilunen, *Doppelgebot*); they probably reflect either scribal harmonization of Luke to Matthew or the later evangelists' common knowledge of another version of our story (see Davies and Allison,
235–36; Evans, 262). The more irenic Markan features, however, are probably
part of the pre-Markan tale, since the question the scribe asks is neither intrinsically hostile nor intrinsically tricky. Markan editing includes the long description
of the scribe's approach at the beginning (12:28) and the significant elaboration
of the ending (12:34), which contains redactional features such as the theme of
perception and the double negative (see the NOTE on "And no one dared ask
him anything anymore" in 12:34). It is also possible that Mark is responsible for
the term "understanding" in 12:33 (cf. the redactional usages of the cognate verb
in 4:12; 6:52; 7:14; 8:17, 21).

The passage falls into three sections of decreasing length: the initial question
and answer (12:28–31), the scribe's response (12:32–33), and Jesus' reaction to this
response (12:34). Contrary to the pattern in the preceding controversy stories
(11:27–12:27), Jesus' reply to the question does not terminate the conversation; our
passage is almost as much about the relationship between Jesus and the scribe as
it is about the great commandment in the Law.

12:28–31: the scribe's question and Jesus' reply. In the previous passage, the
Sadducees questioned Jesus antagonistically on an abstruse and even ridiculous

halakic subject, the application of the Pentateuchal law of marriage in the age to come. Now, however, a perspicacious and not unsympathetic scribe broaches a legal question of far greater significance: "What is the first of all the commandments?" (12:28). The finite verb "asked" is preceded by a string of participles ("coming forward . . . hearing . . . seeing"; cf. the COMMENT on 5:25–34) that emphasizes the attractive power of Jesus, which is potent enough to overpower the resistance that characterizes other scribes in the Markan narrative. The combination of "hearing" and "seeing" might remind Mark's readers of 4:12, but unlike the blinded "outsiders" of that verse or the hostile interrogators of the immediately preceding passages, this scribe sees with insight and hears with understanding.

The question about the most important commandment in the Torah (see the NOTE on "first of all the commandments" in 12:28) takes up an issue that was vigorously debated among Jesus' contemporaries. For example, despite their in-principle commitment to the unity of the Law, the Pharisees and their successors, the rabbis, acknowledged a difference between "heavy" and "light" commandments (cf. Matt 5:19; 23:23; *m. 'Abot* 2:1; 4:2; *m. Ḥul.* 12:5; Loader, *Jesus' Attitude*, 100 n. 193), and this inevitably raised the question of which commandment was weightiest of all. In response, some rabbinic traditions elevate one injunction above the others (e.g., Sabbath observance, circumcision, or avoidance of idolatry), declaring hyperbolically that the chosen statute is "equal to all the other commandments in the Torah" (see, e.g., *Exod. Rab.* 25.12; *b. Men.* 43b; *b. Ned.* 32a; cf. Urbach, *Sages*, 1.347–48). The Markan Jesus, then, is being invited by his friendly interlocutor to enter into an ongoing Jewish discussion.

His response begins with a reference to the famous Shema, the affirmation consisting principally of Deut 6:4–9 that was and remains the basic creed of Judaism. It is significant for exegesis of our passage that, according to the Mishnah, the Shema was recited daily, along with the Decalogue, in the Temple (*m. Tam.* 5:1; cf. the NOTE on "Hear, Israel" in 12:29). The latter is, of course, the setting for our story (11:27; 12:35), and the Decalogue may also be relevant to Jesus' answer (see the NOTE on "second" in 12:31).

The Markan Jesus cites the first two verses of the Shema (Deut 6:4–5), whereas the Matthean and Lukan Jesus cites only Deut 6:5, the command to love the Lord wholeheartedly. This omission by the later Gospels makes sense in a way, since Deut 6:4 is not a command but a proclamation. But the Markan narrative's inclusion of the proclamation of God's oneness (12:29) is significant for Markan Christology, since this whole section of the Gospel (11:27–12:37) answers the question posed in 11:28 about whether Jesus' authority derives "from heaven" or from the sinful human sphere. Mark's answer, which is suggested in various ways throughout the section, is that Jesus' authority comes from God; in the very next passage, indeed, Jesus will come close to placing himself on a par with "the Lord" (12:35–37). To love "the Lord our God" with all one's heart, soul, mind, and strength, then, is at the same time to love and follow Jesus—as the scribe seems nearly ready to do. Mark thus foreshadows a daring Christian reinterpretation of the Jewish idea of divine oneness, a reinterpretation that implies a unity between God and Jesus (cf. 2:7, 10 and the COMMENT on 2:6–10a; Marcus, "Authority").

The Markan Jesus, however, is not just inseparable from the object of the Shema's devotion; he also displays that devotion himself. Throughout the Gospel, indeed, Jesus demonstrates what it means to love God with one's whole being—above all, in the concluding section of the narrative, where he sets his Father's will above his own and submits himself to his God-willed death (14:36; cf. 10:45; 14:24). There is a natural connection between this sort of self-sacrifice and the Shema, as shown by the passage in *b. Ber.* 61b in which R. Akiba expresses his gratitude that his martyrdom is finally enabling him to fulfill the injunction to love God with one's whole *nepeš* ("soul" or "life"). Jesus, then, does not merely call others to love the Lord with heart, soul, mind, and strength; he also demonstrates this obedience to the divine will in costly, self-sacrificial action.

Jesus has been asked about the "first commandment," and by the end of 12:30 he has answered that question; but then he goes on to add a second biblical injunction: "You shall love your neighbor as yourself" (12:31, quoting Lev 19:18). For the Markan Jesus, apparently, the command to love God is indissoluble from the command to love the neighbor (cf. 12:33, in which the scribe runs the two commands together and makes them the subject of the singular verb "is"). Again, however, the Markan Jesus does not just *insist* that his addressees show their love for God through their love for their neighbors; he will also *demonstrate* and make such love possible by giving his life "as a ransom for many" (10:45; cf. 14:24).

The Markan Jesus, to be sure, is not saying anything startlingly novel in finding the essence of the Law in a combination of the Deuteronomic call to love God with the Levitical call to love the neighbor. Deuteronomy itself contains not only the admonition to love God with one's whole heart (Deut 6:5) but also exhortations to treat one's fellow Israelite with justice and mercy (see, e.g., Deut 22:1–4; 24:10–22). The charge to love one's neighbor as oneself in Lev 19:18, similarly, ends with the proclamation "I am the LORD," which is a reminder that the ethical demands of the Torah are linked with the divine claim to wholehearted devotion. Even outside the Israelite/Jewish sphere, many Greek thinkers defined the life of virtue as a combination of *eusebeia* ("piety") and *dikaiosynē* ("righteousness"; see Berger, *Gesetzauslegung*, 142–51), and such ideas were associated with the Torah by Hellenized Jews such as Josephus (see *War* 2.139) and Philo (*Special Laws* 2.63). The pseudepigraphical *Testaments of the Twelve Patriarchs*, similarly, seems to echo Deut 6:5 and Lev 19:18 in exhorting the patriarchs' descendants to love God and the neighbor (*T. Iss.* 5:2; 7:6; *T. Dan* 5:3). And a famous rabbinic story relates that Jesus' contemporary Hillel, when challenged by a Gentile to teach him the whole Torah while he stood on one foot, responded, "What you hate for yourself, do not do to your neighbor. This is the whole Law; the rest is commentary" (*b. Šabb.* 31a). As Davies and Allison (3.245) point out, this negative form of the Golden Rule was considered to be synonymous with Lev 19:18 in Jewish and Christian traditions (see, e.g., *Tg. Ps-J.* Lev 19:18; *Did.* 1:2).

12:32–33: the scribe's response. Jesus' interlocutor, impressed with a response that draws on such a wealth of Jewish tradition, commends Jesus (12:32a) and then goes on to repeat and elaborate on his response, breaking it into two parts, but erasing the division between the biblical passages quoted. He first cites Deut 6:4 ("he is one") and adds his own supplement, a common biblical topos with especially close ties to Isa 45:21–22 ("and there is no other besides him"; see the NOTE on this clause in 12:32). He then fuses Deut 6:5 with Lev 19:18 and again adds a supplement, this time an allusion to 1 Sam 15:22 or Hos 6:6 (obedience to God and mercy are more important than burnt offerings and sacrifices; on the relevance of these passages, see the NOTE on "is greater than all burnt offerings and sacrifices" in 12:33). This procedure of supplementing Pentateuchal verses with quotations from the Prophets (1 Samuel, according to Jewish nomenclature, is in the "Former Prophets") is well known from Jewish liturgical practice (see Acts 13:15–16 and Levine, *Synagogue*, index under "Haftarah reading").

The scribe's additions are particularly revealing. "And there is no other besides him" (12:32) is an important Jewish principle that was frequently used *against* Christians, who were accused of making Jesus equal to God and thus violating the oneness of God proclaimed in the Shema (see, e.g., John 5:18; 8:58–59; 10:31–33; Segal, *Two Powers*, 89, 137–40, 148–49, 152, 232; Marcus, *Way*, 145–46; "Idolatry," 142–44). By quoting this principle in a context that suggests a Jewish scribe's *approval* of Jesus, the Markan narrative implies that the Shema's affirmation of divine oneness is compatible with reverence for Jesus. Similarly, the scribe's assertion that loving God and neighbor transcends the sacrifices performed in the Temple (12:33) shows him to be like-minded with Jesus, who has recently interrupted the sacrificial commerce in the Temple (11:15–17) and will shortly declare that structure to be passé (13:1–2; cf. Loader, *Jesus' Attitude*, 101–2). The accord between Jesus and the scribe, then, delivers a message similar to that of the healing story in 1:40–45 (see the COMMENT on 1:43–45): Jesus' clashes with elements of the Jewish leadership do not make him a bad Jew.

12:34: Jesus' praise of the scribe. Our passage, however, does not conclude with the scribe's praise of Jesus but with Jesus' commendation of the scribe. Seeing that the man has answered intelligently, Jesus tells him, "You are not far from the dominion of God" (12:34a). This penultimate sentence ties up a number of the pericope's themes.

First, it expresses the motif of perception that has loomed large in the passage and the Gospel as a whole. The passage begins with the scribe *seeing* that Jesus has answered the Sadducees well; it concludes with Jesus *seeing* that the man has answered him *intelligently*. In between, the particular form in which the Shema is quoted emphasizes loving God with one's whole *mind* and one's whole *understanding* (12:30, 33; cf. Loader, *Jesus' Attitude*, 100). The God whom Jesus proclaims, therefore, is one who grasps mind as well as heart and thus brings a new type of perception into the world.

Second, the penultimate sentence draws to a close the passage's favorable portrait of the scribe: not only is he intelligent, but he is also close to God's dominion. This portrait would deliver an important message to the Markan community, which seems in general to have suffered at the hands of Jewish leaders (cf. 13:9).

Despite the prevailing hostility, Mark is implying, all is not necessarily lost; some even among the leaders may still be susceptible to God's call (cf. Kertelge, "Doppelgebot," 47). This interpretation is supported by the portrait of Joseph of Arimathea near the Gospel's conclusion: though a member of the ruling council, Joseph piously awaits God's dominion, recognizes its intimate connection with Jesus, and in the end plucks up the courage to identify himself with him (15:43).

Third, however, this sentence orients Jesus' encounter with the scribe to reinforce the Gospel's prevailing theme from 11:27 onward: the authority of Jesus. If the scribe begins by being favorably impressed with Jesus (12:28) and approving his response to a test question (12:32), Jesus ends by being favorably impressed with the scribe ("seeing that he answered intelligently," 12:34a). The language used here seems deliberately to mirror that used in the initial description of the scribe ("seeing that [Jesus] answered them well") in order to underline this reversal. Nor does the Markan Jesus go overboard in his praise of the scribe; the latter is *close* to the dominion of God, but not fully in it (12:34b; cf. Theophylact, *Explanation of Mark* 12:28–34, who says that "the Lord's words of praise bore witness to the fact that the man was not yet perfect"). It is Jesus who judges humanity, not the other way around; and in confirmation of his preeminence the passage concludes with the editorial remark that henceforth "no one dared ask him anything" (12:34c; see the NOTE).

This silencing of opposition is closely related by the context to the advent of the dominion of God (12:34bc), and this juxtaposition is probably deliberate. Jesus' conclusive and discussion-ending reply reflects not just his personal wisdom but the arrival of the eschatological power whereby God regrasps the world for himself (cf. Käsemann, "Righteousness," 182). In view of the Temple setting and the allusions to the Shema in the passage, it is significant that a blessing accompanying recital of that creed in the sanctuary praised "the name of [God's] glorious dominion for ever and ever" (see *m. Tam.* 5:1; *Gen. Rab.* 65.21; cf. Reif, *Judaism*, 83; Kimelman, "Shema"). In the Markan narrative, then, the Shema's acclamation of divine unity is not a static description of a condition that has always existed but an announcement of an *event*, the eschatological fusion of the world below with the world above that occurs as Jesus extends God's dominion from heaven to earth (cf. Zech 14:9: "And the LORD will become king over all the earth; on that day the LORD will be one and his name one").

The Gospel's next passage will use OT images to portray this extension of royal power, and the intimate connection between God and Jesus, by showing Jesus enthroned beside God while the latter crushes enemies under his feet.

JESUS OPPOSES THE SCRIBAL VIEW OF THE MESSIAH (12:35–37)

12 ³⁵And Jesus answered and said, teaching in the Temple, "How do the scribes say that the Christ is the Son of David? ³⁶David himself said in the Holy Spirit, 'The Lord said to my lord, "Sit on my right until I put your enemies under your

feet.'" ³⁷David himself calls him 'lord'; and how is he his son?" And the large crowd heard him gladly.

NOTES

12 35. *answered and said*. Gk *apokritheis . . . elegen*. This seems strange at first, because in the immediate context no one has spoken; indeed, the preceding words emphasize that Jesus' interlocutors have fallen silent ("And no one dared ask him anything anymore," 12:34b). Part of the explanation is that "answered and said" is a biblical idiom frequently employed in our Gospel (see the NOTES on "he answered and said" in 3:33 and "answered and said" in 7:28). The present usage, however, is not just idiomatic: Jesus is responding to the significant silence of his questioners (see the COMMENT).

36. *David himself said in the Holy Spirit*. Gk *autos Dauid eipen en tō pneumati tō hagiō*. Because many of the biblical psalms begin with *lĕdāwîd* ("to/for/of David") and because of David's reputation as a great poet and musician (e.g., 1 Sam 16:18–23; 2 Sam 1:17–27; 22:1–23:7), he is commonly credited in ancient Jewish and Christian literature as the author of the Psalter. As Evans (273) notes, the idea that David was inspired by the Spirit goes back to the OT (2 Sam 23:2), and he is described as a Spirit-inspired prophet in the Dead Sea Scrolls (11QPsᵃ 27:2–4, 11), the NT (Acts 1:16; 4:25), and rabbinic literature (*b. Ber.* 4b; *b. ʿArak.* 15b; etc.). On the close relation between the Holy Spirit and prophecy in Jewish texts, see Schäfer, *Vorstellung*, passim.

The reference to the Holy Spirit here is one of a number of parallels with the pre-Pauline Christological credo in Rom 1:3–4:

Mark 12:35–37	*Romans 1:3–4*
[scribes say that] Christ is the Son of David	descended from David according to the flesh
David himself . . . in the Holy Spirit . . . calls Christ "lord"	Son of God with power according to the Spirit of holiness . . . Jesus Christ our Lord
[God says to Christ], Sit on my right	by resurrection from the dead

The Lord said to my lord, etc. Gk *eipen kyrios tō kyriō mou*, etc. This is a citation of Ps 110:1 [109:1 LXX] that more or less corresponds to the LXX, with the substitution of "under" for "as a footstool," on which see the next NOTE. In the original context, "my lord" is the ruling Davidic monarch, who is symbolically exalted to co-regency with God on the day of his coronation. In postbiblical Judaism, however, this and the other enthronement psalms were interpreted as prophecies of the establishment of God's reign through his Messiah or other eschatological agents (see Dan 7:13–14; 11QMelchizedek 2; *Midr. Psalms* 110.4; cf. Marcus, *Way*, 132–37).

under. Gk *hypokatō*. This word reflects Ps 8:6, "You [God] have subjected all

things under his feet" (*hypokatō tōn podōn autou*), a verse that is frequently conflated with Ps 110:1 in the NT (cf. 1 Cor 15:20–28; Eph 1:20–23; 1 Pet 3:21–22),
perhaps partly because both texts speak of universal subjection to a figure who
has been granted divine authority. In Ps 8:4 this figure is called "man" (*anthrōpos*)
and "son of man" (*huios anthrōpou*) synonymously, a circumstance that facilitated
its application to Jesus, whose favorite term for himself in the Synoptic tradition
is "the Son of Man" (cf. also Heb 2:5–9). The conflation of Ps 110:1 with Ps 8:6
in the Pauline texts and 1 Peter probably reflects early Christian creeds dealing
with Christ's exaltation over angelic or demonic powers (cf. de Boer, *Defeat*,
114–20).

37. *and how is he his son.* Gk *kai pothen autou estin huios*, lit. "and whence is he
his son?" The logic seems to be that no father calls his own son "lord"; therefore if
David calls the Messiah "lord," it is inappropriate to call him "the Son of David"
(cf. *Barn.* 12:11: "See how David calls him 'lord' and does not say 'son' ").

Many exegetes, however, prefer to take their cues from Rom 1:3–4: Christ is
both the Son of David *and* the Son of God (see, e.g., Tertullian, *Against Marcion* 4.38; Novatian, *On the Trinity* 11; Bede, *Exposition of Mark* 12:35–37). The
fourth-century anti-Gnostic writer Adamantius asserts that "how" in Mark 12:35
implies questioning but not denial, as in Deut 32:30; Isa 1:21; 14:12 (*Concerning
True Faith in God*; PG 11.1849–52). A similar conclusion is reached by modern
interpreters such as Lövestam ("Davidssohnfrage," 72–82) and Juel (*Messianic
Exegesis*, 142–44), who take our passage as a rabbinic-style reconciliation of contradictory scriptural expectations (the Davidic descent of the Messiah on the one
hand, his exaltation to heaven on the other).

As Bultmann (407) points out, however, our passage cites only one scripture
(Ps 110:1), not two. Its foil, moreover, is a scribal opinion, and in Mark such opinions are routinely refuted (see 2:6–8; 3:22–27; 7:5–13; 9:11–13; 11:27–33; 15:31–32)
and the scribes as a class negatively evaluated (the scribe in 12:28–34 is an exception). Certainly, as Adamantius claims, *pōs* ("how") and *pothen* ("whence") can
have a variety of meanings, depending on context (cf. de Jonge, "Jesus, Son of
David," 99). But the OT passages he cites in favor of the interrogative interpretation are not apposite (*pōs* introduces exclamations rather than questions), and
the immediate context here suggests that Jesus is aiming at refutation rather than
reconciliation, since, again, no father calls his own son "lord." This would be especially true in the hierarchical Greco-Roman world, where lord" and "son" were
near opposites, the father being, so to speak, the lord of the son (cf. the household
codes in Col 3:18–4:1; Eph 5:21–6:9).

On the face of it, then, our passage seems to be denying that the Messiah is
"the Son of David." Earlier in Mark, however, Jesus was hailed as "the Son of David" by Bartimaeus (10:47–48) and as the restorer of "the dominion of our father
David" by the crowd at the triumphal entry (11:9–10), and in neither case did he
reject the link with David. How, then, is 12:35–37 to be reconciled with these
earlier passages—not to mention the overwhelming OT and Jewish expectation
that the Messiah is to be a descendant of David (see the APPENDIX "The 'Son of
David' Title") and the numerous extra-Markan NT references to Jesus' Davidic

descent (e.g., Matt 1:6; Luke 3:31; Acts 2:30–31; 13:22–23; Rom 1:3–4; 2 Tim 2:8; Rev 3:7; 5:5; 22:16)?

Two answers seem possible: (1) In our passage Mark has preserved a rare historical memory that Jesus was not a Davidide and that he recognized that this deficient ancestry might, in some people's eyes, disqualify him from messiahship (cf. John 7:42). In the development of the Christian tradition, however, this memory of his non-Davidic descent has been overwhelmed by the conviction that since he was the Messiah, he *had* to be descended from David (cf. Burger, *Jesus*, 52–59). (2) The Markan Jesus is not denying the Messiah's physical descent from David but the adequacy of the Davidic image to express his full identity. Explanation (2) seems to be closer to the Markan meaning of the Son of David pericope, and there may be additional factors in the Markan situation that render the Davidic image problematic (see the COMMENT on 12:35–37). But explanation (1) cannot be ruled out as a possible meaning for the original tradition, assuming that it goes back to Jesus. Brown (*Birth*, 505–12) and Meier (*Marginal Jew*, 1.216–19; "Elijah-like Prophet") disagree, pointing out that pagan and Jewish critics of Christianity fail to attack Jesus' lack of Davidic credentials and arguing that it would be difficult to explain the genesis of belief in his messiahship if he was known not to be a Davidide. But the scriptural necessity for the Messiah's Davidic descent might answer some of these objections. After all, many critical scholars, including Brown and Meier, think that Jesus was not born in Bethlehem, despite the agreement of Matthew and Luke that he was (cf. Brown, *Birth*, 513–16; Meier, *Marginal Jew*, 214–16). In that instance, the imperative of conformity with scripture (Mic 5:2) has overwhelmed historical fact to create a pre-Gospel tradition. Could not the same be true of belief in Jesus' Davidic descent?

And the large crowd heard him gladly. Gk *kai ho polys ochlos ēkouen autou hēdeōs.* Evans (275) cites an intriguing parallel from *Ant.* 18.63, where Josephus refers to Jesus as "a teacher of such people as accept the truth with gladness" (*didaskalos anthrōpōn tōn hēdonȩ̄ talēthȩ̄ dechomenōn* [LCL trans. alt.]; on Jesus as teacher, cf. Mark 12:35).

COMMENT

Introduction. Having vanquished his opponents in a series of verbal duels (11:27–12:27; cf. 12:34c), and having asserted his authority over a sympathetic scribe (12:28–34b), Jesus now goes on the offensive against scribes who are *not* sympathetic, first showing the error of their opinions about the Messiah (12:35–37), then denouncing their rapacity and hypocrisy (12:38–40).

The present passage, which concerns the Christological question, is a pre-Markan product that arguably reaches back to the historical Jesus, since it is in tension with the usual view of Jews and Christians that the Messiah must be of Davidic descent, and so would not likely have been an early Christian invention. The conflation of Ps 110:1 with Ps 8:6, however, is frequent in early Christian creeds and may reflect post-Easter exegesis (see the NOTE on "under" in 12:36). Markan redaction is clearly visible only at the beginning (12:35a) and end

(12:37b), two half-verses that are full of redactional vocabulary ("answered and said," "teaching," "large crowd," "heard"; cf. Mudiso Mbâ Mundla, *Führer*, 236–37; Marcus, *Way*, 131).

This short passage is structured chiastically around the citation of Psalm 110:1 (here in italics):

12:35a	And Jesus answered and said, teaching in the Temple,	A
12:35b	"How do the scribes say that the Christ is the Son of David?	B
12:36a	David himself said in the Holy Spirit,	C
12:36b	*'The Lord said to my lord, "Sit on my right*	
12:36c	*until I put your enemies under your feet.'"*	D
12:37a	David himself calls him 'lord';	C′
12:37b	and how is he his son?"	B′
12:37c	And the large crowd heard him gladly.	A′

The outer portion, AA′, provides the narrative frame of Jesus' instruction, and BB′ asserts the problematic nature of Davidic sonship. CC′ explicates the problem: Davidic sonship contradicts what "David himself" said about the Messiah. D, the center of the chiasm, relates the specific scriptural words that create the contradiction.

12:35–37: Davidic sonship and the Messiah. The previous passage ended with Jesus' interlocutors falling silent before him. This silence speaks volumes about his authority, which has been in dispute since 11:27. Now Jesus responds to ("answers") his questioners' silence with a scriptural proof that the Messiah is David's lord (cf. Gundry, 717). This proof is relevant to the issue of Jesus' authority because, for Mark's readers at least, Jesus himself is the Messiah, so any statement about the Messiah is *ipso facto* a declaration about Jesus.

Jesus' monologue takes place as he is teaching "in the Temple" (12:35a), a specification that is superfluous at first sight (it repeats 11:27), but in fact significant. A traditional nexus existed between Jerusalem, the Temple, and the coming Davidic Messiah, who was expected not only to cleanse Jerusalem of its pagan defilements and restore the Temple but also to be a profound expositor of God's word (see esp. *Pss. Sol.* 17:21–46). Within the Markan narrative, Jesus has already entered Jerusalem in triumph, been hailed as the vanguard of David's restored dominion, and asserted his messianic authority over the Temple by an act of symbolic appropriation and purification (11:1–18; cf. Marcus, *Way*, 137–39). So far, therefore, Jesus' actions in Jerusalem and the Temple have conformed to a traditional messianic paradigm (although see the COMMENT on 11:15–19).

This makes all the more surprising what happens next: Jesus seems to go on the offensive, not against pagans, but against Jewish scribes who teach that the Messiah is "the Son of David" (12:35b). Jesus' monologue here begins and ends with a "how" question that is most naturally interpreted as a denial (see the NOTE on "and how is he his son" in 12:37). The following outline, moreover, seems to be the only one that does justice to the argument's progression:

The scribes call the Christ the *Son* of David, implying that David is his
    father,
But David himself calls the Christ his *lord.*
No father calls his own son "lord";
Therefore David is not the Christ's father, and the Christ is not David's son.

The Markan Jesus employs a traditional Jewish exegetical method: establishing
the inferiority of one biblical character to another through ingenious juxtaposition
of scriptural traditions (see, e.g., *Mekilta, Pisḥa* 1 [Lauterbach 1.1] 3 [Lauterbach
1.22]). But the result is innovative, since the opposition between the Messiah and
the Davidic line contradicts not only Jewish messianic expectations but also the
OT itself, which looks for a scion of David—later called the Messiah, or "anointed
one"—to restore David's shattered dynasty (see the APPENDIX "The 'Son of
David' Title"). In Christian sources outside of our passage, moreover, including
Markan ones, Jesus' Davidic descent is affirmed (see 10:47–48 and cf. 11:9–10 and
the NOTE on "and how is he his son" in 12:37). Rather than the inquiry that the
Markan Jesus actually makes, one might well pose the opposite question: How
can he imply that the Messiah is *not* David's son?

Leaving aside the question of what 12:35–37 meant for the historical Jesus (see
the NOTE just cited) and concentrating on its Markan meaning, it seems that
overall the evangelist means both to affirm and to qualify the idea of Davidic
messianism. This ambivalence probably has to do with the Gospel's setting in
the Jewish War against the Romans (see Marcus, "Jewish War," and the INTRO-
DUCTION in vol. 1, pp. 33–37). The latter appears to have been catalyzed and
led by Jewish "messiahs" of Davidic stripe such as Menachem son of Judas the
Galilean and Simon bar Giora (see Josephus, *War* 2.433–34, 444, 652; 4.510,
574–78; 7.29–31). On the one hand, then, Mark wishes to affirm that Jesus rather
than Menachem or Simon was the true "Son of David," as he showed when he entered Jerusalem in triumph and purged the Temple, thereby manifesting his own
and the divine kingship. On the other hand, Mark's embrace of Davidic messianism is equivocal, partly perhaps because Menachem, Simon, and their followers
linked that hope with a nationalistic fervor that was not only anti-Roman but also
anti-Gentile (cf. Psalm 2; *Pss. Sol.* 17; etc.). For Mark, then, Jesus *is* the Davidic
Messiah, but the "Son of David" title does not pluck out the heart of his mystery
(cf. Shakespeare, *Hamlet* 3.2).

That is because, for Mark, Jesus' identity is not defined so much by his relationship to David as by his relationship to God. It is revealing that when the Markan
Jesus uses Ps 110:1 to establish David's inferiority to the Messiah, he quotes more
of the psalm than he needs to for that purpose, citing the picture of "the Lord"
telling "my lord" to sit on his right until he has subdued his enemies (12:36bc).
A seated position on the right hand of a deity implies co-regency with him, as is
confirmed both by ancient iconography (see Keel, *Symbolism,* 253–68; Hengel,
Christology, 175–79) and by Jewish texts (see *b. Sanh.* 38b and cf. Dan 7:9–14).
The imagery of the quoted portion of the psalm, then, implies that "my lord"
stands in a relation of near-equality with God, and the inference for Mark would

seem to be that Jesus is not (just) the Son of David but (also) the Son of God. This implication is consonant both with the continuation of Psalm 110 in the LXX, which speaks of divine begetting (Ps 110:3 [109:3 LXX]; cf. Marcus, *Way*, 141), and with the parallel in Rom 1:3–4, which speaks of the Davidic Messiah as God's Son (see the NOTE on "David himself said in the Holy Spirit" in 12:36).

This conclusion is also consonant with the observations that Adam, too, was "the Son of God" (see Luke 3:38) and that in our passage and elsewhere in Mark's Gospel Jesus may be presented as a new Adam (see the subject index in vols. 1 and 2 under "Adam"; Marcus, "Mark—Interpreter," 3 and n. 11; "Son of Man," 371–77). This Adamic nuance comes to the fore through the conflation of Ps 110:1 with Ps 8:6 (see the NOTE on "under" in 12:36); the latter is, in origin and interpretation, an allusion to Adam as the divinely endowed sovereign of creation (see G. Anderson, "Exaltation"). Jesus, then, is not just a new David but a new Adam, and as such he has power not merely over human adversaries but also over demonic powers of cosmic scope (see again the NOTE on "under" in 12:36)—including the last enemy of all, death (cf. 1 Cor 15:21–28). The Markan Jesus has foreshadowed this Adamic sovereignty in his exorcisms throughout the Gospel, and he will conclusively prove it at the Gospel's end, when he is exalted to God's right hand through the resurrection—the definitive sign of a new creation.

In line with these hints about a renovation of the universe, it is fitting that the passage concludes with the editorial notice that the large crowd heard Jesus gladly (12:37c). Joy breaks forth when the Markan Jesus alludes to the new creation, as joy broke forth when God created the old one (cf. Gen 2:23; Job 38:7). It is significant, moreover, that here, as at other points in his narrative, Mark juxtaposes the crowd's enthusiasm for Jesus with their leaders' opposition (cf. 1:22; 2:6–7, 12; 3:20, 22; 8:1–12; 11:18; 12:12; 14:2). The common people are moving to Jesus' side and away from that of the scribes; a basic realignment of Palestinian politics is taking place as part of the cosmic revolution instigated by David's lord.

In the next passage Jesus will reciprocate this popular support by denouncing the scribes' ruthless exploitation of the people.

JESUS CONDEMNS SCRIBAL OPPRESSION AND HYPOCRISY (12:38–40)

12 ³⁸And in his teaching he said, "Watch out for those scribes who like to go around in long robes, and like greetings in the marketplaces ³⁹and the first seats in the synagogues and the first couches at feasts; ⁴⁰who devour the houses of widows and make long prayers as a pretext. These men will receive greater condemnation."

NOTES

12 38. *those scribes who like to.* Gk *tōn grammateōn tōn thelontōn*, lit. "the scribes the ones liking to." In classical Greek *thelein* usually means "want, desire" rather

than "like, enjoy," and Zerwick (149) identifies its usage here in the latter sense as a Semitism (cf. Lust, *Lexicon*, 203; Jastrow, 1493 [*rṣy*]). As early as Homer, however, there are examples of *(e)thelein* = "like" in Greek uninfluenced by Semitic sources, and the locution is especially common in Epictetus (cf. Schrenk, *Thelō*, 45; BDAG 448 [3]).

The participial clause *tōn thelontōn*, etc. could be interpreted either as an apposition ("the scribes, the ones who like to . . .") or as a restrictive modifier, as is done in the present translation (see Smyth §1158; Robertson, 776, 1106; Goodwin, *Grammar* §959). The latter is the way in which the other Markan constructions of the form plural definite article + noun + plural definite article + adjective/ participle are most naturally interpreted (1:27; 3:22; 6:7; 7:21; 9:42; 13:25). The closest parallel is 3:22, *hoi grammateis hoi apo Hierosolymōn katabantes*, lit. "the scribes, the ones coming down from Jerusalem" = "the scribes who had come down from Jerusalem." This does not imply that *all* scribes came down from Jerusalem, but that Mark is focusing on the subset of them that did. In the present case, the example of the good scribe a few verses earlier (12:28–34) shows that the evangelist does not think that all scribes are of the vainglorious sort he is depicting here.

in long robes. Gk *en stolais.* The Sinaiticus manuscript of the Old Syriac translation reflects the reading *en stoais* ("in stoas," or porches), a difference of just one letter from the usual version, and probably in origin either a mistake or an attempt to create an easier text.

The *stolē* was a long, flowing robe, usually worn on festal occasions; in the LXX the term is used for the garments of priests, especially the high priest, and the king (see, e.g., Exod 28:2; 29:21; 31:10; 2 Chron 18:9; see Rengstorf, "Stolai," 389). The association of *stolai* with priests continues in postbiblical Jewish usage (see Philo, *Embassy to Gaius* 296; Josephus, *Ant.* 3.151–56; 11.80), and this is significant because the NT scribes were probably priests and Levites (see the APPENDIX "The Scribes and the Pharisees" in vol. 1, p. 524). The priestly *stolē* was designed to impress; Josephus, for example, says that the beauty of a priest's robe "is displayed to the beholders' advantage" (*Ant.* 3.155; cf. Sir 50:11 on the glorious robe of the high priest Simon).

greetings in the marketplaces. Gk *aspasmous en tais agorais.* The respectful greeting was valued not only for its own sake but also for the glory it conferred on the recipient in the eyes of bystanders (note the public venue implied by "in the marketplaces"). Jesus' negative attitude toward such signs of distinction is similar to that of R. Yoḥanan ben Zakkai, about whom it is said that "no one ever preceded him in greeting, even a Gentile in the market-place" (*b. Ber.* 17a, my trans.): he did not wait to be greeted, as behooved his dignity, but always greeted others first (cf. Evans, 278).

39. *first seats.* Gk *prōtokathedrias.* Matthew 23:2 acknowledges that "the scribes and Pharisees sit on Moses' seat," a declaration that has been linked with the isolated stone seat found in the ancient synagogues in Delos, Dura Europos, Ḥammat Tiberias, Chorazim, and ʿEn Gedi, which seems to have had

an honorific purpose. Cf. *b. Yeb.* 98a, which mentions a special seat on which R. 'Aqibah sat while he taught (see Davies and Allison, 3.268; Levine, *Synagogue*, 323–27).

first couches. Gk *prōtoklisias.* On the custom of reclining at meals, see the NOTE on "reclining at table" in 2:15. On the importance of who sits where and other matters of precedence in banquets, etc., see Luke 14:7–14; 1QS 6:4–6, 8–9; *b. Ber.* 46b. In 1QS the priest takes precedence at the communal meal; see the NOTE on "in long robes" in 12:38 on the NT scribes as priests.

40. *who devour the houses.* Gk *hoi katesthiontes tas oikias.* Derrett ("Eating Up," 6–8) cites two noteworthy parallels: *Test. Mos.* 7:6–7, "Devourers of the goods of the [poor], saying that they do so on the grounds of their justice, but in reality to destroy them . . ."; and *b. Git.* 52b, in which the trustee of an orphan's property is accused of "eating and drinking out of what is theirs" (my trans.).

of widows. Gk *tōn chērōn.* A few Western and "Caesarean" witnesses (D, W, *f*[13], 28, 565, it) add *kai orphanōn* ("and of orphans"), thus conforming our text to a standard OT phrase (cf. Exod 22:22; Deut 14:29; Isa 1:17; etc.). It is possible that the longer phrase is original and that *kai orphanōn* has dropped out through haplography induced by the homoeoteleuton of the *-ōn* ending (see the GLOSSARY); as Freedman writes, "Surely you would expect orphans to be included in such references." This expectation, however, may explain the scribe's addition rather than the story's original form (cf. Metzger, 111), and the textual evidence for inclusion is weak.

On the general OT attitude toward widows, see the COMMENT on 12:38–40. In view of the identification of NT scribes as priests and Levites (see the NOTE on "in long robes" in 12:38), it is striking that in several Deuteronomic texts, the Levites are included along with widows, orphans, and resident aliens as people who require societal support. This is because their complete devotion to God precludes land ownership and thus reduces them to a humble status (see, e.g., Deut 14:29; 16:14; 26:12). The situation in which rapacious Levitical scribes prey on poor widows is thus a reversal of the God-ordained solidarity between the two groups.

These men will receive greater condemnation. Gk *houtoi lēpsontai perissoteron krima.* As pointed out in the COMMENT on 12:38–40, the OT often threatens with judgment those who oppress widows, orphans, and other helpless persons. In some cases this punishment seems to be a threat that the oppressor will experience a loss of fortune in this life (see, e.g., Deut 27:19 [cf. 28:15–68]; Job 22:9–11), but in later OT texts and postbiblical literature the threatened judgment becomes eschatological (see, e.g., Wis 2:10 in context). It is particularly interesting, in view of the larger Markan context, that the threatened punishments include destruction of a prominent Jerusalem building (the king's palace in Jer 22:3–6; cf. the threatened destruction of the Temple in Mark 13:1–2) and the dispersion of Israel among the nations (Ezek 22:7, 15; Zech 7:10–14; *Tg. Isa.* 10:1–4; cf. Mark 12:9; 13:14).

COMMENT

Introduction. Having refuted the scribes' ideas about the pedigree of the Messiah (12:35–37), Jesus now impugns their character, accusing them bluntly of oppression and hypocrisy.

It is probable that the three passages in 12:28–34, 12:35–37, and 12:38–40 stood together in a pre-Markan collection (see the introduction to chapters 11–13); our text, the last in the series, is connected with the previous two pericopes through the catchword "scribes." Markan redaction is clearly visible only at the beginning, in the introductory 12:38a ("And in his teaching he said . . ."). Despite this pre-Markan provenance, however, the passage fits well into the Gospel's overall narrative.

After the redactional introduction, the pericope consists of three sections, of decreasing length. First, there is a four-part description of things the scribes like (robes, greetings, choice seats in synagogues, choice seats at feasts; 12:38b–39). Next, there is a two-part description of their nefarious activities (devouring widows' estates, masking their rapacity with prayer; 12:40a). Finally, there is a terse clause prophesying their eschatological condemnation (12:40b). As the sections become shorter and shorter, then, the theme grows darker and darker: from frivolous concern with externals (12:38b–39) to oppression and hypocrisy (12:40a) to the prospect of fierce judgment (12:40b).

12:38–40: Jesus' condemnation of the scribes. The first part of Jesus' condemnation of the scribes focuses on their vainglorious concern with the trappings of elite status: long robes, public salutations, and the "first" (*prōto*-) seats at synagogue services and dinner parties (12:38b–39). In the honor-conscious Greco-Roman society, such distinctions would have been important signs of status, but in the Markan context they fall under the judgment that in God's end-time dominion, the first (*prōtoi*) will become last (cf. 10:31). The *prōto*-language, then, already foreshadows the reference to the eschatological assize at the end of the passage (12:40b).

The reason for this harsh judgment becomes plain in 12:40a, where Jesus rips off the scribes' mask of respectability to reveal the brutal, even demonic reality underneath. This contrast between appearance and actuality is reinforced by the transition from "feasts" at the end of 12:39 to "devour" at the beginning of 12:40; while the first word suggests orderly, civilized dining, the second implies the sort of ravenous assault on food that is characteristic of wild animals (cf. BDAG 532). As Miller (*Women*, 121–22) notes, moreover, the only other Markan usage of "to devour" is 4:4, where the subject is birds that are later allegorized as Satan (4:15). As elsewhere, therefore, Mark implies an overlap between Jesus' human opponents and his devilish ones (see the subject index under "Enemies of Jesus, human and demonic"). The very pillars of society, men distinguished as such by dress and universal approbation, are revealed to be demonic abusers of the helpless who use prayer as a means for veiling their assaults.

The specific charge against the scribes is that they "devour the houses of widows" (12:40a). The reference to widows invokes a rich OT background, much of which is relevant to our passage. Widows, along with orphans, resident aliens, and the poor in general are often mentioned in the OT as objects of special concern to God, since they are without the usual social support systems. Their well-being, therefore, is a sacred trust, and to violate it, for example by defrauding them, is an especially heinous crime (see, e.g., Jer 7:6–7; Ezek 22:7; Zech 7:10–14; Mal 3:5). Since, moreover, the widow's house was often the sum total of her inheritance, it was an especially important matter to maintain it for or restore it to her (Ps 68:5–6; cf. Prov 15:25). To deprive her of it, contrariwise, would be a particularly grave transgression, and those who perpetrate outrages against widows are warned in numerous OT texts that they will eventually be punished by the "God of vengeance" (Ps 94:1, 6; see the NOTE on "These men will receive greater condemnation" in 12:40). Many of these themes come together in Isa 10:1–4, a passage with especially striking points of contact to Mark 12:38–40:

> Ha!
> Those who write out evil writs
> And compose iniquitous documents,
> To subvert the cause of the poor,
> To rob of their rights the needy of My people;
> That widows may be their spoil,
> And fatherless children their booty!
> What will you do on the day of punishment,
> When the calamity comes from afar? . . .
> [God's] anger has not turned back,
> And his arm is outstretched still. (NJPS)

Not only is a day of divine punishment decreed against those who abuse widows and other helpless people, as in Mark 12:40b, but the oppressors are said to defraud their victims with "evil writs" and "iniquitous documents"—that is, documents that would come from a scribe. The influence of this OT passage is attested by CD 6:16–17, which links the widows' plunderers with "the wealth of the Temple"—apparently identifying them, therefore, with the Temple priests (cf. Evans, 284) and thus supporting the hypothesis that the scribes in our passage are meant to be understood as priests and Levites (see the NOTE on "in long robes" in 12:38). The Targum on the Isaiah passage is even closer to the language and context of our pericope, since it specifies that the *property* of the widows is plundered and that the threatened judgment will include exile from Israel (cf. Mark 12:9; 13:14).

Given this biblical background, exactly what is the scribal oppression described in Mark 12:40a? Since "house" means not only the building in which one lives but also the property that it contains (cf. 3:27 and BDAG 699 [4]), the reference is probably to appropriation of the estate that the widow's husband has bequeathed to her. The exact mechanism of this appropriation is unclear; Fitzmyer (*Luke* 2.1318) lists six different possibilities, of which he favors Derrett's conjecture that the scribe, acting as a probate lawyer, has cheated the widow out of the estate by overcharging for his services ("Eating"; cf. *b. Git.* 52b, cited in the NOTE on "who devour the houses" in 12:40). Another possibility is that the passage has in view forcible seizure of property by priests, who are also scribes, for nonpayment of tithes (cf. Josephus, *Ant.* 20.206). In either case, the passage's reference to prayer may suggest that the scribe tries to mitigate his guilt by promising to pray for the victim of his legal skullduggery (cf. Evans, 279)—an attempt that only increases his culpability (12:40b). The general atmosphere of sacerdotal extortion here is illuminated by the famous denunciation of high-priestly families in a Talmudic tradition (*b. Pes.* 57a):

> Woe is me because of the house of Boethus, woe is me because of their staves! Woe is me because of the house of Ḥanin, woe is me because of their whisperings! Woe is me because of the house of Kathros, woe is me because of their pens! Woe is me because of the house of Ishmael son of Phabi, woe is me because of their fists! For they are high priests and their sons are [Temple] treasurers and their sons-in-law are trustees and their servants beat the people with staves.

Here the high-priestly clans are accused of violence ("staves," "fists"), stealthiness ("whisperings"), and oppression of the common people ("beat the people")—all characteristics of the Markan scribes in the present context. Significantly, moreover, one of the instruments of this oppression is the *pen*, bringing the Talmudic tradition close to our text's portrayal of rapacious *scribes*.

Like the Talmudic passage, the Markan one unmasks the brutal reality that beautiful robes and impressive-sounding prayer may conceal. The conclusion of the passage, with its announcement of the eschatological verdict on the scribes, exposes the futility of this attempt at camouflage with its spare but terrible words, which are emphasized by asyndeton (see the GLOSSARY): "These men will receive greater condemnation." The word for "greater" here, *perissoteron*, is comparative in form but may have an elative (intensive) nuance, giving it a sense close to that of the Aramaic *yatîrā'* = "very great, extraordinary" (on the elative comparative, see DBF §244; MHT 3.29–32). In the context, however, it is more probable that *perissoteron* is a true comparative: the scribes' attempt to mask their oppression with piety will garner a richer harvest of punishment than the oppression alone would have earned them.

Our passage does not imply that *all* scribes were like this (see the NOTE on "those scribes who like to" in 12:38), nor is it likely that all, or even perhaps the majority, were (see the sympathetic descriptions of priests and Levites in Sanders, *Judaism*, 77–102, 170–89). At the same time, professions do have their besetting sins, and the prophetic consciousness, which was at least a part of Jesus' identity, is a mind-set that perceives seemingly routine corruption to be a matter of earth-shaking importance:

> The world is a proud place, full of beauty, but the prophets are scandalized, and rave as if the whole world were a slum. They make much ado about paltry things,

lavishing excessive language upon trifling subjects. What if somewhere in ancient Palestine poor people have not been treated properly by the rich? . . . Why such immoderate excitement? Why such intense indignation? . . . The prophet is a man who feels fiercely. God has thrust a burden upon his soul, and he is bowed and stunned at man's fierce greed. Frightful is the agony of man; no human voice can convey its full terror. Prophecy is the voice that God has lent to the silent agony . . . God is raging in the prophet's words. (Heschel, *Prophets*, 3–4)

There is thus a sharp contrast between the way things seem to most people most of the time and the way they loom in the consciousness of the prophet. The latter has been vouchsafed not only an agonizingly keen recognition of the evil occurring behind respectable facades but also a hope-creating insight into the transcendent value of tiny, overlooked acts of charity and faith. The following passage will lift the curtain on one of these precious deeds.

JESUS COMMENDS THE POOR WIDOW'S CHARITY (12:41–44)

12 [41]And sitting opposite the treasury, he was watching how the crowd was throwing money into the treasury. And many rich people were throwing in a large amount. [42]And one poor widow came and threw in two *lepta*, that is, a *quadrans*. [43]And calling his disciples, he said to them, "Amen, I say to you, this poor widow has thrown in more than all of those who have been throwing into the treasury. [44]For they all threw in out of their abundance, but she has thrown in out of her scarcity everything she had, even her whole living."

NOTES

12 41. *sitting.* Gk *kathisas.* This is changed to *hestōs* ("standing") in W, Θ, *f*[1, 13], 28, 565, 2542, *pc*, sy[s, hmg] Origen. As Metzger (111) puts it, these scribes "obviously thought that it was more appropriate for Jesus to stand . . . than to sit in the Temple." The sitting, though, could be significant; David sits before the Lord in the Tabernacle in 2 Sam 7:18 = 1 Chron 17:16, and some rabbis concluded that only the Davidic king was allowed to sit in the Temple court (see, e.g., *t. Sanh.* 4:4; *b. Yoma* 69b; *b. Soṭah* 40b, 41b; *Mid. Psalms* 1.2). Other rabbis, however, opined that sitting was forbidden even to him (e.g., *y. Yoma* 3:2 [40b; Neusner, 14.76]; *y. Soṭah* 7:7 [22a; Neusner, 27.197]; *y. Pesaḥ* 5:10 [32d; Neusner, 13.248]). The rabbinic controversy, like the scribal change in our NT text, indicates awareness of the unusualness of sitting in the Temple.

treasury. Gk *gazophylakiou.* This term would normally refer to the treasury storerooms, which lay behind the walls of the inner court and therefore were not accessible to laypeople (see, e.g., 1 Macc 14:49; 2 Macc 3:6; Josephus, *War* 5.200; 6.282; *Ant.* 19.294). Because of this difficulty, exegetes usually interpret our verse as a reference to one of the thirteen trumpet-shaped offering boxes that stood in the

Women's Court, six of which were designated for freewill offerings (see *m. Šeqal.* 6:5 and Thackeray's note on Josephus, *War* 3.260 in LCL; for an archaeological survey of offering boxes in ancient temples, see Kaminski, "Thesauros"). It is claimed by BDAG (186) that these offering boxes could be considered part of "the treasury," since they eventually fed its coffers. There is no direct lexical evidence for this assertion (see Strack and Billerbeck, 2.42), but Balz ("*Gazophylakion*") cites a partial parallel from *m. Šeqal.* 5:6, where reference is made to casting articles into "the Chamber of Utensils," which seems to mean throwing them into an offering box. Since it does not mention the treasury, however, the Mishnaic passage is at best a distant parallel, and Mark 12:41 may simply be one of many unrealistic features in our narrative (see the introduction to the COMMENT).

was throwing . . . were throwing. Gk *ballei . . . eballon.* Codex Bezae leaves out the words between these two instances of *ballein*, so that the reading becomes "he was watching how the crowd was throwing in a large amount." This is probably a case of haplography (see the GLOSSARY), although the similarity between the two words is more impressive in English than it is in Greek.

money. Gk *chalkon.* This word originally denoted not money but the metal out of which it was made (copper, brass, or bronze; see BDAG 1076). Evans (283) points to the parallel in American slang of a century ago, in which money was called "copper."

42. *poor widow.* Gk *chēra ptōchē.* In 2 Macc 3:10 the high priest tries to dissuade the agent of the Seleucid overlord from plundering the Temple treasury by saying that it contains "deposits belonging to widows and orphans," along with other monies. The Temple treasury, then, functioned partly as a bank for widows, among others, but this sort of deposit is to be distinguished from the charitable contribution of the widow in our story, who does not expect to get anything back.

two lepta, that is, a quadrans. Gk *lepta duo ho estin kodrantēs.* On the coinage here, see Marcus, "Jewish War," 444–45; the use of a Latin term to explain a Greek one is not necessarily a sign that Mark was composed in Rome (against Standaert, *Marc*, 470–73; Hengel, *Studies*, 29). The *lepton* was not an official denomination but a general term for lightweight bronze money of little value, much like the Elizabethan word "mite" used in the KJV translation. "Two *lepta*, that is, a *quadrans*," then, is less a translation than a specification of a vague term by a precise one. The *kodrantēs/quadrans*, a Latin loanword found also in Hebrew (see Jastrow, 1324), was equivalent to a quarter of an *as* or one sixty-fourth of a denarius (cf. 12:15) and was known throughout the Roman Empire. It was the least valuable Roman coin, as Plutarch (*Cicero* 29.5) specifically says; its low value gives added emphasis to "until you have paid the last *quadrans*" in Matt 5:26//Luke 12:59 (cf. BDAG 550).

43. *more than all of those [rich people].* Gk *pleion pantōn.* This could be taken either in a distributive sense (more than any of them) or in a collective sense (more than all of them put together). In view of the point being made and the contrast between the single poor widow and the group of many rich donors (see the COMMENT on 12:41–42), the collective sense is to be preferred.

44. *even her whole living.* Gk *holon ton bion autēs. Bios* literally means "life"; by extension, the word can also denote the resources necessary to sustain it (cf. Luke

8:43; 15:12, 30; see BDAG 176–77). In the *Palatine Anthology* an epigram of Julian, a governor of Egypt in the sixth century C.E., records a fisher's dedication of his net to the nymphs, asking them to accept this humble gift because it represents his "whole living" (*holos . . . bios*; see LCL *Greek Anthology*, 6.25.5–6). The fisher's generosity, however, is less impressive than that of the widow in our story, since he describes himself as tired of fishing (6.25.1) and unable to cast his net anymore because of old age (6.26.1–2).

COMMENT

Introduction. Having peered into the future and predicted the eschatological judgment of scribes who devour widows' houses (12:38–40), Jesus now returns his gaze to the present but stays with the theme of the impoverished widow, rendering a positive verdict on the charitable action of one such person. The two passages taken together, then, are an illustration of the age-old motif of the Two Ways (see the COMMENT on 9:41–42); they contrast leaders whose wealth has increased their greed with a destitute woman whose poverty is matched by her generosity.

The present pericope seems to be a historicized parable, for it is hard to understand as a realistic account (for another historicized parable, see the NOTE on "they saw the fig tree withered from the roots" in 11:20). The widow, for example, could not really be throwing her money into the Temple treasury (see the NOTE on "treasury" in 12:41), and unless we presume that Jesus is exercising clairvoyance, which is not mentioned in the account, it is impossible to explain how he could know (*a*) that the woman is a widow, (*b*) the amount she is contributing, and (*c*) the percentage of her livelihood it represents (see Nineham [334–35] and contrast Evans [281–84] for unconvincing rationalizations). In its original, parabolic form, our tradition may have been the twin of the parable in Luke 18:9–14. Both concern a proud person (or people) and a humble one who go up to the Temple; the former is condemned and the latter applauded. It is impossible to say whether it is Mark or the pre-Markan tradition that has historicized the parable; in any case, the evangelist seems to be responsible for its present placement (see the introduction to chapters 11–13). Possible features of Markan redaction include "And many rich people were throwing in a large amount" in 12:41, "that is, a *quadrans*" in 12:42, "And calling his disciples" in 12:43, and "even her whole living" in 12:44.

The passage is divided into two major sections: the description of people coming to contribute to the Temple treasury (12:41–42) and Jesus' comment on the contributors (12:43–44). Overarching this division is a chain structure that alternates attention to the other donors with attention to the widow:

12:41   other donors
12:42   poor widow
12:43   this poor widow
            [more than] all of the other donors
12:44   they out of their abundance
                she out of her scarcity

Rhetorically, then, the widow does not come into the picture until after her rich compatriots have been introduced; in this section of the Gospel, then (cf. 12:38–40), the first becomes last and the last first.

12:41–42: the scene. After a long series of teachings (11:27–12:40), which were presumably delivered from a standing position, Jesus sits down opposite the Temple treasury to observe and draw a lesson from the various contributors to the sanctuary's wealth (12:41a). His rhetorical method here fits into a time-honored prophetic pattern of critical observation and negative comment about what is going on in the Jerusalem Temple (see, e.g., Jeremiah 7 and Ezekiel 8, and cf. Mark 11:11, 17). The act of sitting may itself be significant, both because the position can carry a connotation of judgment (see Dan 7:10; Matt 19:28; 27:19; and the COMMENT on 13:1–2) and because such a posture in the sacred precincts may have been unusual and thus an implicit claim to authority (see the NOTE on "sitting" in 12:41). What Jesus sees from this sitting position is first described in general terms (the crowd throwing money into the treasury, 12:41b), then rendered more precisely (many rich people throwing in a great deal, 12:41c), in accordance with the typical Markan rhetoric of repetition (see Neirynck, *Duality*).

Jesus contrasts the many rich people engaged in ostentatious acts of charity (cf. Matt 6:2) with a lone individual, a poor widow, who inconspicuously arrives, donates her money, and, presumably, departs (12:42). As Malbon ("Poor Widow," 595) notes, this unobtrusive widow is a foil not only to the rich people in the present pericope but also to the scribes in the previous one who seek to draw attention to themselves by their dress, their receipt of salutations, and their place in seating arrangements (12:38–39). The antithesis between her and the rich donors of the present scene is deliberately emphasized:

polloi	*plousioi*	*eballon*	*polla*
many	rich people	were throwing (impf.)	many things [a large amount]
mia	*chēra ptōchē*	*ebalen*	*lepta duo*
one	poor widow	threw (aor.)	two *lepta* [a tiny sum]

This contrast extends to the verb tenses used for the action of tossing contributions into the treasury: imperfect plural for the rich, signifying many individual contributions (perhaps several per person), as opposed to aorist singular for the widow, connoting a single act. The widow throws in her negligible contribution, which employs the smallest coin in circulation (see the NOTE on "two *lepta*, that is, a *quadrans*" in 12:42). One might almost be tempted to accuse her of stinginess.

12:43–44: Jesus' comment. Jesus, however, summons the disciples (12:43a) to render the opposite judgment, a verdict that perhaps prefigures the eschatological one that both the widow and the rich donors will one day hear: she has given more than all of them put together (12:43b; see the NOTE on "more than all of those [rich people]" in 12:43). The introduction of this verdict with the formula "Amen, I say to you" suggests that it is contrary to received opinion and that it requires

Jesus' eschatological insight (cf. Klostermann, 131). The fact that it follows Jesus' summons of the disciples, moreover, could hint that the lesson is particularly important for the members of the Markan community (see 7:14; 8:34; 10:42). Are there perhaps rich people there as well as poor ones, and are the ostentatiousness of the former and their callousness toward the latter among the spiritual dangers besetting Mark's home church (cf. Jas 2:1–17)?

The lesson that Jesus wants his disciples to take away is spelled out in the conclusion of the passage, where he observes that the rich have given out of their surplus, while the poor widow has contributed everything she had (12:44). The traditional way of interpreting this conclusion is that Jesus is holding the widow up for emulation (cf. already *Apostolic Constitutions* 3.1.7; *Instructions of Commodianus* 72; Bede, *Exposition of Mark* 12:43). The crucial thing, we learn, is not the quantity that one gives but the quantity—or rather the scarcity—that one subsequently has left over (see Ambrose, *On Widows* 5.27, and cf. A. Wright, "Widow's Mites," 257); it is more commendable to give out of poverty than out of abundance (see Pseudo-Jerome, *Exposition of Mark* 12:41 [Cahill, 92]: "God notices not how much but from how much"). In this particular case, the depth of the widow's sacrifice is emphasized by the Markan repetition at the end (cf. Lohmeyer, 266): she gives everything she has, even her whole living (12:44bc)—a repetition that balances the double reference to the ostentatious donations of the rich in 12:41bc.

Recently, however, this positive interpretation of the widow's act has been challenged by A. Wright ("Widow's Mites"), Sugirtharajah ("Widow's Mites"), and other exegetes. These commentators argue that Jesus never explicitly praises the widow's donation and that the apparent encomium is in fact a lament over a foolish deed. In the Markan context, Jesus has just excoriated scribes who devour widows' houses (12:40); this poor widow is an example of those who have been so abused, presumably by the scribes who have duped her into contributing her last coins to the Temple. That institution is barren, corrupt, and headed for judgment and ruin (cf. 11:12–20; 13:1–2), so whatever is contributed to it is at best a waste and at worst a prop for a rotten, oppressive, and doomed system. In the discussion of the *korban* vow in 7:9–13, moreover, Jesus has set human need above religious offerings; in neglecting her own exigencies to donate to the Temple, therefore, the widow shows herself to be the victim of a tragic delusion.

Although these interpreters make some good points, overall their reading seems to be catalyzed less by the logic of the text than by a political agenda, namely, encouraging the poor to stick up for themselves against the rich. Laudable as this goal is, it does not seem to be *Mark's* objective; in the end there seems to be no alternative to interpreting the widow's action as praiseworthy and worthy of emulation:

(1) Jesus graphically contrasts the poor widow who gives her all with the rich people who donate out of their surplus: she has given more than all of them put together. This sounds like praise rather than lament; Jesus is exalting the humble widow at the expense of the complacent plutocrats.

(2) That this is the correct interpretation is supported by the fact that it is a commonplace, not only in other Christian writings (e.g., 2 Cor 8:2–3), but also in

philosophic and religious traditions around the world, that the sacrificial giving of the poor is of infinitely greater value than the oblations of the rich (see, e.g., Xenophon, *Memorabilia* 1.3.3; Aristotle, *Nicomachean Ethics* 4.1.19 [1120b]; Horace, *Odes* 3.23; cf. Aufhauser, *Buddha und Jesus*, 13–16, on the parallel in Aśvaghoṣa, *Sūtrālaṃkāra* 4.22 [from around 100 C.E.]).

(3) Our story has particularly close parallels with two rabbinic tales recounted in *Lev. Rab.* 3.5 and *Midr. Psalms* 22.31 (cf. also *b. Men.* 104b). According to the first, King Agrippa asks the high priest to suspend all offerings but his own so that he might sacrifice a thousand oxen in a day. A poor man, however, comes and begs to be allowed to sacrifice two doves. Every day, he says, he catches four doves, sacrifices two, and earns his living with the other two; his livelihood, he asserts, is dependent on this sacrifice (i.e., it is a divine reward for his sacrificial renunciation of half of his small income). The high priest gives way before this demonstration of humble godliness and sacrifices the man's doves. Agrippa is informed in a dream of this contravention of his order, but when the high priest explains what has happened, he, too, is moved by the poor man's piety.

In the second tale, a woman brings to the Temple a handful of flour; the priest on duty expresses contempt for this offering, but in a dream is commanded to accept it, "because it is as if she had sacrificed her life/soul/self (*npšh*)." In the *Midrash on Psalms*, each of these tales is followed by a quotation of Ps 22:24, "For [God] has not despised or abhorred the poverty of the poor person" (RSV alt.).

Although these rabbinic narratives postdate the NT, their similarity to our Gospel story is striking: in each case the main character is a person whose piety moves him or her to sacrifice at the Temple despite extreme poverty, and in the second this character is a widow who is described as sacrificing her very life or soul. These similarities are part of the motivation for Lohmeyer's assertion (267) that "what Jesus says in our passage could also be said by a rabbi; it is Jewish humanitarianism that expresses itself in these sentences"—a brave thing for a German scholar to publish in 1936. For our present purposes, it is significant that the narrators of the rabbinic stories approve of the sacrifices the poor people make, as becomes explicit in the quotation of Ps 22:24 in the *Midrash Psalms* version (cf. Margulies, *Wayyikra Rabbah*, 65). Evans (282–83) tries to distance our passage from the rabbinic tale of the widow by speculating that if the latter derives from an earlier tradition, Jesus "may have deliberately and ironically alluded to it." Nothing about our story, however, suggests an ironic twist.

(4) The Markan reference to the woman giving everything she has, "even her whole living," is telling not only because of the similarity to the positively viewed woman of rabbinic tradition but also because of the parallel to Jesus in Mark. He, too, gives his whole life as a sacrifice (cf. 10:45; 14:22, 24), and this action is a paradigm for all Christians (cf. 8:34–35 and Malbon, "Poor Widow," 597, 601). In 10:21, moreover, Jesus commands the rich man to sell "whatever you have" (*hosa echeis*) and give it away, thus suggesting a positive evaluation of the widow who gives to charity "everything she had" (*panta hosa eichen*).

The traditional interpretation, therefore, seems to be basically right: the widow's generosity is praiseworthy. Why, then, does Mark place her story precisely here, between the excoriation of ravenous scribes and the prophecy of the Temple's destruction? It may be that he does so unconscious of the jangling elements in the context, intent only on the pericope's central message of the importance of whole-hearted devotion and the literary necessity of placing it in a "Temple" section. But it may also be that he uses the story's uneasy relation to its context to express his own mixed attitude toward the Temple. Such ambivalence is not unusual in early Christianity; Luke-Acts, for example, idealizes Zechariah, Elizabeth, Simeon, and Anna, who frequent the Temple as an expression of their piety (Luke 1–2), but it also glorifies Stephen, who excoriates the Temple and predicts its destruction by God (Acts 6:13–7:60; on early Christian ambivalence toward the Temple, see Bauckham, "Parting," 141–48). It is possible, moreover, to recognize the corruption of an institution and the venality of its officers and at the same time to admire the piety of the simple souls who devote themselves to it in innocence and faith.

The poor widow in our story, who gives her "life" to support the Jerusalem Temple, is also a prefigurement of the Messiah who, unbeknownst to her, commends her inconspicuous action. He, too, will give his life to build a Temple, an eschatological sanctuary not made by hands (14:58b), and this combination of self-sacrifice and eschatological construction will confound human ways of knowing (cf. 12:10–11). His death, however, will also be mysteriously intertwined with the destruction of the present Temple (cf. 14:58a; 15:37–38; and Malbon, "Poor Widow," 598), an event that he will prophesy in the very next passage of the Gospel.

INTERLUDE: END-TIME
PROPHECIES AND EXHORTATIONS
(MARK 13:1–37)

◆

INTRODUCTION

There is a natural connection between the end of Mark 12 and the beginning of Mark 14: Jesus commends a poor widow who has devoted "her whole living" to the cause of God (12:44), and subsequently the evangelist begins the painful but ultimately triumphant tale of Jesus' God-willed sacrifice of his life as "a ransom for many" (14:1–2; cf. 10:45). In between, however, comes an interlude, a discourse in which Jesus delivers detailed prophecies and exhortations concerning the terrifying period of eschatological tribulation that will, presumably, follow his death and precede his coming in glory.

This chapter has been subjected to more frequent and detailed exegesis than any other portion of Mark's Gospel, with the possible exception of Mark 4 (for a painstaking review of the history of its interpretation, see Beasley-Murray). It is easy to see why: like Mark 4, it is full of problems. The chief difficulty is an apologetic one—was Jesus wrong about the future? In its context, for example, 13:30, like 9:1, seems to suggest that Jesus expected the end of all things imminently, or at least within a generation of his own lifetime. Moreover, the line of thought within the chapter seems to place the cataclysmic events of the end, including cosmic collapse and Jesus' return on clouds of glory (13:24–27), in a very close temporal relation to the "abomination of desolation" (13:14), which is often associated with the destruction of the Jerusalem Temple (cf. 13:1–2). The Temple was razed in 70 C.E., nearly two thousand years ago; the end described in 13:24–27, however, has still not occurred.

Much exegesis of Mark 13 during the past three centuries of critical study, therefore, has been covertly or overtly designed to protect Jesus from error. "Liberal" and "conservative" exegetes have united in pursuit of this common goal, although they have adopted different strategies for achieving it. Conservative interpreters have often invoked the idea of "prophetic perspective," which was anticipated by patristic commentators but given its definitive shape in the eighteenth century by Bengel (*Gnomon* on Matt 24:29), who wrote that "a prophecy resembles a landscape painting, which marks distinctly the houses, paths, and bridges in the foreground, but brings together, into a narrow space, the distant valleys and mountains, though they are really far apart." Jesus, then, was actually describing widely separated events (the destruction of Jerusalem on the one hand, the end of the world on the other), but "painting" them in such a way that they appeared close to each other. It is interesting to note that this sophisticated hermeneutical strategy did not prevent Bengel from trying to calculate the date of the eschaton himself; he predicted that the world would end in 1836 (see Martin, "Date Setters").

A common "liberal" method of dealing with the difficulty of dominical error is to distinguish between the parts of the discourse that derive from Jesus and those that derive from Jewish or Christian apocalypticists. The correct parts, of course, come from Jesus; the mistaken ones derive from apocalyptic fanatics, including Jesus' own disciples, according to some scholars. A mediating approach is to assert that the various sayings attributed to Jesus in Mark 13 were indeed spoken by him, but not at one time, and that therefore their present order is misleading. For example, the Parable of the Fig Tree, which implies imminent advent (13:28–29), and the statement that "all these things" must happen within a generation (13:30), did not originally refer to the parousia prophecy, which immediately precedes them in the discourse (13:24–27), but to the prediction of the desolating sacrilege and its accompanying distress, which comes earlier (13:14–20).

The "little apocalypse" hypothesis originated by T. Colani (*Jésus Christ*) in the mid-nineteenth century has been a particularly popular version of the view that much of the material in Mark 13 is nondominical. According to this theory, the core of the chapter is a Jewish or Jewish-Christian apocalyptic tract describing the coming of the end in three distinct stages: the "beginning of the labor pains" (13:7–8), the great tribulation (13:14–20), and the eschaton (13:24–27). This emphasis on a discernible progression of eschatological signs is in tension with the stress in 13:32–37 on the suddenness and unexpectedness of the end, and the neat progression of the three stages has been further disrupted by additions to the discourse that are chronologically out of place (e.g., 13:10, 21–22) or are exhortative rather than predictive (e.g., 13:9, 11–13; 33–37). Unsurprisingly, commentators usually ascribe to Jesus the conceptions that are most unproblematic and most like their own, especially the notion that no one really knows the date of the eschaton.

The desire to protect Jesus from error and from eschatological "fanaticism" is not the only reason that commentators have traced some of the sayings in Mark 13 to sources other than him. The material in this chapter is remarkably self-contained, and much of it differs, in its carefully predictive nature, from the rest of Jesus' eschatological teaching (e.g., Mark 9:42–49; Matthew 25; Luke 17:20–37); it is therefore easy to imagine it circulating as an independent eschatological tract (a "little apocalypse"). The reference in 13:14 to the "abomination of desolation," moreover, invokes passages from the OT book of Daniel (9:27; 11:31; 12:11) that speak of the desecration (not the destruction) of the Temple by a foreign king who erects an idolatrous image there. The Danielic "abomination of desolation" was a statue of a pagan god erected by Antiochus Epiphanes in the Jerusalem sanctuary in 168 B.C.E., but the phrase could easily have been reapplied to the Roman emperor Caligula's ambition about two hundred years later, a decade after Jesus died, to erect a statue of himself in the Temple, a campaign that was averted only by the emperor's timely assassination in 42 C.E. Some proponents of the "little apocalypse" theory, therefore, believe that the core of Mark 13 was a tract of apocalyptic warning and exhortation written in the anxious days when Caligula was threatening to desecrate the Temple with his own image (see already Pfeiderer, "Composition").

Since this is a commentary on Mark, not a reconstruction of the thought of the historical Jesus, it is not as vital to know what Jesus said about the eschaton as it is to know how Mark has incorporated and shaped the material at his disposal, whatever its source. Probably this extended discourse, like the other one in Mark 4:1–34, contains a combination of sayings from Jesus and pre-Markan Christian traditions edited by Mark; and the possibility cannot be excluded that some of its features are non-Christian in origin. Markan redaction is most visible, as usual, at the beginning and end of the passage. The scene-setting in 13:1–5a is full of Markan vocabulary and grammatical features (genitive absolutes, "teacher," "look," "privately," "all," "began to say") and reflects a typically Markan desire to situate important instruction for his church within the private teaching of Jesus (cf. 4:10–12; 7:17–23; 9:2–13). The concluding verse, 13:37, makes the application to the Markan community explicit ("And what I say to you I say to all"). Two statements located close together in the body of the discourse may also relate to the Markan situation. Mark 13:10 is disruptive in its context, features distinctively Markan vocabulary, and reflects the Markan preoccupation with the Gentile mission. And the awkward interjection "let the reader understand" in 13:14 suggests that whatever Mark thinks the "abomination of desolation" is, he believes it to be significant for his Gospel's readers.

Mark 13:5–37 is the last and longest extended discourse of the Markan Jesus, and it looks beyond his death to the trials coming upon his followers, urging them to persevere when the eschatological tribulation arrives. It therefore fits the genre of the farewell discourse, a literary form already found in the OT (see, e.g., Genesis 49; Deuteronomy 31–33; 1 Chronicles 28–29) and developed further in intertestamental Jewish circles (see, e.g., Tob 14:3–11; *Testaments of the Twelve Patriarchs*; *1 Enoch* 91–105; 1QWords of Moses) and the NT (see John 14–17; Acts 20:17–35; 2 Tim 3:1–4:8; cf. Stauffer, *New Testament Theology*, 344–47; Brown, 2.598–601; Kurz, *Farewell Addresses*). In several of the intertestamental and NT examples of the genre, the departing figure prophesies eschatological afflictions that include persecution from without and deception from within, bringing the form even closer to that of Mark 13 (see, e.g., *1 En.* 95:7; 100:7; *T. Judah* 21–23; *T. Moses* 7:4; John 15:18–25; Acts 20:29–30). Although Jesus does not begin his speech here with an explicit reference to his approaching demise, as is usual in farewell discourses, the whole chapter, as noted above, is framed by the notion of his sacrificial death. There are especially close parallels between Mark 13 and the Johannine farewell discourses in John 14–16: both emphasize enduring persecution, the name of Jesus, the presence of the Spirit, and living in the time between Jesus' departure and his return (see Moloney, "Johannine Paraclete").

The Markan discourse in its present form gives an impression of structural unity. Van Iersel (*Mark*, 391) has detected a concentric structure:

5–6		pseudoteachers
7–8		wars and disasters
9–13	**Signs**	persecutions
14–20		desecration and flight
21–23		pseudomessiahs
24–25		the clearance of the heavens
26	**The Coming**	the coming of the Son of Man
27		the gathering of the elect
28–29		Parable of the Fig Tree
30–32	**Signs**	day and hour known only by God
33–37		Parable of the Doorkeeper

This sort of structure is fairly common in apocalyptic writings, which frequently do not proceed in a simple chronological sequence but go back over ground already covered in a slightly different manner (see, e.g., Daniel 7; Revelation; 4Q426; cf. Collins, *Scepter*, 158). Confidence in Van Iersel's discernment is increased by the observation that the items at the center of each section seem to be matters of special importance to the author: the persecution of the Markan community (13:9–13), the coming of the Son of Man (13:26), and the unknown date of the eschaton (13:30–32). The careful concentric structure embodies a theological conviction: however chaotic and frightening the present may be, no matter how inevitably the world may seem to be hurtling toward the abyss, the present evil age is nonetheless part of the unfolding plan of the eternal God, who orders all things well, according to his purpose. In the present discussion, however, Van Iersel's literary structure will be altered slightly in order to offer a more thematic division: Jesus' prophecy and the disciples' question (13:1–4), the early signs of the end (13:5–8), persecutions (13:9–13), the abomination of desolation and the accompanying distress (13:14–20), false messiahs (13:21–23), the return of the Son of Man (13:24–27), the Parable of the Fig Tree / imminence of the end (13:28–32), and concluding exhortations to wakefulness (13:33–37).

As exegesis of the individual sections will show in detail, the chapter abounds in echoes of the book of Daniel, especially the apocalyptic sections in Dan 2:27–45 (Nebuchadnezzar's dream), Daniel 7 (the four beasts, the Ancient of Days, and the "one like a son of man"), Dan 9:22–27 (the reinterpretation of Jeremiah's prophecy of seventy years of captivity), and Daniel 11–12 (the wars of the end and the final deliverance of the people of God; cf. Hartman, *Prophecy*, 145–77). The most obvious of these echoes are "when all these things will be accomplished" in Mark 13:4 (cf. Dan 12:6–7), "[these things] have to happen" and "it is not yet the end" in 13:7 (cf. Dan 2:28–29, 45; 12:13), "the 'abomination of desolation' " in 13:14 (cf. Dan 9:27; 11:31; 12:11), and "the Son of Man coming in clouds with great power and glory" in 13:26 (cf. Dan 7:13–14). In contrast to Daniel, however, in Mark the Temple will not be rescued from its "desolation" but destroyed (Mark 13:2; contrast Dan 9:24, 27), the Jewish people will not be gathered in from their dispersion but scattered to the four winds (12:9; contrast Dan 12:7), and the principal enemies of God and the Son of Man are not pagans but the leaders of Israel. Since the Danielic scenario was probably crucial for the Jewish revolutionaries whose activity forms the backdrop to Mark (cf. Hengel, *Zealots*, passim), these reversals may be a deliberate reaction to events and interpretations current in the Markan setting.

JESUS PROPHESIES THE DESTRUCTION OF THE TEMPLE AND IS ASKED ABOUT THE ESCHATON (13:1–4)

13 ¹And as he was coming out of the Temple, one of his disciples said to him, "Teacher, look! Such stones and such buildings!" ²And Jesus said to him, "Do you see these great buildings? There surely won't be left a stone upon a stone here that won't surely be thrown down."

³And as he was sitting on the Mount of Olives, opposite the Temple, Peter and James and John and Andrew asked him privately, ⁴"Tell us, when will these things be? And what is the sign, when all these things will be accomplished?"

NOTES

13 1. *look! Such stones and such buildings!* Gk *ide potapoi lithoi kai potapai oikodomai.* Davies and Allison (3.334) appositely cite Josephus, *War* 5.222: "The exterior of the building wanted nothing that could astound either mind or eye." The stones were especially impressive in size and beauty. As Geva ("Jerusalem," 738) notes, they had dressed margins whose "play of light and shade . . . contributed to the beauty and dramatic appearance of the massive walls," and some of the surviving stones in the retaining wall (part of which is now visible as the "Wailing" Wall) weigh fifty tons or more; one is forty feet long and weighs approximately three hundred tons! These retaining walls towered more than eighty feet above the roadways that circled the structure, and on the south the highest wall of the Temple reached some one hundred seventy-five feet above bedrock. The reaction of amazement at the magnificence of the Temple, therefore, is natural, but it also has a narrative function, namely, to prepare for the prophecy of Temple destruction in 13:2, just as the women's question in 16:3 anticipates the description of the rolled-away stone in 16:4.

2. *a stone upon a stone.* Gk *lithos epi lithon.* "A stone upon a stone here that won't surely be thrown down" is awkward in Greek as well as in English, but this sort of repetition is common in Semitic languages (cf. "eating-group by eating-group" in 6:39 and "cluster by cluster" in 6:40; see Gesenius, 395–96). In ancient Greek texts, the specific phrase *lithos epi lithon* is limited to Hag 2:15 LXX, our passage, its Synoptic parallels, and commentaries on these Synoptic passages. Davies and Allison (3.335), however, cite a striking Hebrew parallel in a late Jewish magical text, *Sepher Ha-Razim* 1.75–76: "Smite it to dust and let it be overturned like the ruins of Sodom and Gomorrah, and let no man place *stone upon stone* on the place" (Morgan trans.).

that won't surely be thrown down. Gk *hos ou mē katalythę*. Depending on whether the retaining wall is considered to be part of the Temple, Jesus' words can be seen either as an unfulfilled prophecy (see the INTRODUCTION in vol. 1, p. 38) or as one that was fulfilled in the destruction of the Temple buildings themselves. In favor of the latter interpretation, the complete demolition of the Second Temple, down to its very foundations, became proverbial in rabbinic circles and was even used to distinguish the second destruction by the Romans from the first destruction by the Babylonians (see, e.g., *b. Giṭ.* 57b; *Exod. Rab.* 35.5; *Lam. Rab.* 5.1).

ou mē katalythę is an example of the construction *ou mē* + aorist subjunctive, which is also used at the beginning of the sentence ("There surely won't be left . . ."). In the NT the form almost never occurs outside of quotations from the LXX, words of Jesus, and the book of Revelation (cf. MHT 3.96). Lagrange (332), therefore, suspects Semitic influence, but unfortunately for this theory, Aramaic and Hebrew have no corresponding idiom. In Mark, the *ou mē* + aorist subjunctive is almost always used in eschatological contexts (see 9:1, 41; 13:19, 30–31; 14:25; cf. 10:15; 14:31).

3. *on the Mount of Olives, opposite the Temple.* Gk *eis to oros tōn elaiōn katenanti tou hierou*. The phrasing recalls that in Zech 14:4, one of only two OT passages that mention the Mount of Olives by name (cf. 2 Sam 15:30): "And his feet shall stand on that day *on the Mount of Olives*, which is *opposite* Jerusalem" (*epi to oros tōn elaiōn to katenanti Hierousalēm*; my trans.). The Zecharian context (Zech 14:1–5) is one that speaks of a war focused on Jerusalem, and this is similar to the context of the Danielic "abomination of desolation" passages (Dan 9:27; 11:31; 12:11), which are alluded to in Mark 13:14 (see the NOTE on "the 'abomination of desolation' " in 13:14). These contexts are probably relevant to the Markan situation, since Mark himself probably assumes or knows that the Temple will be or has been destroyed (cf. 12:9 and the INTRODUCTION in vol. 1, pp. 37–39).

Perhaps in dependence on our passage and its Synoptic parallels, the apocryphal gospels often portray the risen Jesus appearing on the Mount of Olives (e.g., *Ap. John* 2:19; *Sophia of Jesus Christ* 91:20; *Letter of Peter to Philip* 133:15; cf. Pesch, 2.274–75). It is also possible, however, that the motif of the risen Jesus giving eschatological instruction on the Mount of Olives has priority (cf. Acts 1:6–12) and that Mark or a predecessor has transposed this post-Easter scene into Jesus' ministry (cf. Gaston, *No Stone*, 44–46).

Peter and James and John and Andrew. Gk *Petros kai Iakōbos kai Iōannēs kai Andreas.* With regard to Peter's name, the Peshitta and Sinaiticus witnesses to the Syriac text read *Kephā'* (on this Aramaic version of *Petros* = "rock," see the NOTE on "Simon . . . Peter" in 3:16). There is probably a punning connection here with 13:1–2, in which the word used for "stone" is *kiphā'*. In Greek the pun is more distant (*lithos/petros*).

As in 3:16–18, Andrew is separated from his brother Peter by James and John, the sons of Zebedee. This reflects not only Andrew's obscurity in the tradition (see the NOTES on "Simon . . . Andrew" in 1:16 and "Andrew" in 3:18) but also the Gospel principle that the eschatological "family" relativizes the natural one (cf. 3:31–35; 10:29–30).

4. *when will these things be? And what is the sign, when all these things will be accomplished?* Gk *pote tauta estai, kai ti to sēmeion hotan mellē tauta synteleisthai panta.* On the distinction between "these things" and "all these things," see the COMMENT on 13:3–4. The first part of the question is similar to 4QPseudo-Ezekiel[a] (4Q383) 2:3, 9, "When will these things happen?" (*mty yhyh 'lh*). The context in which the question occurs in 4QPseudo-Ezekiel, like that in Mark, is eschatological; as Dimant (*Qumran Cave 4*, 21) points out, 4QPseudo-Ezekiel "outlines a well-defined string of topics" that includes "resurrection as future recompense to the righteous, future events related to the Land of Israel and the people of Israel, a great war involving the nations, [and] the hastening of the time in which Israel receives its inheritance." As Beasley-Murray (387) notes, the terminology in the second half of the question echoes Daniel 11–12, in which an angel prophesies the erection of an "abomination of desolation" in the Temple (Dan 11:31; cf. Mark 13:14). Daniel asks when this and the other portents of the end will happen (Dan 12:6), and the angel replies that "all these things will be accomplished" (*syntelesthēsetai panta tauta*) when Israel's abandonment (LXX) or its dispersion (Theodotion) comes to an end (Dan 12:7). Questions about when "these things"/"all these things" will happen, then, are commonly answered by reference to an eschatological scenario in which Israel triumphs over its enemies. For Mark, by contrast, "these things"/"all these things" will include the destruction of Jewish sovereignty in Palestine (cf. 12:9 and see the NOTE on "on the Mount of Olives, opposite the Temple" in 13:3 and the introduction to chapter 13).

COMMENT

Introduction. The Temple has provided the setting for most of Mark's story since Jesus' entry into Jerusalem in 11:1–11; he has viewed it (11:11), "cleansed" it (11:15–19), and continuously argued in it (11:27–12:44). Now he leaves it, never to return, and pronounces its doom (13:1–2), a prophecy that naturally evokes from his disciples a query about the timing of this event (13:3–4).

This introductory passage is commonly recognized as a Markan composition. It is full of Markan vocabulary and themes (see the introduction to chapter 13) and serves to hook the "little apocalypse," which is presumably pre-Markan, into the evangelist's larger story. This redactional bridge passage, however, probably has a pre-Markan core, Jesus' threat against the Temple (13:2; see the COMMENT on 13:1–2). Mark uses this threat as the occasion for the disciples to ask Jesus privately about the end, and the rest of the chapter constitutes his response; the motif of private instruction is a typical Markan way of emphasizing a subject of vital importance for his community (see 4:10; 7:17; 9:2, 28, 30–31; 10:10).

The passage falls naturally into two sections: the threat against the Temple (13:1–2) and the disciples' question (13:3–4).

13:1–2: the threat against the Temple. Having bested the chief priests, scribes, and elders in argument in the Temple (11:27–12:37), and having then denounced them (12:38–40) and acclaimed the transcendent worth of a poor widow's contribution to the Temple treasury (12:41–44), Jesus now leaves the sanctuary, never to return (13:1a). This departure is probably meant to be understood as an act of judgment against the Temple, comparable to OT descriptions of the deity abandoning that structure. In Ezekiel 10, for example, the glory of God abandons the First Temple before it is destroyed (cf. Evans, 295), and Josephus (*War* 6.300) reports a similar happening before the destruction of the Second Temple: a voice was heard in the inner court, saying, "We are departing [or let us depart] from here" (cf. Dodd, *Parables*, 49 n. 32). Ezekiel's portrait has an intertextual connection with the larger context in Mark 13, since for the prophet the departure of God's glory and the consequent destruction of the Temple are punishments for the *abominations* that the house of Israel has practiced there, "to drive me far from my sanctuary" (Ezek 8:6 JPS). Thus, in a way, Mark 13:1a lays the groundwork for the reference to the "abomination of desolation" in the Temple in 13:14.

Jesus' condemnatory departure from the Temple, however, contrasts with one disciple's apparent desire to linger and admire its magnificent buildings. That disciple expresses his awe at the buildings' splendor, which was indeed overwhelming (see the NOTE on "look! Such stones and such buildings!" in 13:1). He could reasonably expect, therefore, that Jesus would second his enthusiasm.

Indeed, Jesus' response at first seems to do so ("Do you see these great buildings?" 13:2a). But Jesus immediately shifts gears and turns the question about viewing the buildings into a chilling prophecy of their destruction: "There surely won't be left a stone upon a stone here that won't surely be thrown down" (13:2b). As Evans (299) notes, Mark's exact formulation "a stone upon a stone" (*lithos epi lithon*) is used in Hag 2:15 to describe the rebuilding of the (First) Temple; this intertextual allusion, therefore, may suggest that the Second Temple, unlike the First, will remain in ruins.

Jesus' prophecy is probably in its essentials historical; it is independently attested in several different layers of the Gospel tradition and Acts (see Mark 14:58 pars.; John 2:19; Acts 6:14), which also manifest a certain discomfort with the idea of Jesus threatening the Temple. The church, therefore, is unlikely to have fabricated the prophecy (cf. Brown, *Death*, 1.454–60). Nor is a prediction of the Temple's destruction implausible in the setting of Jesus' life. Rabbinic traditions, for example, record prophecies and portents of the Temple's destruction forty years before its demise—that is, in the time of Jesus (see, e.g., *y. Yoma* 6:3 [43c; Neusner, 14.176]; *b. Yoma* 39b; see the COMMENT on 15:38–39). These rabbinic traditions, to be sure, could themselves be prophecies-after-the-fact, but it is more difficult to dismiss Josephus' detailed description (*War* 6.300–9) of another Jesus who prophesied against the Temple in the sixties in a manner amazingly similar to that attributed to his earlier namesake, the Nazarene:

But a further portent was even more alarming. Four years before the war [i.e., in 62 C.E.], when the city was enjoying profound peace and prosperity, there came to the feast at which it is the custom of all Jews to erect tabernacles to God, one Jesus, son of Ananias, a rude peasant, who, standing in the Temple, suddenly began to cry out, "A voice from the east, a voice from the west, a voice from the four winds; a voice against Jerusalem and the sanctuary, a voice against the bridegroom and the bride, a voice against all the people." Day and night he went about all the alleys with this cry on his lips. Some of the leading citizens, incensed at these ill-omened words, arrested the fellow and severely chastised him. But he, without a word on his own behalf or for the private ear of those who smote him, only continued his cries as before. Thereupon, the magistrates, supposing, as was indeed the case, that the man was under some supernatural impulse, brought him before the Roman governor; there, although flayed to the bone with scourges, he neither sued for mercy nor shed a tear, but, merely introducing the most mournful of variations into his ejaculation, responded to each stroke with "Woe to Jerusalem!" When Albinus, the governor, asked him who and whence he was and why he uttered these cries, he answered him never a word, but unceasingly reiterated his dirge over the city, until Albinus pronounced him a maniac and let him go. During the whole period up to the outbreak of war he neither approached nor was seen talking to any of the citizens, but daily, like a prayer that he had practiced, repeated his lament, "Woe to Jerusalem!" He neither cursed any of those who beat him from day to day, nor blessed those who offered him food: to all people that melancholy omen was his only reply. His cries were loudest at the festivals. So for seven years and five months he continued his wail, his voice never flagging nor his strength exhausted, until in the siege, having seen his omen verified, he found his rest. For, while going his round and shouting in piercing tones from the wall, "Woe once more to the city and to the people and to the Temple," as he added a last word, "and woe to me also," a stone hurled from the *ballista* struck and killed him on the spot. So with those ominous words still upon his lips he passed away.

We can note several parallels with the Markan portrayal of Jesus: the prophet predicts the Temple's destruction; this prediction earns him the hostility of the Jewish authorities; the latter arrest and beat him; they then transfer him to the custody of the Roman governor, who interrogates him; he refuses to answer the governor's questions; he is scourged by Roman soldiers (cf. Brown, *Death*, 2.539–40). The context provides an additional point of correspondence, since Josephus' portrayal of Jesus son of Ananias is immediately preceded by a description of protective spirits departing from the Temple shortly before its destruction. Similarly, as we have noted, Jesus' prophecy of the Temple's destruction is immediately preceded by his departure from it, which may signify divine abandonment. As Evans (296–97) points out, moreover, Jesus son of Ananias, like Jesus son of Mary of Nazareth in Mark, is portrayed as alluding to Jeremiah 7 to justify his assault on the Temple (cf. Mark 11:17). These parallels support the plausibility of the Markan portrayal and suggest that Jesus' action and prophecy against the Temple, which fit into a

Jewish apocalyptic framework, may have been decisive factors in turning the Jewish leadership against him (cf. Sanders, *Jesus*, 77–90 and passim).

But what has the Temple done wrong, that Jesus should threaten it with destruction? He makes no explicit charge against it in our passage, but other Markan pericopes help fill in the gap. Earlier in the narrative, Jesus' cursing of a fig tree (11:12–14), which subsequently withered (11:20–21), seemed to symbolize the coming destruction of the Temple by God, since it significantly framed Jesus' act of "cleansing" the Temple (11:15–19). The offenses identified in the latter passage included commercial activity that defiled the sanctuary (cf. 11:15–16) and a militantly nationalistic attitude that transformed the Temple from a "house of prayer for all the nations" into a "den of brigands" (see the COMMENTS on 11:12–14 and 11:15–19). But the prophecy of Temple destruction in the present context is probably also meant to be understood as a judgment on Israel's leaders, especially the Temple hierarchy, for their rejection of Jesus, as in Luke 19:44 and commonly in the church fathers (see, e.g., Tertullian, *Answer to the Jews* 13; Origen, *Homilies on Jeremiah* 13.1.3; Jerome, *Commentary on Matthew* [on 23:38]). A similar connection between rejection of Jesus and destruction of the Temple is suggested by the circumstance that, in 15:37–38, Jesus' death is immediately followed by the tearing of the Temple's curtain (cf. Matt 23:37–39//Luke 13:34–35, in which rejection and murder of God's messengers, culminating in the death of Jesus, causes God to abandon his "house").

13:3–4: the disciples' question. Jesus' symbolic exit from the Temple and his prophecy of its destruction are followed by a third threatening action: he takes a seat on the Mount of Olives, opposite the Temple Mount, and looks back toward the doomed structure (13:3a). The sitting posture is often associated in biblical texts both with teaching and with judgment (see the NOTE on "sitting down" in 9:35), and in 12:36 (cf. 14:62) it is particularly linked with judgment on Jesus' enemies. The proximity to the threatening words of 13:2 and the possibly negative nuance of *katenanti* ("opposite, against") confirm this association, as does the judgmental context of Zech 14:4, which seems to be alluded to here (see the NOTE on "on the Mount of Olives, opposite the Temple" in 13:3).

When Jesus has taken up his judgment seat, he is approached privately by Peter and his brother Andrew, along with James and his brother John—the same four men he chose to be with him at the beginning of his ministry (1:16–20; cf. the NOTE on "Peter and James and John and Andrew" in 13:3). Near its end, then, Jesus' ministry recapitulates its beginning. These four close disciples, whose eschatological curiosity has been piqued by his prophecy of Temple destruction, pose a double-barreled question about it: "When will these things be? And what is the sign, when all these things will be accomplished?" (13:4bc). The privateness of the instruction fits the topic, the secrets of the end-time. In this context, the introduction to that question, "Tell us . . ." (13:4a), may have an exclusive sense: Tell *us*, and not "those outside" (cf. 4:11).

Exegetes have frequently viewed the first part of the disciples' query as a reference to the Temple's destruction (*tauta* = "these things") and the second as a reference to the eschaton (*tauta . . . panta* = "all these things"; see, e.g., Pesch, *Naherwartungen*, 101–5). In favor of this distinction, the phrase "these things" in 11:28 refers to the cleansing of the Temple, which foreshadows the Temple's destruction (cf. Watts, *New Exodus*, 338), and the phrase "all these things" in 13:30 occurs between a description of the eschaton (13:24–27) and a reference to the dissolution of the universe (13:31; cf. Gnilka, 2.184). Although Jesus, then, has prophesied only the destruction of the Temple, not the end of everything, the disciples' question reveals their belief that these two sets of events are conjoined—an impression that the subsequent discourse will do nothing to refute. As Harder ("Geschichtsbild," 71) puts it, the Markan picture is that the Temple will be destroyed by God and the cosmos will be drawn into its downfall.

But *when* will "these things" happen? The disciples' question echoes one that is frequently asked in apocalyptic literature. The answer often given is: (*a*) soon, and (*b*) when you see the following signs. In *4 Ezra* 8:62–9:2, for example, the seer complains that the angel who has been instructing him about the end has not shown him when it will take place. The angel responds, "When you see that a certain part of the predicted signs is past, then you will know that it is the very time that the Most High is about to visit the world that he has made" (Stone trans. alt.; cf. also *4 Ezra* 4:52 and *2 Apoc. Bar.* 25:2). That "very time" is the era in which the author sees himself as standing, and the already-fulfilled signs are a surety for the quick arrival of the rest of them and the eschaton. Similarly, for Mark, the signs that Jesus goes on to list in the first part of the chapter (13:5–23) have already occurred, and this fulfillment provides assurance that the remaining signs, the cosmic events detailed in13:24–27, will shortly come to pass.

There is thus a progression within the "last things," and it is the purpose of this Markan chapter to specify that progression. The next passage will describe the first phase, "the beginning of the labor pains" of the new age.

THE BEGINNING OF THE ESCHATOLOGICAL LABOR PAINS (13:5–8)

13 ⁵And Jesus began to say to them, "Look out, lest someone lead you astray. ⁶Many people will come in my name, saying, 'I am he,' and they will lead many people astray. ⁷But when you hear about wars and rumors of wars, don't be disturbed—they have to happen, but it is not yet the end. ⁸For nation will be raised against nation and dominion against dominion; there will be earthquakes in place after place; there will be famines. These things are the beginning of the labor pains.

NOTES

13 5. *lest someone lead you astray.* Gk *hina mē tis hymas planēsē.* On deceivers as characteristic of the end-time, see 13:6, 21–22; CD 5:20; 1QH 4[12]:7, 16, 20; *T. Moses* 7:4; Acts 20:29–30; 2 Thess 2:9–12; 1 John 2:18, 22; 4:1–4; 2 Pet 2:1;

2 John 7; Rev 13:14; 19:20; *Did.* 16:4; *2 Apoc. Bar.* 70:2 (cf. Braun, *"Planan,"* 241–42). According to *1 En.* 56:4, at the eschaton deceivers will be judged and punished, and they will no longer be able to lead anyone astray.

6. *in my name, saying, 'I am he.'* Gk *epi tǭ onomati mou legontes hoti egō eimi*, lit., "in my name, saying that, 'I am he.'" On the omission of "that" from the translation, see the NOTE on "and saying" in 1:15. As Wellhausen (101) points out, this phrase is difficult because "in my name" suggests that the deceivers are Christian, but "I am he" implies that they see *themselves* (rather than Jesus) as the redeemer. Some scholars therefore suggest, without textual support, that either "in my name" or "saying, 'I am he'" is a gloss (e.g., Klostermann, 133; Gaston, *No Stone*, 14). There are, however, other ways of dealing with the tension.

Many commentators, for example, interpret "coming in my name" as something like "seeking to claim my authority"; the name at issue, then, is the title Christ = Messiah (see already Matt 24:5 and Williams, *I Am He*, 229–41). This, however, is a strained interpretation of "in my name," and it is inconsistent with usage elsewhere in the NT, where *epi tǭ onomati mou* designates people who are on Jesus' side or want to tap into his power (see 9:37–39 pars. and cf. Nineham, 345; Gundry, 761). The deceivers, then, are probably in some sense believers in Jesus.

Boring (*Sayings*, 128–30, 186–95) suggests that they are, specifically, Christian prophets who claim to speak in the name of the Resurrected One (cf. *Odes Sol.* 42:6, where the risen Jesus says that he is with his people "and will speak by their mouths"). According to Boring, the deceivers' "I am" style of speaking is like that used by the prophet of the Apocalypse (Rev 1:8, 17; 2:23; 21:6; 22:16) and by Montanus ("I am the Father and I am the Son and I am the Paraclete"; cf. Aune, *Prophecy*, 314), and "in the name of Jesus" is similar to designations employed by Paul for his own inspired speech (1 Cor 1:10; 5:4; 1 Thess 4:15; 2 Thess 3:6; cf. 1 Cor 14:37). The seer of the Apocalypse, however, does not say "I am" but records visions of the risen Jesus doing so. If, moreover, the deceivers of Mark 13:6 are identical with or similar to the false Christs later in chapter 13, they are claiming to be something more than Jesus' mouthpiece, since the false Christs engender the response "Here is the Messiah!" rather than "The Messiah is speaking through him!" (13:21–22). The Markan deceivers, then, are probably Christians who claim actually to *be* the returning Jesus. We encounter numerous such figures in later Christian history (see Cohn, *Pursuit*, passim), and the Gospel of Mark itself suggests that some first-century Jews could conceive of a legendary figure returning after his earthly life had ended (see 6:14–16; 8:27–28).

7. *But when you hear about wars and rumors of wars.* Gk *hotan de akousēte polemous kai akoas polemōn*, a pun in Greek, since *akousēte* ("hear about") and *akoas* ("rumors") are cognates (cf. Gundry, 738). On wars as a characteristic of the end-time in Jewish and Christian apocalypticism, see Dan 9:26; 11:40–42; Zech 14:1–5; Rev 9:7, 9; 11:7; etc.; *2 Apoc. Bar.* 27:5; 48:37; 70:8; *b. Sanh.* 97a. In the last passage, as Klausner (*Jesus*, 322) points out, the end-time is marked by famines, wars, and "noises" (*qwlwt*), which may mean rumors of wars.

The phrase "wars and rumors of wars" fits the presumed time and circumstances of the Gospel's composition (see the INTRODUCTION in vol. 1, pp. 37–39, for a Markan date of around 70 C.E., in proximity to the Jewish revolt in Palestine). While the Roman empire was basically at peace from the time of Tiberius (14–37 C.E.) to the end of Nero's reign (54–68), this relative calm was shattered by the Jewish War, which began in 66, and the "year of the four emperors," in 68–69 (cf. Hengel, *Studies*, 21–22).

they have to happen. Gk *dei genesthai*, lit. "it is necessary to happen," an allusion to Dan 2:28–29 Theod.; 2:45 Theod. (echoed in Rev 1:1; 22:6). The following phrase also reproduces a Danielic theme; see the next NOTE.

but it is not yet the end. Gk *all' oupō to telos*. The overall purpose of Mark 13 is not to dampen eschatological enthusiasm but to awaken it (see the introduction to chapter 13 and the COMMENT on the present passage). For Mark and his community, the disasters described in 13:7–8 (outbreaks of war, earthquakes, famines) belong to the recent past; though they did not lead *immediately* to the end, the latter is now imminent from the later Markan perspective (see the COMMENT on 13:14–20 and Carroll, *Response*). A similar theme of completed delay is implicit in Dan 12:13 LXX Theod., which seems to be echoed here: "For there are yet days before the fulfillment of the end." For the character Daniel, prophesying in the sixth century B.C., the end is still far away, but for the author of the biblical book, writing pseudonymously during the Maccabean Revolt in the second century B.C., it has come near.

8. *For nation will be raised against nation and dominion against dominion.* Gk *egerthēsetai gar ethnos ep' ethnos kai basileia ep' basileian*. The form "X against X and Y against Y" epitomizes conflict already around 700 B.C.E. in Hesiod, *Works and Days* 25–26 ("Potter is angry with potter, craftsman with craftsman, beggar is jealous of beggar, and singer of singer"). But the closer parallel is in Jewish apocalyptic writings such as 4 *Ezra* 13:31 ("And they shall plan to make war against one another, city against city, place against place, people against people, and kingdom against kingdom") and *Sib. Or.* 3:635–36 ("King will lay hold of king and take away territory; peoples will ravage peoples, and potentates, tribes"; cf. also *Jub.* 11:2). The *Sibylline Oracles* passage goes on to describe the nations' assault on the Temple, which God preempts in an act of fiery judgment, perhaps by sending "a king from the sun who will stop the entire earth from evil war." Both the likeness and the unlikeness to the eschatological scheme in Mark 13 are interesting (see Mark 13:2 for the destruction rather than rescue of the Temple, and Mark 13:26–27 for the climactic coming of the Son of Man in glory). Our chapter, then, seems to be adapting a standard eschatological scheme.

"Nation . . . against nation and dominion against dominion" may expand the reference to international war in the previous verse (i.e., one nation or dominion going to war against another), but it may also suggest internecine conflict (i.e., a nation or dominion pitted against itself). Such internal strife appears frequently in eschatological schemata, since it implies breakdown of the social order and thus is an example of the universal disintegration that characterizes the end-time (see 4 *Ezra* 5:5; 9:3; *T. Jud.* 22:1; 1 *En.* 99:4; cf. Stone, 4 *Ezra*, 111). This interpretation is supported by the striking parallel in Isa 19:2: "And I [God] will stir up Egypt against Egypt, and they will fight, every man against his brother [cf. Mark 13:12] and every man against his neighbor, city against city, kingdom against kingdom." The first clause is rendered in the LXX as *kai epegerthēsontai Aigyptioi ep' Aigyptious* ("and Egyptians will be raised up against Egyptians"). *Epegerthēsontai*, then, is a divine passive, and this is probably the implication of *egerthēsetai* in Mark as well; otherwise, a more common and less awkward verb such as *anistēmi* ("to rise") would probably have been used (cf. Judg 7:9, 15; Isa 21:5; Jer 51:29 [28:29 LXX]; etc.).

earthquakes in place after place . . . famines. Gk *seismoi kata topous . . . limoi.* On the translation of *kata topous* as "in place after place," see BDAG 511 (B1a). On earthquakes and famines as eschatological signs, see Zech 14:4–5; Rev 6:8, 12; 8:5; 11:13, 18:8, etc.; *1 En.* 1:7; *4 Ezra* 9:3; *2 Apoc. Bar.* 27:6–7; *b. Sanh.* 97a; *Signs of the Judgment* 8 (cf. Stone, *4 Ezra*, 295; idem, *Signs*). See also Matt 27:51–53; 28:2, in which earthquakes are linked with Jesus' death and resurrection, which are understood as eschatological events. For a review of major earthquakes in Israel since 100 B.C.E., see Amiram and Arieh, "Earthquakes." Notable "earthquakes in place after place" in the decade or so before the probable composition of Mark included the one in Asia Minor in 61 C.E., in which twelve cities were leveled in a single night (see Pliny, *Natural History* 2.86), and that in Pompeii and Herculaneum in Italy in 63 C.E. (see Seneca, *Natural Questions* 6.1.1–3 and cf. http://urban.arch. virginia.edu/struct/pompeii/). Closer to Mark's probable setting, Dio Cassius (*Roman History* 63.28.1) records an earthquake at the flight of Nero shortly before his death in 68, and Josephus (*War* 4.286) refers to another in Jerusalem during the Jewish Revolt—though it is difficult to tell what is historical in Josephus' theologically molded narrative. But Josephus' references to famines during the same war, especially during the siege of Jerusalem, are doubtless historical at core (see "*limos*" in Rengstorf, *Concordance*, especially the horrifying description of cannibalism in *War* 6.193–213). Earlier in the century, there was a severe famine in the time of Claudius (41–54 C.E.; see Acts 11:28; Tacitus, *Annals* 12.43; Dio Cassius, *Roman History* 60.11), and according to Suetonius (*Life of Nero* 45.1), the Romans suffered hunger under Nero (cf. Hengel, *Studies*, 133 n. 129).

These things are the beginning of the labor pains. Gk *archē ōdinōn tauta.* This sort of statement is common in eschatological timetables; see, for example, *2 Apoc. Bar.* 27:2: "In the first part [of the eschatological era]: the beginning of commotions."

Already in the OT, the suddenness and intensity of labor pains makes them a popular image for divine judgment (see Isa 13:6–8; Mic 4:9–10; cf. Isa 66:7–9), and Isa 26:17–19 uses this image in an eschatological context. Ancient Jewish and early Christian literature extends this OT trajectory, employing birthing imagery for the arrival of the eschaton (see, e.g., *2 Apoc. Bar.* 22:7) and a woman's labor pains for the sudden, brief period of intense suffering that immediately precedes the eschaton (*1 En.* 62:4; 1 Thess 5:3) or the birth of the Messiah (1QH 3[11]:7–10; Rev 12:2; cf. Gal 4:19). Once this period of labor has begun, the hoped-for birth is not far off (*4 Ezra* 4:40–42; cf. Gaventa, "Maternity," 191–94). In rabbinic literature, *ḥblw šl mšyḥ*, "the writhing (= labor pain) of the Messiah," becomes a technical term for this short period of eschatological affliction (e.g., *b. Šabb.* 118a; *b. Sanh.* 98b; *Mekilta Vayassa'* 5 [Lauterbach 2.120]). This phrase is almost always singular, as opposed to Mark's plural *ōdinōn*, though *ḥblw* could be construed as a defectively written plural, and *b. Ketub.* 111a may attest the plural in Aramaic (see Dubis, *Messianic Woes*, 10–13). In view of the pervasive association of the labor-pain image with a short period of intense suffering, it is misleading for Moloney (255) to write that it "indicates that history . . . is still working its painful way to a final end"; the emphasis, rather, is on imminence, as Mark himself makes clear in 13:19–20, 28–29.

The Markan clause, however, is sometimes translated in a way that minimizes the eschatological significance of the "labor pains." See, for example, RSV/NRSV: "This is but the beginning of the birth pangs"—an enticing translation, since it protects Jesus from a mistaken belief in an imminent end. The word "but," however, is absent in the Greek and the ancient versions, and the reasons usually adduced for interpolating it are unconvincing. Gundry (738), for example, points to the asyndeton (see the GLOSSARY) of our clause and the forward position of *archē* ("beginning") as evidence that the word is emphasized. But it is unclear how the absence of a particle leads to supplying the English word "but," and asyndeton is ubiquitous in our passage, which may reflect Aramaic or popular Greek style rather than emphasis (cf. Zerwick, *Markus-Stil*, 21–23). Even if the asyndeton in the present instance *is* emphatic, the stress would apply to the whole clause, not just to the word *archē*, and the forward position similarly pertains to the whole predicate, "the beginning of the labor pains." The appropriate translation, then, is not "These things are *only* the beginning of the labor pains" but "These things are indeed the beginning of the labor pains" (cf. Beasley-Murray, 397). Matthew picks up the Markan nuance when he renders our clause "*All* these things are the beginning of the labor pains" (Matt 24:8, my trans.), thus stressing rather than denigrating the "labor pains," and later in the chapter repeating "all these things" twice in a context that links the phrase with the imminent eschaton (Matt 24:33–34).

COMMENT

Introduction. Jesus begins his response to the disciples' question about the eschatological timetable with an overview of the first part of that schedule.

The substance of the passage seems to be pre-Markan; the only verse showing strong signs of redaction is the introductory one, 13:5. Here "and Jesus began to" + verb of speaking is a typical introductory locution of the evangelist (cf. the NOTE on "began to send them out" in 6:7), and "Look!" (*blepete*) punctuates the whole eschatological discourse (cf. 13:9, 23, 33), reflecting the Markan preoccupation with perception (see the subject index in vols. 1 and 2 under "seeing," and 8:22–26; 9:6, 20, 25, 32; 10:14; 11:13; 12:11, 34; 15:39). It is also possible that the phrase "in my name" in 13:6 is Markan, since it overloads the verse and also occurs in 9:37, 39 (cf. 9:38, 41; 11:9; 13:13; and the NOTE on "in my name, saying, 'I am he,' " in 13:6).

After the introductory 13:5a ("And Jesus began to say to them"), the passage is structured in a trio of double sayings (13:5b–6; 13:7; and 13:8). In each case, the second saying (13:6; 13:7b; 13:8d) is asyndetic (see the GLOSSARY) and helps explain the first saying (13:5b; 13:7a; 13:8abc; on this function of asyndeton, see Smyth §2167 [b]).

13:5–8: the beginning of labor pains. Mark introduces the eschatological discourse, the longest continuous address delivered by Jesus in his Gospel, with a customary locution: "And Jesus began to say to them" (13:5a). Although this introductory formula is often treated as a mere cliché, in this instance it may imply more: Jesus' words address not just the four closest disciples of his earthly ministry but also a subsequent generation of Christians who will live through the prophesied horrors—including the members of the Markan community (cf. 13:14, 37; cf. the NOTE on "began to send them out" in 6:7). Thus, the earthly Jesus "begins to" warn his earliest followers about eschatological horrors, which their successors will be able to endure through the empowerment and instruction that will continue to come to them through the risen Lord (cf. 13:11).

The first sentence of this discourse sounds its *Leitmotif*: "Look out, lest someone lead you astray" (*blepete mē tis hymas planēsę*, 13:5b; cf. 13:9, 23, 33). This introduction, along with the admonition to shun those who say, "I am he" (13:6), echoes the warning in Deuteronomy 13 against false prophets who lead people astray (*planēsai*) with signs and wonders, enticing them to serve another god—language that reappears later in the chapter (Mark 13:21–22). This same Deuteronomic language also appears in Jewish denunciations of Jesus, where he is charged with being a deceiver (*planos*) and a sorcerer who teaches apostasy (see John 7:12, 47; Justin, *Dialogue* 69; *b. Sanh.* 43a; 107b; *T. Levi* 16:3; *Acts of Thomas* 48; cf. Martyn, *History*, 76–83). The introduction to the discourse, then, may be partly defensive—it is not *Jesus* who leads people astray but some of those who come "in [his] name" (13:6). These deceivers do not act autonomously; behind them stands a more sinister power, "*the* Deceiver," that is, Satan (see *Sib. Or.* 3:68–70; *T. Sim.* 3:5; *T. Jud.* 19:4; Rev 12:9; 20:3, 8, 10; cf. 2 Thess 2:11; 1 John 4:6), whose involvement in his lackeys' web of delusion is suggested by the vague word "someone" (*tis*; cf. *tines* in Gal 1:7, and Braun, "*Planaō*," 238, 247–49). Here, then, we see a typically apocalyptic picture of human actors under the sway of superhuman powers—the Devil on the one hand and God on the other (see below on "they have to happen" and "nation will be raised against nation").

But who exactly are the deceivers? The Markan Jesus describes them as people who say, "I am he" (*egō eimi*), a proclamation that, earlier in Mark (6:50), had a divine connotation (see the COMMENT on 6:48–50). Lacking the epiphanic context and the OT echoes present in Mark 6:45–52, however, the declaration ascribed to the deceivers in the present instance is probably not meant to be understood in this way (cf. Williams, *I Am He*, 233). This leaves two main possibilities (see Bede, *Exposition of Mark* 13:6): the deceivers are either Jewish pseudomessiahs or Christians. On balance, the latter option seems preferable (see the NOTE on "in my name, saying, 'I am he' " in 13:6), but in either case, they join the crowded field of sign prophets, "messiahs," and other religious enthusiasts in Palestine and its environs in the years leading up to and including the Jewish War (see Josephus, *War* 2.259, and cf. Braun, *"Planaō,"* 6.241). For an apocalypticist such as Mark, the proliferation of such deceivers is itself an eschatological sign (see the NOTE on "lest someone lead you astray" in 13:5).

Another, more devastating eschatological portent is adduced in the next section of the passage: war (13:7a, 8a; see the NOTE on "But when you hear about wars and rumors of wars" in 13:7). So fearsome is this sign that not only its presence but even the rumor of it strikes terror into hearers ("rumors of wars" also reflects the premodern context, in which it could take weeks or months for word to spread about a war erupting in distant parts). Mark's readers would doubtless think first and foremost of the Jewish revolt against the Romans, which began in 66 C.E. and reached a terrible climax with the destruction of the Temple in 70 (see the NOTE on "But when you hear about wars and rumors of wars" in 13:7). Yet despite the terror of such events, the Markan community is exhorted not to lose heart at them; these things "have to happen (*dei genesthai*), but it is not yet the end" (13:7b). The other Markan usages of *dei* (lit. "it is necessary") are in eschatological prophecies later in this chapter (13:10, 14), in one of the passion predictions (8:31; cf. 9:11), and in Peter's pledge of undying loyalty to Jesus, even to the point of death (14:31). Mark, then, views Jesus' suffering and death, as well as that of disciples who follow him (cf. 8:34), as grim but ultimately redemptive eschatological events enfolded in the providence of God, who is steering history rapidly toward its predestined port. The same divine superintendence is implied by 13:8: "For nation will be raised against nation and dominion against dominion"—*egerthēsetai* probably being a divine passive (see the NOTE on "For nation will be raised against nation and dominion against dominion" in 13:8). Earthly rulers may appear to be in charge, but it is actually God who has the life and death of nations in his hand (cf. 10:42; Dan 4:17, 25, 32).

War will not be the only violent disaster visited upon the earth at this preliminary stage of the eschatological era; earthquakes and famines will also ensue (13:8bc), all three types of disasters being frequently associated with the end time in apocalyptic literature (see the NOTE on "earthquakes in place after place . . . famines" in 13:8). In 2 *Apoc. Bar.* 70:8, for example, the three occur in the same order as in Mark:

> And it will happen that everyone who saves himself from the war will die in an earthquake, and he who saves himself from the earthquake will be burned by fire, and he who saves himself from the fire will perish by famine.

The agreement in order could be coincidental, or due to the fact that wars and earthquakes can lead to famines, but it may also suggest a fixed eschatological scheme. Yet this is not just an outline plucked out of an apocalyptic timetable but one that Mark and his readers would realize fits their own recent past (see the NOTES on "But when you hear about wars and rumors of wars" in 13:7 and "earthquakes in place after place . . . famines" in 13:8), especially the events surrounding the Jewish War. Many of the people involved in that conflagration were themselves eschatological thinkers, and some of them invoked similar scenarios to interpret their times. Josephus (*War* 4.361–62), for example, tells of a rebel leader who fell out with the Zealots and was murdered by them; in his dying moments, he "imprecated upon their heads the vengeance of the Romans, famine and pestilence to add to the horrors of war, and, to crown all, internecine strife." These curses, Josephus adds, were soon realized.

Although such events are not yet the end (13:7b), they are, for Mark, signs that the end is approaching, as the conclusion of 13:8 makes clear by identifying these events with the start of the eschatological labor pains. This is a familiar Jewish image for the brief interval of tribulation immediately preceding the eschaton: when a woman goes into labor, one can be sure that a baby will shortly be born (see the NOTE on "These things are the beginning of the labor pains" in 13:8). Indeed, the whole outline in our passage is strikingly similar to that in apocalyptic Jewish passages such as 2 *Apoc. Bar.* 27; *Signs of the Judgment* (see Stone, *Signs*); *b. Sanh.* 97a, and the remarkable parallel in 4 *Ezra* 9:1–4 (cf. also 5:1–12):

> Measure carefully in your mind, and when you will see that a certain part of the predicted signs are past, then you will know that it is the very time when the Most High is about to visit the world which he has made. So when there shall appear in the world quaking of places, tumult of peoples, intrigues of nations, wavering of leaders, confusion of princes, then you will know that it was of these that the Most High spoke from the days that were of old. (Stone trans.)

The parallels with Mark include earthquakes and civil and international strife; God reclaiming the world that he made (cf. 13:19); and the notion that a certain portion of the eschatological signs have occurred ("the beginning of the labor pains") and the rest will shortly ensue.

In the following passage, the Markan Jesus will specify the powerful personal and communal impact that this "beginning of the labor pains" will have on the members of the Markan community.

THE COMING PERSECUTIONS (13:9–13)

13 ⁹But you, look to yourselves—they will turn you over to councils, and in synagogues you will be beaten, and you will be arraigned before rulers and kings for my sake, as a witness to them. ¹⁰And first the good news must be preached to all the nations. ¹¹And when they arrest you and turn you over, don't think beforehand about what you are to say, but whatever is given you in that hour, say that; for it is not you who are speaking, but the Holy Spirit. ¹²And brother will turn brother over to death, and a father his child, and children will rise up against their parents and have them put to death. ¹³And you will be hated by all for the sake of my name. But the one who endures to the end, he will be saved.

NOTES

13 9. *But you, look to yourselves.* Gk *blepete de hymeis heautous,* an awkward pileup of references to the addressees; *blepete* ("Look!") alone would have been sufficient (cf. 4:24; 12:38; 13:5, 33). This awkwardness helps explain why the words are missing in some manuscripts (D, W, Θ, *f*¹, 27, 565, 700, it syˢ). The emphasis on "you" may reflect Mark's desire to underline the relevance for his community of the prophecies of persecution in 13:9–13 (see the COMMENT on 13:9–11).

councils. Gk *synedria.* On arraignments of Christians before the Jewish ruling council in Jerusalem, the Sanhedrin, in the earliest years of the church, see Acts 4–5 and 22–23; on appearances before Roman councils and assemblies, see Acts 17:6–9; 19:35–41 (though these non-Jewish gatherings are not called *synedria* in Acts). The parallel between being turned over to councils and being beaten in synagogues suggests to most scholars that the councils in our passage are Jewish. The Greek word *synedrion,* indeed, became a loanword in Mishnaic Hebrew and Aramaic (*sanhedrîn, sanhedrê*), designating either the ruling council of seventy leading Jews in Palestine (see the NOTE on "the whole Sanhedrin" in 14:55) or smaller decision-making and judicial bodies in Israel and the Diaspora (cf. *m. Sanh.* 1:6; *t. Sanh.* 3:10; Hare, *Jewish Persecution,* 102–4). Since the present commentary situates the Markan community in geographical and temporal proximity to the Jewish revolt against the Romans of 66–73 C.E., it is interesting to note that Josephus (*War* 4.335–44) speaks of Zealot leaders instituting kangaroo courts during the revolt in order to persecute their enemies; on one such occasion they "issued a peremptory summons to seventy of the leading citizens to appear in the Temple, assigning them, as in a play, the role, without the authority, of judges" (§336; cf. §341). Although this group is not called a sanhedrin, it seems to be acting as one, and the number of its members corresponds to that of the Sanhedrin in the Mishnah (cf. *m. Sanh.* 1:6 and Gibson, "Function," 17–19).

in synagogues you will be beaten. Gk *eis synagōgas darēsesthe.* This prophecy has in view either spontaneous beating or formal synagogue discipline; in view of the juxtaposition with the reference to councils, the latter is more likely (cf. Matt 23:34; Acts 22:19; *m. Mak.* 3:12; Epiphanius, *Panarion* 30.11; Levine, *Synagogue,* 131–32). Already Deut 25:1–3 mentions whipping as a punishment that may be imposed by a judge, but it does not specify for what crimes; it was left to later authorities, therefore, to figure out which infractions deserved the lash (see Elon, *Jewish Law,* 1.201–2). Josephus (*Ant.* 4.238), for example, calls flogging a "most disgraceful penalty" earned by people who have oppressed their neighbors, and the Mishnah (*m. Mak.* 3:1–9) prescribes it for violation of purity rules having to do with sex, forbidden foods, and so on. There is no clear evidence as to what kinds of transgressions subjected early Christians to this sort of synagogue discipline, but Paul says that he received thirty-nine lashes as a "slave (*diakonos*) of Christ" (2 Cor 11:23–24, my trans.)—perhaps an allusion to preaching the good news, which he did "under compulsion" (and hence as a slave) according to 1 Cor 9:16–17. It may be that other early Christians, too, were beaten for disturbing synagogue assemblies with their preaching.

you will be arraigned before rulers and kings. Gk *epi hēgemonōn kai basileōn stathēsesthe.* On arraignments of early Christians before rulers and kings, see Acts 18:12–17; 19:35–41; 21:37–22:29; 23:23–26:32.

as a witness to them. Gk *eis martyrion autois.* The same phrase occurs in 1:44 and 6:11; on positive and negative ways of interpreting it, see the NOTE on this phrase in 1:44. In the present context, the juxtaposition with 13:10 makes the positive meaning probable, but the implication of eschatological judgment later in the chapter (13:24–26) means that a negative nuance ("as a witness against them") cannot be excluded.

10. *first.* Gk *prōton.* From the line of thought in 13:9–10, one might think that this word implies that the good news must be preached universally before the persecution spoken of in 13:9 can occur. Verse 13:11, however, seems to imply that proclamation of the gospel is *a result of* persecution rather than its *cause.* Mark, then, probably means to say that the worldwide proclamation of the gospel has to happen before the final end can come (cf. Matt 24:14), and Mark 13:10 is thus part of the Markan Jesus' answer to the disciples' question as to the timing of the end (13:4). Mark himself has probably created this verse and inserted it here, out of chronological sequence, because of the word "witness" in 13:9 (see the introduction to the COMMENT).

11. *arrest.* Gk *agōsin.* On this nuance of *agein* (lit. "lead, lead away"), see BDAG 16 (2). In 14:42 the Markan Jesus uses the same verb to exhort his sleeping disciples to get up and face the party that is coming to arrest him, thus underlining the relationship between his arrest and that of his followers (see the COMMENT on 13:9–11).

don't think beforehand about what you are to say, but whatever is given you in that hour, say that. Gk *mē promerimnate ti lalēsēte, all' ho ean dothē hymin en ekeinē tē hōrā, touto laleite.* Evans (311) points to the parallels in Exod 4:10–17 and Jer 1:6–10, where Moses and Jeremiah complain that they are not good speakers and God responds that he will put his words in their mouths and teach them what to say (*lalēsai*). *Exod. Rab.* 3.15, interpreting the Exodus passage, says that God was thereby promising that he would make Moses into a new creation—a motif similar to that of the creative, eschatological Spirit in our passage.

for it is not you who are speaking, but the Holy Spirit. Gk *ou gar este hymeis hoi lalountes alla to pneuma to hagion.* On the Spirit as the power of inspired speech, see Num 24:2–3; 2 Sam 23:2; 1 Kgs 22:24; etc. In the later Prophets, intertestamental Judaism, and the NT, this endowment with the Spirit for speaking purposes either points to eschatological events (e.g., Mark 12:36–37) or becomes one itself (e.g., Isa 11:1–2; 42:1; 61:1–2; Joel 2:28; *Pss. Sol.* 17:35–37; Acts 4:8, 31; 13:9–10). In rabbinic traditions, similarly, the Holy Spirit is often the spirit of prophecy (see Schäfer, *Vorstellung,* passim).

13. *But the one who endures to the end, he will be saved.* Gk *ho de hypomeinas eis telos, houtos sōthēsetai.* This is an example of *casus pendens* followed by a resumptive pronoun, an idiom especially characteristic of Semitic prose (cf. 13:11: "but whatever is given you in that hour, say that"). Maloney's argument against Semitic influence in the present instance—that Semitic languages do not use a demon-

strative pronoun in such cases (*Semitic Interference*, 86–90)—is hairsplitting; *houtos* is the normal Greek term for the personal pronoun in the nominative.

COMMENT

Introduction. After briefly sketching the preliminary "labor pains" of the new age, disasters that will occur on an international stage, the Markan Jesus zeroes in on troubles that will afflict the Markan community in particular.

Most of 13:9–13 is probably pre-Markan tradition, but 13:10 should be ascribed to the evangelist himself. This verse interrupts the natural connection between the prophecy of persecution in 13:9 and the instruction about how to respond to this persecution in 13:11 (see the NOTE on "first" in 13:10). All the major words in the intervening verse, moreover, are typically Markan ("first," "good news," "must," "preach," "all," "nations"). Part or all of the awkward introductory exhortation in 13:9a ("But you, look to yourselves") and the corresponding final exhortation in 13:13b ("But the one who endures to the end, he will be saved") may be Markan as well (see the NOTE on "But you, look to yourselves" in 13:9).

The passage forms an alternating pattern of prophecy and encouragement:

13:9a	Exhortation to heedfulness
13:9b–10	Prophecy of arraignment before rulers, leading to worldwide witness
13:11	Exhortation not to plan one's speech in advance in such situations of witness
13:12–13a	Prophecy of betrayal and universal hatred of Christians
13:13b	Exhortation to endure to the end

The call to attentiveness in 13:9a stands as a rubric over the entire pericope, and the exhortations in 13:11 and 13:13b refer directly to the prophecies that precede them. Structurally, therefore, the pericope falls into two major parts, 13:9–11 and 13:12–13.

13:9–11: trials and witness. The initial and overarching exhortation of the passage, "But you, look to yourselves," is a logical continuation from and intensification of the prophecies of wars and natural disasters in 13:5–8: such events may be unsettling, but even worse things are to come, because the wars, earthquakes, and famines are only the *start* of the eschatological childbirth (see 13:8d). While the previous passage, moreover, prophesies disasters that will afflict the whole world, the present one describes tribulations that will specifically torment the Markan Christians; the latter, therefore, had better look to *themselves*. Like "let the reader understand" in 13:14, then, the opening of our passage is designed to call attention to contemporary events of special relevance for the Markan community—in this case persecution by councils, synagogue officials, rulers, and kings. The connection between 13:5–8 and 13:9–13 hints that these persecutions will grow directly out of the international upheavals portrayed in the earlier passage, and this in turn suggests that the reference may be to trials of Christians connected with the Jewish revolt against Rome (see the NOTE on "councils" in 13:9 and Donahue, *Are You*, 217–24; Marcus, "Jewish War," 448).

Jesus' prophecy of persecutions begins with the verb *paradōsousin* ("they will turn you over," 13:9b). This word is significant for two reasons. The first is its background in Isaiah 52–53 LXX, where the Lord's Suffering Servant is "turned over" to an ignominious death but ends up being exalted and glorified (Isa 52:13; 53:12); the verb thus already hints at the salvation that Jesus prophesies at the end of our passage ("But the one who endures to the end, he will be saved"; 13:13b; cf. the NOTE on "handed over" in 1:14 and Marcus, *Way*, 187–90). The second important aspect of *paradidōmi* is its use elsewhere in the Gospel, where it is applied to the arrest of John the Baptist (1:14) but more often to Jesus' own betrayal and death (3:19; 9:31; 10:33; 14:10–11, 18, 21, 41–42, 44; 15:1, 10, 15). The word itself, then, implies what Jesus says explicitly at the end of the verse: the disciples' delivery into the hands of their enemies will be "for my sake." This is just the first in a series of correspondences between what Jesus foretells here and what he himself will soon undergo. Like his followers, he will be betrayed by a "brother" (14:10–11, 43–45), arrested (14:46), turned over to a council (14:53, 55), beaten (14:65; 15:15, 19), stood before a ruler for judgment (15:1–15), exposed to the contempt of the masses (15:16–36), and killed (15:37). In the end, however, he, like them, will be "saved" (16:1–8).

The prophecy about their being turned over to (Jewish) councils (see the NOTE on "councils" in 13:9) is chiastically linked with that about being beaten in synagogues (13:9c), which reflects a form of synagogue discipline attested elsewhere in Jewish and Christian sources (see the NOTE on "in synagogues you will be beaten" in 13:9). It is possible that our prophecy envisages these arraignments before Jewish judicial bodies as preliminary hearings, after which the Christians will be turned over to a higher authority, the ruler or king (cf. Acts 18:12–17; 19:35–41; 21:37–22:29; 23:23–26:32). Here, again, there is a parallel to Jesus' fate (cf. 14:53–15:20).

But God can make the wrath of human beings into an instrument for his praise (cf. Ps 76:10); although the Christians' enemies will intend their persecutorial actions to eradicate the upstart movement, God will use them as a method for spreading the gospel to the ends of the earth (13:9c–10)—as happens, again, in the case of Jesus, whose death elicits the Gentile centurion's conversion (15:39). As Tertullian (*Apology* 50) famously put it: "The blood of Christians is [the] seed [of the church]." Ancient martyrdom accounts show how Christians turned their trials into occasions for testimony to the Christian message, both through what they said and through what they suffered. The way in which such Christian witness might spread to "all the nations" as a result of persecution (13:10) is illustrated by the Lukan portrait of Paul being taken as a prisoner to Rome, the heart of the pagan Empire, to defend himself before the emperor against the Sanhedrin's charges (Acts 25–28), on the way converting the ruler and people of Malta (Acts 28:1–10) and in Rome conducting a successful ministry under house arrest (Acts 28:30–31).

The redactional verse 13:10 places such Christian preaching "to all the nations" in an eschatological context—it is one of the key things that must happen before the end can come (see the NOTE on "first" in 13:10). This idea may represent a broadening of the perspective of the historical Jesus, who may have thought that his message needed to reach all his fellow *Jews*, or at least those in the Holy Land, before the end could arrive (cf. Matt 10:23). When most of Jesus' co-religionists rejected the Christian message, his post-Easter followers turned more and more to the Gentiles, whose evangelization became imbued with a similar eschatological urgency (cf. Rom 11:25–27; Rev 14:6–7). As a member of the Pauline mission (see the INTRODUCTION in vol. 1, pp. 73–75, and Marcus, "Mark—Interpreter"), Mark probably thinks that this eschatological prerequisite of worldwide evangelization is nearly complete (cf. Rom 15:23–24; Col 1:23) and that therefore the end is imminent (cf. the INTRODUCTION in vol. 1, p. 72, and the introduction to chapter 13). Like the redactional verse 7:27, then, the redactional verse 13:10 uses an adverbial *prōton* to delineate the Markan timeline of salvation: the good news has gone to the Jews (7:27; cf. Rom 1:16), then to the Gentiles (13:10)—and now that that has happened, the end will come quickly.

But the wording of 13:10, "And first the good news must be preached to all the nations," is susceptible to misinterpretation: the members of the Markan community might get the mistaken impression that the spread of the gospel message, and hence the arrival of the eschaton, is dependent on their own efforts, as though they could "force the end" by proclaiming the good news far and wide. This sort of activist apocalyptic thinking, which was probably prominent among the Jewish revolutionaries (see Hengel, *Zealots*, 123–27), has already been combated by the Parable of the Seed Growing by Itself in 4:26–29 (see the COMMENT on 4:26–29). It is now further corrected by Jesus' emphasis that proclamation of the gospel is not really a human activity but the work of the Spirit. Jesus' disciples, therefore, are not to premeditate what they should say but to speak what is given them "in that hour" of testimony before the authorities (13:11). Here, as often in the NT, "hour" is a technical term for the time of eschatological testing (see Mark 14:41; John 16:21; Rom 13:11; 1 John 2:18; Rev 3:10; Giesen, "*Hōra*"). This interpretation is appropriate to the context, since the Spirit that will provide utterance "in that hour" is an eschatological gift (see the NOTE on "for it is not you who are speaking, but the Holy Spirit" in 13:11). As often in Mark, then, end-time distress and end-time empowerment go hand in hand (cf. 1 Pet 4:14).

As pointed out in the NOTE on "don't think beforehand about what you are to say, but whatever is given you in that hour, say that" in 13:11, this prophecy of verbal empowerment also echoes the OT stories of Moses and Jeremiah, two leaders who were diffident about their eloquence but promised by God that he would put his words in their mouth. As at earlier critical junctures in Israel's history, so now at the climax of that history, the proclamation of the message is too important to be left to the experts, the talented rhetoricians. Its promulgation, rather, depends on the divine power that delights to employ awkward and unlikely human instruments. By assimilating the Markan evangelists to great figures of Israel's past, Jesus supports and encourages people whose self-image has probably been battered by the fact that, for his sake, they have become "hated by all," including the majority of Israel.

13:12–13: betrayal and endurance. Not only will the Markan Christians experience persecution from outsiders (kings, rulers, synagogue authorities, Sanhedrin members); they will also be betrayed by members of their own families. This betrayal is described in 13:12 (cf. Matt 10:34–36//Luke 12:51–53), in imagery drawn largely from the OT and mediated by later Jewish apocalyptic literature (cf. Allison, "Q 12:51–53"). The eschatological prophecies in Isa 19:2 and Ezek 38:21, for example, depict brothers killing each other (i.e., civil war), and *1 En.* 56:7 echoes the latter passage in a portrayal of end-time mayhem (on Isa 19:2, cf. the NOTE on "For nation will be raised against nation and dominion against dominion" in 13:8). *Sibylline Oracles* 8.84–85, similarly, describes alienation of parents from children, and vice versa, as an illustration of the evil that in the end time will increase "impiety and affliction beyond hope," and the speaker in 1QH 17(9):34–36 complains that his father and mother have abandoned him in the era of eschatological testing (see also *Jub.* 23:19).

Familial alienation as a result of conversion was a trait that early Christianity shared with early Judaism. In *Joseph and Aseneth* 11–12, for example, a convert to Judaism complains movingly, and in terms strikingly similar to those in Mark 13:12–13, about the hostility she has experienced from her family:

> All people have come to hate me,
> and on top of those my father and my mother,
> because I, too, have come to hate their gods . . .
> And therefore my father and my mother and my whole family
> have come to hate me and said, "Aseneth is not our daughter
> because she destroyed our gods."
> And all people hate me . . .
> And now, in this humiliation of mine, all have (come to) hate me,
> and gloat over this affliction of mine. (11:4–6)

The alternation here, as in our passage, between hatred by family members and hatred by "all" may be psychologically significant: people rejected by their families are likely to end up convinced that whole world hates them.

A particularly important background for our passage's interpretation of this theme of familial alienation is found in Mic 7:1–7, where the Septuagintal and Targumic versions are especially striking:

> [2]They all lie in wait for blood, and each *hunts his brother* with a net (*Targum Jonathan:* a man delivers his brother to *destruction*) . . . [5]Put no trust in a neighbor, have no confidence in a friend, . . . [6]for *the son treats the father with contempt, the daughter rises up against her mother,* the daughter-in-law against her mother-in-law; a person's enemies are the people of his own house (LXX: a man's enemies are *all* the men in his house; *Targ. Jon.:* those who *hate* a man

are the men of his own house). ⁷But as for me, I will look to the Lord, I will *wait for* (LXX: *hypomenō*) the God of my *salvation*. (Hartman trans. alt., *Prophecy Interpreted*, 169)

Here family hatred, including brothers delivering each other to death and children rebelling against parents, is part of the disintegration that characterizes the last time. This eschatological dimension is reinforced in *m. Soṭ.* 9:15, where Mic 7:6 is quoted in an eschatological prophecy about the presumption (*ḥûṣpāh*) that will increase "in the footsteps of the Messiah," that is, the time that immediately precedes his coming (cf. *b. Sanh.* 97a; *Pesiq. Rab.* 34.1; Klausner, *Idea*, 442–45; Dubis, *Messianic Woes*, 8–9). But Micah also exhorts his hearers to endure this period of disintegration patiently and to wait for the Lord, for from him, in the end, salvation will arise (cf. the divine passive "will be saved" in Mark 13:13b; Hartman, *Prophecy Interpreted*, 167–69).

The eschatological disintegration of the family is described in Mark 13:12 as a crescendo of horror. Brother betraying brother is unpleasant but not unexpected in a biblical context (cf. Genesis 4 and 37); father betraying son is more unnatural; worst of all, in a patriarchal society, is the prospect of children rising up against their parents and having them put to death. This sort of rebellion not only violates the fifth commandment but also reverses Deut 21:18–21, where the mutinous son is to be executed for his presumption. But the passage may hint at an even more disturbing betrayal, since "brother" is a common early Christian term for "fellow Christian" (see the NOTE on "my brother and sister" in 3:35), and we know that apostate Christians *did* denounce their "brothers and sisters" to the authorities, which sometimes led to the latter's persecution and death (see Tacitus, *Annals* 15.44.5; Pliny, *Epistles* 10.96.5–6).

In view of the searing nature of these betrayals, the conclusion in 13:13a, as already noted, seems psychologically justified, if factually exaggerated: "You will be hated by all for the sake of my name" (cf. the Q parallel Matt 10:22//Luke 6:22). This exaggeration, however, is not unprecedented; the Roman historian Tacitus, for example, writes that the Christians were blamed for the great fire in Rome in 64 C.E. *odio humani generis*, "because of the hatred of the human race" (*Annals* 15.44.2–4). In context, this probably means "because they were perceived to hate outsiders," but Tacitus also gives the impression that the Christians were despised by the populace. These two reactions would be naturally related, since people perceived to be misanthropic—as Jews and Christians commonly were—are usually hated in their turn (cf. John 7:7; 15:18–25; 17:14; 1 John 2:15; 3:13).

Despite this bleak picture of societal alienation, the Markan Jesus concludes the section with a promise: "But the one who endures to the end, he will be saved" (13:13b). As Gnilka (2.192) points out, *telos* ("end") probably has a double sense, referring both to death and to the end of the world, and "saved" is also a double entendre. The continuation of Mark 13 makes it clear that God, to preserve a remnant of his elect people, will "save" some of them from death by cutting short the eschatological tribulation that otherwise would wipe them out (13:20) But others will be cut down before the eschaton can arrive; they will be "saved" in the world to come, but at the cost of their lives in this world (cf. 8:35). No one can tell in advance to which of these two categories he or she may belong; the important thing is to endure the suffering allotted, not allowing "tribulation or persecution on account of the word" to cause spiritual sterility (cf. 4:17), and leaving it up to God to decide whether he will deliver in this life or the next.

In the following passage, Jesus will make clear precisely how bad the suffering of the Markan community, and indeed of the world, will become in the days just before the end, when he describes a time of tribulation such as there has never been since the creation (13:19). Yet the word spoken at the conclusion of our passage also stands as the implicit headline over that picture of unprecedented distress: "But the one who endures to the end . . . will be saved!"

THE ABOMINATION OF DESOLATION (13:14–20)

13 ¹⁴But when you see the "abomination of desolation" standing where he should not—let the reader understand—then let those in Judaea flee to the mountains, ¹⁵and let not the person on the roof come down or go in to get anything out of his house, ¹⁶and let not the person in the field turn back to pick up his garment. ¹⁷And alas for pregnant women and for nursing mothers in those days! ¹⁸And pray that it may not happen during a storm. ¹⁹For those days will be such tribulation, that there has not been such from the beginning of the creation, which God created, until now, and never will be. ²⁰And if the Lord had not shortened the days, no flesh would be saved. But on account of the chosen ones, whom he chose, he shortened the days.

NOTES

13 14. *the "abomination of desolation."* Gk *to bdelygma tēs erēmōseōs*. This mysterious phrase originates in the OT book of Daniel (11:31; 12:11; cf. 9:27), where it refers to an idolatrous statue, an "abomination," that makes God's Temple "desolate" by defiling its holy space and thus causing pious worshipers to avoid it (see Kittel, *"Erēmos,"* 660). Because at least some of Mark's readers probably would have recognized the phrase as a quotation from scripture, the translation puts it in quotation marks. In Daniel itself, the phrase is a coded reference to Antiochus Epiphanes' erection of an image of a pagan deity, the Syrian god Baal Shemayin, on the altar of the Jerusalem Temple in 168 B.C.E. (see 1 Macc 1:54, 59; 6:7; cf. 2 Macc 6:2). The apocalyptically minded author of Daniel believed that this sacrilege would swiftly be followed by an unparalleled time of trouble (Dan 12:1; cf. Mark 13:20), the general resurrection (Dan 12:2–3), and the end of the world (Dan 11:35, 40; 12:13).

The latter events did not occur; a group of Jewish guerrillas, the Maccabees, led a revolt against the Syrians, restored the Temple in 164 B.C.E., and eventually reestablished Jewish rule in Palestine. After the Romans became the overlords of Palestine in 63 B.C.E., however, people began to reinterpret Daniel's "abomination of desolation" as a prophecy of a future desecration of the sanctuary. It is possible that Jesus himself used the term in this way, perhaps without being sure exactly what form the "desolation" would take—though if he also prophesied the Temple's destruction (cf. 13:2), he probably would have linked the two impending events. Some Jews and Christians probably thought that the Danielic prophecy was about to be fulfilled in 39–41 C.E., when the Roman emperor Caligula demanded that his own effigy be set up in the Temple. Many Jews were ready to go to war to prevent this sacrilege, and only Caligula's timely assassination prevented a bloodbath (see Philo, *Legation to Gaius*; Josephus, *War* 2.184–203; *Ant.* 18.261–308; Tacitus, *Histories* 5.9). Some scholars believe that the core of Mark 13 is a Jewish or Christian apocalypse written during the Caligula crisis (see the introduction to chapter 13 and cf. Taylor, "Caligula Crisis").

For Mark, however, writing thirty years afterward, the expected abomination cannot be Caligula's plan to erect his effigy, since that danger was long past. Perhaps (like Jesus before him?) he did not have any specific event in mind, but scholars have generally assumed that he did. Some (e.g., Pesch, *Naherwartungen*, 139–44) argue that for Mark the "desolation" is the destruction of the Temple by Roman legions under Titus in 70 C.E. (cf. Jer 22:5; Hag 1:9; Tob 14:4; *T. Levi* 15:1; Matt 23:38–24:2, all of which relate the Temple's destruction to "desolation"). But the participle *hestēkota* ("standing") is masculine in gender, despite its referent *bdelygma* ("abomination") being neuter, and this suggests that in Mark's eyes the desolating abomination is a *person* rather than an *event* such as the Temple's demise.

Some exegetes (e.g., Brandenburger, *Markus 13*, 82; Lührmann, 222) identify this person with the Roman general Titus, who was responsible for the successful siege of Jerusalem and entered the Temple when it was already in flames to view the holy of holies (see Josephus, *War* 6.260)—a sight prohibited by Jewish law to any Israelite except the high priest on the Day of Atonement, and certainly forbidden to a pagan general. Owen ("One Hundred and Fifty Three Fishes," 53) tries to strengthen the identification with an ingenious gematria (see the GLOSSARY): the numerical value for the Hebrew words *šqwṣ šmm* = "abomination of desolation" from Dan 12:11 is 876, as is the value of the name *Titos*, the Hebrew version of "Titus." Owen's numerological calculations, however, are flawed, since in Hebrew, Titus' name is spelled with a *ṭet* rather than the *taw* Owen presupposes (cf. Jastrow, 530) and the numerical value of Titus' name is thus 94 rather than 876. The main problem with the Titus interpretation, however, is not numerological but chronological: what sense does it make to enjoin flight to the mountains (13:14c) when the Temple and the capital city have already been destroyed and the war effectively lost?

The abomination of desolation is probably related to a desecration that *preceded* the destruction of Jerusalem. The occurrence that best fills the bill is the occupation of the Temple by the Zealots near the beginning of the war (winter of 67–68 C.E.), an event that was coupled with the revolutionaries' usurpation of the high priesthood (Josephus, *War* 4.151–57; 5.5; cf. Sowers, "Pella Flight," 317–19; Lane, 469; Marcus, "Jewish War," 454–55; Balabanski, *Eschatology*, 124–

32). Josephus presents these actions as a desecration of the holy precincts (*War* 4.163, 182–83, 201, 388; 6.95), in one passage (*War* 4.163) even describing them as "abominations" (*agesi*). Mark might, moreover, think that the revolutionaries' nationalistic occupation of the Temple "desolated" it by depriving it of the Gentiles who formerly and rightfully worshiped there (see Mark 11:17). The "abomination of desolation," then, may be a revolutionary leader such as Eleazar son of Simon, who occupied the Temple and stained it with blood, or Phanias, the high priest appointed by the Zealots, whom Josephus describes as mentally defective and not of high-priestly descent—offenses that would have justified the term "abomination." This interpretation of the Markan "abomination of desolation" also solves the timing problem, since flight from Jerusalem was still possible during the winter of 67–68, when the Zealots occupied the Temple and appointed Phanias (see Josephus, *War* 4.377–79, 413).

The Jewish revolutionaries, however, may have had their own interpretation of the Danielic "abomination of desolation" (see Hengel, *Zealots*, 242–45, on the importance of Daniel to the Zealots). According to 4QFlor 1 1:4–6, the Gentiles' presence in the Temple "laid it waste" (*hšmw*); the Zealots' attempt to eradicate Gentile influence from the Temple could therefore be seen as eliminating the "abomination of desolation," which in Daniel itself is a desecration caused by Gentiles (see Marcus, "Jewish War," 450–51). It is possible, then, that the Markan interpretation, in which the abomination is tied to anti-pagan nationalism, is a response to the Zealots' exegesis, in which the abomination is pagan influence—a typical sort of Markan inversion (cf. the NOTE on "The stone that the builders rejected" in 12:10).

let the reader understand. Gk *ho anaginōskōn noeitō*. Although the possibility of a scribal gloss cannot be excluded (cf. Pesch, 2.292), it is more likely that this intrusive clause is an insertion by the evangelist to underline for his addressees the significance of the prophecy of end-time persecution he is transmitting. Cf. Nolland ("Sib. Or. III.265–94," 161) on a comparable grammatical shift in a *Sibylline Oracles* passage as an indicator of contemporary address and relevance.

let those in Judaea flee to the mountains. Gk *hoi en tę Ioudaią pheugetōsan eis ta orē*. On the allusion to Gen 19:17, see the COMMENT on 13:14–18. As Sowers ("Pella Flight," 319) points out, Judaea is a mountainous region itself, and Jerusalem is built on a mountain; the injunction for Judaeans to flee to the mountains, therefore, suggests flight to a *different* mountain range, probably that on the far side of the Jordan Valley. This geographical circumstance connects our passage with the tradition about the Jerusalem church's flight to Pella, which lies in the foothills of the Transjordanian mountain range, before or during the Jewish War (see Smith, *Pella*, 1.83). On the disputed issue of the historicity of the flight to Pella, see Balabanski (*Eschatology*, 101–34), who makes a strong argument in its favor.

15. *let not the person on the roof come down.* Gk *ho epi tou dōmatos mē katabatō*. In ancient Palestinian dwellings, which were usually cramped and poorly ventilated, the flat roof, often cooler than the rest of the house (see Judg 3:20), served as a sort of "bonus room." Biblical passages describe people using their roofs for

activities such as relaxing (Judg 3:20), sleeping (1 Sam 9:25–26; 1 Kgs 17:19), praying (Acts 10:9), and storing goods (Josh 2:6; cf. Evans, 321). In 2 Kgs 4:10, the roof
is converted into a guest room complete with bed, table, and chair. Access was
usually by an outside ladder or stone staircase (see *HBD* 883; Evans, 321; King and
Stager, *Life*, 34–35).

17. *alas*. Gk *ouai*. This is one of only two "woes" in Mark (cf. 14:21). There is,
by contrast, a whole series of woes in Matthew and Luke (Matt 11:21//Luke 10:13;
Matt 23:13–23//Luke 11:42–52; Luke 6:24–26; Matt 18:7//Luke 17:1; Matt 23:25–
30; Matt 24:19//Luke 21:23; Matt 26:24/Luke 22:22). The woe is an OT form that
is especially characteristic of the Prophets (see, e.g., Isa 5:8–24; 10:1–11; Zech
11:17) and is also found in later Jewish literature such as the Dead Sea Scrolls
(e.g., 4QapocrJoshua^a [4Q378] 6 1:7) and rabbinic traditions (see "*Hôy*" in Clines,
Dictionary, 2.504 [2] and Jastrow, 338). The usual form is "alas" + "for X" + threat
of disaster, sometimes followed by a justification of the threat. Woes can imply a
variety of attitudes toward their object, from sorrow (as here) to gloating satisfac-
tion.

pregnant women and for nursing mothers. Gk *tais en gastri echousais kai tais
thēlazousais*. On the traditional background of this woe and its possible background in the Jewish War years, see the COMMENT on 13:14–18. Josephus tells
a particularly horrible story about a mother who, during the terrible famine that
resulted from the siege of Jerusalem, cannibalized her infant son (*War* 6.201–19).

18. *during a storm*. Gk *cheimōnos*, a term that can also mean "during the winter," the season of bad weather (cf. the Latin and Syriac versions and BDAG 1082).
Winter is associated with persecution in a later Syriac text, *The Story of Maryam
(Shamone') and Her Seven Sons*: "Do not tremble before the winter of persecutions" (Bensly and Barnes trans. alt., *Fourth Book*, xxxvi; Syriac text on p. 105, line
8). It is more probable, however, that the reference is to the danger that those fleeing eastward from Judaea would be unable to ford the Jordan because of stormy
weather. Exactly this situation faced Gadarene fugitives trying to cross the Jordan
in the other direction in the spring of 68 C.E. (see Josephus, *War* 4.433; cf. 4.286
and Sowers, "Pella Flight," 319–20).

19. *those days will be such tribulation*. Gk *esontai . . . hai hēmerai ekeinai thlip-
sis*. Mark's phrasing is awkward; one would expect "*in* those days there will be
such tribulation," and both Matthew (24:21) and Luke (21:23) smooth out the
syntax. But the Markan wording accurately conveys the intended meaning; see
the COMMENT on 13:19–20.

that there has not been such. Gk *hoia ou gegonen toiautē*. On the widespread
apocalyptic idea that the eschaton will be preceded by a period of unparalleled
suffering, see the NOTE on "These things are the beginning of the labor pains"
in 13:8, the COMMENT on 13:5–8, and Dubis, *Messianic Woes*, 5–36. The closest OT approximation to Mark's formulation is Dan 12:1 (see the COMMENT
on 13:19–20), but Mark may also be echoing several passages in Exodus that describe the unprecedented severity of the plagues on Egypt (see, e.g., Exod 11:6:
"Then there will be a loud cry throughout the whole land of Egypt, such as has
never been or will ever be again"; cf. Exod 9:18; 10:14). As Beasley-Murray (419)

comments, this is an appropriate echo, since the Egyptian plagues sometimes served as a model for the coming apocalyptic ones (see, e.g., Rev 8:1–11:19; 15:1–16:21; *Apoc. Ab.* 29:14–16; cf. Aune, *Revelation,* 2.499–502). One of these recyclings of the Exodus plague traditions, Rev 16:18, contains a close parallel to Mark 13:19: "a great earthquake such as had never been since people were on the earth" (RSV alt.).

There are also parallels to Mark 13:19 in nonbiblical Jewish literature. *Testament of Moses* 8:1, for example, mentions a visitation of punishment and wrath "such as has never happened to them *from the creation* till that time," and 1QM 1:11–12 prophesies: "That is a time of m[ighty] trouble (*ṣrh*) for the people to be redeemed by God. In all their troubles there was none like it, from its hastening until its completion for an eternal redemption" (Yadin trans.).

from the beginning of the creation, which God created. Gk *ap' archēs ktiseōs hēn ektisen ho theos.* The clause "which God created" is missing from D, Θ, 565, and a few other Greek manuscripts, as well as the Old Latin tradition. The repetition with a cognate verb, however, corresponds to Markan style (see "the chosen ones, whom he chose" in 13:20 and Taylor, 514), and the witnesses for the omission are not particularly impressive. The excision is easily explained as an attempt to iron out an awkward redundancy or an assimilation to Matt 24:21. But even though later scribes disliked it, the repetitiveness of the Markan text is purposeful: it emphasizes that despite the sufferings of the present time, God is not impotent and will soon reassert his control over the world he created; cf. *4 Ezra* 9:2: "Then you will know that it is the very time when the Most High is about to visit *the world which he has made*" (Stone trans., emphasis added). Compare also the first line of the Qaddish prayer ("May his great name be magnified and sanctified *in the world that he has created*") and *T. Abr.* shorter recension (Family E) 7:19; 13:9.

20. *shortened.* Gk *ekolobōsen.* As Davies and Allison (3.351 n. 155) point out, *koloboun* literally means "to amputate" (cf. 2 Sam 4:12; BDAG 556). A close parallel is found in one of the Dead Sea Scrolls, 4QPseudo-Ezekiel (4Q385) 3(4):1–7, where Ezekiel prays, "Instead of my grief make my soul rejoice and let the days hasten quickly, until it may be said by humans, 'Indeed the days are hastening so that the children of Israel may inherit.'" God replies, "I will not re[fu]se you, O Ezekiel! I will cut short the days and the year[s] . . . from tribulation, as you said" (*hn*[*n*]*y gwdd 't hymym w't hšny*[*m*] . . . *mṣ'r k'šr 'mrt;* Dimant trans. alt., *Qumran Cave 4,* 38). Here we find the idea of God abbreviating the time in order to save the elect from tribulation (Dimant, García-Martínez, and Vermes translate *mṣ'r* as "a little," but "from tribulation" is also possible, and better fits the context.)

This Qumran passage fits into a larger pattern; early Jewish and Christian literature frequently expresses the hope or conviction that God will hasten the arrival of the new age (see, e.g., Sir 36:10 = [36:7 Rahlfs]; *LAB* 19:13; *4 Ezra* 4:26; *2 Apoc. Bar.* 20:1; 54:1; 83:1; cf. 1 Cor 7:29). In rabbinic traditions, similarly, circumstances such as excessive oppression by the nations or mass repentance by Israel may hasten the arrival of the eschaton (see, e.g., *Cant. Rab.* 2.7.1; *b. Sanh.* 98a; Jacobson, *Commentary,* 2.645).

The use of the aorist tense *ekolobōsen* ("shortened") twice in our verse is puzzling, since the future seems to be demanded by the sense (cf. 13:19). Some exegetes (e.g., Alford, 240–41; Swete, 290) argue that the aorist reflects Mark's awareness that the tribulation of the Jewish Revolt was short-lived. But for Mark the tribulation must still be in progress, since when it is over, the end will come (cf. 13:24–27). The aorist, rather, should be interpreted on the analogy of the "prophetic perfect" of the OT, which "occurs in the midst of imperfects in descriptions of future events" and "is thought to reflect the prophet's imagined or visionary glimpse of the future as though already accomplished" (Fanning, *Verbal Aspect*, 271, citing LXX passages such as Gen 17:20; Psalm 20:7 [19:7 LXX]; Isa 9:6; 11:9). God, in other words, has decreed that the eschatological tribulation will be shortened, so even if it is ongoing, it is as good as over. As Fanning (*Verbal Aspect*, 273) points out, the usage of the future in the Matthean parallel to Mark 13:20 (Matt 24:22) supports this "prophetic perfect" interpretation. Cf. *Sib. Or.* 5.414–28 (and Collins's note in *OTP*, 1.403 n. y3) for a similar, anticipatory use of aorists in an eschatological prophecy.

no flesh would be saved. Gk *ouk an esōthē pasa sarx. Pasa sarx* is a Semitic idiom for the entirety of the animal kingdom (see, e.g., Gen 6:13, 17, 19), but the focus is usually on humanity (see Gen 6:12; Num 16:22; Ps 65:2; Isa 40:5–6; Jer 25:31). *Esōthē* is an aorist passive verb, so the clause would normally be translated "no flesh would have been saved," but a timeless translation of the aorist is demanded by the context, which refers to a future event (see the NOTE on "shortened" above).

COMMENT

Introduction. Up to this point in chapter 13, Jesus has counseled vigilance (13:5, 9a), dependence on God (13:11), and patient endurance of suffering (13:13b) as the weapons of choice in the first stage of the eschatological battle. Now, however, he identifies the mysterious "abomination of desolation" as the signal that more activism will be called for in the second phase.

Mark 13:14–20 seems to be made up of traditional material from a variety of venues, since there are some internal tensions and the individual parts do not always occur in logical sequence. Verses 13:14, 17–18, for example, presuppose that the eschatological refugees will have time to make a journey of several days, whereas 13:15–16 assume that they will hardly have time to blink. Verses 13:14–16, 18 are instructions for eschatological flight, but the woe on pregnant and nursing women in 13:17 not only has a different form but also lacks an intrinsic connection to flight. It may be an independent logion that Mark has inserted here. Other good candidates for Markan editing are the intrusive exhortation "let the reader understand" in 13:14, which is probably Mark's way of calling attention to a crucial aspect of the traditions he is transmitting (cf. 13:37), and "until now" in 13:19, which has a similar function (cf. the INTRODUCTION in vol. 1, p. 29).

The passage falls into two parts, 13:14–18, which is mostly paraenetic (see the GLOSSARY), and 13:19–20, which is prophetic. The latter grounds the former (see the *gar* = "for" clause in 13:19).

13:14–18: eschatological instructions. Up to this point in chapter 13, the Markan Jesus' warnings about coming distress have been general but clear: there will be wars, rumors of wars, earthquakes, famines, and persecution from authorities and family members. In 13:14, however, the warning suddenly becomes at once more specific and more obscure: the "abomination of desolation" will arise, and this will be the signal for a general egress of Christians from Judaea. But what is this "abomination"?

As detailed in the NOTE on "the 'abomination of desolation' " in 13:14, the phrase is drawn from the OT book of Daniel, where it describes the desecration of the Temple under Antiochus Epiphanes in 168 B.C.E. Mark, however, probably reinterprets it to refer to a first-century event, perhaps the occupation of the Temple and appointment of an unqualified high priest by the Zealots in the winter of 67–68 C.E. Mark signals his reinterpretation of this crucial biblical prophecy, and its relevance to the present situation of his community, by adding the wake-up call "let the reader understand" (13:14b).

The unveiling of the "abomination," Jesus goes on to say, is to be a signal for the Christian community's flight to the mountains (13:14c)—likely a reference to the Jerusalem church's escape to Pella in the Transjordan during the early stages of the war (see Eusebius, *Ecclesiastical History* 3.5.3; Epiphanius, *Panarion* 29.7.7–8; 30.2.7; *Weights and Measures* 15). This flight to the mountains, like the "abomination of desolation," follows a biblical pattern, since Abraham's nephew Lot and his family were warned to flee to the hills from Sodom when it was threatened with divine punishment (see Gen 19:17). Their deliverance became the prototype for eschatological deliverance from judgment in later Jewish and Christian traditions (see, e.g., *Jub.* 16:6; Luke 17:28–32; 2 Pet 2:6–8; Allison, *Intertextual Jesus*, 78–84). Thus, Jesus implicitly links Jerusalem with the archetypically wicked Gentile city (cf. Beasley-Murray, 412), and this is not the only ironic scriptural inversion in our passage (cf. the end of the NOTE on "the 'abomination of desolation' " in 13:14). This particular inversion, however, has a biblical precedent, since Isaiah already compared the rulers and people of Judah and Jerusalem to the citizens of Sodom and Gomorrah (Isa 1:1, 10; cf. *Martyrdom of Isaiah* 3:10–12; Rev 11:8; Kugel, *Traditions*, 350).

The exhortation to head for the hills (13:14c) is followed by more explicit instructions about the necessary haste (13:15–16): one is not to return home to pack one's bags (13:15) or even turn around to pick up a stray garment abandoned in a field (13:16). What is being described, then, is an emergency evacuation, such as becomes necessary when people are confronted with a swiftly advancing army (see Borg, *Conflict*, 208). Josephus uses similar terminology when he says that most of the population of Jericho, anticipating the Roman legions' arrival in June of 68 C.E., fled to the hill country (*War* 4.451). But the exhortations in 13:15–16 also echo the biblical story of Lot, since the Markan Jesus' injunction not to turn around (*mē epistrepsatō eis ta opisō*, 13:16) recalls the way in which Lot's wife's ignored a similar warning, with disastrous consequences (*mē periblepsēs eis ta opisō*, Gen 19:17, 26; cf. Luke 9:62; 17:31–32).

Cross-country flight, however, is harder for some people than for others, and

the next verse singles out two related groups who will find it particularly difficult: pregnant women and nursing mothers (13:17). The "woe" in Mark 13:17,
then, may enshrine a remembrance of a particularly searing aspect of the flight of
Christians from Judaea: young mothers either had to be left behind or, with their
infants, suffered illness and death along the way. But as Evans (321) points out,
this woe also has a traditional background, since pregnant and nursing women
and unweaned children often feature in OT and Jewish oracles of eschatological
judgment (see, e.g., Deut 32:25; Jer 44:7; Lam 2:11; Hos 13:16; *Sib. Or.* 2.190–93;
4 Ezra 6:21). *Fourth Ezra* 16:44–46, moreover, warns against having children during the period of eschatological turmoil, and this warning comes soon after a
description of the eschatological labor pains (*4 Ezra* 16:38–39; cf. Mark 13:8 and
see Balabanski, *Eschatology*, 91; Pitre, *Jesus*, 317). Jesus himself singles out nursing mothers for mention in Luke 23:27–31, another passage linking the horrors of
the Jewish War with the eschatological judgment.

Like the woe on the nursing mothers and pregnant women, the final injunction of the passage, "And pray that it may not happen during a storm" (13:18), may
reflect the Markan situation; Mark and other Jewish Christians from Jerusalem
probably abandoned the city before the spring of 68 C.E., when the Romans tight-
ened the noose and heavy rains made escape across the Jordan difficult or impossible (see the NOTE on "during a storm" in 13:18). The Markan community,
then, may have seen its recent history and propitiously timed flight as signs that
despite the intensity of the tribulation it was experiencing, God's saving presence
was still with it. Thus, in the concluding verses of this subsection (13:17–18) we
see a typically apocalyptic combination of eschatological woe and eschatological
deliverance.

13:19–20: the great tribulation. In the coda to the passage, Jesus describes an
even greater proof of God's grace: he will cut short the time of eschatological tribulation in which the Markan community presently finds itself living (and dying).
The language of the first verse here echoes Daniel once more, indeed is a virtual
citation of Dan 12:1b LXX, which speaks of a tribulation that will be greater than
any that Israel has known from the beginning until "that day" (see Lane, 471).
The Markan wording, however, contains a significant variation from the Danielic
source; Jesus does not say "until that day" but "until *now*." This may be another
of those places in which Mark drops the appearance of transmitting a speech by
the earthly Jesus in the early thirties C.E. and lets his readers see that the body of
chapter 13 is, at least in part, an address by the *risen* Lord to a Markan community
that is currently undergoing tribulation (cf. "let the reader understand" in 13:14).

The passage concludes with a verse that stresses the intensity of this suffering
even more strongly: it will be so grievous that it will threaten to wipe out all living creatures (13:20a; see the NOTE on "no flesh would be saved" in 13:20). On
account of God's chosen ones, however, he will *not* destroy humanity but instead
will shorten the time allotted to the end-time tribulation (13:20b). Here several
different ideas, strongly influenced by a variety of OT texts, coalesce.

First, if God had not decided to restrain his judgment, all humanity would perish in the eschatological tribulation. Although no exact counterpart to this concept is present in the OT or ancient Jewish literature, one certainly gets the impression from passages in the book of Revelation (chapter 6; 8:6–9:21; chapter 16) that the end-time judgments will be so fearsome that the very existence of mankind will be threatened. The OT Prophets, moreover, often convey the idea that God's judgment poses a dire threat to Israel itself (see, e.g., Isa 1:7–9; Zech 13:8; and Amos, passim). One of these prophetic passages, Isa 1:9, is similar to Mark 13:20a in vocabulary and grammatical structure, since both begin with *kai ei mē . . . kyrios*: "*And if the Lord* Sabaoth *had not* left us a seed, we should have been as Sodom, and we should have been made like to Gomorrah" (Brenton trans. alt.). The specter of Sodom's destruction, then, continues to haunt our passage (see above on the echoes of Genesis 19 in Mark 13:14, 16).

This Isaian passage, however, also implies good news: God *has* left a seed, preserved a remnant, and for the sake of that remnant he will spare the people from total destruction (on the concept of the remnant, see Schrenk, *"Leimma"*; Meyer, "Remnant"). The remnant corresponds to the "chosen ones" (*eklektoi*) in our passage (cf. Paul's application of the "remnant" motif to Christians, and his equation of it with "the elect," in Rom 9:27–29; 11:1–7; cf. Rom 8:33; Col 3:12; 2 Tim 2:10; 1 Pet 1:1–2; 2:9). In many LXX and later Jewish passages, to be sure, the *eklektoi* are Israel as a whole (see, e.g., Pss 105:6, 43 [104:6, 43 LXX]; 106:5 [105:5 LXX]; Isa 43:20; *Sib. Or.* 2.174), but some later OT works develop the idea that most of the people have defaulted on their vocation, so that a winnowing of the nation will be necessary. This remnant notion becomes particularly important in the Qumran scrolls, where the "the elect" (*bhyrym*) is a common name for the sect itself (see, e.g., 1QS 8:6; 9:14; 11:16; 1QH 10[2]:13; cf. Sanders, *Paul*, 244–46). Here, then, the "chosen ones" become the faithful remnant, who will survive the fearful judgments that are being sent to try the earth in general and them in particular. An especially significant expression of this idea is found in Isa 65:8–10, where God restrains himself from destroying all of Israel out of consideration for his chosen ones (*eklektoi*; cf. 65:15, 23). In our passage this motif is expanded, so that the chosen ones indirectly rescue not only all Israel but all "flesh"—a parallel to their master's donation of his life "as a ransom for many" (10:45).

Elsewhere in the LXX of Isaiah the deliverance of the faithful remnant from tribulation and destruction is referred to as their salvation (see, e.g., Isa 10:20–22; 33:2; 37:32; 45:20–22; 66:19), and this circumstance also provides a vocabulary linkage with Mark 13:20, where the salvation of the chosen ones is implied. More pertinently, however, the verb *sōzein* ("to save, deliver") also appears in Dan 12:1b, the second half of the verse that, as we have seen, is virtually quoted in Mark 13:19. Here Daniel describes the way in which "everyone who is found written in the book" will be saved (*sōthēsetai*) out of tribulation by the mighty power of God. Similarly, Mark 13:20 speaks of the Lord shortening the time of trial on behalf of his elect people and thereby saving them from tribulation and death.

The concluding verses in our passage, then, use biblical language to express a characteristically apocalyptic two-level vision. On the one hand, things look worse than they ever have: not only are the days *characterized* by "tribulation," but

they actually *are* tribulation (see the NOTE on "those days will be such tribulation" in 13:19). No such time of trial has been experienced on the earth since its
creation. Yet the apparently superfluous reaffirmation that God *did* in fact fashion
this world ("which God created") also hints to the beleaguered Markan community that he has not abandoned the creation he once called into existence—as the
tribulation might tempt them to believe—but that he will soon regrasp it firmly
and decisively (see the NOTE on "from the beginning of the creation, which God
created" in 13:19). Indeed, he has already begun to do so: he has shortened the
days—a point that is also repeated for emphasis (cf. the NOTE on "shortened"
in 13:20). The curtailment of tribulation is fixed in the divine mind, in heaven, if
not yet on earth; and what God purposes will swiftly come to pass "on earth as it
is in heaven."

But in order to interpret this hopeful message rightly, the Markan readers will
need ears to hear and eyes to see, minds undistracted by deceitful appearances. It
is against such deceptions that Mark warns his readers in the next passage.

THE REIGN OF DELUSION (13:21–23)

13 ²¹"And then if anyone says to you, 'Look, here is the Christ!' or 'Look, there!'
do not believe it. ²²For false Christs and false prophets will be raised up and will
give signs and wonders in order to lead astray—if possible—the chosen ones. ²³You
then, look out. See, I have foretold all things to you.

NOTES

13 21. *'Look, here is the Christ!'* . . . *'Look, there!'* Gk *ide hōde ho Christos, ide
ekei.* These proclamations may reflect Jewish conceptions about a Messiah who
is present but hidden (see, e.g., John 7:27; Justin, *Dialogue* 8.4; *b. Sanh.* 98a). The
idea of hidden messiahship, however, is clearer in the Matthean parallel (Matt
24:26).

22. *false Christs and.* Gk *pseudochristoi kai.* These words are missing in Codex
Bezae and a few other manuscripts, but their omission may be due to homoeoarcton (*pseduo-*; on homoeoarcton, see the GLOSSARY).

false prophets. Gk *pseudoprophētai.* As Meeks (*Prophet-King*, 47–55) points out,
the fountainhead for the conception of the false prophet is the Mosaic warning in
Deut 13:1–5; 18:18–22. Deut 13:1–3 speaks of a prophet who hopes to gain credence
through "a sign or a wonder" (*sēmeion ē teras*), and *Tg. Neof.* Deut 13:2 specifically
calls this figure a *"false* prophet" (see Evans, 323). In later Jewish literature, this
conception is developed in a mythological direction, in which Satan becomes the
ultimate source of the false prophet's power (see the COMMENT on 13:21–23).
The false prophets, then, are the demonic imitators of the true prophet Moses,
who also worked signs and wonders (see the next NOTE), and of his successor, the
expected "Prophet-like-Moses" (see Deut 18:15–19; CD 5:17–6:2; Acts 3:19–22).

This Mosaic background may be a link with the Markan situation in the Jewish War, since some Jewish revolutionaries viewed their mission as a reprise of Moses' liberation of Israel from Egyptian bondage (see the NOTE on "sign" in 8:11).

signs and wonders. Gk *sēmeia kai terata.* In the LXX this phrase and its individual components are especially associated with the miracles that God worked through Moses in the exodus from Egypt (see, e.g., Exod 7:3, 11:9–10; Deut 6:22; 7:19; 11:3; 28:46; 29:3; Wis 8:8; Jer 32:20 [39:20 LXX]). These miracles were "signs" because they pointed to God's greatness, though in the present context it may make more sense to think of demonic influence, and "wonders" because they caused amazement and suggested a transcendent source (cf. BDAG 999).

in order to lead astray—if possible—the chosen ones. Gk *pros to apoplanan ei dynaton tous eklektous.* Christian commentators have been bothered by this clause for millennia, both because of the apparent imperfection of Jesus' knowledge (does "if possible" imply uncertainty?) and because of apparent contradiction to the rest of the verse. See, for example, Gregory the Great, *Homilies on Ezekiel* 1.9: "Why however is it said with a doubt, 'If it were possible,' when the Lord knows beforehand what is to be? . . . If they are elect, it is not possible; and if it is possible, they are not elect" (cited in Thomas Aquinas, *Catena Aurea* 2.264). The phrase "if possible" may be an interpolation by Mark or a later scribe to ward off the implication that the elect can lose their salvation.

God's "chosen ones" and the eschatological deceivers form a standard pair in apocalyptic Jewish writings; the latter are those who are *not* chosen by God, and who consequently oppose him by leading others astray (cf. Reiser, *Jesus and Judgment,* 75). The Qumran text 1QH 10[2]:13–16, for example, opposes the "chosen ones of righteousness" (*bḥyry ṣdq*) with the "mediators of error" (*mlyṣy t'wt*) and the "men of deceit" (*'nšy rmyh*).

will give. Gk *dōsousin.* This is replaced in D, Θ, *f*¹³, 28, 565, etc. by "will do" (*poiēsousin*), which is better Greek; the more difficult and better-attested reading "will give," however, follows Semitic idiom (see Taylor, 516) and is probably original.

23. *You then, look out.* Gk *hymeis de blepete.* The grammatically unnecessary *hymeis* is emphatic; see the COMMENT on 13:21–23 and cf. the NOTE on "Give . . . yourselves" in 6:37.

See. Gk *idou.* This word is missing in B, L, W, Ψ, 0235, 28, etc., as well as most Coptic manuscripts, but is present in ℵ, A, C, D, Θ, 0104, *f*¹, ¹³, and the majority of Greek manuscripts, as well as the Latin and Syriac versions and one Bohairic manuscript. There is thus impressive testimony for its inclusion, and its omission in B, L, W, etc. is explicable by its perceived redundancy, which is in line with Markan style; cf. *blepete agrypneite* ("Look out, don't fall asleep!") in 13:33, *horate blepete* (lit. "See! Look out!") in 8:15, and *akouete idou* ("Listen! Look!") in 4:3. In the last case, the Matthean parallel (Matt 13:3) eliminates *akouete,* leaving *idou* by itself, which is exactly what Matthew has done in his redaction of 13:23 (see Matt 24:25) if the original read *blepete idou*; cf. also Matt 16:6, which redacts Mark 8:15 in a similar way.

COMMENT

Introduction. In the previous passage, Jesus warned about a coming period of tribulation more catastrophic than anything the earth had yet experienced. He also
implied, however, that this tribulation would, in a paradoxical way, be a *good* sign,
since it would signal that God was about to save his chosen people by ending their
affliction; according to 13:27 he will do this by sending Jesus to gather the elect
into his dominion. Our passage, however, warns that this sort of eschatological
hope can be delusive: the end-time will also produce false Christs and prophets
who, rather than gathering God's people, will lead them astray through deceitful
signs.

The last verse in this passage is probably redactional; it contains characteristic
Markan vocabulary ("look out," "all things") and is, as Taylor (517) points out,
one of the editorial linchpins of the whole discourse (cf. the calls to attention in
13:5b, 9a, 14b, 33a, 35, 37). It is also possible that "if possible" in 13:22 is a Markan
or post-Markan gloss on a preexistent eschatological discourse (see the NOTE on
"in order to lead astray—if possible—the chosen ones" in 13:22 and, on the "little
apocalypse" theory, the introduction to chapter 13).

Like the previous passage, this one alternates prophecy (13:21ab, 22) with exhortation (13:21c, 23).

13:21–23: false Christs and prophets. The first words of the passage, "And then"
(13:21a), retreat in time a bit from the previous verse, which described God's ab-
breviation of the eschatological tribulation in order to save his elect. The phrase
"and then" winds the narrative clock back to the tribulation itself (cf. 13:19).

In this time of trouble, Jesus predicts, false messiahs and prophets will arise.
The insubstantial nature of the hopes these figures will inspire is already suggested by the fact that the first reference to them concerns mere *rumors* of their
advent ("if anyone says to you, 'Look, here is the Christ!' ") and by the shifting
locale of their putative appearance ("Look, here . . . Look, there!"). There is thus
a parallel to the beginning of the eschatological discourse, in which Jesus spoke
of rumors (13:7) and of deceivers who would claim his identity (13:6). There is
also, however, a progression beyond that earlier passage: if the deceivers in 13:6
claimed to be Jesus, and thus implicitly acknowledged his supremacy, the present deceivers claim to be messiahs and prophets in their own right. If the earlier
deceivers, moreover, merely hoodwinked "many," these deceivers will come close
to bamboozling all (13:22).

Although 13:21 mentions only people who are thought to be the Messiah,
13:22 expands this reference to false Christs and *prophets*, probably reflecting the
coalescence of the figure of the Messiah with that of the Prophet-like-Moses in
first-century Judaism and Christianity. It is especially likely that the Prophet-like-
Moses figure is in view because the latter, unlike the Messiah, was often associated with miracle working, as Moses himself was (see the NOTE on "sign" in
8:11). The false prophet is the demonic counterpart of the true prophet, Moses,
and of Moses' eschatological successor (see the NOTE on "false prophets" in

13:22); the Jewish revolutionary figures whom Mark has in view probably fancied themselves to be the latter, but Mark identifies them as the former. These "false Christs and false prophets" deceive people by means of their "signs and wonders," an OT idiom especially associated with Moses (see the NOTE on "signs and wonders" in 13:22), but "a sign or a wonder" has a negative valence in the classic "false prophet" passage, Deut 13:1–3 (see the NOTE on "false prophets" in 13:22).

The warning in 13:22 is thus firmly rooted both in OT typologies and in first-century realities. Josephus, for example, describes revolutionary prophets who claimed to be able to perform saving miracles (*Ant.* 20.97,170; *War* 2.261), which Josephus calls "signs" (*sēmeia; War* 6.285) or "wonders and signs" (*terata kai sēmeia; Ant.* 20.168). These purported miracle workers had a great influence on the people; Josephus describes them as "deceivers and impostors [who] under the pretence of divine inspiration fostering revolutionary changes . . . persuaded the multitude to act like madmen" (*War* 2.259), fomenting the sort of commotion that ultimately produced the Jewish War (cf. Barnett, "Sign-Prophets"; Gray, *Prophetic Figures*). In the Josephus passages the miracles promised by the "false prophets" relate to hopes for military victory against the Romans through the direct intervention of God (cf. *War* 2.262–63), who was expected to give "signs of salvation" (*sēmeia tēs sōtērias*) such as causing the Jordan to part (*Ant.* 20.97), destroying the walls of occupied Jerusalem (*Ant.* 20.170), and saving the burning Temple from destruction (*War* 6.285). It is likely that the revolutionary leaders of 66–67 C.E. interpreted the military successes of the early months of the Jewish War, too, as miraculous "signs of salvation" similar to those performed on behalf of Moses and the exodus generation. It is plausible, then, that the background of Mark's description of false Christs and prophets performing "signs and wonders" is the tumult of the Great Revolt and the Moses-like figures who spearheaded that struggle.

For Mark, as for other Jewish and Christian apocalypticists, such false messiahs and prophets are themselves a sign of the end-time. Ironically, then, part of the answer to the disciples' question in 13:4 about the "sign" of the end is that false Christs and prophets will perform "signs and wonders" that will deceive the elect. For if the end was expected to be a time of unprecedented suffering, it was also supposed to be one of unparalleled delusion. The keywords of our passage ("false prophets," "signs," "lead astray," "chosen ones") appear again and again in Jewish and Christian apocalyptic literature. *Sibylline Oracles* 2.165–69, for example, describes "deceivers, in place of prophets," who will, through the power of Beliar (= Satan), perform many signs (*sēmeia*), leading to "a confusion of holy chosen (*eklektōn*) and faithful people." Similarly, *Sib. Or.* 3.63–69 describes Beliar himself performing signs, thereby leading countless people astray (*planą*), including "many faithful, chosen (*eklektōn*) Hebrews" (cf. *Asc. Isa.* 4:2–10; Evans, 323). In the NT book of Revelation, likewise, the "false prophet" works demonic "signs" by which he "deceives" the people (Rev 13:13–14; 19:20). And in 2 Thess 2:8–12, Paul or one of his followers warns against an antichrist figure, "the lawless one," in a passage that forms a fascinating counterpart to Mark 13:20–22:

The coming of the lawless one by the activity of Satan will be with all power and with pretended signs and wonders (*sēmeiois kai terasin*), and with all wicked deception for those who are to perish, because they refused to love the truth and so be saved (*sōthēnai*). Therefore God sends upon them a strong delusion (*planēs*), to make them believe a lie, so that all may be condemned who did not believe the truth but had pleasure in unrighteousness. (RSV alt.)

Here, as in the *Sibylline Oracles* and Revelation, Satan produces "signs and wonders" (cf. Mark 13:22) and tries his best to prevent people from being "saved" (cf. Mark 13:20) by sending "delusion" (*planē*), a word cognate with "lead astray" (*planan*) in Mark 13:22. Both 2 Thess 2:11-12 and Mark 13:21, moreover, emphasize the dire results of believing (*pisteuein*) this delusive message. But the Markan scenario is even grimmer than the Pauline one, since Paul describes the delusion of the *damned*, of those who "refused to love the truth" and "had pleasure in wickedness," whereas Mark contemplates the falling away, "if possible," of the elect themselves.

Although Mark is not as explicit as the *Sibylline Oracles* and Revelation about the demonic dimension in the delusive activity of the false Christs and prophets, he probably shares this idea with the other apocalyptic texts. The passive voice of *egerthēsontai* ("will be raised up") is probably a double entendre. On the one hand, its connection with the purpose clause "in order to lead astray . . . the chosen ones" (Mark 13:22) suggests that the false Christs and false prophets are not autonomous actors but agents of "the father of lies" (see John 8:44), "the deceiver of the whole world" (Rev 12:9)—that is, the Devil (cf. also the NOTE on "signs and wonders" in 13:22). On the other hand, however, *egerthēsontai* also functions as a *"divine* passive," implying God's ultimate agency and assuring the Markan community that even the delusion that is assaulting some of its members does not mean it has slipped from God's hand (on the divine passive, see the GLOSSARY and Reiser, *Jesus and Judgment*, 266-73). As Bart Ehrman (private communication) points out, there is an OT analogy to this idea of double agency in Daniel 7, where the winds of heaven (and thus, by implication, God) stir up the sea of chaos out of which the diabolical monsters emerge. Elsewhere in Mark itself, moreover, the agency behind horrific events is presented as complex; in the passion predictions, for example, the "turning over" of Jesus is an action both of Judas and of God (see the COMMENT on 10:33-34).

The phrase "if possible" later in the same verse (13:22b) reinforces the message of divine superintendence by qualifying the initial impression that the elect may stray permanently from the path of God. In the overall Markan context, this (redactional?) phrase foreshadows 14:35, where Jesus asks that "if . . . possible" (*ei dynaton*) the cup might pass from him (14:35). There may be a substantive linkage between these two instances of *ei dynaton*: what prevents the deception of the elect from becoming a reality is Jesus' acquiescence to God's refusal of his request that God spare him from death. Jesus, then, saves others by prescinding from the opportunity to save himself (cf. the COMMENT on 15:29-32).

The mention of God's "chosen ones" (*eklektoi*) at the end of 13:22 leads into the concluding verse of the passage, in which the subject is emphasized: "*You* then, look out" (13:23a; see the NOTE). As Nineham (355) points out, this emphasis helps convey the impression that the three disciples addressed, as well as the Markan readers in general, are among the elite: "See that *you* heed what has been said in verses 14–20 (and 22) about *the elect.*" The message, then, is double-edged: Look out, because your status as God's chosen does not remove you from the realm of demonic opposition (cf. 8:17–18; 1 Cor 10:12). At the same time, however, lift up your heads, because you *are* God's chosen, and you may rest assured that he will ultimately deliver you from that realm.

The Markan Jesus concludes the passage by saying, "See, I have foretold *all things* to you," a partial inclusion (see the GLOSSARY) with the disciples' question in 13:4 ("And what is the sign, when *all these things* will be accomplished?"). This concluding statement would have its most powerful rhetorical impact on addressees who had experienced the sort of events described in 13:6–22; for them the words would imply, "Look, I foretold all the things *that now have come upon you.*" Such a reminder would, in a paradoxical way, generate hope, because it would signal that the terrible things spoken of in those verses are no reason for questioning that God was and remains with Jesus, and through him with the struggling church. It would also induce confidence that the following prophecy, which speaks of the disintegration of the universe and the return of Christ, will be swiftly fulfilled as well.

THE RETURN OF THE SON OF MAN (13:24–27)

13 [24] "But in those days, after that tribulation, the sun will be darkened, and the moon will not give its light, [25] and the stars will be falling from heaven, and the powers in the heavens will be shaken. [26] And then they will see the Son of Man coming in clouds with great power and glory. [27] And then he will send out the angels and he will gather his chosen ones from the four winds, from the end of the earth to the end of heaven.

NOTES

13 24–25. *the sun will be darkened, and the moon will not give its light . . . and the powers in the heavens will be shaken.* Gk *ho hēlios skotisthēsetai kai hē selēnē ou dōsei to phengos autēs . . . kai hai dynameis hai en tois ouranois saleuthēsontai.* See the next NOTE for the suggestion that the heavenly bodies in these verses may be the subject of "will see" in 13:26. Such personification of heavenly bodies is common in ancient literature (see Allison, *Studies*, 21–25, 36–41) and is compatible with the imagery in our verse: a person's eyes can be "darkened" (see Ps 69:23 [68:24 LXX]; Lam 5:17), "will not give its light" implies volition, and "will be shaken" can connote fear (see Ps 13:4 [12:5 LXX]; Eccl 12:3).

26. *they will see.* Gk *opsontai.* This verse echoes Dan 7:13–14, but the only one who *sees* in Daniel 7 is the seer himself (Dan 7:13; cf. 7:2, 4, 6, etc.). Who sees in

Mark? Most scholars (e.g., Swete, 293; Pesch, 2.303; Gundry, 745) take *opsontai* as an impersonal plural, equivalent to "people will see" or "the Son of Man will be seen." This sort of impersonal construction is attested elsewhere in Mark, including chapter 13 (cf. "they will turn you over" in 13:9 and the subject index in vols. 1 and 2 under "Impersonal use of third person plural"), but this sort of exegetical option should be exercised only if a personal reference is nonsensical. Is that the case here? Both the elect and the false Christs and prophets were mentioned a few verses back (13:22), and the elect will immediately be mentioned in 13:27. Of the two groups, however, the false Christs and prophets seem the more likely candidate, since the Markan passage most similar to ours ascribes eschatological seeing to Jesus' enemies (the high priest and his associates, 14:62), and this might suggest that the gospel's opponents, such as the false Christs and prophets, are the seers of 13:26. This possibility is enhanced by history-of-religions parallels; in 1 *En.* 62:2–11, for example, the rulers of the earth "see and recognize" the Son of Man revealed in glory and are filled with dismay at the sight, since they know that his glorious appearance spells their eternal doom, and in *Sib. Or.* 3.556–57, the Sibyl warns the Greeks, "But when the wrath of the great God comes upon you, then indeed you will recognize the face of the great God" (cf. 3.693 and Wis 5:2; 4 *Ezra* 7:78–86; *Apoc. Elijah* 35:17; Rev 11:12; Pesch, 2.438).

But in Mark the opponents who will be dismayed by the sight of the returning Jesus may not be limited to human beings; they may include the shaken heavenly bodies of the immediately preceding verses (13:24–25). This is the most grammatically natural way of taking the third person plural *opsontai* in 13:26, and in ancient contexts it is perfectly normal to think of heavenly bodies as animate and therefore capable of perception, thought, and emotion (see the previous NOTE and cf. Isa 13:10 and Joel 2:10, in which the sun, moon, and stars refuse to shine; Isa 24:21–23, in which the sun and moon are ashamed; and *Apoc. Adam* 5:10, in which "the eyes of the powers of the luminaries" [i.e., the sun and the moon] are darkened). The contrast between the two instances of *dynamis* ("power") in 13:25 and 13:26 is consonant with this interpretation: the inimical *powers* of heaven will be shaken when they know their doom is near, as will immediately be confirmed when they see the Son of Man coming with a *power* greater than their own. Cf. Rashi, who interprets the disappearance of the heavens in Isa 51:6 as God's defeat of their demonic rulers.

the Son of Man coming in clouds with great power and glory. Gk *ton huion tou anthrōpou erchomenon en nephelais meta dynameōs pollēs kai doxēs.* The terminology is drawn from Dan 7:13–14, in which the seer beholds "one like a son of man" coming "with . . . clouds" and being presented to the "Ancient of Days," who bestows his own authority, glory, and dominion upon him. The imagery probably goes back to Canaanite mythology, in which the young storm god Baal, the "rider on the clouds," is enthroned in the council of the old god, 'El (see Emerton, "Origin" and Collins, *Daniel,* 286–94). Although the figure in Daniel 7 is not designated the Messiah, he is so identified in subsequent Jewish tradition (already 1 *En.* 48:10; 52:4), and the Messiah is even dubbed "Cloud-Man" (*'nny*) in some rabbinic texts on the basis of Daniel (e.g., *Tanḥuma* [Buber] *Toledot* 6.20

[Townsend, 1.167]; *Tg. 1 Chronicles* 3:24; cf. Vermes, *Jesus*, 171–72; Collins, *Daniel*, 311). In the NT and some rabbinic traditions, however, the direction of movement is reversed: instead of *ascending* with the clouds to God, as in Dan 7:13–14, the Son of Man *descends* with the clouds from heaven to earth (cf. Mark 14:62; *b. Sanh.* 98a; Perrin, *Rediscovering*, 164–85). This reversal presumably expresses the hope that *this world* will be transformed at the eschaton.

In Mark 13:26 the Son of Man comes "in clouds." In the MT of Dan 7:13, however, the "one like a son of man" comes *with* (*'im*) the clouds, and this wording is followed by Theodotion, the Vulgate, and various Jewish and Christian texts (e.g., Mark 14:62; Rev 1:7; *4 Ezra* 13:3; Justin, *Dialogue with Trypho* 31). The LXX, however, has "*on* (*epi*) the clouds," and this wording is followed in the Peshitta and Matt 24:30; 26:64; Rev 14:14; Justin, *1 Apology* 51 (cf. Collins, *Daniel*, 311). Probably both Mark's "in the clouds" and the LXX's "on the clouds" are attempts to make sense of the vague and confusing Masoretic reading, "with the clouds."

27. *the angels.* Gk *tous angelous.* Significant manuscripts, including ℵ, A, C, Θ, Ψ, 0104, *f*[1, 13], the Majority Text, and most Latin and Syriac versions add *autou* ("*his* angels"), as does the Matthean parallel (Matt 24:31). This addition, however, is in accord with Matthean Christology/angelology (cf. Matt 16:27) and with later Christology in general (cf. Hebrews 1–2 on Christ's sovereignty over the angels) and is probably a harmonization to Matthew. The shorter reading is attested by B, D, L, W, 0235, as well as some Bohairic manuscripts.

his chosen ones. Gk *tous eklektous autou.* Some of the same manuscripts that omit "his" (*autou*) before "[the] angels" (D, L, W, it; also Ψ, *f*[1], 28, etc.) also omit it before "[the] chosen ones," but this time the important witness of Vaticanus (B) joins ℵ, A, C, Θ, 083, *f*[13], 2427 Majority Text lat syr in attesting the longer reading.

from the end of the earth to the end of heaven. Gk *ap' akrou gēs heōs akrou ouranou.* Pesch (2.304) explains this unparalleled construction as a conflation of two biblical expressions: "from one end of heaven to the other" (*ap' akrou tou ouranou heōs akrou tou ouranou*; see Deut 30:4; Ps 19:6 [18:7 LXX]; cf. Deut 4:32) and "from one end of earth to the other" (*ap akrou tēs gēs heōs akrou tēs gēs*; see Deut 13:8; 28:64; Jer 12:12; cf. Jdt 11:21). It is possible, however, that Mark would interpret it as implying a distinction between the elect gathered "from the end of the earth" = those still alive at the parousia and the elect gathered "from the end of heaven" = those already dead when Jesus returns. Cf. *1 En.* 39:3–7, where the abode of the sainted dead, "the righteous and elect," is "at the ends of heaven" (cf. 70:1–4). Mark 13:27, then, may picture something like 1 Thess 4:15–17: Christ descends from heaven, both living and deceased believers rise to meet him, and subsequently both groups are forever "with the Lord" in the air.

COMMENT

Introduction. The last section ended, "See, I have foretold all things to you" (13:23), and readers might therefore suppose that Jesus had reached the end of his eschatological instruction. As it turns out, however, this declaration leads into the

climactic section of the chapter, in which Jesus prophesies the disintegration of
the universe and the return of the Son of Man in glory.

It is hard to identify Markan redactional activity in this passage, though "in
those days" in 13:24 (cf. 1:9; 13:17, 19) may be editorial. The pericope divides
neatly into two halves of equal length: 13:24–25, which describes the cosmic catastrophes that precede the Son of Man's advent, and 13:26–27, which portrays
the advent itself.

13:24–25: *cosmic signs*. In the previous passage, Jesus has depicted false Christs
and prophets who will perform specious "signs and wonders" designed to deceive
the elect into thinking that the Messiah has arrived. He now proceeds to describe
the *true* signs and wonders that presage the Son of Man's arrival: the dimming of
the sun and moon, the falling of the stars, and the shaking of the heavenly powers
(cf. Joel 2:30–31, which describes the dimming of sun and moon as "wonders,"
and the Targum on that passage, which calls them "signs"; cf. Hartman, *Prophecy
Interpreted*, 157 n. 35).

The passage begins with the loaded biblical phrase "But in those days," which
already in the OT can refer to an eschatological event of signal importance (see,
e.g., Jer 31:29; 33:15–16; Joel 2:29; 3:1; Zech 8:23; cf. Mark 13:17, 19; and Evans,
327). The eschatological nuance is confirmed by the immediately following
words, "after that tribulation" (13:24a), since elsewhere in apocalyptic literature,
including Mark 13:19, unprecedented tribulation is the immediate prelude to the
turn of the ages (see 13:19 and the NOTES on "These things are the beginning of
the labor pains" in 13:8 and "that there has not been such" in 13:19).

The post-tribulation events begin with a cosmic catastrophe that is described
through a pastiche of OT eschatological prophecies. Amos 5:20 already spoke
of "the day of the LORD" as a time of darkness; in some later prophetic passages
this metaphorical description is interpreted literally, as a darkening of the sun,
moon, and stars (see, e.g., Isa 13:10; 24:21, 23; 34:4; Ezek 32:7–8; Joel 2:10, 31;
3:15; cf. Aune, *Revelation*, 2.414). These prophecies are frequently accompanied
by descriptions of heaven and earth shaking (see, e.g., Isa 13:13; 24:18–19; Joel
2:10; cf. Hag 2:6, 21) and usually by portraits of the judgment of the wicked, that
is, the enemies of Israel, and salvation for Israel through a climactic manifestation
of the glory of God. This biblical tradition continues in postbiblical Judaism (see,
e.g., 4 *Ezra* 5:4–5; 7:39; *Sib. Or.* 2.194–202; 3.796–803; 5.344–50; *T. Levi* 4:1; *Ass.
Moses* 10), as well as in Christian works such as the *Epistle of Barnabas* (15:5) and
the book of Revelation:

> When he opened the sixth seal, I looked, and there came a great earthquake;
> the sun became black as sackcloth, the full moon became like blood, and the
> stars of the sky fell to the earth as the fig tree drops its winter fruit when shaken
> by a gale. The sky vanished like a scroll rolling itself up. (Rev 6:12–14a)

Here, as in our Markan passage, we see the sun and the moon darkening, the stars
falling to earth, and the heavens shaking (the earthquake, too, is reminiscent of

the larger Markan context; cf. Mark 13:8). The next Markan passage, moreover, will use the growth of the fig tree as a metaphor for the arrival of the eschaton (Mark 13:28–29). The Markan Jesus, then, seems to be drawing on well-known apocalyptic traditions about cosmic collapse but reconfiguring them in an original manner. The "punishment of the nations" theme, for example, is absent from our passage, and indeed from the whole eschatological discourse; the only mention of the nations is in 13:10, where they are to be an object of mission rather than condemnation. This reversal may reflect an emphasis of the historical Jesus (cf. Matt 8:11–12//Luke 13:28–29), but it probably also mirrors the Markan situation, in which the Christian message has been rejected by Jews but embraced by Gentiles (see the COMMENT on 12:1–12).

Jesus' prophecy begins with a reference to the darkening of the sun and the moon (13:24). Gundry (782) suggests that this returns the universe to the situation before the fourth day of creation (Gen 1:14–19), and Davies and Allison (3.358) point out that this idea is supported by Jer 4:23 (the heavens go black and the earth becomes "waste and void," as in Gen 1:2) and *Liv. Pro.* 12:13 ("pursued by the serpent in darkness as from the beginning"). There is also internal Markan evidence to support this idea of reversion to primordial chaos, since 13:19 speaks of a tribulation so great that it is unparalleled "from the beginning of the creation" (see Evans, 328). This "beginning time/end-time" typology may continue in the description in 13:25 of the stars falling from heaven and the heavenly "powers" being shaken, since the stars, too, were created on the fourth day, and the Genesis account emphasizes their orderly placement in the "firm structure" of the sky to serve as signs of "seasons and days and years" (cf. Philo, *On the Creation* 36; Clement of Alexandria, *Eclogae propheticae* 52.2; *Gen. Rab.* 4.2; Bertram, "*Stereos*," 609–11). Now that firm celestial edifice is shaking, the stars are consequently falling, and the space-time universe structured by "seasons and days and years" is dissolving. *Ecclesiastes Rabbah* 1.2.1 confirms that the eschatological dimming of sun and moon and the shaking of the firmament could be seen as a reversal of the work of creation:

> R. Judah b. R. Simon said: The seven "vanities" mentioned by Koheleth correspond to the seven days of creation. On the first day, "In the beginning God created the heavens and the earth" (Gen 1:1), but it is written, "For the heavens shall vanish away like smoke, and the earth shall wax old like a garment" (Isa 51:6). On the second day, "Let there be a firmament" (Gen 1:6); but it is written, "And the heavens shall be rolled together like a scroll" (Isa 34:4) . . . On the fourth day, "Let there be lights in the firmament of the heaven" (Gen 1:14), but it is written, "Then the moon shall be confounded and the sun ashamed." (Isa 24:23)

But our passage does not just describe a reversion to chaos; it also hints at a victory over it. In OT, Jewish, and Christian sources, the eschatological dimming of the sun, moon, and stars is often portrayed as a climactic event in the cosmic battle between God and the forces of evil (e.g., Isa 13:10–13; 14:12–13; 24:17–23;

Sib. Or. 3.801–7; Ignatius, *Eph.* 19:2–3; *Mekilta,* Shirata 5 [Lauterbach 2.38]; *Tanḥuma* [Buber] Bereshit 1.12 [Townsend, 1.8]). This is because the heavenly bodies are considered to be animate; the expulsion of Satan and the demons from heaven, for example, is compared to the falling of stars (see *1 En.* 16:2–3; 54:4–5; 90:21, 24; Luke 10:18; Rev 12:7–12; *T. Sol.* 20:16–18), and evil cosmic spirits are designated "powers," linked with heavenly bodies, and pictured as residing "in the heavenly places" (e.g., Job 1:6; *T. Levi* 3:1–3; *Asc. Isa.* 7:9; 10:29–30; Philo, *On the Giants* 6; Rom 8:38; Eph 1:21; 2:2; etc.). In Mark itself, the idea of power (*dynamis* and its cognates) has been associated with the struggle between God and Jesus on the one hand and Satan and the demons on the other (see 3:23–27; 5:3; 9:22–23, 28–29), and the latter have shown their panic that Jesus' advent spells their destruction (1:24; cf. 5:7). If we now read of heavenly *powers shaking* and in the next verse of the Son of Man coming in clouds "with great *power*," the shaking motif correlates with the fear of the demons, and the juxtaposition of the two usages of *dynamis* suggests that one supernatural power is displacing the other. The underlying conception of Mark 13:25b, then, may have been rightly divined by Eusebius (*Commentary on Isaiah* 2.7), who used the language of Eph 6:12 to present our passage as a reference to the eschatological defeat of the "principalities and powers . . . the world rulers of this present darkness . . . the spiritual hosts of wickedness in the heavenly places" (cf. *Pistis Sophia* 1.2).

13:26–27: *the glorious advent of the Son of Man.* Given this context of cosmic battle and the grammatical linkage between the last clause in 13:25 and the beginning of 13:26, it makes sense to take the implied subject of *opsontai* ("they will see") as the shaken "powers in the heavens": those who will see the Son of Man coming in clouds will, in the first instance, be the personified celestial powers through whose realm he will make his triumphal descent (cf. *Asc. Isa.* 10:29–31; *Epistula Apostolorum* 13; *Pistis Sophia* 1.28; cf. the NOTE on "they will see" in 13:26). This descent is described using imagery drawn from Dan 7:13–14, except that the direction of movement is reversed: instead of ascending in the clouds to God, the Son of Man will come in the clouds from heaven to earth (see the NOTES on "the Son of Man coming in clouds with great power and glory" in 13:26 and "the Son of Man . . . coming with the clouds of heaven" in 14:62). His arrival "in clouds" is significant, since clouds frequently accompany theophanies (see, e.g., Deut 33:26; 2 Sam 22:12; Ps 68:4 [67:5 LXX]; Ezek 1:4; cf. Davies and Allison, 3.362), and in Daniel 7 itself the cloud accompaniment suggests that the "one like a son of man" is a divine figure (see Collins, *Daniel,* 290). The advent in clouds, therefore, is one of several ways in which the returning Son of Man in Mark is like God (see below on his sending out of the angels and his gathering of the elect). "Power" and "glory" are also divine attributes, and the nuance of radiance in the latter contrasts vividly with the darkened backdrop of 13:24–25 (cf. Gnilka 2.201).

The importance of Daniel 7 for our passage, however, transcends individual motifs. For one thing, the Danielic vision is probably relevant in the Markan situation, since it is likely that it inspired the Jewish revolutionaries with its vision of the overthrow of evil Gentile empires and the transfer of earthly dominion to a purified Israel (cf. Hengel, *Zealots*, index). Moreover, the Danielic scene includes a description of myriad angels serving God (Dan 7:10) and associates the "one like a son of man" with a chosen group of people, "the people of the holy ones of the Most High" (Dan 7:27). This linkage continues in postbiblical literature; in *1 Enoch* 37–71, for example, the Son of Man figure, who is called "the Chosen One," is frequently linked with the saints, who are called "the chosen ones" (39:6; 40:5; 45:3–5; 49–50; 51:3–5), and *1 En.* 62:14–15 describes the destiny of the latter as eternal communion with the former. Both "the Chosen One" and "the chosen ones," moreover, are connected with angels (see, e.g., *1 En.* 39:4–7; 61:9–12; cf. Marcus, *Way*, 169–71). When the Markan Jesus speaks of the returning *Son of Man* sending out *the angels* and gathering *his chosen ones*, therefore, his close association with both groups, especially the latter ("*his* chosen ones"), is consonant with Daniel 7 and its reinterpretation in *1 Enoch* 37–71. This, then, is the reverse side of the Markan disciples' union with the Son of Man in suffering (see 8:31–38; 10:32–40; 13:9–13), and the culmination of the "being with him" motif that has been present since the constitution of the Twelve as a group (see 3:14 and cf. Stock, *Boten*): as they have trodden the way wearily with Jesus "in the days of his flesh" (Heb 5:7), they will also fly exultantly with him in the air on the day of his triumphant return (see the NOTE on "from the end of the earth to the end of heaven" in 13:27).

Jesus' gathering of the elect, with which the passage concludes (13:27), relates both to the narrow Markan context and to larger biblical conceptions. On the one hand, it defeats the malign scheme of the false Christs and prophets, who have done everything they could to lead the elect astray (13:22). On the other hand, the phrase about "gather[ing]" the elect brings in the biblical notion that the dispersed people of God will at the end be garnered from the four corners of the earth (see, e.g., Deut 30:4; Isa 43:5–6; Zech 2:6). But the Markan Jesus tweaks the biblical scenario by picturing himself, rather than God, as the figure who will do this gathering, and it is his advent rather than God's that will be accompanied by the dimming of the heavenly lights (cf. Hartman, *Prophecy Interpreted*, 158). While Jesus, then, will shortly distinguish himself from "the Father" by his lack of precise knowledge about eschatological *timing* (13:32), our passage establishes that when it comes to knowledge about the eschaton's *nature*, he is supremely well informed, and that he will share many of the attributes of God himself when he returns at the parousia.

The eschatological scenario that Jesus has been unveiling since 13:5 has now been fully disclosed; "all these things" that the disciples asked about in 13:4 have been revealed. In the next passage, therefore, Jesus can return to their original question of *when* "all these things" will transpire.

THE IMMINENCE OF THE END (13:28–32)

13 ²⁸"From the fig tree, learn the parable. When its branch is already becoming tender and putting forth leaves, you know that the harvest is near. ²⁹So you also, when you see these things happening, you know that he is near, at the doors. ³⁰Amen, I say to you, this generation will not pass away before all these things come to pass. ³¹Heaven and earth will pass away, but my words will never pass away. ³²But concerning that day or hour no one knows—neither the angels in heaven nor the Son—except the Father.

NOTES

13 28. *From the fig tree, learn the parable.* Gk *apo de tēs sykēs mathete tēn parabolēn.* The use of the growth of a plant as a metaphor for the manifestation of the dominion of God is one of several links between 13:28–29 and the parabolic discourse in 4:1–34. Both use harvest as a metaphor for the imminent eschatological consummation (cf. 4:29) and presuppose that parables require interpretation (cf. 4:33–34).

When its branch is already becoming tender. Gk *hotan ēdē ho klados autēs hapalos genētai.* Swete (295) points out that *hapalos* and a cognate noun are used for young vegetation in Lev 2:14 Aquila and Ezek 17:4, adding that in our passage the adjective "denotes the result of the softening of the external coverings of the stem, as it grows succulent under the moisture and sunshine of spring." Hepper (*Encyclopedia,* 111) specifies that "by 'tender' [Jesus] may have been referring to the abundance of milky latex present in the thick twigs during the spring" (on this latex, cf. Condit, *Fig,* 25). The fig was proverbial for this substance; cf. the story in *Tanhuma* [Buber] Tezaveh 8.10 (Townsend, 2.144–45) about R. Jonathan, son of Eliezer, "who was sitting beneath a fig tree in the summer and the fig tree was full of beautiful fruit. Dew descended and the figs exuded honey." Rabbi Jonathan goes on to compare this spectacle to the world to come. Cf. *4 Bar.* 5:4, 24–31, in which the fact that the figs are still dripping milk is a sign that the time for redemption has not yet come. On the traditional connection between the fig tree and the eschaton, see the COMMENT on 13:28–29 and cf. Goor, "History," 130.

the harvest. Gk *to theros.* This is a standard OT, Jewish, and Christian metaphor for the eschatological consummation, and it often has connotations of judgment (cf. 4:29 and the COMMENT on 4:26–29). In the immediate Markan context, however, the image is optimistic, since it recalls 13:27, in which the returning Son of Man gathers (*episynaxei*) the elect from the four winds (cf. Matt 25:24, 26; John 4:36, which use the cognate verb *synagein* for reaping).

The fig blooms in the spring and is ready to be harvested in the summer, the Hebrew term for which is *qayiṣ.* The word for "end" is the similar-sounding *qēṣ.* A pun between the two words is already employed in the oracle of doom in Amos 8:1–2 and may be part of the background for our parable (see Hepper, *Encyclopedia,* 111–12; Pesch 2.307).

29. *these things.* Gk *tauta*. This term is distinct from "all these things" (*tauta panta*) in the next verse; cf. 13:4, where "these things" probably refers to the destruction of the Temple and "all these things" to the eschaton (see the COMMENT on 13:3–4). A similar distinction may apply here: "these things" are occurrences in the Markan present and recent past, beginning with the "abomination of desolation" in the Temple (13:14), which show that the great tribulation is under way and that God's decisive intervention ("the harvest") is near. "All these things" in 13:30, by contrast, refers to the entire eschatological timeline laid out in 13:5–27, including the cosmic signs in 13:24–25, the return of the Son of Man in 13:26, and the "harvest" of the elect in 13:27 (see the previous NOTE and the NOTE on "Amen, I say to you, etc." in 13:30 and cf. Pesch, *Naherwartungen*, 186). Thus, when Jesus' disciples see "these things," they will know that the end is *near* (13:28–29), but when they see "all these things," including the disintegration of heaven and earth (13:30–31; cf. 13:24–25), they will know that it has *arrived.*

he is near, at the doors. Gk *engys estin epi thyrais*. There is no pronoun in the Greek, so the referent could be either the Son of Man (the subject in 13:26–27) or the harvest, which was just referred to in 13:28. The latter stands in closer grammatical proximity to 13:29, but the personal dimension of the former comports better with the image of standing at the doors (cf. Luke 12:35–38; Rev 3:20; cf. Ernst, *Markus*, 389). The ambiguity may be deliberate: the coming of the Son of Man will be the eschatological harvest. The plural "doors" is a frequent idiom; cf. Jas 5:9: "The Judge is standing at the doors (*pro tōn thyrōn*)." In the LXX the plural of "door" can alternate with the singular, with no apparent difference in referent (see Exod 40:5–6; Lev 1:3, 5; etc.; cf. Beasley-Murray, 438 n. 188). The plural does not necessarily imply a plurality of openings; the plural, rather, is frequently used for "certain concrete substantives, originally to denote what is long or wide, or mysterious powers" (BDF §141[4]). Other examples are "heavens" (*ouranoi*, so frequently), "worlds" (*aiōnes*, e.g., Heb 1:2; 11:3), and "gates" (*pylai*, e.g., Matt 16:18).

30. *Amen, I say to you, this generation will not pass away before all these things come to pass.* Gk *Amēn legō hymin hoti ou mē parelthȩ̄ hē genea hautē mechris hou tauta panta genētai.* Compare Mark 9:1 and Matt 10:23 (see figure 40), all of which have the same structure: "Amen, I say to you" + statement using *ou mē* about what will not happen + statement using *heōs an* ("before") setting a time limit for the first statement. Exegetes debate whether Mark 9:1 is a reformulation of Mark 13:30 (e.g., Beasley-Murray, 444) or the other way around (e.g., Schlosser, *Règne*, 1.324–27), and whether Matt 10:23 is a Matthean revision of Mark 9:1 or a variant form of the logion preserved independently in Mark (see Davies and Allison, 2.187–90). In any case, the similarity in form suggests that the three passages may be mutually illuminating, and this supports the contention that "all these things" in 13:30 include the parousia, since that is the temporal limit in Mark 9:1 and Matt 10:23.

The most natural way to interpret "this generation" is as a reference to those living at the time of Jesus' speech (see BDAG 191 [2]); they will not all die before the end arrives (cf. again Mark 9:1). An even more precise calculation of the length of

Figure 40: Mark 9:1, Mark 13:30, and Mathew 10:23

Mark 9:1	*Mark 13:30*	*Matthew 10:23*
Amen, I say to you	Amen, I say to you	Amen, I say to you
there are some of those standing here who will not taste death	this generation will not pass away	you will not completely traverse the cities of Israel
before they see the dominion of God fully come in power	before all these things come to pass	before the Son of Man comes

"this generation" is possible, since the phrase recalls the wilderness wanderings of the children of Israel, which lasted forty years (see the NOTE on "this generation" in 8:12). The reckoning of a generation as forty years is also in line with a Greek way of counting that goes back to Hecataeus of Miletus in the sixth century B.C.E. (see Meyer, *Forschungen*, 170–72). Moreover, the idea of a forty-year gap between the beginning of the redemption and its completion is attested elsewhere in Jewish apocalyptic literature (see CD 20:13–15).

This temporal interpretation of "this generation," however, poses a hermeneutical difficulty, since it foresees the end of the world as occurring within forty years or so of Jesus' death. This is probably the way Mark saw things; he expected the end of the world to come soon (see the COMMENT on 13:30–31). Many later Christian interpreters, however, have found this exegesis difficult because it means ascribing error to Jesus, and instead they have chosen to interpret "this generation" in an atemporal manner: as a reference to the Jewish people, or to the Christians, or to the human race in general (see Aquinas, *Catena Aurea* on Mark 13:28–31; Kunzi, *Naherwartungslogion*, 214–221). None of these interpretations is supported by the context, which does contain a clear reference to the idea of eschatological imminence (the Parable of the Fig Tree in 13:28–29; cf. Lövestam, *This Generation*, 81–84). As Beasley-Murray puts it, moreover, "While admittedly *genea* in earlier Greek meant birth, progeny, and so race, in the sense of those descended from a common ancestor, in the LXX it most frequently translated the Hebrew *dôr*, meaning age, age of humankind, or generation in the sense of contemporaries" (444). He goes on to point out that all of the other Gospel usages of "this generation" occur on Jesus' lips and refer to his contemporaries, usually in a threatening way. A close parallel is provided by Matt 23:36 (cf. Luke 11:51): "All these things will come upon this generation" (NRSV alt.)—an apparent reference to the destruction of Jerusalem and its Temple (cf. Matt 23:38).

31. *Heaven and earth will pass away, but my words will never pass away.* Gk *ho ouranos kai hē gē pareleusontai, hoi de logoi mou ou mē pareleusontai.* There is a variant of this saying in Matt 5:18//Luke 16:17 = Q, but there it is the *Law* rather than Jesus' words that will remain in force "until heaven and earth pass away," that is, forever (cf. Job 14:12), an idea consonant with mainline Jewish teaching on the eternity of the Torah (e.g., Bar 4:1; Philo, *Life of Moses* 2.14; *Deut. Rab.* 8.6;

cf. Moore, 1.269–70). Our passage, however, trumps this traditional motif: even if heaven and earth *do* pass away, Jesus' words will endure (*Gen. Rab.* 10.1 makes a similar claim for the Torah). For the background to this verse in Isa 51:6, see the COMMENT on 13:30–31. In view of 13:24–27, in which the heavenly bodies are personified cosmic powers opposed to and vanquished by Jesus (see the NOTES on "the sun will be darkened, etc." in 13:24–25 and "they will see" in 13:26, and the COMMENTS on 13:24–25 and 13:26–27), the implication may be that Jesus' words will play an active role in the destruction and renewal of the cosmos (see the COMMENT on 13:30–31). The medieval Jewish exegete Rashi, similarly, interprets the disappearance of the heavens in Isa 51:6 as God's defeat of their demonic rulers.

32. *nor the Son.* Gk *oude ho huios.* This is the only Markan instance of the title "the Son" without the genitive "of God" either being added or directly implied, though it is indirectly implied by the contrast with "the Father" = God. The absolute form "the Son" also occurs in Matt 11:27 and frequently in the Gospel of John (3:17, 35–36; 5:19–27; etc.), but in these passages the emphasis is usually on the reciprocity and commensurability between the Father and the Son, never on their distinction, as in our passage. There is, however, an interesting overlap with the absolute use of "the Son" in 1 Cor 15:28: "When all things are subjected to him, then the Son himself will also be subjected to the one who put all things in subjection under him, so that God may be all in all." Here, as in our passage, the term "the Son" occurs "in a highly apocalyptic context with a pronounced subordinationist ring" (Schweizer, "*Huios,*" 371).

Jesus' apparent denial of knowledge about the day and hour of the end was felt to be a severe problem by later orthodox theologians; as Jerome (*Commentary on Matthew* 4) puts it, our verse makes "Arius and Eunomius rejoice," because it seems to support their position that the Son is inferior to the Father. Seemingly in response to this Christological problem, Luke leaves out all of Mark 13:32, and some later manuscripts (e.g., X) omit "nor the Son" from our passage and frequently from its Matthean parallel (it is absent in the Vulgate, most Syriac and Coptic witnesses, and the Majority Text; the omission, moreover, is already attested by Origen; see Ehrman, *Textual Corruption,* 91–92). For similar reasons, some church fathers assert unconvincingly that "nor the Son" was not part of the original text but had been introduced into it by the Arians (see, e.g., Ambrose, *On Faith* 5.16.191–93; Jerome, *Commentary on Matthew* 4).

The phrase "nor the Son," however, was too firmly rooted in Christian memory to be dealt with in this cavalier manner, so other hermeneutical strategies became necessary. As Luz (*Matthew,* 3.213–14) notes, later church interpreters are almost unanimous in claiming, on the basis of passages such as Matt 11:27; John 10:15; 16:15; and Acts 1:7, that Jesus *did* know the time of the end (cf. the survey in Oden and Hall, 191–93, and especially the fascinating article by Madigan, "Christus Nesciens"). After all, he knew the signs of the future judgment, so he must have known its day and hour as well (see, e.g., Ambrose, *Exposition of Luke* 8.35; *On Faith* 5.16.206–7). Many, like Augustine (*On the Trinity* 1.12.1), assert that the meaning of the verse is that although Jesus himself knew the "hour," he withheld knowledge of it from his disciples. One of most common proof texts is Acts 1:7, "It is not for you [disciples] to know the times or periods": Christ does not say, "It is not for *me* to know" but "... not for *you* to know," implying that he himself *does* know (see Ambrose, *On Faith* 5.17.212; Jerome, *Commentary on Matthew* 4; Augustine, *Question* 60). A less frequent solution is that of Athanasius (*Four Discourses Against the Arians* 3.46), who claims that Christ knew the hour in his divine nature but not in his human one. These interpretations all fly in the face of the plain sense of the verse, but for orthodox theologians it was "simply not imaginable that the text could mean what it states, nor could Jesus mean what he explicitly declares" (Madigan, "Christus Nesciens," 261). As the Arians realized, however, and as theologians in our own day have rediscovered, the admission of ignorance in Mark 13:32 has its own theological importance; Ebeling (*Dogmatik* 2.473), for example, understands Jesus' ignorance of the day and hour as a necessary part of his participation in the limitations of human existence.

Present-day historical critics are divided about whether 13:32 was actually spoken by Jesus. On the one hand, the denial of omniscience seems to some to point toward genuineness; would the church have made up a saying in which Jesus disclaimed eschatological insight (see Davies and Allison, 3.378–79)? On the other hand, the fact that Jesus speaks of himself as "the Son" here is taken by some (e.g., Luz, *Matthew*, 3.212) as a sign of later composition by Christians concerned to dampen apocalyptic speculation in the name of the Lord. This is possible, but it seems more likely that Jesus did think of himself as, in some special sense, God's Son (cf. the NOTE on "*Abba* [Father]" in 14:36) but nonetheless recognized that he did not possess any special insight into the exact date of the end.

COMMENT

Introduction. In the previous passage, Jesus prophesied that the time of great tribulation—the era in which the Markan community now finds itself living— would be followed by a cosmic collapse and the return of the Son of Man in glory. This prophecy, however, left open the question of when those climactic events would occur, and that is the conundrum addressed by the present text.

This passage seems to be made up of independent units, some of which fit together uneasily and variants of which appear in different contexts elsewhere: the Parable of the Fig Tree and its interpretation (13:28–29; cf. 11:13–14), the prophecy of eschatological consummation within a generation (13:30; cf. 9:1), the prophecy that Jesus' words will outlast the present universe (13:31; cf. Matt 5:18// Luke 16:17), and the assertion that no one except the Father knows the timing of the end (13:32). While 13:28–30 emphasizes the imminence of the eschaton, 13:32 asserts that no one knows its hour, and 13:31 seems to have no relevance to the issue of imminence at all but to be loosely connected to 13:30 by the notion of things passing away (cf. Kümmel, *Promise*, 91). It is possible that Mark himself is responsible for this catchword association, though it may also be a pre-Markan linkage. It is more likely that Mark is responsible for introducing into the present context the warning that no one knows the hour (13:32), which forms a transition to the next and final pericope in the eschatological discourse. Matching this redactional activity at the end of our passage is a probable editorial touch at the beginning, "From the fig tree, learn the parable" (13:28a), which corresponds to the Markan emphasis on parables as a teaching tool for insiders (4:10–12, 33–34).

The passage is divided into three parts: the Parable of the Fig Tree and its interpretation (13:28–29), the sayings about things passing away (13:30–31), and the concluding warning that no one knows the hour (13:32).

13:28–29: the Parable of the Fig Tree. The penultimate section of the eschatological discourse begins with a parable about a fig tree—a symbol that has already been used earlier in the Gospel in an enacted parable concerning the eschatological fate of Israel (11:12–14, 20–21). Unlike most trees that grow in Israel, the fig tree is deciduous, losing its leaves in the winter and budding again in late spring (see Davies and Allison, 3.365). Ancient farmers knew all about these processes and could easily predict how long it would take for the fruit to develop and become ready for harvest; *t. Šeb.* 4.20, for example, subdivides the maturation period thus: "From the time the leaves appear until the young fig is formed—fifty days . . . From the time the fig appears till the fig is fully formed—fifty days" (cf. Goor, "History," 130).

Because it goes through these regular and predictable changes, the fig is a suitable metaphor for the final stages in the outworking of the divine plan for history. This potential is already exploited in Isa 34:4, especially in the version found in the LXX according to Codex Vaticanus and the Lucianic recension. This OT passage has a strong connection to the larger Markan context, in that the development of the fig tree's leaves is linked with the coming of the eschaton and the disintegration of "the powers in the heavens":

> And all the powers of the heavens (*hai dynameis tōn ouranōn*) shall melt (cf. Mark 13:25b), and the sky shall be rolled up like a scroll; and all the stars shall fall (cf. Mark 13:25a) like leaves from a vine, and as leaves fall from a fig tree. (cf. Mark 13:28–29)

This Isaian passage was used in later eschatological prophecies, for example, Rev 6:13–14 (see the COMMENT on 13:24–25); and a later rabbinic midrash on it, *Pirqe R. El.* 50[51], contains features that strengthen the link with the Markan context (cf. Telford, *Barren Temple*, 185):

> "And all the host of heaven shall be dissolved" (Isa 34:4). Just as the leaves fade from off the vine and the fig tree, and the latter remains standing as a dry tree, and again they blossom afresh and bear buds and produce new leaves and fresh leaves, likewise in the future will all the host of heaven fade away like a vine and a fig tree, and they will again be renewed before Him to make known that there is passing away (which) does not (really) pass away. No more shall there be evil,

and no more shall there be plague, and (there shall) not be the former misfortunes, as it is said, "For behold, I am creating new heavens and a new earth" (Isa 65:17). (from Friedlander, *Pirkê*, 411–12, trans. alt.)

Here not only the fig tree's loss of leaves, as in Isa 34:4, but also its budding and production of new leaves, as in Mark 13:28–29, become eschatological metaphors, and this happens in a context that uses the Isaian image of the heavenly bodies disintegrating, as in Mark 13:24–25, and speaks in Isaian terms of the creation of a new heaven and a new earth (cf. Isa 65:17), implying that the old ones have "passed away" (cf. Isa 51:6), as in Mark 13:31. It seems, then, that Isaian passages and their traditional interpretations have exerted a strong influence on the entire Markan section from 13:24 to 13:32 (see figure 41; is it just a coincidence that the Isaian passages occur here basically in sequence?). This emphasis is in accord with an overall Markan tendency to interpret the good news as a fulfillment of what was "written in Isaiah the prophet" (see the COMMENT on 1:2–3).

The point of all of this OT imagery in the parable is that the eschaton is imminent—just as a fig tree's budding is a sign that the harvest, a standard OT metaphor for the end, is at hand (13:28b; see the NOTE on "the harvest" in 13:28). After having uttered this eschatological parable, therefore, Jesus interprets it for his disciples (in line with "parable theory" enunciated in 4:10–12, 33–34): when

Figure 41: Isaian Motifs in Mark 13:24–32

Mark 13:24–32	*Isaiah*
24: the sun will be darkened, and the moon will not give its light *(ou dōsei to phengos autēs)*	13:10: the sun will be dark at its rising, and the moon will not give its light *(ou dōsei to phōs autēs)*; cf. 24:23
25: and the stars will be falling from heaven	34:4c: and all the stars will fall
and the powers in the heavens will be shaken	34:4a: and all the powers of the heavens will melt
28: Coming of end compared to fig tree's leaves budding	34:4d: Coming of end compared to fig tree's leaves falling off; cf. midrash on this passage in *Pirqe R. El.* 51: coming of end compared to fig tree's leaves falling off and budding
31: heaven and earth will pass away, but my words will never pass away	51:6: for the heavens will vanish like smoke, and the earth will wear out like a garment, . . . but my salvation will be forever, and my deliverance will never be ended; cf. 65:17: new heavens and a new earth

his followers see "these things"—the tribulations described in 13:14–23, through which the Markan community is presently passing—they will know that the Son of Man or the harvest (*to theros*) is near, at the very doors (*epi thyrais*, a pun on *theros*; see the NOTE on "he is near, at the doors" in 13:29). The message of Mark 13:28–29, therefore, is similar to that of a later Jewish apocalyptic passage, *4 Ezra* 9:1–2: "When you see that a certain part of the predicted signs are past, then you will know that it is the very time when the Most High is about to visit the world." The Markan community knows that "a certain part of the predicted signs are past," because its members have experienced "these things": the Jewish war, the associated persecution of Christians, the flight from Judaea, and tribulation such as has never before existed. But by placing these sufferings near the end point of the eschatological timeline, the parable relativizes them; they are not the ultimate reality but only an interim one that will swiftly pass away. What they show, in fact, is not that the powers of evil have triumphed—as the hard-pressed Markan community might be tempted to think—but that "it is the very time when the Most High is about to visit the world" (*4 Ezra* 9:2).

13:30–31: what will last and what will not. The next verse confirms this eschatological expectation: "all these things," which include the eschatological culmination, will come to pass within a generation of Jesus' Olivet speech. Since a biblical "generation" is about forty years (see the NOTE on "Amen, I say to you, etc." in 13:30), and since Jesus died in the early thirties C.E., our passage places the coming of the end squarely within the time frame of the Markan present (around 70). For Mark, therefore, the eschatological timer is ticking, and the explosion could come at any time.

As already emphasized in 13:24–25, the arrival of the eschaton will have radical consequences not only for human life on earth but also for the entire universe, because the fate of humanity is bound up with that of the cosmos; both stand under the grace and judgment of God (cf. Rom 8:19–23). When the longed-for eschatological consummation happens, therefore, not only human evil but also "heaven and earth will pass away" (13:31a), probably to be replaced by "a new heaven and a new earth" (cf. Isa 65:17). The words of Jesus, however, will remain (13:31b), and thus constitute a bridge between the present evil age and the age to come.

But they are more than that; as the Parable of the Mustard Seed implies, they are also in a certain sense the instrument for bringing that new age into being (cf. 4:14, 30–32; see the COMMENT on 4:30–32) and demolishing the old one (cf. the NOTE on "Heaven and earth will pass away, but my words will never pass away" in 13:31). Jesus' words thus have the destructive and creative potency of the divine utterance placed in the prophet's mouth in Jer 1:9–10. Indeed, what is being implied is not just that Jesus' words will outlast heaven and earth but that they will be God's potent weapons for the demolition and renewal of the cosmos. Other early Christians exalted Christ as the instrument for God's creative work "in the beginning" (see John 1:3; Col 1:16); Mark is praising him as the instrument for the destructive and re-creative work at the end. Despite the partial anal-

ogy with Jeremiah, then, a higher claim is being made than that Jesus' words
are filled with prophetic power. Jesus is being placed in a position analogous to
that of God: "For the heavens will vanish like smoke, [and] the earth will wear
out like a garment . . . but *my salvation* will be forever, and *my deliverance* will
never be ended" (Isa 51:6; on the imperishability of God's word, see Isa 40:8 and
Ps 119:89).

13:32: no one knows the hour. Just when the Markan text seems ready to suggest
Jesus' commensurateness with God, however, it also registers a reservation, contrasting him with God in a way that later theologians found difficult to reconcile
with their belief in his divinity. Only God himself, Jesus adds, knows the day and
hour of the eschaton's arrival; this knowledge is withheld from all lesser beings,
including the angels and the Son himself. Early exegetes were concerned about
the thorny Christological problems created by this statement (see the NOTE on
"nor the Son" in 13:32), and latter-day interpreters have been equally occupied
with its eschatological ramifications. Many claim that the emphasis that no one,
including Jesus, knows the eschatological hour qualifies or neutralizes the element of imminence found in the previous verses (see, e.g., Hooker, "Trial and
Tribulation"; Juel, *Mark*, 184; cf. the survey of German scholarship in Strobel,
Kerygma, 16–30).

This is a beguiling line of argument, since it protects Jesus from being mistaken
about the time of the end; unfortunately, however, its presupposition is mistaken,
since many Jewish apocalyptic texts seamlessly combine the idea that knowledge
of the "hour" is restricted to God with the conviction of that hour's imminence
(see Strobel, *Kerygma*, 85–88). The author of the *Psalms of Solomon*, for example,
believes that the end-time is at hand (see 2:25–26 and cf. *OTP*, 2.645), yet he asserts that the Messiah will arise only "in the time known to you, O God" (17:21).
Similarly, the interpreting angel in *4 Ezra* 4:51–52 confesses that he does not
know whether Ezra will live to see the end, but it is apparent from 14:10–12 that
the author feels himself to be living in the final phase of world history (cf. Strobel,
Kerygma, 86). And *2 Apocalypse of Baruch* repeatedly emphasizes that only God
knows the exact point of the end (21:8; 48:3; 54:1), but it also stresses time and
again that the eschaton is near (23:7; 82:2; 83:1). This is not a contradiction but, as
Gunkel ("Vierte Buch Esra," 359) points out, a reflection of the double concern of
apocalyptic writers: to proclaim the good news that the sufferings of the present
are almost over and to warn against a pretension to eschatological knowledge so
precise that it compromises the sovereignty of God.

This combination—the intensification of end-time expectation on the one
hand and the warning against apocalyptic hubris on the other—lays the groundwork for the chapter's final passage, which calls the Markan community to un-
ceasing eschatological vigilance.

A CALL TO ESCHATOLOGICAL VIGILANCE (13:33–37)

13 ³³"Look out, don't fall asleep!—for you don't know when the time is. ³⁴It is like a man away from home, who has left his house and has given his slaves authority, to each his work, and the doorkeeper he has commanded to keep awake. ³⁵So keep awake!—for you don't know when the lord of the house is coming, whether at evening or midnight or cockcrow or early in the morning, ³⁶in case he comes suddenly and finds you sleeping. ³⁷And what I say to you I say to all: Keep awake!"

NOTES

13 33. *don't fall asleep.* Gk *agrypneite.* Both *agrypneite* and *grēgoreite* (13:34–35, 37) have the basic meaning of keeping awake.

34. *it is like.* Gk *hōs.* On this typical introduction to Gospel and rabbinic parables, see the NOTES on "as if" in 4:26 and "It is as" in 4:31.

a man away from home. Gk *anthrōpos apodēmos.* As noted in the exegesis section of the COMMENT, for Mark this man is Jesus. For the historical Jesus himself, however, the man may well have been God, for whose near advent (the dominion of God) Jesus was preparing his hearers (cf. Jeremias, *Parables*, 53–55; Hultgren, *Parables*, 265).

and has given his slaves authority, to each his work. Gk *kai dous tois doulois autou tēn exousian hekastō to ergon autou.* Some Greek manuscripts (e.g., A, Cᶜ, Majority Text, K, M, *f*¹, ¹³) and some ancient and modern translations (e.g., Latin Syᵖ, ʰ, KJV) add "and" after "authority." With this reading, which is a scribal amelioration, the master gives his slaves two separate things, authority and a task; cf. Swete (298): "The authority is committed to the servants collectively . . . the task is assigned individually." It may be, however, that Mark's awkward wording implies a closer connection between *exousia* and *ergon* than Swete recognizes; the divine gift of authoritative power brings with it a task whose fulfillment it enables.

doorkeeper. Gk *thyrōrō.* The doorkeeper's tasks were to exclude unwanted visitors (see Josephus, *Ant.* 17.90) and to admit others on their arrival (see John 10:3), including the master himself (see Luke 12:36), since doors were locked from the inside (see Lövestam, *Wakefulness*, 80–82; King and Stager, *Life*, 80–83). Dereliction of duty could have grave or even fatal consequences for the inhabitants of the house (see 2 Sam 4:6–7 LXX; Esth 2:21); the position thus required a person in whom one could repose absolute trust. At the same time, the doorkeeper was normally a slave, so the role combined humility and responsibility; cf. Ps 84:10: "I would rather be a doorkeeper in the house of my God than live in the tents of wickedness."

In the fuller Lukan version of our parable (Luke 12:35–38), all the slaves, not just the doorkeeper, remain awake, but Jeremias (*Parables*, 54) considers this an allegorizing trait, reflecting the application of the parable to the community of the church. Hultgren (*Parables*, 267) asserts the opposite: "One would expect, as in Luke's account, that all the slaves should be vigilant." On balance, however,

Jeremias' opinion seems more compelling, since a situation in which the door-keeper alone stays up to welcome a master who may or may not arrive is more realistic than one in which all slaves are sleep deprived and therefore less fit for their duties the next day.

35. *whether at evening or midnight or cockcrow or early in the morning.* Gk *ē opse ē mesonyktion ē alektorophōnias ē prōi.* Martin ("Watch") argues that these four time designations are a modification of the four watches of the night in the Roman system, in which the first watch begins around 6:00 P.M., the second around 9:00, the third around midnight, and the fourth around 3:00 A.M. (Time telling was mostly by sundials, but water clocks were used at night; see Toomer, "Clocks.") By the first century this modified four-watch system had been adopted by the Jews of Palestine (see Mark 6:48; Luke 12:38; Josephus, *Ant.* 18.356; *War* 5.510–11), more or less replacing the three-watch system in the OT and earlier Jewish sources (see, e.g., Judg 7:19; *Jub.* 49:10–12; cf. *b. Ber.* 3b for Talmudic awareness of both systems).

37. *Keep awake!* Gk *grēgoreite.* On the alternation in our passage between this word and *agrypneite* in 13:33, see the NOTE on "don't fall asleep" in 13:33. The fact that the repeated command to keep awake is immediately followed by a refer-ence to the Passover (14:1) is probably not simply fortuitous, since the Passover is called a night of vigil (lit. "night of watching") in Exod 12:42, and at least by the time of the Tannaim some Jews were in the habit of staying up all night to cel-ebrate it (see *t. Pes.* 10:12 and Glatzer, *Haggadah*, 22–25; cf. Bar-Ilan, "Tiqun," nn. 20 and 21). Jewish exegetes, moreover, connect the "night of watching" with their hope for a future redemption at Passover (see, e.g., *Tg. Neof.* Exod 12:42; *b. Roš. Haš.* 11b; cf. *Tg. Lam.* 2:22 and Le Déaut, *Nuit*, 253; Jeremias, *Eucharistic Words*, 206–7). It is appropriate, therefore, that the transition between the eschatological chapter 13 and the story of Jesus' death at Passover time is a command to keep awake.

COMMENT

Introduction. After the hints throughout chapter 13 that the eschaton is immi-nent, the eschatological discourse concludes with an exhortation to remain alert, because the Lord could return at any time. No one, to be sure, knows the exact hour of his advent, but in the view of the Markan Jesus it will certainly be soon.

This concluding passage, like the initial scene setting in 13:1–4, seems to be ba-sically a composition of the evangelist, although some traditional material, such as the parable in 13:34, has been employed. The first and last verses (13:33, 37) appear redactional; they abound in Markan terms ("look out," "know," "time," "keep awake"), and 13:33 features a typically Markan *gar* ("for") clause, which ap-plies the thought of 13:32 to the disciples and, by implication, to the Markan com-munity, an expansion of audience that 13:37 makes explicit. Mark 13:34 appears to be a condensed version of the Parable of the Doorkeeper in Luke 12:35–38 ("authority," a favorite Markan word, may be an editorial addition). The Markan version lacks the expected conclusion, in which the man comes back (at midnight? cf. Matt 25:6) to find the doorkeeper sleeping, although the gist of that conclusion is incorporated into the interpretation in 13:35–37, which also contains much redactional vocabulary ("keep awake," "know," "house," "come," "early in the morning," *gar* clause). The passage, then, is substantially Markan, which is what one would expect at such a major transition point.

The passage is structured around three plural imperatival phrases: "Look out, don't fall asleep!" in 13:33, "So keep awake!" in 13:35, and "Keep awake!" in 13:37. Each of the first two imperatival phrases is followed by a *gar* clause explaining the necessity of wakefulness (13:33b, 35b) and then by the Parable of the Doorkeeper (13:34) and its interpretation (13:35c–36) respectively.

13:33–37: *concluding call to alertness.* Jesus begins the final section of his last extended Markan discourse with a call to attention ("Look out, don't fall asleep!" 13:33a), thus signaling the importance of what is to follow. He then connects this section to the previous paragraph through an implicit argument from the greater to the lesser: if he himself does not know the exact hour of the end, how much less will his disciples be able to determine it (13:33b)! All human beings thus find themselves in the same state of radical eschatological indeterminacy, and they therefore share a common imperative of apocalyptic vigilance.

Jesus hammers this point home with the Parable of the Doorkeeper (13:34), which outlines a scenario familiar from other dominical parables: a wealthy man goes away and leaves his slaves in charge of his property (cf. Mark 12:1–12 pars.; Matt 24:45–51//Luke 12:42–46; Matt 25:14–30; Luke 19:12–27). The master's departure poses an implicit test: will the servants be faithful to their absent lord? Mark's emphasis in the present passage shifts from the slaves in general (13:34b) to the doorkeeper in particular (13:34c), whose task it is to keep awake and open the door when the master returns, even if the latter arrives in the middle of the night (cf. the NOTE on "doorkeeper" in 13:34). The parable, then, reduces the encounter between master and slave to its starkest terms: the master returns and knocks, and the question is whether or not the slave will be awake to open the door for him (cf. Rev 3:20). In the allegory of the parable in its Markan context, this "lord" (*kyrios*) is Jesus, who will soon go away, ascending to heaven at his resurrection, but returning at the parousia to gather his elect and judge the world (cf. 12:35–36; 13:26–27; 14:62; but see the NOTE on "a man away from home" in 13:34).

The time of this return, however, is unknown, so Jesus calls his hearers to wakefulness a second time ("So keep awake!" 13:35a) and then interprets the parable with the observation that no one knows at what hour of the night the master will return (13:35bc). As Lövestam notes (*Wakefulness*, 82–89), the parable here makes the seemingly uncalled-for assumption that the master will return by night rather than by day. *Sibylline Oracles* 2.177–83 provides an instructive comparison and contrast:

The Most High, who oversees all, living in the sky,
will spread sleep over people, having closed their eyes.

O blessed servants, as many as the master, when he comes,
finds awake; for they have all kept awake
all the time looking expectantly with sleepless eyes.
For he will come, at dawn, or evening, or midday.
He will certainly come, and it will be as I say. (*OTP* trans. alt.)

Here, as in Mark 13, the greater part of humanity is led astray by supernatural
forces (cf. the COMMENT on 13:21–23) and plunged into a "sleep" of eschatological inattentiveness. A few, however, manage to maintain their alertness, seemingly by God's grace, until the master arrives. The possible times of his coming in
Sibylline Oracles 2, however, are dawn, noon, and evening, rather than the four
night-watch hours listed in Mark. Why this difference?

Arrival at night is unusual, though not unprecedented (cf. Luke 11:5), since
ancient people were reluctant to travel after dark because of brigands and other
highway dangers (cf. Lövestam, *Wakefulness*, 82–83). It may be that this feature
reflects an earlier version of the parable in which a doorkeeper was caught napping
when his master returned late at night (see the introduction to the COMMENT).
But the nighttime return of the master also has a theological dimension, based on
the common Jewish notion that this age is like night and the age to come like day
(see, e.g., 1QM 1:8–9; *1 En.* 58:3–5; *Mekilta, Beshallaḥ* 7 [Lauterbach 1.253–54];
Ruth Rab. 6.4). Jesus, then, will come like a thief in the night (cf. 1 Thess 5:2; Matt
24:43), and in his coming the darkness will turn to light, bringing joy to those who
are "children of the day" (cf. 1 Thess 5:5).

But with this good news comes an implicit threat: "in case he comes suddenly
and finds you sleeping" (13:36). In Mark, unlike *Sibylline Oracles* 2, being a believer in God, even one of the "elect," is no guarantee that one will remain awake
until the master returns (cf. 13:22; contrast *Sib. Or.* 2.180–81). This danger of
eschatological slumber, Jesus goes on to imply, pertains not only to the four disciples who are immediately being addressed (13:3–4) but to all those who will
hear Jesus' story through them, including first and foremost the members of the
Markan community (13:37a). As in 13:14, it is probable that this movement to
address the Markan audience directly and inclusively reflects the evangelist's concern about a matter of the utmost significance for the survival of his community.
Indeed, if 13:22 is taken seriously, the majority of the Markan Christians will be
enmeshed in the realm of demonic delusion—perhaps not only a tendency to follow false Christs (13:22) but also a related propensity to despair over the delayed
return of the true one (cf. 4:38; 6:48; in the latter, Jesus comes at the last possible
minute—the fourth watch of the night!—to save his struggling disciples).

The disquieting prospect of being caught napping at the parousia elicits a third
and final call to attention, with which the passage ends ("Keep awake!" 13:37b).
This extraordinary repetition of the imperative of wakefulness (the fourth instance of a synonymous verb within five verses) is probably a double entendre. On
the one hand, it is a last call to adopt the attitude of eschatological vigilance that
has been the urgent burden of the pericope. This attitude, Mark implies, means
living one's life with eyes wide open. Scoffers may disparage as dreamers people

whose attention is fixed on future events (cf. Gen 37:19; 2 Pet 3:3–4; cf. Jude 8), but Mark implies that it is these dreamers who really have their eyes peeled. The "realists," on the other hand—who think that the world will continue indefinitely on its accustomed course—are simply dreaming.

But it is also significant that this concluding call to attention immediately precedes the final section of the Gospel, which contains the narratives of Jesus' passion (chapters 14–15) and of the discovery of the empty tomb (16:1–8). For these events of passion and resurrection are at least a partial fulfillment of the eschatological prophecies in chapter 13: in them the end has come. The elect fall asleep (14:37, 40–41) and go astray (14:50–52, 66–72), the sun is dimmed (15:33), the Temple suffers damage that portends its destruction (15:38), and the Son of Man passes through an all-night vigil until finally, on the other side of cosmic death, he returns as the herald of new life and a new age (cf. Lightfoot, *Gospel Message*, 48–59). If the Markan Jesus, then, exhorts his disciples to keep their eyes open, he is calling their attention not only to the signs of the times in Mark's day but also to the last act of the eschatological drama of Jesus' life, which is about to unfold in the gripping conclusion of the Gospel.

SIXTH MAJOR SECTION
(MARK 14:1–15:47)

◆

INTRODUCTION
DYING: THE PASSION NARRATIVE

There is a large element of truth in Kähler's famous exaggeration (*So-Called*, 80 n. 11) that the Gospels are "passion narratives with extended introductions." In the case of Mark, the evangelist has been preparing for the climactic section of the Gospel, the account of Jesus' passion (= suffering), since 2:20, where Jesus spoke allusively of himself as a bridegroom destined to be taken away (= killed), and 3:6, where the narrator described a Pharisaic/Herodian plot to destroy him. Nothing that Jesus has done in the interim has been calculated to lessen this deadly enmity, and in 12:12a the chief priests, the scribes, and the elders (cf. 11:27) have manifested a purpose similar to that of the Pharisees and the Herodians, although the plot has been thwarted by popular support for Jesus. Now at last this long-delayed conspiracy is set into motion, and Mark tells with economy and power the story of Jesus' death.

Structure. This narrative seems carefully constructed. It is divided into two main sections with six subsections, as shown in figure 42. These subections alternate in a regular pattern: a three-scene "sandwich" (see the subject index in vols. 1 and 2 under "sandwich structure") followed by two two-scene subsections. In the first main section, which ends with Jesus' arrest, the chief characters are Jesus and the disciples. In the second main section, which ends with his burial, the chief characters are Jesus and his opponents. This division, to be sure, is not hard and fast; Jesus' opponents, who now include Judas, frame the story of his anointing at the beginning of Part I, and the tale of his denial by one of his disciples, Peter, frames the story of his Jewish trial at the beginning of Part II (the juxtaposition of Judas and Peter is probably not accidental). But there is clear structural evidence to make the suggested structure plausible.

Pre-Markan passion narrative? Who is responsible for this carefully structured narrative—Mark, or some anonymous Christian author before him? The answer is probably not an "either/or" but a "both/and"; Mark may have used a source with a discernible structure, but he probably extended and altered that structure in line with his own tendencies and purposes. The three-scene sandwich, for example,

Figure 42: The Structure of the Markan Passion Narrative

Part I: Jesus at Large

  1. Prologue: Plot and anointing (14:1–11)—THREE-SCENE SANDWICH
     A. Plot against Jesus (14:1–2)
     B. Anointing of Jesus (14:3–9)
     A'. Plot against Jesus (14:10–11)
  2. Last Supper (14:12–31)—TWO SCENES
     A. Preparation for supper (14:12–16)
     B. Last supper itself (14:17–31)
  3. Events in Gethsemane (14:32–52)—TWO SCENES
     A. Agony (14:32–42)
     B. Arrest (14:43–52)

Part II: Jesus in Captivity

  1. Jewish trial (14:53–72)—THREE-SCENE SANDWICH
     A. Peter as onlooker (14:53–54)
     B. Hearing before the Sanhedrin (14:55–65)
     A'. Peter's denial (14:66–72)
  2. Roman trial (15:1–20a)—TWO SCENES
     A. Hearing before Pilate (15:1–15)
     B. Mockery (15:16–32)
  3. Death and burial (15:33–47)—TWO SCENES
     A. Death (15:33–41)
     B. Burial (15:42–47)

is a typically Markan format, but John 18:15–27 suggests that it may have had its prototype in a pre-Markan source.

Most scholars, indeed, think that in composing his passion story Mark is dependent on a pre-Markan passion account that had been passed down in the church, either in oral or written form (see the summary of scholarship in Brown, *Death*, 46–57, and Soards, "Question"). The alternative is to believe that Mark himself essentially created the passion narrative, either out of whole cloth or, more likely, out of preexistent snippets of tradition (see, e.g., Matera, *Kingship*, and Mack, *Myth*, 249–312). Such views, however, do not on balance seem as likely as the hypothesis that Mark is significantly dependent on a pre-Markan source:

(1) The church would have needed an account of Jesus' passion from a very early stage of its existence, in order to answer the pressing question of how it came about that Jesus, its proclaimed Messiah, had suffered and died. As Mark itself makes clear, the idea of a suffering and dying Messiah was at least unusual, and possibly unprecedented, in Judaism (see especially 8:31–32 and cf. Mowinckel, *He That Cometh*, 325–33, 410–15). The proclamation of a crucified Savior was a scandal to non-Christian Jews and Gentiles alike (see, e.g., 1 Cor 1:23; Origen, *Against Celsus* 2.35, 44). A Messiah "crucified in weakness" (2 Cor 13:4), therefore, was a contradiction in terms, and Christians would have needed a passion narrative early on in order to answer the question of how Jesus ended up that way.

(2) In other parts of the Gospels, John departs radically from the Synoptics; most of the Synoptic stories are missing from John, and most of the Johannine ones are absent in the Synoptics. It is only in the passion narrative that considerable overlap exists. Since John does not seem to be directly dependent on the Synoptics (see the INTRODUCTION in vol. 1, pp. 53–54), this pattern may be explained by a common dependence of John and the Synoptics on a pre-Gospel passion narrative.

(3) In other parts of Mark, time indications are generally nonexistent, or vague (e.g., "several days later," 2:1; "in those days," 8:1), or puzzling (e.g., "after six days" in 9:2). Only in the passion narrative do we get a series of connected time notices that structure the narrative and help readers follow the developing story of Jesus' last hours (see figure 33 in the introduction to chapters 11–13). This anomaly is explicable on the theory that the passion narrative, in contrast to the rest of the Gospel, was already a connected account before its Markan appropriation.

(4) Some of the passages in the Markan passion narrative do not make sense as individual units, but only as part of a consecutive text. The story of the preparation for the Passover meal (14:12–16), for example, necessitates the immediately subsequent narrative, which describes the meal itself (14:17–25). Similarly, it is hard to imagine that the scene in which Jesus prophesies Peter's denial (14:29–31) ever existed apart from the scene in which that prophecy is fulfilled (14:66–72).

It is theoretically possible that in these instances Mark created both of the linked stories and therefore was not dependent on a preexistent passion source. But in at least one case this hypothesis appears unlikely. In the complex having to do with Peter's denial, one of the verses in the prophecy scene, 14:28, appears to be redactional—a Markan addition to a pre-Markan narrative (see the introduction to the COMMENT on 14:26–31). There was, then, a *pre-Markan* scene in which Jesus prophesied Peter's denial, which was hooked to a *pre-Markan* scene in which Peter denied Jesus (see Scroggs in Kelber et al., *Reflections*, 509–13, 523–28).

How extensive was the pre-Markan passion narrative? John lacks parallels to most of the Synoptic stories about Jesus' Jerusalem ministry (Mark 11–13 and parallels), although he does have the triumphal entry (John 12:12–19), the cleansing of the Temple, though in a different place (John 2:13–17), and occasional echoes of other Synoptic stories (compare e.g. John 2:18 with Mark 11:28, and John 14:26 with Mark 13:11). John also lacks parallels to important sections of Mark 14:1–42, such as Jesus' eucharistic action at the Last Supper and his agony in Gethsemane (Mark 14:22–25, 32–42), though he includes the leaders' plot against Jesus (John 11:45–52), the anointing at Bethany (John 12:1–8), and Jesus' prophecies that one of his followers would betray him (John 13:18, 21–30) and Peter would deny him (John 13:36–38). Some of the Johannine omissions might be deliberate; in John 12:27, for example, the evangelist seems to know but reject the tradition that Jesus prayed to escape the cup of suffering (Mark 14:36 pars.), and the realized eschatology in his last discourse (John 13–17) could be an intentional revision of the sort of imminent eschatology found in Mark 13 and its Synoptic parallels. It is also possible that the Johannine footwashing scene (John 13:1–17) acts out the theme of Jesus' eucharistic words in the Synoptics (cf. Smith, *John*, 254–55).

Other Johannine omissions, however, are harder to explain if John knew Mark or a Markan-type passion narrative, especially the lack of the narrative about finding the colt for Jesus' triumphal entry (Mark 11:1–6) and the parallel scene of the disciples' discovery of the room for the Last Supper (Mark 14:12–16). Both of these imply Jesus' clairvoyance and probably would have been included if John had known them, since Jesus' prevision of his fate is such an important Johannine theme (see Smith, *John Among*, 214, 228). Many scholars, therefore, think that the earliest form of the passion narrative began at a later point in the story, perhaps with Jesus' arrest, where the parallels with John become more numerous (see the survey by Soards, "Question"). It may be, however, that Jeremias (*Eucharistic Words*, 96) is right when he posits that this early, short account of Jesus' passion was subsequently extended backward to the triumphal entry.

Historicity? The cumulative evidence for a pre-Markan passion narrative does not necessarily imply that Mark's account of Jesus' last days is historically accurate. Crossan (*Cross*), indeed, asserts that the Markan passion-and-resurrection account is derivative of the story of Jesus' death in the so-called Cross Gospel, a source that he reconstructs from the second-century *Gospel of Peter* and that, in his view, is totally based on OT prophecies, anti-Judaism, and other Christian theological motifs. Mark has made this narrative more realistic, getting rid of fantastic details such as the earthquake that occurs when Jesus' corpse is laid on the ground and the speaking cross that follows him when he emerges from the tomb. But since he is totally dependent on this Cross Gospel, and since it is patently unhistorical, his own passion narrative is divorced from historical reality. This hypothesis has been subjected to sharp criticism from Brown ("Gospel of Peter" and *Death*, 2.1317–49) and Schaeffer ("Gospel of Peter"), and it seems intrinsically unlikely that the fantastic account in the *Gospel of Peter*, which is after all a second-century document, should be the source for Mark's sober, first-century narrative. Still, Crossan is right that priority does not necessarily imply historicity.

Although the present commentary is primarily an exposition of the Markan text, not an attempt to determine what actually happened in the final days of Jesus' life, such historical questions will occupy us in this final section more frequently than in previous parts of the Gospel—partly because the stakes here are so high (see, e.g., the discussion of anti-Judaism below). The basic point of view adopted is middle of the road. The Markan passion narrative, like the Markan Gospel in general, is a mixture of memory and theological insight, a "two-level drama" (cf. Martyn, *History*, 42, 85–89). On the one hand, it contains features that were embarrassing to later Christians, such as Jesus' despair in Gethsemane, his denial by Peter, his abandonment by the other members of the Twelve, and his cry of dereliction from the cross. These embarrassing features are unlikely to have been invented by early Christian storytellers. At the time and place that Mark was composed (Syria around 70 C.E., according to our reconstruction), moreover, there were probably people still around who remembered the general contours of Jesus' public life, including his passion and death, and who could correct an account that was outlandishly inaccurate. It is to be expected, then, that the Markan passion narrative preserves remembered events. On the other hand, it is also probable that Mark, like the other Gospel writers, has fleshed out his passion narrative in order to bring its significance home to his readers.

As we shall see, for example, many features of the Markan passion narrative echo famous OT passages (cf. Marcus, *Way*, 153–98). The ancient church had no problem in affirming that these scripturally plotted narratives were historical, and indeed saw them as proof of the miraculous nature of Jesus' ministry: the same God who had caused him to live, die, and rise again for the sake of humanity had also provided previews of these wonderful events in the prophetic writings hundreds of years before. But the extent of OT allusion in the passion narrative causes some modern scholars to wonder, as Crossan (*Who Killed*, 1–13) puts it, whether we are dealing with history remembered or with prophecy historicized.

It seems very probable that, in some instances, the Gospel writers or their sources *did* historicize prophecy, creating narrative features out of OT motifs. The Markan account of Jesus' crucifixion, for example, is strongly reminiscent of the description of the Righteous Sufferer in Psalm 22 (see the COMMENTS on 15:20b–27, 29–32 and 15:33–34, 38–39). Matthew, in editing this Markan text, adds an explicit echo of the same psalm when he has the mockers say, "He trusts in God; let God deliver him now, if he desires him" (Matt 27:43 RSV; cf. Ps 22:8). Matthew probably does not possess an additional historical datum about this incident; rather, he realizes that the Markan narrative is suffused with allusions to Psalm 22 and extends this tendency with an explicit quotation of the same psalm. And if Matthew thus historicizes prophecy in editing Mark, it is possible that Mark or his sources have already done the same. The placement of the women at a distance in Mark 15:40 may be an example; John 19:25–26, by contrast, has them close enough to carry on a conversation with Jesus. This closer placement may be historical (see Brown, 2.204, 222); Mark or his source may have moved them away in order to emphasize Jesus' isolation (a major theme of the Markan passion narrative) and to fulfill Ps 38:11: "My friends and companions stand aloof from my affliction, and my neighbors stand far off" (cf. Marcus, "Role," 212–13). Conversely, it is also possible that Mark's more distant placement of the women is historical and that John has moved them closer for the sake of a conversation with Jesus that he has invented (see Brown, *Death*, 2.1028–29).

Indeed, a rough consonance with OT scripture does not necessarily mean that a Gospel narrative is unhistorical. It is conceivable, rather, that some of the words spoken and actions performed in the last act of Jesus' life actually *did* correspond to OT texts, especially since both Jesus and his opponents were well versed in the scriptures, or were remembered in a way that was influenced by scripture without having been created by it. It seems unlikely, for example, that Christians would have ascribed to the crucified Jesus the words of Ps 22:1 ("My God, my God, why have you forsaken me?") if he had not spoken them, or at least expressed despair in some way. Crossan's dichotomy between "history remembered" and "prophecy historicized," therefore, is a false one; at certain points in the passion narrative, rather, we are probably dealing with "history scripturized" (see Goodacre, "Prophecy").

Anti-Judaism? This conclusion has important implications for the most troubling aspect of the passion narrative: its portrait of Jewish culpability in Jesus' death. Because of the role this portrait has played in fanning hatred of Jews, the subject is rightly a sensitive one. Exegetes such as Crossan (*Who Killed*) and W. Stegemann ("Beteiligung") have argued that the Gospel portrait of Jewish culpability is an invention of primitive Christian anti-Judaism, an ancient lie that leads ultimately to the Holocaust. According to these scholars, it was the Roman governor Pontius Pilate and his henchmen, not the Jewish authorities, who were solely responsible for Jesus' death. They point out that the oldest pagan witness to Jesus, the second-century Roman writer Tacitus, does not mention a Jewish role in his execution, only a Roman one (*Annals* 15.44.2–3). Moreover, at least two of the later Gospels, Matthew and John, show a clear tendency to increase Jewish culpability in an unhistorical and tendentious manner (e.g., Matt 27:24–25 and John 19:12–16), and this raises the suspicion that the Markan portrait of a Jewish role may also be the result of polemic rather than historical memory. Christians may have had a political motive for heightening the Jewish role and lessening the Roman one in Jesus' execution, namely, to demonstrate that they and their founder were friends of the Roman order, unlike the frequently seditious Jews.

Despite these arguments, however, the conclusion that Jewish personages and groups played no role in bringing about Jesus' death is doubtful (see Schwemer, "Antijudaismus"). Tacitus need not mention Jewish involvement in Jesus' death, because his purpose is to show what scoundrels Christians have been in Roman eyes—not Jewish ones—from the beginning. The basic Gospel presentation of Jewish initiation and Roman execution of the plot against Jesus is congruent with the Jewish historian Josephus' famous testimony about him (*Ant.* 18.64), which probably is *not* a total Christian interpolation (see Meier, *Marginal Jew*, 57–69; Van Voorst, *Jesus*, 81–104; against Olson, "Eusebius"). Second- and third-century Christian writings, moreover, quote Jews who say that their forefathers were right to put Jesus to death (Justin, *Dialogue* 108; Origen, *Against Celsus* 2.4, 9), and rabbinic traditions forthrightly portray Jewish involvement in his execution (see, e.g., *b. Sanh.* 43a). And the potential motivation for later Christians to overemphasize Jewish culpability needs to be balanced against a potential reason to downplay it, since it reflected poorly on the Christians' supposed Messiah that the religious leaders of his own people had rejected him (see, e.g., Origen, *Against Celsus* 1.52, 61; 2.4–5, 39, 78). The Markan portrayal of a Jewish role in Jesus' death, therefore, cannot simply be written off as anti-Jewish polemic.

All of this is not to deny that, at various points in the passion narrative, Mark or his predecessors may have dramatized and sharpened the portrait of Jewish culpability. It is uncertain, for example, how much reliable information the early Christians had about what went on at Jesus' hearing before the high priest and other Jewish authorities, though the closed nature of such proceedings does not preclude that news about it leaked out. Some of the Markan narrative, such as the combination of the three most important Christological titles in Mark (14:61–62), reads like a dramatization of basic Christian convictions rather than a historical account (cf. Schwemer, "Antijudaismus," 14), and it is likely that early Christian storytellers similarly colored the story with their own convictions about the perfidy of anyone who would oppose Jesus (see, e.g., the Sanhedrin's conduct in 14:55, 59) and with their own experiences with Jewish courts (cf. the parallel between the conclusion of Jesus' trial in Mark 14:61–65 and the conclusion of Stephen's trial in Acts 7:55–58). While it is probable, moreover, that some members of the Jewish hierarchy pressed Pilate to put Jesus to death (Mark 15:1, 3, 11), and while a revolutionary ringleader may have been released at about the same time that Jesus was condemned, the Markan description of the Barabbas incident presupposes an implausible Roman custom for which no external evidence exists (15:6–8). This account may partly betray a theological interest, to depict the human perversity that valued a murderer's life above that of God's Son, and it may partly reflect the later Markan situation, in which some Christians have suffered from the violence of revolutionaries who, in their own day, have usurped the leadership of the Jewish community (see the COMMENT on 12:6–9).

Whatever the precise cause, the Markan passion narrative does evince bitterness toward the Jews involved in Jesus' death—a generalization that is even truer of the more extreme depictions of Jewish culpability in Matthew and John. But in the case of Mark, at least, the bitterness is directed primarily against the Jewish leaders rather than the people as a whole (cf. Schwemer, "Antijudaismus," 12, 22). Throughout the Gospel, the leaders' negative reaction to Jesus is contrasted with the people's positive one, an opposition that becomes explicit in 12:12, where the leaders refrain from arresting Jesus for fear of the crowd, and in 14:1–2, where they plot to take him into custody secretly, lest there be a disturbance among the people. It is only at the very end that they succeed in manipulating the crowd into colluding in their plot to put Jesus to death (15:11–13; cf. the NOTE on "crowd" in 14:43).

While we cannot completely absolve Mark from the charge of anti-Judaism, then, we should note that it is a restricted sort of negativity, and that much of it and of NT anti-Judaism generally flows out of conflicts in which Jesus and his earliest followers suffered persecution from their own people. It is vital to keep this situation in mind in asking how this NT polemic should be interpreted in our own radically different context—a context in which, for the past seventeen hundred years, it has generally been Christians persecuting Jews rather than the other way around.

Eschatology. Besides OT prophecy and the evangelist's own situation, one other factor has pervasively influenced the Markan retelling of the narrative about Jesus' suffering and death: the conviction, already noted in the COMMENT on 13:33–37, that the events of his passion and resurrection were the decisive act in an eschatological drama that would soon be completed by his glorious return. These three factors, indeed, go together. The horrific experiences of Mark's time, including the Jewish War against the Romans, the consequent civil war within Israel, and the associated persecution of Christians, have helped convince the evangelist that he is dwelling in the last days. And because he believes himself and his community to be living in the dawning eschaton, he also believes his era to be the one in which the promises and threats encoded long ago in the scriptures are coming true.

THE PLOT AGAINST AND ANOINTING OF JESUS (14:1–11)

14 ¹And the Passover and the Feast of Unleavened Bread was to come after two days, and the chief priests and the scribes were seeking how they might stealthily seize and kill him. ²For they were saying, "Not during the feast, lest there be a disturbance among the people."

³And while he was in Bethany in the house of Simon, the man with scale-disease, as he was reclining there, a woman came, having an alabaster jar of perfume of pure, precious nard; and breaking the alabaster jar, she poured the perfume over his head. ⁴But there were some who were expressing their indignation to each other: "Why has this waste of perfume occurred? ⁵For this perfume could have been sold for more than three hundred denarii and given to the poor!" And they were outraged at her. ⁶But Jesus said, "Leave her alone! Why are you bothering her? She's done a good deed to me. ⁷For the poor you always have with you, and whenever you want to you can do them good; but me you won't always have. ⁸She has done what she could; she has come beforehand to anoint my body for burial. ⁹Amen, I say to you, wherever the good news is proclaimed in all the world, what she has done will also be spoken of, as a memorial for her."

¹⁰And Judas Iscariot, one of the Twelve, went away to the chief priests in order to turn him over to them. ¹¹And when they heard, they were glad, and they promised to give him money. And he was seeking how he might find the right time to turn him over.

NOTES

14 1. *the Passover.* Gk *to pascha*. This is a transliteration of the Aramaic term for "Passover," *pishā'* or *pashā'* (BDAG 784; cf. Sokoloff, *Palestinian Aramaic*, 439). It appears in the LXX as the regular rendering for the Hebrew *pesaḥ* = "Passover" (Exod 12:11, 21, 27, etc.), which suggests that the Aramaic term had already established itself throughout the Jewish world by the time the LXX was translated (cf. Jeremias, "*Pascha*," 896–97). It likewise became a technical term in early Christianity and is not glossed in its Matthean usages (Matt 26:2, 17, 18, 19) or other NT passages (Acts 12:4; 1 Cor 5:7; Heb 11:28; though cf. the explanations in Luke 22:1; John 6:4; Josephus, *Ant.* 3.249). The word has a range of meanings: (*a*) the Passover celebration on the night of the fifteenth of Nisan, in which a lamb was festively eaten and the exodus from Egypt recalled (most OT passages;

perhaps also Mark 14:16); (*b*) the Passover lamb itself (e.g., Exod 12:21 LXX; Josephus, *Ant.* 3.248; Mark 14:12; 1 Cor 5:7); (*c*) the seven-day holiday that began on the night of the feast (the usual NT meaning); and (*d*) in Christian circles, Easter (e.g., Hippolytus, *Refutation of All Heresies* 8.5). Christian adoption of the term, and the association of Jesus with the Passover lamb, was aided by the closeness of *pascha* to the Greek word *paschein* = "to suffer" (see, e.g., Tertullian, *Answer to the Jews* 10; Irenaeus, *Against Heresies* 4.10.1).

and the Feast of Unleavened Bread. Gk *kai to azyma*, lit. "and the unleavened things"; cf. the parallel in 1 Esd 1:19: "They celebrated the Passover and the Feast of Unleavened Bread for seven days." Originally the Passover, a one-night feast, and the seven-day holiday of unleavened bread (*maṣṣôt*) were two separate spring festivals, but they merged already in OT times (see de Vaux, *Ancient Israel*, 2.484–93), and the whole holiday was often simply called "Passover" (see the previous NOTE); the perceived redundancy of the Markan text may explain why Bezae and some other manuscripts omit "and the Feast of Unleavened Bread." The *kai* may be epexegetical, explaining the Aramaic term *pascha* ("the Passover, i.e., the Feast of Unleavened Things"); in favor of this interpretation is the parallel in Luke 22:1 ("the Feast of Unleavened Bread that is called Passover," my trans.). Or Mark may be treating "Passover" and "unleavened things" as two separate aspects of the same holiday, in line with their separate origin; cf. Josephus, *Ant.* 3.249: "The Passover is followed up by the Feast of Unleavened Bread, lasting seven days" (LCL trans. alt.).

was to come after two days. Gk *ēn . . . meta duo hēmeras*, lit. "was after two days." Here *ēn* ("was") has to mean something like *ēmellen* ("was about to be"; cf. Swete, 300), an unusual usage that is altered in Matt 26:2 and Luke 22:1. Mark's "after two days" may owe more to a desire to create a "holy week" and an OT allusion than to historical memory; at a comparable point in his narrative, John has "six days before the Passover" (John 12:1), which is more plausible (see the introduction to the COMMENT). The only instance of "after two days" in the LXX is the eschatological prophecy in Hos 6:2, which was an important scriptural testimony in early Christianity and is relevant to the larger Markan context, since it speaks of resurrection on the third day (see Dodd, *According*, 76–77).

the chief priests. Gk *hoi archiereis.* On the identity of this group, see the APPENDIX "The Jewish Leaders in Mark."

stealthily . . . kill. Gk *en dolǭ . . . apokteinōsin.* Biblically literate readers might recognize an allusion to the Psalms here; in Ps 10:7–8 [9:28–29 LXX] a reference to the *dolos* ("stealth") of the enemy is immediately followed by a description of his intention to kill (*apokteinai*) his innocent victim.

2. *Not during the feast.* Gk *mē en tę̄ heortę̄.* The Jewish leaders' intention is thwarted, since Jesus, according to Mark and the other Synoptics, was executed on the first day of Passover (cf. 14:12). The leaders' words here, however, may be evidence for a pre-Markan tradition in which Jesus died on the day *before* Passover, as in John 19:14, 31, 42 (see the NOTES on "coming in from the country" in 15:21 and "since it was the Preparation Day [that is, the day before the Sabbath]" in 15:42; cf. Dibelius, 181; Theissen and Merz, *Jesus*, 426–27). Mark himself, how-

ever, may wish to imply that the Jewish authorities intended to arrest Jesus out-side the Passover season, but that events—and the will of God—forced their hand (cf. Schenke, *Studien*, 49).

Jeremias (*Eucharistic Words*, 71–73) deals with the discrepancy differently, by interpreting *mē en tę heortę* as "not in the presence of the festal crowd." He cites John 2:23; 7:11; Ps 74:4 [73:4 LXX]; 118:27 [117:27 LXX]; and Plotinus, *Ennead* 6.6.12 as other passages in which *heortē* means "festal crowd" rather than "the time of the feast" (cf. Luke 22:6) and argues that this interpretation makes the most sense of the *gar* ("for") clause in 14:2. Of the passages Jeremias cites, how-ever, only the one from Plotinus is unambiguous, since it puts *heortēn* in parallel with *ochlon*, *straton*, and *plēthos* ("crowd," "army," and "multitude"). Two Johan-nine passages Jeremias does *not* mention, in contrast, plainly ascribe a temporal meaning to *en tę heortę* (John 4:45; 12:20), as do several LXX usages (Deut 16:16; 31:10; 2 Chron 5:3; 8:13 [*en tę heortę tōn azymōn*]; Tob 2:1); and the rest of the LXX instances seem to interpret *heortē* as "feast" rather than "festal crowd." Lacking the sort of contextual clues that point in the Plotinus passage to an unusual usage, one would assume that the Markan passage is about the leaders' desire to arrest Jesus outside *the time of* Passover, and this is indeed the way the Latin and Syriac translators render it. As Theissen (*Gospels*, 167 n. 3) points out, moreover, the larger context in Mark supports this reading, since 14:11 speaks of Judas seeking to turn Jesus over to the authorities at "the right time" (*eukairōs*).

3. *Bethany*. Gk *Bēthanią*. On this village on the outskirts of Jerusalem, see the NOTE on "Bethany" in 11:1.

the house of Simon, the man with scale-disease. Gk *en tę oikią Simōnos tou lep-rou*. This man is otherwise unidentified, and the name was a very common one (see the NOTE on "Simon . . . Peter" in 3:16). He is called a *lepros*, but this term is not identical with what modern people call leprosy (see the NOTE on "a man with scale-disease" in 1:40). It was, however, considered to be ritually defiling, so Jesus' residence at his house is of a piece with his association with tax collectors and sinners (see the NOTES on "tax collectors" and "and sinners" in 2:15).

reclining. Gk *katakeimenou*. This probably means reclining on a banqueting couch for a meal (see the NOTE on "reclining at table" in 2:15 and cf. John 12:2: "gave a dinner for him"). In OT times, by way of contrast, people usually dined in a sitting position, even if they were prominent or royal (see Gen 37:25; Judg 19:6; 1 Sam 20:5, 25, etc.); reclining on a banqueting couch is viewed in Amos 6:4–7 as a sign of culpable luxury (cf. Dentzer, "Origines," 226–27). Under Greek influ-ence, however, reclining to eat became common in Palestine (cf. Jdt 12:15; *t. Ber.* 4:8), and it is ubiquitous in the Gospel references to meals (see Mark 2:15; 14:18; Matt 8:11//Luke 13:29; Matt 23:6//Luke 14:7–8; etc.; cf. *NewDocs*, 1.9). With the exception of the outdoor scene in Mark 6:39, however, the Gospel references pre-sume that the meal under discussion is a special feast and/or taking place in a rich person's home; common people did not have the space or the money for banquet-ing couches and usually ate sitting on the floor (see Bokser, *Origins*, 130 n. 48; Hirschfeld, *Dwelling*, 274–75; Leyerle, "Meal Customs," 30–31). The household in our story, then, is presumably well-to-do.

a woman. Gk *gynē.* John (12:1–3) specifies her as Mary, the sister of Lazarus, and the incident seems to take place in her house; a few verses later he speci- fies that the objector to her extravagant act is Judas (see the NOTE on "some" in 14:4). In both cases the Johannine specification may reflect a later narrator's desire to give anonymous characters a concrete identity rather than solid histori- cal information (on this narrative process, see Dibelius, 114; Bultmann, 67–68; Metzger, "Names"). This thesis is supported by the observation that in John 11:2 the author's labeling of the anointing woman as Mary seems to be a novel identi- fication that he does not expect his readers to know.

perfume of pure, precious nard. Gk *myrou nardou pistikēs polytelous.* The first three Greek words also appear in John 12:3, a rare example of Johannine termi- nological agreement with the Synoptics. This agreement is especially striking because *pistikēs* ("pure") is a rare and puzzling word, which elsewhere means "faithful." Scholars have suggested various emendations, such as *Pisidikēs* ("of Pisidia"), *spikatēs* ("of spikenard"), or *pistakēs* ("of pistachio"); the last may be the way the word is taken already by syrˢ, which transliterates rather than translating it (see Bennett, "St. John xii. 3"; Nestle, "Narde"; Jannaris, "NARDOS PISTIKĒ"; Van Rompay, "Griekse Woorden," 178–79). The agreement of John with Mark does not necessarily mean that John is dependent on Mark, since Mark's word for "precious," *polytelēs,* is more common than John's word *polytimos* and hence may have displaced the latter; in this particular, then, the Johannine version seems to be more primitive than the Markan one, and both may be relying on common oral tradition.

Despite the similarity in sound, *myron* is not related to myrrh, which comes from the Hebrew *mōr* and refers to the resinous gum of a particular plant, but to the Greek root *myr,* which means "to anoint." *Myron,* then, is a general term for perfume (see LSJ 1155; Michaelis, "*Myron,*" 800 n. 2; against RSV, NRSV, and NIV, which translate *myron* in Rev 18:13 as "myrrh"). Greek speakers wishing to refer to myrrh in particular would have used a different word, *smyrna* (see Matt 2:11; John 19:39; cf. *esmyrnismenon oinon,* "myrrhed wine," in Mark 15:23).

As Dayagi-Mendeles (*Perfumes,* 96) points out, most ancient perfumes were oil based, unlike modern perfumes, which are alcohol based; and the fattier the base, the more stable the perfume. They were, therefore, thicker than modern perfumes, and this may be part of the reason that *myron* is usually translated "oint- ment" in modern English. But a more important reason may be that translators are uncomfortable with the idea of a heavily perfumed Jesus!

breaking the alabaster jar. Gk *syntripsasa tēn alabastron.* An *alabastron* was a jar with a long, narrow neck, usually made out of alabaster, and frequently used for holding perfumes (see the beautiful photos in Dayagi-Mendeles, *Perfumes,* 95, 99). Commentators generally assume that the breaking of the jar's neck was a common practice, but no archaeological or literary evidence supports this thesis; rather, the neck of the *alabastron* was usually stoppered with a piece of cloth, parchment, or papyrus, the removal of which would allow the valuable and potent perfume to flow out in a thin stream or drop by drop (see Veldhuizen, "Flesch" and Dayagi-Mendeles, *Perfumes,* 101, 105, 106). The woman's breakage of the jar allows the perfume to flow out in a greater quantity than usual (see "poured" in 14:3 and "Why . . . this waste of perfume?" in 14:4). It also perhaps indicates that she does not wish to reuse for another purpose a jar whose contents have been devoted to Jesus (cf. Gundry, 813).

4. *some.* Gk *tines.* Matthew 26:8 and some manuscripts of Mark (D, W, Θ, 565, *f*¹³, it) make the objectors into disciples, and John 12:4 specifies that the complainer was Judas, whereas Luke 7:39, in a story related to ours, makes him an anonymous Pharisee (there is a similar movement toward specification of protagonists in the retellings of 14:3 and of the story of Jesus' arrest; see the NOTES on "a woman" in 14:3 and "of those who were present" in 14:47). It is probable that our tale originally intended to speak about anonymous objectors, but Mark, like Matthew and John, may understand them as disciples, since from 12:43 until his arrest in 14:46 Jesus is constantly with the latter group. This interpretation accords with the general Markan emphasis on apostolic misunderstanding.

who were expressing their indignation to each other. Gk *aganaktountes pros heautous.* It is debatable whether the onlookers express their indignation orally and publicly or internally and privately; the phrase could also be rendered "who were indignant within themselves," and in favor of this translation is the fact that it appears here in conjunction with a verb that generally indicates an internal state. Elsewhere in Mark, however, *pros heautous* always means "one another" or "among themselves" (1:27; 9:10; 10:26; 11:31; 12:7), and if the onlookers' reaction were purely internal, Jesus' response, "Leave her alone! Why are you bothering her?" would be a bit strange, since their reaction would be invisible to the woman. It is worrisome that the reaction of these onlookers, who are probably meant to be understood as disciples (see the previous NOTE), is so close to that of the scribes in 2:6.

waste. Gk *apōleia.* Although this is a word for "waste" or "loss" from Aristotle on, it is much more commonly employed in the NT for death and eschatological destruction (Matt 7:13; John 17:12; Acts 8:20; Rom 9:22; etc.; see BDAG 127), and the cognate verb *apollymi* is used in Mark 3:6; 11:18 for the Jewish leaders' plot against Jesus' life. Already in 14:4, then, the narrator foreshadows the linkage made in 14:8 between the "waste" of the perfume and the loss of Jesus' life.

5. *three hundred denarii.* Gk *dēnariōn triakosiōn.* According to Matt 20:2, a denarius was a typical wage for a Palestinian agricultural worker for a day's work, and this seems to be the case for Egypt as well (see N. Lewis, *Life,* 208); the perfume in our story, therefore, is worth about a year's wages. Pliny (*Natural History* 12.43) lists the price of the most expensive nard as only one hundred denarii to the Roman pound (= about three-quarters of a modern pound), but he describes an unguent of cinnamon that can fetch up to three hundred (13.15).

6. *a good deed.* Gk *kalon ergon.* This phrase is not employed in the LXX but is frequently encountered, in both singular and plural, in pagan literature (e.g., Plato, *Symposium* 178d; Xenophon, *Memorabilia* 2.1.31; Plutarch, *Life of Alexander* 5.7), Jewish pseudepigrapha (e.g., *Let. Aris.* 18; *T. Naph.* 8:5; *3 Bar.* 15:2), the NT (Matt 5:16; John 10:32; 1 Tim 5:25), and rabbinic traditions (*ma'asîm*

tôbîm; cf. Strack-Billerbeck, 4.1.536–37). On burial as a good deed, see Tob 1:16–17, where Tobit's acts of charity (*eleēmosynas*) include the burial of strangers; *b. Soṭ.* 14a, where God's interment of Moses in Deut 34:6 is a model for "deeds of lovingkindness"; and the discussion of the *mēt miṣwāh* = "good deed of burial of the dead" in *b. Meg.* 3b (cf. Daube, *New Testament*, 315; Fitzmyer, *Tobit*, 118). Jesus' prophecy of a lasting memorial for a woman who has performed a good deed is somewhat reminiscent of Prov 31:10–31, where the "woman of valor" stretches out her hand to the needy (31:20), and her deeds "praise her in the gates" (31:31).

to me. Gk *en emoi*, lit. "in me." This idiom probably reflects Hebrew/Aramaic *bĕ*, which can mean either "in" or "to" (for the latter nuance in combination with the verbs *'sh* and *'bd* [= "to do" or "to make"] see Esth 9:5; Neh 9:24; Jer 18:23 [cf. LXX]; Dan 11:7 [cf. Theodotion]; *Tg. Gen.* 31:43 [Genizah]; cf. Black, 301; Brockelmann, 504).

8. *She has done what she could.* Gk *ho eschen epoiēsen*, lit. "what she had, she has done." In 12:42–44 another anonymous woman donor throws all she has (*panta hosa eichen*) into the Temple treasury; see the COMMENT on 14:3–9.

she has come beforehand. Gk *proelaben*, lit. "she has taken before." In classical Greek *prolambanein* can mean "to be beforehand with, anticipate," and is occasionally used as an auxiliary verb (see LSJ 1488), but the idiom also corresponds to the Hebrew/Aramaic *qdm* ("to do beforehand"), which is frequently used as an auxiliary (see, e.g., syr[s] of our passage and Jonah 4:2; cf. Lagrange, 369; Koehler-Baumgartner 2.1069 [4]; Sokoloff, *Babylonian Aramaic*, 985). It is possible, then, that *proelaben myrisai* is a Semitism (cf. Taylor, 533).

to anoint. Gk *myrisai*. Lamarche (312–13) suggests that the woman's anointing of Jesus points to his status as the Anointed One (Hebrew *māšîaḥ* = "Messiah" / Greek *Christos* = "Christ"; cf. the APPENDIX "The Meaning of Christ = Messiah"), citing the juxtaposition with the worldwide proclamation of the good news (14:9), which Lamarche interprets as the announcement of an enthronement (see the COMMENT on 1:1). Davies and Allison (3.445), similarly, point to OT passages in which oil is poured over the head of a person in order to indicate his consecration to kingship (1 Sam 10:1; 2 Kgs 9:3, 6); we may also note 1 Kgs 10:2, 10, where spices are among the gifts that the Queen of Sheba brings to King Solomon in Jerusalem. It is problematic for the messianic interpretation, however, that *myrisai* rather than *chrisai* is used for the act of anointing.

9. *Amen, I say to you,* etc. Gk *amēn de legō hymin*, etc. The accolade in this verse is probably redactional (see the introduction to the COMMENT); "Amen, I say to you . . ." sometimes introduces redactional insertions by the evangelist (e.g., 9:1; 10:15; 11:23), and the "Amen" saying is missing in the Johannine version of our story. This omission supports the thesis of Johannine independence of Mark; as Brown (1.453) points out, "If John were dependent on Mark, the omission of this praise would be hard to understand, since 11:2 presumes that Mary was well known precisely because she anointed Jesus."

as a memorial for her. Gk *eis mnēmosynon autēs*. On the idea of being remembered for a good deed, see Neh 13:14, 22. *Eis mnēmosynon autēs*, however, probably has a more specific nuance, since it is close to the formula *eis mneian/mnēmēn* + genitive ("as a memorial for X"), which is frequently found in funerary contexts such as gravestone inscriptions and descriptions of memorial meals (e.g., 4 Macc 17:8; cf. BDAG 654–55; Bernard, *Paneion*, 146). The feminine counterpart of our word *mnēmosynon* is present on an ancient Bulgarian headstone erected by a husband for his wife and called *mnēmosynēs stēlē* ("stone of memorial"; see Mihailov, *Inscriptiones* 2.814). In *Gos. Pet.* 12:54, moreover, the women approaching Jesus' tomb on Easter morning decide to leave the burial paraphernalia at the entrance of the tomb *eis mnēmosynēn autou* ("as a memorial for him")—a near-duplicate of our formula. See also the Hebrew grave inscription in Tarent, Italy: *nzkr ṣdyq lbrkh* ("the righteous one is remembered for a blessing"; *CIJ* 629b; cf. Jeremias, "Mc 14,9," 105–6). Our phrase, therefore, reproduces funerary terminology, which is transposed into an eschatological key in *1 En.* 99:3, where the prayers of the righteous and the sins of the wicked become a memorial (*eis mnēmosynon*) before God at the judgment.

Another possible nuance of *mnēmosynon* is liturgical, since the term is used in Lev 2:2, 9, 16 for a memorial sacrifice, that is, a cereal offering made with the intent that God should remain mindful of the sacrificer. This concept is employed figuratively in Acts 10:4: "Your prayers and your alms have ascended as a memorial [offering] (*eis mnēmosynon*) before God" (see further liturgical usages in Sir 45:9, 11, 16; 50:16; cf. *EDNT* 436).

10. *one of the Twelve.* Gk *ho heis tōn dōdeka*, lit. "the one of the Twelve." This is a Markan and a NT *hapax* (see the GLOSSARY); later in the chapter (14:20, 43) *heis tōn dōdeka* ("one of the Twelve") occurs twice without the definite article *ho* ("the"). The presence of the definite article in our passage makes the expression awkward, but *ho heis* is sometimes attested in the papyri (cf. Taylor, 534), where it seems to mean either "one of the previously referred-to group" (BGU 2.614; 4.1124; *P.Tebt.* 1.138) or "the only one of the group" (*P.Lond.* 7.2007). The latter nuance makes more sense in the present context (cf. Swete, 307: "that one, the only one, of the Twelve who proved a traitor or was capable of the act").

went away. Gk *apēlthen.* An obvious verb to use, but in the present context also probably one with connotations of apostasy (cf. John 6:66).

COMMENT

Introduction. The passion narrative begins with an effective example of Markan sandwich structure that counterposes the lethal machinations of Jesus' enemies with his clear-eyed prophecy of his own death.

Although this sandwich structure is probably, as usual, the work of the evangelist himself, that does not mean that every part of the sandwich is a Markan invention. Verse 14:2b, for example ("Not during the feast"), seems odd, since, according to Mark Jesus *did* die during the Passover holiday, and the leaders' intention to arrest him before the holiday is implausible, since they are giving themselves only a day or so to apprehend him (contrast John 11:45–53, where the plot is hatched long before Passover). Verse 14:2b, therefore, may be a remnant from a pre-Markan tradition, a view that is strengthened by its consonance with the Johannine dating of Jesus' death, which in this case may be accurate (see the NOTES on "was to come after two days" in 14:1 and "Not during the feast" in 14:2; cf. Myllykoski, *Letzten Tage*, 1.182). Aside from 14:2b, however, the "sandwich" in 14:1–2, 10–11 is probably a Markan composition, as is shown by its plethora of Markan terms and the notable parallel between 14:1b and 14:11b (see the end of the COMMENT).

Brown (1.449–54) provides a helpful chart of the Markan, Johannine, and Lukan versions of the intercalated story of the woman who anoints Jesus (the Matthean version is an abbreviated form of the Markan one), which is reproduced in figure 43. He concludes that these passages go back to two independent traditions, one about a repentant woman who weeps at Jesus' feet, as in Luke, and the other about a woman who anoints Jesus' head with expensive perfume, as in Mark. Certain Markan differences from the Johannine story look like secondary embellishments, such as the note that the perfume is worth *more than* three hundred denarii (14:5; contrast John 12:5) and the prophecy that the woman's deed will be proclaimed throughout the world (14:9, a redactional verse that is replete with Markan vocabulary; cf. also the NOTE on "Amen, I say to you, etc." in 14:9). It is also probable that Mark has reversed the order of the "poor always with you" and "anoint for burial" statements, so that the latter may lead into a triumphant ending on a note of worldwide proclamation.

The passage falls naturally into three parts: the short description of the Jewish leaders' plot (14:1–2), the long tale of the woman anointing Jesus (14:3–9), and the short description of the agreement between Judas and the Jewish leaders (14:10–11). The story about the woman further subdivides into her action (14:3), the onlookers' objection (14:4–5), and Jesus' response (14:6–9). The length of the last subsection is indicative of the weight of emphasis.

14:1–2: the religious leaders' plot. Jesus has just finished warning his inner circle of disciples that they must remain spiritually awake, since they do not know the moment of the Son of Man's glorious advent (13:33–37). This is primarily a prophecy of Jesus' postresurrectional return in the clouds (cf. 13:26–27), but as noted in the COMMENT on 13:33–37, the Markan Jesus is also calling readers to pay attention to the coming section of the Gospel, which will portray his death and resurrection as eschatological events. This interpretation is supported by the immediately following words, which solemnly inaugurate the Markan passion narrative: "And the Passover and the Feast of Unleavened Bread was to come after two days" (14:1a). This linkage is significant because Passover is called a night of vigil (lit. "night of watching") in Exod 12:42, because some Jews expected the final redemption to occur during the Passover holiday, and because "after two days" recalls Hos 6:1–2, which is a prophecy of eschatological succor from the Lord (see the NOTES on "Keep awake!" in 13:37 and "was to come after two days" in 14:1). Through a web of allusions, then, Mark implies that the moment of apocalyptic crisis, the eschatological "night of watching," is nearing as the plot against Jesus begins to take shape.

Figure 43: The Gospel Accounts of the Anointing of Jesus
(adapted from R. E. Brown, *The Gospel According to John*, 1.450)

Mark 14:3–9	*John 12:1–8*	*Luke 7:36–38*
2 days before Passover	6 days before Passover	during the ministry
Bethany	Bethany	Galilean setting
house of Simon, the man with scale-disease	not specified	house of Simon, the Pharisee
unnamed woman	Mary of Bethany	sinner woman
with alabaster jar	with a pound	with alabaster jar
perfume of pure, precious nard (*myrou nardou pistikēs polytelous*)	perfume of pure, expensive nard (*myrou nardou pistikēs polytimou*)	perfume (*myrou*)
		weeps on feet
		dries them with hair
pours perfume on head	anoints feet	anoints feet
	dries them with hair	
some (disciples) angry	Judas angry	Jesus criticizes Simon (7:44–46)
value: more than 300 denarii	value: 300 denarii	
Jesus defends woman	Jesus defends Mary	Jesus forgives woman (7:48–50)
"Leave her alone"	"Leave her alone"	
"Poor always with you, but me not always"	"Keep perfume for burial"	
"Has anointed me for burial"	"Poor always with you, but me not always"	
"Will be proclaimed in all the world"		

Blind to the end-time drama that is unfolding through them, however, and catalyzed by the approach of Passover, the chief priests and the scribes swing into action, determined to do away with Jesus before the festival arrives, lest they risk a popular revolt (14:1b–2). This is a reasonable fear, since during the Passover season the population of the .75–square-mile city of Jerusalem swelled several times to perhaps half a million, producing a volatile situation that was aggravated by the tantalizing memory of liberation from Egyptian bondage at Passover and the belief that the eschatological redemption would be accomplished at the same season (see Sanders, *Judaism*, 126–28). Not surprisingly, therefore, the Jewish historian Josephus mentions several popular disturbances and uprisings during this season in Jerusalem, and specifically in the priestly power base, the Temple (*Ant.* 20.105–12; cf. *War* 2.10–13; *Ant.* 17.213–18; 18.29–30). Such disturbances would have threatened the position of the chief priests and the scribes, who were also priests (see the APPENDIX "The Scribes and the Pharisees" in vol. 1, pp. 523–24), not only because of the possibility of a direct assault on the Temple (cf. 11:15–19) but also because the Romans held the Jewish elite responsible for maintaining public order, and any breach in that order was likely to be taken out on them (cf. John 11:47–48 and Sanders, *Judaism*, 321–22). The priestly anxiety over the consequences of "a disturbance among the people," therefore, is understandable.

14:3–9: the woman's anointing of Jesus. From the specter of a commotion in the public sphere, the scene shifts to the intimacy of the private one: Jesus is in Bethany, on the outskirts of Jerusalem (see the NOTE on "Bethany" in 11:1), in the house of Simon, a man with scale-disease (see the NOTE on "the house of Simon, the man with scale-disease" in 14:3). The mention of this disease, in proximity to the reference to the religious authorities, is perhaps meant to recall 1:40–44, where Jesus "cleanses" a scale-diseased man and sends him to the local priest to confirm the healing, thus suggesting that the authorities' subsequent hostility to Jesus is not his fault. But the presence of a man with this same illness in a scene that foreshadows Jesus' death would also perhaps remind readers that some disorders, such as Simon's form of the disease and the deadly hostility of the chief priests and the scribes, are too deep-seated to be dismissed with a single healing touch.

But other influences are at work as well, including the extravagant generosity of an anonymous woman, apparently an outsider to Simon's family (see the NOTE on "a woman" in 14:3), who comes into the room where Jesus is reclining at table, breaks a bottle of precious, perfumed ointment, and anoints Jesus' head with it (14:3b). This action is unsettling on several fronts. First of all, the very presence of am unattached female character may raise eyebrows, and the act of anointing Jesus with expensive perfume increases the hint of scandal, since in ancient documents perfume, anointing, and a recumbent posture are usually associated with luxury and sex (see the NOTE on "reclining" in 14:3 and cf. Corley, *Private Women*, 104). To be sure, the woman in our story does not lie down with Jesus, anoints his head rather than his lower extremities (contrast Luke 7:38), and does not, like the woman in Luke 7:36–50, earn the sobriquet "sinner"; sexuality, therefore, remains only an undercurrent here.

Rather, the explicit objection to the woman's action by the bystanders, who are probably meant to be understood as disciples (see the NOTE on "some" in 14:4), is that she has wasted a lot of expensive perfume (14:4), whose sale could have raised for the poor more than three hundred denarii (approximately a year's wages; see the NOTE on "three hundred denarii" in 14:5). Emotive phrases surround this objection ("expressing their indignation . . . they were outraged"), and the indignant response creates a parallel with that of Jesus' sworn enemies in 14:1–2: both are more concerned about a commotion during a feast than they are about the well-being of Jesus (for another parallel, see the NOTE on "who were expressing their indignation to each other" in 14:4). The mention of three hundred denarii, more-over, echoes the reference to two hundred denarii in the sarcastic question in 6:37, and both passages show the disciples to be overly concerned with finances, despite Jesus' teaching elsewhere (10:17–27). But the parallel with chapter 6 may also work to the disciples' advantage, for there Jesus' directive ("Give them something to eat yourselves") and the subsequent feeding hint at a continuing presence that will transcend the boundaries of death and empower his followers to feed a hungering world. Here, similarly, his response points to the post-Easter victory march of the gospel ("wherever the good news is proclaimed in all the world"; 14:9) and to the disciples' continuing role as instruments of his compassion (see "whenever you want to you can do them good" in 14:7 and cf. Henderson, *Christology*).

Jesus' response to the disciples' emotional objection ("they were outraged") starts out on the emotional level as well: "Leave her alone! Why are you bothering her?" (14:6a). He then gives his reasons for defending the woman, beginning with the assertion that, far from neglecting her duty to perform charitable works, she has performed a good deed by anointing him (14:6b; see the NOTE on "to me" in 14:6). As he will reveal presently (14:8), this is because her anointing of his body with costly perfume prepares it for burial and thus fits into a classic Jewish pattern of charitable deeds (see the NOTE on "a good deed" in 14:6).

Granted, however, that both the donation of money to the poor and the anoint-ing of Jesus are charitable acts, why does the latter take precedence over the for-mer? Jesus answers this implicit question by hinting at his coming death: assistance to the poor will remain possible in the coming days, but the time for service to the earthly Jesus is rapidly drawing to a close (14:7). The first part of Jesus' statement here echoes Deut 15:11: "For the poor will never cease out of the land" (RSV)—a verse that goes on to commend openhandedness to the poor. Jesus is not, then, devaluing service to the poor but assuming that it will remain a continuing duty in the coming period. He is also, however, pointing toward a more pressing cir-cumstance in the immediate future: his own approaching death.

The latter is referred to allusively ("but me you won't always have," 14:7b), then more explicitly ("she has come beforehand to anoint my body for burial," 14:8b; cf. the similar progression in John 16:16–28). In between, Jesus says that the woman has done what she could (14:8a), a statement that is reminiscent of his praise of another anonymous female donor in 12:44 (see the NOTE on "She has done what she could" in 14:8). Right before chapter 13, then, Jesus praises an anonymous woman who "[gave what] she had" to the Temple; right after it he praises an anonymous woman who "[did] what she could" (lit. "had") by anoint-ing his body for burial. These two examples of humble, self-giving female service form a stark contrast to the greedy and destructive actions of the men in each context (12:38–40; 14:1–2, 10–11; for another example of juxtaposed anonymous women who are positive role models, see the COMMENT on 5:25–34).

The perfume the woman pours on Jesus, then, is a prelude, not to sexual intercourse, but to burial—the other major usage for perfume in ancient times (see Connolly, "Frankincense," 130, and cf. the NOTE on "bought spices in order that they might come and anoint him" in 16:1). Since rabbinic discussions suggest that the duty of burial overrides other obligations (see, e.g., *b. Ber.* 14b; *b. Meg.* 3b), including perhaps almsgiving (see *b. Suk.* 49b and cf. *t. Pe'ah* 4:19; Jeremias, "Salbungsgeschichte"), the halakic relevance of Jesus' defense of the woman's action is clear: the three hundred denarii are better spent on Jesus than on the poor, since the importance of burial supersedes that of almsgiving.

But the Markan Jesus does not end the pericope on this bittersweet note, as happens in John; instead, he appends a saying that prophesies the triumphant proclamation of the good news throughout the world and completes the vindication of the woman by alluding to the role that her action will play in the kerygma (14:9; for "kerygma," see the GLOSSARY). Already the introduction of this saying, "Amen, I say to you" (14:9a), reasserts the authority of Jesus in the teeth of the death he has just prophesied (on the "Amen" sayings, see the NOTE on "Amen" in 3:28 and the COMMENT on 3:28–30). And the prophecy that follows of the worldwide proclamation of the good news suggests that Jesus' death will not be the end, or the news would not be good. The woman's action, therefore, is the prelude not only to the last sad episode of the old age but also to the first triumphant chapter of the new one.

This subsection concludes, then, by transposing Jesus' praise of the generous, anonymous woman into another key: not only has she done a good deed for him, but it will be mentioned wherever the gospel is proclaimed, "as a memorial for her." The Markan Jesus is here probably employing a standard formula found on gravestones and in other memorial contexts (see the NOTE on "as a memorial for her"). This formula fits into the general context, in which Jesus has been talking about his own death and burial; in an unexpected twist, however, he now speaks of a memorial not for himself but for the woman who has just anointed him. This twist points to the surprising reversal implicit in the conclusion of the subsection: the burial of Jesus will not be an end but a beginning. He will not require a memorial, because he will not remain dead, and the power that his resurrection will unleash in the cosmos will transform the deeds of those who serve him into episodes in the worldwide triumph of the good news. Although the primary nuance here is a reference to the post-Easter period and the Markan community's preservation of the memory of the anonymous woman's deed, Jeremias ("Mc 14,9") is probably right to discern also a nuance of eschatological remembrance before God: what she has done will be mentioned at the Last Judgment, and God will remember her for good (see the NOTE on "as a memorial for her" in 14:9). This interpretation is supported by the implicit contrast between the woman and Judas Iscariot, who is conspicuously named in the next verse. Whereas she gives freely of her substance to do Jesus good, he takes money to betray him; whereas she will be remembered for good at the Last Judgment, it would be better for him if he had never been born (cf. 14:21).

14:10–11: Judas' compact with the chief priests. Mark completes his literary sandwich by reintroducing Judas (last mentioned in 3:19) into the narrative. Judas' agreement to turn Jesus over to the chief priests (14:10) enables them to fulfill the murderous intent they expressed in 14:1–2. His "going away" to join these enemies of Jesus probably has an implication of apostasy (cf. John 6:66). Verse 14:11a mentions their promise to give Judas money for his treachery, but it is unclear in the Markan narrative whether finances are his main motivation (as in John 12:6) or merely a side effect of a betrayal pursued for some other purpose. Perhaps Mark deliberately leaves Judas' motivation in the shadows; it is part of "the mystery of iniquity" (cf. 2 Thess 2:7) and ultimately reflects the unfathomable will of God (see 14:21a). This interpretation is supported by the seemingly deliberate parallel between 14:1 and 14:11b:

14:1	*14:11b*
and the chief priests and the scribes were seeking (*ezētoun*)	and he [Judas] was seeking (*ezētei*)
how him (*pōs auton*)	how him (*pōs auton*)
stealthily (*en dolǭ*)	opportunely (*eukairōs*)
they might seize and kill (*kratēsantes apokteinōsin*)	he might turn over (*paradoi*)

This parallelism emphasizes the terrifying extent of Judas' corruption, which is so complete that his will has blended with that of Jesus' enemies; but it also suggests that there is another, superhuman purpose at work shaping events for its own ends. The alert reader will recall that Jesus himself has prophesied three times that he will be turned over to the hands of his enemies but that this treachery, which fulfills a divine plan, will end in his resurrection (8:31; 9:31; 10:33–34). When, therefore, readers hear of Judas seeking "the right time" to turn Jesus over (14:11b), they may well reflect on the overlap and tension between "the right time" from the point of view of Jesus' opponents (cf. 14:2) and from the point of view of God.

At the beginning of the next passage, Mark's readers will receive another hint about which of these viewpoints will ultimately win out: despite the desires of the chief priests and scribes ("not during the feast," 14:2), Jesus is turned over "on the first day of . . . Unleavened Bread" (14:12).

THE PREPARATION FOR THE PASSOVER MEAL (14:12–16)

14 ¹²And on the first day of the Feast of Unleavened Bread, when they sacrificed the Passover, his disciples said to him, "Where do you want us to go out and prepare, so that you may eat the Passover?" ¹³And he sent out two of his disciples and said to them, "Go into the city, and a man will meet you carrying a ceramic water jar. Follow him, ¹⁴and wherever he goes in, say to the master of the house,

'The teacher says, "Where is my lodging, where I may eat the Passover with my disciples?"' ¹⁵And he will show you a large upper room, furnished and prepared; and there prepare for us." ¹⁶And the disciples went out and went into the city and found it just as he had told them, and they prepared the Passover.

NOTES

14 12. *on the first day of the Feast of Unleavened Bread.* Gk *tę̄ prṓtę̄ hēmerą tōn azymōn.* In the larger Greco-Roman world, the day was considered to begin either at midnight or, more frequently, at sunrise (see Pliny, *Natural History* 2.79.188). Jews, however, usually reckoned that the day started at sundown, and Mark shows awareness of this method of computation in 1:32; 4:27; and 15:42 (see the NOTES on "When evening had come, etc." in 1:32 and "sleep and rise night and day" in 4:27). In this Jewish system the slaughter of the Passover lambs did not occur on the first day of the Passover holiday (Nisan 15), as Mark says here, but on its eve (see Philo, *Special Laws* 2.149; *m. Pes.* 5:1), sometime in the afternoon of Nisan 14 (see the next NOTE). By the Greco-Roman sunrise-to-sunrise method of reckoning, however, this afternoon slaughter of the lambs occurred on the same day as the evening Passover meal (or "seder"). Some scholars, therefore, have used the phrase "on the first day of the Feast of Unleavened Bread, when they sacrificed the Passover" as an argument against the evangelist's Jewishness (e.g., Bultmann, 264: "quite impossible in Jewish usage"; cf. the INTRODUCTION in vol. 1, p. 20). But Jews sometimes employed the sunrise-to-sunrise delimitation of days (see Bacchiocchi, *Time*, 65–89), and there are ancient examples of them doing so precisely in relation to Passover (see Philo, *Special Laws* 2.149; Josephus, *Ant.* 3.248; *m. Pes.* 5:1). Mark's inconsistency about when day begins, then, is not un-Jewish; both the OT and the writings of the Jewish historian Josephus show similar discrepancies (compare Josephus, *Ant.* 3.248 with *War* 4.582; for OT passages, see the INTRODUCTION in vol. 1, p. 20).

    when they sacrificed the Passover. Gk *hote to pascha ethyon.* The Passover lambs (or goats) were sacrificed in the Temple on the eve of the holiday from noon or midafternoon until sundown (see *Jub.* 49:10; Josephus, *War* 6.423; Philo, *Questions and Answers on Exodus* 1.11; *Special Laws* 2.145; *m. Pes.* 5:1, 3; cf. Brown, *Death*, 1.847). Casey (*Aramaic Sources*, 222–23) envisages a situation in which Jesus, in the Temple, is slaughtering a lamb on behalf of himself and his disciples and simultaneously answering their question about where to prepare it. But what sense would it make for Jesus, standing in the Temple in the center of Jerusalem, to tell his disciples to "go into the city" (cf. ibid., 227)? The plural, then, is probably impersonal ("when people sacrificed"), and the imperfect recognizes that the slaughter of so many animals took several hours (imperfect of continuous action), though it might also refer to the yearly slaughter of the Passover lambs and goats as a thing of the past (imperfect of repeated action), in which case it would be compatible with a Markan dating after the destruction of the Temple in 70 C.E. (cf. the INTRODUCTION in vol. 1, pp. 37–39).

    13. *Go into the city.* Gk *hypagete eis tēn polin.* It is presumed that the setting

of this instruction is Bethany, on the outskirts of Jerusalem (see the NOTE on "Bethany" in 11:1); Jesus is giving the disciples guidance in finding a place to eat in the city itself, since the Passover lamb had to be consumed within its precincts. Although Passover began as a domestic ritual, in which the animal was slaughtered and consumed at home (Exod 12:1–13), the Josianic reform in the seventh century B.C.E. transformed it into a pilgrimage festival and the Passover lamb into a sacrifice that had to be slaughtered and eaten in "the place that the LORD your God will choose as a dwelling for his name," that is, the Temple (Deut 16:5–7; cf. Bokser, *Origins*, 17). This restriction is reasserted in *Jub.* 49:15–21 and 11QTemple 17:8–9, although rabbinic traditions widen the eating area to include all of Jerusalem (see *m. Pes.* 7:12; *Sipre Num.* 69:3; cf. Jeremias, *Eucharistic Words*, 42–43). Jews outside Jerusalem presumably celebrated Passover as well, and Philo (*Special Laws* 2.145, 148; *Questions on Exodus* 1.10) implies that this celebration included the slaughter and consumption of lambs (cf. Josephus, *Ant.* 2.312; Sanders, *Judaism*, 133–34; Martola, "Eating"; against Tabory, *Passover Ritual*, 78–92). A pilgrim whose lamb was slaughtered in the Temple, however, would have been obligated to eat it within the city limits, since anything else would have violated the concept of pilgrimage.

a man . . . carrying a ceramic water jar. Gk *anthrōpos . . . keramion hydatos bastazōn.* It is regularly asserted in scholarly literature (e.g., Evans, 374) that this would be an unusual sight, and hence perhaps a prearranged signal, since women usually carried water in earthenware jugs, while men carried it in skins. This suggestion goes back to Lagrange (373), who lived in Jerusalem at the turn of the twentieth century, and it is based on nothing more than his observation of Palestinian habits in his own day ("if one can judge from modern custom"). It is true that in the OT carrying water is sometimes described as women's work (Gen 24:11–21, Exod 2:16; 1 Sam 9:11), but there are also OT passages that speak of men carrying water (e.g., Deut 29:10–11; Josh 9:21–27). Greco-Roman artists regularly depict male slaves carrying jugs of wine (e.g., Rostovtzeff, *History*, 288: Plate XLVI, #1) or of water (e.g., the many portrayals of Aquarius, the juvenile Water Carrier), and there is no reason to think that Jewish custom was different; Jeremias (*Jerusalem*, 8) suggests that the man in our story is either a domestic servant or a water seller. The theory that the disciples follow the man because they see him engaged in an unusual activity is also belied by the circumstance that it is *he* who approaches *them* ("a man will meet you"; on the initiative implied by *apantan*, see LSJ 178[I]: "move from a place to meet a person").

14. *Where is my lodging.* Gk *pou estin to katalyma mou.* The papyri contain several examples of an official requesting or demanding a *katalyma* when he comes on state business; see, for example, *PSI* 4.341.8 and *P.Cair.Zen* 2.59254.3. "My lodging" thus implies Jesus' authority (see the COMMENT on this passage), but it may also fulfill 10:29–30: like those he commends, Jesus has abandoned his home for the sake of the dominion of God, but he has gained the homes of others.

15. *upper room.* Gk *anagaion.* Israelite houses often had a second floor reached by an exterior stone staircase or an interior wooden ladder; this floor frequently served as the main living area of the family (see King and Stager, *Life*, 28–35). In

Hellenistic and Roman times, storerooms and water installation often occupied the ground floor of a house, so that, similarly, the living areas and banqueting rooms (*triclinia*) were often on an upper floor reached by an interior or exterior staircase (see Hirschfeld, *Dwelling*, index under "Upper-story, Upper-room").

furnished and prepared . . . there prepare. Gk *estrōmenon hetoimon . . . ekei hetoimasate.* If the room is already prepared (*hetoimon*), why do the disciples need to prepare there (*hetoimasate*)? Taylor (538) responds: "To some extent preparations have already been made . . . and the two disciples are to complete them." Perhaps the room is already prepared but the meal is not. It is also possible, however, that the juxtaposition betrays Markan editing (see the introduction to the COMMENT).

COMMENT

Introduction. After the triptych of 14:1–11, in which a scene featuring Jesus and his disciples is framed by two scenes featuring his enemies, the focus shifts for the last time in the Gospel to Jesus' fellowship with his followers. It will remain there for thirty-one verses (14:12–16, 17–21, 22–25, 26–31, 32–42)—as though the evangelist were lingering over the disciples' last moments with their Teacher. The first part of this valedictory section describes the disciples' preparations for what will turn out to be Jesus' last supper (14:12–16).

This scene is framed by two instances of the combination "disciples . . . prepare[d] . . . the Passover" (14:12, 16; cf. Davies and Allison, 3.458), a repetition emphasizing that things are unfolding as Jesus predicted, as is explicitly stated in 14:16 ("and found it just as he had told them"). In between come detailed instructions about finding a site for the seder (14:13–15), which imply movement to a progressively more interior place: into the city (14:13), into the house (14:14), and into the upper room (14:15). The atmosphere of mystery this movement imparts is heightened by the appearance of two enigmatic, anonymous characters, the man carrying a water jar (14:13) and the master of the house (14:14). The inward movement is matched syntactically by the depth of quotation in 14:13–15: Mark is quoting Jesus telling his disciples what they are to say, which includes a direct quotation of Jesus.

This scene is strikingly parallel to that of the finding of the colt in 11:1–6 (see the introduction to the COMMENT on 11:1–11 and figure 35); indeed, as Hooker (332) points out, eleven consecutive words in 11:1–2 and 14:13 are identical. This similarity, along with the lack of a Johannine counterpart and the implication of Jesus' omniscience, suggests to some that both stories are fictional (see, e.g., Bultmann, 261–64; Nineham, 295, 376). This judgment, however, is not a necessary one; in both cases there may have been prearrangement between Jesus and some confederates in Jerusalem (see below).

It is difficult to identify Markan redaction in the passage. The tension between "furnished and prepared" in 14:15b and "there prepare" in 14:15c may suggest a redactionally expanded tradition, though the tension is not an outright contradiction; different aspects of the preparation could be in view (see the NOTE on "furnished and prepared . . . there prepare" in 14:15). The case for redaction, however, is strengthened by the observation that "with my disciples" in 14:14, "there prepare" in 14:15, and "and they prepared the Passover" in 14:16 reflect the typical Markan theme of the disciples' involvement in Jesus' ministry (see Henderson, *Christology*). Markan expansion of a pre-Markan tradition, then, is probably responsible for the ambiguity about whether or not the room is already prepared.

The passage is composed of three unequal parts: the disciples' question (14:12), Jesus' response (14:13–15), and the disciples' fulfillment of his directive (14:16). The first and third sections are extremely short. The important thing is Jesus' carefully detailed instructions; it almost goes without saying that these will be heeded and Jesus' prophecies fulfilled (cf. Lohmeyer, 298).

14:12–16: the preparation for the seder. In the space of eleven verses the story has rushed through two days (cf. 14:1–2), but Mark now applies the narrative brakes, taking 108 verses to describe the next twenty-four hours, which will be the setting for Jesus' last supper, arrest, trials, crucifixion, death, and burial (14:12–15:47). We have arrived at the heart of the Markan Gospel.

This crucial section begins with the scene of preparation for the Last Supper, which is strikingly parallel to the scene of preparation for Jesus' triumphal entry into Jerusalem (11:1–6). Both stress the supernatural omniscience and sovereignty of Jesus. As Lohmeyer (300) points out, it is not accidental that these premiere demonstrations of clairvoyance appear precisely in relation to the events of Holy Week. It was those events that most seriously called Jesus' sovereignty into question; if he was God's all-knowing Messiah, how did he end up nailed to a Roman cross? Mark's answer is that a divine necessity stood behind this apparent outrage (cf. 8:31; 9:12, 31; 10:33–34); the plot of Judas and the Jewish leaders against Jesus (14:10–11) succeeded only because God had planned things that way from the beginning (cf. 14:21, which interweaves Judas' accountability and divine providence). The parallel with 11:1–6 also underlines the Markan point that although Jesus is the Davidic Messiah, as the triumphal entry has already demonstrated (see 11:9–10), he will manifest this messiahship precisely through his suffering death, to which his words at the Last Supper allude (14:21–25). Suffering and regal authority thus coincide in the person of Christ.

The disciples ask Jesus where he wants them to prepare "so that you may eat the Passover" (14:12b). Their present abode, in the Jerusalem suburb of Bethany (14:3), is not an option, since pilgrims were required to eat the meal in the city itself (see the NOTE on "Go into the city" in 14:13). The use of the second person singular ("so that *you* may eat"), when the first person plural might be expected ("so that *we* may eat"), emphasizes Jesus' centrality and the disciples' reverence for him: it is crucial that *he* should consume the festal meal. Presumably they will eat as well, but they modestly refrain from mentioning this.

In a further demonstration of this sovereignty, Jesus now sends two of the disciples ahead to prepare the way for him (cf. 1:3)—a recapitulation of the occurrence at the beginning of the triumphal entry scene (11:2). Jesus' present instructions, however, have greater weight than his earlier ones, since he sends them into the capital rather than one of its suburbs. In the city, Jesus tells them, they will be approached by a man carrying a ceramic water jar (see the NOTE on "a man . . . carrying a ceramic water jar" in 14:13). They are to follow him through the streets, enter the house he enters, and greet its master with the report that "the teacher" says, "Where is my lodging, where I may eat the Passover with my disciples?" (14:13c–14). This query augments the emphasis on the sovereignty of Jesus and forms a notable parallel with 11:2–6, where Jesus impresses an apparent stranger's donkey into his service; here, similarly, he appropriates a man's house for his own use ("*my* lodging"; cf. the NOTE on "Where is my lodging" in 14:14). This implication of sovereignty is underlined by the use of the first person singular ("where *I* may eat") as well as by the title "teacher," since from the beginning of the Gospel the evangelist has associated this and cognate terms with Jesus' unparalleled authority (see 1:21–22, 27; 4:38–39; 6:2–3; 11:18; cf. Lohmeyer, 299; Ambrozic, "New Teaching").

Despite this emphasis on Jesus' sovereignty, however, his words to the homeowner, as well as his final instructions to the disciples, also imply his identification with his followers, since he speaks of eating the Passover "with my disciples" and tells the latter to "prepare for *us*" (14:14b–15). In the progression of our passage, therefore, we move from the disciples' subordination of themselves to Jesus ("that *you* may eat the Passover") to Jesus' association of himself with them. This progression makes sense in the Markan context, since, earlier in the Gospel, Jesus announced that those who humbled themselves would be exalted (9:35).

Jesus' instructions conclude with the prophecy that the homeowner will, in response to the disciples' question, show them an upper room furnished for the paschal meal (14:15ab). Here they are to finish their preparations, perhaps by setting out the essential elements of lamb, unleavened bread, and bitter herbs (cf. *m. Pes.* 10:5 and the NOTE on "furnished and prepared . . . there prepare" in 14:15). The passage terminates with the evangelist's observation that the two disciples went out and did as Jesus had asked, finding everything just as he had told them (14:16).

This whole chain of events could be interpreted in a non-supernatural manner, as reflecting prearrangement between Jesus and the owner of the room (cf. the COMMENT on 11:1–6). Jesus was a wanted man, and it may have been necessary for him to communicate clandestinely with an accomplice in Jerusalem in order to make a Passover seder there possible. Both Jesus' vague designation of himself as "the teacher" and his question about the whereabouts of "my lodging" might be codes designed to signal a confederate but to mystify untrustworthy servants. As Taylor (537–38) notes, had there been no prior communication, it is hard to see why the householder would have reacted in the way described.

This reading, however, misses the point, as far as Mark is concerned. The Markan story emphasizes that Jesus' clairvoyance extended to the whole series of events leading up to his last supper and hence to the shattering occurrences that ensued from it. The Markan community, whose members were being turned over to suffering and death (cf. 13:9–13), was doubtless in particular need of assurance that such a fate was compatible with divine leading. The theme of providence might by reinforced for some readers by the parallel with 1 Sam 10:1–5, in which the anointing of Saul to be king over Israel (cf. Mark 14:1–9) is followed by a confirmatory sign having to do with people he will meet, including one who carries a wineskin (cf. Evans, 374). The point of the Markan narrative, like that of 1 Samuel, is that God is with this anointed king (cf. 1 Sam 10:7). In Mark this theme is epitomized by the climactic words of the pericope, "the disciples . . . found it just as he had told them" (14:16a).

The evangelist, however, does not record any amazement on the disciples' part; by this point in the narrative they, and the reader, have grown accustomed to miracles occurring when Jesus is around. There is something beautiful about the story's economy here; instead of exclaiming about Jesus' extraordinary second sight, his faithful disciples simply get down to work and prepare his meal for him (14:16b). There is no time for superfluous exclamations; the moment of crisis is approaching, and Mark probably means the disciples' simple, faithful response to be a paradigm for the Christians in his community.

But this is the last such praiseworthy response to Jesus by members of his inner circle; from here on out their path will run sharply downhill. The very next passage, indeed, will focus on Jesus' prophecy that one of them will betray him.

JESUS PROPHESIES HIS BETRAYAL (14:17–21)

14 [17]And when it was evening, he came with the Twelve. [18]And as they were reclining and eating, Jesus said, "Amen, I say to you, one of you will turn me over, the one eating with me." [19]They began to grieve and to say to him one after the other, "It's not me, is it?" [20]But he said to them, "One of the Twelve, the one dipping with me in the one bowl. [21]For the Son of Man is going away, as it has been written concerning him, but alas for that man through whom the Son of Man is being turned over. It would have been better for that man if he had never been born."

NOTES

14 18. *reclining.* Gk *anakeimenōn.* On the custom of reclining at meals, see the NOTE on "reclining" in 14:3. In the present case, the reclining is associated with the Passover setting (cf. 14:12). Despite Exod 12:11, which stipulates that the Passover sacrifice should be eaten in haste and readiness to depart, later Jews stretched the Passover meal, or seder, into a banquet in which the exodus from Egypt was recounted in a leisurely manner and participants reclined as a sign of their status as free people (see *m. Pes.* 10:1–9; cf. Jeremias, *Eucharistic Words,* 48–49).

will turn me over. Gk *paradōsei me.* The same verb is used in the passive voice in 14:21 and thus brackets the discussion. The LXX often employs it for God's delivery of people to death, an action that is either acclaimed, if they are Israel's enemies (as frequently in the Deuteronomic history and 2 Chronicles), or bemoaned, if they are Israel or the speaker (as frequently in Jeremiah, Ezekiel, and the psalms of the Righteous Sufferer). Since the continuation of the verse contains an allusion to Psalm 41, which is one of the Righteous Sufferer psalms (see the next NOTE), it is particularly relevant that these psalms, including Psalm 41, use active and passive voices of *paradidonai* to speak of God delivering the speaker to his enemies (Pss 27:12 [26:12 LXX]; 41:2 [40:3 LXX]; 74:19 [73:19 LXX]; etc.). Similarly, Isa 53:6 LXX uses the active voice of *paradidonai* to speak of the Lord giving up his Suffering Servant to death, and 53:12 expresses the same thought through two usages of the passive voice of the verb. Although the subject in our verse is a human being rather than God, God as well as Judas may be in view in 14:21 (see the NOTE on "through whom the Son of Man . . . is being turned over" in 14:21).

the one eating with me. Gk *ho esthiōn met' emou.* Translations usually omit the definite article or adopt other expedients to mitigate the awkwardness of this belated phrase, but the awkwardness may be a sign that Ps 41:9 [40:10 LXX] is being echoed: "For even my close friend (lit. "the man of my peace"), in whom I trusted, the one eating my bread (*ho esthiōn artous mou*), has lifted up his heel against me" (my trans.; cf. John 13:18). Psalm 41:9 is also quoted in 1QH 5:23–24, which, like the Gospels, refers it to a person within the elect community. The Qumran text goes on to imply that, as in our passage, this act of eschatological treachery reflects both divine providence and human malice (see the previous NOTE; cf. Marcus, *Way,* 172–73, 178).

19. *one after the other.* Gk *heis kata heis.* This unusual locution, which recurs in John 8:9, is probably "the result of a mixture of the Semitic idiom in which the cardinal is repeated [cf. *dyo dyo* = 'two by two' in Mark 6:7], and the Hellenistic pronominal expression *katheis/kata heis,* 'one by one, each one' " (Maloney, *Semitic Interference,* 154).

It's not me, is it? Gk *mēti egō.* The *mē* indicates that the question expects a negative answer (see BDAG 3a). Eusebius (*Demonstration of the Gospel* 10.3) thinks that the speakers included Judas, who thus displayed the guile prophesied in Ps 109:2.

20. *the one dipping with me in the one bowl.* Gk *ho embaptomenos met' emou eis to hen tryblion.* Most manuscripts have simply "in the bowl" (*eis to tryblion*), but "in the one bowl" (*eis to hen tryblion*), which may be a Semitism (see Casey, *Aramaic Sources,* 250), has the support of B, C*, θ, 565, and one Georgian manuscript—a fairly diverse sampling, which includes some weighty manuscripts. Greeven and Güting (659), however, prefer the shorter text, arguing that the longer one is an attempt to add color to the story, and citing other exegetes who think that it reflects contamination from Matthew's *en tō trybliǭ* ("in the bowl"; *en* = "in" and *hen* = "one" are spelled identically, while Mark uses a different word for "in," namely, *eis*). Also favoring the shorter text, David Adams suggests that the longer rendition could be a scribal assimilation to the repeated use of "one" in 14:18–20 ("one of you will turn me over . . . one after the other . . . one of the Twelve").

None of these arguments, however, is compelling. Scribes are more likely to remove colorful expressions than to add them, especially if, like this one, they are awkward. Contamination from Matthew would probably result in replacement of *eis* with *en*, not an amalgamation of the two words. As for the point about the other instances of "one" in the passage, this could just as well be an argument for its original usage here as a reason for attributing its presence to a later scribe, and its elision may be explained by a scribal feeling that the passage is overloaded with instances of "one," especially after the previous phrase, "one of the Twelve" (cf. Gundry, 837).

Dipping food in sauces and relishes was a common feature of Greco-Roman meals (see Leyerle, "Meal Customs," 34–35) and became a fixed part of the Passover seder: "On all the [other] nights we dip once, this night twice" (*m. Pes.* 10:4). In first-century seders the important thing was probably not *what* was dipped but the number of dippings, since repeated dippings epitomized the leisurely dining characteristic of free people (cf. Elias, *Haggadah*, 63, and the NOTE on "reclining" in 14:18).

Partly on the basis of John 13:26, some exegetes (e.g., Jerome, *Commentary on Matthew* 26:23, 25; Swete, 313) have suggested that "the one dipping with me in the one bowl" is meant to single out Judas, that is, that he was the one dipping his food at that moment. In the following chart, however (adapted from Lane, 502), the left-hand phrases appear to be synonymous, and therefore the right-hand ones probably are as well:

| 14:18 | one of you | the one eating with me |
| 14:20 | one of the Twelve | the one dipping with me in the one bowl |

Neither "the one eating with me" nor "the one dipping with me in the one bowl" singles out a particular person; both are probably examples of the Semitic use of the article with indefinite nouns (see the subject index in vol. 1 under "Definite article, with indefinite noun or adjective"). If Jesus was openly identifying Judas as his future betrayer, one would expect a reaction from the other members of the Twelve.

21. *going away.* Gk *hypagei*. Death as a journey to the other world is a very old metaphor. Hauck and Schulz ("*Poreuomai*," 567–69) give examples from the ancient Near Eastern and Greek literature, although in the latter the term is usually *poreuesthai* rather than *hypagein*, and this pattern continues in the LXX (e.g., 1 Kgs 2:2; Job 10:21; 16:22; Eccl 9:10; 12:5; cf. *T. Reuben* 1:3). The metaphorical use of "going" for death is also attested in non-Greek Jewish texts such as *Jub* 36:1; *4 Ezra* 8:5; *2 Apoc. Bar.* 14:11; 21:9; 48:15. The metaphor appears in conjunction with the phrase "son of man" in a rabbinic saying that speaks of dying and being resurrected: "Not as a son of man goes away ('*zl*) does he come back" (*y. Ketub.* 12:3 [35a; Neusner, 22.345]//*y. Kel.* 9:3 [32b; Neusner, 4.271]; *Gen. Rab.* 100.2; cf. Casey, *Aramaic Sources*, 233–36). John 14:28, similarly, speaks about Jesus going away (dying) and returning (coming back in the form of the Spirit; cf. John 7:33; 8:21–22; 13:3, 33, 36; etc.). See also the Pauline metaphor of "leaving home" (*ekdēmein*; 2 Cor 5:6, 8, 9), which is close to the use of *apodēmein* as a metaphor for death in Plato, *Apology* 40E–41A.

but alas for that man . . . It would have been better for that man if he had never been born. Gk *ouai de tǭ anthrōpǭ ekeinǭ . . . kalon autǭ ei ouk egenēthē ho anthrōpos ekeinos*, lit. "It would have been good for him if had not been born that man." Aside from its awkwardness, this sort of literal translation might misleadingly imply to readers of English that "him" and "that man" were two different people. On the Semitic use of the absolute for the comparative, see the NOTE on "better" in 9:42. Despite the skepticism of Maloney (*Semitic Synax*, 121–26), Jeremias (*Eucharistic Words*, 183–84) is probably right that the pleonastic (see the GLOSSARY) usages of *ekeinos* here are also Semitisms (cf. Casey, *Aramaic Sources*, 243). The delay of the subject until the end ("if had not been born that man") is another Semitic characteristic (see Black, *Aramaic Approach*, 50–51; Maloney, *Semitic Interference*, 51–53).

through whom the Son of Man is being turned over. Gk *di' hou ho huios tou anthrōpou paradidotai*. This is usually translated "*by* whom the Son of Man is being turned over," but the more literal rendering adopted here reflects an important theological point: Jesus is delivered to the authorities through the treachery of Judas, but God is ultimately responsible for his death (see "as it has been written" in the previous clause). Origen (*Commentary on Matthew* 83), however, sees the use of "through" rather than "by" as implying that *Satan* is the catalyst for Judas' betrayal of Jesus, and this implication is in line with passages from other Gospels (Luke 22:3; John 6:70–71; 13:2, 27) and the heavy emphasis on Satan elsewhere in the Markan narrative (see the subject index in vols. 1 and 2 under "Satan" and cf. 1QS 3:15–26, which links God, the "Angel of Darkness," and the "children of deceit" in the production of human wickedness).

COMMENT

Introduction. After the narrative describing the supernaturally guided preparations for Jesus' Last Supper with his disciples (14:12–16), the supper itself unfolds in two subsections, the present one in which Jesus predicts his betrayal, and 14:22–25, in which he proleptically enacts his death on behalf of "many" through broken bread and shared cup. Thus, the whole narrative of the supper is dominated by the theme of Jesus' "going away" (cf. 14:21).

Although the scene of Jesus predicting his betrayal was probably part of the pre-Markan passion narrative (cf. John 13:21–30), it has undergone substantial Markan editing. The introductory verse (14:17) is full of redactional vocabulary, and in the next verse (14:18) the genitive absolutes "as they were reclining and eating" and the belated phrase "the one eating with me" may be Markan. The next three verses (14:19–21) also contain typically redactional elements ("began to" + infinitive, "one of the Twelve," *meta* + genitive for "with me," and "as it has been written"). At the same time, the allusions to Ps 41:2, 9 are paralleled in John 13:18, 21 (see the NOTE on "the one eating with me" in 14:18), and the passage is full of Semitisms, which may reflect pre-Markan tradition (see the NOTES on "one after the other" in 14:19, "the one dipping with me in the one bowl" in 14:20, and "but alas for that man. . . . It would have been better for that man if he had never been born" in 14:21). Perhaps the pre-Markan story consisted of Jesus' psalm-influenced prophecy of betrayal, his disciples' worried reaction, and his woe about the betrayer.

The passage is dominated by repeated terms: "the Twelve," "Son of Man," "man," and especially "turn over" (*paradidonai*). It falls into three parts: first prophecy of betrayal + disciples' reaction (14:17–19); second prophecy of betrayal (14:20); and prophecy of death + woe on betrayer (14:21). The first and third parts are bipartite and have almost exactly the same number of words, while the second contains half as many. But the first two parts are also structurally parallel to each other (see the NOTE on "the one dipping with me in the one bowl" in 14:20). The third has an internal structure that alternates "Son of Man" with "man" (cf. Davies and Allison, 3.462):

> the *Son of Man* is going away . . .
>> alas for *that man*
> through whom *the Son of Man* is being turned over
>> better for *that man* if he had never been born

14:17–21: prophecy of betrayal. The story of the Last Supper begins with the arrival of Jesus and the Twelve at the upper room (see the NOTE on "upper room" in 14:15) "when it was evening" (14:17). This is a typical Markan time designation (cf. 1:32; 4:35; 6:47; 15:42), but here it takes on additional significance, since the evening hour means that the Passover holiday is beginning (see the NOTE on "on the first day of the Feast of Unleavened Bread" in 14:12). The arrival of night may have not only a chronological significance but a symbolic one as well (cf. "And it was night" in John 13:30): the cosmic darkness of the time of eschatological trial is looming, as will immediately become clear through Jesus' prophecy of betrayal (cf. the COMMENT on 16:1–4 on the symbolic resonance of the dawn setting of the empty tomb narrative). As the earliest commentary on Mark puts it: "The evening of the day points to the evening of the world" (Pseudo-Jerome, *Exposition of Mark* 14:17 [Cahill, 104]).

Another seemingly prosaic detail with special significance immediately follows: upon arrival, Jesus and the Twelve assume a reclining posture and begin to eat (14:18a). The reclining posture has a special importance here because in the paschal setting it is a ritual duty to recline, as befits a free person (see the NOTE on "reclining" in 14:18). In some Jewish circles the Messiah was expected to appear at Passover time to recapture this promise of freedom for the present (see the NOTE on "Keep awake!" in 13:37), and the following passage will extend the Passover theme by suggesting an analogy between Jesus and Moses, the great liberator at the first Passover (see the NOTE on "This is my blood of the covenant" in 14:24 and the COMMENT on 14:23–24). Unlike Moses, however, Jesus will shed his own blood—not that of sacrificial animals or Israel's enemies.

In 14:18, similarly, Mark jarringly juxtaposes an image of paschal liberty (reclining) with Jesus' solemn declaration that one of the Twelve will turn him over to death (*paradōsei*, 14:18b). The use of *paradōsei* may be ironic, since the LXX frequently employs this verb for the covenant God's delivery of his enemies into the hand of his chosen people, and 4Q246 2:1–9 individualizes this hope in terms of God's delivering them into the hands of his Son (probably the Messiah; see the NOTE on "the Son of Man is being turned over to the hands" in 14:41). To paraphrase Bultmann (*Theology*, 1.33), in Markan theology the deliverer-to-death becomes the one delivered to it.

But there is an additional scriptural source for the latter thought. For *paradidonai* is also used frequently in the psalms of the Righteous Sufferer, where the speaker complains that, despite his innocence, he has been turned over to the hands of his enemies (see the NOTE on "will turn me over" in 14:18). The Markan Jesus immediately echoes one of these psalms when he specifies his betrayer as "the one eating with me," an apparent allusion to Ps 41:9 [40:10 LXX] (see the NOTE on "the one eating with me" in 14:18). It is perhaps relevant that this psalm, like several other Righteous Sufferer psalms, is headed *eis to telos* = "for the end" in the LXX. It could easily be taken, therefore, as a reference to death or an eschatological prophecy—as indeed happens at Qumran (see 1QH 5:23–24 and cf. Marcus, *Way*, 177–78). Jesus' betrayal, correspondingly, is for Mark the beginning of a climactic apocalyptic drama that will end with Jesus' death and resurrection.

Jesus' prophecy of this eschatological act of betrayal, however, does not specify a precise agent, only that the perpetrator will be one of those sharing his meal. In response, therefore, each of the disciples begins to ask whether he will turn out to be the culprit (14:19). The Greek word that Mark uses to introduce their question, *mēti*, suggests that each considers himself an unlikely candidate—or at least wants the others to think so (see the NOTE on "Not me, is it?" in 14:19).

In response to the disciples' inquiry about the identity of the betrayer, Jesus reiterates his prophecy, this time speaking of the culprit as "the one dipping with me in the one bowl" (14:20). This description is not really any more specific than the earlier one but merely another reference to the Passover setting shared by Jesus and his disciples; the dipping of the participants' food, like their reclining posture, was a standard part of the Passover service. It functioned as a sign of the luxury that was withheld from slaves but conferred on free people and thus was one of the privileges that accrued to covenant members (see the NOTE on "the one dipping with me in the one bowl" in 14:20). This association makes all the more terrible the culinary dipping of the man who is about to betray the Messiah and the new covenant he will inaugurate; his perfidy is highlighted by his intimacy with Jesus, which is graphically illustrated by their shared bowl (cf. Ruth 2:14). A similar and even more searing example of this abuse of intimacy will soon emerge in the "Judas kiss" incident (14:45; cf. Clement of Alexandria, *Pedagogue* 2.8, who links the two passages).

Having twice prophesied his betrayal, Jesus concludes by sketching its consequences, first, laconically, for himself, then, more expansively, for his betrayer (14:21). The result for himself will be "going away," a euphemism for death that has a long background in the history of religions (cf. the NOTE on "going away" in 14:21). The metaphor is paradoxical, since it ascribes volition to an involuntary act and motion to a state that occurs only when the subject has, to all appearances, become immobile. Since the Middle Ages, exegetes have argued that its usage here emphasizes the voluntary nature of Christ's sacrifice (see Aquinas, *Catena Aurea* on Mark 14:17–21), but this interpretation reads too much into the metaphor, which in fact is compatible with the notion of involuntary decease, as is illustrated by *4 Ezra* 8:5 (Syr): "For you entered the world involuntarily, and are leaving it (*w'zl'*) without your consent" (J. Myers trans., *I & II Esdras*; cf. *2 Apoc. Bar* 14:11; 48:15). In the Markan context, similarly, the subsequent words imply an element of divine compulsion (see Gundry, 838–39); Jesus' "going away" is willed by God, since it will happen "as it has been written" in OT passages such as those echoed in the previous verses (cf. the NOTE on "through whom the Son of Man is being turned over" in 14:21b).

These passages include allusions to Jesus' betrayal by Judas, which is therefore a fated action; despite this fatedness, however, Judas remains personally culpable, as Jesus implies in 14:21bc, where he refers to the punishment that his actions will earn for him ("alas for that man . . . It would have been better for that man if he had never been born"). The day of reckoning will be the eschatological assize, as is suggested not only by the parallel to the "it would be better" formula in Mark 9:42–47 but also by the similarity to the graphic portrayal of end-time judgment in *1 En.* 38:2. Here sinners are driven away to eternal punishment for their sins, above all the sin of having "denied the name of the Lord of spirits," and the verdict pronounced on them is that "it would be better for them if they had never been born" (Black trans. alt.; on the "it would be better" formula, see also *m. Ḥag.* 2:1). Judas' eschatological fate, then, is the one that is appropriate to apostates.

In the Markan case, however, as in the Enochic one, this judgment appears problematic because the perpetrator seems predestined to sin and therefore to destruction (see, e.g., the ascription of human sin to the influence of evil angels in *1 Enoch* 69). Medieval and modern exegetes have fought mightily against this conclusion, for example, by arguing that "as it has been written" applies only to the fact of Jesus' death, not to the manner of its accomplishment (see Theophylact, *Explanation of Matthew* 26:23–25). These efforts, however, founder in 14:18, 20, verses that echo scriptural texts and speak of betrayal; biblically literate readers, therefore, would probably think that Jesus' scripturally foretold "going away" included the betrayal that led up to it. As Calvin observes, Jesus does not free Judas from blame merely because he does what God appoints (*Harmony* on Matt 26:24), and our text is a classical expression of the mysterious interpenetration between divine sovereignty and human responsibility—a gray area that fascinated ancient Jews and Christians alike (see, e.g., Josephus, *War* 2.162–63; *Ant.* 18.13; *m. 'Abot* 3:15[16] and early commentaries on our passage; cf. Davies and Allison, 3.462 n. 54). Drury ("Luke," 437) eloquently expresses the tension implicit in our passage:

The colon [between the two halves of the verse] . . . divides the two opposing insights which together grip our minds in the face of tragedy: that fate is irresistible and that nevertheless we are culpable. And the last line, echoing Job [3:3], faces us with the morally destructive possibility of a life not worth living at all. Where is goodness in such a world?

The existential depth of this question should not be dodged, and for Mark it is not just Judas' problem, since all human beings find themselves caught in the sticky nexus between free will and determinism, as the scripturally prophesied abandonment of Jesus by the other disciples will attest (see 14:27, 49–52, 66–72). Nevertheless, to the question of where goodness is to be found, it is probable that Mark would point to Jesus himself, who, unlike the author of 1 Enoch, bewails rather than gloats over the punishment he foresees for his denier (cf. Theophylact, *Explanation of Matthew* 26:23–25). As we discovered with regard to chapter 13, therefore (see the COMMENT on 13:24–25), the Markan text mutes, though it does not eradicate, the characteristic apocalyptic note of retribution.

This Markan tendency to emphasize the positive and world-embracing aspect of Jesus' messiahship will continue in the next passage, where Jesus will speak not of killing his enemies but of dying a liberative death on behalf of "many" (14:24).

JESUS INTERPRETS THE BREAD AND WINE OF THE LAST SUPPER (14:22–25)

14 ²²And as they were eating, he took bread, blessed, broke, and gave it to them, and said, "Take, this is my body." ²³And taking a cup and giving thanks, he gave it to them, and they all drank from it. ²⁴And he said to them, "This is my blood of the covenant, which is poured out on behalf of many. ²⁵Amen, I say to you, I will never again drink from the fruit of the vine until that day when I drink it anew in the dominion of God."

NOTES

14 22. *And as they were eating.* Gk *kai esthiontōn autōn.* In Judaism, blessings are usually pronounced at the beginning and end of meals, not in the middle (see the NOTE on "said the blessing" in 6:41), and bread is usually broken at the start of a repast (see Jeremias, *Eucharistic Words,* 49). In our narrative, however, the blessing and breaking of the bread and the blessing of the wine take place well into the meal (see "as they were [. . .] eating" in 14:18 and 14:22). Jeremias (*Eucharistic Words,* 85–88) sees this odd circumstance as a sign that we are dealing with a Passover seder, in which a preliminary course without a grace (green herbs, bitter herbs, and fruit purée) precedes the liturgy and the main meal, when graces are said. We have no hard evidence about the order of events in first-century seders— Jeremias bases his view on later evidence such as the Mishnah (*m. Pes.* 10:3)—but he at least provides a possible explanation for an unusual phenomenon.

this is my body. Gk *touto estin to sōma mou.* Jesus' interpretation of the bread as his body may build on the Jewish seder custom of offering an explanation for the special foods consumed there (see *m. Pes.* 10:5 and cf. Jeremias, *Eucharistic Words,* 55–56). To be sure, not only is the evidence for first-century seders fragmentary (see the previous NOTE), but it is also debatable whether the Last Supper actually was a seder or instead occurred on Passover eve (see the introduction to the COMMENT and the NOTE on "Not during the feast" in 14:2). Mark, however, portrays it as a seder (14:12, 16), so the customs of Passover are at least relevant for exegesis of his account. On the level of the historical Jesus, even if his last meal occurred on Passover eve rather than the holiday itself, the paschal ritual probably would have been on his and his disciples' minds already, so Passover symbolism would not have been out of place at the supper, any more than turkey talk would be unexpected on the day before Thanksgiving.

Scholars who assume that the "bread word" is basically historical have argued about the Aramaic original underlying *sōma,* since there is no common term for "body" in the Aramaic of the time (see Casey, *Aramaic Sources,* 239, for some of the guesses, e.g., *gûph, pigrā',* and *gešem*). The most popular theory, however, is that Jesus originally identified the bread not with his body but with his flesh (Aramaic *biśrā'* = Hebrew *bāśār*). "Flesh" *is* a common term, both in the Bible and in later Hebrew and Aramaic, and its OT usages are frequently translated with *sōma* in the LXX (e.g., Lev 15:2, 3, 11, etc.; 1 Kgs 13:22, 24, 28, 29). Cf. also the parallel to the "bread word" in John 6:51: "The bread that I will give . . . is my *flesh*" (cf. Bonsirven, "Hoc Est"; Jeremias, *Eucharistic Words,* 198–201).

23. *a cup.* Gk *potērion.* The cup contains wine, as is clear from the term "the fruit of the vine" (14:25). It is probably red wine, as the comparison to blood in 14:24 suggests, although both red and white wines were known in ancient Palestine (see Hirsch and Eisenstein, "Wine"). Wine played an important role in Second Temple Passover rituals, though it is not mentioned in the OT Passover accounts. It does, however, appear in *Jub.* 49:6 as part of the description of the Israelites' celebration of their imminent redemption from Egyptian bondage, and this description may well reflect the use of wine in Passover celebrations at the time of the composition of *Jubilees* (second century B.C.E.). By the time of the Mishnah, three centuries later, the consumption of four cups of wine at the seder had become a religious requirement (*m. Pes.* 10:1, 2, 4, 7). *Tosefta Pes.* 10:4 gives the reason for this drinking as the necessity of being joyful on the holiday. Later traditions, such as *Gen. Rab.* 88.5, ascribe eschatological significance to these cups (see Bokser, *Origins,* index under "Wine"), and this may already have been the case in Jesus' time. (In modern seders, the two cups of wine before the meal look back to the redemption under Moses, whereas the two cups after the meal look forward to the redemption brought by the Messiah.) The term "cup" itself has an eschatological connotation in the OT, although the image is usually negative (the cup of judgment or wrath, e.g., Isa 51:17–23; Jer 25:15, 1QpHab 11:14–15; cf. Patsch, "*Potērion,*" 142, and the NOTE on "cup" in 14:36). But the OT also provides the raw material for a positive usage of the cup image (see, e.g., "cup of salvation" in Ps 116:13). See also the remarks on the eschatological symbolism of wine in the Qumran literature in the NOTE on "anew" in 14:25.

Some abstainers from alcohol maintain that Jesus was a teetotaler and that the wine he and his disciples drank at the Last Supper was what the Bible calls "new wine," which they identify with unfermented grape juice. This "two-wine theory," however, is a result of piety rather than historical evidence (for an amusing refutation, see Homan and Gstohl, "Jesus the Teetotaler"). Throughout the OT, the power of wine to make people happy, and even to intoxicate them, is assumed (e.g., Gen 9:21; Prov 31:6–7; Jer 51:7; Zech 10:7), even if it is *tîrôš*, which is sometimes translated "new wine" (see Hos 4:11; Acts 2:13; cf. Ross, "Wine," 849). This exhilarating effect is the reason that wine is frequently mentioned in connection with the eschatological banquet (e.g., Isa 25:6–10; Joel 3:18; 1QSa 2:18–22; *2 Apoc. Bar.* 29:5), an image that provides part of the background for our passage (see the COMMENT on 14:25). It is also the reason that, by the time of Jesus, wine had probably become a regular part of the Passover celebration (see the previous paragraph). It makes sense, therefore, that the wine used at the Last Supper was the normal, alcoholic sort (cf. also John 2:1–11).

they all drank from it. Gk *epion ex autou pantes.* Special emphasis is placed on the circumstance that *all* of the participants (thus including Judas) drink, and this detail entered into later discussions of the participation of unworthy communicants in the Eucharist (see, e.g., Theophylact, *Explanation of Mark* 14:22–25). In the present context, however, Judas may not be particularly in view; Mark may, rather, intend a contrast between the generality of the drinkers ("they *all* drank") and the more limited number of those for whom this drinking availed ("poured out on behalf of *many* "). As Pseudo-Jerome puts it, "The blood of the New Testament, which is shed for many, does not cleanse all" (Pseudo-Jerome, *Exposition of Mark* 14:23 [Cahill, 106]).

24. *This is my blood of the covenant.* Gk *touto estin to haima mou tēs diathēkēs.* On the association of wine with blood, see Gen 49:11 and Deut 32:14, where it is called "the blood of grapes" (cf. Isa 63:3; Sir 39:26; 50:15; Rev 14:20; J. Segal, *Hebrew Passover,* 35 n. 7). Our saying most directly recalls Exod 24:8 (see the COMMENT on 14:23–24). But the Markan Jesus may also be alluding to Zech 9:11, which itself echoes Exod 24:8 (see Meyers and Meyers, *Zechariah 9–14,* 138) and is the only OT passage to conjoin the words "blood," "my", and "covenant": "Because of the blood of my covenant with you, I will set your prisoners free" (NRSV). In Targum Jonathan this passage is understood as an allusion to the exodus events, thus linking it with the Passover context of Mark 14:24.

poured out on behalf of many. Gk *ekchynomenon hyper pollōn.* The idea of a person's death functioning as an atoning sacrifice on behalf of "many" is similar to the picture in Isa 53:11–12, though the only vocabulary linkage is the term "many." This concept of atoning death was picked up in postbiblical Judaism, partly under the impact of the martyrdoms in the Maccabean and later periods, which raised the question of why God let pious people suffer such a terrible fate; one influential answer was that their suffering atoned for the sins of the rest of the people and thus would deliver them from eschatological wrath (see 2 Macc 7:37–38; 4 Macc 6:28–29; 17:21–22; 1QS 8:3–4).

25. *I will never again drink.* Gk *ouketi ou mē piō,* lit. "no longer, I will never drink." Jeremias (*Eucharistic Words,* 207–12) argues that Jesus distributes the cup of wine but does not drink from it himself, because he has taken a Nazirite-like

vow of abstinence (cf. Num 6:1–4). Under this interpretation, "I will never again drink" casts a backward glance on Jesus' lifetime of wine drinking, which he is now suspending in fulfillment of his vow. The more natural interpretation, however, is that Jesus is saying that although he has just drunk wine, he will do so no longer. It seems unlikely that he would give thanks for the wine but refuse to drink it.

the vine. Gk *tēs ampelou.* Like wine and the cup (see the NOTE on "a cup" in 14:23), the vine can be an eschatological symbol (see Roth, "Symbols" and Rordorf, "Vigne," 498–503), and this may be why it, like the cup, often appears on coins from the First Jewish Revolt (for examples, see Meshorer, *Coinage,* vol. 2, plates 17–18). The vine leaf on these coins may have a specifically messianic nuance, based partly on Gen 49:11 (see 2 *Apoc. Bar.* 39:7; *Did.* 9:2; cf. Hengel, *Zealots,* 116 n. 214) and partly on its attachment to a branch, which recalls the "branch" prophecies of Isa 11:1; Jer 33:15; Zech 3:8; 6:12 (see Roth, "Symbols," 161–62). On the importance of Genesis 49 in Mark, see the COMMENT on 14:23–24.

anew. Gk *kainon.* This neuter accusative singular adjective is usually taken to refer to *genēmatos* = "fruit (of the vine)"; according to this reading, Jesus will drink "new wine" at the eschaton. This reading is supported by 2:22, where "new wine" is a symbol for the eschatological originality of Jesus' ministry, although a different term for "new" is used. This passage and ours may pick up on preexistent associations of "new wine"; in 1QSa 2:17–20, for example, the Messiahs bless the bread and the new wine (*tyrwš*) when the eschatological community gathers. The Temple Scroll, moreover, describes a "Festival of New Wine" (*mw'd htyrwš*; 11QTemple 19:11–21:10; 43:7–9), which seems to have an eschatological orientation and to be connected with atonement (*kpr,* 21:8; cf. Yadin, *Temple Scroll,* 1.108–11). "New wine," therefore, is linked at Qumran with the eschaton, the Messiah, and atonement.

But neuter accusative adjectives may also function as adverbs; Wallace (293) cites NT usages such as *prōton* = "first" (e.g., Matt 6:33), *perisson* = "abundantly" (John 10:10), and *loipon* = "at last" (Acts 27:20). Under an adverbial reading, which is grammatically smoother than the adjectival one, *kainon* modifies "I drink" rather than "fruit of the vine," and Jesus is saying that when the dominion of God arrives, he will imbibe again or in a new way. The translation of *kainon* as "anew" best fits the context, which seems to imply temporal interruption followed by resumption ("never again . . . until . . . I drink it *kainon*"). The adverbial interpretation is supported by the two earliest Syriac witnesses, Sinaiticus and Peshitta, both of which read *ḥadtā'yit,* an adverbial form that means "again," "recently," or "in a new manner" (see Payne Smith and Brockelmann).

COMMENT

Introduction. Hard on the heels of Jesus' prophecy of betrayal to death in 14:17–21, he now employs a resonant ritual action that presents this imminent demise as an atoning sacrifice.

We are in the fortunate position of having an independent attestation of this tradition, Paul's account in 1 Cor 11:23–25, which is similar to most manuscripts of Luke 22:15–20 (see figure 44). Either Luke himself has been influenced by this

Figure 44: The Lord's Supper Tradition

Mark 14:22–25	Matthew 26:26–29	Luke 22:15–20 D, etc.	Luke 22:15–20 Majority Text	1 Corinthians 11:23–25
				. . . that the Lord Jesus on the night on which he was turned over
		And he said to them, With desire I have desired to eat this Passover with you before I suffer	And he said to them, With desire I have desired to eat this Passover with you before I suffer	
		For I say to you that I will never any longer eat it	For I say to you that I will never any longer eat it	
		until it is fulfilled in the dominion of God	until it is fulfilled in the dominion of God	
		And having grasped the cup	And having grasped a cup	
		having given thanks	having given thanks	
		he said, Take this, distribute it among yourselves	he said, Take this and distribute it to yourselves	

		for I say to you, I will never drink from now on from the fruit of the vine until the dominion of God comes	for I say to you that from now on I will never drink from the fruit of the vine until the dominion of God comes	
And as they were eating	As they were eating			
having taken bread	Jesus having taken bread	And having taken bread	And having taken bread	took bread
having blessed	and having blessed	having given thanks	having given thanks	and having given thanks
he broke	broke	he broke	he broke	broke
and gave to them and said,	and having given to the disciples said,	and gave to them saying,	and gave to them saying,	and said
Take	Take, eat			
this is my body	this is my body	This is my body	This is my body	This is my body
			which is given on your behalf	which is on your behalf
			Do this as my memorial	Do this as my memorial
And having taken a cup	And having taken a cup		And likewise the cup after dinner, saying,	Likewise also the cup after dining, saying,
having given thanks	and having given thanks			

Figure 44: The Lord's Supper Tradition (continued)

Mark 14:22–25	Matthew 26:26–29	Luke 22:15–20 D, etc.	Luke 22:15–20 Majority Text	1 Corinthians 11:23–25
he gave to them and they all drank from it	he gave to them saying, Drink from it, all of you			
And he said to them, This is my blood of the covenant	for this is my blood of the covenant		This cup is the new covenant in my blood	This cup is the new covenant in my blood
				Do this, as often as you drink, as my memorial
which is poured out on behalf of many	which is poured out on behalf of many		which is poured out on your behalf	
	for the forgiveness of sins			
Amen, I say to you	I say to you			
that I will never any longer drink from the fruit of the vine	I will never drink from now on from this fruit of the vine			
until that day	until that day			
when I drink it new(ly) in the dominion of God	when I drink it with you new(ly) in the dominion of my father			

Pauline tradition or a later scribe has interpolated it into Luke's text (it is absent from Codex Bezae). In any case, the Pauline version parallels most of the important elements of the Markan one (taking bread, blessing, breaking, "this is my body," and identification of the cup with a covenant sealed in Jesus' blood). The most important Markan pluses in relation to Paul are "as they were eating"; Jesus' command to *take* the bread and the description of his *giving* it; the blessing, distribution, and drinking of the cup; and Jesus' vow not to drink the fruit of the vine again until the arrival of the dominion of God. Of these differences, however, only "as they were eating" seems a likely Markan addition, since it evinces Mark's love for the genitive absolute and adapts this passage to the previous one, which begins with a similar formula (see 14:18). The other Markan plusses may reflect the development of the Last Supper tradition in pre-Markan, liturgical contexts.

The reconstruction and interpretation of the "historical" Last Supper have been a storm center in modern scholarship (for an accessible summary, see Theissen and Merz, *Historical Jesus*, 405–39). There is controversy partly because Jesus here uses liturgical actions to prophesy his death, and those who are skeptical that he foresaw the latter, and who suspect that the church retrojected its own eucharistic practice into the pre-Easter period, regard the tradition as largely unhistorical (see, e.g., Funk and Hoover, *Five Gospels*, 118). The Passover setting of the tradition has also been challenged, since it is mentioned only in the larger context (14:12, 16), not in the eucharistic account itself, and Paul says only that Jesus performed the ritual "on the night in which he was turned over" (1 Cor 11:23, my trans.), not "on Passover." Moreover, the Johannine chronology and certain details from the Markan account itself seem to contradict the thesis that the meal was, strictly speaking, a seder (see the NOTE on "Not during the feast" in 14:2). Scholars have therefore related the Last Supper actions to a variety of other history-of-religions backgrounds, from the repasts of pagan mystery cults, to Jewish *tôdāh* (thanksgiving) meals and the suppers of the Qumran community, to Christian *agapē* (fellowship) celebrations. Some have argued that Jesus' original meal, which was eschatological but not expiatory in character (cf. *Didache* 9–10), mutated in the early church into a commemoration of his atoning sacrifice.

It is impossible to sort out these complicated questions here (or perhaps anywhere); the church *may* have retrojected its own eucharistic ceremony onto Jesus, but then again it may have gotten the rudiments of the Eucharist from the memory of what Jesus had done "on the night in which he was turned over," as Paul says it did. Categorical pronouncements about historicity are out of place, but so are categorical pronouncements about fictitiousness; even if, as seems likely, the Last Supper occurred on the night before Passover officially began, as in John (19:14, 31, 42), it was probably still deeply imbued with the atmosphere of the holiday, and the Passover symbolism that is emphasized in the Synoptics is apropos (cf. the NOTE on "this is my body" in 14:22).

The Markan form of the passage falls into three parts: the blessing, distribution, and interpretation of the bread (14:22); the blessing, distribution, and interpretation of the wine (14:23–24); and the vow not to drink wine again until God's dominion arrives (14:25).

14:22: the actions over the bread. The passage begins with Jesus' blessing, division, and distribution of the bread (14:22a). These actions are introduced by the genitive absolute *kai esthiontōn autōn* = "and as they were eating," which repeats 14:18 almost word for word. Both passages go on to speak of Jesus' death, but as Davies and Allison (3.464) note, the atmosphere has now changed from the tragic to the redemptive.

The redemptive note is integrally connected to the bread symbolism—Jesus links his body with bread, which is consumed and hence destroyed (an allusion to his approaching death) but which also nourishes those who eat it. The bread here is blessed in the middle of the meal ("as they were eating"), an unusual placement that may be explained by the order of the Passover seder (see the NOTE on "And as they were eating" in 14:22). If this incident is historical, the blessing would probably have been the one that Jews still invoke over bread: "Blessed are you, O Lord our God, king of the universe, who brings forth bread from the earth" (cf. *m. Ber.* 6:1). Jesus' body, which he identifies with bread, will also be "brought forth from the earth" by a creative act of God (cf. 16:6).

The bread consumed at Passover (and perhaps at Jesus' last supper, even if it was not a seder) was not the normal, leavened kind but flat, unleavened cakes—in Hebrew, *maṣṣāh*. This special Passover bread is associated in the Haggadah (the retelling of the exodus story) with both affliction and redemption—linkages that are peculiarly appropriate to the context of Jesus' last meal. The association with affliction arises out of the fact that *maṣṣāh* was not a luxury item but the sort of rough-and-ready food eaten by slaves and the poor (see *b. Pes.* 115b-116a; *Mekilta, Pisḥa* 10 [Lauterbach 1.80–81]); it is thus, in the words of Deut 16:3, a "bread of affliction" (*lḥm 'ny*; cf. Routledge, "Passover," 212). The latter phrase is reflected in a hard-to-date Aramaic saying that eventually became part of the Passover ritual: "This is the poor bread (*lḥm' 'ny'*) that our forefathers ate in the land of Egypt." The latter, in turn, may be echoed in Jesus' declaration, "This is my body" (cf. Jeremias, *Eucharistic Words*, 60–61). Jesus' bread, too, is a "bread of affliction," since it symbolizes the death he is about to suffer.

At the same time, however, the *maṣṣāh*, like Jesus' body, is associated with redemption, since it serves as a reminder of the day of liberation from Egyptian bondage, when the Israelites had to move so fast that their bread did not have time to rise (cf. again Deut 16:3). This association between the *maṣṣāh* and the deliverance of the Israelites becomes explicit in the Mishnah: "[We eat] *maṣṣāh* because they were redeemed" (*m. Pes.* 10:5). Already in the time of Jesus, moreover, some Jews may have linked the *maṣṣāh* not only with the past deliverance from Egypt but also with the coming end-time redemption, especially since they connected the Passover setting to the manna miracle, which was expected to be renewed at the end of days (see the NOTE on "broke the loaves, etc." in 6:41 and cf. Hoffman, "Symbol," 111–15). The bread saying, then, suggests not only Jesus' death but also its redemptive results, hinting at their eschatological nature.

In the history of interpretation, Jesus' words of institution over the bread here and over the wine in 14:24 have generated tremendous theological controversy: how realistically did Jesus mean them to be taken? Martin Luther, in defending the notion of a "real presence" of Christ in the Eucharist, famously drew a circle on a table with a piece of chalk and wrote the words "This is my body" in its center—as if that settled the matter (see Bainton, *Here I Stand*, 249). By contrast, his erstwhile colleague Carlstadt, who opposed the idea of real presence, hypothesized that when Jesus said these words he was pointing at himself, not at the bread (see Sider, *Karlstadt*, 293 n. 355). Even if one rejects such imaginative hypotheses, the exact meaning of "this is my body" is not clear; "this is . . ." language *may* imply complete identification of the signifier with the thing signified, but does not necessarily do so (see, e.g., John 15:1–6). Whether one interprets the words of institution as implying total identification, mere symbolism, or something in between will depend on larger doctrinal and hermeneutical considerations that cannot be decided by exegesis.

It is certain, however, that the Passover seder itself has from very early on been imbued with an idea of remembrance that involves not just a disinterested review of bygone events but a reliving of them (see, e.g., Exod 12:14; 13:3, 9; Deut 16:3; *Jub.* 49:7; Josephus, *Ant.* 2.317; cf. Hofius, "Lord's Supper," 104 n. 164). As the Passover Haggadah says, basing itself on a saying attributed to Rabban Gamaliel in *m. Pes.* 10:5 and extending a theme already present in the biblical passages it quotes:

> In every generation a person ought to look on himself as if *he* came forth from Egypt.
> As it is said: "And you shall tell your son in that day saying, It is because of what the Lord did for me when I came forth from Egypt." (Exod 13:8).
> It was not only our fathers that the Holy One, blessed be he, redeemed, but us as well he redeemed along with them.
> As it is said: "And he brought us forth from there, that he might bring us in, to give us the land which he swore to our fathers." (Deut 6:23; Glatzer trans. alt.).

In a similar way Christians are meant to recall Jesus' words of institution, and the whole passion narrative, as though they themselves had actively participated in them. The probability that the words of the Last Supper were known to the Markan Christians from their own celebrations of the Eucharist (they were already well known to Paul and the Corinthians twenty years earlier) would encourage such identification. The genius of this and other parts of the passion narrative, then, is that of the African American spiritual: "Were you there when they crucified my Lord?"

14:23–24: the actions over the wine. This atmosphere of remembrance also permeates Jesus' actions over the cup, which recall the activities of Moses at the inauguration of the Sinai covenant. Jesus handles the cup in a similar way to the bread, taking it (14:23a), blessing it (14:23b), and then interpreting it (14:24; see figure 45). This studied repetition reinforces the impression that these ritual actions are meant to be recollected and repeated in their turn.

If this account is historical, the blessing Jesus used may well have been the simple one still employed in Jewish homes: "Blessed are you, O Lord our God, king of the universe, who creates the fruit of the vine." This "fruit of the vine," that is, wine, was a natural part of the Passover seder, since that ceremony commemorated a great and joyful event of liberation in the past and anticipated an even greater and more joyful one in the future (see the NOTES on "Keep awake!" in 13:37, "a cup" in 14:23, and "anew" in 14:25). But Jesus' interpretation of this shared wine as "my blood of the covenant" rings a typically Markan change on this eschatological expectation by identifying the new-age wine with Jesus' blood and hence with his death.

This linkage is supported by a web of OT allusions. The "cup word" begins by echoing the scene in which Moses splashed sacrificial blood on the Israelites at Sinai and declared to them, "This is the blood of the covenant that the LORD now makes with you" (Exod 24:8 NJPS). In the OT passage the splashed blood signifies that the Israelites will incur blood guilt if they break God's covenant with them, but by the first century it may have been interpreted as a reference to sacrificial atonement. *Targums Onkelos* and *Pseudo-Jonathan*, for example, understand "on the people" as "on the altar to atone for the people" (cf. Kugel, *Traditions*, 667). The Targums thus offer a close parallel to our verse, in which "my blood of the covenant" acts as an expiatory sacrifice ("on behalf of many"). The inserted word "my," however, helps turn this memory of the past atonement under Moses into an expectation of future redemption, since it echoes the eschatological prophecy in Zech 9:11 (see the NOTE on "This is my blood of the covenant" in 14:24). And "which is poured out on behalf of many" specifies the means of eschatological liberation by echoing Isa 53:12: the Lord's Suffering Servant will save his people

Figure 45: Actions and Words over Bread and Wine in Mark 14:22–24

Bread	*Wine*
and as they were eating	and
taking bread	taking a cup
having blessed	having given thanks
he broke	
and gave it to them and said	he gave it to them
	and they all drank from it
	and he said to them
"This is my body"	"This is my blood of the covenant poured out on behalf of many"

by pouring his soul out to death on their behalf (see the NOTE on "poured out on behalf of many" in 14:24). This linkage between eschatological triumph and atoning death is not a total NT innovation, since already in Deutero-Isaiah the expiatory suffering of the Lord's Servant becomes the means to holy-war victory (cf. Marcus, *Way*, 190, 196).

One other OT passage may lie in the background of Jesus' interpretation of the wine: the reference in Gen 49:8–12 to a descendant of Judah who will bind his foal to a vine and wash his garments in wine. This passage, which was already echoed in Mark 11:4 (see the NOTE on "a colt tied up . . . in the street" there), is commonly interpreted as a messianic testimony in Second Temple and later Jewish texts (see, e.g., 4QCommGenA [4Q252] 5:1–7; *T. Judah* 24:5–6, and the Targums). The church fathers see it as a prophecy of Jesus' messianic status and bloody death, sometimes linking it with the "cup word" from the Last Supper tradition (see, e.g., Justin, *1 Apology* 32:1–8; Tertullian, *Against Marcion* 4.40; Eusebius, *Demonstration of the Gospel* 8.1.72–78). The linkage is logical, since the passage associates the coming scion of Judah with several images connected to our passage: the vine; wine, which is called "the blood of grapes"; and the scepter, which is paraphrased in some of the Jewish texts as "dominion" (*malkûtā'/basileia*)—all of which is reminiscent of the vocabulary of Mark 14:23–25. The Palestinian Targums, moreover, interpret the "the blood of grapes" as a reference to literal blood and link it with the Messiah (see McNamara, *New Testament*, 230–33; Syrén, *Blessings*, 102–11; Aune, *Revelation*, 1049–50).

Unlike our passage, however, the Palestinian Targums on Genesis 49 identify the blood as that of God's enemies, who are slaughtered by the Messiah. This sort of militant, messianic construal may also be reflected in coins from the Jewish revolt against the Romans that picture either a chalice or a vine branch with leaf (see the NOTE on "the vine" in 14:25). Jesus' "cup word" and the concluding oath of the Last Supper pericope, then, may take up a well-known association of the Messiah with vine, wine, blood, and kingship, but change the blood into that of the Messiah himself (not his enemies) and the kingship into one that is established by his death (not theirs).

14:25: the vow not to drink again. In stark contrast to the "cup word," in which the Markan Jesus speaks of the benefits to *many* people of his redemptive act, the concluding statement of the whole passage begins with a reference to its cost to *one* person, namely, Jesus himself: "Amen, I say to you, I will never again drink from the fruit of the vine . . ." (14:25a). As Davies and Allison (3.475) point out, this "prophecy of abstinence is in effect another passion prediction"; in saying that he will no longer drink wine, Jesus implies that he will no longer eat or drink anything—until "that day" when he does so in the dominion of God.

This renunciation is in some ways similar to the Nazirite vow, which included abstention from wine (see Num 6:1–4), and to the holy manner of life of the Rechabites, who also avoided alcohol (see Jeremiah 35). But it has an eschatological horizon not present in these OT prototypes: Jesus swears off wine until God brings the divine dominion to earth (14:25b), partly perhaps in order to induce God to act in the desired manner (see Jeremias, *Eucharistic Words*, 214–16). In any event, Jesus' concluding vow turns attention to the eschatological future; it is of a piece, therefore, with Paul's statement that when Christians eat the eucharistic bread and drink the cup, they proclaim the Lord's death "until he comes" (1 Cor 11:26). It is also in accord with the spirit of Passover, which not only commemorates the redemption accomplished under Moses in the past but also looks forward to the messianic redemption in the future, thus melding the memory of the exodus with the hopeful anticipation of the eschatological banquet (see the NOTES on "Keep awake!" in 13:37 and "a cup" in 14:23).

Against all hope, then, and according to a divine necessity, the Messiah must suffer and die; but against all expectation, this demise will signal not defeat but victory. In order for this mysterious chain of events to be set in motion, however, Jesus will have to be abandoned by his closest followers—a desertion that he will prophesy in the next pericope.

JESUS PROPHESIES HIS DESERTION BY THE TWELVE (14:26–31)

14 ²⁶And after singing a hymn, they went out to the Mount of Olives. ²⁷And Jesus said to them, "You will all be tripped up, for it has been written, 'I will strike the shepherd, and the sheep will be scattered.' ²⁸But after I have been raised up, I will go before you into Galilee." ²⁹Peter said to him, "Even if all will be tripped up, I won't." ³⁰And Jesus said to him, "Amen, I say to you: Today, in this night, before the rooster crows twice, you will deny me three times." ³¹But he kept speaking vehemently: "If I have to die with you, I will never deny you." And they all also said likewise.

NOTES

14 26. *after singing a hymn.* Gk *hymnēsantes.* When the Second Temple was standing, the scriptural portion known as the Hallel ("Praise"), which consists of Psalms 113–18, was sung there at Passover (cf. *m. Pes.* 5:7), as it was at Tabernacles, Hanukkah, and Weeks (see the NOTE on "Blessed is he who comes in the name of the Lord!" in 11:9). Probably already in Second Temple times Jews began singing the Hallel at the conclusion of the Passover seder as well (see *m. Pes.* 10:6–7 and Goldschmidt, *Haggadah*, 62 n. 6; Bokser, *Origins*, 43–45); cf. the references to "praising and blessing and glorifying the Lord" at Passover in *Jub.* 49:6 and to the singing of hymns (*hymnōn*, a cognate of *hymnēsantes*) at Passover in Philo, *Special Laws* 2.148.

27. *You will . . . be tripped up.* Gk *skandalisthēsesthe.* On this word, which is rendered "fall away" in 4:17, "were scandalized" in 6:3, and "offends" in 9:42–43, 45, 47, see the NOTES on "fall away" in 4:17, "were scandalized" in 6:3, and "offends" in 9:42. The root meaning is to set a trap for someone to fall into (cf. Moulton,

"*Skandalon*"), and the verb often has an eschatological nuance. Mark does not specify an agent for this entrapment, and it is possible that the idea is that the disciples' own stupidity or fear will cause them to stumble. But the next sentence speaks of the agency of God ("I will strike the shepherd"), and in apocalyptic contexts God often operates through Satan, who is frequently described as leading people astray (see the COMMENT on 13:5–8).

I will strike the shepherd, and the sheep will be scattered. Gk *pataxō ton poimena kai ta probata diaskorpisthēsontai.* This is a citation of Zech 13:7, which is especially close to the version of the LXX represented by A and Q; some texts of our verse, such as K, make the similarity even greater by adding "of the flock" after "sheep." The most significant departure of Mark from the LXX is that in the latter God commands his sword, "Strike the shepherd . . . !" whereas, in Mark, God himself says, "*I* will strike the shepherd. . . ." God is still ultimately responsible for the smiting of the shepherd in the LXX, so Mark is making explicit what the LXX implies, but he may also be bringing in an allusion to Isaiah 53, in which God's people, who are compared to sheep, go astray, yet the Lord lays their sins on his righteous Servant, whom he causes to suffer for their sake (Isa 53:4, 6, 10). The reference to sheep in the larger Isaian context is perhaps part of the reason that these two passages were brought together in the first place (cf. 1 Pet 2:25 and Lindars, *Apologetic*, 127–32).

The quotation of Zech 13:7 in Mark 14:27 is part of a cluster of allusions to or connections with Zechariah 9–14 in Mark 14:24–28 (see Marcus, *Way*, 154–64):

Mark		*Zechariah*
14:24	my blood of the covenant	9:11
14:25	that day, dominion of God	14:4, 9
14:26	Mount of Olives	14:4
14:27	strike the shepherd, and the sheep will be scattered	13:7
14:28	restoration of scattered sheep	13:8–9

In later Jewish exegesis, moreover, the earthquake on the Mount of Olives in Zech 14:4–5 allows the dead to arise through the cleft that is created (*T. Canticles* 8:5; Dura Europos synagogue; cf. the Reuchlin ms. of *T. Zech* 14:4, on which see Cathcart and Gordon, *Targum*, 223 n. 7). There is thus a possible connection between this section of Zechariah and the theme of resurrection in Mark 14:28.

Why this plethora of allusions to Zechariah 9–14 in these few verses? It is possible that Jesus himself was reminded of this section of Zechariah, which deals with the eschatological climax, as he moved from the upper room to his own approaching crisis on the Mount of Olives. But this may also be an example of Christian reflection on a section of the OT contributing to a Gospel narrative (see the section on historicity in the introduction to chapters 14–15). In his retelling of the passion narrative, Matthew extends the allusions to Zechariah 9–14 by introducing the narratives about the thirty pieces of silver (Matt 27:3–10; cf. Zech 11:12–13) and the earthquake at Jesus' death (Matt 27:51–53; cf. Zech 14:4–5 and Allison, *End*, 33–36; Marcus, "Role," 218–20). Perhaps both processes are involved: early Christians remembered Jesus' exegesis of a crucial OT corpus, but they also extended it.

28. *I will go before you.* Gk *proaxō hymas. Proagein* can mean either "lead" or "go before" (see BDAG 864). The latter nuance seems sure in other Markan passages (6:45; 11:9), is supported by the Latin and Syriac versions, and fits the context here and in the related 16:7 better than "lead"; Jesus is not saying that he will pilot the disciples to Galilee but that when they get there, they will find that he has already arrived (cf. John 21:1–14). In view of the shepherd imagery of the previous verse, however, there may be a secondary connotation of leading (cf. the use of *agein* with "sheep" in John 10:16). In 4Q521 2 2:11–13, either God or his Messiah not only heals the sick, raises the dead, and preaches good news to the poor but also leads (*ynhl*) them.

On the theory that 14:28 and 16:7 are references to the parousia, see the NOTE on "There you will see him" in 16:7.

30. *Today, in this night.* Gk *sēmeron tautē tē nukti.* This is in accordance with the common Jewish way of reckoning time, whereby the new day began at sundown (see the NOTE on "on the first day of the feast of Unleavened Bread" in 14:12).

before the rooster crows twice. Gk *prin ē dis alektora phōnēsai.* In Mark the rooster crows only once—but this crowing is designated the second one (14:72). On the problem, see the NOTE on "forecourt" in 14:68.

31. *kept speaking.* Gk *elalei.* The imperfect tense could simply reflect the normal linearity of speech (cf. 2:2; 7:35; 8:32), but in view of the repetition of the substance of 14:29, the word here is probably iterative (cf. 4:33–34).

COMMENT

Introduction. Jesus' inauguration of the eschatological sacrament of bread and wine is followed by a warning about eschatological testing: the Twelve will be weighed in the balance and found wanting (cf. Dan 5:27). The comment of Davies and Allison (3.488) about the corresponding passage in Matthew is also applicable to Mark: it is "almost an outline of the remainder of the Gospel," since it prophesies the disciples' abandonment of Jesus, Peter's denial of him, and his death and resurrection. It is particularly important that Jesus utters this detailed prophecy right before the Gethsemane scene; no matter how deep his suffering will become there, his fate is one that he has foreseen and chosen.

Of the verses in the passage, 14:28 stands out as a Markan addition. The prophecy of apostolic abandonment in 14:27 connects smoothly with Peter's protest in 14:29, but the intervening prediction of resurrection in 14:28 moves in a different direction and is ignored by Peter. Much of the vocabulary of this short verse, moreover, is typically Markan (*meta to* + infinitive, *proagein* ["lead, go before"], "Galilee"), and much of it is reproduced in 16:7—another verse that is disruptive in its context and seems to be redactional (see the introduction to the COMMENT on 16:1–8). Verse 14:31b ("And they all also said likewise") may also be redactional, since it contains one of Mark's favorite words (*pantes* = "all") and stresses one of his favorite subjects, the disciples' collective fallibility.

The pericope consists of a transitional description of travel (14:26); Jesus' prophecy of abandonment by the disciples (14:27–28); Peter's exemption of himself from that prophecy (14:29); Jesus' prediction of Peter's denial (14:30); and Peter's renewed protestation that he will remain faithful, which is echoed by the Eleven (14:31). The focus, then, shifts from the disciples in general to Peter in particular and back again, making Peter here, as elsewhere, a paradigmatic figure (cf. 8:29; 9:5–6; 14:37–38), linked with the rest of the disciples by the regularly recurring word *pantes* ("all," 14:27, 29, 31).

14:26–28: Jesus' prophecy of abandonment by the disciples. In 14:22–25, Jesus used the unleavened bread and wine of the Passover seder as the point of departure for a prophecy of his atoning death. He and his disciples now sing a hymn as they depart from the upper room for the Mount of Olives (14:26). This practice, too, is in accordance with Passover customs, since the seder ends with the recitation of the Hallel (Psalms 113–18; see the NOTE on "after singing a hymn" in 14:26). These psalms are peculiarly appropriate in the present context, since they speak of the righteous person feeling the tug of the underworld, falling into distress and sorrow, and calling on God to save his life (116:3–4; cf. Mark 14:32–42). Yet they also promise that the death of the Lord's faithful ones is precious in his sight, that the living rather than the dead will praise him (115:17–18), and that God will raise the lowly from the dust (113:7) and free them from death (116:8). Near its conclusion, the final Hallel psalm proclaims: "I shall not die but live, and declare the works of the Lord," because "the Lord . . . has not delivered me to death," and "the stone that the builders rejected has become the cornerstone" (118:17–18, 22–23; my trans.)—the last being words that the Markan Jesus quoted two chapters earlier in reference to his resurrection (Mark 12:10–11).

The concluding psalms of the Passover seder, then, prefigure the story of suffering and triumph that is about to unfold; but scriptures that are now quoted or alluded to also foreshadow or prophesy his abandonment by his closest followers. In 2 Sam 15:16, 30–31, for example, King David and his retainers leave (*exēlthon*) Jerusalem and ascend the Mount of Olives, where David learns that he has been betrayed by a trusted counselor, weeps, and prays to God for a reversal of his situation. Similarly, in our passage Jesus, the "Son of David" (10:47–48), goes out (*exēlthon*) of Jerusalem with his followers to the Mount of Olives (14:26b), where he will suffer deadly sorrow, pray for deliverance, and finally be betrayed by one of his intimate circle (14:32–45; cf. Brown, *Death*, 1.125).

The other OT reference to the Mount of Olives, Zech 14:4, also provides relevant background, since it is part of a series of prophecies of eschatological judgment and redemption (Zechariah 9–14) that have strongly influenced this section of the Gospel (see the NOTE on "I will strike the shepherd, and the sheep will be scattered" in 14:27). The Markan Jesus goes on to quote another of these passages in the very next verse, where he prophesies that the Twelve will be "tripped up" (by themselves? by God? by Satan?—see the NOTE on "You will . . . be tripped up" in 14:27): Jesus supports this prophecy scripturally by adding, "for it has been written, 'I will strike the shepherd, and the sheep will be scattered,'" a citation of Zech 13:7. The original, however, does not read "I will strike the shepherd" but instead has God addressing his own sword with the imperative "Strike . . . !" (see the NOTE on "I will strike the shepherd, and the sheep will be scattered" in 14:27 and cf. Marcus, *Way*, 154). The sense in both LXX and Mark is that God is responsible for the smiting of the shepherd, but Mark accentuates this implication by changing the imperative to a future indicative, perhaps reflecting the influence of Isa 53:4, 6, 10: if Jesus will suffer, it is because "it pleased the LORD to bruise him; *he* has put him to grief" (Isa 53:10 RSV alt.). Although the emphasis on direct divine responsibility for Jesus' death may seem cruel, the context of the Isaian passage, which speaks of the redemptive nature of that suffering, is also germane: "All we like sheep have gone astray . . . and the LORD has laid on him the iniquity of us all" (Isa 53:6). Nor is this the only time in the immediate context that Isaiah 53 is conflated with Zechariah 9–14, since Jesus' words over the cup in 14:24 fuse allusions to Isa 53:11–12 and Zech 9:11 (see the COMMENT on 14:23–24 and Marcus, *Way*, 162–63).

But if the sheep stumble and are subsequently scattered, they can also be regathered, as Zechariah also makes clear. Throughout Zechariah 9–14, the imagery of shepherd and sheep is used to speak not only of the destruction that Israel suffers as a result of her worthless shepherds (Zech 11:4–17) but also of the care that the Lord, her true shepherd, has for her (Zech 9:16; 10:3). Two verses after the prophecy of the flock's scattering in 13:7, for example, we read of a time of testing that will come upon Israel, at the end of which a remnant of the people will be restored, and in 10:6–12 it is said that the Lord who has scattered the people in his anger will regather them in his compassion. The scattering of Zech 13:7, therefore, will be followed by a restoration that is strikingly comparable to the prophecy in Mark 14:28 of Jesus again shepherding his flock of disciples (cf. Marcus, *Way*, 155). A postresurrectional resumption of discipleship in Galilee is thus implied, a new beginning in which Jesus will return to the place where his career started and display the same compassion for lost sheep that marked his ministry there (see 6:34).

In interpreting the Zecharian texts in this way, the Markan Jesus seems to be following a way of reading them that was common in apocalyptic circles. Brown (*Death*, 1.129), for example, notes that the Qumran *Damascus Document* is similar to our passage in reading the smitten shepherd/scattered sheep text in Zech 13:7 as a reference to a future, eschatological event (CD 19:7–9) and in referring to the notion of a preserved remnant in the larger context (CD 19:10). This context, moreover, speaks of the "coming" of "the messiah of Aaron and Israel," a partial analogue to the reference to the resurrection and renewed leadership of Jesus in Mark 14:28. But there is also a significant difference: in the *Damascus Document*, "the messiah of Aaron and Israel" is a militant figure, who will deliver the wicked to the sword (CD 19:10–11); in Mark, the sword will strike the Messiah himself.

14:29–31: *Petrine protest, dominical response.* The smiting of "the shepherd," however, will not be the end for him; Jesus concludes his prophecy by alluding in 14:28 not only to his own resurrection but also to the resurrection of his relationship with the Twelve. Peter does not seem to pay attention to this prophecy of resurrection and restoration (cf. 8:32, where he also ignores a prophecy of resurrection); instead, with an air of injured innocence, he picks up Jesus' prophecy of apostolic abandonment, fixating on the word "all" (*pantes*). Peter's response is that even if *all* fall away, *he* certainly will not (14:29). This is a dangerous sort of prophecy to make, especially if one uses the word "never," as Peter goes on to do (14:31); in literature generally, a character's wish or assertion that all will be well is often a sign of impending disaster (see, e.g., Lull, *Richard III*, 73).

Jesus' response to Peter's assertion is a detailed prophecy of Peter's denial. Perhaps because of the importance of this prophecy, it breaks the usual Markan pattern of double time designations (cf. Neirynck, *Duality*), instead incorporating three, and the number of words increases each time, thus artfully heightening the tension:

Today	1 word
in this night	3 words
before the rooster crows twice	5 words

Then comes the stunning three-word denouement, which prophesies a triple denial and saves the point of emphasis for last: "Three-times me you-will-deny."

The word *aparnēsē* ("you will deny") cuts Peter to the heart; he responds indignantly that he will never deny Jesus, even if he has to die with him (14:31a). This asseveration echoes 10:35–45, in which James and John attempted to distinguish themselves from the other disciples and were directed to Jesus' slave-like death; and it contrasts with 8:31–33, in which Peter rebuked Jesus for prophesying that death. Peter has at least learned by now that "being with Jesus" (cf. 3:14) may ultimately mean "dying with him" (the latter expression would probably remind Mark's readers of Christian baptism; cf. Rom 6:4; Col 2:12). But he has yet to learn that this co-dying, and the discipleship of which it is a part, cannot be accomplished by the zealousness of the human will but is a gift bestowed on the far side of betrayal (14:28; 16:7; cf. John 21:18–19). While 8:32, then, revealed a faulty Christology, 14:31 reveals a lack of self-knowledge, and these two misperceptions are related: if humans *could* be faithful to God under their own steam, a suffering Messiah would not be necessary (cf. Gal 2:21). For the Markan readers, who probably live after Peter's martyrdom in 64 C.E., his words in 14:31 contain an ironic mixture of truth and falsehood: Peter did eventually "die with" Jesus, even suffering crucifixion for his sake (cf. John 21:18–19), but in the short term he deserted him (cf. Mark 14:66–72).

Peter, however, is not the only one of the Twelve engaged in the self-deception of thinking himself a perfectly faithful follower of Jesus. He is linked with the Eleven by the word "all," which appears near the beginning, middle, and end of the passage, in another significant progression:

27   Jesus: "You will *all* be tripped up"
29   Peter: "Even if *all* will be tripped up, I won't"
31   Narrator: They *all* also said likewise

The progression is ironic: Peter objects to being included in the "all" of Jesus' prophecy, but the finale undermines his protest by including the Eleven along with him in a wrongheaded assertion of innocence.

The passage thus ends on a somber and ironic note, with Peter and the other disciples vying for the title of "more-faithful-than-thou," blind to the precariousness of their spiritual position. Nothing, it seems, can stop the onrushing power of darkness, which will entrap even those who wish to remain loyal to Jesus. Indeed, in the next passage, the shadows will begin to fall on Jesus himself.

JESUS SUFFERS AND PRAYS IN GETHSEMANE (14:32–42)

14 ³²And they came to a place named Gethsemane, and he said to his disciples, "Sit here while I pray." ³³And he took Peter and James and John with him, and he began to be overwhelmed and anxious, ³⁴and he said to them, "My soul is very sad, to the point of death. Stay here and keep awake." ³⁵And going forward a bit, he fell on the ground and began to pray that, if it were possible, the hour might pass from him; ³⁶and he said, "*Abba* (Father), all things are possible for you—take this cup from me! But not what I want, but what you want." ³⁷And he came and found them sleeping, and he said to Peter, "Simon, are you sleeping? Didn't you have the strength to keep awake one hour? ³⁸Keep awake and pray, so that you may not enter into testing; the spirit is willing, but the flesh is weak." ³⁹And again he went away and prayed, saying the same thing. ⁴⁰And again he came and found them sleeping, for their eyes were weighed down; and they didn't know what to answer him. ⁴¹And he came a third time and said to them, "Do you intend to sleep away the rest of the night, and take your rest? Is the hour far away? It has come; look, the Son of Man is being turned over to the hands of the sinners. ⁴²Get up, let's go! Look, the one who will turn me over has come near."

NOTES

14 32. *Gethsemane.* Gk *Gethsēmani.* This place-name is not mentioned in ancient Jewish sources. The etymology of the word, *gat šĕmānî* = "oil press," probably reflects the site's function at one time.

33. *to be overwhelmed and anxious.* Gk *ekthambeisthai kai adēmonein.* As Brown (*Death*, 1.153) points out, *ekthambeisthai* "indicates a profound disarray, expressed physically before a terrifying event: a shuddering horror," whereas *adēmonein* "has a root connotation of being separated from others, a situation that results in anguish." On the Markan emphasis on Jesus' isolation, see the introduction to the COMMENT, and on the other Markan usages of *ekthambeisthai* see the COMMENT on 14:32–36.

34. *My soul is very sad, to the point of death.* Gk *Perilypos estin hē psychē mou heōs thanatou.* The first part of this statement fuses Ps 6:3 ("My soul [*hē psychē mou*] is greatly harassed") with the refrain from Pss 42:5, 11; 43:5 [41:6, 12; 42:5

LXX] ("Why are you so very sad [*perilypos*], O my soul?"; cf. Moo, *Old Testament*, 240; Marcus, *Way*, 173). Feldmeier (*Krisis*, 154) also points to Sir 37:2, where *lypē . . . heōs thanatou* ("sadness unto death") is the result of a companion becoming an enemy (cf. Mark 14:42). Gnilka (2.259) suggests that Jesus' statement also echoes Jonah 4:8–9 LXX, where the OT prophet says he is so sad that he wants to die, and "very sad, to the point of death" (*sphodra lelypēmai . . . heōs thanatou*); "to the point of death," therefore, would mean that Jesus' suffering is of such intensity that he craves death. But in 14:36 Jesus asks that God not make him drink from the cup, the beaker of death (see the NOTE on "cup" in 14:36), so it does not seem that he wants to die. "To the point of death," rather, is an emphatic image for the deepest sorrow: Jesus' suffering is intense enough to kill him.

Psalms 6 and 42/43, like other Righteous Sufferer psalms, are interpreted eschatologically in postbiblical Jewish exegesis (cf. Marcus, *Way*, 177–79); see, for example, the allusion to Ps 42:6 in 1QH 8:32, which adds "to death" to "my soul within me languishes," thus increasing the likeness to our passage. The exegesis of Ps 6:1–4 in 4QCatena[a] (4Q177) 4:7–16 [12–13 1:2–11] is also illuminating:

> [7] . . . for the last [d]ays, as David said: "YH[W]H, do not sc[old me] in anger. [Take pity on me YHWH, fo]r I am collapsing. [8] [. . .] My soul is very troubled; and now, YHWH, how long? Take pity on me, save [my] li[fe . . ."] . . . [12] [. . .] The angel of his truth will rescue all the children of light from the power of Belial . . . [13]This is the period of distress (*'t 'nwt*) . . . [14]The [j]ust person will flee and God's great hand will be with them to rescue them from all the spirits of [Belial] . . . [16][. . . Be]l[ia]l and all the people of his lot will be fin[ished] forever, and all the children of li[ght] will be reunited (García-Martínez trans. alt.)

Here David, the ancestor of the Messiah, on the point of collapse, complains that his soul is troubled and asks God to save his life. The suffering of David, moreover, is interpreted as a foretaste of the end-time tribulation, in which Belial = Satan will attack God's people and try to gain control over them (cf. 1QH 13[5]:30–39). But Belial's ultimate destruction is assured, since God and his angels will fight on the side of the children of light and deliver them.

keep awake. Gk *grēgoreite*. This verb will be employed again in 14:37, 38; and two out of these three instances are in the second person plural imperative. Similarly, it is used three times in 13:34, 35, 37, and two out of those three are second person plural imperatives (see figure 46). This grammatical correlation strengthens the thematic linkage between the two passages (see the COMMENT on 14:32–36).

35. *going forward a bit.* Gk *proelthōn mikron.* But if the disciples were separated from Jesus by some distance (a stone's throw, according to Luke 22:41), and if they were sleeping by the time Jesus finished his prayer (Mark 14:37), how could they or anyone else know what he prayed? Although Brown dismisses this as a "village atheist question" (*Death*, 1.174), it has engaged interpreters who were neither atheists nor idiots. Some of the answers have been tendentious: for example, that

**Figure 46: The Conclusion of the Eschatological Discourse (Mark 13:32–37)
and the Gethsemane Scene (Mark 14:32–42)**

Mark 13:32–37	*Mark 14:32–42*
32: no one knows the hour	35: Jesus prays that the hour might pass
34: the doorkeeper he has commanded to keep awake (*hina grēgorę*)	37c: Didn't you have the strength to keep awake (*grēgorēsai*) . . . ?
35ab: keep awake (*grēgoreite*)!—for you don't know when . . . he comes (*erchetai*)	34, 37a: keep awake (*grēgoreite*)! . . . he comes (*erchetai*)
35c: whether at . . . cockcrow	[72: cockcrow—setting of Peter's denial]
36: in case coming (*elthōn*) . . . he finds (*heurę̄*) you sleeping (*katheudontas*)	37a: and he comes (*erchetai*) and finds (*heuriskei*) them sleeping (*katheudontas*)
37: Keep awake (*grēgoreite*)!	38: Keep awake (*grēgoreite*)!

Jesus divulged the content of the prayer in one of his resurrection appearances
(e.g., Theodore of Mopsuestia, *Commentary on Luke* 22:39–47 [PG 66.725];
Luther, WA *Tischreden* 5.255; cf. Feldmeier, *Krisis*, 137). Another attempt to salvage historicity is to posit that Jesus, like most ancient people, was praying aloud
(Davies and Allison, 3.493 n. 13) and the distance was small (not more than forty
or fifty yards according to Alford, 273), so the disciples "might well catch the leading words of our Lord's prayer, before drowsiness overpowered them" (ibid.). But
Jesus would have to have been praying extremely loudly to be understood from
fifty yards away, and, if he was, his agonized cries probably would have kept the
disciples awake.

It is more likely that either the sleeping motif or the content of the prayer has its
roots in narrative art and early Christian theology rather than historical memory.
Davies and Allison argue that the sleeping motif is redactional, since it accords
with the Markan emphasis on apostolic incomprehension. The potentially scandalous nature of the picture of Jesus seeking to avoid death, moreover, has impressed many, beginning with Origen (*Against Celsus* 2.24), as an argument for its
basic historicity; would the church have invented a portrayal that was so embarrassing and so useful to its enemies? But it also seems likely that the content of the
prayer has been elaborated on the basis of later insight, since it appears to echo
not only OT scripture (which was well known to Jesus) but also the Lord's Prayer
and other early Christian liturgical language (see the NOTE on "Abba [Father]"
in 14:36 and the COMMENT on 14:32–36).

Perhaps a compromise solution is possible, since Heb 5:7 paints a picture
much like that of the Gethsemane scene but describes Jesus' prayer for deliverance as a frequent practice rather than a one-time event (see the COMMENT on
14:32–36). This may be substantially correct: Jesus, toward the end of his minis-

try, was frequently observed by his followers to struggle with God in prayer over the question of his fate, and when they later tried to piece together what he had prayed in Gethsemane, they filled in the blanks from their memories of this practice in combination with the scriptures, the Lord's Prayer, and the liturgy of the church.

he fell on the ground. Gk *epipten epi tēs gēs.* In the OT, those who pray frequently prostrate themselves before God as a sign of submission to the divine will, and some of these instances use expressions such as "he fell on his face" (e.g., Num 16:22, 44–45; 20:6), a locution that reappears in intertestamental literature (e.g., Jdt 9:1; see Gruber, *Aspects,* 123–38, 140–45; Ehrlich, *Nonverbal Language,* 37–40). In the present instance, there may be an added dimension to the gesture, since in the Bible and related literature falling to the ground is often the result of divine judgment, and the gesture is frequent in eschatological contexts (see, e.g., 2 Chron 20:24; Ezek 38:20; Amos 3:14; 2 Macc 3:27; Acts 9:4; Rev 6:13; 9:1; cf. Feldmeier, *Krisis,* 163–64, 190–91). There is a noteworthy OT parallel in the story of King Saul hearing a prophecy of his violent death and collapsing on the ground (*epesen . . . epi tēn gēn*) in great fear (1 Sam 28:20 LXX). The parallel is especially striking because Saul is the Lord's anointed (1 Sam 10:1, etc.), but God has now rejected him and refuses to hear his prayer (1 Sam 28:6), and he will subsequently be "turned over to the hands" of his enemies (1 Sam 28:19) to be killed.

hour. Gk *hōra.* This can be a synecdoche (see the GLOSSARY) for the appointed time of death, as, for example, in John 2:4; 7:30; 8:20; etc., but it can also be a term for the predestined eschatological crisis, as in Esth 10:3 LXX; Dan 11:40, 45 LXX; Mark 13:32; Rom 13:11; and Rev 3:10 (see Gnilka, 2.261; Davies and Allison, 3.501). The last passage, like ours, conjoins the notion of the hour with that of eschatological testing (*peirasmos*). The usage of "hour" here is one of many linkages between our passage and Mark 13 (see figure 46 and the COMMENT on 14:37–42).

36. *Abba (Father).* Gk *abba ho patēr.* On *Abba* see Fitzmyer, "Abba," and Brown, *Death,* 1.172–75. The phrase *abba ho patēr* also appears in Rom 8:15 and Gal 4:6, and in all three instances the expression is employed vocatively, that is, as an address to God, even though the nominative *patēr* rather than vocative *pater* is employed (cf. Fitzmyer, "Abba," 19, for other examples of the nominative replacing the vocative). The two Pauline instances occur in a liturgical context ("crying"); apparently Jesus' use of *Abba* was considered important enough not only to be translated into Greek but also to be transmitted in the original Aramaic in early Christian liturgy.

The Aramaic word *'abbā'* is the emphatic (definite) form of *'ab* = "father" and thus is appropriately translated with the Greek *ho patēr* ("the father"); this definite form can be equivalent to "my father," as is shown by *m. Sanh.* 4:5, " 'Abbā' is greater than your father." Contrary to Jeremias (*Prayers,* 58), however, *'abbā* is not normatively a child's word (cf. Barr, " 'Abbā"). In *m. 'Ed.* 5:7, for example, the speaker is a grown man, in *m. Sanh.* 4:5 he is any human being, and in the earlier Aramaic of Jesus' time, *'abbā',* in its few attested instances, is either a proper name, a patronymic, a title, or possibly a formal term for "father" (see Fitzmyer, "Abba," 21–22). Yet it is undeniable that 'abbā' can *sometimes* have the implication of childlike intimacy that Jeremias saw in it, as in the delightful baraitha (see the GLOSSARY) in which Ḥoni the Circle-Drawer is compared to a spoiled but beloved child who gets whatever he demands from his doting father (b. Tan. 23a).

This idea of God as a father has deep roots already within the OT, though the context is usually corporate: God is the Father of Israel as their Creator, Lord, and Savior (see, e.g., Deut 32:6; Isa 63:16; Jer 3:19). This corporate nuance is retained both in Jewish prayers (e.g., the common invocation 'Abînû malkēnu, "Our Father, our King") and in the prayer that Jesus teaches his disciples in Matt 6:9 ("Our Father in heaven"; cf. Luke 11:2). But the OT/Jewish tradition also contains personal address to the heavenly Father; in Ps 89:26, for example, David or the king addresses God as "*my* Father," and an individual invokes God as Father in the LXX version of Sir 23:1, 4 (cf. Wis 2:16; 14:3, and Winston, *Wisdom*, 265–66). Closer to the time of Jesus, two Qumran texts, 4Q460 5:5 [9 1:6] and 4Q372 1:16, have individuals addressing God as 'abî = "my father"; the latter is an interesting parallel, because here Joseph invokes "the powerful God," whom he subsequently addresses as "my father," to save him from "the hands" of the Gentiles. By way of comparison and contrast, the Markan Jesus, after praying for deliverance to the "Father" for whom all things are possible, is "turned over to the hands of . . . sinners" (14:41). These passages vitiate the claim of Jeremias (*Prayers*, 29) that in ancient Palestinian Jewish sources "my father" is never used as a personal address to God, and the even more tendentious assertion of Hahn (*Titles*, 307) that Jesus' use of *abba* is "absolutely unthinkable in the prayer language of contemporary Judaism." It is also true, however, that scholars have not yet discovered a pre-Christian text in which an individual addresses God as 'abbā', so there may have been something distinctive about Jesus' idiom (see Brown, *Death*, 1.173).

cup. Gk *potērion*. On this image, see the NOTES on "the cup" in 10:38 and "a cup" in 14:23. A metaphor for one's portion in life, "the cup" can have a positive connotation (e.g., "cup of salvation" in Ps 116:13) but is usually negative. In the OT (e.g., Ps 75:8; Jer 25:15–29; Ezek 23:31–34; Hab 2:16) and intertestamental literature (e.g., *Pss. Sol.* 8:14–15; 1QpHab 11:10, 14; 4QpNah 4:5–6) it is overwhelmingly associated with God's eschatological judgment, which will be visited upon the sinful world (cf. Rev 14:10). In later Jewish texts the symbol can also be used for the death of individuals (see, e.g., "the cup of death" in *T. Ab.* 1:3; 16:11; *Tg. Neof.* Gen 40:23 and Deut 32:1). Our passage seems to combine both aspects: the individual demise of Jesus is in view, but there is some sort of relationship between that death and the judgment God renders on others (cf. 14:23–24, where the cup symbolizes "my blood of the covenant . . . poured out on behalf of many," and Feldmeier, *Krisis*, 176–85).

not what I want, but what you want. Gk *ou ti egō thelō alla ti sy*. This may be an echo of the third petition of the Matthean version of the Lord's Prayer, "Your will (*to thelēma sou*) be done" (Matt 6:10). For other links between the Gethsemane story in the Gospels and the Lord's Prayer, see Walker, "Lord's Prayer." It is natural that Christians, in retelling the story of Jesus' struggle with his fate, should portray him as echoing the familiar prayer that he taught his disciples (though he teaches it directly only in Matthew and Luke, not in Mark or John). For another possible Markan echo of the Matthean version of the Lord's Prayer, see the NOTE on "so that your Father in heaven may also forgive you your transgressions" in 11:25.

37. *he came and found them sleeping.* Gk *erchetai kai heuriskei autous katheudontas.* From the flow of the narrative, "them" here is probably the inner group of three whom Jesus separated from the main body of twelve disciples and exhorted to stay awake with him in 14:33–34. By the end of 14:42, however, he seems to be addressing the whole body of disciples again—a possible indication of a redactional seam (see the introduction to the COMMENT).

Simon. Gk *Simōn.* As Smith (*Petrine*, 177) points out, this is the last time that Jesus will address Peter in Mark, and Smith, like many interpreters, thinks it "surely significant that the writer has Jesus call him by his 'pre-Christian' name: Peter is denied his name of 'Rock' because his behavior up until now, and even more so during the passion-narrative, shows him to be somewhat less than Rock-like." Swete (325) compares the use of "Simon son of John" in a Johannine context having to do with rehabilitation of the fallen disciple (John 21:15–19). Brown (*Death*, 1.195), however, points out that Mark also uses the name "Peter" here and continues to employ it in the scenes that follow (14:54, 66–72; 16:7). Matthew 16:17, moreover, employs "Simon" in a very favorable way. Even in Mark, the implication of the name may not be entirely negative, since Jesus will immediately exhort the disciples to renewed alertness (14:38), and *Šim'ôn* comes from a root meaning "to hear, obey."

38. *testing.* Gk *peirasmon.* See the COMMENT on 14:37–42 for a discussion of the eschatological dimension of this term, which is closely connected in the history-of-religions parallels with the idea of demonic attack (see Rev 2:9–10 and cf. 4QFlor 1–3 2:1–2; 1 Pet 4:12–5:8; Rev 3:9–10). It is likely that the *peirasmos* of the Markan Gethsemane scene also has a demonic dimension (cf. Kuhn, "New Light," 94–95). The first Markan use of the cognate verb *peirazein* (1:13) has Satan as its implied subject, and a demonic nuance is detectable in subsequent instances as well (see the NOTE on "testing" in 8:11 and the COMMENT on 10:1–4). Elsewhere in the NT, Satan is known as *ho peirazōn* ("the tester" or "tempter"; see Matt 4:3 and 1 Thess 3:5, and cf. 1 Cor 7:5), and in Matt 6:13, "Deliver us from the evil one" is parallel to, "Lead us not into *peirasmos*" (RSV).

the spirit is willing, but the flesh is weak. Gk *to men pneuma prothymon hē de sarx asthenēs.* This contrast does not reflect Greco-Roman dualism, where the usual opposition is between the soul and the body, as much as Jewish apocalypticism; the closest analogies are in two texts from the Dead Sea Scrolls, 1QH 12[4]:29–32 and 7[15]:24–25, where "flesh" is the seat of the human propensity to sin and "spirit" is the God-given capacity to overcome this natural inclination, direct one's steps rightly, and perform deeds of righteousness. Similarly, in our passage, the flesh—the corporeal, mortal, instinctually self-seeking dimension of humanity—is "weak," open to attack by invasive hostile forces and easily led into opposition to God; the spirit, by way of contrast, is the part of human beings that is capable of prompting them to act in accordance with God's will (cf. Rom 7:22–8:10). This spirit, however, is not identical with the Holy Spirit, which in Mark is the effective opponent of the unclean spirits (see the COMMENT on 1:7–8) and is usually an eschatological gift reserved for Jesus and his postresurrectional followers (see Mark 1:8, 10, 12; 3:29; 13:11; but cf. 12:36). Similar to the situation in some Qumran texts, rather, "the spirit" of 14:38 seems to be an endowment of every human being at creation (cf. 1QH 9[1]:15, 27–31; Kvalvaag, "Spirit").

It would be a mistake, however, to make too sharp a distinction between the human spirit and the Holy one when it comes to Jesus and his postresurrectional disciples. In 1:10 the Holy Spirit descends upon (lit. "into") Jesus at his baptism, in 2:8 Jesus knows his enemies' secret thoughts supernaturally "in his spirit" (cf. 8:12), and in 13:11 the Holy Spirit will speak through his followers; in these cases, the line of demarcation between "the Holy Spirit" and the human one seems to grow thin. These passages are perhaps illuminated by 1QH 12[4]:31, which appears to speak of a re-creation of the human spirit by an act of God, and 1QS 4:20–22, which describes a cleansing of the human interior through the Holy Spirit (cf. Kvalvaag, "Spirit," 174). Another Qumran document, 4QCatena^a (4Q177), may link the *testing* of the elect community with their refinement by means of the [*Holy*] *Spirit*, thus bringing together two of the significant terms from Mark 14:38 in an eschatological context (but contrast Tov, *Electronic Library* [4QCatena^a (4Q177) 10–11:9–11], which does not support the linkage). It is doubtful, moreover, whether Mark's Christian readers could have heard the sentence "The spirit is willing, but the flesh is weak" without thinking of their own continuing battle with "the flesh" and support by the Holy Spirit (cf. Gal 5:17).

41. *Do you intend to sleep away the rest of the night, and take your rest?* Gk *katheudete to loipon kai anapauesthe*. On the conative (intentional) use of the present tense, see Smyth §1878; Robertson 562. *To loipon* might also be translated "from now on," "henceforth," or "meanwhile" (see BDAG 602 [3a]), but the literal meaning "the remainder [of the night]" works in the context and is to be preferred. The clause might also be interpreted as a statement ("You are sleeping on and taking your rest") or a command ("Sleep on and take your rest!"). The latter, however, seems unlikely in the present context, because it is immediately followed by the command to get up (14:42). The difference between the declarative interpretation and the interrogative one is negligible, but the latter makes for a smoother sentence and parallels the question in Luke 22:46 (cf. Brown, *Death*, 1.208).

Is the hour far away? It has come. Gk *apechei ēlthen hē hōra*, lit. "Is it far away? The hour has come," but for clarity the translation has transposed "it" and "the hour."

Apechei is a famous crux; for surveys of the history of interpretation see Feldmeier, *Krisis*, 209–15; Brown, *Death*, 2.1379–83. The word is usually taken as a statement rather than a question, and many interpreters follow the lead of Jerome, who translates it with *sufficit* ("it is enough") in the Vulgate. The reference, then, would be to Jesus' threefold prayer and the threefold failure of the disciples. The external attestation for *apechei* meaning "it is enough," to be sure, is meager; there are no pre-NT examples, and the post-NT ones are debatable. But it is close to the commonest definition of *apechein* in the papyri, "to receive the money in full." Some interpreters have applied this nuance literally to Judas, who has now received the money promised him in 14:11 (cf. the reference to him in 14:42). That verse, however, is rather far from the present one, and nothing in the immediately preceding context would signal to readers that financial matters or Judas were being discussed.

An attractive alternative, and the one adopted here, is to render *apechein* by another of its common meanings, "to be distant." Black (225–26) mentions the reading of Codex Bezae, *apechei to telos kai hē hōra* ("far-off is the end and the hour"), which uses this meaning but which, he says, is "the very opposite of what the context requires." Black postulates that *apechei* is the Greek rendering for the Aramaic *rĕḥîq*, which could easily be a corruption of *dĕḥîq* = "pressing," a word that would fit the context. But the hypothesis of textual corruption and resort to the Bezae reading are unnecessary if one takes *apechei* as a question, matching the question in the previous sentence (cf. the NOTE on "Do you intend to sleep away the rest of the night, and take your rest?" at the beginning of the present verse). *Apechei*, then, would mean "Is it far away?"—"a question answered immediately by '(No), the hour has come' " (Brown, *Death*, 2.1381; cf. Hudson, "Irony").

the Son of Man is being turned over to the hands. Gk *paradidotai ho huios tou anthrōpou eis tas cheiras.* In the next verse, Judas' act of betrayal is specifically mentioned, so the passive *paradidotai* in our verse ("is being turned over") probably implies his agency, but it may also include a nuance of "divine passive" (see the GLOSSARY and the subject index in vols. 1 and 2 under this concept): the human betrayal reflects the divine will. Feldmeier (*Krisis*, 224) notes that in the Pauline correspondence "God turned [Jesus] over" (Rom 8:32) and "he was turned over" (Rom 4:25; 1 Cor 11:23) seem to be equivalent expressions. There may also be a nuance of "demonic passive"; see the COMMENT on 14:37–42.

of the sinners. Gk *tōn hamartōlōn.* The parallel in 9:31 speaks of the Son of Man being turned over to the hands of human beings (*anthrōpōn*)—a word that can, in some Markan contexts, approximate "sinners" (see 7:7–8, 8:33, and the COMMENT on 7:6–8). In many OT and Jewish texts, the enemies to whom the righteous are delivered, but who will eventually be delivered into the hands of the righteous, are hostile Gentiles (see the COMMENT on 14:37–42), and elsewhere "sinners" can be nearly synonymous with "Gentiles" (see, e.g., Ps 96:10 LXX; *Pss. Sol.* 17:23–25; 1 Macc 1:34; cf. Rengstorf, "*Hamartōlos*," 325–26). But in our immediate context the "sinners" to whom Jesus is delivered are Judas and the arresting party sent by the chief priests, the scribes, and the elders, who are all Jews—though the Jewish authorities will subsequently turn Jesus over to the Roman governor (15:1), who will eventually turn him over to the executioners (15:15). Verse 10:33, similarly, speaks of the turning over of the Son of Man to the chief priests and the scribes, who will then turn him over to the Gentiles. "Sinners" in 14:41, therefore, probably includes both Jesus' Jewish enemies and his Gentile ones, though the former are the more immediate referent.

COMMENT

Introduction. In 14:26–31, the Markan Jesus has forthrightly prophesied his death and resurrection one last time, and his twelve closest followers have proclaimed their undying loyalty to him. Now, however, in the famous Gethsemane scene, both Jesus' resolve and theirs seem to crumble.

The passage is carefully structured to bring out its distinctive themes. It is, for example, full of vocabulary concerning strength, ability, and weakness: "if it were possible" (*dynaton*, 14:35); "all things are possible" (14:36); "Didn't you have the strength . . . ?" (*ouk ischysas*, 14:37); "the flesh is weak" (14:38). As Brown (*Death*, 1.202–3) points out, structurally it consists of two triplets—three movements of Jesus forward, toward prayer (14:32, 33–34, and 35–36), and three movements back to the disciples (14:37–38, 39–40, and 41–42)—both of which emphasize Jesus' increasing isolation: he moves progressively further from human company, and his efforts to secure companionship repeatedly fail. Jesus' speech is even more prominent than his movements; he is described as "speaking" (*legein*) five times (14:32, 34, 36, 37, 41) and as "praying" (*proseuchesthai*) twice (14:35, 39; cf. Davies and Allison, 3.491). Jesus' prayers are rendered more and more tersely as the passage progresses:14:35–36 gives a full account of the first prayer, 14:39 is just a note about Jesus "saying the same thing," and the third prayer is not even described, but must be inferred from the context in 14:41 (cf. Dibelius, "Gethsemane," 254). The center of gravity, then, is the first prayer, together with the anguish that precipitates it, both of which are summarized by the narrator (14:33b, 35) before being expressed in Jesus' own words (14:34a, 36; cf. Brown, *Death*, 1.135–36).

Many scholars have seen the doublets in the passage (e.g., Jesus' prayer in both indirect and direct discourse in 14:35–36; also 14:32/33 and 14:41/42) as a sign that multiple sources have come together here (see, e.g., Kuhn, "Jesus"). Those averse to source analysis, such as Brown, respond that the repetitions are narratively effective and may therefore have been composed by a single author. It is also possible, however, that a redactor combined his sources in a rhetorically effective way, and there are certain features of the passage that seem to point toward a literary history (see, e.g., the return to the disciples in 14:41, which is not preceded by a departure in 14:40, and the shifting indications as to whether those Jesus finds sleeping in 14:37–42 are the Twelve or just Peter, James, and John; see the NOTE on "he came and found them sleeping" in 14:37). It is a separate question whether Mark combined the putative sources or whether they were already fused in the pre-Markan tradition; the only verses that seem to bear his fingerprints are 14:33a (the separation of Peter, James, and John) and 14:40bc, which echoes the redactional 9:6.

The passage falls into two roughly equal halves: the first prayer (14:32–36), and the second and third prayers and the returns to the disciples (14:37–42).

14:32–36: the first prayer. The passage begins with "And they came" (*kai erchontai*, 14:32a), the first of a series of usages of *kai* ("and") plus *erchesthai* ("to go or come") to indicate Jesus' shuttling back and forth from isolation to contact with his disciples (see 14:32, 35, 37, 39, 40, 41). As this enumeration indicates, the shuttling becomes more frantic toward the end of the passage. The goal of the "coming" in the present verse is "a place named Gethsemane," which presumably was on the Mount of Olives (cf. 14:26). Although nowadays this site is usually called "the garden of Gethsemane," the Synoptics call it Gethsemane but not a garden, whereas John refers to it as a garden but not Gethsemane (John 18:1).

Arriving at this site, Jesus leaves the main body of the disciples near its entrance (14:32) and proceeds into the interior with his three most intimate followers (14:33a). The interior, the private place, is often in Mark the locus for divine revelation or other manifestations of miraculous power (cf. 4:10, 34; 7:33; 9:2, 28; 13:3); here, too, there will be a revelation, but of a different nature. Jesus' three companions, Peter, James, and John, are the first disciples mentioned in the list in 3:16–19, and on two previous occasions, the raising of Jairus' daughter (5:37) and the transfiguration (9:2), he segregated himself with them. The transfiguration provides a particularly close parallel to our narrative; in both, Jesus "takes" (*paralambanei*) the three with him (9:2; 14:33) and is shown to be God's Son (9:7; 14:36), and in both the disciples "do not know what to answer him" (9:6; 14:40; cf. Brown, *Death*, 1.151–52). The three have thus been witnesses of Jesus' life-giving power and transcendent glory; now they become observers of his human frailty (cf. Theophylact, *Explanation of Mark* 14:32–42).

In Mark there is the closest possible connection between these two aspects of Jesus, and this paradoxical coexistence is stressed by the application to him of the peculiarly Markan term "to be overwhelmed" (*ekthambeisthai*, 14:33b). Elsewhere Mark uses forms of (*ek*)*thambeisthai* to portray Jesus overwhelming *others* by the divine power manifest in his words (10:24), his healing miracles (1:27), his radiant countenance (9:15), and, ultimately, his rising from the dead (16:5–6). In 10:32, moreover, the disciples were overwhelmed by the prospect of going up to the city where Jesus had implied that he would die (see the reference to the chief priests in 8:31, and cf. 9:31), while he calmly reiterated that prophecy (10:33–34). Now, however, Jesus himself is overwhelmed and anxious as he faces death, and in a moment he will ask God to take away the "cup" that he previously accepted (cf. 10:38; 14:23–24; cf. Brown, *Death*, 1.170). These features contradict both Jesus' previous behavior and the stalwart way in which martyrs, including Christian ones, were expected to face death and thus to testify to a higher truth (see, e.g., 2 Macc 6:18–7:42; 4 Macc 6:1–18:23; Mark 8:35; Acts 6:8–7:60; *Mart. Pol.* 5; Origen, *Against Celsus* 2:23–24; cf. Feldmeier, *Krisis*, 145–46; Davies and Allison, 3.492–93).

Jesus' first words in the scene, "My soul is very sad, to the point of death" (14:34a), begin to place these puzzling reversals into a scriptural context. On the one hand, they express desperate sorrow, but on the other they echo two of the psalms of the Righteous Sufferer, Psalms 6 and 42/43 (see the NOTE on "My soul is very sad, to the point of death" in 14:34). This allusion is part of a persistent pattern, since the Righteous Sufferer psalms are echoed throughout the Markan passion narrative (see figure 47). In these psalms, the speaker complains about the pain and persecution he is suffering, protests his innocence, and affirms his trust in God's

Figure 47: The Markan Passion Narrative and the Psalms of the Righteous Sufferer

Mark		Psalms
14:1	stealthily . . . kill	10:7–9
14:18	the one eating with me	41:9
14:34	very sad	6:3; 42:5, 11; 43:5
14:41	turned over to the hands of sinners	140:4, 8
14:54	following from a distance	38:11
14:55	sought to put him to death	37:32
14:57	false witnesses rose up	27:12; 35:11
14:61; 15:4–5	silence before accusers	38:13–14
15:3	vehement verbal attack	109:3
15:24	division of garments	22:18
15:29	mockery, shaking of heads	22:7
15:30–31	Save yourself!	22:8
15:32	reviling	22:6
15:34	cry of abandonment	22:1
15:36	gave him vinegar to drink	69:21
15:39	worshiped by Gentiles	22:27
15:40	watching from far away	38:11
15:43	dominion of God	22:28

goodness and eventual vindication. Jesus' complaint about his depression thus stands within a biblical context of ultimate trust in God's purposes. Moreover, the complaints of the Righteous Sufferer were by the first century being interpreted as references to the eschatological tribulation of the elect, who in the end-time would be assailed by Satan's hosts but ultimately delivered by God (see again the NOTE on "My soul is very sad, to the point of death" in 14:34). A similar eschatological context can be inferred from our passage, which as we shall see is full of words that have an apocalyptic nuance elsewhere in Mark, the rest of the NT, and ancient Jewish literature (e.g., "keep awake," "hour," "cup," "sleeping," and "has come near"). Jesus, then, is engaged not just in a personal confrontation with his own death but in eschatological warfare against cosmic forces of evil, and his anguish is part of an ongoing battle for the salvation of the world.

Faced with this eschatological challenge, Jesus urges his closest followers to keep awake (grēgoreite, 14:34b), as he himself will do—the first of three instances of this verb in our pericope (cf. 14:37, 38). Grēgorein was employed eschatologically three times at the end of chapter 13, and this is just one of a series of vocabulary and thematic connections between that section and the present one (see the NOTE on "keep awake" in 14:34 and the COMMENT on 14:37–42 below), all of which suggest that the end-time nuance from chapter 13 is meant to carry over here. The injunction to stay awake has both a literal and a metaphorical meaning, the first of which the disciples will violate by falling asleep, the second by being unprepared when disaster strikes. Jesus himself, however, takes his own advice and stays awake, and his spiritual distance from the disciples is complemented by a physical one, as he moves beyond them (14:35a), apparently seeking the privacy necessary for communion with his "Father."

He does not, however, get very far, going forward only "a bit" (*mikron*) before he falls on the ground (*epipten epi tēs gēs*, 14:35b), a gesture reminiscent of the tragic story of the anointed but rejected king of Israel, Saul (see the NOTE on "he fell on the ground" in 14:35). Unlike Saul, however, Jesus, though literally floored by anguish, nevertheless remains active, doing the one thing left to him, and to all who find themselves in similar situations: he prays. The prayer is repeated for emphasis: Jesus asks (in indirect discourse) that "the hour" might pass from him (14:35c) and then (in direct discourse) that God would remove "this cup" (14:36a); the indirect request is qualified by "if it were possible," while the direct one is modified by "But not what I want, but what you want" (Brown, *Death*, 1.166). Both "hour" and "cup" are common metaphors for death but also have an eschatological dimension: "the hour" is the appointed time of eschatological testing, tribulation, and deliverance, as already in Mark 13:32, and "the cup" is the beaker of divine wrath that is to be poured out on the recalcitrant earth in the end-time (see the NOTES on "hour" in 14:35 and "cup" in 14:36). This context of eschatological judgment is probably part of the explanation for Jesus' anguished reaction to the prospect of his death: he quails not just before the termination of his life but also before the prospect of the outpouring of the divine wrath (cf. Feldmeier, *Krisis*, 144–46). A similar nuance of divine judgment is conveyed by the implied setting in night and darkness (cf. Luke 22:53; John 13:30), the description of Jesus falling to the ground (see the NOTE on "he fell on the ground" in 14:35), and his climactic words about being delivered into the hands of sinners (see the NOTES on "the Son of Man is being turned over to the hands" and "of the sinners" in 14:41). The true horror is not just to face death but to face it under the wrath of God.

No wonder, then, that Jesus petitions God, his heavenly Father (see the NOTE on "*Abba* [Father]" in 14:36), to grant that this experience of eschatological tribulation ("the cup") may pass from him (14:36a). He ends up acknowledging, however, that things need to fall out according to God's will rather than his own. These features are similar to aspects of the Lord's Prayer, especially in its Matthean version: "Our Father . . . may your will be done . . . do not lead us into testing" (Matt 6:9–15, my trans.; cf. Luke 11:2–4), and it is possible that this prayer was known to Mark's community, even though he never quotes it explicitly; the parallels here and elsewhere in Mark make the hypothesis at least a strong possibility (cf. the NOTES on "so that your Father in heaven may also forgive you your transgressions" in 11:25 and "not what I want, but what you want" in 14:36). If so, Mark's addressees may grasp that Jesus, in asking for the removal of the cup, was only putting into practice what he elsewhere instructed others to do; the terrors of the end-time may be a necessary part of the unfolding divine plan, but it is natural to want to avoid them, and Jesus does.

From earliest times, however, critics of Christianity, as well as some Christians, have treated as problematic the Markan portrait of Jesus' attempt to escape from death in Gethsemane. The late-second-century pagan critic Celsus, for example, regarded Jesus' lamentation and prayer as proof that he was not divine (Origen, *Against Celsus* 2.24). Christians had similar qualms; Luke, for example, omits the Markan references to Jesus being overwhelmed, anxious, and sorrowful, softening the impact of the scene further by having Jesus *kneel* on the ground rather than *falling* on it and by having him pray only once (Luke 22:39–42, 45–46); Matthew makes subtler changes to Mark 14:35 that also attenuate its impact (Matt 26:39; see Ehrman and Plunkett, "Angel," 411; Brown, *Death*, 1.165). John goes even further, since his Jesus seemingly contradicts, at the same time that he echoes, the core of the Gethsemane tradition: "Now my soul is troubled. And what should I say—'Father, save me from this hour'? *No!*—it is for this reason that I have come to this hour!" (John 12:27 NRSV alt.).

Subsequent Christian interpreters have often followed in the footsteps of these later Gospels by toning down the rough edges of the Gethsemane tradition through ingenious exegesis. Origen, for example, making much of a Markan stylistic quirk, notes that the text says that Jesus *began* to be overwhelmed and anxious—not, Origen concludes, that he actually *arrived* at such a state (*Commentary on Matthew* 90; on Mark's "began to" idiom, see the NOTE on "began to send them out" in 6:7). Others have argued, against the plain sense of the text, that Jesus' sorrow in Gethsemane was not for himself but for Judas and/or the Jewish people, who had rejected him (e.g., Jerome, *Commentary on Matthew* on 26:37). The motivation for such exegetical softenings is both Christological and paraenetic (see the GLOSSARY). Hilary of Poitiers asserts that only heretics say that Jesus feared death, since such an opinion contradicts the truth that he was consubstantial with the Father (*Commentary on Matthew* 31.3), and Origen claims that a portrait of a fearful Jesus would undermine Christian willingness to endure martyrdom: "If he showed fear . . . who will be always brave?" (*Exhortation to Martyrdom* 29; trans. Smith, *Ante-Nicene Exegesis*, 5.327).

But there is another side to the issue, and this is probably the aspect that Mark wants to emphasize. When Christians feel weak and fearful at the prospect of imminent death and other suffering—as many in the persecuted Markan community probably did—they may be empowered by remembering that their Lord also struggled with tribulation, but thereby overcame the world (cf. John 16:33). Thus some interpreters have seen the portrait of Jesus' agony in Gethsemane as significant precisely because it shows him to be human (see already Justin, *Dialogue* 99), and the depiction of him both seeking to avoid the cup and accepting it has often been cited as proof that he had both a human will and a divine one (see, e.g., Aquinas, *Summa Theologica* 3.18.1, cited by Brown, *Death*, 1.170–71). And because Jesus is shown here to share in human weakness, he is also a model for the way in which feeble and wavering Christians may be strengthened through the grace of God (cf. Dormeyer, *Passion*):

> In the days of his flesh, he offered up prayers and supplications, with loud cries and tears, to the one who was able to save him from death, and was heard because of his reverent submission . . . For we do not have a high priest who is un-

able to sympathize with our weaknesses, but one who in every respect has been tested as we are, yet without sin. Let us therefore approach the throne of grace with boldness, so that we may receive mercy and find grace to help in time of need (Heb 5:7; 4:15–16 NRSV alt.)

"Grace to help in time of need": this is the hidden message of the searing Markan depiction of Jesus in Gethsemane.

14:37–42: the second and third prayers and the returns to the disciples. From his followers, however, the Markan Jesus does not get help in his time of need. The second half of the pericope is dominated by the story of his fruitless attempts to rouse them to keep him company and guard their own spiritual health.

This quest begins when Jesus returns from his *Abba* prayer to find the disciples sleeping (14:37a). This is a second hint (the first was the conclusion of the prayer itself) that the answer to that prayer will be no; God will not remove the cup of suffering from Jesus, any more than he will provide him with companionship for his ordeal. As Cranfield (434) puts it: "The only answer Jesus receives to his prayer is the hard answer of events." This section of the Gethsemane narrative, then, has been aptly titled, "The Silence of God" (Feldmeier, *Krisis*, 186). In this terrible divine silence, and confronted with the slumbering group of erstwhile devotees, Jesus addresses Peter with words meant for all disciples, as is evident from the shift from the second person singular in 14:37bc to the second person plural in 14:38; Peter thus continues to be the representative disciple (cf. the introduction to the COMMENT on 14:26–31). He represents, however, an apostolic group teetering on the edge of apostasy, as will become evident in the following scenes, when the Twelve flee at Jesus' arrest (14:50; cf. also 14:52) and Peter himself denies him (14:66–72). It may be that Jesus' address of Peter with his old name, "Simon," hints at this incipient apostasy; instead of being "the Rock," the ecclesiastical foundation of Jesus' new-age edifice, Peter is in danger of slipping back into the old age where Satan holds sway (cf. the COMMENT on 8:31–33 and the NOTE on "Simon" in 14:37).

Jesus' approach to the disciples begins with words that both awaken Peter and apprise him of his condition: "Are you sleeping? Didn't you have the strength to keep awake one hour?" (14:37bc). Peter has been sleeping in more than one sense. He and the others have literally been nodding off, but sleep in the NT may also be a symbol for a state of mind that insensately takes its cues from the darkness of the old age rather than the light of the new (see Rom 13:11–14; Eph 5:11–14; 1 Thess 5:4–10; cf. Maurer, "*Hypnos*," 554). This eschatological nuance is enhanced by the verbal links between our passage and the end-time prophecies at the close of chapter 13, where Jesus warned his followers to keep awake lest the master "come" and "find [them] sleeping." Jesus repeats the exhortation to stay awake in 14:34, but shortly thereafter "the master" does indeed come and find his disciples sleeping, not once but three times (14:37a; cf. 14:40, 41), suggesting that the prophesied hour of crisis has arrived. The phrasing in 13:32–37 and 14:32–42 is strikingly parallel (see figure 46), suggesting that Mark has deliberately fashioned the pres-

ent narrative as an echo of the eschatological prophecies in chapter 13. Jesus'
question to Peter, therefore, contains a double entendre similar to that of God's
"Where are you?" to Adam in Gen 3:9. It is not only a question about where Peter
stands physically—in a state of physical wakefulness or slumber—but also one
about where he is situated in relation to the tremendous collision of ages that will
soon occur in Jesus' death and resurrection.

Moving from reproach to remedy, Jesus prescribes watchfulness and prayer, "so
that you may not enter into testing (*peirasmon*); the spirit is willing, but the flesh
is weak" (14:38ab). Here again, a manifestly eschatological locution is employed;
peirasmos, especially in conjunction with *hōra* ("hour," 14:35, 41), is a technical
term for "the hour of testing that is coming on the whole world, to test the inhabitants of the earth" (Rev 3:10 NRSV alt.; cf. Rev 2:9–10; 1 Pet 4:12; Acts 20:19;
Matt 6:13//Luke 11:4; 4QCatena[a] (4Q177) 2:10–11; 4QFlor 1 2:1; Brown, *Death*,
1.159–61). Kuhn ("Temptation") has pointed out the striking similarities between
this Markan picture of eschatological testing and that at Qumran; in both, the entrance point for the attacking forces is "the flesh," that is, humanity's corporeality,
self-absorption, and vulnerability to sin (see, e.g., 1QM 4:3; 1QS 11:7–12), whereas
the chief weapon of resistance is the spirit that God has implanted in the world
(see the NOTE on "the spirit is willing, but the flesh is weak" in 14:38). Both at
Qumran and in Mark, however, the victory of the spirit is by no means assured;
the vulnerability of "the flesh" to attack results not only in strife between the
elect community and outsiders but also in apostasy and internal division within
the elect group itself (cf. Marcus, "Epistemology," 567–70). The ultimate source
of these tribulations is demonic assault (see the NOTE on "testing" in 14:38); as
Dostoyevsky's character Dmitri Karamazov famously puts it: "God and the devil
are fighting for mastery, and the battlefield is the heart of man" (*Brothers Karamazov*, 124 [1.3.3]).

This framework of eschatological warfare helps explain the increasing frenzy
implicit in Jesus' movements toward the end of the scene (see the introduction to
the COMMENT). This accelerated movement begins with Jesus going away to
pray a second time, using the same words as before (14:39); he is still, therefore,
seeking escape from "the hour" and "the cup." When he returns to the disciples
again, he finds their eyes "weighed down" (14:40), another probable indication of
eschatological tribulation and Satanic oppression (cf. the use of "weighed down"
in an eschatological context in Luke 21:34, and the introduction to the COM-
MENT on 8:27–33 on Satan as a blinder). Still suffering from his isolation and the
weight of the eschatological crisis, therefore, Jesus presumably wakes the disciples
again, though this is not narrated. Their befuddled response ("and they didn't
know what to answer him," 14:40c) echoes the scene of the transfiguration ("For
he did not know what to answer; for they had become afraid," 9:6): they understand
neither Jesus' transcendent glory nor his human vulnerability, although these are
inseparable characteristics of God's new age. The next verse (14:41a) implies that
Jesus, unable to rouse them to action, goes away to pray a third time; attentive
readers may thus link Jesus' Gethsemane experience with a biblical pattern of
earnest, threefold petition (see Ps 55:17; 2 Cor 12:8–9; cf. *b. Yoma* 87a; Davies and

Allison, 3.500). Of these parallel passages, 2 Cor 12:8–9 is most instructive, since it consists of a triple petition by Paul that is rejected by the risen Lord; in the end, however, Paul understands that while Jesus does not intend to relieve his suffering, he will give him the strength to bear it, since Jesus' eschatological power is perfected in arenas of old-age weakness. Something similar may be inferred with regard to Jesus himself at the end of our passage (14:41b–42); we do not hear, as we did in 14:39, that he is "saying the same thing," and his concluding words manifest an acceptance of his fate.

This weighty concluding announcement has several important aspects. First, it proclaims eschatological advent: "The hour has come!" (14:41b; see the NOTE on "hour" in 14:35). Second, it links this advent with the "turning over" (*paradidotai*) of the Son of Man to "sinners," presumably to be killed (14:41c; cf. 9:31; 10:33–34). Mark probably thinks of this "turning over" as both a divine and a human action, and Satanic influence may also be implied, in view of the implications of demonic agency in the context (cf. the NOTES on "You will . . . be tripped up" in 14:27, "testing" in 14:38, and "the Son of Man is being turned over to the hands" in 14:41).

The central theological conundrum of the passage, however, is that it speaks of the Son of Man being "turned over to the hands of . . . sinners" (14:41c). The expression "turn over to the hands" is not found in secular Greek but is frequent in the OT and intertestamental Judaism (see the survey of usage in Popkes, *Christus Traditus*, 1–129). The explicit or implied subject is usually God, who gives Israel's foes into their hands in holy war (e.g., Josh 2:24; 6:2, 16; *1 En.* 38:5; 48:9; 63:1) or turns Israel over to their enemies when they have sinned and deserve punishment (especially in Jeremiah and Ezekiel; see, e.g., Jer 21:10; 22:25; 46:24 [26:24 LXX]; Ezek 7:21; 11:9; 16:39; cf. *Jub.* 1:13, 19, 21–22; *T. Ash.* 7:2; *Par. Jer.* 4:6–7). "Turning over to the hands," therefore, is the opposite of salvation and equivalent to judgment, an equivalence made explicit in Ezek 11:9 and 4Q171 2:20 [1–10 2:20]. For this reason, what Jesus prophesies is the opposite of what the faithful hoped for; the psalmist, for example, prays, "Do not turn me over, O Lord . . . to the sinner" (*mē paradǭs me kyrie . . . hamartōlǭ*, Ps 140:8 [139:9 LXX]). When such things happen, the righteous can justly protest against them (see, e.g., Isa 25:5 LXX), and at the eschaton such outrages will cease; sinners, instead, will be delivered into the hands of the righteous for judgment (see *1 En.* 91:12; 95:3, 7; cf. 38:5; 98:12; 1QpHab 9:9–12; 4Q171 4:7–10 [1–10 4:7–10]). Our passage, then, represents a reversal of what was normally expected for the eschaton: sinners should be turned over to the righteous, not the other way around.

It is even more paradoxical to speak of *the Son of Man* being delivered into the hands of sinners. This is a striking reversal of Dan 7:13–14, in which the "one like a son of man" is "given dominion and glory and kingship, that all peoples, nations, and languages should serve him," including the evil nations that have oppressed Israel. (For another Markan reversal of this passage, see the NOTE on "the Son of Man did not come to be served but to serve" in 10:45.) In a later midrash on Daniel 7, 4Q246 2:1–9, the Son of Man figure is called "the Son of God" (2:1), and it is said that "the great God . . . will wage war for him; he will give the peoples into his hand" ('*mmyn yntn bydh*; García Martínez trans. alt.; cf. Collins, *Scepter*, 159). The Hebrew/Aramaic idiom employed here, *ntn byd*, is usually translated by the LXX with *paradidonai eis (tas) cheiras* ("to turn over to the hands"). Thus, the OT and Qumran expectation is that God will deliver sinful nations into the hands of the Son of God/Son of Man, and it is likely that the Jewish revolutionaries whose militant theology forms the backdrop for our Gospel fervently embraced such expectations. Jesus in our passage, however, announces the opposite: the Son of Man is about to be delivered into the hands of sinners. By so doing, he will accomplish a different kind of salvation, taking upon himself the divine judgment that, as we have seen, is intrinsic to the idea of being "turned over to the hands of . . . sinners." Verse 14:41, therefore, expresses the same basic thought as 10:45 and 14:24, and that Paul points to when he speaks about Christ being "made sin" for humanity's sake (2 Cor 5:21).

But in order for Jesus to accomplish this salvation, he must die; and in order for that to happen, he must be turned over to the authorities by a member of his inner circle. That betrayal is announced as imminent at the conclusion of our passage (14:42b) and will immediately occur in the next one.

JESUS IS ARRESTED (14:43–52)

14 ⁴³And immediately, as he was still speaking, Judas, one of the Twelve, arrived; and with him a crowd with swords and clubs from the chief priests and the scribes and the elders. ⁴⁴The one who was turning him over had given them a signal, saying, "Whoever I kiss, he's the one; seize him and lead him away securely." ⁴⁵And when he arrived, he immediately went up to Jesus and said to him, "Rabbi!" and kissed him. ⁴⁶And they laid hands on him and took him into custody. ⁴⁷But a certain one of those who were present drew a sword and struck the high priest's slave and cut off his ear.

⁴⁸And Jesus answered and said to them, "Have you come out as against a brigand to apprehend me? ⁴⁹During the daytime I have been with you, teaching in the Temple, and you did not seize me. But in order that the scriptures may be fulfilled . . ."

⁵⁰And abandoning him, they all ran away. ⁵¹And a certain youth was following along with him, clothed with a linen cloth over his nakedness; and they seized him. ⁵²But he, abandoning the linen cloth, ran away naked.

NOTES

14 43. *crowd.* Gk *ochlos.* The exact nature of this crowd is difficult to determine (see Brown, *Death*, 1.247); the word can designate a disorganized mob, and this nuance coheres with the wooden clubs (*xyloi*) that its members carry, which could be the sort of "pickup" weapons used by civilians, though soldiers sometimes wielded clubs as well (cf. Josephus, *War* 2.176). The crowd also brandishes swords (*machairai*), which were usually carried by soldiers or police, but sometimes by

civilians (cf. Luke 22:49; John 18:10). The reference to the crowd having come "from the chief priests and the scribes and the elders," however, seems to tip the balance toward a commissioned group (cf. John 18:3). Practically speaking, more-over, it is questionable that the Jewish authorities would have left the arrest of Jesus to the discretion of a mob. It may be that the historical reality was arrest by a delegation of police and/or other agents of the authorities, but Mark uses the vague word "crowd" because he wishes to broaden the responsibility and thus to foreshadow 15:11, where the Jerusalem populace turns against Jesus.

44–45. *kiss . . . kissed.* Gk *philēsō . . . katephilēsen.* The treacherous kiss has background in the OT; see, for example, Prov 27:6 ("profuse are the kisses of an enemy") and 2 Sam 20:9–10, where Joab purports to greet the unsuspecting Amasa with a kiss and then stabs him to death. The kiss, indeed, is not infre-quently associated with death (cf. our expression "kiss of death"); see, for example, *T. Job* 52:8, where Death's kiss kills Job; the tradition in *b. B. Bat.* 17a about the biblical saints who died from a "kiss of God"; and the medieval Christian idea of the "death of the kiss" (cf. Allison, *Testament of Abraham*, 395–97; Perella, *Kiss*, index under "Death, and kiss").

In the OT, people frequently kiss each other as a sign of greeting (e.g., Gen 33:4; Exod 4:27; 2 Sam 15:5); if in Jesus' time the kiss was still a normal mode of salutation, Judas' kiss may have been an inconspicuous action designed to iden-tify Jesus to the arresting party without alarming him or the Eleven. Some schol-ars, however, cite rabbinic passages such as *Gen. Rab.* 70.12 in support of the counterclaim that the salutatory kiss had lapsed among first-century Palestinian Jews (see, e.g., Klassen, "Kiss," 4.91). If this were the case, Judas' kiss may have ap-peared to onlookers to be something more than a greeting, perhaps an expression of the strong emotional attachment of a disciple for his master (cf. *m. Roš Haš* 2:9; *b. Ketub.* 103b; Brown, *Death*, 1.254–55). In line with this interpretation, Taylor (559) argues that the compounded form *katephilēsen* in 14:45, in distinction from the simple *philēsō* in 14:44, should be translated "kissed fervently" (cf. Xenophon, *Memorabilia* 2.6.33).

These arguments, however, are unconvincing. As with many other verbs, the classical distinction between the simple and compounded forms of *philein* does not seem to hold in koine Greek (see Robertson, 606; Voelz, "Language," 938); *kataphilein*, for example, is used in Gen 31:28, 55; Exod 4:27 for formal kisses of greeting and farewell rather than for fervent ones. The shift from *philēsō* in 14:44 to *kataphilēsen* in 14:45, therefore, may just be stylistic (see Stälin, "Phileō," 140 n. 240). As for the argument that salutatory kissing had disappeared among first-century Jews, Luke 7:45 seems to presuppose the formal greeting kiss (see Stählin, "Phileō," 138), and Philo (*Who Is the Heir* 41) speaks of it explicitly (though he was a Diaspora Jew, not a Palestinian one). The later rabbinic strictures against kiss-ing, moreover, are directed against contemporary customs and thus are a witness to the very thing they oppose. The greeting kiss, then, was not unusual in Jesus' world. Still, the early Christians and perhaps already the circle of Jesus may have expanded the use of the kiss out of a sense that all Christians were brothers and sis-ters and that kissing was permitted within this Christian "family" (cf. the Pauline references to the "holy kiss" in Rom 16:16; 1 Cor 16:20; 2 Cor 13:12; 1 Thess 5:26; and Phillips, *Ritual Kiss*, 15).

On what part of Jesus' body would Judas have kissed him? In the Greco-Roman world, non-erotic kisses could be placed on various parts of the body, but the kiss of honor was usually directed to the hands (see Stählin, "*Phileō*," 120–21). Rabbinic sources speak especially about kisses on the head (the context is usually a teacher kissing his student, and we are probably to imagine the student bowing his head and the teacher kissing the top of it), but also about kisses on the hand, mouth, knee, or foot (cf. Strack-Billerbeck, 1.995–96). In the present case a kiss on the lower extremities can safely be ruled out, because it would be hard to see in the crowd, but beyond that it is impossible to determine the precise location (lips, head, hand, perhaps even shoulder or chest). In Christian art, however, a kiss on the face is almost always portrayed, presumably because of its dramatic potential.

Some have questioned the historicity of the Judas kiss because of its absence from John. Stählin ("*Phileō*," 141), however, points out that the Fourth Gospel's stress on Jesus' sovereignty provides a plausible motive for omission: by announcing, "I am he" (John 18:5–6), Jesus identifies *himself* rather than being singled out by Judas' kiss. As Smith (*John*, 330) observes, moreover, "The absence of Judas's kiss fits with John's sense of the dignity and authority of Jesus: the one who is betraying Jesus does not touch—much less kiss—him."

44. *lead him away securely.* Gk *apagete asphalōs.* BDAG (147) defines *aspahlōs* as "in a manner that assures continuing detention." Matthew omits the clause; Davies and Allison (3.508) speculate that he may have found troublesome the implication that Jesus might flee or resist arrest. *Asphalōs*, however, could also be translated "safely," and perhaps Matthew was bothered by the overly sympathetic impression that *apagete asphalōs* might leave of Judas—as though he were trying to protect Jesus.

45. *Rabbi.* Gk *rabbi.* On this honorific term, see the NOTE on "Rabbi" in 9:5, where its special connection with the teaching office is noted; that connection continues in our passage (cf. "teaching in the Temple" in 14:49).

46. *laid hands on him.* Gk *epebalon tas cheiras autọ.* On the OT background of this phrase, see the COMMENT on 14:43–47. One of the echoes is Gen 22:12, in which Abraham is ordered not to lay his hand on his son Isaac (cf. Huizenga, "Jesus," 87; on the analogy between the sacrifice of Jesus and that of Isaac, see the NOTES on "beloved" in 1:11 and "He still had one, his beloved son" in 12:6). In our passage, however, no heavenly voice intervenes to stop hostile hands from seizing Jesus.

took . . . into custody. Gk *ekratēsan.* This verb is translated "seized" in 14:44, 51; it can be used either for the physical action of laying hands on a person or for the more abstract idea of gaining control over him. In the present case the latter is meant, since otherwise *epebalon tas cheiras autọ kai ekratēsan auton* would be tautologous.

47. *But a certain one.* Gk *heis de tis.* *Heis* alone, which is the reading of some texts, would also mean "a certain one," as would *tis* alone; *heis . . . tis* may therefore have struck a scribe as redundant and awkward, or the omission may have

occurred through homoeoteleuton (*he<u>is</u> ... <u>tis</u>*; on homoeoteleuton, see the GLOSSARY). The reading *heis ... tis* is supported by the majority of manuscripts, including B, C, D, Θ, Ψ, *f*¹³, a, l, vg, sy^h. The attestation for the omission, to be sure, is also strong (e.g., ℵ, A, L, 579, 700, 2427, aur, f, sy^{p, s}), and *tis* could be a marginal gloss or an assimilation to Luke 22:50 (contrast Matt 26:51, which has *heis* alone). But *heis* is probably not ambiguous enough to be glossed, and assimilation to an awkward Lukan text is less likely than assimilation to a smooth Matthean one.

If *heis de tis* is the original reading, one way of construing it is as a reference to someone whom the author knows but does not wish to mention (see, e.g., Sophocles, *Oedipus the King* 118). In line with this construal, Lagrange (394) thinks that Mark knows that the swordsman is Peter, as in John 18:10, but suppresses the name for prudential reasons. Theissen (*Gospels*, 184–89), who rejects the historicity of the identification with Peter (later traditions often fill in the names of anonymous characters), still thinks it likely that the anonymity of the swordsman in 14:47 and the young man who runs away naked in 14:51–52 is a protective device for still-living followers of Jesus and thus an indication of the early provenance of the pre-Markan passion narrative. This may be, but *heis de tis* may also indicate someone who stands out from a group that has previously been mentioned (cf. John 11:49; Josephus, *Ant.* 3.297; 13.291; *Life* 290); understood in this way, the swordsman could be a member of the arresting party who had suddenly changed his mind (see the next NOTE). It is also possible that this is simply an example of the pleonasm of koine Greek (see the GLOSSARY; Robertson, 675; BDAG 292 [3c]; cf. Jdt 2:13; *Acts of John* 60, 63).

of those who were present. Gk *tōn parestēkotōn.* A *parestēkos* can be either an innocent bystander or a person involved in the action (see BDAG 778 [2ba]). Most scholars assume that the attacker is one of the disciples, since that is how Matthew, Luke, and John interpret him (Matt 26:51; Luke 22:49–50; John 18:10), and it seems logical that one of Jesus' entourage might resist his arrest. Brown (*Death*, 1.266), however, advocates the bystander interpretation: Mark would have made the man's status clear if he had meant him to be a disciple, and none of the other instances of *parestēkos* in the Markan passion narrative denotes a follower of Jesus (14:69, 70; 15:35, 39). But later in the narrative, where these instances occur, the context has shifted to a more public setting, in which the presence of uninvolved bystanders is more plausible than it is in the scene of Jesus' arrest. Our story, moreover, otherwise assumes the presence only of Jesus, his disciples, and the arresting party. And if the swordsman was one of the disciples, Mark or the pre-Markan tradition might have a motivation for obscuring this fact and the identity of the assailant (see the COMMENT on 14:48–49). There are other possibilities, such as that Mark understands the swordsman as a repentant member of the arresting party (see the previous NOTE and Lamarche, 339), but all in all the disciple interpretation seems the most likely one.

49. *During the daytime.* Gk *kath' hēmeran.* This phrase can mean either "day after day" or "during the daytime" (LSJ 883, B, II, 2, and VII). In the NT it usually means "day after day" (see, e.g., Luke 9:23; 11:3; Acts 2:46–47; 3:2; 1 Cor 15:31;

2 Cor 11:28; Heb 7:27; 10:11; cf. BDAG 512 [2c]). This interpretation, however, conflicts with the Markan chronology, in which Jesus teaches in the Temple for two days only (11:17; 11:27–12:44; cf. figure 33 and Lohmeyer, 227). It is more likely that Mark interprets *kath' hēmeran* as "during the daytime," a meaning supported by the Lukan parallel (Luke 22:53; cf. 21:37 and Argyle, "Meaning"; BDAG 512 [2a]). This nuance fits the Markan context, in which Jesus is arrested at night and denies that he is a brigand—that is, the sort of person who operates under cover of darkness (cf. Obadiah 5; Philo, *Embassy to Gaius* 122; Chariton, *Chaireas and Callirhoe* 3.10.2; 8.8.1; Epiphanius, *Panarion* 69.44.1).

   But in order that the scriptures may be fulfilled . . . Gk *all hina plērōthōsin hai graphai.* As in 9:12, no specific OT passage is cited, and the use of the plural *graphai* ("scriptures") may suggest that more than one passage is in view. Since the reference is to Jesus' arrest through "the one . . . turning him over" (*ho paradidous*), which will lead to his death, one of those passages is probably Isa 53:12 LXX: "His soul was turned over (*paredothē*) to death." Another may be Zech 13:7, which speaks of the shepherd being struck and his sheep scattered, especially since the following Markan verses allude to the dispersal of the disciples (14:50–52; see Moo, *Old Testament,* 109–10).

   50. *they all ran away.* Gk *ephygon pantes. Pheugein* is frequently used in the OT and later writings to speak about the panicked flight that will characterize the coming crisis or the last days (see, e.g., Isa 10:18, 30; 13:14; Amos 5:19; 9:1; Nah 2:5; Zech 2:6; 1 *En.* 62:10; cf. Gnilka, 2.267). As in our passage, some of these texts combine *pheugein* with forms of *pas* ("all"; see Isa 22:3; 43:14; Rev 16:20; cf. the idea of general or universal flight in Isa 24:18; 30:17; Jer 46:21 [26:21 LXX]; 50:16 [27:16 LXX]). In the NT *pheugein* is particularly prominent in eschatological passages (see Mark 13:14 pars.; Matt 3:7//Luke 3:7; Matt 10:23; 23:33; Rev 9:6; 12:6; 16:20; 20:11).

   51. *clothed with a linen cloth over his nakedness.* Gk *peribeblēmenos sindona epi gymnou.* The term *sindōn* can be used for either an outer or an inner garment (see Jackson, "Youth," 279), but here the reference is apparently to a loincloth (see Edwards, "Dress," 236). Smith (*Clement,* 176), citing Diogenes Laertius, *Lives* 6.90, asserts that this is not a "proper" garment, that is, the sort of thing one would normally wear in public. Neither, however, is it a rag; linen was costly (cf. Neirynck, "Fuite," 237), and among Jews it was especially associated with priestly garb (see Exod 28:39, 42; Lev 16:4, 32; etc.). Indeed, the theme, though not the vocabulary, of our passage recalls the description of priestly clothing in Exod 28:42: "And you shall make them linen leggings to cover the shame (= nakedness) of their flesh" (my trans.).

   The words *epi gymnou* ("over his nakedness") are omitted by a small number of manuscripts (W, f^1, c, k, sy^s, sa^{mss}), and Neirynck ("Fuite," 62–64) thinks them a scribal addition. But *epi gymnou* is the harder reading, and it has the clear purpose of preparing for *gymnos* in 14:52 (see Jackson, "Youth," 278). It is more likely that this phrase was omitted by scribes because of its grammatical awkwardness or potentially scandalous implications (cf. Smith, *Clement,* 91, 185) than that it was added by scribes out of a desire to make sure that readers understood *gymnos* in

14:52 as literally "naked" (so Neirynck; on possible translations of *gymnos*, see the NOTE on "abandoning the linen cloth, ran away naked" in 14:52). A few manuscripts (Θ, *f* [13], 565, pc, sy[p], sa[ms]), moreover, read *peribeblēmenos sindona gymnos*, "wearing a linen cloth, naked," and one (H) reads *peribeblēmenos sindona en gymnou*, which is impossible to translate, but both of which may be corruptions of *epi gymnou* (cf. Jackson). Cranfield (438) thinks, on the contrary, that *epi gymnou* may be a correction of *gymnos*, which in turn resulted from the copyist's eye skipping from *sindona* in 14:51 to *sindona gymnos* in 14:52. But this would make *epi gymnou*, which is attested in the earliest and best manuscripts (א, B, D, L, Δ, Ψ, etc.), dependent on a reading that is first attested in Greek in the ninth century. The reading with *epi gymnou*, therefore, best explains the other texts and is to be preferred.

52. *abandoning the linen cloth, ran away naked.* Gk *katalipōn tēn sindona gymnos ephygen.* Some (e.g., Neirynck, "Fuite," 63–65) have argued that *gymnos* here means "in his underwear," that is "with only a chiton on" (on this garment, see the NOTES on "two tunics" in 6:9 and "throwing off his garment" in 10:50). This is a possible meaning of *gymnos* (see, e.g., Demosthenes, *Against Midias* 216; cf. M-M 133; Neirynck, "Fuite," 64 n. 287; BDAG 208[3]) and may be its nuance in John 21:7 (cf. Dio Chrysostom, *Orations* 72.1); an English equivalent would be "stripped," which can mean either completely naked or uncovered to one's underwear. But "over his nakedness" (*epi gymnou*) in 14:51 seems to belie this modest interpretation (on the place of these words in the text, see the NOTE on "clothed with a linen cloth over his nakedness" in 14:51).

As Pseudo-Jerome, the first commentator on Mark, realized (*Exposition of Mark* 14:51–52 [Cahill, 109]), the description in our verse is reminiscent of that of Joseph, whom Potiphar's wife pressured to have adulterous relations but who left his clothes in her hands and ran away (*katalipōn ta himatia autou en tais cheirsin autēs ephygen,* Gen 39:12). The similarity is even greater to *T. Jos.* 8:3 (*kratei mou ton chitōna kataleipsas auton ephygon gymnos,* "She grabbed my garment; I abandoned it and ran away naked"). Waetjen ("Ending," 117–20) concludes that this similarity is part of a pervasive Joseph typology in Mark, but Fleddermann ("Flight," 415) finds no Joseph typology elsewhere. This is not entirely true (see the NOTE on "Come on, let's kill him" in 12:7 and the APPENDIX "History-of-Religions Backgrounds to the Transfiguration"), but a more pressing objection to Waetjen's thesis is that Joseph's flight is commendable, whereas that of the Markan youth is disgraceful. There does, then, seem to be a verbal echo of the Joseph story, but it is difficult to know what to make of it (cf. Jackson, "Youth," 283 n. 26).

COMMENT

Introduction. With Jesus' arrest, the character of the Markan narrative changes. Jesus himself begins to play a more passive part—the sort of role he will assume for the remainder of the Gospel. While previous to 14:43 he has been the subject of most main verbs in any given pericope, from this point on he will be the grammatical object of most action (as in 14:45–46, 50) or the passive focus around which it revolves (as in 14:43–44, 47, 51–52). In our passage, as in the following one, to be sure, this passivity is interrupted by a striking dominical pronouncement that comes, in each case, about two-thirds of the way through (14:48–49, 62). In general, however, from the present scene on, Jesus' speech plays a diminishing role in the narrative: while he uttered about 80 words at the Last Supper (14:22–31), or about 135 if the prophecy of betrayal in 14:18–21 is included, and 85 words in Gethsemane (14:32–42), he voices only about 30 in the present scene (14:43–52), only about 20 at the "Jewish trial" (14:53–72), only 2 at the "Roman trial" (15:1–15)—and then does not speak at all until his final words from the cross. From his arrest on, then, Jesus is falling into silence—which makes his rare utterances even more striking than they would otherwise be. From one point of view, this increasing silence and passivity are not surprising, since in the previous passage Jesus resigned himself to accomplishing not his own will but the will of his Father (14:36).

The episode of Jesus' arrest may once have been handed down independently of the foregoing narratives. In its present context, the designation of Judas as "one of the Twelve" highlights the pathos of the incident and the fulfillment of Jesus' prophecy of betrayal by one of his inner circle (14:18, 20), but it could also be a remnant of an earlier stage in the development of the tradition, in which the identification was necessary because Judas had not yet been introduced. In the previous Markan passages, moreover, it was not said that Judas removed himself from Jesus and the Eleven (contrast John 13:30), so now his rejoining them comes as a surprise (cf. Davies and Allison, 3.507 n. 6). An earlier version of the story may not have included Jesus' utterance in 14:48–49, which sounds like apologetics and ill suits the context: the words would be more appropriate for the Jewish leaders than for their emissaries (see Bultmann, 268–69). When 14:48–49 is omitted, moreover, the story forms a logical progression: one of the disciples commits a desperate act of violent resistance (14:47), then he and his companions take fright and flee for their lives (14:50). The secondary statement in 14:48–49 may well represent Markan redaction; many of the terms and themes are typical of the evangelist ("answered and said"; "com[ing] out," distinguishing Jesus from "brigands" [cf. 11:17; 15:27]; teaching in the Temple [cf. 12:35, 38]; fulfillment of scripture). Also possibly redactional are the typically Markan double time notice in 14:43, which includes Mark's favorite word "immediately" and one of his favorite constructions, a genitive absolute; and the designation of the senders as "the chief priests and the scribes and the elders" (14:43), another typically Markan combination (cf. 8:31; 11:27; 14:53; 15:1).

The passage in its present form is structured in three parts: the arrest itself (14:43–47), Jesus' pronouncement (14:48–49), and the flight of the disciples (14:50–52). Fittingly, the arrest receives most of the attention, but Jesus' pronouncement, because of its central position, illuminates the other two parts.

14:43–47: the arrest of Jesus. Jesus has just warned his disciples that his betrayer is approaching (14:42); now, "immediately, as he was still speaking," Judas appears (14:43a). Already at the very beginning of the passage, then, Jesus is shown to be a prophet—a theme that is underlined by the reference to Judas as "one of the Twelve," which recalls 14:18, 20, where Jesus had prophesied that a member of this group would betray him.

Judas comes, however, not alone, but accompanied by a crowd whose members are doubly armed, with swords and clubs on the one hand, and the authority of the chief priests, the scribes, and the elders on the other (14:43b; on the identity of this mob, see the NOTE on "crowd" in 14:43). They do not seem to know Jesus by face, since they need Judas to identify him—an indication that Jesus may not have been as well known as the Gospel narratives sometimes imply (e.g., Mark 1:5; 3:7–8; 11:1–10; John 11:45–48). Judas tells these confederates that he will identify Jesus by kissing him; they are then to "lead him away securely," that is, under guard (14:44)—displaying the betrayer's anxiety that Jesus may try to flee or that his followers may attempt to liberate him. These apprehensions are not entirely groundless, though they reflect misunderstanding; in Gethsemane Jesus prayed to escape from death (14:36, 39) but ended up ready to die according to God's will (14:41–42), and in the present pericope one of his disciples will try to prevent his arrest but will be implicitly rebuked (14:47–48).

Upon encountering Jesus and the Eleven, Judas immediately delivers the betrayal kiss (14:45). The kiss may have been a recognized gesture of greeting in first-century Judaism, but use of the greeting kiss seems to have expanded in early Christian communities, and perhaps already in the circle of Jesus' disciples, as a sign of shared membership in the new, eschatological family (see the NOTE on "kiss . . . kissed" in 14:44–45). Judas' kiss of Jesus, however, betrays this new familial relationship and thus in a way fulfills Jesus' prophecy that in the time of eschatological crisis, brother will turn brother over to death (13:12; on other fulfillments of chapter 13 in this section of Mark, see figure 46 and the COMMENT on 14:32–42).

Christian commentators have always been filled with fascinated horror at the monstrosity of this betrayal (see Perella, *Kiss*, 39; Penn, "Mouth," 229; cf. 231–32). As the first commentary on Mark puts it, "the poison of deceit" accompanies Judas' kiss (Pseudo-Jerome, *Exposition of Mark* 14:43 [Cahill, 109]). The offense is felt to be especially rank because the gesture of the kiss is associated with affection and even the impartation of life (on the latter, see Gen 2:7; John 20:22; *Jos. Asen.* 19:10–11; *Odes Sol.* 28:7–8; cf. Stählin, "*Phileō*," 125–26; *OTP*, 2.233 n. m). In our passage, however, this gesture of life becomes the vehicle for delivery to death— an inversion with precedent in the OT (see again the NOTE on "kiss . . . kissed" in 14:44–45). A similar double message is conveyed by the way in which Judas calls Jesus "Rabbi," since this is an honorific title meaning "my great one" and implying personal adherence (see the NOTE on "Rabbi" in 9:5). Both inversions, however, are consistent with an ironic and paradoxical Gospel in which God's anointed king triumphs and ultimately rises to life by ignominiously dying on a cross (cf. Lamarche, 338–39, and Camery-Hoggatt, *Irony*).

The "Judas kiss" accomplishes its purpose: the members of the arresting party lay hands on Jesus and take him into custody (14:46). The OT phrase "to lay hands on" (*epiballein tas cheiras*) denotes a hostile action, often ending in death (e.g., 2 Sam 18:12; 1 Kgs 20:6; Acts 4:3; Josephus, *War* 2.491; cf. Davies and Allison, 3.510), and has, in many instances, a nuance of judgment (e.g., Exod 7:4; Isa 5:25; 11:14–15; 25:11). Mark's usage of this idiom thus continues a theme that undergirded the Last Supper and Gethsemane scenes: Jesus' passion is the hour of eschatological tribulation and judgment (cf. the NOTE on "a cup" in 14:23 and the COMMENT on 14:32–42). The phrase also fulfills another prophecy of Jesus, since in 9:31 he predicted that the Son of Man would be turned over "to the hands of human beings" (cf. Davies and Allison, 3.506). By such means, then, Mark reinforces the impression that a mysterious divine purpose is working itself out through Jesus' arrest.

An unnamed bystander, however, tries to interrupt this seemingly unstoppable series of events by drawing a sword and cutting off the ear of the high priest's slave, who is apparently a part of the arresting party (14:47). Unlike the parallel narratives in the other Gospels, this one records no direct reaction from Jesus or anyone else. The swordsman is not named, and it is not entirely clear whether he is a disciple or a repentant member of the arresting party, although the former seems more likely. Here, then, as in 14:51–52, Mark describes a cryptic and desperate act by an anonymous character without explicit motivation or consequences. Although there may be prudential reasons for this lack of specification (see the NOTE on "of those who were present" in 14:47), in the present context it may also be symbolic: as the world descends into apocalyptic chaos, not even the motives or identities of the *dramatis personae* remain clear.

14:48–49: Jesus' response. The bystander's violent response to Jesus' arrest could easily be interpreted as an act of revolutionary violence. Jesus, however, immediately dissociates himself from any such action, denying that he is a brigand and implicitly criticizing the swordsman (14:48). This response probably reflects early Christian apologetics; "brigand" was often used as a code word for the sort of religiously motivated revolutionary who unsettled Palestine in the last century B.C.E. and the first century C.E. (see, e.g., Mark 15:2; Luke 23:2–23; John 18:33–38; cf. Marcus, "Jewish War," 449–51), and Christians felt themselves constrained to defend Jesus against the charge of having been one, since he had been executed by the Romans as a putative "king of the Jews." Moreover, such features as Jesus' popular support, his embrace of the poor, and his proclamation of the exclusive sovereignty of God lent themselves to the view that he was a social and political revolutionary (modern advocates of this view include Brandon, *Jesus*, and Horsley, *Jesus*; opponents include Hengel, *Revolutionist*). The Markan Jesus, however, implies that "brigand" is an inappropriate term for him; he is a teacher, as Judas has just indicated by calling him "Rabbi" (see the NOTE on "Rabbi" in 14:45). He has not skulked about in the darkness, as was the wont of brigands (see the NOTE on "During the daytime" in 14:49); he has taught openly in the Temple by day without being arrested.

This riposte would also convey to the Markan readers that Jesus' nighttime arrest is evidence of his popular support: his enemies have to arrest him covertly because they dare not proceed against him openly (cf. 12:12; 14:1–2). But the Markan Jesus is also suggesting that there is a divine dimension both to the fact that he has not hitherto been arrested ("you did not seize me"; 14:49b) and to the fact that he is now being taken into custody ("But in order that the scriptures might be fulfilled"; 14:49c; cf. Theophylact, *Explanation of Mark* 14:43–49). In this context, the length of Jesus' speech is itself significant, since it underlines his dominance of the arrest scene. His word seems to stop the chaotic action swirling around him; although already in the hands of his enemies, he boldly exposes their duplicity and implies that he is only submitting to them because his delivery to death is God's will and a fulfillment of scriptural prophecy (see the NOTE on "But in order that the scriptures may be fulfilled . . ." in 14:49). This is an important point for the Markan narrative to emphasize, since Jesus' arrest was a major emphasis of anti-Christian polemic (according to Origen, *Against Celsus* 2.31, Celsus called it "disgraceful"). The urgency of the counterpolemic is suggested by the fact that this is the fourth time that our passage has invoked the theme of fulfillment of prophecy (cf. 14:43, 44, 46).

14:50–52: the flight of the disciples. The statement about scriptural fulfillment in 14:49, however, is a double entendre; it not only looks backward, to the immediately preceding reference to Jesus' delivery to death (14:49ab), but also forward, to the immediately following story of apostolic abandonment (14:50–52), which fulfills an OT prophecy that Jesus cited a few verses back (Zech 13:7 = Mark 14:27). That abandonment is now described, first in a general way (14:50), then by a specific example (14:51–52). Both parts use the verb "ran away" (*pheugein*), which also appears in the reference to eschatological flight in 13:14. This overlap with chapter 13 probably reflects the Markan conviction that Jesus' arrest inaugurates the last days (see the NOTE on "they all ran away" in 14:50). The general notice that "they *all* (*pantes*) ran away" (14:50) ties in both with the apocalyptic idea of universal panic and with the specific prophecy in 14:27, "You will *all* be tripped up" (cf. Senior, *Passion*, 84). Once again, the circumstances of Jesus' arrest fulfill prophecy; nothing is happening that he has not foreseen, including his abandonment by his followers. The motif of abandonment, however, also increases the pathos of the scene by underlining Jesus' aloneness.

The pathos is further heightened by the immediately following story of the young man who flees naked (14:51–52). As Jackson ("Youth," 280) puts it, here, as in similar depictions in Greco-Roman literature (e.g., Lysias, *Oration* 3.12; Demosthenes, *Oration* 21.215–17), "the loss of the garment to the clutches of the captor and the naked flight of a person stripped to the undignified level of an animal" create a sudden, unpleasant sensation. As Jackson (ibid., 280–85) also points out, these depictions are realistic, since garments such as the *sindōn* were generally wrapped or draped around the body without fasteners and easily came off, especially under the influence of violent motion. Our narrative, therefore, may enshrine a historical memory (or, as Dodd punningly puts it, "a bare matter of fact"); Mark's community may even have known the man in question (see Davies and Allison, 3.516).

But although the incident may at base be historical, as retold by Mark it probably has symbolic dimensions as well (on the history of its interpretation, see the APPENDIX "The Youth Who Ran Away Naked [Mark 14:51–52]"). One of these has to do with discipleship; the youth who runs away naked is the negative counterpart of the ideal disciple portrayed elsewhere in the Gospel. For example, he is described as "following along with" Jesus (*synēkolouthei*). The only other Markan instance of this compound verb, in 5:37, relates it to Peter, James, and John, who are given a foretaste of resurrection power when they see Jesus raise a young girl from the dead. Our passage now applies the same verb to a youth who, like the Twelve, is called to follow Jesus to the death that is the ultimate source of that power but who instead, like them, forsakes him. Moreover, as Brown (*Death*, 1.303) points out, in 10:28 Peter reminds Jesus that he and the other members of the Twelve have left all things to follow Jesus—a form of adherence that Jesus praises. Later in the same chapter this sort of apostolic self-sacrifice is graphically illustrated by the case of Bartimaeus, who leaves his garment behind to follow Jesus (10:50–52; cf. Jackson, "Youth," 288–89). In contrast to these two positive images of following, the youth in our story leaves everything, including his garment, to *flee* from Jesus. As a negative example, this "certain youth" (*neaniskos tis*) corresponds to the "certain one" (*heis . . . tis*) in 14:47: the one abandons discipleship by trying to stop Jesus' arrest with violence, while the other abandons it by running away in panic. Apostasy and Zealotism, therefore, are mirror images of each other and twin dangers confronting the Markan community (cf. the INTRODUCTION in vol. 1, pp. 25–39); both undermine the theology of the cross.

Besides the theme of discipleship failure, the Markan vignette about the fleeing youth also invokes the sort of apocalyptic framework that is so important for understanding the passion narrative and the Gospel as a whole. The text would probably remind some readers of the eschatological prophecy in Amos 2:16: "And even the one who is stout of heart among the mighty shall flee away naked in that day" (RSV alt.). Closer to home, it also recalls the eschatological prophecy in Mark 13:14–16, since the latter includes not only the idea of end-time flight but also the instruction not to turn back to retrieve one's garment. Although 13:14–16 is an instruction about what one *should* do in the end-time emergency, whereas 14:51–52 is an example of what one should *not* do, the overlap between the two passages reinforces the echo of Amos: Jesus' arrest is part of the eschatological crisis.

That crisis, in the standard scenario, involves judgment, which often is to be executed by the Messiah or the Son of Man (e.g., Isaiah 11; Daniel 7; *Pss. Sol.* 17; *1 Enoch* 37–71). But in the upside-down world of the Markan Gospel, judgment will in the first instance be rendered *against* the Messiah rather than *by* him. The next passage, correspondingly, will describe the first of the two judicial procedures against "the Christ, the Son of the Blessed One."

THE SANHEDRIN CONDEMNS JESUS FOR
BLASPHEMY (14:53–65)

14 [53]And they led Jesus away to the high priest, and all the chief priests and the elders and the scribes gathered together. [54]And Peter was following from a distance into the inside, into the courtyard of the high priest, and he was sitting with the attendants and warming himself at the light.

[55]And the chief priests and the whole Sanhedrin were seeking testimony against Jesus, in order to kill him, and they weren't finding it. [56]For many people were bearing false witness against him, and their testimonies were not agreeing. [57]And some people were rising up and bearing false witness against him, saying, [58]"We heard him saying, '*I* will destroy this Temple made by hands, and within three days I will build another that is not made by hands.' " [59]And even then their witness did not agree. [60]And the high priest rose up into the middle and asked Jesus, saying, "You make no reply? Why are these people testifying against you?" [61]But he was silent, and he did not answer anything.

And again the high priest asked him and said to him, "You are the Christ the Son of the Blessed One!?" [62]And Jesus said, "*You* have said that I am; and you will see the Son of Man sitting on the right hand of the Power and coming with the clouds of heaven!" [63]But the high priest tore his garments and said, "Why do we need additional witnesses? [64]You have heard the blasphemy. What does it seem to you?" And they all condemned him as deserving death. [65]And some began to spit on him and to cover his face and to hit him and to say to him, "Prophesy!" And the attendants received him with slaps.

NOTES

14 53. *to the high priest.* Gk *pros ton archierea*, that is, to the house of the high priest, as Luke 22:54 correctly interprets it (see Fortna, "Jesus and Peter," 373). This house may be the Palatial Mansion, a large Herodian structure of nearly two thousand square feet built on the ruins of a Hasmonean dwelling on the eastern slopes of the Upper City (see Avigad and Geva, "Jerusalem," 733, for floor plan and reconstruction). The house's location overlooking the Temple Mount, the grandeur of its construction, and its many ritual baths suggest that it belonged to an important priestly family. The excavated structure has a central courtyard of about 25 × 25 feet, to the west and north of which is a large hall of about 20 × 35 feet that is plastered with white molded stucco. The former could be the location of Peter in our story (14:54, 66), while the latter could be the place where the Sanhedrin assembles. There is one difficulty with this identification, however: Mark 14:66 implies that the central courtyard was below the hall where the Sanhedrin gathered, whereas the two rooms in the archaeological excavation are on the same level.

The high priest in question is identified as Caiaphas in Matt 26:3 and John 11:49; 18:13, 24. According to Josephus (*Ant.* 18.35), this man's first name was

Joseph. "Caiaphas" was apparently a patronymic; in 1990 an elaborate ossuary, apparently his, was discovered in the Abu Tor section of Jerusalem with the inscription "Jehoseph (= Joseph) son of Qapā'/Qaypā' " (for a picture, see Geva, "Jerusalem," 756). Caiaphas, who succeeded his father-in-law Annas, had the longest tenure of any high priest in the first century, from 18 C.E. to 37; he was apparently very successful in working out a *modus operandi* with the Romans, which suggests one plausible cause for his anxiety about firebrands such as Jesus (cf. John 11:47–50). He was removed from office shortly after his Roman patron, Pontius Pilate, was fired as a result of disturbances among the Samaritans at the end of 36 C.E. (Josephus, *Ant.* 18.58–59, 95).

54. *into the inside, into the courtyard of the high priest.* Gk *heōs esō eis tēn aulēn tou archiereōs.* But how did Peter gain access to this interior space within the high priest's house (cf. the NOTE on "to the high priest" in 14:53)? The author of the Fourth Gospel seems to be aware of this problem, since he relates that another disciple, who was known to the high priest and his servants, gained access for him (John 18:15–16).

attendants. Gk *hypēretōn.* A *hypēretēs* is an assistant of any sort, here of the Sanhedrin described in 14:53, 55.

light. Gk *phōs.* This is not a common term for a fire (cf. however Xenophon, *Hellenica* 6.2.29; 1 Macc 12:28–29; BGU 4.1201.10). As Gnilka (2.275) points out, the unusual usage here prepares for 14:67, where a slave girl recognizes Peter by the light of the fire; it may also, however, have symbolic dimensions (see the COMMENT on 14:53–54). At the corresponding point in his story, John uses the less evocative term *anthrakian* ("coal fire," John 18:18).

55. *the chief priests.* Gk *hoi . . . archiereis.* *Arichiereis* is the plural of *archiereus,* the word translated "high priest" in 14:63. On the relation of the chief priests to the high priest, see the APPENDIX "The Jewish Leaders in Mark."

the whole Sanhedrin. Gk *holon to synedrion.* Sanders (*Judaism,* 472–88) and McLaren (*Power and Politics,* 213–22) argue that in earlier sources (Josephus and the NT), as opposed to the Mishnah, *synedrion* is not a technical term but a loose designation for a consultative or judicial body called together on an *ad hoc* basis by a leader, and that it had neither a fixed membership nor fixed meeting times. McLaren (216), however, acknowledges that the frequent use of the definite article in the NT (Mark 14:55; 15:1; Matt 26:59; Acts 4:15; 5:21; 6:12; 22:30; cf. Josephus, *Ant.* 14.167) suggests a permanency that is somewhat at odds with this description; this is even more true in the present case, in which "Sanhedrin" is modified by "the whole," suggesting the complete roster of membership of the group.

57. *were rising up.* Gk *anastantes.* This verb, which is repeated with reference to the high priest in 14:60, often has a judicial connotation; witnesses and judges arise to execute justice (see Deut 19:17; Isa 3:13; Dan 12:1–3; *Jub.* 18:9; 48:9; Nickelsburg, *Resurrection,* 11–12). The irony in the present instance is that the witnesses and the high priest are arising to pervert justice, an offense for which they will, at the eschaton, be judged themselves (14:62).

58. *I will destroy.* Gk *egō katalysō.* On the emphatic nuance of this superfluous personal pronoun, see the COMMENT on 14:55–61a and cf. the NOTE on

"Give . . . yourselves" in 6:37. Explicit evidence for an OT and Jewish expectation that the Messiah would destroy the Temple is hard to find (see Juel, *Messiah*, 197, and Chester, "Sibyl," 55). If the Temple was to be destroyed, this destruction was usually expected to be the work of God (see, e.g., 2 Chron 36:17–21; Jeremiah 26; Ezek 9:7–8; 10:18–19; 11:22–23; *1 En.* 90:28). Similarly, in Jesus' own forecast of Temple destruction (Mark 13:2), the crucial verb "be thrown down" (*katalythȩ̄*) is a divine passive (see the GLOSSARY and the COMMENT on 13:1–2). But Dan 9:26–27 Theod. contains the cryptic prophecy that an "anointed one" (*chrisma*) will destroy "the city and the sanctuary," apparently before being destroyed himself (cf. Pitre, *Jesus*, 374 n. 364).

this Temple made by hands. Gk *ton naon touton ton cheiropoiēton*. Greco-Roman thinkers often ridicule the superstition of the masses, who treat God as though he were a material being who abides in sanctuaries made by humans and requires sacrifices (see, e.g., Plutarch, *On Stoic Self-Contradictions* 1034B6; Lactantius, *Divine Institutes* 2.2.14). They do not in this connection use *cheiropoiētos* ("made by hands"), a word indicating what is manufactured by humans in distinction from what is natural (see Paesler, *Tempelwort*, 210), but this term is consistently linked with idolatry in Jewish sources such as the LXX (see Lev 26:1, 30; Jdt 8:18; Isa 2:18; etc.) and intertestamental literature (see, e.g., *Sib. Or.* 3.604–6, 616–18, 722–23; 4.28; Philo, *Life of Moses* 2.168; cf. Van der Horst, "New Altar," 33; Paesler, *Tempelwort*, 211–12). Somewhat surprisingly, Philo also applies *cheiropoiētos* to the Jerusalem Temple without a negative connotation, and it is possible that *mqdš 'dm* ("a temple of man") in 4QFlor 1 1:6 has a similar nuance (a Temple made by human beings; see Schwartz, "Three Temples"); this phrase, however, might instead indicate a Temple composed of human beings (see Dimant, "*4QFlorilegium*"). In 4QFlor both this "temple of man" and the original Temple, which foreigners "made desolate" by their sins (4QFlor 1 1:5–6; cf. Mark 13:14), are distinguished from the Temple that YHWH's hands will establish at the end of days (4QFlor 1 1:2–3); cf. *4 Ezra* 10:54, which speaks of the earthly Temple as "a work of man's building" (*opus aedificii hominis*) that will not outlast the revelation of the city of God (cf. Rev 21:22).

Apocalyptic Jewish texts such as 4QFlor and *4 Ezra* 10 thus bear a certain resemblance to Mark 14:58, in that the present Temple, which is associated with or made by humans, is distinguished from a permanent Temple or city made by God. The present Temple, however, is not as negatively judged in these Jewish texts as it is in Mark and in Stephen's speech in Acts. In the latter passage, God, whose hand made everything, is contrasted to things made by human hands, such as the Temple, whose construction was a primal act of rebellion against the divine will (Acts 7:47–51; cf. 17:24). Here, then, as perhaps in our passage, *cheiropoiētos* bears its usual LXX nuance of idolatry, and, as Barrett (1.373) observes, "To associate such language with the Temple must have been highly offensive in Jewish ears." The more usual Jewish attitude is exemplified by *Sib. Or.* 3.718–23, which *contrasts* "things made by hands, idols, and statues of dead men" with the Temple of the one true God.

within three days I will build another that is not made by hands. Gk *kai dia*

triōn hēmerōn allon acheiropoiēton oikodomēso. Although the evangelist calls this
a false testimony, he probably thinks it has an element of truth in it: Jesus did on
the third day found the church, a Temple not made with hands, by rising from the
dead (see the COMMENT on 14:55–61a). Cf. manuscripts D, W, it, which add
something similar to this clause to Jesus' prophecy in 13:2, thus making the witnesses' statement even less false.

61. *But he was silent, and he did not answer anything*. Gk *ho de esiōpa kai out
apekrinato ouden*. Jesus' silence echoes scriptural passages about the patient suffering of the just person (see Pss 38:12–15; 39:9; Lam 3:28–30; and Isa 53:7, which
Acts 8:32–35 applies to Jesus). As Brown (*Death*, 1.464) points out, however, the
vocabulary of silence in our passage is not the same as that in these OT texts, and
the middle voice *apekrinato* is technical legal language, so this is not simply an
instance of "prophecy historicized" (against Crossan, *Who Killed*, 1–13). Brown
(*Death*, 1.464) argues that in Mark and Matthew Jesus' silence shows his superiority to and contempt for those who prejudicially judge him. It may also, however,
reveal a reluctance to deny categorically the Temple charge, which has just been
made (see the COMMENT on 14:55–61a and Davies and Allison, 3.527). This
interpretation is strengthened by comparison with Achilles Tatius, *Leucippe and
Clitophon* 7.4.2.4, in which an innocent bystander "was silent and said nothing"
(*esiōpa kai elegen ouden*) when asked about the details of a murder he had witnessed, since he feared that a more forthcoming response would be taken as an
admission of collaboration. The Markan Jesus, similarly, may keep silence partly
because an affirmative response, while partially justified, might leave a mistaken
impression.

asked him and said to him. Gk *epērōta auton kai legei autǭ*. This is a frequent
Markan locution (cf. 8:27; 9:11; 12:18; 15:4), corresponding to an OT idiom
(cf. BDB 981), but this is the only Markan instance in which *legein* is a finite
verb rather than a participle and in which the object pronoun is repeated. This
distinctive formulation may suggest that in the present instance Mark intends the
phrase as something more than a cliché. This is consonant with the context, in
which Jesus interprets the high priest's skeptical question as a statement, though
it is clearly meant as a question; "asked him and said to him," then, may be meant
literally (see the COMMENT on 14:61b–65).

the Christ the Son of the Blessed One. Gk *ho Christos ho huios tou eulogētou*.
"The Blessed One" is a Jewish circumlocution for God; rabbinic traditions frequently speak of the deity as "the Holy One, blessed be He," and a synagogue
inscription of 41 C.E. from Gorgippia on the Black Sea is dedicated "to the Most
High God, Almighty, Blessed One" (*eulogētǭ*; cf. Levine, *Synagogue*, 114). "The
Christ the Son of the Blessed One" is thus equivalent to "the Christ the Son of
God"; some manuscripts, indeed, combine the two terms (e.g., A, Y, K, Π, 1346)
or follow the lead of Matt 26:63 in substituting "God" for "the Blessed One" (e.g.,
א, 579).

But how are the titles "Christ" and "Son of God" related in Mark 14:61? They
are usually taken to be an instance of nonrestrictive apposition, that is, as syn-

onyms. This is more likely, however, a case of restrictive apposition, in which the second term qualifies the first (cf. the rabbinic distinction between the-Messiah-the-son-of-David and the-Messiah-the-son-of-Joseph; see Marcus, "Mark 14:61"). This limiting function of the second appositive corresponds to the general pattern of Markan duality (see Neirynck, *Duality*); a comparable instance is Mark 6:15, in which "a prophet" is clarified and intensified by the qualification "like a prophet [in the Scriptures]." It also comports with the observation that in first-century Judaism Christ = Messiah = "anointed one" was ambiguous and could refer to a priestly figure as well as to a Davidic one (see Marcus, "Mark 14:61"; Dahl, "Messianic Ideas," 383–89; cf. Theophylact, *Explanation of Mark* 14:61–65: "For there were many christs, that is, anointed ones, such as the kings and the high priests").

62. **You** *have said that I am.* Gk *sy eipas hoti egō eimi.* The majority of texts do not have *sy eipas hoti* ("*You* have said that . . .") but simply *egō eimi* ("I am"). The longer reading is poorly attested, but it does have an early witness in Origen (*Commentary on John* 19.20.28), whose text is supported by some later Greek manuscripts and versions that are mostly of a Caesarean type (θ, *f*[13], 472, 565, 700, 1071, Geo. Arm.). According to this reading, which is favored by Streeter (*Four Gospels*, 322) and Taylor (568), the Markan Jesus replies indirectly by affirming his interrogator's words, as also happens in the interview before Pilate in 15:2 ("*You* are saying it").

The strongest point in favor of this reading is its agreement not only with the vocabulary of Matt 26:64, where Jesus' reply takes the form *sy eipas* ("You [sg.] have said it"), but also with the substance of Luke 22:70, where he says *hymeis legete hoti egō eimi* ("You [pl.] say that I am"). The longer reading also adds to the numerous doublets between our scene and the trial before Pilate (cf. figure 52 in the APPENDIX "Historical Problems in the Markan Sanhedrin Trial"). As Taylor (568) notes, moreover, it is in accord with the Markan theory of the messianic secret, according to which Jesus' identity cannot be truly revealed until his death (see the APPENDIX "The Messianic Secret Motif" in vol. 1).

The alternative explanation is that Mark originally wrote, "I am," that both Matthew and Luke independently changed this direct statement to an indirect reply that parallels Jesus' response to Pilate (15:2), and that a later scribe assimilated the Markan text to Matt 26:64 (cf. Kempthorne, "Marcan Text," 206–7). This is possible, but it is puzzling that Matthew and Luke would conform the clear reply in Mark 14 to the obscure one in Mark 15 rather than the other way around. Evans (450) suggests that Matthew, Luke, and the later scribe behind the longer text of Mark may all have wanted to tone down the apparent presumptuousness of the bald "I am" response, which could have offended Jewish Christian readers (cf. *b. Sanh.* 93b, in which Bar Kochba is discredited for claiming, "I am the Messiah"). It seems more likely, however, and more in line with the sort of alterations that normally occur in NT manuscripts, for a Markan scribe to change an ambiguous Christological reply to an explicit one (cf. Streeter, *Four Gospels*, 322; Dunn, "Messianic Secret," 127). Against Evans, NT scribes are not known for their pro-Jewish proclivities—in fact, the tendency is more often the opposite (see Epp, *Tendency*)—but they *are* known for altering passages in the direction of a higher or more explicit Christology. "I am," then, may the sort of "orthodox corruption of scripture" described by Ehrman (*Orthodox Corruption*, passim).

Kempthorne ("Marcan Text," 204–5) argues that the short text gives a more appropriate answer to the actual question asked in 14:61 and comports better with the continuation in 14:62b–63, which seems to assume that Jesus has just affirmed his messianic divine sonship and has thus incurred a charge of blasphemy. The Markan Jesus, however, often refuses to answer questions directly or gives ambiguous responses to spoken or unspoken queries or objections (see 2:8–9; 4:11–12; 8:17–21; 11:29–30; 12:15–17; 15:2). The longer text of Mark 14:62a, moreover, is an affirmation, though an indirect one, and therefore is an appropriate response in the context.

Some scholars, to be sure, argue that the "You say/have said so" locutions in the Gospels reject the question totally ("*You* have said it, and you're wrong") or express reserve about the way in which it is framed ("That's your way of putting it, not mine") or try to evade it ("Those are your words, and I make no comment"; cf. the outline of the history of interpretation in Catchpole, "Answer"). It is more likely, however, that they are meant to be affirmative ("You yourself have just now rightly said that . . ."), as Catchpole and Brown (*Death*, 1.489–92) argue. The other NT usages of the locution bear out this exegesis. For example, in Matt 26:25 Jesus' reply *sy eipas* to Judas' "Is it I, Rabbi?" (my trans.), cannot be negative; Judas certainly *is* the one who will betray Jesus. Similarly, the Lukan Jesus' response to the Sanhedrin's question whether he is the Son of God—"You say that I am" (Luke 22:70)—is not sarcastic or reserved, since the reader of the Gospel has known from 1:35 on that Jesus was the Son of God. In Mark itself, although the evangelist might harbor some ambivalence about the term "Christ" = "Messiah," when it is combined with "Son of God" it becomes a fitting title for Jesus, since the latter is a designation that God himself has used for Jesus on two occasions (1:11; 9:7). Matthew 26:64 and John 18:37 are also consistent with the affirmative interpretation. In Matthew, "You have said so" is followed by *plēn* ("but"), which often has an adversative sense, but can also be asseverative (cf. Matt 11:22), and the latter nuance better fits the context. In John, "You say that I am a king" is not a denial of kingship, since Jesus has just acknowledged that he possesses a royal dominion, though not one that comes from this world (John 18:36).

you will see. Gk *opsesthe*. Hirshman (*Rivalry*, 15–16) points to passages in rabbinic texts (e.g., *Cant. Rab.* 7.3.3 [7.8]; *Gen. Rab.* 83.5) in which the formula "and then we shall see"/"and then you will see" is used to refute Christian claims to be the true Israel; at the eschaton, according to these passages, the Christians will be forced to acknowledge that the Jews are the real children of God. Thus, both sides in the dispute between early Christians and non-Christian Jews held that at the eschaton their opponents would see the error of their ways—but then it would be too late to repent.

sitting on the right hand. Gk *ek dexiōn kathēmenon*. This is an allusion to

Ps 110:1 [109:1 LXX], on which see the NOTE on "The Lord said to my lord, etc." in 12:36. The psalm borrows an image from Egyptian literature and iconography, which frequently portrays the king enthroned at the god's right hand, the side of strength. This co-enthronement signifies the king's co-regency with the god and the latter's support for his rule. The relationship may have been ritually enacted in the fall kingship festival of ancient Israel, when the monarch mounted a throne placed on the right of the ark: " 'Sitting at the right hand of God,' then . . . has a very definite meaning: the king is installed into an associate rulership (cf. 1 Kings 2:19); in this position of honor in the power structure of God he becomes a participant in Yahweh's strength in battle and victory" (Kraus, *Psalms*, 2.348–49)—a description well suited to the Markan context, in which Jesus is prophesying his eschatological triumph over the enemies now persecuting him. The psalm may also allude to the fact that the Judahite king's royal palace was situated on the right, or south, side of the Temple, a placement that was "a monumental expression of the fellowship of God and king" (Keel, *Symbolism*, 263–64).

of the Power. Gk *tēs dynameōs.* God is associated with power in the OT (see, e.g., 1 Chron 29:12; Job 26:12; Pss 62:11; 65:6; Isa 40:10), and Ps 54:1 parallels God's name, which is almost a divine hypostasis (see the GLOSSARY), with his power: "O God, save me by your Name, and vindicate me by your Power" (Morray-Jones trans. alt., "Mysticism," 4). This association of power with God continued in intertestamental Judaism; Philo, for example, speaks of God as "the highest and greatest *dynamis*" (*Life of Moses* 1.111), and the author of the Qumran Hodayot praises him because "you have revealed yourself to me in your power as perfect light" (1QH 12[4]:23; Morray-Jones trans. alt., "Mysticism," 3). Postbiblical Jews personified such attributes of God, sometimes in throne-room settings; in the Greek version of *1 En.* 14:20, for example, "the Great Glory" seats himself upon his throne (see Flusser, "Right Hand," 44 n. 8). Rabbinic traditions, similarly, refer to God as "the Power" (*haggĕbûrāh*), especially in the context of the revelation of his royal might at Sinai (see, e.g., *b. Šabb.* 87a, 88b; *b. 'Erub.* 54b; *b. Yeb.* 105b; Goldberg, "Sitzend"; Brown, *Death*, 1.496–97), and Acts 8:10 quotes Samaritans who speak of "that Power of God which is called Great" (RSV alt.). As for the association of the Messiah with the power of God, Isa 9:6 [9:5 Heb] refers to the coming Davidic ruler as a wonderful counselor and *'El Gibbôr* ("God, the Powerful One"); 1QH 11[3]:10 reinterprets this passage as a reference to a person who will be a "wonderful counselor with his [= God's?] power" (see Flusser, "Right Hand," 44–45).

the Son of Man . . . coming with the clouds of heaven. Gk *ton huion tou anthrōpou . . . erchomenon meta tōn nephelōn tou ouranou.* Jesus does not explicitly claim to be the coming Son of Man he describes here, but the high priest has asked him whether he is the Christ = Messiah, a title to which "Son of Man" is sometimes equivalent (see the COMMENT on 14:61b–65 and the APPENDIX "The Son of Man" in vol. 1), and the high priest's ensuing charge of blasphemy probably picks up not only Jesus' implicit affirmation of his divine sonship but also what he says about the Son of Man's elevation to God's right hand (see the NOTE on "blasphemy" in 14:64). The Markan Jesus, then, seems to be affirming, in a way understood by his interlocutor, that he is not only the Son of God but also the Son of Man.

On the cloud as a means of transport, see Dan 7:13; Acts 1:9; Rev 11:12; 14:14; *T. Abraham* 9:8, and later texts listed in Allison, *Testament of Abraham*, 213. The Markan text is very close to the Greek versions of Dan 7:13, especially Theodotion, in which "one like a son of man" (*hōs huios anthrōpou*) comes (*erchomenos*) with the clouds (*meta tōn nephelōn*) into the heavenly throne room, where he is enthroned alongside God (7:14)—thus making the scene very similar to Ps 110:1, with which the passage is conjoined in our Markan text. The direction of movement in Dan 7:13, however, is upward, into the heavenly throne room, whereas in Mark it seems to be downward, since "sitting at the right hand of the Power" precedes "coming with the clouds." One of the Qumran texts has a rereading of Daniel 7 similar to that of Mark, since it speaks of "the ruler of the heavens" descending to earth and being enthroned there (4QBook of Giants[b] [4Q530] 2:16–19; see Stuckenbruck, "Throne-Theophany").

63. *tore his garments.* Gk *diarrēxas tous chitōnas autou.* On the meaning of *chitōn*, see the NOTE on "two tunics" in 6:9. In the Mishnah, *m. Sanh.* 7:5 prescribes that one should tear his or her garments upon hearing an utterance of blasphemy. The high priest's action, however, may have an ironic dimension, since this functionary is expressly forbidden to tear his sacral vestments by Lev 21:10, as Pope Leo the Great (Leo I) noticed in commenting on the trial scene (*Sermon* 57, *Concerning the Passion* 2). It may be that Mark is unaware of this interdict, or he may want to suggest that the high priest is not in uniform; but it is also possible, as Davies and Allison (3.533) suggest, that the evangelist wishes to imply another violation of the Law by a chief justice who has not flinched at conducting Jesus' trial in a blatantly prejudicial manner.

64. *blasphemy.* Gk *blasphēmias.* Exodus 22:28 warns against reviling God, and Lev 24:10–23 prescribes the death penalty for the person who pronounces God's name and curses. Taking its cues from the latter passage, the Mishnah stipulates that a person is not guilty of blasphemy unless he pronounces the divine name (*m. Sanh.* 7:5; cf. Philo, *Life of Moses* 2.206), but this rule is not followed in our passage (see the APPENDIX "Historical Problems in the Markan Sanhedrin Trial"). As a matter of fact, both the high priest and Jesus use circumlocutions for God ("the Blessed One" and "the Power"), and the Talmud specifically excludes such circumlocutions from its definition of blasphemy (see, e.g., *y. Sanh.* 7:8 [25a; Neusner, 31.231–32] and *b. Sanh.* 60a).

Why, then, does the Sanhedrin convict Jesus of blasphemy in Mark? It is probable that his blasphemy consists of implicitly placing himself on a par with God through his usage of Ps 110:1 in 14:62. This interpretation corresponds to the scribal charge of blasphemy in 2:7 (see the COMMENT on 14:61b–65), as well as to what we see in some postbiblical Jewish passages. Philo (*On Dreams* 2.129–31; *Decalogue* 61–69; *Embassy to Gaius* 353, 357, 367–68) denounces as blasphemers those who claim to be like God, who give the Creator and the creature equal honor, or who "worship those who are our brothers by nature." In *b. Sanh.* 38b, similarly,

R. Jose denounces R. Aqiba for profaning the divine presence by interpreting the plural "thrones" in Dan 7:9 as a reference to the Messiah's enthronement beside God. In *y. Ta'an.* 2:1 (65b; Neusner, 18.183) R. Abahu condemns any person who claims to be a god, to be the Son of Man, or to go up to heaven. This sort of stretching of biblical monotheism is linked with the motif of someone besides God *sitting* in heaven in 3 *En.* 16:2–3: "When he saw me seated upon a throne like a king, with ministering angels standing beside me as servants . . . he opened his mouth and said, 'There are indeed two powers in heaven!' " (cf. *b. Ḥag.* 15a; *Gen. Rab.* 65.21; Alexander, "3 Enoch," 54–66; "Family," 292). 3 *Enoch* and the rabbinic traditions postdate the NT, but the same idea is expressed in a Qumran text, 11QShirShabb (11Q17) 7:4 "In his glorious shrines they do not sit" (my trans.; cf. Newsom, *Songs*, 308–9). This proscription has to do with the notion that inferiors stand while superiors sit (cf. Mark 4:1; 10:37).

Bock (*Blasphemy*, passim), to be sure, shows that Jewish legends praise human figures such as Adam, Abel, Abraham, Job, Moses, and David, who are exalted to heaven. Sometimes one of these figures sits on a separate throne in the heavenly throne room (see, e.g., David in 4QDibHam^a [4Q504] 1–2 4:7 [17:8]) or on God's throne after he has vacated it (see, e.g., Moses in Pseudo-Ezekiel, *Exagogē* 68–89). In *1 Enoch*, moreover, the Elect One/Son of Man, who is later identified with Enoch (71:14), sits on God's throne, perhaps while God is still enthroned there (51:3; 55:4; 61:8; cf. Rev 3:21 RSV alt.: "to sit down with me on my throne, as I myself . . . sat down with my Father on his throne"). In Jewish traditions, then, human beings can sit on a heavenly throne without incurring a charge of blasphemy. But as Collins ("Charge," 399) points out: "To envisage Enoch, Moses, an angel or a heavenly Messiah sitting on God's throne . . . is a very different thing from confronting a living human being who predicts that he himself will be so enthroned. Such a prediction might seem close to Gaius's claim to be a god or the governor of Egypt's claim to be 'constraining destiny,' claims that so offended Philo."

65. *Prophesy!* Gk *prophēteuson.* Both Matthew (26:68) and Luke (22:64) add here, "Who is it that struck you?" (*tis estin ho paisas se*)—one of the most impressive of the "minor agreements" (see the INTRODUCTION in vol. 1, pp. 45–47). Some texts of Mark have the addition as well (e.g., N, W, X, Θ, *f*^13), and it has some support from the early non-Greek versions of Mark, so that Streeter (*Four Gospels*, 325–26) concludes that it "is influentially supported in each of the three main streams of textual tradition," but the attestation for the shorter text is far more impressive (ℵ, A, B, C, D, etc., lat sy^p). It is possible, then, that the words in question were originally part of the Markan text and fell out by accident, but more likely that they were originally absent from either Matthew or Luke and later added by assimilation. Although assimilation to Matthew is far more common in general, in this instance several scholars (e.g., Streeter; Neirynck, "*Tis Estin*," 29–32; Davies and Allison, 3.536) favor assimilation to Luke because of "the oddity of Matthew's sequence: although there is no blindfolding, Jesus is asked who has hit him, as though he cannot see" (Neirynck).

received him with slaps. Gk *rapismasin auton elabon.* On this colloquialism, see BDAG 584 (5).

COMMENT

Introduction. Jesus' arrest is immediately followed by his trial before the Jewish authorities, which is certainly one of the climactic moments in the Gospel and one of its richest theologically.

The extent to which Mark is relying on pre-Markan tradition in this passage is debated. In both Mark and John, Jesus' interrogation by the high priest is sandwiched between two sections of the narrative of Peter's denial. The sandwich technique is often a sign of Markan redaction, and some think that this is the case here and thus evidence that John is dependent on Mark (see, e.g., Perrin, "Christology," 128). In general, however, we have rejected the thesis of Johannine dependence on Mark (see the INTRODUCTION in vol. 1, pp. 53–54), and in the present instance the Johannine narrative often seems less elaborate than the Markan one both stylistically and theologically, so it is hard to see John as a revision of Mark (compare Mark 14:54b, 55–59, 61b–62, 68a, 71, 72 with their Johannine counterparts in figure 48, and cf. the NOTE on "light" in 14:54). The sandwich structure alone is not enough to prove dependence, and it is possible that the structure was already present in the pre-Markan passion narrative (see Fortna, "Jesus and Peter"), which was the inspiration for Mark's pervasive use of the pattern.

The introductory 14:53–54 seems to be based on a pre-Markan tradition (see again figure 48), but certain features are probably redactional: the list of opponents in 14:53b (the typical Markan triumvirate of chief priests, elders, and scribes), the allusion to Peter following "from a distance into the inside" in 14:54a (cf. 15:40), and the reference to him warming himself "at the light" in 14:54b. It is more difficult to separate tradition from redaction in the rest of the passage, where Mark and John diverge radically, but because 14:61–62 offers a veritable compendium of Markan Christological titles (cf. Dautzenberg, *Studien*, 222–39), whereas the Johannine dialogue with the high priest is theologically less weighty and intrinsically more plausible, substantial Markan redaction may have occurred here as well. John, indeed, does not present Jesus' appearance before the Jewish authorities as a trial at all but as an interrogation by the high priest and a few of his associates; this, again, seems more plausible than the Markan picture of a full-blown judicial procedure, complete with witnesses and the imposition of a death sentence, on the first night of Passover (cf. the APPENDIX "Historical Problems in the Markan Sanhedrin Trial"). And although the "Temple charge" (14:58) may have come up when Jesus was interrogated by the religious authorities, the Markan version of this saying may well have been influenced by early Christian thought and vocabulary, especially in the contrast between the Temple made by human hands and one not made by hands (cf. Acts 7:48; 17:24; 2 Cor 5:1; Eph 2:11; Col 2:11; Heb 9:11, 24).

Our passage is divided into three parts: stage-setting (14:53–54), the Temple charge (14:55–61a), and the question about messianic identity (14:61b–65); the latter subsections contain about ninety words each, whereas the first is about half as long. As pointed out in the introduction to the COMMENT on the previous

Figure 48: The Hearing before the High Priest and Peter's Denials in Mark and John

Mark 14:53–72

John 18:13–27 (passages in small print depart from Markan order)

53a: And they led Jesus away to the high priest [= Caiaphas]

13: And they led him to Annas (the father-in-law of Caiaphas, the high priest) first

53b: And all the chief priests and the elders and the scribes gathered together

54a: And Peter was following from a distance into the inside, into the courtyard of the high priest

15–16: And Simon Peter was following Jesus, along with another disciple (*who secures entrance to the courtyard of the high priest for himself and Peter*)

17: *Slave-girl doorkeeper identifies Peter; Peter issues his first denial* [see below]

54b: And he was sitting with the attendants and warming himself at the light

18: And the slaves and the attendants had made a charcoal fire, because it was cold, and were warming themselves; and Peter also was standing with them and warming himself

55–59: *Chief priests and whole Sanhedrin seek testimony against Jesus; false witnesses testify:* "We heard him saying, 'I will destroy this Temple made by hands, and within three days I will build another that is not made by hands' "

2:19: *Jesus answers those who challenge him about the Temple cleansing:* "Destroy this Temple, and in three days I will raise it."

60–61a: *High priest [= Caiaphas] asks Jesus about witnesses' testimony; Jesus is silent*

61b: *High priest asks Jesus whether he is the Christ the Son of the Blessed One (= God)*

19: *High priest [= Annas] asks Jesus about his disciples and teaching*

62: *Jesus answers that the high priest himself has said that he is and prophesies the Son of Man's coming with the* clouds

20–21: *Jesus answers that he has spoken openly in synagogues and in the Temple*

63–64: *High priest accuses Jesus of blasphemy, and he and the other Sanhedrin members condemn him to death*

65a: *Some spit on Jesus, cover his face, hit him, and ask him to prophesy*

Figure 48: The Hearing before the High Priest and Peter's Denials in Mark and John (continued)

Mark 14:53–72

John 18:13–27 (passages in small print depart from Markan order)

65b: And the attendants (*hypēretai*) received him with slaps (*rapismasin*)

22: One of the attendants (*heis . . . tōn hypēretōn*) gave Jesus a slap (*edōken rapisma tǭ Iēsou*)

23: *Jesus asks the attendant why he has slapped him*

24: *Annas sends Jesus bound to Caiaphas*

66–67a: And as Peter was in the courtyard below, one of the slave girls of the high priest came and saw Peter warming himself

25a: And Simon Peter was standing and warming himself

67b: And looking intently at him, she said, "You too were the Nazarene, Jesus"

17a: Then the slave girl, the doorkeeper, said to Peter, "Aren't you one of the disciples of that man?"

68a: But he denied it, saying, "I don't know or understand what you're saying"

17b: He said to her, "I am not"

68b: And he went outside into the forecourt

69: And the slave girl, seeing him, began to say again to the bystanders, "This man is one of them"

25b: And they said to him, "Aren't you one of his disciples?"

70a: But he denied it again

25c: He denied it and said, "I am not"

70b: And a little later the bystanders again said to Peter, "You really are one of them, because you're a Galilean"

26: One of the slaves of the high priest, who was a relative of the man whose ear Peter cut off, said, "Didn't I see you in the garden with him?"

71: But he began to call down curses and to swear: "I don't know this man that you're talking about!"

27a: Peter denied it again

72a: And immediately the rooster crowed for the second time

27b: And immediately the rooster crowed

72b: And Peter remembered the word that Jesus had said to him, "Before the rooster crowds twice, you will deny me three times"

72c: And rushing outside, he wept

passage, the two pericopes are similarly structured: in each case Jesus is, for the most part, the passive object of others' actions but breaks through that passivity to make a striking pronouncement about two-thirds of the way through (14:48–49, 62). In the present instance, the pronouncement is the climax of the passage and one of the most Christologically freighted statements in the Gospel.

14:53–54: stage-setting. The first two verses set the stage for the action to follow: 14:53 for Jesus' trial before the Jewish authorities (14:55–65), 14:54 for Peter's denial (14:66–72; cf. Brown, *Death*, 1.589, 592). In the first verse, three groups of hostile agents are identified: the impersonal "they" who lead Jesus to the high priest (apparently the arresting party from the previous passage), the high priest himself, and the chief priests, elders, and scribes who gather to assist the high priest in his deliberations.

Despite this mustering of hostile forces, the following verse reveals that Jesus has not been totally abandoned by his followers. Peter is still there, following "from a distance" (*apo makrothen*, 14:54a)—the same expression that will be used later for the women who watch him die (15:40). This expression implies a criticism (cf. Bede, *Exposition of Mark* 14:54), and the critical nuance is strengthened by the echo of Ps 38:11 [37:12 LXX], where the speaker complains that his closest friends stand at a distance (*apo makrothen*) from his travail. The psalmist goes on to say that he does not open his mouth in complaint (38:14 [37:14 LXX])—a feature that appears later in the Markan narrative (14:61a). Seen in this biblical context, Peter is a shadowy figure, flirting with defection though still trying to follow "the light"—a theme suggested by the unusual choice of *phōs* to describe the fire beside which he attempts to warm himself (see the NOTE on "light" in 14:54). But he is gradually being pulled into the dark orb of his master's enemies, as is emphasized by the typically Markan double expression "into the inside, into the courtyard of the high priest."

14:55–61a: the Temple charge. The scene now shifts from the courtyard to the inner recesses of the high priest's house (on the geography of this building, see the NOTE on "to the high priest" in 14:53). Here Jesus is arraigned in a trial with a predetermined verdict: "And the chief priests and the whole Sanhedrin were seeking testimony against Jesus, in order to kill him . . ." (14:55a). This seems to echo another Righteous Sufferer psalm, 37:32 [36:32 LXX]: "The sinner watches the righteous, and seeks to kill him." The context within the psalm seems at first to contradict the Markan passion narrative, since the next verse says that the Lord will not leave the righteous person in the hands of the wicked one, "nor by any means condemn him when he is judged" (37:33 [36:33 LXX]). In Mark, by contrast, Jesus *does* remain in his enemies' hands (cf. 14:41), and he *is* condemned in judgment (cf. 14:64), which seems to undermine the conviction that God will deliver the righteous. But this is the paradox of Markan theology: Jesus *will* ultimately be vindicated by God, and his enemies will see him triumph (cf. 14:62), but this triumphal procession must pass through the way of the cross.

The specific means by which the chief priests and their allies try to entrap Jesus is the testimony of false witnesses, who "rise up" against him (14:55–57)—still another echo of the Righteous Sufferer psalms (27:12 [26:12 LXX]). Convicting him, however, does not prove easy, and Mark's readers would probably surmise that this is because he has done nothing wrong. The specific testimony that the witnesses cite is the famous "Temple charge" (14:58), according to which Jesus said that he would destroy the Temple made by human hands (the present sanctuary in Jerusalem) and within three days build another not made by hands (cf. Matt 26:61; John 2:19; Acts 6:14).

Mark designates this a false testimony (14:57), so there must be something erroneous about it in his eyes, but it does not necessarily follow that it is entirely mistaken. As Brown (*Death*, 1.446) points out, later in the narrative Jesus is mocked both as Messiah and as the destroyer and rebuilder of the Temple, and there is no indication that one charge is completely true while the other is entirely false (15:29–32); indeed, elsewhere in the Markan story such derision reinforces the truth of mockers' sarcastic statements (cf. 14:65; 15:16–19, 26). Jesus, moreover, does not respond when the high priest asks him why he makes no reply to the charge (14:60–61a), and this lack of response may be a tacit admission that it is, in a sense, true (see the NOTE on "But he was silent, and he did not answer anything" in 14:61).

But in what sense is it true, and in what sense false? Mark and his community probably know about, or at least can foresee, the destruction of the Jerusalem Temple in 70 C.E., and they probably, in common with many early believers in Jesus, view the Christian community as the eschatological Temple that replaces the old structure (see 1 Cor 3:16–17; 2 Cor 6:16; Eph 2:18–22; 1 Pet 2:5)—a view with strong roots in the OT and pre-Christian Judaism (see, e.g., 2 Sam 7:11b–16; 1QS 8:4–10; 4QFlor 1 1:1–13; cf. Gärtner, *New Temple*). The Temple charge is thus true in that the Temple *will* be destroyed and replaced by a new one. But it is also false, perhaps because the destruction and reconstitution of the Temple will not be an autonomous act of Jesus (contrast the emphatic *egō* in "*I* will destroy") but a miracle that "come[s] from the Lord, and . . . is amazing in our eyes" (12:11; cf. Brown, *Death*, 1.439, 447–48).

This expectation of destruction and rebuilding has some precedent in Jewish eschatological expectations, which often include the idea that in the end time there will be a renovation or re-erection of the Temple (see, e.g., *1En.* 90:28–29; 4QFlor 1 1:1–13; 11QTemple 29:8–10; *Sib. Or.* 5.414–433; cf. Sanders, *Jesus*, 77–90; Chester, "Sibyl"). The "made by hands/not made by hands" dichotomy is also at home in apocalyptic Judaism; *Sib. Or.* 3.618, for example, prophesies that in the end time, all "things made by hands" (*cheiropoiēta*) will perish, and a classic biblical passage associates the new age with a "stone . . . cut out . . . without hands" (*aneu cheirōn*, Dan 2:34, 45). It is still striking, however, that our pericope links the Jerusalem Temple with the negatively judged, even idolatrous, "made-by-hands things" of the old age.

It could be dangerous for a first-century Jew to belittle or threaten the Temple with dissolution in this way. Josephus, for instance, relates the story of a "rude peasant," Jesus son of Ananias, who announced God's coming judgment against Jerusalem and its Temple four years before the Great Revolt began in 66 C.E. (*War*

6.300–9; for the text, see the COMMENT on 13:1–2). There are arresting parallels to the story of Jesus of Nazareth here: the leading citizens, incensed by the son of Ananias' "ill-omened words," arrest and chastise him, and when he refuses to cease prophesying destruction, they turn him over to the Roman governor, who has him "flayed to the bone with scourges." This Jesus, moreover, like ours, refrains from speaking to the Jewish authorities and the governor, and refuses to answer the latter's direct question. Yet the differences between the two cases are also significant: unlike the Markan Jesus, the Josephan one does not promise the erection of a new Temple, and the upshot of his interview with the Roman governor is not that he is crucified but that he is pronounced mad and released.

These two differences may be linked via the messianic implications of establishing a new Temple—implications that are lacking in the case of Jesus son of Ananias and that point toward a higher self-claim on the part of Jesus. A generative OT text for later Jewish messianism, 2 Sam 7:13–14, prophesies that David's descendant, who will become God's son, will build the Temple (cf. Zech 6:12). A Qumran composition that is largely a midrash on this scriptural passage, 4QFlor, implicitly criticizes the present Temple for its impurity and looks forward to the construction of an eschatological sanctuary by God's hands alone, associating this new edifice both with the inauguration of the dominion of God and with the revelation of God's son, the "Shoot of David" or Messiah (4QFlor 1 1:1–13; see Flusser, "Two Notes," 99–104; Dimant, "*4QFlorilegium*"). This sort of hope for a messianic rebuilding of the Temple was still alive in later times; *Sib. Or.* 5.414–33, for example, describes how a "blessed man . . . from . . . heaven," with a scepter in his hand, founds a new Temple, and *Tg. Isa.* 53:5 and *Tg. Zech.* 6:12 speak of the Messiah building the Temple of the Lord. Bearing this complex of ideas in mind, the transition between our subsection and the next one is logical: a reported claim to be the builder of the eschatological Temple raises the question whether the claimant thinks that he is the Messiah/Son of God (see Betz, *What Do We Know*, 90; Juel, *Messiah*, 170–209).

Confronted with the high priest's question about the Temple charge, however, Jesus remains silent—partly in fulfillment of his role as the Suffering Just One of the Psalms and Isaiah 53, but partly perhaps because the Temple charge is in a way true: God will, within a generation, destroy the present Temple. This destruction will be related to the fate of Jesus. God will, through Jesus, build a new Temple, which will consist of those who adhere to him as the new locus of holiness on earth (cf. the NOTE on "But he was silent, and he did not answer anything" in 14:61). And this building project will begin in three days.

14:61b–65: the clash over Jesus' messianic identity. The high priest, noting Jesus' significant silence, now sharpens his question: "You are the Christ the Son of the Blessed One!?" (14:61b). The question is introduced by the words "And again the high priest asked him and said to him." "Again" (*palin*) and "asked . . . and said" are both frequent Markan idioms, which usually cannot be pressed, but in this case "again" coheres with the fact that the high priest's question about Jesus' messianic identity (14:61b), as we have seen, is a balder form of his question about the Temple charge (14:60). "Asked him and said to him" is also significant, since it suggests that the high priest's words can be interpreted as both a question and a statement—which is what Jesus proceeds to do. This, then, is one of several ironic instances in the Markan passion narrative in which the enemies of Jesus inadvertently proclaim the very Christological truths they abhor (cf. 14:2, 65; 15:2, 18, 26, 29–32).

The high priest, then, means his words skeptically, even sarcastically, but Jesus turns them around and interprets them as an asseveration: "*You* have said that I am . . ." (14:62a; see the NOTE on "*You* have said that I am" in 14:62). This form of response is illuminated by rabbinic parallels; in *t. Kelim B. Qam.* 1:6, for example, R. Simeon at first responds with silence to a challenging question from R. Eliezer because a more forthcoming response would help the latter's case, but he then reacts positively to a further question, which is phrased as a statement, by saying, "You have said it" (cf. *Eccl. Rab.* 7.12). The Markan Jesus, similarly, remains silent when the high priest presses him on the Temple charge, since that charge is at least partly true, then indirectly affirms a question about his messianic divine sonship, which is phrased as a statement, by saying, "You have said that I am." The messianic secret is thereby preserved: Jesus does not proclaim his messianic divine sonship but lets his enemies announce it for him. And that they do so, even against their will, is one of the subtle signs in the Markan passion narrative that, despite Jesus' apparent subjection to their power, God is still in control and his victory march ongoing. The passage, moreover, is reminiscent of earlier Markan pericopes in which the demons shouted out Jesus' identity (1:24; 3:11; 5:7), and indeed the phrasing of the high priest's question ("You are the Christ the Son of the Blessed One!?") is almost identical with that of the demons in 3:11 ("You are the Son of God!"; cf. Danker, "Demonic Secret," 62). The high priest is therefore unmasked by his own question; it is not Jesus who is on the side of Satan, but the high priest and his collaborators (cf. the COMMENT on 3:28–30).

Nor is this the last time that the high priest and his allies will involuntarily bear witness to the one whom they now presume to judge; the Markan Jesus terminates his words to them with the prophecy that, at the eschaton, they will see the high priest's unwitting testimony confirmed when they behold Jesus enthroned at God's right hand and coming "with the clouds" to execute judgment (14:62b). This prophecy reflects a standard martyrological motif: the witness to the divine truth throws in his enemies' face that, although they are now persecuting and presuming to judge him, the tables will soon be turned and they will see God vindicate him and send them off to eternal punishment (cf. Wis 5:2; *1 En.* 62:3–5; *Apoc. Elijah* 35:17; Rev 11:12; Marcus, *Way*, 166–67; and the NOTE on "you will see" in 14:62).

The Markan variation on this motif, which draws on Ps 110:1 and Dan 7:13–14, accords, at least in part, with preexistent Jewish interpretations of these passages that speak of the eschatological triumph of the Messiah. A fragmentary Qumran text, for example, uses imagery borrowed from Daniel 7 to speak of "the Son of God"—apparently the Davidic Messiah—crushing God's enemies and establishing his eschatological dominion on earth (4Q246 2:1–10; see Collins, *Scepter*, 154–72). Another fragmentary text, 11QMelchizedek, presents a similar scenario in a passage apparently influenced by Psalm 110 (see Kobelski, *Melchizedek*, 152–

55; Marcus, *Way*, 133). Yet the differences are no less remarkable: immediately after predicting his triumph, the Markan Jesus, rather than proceeding to annihilate his enemies, is instead condemned, mocked, and beaten by them (14:64–65). Once again the Markan theology of the cross transforms but does not obliterate a standard eschatological scenario.

The key to the Markan Jesus' condemnation by the Sanhedrin lies in the way in which he implicitly identifies himself with Psalm 110's portrait of a figure enthroned beside God and with the Danielic description of the Son of Man coming for judgment in theophanic clouds of glory. These passages are biblical expressions of the royal theology of ancient Israel, which sometimes blurred the line between God and the king, but about which many Jews by the first century had developed reservations, because its portrait of a human being enthroned beside God seemed to infringe on the uniqueness implied by the first commandment and the Shema (see the NOTE on "blasphemy" in 14:64). It is not surprising, therefore, that the high priest responds to Jesus' prophecy by tearing his garments (14:63a), an action prescribed by the Mishnah (*Sanh.* 7:5) when a blasphemy is heard. This symbolic self-mutilation is a biblical sign of grief (see, e.g., Gen 37:34; 2 Sam 1:11–12; cf. Josephus, *War* 2.316), and already in 2 Kgs 18:32–19:1 it is performed in response to a blasphemous assertion that belittles the God of Israel. In the NT itself, moreover, Barnabas and Paul tear their garments in dismay when the people of Lystra identify them as gods and start to perform sacrifices to them (Acts 14:14–15). Here, as in our passage, the tearing of garments is a response to people who are trying to efface the essential boundary between God and humanity ("Why are you doing this? We also are human beings, of like nature with you," Acts 14:15 RSV alt.). An earlier Markan use of the cognate verb confirms this definition of blasphemy: in 2:7 the scribes object to Jesus' pronouncement of forgiveness by saying, "He is blaspheming! Who can forgive sins except One, that is, God?"

For the members of the Markan community, however, the high priest's action is itself blasphemous because Jesus *is* the Son of God, and that title implies participation in the divine glory and liberative eschatological action (cf. 8:38; 9:2, 7). The real blasphemy is *not* to recognize Jesus' words and deeds as the saving activity of God (cf. 3:29–30; 15:29–30). The narrative thus deconstructs the high priest's protestation of concern for God's honor, and it exposes his injustice further by having him declare Jesus' guilt *before* polling his fellow justices (14:64b). The farcical logic of the Markan Sanhedrin trial, then, approaches that enunciated by the Red Queen: "Sentence first—verdict afterwards" (L. Carroll, *Alice*, chapter 12). The other members of the Sanhedrin go along with this mockery of justice, chiming in with a unanimous death sentence (14:64c).

The passage concludes with a description of physical abuse (14:65), which may have reminded some of Mark's readers of Isa 50:6 LXX, which speaks of the Lord's righteous Servant being subjected to spitting and slapping (it also describes scourging, which is mentioned along with spitting in Mark 10:34; cf. Marcus, *Way*, 189–90). This physical mistreatment is accompanied by mockery, as Jesus' tormentors urge him to prophesy—a reference to his prediction a moment earlier, in which he has presented himself as a powerful eschatological figure, and probably to the

Temple charge, for which he will be jeered in 15:29. In the mockers' eyes, Jesus'
claim to be the eschatological redeemer and rebuilder of the Temple is vitiated
by his present state of helplessness and subjection to their will. For the evangelist
and biblically literate readers, however, the echoes of the Suffering Servant passages in Isaiah 50–53 (silence before judges, spitting, slapping) may suggest that
this absorption of abuse is actually effecting the defeat of the rulers of this world.
Jesus, then, is not being vanquished but triumphing in his very humiliation. And
that he is indeed a prophet, contrary to the mockers' sarcasm, will immediately be
confirmed when Peter denies him three times (14:66–72), just as Jesus predicted
(14:30). The taunting command that Jesus prophesy is thus another example of
his enemies unwittingly proclaiming the truth about him.

All appearances to the contrary, then, the Suffering Servant has now embarked
on his victory march. Haled before the Sanhedrin, he has made "the good confession," as a disciple of Paul put it a generation or two later (1 Tim 6:12), and he is
about to receive a world-conquering cross as his reward. This fearless testimony to
the truth of God would probably resonate with the members of the Markan community, who are themselves being haled before sanhedrins and called to make a
"good confession" (cf. 1 Tim 6:13)—forced to choose between the suffering Jesus
and more plausible-seeming, militant messiahs (Mark 13:6, 22), between death
for the good news and life without it (13:9–13).

This choice will be starkly illustrated through the example of Peter in the Gospel's next passage.

PETER DENIES JESUS THREE TIMES (14:66–72)

14 ⁶⁶And as Peter was in the courtyard below, one of the slave girls of the high
priest came ⁶⁷and saw Peter warming himself, and looking intently at him, she
said, "You too were with the Nazarene, Jesus." ⁶⁸But he denied it, saying, "I don't
know or understand what you're saying." And he went outside into the forecourt.
⁶⁹And the slave girl, seeing him, began to say again to the bystanders, "This man
is one of them." ⁷⁰But he denied it again.

And a little later the bystanders again said to Peter, "You really are one of them,
because you're a Galilean." ⁷¹But he began to call down curses and to swear, "I
don't know this man that you're talking about!" ⁷²And immediately the rooster
crowed for the second time. And Peter remembered the word that Jesus had said
to him, "Before the rooster crows twice, you will deny me three times." And rushing outside, he wept.

NOTES

14 67. *You too were with the Nazarene, Jesus.* Gk *kai sy meta tou Nazarēnou ēstha
tou Iēsou.* The force of "You too" is obscure, since no one else has been identified
as a follower of Jesus in the scene. This oddity may reflect the shaping of the passage by the experiences of the early church; in the account of the interrogation of

a second-century believer, for example, the examining prefect asks, *kai sy Christianos ei* ("Are you too a Christian?")—phrasing remarkably similar to ours (*Acts of Justin* 3; cf. Pliny, *Epistles* 10.96.3; Lampe, "Denial," 350–51).

68. *denied.* Gk *ērnēsato*. On the important usages of this verb in accounts of later Christians renouncing Jesus, see the COMMENT on 14:66–70a. The Syriac versions use the verb *kĕphār* ("denied") here and in 14:70, 72; and Sinaiticus and the Peshitta use *Ki'phā'* (= Cephas), the Syriac form for "Peter," at various points in 14:66, 70, 72. An earlier, Aramaic version of the passion narrative may have been built on the pun *kĕphār Kêphā'* ("Peter denied").

I don't know or understand what you're saying. Gk *oute oida oute epistamai sy ti legeis.* As Davies and Allison (3.545–46) point out, with a different punctuation we could translate the Greek, "I neither know nor understand. What do you mean?" The translation chosen, however, is less awkward, as well as being similar to Jewish denial formulas such as *m. Šeb.* 8:3, 6 ("I don't know what you're saying" [my trans.]) and *T. Jos.* 13:2 ("I pray you, my lord, I don't know what you are saying" [*ouk oida ho legeis*; OTP trans. alt.]). The latter is a particularly close parallel to our passage, since in both cases the person issuing the denial is afraid that a candid answer will lead to punishment.

forecourt. Gk *proaulion*. For Mark the *aulē* (14:54, 66) seems to be a hall or court within the building, while the *proaulion* is the forecourt leading to this *aulē* (cf. Brown, *Death*, 1.593–94). It seems, therefore, to correspond to the vestibule in the Palatial Mansion in Jerusalem (see the NOTE on "to the high priest" in 14:53), which is within the house but on the way out from the central courtyard (cf. the drawings in Avigad, "Jerusalem," 733).

The clause about Peter's exit into the forecourt is followed, in important witnesses such as A, C, D, Θ, *f*[1, 13], sy[p, h], Eus, by "and the rooster crowed" (*kai alektōr ephōnēsen*). The witnesses for omission, however, are weightier (ℵ, B, L, W, Ψ, 892, c, sy[s], sa[mss], bo, Diatessaron), and it is plausible that a later scribe would have introduced a first cockcrow to prepare for the reference to a second one in 14:72. Matthew and Luke deal with the same awkwardness by eliminating "twice" and "a second time" from their parallels to 14:30 and 14:72, and some scribes of Mark follow suit.

69. *the slave girl.* Gk *hē paidiskē*. Exegetes in the precritical era, such as Bede (*Exposition of Mark* 14:69–70), tried to reconcile Mark with the better-known Gospel of Matthew by interpreting this as a reference to a second slave girl (cf. Matt 26:71). The second slave girl, however, appears to be a creation of Matthew, who may think that two independent sightings of Peter make for a more dramatic story and who elsewhere shows a propensity to double Markan characters (cf. Matt 8:28; 20:29–34; 21:1–11; Davies and Allison, 1.87).

70. *because you're a Galilean.* Gk *kai gar Galilaios ei*. Mark does not specify how the bystanders are able to guess Peter's regional identity, but Matt 26:73 supplies a plausible guess: he is recognized by his Galilean accent (cf. Acts 2:7; *b. 'Erub.* 53b; Beyer, *Aramaic Language*, 39).

71. *to call down curses and to swear.* Gk *anathematizein kai omnyein.* The object of these verbs is not stated, so Peter is cursing either himself or someone else. In

the history of interpretation, exegetes have usually opted for the first alternative, but elsewhere *anathematizein* always seems to be transitive rather than reflexive (Merkel, "Peter's Curse," 67–68; Lampe, "Denial," 354). And since Peter has been asked about his association with Jesus, the object of his curse is probably also Jesus, whose name may have been suppressed for reverential reasons. On the way in which Peter's action foreshadows later Christians cursing Christ under duress, see the COMMENT on 14:70b–72.

I don't know this man that you're talking about! Gk *ouk oida ton anthrōpon touton hon legete.* Some early commentators, concerned to defend the honor of Jesus' first disciple, fancifully exploit the wording here, which might be translated, "I don't know this one whom you're calling a man," to assert that Peter could without offense deny Jesus as a human being because he knew him as the Son of God (Matt 16:16; cf. Hilary, *Commentary on Matthew* 31.5; 32.4; Ambrose, *Exposition of Luke* 10.82).

72. *the rooster crowed.* Gk *alektōr ephōnēsen.* Brown (*Death,* 1.606–7) has an amusing couple of pages about scholarly investigations into the Gospel cockcrowings. These researches have attempted to answer questions such as whether the reference to the cockcrow is merely a conventional way of designating the hours from midnight to 3:00 A.M. (cf. 13:35; but the explanation does not fit our passage), whether roosters were allowed in Jerusalem (*m. B. Qam.* 7:7 seems to forbid them, but *m. 'Ed.* 6:1 acknowledges their existence), whether they were allowed in the vicinity of priests (*m. B. Qam.* 7:7 forbids priests to raise them, but says nothing about their neighbors), and when exactly Jerusalem roosters are accustomed to crow at Passover time. Lagrange, a late-nineteenth-/early-twentieth-century scholar who resided in Jerusalem, once stayed up all night to investigate the latter question (he reported an early crowing at 2:30 A.M. but said that most occurred between 3:00 and 5:00 A.M.). Brown, however, rightly lets the Roman author Cicero have the last word: "Is there any time, night or day, that roosters do not crow?" (*On Divination* 2.26.56).

for the second time. Gk *ek deuterou.* As Brown (*Death,* 1.137) points out, in Greco-Roman sources dawn was associated with the *second* cockcrow (see, e.g., Aristophanes, *Ecclesiazusae* 30–31, 390–91; Juvenal, *Satires* 9.107–8), so it is fitting that the present reference to the second cockcrow is immediately followed by a reference to the arrival of morning (15:1).

Peter remembered. Gk *anemnēsthē ho Petros.* Once before in the Gospel, Peter "remembered" a prophecy of Jesus, a curse on a fig tree that stood for the leaders of Israel who had rejected him (cf. 11:14, 21). Now Peter himself appears to have sided with this clique by cursing and denying Jesus, although this is not the Gospel's last word about him (see the COMMENT on 14:70b–72).

And rushing outside, he wept. Gk *kai epibalōn eklaien.* The force of *epibalōn* is much disputed. The word's basic meaning is "to throw upon," and all the other Markan usages seem to have this literal nuance (4:37: waves attacking a ship; 11:7: disciples throwing their clothes on a donkey; 14:46: the arresting party laying hands on Jesus). This nuance, however, does not fit the present context unless the participle is understood reflexively (Peter began attacking himself, e.g., by beating his breast; cf. Boomershine, "Peter's Denial," 59), in which case, however, *heau-ton* ("himself") or something similar would be expected. The verb is commonly used elsewhere for putting on clothing, so some think Peter covers his head with his garment, but in this case a word such as *himation*, as well as a mention of the head, would probably be present (see BDAG 367 [2]). Another possibility is that *epibalōn* has the meaning of "began to," as in the variant reading found in D, Θ, 565, latt, sa^mss. One of the passages commonly cited for this meaning, P.Tebt 50.12, actually works better with the regular nuance "to attack," but another, Diogenes Laertius, *Lives* 6.27, does seem to support it (*epebale teretizein* = "he began to whistle"; see G. Lee, "St. Mark xiv. 72" and "Mark 14,72"). But even if *epibal-lein* has the nuance of "begin" in one or two passages, this meaning is rare, and one is left wondering why, if Mark wanted to indicate that Peter began to cry, he did not use his favorite expression *ērxato* + infinitive (cf. Schwarz, "Begann," 19). Another possibility is that *epibalōn* means "he threw [it into his mind]," that is, he thought about Jesus' prediction (cf. Lampe, *Lexicon*, 517 [4] for examples of *epiballein* meaning "to think about, consider"). Brown (*Death*, 1.610) finds this nuance tautological after *anemnēsthē* ("he remembered"), but Markan style is often repetitious (cf. the subject index under "Double expressions"); *epibalōn* is separated from *anemnēsthē* by a long clause, and the overall sentence may not be as tautologous as Brown thinks (cf. Danson, "Fall": "Peter first remembers the word, then reflects thereupon, and finally weeps").

The most likely interpretation, however, is the one shared by Matthew (26:75) and Luke (22:62): Peter cast himself forth out of the house. This exegesis fits fairly well with the literal meaning of *epiballein* (although the word must again be taken reflexively) and accords with the geographical progression implied in the passage: Peter starts in the inner courtyard (14:66), moves out to the vestibule (14:68), and finally runs out of the house altogether. It also explains what would otherwise be puzzling, namely, how Peter manages to avoid arrest if his tears clearly identify him as a follower of Jesus: he is already out of the house by the time he breaks down.

COMMENT

Introduction. The description of the trial of Jesus (14:53–65) is immediately followed by one of the informal "trial" of Peter, which is the opposite of Jesus' ordeal in several ways (see Reinbold, *Bericht*, 155). Indeed, it seems that the two scenes unfold simultaneously in a sort of upstairs/downstairs scenario: while on the upper level false witnesses accuse Jesus, who stoutly confesses the truth and pays for it with his life, on the lower level trustworthy witnesses accuse Peter of adherence to Jesus, a charge that he vehemently denies.

As argued in the introduction to the COMMENT on 14:53–65, the way in which this denial surrounds Jesus' trial before the high priest, although consonant with the Markan purpose of contrasting the two stories, is probably not a Markan invention but an inheritance from the pre-Markan passion tradition. The Johannine parallel (John 18:13–27) supports this, although in John the first denial precedes rather than follows the trial (John 18:17; see figure 48). It seems more likely that John has moved the first denial to a position before the trial than that Mark has consolidated dispersed denials; John 18:25a reads like a redactional repetition of 18:18b necessitated by such a move (cf. the introduction to the COMMENT on 3:7–12), and it makes sense that John would have wanted to accentuate the contrast between Jesus and Peter by having the latter's denials surround the former's fearless self-defense. Comparison with John also helps us identify some Markan editorial work: the Markan motif of "being with Jesus" in 14:67b (cf. Stock, *Boten*, 18–19), the typically epistemological language having to do with seeing and understanding (14:67–69, 71), and the evocative terms of Peter's self-curse in 14:71, which probably echo experiences of the Markan community (see below). As often happens, redactional expansion may also have occurred at the beginning and end of the passage, in 14:66a and 14:72bc, which lack Johannine counterparts, are full of Markan features and motifs (genitive absolute, Jesus' word, and Peter's remembering [cf. 11:21]), and create at least one awkwardness (the repetition of "Peter" in 14:66–67a).

The passage may be divided into two sections of approximately equal length (60–65 words): the two identifications by the slave girl + Peter's first two denials (14:66–70a); and the identification by the bystanders + Peter's third denial, remembrance of Jesus' words, and repentance (14:70b–72).

14:66–70a: first two denials. As the lights go down on the scene in the great hall of the high priest's house, where Jesus is being tormented with spitting and slaps, they go up on Peter, who has been standing below in the courtyard of the same house all during Jesus' hearing (cf. 14:54). Now, as if catalyzed by the negative verdict on Jesus, one of the high priest's servants, a slave girl, suddenly peers at Peter (*emblepsasa autō*) and recognizes him as a man who has "[been] with" Jesus (14:66–67). In the earlier portions of the Gospel, this would have been a positive designation (cf. 3:14–15; see also Acts 4:13), but now, because of Jesus' condemnation by the authorities, it has become a dangerous thing to admit.

It is, nevertheless, true of Peter, and the slave girl sees its truth, as is supported by Mark's usage of the verb *emblepein*, which in its previous Markan instances has had a nuance of revelation (see 8:25; 10:21, 27). The two usages in chapter 10 occur in a context having to do with discipleship, and the second is immediately followed by Peter's assertion that he and the other members of the Twelve have left everything to follow Jesus (10:28); this assertion is about to be rendered deeply ironic as Peter denies Jesus three times. Yet the echoes of chapter 10 hold out hope as well as remonstrance, since Jesus responds to the disciples' despair by saying that what is humanly impossible can become a reality through the grace of God (10:27). In the end, that grace, rather than his own faithfulness, will be the basis for Peter's hope.

The theme of discipleship is also invoked by the way in which the slave girl, as already noted, identifies Peter as someone who has been "with the Nazarene, Jesus" (14:67b). Mark's readers would probably be reminded of Jesus' call of the Twelve "in order that they might be with him," a fellowship that was the basis for their missionary activity (3:14–15; cf. Stock, *Boten*, 18–19); and these words would resonate with the Markan audience's own experience of "being with Jesus" through prayer, sacrament, and encounter with the preached word (see the COMMENT on 3:13–15). The persecutors of the early church, moreover, sometimes asked suspects whether they too were adherents of Jesus—and executed them if they answered in the affirmative (see the NOTE on "You too were with the Nazarene, Jesus" in 14:67); the slave girl's initial identification of Peter, then, probably echoes the Markan community's own experience. The narrative of Peter in the high priest's house seems to be deliberately shaped to induce the Markan hearers to read themselves into the story and to ask, "What would *I* have done?" One possible answer, and a sobering one, is, "I would have denied Jesus, as Peter did." Mark's use of the loaded term "denied" (*ērnēsato*) to describe Peter's response to the girl's first accusation again foreshadows the experience of later Christians, who were often required by the authorities to "deny" Jesus publicly in order to escape martyrdom (see, e.g., *Martyrdom of Polycarp* 9:2–3; Justin, *1 Apology* 31.6; Lampe, "Denial," 353; BDAG 132 [3b]).

The Markan Peter, too, probably fears for his life, but the text never specifies this motive, and other interpretations are possible; he may, for example, be trying to buy time by his lie because he hopes somehow to rescue Jesus from his captors. The roots of his behavior thus lie in a narrative "gap" (see the COMMENT on 4:3–8), the sort of "strategic opacity" that creates a greater sense of depth in the character and involvement in the reader than spelling everything out with "familiar, reassuring explanations" (see Greenblatt, *Will*, 323–24). This sort of "strategic opacity" is common in Mark; at key points, characters, including Jesus, speak and act for reasons that are not entirely explicable and for that very reason hint at great psychological depth (see, e.g., 1:36, 41; 4:12; 6:3, 6, 20, 27; 8:17–21, 30; 14:61; 15:5, 34).

In the present case, as in many of these others, the lack of a specified motive may be designed not only to deepen readerly involvement but also to suggest that a hidden divine purpose is the underlying force for the events taking place (see Auerbach, *Mimesis*, 3–23). This view is supported by Peter's use of the double epistemological phrase "I don't know or understand what you're saying" (14:68a), which expands a standard formula of denial in a characteristically Markan way to echo the language of 4:11–12 about the mystery of the dominion of God afflicting "those outside" (*hoi exō*; cf. 8:17–21) with perceptual blindness, that "they may look but not *see*, and . . . hear but not understand." It is perhaps no accident, therefore, that Peter, immediately after his first denial, goes *outside* (*exō*) into the forecourt. Despite this drift toward "the outside," however, Peter has not yet become an apostate; he still remains inside the building where Jesus is suffering and seems unable either to come to his aid or to abandon him completely. As Davies and Allison (1.546) comment, "Even his retreat is half-hearted." But it is also true that a full retreat would be a safer option than lingering in the forecourt; Peter still experiences both the tug of Jesus' call to follow him (cf. 1:16–17) and the natural human inclination to save his own life.

In this divided condition, Peter is again confronted by the slave girl, who follows him out into the forecourt for another look and then accuses him again of being an adherent of Jesus (14:69). This time the charge is public, and its words would again be familiar to readers who themselves were veterans of persecution: "This man is one of them." The note of hostility ("one of *them*") is palpable. Peter issues a second denial but does not leave the premises; he remains a man in the middle (14:70a).

14:70b–72: third denial and repentance. The passage now hurtles toward its climax, as both the accusation and the denial increase in gravity. So far Peter has been confronted by a single witness of low social status (female and enslaved), who has accused him privately and then publicly. Now, however, the chorus of accusation grows louder and is accompanied by corroborative proof, as a group of bystanders reasserts that Peter is "one of them" (i.e., a follower of Jesus) and that his Galilean identity, as shown perhaps by his accent, proves it (see the NOTE on "because you're a Galilean" in 14:70). This third accusation continues the pattern of the previous two by opening out onto the Markan situation; both Pliny, *Epistles* 10.96.3 and *Martyrdom of Polycarp* 9–10 attest threefold interrogations of Christians (cf. Lampe, "Denial," 352).

The moment of truth for Peter, then, has arrived; he can no longer pretend to be an innocent spectator but must either declare his allegiance to Jesus or break his ties with him. He chooses the latter course, not only denying Jesus for a third time but also cursing him (14:71). This third and final denial, like the previous two, would have a topical relevance for Mark's readers, since suspected Christians were required to curse Jesus in order to prove that they were not his adherents—an act, Pliny says, that real Christians cannot be forced to perform (*Epistles* 10.96.5; cf. Justin, *1 Apology* 31.6). Peter, however, does perform it, and with alacrity; and the words of his denial are an escalation beyond the previous ones, since he now denies not only the accusation but Jesus himself, and in an extremely distancing way: "I don't know this man that you're talking about!"

Now ambiguity seems to be left behind; these are the actions and words of an apostate, and they are all the more serious because of Jesus' earlier prophecy that anyone who was ashamed of him would himself become an object of shame at the eschaton (8:38; cf. the NOTE on "denied" in 14:68). By his physical movements within the pericope, moreover, Peter has appeared to confirm the impression that he is an "outsider" to the faith. There does seem to be evidence, then, for the position of Dewey ("Peter's Curse") that the Markan Peter is cursed and that the main message of the pericope is to avoid acting like him and thus sharing his fate.

But this is not the whole story, because now, at the climax of the passage, just when things seem to be at their blackest, the crow of a rooster announces the coming of dawn (14:72a), and this announcement may hint at a coming reversal in Peter's spiritual condition. It also suggests that his denials are part of the divine plan, since the second cockcrow happens "immediately" after Peter's third denial, just as Jesus has prophesied; at the very moment, then, that Jesus is being mocked as a prophet (14:65), his prophecy of Peter's denial (14:30) is coming to pass, as

Peter confirms by recalling it word for word (14:72b; cf. Juel, *Messiah*, 67–72). Importantly for the question of Peter's fate, this prophecy was embedded in a graceful context: Jesus foretold that Peter and the other disciples would abandon him, but he added the coda that he would later lead them back into battle at his side (14:28)—a prophecy that the angel will repeat in the very last scene of the Gospel (16:7). All has been foreseen, even Peter's denial, but that faithless act is not the last word; Mark's readers would know that after Jesus' resurrection there had been such a reversal of Peter's apostate status that he had died a martyr for the cause (cf. Gnilka, 2.254). Throughout church history, exegetes have cited Peter's example to confound rigorists who insist that sin after baptism automatically disqualifies one from salvation (see, e.g., Theophylact, *Explanation of Mark* 14:66–72). Peter, like King Manasseh of Judah (2 Chron 33:12–13, 19), shows that the doors of repentance are always open (cf. Epiphanius, *Heresies* 59.7.7 [59.1.8]).

This hopeful implication may, like so much else in the passage, reverberate loudly in the Markan situation in the Jewish War, in which some Markan Christians have apparently responded to persecution and pressure by renouncing Jesus to embrace other "messiahs" (cf. 13:6, 22). While Mark regards the acts of such turncoats with abhorrence, he probably does not give up all hope for them; the example of the Prince of the Apostles shows that one act of renunciation, or even three, do not an apostate make but may be the prelude to repentance, restoration, ecclesiastical leadership, and martyrdom. Christians, in the Markan view, are not supermen but stumbling, often exasperatingly inconsistent, "fallible followers" (cf. Malbon, "Fallible Followers"). As Paul suggests, however, such fallibility rather than spiritual correctness is the human material that God prefers to work with, "so that the superabundance of power might be of God and not from ourselves" (2 Cor 4:7; my trans.).

This hopeful implication does not change the fact that the last remnant of Jesus' inner circle has now abandoned him and he has been condemned to death by the highest religious authority in Palestine. In the next passage this sentence will be ratified by the Roman governor and Jesus will be turned over to executioners.

PILATE CONDEMNS JESUS TO DEATH (15:1–15)

15 [1]And immediately, early in the morning, the chief priests, having taken counsel with the elders and the scribes and the whole Sanhedrin, bound Jesus and led him away and turned him over to Pilate. [2]And Pilate asked him, "*You* are the king of the Jews?" But he answered him, saying, "*You* are saying it." [3]And the chief priests accused him of many things. [4]And Pilate asked him again, saying, "You make no reply? See what great things they are charging you with!" [5]But Jesus did not answer anything anymore, so that Pilate was amazed.

[6]But during the feast he used to release to them one prisoner whom they had requested. [7]Now there was a man called Barabbas who was bound together with the insurrectionists who had committed murder in the insurrection. [8]And the

crowd went up and began to ask him to act as he was accustomed to do for them. [9]But Pilate answered them, saying, "Do you want me to release to you the king of the Jews?" [10]For he knew that the chief priests had turned him over out of envy. [11]But the chief priests stirred up the crowd to ask that he might release Barabbas to them instead. [12]But Pilate again answered them, saying, "What then shall I do with the one whom you call the king of the Jews?" [13]They cried out again, "Crucify him!" [14]But Pilate said to them, "What has he done wrong?" But they cried out even more, "Crucify him!" [15]And Pilate, wishing to satisfy the crowd, released Barabbas to them and turned Jesus over, after flogging him, in order that he might be crucified.

NOTES

15 1. *the chief priests, having taken counsel with the elders and the scribes and the whole Sanhedrin.* Gk *symboulion poiēsantes hoi archiereis meta tōn presbyterōn kai grammateōn kai holon to synedrion.* This is one of the many doublets between the Sanhedrin trial (14:53–65) and the trial before Pilate (15:1–20; see figure 52 in the APPENDIX "Historical Problems in the Markan Sanhedrin Trial"); both mention a deliberation of "the whole Sanhedrin" about Jesus. For Mark himself, however, it may function not as a doublet but as a back-reference to the first trial from within the second (see Brown, *Death*, 1.417–20, 631–62); for a similar back-reference in an apparent doublet, see the NOTE on "having given a loud cry" in 15:37.

bound. Gk *dēsantes.* In Cicero, *Rabirius* 13, a Roman officer charged with carrying out sentences is told to "bind his hands, veil his head, [and] hang him on the tree of shame!"—apparently a customary formula (see Hengel, *Crucifixion*, 44). The Markan Jesus' head is veiled (14:65), his hands are bound (15:1), and he is crucified (15:24–25). The veiling and binding occur before he has been sentenced to crucifixion, but the correspondence of the three elements is striking nonetheless.

Pilate. Gk *Pilatǭ.* Pontius Pilate was the prefect or governor of Judaea from 26 to 36 C.E.—not its procurator, as is sometimes erroneously stated on the basis of Tacitus, *Annals* 15.44 (see the "Pontius Pilate" inscription discovered in Caesarea and described in *NEAEHL* 1.273–74). During the time of Jesus, a procurator was an emperor's representative in fiscal affairs, whereas a prefect was his agent for civil and criminal matters (see Brown, *Death*, 1.336–37). Pilate was therefore the Roman official directly responsible for Jesus' execution. For a sifting of the little that is known about his career, see Schwartz, "Pilate," and Brown, *Death*, 1.693–705. Already by Mark's time, apparently, he had become so firmly connected in Christian memory with Jesus' death that the evangelist did not need to explain his identity to his audience. The most important point about him for Christian history is that he, rather than the Jewish authorities in Jerusalem, had the authority to impose the death sentence in Judaea; Josephus sums up the extent of his jurisdiction by saying that he had the power "even to execute" (*War* 2.117, my trans.).

Mark describes Pilate as disinclined to exercise this power on Jesus, and the later evangelists paint him as even more reluctant to do so (see Matt 27:19, 24;

Luke 23:4, 13–16; John 18:29–31, 38; 19:4–8, 12). While there may be an element of truth in this portrayal, it also helps the evangelists shift blame to the Jews
(see the section on anti-Judaism in the introduction to chapters 14–15) and show
Greco-Roman readers that Christianity is politically unobjectionable. Luke extends the latter tendency in Acts, where governmental authorities are frequently
sympathetic or at least indifferent to the Christian movement (see, e.g., Acts
19:35–41; 23:26–30; 26:28–31; 28:31). As Schwartz points out, a similar tendency
to exculpate a political leader is evident in the Gospels' depiction of Herod Antipas only reluctantly consenting to his wife's murder plot against John the Baptist
(see Mark 6:14–29). Josephus more plausibly describes Antipas as calculating that
"it would be much better to strike first and be rid of [John] before his work led
to an uprising" (*Ant.* 18.118)—reasoning that might also have been operative in
Pilate's relation to Jesus. The tendency to rehabilitate Pilate developed further in
post-NT Christianity (see Jensen, "How Pilate Became a Saint").

Brown, however, argues that we should not think of the historical Pilate as a
bloodthirsty monster whom the Gospels have thoroughly whitewashed. The picture of him that emerges from Josephus and other sources, rather, is of a governor
who was as corrupt as most provincial officials, and ruthless when threatened
with upheaval (see, e.g., the violence against a protesting crowd in Josephus, *War*
2.175–77, and cf. Luke 13:1–2), but who usually antagonized his Jewish subjects
more out of ignorance than out of malignity and sometimes relented under popular pressure (see, e.g., Josephus, *War* 2.169–74, and Philo, *Embassy to Gaius* 299–
305; cf. Reinbold, *Bericht*, 259–60).

2. **You are the king of the Jews?** Gk *sy ei ho basileus tōn Ioudaiōn.* In the NT
the title "king of the Jews" appears with one exception (John 19:21) on the lips of
non-Jews (the Jewish counterpart is "king of Israel," as in Mark 15:32). In passages
from Josephus, however, Jews call two earlier Jewish leaders, Alexander Jannaeus
and Herod the Great, the "king of the Jews" (*Ant.* 14.36; 15.373; 16.311), and the
title also appears on wine amphoras imported from Italy and found in the palace
of Herod the Great (see Mendels, *Rise*, 217). As Brown (*Death*, 1.731) observes,
therefore, in first-century Palestine "the charge that Jesus was claiming that title
might well be understood by the Romans as an attempt to reestablish the kingship over Judaea and Jerusalem exercised by the Hasmoneans . . . and Herod the
Great."

You *are saying it.* Gk *sy legeis.* On the boldness of this reply to the Roman ruler
of Judaea, see the COMMENT on 15:1–5; on Hellenistic respect for *parrēsia*
("boldness in speech"), cf. the NOTE on "You're not allowed to marry your brother's wife" in 6:18. For a similar instance of Jesus' audacity to a political ruler, see
his message to "that fox" Herod Antipas in Luke 13:32.

4–5. *You make no reply? . . . But Jesus did not answer anything anymore.* Gk
ouk apokrinē ouden . . . ho de Iēsous ouketi ouden apekrithē. Jesus' silence before
his accusers echoes biblical passages such as Isa 53:7 and Ps 38:13–14, but it also
is similar to Josephus' story about Jesus son of Ananias, who prophesied against
the Temple in the years before the Great Revolt broke out in 66 C.E. but fell mute
when interrogated by Jewish officials and the Roman governor (*War*, 6.302–5; for

the text from Josephus and other parallels between the son of Ananias and Jesus of Nazareth, see the COMMENT on 13:1–2).

6. *But during the feast he used to release to them one prisoner whom they had requested.* Gk *kata de heortēn apelyen autois hena desmion hon parētounto.* We have no evidence outside Mark and Matthew for such a paschal amnesty, and indeed the institution seems unlikely: would the Romans have agreed to release, on a regular basis, just *any* prisoner whom the Jewish populace requested, even a murderous revolutionary such as Barabbas? Moreover, as Gnilka (2.304) points out, if there had been such a custom, Josephus, who usually tries to portray the Romans in the best light, would probably have mentioned it. The Gospel of John presents a more plausible picture, since the Johannine Pilate ascribes the institution of the Passover amnesty to the Jews rather than the Romans ("But *you* have a custom that I release someone for you at the Passover," John 18:39). It is plausible that the Jews would regularly have asked the Romans to release prisoners at Passover time, since that holiday celebrated a famous instance of liberation from foreign servitude, and it is also plausible that the Romans would occasionally have granted such requests in order to increase their popularity (see Brown, *Death,* 1.817).

7. *a man called Barabbas.* Gk *ho legomenos Barabbas,* lit. "the one called Barabbas." Nothing is known about this man apart from the terse notices in the Gospels. The name given here is a patronymic meaning "son of Abbas" (cf. "Bartimaeus" in 10:46) and is attested in Jewish sources (see, e.g., *b. Ber.* 18b). Since Abba itself means "father," the narrative may intend to imply a contrast between Barabbas = "son of the father" and Jesus, the true son of the (heavenly) Father (cf. 14:62). While Mark does not make this contrast explicit, his readers would not need to be Aramaic speakers in order to get the point, since they would be able to piece together the components of Barabbas' name from the translations provided in 10:46 and 14:36.

Some texts of Matt 27:16–17, mostly of a Caesarean type (e.g., Θ, *f*[1], 700*, sy[s]), read "Jesus Barabbas" rather than "Barabbas," and Origen acknowledges that some of the manuscripts known to him attest this reading (*Commentary on Matthew* 121 [on 27:16–18]). Many scholars think that "Jesus Barabbas" was the original reading in Matthew and that the forename was later suppressed by reverential scribes who felt, as Origen did, that no sinner should bear the name of Jesus (see Metzger, 68; Brown, *Death,* 1.798). This theory is made more plausible by the observation that the forename has been erased from several manuscripts (see Burkitt, *Evangelion,* 2.277).

Some exegetes, such as Taylor (581), even argue that "Jesus Barabbas" may have been the original reading in Mark, since "the one called Barabbas" is awkward, and elsewhere *ho legomenos* is usually preceded by a personal name and followed by a descriptive title or nickname (Matt 1:16; 4:18; 10:2; 27:17, 22; John 11:16; 20:24; 21:2; Col 4:11). There are instances, however, in which *ho legomenos* is not preceded by the personal name (Matt 26:3, 14; Luke 22:47; John 4:25; 9:11; 19:17), and awkward expressions are common in Mark (see, e.g., the NOTE below on "to ask him to act as he was accustomed to do for them" in 15:8). Taylor's theory, which lacks any textual support, is therefore dubious.

insurrectionists . . . insurrection. Gk *stasiastōn . . . stasei.* These terms usually imply revolutionary activity (see BDAG 940), an implication confirmed by the Vulgate, which translates them with *seditiosis* and *seditione,* and by the larger Markan context, in which Barabbas' counterpart Jesus is described as "the king of the Jews" and crucified between two *lēstai,* the word Josephus uses to designate Jewish revolutionaries (cf. John 18:40, which describes Barabbas himself as a *lēstēs*). Brown (*Death,* 1.787, 796–97), however, downplays the political dimension of *stasis* and *stasiastēs,* preferring to translate them "riot" and "rioter," and claiming that *stasiastēs* is employed by Josephus "to describe a range from a troublemaker to a rebel" (citing *Ant.* 14.8; *War* 6.157). But the great majority of Josephan usages of the term refer to insurgents (see Rengstorf, *Concordance,* 2.1732–35, and cf. Hengel, *Zealots,* 382 n. 9), and even in the passage that Brown cites for the "troublemaker" meaning, *Ant.* 14.8, the troublemaker in question is Herod the Great's father, Antipater, whose agitation against the Hasmonean king Aristobulus eventually led to civil war. The three instances of the cognate verb *stasiazein* in the LXX, moreover, speak of insurrections (Jdt 7:15; 2 Macc 4:30; 14:6). The strongest argument for Brown's nonpolitical translation of *stasis* is Acts 19:40, where no revolutionaries are in sight, but here the riot is catalyzed by a religious disagreement. While *stasis,* therefore, need not refer to a full-scale war of liberation, it usually connotes civil unrest with a political and/or religious dimension absent from more neutral terms such as *thorybos* ("disturbance"; see 14:2).

Our passage refers to the fracas in which Barabbas was involved as "*the* insurrection"; Mark presents it, therefore, as a well-known incident, but it has proved difficult for modern historians to identify. The biggest and best-known previous rebellions against the Romans, which erupted in the wake of Herod the Great's death in 4 B.C.E. (*War* 2.55–65; *Ant.* 17.269–85; Acts 5:36–37), seem too far away in time for Barabbas still to be languishing in prison thirty-five years later. As for later rebellions, Tacitus' statement (*Histories* 5.9.2) that under Tiberius (the emperor from 14 to 37 C.E.) all was quiet in Palestine has caused some scholars to think that Mark is making things up. As Price (*Jerusalem,* 6) emphasizes, however, Tacitus, writing in Rome around 110 C.E., demonstrates a very sketchy knowledge of Palestine eighty years before, and we know from Josephus and Philo that all was in fact not quiet there during this period.

Two incidents mentioned by the latter two writers might qualify as "the insurrection" of Mark 15:7: the riot over Pilate's plan to build an aqueduct in Jerusalem with Temple funds (see Josephus, *War* 2.175–77; *Ant.* 18.60–62) and the protest over his introduction of golden shields into the city (see Philo, *Embassy to Gaius* 299–305). Josephus calls the aqueduct incident a *stasis* (*Ant.* 18.62), and Philo reports that the shield protestors warned Pilate *mē stasiaze* ("Do not arouse sedition"; *Embassy to Gaius* 301). Both incidents, moreover, seem to have occurred around the time of Jesus' crucifixion; if the *Testimonium Flavianum* is authentic, Jesus' ministry and death happened at "about the same time" (*kata touton ton chronon*) as the aqueduct incident (*Ant.* 18.63), and Brown dates the shields protest to around 31 C.E. (*Death,* 1.701). While neither Josephus nor Philo describes the protestors in these incidents as spilling the blood of Romans or their collaborators, Josephus reports that the reverse happened in the aqueduct riot, and his presentation of the violence as one-sided may reflect his desire to present the Jews as generally peaceable.

8. *to ask him to act as he was accustomed to do for them.* Gk *aiteisthai kathōs epoiei autois*, lit. "to ask as he used to do for them." The syntax is awkward. Taylor (583) mentions the possibility that *epoiei* should be taken impersonally: "just as one was wont to do for them." The narrative flow, however, makes it more likely that the implied subject is Pilate. Either something has dropped out of the text, such as *poiein* ("to do") after *aiteisthai*, or this is an example of ellipsis (see the GLOSSARY).

11. *But the chief priests stirred up the crowd.* Gk *hoi de archiereis aneseisan ton ochlon.* The Markan portrayal of the capriciousness of the Jerusalem crowd (contrast their support for Jesus in 11:1–11; 12:12; 14:2) corresponds to a common ancient trope; see, for example, Gruen (*Heritage*, 176), who describes the crowd in the Susanna story as "fickle, malleable, and readily manipulated" by the corrupt elders of the nation (cf. Yavetz, *Plebs*, 9–37, for a survey of the mostly negative passages about crowds in Roman sources). But there may be a kernel of historical truth here, as Theissen and Merz (*Historical Jesus,* 179) point out: Jesus may have been hailed by his fellow pilgrims, who came up to Jerusalem with him (11:1–11, etc.), but rejected by the inhabitants of the city, many of whom were dependent on the Temple for their livelihood and hence provoked by his prophecy against it.

12. *whom you call the king of the Jews.* Gk *hon legete ton basilea tōn Ioudaiōn.* The first two Greek words ("whom you call" in the translation) are missing in some important witnesses (A, D, W, Θ, *f*[1, 13], lat, sy[s], sa, etc.) but were probably original to the text; they seem to be ameliorated by Matt 27:22 (cf. Metzger, 118) and might have dropped out because a scribe realized the logical difficulty that the Jewish authorities have not previously called Jesus "the king of the Jews." The alternative theory, that the words have been added "in order to throw the onus for the use of the title 'The King of the Jews' upon the high priests" (Metzger, ibid.), is unconvincing, since the logical place for the introduction of the qualification would be 15:9 rather than 15:12.

13. *cried out again, "Crucify him!"* Gk *palin ekraxan staurōson auton.* The crowd calls for Pilate to crucify Jesus, but they do not expect him to perform the execution himself, merely to give the order; cf. the NOTE on Herod's phrase "The one I myself beheaded" in 6:16.

Palin ("again") is difficult, since this is the first time that the crowd has called for Jesus' crucifixion; the same difficulty is present in John 18:40, suggesting some relation between the Markan tradition and the Johannine one (both Matthew and Luke omit *palin*). It may be that the word reveals a redactional seam, or it may mean "in turn" or "back" (see BDAG 753 [5]). Black (112) suggests mistranslation from Aramaic *tûb*, which can mean both "again" and "thereupon." The literal meaning "again," however, may be ironically relevant as an allusion to 15:9 (see the COMMENT on 15:6–15).

On the possibly demonic nature of this cry, see the COMMENT on 15:6–15, and cf. the Satanic inspiration of Judas' betrayal of Jesus according to Luke 22:3

and John 13:2, 27. The linkage between crucifixion and demons is not accidental, since this horrible mode of execution had an atmosphere of the uncanny about it; see, for example, *Liber Hermes Trismegisti* 26 (in Gundel, *Texte* 79, lines 30–31), in which dying from demons is parallel to dying fastened to a cross (cf. Hengel, *Crucifixion*, 78); *Martyrdom of Pionius* 13.8, which records the slur that Jesus performed necromancy and spirit divination with the cross; and the use of nails and other paraphernalia from crucifixions in magical spells (e.g., Pliny, *Natural History* 28.11.46; Lucan, *Civil War* 6.547; *m. Šabb.* 6:10; *Geniza* 23.2.18 [Naveh and Shaked, *Magic Spells*, 220–21]; cf. Fulda, *Kreuz*, 186).

14. *even more.* Gk *perissōs.* On this translation, see the NOTE on "even more" in 10:26.

15. *wishing to satisfy the crowd, released Barabbas to them and turned Jesus over, after flogging him.* Gk *boulomenos tǭ ochlǭ to hikanon poiēsai apelysen autois ton Barabban kai paredōken ton Iēsoun phragellōsas.* As Brown (*Death*, 1.850) notes, *to hikanon poiēsai* ("to satisfy," lit. "to do enough for") and *phragellōsas* ("after flogging") are Latinisms corresponding to *satisfacere* and *flagellare,* "so this is probably a deliberate imitation of Latin style to supply atmosphere for the Roman governor's legal decision." Although there is no extra-NT corroboration for the yearly Passover amnesty described in 15:6 (see the NOTE on "But during the feast he used to release to them one prisoner whom they had requested" in 15:6), there is some evidence for occasional pardons, and one example from the papyri (P.Flor 61.59–63) contains a striking verbal parallel to our passage: "You have been worthy of scourging, . . . but I am granting you to the crowds" (*tois ochlois*; see Deissmann, *Light*, 269).

On flogging as the usual preliminary to crucifixion, see Dio Chrysostom, *Discourses* 4.67; Philo, *Against Flaccus* 72; Josephus, *War* 2.306; 5.449. The governor would not have flogged the prisoner directly but would have left the task to the soldiers; "after flogging him," like "Crucify!" in 15:13–14, is probably a causative usage of an active verb (= after having him flogged; for other Markan examples of this grammatical phenomenon, see "beheaded" in 6:16, "arrested" and "bound" in 6:17, and perhaps "rolled" in 15:46; cf. Smyth §1711; Wallace, 411–412). Blinzler (*Trial*, 222) describes the different types of implements that might be used in flogging: rods for free people, sticks for soldiers, but whips for slaves and other noncitizens, "the leather thongs of these being often fitted with a spike or with several pieces of bone or lead joined to form a chain." The physical cost of punishment with such implements usually shortened the time it took for the condemned prisoner to die (cf. 15:44), and executioners wishing to extend the torture of crucifixion might forgo the flogging (see Sallust, *Histories* fr. 3.9 on the punishment of pirates; cf. Hengel, *Crucifixion*, 29, 40–41 n. 5).

COMMENT

Introduction. The second of Jesus' two trials, his hearing before the Roman governor Pontius Pilate, follows Peter's denial (14:66–72) and is amazingly similar to the first trial before the Jewish Sanhedrin (14:53–65). The APPENDIX "His-

torical Problems in the Markan Sanhedrin Trial" suggests a source-critical explanation for these parallels, namely, that Mark or a predecessor has fashioned
the Sanhedrin trial narrative on the model of the trial before Pilate. For Mark,
who has deliberately included both narratives in his Gospel, there is probably a
theological point to this parallelism: the same inimical power that masterminded
Jesus' condemnation by the Jewish authorities is now bringing about his condemnation by the Gentiles in a strikingly similar manner. Behind that power of evil,
however, lies the overarching will of God (see 8:31 and 9:12, and for the coexistence of divine and demonic determinism, 1QS 3:15–26).

As implied above, there was probably a preexistent account of Jesus' trial before
Pilate, which served as the basis for the construction of the Sanhedrin trial as well.
In an earlier, more naive age, this account of the Pilate hearing was sometimes
traced back to a Roman transcript of the trial (see already Justin, *1 Apology* 1.35, 48),
but this theory is now generally dismissed because such transcripts, along with the
other paraphernalia of a prescribed legal process, were not customarily employed
for non-elite prisoners in provincial settings. The governor, rather, had a free hand
to conduct a simple *cognitio*, or investigation, determine the prisoner's innocence
or guilt with little attention to legal niceties, and impose whatever sentence he
deemed fit, up to and including the death penalty (see Brown, *Death*, 1.712, 715–
16). The Markan account of the trial before Pilate, which contains several improbabilities (the paschal amnesty custom, the release of a murderous revolutionary,
and the governor's sympathy for Jesus), probably does not go back to eyewitness
testimony but to Christian reconstruction of "what must have happened."

Nevertheless, there seems to be a pre-Markan substratum to the scene, as suggested by details such as the apparent superfluity of the Sanhedrin's deliberation
(15:1) after it has already tried and condemned Jesus to death (14:63–64; cf. the
first NOTE on 15:1) and the general correspondences between Mark and John
(cf. Reinbold, *Bericht*, 258–59). This pre-Markan substratum probably would
have included, at a minimum, the "You are the king of the Jews?" question, the
"You are saying it" answer, Jesus' silence before subsequent questioning, the offer
to release "the king of the Jews," the crowd's choice of Barabbas rather than Jesus,
their repeated cry to crucify Jesus, and the delivery of Jesus to crucifixion—in
other words, the bare bones of the narrative. Markan features include the list of
opponents and use of *euthys* ("immediately") and *paradidomi* ("to turn over") in
15:1; the double negative in 15:5; the *gar* ("for") clause in 15:10, which includes
paradidomi again; and perhaps the speculation about Pilate's motive in 15:15a
("wishing to satisfy the crowd").

The passage is divided into two parts of unequal length: the short scene of
Pilate's interrogation of Jesus (15:1–5), and the long scene of his negotiations with
the crowd about Jesus and Barabbas (15:6–15). The unequal length is significant:
it takes Pilate just moments to conclude that Jesus is innocent, but he is so impressed by this brief encounter that he mounts a protracted effort to free him.
He does not succeed, however, and a sad inclusion results: in 15:1 the Sanhedrin
turns Jesus over to Pilate, and in 15:15 Pilate turns Jesus over to the soldiers to be
crucified (see Gnilka, 2.298).

15:1–5: Pilate interrogates Jesus. After the interlude of Peter's denial (14:66–72), the focus returns to Jesus, whom the Jewish leaders bind and turn over to Pontius Pilate, the Roman governor (15:1; on his career, see the NOTE on "Pilate" in 15:1). Although they have technically ceded control of Jesus, these leaders lurk in the background, providing an audience for the subsequent interrogation and remaining ready to spring into action.

The portrayal of the bound Jesus prepares for the sarcastic tone of Pilate's initial question: "*You* are the king of the Jews?" (15:2a). Although titles with related connotations such as "Christ" and "Son of David" have appeared throughout Mark, "king of the Jews" does not occur until this point in the narrative, where Jesus encounters the Roman authorities, and it then appears five times (15:2, 9, 12, 18, 26) and becomes the leitmotif of the section (cf. Matera, *Kingship*, 147–49). In this first appearance, however, it seems to come out of nowhere; one must presuppose that between 15:1 and 15:2 the Jewish leaders have informed Pilate of the charge against Jesus—a narrative gap that Luke 23:2 fills in. In Mark itself, the obscurity is cleared up later in the narrative, when Pilate refers to Jesus as "the one whom you [the Jewish leaders or crowd] call the king of the Jews" (15:12); Pilate, therefore, asks Jesus about his kingship because the Jewish authorities have reported his royal pretensions and/or reputation.

In the present circumstances, however, such pretensions seem outlandish, since the state of impotence symbolized by Jesus' bound condition is the opposite of the unfettered power associated with kingship; as 3:27 illustrates, a bound person lies in the control of another, who can use him as he will. Despite this outward appearance of impotence, however, the Markan Jesus seems anything but powerless as he replies ironically in turn to Pilate's ironic question about kingship, showing the same sort of panache that he had demonstrated before the high priest in 14:62: "*You* are saying it" (15:2b). As in the answer to the high priest, this reply exploits the fact that Pilate's question could be construed as a statement; Jesus himself has no need to affirm his kingship, because Pilate has already done so for him. Whereas, however, the response in 14:62 was couched in the aorist tense (*sy eipas*, "You have said"), the current one is expressed in the present (*sy legeis*, "You are saying"), a change that anticipates the way in which the governor will side with Jesus and repeatedly refer to him as "the king of the Jews" (15:9–14).

At the present point, however, Pilate's partisanship of Jesus is anything but a foregone conclusion, since Jesus' reply affirms his claim to the title "king of the Jews"—a title that made the Romans extremely nervous (see the NOTES on "*You* are the king of the Jews?" and "*You* are saying it" in 15:2). There had not been a Jewish king in Palestine since 4 B.C.E., when Herod the Great died, although several of his sons and several revolutionary leaders aspired to kingship in the wake of his death (see Josephus, *War* 2.55–65). Eventually the Roman emperor Augustus appointed Herod's son Archelaus ethnarch of Judaea and promised to make him king if he proved worthy (*War* 2.93; *Ant.* 17.317); in fact, however, Archelaus turned out to be a terrible ruler and was removed in 6 C.E., instituting a period of direct Roman rule. This was interrupted only by the short-lived kingship of Agrippa I (41–44 C.E.) and the revolts of 66–73 and 132–135, which seem to have been led by "kingly," that is, messianic, figures (cf. Schürer, 1.330–484; Marcus, "Jewish War," 458–59; Brown, *Death*, 1.682–84). The term "king of the Jews," therefore, had a revolutionary, anti-imperial potential that goes a long way toward explaining the Roman reluctance to let Jewish leaders call themselves kings (cf. John 19:12). Indeed, in the Roman world at large, a claim to be king, or a real or imagined slight to the emperor, even in jest, was sometimes enough to get a person crucified (see, e.g., Petronius, *Satyricon* 53.3; *Sententiae of Paulus* 5.21.3–4). The emperor in Jesus' day, Tiberius, was especially sensitive to such perceived insults, which cost people their lives for matters as slight as changing one's clothes near a statue of Augustus, carrying into a privy or brothel a ring or coin stamped with his image, or accepting an honor on the same day that he got one (see Suetonius, *Life of Tiberius* 58, and cf. Hengel, *Crucifixion*, 49 n. 11, 59, 75). In later times, offenders against the majesty of the emperor were defined to include people who claimed offices that did not belong to them and kings of foreign nations who failed to submit to the will of the Roman people (Justinian, *Digest* 48.4.3–4; cf. Brown, *Death*, 1.719).

The substance of Jesus' reply, therefore, is not calculated to induce sympathetic feelings in the emperor's subordinate, and its manner is just as bad, since it cheekily shifts the responsibility for a positive evaluation of Jesus' kingship onto Pilate himself. Jesus employs none of the respectful rhetoric ("my lord," etc.) that might be expected from a low-class provincial on trial for his life before the supreme Roman official in Palestine (contrast the deferential address to officials from Christians in the trial scenes in Acts 24:10; 26:2–3, 19, 25–27). By "answering back," rather, he displays the very royal consciousness that he is being interrogated about, since no one would dare to answer a ruler in this way unless he felt himself to be somehow his superior. The edginess of the response is increased by the fact that it is delivered in the presence of members of the Jewish elite, before whom Pilate risks losing face if he does not react strongly (cf. Scott, *Domination*, 202–27).

A punishing retaliation from the governor, therefore, is to be expected (cf. Acts 23:2), but in fact none occurs—an indication, perhaps, that Pilate has already begun to feel partial toward Jesus. The chief priests, however, do not, and Pilate's surprising reluctance to condemn him awakens them out of their dormancy and spurs them to accuse Jesus of "many things" (15:3). Mark does not specify these "things," and his silence may be significant, since they would presumably be political in nature, as are the charges detailed in Luke 23:2 ("perverting our nation, forbidding us to pay taxes to the emperor, and saying that he himself is the Messiah, a king"). Neither does Mark directly describe Jesus' reaction to these charges; we learn obliquely, from Pilate's query (15:4), that his first response is silence, and, from the narrator, that his subsequent response to Pilate's further questioning is silence as well (15:5a).

This very lack of response, however, like the audacious reply in 15:2, shows Jesus' sovereign self-possession; he does not defend himself or try to escape from the brutal fate that hangs over him, but risks antagonizing Pilate by his repeated refusal to answer direct questions. Yet instead of provoking Pilate's wrath, Jesus' unintimidated silence instead elicits his amazement (15:5b), since, as Bengel puts it, "No one is wont to be silent when his life is at stake" (*Gnomon* on Matt 27:14). This is typical of martyr stories, in which examining authorities are often amazed at the steadfastness of the martyr, who disdains the chance to save himself and sometimes even goes out of his way to antagonize them (see, e.g., 2 Macc 7:11–12). Pilate's reaction is akin to awe, and thus is similar to that of the magistrates in Josephus' *Jewish War* (6.302–5), who conclude from the refusal of another Jesus to answer their questions that he is acting under a supernatural impulse (see the COMMENT on 13:1–2).

As in earlier Markan passages (e.g., 1:16–20; 2:13–14; 8:14–21), Jesus refuses to give the required explanations for his deeds and words; and the fact that, lacking such explanations, people still find themselves drawn to and even overwhelmed by him testifies that a divine power is at work in him even as he moves inexorably toward death. This impression is reinforced by the narrative's echo, here and in 15:44, of the famous scriptural prophecy about the Lord's Suffering Servant, who is silent before his accusers (Isa 53:7) and at whom nations are amazed (*thaumasontai*) and kings shut their mouths (Isa 52:15 LXX). The Isaian echo deepens the Markan picture of a paradoxical reversal of appearances: instead of being defeated by the worldly authorities who presume to judge him, the bound and seemingly powerless Jesus is actually advancing toward holy-war victory.

15:6–15: Jesus or Barabbas? That victory, however, will be won through the Suffering Servant's death, which according to Isaiah 52:13–53:12 is the will of God; and no human power, not even that of a sympathetic governor, can stand in the way of the accomplishment of that will. Pilate's efforts, therefore, like the similar endeavor of Herod Antipas to preserve John the Baptist (6:14–29), turn out to be ineffectual and thus demonstrate the hollowness of worldly authority, which only *appears* to rule in the world of humans (10:45; cf. Dan 4:17; 5:21 and the COMMENT on 6:14–16). Although, therefore, the second and longer part of our pericope is dominated by the verb "to release" (*apolyein*), which always has Pilate as its subject (15:6, 9, 11, 15), this is precisely what Pilate *cannot* do (cf. Gnilka, 2.298).

Pilate's lack of control is already suggested by the roundabout way in which he attempts to save Jesus, utilizing a supposed Roman custom of releasing at Passover a single prisoner selected by the Jewish populace (15:6). We have no other evidence for such a yearly paschal amnesty, and it strains credulity to think that the Romans would commit themselves to such an institution (see the NOTE on "But during the feast he used to release to them one prisoner whom they had requested" in 15:6). It may be, rather, that Mark or his source has generalized an occasional Roman practice in order to explain how a governor so partial to Jesus ended up executing him—he could pardon only one man, but the crowd demanded Barabbas rather than Jesus (cf. Reinbold, *Bericht*, 264, 267). The crucial thing for Mark, however, is not the paschal amnesty but the comparison and contrast between Jesus and Barabbas, the revolutionary leader who ends up being freed. Both Jesus and Barabbas are bound (15:1, 7), and the militant connotation of "king of the Jews" suggests that Jesus, like Barabbas, is being depicted by his enemies as a revolutionary figure. The comparison becomes even closer if Mark's hearers realize that Barabbas' name, which contains the word "Abba," means "son of the father" (see the NOTE on "a man called Barabbas" in 15:7) and if they remember that a few passages back Jesus prayed to *his* Father, calling him "Abba." But Mark also wants to show that this comparison is mistaken: Barabbas is an insurrectionist and a murderer, whereas Jesus bestows health and life (5:23; cf. 9:43, 45; 10:17, 30) and does not pose a threat to the *pax Romana* (cf. 12:13–17). One "son of the father," then, has tried in vain to usher in the heavenly *Abba's* dominion through revolutionary violence against the Romans; the other succeeds in doing so by dying on a Roman cross. The genius of our scene is well expressed in Samuel Crossman's Good Friday hymn: "A murderer they save; the Prince of Life they slay" ("My Song Is Love Unknown," 1664).

Pilate, at least, seems to have an inkling of this difference between Barabbas and Jesus, and when the crowd requests that he perform the customary Passover amnesty (15:8), he seizes the opportunity and proposes that its object this year be the latter, whom he calls "the king of the Jews" (15:9). His motivation for wanting to free Jesus, and the priests' inducement for wanting him dead, are now explicitly stated: "For he knew that the chief priests had turned him over out of envy" (15:10). This envy presumably reflects Jesus' popularity among the people, which up to this point has prevented the elite from moving against him (see 12:12; 14:2) and which is encapsulated in the title "king of the Jews"; even though kingship has lapsed in Israel, Jesus is the sort of person whom the populace would choose for their king, as they have demonstrated by feting him royally when he entered Jerusalem (11:1–11).

Given this prior support for Jesus, however, it is puzzling that the crowd is now so easily manipulated into abandoning him and demanding the freedom of Barabbas instead (15:11). As in previous instances of sudden, otherwise inexplicable opposition (5:17; 6:2–3), this radical reversal may be traceable to the influence of malignant spirits, who have popped up suddenly throughout the Gospel, seemingly out of nowhere, in order to convulse people (see 1:26; 9:26) and cause them to oppose Jesus (see 1:23–24; 5:6–7; 8:33). There is an analogy, moreover, between our scene and the exorcism of the Gerasene demoniac in 5:1–20, in which the demons are thwarted in their direct attempt to repulse Jesus but succeed in driving him from the country by working indirectly through the local populace (see the COMMENT on 5:14–17). In our scene, similarly, the priests' direct approach fails, but the indirect one through the crowd succeeds.

This demonic explanation for the populace's sudden indifference to Jesus' fate is supported by the conclusion of the story, in which they go further and demand his crucifixion—this time without incitement from the priests. The first expression of this demand is precipitated by Pilate's query as to what they want him to do with "the one whom you call the king of the Jews" (15:12). Operating under the assumption that Jesus' reputation for kingship flows from his popular support, the governor attempts to exploit this allegiance by putting Jesus' fate up to a vote (a procedure that seems historically dubious; see Brown, *Death*, 1.720–22, 814–20). The appalling reply comes back: "Crucify him!" (15:13). As Brown (*Death*, 824) comments: "Even though the chief priests have been active, the brutal imperative of the shout of the crowd against Jesus in 15:13 is shocking in the flow of the story." This is especially true because the description of the crowd "crying out (*ekraxan*) again" pushes the reader's memory back to the last time this word was used—when a Jerusalem crowd rained blessings on Jesus as "he who comes in the name of the Lord," the successor of King David (11:9; cf. Brown, *Death*, 1.824). Now the same Jerusalem crowd demands instead that "the king of the Jews" be crucified—the first time that *stauroun* has been used in the narrative. This shocking, uncanny change defies human explanations, even the manipulation of the chief priests; a more powerful malignity than theirs, rather, appears to be at work, as is confirmed by the frequency with which Mark refers *krazein* to the shouts of demons (3:11; 5:5, 7; 9:26; cf. the NOTE on "cried out again, 'Crucify him!' " in 15:13). But an acme of demonic activity, including demonic hatred, is to be expected in the end-time (cf. 1QH 13[5]:5–39; Rev 11:9–10; 12:10–12; etc.). As previously Jesus has been (13:13), so in the coming tribulation the members of the elect community will be "hated by all" (cf. the COMMENT on 13:33–37 and 14:32–36 for other parallels between the passion narrative and the eschatological prophecies in chapter 13). The hatred that the crowd displays in 15:13–14, then, is a sign that the darkness of the last days is descending on this spring morning in Jerusalem.

Pilate, taken aback by the ferocity of the crowd's hatred, asks the logical question: "What has he done wrong?" (15:14a). Significantly, this question receives no response. There *can* be none, since Jesus has done nothing but good; in a benighted, morally upside-down world, however, this is precisely the reason that he must be opposed, slandered, and finally killed (cf. Plato, *Republic* 7.517). The same blind, demonic hatred is at work that caused Jesus' gracious healings to be ascribed to the devil (3:22) and turned them into occasions for plots against his life (3:1–6). The crowd, therefore, ignores Pilate's question and simply shouts out all the more fiercely, "Crucify him!" (15:14b). Confronted by this intense, illogical, and persistent hatred, Pilate suddenly caves in and turns Jesus over to be crucified out of a desire to appease the crowd (15:15). He thus repeats the behavior of Herod Antipas when confronted by John the Baptist: although awestruck by his otherworldly prisoner (15:5; cf. 6:20), he nevertheless delivers him to death in order to gratify others (15:15ab; cf. 6:26; Moloney, 315). The apocalyptic situation described by Mark is similar to that depicted in Yeats' famous poem "The Second Coming": "The best lack all conviction, while the worst / Are full of passionate intensity." Pilate's moral collapse is, again, probably due not just to a weakness in his character but to the action of the superhuman forces that we have traced throughout our passage; a sudden switch from siding with God and Jesus to siding with "the things of human beings" can only be the work of the devil (cf. 8:29–33).

Both what Mark includes and what he excludes from his description of Pilate's delivery of Jesus to death are significant. Although he alludes to the flogging that was the general prelude to crucifixion (see the NOTE on "wishing to satisfy the crowd, etc." in 15:15), a detail that might again remind readers of the Suffering Servant of Isaiah (see Isa 50:6), he does not relate the details of the sentence. This omission is of a piece with his failure to specify the accusation against Jesus by the Jewish authorities (15:1–2) and probably reflects Christian embarrassment at the political nature of the charge for which Jesus was executed (see Reinbold, *Bericht*, 260–61). This inference is supported by H. Kuhn's observation that, insofar as we know, in Palestine during the entire period from the Roman conquest (63 B.C.E.) until shortly before the outbreak of the revolt (66 C.E.), only reputed revolutionaries and their sympathizers were subjected to crucifixion ("Kreuzesstrafe," 274).

In the Markan situation, the necessity of distinguishing Jesus and his followers from such revolutionaries has probably been increased by the recent open rebellion in Palestine. Indeed, for Mark's readers the freeing of Barabbas and condemnation of Jesus are probably part of a two-level drama that has frequently recurred in their own day: Jesus and his followers have been rejected and killed, whereas people who have committed revolutionary violence have been embraced, with disastrous results (cf. 13:9–13, 22). Nevertheless, despite the Markan desire to distinguish Jesus from the sort of revolutionary hopes that would lead his countrymen to disaster, it is also important for the evangelist to affirm that Jesus truly *is* "the king of the Jews"—a king whose dominion is won by suffering rather than inflicting violence, a pierced rather than a piercing Messiah (contrast 4Q285 5[7]:2–5; see Abegg, "Messianic Hope").

In the Gospel's next passage this king will be clad in royal robes (by taunting soldiers), crowned (with thorns), and hailed as "king of the Jews" (in mockery) by people who "look and look but never see, hear and hear but never understand" (cf. 4:12) the truth of what they say and do.

THE MOCKERY AND CRUCIFIXION OF "THE KING OF THE JEWS" (15:16–32)

15 [16]Then the soldiers led him away, into the courtyard—that is, of the praetorium—and they called together the whole cohort. [17]And they put purple clothes on him and wove and placed on him a crown of thorns. [18]And they began to salute him: "Hail, king of the Jews!" [19]And they were beating his head with a cane, and they were spitting on him and bending the knee and bowing down to him. [20]And when they had mocked him, they took the purple clothes off him and put his own clothes on him.

And they led him out in order to crucify him. [21]And they pressed into service a certain passerby, Simon of Cyrene, who was coming in from the country, the father of Alexander and Rufus, in order that he might carry his cross. [22]And they bore him away to the place called "Golgotha," which is translated "The Place of the Skull." [23]And they were trying to give him myrrhed wine, but he would not accept it. [24]And they crucified him, and they divided his clothes, casting lots for them, to see who would get what. [25]It was the third hour, and they crucified him. [26]And the inscription of the charge against him was inscribed, "The King of the Jews." [27]And with him they crucified two brigands, one on his right and one on his left.

[29]And the passersby were blaspheming him, shaking their heads and saying, "Ha! You who destroy the Temple and build it in three days, [30]save yourself by

coming down from the cross!" [31]Likewise the chief priests were mocking him to each other, along with the scribes, saying, "He saved others; himself he cannot save. [32]The Christ, the king of Israel? Let him now come down from the cross, in order that we might see and believe!" And those who were crucified along with him were railing against him.

NOTES

15 16. *into the courtyard—that is, of the praetorium.* Gk *esō tēs aulēs ho estin praitōriou.* This reading involves a textual emendation. The last word in all manuscripts is *praitōrion,* the neuter singular accusative, and with this reading the phrase is usually construed to mean "into the palace—that is, the praetorium." Here *aulē* and *praitōrion* are taken as synonyms, with *aulē* meaning "palace." It seems strange, however, that Jesus should be led into Pilate's palace *after* he has been tried by him. And while *aulē* can mean a royal palace, it usually denotes a courtyard (see M-M 91–92; BDAG 150), and this seems to be the word's meaning in its two other Markan appearances (14:54, 66). The courtyard of a palace also seems like a more suitable place to assemble a large number of soldiers (see the next NOTE) than its interior. It is possible, then, that *praitōrion* is a corruption of an original *praitōriou,* the neuter singular genitive, which differs from *praitōrion* only by the final letter. This conjecture is supported by the Vulgate and Latin manuscripts c, ff, l, which read *in atrium praetorii* ("into the courtyard of the praetorium"; see Blass, "Mark xii. 42," 186).

the whole cohort. Gk *holēn tēn speiran.* A cohort was one-tenth of a legion and normally consisted of six hundred men (see Brown, *Death,* 1.248); Josephus (*War* 3.67), however, says that ten of the twenty-three cohorts present in Judaea during the Great Revolt had a thousand infantry apiece. (During Jesus' time there were fewer Roman troops in Palestine; Josephus [*Ant.* 19.365] gives the number during the forties C.E. as five cohorts.) It is likely that one cohort was stationed permanently in Jerusalem (see Acts 21:31–32). As Brown (*Death,* 1.701 n. 64) notes, these cohorts were mostly made up of non-Jewish soldiers from the Syro-Palestinian region (cf. Josephus, *Ant.* 14.204; 19.365), many of whom may have been anti-Jewish because of the constant friction between Jews and Gentiles in the area (cf. Theissen, *Gospels,* 61–80). The assembly in the courtyard of the praetorium of the whole cohort, that is, of all of the Roman troops quartered in Jerusalem, seems implausible; even if they could all fit there, Pilate would probably have wanted at least some to be stationed in other parts of the city to prevent disturbances (see the COMMENT on 15:16–20a).

17. *purple clothes.* Gk *porphyran.* Although the wearing of purple was not restricted by law to royalty in the first century, the higher grades of purple dye, which were formed from enormous numbers of tiny mussels, were so difficult to produce and consequently so expensive (see Pliny, *Natural History* 9.60–64) that they are especially associated with royalty both in the OT (see, e.g., Judg 8:26; Esth 8:15) and in Greco-Roman literature (see, e.g., Horace, *Odes* 1.35.12; Plutarch, *Life of Tiberius Gracchus* 14.2; Strabo, *Geography* 14.1.3), including

Jewish texts of the period (see, e.g., 1 Macc 8:14; 10:20; Josephus, *Ant.* 17.197). The phrase "royal purple," therefore, became a commonplace (see, e.g., Cicero, *Scaurus* 45; Appian, *Mithraditic Wars* 1.5). Cheaper purple dyes, however, were available and were popular because of the social cachet of the color (see Reinhold, *History,* passim, citing Luke 16:19 and Acts 16:14, among other passages); it is thus not impossible that a purple robe would have been available to Jesus' executioners. Matthew 27:28, however, increases the plausibility of the scene by changing the garment to a scarlet cloak, the normal garb of a Roman soldier (see Davies and Allison, 3.602).

19. *with a cane.* Gk *kalamǭ.* This word usually signifies a reed, but it can sometimes denote a staff or cane; see, for example, Artemidorus, *Oneirocritica* 2.48: "It is bad luck to be beaten [in a dream] . . . by a cane (*kalamǭ*) because of the noise that it makes" (cf. BDAG 502 [2]). The normal word in such cases, however, is *rabdos* (= rod, staff, stick), so *kalamǭ* may be an allusion to the "bruised reed" of Isa 42:3 (see the COMMENT on 15:16–20a).

20. *put his own clothes on him.* Gk *enedysan auton ta himatia autou.* Blinzler (*Trial,* 244 n. 17) and Davies and Allison (3.605) contrast passages from Dionysius of Halicarnassus (*Roman Antiquities* 7.69.2), Josephus (*Ant.* 19.270), and perhaps Valerius Maximus (*Memorable Doings* 1.7.4) that imply that prisoners were led to execution naked. The executions described by these authors, however, took place in Rome; it may be that in Palestine the Romans avoided nudity, even in condemned prisoners, out of consideration for Jewish sensibilities (cf. *Jub.* 3:30–31; 7:20; *m. San.* 6:3; Brown, *Death* 2.953).

led him out. Gk *exagousin auton.* Since the soldiers led Jesus *into* the courtyard of the praetorium at the beginning of our passage (15:16), it would make sense to take *exagousin* as a reference to them leading him *out* of that building at the end of the subsection. But since the place of execution was outside the city walls, a fact well known to Christians (cf. Heb 13:12), it is also possible to interpret *exagousin* as a reference to Jesus' crucifixion outside Jerusalem (cf. Chrysostom, *On the Cross and the Thief* 1).

21. *Simon of Cyrene.* Gk *Simōna Kyrēnaion.* As his personal name shows, this man is a Jew, though obviously from the Diaspora. Despite this, some medieval commentators such as Hilary of Poitiers demonstrate their anti-Judaism by claiming that he was a Gentile, "for a Jew was not worthy to bear Christ's cross" (*Commentary on Matthew* 33.4). Cyrene was the capital of the North African province of Cyrenaica, which corresponded to modern Libya; Jews formed an important part of its population from the time of Ptolemy I (late fourth–early third centuries B.C.E.; see Gasque, "Cyrene"). Simon was far from the only Cyrenian Jew to live in Jerusalem in the first century (see Acts 2:10; 11:19–20); the Cyrenians, in fact, were numerous enough to have their own synagogue (see Acts 6:9).

Another curious exegetical opinion about Simon is the view of the Gnostic Basilides that he was crucified in Jesus' place. Theologically this opinion rests on Gnostic embarrassment at the suffering death of Jesus (cf. Irenaeus, *Against Heresies* 1.24.4), but grammatically it may have exploited an ambiguity in the Markan account; since the proper name "Jesus" is not employed between 15:15 and 15:34, and since Simon is the subject of 15:21, he could also be the subject of the description of crucifixion in 15:22–27 (cf. Grant, *Earliest Lives*, 10).

coming in from the country. Gk *erchomenon ap' agrou*. *Ap' agrou* can mean either "from the country" or "from the field" (see BDAG 15–16), and either interpretation poses a problem for the Synoptic dating of Jesus' crucifixion on the first day of Passover. If the expression means "from the field," then Simon has broken the commandment against working on the holiday (see Exod 12:16). If it means "from the country," Simon may have transgressed the proscription on journeys of over two thousand cubits = three thousand feet on the Sabbath and holidays such as Passover (on the Sabbath day's journey, see Acts 1:12 and *m. 'Erub*. 4:3). Simon's journey from the field or country, then, is another piece of evidence that Jesus was not actually crucified on Passover but on its eve (cf. Theissen, *Gospels*, 167, and cf. the NOTE on "Not during the feast" in 14:2).

the father of Alexander and Rufus. Gk *ton patera Alexandrou kai Rouphou*. On Alexander and Rufus as members of the Markan community, see the INTRODUCTION in vol. 1, pp. 27–28; on the identity of Rufus, see the INTRODUCTION, p. 32. In 1962 N. Avigad published the inscriptions from a first-century ossuary in the Kidron Valley that reads, on the side, "Alexander, the son of Simon" in Greek and, on the lid, *'lkśndrws qrnyt* in Hebrew, which may mean "Alexander the Cyrenian." It is possible that this is the ossuary of Alexander, the son of Simon the Cyrenian (see van der Horst, *Epitaths*, 140–41).

in order that he might carry his cross. Gk *hina arȩ ton stauron autou*. The ordinary pattern was for the prisoner to carry his own cross, or more usually the crossbeam, to the place of execution, the public humiliation of the journey forming part of the punishment (see the APPENDIX "Crucifixion"). See, for example, Chariton, *Chaereas and Callirhoe* 4.2.7: "They were brought out chained together at foot and neck, each carrying his cross—the men executing the sentence added this grim public spectacle to the inevitable punishment as an example to frighten the other prisoners" (B. Reardon trans., *Novels*, 67). According to the Synoptic Gospels, however, Simon of Cyrene carried Jesus' cross. A porter was presumably necessary because of the toll taken by Jesus' scourging and other mistreatment (see 14:65; 15:15, 19). John 19:17, however, emphatically asserts that Jesus carried his *own* cross, a portrait that fits John's general tendency to avoid any implication of weakness in depicting Jesus' passion (see Brown, *Death*, 916–17). Precritical commentators such as Jerome (*Commentary on Matthew* 27:32) harmonize the Johannine account with the Synoptic one by asserting that Jesus began by bearing his own cross but that afterward, when he faltered, Simon was pressed into service. This harmonization, which is now enshrined in the stations of the cross and numerous Hollywood movies, is ingenious but unconvincing; John shows no awareness of Simon of Cyrene but leaves the impression that Jesus bore his cross all the way, while the Synoptics give no indication that Jesus carried his cross but leave the impression that only Simon did.

22. *they bore him away.* Gk *pherousin auton*. *Pherein* can be used for bringing or leading a person from one place to another, and this is what the verb usually connotes in Mark (see 1:32; 2:3; 7:32; 8:22; 9:17, 19–20; cf. BDAG 1051 [2bb]). Its

literal meaning, however, is "to carry" or "to bear." In view of the context, this literal meaning cannot be excluded: not only was Jesus too weakened by torture to carry his cross (15:15–19, 21), but he was also too enfeebled to walk (cf. Boring, *Truly Human*, 53).

the place called "Golgotha," which is translated "The Place of the Skull." Gk *ton Golgothan topon, ho estin methermēneuomenon Kraniou Topos*, lit. "the 'Golgotha' place, which is translated 'The Place of the Skull.' " On the location of this hill, see Corbo, "Golgotha"; Brown, *Death*, 2.937–40; Murphy-O'Connor, *Holy Land*, 45–48. The two most common suggestions are the Church of the Holy Sepulchre and the Garden Tomb, with the former receiving much greater support from scholars, partly because of the antiquity of the tradition favoring it; already in the early fourth century, when Constantine's architects wanted to build a church on the site of Jesus' crucifixion and burial, this location was well established by a local tradition that may have gone back to the earliest church. The Garden Tomb, by contrast, contains two burial chambers laid out in a manner typical of tombs of the ninth–seventh centuries B.C.E., so it is unlikely to be the "new tomb" mentioned in John 19:41. In the Byzantine period, moreover, the benches in this tomb were destroyed to make rock sarcophagi, which "clearly indicates that Christians of the fourth to sixth century did not believe that this tomb was the burial place of Christ" (Murphy-O'Connor, *Holy Land*, 141).

The reason for the name "Golgotha," which means "skull" in Aramaic, is something of a mystery. (The Latin word for "skull" is *calvaria*, from which we get "Calvary," the common English term for the place.) Jerome (*Commentary on Matthew* 27:33) rejects the belief of many of his contemporaries that it derives from the burial of Adam's skull there; while Jerome's exegetical instinct is sound, the Adam/Christ typology embodied in this belief is interesting (cf. Marcus, "Son of Man"). Jerome favors another theory, which some modern scholars have adopted, that the name derives from the site's reputation as a place of execution in which the unburied bones of the dead, including skulls, could be seen. Because bones were ritually unclean, however, it seems unlikely that they would have been left unburied or their presence commemorated in an Aramaic place name (cf. Clark, "Golgotha"). The other major scholarly theory is that the hill, which is a rounded knoll arising from the surrounding surface, looked skull-like, an appearance that may have been accentuated by the shadowy entrances to the tombs in its side. (see Brown, *Death*, 2.937). It is possible that both theories contain an element of truth; Golgotha was a place of death, for which a skull is a good symbol, and the identification with the skull was reinforced by the hill's rounded, indented shape.

23. *myrrhed wine.* Gk *esmyrnismenon oinon.* This sort of drink was given to condemned prisoners as an act of mercy, to render them insensible to the pain of execution; see, for example, the succor provided by the noble women of Jerusalem and the friends of a condemned Christian in *b. Sanh.* 43a and Tertullian, *On Fasting* 12.3 respectively (see the COMMENT on 15:20b–27). Brown (*Death*, 1.941–42) notes that in such background texts the assistants who provide the anesthetic wine are usually family, friends, or pious helpers of the condemned,

whereas in our passage it is provided by the Roman soldiers. Lamarche (386) therefore finds the picture unrealistic and thinks that it reflects the evangelist's desire to exculpate the Romans. Certainly the usual goal of the executioners at crucifixions was to increase rather than alleviate the suffering of the condemned (see Fulda, *Kreuz*, 158), and this may be part of the reason that Matthew changes the merciful Markan drink of myrrhed wine to a tormenting one of wine mixed with gall (Matt 27:34). But if there is some historicity to the Gospels' depiction of Pilate's sympathy for Jesus (see the NOTE on "Pilate" in 15:1), the governor may have ordered that special consideration be shown to Jesus.

24. *divided his clothes, casting lots for them.* Gk *diamerizontai ta himatia autou ballontes klēron ep' auta.* This is a condensation of Ps 22:18 [21:19 LXX], *diemerisanto ta himatia mou heautois kai epi ton himatismon mou ebalon klēron* ("They divided my clothes among themselves, and for my garments they cast lots"). The prisoner's clothes were apparently one of the perquisites of executioners in the first century, although in the second century Hadrian exempted them from confiscation (Justinian, *Digest* 48.20.6; cf. Brown, *Death*, 2.955). Brown (*Death*, 1.952–53) discusses whether the division of Jesus' clothes among the executioners means that he was crucified naked, or whether he would have been allowed to retain a loincloth, as he is usually portrayed in Christian art (cf. *Acts of Pilate* 10:1). Artemidorus (*Oneirocritica* 2.53) states categorically that people are crucified naked. It is possible, however, that here as in the procession to the cross the Romans made a concession to the Jewish abhorrence of nakedness (cf. the NOTE on "put his own clothes on him" in 15:20). A man whose *himation* had been taken from him might retain some sort of covering; blind Bartimaeus, who casts his *himation* aside to approach Jesus (10:50), presumably does not leave himself naked in so doing. Still, in 15:24 Mark does not use the singular *himation*, which denotes the outer garment in particular, but the plural *himatia*, which means clothing in general (see BDAG 475), and, as Brown notes, the Johannine parallel (John 19:23–24) "is so specific about every item of clothing [stripped from Jesus] that one would have the impression that nothing was left."

25. *It was the third hour, and they crucified him.* Gk *ēn de hōra tritē kai estaurōsan auton.* The "third hour" was 9:00 A.M., since the Roman day began at 6:00 A.M. (see the NOTE on "on the first day of the feast of Unleavened Bread" in 14:12)—a rather early hour for an execution (cf. Brown, *Death*, 2.960). The Fourth Gospel is more plausible in this instance, since there Jesus is delivered to crucifixion at "about the sixth hour," that is, at around noon (John 19:14, RSV). The Markan scheme of third, sixth, and ninth hours (cf. 15:33–34) probably reflects the theological conception that the precise progression of events testifies to the purposefulness of divine providence in bringing about Jesus' death (cf. the NOTE on "whether at evening or midnight or cockcrow or early in the morning" in 13:35).

27. *brigands.* Gk *lēstas.* The KJV and the RSV translate this word "thieves" and "robbers" respectively, but a *lēstēs* is usually something more than a thief or robber, and as Lane (568) points out, neither theft nor robbery was a capital crime in Roman law. In the present context, rather, it is probably a code word for a revo-

lutionary, as elsewhere in Mark (see the NOTE on "den of brigands" in 11:17); cf. the reference to insurrectionists and insurrection in 15:7 and the NOTE on "insurrectionists . . . insurrection" there. If so, they are almost certainly Jews (cf. the COMMENT on 15:42–45).

After 15:27, many manuscripts add 15:28, *kai eplērōthē hē graphē hē legousa kai meta anomōn elogisthē* ("And the scripture was fulfilled that says, 'And he was numbered with the lawless ones,' " my trans.). This clause echoes Isa 53:12 (cf. LXX: *kai en tois anomois elogisthē,* "and he was numbered among the lawless ones," my trans.) but is not found in the earliest and best Alexandrian and Western manuscripts of Mark, and it is probably an assimilation to Luke 22:37, with which the last four Greek words agree exactly.

29. *You who destroy the Temple and build it in three days.* Gk *ho katalyōn ton naon kai oikodomōn en trisin hēmerais.* The mockery of Jesus as the destroyer and rebuilder of the Temple is linked with the mockery of him as "the king of the Jews" (15:26, 32). On the expectation that the Messiah would (destroy and?) rebuild the Temple, see the COMMENT on 14:55–61a.

30. *coming down from the cross.* Gk *katabas apo tou staurou.* Other ancient literature knows the motif of people coming down from the cross. In Chariton's romance *Chaereas and Callirhoe,* for example, Chaereas, like Jesus, is told to come down (*katabēthi*) from the cross, and he does "come down from the cross" (*katebaine tou staurou*) when rescued by the timely intervention of the man who had condemned him to death (4.3.6). Josephus (*Life,* 420–21) describes interceding for three crucified friends with the Roman general Titus, who immediately gave orders that they should be taken down and receive treatment. But the analogy to our passage is inexact, because Chaereas and Josephus's friends descend from the cross through the help of others, whereas if Jesus is to descend from the cross, he must do so unassisted or with supernatural help (15:36b).

32. *And those who were crucified along with him were railing against him.* Gk *kai hoi synestaurōmenoi syn autō ōneidizon auton.* Matthew 27:44 follows the Markan story here, but in Luke 23:39–43 only one of the brigands berates Jesus. The other rebukes the rebuker and asks Jesus to remember him when he comes into his dominion. Jesus in turn promises him, "Today you will be with me in Paradise"—a fine expression of the Lukan themes of human repentance and dominical compassion. In an influential harmonization, however, Jerome resolves the conflict between the Markan/Matthean and Lukan depictions by suggesting that at first both brigands railed against Jesus but later, after the cosmic signs (cf. Mark 15:33// Matt 27:45; Matt 27:51–53//Luke 23:44–45), one of them repented and turned toward him in faith (*Commentary on Matthew* 27:44). For a similar harmonization, see the NOTE on "in order that he might carry his cross" in 15:21.

The railing at Jesus by his fellow prisoners may be a historical memory, but it also serves the Markan purposes of highlighting his isolation and distinguishing him from the sort of revolutionary brigand that the Romans apparently took him to be. It may also be a window on the situation of the later Markan Christians who were rejected by the Jewish revolutionaries even as the latter, like them, were suffering at the hands of the Romans.

COMMENT

Introduction. Pilate's effort to save Jesus having failed, the latter is now delivered into the hands of the executioners, who mock him (15:16–20a) and affix him to a cross (15:20b–27), where he is mocked again (15:29–32).

The attempt to discover the editorial history of our passage begins with the observation that it contains a number of doublets (see figure 49). The mockery at the conclusion of the Roman trial, for example (15:16–20a), is similar to that at the conclusion of the Jewish trial (14:65), and it has the title "king of the Jews/of Israel" in common with the mockery after the crucifixion (15:32); the mockings in 15:29–30 and 15:31–32, moreover, are similar to each other in theme and vocabulary. In the description of the crucifixion, "It was the third hour, and they crucified him" (15:25) seems repetitious after 15:24 ("And they crucified him"), and the drink in our passage (15:23) is matched by the drink in the next pericope (15:36), which also contains two cries (15:34, 37). Bultmann (273), Taylor (649–51), and others think that most of these repetitions result from the interweaving of different passion sources (cf. the APPENDIX "Historical Problems in the Markan Sanhedrin Trial"), but some of them may be due to Markan redaction or even to historical memory (is it implausible that Jesus would have been mocked as a king both at the conclusion of his trial and on the cross?). As for Markan editing, the repetitious "It was the third hour, and they crucified him" in 15:25 and the scheme of third, sixth, and ninth hours may be Markan inventions designed to underline the solemnity and divine purposefulness of Jesus' crucifixion (see the COMMENT on 15:21b–27 below and cf. Bultmann, 273–74). In 15:31 the awkward phrase "along with the scribes" reflects a typically Markan motif, and in 15:32 "in order that we might see and believe" is probably a deliberate Markan echo of 4:12.

Our passage is usually divided into two or three different pericopes (15:16–20a and 15:20b–32, or 15:16–20a, 15:20b–27, and 15:29–32), probably out of a desire to give the crucifixion scene the independence that it is thought to deserve theologically. For Mark, however, the main point of the passage is the mockery of Jesus, which both precedes and follows the crucifixion itself, and in both parts of which his royal pretensions are held up to scorn. In both instances this mockery ridicules the idea that Jesus is the king of the Jews or of Israel—the title that is also highlighted in the crucifixion segment (15:26). Mark 15:16–32, therefore, is best viewed as a unified, three-part passage on the mockery of Jesus' kingship.

15:16–20a: Jesus is mocked by the soldiers. The first stage of this mockery occurs at the hands of the Roman soldiers in the praetorium, the governor's palace (see the NOTE on "into the courtyard—that is, of the praetorium" in 15:16). It begins with him being led away into the courtyard of this building (15:16a), where the group of soldiers to whom he has been entrusted unselfishly call "the whole cohort" together, in order to give them a chance of joining in the fun of tormenting the prisoner (15:16b; on the meaning of "cohort," see the NOTE on "the whole cohort" in 15:16). The mobilization of an entire cohort for this purpose seems implausible, and the phrase is probably a generalization of guilt, like "the whole

Figure 49: Doublets in the Markan Crucifixion and Death Scenes

15:23: And they were trying to give him myrrhed wine . . .	15:36a: And one of them ran and filled a sponge with vinegar and put it around a reed and tried to give it to him to drink . . .
15:24: And they crucified him.	15:25: It was the third hour, and they crucified him.
15:29–30: And the passersby were blaspheming him, shaking their heads and saying, "Ha! You who destroy the Temple and build it in three days, save yourself by coming down from the cross!"	15:31–32: Likewise the chief priests were mocking him to each other, along with the scribes, saying, "He saved others; himself he cannot save. The Christ, the king of Israel? Let him now come down from the cross, in order that we might see and believe!"
15:34: And at the ninth hour Jesus cried out with a loud voice . . .	15:37: But Jesus, having given a loud cry . . .
15:35, 36b: [Response to cry:] And some (tines) of those who were standing about, hearing it, said, "Look, he is calling Elijah . . . Let's see if Elijah is going to come to take him down!"	15:36a: [Response to cry:] "Let me be!" + offer of vinegar; see above

Sanhedrin" in Mark 14:55; 15:1 (see Brown, *Death*, 1.864). The Jewish authorities and the Roman soldiers, then, collude in mocking Jesus and delivering him to death.

There is a deeper level to this action of calling together the cohort, however, as there is to all of the soldiers' doings throughout the passage; although they certainly do not think that Jesus is a king, their ridicule unwittingly points to this identity. As Davies and Allison (3.598) note, the fact that it is *soldiers* who clothe, crown, and hail Jesus is itself significant, since, as Cyril of Jerusalem points out, "Every king is proclaimed by soldiers" (*Catechetical Lectures* 13.17; see, e.g., *Historia Augusta*, Julianus 2.6–7; Tacitus, *Histories* 2.79–81; Josephus, *War* 1.670//*Ant.* 17.195).

The military identity of the mockers, therefore, is important; but the details of the mockery are even more so. Schmidt ("Mark 15.16–32") has argued that these particulars reflect Roman triumphal processions, in which victorious generals were sometimes crowned, dressed in purple, and acclaimed by their soldiers; our passage, then, depicts a sort of "anti-triumph." These processions, to be sure, did not usually involve the central element of Mark 15:16–20a, the manifestation and acknowledgment of kingship; ancient rituals of accession to kingship provide the more proximate background to the Markan portrayal of Jesus' mockery. Roman emperors, who were not themselves kings, usually took a dim view of others who claimed royal status (cf. John 19:15; Acts 17:7), but client-kings still existed within the empire, even from time to time in Palestine (Herod the Great and Agrippa I and II were all kings, and Archelaus was conditionally promised kingship by the Romans; see the COMMENT on 15:1–5). In addition to the occasional practice of kingship, the *memory* of kingship was also a powerful factor, both among Jews (see Horbury, *Messianism*) and in the non-Jewish sphere.

The paradigmatic example in the latter was Alexander the Great, who had taken upon himself the trappings of an Oriental monarch, including enthronement, investment with a purple robe and diadem, and the genuflection of attendants (see Quintus Curtius, *History of Alexander the Great* 6.6.2–4; Pseudo-Callisthenes, *Romance of Alexander the Great* 95 [Wolohojian ed., p. 55]). The memory of such events was transmitted on the popular level partly through the theater; Plutarch, for example, speaks of stage actors who counterfeited Alexander's majesty and pomp, including his purple clothing and double-mitered, broad-brimmed, hat (*Life of Demetrius* 41.3–4), and Philo (*Flaccus* 38) describes the royal mockery of the lunatic Carabas (see below) as resembling a theatrical farce. While the Roman emperor was not technically a king, moreover, he could be popularly called one (see again John 19:15; Acts 17:7), and he was sometimes depicted in ways that were redolent of kingship, especially outside Rome (see Zanker, *Power*, 230–38). For example, the famous Gemma Augustea, a low-relief cameo carved on an onyx stone during or slightly after the reign of Augustus, portrays the emperor enthroned as Jupiter, the king of the gods, being crowned by a personification of the inhabited world, holding a scepter in his left hand, and surrounded by images of prosperity, victory, and the subjugation of enemies (cf. Kähler, *Dissertatio*). The image of royal coronation was still very much alive in the Roman empire of Jesus' time.

Our passage, however, is a mock rather than a real coronation. Such mockery could itself be a ritualistic activity (see, e.g., the description of the Sacaean feast in Dio Chrysostom, *Discourses* 4.67–70 and of the Saturnalia in Seneca, *Apocolocyntosis* 8.2 and the anonymous *Martyrdom of Dasius* 1). But more often such parodies were triggered by local political events. A Jewish mob in Jerusalem, for example, angered by the behavior of the half-Jewish king Agrippa I, mocked him with the parodic enthronement of the madman Carabas, whom they "set up on high, to be seen by all," crowned with a piece of papyrus for a diadem, invested with a rug for a royal robe and a papyrus scepter (cf. Matt 27:29), surrounded with a mock bodyguard of young men carrying sticks, and hailed and supplicated as "lord" (see Philo, *Flaccus* 36–39). The mockery of Jesus, which was so similar to that of Carabas, may also have been a response to a local event, an insurrection (see the NOTE on "insurrectionists . . . insurrection" in 15:7), with which the soldiers probably linked the so-called king of the Jews (cf. 14:48). What better way to obtain revenge for past revolutionary violence and deter future activity of the same sort than by torturing and mocking its supposed ringleader, thereby exposing the emptiness of his pretensions to kingship?

In Jesus' case, as in that of Carabas, the parody begins with a mock robing and crowning, which is followed by a royal acclamation (15:17–18); in both instances, the victim receives the livery of a king before being hailed as one. Jesus is robed with a garment of purple, a color that was especially associated with royalty (see the NOTE on "purple clothes" in 15:17), as were crowns; Davies and Allison (3.602–3) suggest that Jesus' crown of thorns may have reminded first-century readers both of royal wreaths or diadems and of the light rays that emanate from the heads of rulers on Ptolemaic, Seleucid, and Roman coins. The only element here that seems odd is the beating of Jesus' head with a cane (*kalamǭ*), since this word usually means "reed" (see the NOTE on "with a cane" in 15:19). It may be that *kalamǭ* is inserted here to allude to Isa 42:1–4, a passage that speaks of a "bruised reed" and has several other thematic connections to our section of the Gospel: the Lord's Servant, who is identified with Israel (cf. the "king of the Jews/of Israel" title), does not make his voice heard (14:61; 15:5) but brings judgment to the earth (15:38) and is believed in by Gentiles (15:39; cf. 15:5, 9, 14?). This linkage seems especially plausible because a later Isaian passage about the Lord's Servant, Isa 50:6 LXX, also parallels the Markan context significantly: "I gave my back to *scourges* (cf. Mark 15:15), and my cheeks to *slaps* (cf. Mark 14:65); and I did not turn my face away from the shame of *spitting*" (cf. Mark 14:65; 15:19). As elsewhere in Mark, therefore, the image of the powerful royal Messiah is strangely fused with that of Isaiah's tormented "man of sorrows" (cf. 8:27–33).

When the soldiers have had their fun with Jesus, they remove the purple garments with which they have mockingly invested him and return his own clothes to his back (15:20a; see the NOTE on "put his own clothes on him" in 15:20). The stage is now set for the crucifixion itself.

15:20b–27: the crucifixion. There is a problem that the soldiers must overcome, however, in order to accomplish their task: apparently Jesus has been so weakened by his mistreatment that he is unable to carry his cross, or rather the crossbeam, the short distance to the place of execution, as the liturgy of punishment requires (see the NOTE on "in order that he might carry his cross" in 15:21). The soldiers, therefore, compel a passing stranger, a Jew named Simon from the North African city of Cyrene (near the village of Shahat in modern-day Libya), to bear it (15:21). Mark probably understands this as a paradigmatic act; the Christian disciple is to take up his cross and follow his Lord in the way of crucifixion (cf. 8:34; 10:52; Luke 23:26 makes the connection more explicit by adding "behind Jesus"). For the Markan readers, this interpretation of Simon as an honorary disciple probably would have been helped by the circumstance that his sons, Alexander and Rufus, later became members of the Markan community (see the INTRODUCTION in vol. 1, pp. 27–28).

Jesus, then, is already losing ground against the advancing power of death; indeed, not only can he not carry his cross, but he also may be unable to carry *himself* to the place of execution, and must be borne or dragged there by the soldiers (see the NOTE on "they bore him away" in 15:22). The place toward which they transport him is called "The Place of the Skull," either from its shape or from the bones of the executed criminals (see the NOTE on "the place called 'Golgotha,' etc." in 15:22); in either case the Jewish association between bones and impurity would have lent it an atmosphere of ritual uncleanness, and the skull was especially associated with impurity (cf. *t. 'Ohal.* 4:2) and even fatal retribution for past sins (cf. *m. 'Abot* 2:7).

In the midst of this scene of death and pollution, Jesus now performs an act of resistance, refusing to drink the myrrhed wine that the soldiers offer him (15:23). This sort of drink was given to condemned prisoners in order to reduce the pain of their ordeal; *b. Sanh.* 43a, for example, records that "when one is led out to execution, he is given a goblet of wine containing a grain of frankincense, in order to addle his wits, for it is written, 'Give strong drink to one who is perishing, and wine to those in bitter distress' [Prov 31:6]" (Soncino trans. alt.). Jesus' refusal of this sort of alleviation may have several dimensions. On a practical level, the drugged wine worked by inducing extreme drunkenness; Tertullian (*On Fasting* 12.3), for example, tells the story of a Christian martyr who was so "medicated" by his friends that he could only hiccough and belch when asked by the examining officer which Lord he confessed. Jesus may have abstained partly because he believed that such undignified behavior would injure the cause for which he was sacrificing his life. Another dimension of the refusal may be soteriological: the Markan Jesus is giving his life "as a ransom for many" (10:45), and any attempt to lessen the pain of his demise may be suspect as a betrayal of his mission to undergo "the suffering of death, so that by the grace of God he might taste death for everyone" (Heb 2:9; cf. Gnilka, 2.316, and Brown, *Death*, 1.941–42). Another possible dimension is eschatological: at the Last Supper, Jesus swore a vow, similar to that of a Nazirite, that he would no longer drink from "the fruit of the vine" until he imbibed it anew in the dominion of God (cf. the COMMENT on 14:25 and Lamarche, 386). The refusal may also have a messianic dimension. As we have just seen, Prov 31:6 is linked in the Talmud with the practice of the anesthetizing drink, and *Num. Rab.* 10.4 even claims that the Sages derived the practice from that verse. It may be relevant, therefore, that the immediately preceding passage in Proverbs warns that "it is not for kings to drink wine, or for rulers to desire strong drink" (Prov 31:4)—a text that Jesus or his followers may have interpreted messianically.

Perhaps, then, a confluence of reasons, from the mundane to the messianic, drives the Markan Jesus to refuse the palliative drink he is offered. Having made this refusal, he is crucified without further ado. Mark describes this momentous event with the utmost simplicity: "And they crucified him" (15:24a). In contrast to modern novelistic and cinematic depictions, therefore, Mark and the other Gospels eschew the gory particulars of the crucifixion, simply narrating that it occurred and leaving the details to the reader's imagination (for a review of the basic facts about the procedure, which would have been well known to the Markan audience, see the APPENDIX "Crucifixion"). Here, if anywhere, the Markan narrative is "fraught with background" and all the more powerful for its heartbreaking restraint (see Auerbach, *Mimesis*, 15).

Despite the lack of detail, however, crucifixion is strongly emphasized; indeed, the verb *stauroun* ("to crucify") and its compound *systauroun* ("to crucify along with") occur five times in 15:20b–32 (15:20, 24, 25, 27, 32), and the noun *stauros* ("cross") appears three times (15:21, 30, 32). Mark's emphasis on the cruciform death of Jesus may partly have to do with the fact that this mode of execution was understood to burlesque kingship rituals, even apart from Christianity (see the APPENDIX "Crucifixion"). Ensconced on the royal seat of the cross, the crucified person was a king of fools; but the supreme irony for Mark is that in the present instance this laughingstock of a "king" is indeed being installed as the monarch of the universe. Having been clothed, crowned, and hailed as a king in the previous section, Jesus is now royally enthroned—on a cross.

After mentioning Jesus' crucifixion, Mark hurries on to describe the division of his garments (15:24b), a procedure to which he devotes four times as many words as he does to the crucifixion itself. This distribution was of some importance to the executioners, since clothes were expensive in preindustrial societies, and in the Greco-Roman world they were often the most valuable thing a person owned (see Meggitt, *Paul*, 60–62). Mark highlights the Roman soldiers' opportunism and callous indifference to their victim's fate by adding the words "to see who would get what" (*tis ti arę*) to an echo of Ps 22:18 (see the NOTE on "divided his clothes, casting lots for them" in 15:24). This stripping added to the dehumanization of the execution process, especially for Jews, who had a horror of nakedness (see the NOTES on "put his own clothes on him" in 15:20 and "divided his clothes, casting lots for them" in 15:24). It is not surprising, therefore, that in Ps 22:18, the OT passage echoed by Mark 15:24b, the reference to the division and raffling of the clothes immediately follows a description of the Sufferer's foes gloating over him; the psalm thus accentuates the victim's sense of being laid bare and exposed to the hostile gaze of enemies. This is only the first of several allusions to Psalm 22 in the Markan crucifixion and death scenes (see figure 47), and Mark apparently expects his readers to recognize it as a biblical echo; at the same time that the evangelist highlights the shame of Jesus' crucifixion experience, he also implies that it has been prophesied in the scriptures and is part of the divine plan.

That implication is strengthened by the reference to the time of crucifixion as the third hour, that is, 9:00 A.M. (15:25)—the first of three such time notices in the crucifixion and death scenes, the other two being the allusion to the cosmic darkness that descends at the sixth hour (15:33) and to Jesus' cry of dereliction at the ninth (15:34). All three are "negative" events, which might leave the impression that a cosmic catastrophe is under way; but the orderly progression of third, sixth, and ninth hours, like the series of sevens in the book of Revelation, implies that this dark epoch is nevertheless under the firm control of an all-powerful God.

The world has not wandered out of divine superintendence, because for Mark Jesus' death is an inseparable part of, indeed the central act in, the manifestation of his and God's kingship. The present subsection, accordingly, ends with two details that emphasize the royal theme: the inscription over Jesus' cross (15:26) and the description of his crucifixion between two brigands, "one on his right and one on his left" (15:27). From the point of view of the soldiers, of course, the "King of the Jews" inscription is a mockery; Jesus' crucifixion shows that he is certainly *not* royal, as he claims to be. For the Christian reader, however, the opposite conclusion would emerge: the mocking inscription unwittingly expresses the truth. It is probable that Jesus' placement between two brigands would also be understood by Mark's readers as part of the royal pageantry of the event, since the co-crucified criminals on his right and left could be seen as the retinue of a king (see Hare, *Matthew*, 320). This suggestion is supported by comparison with 10:35–40, where places at Jesus' right and left imply participation in his royal glory, and Philo, *Flaccus* 38, where the ridicule of Carabas as king includes that "young men carrying rods on their shoulders as spearmen *stood on either side of him* (*hekaterōthen heistēkesan*) in imitation of a bodyguard."

15:29–32: *the mockery of the crucified Jesus.* Jesus has now been nailed to the cross as the climactic event in a sick parody of royal coronation. The frenetic movement that has characterized him through most of the Gospel is at last at an end. Indeed, the victim's immobility was one of the most dreaded aspects of death by crucifixion; the prisoner is often described as being "fixed to the cross" (see, e.g., Menippus, *Fragment* 25; Tacitus, *Annals* 15.44.4), and he could not even avoid the dogs and birds of prey who, sensing his helplessness and closeness to death, came to dine on his flesh (see, e.g., Eusebius, *Ecclesiastical History* 5.1.41). Jesus' immobility is mocked by the passersby (15:29–30) and the chief priests (15:31–32), all of whom challenge him to come down from the cross. In their view, his paralysis demonstrates the hollowness of his claim to be king; far from possessing the limitless freedom of a monarch, he is transfixed and helpless. A contrast is provided by the first group of mockers, whose freedom of movement is emphasized: they are those who pass by, wagging their heads as they do so (15:29a).

This language is reminiscent of Ps 22:7–8 [21:7–8 LXX], so that the present subsection begins with another echo of the psalm that was already alluded to in the reference to the division of Jesus' clothes (15:24). This echo, like that one, helps assure scripturally literate readers that the indignities Jesus is suffering are within the divine plan. Unlike the mockers in the psalm, though, who call on God to save the innocent Sufferer, those in Mark call on *Jesus* to save *himself*. This discrepancy, however, makes a theological point: the mockers do not realize that Jesus and God are so intertwined that Jesus' salvific power *is* the power of God (cf. the COMMENT on 5:18–20) and that Jesus' kingship, far from being a joke, participates in that of God. Mark accuses these mockers of "blaspheming," and while on the surface this term simply conveys the idea of abuse (see BDAG 178 [e] and cf. the NOTE on "abusive speech" in 7:22), Mark's readers might discern a deeper nuance: those who oppose Jesus are guilty of the "blasphemy" of separating Jesus from God and of seeing his present powerlessness as an indication of permanent divine abandon (contrast 14:61b–64, where Jesus is convicted of blasphemy for associating himself too closely with the throne room and royal power of God).

The royal theme, and the irony that it is proclaimed by Jesus' enemies, continue to the end of the passage. The "blasphemy" of the passersby is to call Jesus the destroyer and rebuilder of the Temple, and "likewise" the chief priests and the scribes deride him as "the Christ, the king of Israel" (15:29–32a). The "likewise" here makes sense in the Markan context because Jesus will indeed, through his death and resurrection, set the stage for the destruction of the Jerusalem Temple, inaugurate a new, spiritual sanctuary, and thus show himself to be the Messiah, the king of Israel (see the COMMENTS on 12:10–12, 14:55–61a, and 15:38–39). In their blind mockery, however, the chief priests and scribes miss the salvific drama unfolding before their eyes and call for Jesus to come down from the cross. In contrast to the plebian passersby, these elite leaders do not address Jesus directly with their ridicule but rather each other, and, as Gnilka (2.320) points out, this grammatical difference underlines their scorn for him.

The chief priests and the scribes say that Jesus should descend from the cross "in order that we might see (*hina idōmen*) and believe" (15:32a). The phrasing here ironically recalls that of 4:12, which in turn used the language of Isa 6:9–10—an OT passage that takes place in the throne room of God—to speak of God's purpose to blind outsiders "in order that 'in their looking they may look but not see' " (*ina . . . mē idōmen*). Even the blind derision of Jesus as king, therefore, reflects the kingship of God and thus, by implication, that of Jesus. The "looking" of the priests and scribes is a form of myopia—blindness to the upside-down way in which God's purposes work themselves out in a world where a cross may truly become a throne (see Marcus, "Epistemology," 570–71). And the leaders' demand that a miracle be performed in order that they may "believe" reverses the Markan and NT dynamic in which faith in God's dominion, which sometimes hides under a contrary appearance, precedes the miracle that brings it into the light (see 2:5; 5:34, 36; 9:23–24; 10:52; 11:22–24; cf. Theissen, 132).

Despite their blindness, the chief priests and the scribes do acknowledge one aspect of Jesus' redemptive role when they admit that he has "saved" (i.e., cured) others (15:31b). Earlier in the Gospel, Jesus' "salvation" of blind Bartimaeus established the truth of the latter's acclamation of him as the "Son of David" (10:46–52), a title synonymous with "Messiah" or "king of Israel." But the chief priests and scribes imply that Jesus cannot be "the Christ, the king of Israel," because he cannot save himself. For the evangelist, however, Jesus' refusal to "save himself" is not a contradiction but a confirmation of his royal status, since kings (who were often called "saviors" in Hellenistic times) demonstrated their royalty by conferring benefits on their people and saving them from their enemies (cf. Ezek 34:1–10; *Let. Aris.* 187–88, 190, 289–92; Cicero, *Republic* 1.35.54; 2.26.47; Mendels, *Rise*, 55–79; Blumenfeld, *Paul*, 207, 222–23, 228, 237–38, 250). As Juel (*Messiah*, 48) points out, the mockery in 15:31–32a ironically expresses the deepest secret of Markan soteriology: the compassionate deliverer of his people, "the Christ, the king of Israel," must save others through his atoning death, and therefore he *cannot* save himself by descending from the cross.

But there is a huge price to be paid for such relentless, all-consuming love, which involves not only dying for but also entering into proximity to godforsaken human beings and thus risking rejection by them. This is, indeed, what happens at the end of our passage, where Jesus ends up being mocked, not only by the Jewish leaders and the passersby, but also by the brigands who are sharing in the horrible fate of crucifixion and from whom he therefore might hope for some sympathy. Instead they rail against him (15:32b), which suggests that Jesus is not one of them, not a brigand, and thus a different sort of "king of the

Jews" from the revolutionary leaders who would later, in Mark's time, lead the people to a disastrous military confrontation with Rome (see the NOTE on "And those who were crucified along with him were railing against him" in 15:32). But their verbal attacks also convey a sense of the terrible isolation in which Jesus dies.

In the next passage that sense will be deepened as Jesus enters not only into proximity to godforsaken human beings but also into the experience of godforsakenness itself.

THE DEATH OF JESUS (15:33–41)

15 ³³And when the sixth hour arrived, there was darkness over the whole earth until the ninth hour. ³⁴And at the ninth hour Jesus cried out with a loud voice, "*Elōi, Elōi, lama sabachthani*," which is translated, "My God, my God, why have you abandoned me?"

³⁵And some of those who were standing about, hearing it, said, "Look, he is calling Elijah!" ³⁶And one of them ran and filled a sponge with vinegar and put it around a reed and tried to give it to him to drink, saying, "Let me be! Let's see if Elijah is going to come to take him down!" ³⁷But Jesus, having given a loud cry, expired.

³⁸And the veil of the sanctuary was ripped in two from top to bottom. ³⁹And the centurion who was standing opposite him, seeing that he expired in this manner, said, "Truly this man was God's son!"

⁴⁰And there were also women watching from far away, among whom were Mary the Magdalene, and Mary the mother of James the Small and of Joses, and Salome, ⁴¹who used to follow him when he was in Galilee and used to serve him, and many others who had come up with him to Jerusalem.

NOTES

15 33. *there was darkness over the whole earth.* Gk *skotos egeneto eph' holēn tēn gēn.* Contrary to BDAG 196(3), *holēn tēn gēn* probably means "the whole earth" rather than "the whole land [of Palestine]." As Gundry (964) points out, in the LXX and NT, *holē hē gē* and the synonymous *pasa hē gē* "almost always mean the whole earth except when qualified by an additional phrase such as 'of Egypt.' " In Mark itself, moreover, if *gē* does not refer to soil or seashore (as in 4:1, 5, 8, etc.; 6:47, 53; etc.), it always means the earth as opposed to the heavens (see 2:10; 9:3; 13:27, 31), never a particular country. To be sure, Exod 10:21–23 describes one of the exodus plagues as darkness "over all the land of Egypt" (NRSV alt.; LXX: *epi pasan gēn Aigyptou*), and the Passover context here forms a link with our passage; the *Gospel of Peter* parallel to the latter, moreover, explicitly speaks of darkness falling on all of Judaea (*Gos. Pet.* 5:15). Brown (*Death*, 2.1035–37), however, ascribes the *Gospel of Peter* restriction to Judaea to the "fierce antiJudaism" of that work and reasons that Mark may think that the divine judgment in relation to Jesus should be greater than that produced under Moses. The closest background to our passage is in OT descriptions of "the day of the LORD," which seem to envisage an obscuration that affects the entire world, not just a particular country (see Joel 2:1–2, 10, 30–31; Amos 8:9–10).

Luke 23:45 clarifies the Markan expression with *tou hēliou eklipontos*, which probably means "the sun having been eclipsed" (see Brown, *Death*, 2.1038–43). As an explanation of the darkness at Jesus' death, however, this gloss fails, since a solar eclipse occurs when the moon is new, while at the beginning of Passover it is full—a point already noted by Julius Africanus in the third century (quoted by George Syncellus, *Chronicle*, 610; cf. Allison, *Studies*, 91 n. 51). Full solar eclipses, moreover, last less than eight minutes, whereas the Markan darkness extends for three hours, as already observed by Chrysostom (*Homilies on Matthew* 88 [on Matt 27:45–48]), and it is probable that no solar eclipse occurred within four months of Jesus' death (Brown, *Death*, 2.1376 locates the crucifixion on either 7 April 30 C.E. or 3 April 33 C.E.; for the eclipses within a few years of those dates, see ibid., 2.1041–42). A solar eclipse, moreover, would not cover the entire earth, only a narrow band of it, as noted already by Erasmus (*Annotations on Matthew* 27:45) and Calvin (*Harmony* on Matt 27:45). Other rationalistic explanations of the darkening of the sun at Jesus' death have been proffered, such as the effects of clouds, sirocco winds, or distant volcanic eruptions (cf. Allison, *Studies*, 88–96), but none of these phenomena would explain a worldwide three-hour darkness unnoticed by ancient historians.

until the ninth hour. Gk *heōs hōras enatēs*. This probably means that the darkness extends up to and includes the moment Jesus cries out and dies at the ninth hour (cf. Brown, *Death*, 2.1034). *Heōs* sometimes connotes extent in space or time that includes its terminus; see, for example, Mark 6:23 ("up to [and including] half my kingdom"); 13:19 (" until now, and never will be"); and 13:27 ("from the end of the earth to [lit. "until"] the end of heaven"). To be sure, the word may also be used in contexts in which the terminus is specifically excluded; see, for example, 14:25 ("I will never again drink from the fruit of the vine until that day when I drink it anew in the dominion of God"). Some (e.g., Gundry, 964) have therefore argued that in Mark the darkness ends *before* Jesus dies. But the lingering effects of the cosmic darkness are suggested by Jesus' loud, perhaps demonic cry, his complaint about abandonment, and his death. Cf. *Gos. Pet.* 6:22, in which the suns begins to shine again after Jesus' death.

34. *Elōi, Elōi, lama sabachthani.* This corresponds roughly to the Targum on Psalms and the Peshitta of Ps 22:1 [22:2 Heb]; the main difference is in the word for "why" (*lêmānā'* in the Peshitta, *mṭûl mah* in the Targum). There are many variants of the transliteration in the Greek manuscripts (see Swanson, *Mark*, 258 and cf. Brown, *Death*, 1051–52; Williams, "Background"). Some texts, for example (‫א‬, C, L, Δ, Ψ), have *lema* rather than *lama*, which is better Aramaic and identical with Matt 27:46. For these very reasons, however, *lema* is probably a secondary reading; the original Markan text may have been a mixture of Hebrew (*lama*) and Aramaic (*Elōi, sabachthani*). Matthew also mixes the two languages, but in a different way; his word for "my God," *Ēli*, is Hebrew, but *lema* is Aramaic. Some

of these differences may be due to scribes who had a smattering of one language or the other. It is also possible that the word would have been pronounced *lāmā'* in some Aramaic dialects or by some speakers. *Elōi* (= *'Elāhî*) and *sabachthani* (= *šĕbaqtānî*) follow standard patterns of transliteration of Aramaic and Hebrew into Greek (cf. Williams, ibid.).

My God, my God, why have you abandoned me? Gk *ho theos mou ho theos mou eis ti enkatelipes me.* This is identical with the LXX except that the latter has *hina ti* (lit. "in order that what") rather than *eis ti*.

Codex Bezae and other Western witnesses (c, i, k, syr[h], Porphyry) read *ōneidisas* ("you have reviled") rather than *enkatelipes* ("you have abandoned"). Harnack ("Probleme," 97–101) considers this reading original because the agreement of Bezae with Porphyry and Old Latin manuscripts attests wide circulation in the second century, and it is easier to explain a scribal change to *enkatelipes* as an assimilation to Matt 27:46 and Ps 22:1 [21:2 LXX] than it is to explain a change to *ōneidisas.* The overwhelming weight of textual evidence, however, is in favor of *enkatelipes,* and Ehrman (*Orthodox Corruption,* 143–45) suggests that orthodox scribes may have changed this text because it was used by the Gnostics to support their contention that the divine Christ departed from the human Jesus on the cross (*Gos. Phil.* 68:27–29; Irenaeus, *Against Heresies* 1.8.2.3–4; 3.11.7; cf. *Gos. Peter* 5:19).

36. *vinegar.* Gk *oxous.* As Brown (*Death,* 2.1062) points out, Plutarch, *Cato Major* 1.7 establishes that *oxos* can denote a vinegary wine that is an effective thirst-quencher (cf. Num 6:3; Ruth 2:14).

tried to give. Gk *epotizen.* On the conative use of the imperfect, see BDF §326 and Burchard, "Markus 15,34," 9 n. 39, and cf. the conative imperfect with regard to the drink in 15:23. The adversative *ho de Iēsous* ("*But* Jesus, having given a loud cry, expired") in 15:37 indicates that the attempt to make Jesus drink is unsuccessful: instead of receiving the vinegar, which is arguably intended to prolong his life (see the next NOTE), Jesus cries out and expires.

saying, "Let me be! Let's see . . ." Gk *legōn aphete idōmen.* As Brown (*Death,* 2.1060) remarks, the story line is difficult to analyze: "It is not clear . . . why (mistakenly) hearing a cry to Elijah should cause someone to offer vinegary wine to Jesus . . . or whether and why that offering is involved with pausing to see whether Elijah comes to take Jesus down." *Aphienai* literally means "leave, let be," which is the way Matt 27:49 interprets it. In commenting on the Matthean text, Goguel (*Life,* 543), following Renan, suggests that the drink is intended to hasten Jesus' death, and that the other bystanders are trying to prevent his decease long enough to see whether Elijah will come to his aid. Renan's theory of a harmful drink, however, is based neither on medical evidence nor on ancient testimonies but on a fourteenth-century gloss from Nicholas of Lyra and two anecdotal nineteenth-century accounts in which an impaled man and a crucified one died after being given a drink. Renan was already challenged in his lifetime by a physician friend, who opined that in the two nineteenth-century cases the conjunction of the drink with death was probably a coincidence (see Pommier, "Société Ernest Renan"). If we discount the theory of a harmful drink, the sense of the Matthean narrative may be that the bystanders think that Elijah can intervene only at the moment of death and do not want to delay that moment by a sustaining drink.

The Markan narrative is even more difficult to follow than the Matthean one, because the person saying "Let me be! Let's see . . ." is the same as the one offering Jesus the drink of vinegar. This is confusing because, as Brown (*Death*, 2.1064) puts it, "Whom would the 'someone' be stopping since he is the only one who is acting?" Some sense can be made of the narrative flow if *aphete* functions as an auxiliary verb (Taylor, 595) or means "leave it to someone to do something" (BDAG 157 [5]), and if we postulate that the man with the sponge is trying to extend Jesus' life long enough to give Elijah time to act. The latter makes most sense in the Markan context, but the man is probably not being portrayed as believing in the possibility of Elijan rescue, any more than the chief priests and scribes in 15:32 believe in the possibility of Jesus' descent from the cross; like them, rather, his action is a mocking one.

The narrative, however, is sufficiently murky to support the theory of Taylor (595) that "in 35f. Mark is combining two separate traditions: an account of the bystanders in 35, 36b who cried, 'Let us see if Elijah will come to take him down,' and in 36a the story of a compassionate soldier who offered Jesus wine shortly before the end."

37. *having given a loud cry.* Gk *apheis phōnēn megalēn.* This phrase, which virtually repeats 15:34 (*eboēsen . . . phōnē megalē*, "cried out with a loud voice"), probably does not denote a second shout but is a back-reference to the cry of dereliction in 15:34 (see Brown, *Death*, 2.1079). Like the repetition of "they crucified him" in 15:24–25, however, this doublet may result from the weaving together of two versions of the same narrative (see the previous NOTE and the introduction to the COMMENT on 15:16–32).

expired. Gk *exepneusen.* Like the English translation, *exepneusen* literally means "he breathed out"; the underlying idea is that, with one's last gasp, one exhales the breath of life and hence dies (see Allison, *Testament of Abraham*, 395–96). While Hebrew and Aramaic lack a comparable verb, they have a similar idiom; the Harklean Syriac version of our verse, for example, says that Jesus' "breath went out" (*npqt nšmth*; cf. *m. Šabb.* 23:5; Kramer, *Meanings*, 24).

38. *the veil of the sanctuary.* Gk *to katapetasma tou naou.* Exegetes debate whether this phrase denotes the inner veil, which separated the holy of holies from the rest of the Temple (Exod 26:31–35; Lev 16:2; *m. Yoma* 5:1), or the outer curtain, which separated the Temple proper from its forecourt (Exod 26:37; 38:18; Num 3:26; *Letter of Aristeas* 86). Both can be called a *katapetasma* ("veil," "curtain," or "screen"), but the term is more often used for the inner veil (see Brown, *Death*, 2.1111). *Naos*, moreover, generally designates the inner shrine, whereas *hieron* usually means the Temple complex as a whole (cf. Mark 11:11, 15–16, 27; 12:35; 13:1, 3; 14:49). Sometimes, however, *naos* denotes the whole structure (e.g., Mark 14:58; 15:29; cf. 13:2).

Of the two *katapetasmata*, the inner one was more significant theologically, since it screened the holy of holies, in which God's radiant presence was believed to dwell, from profane sight or access (see Exod 26:33; 40:3, 21; Heb 10:19–22) and protected those outside from the potentially disastrous consequences of an irruption of divine power (cf. Exod 19:20–23). This sort of curtain was familiar to pagan as well as Jewish readers, since in Hellenistic temples the deity was often curtained off from view, and the removal of this veil was an act of revelation (see, e.g., *CIG* 2.2886; Ovid, *Fasti* 2.563; Apuleius, *Metamorphoses* 11.20; cf. Schneider, "*Katapetasma*"). In the case of the Jerusalem Temple, however, the outer curtain was also significant, and it was a readily visible and striking sight: rising to a height of fifty-five cubits (= eighty-one feet), this curtain was embroidered with a magnificent depiction of the heavens woven from threads of blue, scarlet, purple, and fine white linen (see Josephus, *War* 5.212–14). For Ulansey ("Heavenly Veil"), this astronomical imagery, though unmentioned in the Gospels, is a decisive argument in favor of the outer curtain hypothesis, since the scene of Jesus' death is evidently meant to parallel that of his baptism (1:9–11), in which the *heavens* are sundered. But the parallel with the baptismal scene provides equally strong evidence for the other theory, since at the baptism the dividing of the heavens allows something to emerge from behind them in a revelatory act, and this may be similar to what happens in 15:38–39 if the torn curtain is the inner one (see the COMMENT on 15:38–39, and cf. Tacitus, *Histories* 5.13). All in all, the vocabulary considerations and greater religious importance of the inner veil make it a more likely candidate for the reference here (cf. BDAG 524).

39. *centurion.* Gk *kentyriōn.* In the Roman army a centurion commanded a group of a hundred men, or century; centurions were the backbone of the military and were prized for their ability to lead, obedience to superiors, and calmness under pressure (cf. Polybius, *History* 6.24.9). One of their main responsibilities was discipline, including the exacting of punishments; for this reason, the emblem of the centurion was the vine-staff, "which he knew how to use on the backs of his men" (Gealy, "Centurion"). The centurion's position as the crucial link in the military hierarchy is well summarized in the Q saying Luke 7:8 (cf. Matt 8:9): "For I also am a man set under authority, with soldiers under me; and I say to one, 'Go,' and he goes, and to another, 'Come,' and he comes, and to my slave, 'Do this,' and he does it" (NRSV alt.). This respect for hierarchy and critical role in the chain of command that ultimately derives from the emperor, who could be termed "the son of God" (see the COMMENT on 15:38–39), makes a centurion an unexpected character to enunciate the radical inversion of values that sees a dying criminal as God's true Son.

standing opposite him. Gk *parestēkōs ex enantias autou.* Although the tearing of the Temple veil in 15:38 seems to be related to the centurion's confession in 15:39, it is hard to imagine the scene physically: if the centurion was facing Jesus, who was crucified outside the city walls on Golgotha to the north of the city, he was probably turned away from the Temple, which was on the east end of the city and was oriented eastward; and even if he was turned the right way, and the torn veil was the outer curtain of the Temple rather than the inner one, his vision would have had to penetrate intervening objects such as the city wall (see Burchard, "Markus 15,34," 11 n. 49; Gundry, 970). Jackson ("Death," 24–25) suggests that Mark may have understood Golgotha to be on the Mount of Olives, which is east of the city and sufficiently elevated that an observer standing on it would be able to see the Temple's outer curtain, and Gundry (955) supports this opinion by linking a strained etymology of Golgotha as "the place for counting heads" with the tradition that a "mustering or counting altar" (*mĕpāqēd*) was located on the Mount of Olives (cf. Martin, *Secrets*, 12–19, 58–64). But aside from the strong tradition linking Golgotha with the Holy Sepulchre site and the lack of one associating it with the Mount of Olives (see the NOTE on "the place called 'Golgotha,' which is translated 'The Place of the Skull' " in 15:22), Mark would probably have been explicit about the Mount of Olives if he had had it in mind, since this mountain is frequently identified elsewhere in the Gospel, and it would have served Mark's purposes to remind his readers that Jesus was crucified on the same hill from which he had entered the city in triumph (11:1), prophesied the Temple's destruction (13:3), and on which he had prayed on the night before his death (14:26). The physical setting of the centurion's confession, therefore, remains a problem; Mark may have been uninformed about the geography of Jerusalem or may have ignored it.

Truly this man was God's son! Gk *alēthōs houtos ho anthrōpos huios theou ēn.* *Huios theou* contains no definite article, so the clause might be translated "this man was *a* son of God." But when, as here, a predicate nominative ("son of God") precedes a copulative verb (*ēn* = "was"), it may be definite, despite the absence of the article (see Colwell, "Definite Rule"); the clause, then, could also be translated "this man was *the* Son of God." As Harner ("Predicate Nouns") shows, Greek has unambiguous ways to express either a definite or an indefinite predicate nominative, and Mark uses these forms frequently elsewhere (cf. 1:11; 3:11; 8:29; 10:44 etc.); since he does not do so here, he may wish to be ambiguous, employing a locution that could be interpreted either as implying that Jesus was God's unique Son or that he was one of many divine children. It may be, then, that the centurion's confession is ironic; *he* simply thinks that he is identifying Jesus as "*a* son of God," that is, a divine man, but the reader knows that he is actually identifying him as *the* Son. (As Burchard ["Markus 15,34"] points out, the centurion's "was" may also reflect misunderstanding, since Jesus' divine sonship has certainly not ceased with his death.) The centurion, then, would join a long list of characters in the Markan passion narrative who say more than they know.

Goodacre (*Case*, 160 n. 28) goes further: the centurion's confession is not just unintentionally ironic but deliberately sarcastic; for the centurion, Jesus' humiliating death on the cross disproves any claim he might have to be called a son of God. In favor of this suggestion, the other Roman personnel in chapter 15, Pilate and the soldiers, have challenged or mocked Jesus' pretensions to kingship (15:2, 16–20), as have all the bystanders mentioned up to this point (15:29–32, 35–36). Mark, moreover, links the centurion's words specifically with the manner in which Jesus expires, and the latter might be considered particularly discreditable, especially if the link between Jesus' loud cry (*phōnēn megalēn*, 15:37) and those of the demons (1:26; 5:7) is given weight (see the COMMENT on 15:33–34). The short time Jesus spends on the cross (cf. 15:44–45) could also be considered dishonorable, since he does not last long on the cross, and his quick death thus shows him to be a weakling. Even the detail that the centurion stands *ex enantias* ("opposite") Jesus might be cited in favor of the sarcastic interpretation of his words, since *enantios* frequently suggests hostility (see, e.g., Acts 26:9; 28:17; 1 Thess 2:15; Tit 2:8; cf. BDAG 331 [2]). Such an interpretation might also be considered compatible with the messianic secret motif (see the APPENDIX "The Messianic Secret Motif" in vol. 1), since the secret is thereby maintained at the cross, and this would accord with 9:9, which sets the secret's time limit as the resurrection rather than the crucifixion.

These arguments, however, are not decisive. With regard to the messianic secret, its disclosure at Jesus' death is consonant with Markan Christology: now that Jesus' messiahship and divine sonship have been decisively qualified by his crucifixion, it is appropriate for them to be revealed (cf. Cranfield, 444). Against a sarcastic interpretation of the centurion's words, moreover, is the linkage that the narrative forges between him and the watching women (see the COMMENT on 15:40–41). The story places the centurion alongside the women after Jesus' death, not alongside the mockers before that event. The women are sympathetic to Jesus, though physically removed from him (see the COMMENT on 15:40–41), and it seems logical that the centurion, though standing opposite Jesus, should be sympathetic as well. Furthermore, the centurion's confession is one of three architectonic acclamations of Jesus as Son of God, which are similar in form and seem to structure the whole Gospel, appearing significantly at its beginning, middle, and end; since the other two (1:11; 9:7) come from the mouth of God, it makes sense that the third is revelatory as well.

40. *Mary the Magdalene, and Mary the mother of James the Small and of Joses, and Salome.* Gk *Maria hē Magdalēnē kai Maria hē Iakōbou tou mikrou kai Iōsētos mētēr kai Salōmē.* We know virtually nothing about these women. Luke 8:2 makes all three of them recipients of Jesus' healing power, including the Magdalene, from whom seven demons had been cast out, but this tradition is probably more indebted to the Lukan view of Jesus as a compassionate healer than to historical memory. Later Christian piety conflated the exorcised Magdalene of Luke 8:2 with the sinful woman of the previous chapter (Luke 7:36–50) and then with Mary of Bethany, the sister of Martha and Lazarus, about whom a similar story is told (John 12:1–8). The Magdalene became a prostitute in the popular imagination because her transgressions were public and flagrant enough to earn her the title *hamartōlos* ("sinner"). In some of the Gnostic Gospels her role is greatly expanded, and she is described in the late-third-century *Gospel of Philip* (59:8–9; 63:33–36) as Jesus' closest disciple, whom he frequently kissed—the source for the fantasy about her marriage to Jesus that forms the basis for the popular novel *The DaVinci Code* (cf. Ehrman, *Truth*, 141–62).

All we know for sure about Mary Magdalene, however, is that she came from a place called Magdala, which is usually identified with the town called Migdal Nûnnaya ("Tower of Fish") in the Talmud (cf. *b. Pesaḥ* 46b). This Aramaic designation corresponds to the Greek place name Tarichaeae or Tarechaeae ("Salted Fish"). According to Josephus (*War* 2.634; 3.445–502), the latter was a Galilean town that was the center of the Great Revolt against Rome; its site lies on the western shore of the Sea of Galilee, about a mile north of Tiberias—a location that renders dubious the traditional identification of the Magdalene with Mary of Bethany (cf. the NOTE on "Bethany" in 11:1).

It is not surprising that the second woman should also be named Mary and that the third is called Salome, since about half of the Jewish women in Palestine in the Second Temple and Mishnaic periods bore these names (see Ilan, "Notes," 191–92). Some scholars (e.g., Crossan, "Relatives," 105–10; Gundry, 977) have thought that the second Mary is the mother of Jesus, who had two other sons named James and Joses (see 6:3) and who, according to John 19:25–27, was present at Jesus' death. It would be extraordinary, however, for Mark to identify this Mary through her sons James and Joses rather than Jesus or to refer to Jesus' brother, who became the head of the Jerusalem church and was commonly known as "James the Just," by the unimpressive sobriquet "James the Small" (cf. France, Mark, 664). The counterargument is that the Markan Jesus has identified his real mother as the one who does the will of God rather than his physical one (3:31–35), and the centurion has just acclaimed Jesus as God's Son (15:39), so Mark may be trying to deemphasize physical relationship and to keep the focus on divine sonship by referring to Jesus' brother slightingly as "James the Small" (see Gundry, 977). But there is no other evidence that the brother of the Lord was known as "James the Small," and it seems more likely that the latter designation was designed to distinguish this James from the better-known Jameses, the brother of the Lord and the son of Zebedee. Later Christian tradition identifies James the Small with the son of Alphaeus (cf. 3:18) and contrasts him with "James the Great," the son of Zebedee (see 1:19; 3:17; cf. Bauckham, Jude, 14, 20; Hagner, "James"). This plethora of Jameses already confused people in the early church (see Hagner, "James").

The Markan names for the women may represent an effort to reconcile the lists in the preexistent traditions that speak of Jesus' burial (15:47) and the discovery of his empty tomb (16:1; see figure 50 and Taylor, 651–53). Mark 15:47 describes the second Mary as "Mary of Joses," while 16:1 speaks of her as "Mary of James." The pattern of female name + male name in the genitive usually identifies the specified woman as the wife of the specified man (see BDF §162[4]), but since the lists have two different names for the man, Joses and James, the evangelist may make Mary their mother rather than their wife. His aim in reconciling the lists would be to ensure that, to the extent possible, the same women witness Jesus' death, his burial, and his empty tomb, so that the reports of all three events become mutually authenticating.

Figure 50: Women at the Crucifixion, Burial, and Empty Tomb

Mark 15:40–Crucifixion	Mark 15:47—Burial	Mark 16:1—Empty Tomb
Mary the Magdalene	Mary the Magdalene	Mary the Magdalene
Mary the mother of James the Small and of Joses	Mary [the wife] of Joses	Mary [the wife] of James
Salome		Salome

COMMENT

Introduction. The Markan account of Jesus' last hours alternates between descriptions of cosmic and earthly wonders (15:33, 38), the death-cry and decease of Jesus (15:34, 37), and the reactions of bystanders to his death and dying (15:35–36, 39–41), with the third element occupying the most space. Before Jesus' death, the reactions are dominated by mockery; afterward, by sympathy and awe.

There are several indications in our passage that the narrative of Jesus' death has grown in the telling—which is only to be expected for such a crucial part of the Christian story. The detail of Jesus crying out with a loud voice is repeated (15:34, 37), and the reaction to the first cry is hard to follow, perhaps because it combines two different traditions—one in which the response is a compassionate offer of a drink (15:36a), the other in which it is mockery having to do with Elijah (15:35, 36b; cf. the NOTE on "saying, 'Let me be! Let's see . . .'" in 15:36). Mark himself may be responsible for these amalgamations, and he is probably behind the schema of sixth and ninth hours at the beginning of the passage, with which the first loud cry is linked (see Bultmann, 274, and Myllykoski, *Letzen Tage*, 2.125). He is probably also responsible for 15:40–41 at the end: the theme of "watching from far away" (15:40a) coheres with the strong Markan emphasis on Jesus' isolation in the passion narrative; the list of women in 15:40b seems to combine those in 15:47 and 16:1 (see the NOTE on "Mary the Magdalene, and Mary the mother of James the Small and of Joses, and Salome" in 15:40); the terms "follow" and "Galilee" are often redactional, their combination is redactional in 3:7 (cf. 6:1), and the redactional 14:28 and 16:7 combine "Galilee" and "go before," which implies following; and the theme of the service of women frames the whole Gospel (cf. 1:31). Mark's redactional interventions in this crucial scene, therefore, seem substantial.

The passage falls into two main parts: the events leading up to and including Jesus' death (15:33–37) and the events immediately following it (15:38–41). Each of these sections can be subdivided: the first into the cry of dereliction (15:33–34) and the bystanders' misunderstanding and Jesus' death (15:35–37); the second into the reaction of the centurion (15:38–39) and the watching women (15:40–41).

15:33–34: the cry of dereliction. The subsection that will terminate with Jesus' death begins, appropriately enough, with darkness falling over the whole world. This darkness is probably not a historical reminiscence but a symbolic feature with several dimensions. It may be a sign of Jesus' stature; eclipses and other unusual astronomical events were often associated with the death of great people, such as Julius Caesar (see Virgil, *Georgics* 1.466–68; Plutarch, *Caesar* 69.3; Josephus, *Ant.* 14.309). They could be a sign that God or nature was mourning the deceased (see, e.g., Diogenes Laertius, *Lives* 4.64) or that the latter had been divine or was in the process of becoming so (see Plutarch, *Romulus* 27.6–7; Dio Cassius, *Roman History* 56.29.3–6 [on Augustus]; *T. Adam* 3:6). The supernatural darkness, therefore, may be one of the reasons that the centurion acclaims Jesus as God's son (see Collins, "Son of God Among Greeks," 94).

More important, the darkness suggests that Jesus' death is a turning point in salvation history. This interpretation is in line with both pagan and Jewish conceptions. Virgil, for example, claims that at the death of Julius Caesar the sun "veiled his shining face in dusky gloom, and a godless age feared everlasting night" (*Georgics* 1.466–68); Caesar's contemporaries, then, were afraid that the eclipse indicated that an era of divine judgment was setting in. In Jewish and Christian contexts such conceptions often become eschatological in character. Earlier in Mark's Gospel, for example, the darkening of the sun was described as part of the eschatological woes (13:24), and there are similar motifs in Jewish literature (see, e.g., *Sib. Or.* 5.346–47; *T. Moses* 10:5; *LAB* 19:13) and the book of Revelation (8:12; 9:2; 16:10).

This eschatological interpretation of the darkness in Mark 15:33 is supported by the observation that the verse appears to echo an OT text, Amos 8:9–10, whose similarities to our passage have been noted by commentators since the second century (see Allison, *Studies*, 80–81, and cf. the NOTE on "on that day" in 2:20 for an earlier Markan allusion to the Amos text). This passage describes the day of judgment:

> On that day, says the Lord GOD, I will make *the sun go down at noon*, and *darken the earth in broad daylight*. I will turn *your feasts* into mourning, and all your songs into lamentation . . . I will make it like the mourning for *an only son*. (MT *yāḥîd*; LXX *agapētou* = "beloved one")

Here the sun is darkened at noon, which in the Roman method of counting would be the sixth hour (see the NOTE on "on the first day of the feast of Unleavened Bread" in 14:12)—the setting for the event in Mark 15:33. In Amos, moreover, this obscurity occurs in the middle of a feast (compare the Passover setting in Mark) and is likened to the mourning for a *yāḥîd* ("only son"; cf. Pesch, 2.493–94). The latter word is redolent of the biblical story of Abraham's intended and, in some later retellings, accomplished sacrifice of his beloved son Isaac (Gen 22:2, 12, 16), a sacrifice to which atoning power is frequently ascribed; moreover, it is translated in the LXX with *agapētou* ("beloved"), the term that the divine voice applies to Jesus in Mark 1:11 (see the NOTE on "beloved" in 1:11). These intertextual echoes suggest that while Jesus may feel abandoned by God, he remains the cherished offspring of a loving father, and his innocent death has a salvific purpose in the unfolding drama of redemption.

The Amos passage goes on to imply that the "day of the Lord" is one also of spiritual gloom, in which people will not only mourn for an "only son" but will also find it impossible to hear the word of God (Amos 8:11–12). The darkness, then, is not just a freak of nature but a judgment like that described in the plague narrative of Exod 10:21, "a darkness that can be felt"—and Jesus feels it. It is no accident, therefore, that the description of world-enveloping darkness (15:33) is immediately followed by an account of Jesus' cry of dereliction (15:34; cf. Burchard, "Mark 15,34," 6). The judgment predicted by the Prophets has fallen on the crucified Jesus.

As the context of the Amos passage makes clear, God is behind this act of judgment, but in the overall Markan narrative, in which demonic agency has been so strongly emphasized, it may involve the intermediacy of Satan, "the Angel of Darkness" (see 1QS 3:17–26; cf. 1QM 13:4–6; 16:11; Eph 6:12), who was sometimes believed to be responsible for strange astronomical phenomena (see, e.g., *Asc. Isa.* 4:5, in which he causes the moon to appear "at the sixth hour"). Satan can also be blamed for the depression that darkens the mood of God's chosen ones; in 1QH 13(5):24–34, for example, the speaker complains that because of the derisive words of his enemies, who are "men of Belial [= Satan]," "the light of my face has become gloomy with deep darkness, my countenance has changed into gloom." One of Satan's most important tasks, moreover, is to convince people that God has abandoned them, so that they curse him and die (cf. Job 1:11; 2:5, 9, and Garrett, *Temptations*, 131–32). If the Markan Jesus does not curse God, he will in a moment complain searingly about God's apparent abandonment of him (15:34), something that he has *not* done previously, even in the agony of Gethsemane. And if Jesus will cry out "with a loud voice" here and in 15:37, that is exactly what people who are demonized—and only they—do elsewhere in the Gospel (1:26; 5:7; cf. 9:26 and Strelan, "Recognizing," 493–501). Although Mark does not say so explicitly, therefore, the inference from his narrative may be that Jesus, on the cross, suffers such a sudden and intense Satanic assault that he becomes in some ways like a man possessed (cf. Danker, "Demonic Secret").

Having described the circumstances of Jesus' anguished cry in 15:33–34a (worldwide darkness, ninth hour, loud sound), Mark proceeds to cite its words in 15:34b. These are a quotation of the opening verse of Psalm 22, which Mark renders in Aramaic, then translates into Greek that corresponds to the LXX (see the NOTES on *"Elōi, Elōi, lama sabachthani"* and "My God, my God, why have you abandoned me?" in 15:34). This psalm has previously been alluded to in the narratives of the division of Jesus' garments (15:24; cf. Ps 22:18) and of the mockery of the crucified (15:29–32; cf. Ps 22:6–8), and it was interpreted in the Second Temple period as a prophecy of the sufferings of the righteous in the end-time (see Marcus, *Way*, 177–79). As the psalm continues, moreover, the speaker complains of God's sudden distance from him ("Why are you so far away from my salvation? . . . Do not be far from me!" 22:1b, 11, my trans.), which is congruent with the divine absence implied by the Markan darkness. As Williams ("Background," 10–11) points out, therefore, something of the psalm's context seems to be evoked by the citation of its first verse.

But how much of the context? Some recent exegetes have noted that Psalm 22 ends triumphantly, with the proclamation of God's dominion to the ends of the earth (22:27–28), and some have sought to lessen the difficulty of our verse by positing that when Jesus quoted the first verse, he had the triumphant ending in mind (see, e.g., Gese, "Psalm 22," 192–96; Pesch, 2.494; Trudinger, "Eli"). But while it seems likely that the psalm's ending was in *Mark's* mind as he continued his story (see the COMMENT on 15:38–39), that victorious ending must not be allowed to override its distressed beginning in exegesis of Jesus' cry of dereliction. This psalm, like several other Righteous Sufferer laments (e.g., Psalms 6, 31, 69, 71, and

130), has near its end a transition point from complaint to praise; the confidence that the speaker possesses at the termination is not available to him at the start, but only comes into being through an act of God in response to his troubled prayer. The Markan Jesus does not quote Psalm 22's ending but its beginning, and that agonized incipit corresponds perfectly to the situation of torment in which a crucified person finds himself (see Rossé, *Cry*, 103–7; Luz, *Matthew 21–28*, 550–51).

That situation, in the case of Jesus, is one of real forsakenness. Earlier in the passion narrative, Jesus was abandoned by his closest associates (14:50–52; cf. *katalipōn* in 14:52), and in the crucifixion scene he was shown to be bereft of sympathy even from his fellow criminals (15:29–32). Now, climactically, he seems to have been abandoned (*enkatelipes*) by God as well. This last abandonment contradicts conventional notions of royalty; kings were supposed to have God as their helper, not their foe (cf. Matt 27:42–43; Josephus, *Ant.* 17.195). As throughout the rest of chapter 15, therefore, the narrative's assertion of Jesus' kingship occurs in the teeth of circumstances that seem to call it radically into question.

While some Christians have been troubled by this cry of dereliction, others have seen it as an indication of Jesus' identification with humanity and thus as a source of comfort and empowerment. Jesus, at the nadir of his existence, experiences the same sense of divine abandonment that so often characterizes our lives; as Augustine puts it, he "took on the speech of our infirmity" (*Letter* 140, to Honoratus 5). A papyrus fragment from the third or fourth century, which was probably used in an amulet, even includes the cry in a series of names and attributes that express God's grace, salvation, and loving fatherly care (P.Heid.Inv.G 1359 = VHP 1.5; see Deissmann, *Light*, 405). Paradoxically, then, the cry of dereliction becomes good news, and this probably has to do with Mark's Pauline soteriology: through identifying with human lostness, the Son of God points a way out of it (cf. 2 Cor 5:21 and Marcus, "Mark—Interpreter"). Jesus enters the darkness of the old age in order that humanity might live in the light of the new; he gives his life as a "ransom for many" (10:45; see Marcus, "Epistemology," 571–72). With his cry, and with the death that follows, Jesus has achieved the purpose of his mission: complete identification with humanity's slave-like, accursed condition, and a corresponding form of decease, "even death on a cross" (cf. Phil 2:7–8). The cry of dereliction, then, is in a strange way the Markan counterpart to the Johannine cry of triumph, "It is finished!" (John 19:30)—the goal has been achieved, humanity has been redeemed, and Jesus can therefore die.

15:35–37: misunderstanding and death. Before his final expiration can occur, however, one last instance of human incomprehension supervenes. Hearing Jesus call out to God (*'Elāhi*, which Mark transliterates *Elōi*), some of the bystanders think that he is addressing Elijah (*'Eliyāhû*), who was probably expected to precede the Messiah (see the NOTE on "Why then do the scribes say that Elijah must come first?" in 9:11) and was popularly regarded as a kind of St. Jude, a patron saint for pious people in dire straits (see, e.g., *b. B. Qam.* 60b, and cf. Strack-Billerbeck, 4.2.769–73). Perhaps for both these reasons, Jesus' cry raises the expectation that Elijah may save him from the cross (15:35–36). The Markan reader, however, knows that this expectation also rests on a misunderstanding: Elijah has *already* come, in the person of John the Baptist, but instead of saving Jesus from the cross, he has gone before him in the way of suffering and death— which Jesus himself must now tread to the end (see the COMMENT on 9:11–13 and cf. Burchard, "Markus 15,34," 9).

Unaware of this, a bystander quickly fills a sponge with vinegar and tries to give it to Jesus to drink by attaching it to a reed and lifting it to his lips (15:36a), explaining or excusing his action by saying, "Let me be! Let's see if Elijah is going to come to take him down!" (15:36b). This seemingly compassionate act, however, seems to be motivated by derision; the man does not really believe that Elijah will come to Jesus' rescue but merely wants to prolong his agony (see the NOTE on "saying, 'Let me be! Let's see . . . ' " in 15:36). His exhortation, which begins with the words "Let me be! Let's see," is another illustration of the Markan theme of "looking without seeing" (cf. 4:12; 8:18), which was just epitomized by the mockery of the chief priests and the scribes (15:32; see the COMMENT on 15:29–32 and Marcus, *Way*, 183–84). But this is also an instance in which a passion narrative character says and does more than he knows, since the offer of vinegar unwittingly invokes another Righteous Sufferer psalm:

> Insults have broken my heart,
>> so that I am in despair.
> I looked for pity, but there was none;
>> and for comforters, but I found none.
> They gave me poison for food,
>> and for my thirst they gave me vinegar to drink. . . .
> Let their eyes be darkened so that they cannot see. (Ps 69:20–23a)

Like the speaker in Psalm 69, the Markan Jesus is insulted by those around him; is in, or at least close to, despair; finds no comforters; and is given vinegar to drink. The psalmist, moreover, calls for the mockers' eyes to be darkened, so that they cannot see; in the Markan narrative, similarly, the mockers speak of "seeing" but are really blind.

The world, then, has become so twisted, and people so blinded, that what at first seems like an act of succor turns out to be motivated by derision. But it is now too late for deeds of kindness, even derisive ones; Jesus' cry of forsakenness is his death shout, and having uttered it, he gives up the ghost (see the NOTE on "having given a loud cry" in 15:37). The way in which he does so is unusual, since a crucified person normally died of asphyxia, and probably would not have had enough breath to expire with a loud cry (see the APPENDIX "Crucifixion," and cf. Origen, *Against Celsus* 2.55, where Jesus' loud death-cry is one of the supernatural elements in the scene). Jackson ("Death," 27–28), therefore, argues that *exepneusen* ("expired," lit. "breathed out spirit") refers to "God's Spirit, working in the expiration of Jesus' breath with a great cry"; it is this powerful expulsion of Jesus' breath that causes the Temple curtain to rip in two. Gundry (947–48, 970) consequently regards Jesus' last cry as a shout of divine victory. But the foregoing narrative points in the opposite direction: Jesus dies forsaken, derided by his enemies and abandoned by his friends, and his last cry, which may be demonic, expresses his perceived distance from God.

15:38–39: the tearing of the Temple veil and the reaction of the centurion. But this cry and death of dereliction are not the narrative's last word; the rest of the pericope is taken up with supernatural (15:38) and human (15:39–40) reactions to Jesus' death, which transform the bleak landscape into a scene of revelation. The first act is the ripping of the Temple curtain (15:38), a tear that moves from top to bottom: it comes, then, "from above," that is, from God (cf. John 3:3, 7, 31; 19:11). But what does this divine action convey?

Here again, as in the darkness at noon, the imagery probably contains several dimensions. Given its violent destructiveness, one aspect of the rip is judgmental: it anticipates the demolition of the Temple by the Romans some forty years after Jesus' death. The Markan Jesus has predicted the Temple's destruction (13:2), and the narrative has linked this prediction with Jesus' trial (14:58) and crucifixion (15:29). In the Parable of the Vineyard (12:1–9), moreover, Jesus has prophesied that the vineyard (= Israel), including its tower (= the Temple?), will be destroyed as punishment for the death of "the beloved son" (cf. the NOTE on "dug out a wine vat, and built a tower" in 12:1). This "prophecy" may be an early instance of the Christian notion that the Temple's destruction was a recompense for the rejection of Jesus (see the COMMENT on 13:1–2). It would be consonant with this judgmental theology that the death of Jesus is accompanied by a sign pointing toward the Temple's doom. This interpretation coheres with the fact that the high priest and the chief priests have been Jesus' principal opponents throughout the passion narrative (see 14:1, 10, 43, 47, etc.); it makes sense, therefore, that God's judgment should fall on their power base, the Temple. Evidence from Jewish literature corroborates this interpretation; Josephus (*War* 6.288–300) and rabbinic traditions (e.g., *b. Yoma* 39b; *y. Yoma* 6:3 [43c; Neusner, 14.176]) report portents of the Second Temple's destruction that occurred in the years before that event, including the spontaneous opening of its gates. The rabbinic traditions date these portents to forty years before the Temple's actual demise—that is, about the time of Jesus' death.

Events of divine judgment, however, can also be acts of divine mourning (cf. Heschel, *Prophets*), as illustrated by rabbinic traditions that speak of God tearing his purple garment in grief at the sack of Jerusalem (e.g., *Pesiq. Rab Kah.* 15.3; *Lam. Rab.* 1.1.1; 2.21; *Lev. Rab.* 6.5)—an evident allusion to the destruction of one or the other of the Temple's curtains (cf. Exod 26:31–35; 38:18). In the Markan case, divine mourning is further suggested by the parallel between the ripping of the Temple veil and the high priest's act of tearing his garment in grief and anger at Jesus' "blasphemy" of putting himself on a level with God (14:61–63; cf. Daube, *New Testament*, 23–24). God himself now refutes the high priest's accusation by tearing his own garment at the death of the one whom the centurion will laud as God's son (15:39). As Carol Shoun points out in a private communication, while such human tearing is a response to people who are trying to efface the essential boundary between God and humanity (see the COMMENT on 14:61b–65c), the divine tearing is a response from a God who is graciously—and legitimately— *choosing* in some measure to efface that boundary.

As this comment already implies, the negative aspects to the tearing of the Temple curtain are not the full story; apocalyptic thinkers look forward to eschatological acts that will bring not only mourning and judgment (to the ungodly) but also revelation and joy (to the righteous; see, e.g., Dan 12:2; 1 Cor 1:18; Rev 12:12; 18:20). Both sides of this apocalyptic equation are probably implied by the tearing of the Temple veil, especially if, as seems likely, the torn curtain is the inner veil of the sanctuary, behind which the divine glory was believed to dwell (see the NOTE on "the veil of the sanctuary" in 15:38). In this case, its ripping is bound to be revelatory as well as destructive: the veil is rent asunder, the glory of God hidden behind it begins to radiate out into the world, and as an initial reflection of this unveiling, a human being, and a Gentile at that, acclaims Jesus' divine sonship for the first time in the Gospel. This interpretation is supported by *T. Benj.* 9:3(4), which is evidently intended as a comment on our passage: "The curtain of the sanctuary (*naou*) will be ripped apart (*schizomenon*), and the spirit of God will pass on to the Gentiles, as a fire that is poured out" (Hollander and de Jonge trans. alt.). The same interpretation of our passage is presupposed in Ephrem, *Hymns on the Nativity* 25:16: "The Spirit in the Temple longed to exalt him, and when he was crucified it tore [the veil] and went out" (McVey trans. alt.).

This revelatory interpretation of the tearing of the Temple curtain is also consonant with the other Markan use of the verb *schizein* ("to rip"), which occurs at Jesus' baptism, where the heavens are ripped apart, the Spirit descends on Jesus like a dove, and a heavenly voice declares him to be God's Son (1:10–11); here the result of the heavenly curtain being torn is that something comes out from behind it (cf. Motyer, "Rending"). As in Rev 21:22–27, therefore, the radiance of God, which was formerly confined to the protective shell of the Temple's interior, emerges into public manifestation at the dawning of the new age, so that not only Jews but also the nations—as epitomized by the Gentile centurion—may walk in its light. While the other witnesses to Jesus' death have looked and looked without seeing, the mystery of the dominion of God is now imparted to the centurion (cf. 4:11–12); he alone sees *alēthōs* ("truly"). In the passion narrative there has been much acclamation of Jesus that has *not* been truthful but derisive. His enemies have mocked him as a prophet and "the king of the Jews" (14:65; 15:2, 16–20, 29–32) and have subjected him to a form of punishment that was viewed in the Greco-Roman world as a burlesque on claims to exaltation and kingship (see the APPENDIX "Crucifixion"). If now the centurion, seeing the way Jesus dies, proclaims that he truly *was* the son of God, this affirmation implies that he was in fact the one whom his enemies have mockingly depicted him to be.

The centurion's acclamation of Jesus thus challenges those for whom the sight of an impaled, degraded, dying prisoner mocks the very notion of sovereignty, with which the term "son of God" was intimately connected; indeed, both the Jewish Messiah and the centurion's erstwhile lord, the emperor, could be dubbed God's son (see Collins, "Son of God Among Jews" and "Son of God Among

Greeks," 94–96). But the local representative of Roman power now sees that it is neither the emperor nor his revolutionary opponents but "*this* man," who has just died in agony on a Roman cross, who is the true revelation of divine sonship and hence of royal sovereignty. This message would be timely for the Markan community, which has probably been caught in the cross fire of the Jewish revolt against the Romans, an insurrection perhaps led by messianic pretenders (see the INTRODUCTION in vol. 1, pp. 33–37). The revolt, moreover, had been crushed by Vespasian (r. 69–79), who may well have been reigning as emperor when Mark wrote his Gospel. The royal power disclosed at the cross is thus the opposite of imperial coercion, which overcomes humanity by force, and of its equal and opposite reaction, revolutionary violence.

The revelation that occurs at Jesus' death also overcomes the dualism that has previously pervaded the Gospel, in which God and humanity have been at odds, and humanity has been under the power of Satan (see 7:7–8; 8:33). Now, through Jesus' exorcistic death on the cross, a blessed, apocalyptic paradox comes into being, in which the radiance of the new age breaks forth out of the depths of human weakness and pain, and a suffering *man* is revealed to be the Son of *God* (cf. Davis, "Paradox"). By his recognition of this profound Christological paradox, the centurion, an "alien from the commonwealth of Israel," a "stranger to the covenants of promise" (cf. Eph 2:12), a pagan from a distant land, becomes the first human in the Gospel to grasp the height and depth of Jesus' identity. In so doing, he unwittingly fulfills the triumphant ending of the psalm whose searing words have punctuated the Markan death scene (cf. 15:24, 29–32, 34):

> All the ends of the earth shall remember
> > and turn to the LORD;
> and all the families of the nations
> > shall worship before him.
> For dominion belongs to the LORD,
> > and he rules over the nations. (Ps 22:27–28)

15:40–41: *the watching women.* After the centurion's climactic confession, the focus shifts to the other witnesses to Jesus' death, a group of reverent women (15:40–41). Although these women are presumably sympathetic, as their subsequent actions confirm (15:42–47; 16:1–8), the description of them as "watching from far away" (*apo makrothen,* 15:40a) introduces a note of editorial reserve, since it portrays them as unable or unwilling to come to Jesus' aid in his hour of distress, perhaps out of fear of being associated with a condemned criminal (cf. Davies and Allison, 3.637 n. 150). The description of the women looking on from afar thus paves the way for the end of the Gospel, in which they will flee in terror from the site of Jesus' resurrection (16:8). It also echoes a Righteous Sufferer psalm whose larger context again has connections with the Markan death scene:

> My heart is troubled, my strength has forsaken me;
> > and the light of my eyes is not with me.

> My friends and my neighbors drew near opposite me and stood,
>   and my nearest ones stood far away. (Ps 38:10–11 [37:11–12 LXX], my trans.)

Here we have not only the obvious connection with the picture of Jesus' acquaintances looking on from afar (*makrothen*) but also the portrayal of onlookers standing opposite him (*ex enantias mou*; cf. 15:39) and of the Sufferer troubled, abandoned (*enkatelipen*; cf. 15:34), and entering into darkness (cf. 15:33–34).

But the depiction of the women is not primarily negative. These same figures will reappear in the Gospel's two remaining passages, where they will witness not only Jesus' burial (15:42–47) but also the empty tomb that will proclaim his resurrection (16:1–8); they are thus, as Davies and Allison (3.637) put it, "eyewitnesses to the kerygmatic triad: Jesus died, was buried, was raised" (cf. 1 Cor 15:3–5). Mark carefully lists their names, so that his readers may recognize these connections (15:40b; see the NOTE on "Mary the Magdalene, and Mary the mother of James the Small and of Joses, and Salome"). He then goes on to offer a wide-ranging flashback about the women's earlier experience with Jesus, which significantly qualifies the negative impression left by the portrayal of them as remote from his suffering: they followed Jesus when he was in Galilee (15:41a), served him there (15:41b), and went up with him to Jerusalem (15:41c).

These details parallel the descriptions of the male disciples in several ways: both groups follow Jesus (cf. 1:16–20; 6:1; 10:28, 32), both are associated with his ministry in Galilee (cf. 1:16, 28–29; 9:30; 14:28; 16:7), and both go up with him to Jerusalem (cf. 10:32–33). Like the twelve men, moreover, the three women are the core of a larger group of many followers (cf. 3:7, 13–14; 4:10). But unlike the men, who fled when Jesus was arrested (14:50–52), and like the anonymous anointer of 14:1–9, these women are linked with Jesus' own ultimate act of service, his death (cf. 10:45). The service of women to Jesus thus brackets the entire Gospel (cf. 1:31), and it may be that the previous ministry of the two Marys and of Salome is mentioned only here, after Jesus' life has ebbed away, because their service is mysteriously intertwined with Jesus' own act of self-sacrifice (see Malbon, "Fallible Followers," 41; Miller, *Women*, 169–73).

Unexpectedly, however, it will not be these women, whose continuous attachment to Jesus has just been emphasized, but a member of the Jewish elite, which has hitherto been overwhelmingly hostile, who, in the Gospel's next passage, will take up the charitable task of burying him.

THE BURIAL OF JESUS (15:42–47)

15 [42]And when it was already evening, since it was the Preparation Day (that is, the day before the Sabbath), [43]there came Joseph from Arimathaea, a prominent member of the council, who was also himself expecting the dominion of God. Plucking up his courage, he went in to Pilate and requested the body of Jesus. [44]But Pilate wondered whether he could already have died and, summoning the centurion, asked him whether he had already died. [45]And having found out from the centurion, he granted the corpse to Joseph. [46]And having bought a linen cloth, he took him down and wrapped him in the linen cloth and placed him in a tomb that had been hewed out of a rock, and he rolled a stone against the door of the tomb. [47]And Mary the Magdalene and Mary of Joses beheld where he had been laid.

NOTES

15 42. *when it was already evening.* Gk *ēdē opsias genomenēs* It would be possible to translate this "when evening was already coming," and that would be logical, since Joseph's motivation seems to be to get Jesus buried before Sabbath arrives at sundown. Elsewhere in Mark, however, the genitive absolute construction with *genomenou/genomenēs* usually indicates the arrival of a point in time rather than its approach (cf. 1:32; 4:17; 6:2, 21, 35, 47; 15:33), although in 14:17 "when evening was coming" is a possible translation for *opsias genomenēs*. But even if our passage is taken to imply the arrival of *opsia*, Joseph's burial of Jesus is not necessarily a violation of Jewish law. As Brown (*Death*, 2.1211–12) points out, this word can designate not only the time after sunset (see Matt 14:23; 16:2) but also late afternoon (see Matt 14:15; 20:8; cf. BDAG 746 [2]). "When it was already evening, since it was the Preparation Day," therefore, may be one of Mark's typical double expressions, in which the second member qualifies the first (see Neirynck, *Duality*): it is already *opsia* but not yet dark, and hence the Sabbath has not yet begun.

since it was the Preparation Day (that is, the day before the Sabbath). Gk *epei ēn paraskeuē ho estin prosabbaton. Paraskeuē* can denote the day of preparation either for the Passover (e.g., John 19:14) or for the Sabbath (e.g., Josephus, *Ant.* 16.163; John 19:31). In the pre-Markan tradition it probably indicated the former, since the likelihood is that Jesus was crucified on the day before Passover (see the NOTE on "Not during the feast" in 14:2 and cf. Theissen, *Gospels*, 167). "That is, the day before the Sabbath," therefore, may be a Markan gloss designed to bring the tradition into line with the evangelist's own chronology. This theory explains the fact that Joseph is able to purchase a linen cloth, when commercial transactions would normally be forbidden on Passover (see Lev 23:7–8; Neh 10:31; Amos 8:5).

43. *Joseph from Arimathaea.* Gk *Iōsēph apo Arimathaia.* Some texts (e.g., B, D, the Sinaiticus Syriac, and some Bohairic witnesses) have the definite article *ho* ("the one") before *apo* ("from"), but the meaning is still definite even if the article is absent. On the location of Arimathaea, see Pattengale, "Arimathea"; Eusebius (*Onomasticon* 144.28) and Jerome (*Commentary on the Books of Kings*, incipit) identify it with Ramah ("height"), the birthplace of Samuel, a town in the hill country of Judaea about twenty miles east of modern Jaffa. This identification makes philological sense; in 1 Sam 1:19 Hannah, having conceived Samuel, returns *Hārāmāta* ("to Ramah"), which the LXX renders *Armathaim* (1 Sam 1:19). Interestingly, after Samuel is born in Ramah/Arimathaea, Hannah praises God for raising people up from Sheol (1 Sam 2:6)—which is exactly what God will do for Jesus in the next passage in Mark.

prominent member of the council. Gk *euschēmōn bouleutēs. Bouleutēs* probably identifies Joseph as a member of the *boulē*, the ruling council of Jewish Palestine, which Mark elsewhere calls the Sanhedrin (see 14:55; 15:1, and cf. Josephus, *War* 2.405; on the synonymy of the two words, see the APPENDIX "The Jewish Leaders in Mark"). He may avoid using "Sanhedrin" here because the word is tainted by that body's hostility to Jesus. *Euschēmōn* carries the implication of "noble," "influential," or "wealthy," as in Acts 13:50; 17:12, and the papyri (see M-M, 266; Taylor, 600; Gnilka, 333); the description of Joseph as *plousios* ("rich") in Matt 27:57, therefore, is a logical inference from Mark. For another indication of Joseph's wealth, see the NOTE on "he rolled a stone against the door of the tomb" in 15:46.

who was also himself expecting the dominion of God. Gk *hos kai autos ēn prosdechomenos tēn basileian tou theou.* The sense of *kai autos* ("also himself") is obscure: who else in the immediate context is, like Joseph, expecting God's dominion? Probably not the other members of the Sanhedrin, though they are implicitly invoked by the reference to Joseph as "a prominent member of the council." Lührmann (267) suggests that the reference is to Jesus and his disciples; although not one of the latter, Joseph, like them, is looking forward to the onset of God's reign. The disciples, however, have not been spoken of since they fled in 14:50–52. The more immediate referent is the women mentioned in the preceding passage, who followed Jesus, served him in Galilee, and came up with him to Jerusalem (15:40–41)—presumably because they expected the dominion of God to be revealed in the holy city through his messianic words and deeds (cf. Isa 2:2–3; *Pss. Sol.* 17:30–34).

45. *the corpse.* Gk *to ptōma.* Many manuscripts (A, C, W, Ψ, 083, *f* [1, 13], 33, as well as the Majority Text, and the Latin, Coptic, and Syriac witnesses except for Sinaiticus) read *sōma* ("body") here, as in 15:43. But a powerful combination of manuscripts, including Sinaiticus (Greek and Syriac), Vaticanus, and Bezae, as well as L, Θ, 565, agree in reading *ptōma.* This is the preferable text, especially since a scribal change from *ptōma* to *sōma* is easier to imagine than the other way around; *ptōma* is a harsh term referring to a corpse, especially one killed by violence, whereas *sōma* is a more dignified word referring to a dead or living body (see BDAG 895). The variation between *sōma* in 15:43 and *ptōma* in 15:45 is adduced by Schonfield (*Passover Plot*, 161) as evidence that Jesus was taken down from the cross alive but in a state of suspended animation (see the COMMENT on 15:42–45): Joseph, who knew that Jesus was still alive, requested his *body*, but Pilate, who did not, granted Joseph his *corpse* (on the theory of suspended animation, see the APPENDIX "The Empty Tomb"). The variation, however, is more likely to reflect Joseph's reverence for Jesus.

46. *placed him in a tomb.* Gk *ethēken auton en mnēmeiǭ.* In typical Jewish tombs from Roman Palestine, a short entranceway leads into one or more burial chambers, which are low (about three feet in height) but relatively spacious in their horizontal dimensions (the two chambers in Tomb 1 at Giv'at ha-Mivtar, for example, are each about ten feet square). The most popular mode of burial in Hellenistic and Roman times was in *loculi or kôkîm*, which Brown calls "deep pigeon holes."

In this method, long, narrow burial niches, typically about 2 × 2 × 6 feet in size, were cut horizontally into the walls of the burial chamber, and the bodies were placed in them headfirst. This is probably the mode of burial we should imagine in the case of Jesus, especially since the ancient Jewish graves found within sixty feet of the Holy Sepulchre are of the *loculus* type. After a year, when the flesh had decomposed and fallen away, the bones were gathered up and placed in ossuaries, or bone boxes (see Brown, *Death*, 2.1248–49; McCane, *Stone*, 32–34, 39–46).

Mark does not say, as Matt 27:60 does, that the tomb in question is Joseph's own, and the fact that he is identified as an Arimathaean rather than a Jerusalemite might suggest the contrary. France (*Mark*, 666), however, argues that Matthew is probably correct about Joseph's ownership of the tomb, since it is difficult to see how else he could have gained access to an elite burial place on such short notice (on the upper-class nature of the tomb, see the next NOTE). It seems strange, to be sure, to have an elite burial site near a place of execution, but as Brown (*Death*, 2.1250–51) points out, it is possible that being close to the holy city made up for this disadvantage; a parallel, he suggests, is presented by the impressive first-century tombs located in the Kidron Valley despite its proximity to the undesirable Valley of Hinnom (Gehenna).

he rolled a stone against the door of the tomb. Gk *prosekylisen lithon epi tēn thyran tou mnēmeiou.* Most Second Temple cave-tombs in and around Jerusalem are sealed with square or rectangular stones; only four of the nine hundred–plus tombs so far discovered are sealed with circular stones, and these tombs apparently belonged to rich and prominent people (most famously, the Herodian family and Queen Helena of Adiabene). The rectangular stones, weighing roughly five hundred pounds, are chiseled to fit like stoppers into the tombs' openings and would have been difficult to maneuver into position (see Kloner, "Rolling Stone"; McCane, *Stone*, 33). The round, disk-shaped stones, though much more massive (some fifteen hundred to three thousand pounds, by Kloner's estimate), are set upright in transverse channels, which would have facilitated their rolling into place with the aid of levers (cf. Finegan, *Archeology*, 202).

Kloner ("Rolling Stone"), however, noting the overwhelming predominance of the square or rectangular type, suggests that this is what our passage has in mind; *prosekylisen* ("rolled against"), he asserts, does not necessarily imply that the stone was round. Allison (*Resurrecting Jesus*, 363 n. 641), in support of this idea, points to Diodorus Siculus, *Library of History* 17.68.2; Josh 10:18; and 2 Kgs 9:33 as passages in which *kylioun* may refer to "rolling or moving an unrounded object." Still, *kylioun* usually implies rolling a rounded object, and may do so in the first two passages cited by Allison, and since circular rolling stones are attested in Second Temple times in well-known tombs, it seems wisest to picture the stone in our passage as of this sort. It is not implausible that Joseph would possess an elite tomb with such a state-of-the-art seal, since he is portrayed as a leading citizen of Jerusalem (see the NOTE on "prominent member of the council" in 15:43).

There is some doubt, however, whether Joseph would be able to move such a stone by himself, as a literal reading of 15:46 might be taken to imply. Most of the circular stones are at least four feet in diameter, and the one from the Herodian tomb is more than two and a half feet thick. Even with the aid of levers, such massive stones would be difficult for a single person to maneuver into place. This impression is supported by the literary references apart from Mark 15:46. A bit later in Mark's own narrative, the three women who come to the tomb on Easter morning think that they cannot move the stone by themselves (16:3), and the plural *ethēkan* ("they laid him") in 16:6 may contain a remembrance that Joseph had helpers (cf. John 19:38–42, where he is assisted by Nicodemus). In Codex Bezae, Luke 23:53 says that twenty men moved the stone with difficulty, and *Gos. Pet.* 8:31 asserts that moving it required the efforts of "all who were there together" (Elliott trans.). Although some of these passages may be intended to refute the charge that Jesus' disciples broke into his tomb and stole his body, they may also be based on real observations or inferences.

How, then, did Joseph move the stone? One possible answer is that Mark does not really mean to imply that he did so by himself. *Prosekylisen*, rather, may reflect a Markan tendency, especially when dealing with officials, to use active verbs causatively (cf. Lagrange, 442, and the NOTE on "wishing to satisfy the crowd, released Barabbas to them and turned Jesus over, after flogging him" in 15:15).

COMMENT

Introduction. In the last few chapters Jesus has passed from the nearly constant motion that characterized him throughout most of his ministry to the constrained movement of a prisoner, to the transfixed immobility of the crucified, and finally to the absolute inertia of death. Other characters, therefore, must now become the subjects of the action. The dominant figure here is Joseph of Arimathaea, who is suddenly introduced in 15:42–43; the passage is entirely taken up with his energetic deeds and people's reactions to them. But two of the three women who were mentioned at the end of the previous passage reappear at the close of this one, and here they function as witnesses to confirm what men have said and done.

Our passage seems to incorporate a terse pre-Markan burial tradition, which both Mark and John (19:38–42) have taken up and edited in their own ways (cf. Reinbold, *Bericht*, 175–76). One pre-Markan element is the description of Joseph as a "prominent member of the council," that is, a Sanhedrist, which contains two Markan *hapax legomena* (see the GLOSSARY) and conflicts with the evangelist's portrayal of "the whole Sanhedrin" participating in Jesus' condemnation (14:55; 15:1). The presence of tradition is also suggested by the names of the women at the end (15:47; see the NOTE on "Mary the Magdalene, and Mary the mother of James the Small and of Joses, and Salome" in 15:40). The explanatory clause in 15:42, moreover ("that is, the day before the Sabbath"), appears to be a Markan gloss on a preexistent statement ("since it was the Preparation Day"); the typically Markan genitive absolute time notice at the beginning (*kai ēdē opsias genomenēs* = "And when it was already evening") transforms this into a characteristic double temporal expression (cf. the other redactional instances of *opsias genomenēs* in 1:32; 4:35; and 14:17). It is also possible that Pilate's question and answer to the centurion in 15:44–45a are Markan; as Gnilka (2.331) points out, they contain indirect discourse and several typically Markan words ("wondered," "summoning," "asked," "having found out").

The first section of the passage (15:42–45) concerns Joseph's request to Pilate for Jesus' body, the second and shorter section (15:46–47) his burial of Jesus.

15:42–45: the request to Pilate. With Jesus' death at 3:00 P.M., according to the Markan reckoning (cf. 15:34), a time pressure is introduced into the narrative: if he is to be buried before the Sabbath starts and work proscribed, he must be interred before sundown (see the NOTE on "since it was the Preparation Day [that is, the day before the Sabbath]" in 15:42). This task falls to an abruptly introduced character named Joseph. The only background we are given about this figure is the name of his hometown (see the NOTE on "Joseph from Arimathaea" in 15:43), that he is "a prominent member of the council" (*euschēmōn bouleutēs*), and that he is "expecting the dominion of God."

What exactly do these phrases convey? Unlike Matthew (27:57) and John (19:38), Mark does not say that Joseph is a disciple of Jesus, and Brown (*Death*, 2.1214–19) argues that he may not even have been a sympathizer; if he were, there would probably be some indication of cooperation between him and the women. Joseph, moreover, is probably being portrayed as a member of the Sanhedrin, the judicial body that convicted Jesus on a capital charge (see the NOTE on "prominent member of the council" in 15:43), and Mark, unlike Luke 23:51, does not mention an exceptive clause in Joseph's case, emphasizing in earlier passages that "the whole Sanhedrin" collaborated in the condemnation (see 14:55; 15:1). This theory of Joseph's hostility is supported by Acts 13:27–29, which seems to imply that Jesus was buried by his enemies. For Brown, therefore, Joseph's actions were not inspired by commitment to Jesus but by a desire to avoid the shame of having a fellow Jew, albeit a sinful one, remain on the cross over the Sabbath (cf. Deut 21:22–23; Josephus, *War* 4.317; *m. Sanh.* 6:4). In this view, Joseph resembles Tobit, who is ready to risk antagonizing the authorities in order to perform the good deed of burying his slain co-religionists (see Tob 1:16–20; 2:1–7).

In line with his negative interpretation of Joseph's motive, Brown characterizes Jesus' burial as dishonorable. Burial of this nature was frequent for people who had been condemned by Jewish courts (see, e.g., Josephus, *Ant.* 5.44; *t. Sanh.* 9:8) or executed by the Romans (see, e.g., Tacitus, *Annals* 6.29; Eusebius, *Ecclesiastical History* 5.1.61–62). McCane (*Stone*, 89–108) supports the thesis of dishonorable burial by pointing out that the Markan account is missing two indispensable features of honorable entombment, namely, mourning rites and placement in a family sepulchre, and that it depicts only minimal preparation of the body.

But the data can also be interpreted as suggesting that Joseph respected Jesus. The Romans sometimes permitted honorable burial of those whom they had executed, including the crucified, as is shown both by literary evidence (see, e.g., Philo, *Flaccus* 83; Justinian, *Digest* 48.24) and by the archaeological remains of the crucified man of Giv'at ha-Mivtar, who was interred in a family tomb (see

Kuhn, "Gekreuzigte"). The approach of the Sabbath rather than a desire to dishonor Jesus may explain the abbreviated nature of Joseph's burial rites (see the
COMMENT on 15:46–47). As Craig ("Reflections," 407) points out, moreover,
failure to bury Jesus in a family tomb does not necessarily indicate dishonorable
burial; Jesus was not a native of Jerusalem but of faraway Nazareth, and those who
died far from home were usually interred where they died (cf. Gen 35:8, 19–20).
With regard to Jerusalem in particular, Matt 27:7 suggests that pilgrims who died
in the holy city were buried there rather than being shipped back to their ancestral homes. And it is not clear that dishonorable burial ever meant interment in
a tomb, as happened with Jesus; the biblical incidents we know of, rather, seem
to involve "the corpse's being cast on or into the ground and covered by dirt or
stones" (Craig, "Reflections," 403; cf. Josh 7:25–26; 8:29; 2 Sam 18:17; Jer 22:19;
26:23).

It seems unlikely, therefore, that Jesus' burial was shameful, and this increases
the possibility that the man responsible for it was a sympathizer, even if he was a
member of a judicial body that had been overwhelmingly hostile to Jesus. Joseph's
willingness to run a risk in order to bury Jesus (cf. "plucking up his courage" in
15:43c), while possible for a non-adherent (cf. Tob 1:19), is more plausible in the
case of a sympathizer, and the fact that he buried Jesus in an expensive, individual
rock tomb rather than a common grave for executed criminals suggests that he
did not regard him as a transgressor (cf. France, *Mark*, 666, and the NOTE on
"he rolled a stone against the door of the tomb" in 15:46). Joseph's charitable act
of burial, moreover, did not embrace all three of the crucified Jews but only Jesus,
even though the other two may have died at the same time (cf. John 19:31–33), and
this probably indicates a special solicitude for Jesus (on the Jewish identity of the
"brigands" crucified with Jesus, see the NOTE on "brigands" in 15:27).

Whether or not the historical Joseph of Arimathaea was a sympathizer with
Jesus, however, it is virtually certain that *Mark* depicts him as such. The evangelist's description of Joseph as one "expecting the dominion of God" links him with
the revelation of divine kingship that occurred earlier in chapter 15, where Jesus
was crucified as "The King of the Jews" and where the centurion's confession, in
conjunction with Ps 22:27–28, identified his death as the inauguration of God's
rule (see the COMMENT on 15:38–39). Joseph may not be a full disciple, but he
is something more than a pious Jew; like the perceptive scribe in 12:34, he is "not
far from the dominion of God." By his willingness to risk connection with the executed Jesus, he situates himself beneath the promises of 8:34–9:1 and 10:23–31,
which link hazard and loss for Jesus' sake with entering the dominion of God. As
Senior (*Passion*, 133) puts it: "Mark portrays Joseph doing something the disciples
had feared to do: he associates himself with the crucified Jesus." While it might be
possible, therefore, to take the Markan picture of Joseph "expecting the dominion
of God" in a negative, ironic sense—Joseph is oblivious to the fact that God's
rule has already arrived through Jesus' death—it is more likely that Mark means
it positively: Joseph has begun to be grasped by the divine dominion he had been
awaiting (cf. Ambrozic, *Hidden Kingdom*, 240–43).

Plucking up his courage and boldly requesting Jesus' body from Pilate (15:43c),

Joseph demonstrates both his incipient allegiance to Jesus and the surprising initiative that arises when God's dominion appears on the scene. Such a request would have required audacity, since Jesus had been crucified as an enemy of the state, and any charitable act toward him might identify the benefactor as a member of a subversive group (cf. Brown, *Death*, 2.1217). The Markan Pilate, however, instructed perhaps by his own positive feelings toward Jesus (see the COMMENTS on 15:1–5, 6–15), does not take umbrage but instead expresses amazement that Jesus is already dead (15:44a). The verb used here, *thaumazein*, is the same as that employed in 15:5 for Pilate's awe at Jesus' refusal to answer. The latter passage recalls the famous Isaian testimony about the Lord's Servant, who suffers mutely before his tormentors (see Isa 53:7); the Roman governor's whole appearance in the Gospel, therefore, is framed by his astonishment at Jesus and therefore fulfills an earlier part of the same OT text: "Thus shall many nations wonder at him (*thaumasontai . . . ep' autǭ*), and kings shall shut their mouths" (Isa 52:15 LXX; Brenton trans. alt.). Because of the thickness of allusion to the Suffering Servant passage here, it is possible that the description of Joseph as *euschēmōn*, which has an implication of wealth (see the NOTE on "prominent member of the council" in 15:43), echoes the same text, since according to Isa 53:9 the Lord's Servant will make his grave with the rich (cf. Gnilka, 2.334).

The specific cause of Pilate's wonder in the present case is that Jesus has died so quickly—a notice that Matthew (27:58) and Luke (23:52) omit. As Senior (*Passion*, 134) points out, the verb "to die" occurs twice in 15:44, and Jesus' decease is then confirmed by the centurion in 15:45. This stress on the reality of Jesus' death may result from Mark's desire to refute the rumor that he was taken down alive from the cross (see the APPENDIX "The Empty Tomb"); Mark implicitly acknowledges this rumor at the same time that he tries to lay it to rest by emphasizing that the centurion, who doubtless had presided at many executions and knew a dead body when he saw one, confirmed Jesus' decease. Matthew and Luke, however, presumably think it preferable not to raise a red flag and therefore do not mention the matter at all.

After confirming Jesus' death, the centurion, who played such an important role in the previous passage, slips quietly into the background. Pilate himself, after receiving the centurion's attestation, grants Jesus' body to Joseph (15:45) and silently exits from the narrative as well. The representatives of imperial power, therefore, fade into the woodwork in a surprisingly inconspicuous manner, perhaps in illustration of the Markan view that they only *seem* to rule (cf. 10:42). Another sort of empire is about to assert its dominance over the world (16:1–8).

15:46–47: the burial. First, however, Jesus' body must be deposited in a tomb, and this action is described tersely in 15:46. The vocabulary used for Jesus' body changes here from that employed in 15:43–45: whereas Joseph requested *the body* of Jesus, and Pilate granted him *the corpse*, Joseph now takes *him* down, wraps *him* in the burial shroud, and places *him* in the tomb. This change may just reflect stylistic variation, but it is possible that it has a deeper significance: while Joseph and Pilate consider that Jesus has been reduced to the status of a corpse, the narrator views him as still an animate personality—a view in line with the common OT phrase "he was gathered to his people/his fathers" (Gen 25:8, 17; 49:29; Judg 2:10; etc.) and with the Jewish practice of secondary burial (see Meyers, *Ossuaries*, 13–14 and passim). The thrice-repeated masculine pronoun, therefore, may foreshadow Jesus' resurrection.

Mark describes what we might term a "bare bones" burial: Joseph buys a linen cloth for a winding sheet, takes Jesus' body down from the cross, wraps it in the cloth, and places it in the tomb that he believes will be its final resting place (15:46a). Customary rites of corpse preparation, such as washing and anointing with perfumes (cf. Acts 9:37; *m. Šabb.* 23:5), go unmentioned (contrast John 19:39–40), and some have seen this omission as a sign of Joseph's disrespect for Jesus (see, e.g., Brown, *Death*, 2.1243–46). The necessity of having Jesus buried before sundown, however, may have prevented the usual obsequies; although *m. Šabb.* 23:4–5 permits corpse preparation on the Sabbath, it forbids moving or burying the body. Burial, to be sure, could have been delayed until the Sabbath was ended; Brown points to *Sipre Deut.* §221 (cf. *m. Sanh.* 6:5), which indicates that "it can be better to leave the body exposed all night than to bury it without proper preparation." He acknowledges, however, that such permissiveness may not have applied in the holy city of Jerusalem. And to delay Jesus' burial for another day and a half may not have been advisable because of the political sensitivity of Jesus' death and the hostility to him of the majority of the Sanhedrin.

There simply may not have been time on Friday afternoon, therefore, for a proper washing and anointing of Jesus' body. In the Markan story, however, this deficit is offset in two ways. First, Jesus' body has already been anointed by the woman in Bethany, who poured precious ointment over his head two days before his death (cf. 14:8). Second, the women who witness Joseph's actions will attempt to compensate for his omission by going to the tomb to anoint Jesus' corpse when the Sabbath is over, two days after his death (16:1).

After the terse description of the preparation of the body, the tomb itself receives attention: Mark informs us that it was "hewed out of a rock" (15:46b). This was the normal form of tomb construction in early Roman Palestine; tombs were cut into the soft limestone bedrock that is so common in the area. People were usually interred in burial niches (*loculi*) that were dug horizontally into the walls of these tombs (see the NOTE on "placed him in a tomb" in 15:46). Typically these were family burial places; nearly half of the Jewish tombs excavated in Roman Palestine are single-chambered, and inscriptions usually indicate that these tombs, as well as some of the multichambered ones, were used by a single group of relations. As McCane puts it, therefore, "Jewish burial in Roman Palestine was a family affair: the deceased were customarily laid to rest with their nearest relatives" ("Jews, Christians, and Burial," 56–57). Jesus' burial in a stranger's tomb partly results from the fact that he dies far away from his ancestral home (cf. the reference to the "field for the burial of strangers" in Matt 27:7), but it also accentuates the isolation that has characterized him throughout the Markan passion narrative.

We should imagine, then, that Joseph places the body of Jesus, wrapped in its shroud, inside the burial niche, and then rolls a stone against the opening of the tomb to seal it (15:46c; see the NOTE on "he rolled a stone against the door of the tomb" in 15:46). Jesus' body is thus triply and seemingly securely enclosed by shroud, *loculus*, and stone-shut tomb, and the description of Joseph's actions has an air of finality. But the termination of the passage with the notice about the two Marys seeing where Jesus has been deposited (15:47) hints that there is something more to come and looks toward the Gospel's final passage.

In that passage, these same women will return to the tomb on Sunday morning to complete the corpse preparation that Joseph has left unfinished—but will be unable to do so. On the way, they will worry about how they will get into the sealed sepulchre—but that will not turn out to be a problem. And this will not be the last surprise that awaits them at the tomb of Jesus.

EPILOGUE (MARK 16:1–8)

◆

THE EMPTY TOMB

16 ¹And when the Sabbath had passed, Mary the Magdalene and Mary of James and Salome bought spices in order that they might come and anoint him. ²And very early in the morning, on the first day of the week, they came to the tomb after the sun had risen. ³And they said to each other, "Who will roll the stone away from the door of the tomb for us?" ⁴And looking up, they beheld that the stone had already been rolled away (for it was very large).

⁵And going into the tomb, they saw a young man sitting on the right, dressed in a white robe, and they were astounded. ⁶But he said to them, "Do not be astounded. You seek Jesus the Nazarene, the crucified one. He has been raised; he is not here. See the place where they laid him! ⁷But go, say to his disciples (and to Peter), 'He is going before you into Galilee. There you will see him, just as he said to you.' " ⁸But they went out and fled from the tomb, for trembling and astonishment had taken hold of them. And they did not say anything to anyone, for they were afraid.

NOTES

16 1. *bought spices in order that they might come and anoint him.* Gk *ēgorasan arōmata hina elthousai aleipsōsin auton.* On the use of perfumes and spices to prepare bodies for burial, see 2 Chron 16:14; *m. Šabb.* 23:5; *b. Ber.* 53a. The last passage says that the spices are used to remove bad smells; this was a service not only to the dead but also to their survivors, who would have to spend time with the corpse in the burial chamber as part of the funeral ceremony (see Dayagi-Mendeles, *Perfumes,* 125–33).

3. *Who will roll the stone away from the door of the tomb for us?* Gk *tis apokylisei hēmin ton lithon ek tēs thyras tou mnēmeiou.* On the massiveness of the sort of stone used to seal Jesus' tomb, see the NOTE on "he rolled a stone against the door of the tomb" in 15:46. As Lagrange (445) notes, the women would probably have lacked the necessary equipment (levers, etc.) for shifting it. And even if they had had the equipment and were physically capable of doing the job, moving such a heavy stone would probably not have been considered "women's work" (cf. Ilan, *Jewish Women,* 184–90, on women's work in Second Temple Judaism).

The women's utterance may be more a lament than a real question; see BDF §496 on the use of rhetorical questions to express vivid emotion, and cf. the Syriac translations, in which the note of lament is explicit (see Van Rompay, "Wings"). Interpreting the women's question in this way helps address the difficulty of why they did not think of the problem before. An analogy is provided by OT clauses beginning with *mi yitten* ("Who will give?"/ "Who would give?"), which "most often [express] the painful awareness of the absence of a person, thing, state, or event" and are equivalent to exclamatory clauses (Van Rompay, "Wings"). The *mi yitten* structure is sometimes rendered in the LXX by means of *tis* + future tense verb (see Deut 5:29; Ps 55:6 [54:7 LXX]; Jer 9:1).

Wilfand ("End," 7–8) points out that three of the four LXX usages of the verb *apokyliein* ("to roll away") occur in Gen 29:3–10 and that in both stories a stone is in place, a small group laments its inability to move it, and the stone is shifted by divine intervention.

5. *a young man.* Gk *neaniskon.* This youth is probably meant to be an angel (cf. Schenke, *Auferstehungsverkündigung,* 64). In the OT, ancient Jewish sources, and the NT, angels have the appearance of human beings and can be mistaken for them (see, e.g., Gen 18:2, 16, 22; 19:1; 2 Macc 10:29–31; 11:8–12). In Judg 13:6 an angel is called "a man of God," and in Acts 1:10–11 a pair of interpreting angels is referred to as "two men in white robes." In 2 Macc 3:26, 33 and Josephus, *Ant.* 5.277, moreover, angels are called *neaniai* ("young men"), and on icons angels characteristically have a youthful appearance (cf. Allison, *Testament of Abraham,* 95). Furthermore, our passage is formally similar to the angelophanies in Dan 10:2–14; Matt 1:18–25; *Apoc. Abr.* 10:1–17; and *2 En.* 1:3–10, which include an introductory identification of the recipients, a description of the angel appearing, a reference to the recipients' fear, a word of consolation from the angel, a word of revelation, and usually a word of command (see Davies and Allison, 2.660–61). One typical component, however, is conspicuously missing in the Markan case: the recipients' obedient response to the command.

On the theory that the young man of 16:6–7 is identical with the youth of 14:51–52, see the APPENDIX "The Youth Who Ran Away Naked [Mark 14:51–52]").

6. *the Nazarene.* Gk *ton Nazarēnon.* These words are missing from the original of Sinaiticus and from Bezae; possibly a scribe's eye skipped from this instance of *ton* ("the") to that before *estaurōmenon* ("crucified one").

He has been raised. Gk *ēgerthē,* an aorist passive indicative verb. The aorist can be used for an action that has just occurred (see Robertson, 841–43; MHT, 1.135), and the sudden switch from the perfect *estaurōmenon* ("crucified one") supports this interpretation in the present instance (see Taylor, 607). The narrative context is in favor of it as well, since the third day after Jesus' death has just dawned, and the prophecies of his resurrection (8:31; 9:31; 10:34) situated that event "after three days" (= on the third day; see the NOTE on "after three days" in 8:31). This is also the way in which the author of the Longer Ending of Mark interpreted *ēgerthē,* since 16:9 speaks of Jesus rising "early in the morning (*prōi*) on the first day of the week" (cf. the Postscript on the Markan ending).

7. *to his disciples (and to Peter).* Gk *tois mathētais autou kai tō Petrō.* On Mark's use of the particularizing *kai,* see the NOTE on "and sinners" in 2:15, and on

the double entendre here ("especially/even to Peter"), see the COMMENT on 16:5–8. Mark's phrasing partly reflects Peter's status as the first male disciple to experience a resurrection appearance (cf. Luke 24:34, which mentions an appearance to him alone). Like Mark, Paul distinguishes Peter from the group of twelve disciples in describing resurrection appearances: "He appeared to Cephas, then to the twelve" (1 Cor 15:5).

He is going before you. Gk *proagei hymas.* Cf. the NOTE on "I will go before you" in 14:28, where it is pointed out that *proagein* can mean "to lead" as well as "to go before." In 2 Macc 10:1 the same verb is used for the Lord leading Judas Maccabaeus and his followers into Jerusalem to recover the Temple from the Syrians. In our passage, by contrast, Jesus goes before/leads his disciples *out* of Jerusalem and puts them on the road toward Galilee, where their life with him will begin again (see the COMMENT on 16:5–8).

There you will see him. Gk *ekei auton opsesthe.* Lohmeyer (356; cf. *Galiläa,* 11), who is followed by Perrin ("Interpretation," 26–27) and others, argues that this is a reference to the parousia rather than resurrection appearances; cf. 14:62, where *opsesthe* (the second person plural future middle of *horan*) *is* used in a prophecy of Jesus' enemies "seeing" him at the Second Coming, and 13:26, where the third person plural of the same verb is employed in a parousia context. For Lohmeyer, the future middle form of *horan* is a technical term for beholding Jesus at the parousia (cf. John 16:16, 17, 19; 1 John 3:2; Rev 1:7; 22:4), whereas the aorist passive is a technical term for a resurrection appearance. As Seal (*Parousia,* 173–77) demonstrates, however, this analysis is simplistic; the usages of *opsesthe* in John 16:16, 17, and 19, for example, are references to postresurrectional communion with the risen Jesus, not to the parousia. Moreover, our passage speaks of Jesus being seen only by Peter and the Twelve. This is consonant with the tradition that the risen Jesus appeared first "to Cephas, then to the twelve" (1 Cor 15:5), but it differs from the sort of universal audience envisaged in parousia prophecies such as 13:26 and 14:62.

8. *trembling and astonishment had taken hold of them.* Gk *eichen gar autas tromos kai ekstasis.* On fear as a typical biblical reaction to a theophany or angelophany, see the NOTE on "a young man" in 16:5 and the COMMENT on 16:5–8. For trembling (*tromos*) and the cognate verb in particular, see Exod 15:15–16; 1 Esd 4:36; Ps 104:32 [103:32 LXX]; Dan 4:37a; 6:26 [6:27 Theod.]; 10:11; 2 Macc 15:23; 4 Macc 4:10. For astonishment (*ekstasis*) see Gen 15:12; 1 Sam 14:15; 2 Chron 14:14; 15:5; Zech 14:13. The latter word often has a negative connotation—the evil are shocked by God's punishment—but sometimes a nuance of godly fear, as in Pss 30:1 LXX and 31:22 (30:23 LXX), and Dan 7:28. In Gen 15:12, moreover, as Wilfand ("End," 17–18) points out, Abraham responds to a covenant-inaugurating theophany with *ekstasis* ("astonishment") and *phobos* ("fear"; cf. Mark 16:8), and in Dan 7:28 Daniel's visions cause *ekstasis* but are not revealed to outsiders. See also Dan 10:7 Theod., in which *ekstasis* falls on the men present at Daniel's vision, who flee in fear (*kai ephygon en phobō*).

they did not say anything to anyone. Gk *oudeni ouden eipan.* When God or an angel appears in the Bible, the recipient of the appearance sometimes becomes mute, either because of shock (e.g., Dan 10:15), as a judgment (e.g., 2 Macc 3:29), or as a prophetic sign (e.g., Ezek 3:26). Similarly, in Luke 1:20–22, Zechariah's muteness is "both a punishment for unbelief and a means of preserving the content of the revelation to Zechariah from the people at large" (Marshall, *Luke*, 61). In our passage, however, the implication does not seem to be that the women are unable to speak but that they choose not to do so (cf. Dan 7:28, on which see the previous NOTE).

For the past hundred years or so, the motif of the women's silence has frequently been interpreted as a later-first-century attempt to explain why no one had previously heard the story about the empty tomb, which according to this theory had recently been concocted, either by Mark or by a predecessor (see the history of this interpretation in Neirynck, "Tombeau," 247–51). Gundry (1013) objects that if the motif had been intended to explain the belatedness of the account, the angel would have instructed the women to tell the disciples about the empty tomb, not about their forthcoming meeting with Jesus in Galilee. This objection is not totally convincing, since the women do not relate *anything* they have experienced at the tomb, including the fact that it was empty. But Gundry is probably correct that the silence motif (which here seems to be redactional; see the introduction to the COMMENT) is not apologetic; it fits in, rather, with the messianic secret motif, which is not apologetic but kerygmatic in nature (see the APPENDIX "The Messianic Secret Motif" in vol. 1).

for they were afraid. Gk *ephobounto gar.* On the question whether a book can end with *gar* ("for"), see the Postscript on the Markan ending. The terminology is strikingly similar to that in Gen 18:15. Here one of the two "men" = angels who have suddenly appeared to Abraham prophesies that within a year his aged wife Sarah will bear a son. Sarah, listening at the tent flap, laughs in disbelief, but when God through the angel asks why, she denies that she has done so, *ephobēthē gar* ("for she was afraid"). Here, as in our pericope, there is a divine promise of life springing out of deadness, a promise that human incredulity, which is linked with fear, finds impossible to accept. Moreover, the son whose miraculous birth is promised, Isaac, is elsewhere in Mark an image for Jesus (see the NOTES on "beloved" in 1:11, "turning and looking at his disciples, rebuked Peter" in 8:33, "take up his cross" in 8:34, "He still had one, his beloved son" in 12:6, and "laid hands on him" in 14:46; and the COMMENT on 15:33–34). Note also the similarity between the anthropomorphic description of the angels as "men" and that of the angel in our passage as "a young man" (see the NOTE on "a young man" in 16:5).

COMMENT

Introduction. At the end of the previous passage, two of the three women who had seen Jesus die also observed the place where Joseph of Arimathaea interred his corpse. Now all three return to the tomb in order to complete the funeral rites that were abbreviated by the arrival of the Sabbath. But their own rites are cut off even before they can get started by the astonishing sight that greets them.

This narrative of the empty tomb is probably not a Markan invention (against Kirby, "Case"). John 20:1–13, which seems to be literarily independent of the Synoptics, tells the same basic story, and in a way that is in some respects more primitive (e.g., one woman rather than three, no angelic interpreter; cf. Brown, *Virginal Conception*, 120–21). Moreover, Mark 16:7, which is probably redactional (cf. its close parallel to the editorial 14:28 and its plethora of Markan vocabulary; see the introduction to the COMMENT on 14:26–31), interrupts the story in which it occurs, since it begins with a disjunctive *alla* ("but") and disrupts the natural progression from the women's sight of the empty tomb and reception of the announcement of Jesus' resurrection (16:5–6) to their reaction of fear and flight (16:8). Mark, then, has probably inserted this disruptive verse into an existent narrative. The list of names in 16:1 also bears witness to the pre-Markan provenance of the passage, since the redactional 15:40 appears to be an attempt to reconcile this list with the one in 15:47 (see the NOTE on "Mary the Magdalene, and Mary the mother of James the Small and of Joses, and Salome" in 15:40, and Bode, *First Easter*, 21). Besides 16:7, other redactional features in the passage may include "very early in the morning" in 16:2, which makes this into a typically Markan double time expression and uses words that are redactional elsewhere in Mark, and the last sentence in 16:8 ("And they did not say anything to anyone, for they were afraid"), which employs a characteristically Markan double negative and *gar* ("for") clause, repeats the theme of fear from 16:8a, and emphasizes the Markan secrecy motif (cf. Gnilka, 2.338–39).

The passage is divided into two main parts: the women's trip to the tomb (16:1–4) and their encounter with the young man (16:5–8). Each part consists of conversation (16:3b, 6–7) enclosed in narrative (16:1–3a + 4 and 16:5 + 8), and the second conversation implicitly answers the question posed by the first: the God who has raised Jesus from the dead has solved the women's problem by removing the stone from the mouth of the tomb.

16:1–4: the journey to the tomb. The Sabbath being over, it is time for those who care about Jesus to spring into action. The three women mentioned in 15:40, who saw Jesus die, and two of whom also witnessed his interment by Joseph of Arimathaea (15:47), buy aromatic spices when commerce resumes on Saturday night (16:1). Very early the next morning, just after sunrise, they visit the tomb (16:2). The time notice is a realistic detail—it would be best to prepare the body, which had already been lying in the ground for over a day, before the temperature rose. The soul, moreover, was thought to linger near the body for three days after death (see, e.g., *y. Moʻed Qaṭ.* 3:5 [82b]), so funeral rites would still be in order on the third day (see Kramer, *Meanings*, 20–21, 82–84). But the belated and therefore emphatic position of the genitive absolute *anateilantos tou hēliou* ("after the sun had risen") suggests that the reference to the sun is also a symbolic detail, a metaphor for Jesus' own rising. In the Markan context, the ascent of the sun at Jesus' resurrection reverses the darkness of his crucifixion (cf. 15:33).

The connection of the empty tomb narrative with the rising sun also has significant OT background; it is a sign that the sun of righteousness has begun to arise with healing in its wings (Mal 4:2). *Prōi*, early morning, is in the OT and Jewish texts the time of God's deliverance, when the forces of darkness fall back before the onslaught of "the dominion of light" (1QS 10:1); as Ps 30:5 puts it, "Weeping may linger for the night, but joy comes with the morning" (*eis to prōi*; cf. Pss 59:16; 90:14; 143:8; Gnilka, 2.341). In the LXX, *prōi* is the time when God reveals himself (see, e.g., Exod 34:2) and rescues the elect from the hands of their enemies (see, e.g., Gen 19:27–29; Judg 6:28; 1 Sam 5:4; Isa 37:36; 1 Macc 3:58). It is also the time when he delivers Daniel from the tomblike lion's den that has been sealed with a great stone and when that Jewish sage, like Jesus, is found against all odds to be alive (Dan 6:17, 19–20).

Even more relevantly, David's last words compare the Davidic monarch to the light of morning at sunrise (2 Sam 23:1–4), and in the LXX the king thanks God for having raised him up (*anestē*) to be an anointed one (*christos*) and links this "resurrection" with the sun rising in the morning (*anateilai hēlios to prōi*). Similarly, the messianic oracle in Num 24:17 speaks of a star rising (*anatelei*) out of Jacob, and Luke 1:78 picks up this language to speak of the Messiah as the "rising light (*anatolē*) from on high" (my trans.). Brown (*Birth*, 390–91), citing the use of the same word in Matt 2:2 ("his star at its *rising*"), argues that the Messiah's advent was widely associated with a rising light (cf. Rev 22:16; *T. Levi* 18:1–3; Justin, *Dialogue* 121.2)—a linkage that continued in early Christian art (see Jensen, *Understanding*, 42–44).

The three women, however, despite their devotion to Jesus, are oblivious to the messianic promise implied by the sunrise that is lighting their pathway to his tomb. They are not thinking of Jesus as the Davidic Messiah whom *God* has anointed but as a corpse that needs to be anointed *by them*—apparently unaware that a couple of days before Jesus' death, an anonymous woman had made their action redundant (cf. 14:8). They suddenly recall, however, that there is a more practical obstacle to the last service they intend to perform for Jesus: "Who will roll the stone away from the door of the tomb for us?" (16:3)—an utterance that is probably more a lament than a question (see the NOTE on "Who will roll the stone away from the door of the tomb for us?" in 16:3).

This exclamation highlights the problem the women face, and it also serves as a foil to the sight they catch in the next verse (16:4): the stone has *already* been rolled away, despite the fact that it is very large. The women's sight of the displaced stone is preceded by their looking up (*anablepsasai*), a word that echoes 6:41 and 7:34, where Jesus turned his gaze heavenward before performing a miracle; in all three cases, the word anticipates a revelation of divine power through Jesus (cf. 8:24, where it is associated with Jesus' healing of a blind man). An action of God, then, has accomplished what was beyond the women's capacity. Our passage is thus reminiscent of 4:35–41, which was structured on three instances of *megas* ("large, great"): the large storm is replaced by a great calm, and this manifestation of divine power produces a great fear in the disciples (see the introduction to the COMMENT on 4:35–41). In the present instance, too, divine power has removed an obstacle that was very large (*megas sphodra*), and this produces overwhelming fear in its human witnesses (cf. 16:5, 8).

16:5–8: the encounter with the angel. This fear begins to grip the women as they enter the burial chamber (on first-century Jerusalem tombs, see the NOTE on "placed him in a tomb" in 15:46). Here they see a young man clad in a white robe, sitting on the tomb's right-hand side (16:5), a position traditionally associated with power, victory, and auspiciousness (cf. Mark 12:36; 14:62; 1 Kgs 2:19; Xenophon, *Cyropaedia* 2.1.1; *b. Hor.* 12a; Gornatowski, *Rechts*; Grundmann, "*Dexios,*" 37–38). Although Mark does not call this youth an angel, that is probably what he understands him to be, since biblical angels have the appearance of human beings (see the NOTE on "a young man" in 16:5). That the angel is called a *young* man (*neaniskon*) is significant as well; his youthful appearance suggests the freshness and vigor of the new era that has just dawned (see Peter Chrysologus, *Sermon* 82 and cf. 2 Macc 3:26, 33). It is unclear, however, whether the women recognize him as a supernatural being; when angels are called "men" or "youths" in the Bible, that is usually because they appear human to the people who encounter them. It is possible, then, that the women's initial astonishment has to do with finding a living being in the tomb rather than with immediately recognizing him as an angel. But it seems more likely that they do perceive him as an angel, since their reaction of fear, and his reassurance, correspond to a typical pattern in biblical angelophanies (see, e.g., Judg 6:22–23; Dan 8:17; 10:7, 12; Tob 12:16–17; Luke 2:9–10; Rev 1:17).

In any event, the "youth" detects the women's shock and moves to reassure them (16:6a). But his reassurance only increases their amazement, because he goes on to inform them that the one whom they seek is not where they had left him two days ago (16:6b); instead of his body, they are greeted by an empty space, at which they are invited to gaze (16:6c). Here absence suggests presence, or rather divine action; the reason for the emptiness of the tomb, and for the futility of the women's quest, is that Jesus of Nazareth, the crucified one, has been raised from the realm of the dead (see the NOTE on "He has been raised" in 16:6). The phrases "the Nazarene" and "the crucified one" are formal sounding and superfluous in the context, which suggests that the Markan angel is reproducing a primitive Christian confession along the lines of "Jesus the Nazarene, the crucified one, has been raised" (cf. Acts 2:22–24; 3:15; 4:10; 5:30; 10:39–40; Rom 4:25; 1 Cor 15:3–4; Lohmeyer, 354; Taylor, 607; Allison, *Resurrecting Jesus*, 230–31). The Markan version of this confession uses the theologically weighty perfect passive participle for Jesus' crucifixion (*estaurōmenon*), as does Paul in 1 Cor 1:23; 2:2; Gal 3:1 (cf. Gal 6:14); Jesus remains the Crucified One even after his resurrection (cf. Lagrange, 416). But he also remains the man from Nazareth (cf. Gnilka, 2.342), and so the combination *ton Nazarēnon ton estaurōmenon* reveals both similarity to and difference from Paul; like Paul, Mark concentrates on the continuing significance of Jesus' death, but unlike Paul, he also writes a Gospel that provides an extended introduction to the Nazarene's passion (cf. Kähler, *So-Called*, 80 n. 11).

The women, however, are not to remain fixated on the empty space where Jesus' body had been; instead (*alla* = "but") the angel commands them to leave the tomb to go out and proclaim the resurrection message to his disciples (16:7a). This, again, is typical of angelophanies, whose purpose is often to deliver a divine commission (see, e.g., Judg 6:25–26; 13:13–14; Tob 12:20; Rev 1:19; Moore, *Tobit*, 272). In this particular commission, the sly addition of "and to Peter" is probably a double entendre. On the one hand, the women are to announce the news *especially* to Peter, the first disciple to be called (1:16–18), the first to recognize Jesus' messiahship (cf. 8:29), and the one who, in the near future, will be granted the first resurrection appearance (cf. "there you will see him" in 16:7c and 1 Cor 15:5). On the other hand, however, they are to proclaim the message *even* to Peter—the disciple who followed his confession of Jesus' messiahship with an outburst that earned him the epithet "Satan" (8:33), and his protestation of eternal faithfulness (14:29–31) with three denials of knowing Jesus (14:66–72). But it is precisely to this wayward disciple, who recognized neither the necessity of Jesus' suffering nor the human sinfulness—including his own—that makes it imperative, that the hand of reconciliation from beyond the grave is outstretched.

The angel's message is that Jesus is going before the disciples into Galilee, where they will see him as he had promised (16:7bc). This announcement evokes several earlier Markan passages. Most obviously, it recalls 14:27–28, where Jesus foretold his death ("I will strike the shepherd"), the dispersion of his followers ("and the sheep will be scattered"), his resurrection ("But after I have been raised up"), and his postresurrectional victory march into his homeland ("I will go before you into Galilee"). The earlier prophecy, however, did not speak explicitly of the disciples *seeing* Jesus in Galilee. But our passage is also resonant of the Galilean walking-on-water scene in 6:45–52, which itself had a resurrectional atmosphere and took place near dawn, and in which Jesus appeared intent on going before the disciples to the opposite shore (see the COMMENT on 6:48–50). There the disciples did see Jesus—and were shocked at the sight. The present reference to seeing Jesus in Galilee, however, gives a positive resonance to the region, which was especially associated with the beginning of Jesus' ministry (see the NOTE on "Galilee" in 1:14), now about to begin anew.

Jesus, then, is on the move again, having overcome the immobility of his fixation to the cross (see the COMMENT on 15:29–32); he is now headed toward the place where the Christian mission will resume. As Catchpole ("Silence," 5) points out, this notion of a heavenly being in motion corresponds to a biblical prototype (see, e.g., Gen 18:1–16a; 24:7; Exod 23:20; 33:2; Tob 5:10; Mark 6:45–52; Luke 24:13–35). In Gen 24:7 and Exod 23:20, moreover, the "going before" of the heavenly being guarantees the success of a project that otherwise would be hopeless. In NT theology, similarly, the active power behind Christian mission is the movement of Jesus himself (cf. Phil 1:12 and Martyn, *Galatians*, 210). The first requirement for being incorporated into this divine victory march is an encounter with the risen Lord, and this is what the angel promises to the disciples through the message he entrusts to the women in 16:7c.

But they do not deliver it; instead they flee from the tomb in terror and say nothing to anyone (16:8). As in 5:14–15, then, human beings fear and flee rather than thanking God for the miracle he has performed (cf. the COMMENT on 5:14–17). In our passage fear is mentioned twice in the concluding verse; it is both the reason for the women's flight and the motivation for their silence. The flight is easy to understand; the women have just encountered an angel, and they have seen a rolled-away rock and an empty tomb where they expected a sealed and full one. The sheer unexpectedness of these events and the impression of supernatural power at work help explain their trembling and astonishment. Their silence is more difficult to explain, though it seems to be ironically related to that which Jesus enjoined earlier in the Gospel, when the time for revelation had not yet arrived. Then, people disobeyed the command to silence and told the news (1:44–45; 7:36); now, when the time for secrecy is over (cf. 9:9), the angel calls for open proclamation—but the women run away and tell their news to no one (cf. Lincoln, "Promise," 290–91). Apparently, "the mystery of the dominion of God" (cf. 4:11–12), according to which the new age has arrived without obliterating all traces of old-age fear, misunderstanding, and opposition to the divine will, continues after the resurrection, and this paradox affects not only the outside world but also the followers of Jesus (cf. Marcus, "Epistemology," 574).

But what exactly is the fear that is spoken of in the final clause ("for they were afraid"), and how does it explain the women's silence? As we have previously observed, fear is a typical reaction to a theophany or angelophany, and muteness can result from such encounters as well. But, as pointed out in the NOTE on "they did not say anything to anyone" in 16:8, the muteness of the women in our story seems to arise not from inability to speak but from unwillingness to do so. Since there is no clear narrative reason for this silence, since the sentence in which it occurs seems to be redactional, and since the women's secrecy concerns the resurrection kerygma, which Mark believes must now be proclaimed to the whole world (13:10), perhaps the explanation for the motif is to be sought on the level of the Markan community, where fear of persecution is creating a temptation to squelch the gospel message (cf. 13:9, 11–13). The import of 16:7–8, then, may be similar to that of the Q passage in Matt 10:26–33//Luke 12:2–9, which combines a call to open confession of Jesus with an exhortation not to fear those who will persecute the confessors to death.

Unlike the Q passage, however, ours ends not on a note of bold proclamation but on one of fearful silence and flight, which shows that the women are not essentially different from the male disciples to whom the angel has attempted to dispatch them (cf. Malbon, "Fallible Followers"). Could this reaction of theirs be the intended ending of Mark's Gospel? Or has the original ending been lost? We will explore this question in the Postscript that follows.

POSTSCRIPT: THE MARKAN ENDING

◆

SECONDARY ENDINGS

The greatest puzzle of Mark's enigmatic Gospel comes at its conclusion: how did the story originally terminate? Most scholars agree that 16:9–20 is non-Markan and subscribe to one of three theories: that the original ending has been lost, that Mark was somehow prevented from finishing his Gospel, or that he intended for it to end with the women running away from the tomb on Easter morning, saying nothing to anyone, "for they were afraid" (16:8).

This may come as a surprise to readers who are used to printed editions in which 16:8 is followed by a series of resurrection appearance stories (16:9–20, the so-called Longer Ending):

16 [9]But having risen early in the morning on the first day of the week, he first appeared to Mary the Magdalene, from whom he had cast out seven demons. [10]She went and announced it to those who had been with him, as they were mourning and weeping. [11]But they, when they heard that he was alive and had been seen by her, did not believe. [12]But after these things he was manifested in another form to two of them as they were walking, traveling into the country. [13]And they went away and announced it to the others. But they did not believe them either.

[14]But later, as they were reclining at table, he was manifested to them, the Eleven, and he rebuked their unbelief and hardness of heart, because they had not believed those who had seen him after he had been raised. [15]And he said to them, "Go into the whole world and proclaim the good news to every creature. [16]The one who has believed and has been baptized will be saved, but the one who has not believed will be condemned. [17]And these signs will follow those who have believed: in my name they will cast out demons; they will speak with new tongues; [18]they will lift up snakes; even if they drink any poison it will never hurt them; they will lay hands upon the sick, and they will recover."

[19]But the Lord Jesus, after he had spoken to them, was taken up into heaven and sat down at the right hand of God. [20]But they, going out, proclaimed the news everywhere, the Lord working with them and confirming the word through the signs that followed.

These verses are found in the overwhelming majority of manuscripts and in all major manuscript families and are attested already by Irenaeus (*Against Heresies* 3.10.5) in 185 C.E. and perhaps, even earlier, by Justin (*1 Apology* 45, around 155 C.E.). But they were almost certainly not penned by Mark, nor were they the original ending of the Gospel. Matthew and Luke follow Mark's narrative closely up to 16:8, whereas beyond it they diverge radically, suggesting that their version of Mark did not contain anything subsequent to 16:8 (see Lane, 601). Verses 9–20, moreover, do not exist in our earliest and best Greek manuscripts, Sinaiticus and Vaticanus, both of which terminate at 16:8, as do the Sinaitic Syriac, about a hundred Armenian manuscripts, the two oldest Georgian manuscripts (from 897 and 913 C.E.), and all but one manuscript of the Sahidic Coptic (Metzger, 122–23; cf. Birdsall, "Review," 154). When verses 9–20 *do* appear, moreover, they are often separated from 16:8 by scribal signs (asterisks or obeli) or by notations that state or suggest that what follows is not found in some witnesses (see Aland, "Markusschluss," 442–46). Several church fathers corroborate the secondary nature of the Longer Ending; Eusebius, for example, asserts in *To Marinus* that "the accurate ones of the copies" of Mark end with the women running away from the tomb, and this testimony is seconded by Jerome (*Letter* 120.3), Hesychius of Jerusalem (*Collection of Difficulties and Solutions* [PG 93.1440]), and Severus of Antioch (*Homily* 77; cf. Kelhoffer, "Witness," 83–91). In a catena attributed to Victor of Antioch (ca. 500), who takes the other side, the author admits that even in his day most copies of Mark lack the Longer Ending (see Kelhoffer, "Witness," 104).

In some manuscripts, moreover, the Longer Ending does not follow 16:8 immediately but is preceded by the so-called Shorter Ending:

> And all the things that they had been commanded they promptly announced to those around Peter. And after these things Jesus himself also sent out through them, from east to west, the sacred and imperishable announcement of eternal salvation.

The Shorter Ending, however, is itself demonstrably late. It occurs on its own in one Old Latin manuscript (k), but neither in this form, nor in combination with the Longer Ending, does it have any support from the church fathers. Its vocabulary is non-Markan; eight of the twelve words that are not prepositions, articles, or names are Markan *hapax legomena* (see the GLOSSARY), and half of them are paralleled within the NT predominantly or exclusively in the epistolary literature. The phrase "those around Peter" in the first sentence seems to be a deliberate attempt to assert Peter's primacy and thus to counteract both the negative implication of Mark 16:7 and later pagan criticism of Peter (see Kannaday, *Apologetic Discourse*, 192–93). The concluding sentence, moreover, with its abstract, enthusiastic, and Hellenistically flavored language ("the sacred and imperishable announcement of eternal salvation") breathes an atmosphere very different from the rest of Mark (see Westcott and Hort, *Introduction* 2.38, 44). But manuscripts that have this late ending *before* the Longer Ending are evidence that the latter is not an original part of Mark; if it had been, the Shorter Ending would have appeared after the Longer Ending, where it belongs contextually (cf. Aland, "Markusschluss," 447–48).

Transcriptional probabilities and vocabulary and stylistic considerations also argue against the Longer Ending. There would be every reason in the world for later scribes to create such a list of resurrection appearances and such a description of the rehabilitation and recommissioning of the Eleven, whereas there would be little motive for deleting it; if scribes objected to the clauses about snake handling and poison drinking, as Farmer suggests (*Verses*, 65–72), they could have eliminated 16:18ab rather than taking the drastic step of excising the whole passage. The Longer Ending, moreover, is full of Markan *hapax legomena* (e.g., *poreuesthai* = "go, walk" in 16:10, 12, 15; *theasthai* = "see" in 16:11; *heterea* = "another" in 16:12; *hysteron* = "later" in 16:14) and other usages that depart from normal Markan style (see Elliott, "Text," and Thomas, "Reconsideration," 410–12). And the transition between 16:8 and 16:9 is rough; the subject in the former is the women, whereas the implied subject in the latter is Jesus. Given the change of scene and of subject, one would expect an iteration of his name (see Metzger, 125).

Overall, 16:9–20 gives the impression of being a compressed digest of resurrection appearances narrated in other Gospels (John 20:14–18; Luke 24:13–43; John 20:27–29; Matt 28:18–20; Luke 24:50–51; Acts 1:9–11). Theoretically, to be sure, the resurrection narratives in the other Gospels could be *expansions* of the notices in Mark 16:9–20. But Mark is generally more detailed than Matthew and Luke in the passages that all three share. By contrast, the narratives in 16:9–20 are sketchy, and at least one of them, the story of the appearance to two travelers "in another form" (Mark 16:12–13), is so compressed that it would not make sense to readers who did not know Luke's Emmaus story (Luke 24:13–35; cf. Kelhoffer, *Miracle*, 87–89).

Before leaving the subject of the Longer Ending, it should be noted that Washingtoniensis, a fourth—to fifth-century manuscript housed in the Freer Gallery of Art in Washington, D.C., includes in its version of the Longer Ending an interesting saying between 16:14 and 16:15. This "Freer Logion" runs as follows:

> And they [the Eleven] were excusing themselves, saying, "This age of lawlessness and disbelief is under Satan, who does not allow the unclean things under the spirits [= those under the unclean spirits?] to grasp the truth of God [and his] power. Therefore, reveal your righteousness, already!" they said to Christ. And Christ foretold to them, "The limit of the years of the rule of Satan has been fulfilled, but other terrible things are drawing near. And on behalf of those people who had sinned I was handed over to death, in order that they might turn to the truth and no longer sin, in order that they might inherit the spiritual and imperishable glory of righteousness in heaven."

This saying is stylistically and thematically different from the rest of the Longer Ending, and it is very unlikely that it formed an original part of that passage. But it is interesting both for its apocalyptic urgency and for the way in which it portrays the disciples citing Satanic oppression as an excuse for their faithlessness in abandoning Jesus (see Gregory, *Freer-Logion*). Although Mark would probably be unhappy with the whiny tone the disciples adopt here, he would agree both with the apocalyptic tenor of the passage and with the view that the apostolic abandonment of Jesus reflected demonic influence (see 8:33 and the COMMENT on 14:37–42).

But is 16:8 the end? But if the Longer Ending, with its list of resurrection appearances and its commissioning narrative, is secondary, did Mark originally end with 16:8? Many exegetes, convinced that the Gospel could not have terminated with the women running away and remaining silent, have hypothesized either that Mark was prevented from finishing his narrative by illness, arrest, or some other mishap, or that an original ending describing the resurrection appearance prophesied in 14:28 and 16:7 has been lost. One difficulty with both theories is that 16:8 seems to be the termination of the pericope that began in 16:1, where the women travel to the tomb to anoint Jesus' corpse; now, in a symmetrical conclusion, they flee from the tomb after hearing the message of his resurrection. It seems a bit too convenient that Mark should have been arrested or have gotten ill immediately after finishing a passage, or that a page should have ended or have been torn off precisely at this point of closure (though see below for later manuscripts in which this apparently happened). With regard to the arrest/illness hypothesis, moreover, one may wonder why, if Mark was suddenly removed from the scene, a member of his community did not complete the Gospel for him.

The lost ending hypothesis has more to be said for it. Bultmann (*John*, 705 n. 5) and Smith (*John*, 390) have even suggested that the missing appearance story may now be found in the secondary ending of John (21:1–14); Smith points out that while nothing in John prepares for this narrative, it answers to the expectation created by Mark 16:7 for an appearance in Galilee in which the disciples—and especially Peter—will be restored to Jesus' favor. The style of John 21:1–14, however, is basically Johannine. The characteristic Markan parataxis is not employed, and there are only a few terms that are atypical of John but common in Mark (*syn* = "with," *ischyein* = "to be able," and partitive *apo* = "from"; cf. Brown, 2.1079–80). If there is a Markan source here, it has been thoroughly worked over by the Johannine redactor. But whether or not one believes that John 21 contains the rudiments of the missing Markan narrative, it is not *prima facie* improbable that the ending of Mark was lost. The list of *Codices graeci et latini in hac editione adhibit* in the Nestle-Aland edition of the NT text confirms that ancient codices frequently lack their beginnings and/or endings. Apropos of Mark in particular, Croy (143) points out that two ancient manuscripts, 2386 and Rom. Vat. Arab. 13, break off precisely at Mark 16:8 because the following leaves are missing.

Bart Ehrman has remarked to me, however, that textual mutilation generally results from decades or even centuries of wear and tear, whereas in the present case we would have to posit a loss that occurred within a decade or so of composition, before Matthew and Luke had gotten their hands on Mark's work. Croy, to be sure, cites an example that, in his view, goes some way toward meeting this sort of objection (140–41): a papyrus discovered in the twentieth century (P.Oxy. 412) that has on one side the conclusion of the eighteenth book of Julius Africanus' *Kestoi* ("Embroiderings"), which was probably written around 230 C.E., and on the other a document dated to the reign of the emperor Claudius Tacitus (275–76; cf. Vieillefond, *Cestes*, 277–83). Bauer (*Orthodoxy*, 159) concludes from this document that "it was possible for a manuscript to be separated into its component parts within a generation of its original production" (cf. Grenfell and Hunt, *Oxy-*

rhynchus Papyri, 3.36–37). It is debatable, however, that an account of Jesus' life would have been treated in as cavalier a manner as the eccentric, miscellaneous text of Julius Africanus.

The mutilation thesis, then, combines two improbabilities—extremely rapid deterioration or dismemberment and mutilation precisely at the end of a pericope. Against these must be weighed the alleged improbability of an intended ending at 16:8. Croy points out that before the 1960s the "jarring lack of closure" of a termination at 16:8 induced most scholars to conclude that Mark's ending had been lost. He attributes the subsequent shift in the consensus not to scientific factors but to changes in literary fashion such as the rise of the "New Criticism," with its emphasis on a fixed text, and the "gloomy and jaded mood of the post-depression and post-World War II era." The latter produced an antipathy to classical ideas of closure and happy endings, which is visible, for example, in the popularity of film noir, of the plays of Samuel Beckett—and of 16:8 as the intended ending of Mark (*Mutilation*, 33–44). For Croy, however, the weirdness of an ending at 16:8 is too pronounced for such a conclusion to be plausible in an ancient text; he cites, among other features, the stylistic eccentricity of terminating a book with *gar* ("for"); the thematic peculiarity of concluding a proclamation of good news with flight, fear, and silence; and the logical contradiction between such an ending and the text's implication that the disciples *did* see Jesus in Galilee (14:28; 16:7). By contrast, "if Mark's narrative continued in a now lost ending, the continuation could easily have made plain that the silence was not permanent" (*Mutilation*, 45–71, here 57).

The question of the Markan ending will probably never be decided with certainty, and Croy has done as good a job as possible of arguing the case against termination at 16:8. But many of his points are open to challenge. As he himself recognizes, the fact that *gar* is the last word in 16:8 does not conclusively refute the thesis that this is the intended end of the Gospel. Many Greek sentences terminate with *gar* (for an important biblical example, see the NOTE on "for they were afraid" in 16:8), and there are other instances in which it concludes a chapter (e.g., Musonius Rufus, *Essay* 12.48; Lucian, *Dialogue of the Courtesans* 6.4) or even a book in its present form (Plotinus, *Ennead* 5.5; see van der Horst, "Can"; Croy, *Mutilation*, 47–50, 180–85; Denyer, "Mark 16:8"). As Denyer points out, moreover, the twenty-five-hundred-word speech of Protagoras in the Platonic dialogue of the same name ends with a two-word sentence, the second word of which is *gar* (Plato, *Protagoras* 328D). Plato's Socrates records his reaction to this abrupt ending as one of entrancement; after the long, "virtuoso performance" of the speech, "I still kept on looking at [Protagoras], expecting that he would say something, and yearning to hear it." According to Denyer, it is possible that Mark chose a similar means for "leaving the reader in what is, after all, a proper frame of mind for someone who has just read a Gospel: thinking that the story of the risen Christ cannot be over yet, and yearning to hear more."

An ending with *gar*, therefore, would be unusual, but not impossible. And Croy does not take seriously enough the point that in many ways Mark's text *is* unusual, so that an idiosyncratic, open ending it not anomalous. This evangelist can paint a picture of naked flight so weird that Matthew and Luke choose to omit it (14:51–52) and can express the moral of another narrative with an editorial comment that has mystified commentators to the present day (6:52). He can portray Jesus getting angry at a man who asks to be cured, and throwing him out after he has healed him (1:41–43); refusing initially to perform, or being initially unsuccessful with, other healings (6:5; 7:27; 8:23–24); speaking to the crowds in parables, not in order to instruct them, but in order to addle their wits (4:10–12); rebuking his disciples for their failure to grasp opaque numerical symbolism (8:17–21); cursing a tree because he does not find the expected fruit on it (11:12–14); and frequently being secretive, even in the absence of a clear motivation or hope for success in doing so (1:44; 3:12; 5:43; etc.). If Mark can create such cryptic and even shocking scenes, can we be sure that he did not choose to end his work in an abrupt but suggestive manner, with a story that alludes to resurrection appearances without describing them, and ends in *gar*?

A Markan ending at 16:8, moreover, would correspond to characteristic Markan concerns about faith, fear, and silence (cf. the COMMENT on 16:5–8). Fear, and specifically anxiety about the persecution that may result from proclamation of the Christian message, seem to be a concern for the Markan community (see 13:9–13), whose emotional state is probably mirrored by the picture in 4:35–41 of storm-tossed disciples, surrounded by darkness and rising waves, and afraid that they are about to perish (see the COMMENT on 4:37–39). An ending at 16:7–8, which prescinds from describing resurrection appearances, simultaneously reflects this fear, affirms Jesus' resurrection, and leaves room for doubt, thereby corresponding to the situation of a Christian community that believes in the Easter kerygma but has not seen the risen Jesus with its own eyes (cf. John 20:29). In such a context, the fleeing women provide an image of what not to do, as they run away in fear and squelch the marvelous tidings of resurrection. But they also suggest the possibility of an opposite reaction: to stop in one's tracks, face down one's terror, and proclaim the good news whatever the cost. The women may thus mirror the situation of some in the Markan community, who find themselves poised between fear and faith, tempted to flee to the safety of the world yet haunted by the message of the resurrection (cf. Boomershine, "Mark 16:8," 238).

Markan composition of such an open ending is more plausible if other premodern narratives end in a comparable manner, as Magness has argued that they do (*Sense*, 25–85). The biblical parallels are particularly impressive; several OT and NT narratives have suspended endings, and some of them conclude by alluding to but not describing important events that occur after the end of the narrative but, from the later perspective of their authors and original readers, have already taken place. The Deuteronomic history stretching from Deuteronomy to 2 Kings, for example, does not terminate on the triumphant note of the Jews coming back from their Babylonian captivity, although the author and his readers probably know about this momentous event, but with a description of the Babylonian monarch freeing the Judahite king from prison and seating him in his court (2 Kgs 25:27–30)—a conclusion that foreshadows Israel's return from Babylon without narrating it. In the NT, similarly, the author of Acts does not describe Paul's execution in Rome under Nero, although Paul himself delivers a veiled prophecy of this event to the elders of Ephesus in 20:17–38. Instead Luke ends his two-volume work with Paul living in Rome under house arrest "for two whole years at his own expense, welcom[ing] all who came to him, and preaching the dominion of God and teaching about the Lord Jesus Christ quite openly and unhindered" (my trans.). Luke does not say what happened at the end of those "two whole years," but his readers would know that Paul's open preaching led to his martyrdom; the ending, then, alludes to his execution without describing it.

The most suggestive biblical parallel of all is the conclusion of the OT book of Jonah. Even Croy (*Mutilation*, 95–96) admits that this termination is abrupt and puzzling. Jonah, having initially rejected God's commission to preach repentance to Israel's ancient enemy, Nineveh, himself repents in the belly of the sea creature, is given a second chance, fulfills his commission—and then becomes so enraged when God fails to destroy the penitent city that he asks to die. God responds, in the book's concluding words, by alluding to the *qîqâyôn* (= castor oil?) plant that he had sent to protect Jonah from the sun:

> You pity the plant, for which you did not labor, nor did you make it grow, which came into being in a night, and perished in a night. And should not I pity Nineveh, that great city, in which there are more than a hundred and twenty thousand persons who do not know their right hand from their left, and also much cattle? (4:10–11, RSV)

What sort of ending is "also much cattle"? Is it any more conclusive than Mark's "for they were afraid"? Not surprisingly, many ancient and medieval readers seem to have been perturbed by Jonah's abrupt conclusion and therefore devised more satisfactory, "closed" endings, as Matthew and Luke did for Mark. Josephus (*Ant.* 9.214), for example, omits the whole *qîqâyôn* episode and instead records that Jonah prophesied the end of the Assyrian empire and then went home (cf. Knox, "Ending," 22). *Yalquṭ Shimoni* has Jonah respond to God's question by falling on his face and begging him to direct the world according to the attribute of mercy. As Sasson (*Jonah*, 320 n. 24) notes, these and similar retellings (e.g., 3 Macc 6:8; *Liv. Pro.* 10:1–11) "tak[e] the story a few . . . steps beyond the account in Scripture" and thus reveal dissatisfaction with the latter.

These correctives are understandable, since the original ending of Jonah does not tie up all the loose ends, although it does point to the major theme of the book, God's graciousness to undeserving and ignorant humanity (and even dumb animals). But it leaves unanswered the question whether Jonah eventually came to realize that God had the right to pardon whom he would, including Israel's enemies, or whether he remained resistant to the extremity of the divine gracious-ness. Ancient readers who assumed that the biblical book came from Jonah him-self would probably conclude that in the end the Israelite prophet had been won to the side of divine grace, but the author does not say so. A Markan ending at 16:8, similarly, leaves open the question whether the women eventually overcame their fear and told the disciples about the meeting in Galilee, to which they then went and were restored to fellowship with Jesus. The mere existence of the narrative suggests a positive answer. But both the OT and the NT writer prescind from portraying the conversion of their deeply flawed characters—perhaps partly because these authors want to put the emphasis on divine compassion rather than the human ability to change (cf. Craig, *Poetics*, 164–65).

Croy (95–96) disputes the relevance of the Jonah parallel, arguing that the ending of Jonah does not "subvert the book's trajectory and constitute an anticlimax as Mark 16:8 does," and quoting W. Knox's conclusion ("Ending," 22) that Jonah is no precedent for a Markan ending at 16:8, since Jonah's author had completed his story whereas Mark 16:8 stops just before his narrative's climax. But this begs the crucial question: would a termination at 16:8 really be anticlimactic? Wellhausen (137) did not think so, famously suggesting that the present ending "lacks nothing; it would be a shame if anything else came afterwards." In support of this view, the theological fulcrum of Mark's Gospel, the point of lasting significance, is not so much Jesus' resurrection as his suffering and death—a thesis borne out both by the greater concentration on the negative elements in the passion-and-resurrection predictions (8:31; 9:31; 10:33–34) and by the use of the perfect tense for crucifixion, versus the aorist for resurrection, in 16:6 (see the COMMENT on 16:5–8). This does not mean that the resurrection is unimportant to Mark (cf. 9:9); the main point of 16:1–8 is that Jesus has been raised from the dead, an event that explains his body's absence from the tomb. But a detailed account of resurrection appearances is not a *sine qua non* for establishing the reality of the resurrection. None of the passion predictions ends with a reference to such appearances, just with an allusion to the fact of Jesus' resurrection—which is established in Mark's narrative by the empty tomb story. An ending at 16:8, therefore, makes sense, because the decisive events in the history of salvation have occurred, and the prophesied appearances will only confirm what the angel has already proclaimed, that Jesus has been raised and yet remains the Crucified One.

Despite the lack of resurrection appearance narratives, these appearances are evoked by the allusion in 16:7 ("There you will see him"). Indeed, allusion can be a more powerful mode of reference than outright description since, as Booth says, it "creates a sense of collusion against all those, whether in the story or out of it, who do not get the point" (*Rhetoric*, 304; cf. Allison, *Jesus Tradition*, 117–19). The way in which such collusion works may be seen by imagining a film about the life of John F. Kennedy that concludes with footage of the fateful visit to Dallas on November 22, 1963. The motorcade threads its way through the streets of downtown Dallas; President and Mrs. Kennedy sit in an open convertible, waving happily to the crowds in the bright sunshine—and there the movie ends. There is no depiction of the gunshots ringing out, of the President slumping forward, of the limousine suddenly picking up speed, of the First Lady cradling the President's head in her lap. But these events are all the more powerfully evoked by not being portrayed, because *everyone knows what will happen next.*

It may be that Mark's ending is meant to function in a similar way. Everyone in the Markan audience knew that the reunion in Galilee prophesied in 14:28 and 16:7 had actually taken place. Stories of resurrection appearances were in common circulation at least by the time Paul wrote 1 Corinthians 15 in the fifties and were surely well known when Mark wrote his Gospel in the late sixties or early seventies. Mark's hearers would have understood that the appearance to Peter and other members of the Twelve had turned them from pusillanimous renegades to courageous proclaimers of the gospel; by the time Mark was written, at least two of the Twelve, including Peter himself, had died martyrs' deaths (on Peter's death under Nero, see Tertullian, *Scorpiace* 15, Eusebius, *Ecclesiastical* History 2.25.5–6; cf. 1 Clem 5:4; Kirsch, "Peter"; on the martyrdoms of James and perhaps John, see the NOTE on "James the son of Zebedee and his brother John" in 1:19 and the COMMENT on 10:35–40). The audience would have recognized that human disobedience and fear had not been allowed to have the last word in the matter of Jesus' relation to his disciples.

Still, we cannot be dogmatic: there is not enough evidence to say definitively whether Mark intended his work to end at 16:8. But that is where it concludes in our earliest and best manuscripts, and so it behooves us, as even Croy (169–70) acknowledges, to try to make sense of that ending as it stands. Again, a cinematic analogy may be helpful. If a film were to be made of Mark's Gospel, the camera, at the end, would record the women running away from the door of the tomb in panic. It would then, however, remain fixed on that dark aperture for a long time before the fadeout. The women run away, disappear from the screen, and the sound of their rapid footfalls and terrified cries gradually fades away; but viewers are left confronting the awful mystery of the gaping tomb. Its open door confronts them, not with "evidence that demands a verdict" (cf. McDowell, *Evidence*), but with questions. What does it all mean? Why was all this suffering necessary? Does Jesus' empty tomb point toward a triumph over death, even while it acknowledges death's terrible reality? Does Jesus' absence from the sepulchre mean that he is present somewhere else, perhaps wherever his story is retold and heard with faith?

Since Mark does not wrap up all the loose ends, we have no alternative but to return to the inception of his narrative, "the beginning of the good news of Jesus Christ" (1:1), and to start to read it again as *our* story (cf. Bartlett, *Fact and Faith*, 104). Mark's Gospel is just the *beginning* of the good news, because Jesus' story has become ours, and we take it up where Mark leaves off.

APPENDICES

◆

THE JEWISH LEADERS IN MARK

◆

There are four major groups of Jewish leaders in Mark: the scribes, the Pharisees, the chief priests, and the elders. For a fifth group, the Herodians, see the NOTES on "the Herodians" in 3:6 and 12:13. For charts on the occurrences of these terms, see figure 51.

In the first half of the Gospel, Jesus' main human opponents are the scribes and the Pharisees, who sometimes act in concert with each other. As described in the APPENDIX "The Scribes and the Pharisees" in vol. 1, the **scribes** were professional interpreters of the Law, probably from the ranks of the priests and Levites. The **Pharisees** were also famous for biblical interpretation, but they were a sect rather than a profession. Besides exegesis, they were also renowned for their stress on such matters as ritual purity and Sabbath observance, and this emphasis partly explains the conflicts with Jesus that the Gospels report.

In the second half of Mark's Gospel, however, a striking change occurs: the Pharisees, featured so prominently in the first half (ten usages between 2:16 and 8:15), fade from view, showing up only twice, and not appearing at all after 12:13. This is at first surprising, because other sources speak of Pharisaic activity in Jerusalem; Josephus, for example, describes their intrigues during the reign of John Hyrcanus, Alexandra Salome, and Herod the Great, and they are also prominent in the Jerusalem portion of Acts. But they do not seem to have played a crucial role in the Sanhedrin, which before 70 C.E. was dominated by their opponents, the Sadducees (see the APPENDIX "The Sadducees" and Sanders, *Judaism*, 458–90). Since most of the references to Jewish leaders in the second half of the Gospel have to do with the Sanhedrin's plot against Jesus' life, the fading away of the Pharisees from the narrative makes sense (cf. Brown, *Death*, 2.1432).

The disappearance of the Pharisees is balanced by the arrival on the scene of the chief priests and the elders. Neither of the latter two groups is mentioned before the first passion prediction in 8:31 ("elders" in 7:3, 5 has a different meaning, namely, the ancients from whom the Pharisees supposedly received their tradition); from then on, "chief priests" are named fourteen times and "elders" five. The only oppositional group that is prominent in both halves of the Gospel is the scribes, who appear fairly frequently (six times) in the first half, where they are conjoined with the Pharisees half of the time (2:16; 7:1, 5), and who in the second half appear very frequently (fifteen times), and are linked with the chief priests and the elders a third of the time (see again figure 51).

Figure 51: Jesus' Collective Human Opponents in Mark

1:22 Jesus teaches as one who has authority, and not as the *scribes*
2:6 *scribes* think Jesus is blaspheming
2:16 *scribes* of the *Pharisees* object to Jesus eating with tax collectors and sinners
2:18 disciples of John and of the *Pharisees* fast
2:24 *Pharisees* object to Jesus' disciples plucking grain on Sabbath
3:6 *Pharisees* go out with *Herodians* and conspire to kill Jesus
3:22 *scribes* who come down from Jerusalem say Jesus has Beelzebul
7:1 *Pharisees* and some of the *scribes* from Jerusalem gather together
7:3 *Pharisees* and all Jews wash before eating, according to tradition (of *elders*)
7:5 *Pharisees* and *scribes* ask Jesus why his disciples don't follow tradition (of *elders*)
8:11 *Pharisees* seek a heavenly sign from Jesus
8:15 "Beware of the leaven of the *Pharisees* and of Herod"
8:31 "Son of Man will be rejected by *elders* and *chief priests* and *scribes*"
9:11 "Why do *scribes* say that Elijah must come first?"
9:14 *scribes* argue with Jesus' disciples
10:2 *Pharisees* ask if it's permissible for a man to divorce his wife
10:33 "Son of Man will be turned over to *chief priests* and *scribes*"
11:18 *chief priests* and *scribes* hear Jesus justify Temple cleansing and seek to kill him
11:27 *chief priests* and *scribes* and *elders* question Jesus' authority
12:13 "they" send some *Pharisees* and *Herodians* to trap Jesus verbally
12:28 one of the *scribes* asks Jesus about the greatest commandment
12:32 this *scribe* approves of Jesus' answer
12:35 "How do the *scribes* say that the Christ is the Son of David?"
12:38 "Watch out for *scribes* who go around in long robes . . ."
14:1 *chief priests* and *scribes* seek to kill Jesus
14:10 Judas goes to *chief priests* to arrange Jesus' betrayal
14:43 Jesus confronts Judas and an armed crowd from *chief priests* and *scribes* and *elders*
14:53 *chief priests* and *elders* and *scribes* congregate with high priest to try Jesus
14:55 *chief priests* and whole Sanhedrin seek testimony against Jesus
15:1 *chief priests*, after counsel with *elders* and *scribes* and whole Sanhedrin, deliver Jesus to Pilate
15:3 *chief priests* denounce Jesus to Pilate
15:10 Pilate knows that *chief priests* have delivered Jesus out of envy
15:11 *chief priests* stir up crowd to ask that Barabbas, not Jesus, be spared
15:31 *chief priests* with *scribes* mock Jesus

Figure 51: Jesus' Collective Human Opponents in Mark (continued)

	Scribes	Pharisees	Herodians	Elders	Chief Priests
1:22	•				
2:6	•				
2:16	•	•			
2:18		•			
2:24		•			
3:6		•	•		
3:22	•				
7:1	•	•			
7:3		•		(•)	
7:5	•	•		(•)	
8:11		•			
8:15		•	(•)		
8:31	•			•	•
9:11	•				
9:14	•				
10:2		•			
10:33	•				•
11:18	•				•
11:27	•			•	•
12:13		•	•		
12:28	•				
12:32	•				
12:35	•				
12:38	•				
14:1	•				•
14:10					•
14:43	•			•	•
14:53	•			•	•
14:55					•
15:1	•			•	•
15:3					•
15:10					•
15:11					•
15:31	•				•

Of the three oppositional groups that dominate the Gospel's second half—the chief priests, the elders, and the scribes—the most important is the **chief priests**, who from 10:33 on are mentioned more often than any other group, and who almost always appear either alone (14:10, 55; 15:3, 10, 11) or at the head of the list of opponents (10:33; 11:18, 27; 14:1, 43, 53; 15:1, 31; the only exception is 8:31). The

Greek term for "chief priests," *archiereis*, is the plural of *archiereus* = high priest and seems to refer to the high priest, any former high priests, and the adult male members of their elite families (see Acts 4:5–6; Josephus, *War* 6.114; cf. Schürer, 2.232–36; Sanders, *Judaism*, 327–32; BDAG 139). The paramount role played by the chief priests in the passion narrative, therefore, corresponds to their predominant position in Jewish society.

The chiefest of chief priests, the **high priest**, was the most prestigious religious authority in Second Temple Jewish Palestine, being the supreme officiant at the Jerusalem Temple and the head of its vast economic, social, and political power (on the history of the high priesthood in the Second Temple period, see VanderKam, *Joshua to Caiaphas*). Because the Jews were generally prevented from having a king by their imperial masters during this period, the high priest was usually the most important Jewish political official as well, and the Romans held him responsible for maintaining public order (see John 11:47–55). Some of the prestige and influence that accrued to this figure as a result of his office still clung to him if he was deposed (a fate that befell many high priests, especially under Roman rule). Thus, a former high priest, as, for example, Annas in Acts 4:6, could still be designated "the high priest," much as a former U.S. president can be addressed as "Mr. President"; and Annas seems to have retained considerably more power than erstwhile American presidents usually do (see Schürer 2.227–36; Sanders, *Judaism*, 319–27).

In the extant sources, most importantly the NT and the writings of the Jewish historian Josephus, the current high priest and the other chief priests form the core of a ruling Jewish council that is known by various Greek terms such as *synedrion*, *gerousia*, and *boulē*, all of which can be translated "council." The commonest NT term for this body is *synedrion* (lit. "the group that sits together"), a word whose Hebrew form, *Sanhedrin*, is found in rabbinic sources from the Mishnah on. In the Mishnah, "the Great Sanhedrin" consists of seventy-one members (see, e.g., *m. Sanh.* 1:6), and this number basically agrees with the seventy-member ruling bodies set up during the Jewish War according to Josephus (*War* 2.570–71; 4.334–44). It is unlikely, however, that in Second Temple times the Sanhedrin regularly had seventy or seventy-one members, or a fixed membership at all; it seems, rather, to have been an informal advisory group that was convened by the high priest on an *ad hoc* basis as need arose (see Schürer, 2.199–226; McLaren, *Power and Politics*, passim; Saldarini, "Sanhedrin"; Sanders, *Judaism*, 472–88; Brown, *Death*, 1.339–72). Thus, it is wrongheaded to try to harmonize rabbinic traditions with the Greek evidence by postulating two or three fixed sanhedrins (one "political," a second "religious," a third a city council for Jerusalem), as earlier generations of scholars sometimes did (see the review of literature in Mantel, *Studies*); it is wiser, rather, to take our cues from Josephus and the NT and to regard the rabbinic reports as anachronisms or idealizations.

Clearly the Second Temple Sanhedrin was dominated by sacerdotal interests. In Acts 4:5–7, for example, Peter and John are interrogated by a gathering of Jewish officials that includes four groups: (*a*) "rulers," "elders," and "scribes"; (*b*) the former high priest Annas and his son-in-law Caiaphas, the current high priest; (*c*) John, who may have been Caiaphas' son and a future high priest, and an otherwise unknown Alexander; and (*d*) "as many as were of high-priestly descent" (*hosoi ēsan ek genous archieratikou*; my trans.). The council thus seems to be dominated by men from high-priestly circles (*b*, *d*, and probably *c*), that is, what the NT usually calls "chief priests," but also to contain people from outside those circles (*a*). But even group *a* probably includes priests, since the scribes were mostly likely "priests and Levites" (see the APPENDIX "The Scribes and the Pharisees" in vol. 1, pp. 523–24). Their expertise in the Jewish law was undoubtedly an invaluable asset for the council's efforts to govern Judaea, where political power was intertwined with religious legitimacy and hence with biblical exegesis.

Despite the dominance of sacerdotal interests in the Sanhedrin, it evidently also included prominent laymen. In the NT the latter are usually called *presbyteroi* = **elders**, a term that literally means "old men" and reflects the fact that ancient Israel, like other traditional societies, looked to elderly males for wisdom and leadership. In the OT, for example, *presbyteros* usually designates a rich, respected, powerful person, typically an older man (see Campbell, *Elders*). In the late OT book of Ezra (5:5, 9; 6:7–8, 14; 10:8) such influential personages make up a Jewish self-governing assembly that in later texts is termed the Gerousia or Senate, both of which mean "council of old men" (see, e.g., 1 Macc 12:6; 2 Macc 1:10). This ruling group of "elders," which was the forerunner of the Sanhedrin of NT times, consisted of both priests and members of the lay aristocracy (cf. 2 Chron 19:8; 1 Macc 7:33; 11:23; 14:28). By NT times, however, the term "elders" was usually restricted to the lay members. In Markan passages (8:31; 14:43, 53; 15:1), for example, the Sanhedrin consists of the chief priests, the scribes (who also were priests), and the elders (who presumably were laymen; see Jeremias, *Jerusalem*, 222–32; Schürer, 2.200–9; Brown, *Death*, 2.1428–29). Similarly, at Qumran the elders are distinguished from both the priests and the remainder of the people (1QS 6:8–9). Nevertheless, the terminology in NT times was still fluid; Luke 22:66, for example, uses *presbyterion* ("council of elders") for an elite group that *includes* chief priests and scribes. *Presbyteroi*, then, remains a somewhat vague term, similar in ways to general designations by Josephus for the elite such as "the prominent people" (*hoi gnōrimoi*) and "the powerful" (*hoi dynatoi*). Despite their elite standing, and perhaps in part because they were usually laymen, elders sometimes appear in the sources as representatives of the nation at large (see "the elders of the people" in 1 Macc 7:33; Matt 21:23; 26:3, 47; 27:1; "the elders of Israel" in 1 Macc 11:23; and "the elders of the country" in 1 Macc 14:28; cf. Jeremias, *Jerusalem*, 222–32).

From the foregoing it should be clear why the chief priests and the elders come to prominence at the point in Mark's story where attention turns to Jerusalem and Jesus' forthcoming death there. The Temple was in Jerusalem, and it was the power base of the chief priests; the ruling council to which both the chief priests and the elders belonged, and which is portrayed in Mark as deciding on the necessity of Jesus' death, also normally met in Jerusalem. Some scribes also belonged to this group, although others were local priests scattered through Palestine; hence the Markan scribes are found in both Galilee and Jerusalem.

THE MEANING
OF CHRIST = MESSIAH

◆

"Christ" is the English rendering of *Christos*, which means "anointed" or "anointed one" and is the Greek translation of the Hebrew *māšîaḥ* and the Aramaic *mešîḥā'*. These terms are used in ancient Jewish and Christian literature for a future monarch from the line of David who will play a vital role in the eschatological redemption.

The OT itself, however, does not use "Messiah" in this way. In ancient Israel both kings and high priests entering their office were anointed with oil as a sign of divine favor; *māšîaḥ*, therefore, usually refers in the OT to either the current high priest (Lev 4:3, 5, 16; 6:22 (6:15 Heb]) or a reigning monarch such as Saul (1 Sam 24:6, 10 [24:7, 11 Heb]; 26:16; 2 Sam 1:14, 16), David (2 Sam 19:21 [19:22 Heb]; 23:1), or a later Davidic king (Ps 2:2). It is even used by Deutero-Isaiah in a figurative sense for a foreign ruler, the Persian monarch Cyrus, who is "anointed" by God for the task of ending Israel's exile (Isa 45:1; perhaps also 61:1–4).

Several OT passages *do* speak of hopes for a future Davidic ruler who will throw off Israel's foreign yoke and inaugurate an era of worldwide peace, prosperity, and fulfillment of God's will (e.g., Isa 9:1–7; 11:1–10; Jer 23:5–6; Mic 5:2–4; Zech 9:9–10); these passages, however, do not term this coming king "anointed." This step is taken only in post-OT Jewish writings and traditions (e.g., *Pss. Sol.* 17:32; 18:5, 7; *1 En.* 48:8–10; 52:4; *2 Apoc. Bar.* 29:3; 30:1; *4 Ezra* 7:28–29; 12:32; rabbinic traditions) and in the NT. In the Jewish traditions, the coming "anointed one" is usually an ideal king from the line of David, though some circles, such as the Qumran sect, also expected an anointed priest from the line of Aaron (e.g., 1QS 9:11); indeed, at Qumran this priestly Messiah is the more important figure (on Qumran messianism, see Collins, *Scepter*). This dual expectation, which is also present in the apocryphal *Testaments of the Twelve Patriarchs* (*T. Levi* 18; *T. Judah* 24), reflects passages in the OT prophet Zechariah that envisage the joint rule of a Davidic king and an Aaronite high priest (Zech 3:6–8; 4:13–14; 6:9–13; on this "biblical diarchy," see Talmon, "Concepts," 106–7). Later rabbinic traditions also expect two Messiahs, though the second is descended from Joseph rather than Aaron (on the Messiah-Son-of-Joseph, see Klausner, *Idea*, 483–501).

Most first-century Jews, however, even the members of the Qumran sect, would probably have thought in terms of a Davidic figure when they heard the absolute title "*the* Anointed One." Admittedly, this absolute usage does not occur in extant extra-NT Jewish literature before the end of the first century C.E., aside from a questionable instance in a fragmentary Qumran text (1QSa 2:11–12; but cf. "the anointed one of righteousness" in 4QCommGenA [4Q252] 5:3–4, and, from later in the century, *4 Ezra* 12:32; *2 Bar.* 29:3; 30:1). The similar expressions "the Lord's anointed" and "my/his anointed" do, however, occur frequently (e.g., *Pss. Sol.* 18:5; *1 En.* 48:10; 52:4; *2 Bar.* 39:7; 40:1; 72:2), and a royal nuance is almost always obvious, as is also the case in the OT usages of these phrases (e.g., 1 Sam 2:10, 35; Ps 2:2). In the NT, similarly, the Anointed One or Messiah = *Christos* is the expected eschatological king from the line of David (see, e.g., Matt 1:1; Mark 10:47–48; 11:9–10; Rom 1:3). As de Jonge ("Use," 147) puts it, therefore, in the time of Jesus the term "anointed" was "on the way to becoming a standard expression" for the coming Davidic figure (cf. Horbury, *Messianism*).

Some Jews, to be sure, could and did dream of God's future redemption of the world without assigning primary importance to a Davidic Messiah or even without invoking him at all. Sometimes the eschatological high priest or a chief angel was expected to be more important (e.g., Dan 10:12–13; 12:1; *1 Enoch* 10; 1QSa 2:12–14; 11QMelchizedek; *T. Levi* 18), sometimes the return of an OT hero such as Elijah was anticipated (e.g., Mal 4:5–6; Sir 48:10), and sometimes it was believed that God would accomplish the redemption without an intermediary (e.g., *1 Enoch* 1; see Smith, "Variety"). Nevertheless, among expected eschatological figures, the Davidic Messiah was probably the most famous, and this prominence helps explain why Jesus was identified as Messiah despite a career that was in many ways nonmessianic (see below).

In the OT and ancient Judaism, the Davidic Messiah is often associated with political elements of an ancient king's role, including military success. This is partly because an important aspect of the Davidic image, from the story of David and Goliath on, is skill in battle (1 Samuel 17; 2 Samuel 8 and 22; etc.). Similarly, in Psalm 2, which became a fountainhead passage for later messianic conceptions, the kings of the earth revolt against the Lord and "his anointed one," the reigning Davidic monarch, but are crushed by the latter's rod of iron. Other OT and Jewish traditions about the coming scion of David also emphasize the military aspect (e.g., Isa 11:4; *Pss. Sol.* 17:22–25; 4Q285 5:2–6; *2 Apoc. Bar.* 39–40; *4 Ezra* 13:3–11). Because of this association with militarism, Davidic messianism was probably an important factor in sparking the great Jewish revolts against the Romans in the first and second centuries (cf. Hengel, *Zealots*; Horsley and Hanson, *Bandits*; Wilson, *Strangers*, 6). The military and political orientation of Davidic messianism is also reflected in some NT passages (e.g., Acts 1:6; Rev 19:11–21), though reserve about it is also expressed (e.g., John 6:15).

But it would be a mistake to reduce Davidic messianism to religious militancy; the Davidic king of Isa 11:1–10 is not only a successful warrior but also a righteous judge on whom the spirit of wisdom rests, and the "Christ" of *Psalms of Solomon* 17 not only crushes hostile Gentile armies but also has mercy on the nations and shepherds his own people in holiness. As de Jonge ("Use," 136) puts it: "The main emphasis [in the *Psalms of Solomon* passage] is laid upon the spiritual aspects of his reign." Nor is the Davidic Messiah invariably a "this-worldly" character, as some scholars have argued (e.g., Jenni, "Messiah, Jewish," 364); in *4 Ezra*, for example, he is preexistent (12:32; 13:25–26), and in 13:1–4 he flies with the clouds of heaven like the Son of Man figure in Daniel 7. *First Enoch* 37–71, too, melds the features of the Danielic Son of Man with those of the Davidic Messiah, and the subject of 4Q521 2 2:1–2, who may be the Davidic Messiah (see Puech, "Apocalypse"), commands the obedience not only of humans but also of heaven and earth (for other interpretations of this fragmentary text, see Stegemann, *Library*, 31–32; Collins, *Scepter*, 118–22; Niebuhr, "Psalm"; Puech ["Remarks"] now reads *lmšyḥw* as a plural and suggests a reference to the royal and priestly Messiahs). Even rabbinic traditions, which generally picture the Messiah as a figure with human lineaments, can upon occasion speak of his exaltation to a quasi-divine status (e.g., *b. Sanh.* 38b). These "high" portrayals of the Messiah ultimately go back to the exalted conception that the ancient Israelites had of their kings, and they continue a tradition of the exegesis of OT texts that is evident in the LXX (see, e.g., Num 24:17; Pss 72:17 [71:17 LXX]; 110:3 [109:3 LXX]; Isa 9:6) and continues in the Targums (see Horbury, *Messianism*, passim).

One idea that does *not* seem to be prominent in pre-Christian Judaism is that of the suffering Messiah; no early Jewish text speaks of such a figure. To Christians the idea of a suffering Messiah seems natural, but that is because it is so deeply rooted in a *Christian* understanding of the OT. In Judaism, however, the Davidic Messiah is associated with triumph, not defeat and death; Peter's shocked reaction to the Markan Jesus' announcement of his coming passion (Mark 8:31–32), therefore, is realistic. Deutero-Isaiah, to be sure, speaks of the Lord's Servant, who suffers and dies an atoning death (Isa 50:4–9; 52:13–53:12), but this figure is not identified with the Messiah. Indeed, while the Targum sees references to the Messiah in Isaiah 53, it assigns the suffering in the Isaian passage to the Messiah's *enemies* rather than the Messiah himself (cf. Mowinckel, *He That Cometh*, 330–33). The later rabbinic traditions that speak of the death of the Messiah-Son-of-Joseph were probably influenced by Christianity and/or the death of the leader of the Second Jewish Revolt, Bar Kochba, rather than by a preexisting Jewish concept of a suffering Messiah (cf. Klausner, *Idea*, 483–501). The NT notion of suffering messiahship, therefore, is a mutation of previous Jewish messianism rather than a straightforward continuation of it (cf. Brown, *Christology*, 160).

But why was Jesus identified as the Messiah at all, if he did not fit the standard scenario? Some (e.g., Bultmann, *Theology*, 1.26–32) have theorized that this evaluation arose only after the resurrection, and resulted from the perception that God had vindicated Jesus in that event. This does not seem to be a sufficient explanation, however, since there is no known ancient Jewish expectation that the Messiah will rise from the dead, and other pious figures who were believed to have transcended death were not identified as the Messiah (e.g., Elijah, Jeremiah, and John the Baptist, according to the opinions cited in Matt 16:14; or Isaac, according to some versions of the *ʾăqēdāh* legend, on which see Spiegel, *Last Trial*, chapter 4). It seems more likely that Jesus was already identified as Messiah by popular opinion during his lifetime; this would at least explain why he was crucified by the Romans as "the King of the Jews" (see Dahl, "Crucified Messiah").

Exactly *why* he was so identified, however, is a complex question. There was no fixed scriptural expectation that the Messiah would work miracles, but 4Q521 *may* speak of the Messiah accomplishing healing miracles, and Matt 11:2–6// Luke 7:18–23 seems to regard such miracles as proof of messiahship; Jesus' reputation for wonder working, therefore, may have suggested a messianic status to some observers (see the NOTE on "sign" in 8:11). Another factor may have been that Jesus' clashes with the authorities aroused political hopes concerning him, and these hopes were attracted to the magnet of the Davidic image—an attraction that would have been increased if Jesus was of Davidic stock, as the NT asserts. A reputation for charismatic teaching and for association with the poor may also have played a role, since these factors are prominent in the description of the coming king in the important OT passage Isa 11:1–5. It is more difficult to say whether Jesus himself shared in this messianic assessment of his ministry, as Mark 8:27–30 and 14:61–62 imply.

HISTORY-OF-RELIGIONS
BACKGROUNDS TO
THE TRANSFIGURATION

◆

Many different parallels from the history of religions have been invoked to elucidate the transfiguration narrative. In what follows, they will be treated in three categories: general motifs (epiphanies of gods, deification of human beings, etc.), particular Old Testament and Jewish figures (the Messiah, Moses, etc.), and a Jewish holiday (Tabernacles).

GENERAL MOTIFS

Epiphanies of gods, goddesses, or angels in human form. Mark uses the verb *metamorphousthai* ("to be transformed") to convey the change that Jesus' body and clothing undergo (9:2). In the Greco-Roman sphere this verb and the cognate noun, *metamorphōsis*, are employed for all sorts of magical changes (see, e.g., Ovid's *Metamorphoses*), including incidents in which gods transform themselves into human beings and back again. Zeller ("Métamorphose," "Bedeutung") regards such tales as offering the closest parallels to the Markan transfiguration narrative.

In these stories the disguised divinities, when about to return to heaven at the end of their earthly sojourn, often reveal their true nature through *a physical transformation* or epiphany; as the scholion (see the GLOSSARY) to Homer, *Iliad* 2:791 puts it: "When the transformed gods depart, they usually leave a sign of themselves behind." These signs can include growing to enormous size (e.g., Nonnos, *Dionysiaca* 45:133–35) or displaying an *unearthly* attractiveness and *radiant* eyes (e.g., Virgil, *Aeneid* 5.647–49), and the human witnesses usually react with *terror*. A superb example of the genre is provided by the Pseudo-Homeric *Hymn to Demeter* 268–69, 275–83:

> "*I am Demeter* the honored, the greatest
> benefit and joy to undying gods and to mortals . . ."
> With these words the goddess *changed her* size and *form*
> and sloughed off old age, as beauty was wafted about her.
> From her *fragrant veils* a lovely smell
> emanated, and from the immortal skin of the goddess *a light*
> shone afar, as her blond hair streamed down over her shoulders,
> and the sturdy mansion was *filled with radiance as if from lightning.*

Out she went through the mansion. The queen *staggered,*
and she remained *speechless* for a long time, forgetting
to pick her growing child up from the floor. (Athanassakis trans., *Homeric
   Hymns*)

Here, as in Mark 9:2–8, the identification of a divine being (here a self-identifica-
tion) is accompanied by a metamorphosis that includes a magical transformation
of clothing and an irruption of supernatural light; in both cases, moreover, the
reaction of the human observer is shock. A Jewish example of the same genre with
several similarities to Mark 9:2–8 occurs in Tob 12:6–22: the archangel Raphael,
who has accompanied Tobias on his wanderings disguised as a human, *initiates
a private interview* with Tobit and Tobias (Tob 12:6; cf. Mark 9:2), *exhorts them*
to continue in the path of righteousness (Tob 12:6–10; cf. Mark 9:7), and *reveals
his identity* (Tob 12:15; cf. Mark 9:7). They are *overcome with fright* (Tob 12:16;
cf. Mark 9:6), and *the angel vanishes* (Tob 12:21; cf. Mark 9:8 and see Frenschkowski, *Offenbarung,* 2.38–45).

Zeller acknowledges that Jesus' transfiguration does not occur at the *end* of his
earthly sojourn, as is usual in such epiphany stories, but he points to a parallel in
Iamblichus, *Life of Pythagoras* 91–93, in which the philosopher-sage in midlife
reveals his divinity to a disciple by displaying his golden thigh.

Deification of human beings. Not only do gods and angels temporarily assume
human shape and then revert to form, but human beings can also be deified.
These deifications usually occur at the end of the hero's life, when he is taken
up into heaven (see the next section). But not always. The mystery religions, for
example, seem to have promised their adherents that they could, by undergoing
a symbolic rite of death and regeneration, attain immortality and a divine status
already in *this* life, as is shown, for example, by the language of rebirth in Apuleius
(*Metamorphoses* 11.16.2; 11.21.6), the same author's reference to a new birthday
(11.24.5), and the inscription from the Santa Prisca Mithraeum in Rome, "One
that is piously reborn" (see Reitzenstein, *Mystery-Religions,* 333–37; Burkert, *Mystery Cults,* 99–101;. Meyer, "Mystery Religions"). Lucius' "metamorphoses" in
Apuleius' novel of the same name provide the most interesting parallels to Mark
9:2–8, starting with the word "metamorphosis" itself, a cognate of which Mark
employs in 9:2 to describe the altered appearance of Jesus. In Apuleius the trans-
formations of the hero reach their climax in his initiation into the Isis cult, the full
mystery of which he is *forbidden to reveal to outsiders.* He can only impart that

I drew *near to the confines of death* . . . and before returning I journeyed through
all the elements. At dead of night I saw the sun gleaming with *bright brilliance.*
I *stood in the presence of the gods* below and the gods above, and worshipped
them from close at hand. (Walsh trans., *Golden Ass,* 11.23.8)

Subsequently Lucius is *robed in garments* that seem to imply his *deification* (the
robe is "Olympian," and the garland around his head has projecting palm leaves

that resemble the sun's rays in portraits of the gods), and for days he *lingers in the precincts* of Isis' temple because of "the indescribable pleasure of gazing on the divine statue" (ibid., 11:24–25). The similarities to Jesus' transfiguration include the motifs of secret revelation to a select few (Mark 9:2, 9), unnatural brilliance, glorious robing (9:2–3), dealings with divine beings (9:4), and the yearning to stay at the place of revelation (9:5). There is also in the Markan passage, as in the Apuleian one, a linkage with the theme of death, through the juxtaposition with the passion prophecy in 8:31.

Another close parallel to Mark 9:2–8 is found in the account of a disciple's words to the neo-Platonic sage Iamblichus:

> A rumor has reached us . . . that when you pray to the gods you soar aloft from the earth more than ten cubits to all appearance; that your body and *your garments change to a beautiful golden hue*; and presently when your prayer is ended your body *becomes as it was before* you prayed, and then *you come down to the earth and associate with us.* (Eunapius, *Lives of the Philosophers*, 13 [458]; LCL trans., emphasis added; cf. Zeller, "Métamorphose," 183–85)

Here, as in the Markan transfiguration, a metamorphosis that includes radiant garments is followed by a return to normal existence that is described as a descent and involves the resumption of discourse with disciples.

Ascents to heaven. Deification is sometimes associated with an ascent to heaven, and Fossum ("Ascensio") has suggested that stories of such ascensions provide a close parallel to the Markan transfiguration. These narratives occur frequently in the pagan world, where eternal gods such as Zeus are often contrasted with "immortals" such as Hercules or Dionysus, who are usually the product of the intercourse between a god and a human being and who at their death are apotheosized and taken up to heaven (see Talbert, *What*, 26–35). The translation of the hero may be either witnessed directly (e.g., Suetonius, *Augustus* 100.4; Justin, *1 Apology* 21) or inferred from the fact that he leaves behind no physical remains (e.g., Diogenes Laertius, *Empedocles* 8.67–68; Philostratus, *Life of Apollonius of Tyana* 8.30).

Fossum, however, concentrates not on such pagan examples but on Jewish narratives of postmortem journeys to heaven. These ascents sometimes include the motif of enthronement (implied, e.g., by the crowns in *Asc. Isa.* 7:22; 9:24–25) and/or investiture with a new robe (e.g., *Asc. Isa.* 7:22; 8:14–15; 9:24–25; *2 En.* 22:8–10). In *3 En.* 12:1–5 moreover, Enoch's reception from God of "a *garment of glory* on which were fixed all kinds of *lights*" (Fossum trans., emphasis added) is linked with his installation as *God's vice-regent* in heaven. The combination of ascent, reception of a radiant robe, and enthronement recalls Jesus' ascent of the mountain, his glorious clothing, and his acknowledgment as God's Son (a royal title; see the NOTE on "You are my . . . son" in 1:11).

Resurrection appearances. The motif of ascent to heaven is related to that of resurrection; indeed, for some NT authors, Jesus' resurrection from the realm of the dead and his postmortem appearances on earth mark the first stop on his transit to heaven (see John 20:17; Acts 1:1–11). Several scholars (e.g., Bultmann, 259–61; Weeden, *Traditions*, 118–26; Schmithals, "Markusschluss"; Robinson, "Jesus," 8–9) have found the parallels between the transfiguration and resurrection appearances so striking that they see the transfiguration as a resurrection appearance story that has been retrojected into Jesus' ministry. The two types of revelatory event have in common a mountaintop location (Mark 9:2; cf. Matt 28:16), the luminosity of Jesus (Mark 9:3; cf. Acts 9:3–4; Rev 1:14–15; *Letter of Peter to Philip* 134:9–13), the use of the term *ōphthē* = "appeared" (Mark 9:4; cf. Luke 24:34; 1 Cor 15:5–8), the cloud (Mark 9:7; cf. Acts 1:9), and the designation of Jesus as Son of God (Mark 9:7; cf. John 20:28; Rom 1:4). Second Peter 1:16–18, moreover, identifies Jesus' transfiguration with the occasion on which he received "honor and glory" from God—words suggestive of the postresurrectional state (see John 17:5; Rom 2:7, 10; Rev 4:11). And the presence of Elijah and Moses with Jesus might point in the same direction, since in the biblical account Elijah was taken up alive to heaven (2 Kgs 2:11), and some later Jews such as Josephus (*Ant.* 4.326) seem to have believed that Moses "returned to the divinity" without dying (see Begg, "Portrayal").

Eschatological light, stars, and angels. Jesus' resurrection, of course, is an anticipation of the general resurrection; and his shining garments and personage may therefore also be seen as a foretaste of the glory the elect will experience at the eschaton. The idea that the saints will shine in eschatological glory has roots in the OT and Jewish traditions. According to Dan 12:3, in the new age the wise "shall *shine like the brightness* of the sky, and those who lead many to righteousness, like the stars forever and ever"—a verse that left its mark on Jewish texts (e.g., *1 En.* 39:7; 104:2; 108:13; *4 Ezra* 7:97, 125), on the NT (e.g., Matt 13:43), and on later Christian literature (e.g., *Apoc. El.* 4:19). In *1 En.* 62:15, moreover, the elect will be clothed with *"garments of glory,"* and in the book of Revelation they are often described as wearing *white* robes (Rev 3:4, 5, 18; 4:4; 6:11; 7:9, 13–14), two features shared by the transfigured Jesus. The idea of shining saints is sometimes conflated with that of astral immortality, that is, the notion that the righteous dead become stars or starlike at their death (see again Dan 12:3 and cf. *LAB* 33:5; *T. Moses* 10:9; *1 En.* 104:2; *2 Bar.* 51:10; *4 Macc* 17:5), and it is also related to the widespread idea that the future state will be like that of the angels (see Mark 12:25; *1 En.* 104:4; *2 Apoc. Bar.* 51:5, 10; *T. Isaac* 4:38–43). The latter are often described as or assumed to be *luminous* (see, e.g., Dan 10:6; *T. Job* 3:1; 4:1 [cf. 5:2]; Matt 28:3; Acts 6:15; 2 Cor 11:14) or are equated with stars (see, e.g., Dan 8:10; *1 En.* 43:1–4; 86:1–6; 90:20–27; Rev 1:20; 9:1–2; 12:4; cf. Allison, "What Was," 63 n. 7, and *Jesus*, 178 n. 35). The transfigured Jesus, therefore, is like an angel, and angelic glory is like the splendor of the elect at the eschaton; Jesus thus shows his followers the glory that will be theirs in the new age.

Royal epiphanies. The way in which Jesus' transfiguration foreshadows his resurrection also points toward a possible background for the former in royal traditions, since in some early Christian traditions the resurrection is understood as an enthronement at God's right hand (e.g., Mark 14:62; Acts 2:32–36; Rom 8:34); interpreting the transfiguration as a foretaste of the resurrection, therefore, is akin to depicting it as an enthronement or demonstration of royal power. An additional reason for seeing royal imagery in the transfiguration is its similarity to ancient accounts in which kings or would-be monarchs make awe-inspiring public appearances. Such appearances can occur on the king's accession to the throne, on his birthday, or on his arrival in a distant province (see Price, *Rituals*, passim). As Horbury (*Messianism*, 134–35) points out, these manifestations are recorded not only of Roman emperors but also of Jewish figures from the Herodian period such as Archelaus and Agrippa I (see, e.g., Josephus, *War* 2.1–2; 7.29–31; *Ant.* 17.200–202; 19.343–46; Philo, *Flacc.* 37–39; Acts 12:20–23). The passages mention the *brilliant vesture* of the king, his *enthronement*, and the *acclamations* he receives from the crowd, sometimes including the *bestowal of titles*—all features that are present in the Markan transfiguration narrative.

The description in *Ant.* 19.343–50 of Agrippa I's appearance in Caesarea in 44 C.E. is particularly appropriate for comparison with Mark 9:2–8:

> On the second day of the spectacles, clad in *a garment* woven completely of silver so that *its texture was indeed wondrous*, he entered the theatre at daybreak. There the silver, *illumined* by the touch of the first rays of the sun, was *wondrously radiant* and *by its glitter inspired fear and awe* in those who gazed intently at it. Straightaway his flatterers raised their voices from various directions—though hardly for his good—addressing him *as a god*. "May you be propitious to us," they added, "and if we have hitherto *feared you* as a man, yet henceforth we agree that you are *more than mortal in your being*." (cf. Acts 12:20–23)

Here, as in the Markan transfiguration narrative, a royal figure's radiant vesture inspires awe, and this is coupled with an acknowledgment of his divine status. Josephus' description of the epiphany of the Jewish revolutionary leader Simon bar Giora at the end of the revolt against the Romans (*War* 7.29–31) also probably reflects traditions about royal appearances: Simon clothes himself in *white tunics*, buckles over them a *purple mantle* (implying royal status), and *"pops up out of the ground"* on the site of the ruined Temple; the spectators to this epiphany, including the Roman soldiers, are at first *seized with awe* (they quickly recover, however, and arrest Simon). The white garments, the implication of royalty, the magical atmosphere ("popped up out of the ground"), the hilltop location (the Temple Mount), and the reaction of awe are all similar to the Markan transfiguration narrative.

PARTICULAR OLD TESTAMENT AND JEWISH FIGURES

The Messiah. The Simon incident is also related to our second category of background material, traditions about particular Old Testament and Jewish figures, since Simon's appearance in royal robes was probably connected with his messianic self-consciousness (see Marcus, "Jewish War," 458–59). And it is logical to look for background to the Markan transfiguration narrative in Jewish expectations about the Messiah, since at the climax of the narrative the Markan Jesus is hailed by the divine voice as "my . . . Son," and "Son of God" was a messianic title (see again the NOTE on "You are my . . . son" in 1:11).

Jewish traditions about the Messiah have other points of contact with the Markan picture of the transfigured Jesus. The Messiah is regularly associated with light, especially that of the rising sun. This association stems partly from Num 24:17, which speaks of a star rising out of Jacob and smashing Israel's enemies; so influential did this oracle become that the nickname of a second-century Jewish messiah, Bar Kochba ("son of a star"), derived from it. Christian sources continue this association of the Messiah's advent with light (see, e.g., Rev 22:16; *T. Levi* 18:1–3; *Apoc. El.* 3:3; *Epistula Apostolorum* 16; cf. the COMMENT on 16:1–4).

Although it is late, the long description of the Messiah in *Pes. Rab.* 37:1–2 makes for a particularly interesting comparison with Mark 9:2–8, since it includes the prophecy that at the eschaton God will *exalt* the Messiah to the heaven of heavens, spread the *brightness* of his glory over him, and *clothe him* with "a garment whose splendor will stream forth from world's end to world's end" (Braude trans.). God will also make for him seven *canopies* of precious stones, and all the righteous *of every generation* will gaze at him. The theme of exaltation here is similar to the motif of Jesus' ascent of the mountain, and the Messiah's shining garment corresponds to the Markan Jesus' radiant clothing. The seven canopies, moreover, are reminiscent of Peter's suggestion that the disciples make three tents (Mark 9:5), and the way in which the Messiah is viewed by people from all generations recalls Jesus' communion with worthies of the past (Elijah and Moses, 9:4).

Adam. According to Rubin and Kosman ("Clothing," 169–73), the section from *Pesikta Rabbati* just described ascribes an added significance to the Messiah's glorious clothing: it is the radiant garment of Adam, which humanity lost through the fall but which will be restored through Adam's eschatological descendant, the Messiah—an idea that is taken up in other Jewish and Christian texts (see, e.g., *Tg. Neof./Ps.-J.* Gen. 3:21; *Gen. Rab.* 12.6; Ephrem, *Commentary on Genesis* 2.4 [on Gen 2:7]; cf. Scroggs, *Last Adam*, 31, 55; G. Anderson, "Garments"; Brock, *Eye*, 85–97). This points toward another facet of the Markan transfiguration narrative, its similarity to the depiction of the pre-fall Adam in Jewish legends; the idea would seem to be that the Messiah recovers what Adam forfeited. Jewish traditions associate Adam with light generally (*y. Šabb.* 2:6 [5b; Neusner, 11.114], etc.) and dwell almost obsessively on his radiant clothing (e.g., the Targumim on Gen 3:21; *Gen. Rab.* 20.12; *Pirqe R. El.* 14), a motif that may already be implicit in Ezek 28:13, where the primal man is covered with a garment of precious jewels (cf. Sir 49:16, which implies Adam's splendor; CD 3:20; 1QS 4:23, which mention his glory; and *T. Ab.* 11:8–9, which speaks of his being "appareled in glory"; see Allison, *Testament of Abraham*, 249). This same OT passage places the first human on *"the holy mountain of God"* (Ezek 28:14), a location that is also picked up by later Jewish and Christian retellings of Genesis 1–3 (e.g., *1 En.* 24:3–4; 25:4–5; *Jub.* 4:26; 8:19; *Targum Ps.-J.* Gen 2:15; Ephrem, *Hymns of Paradise* 1:4). Thus, the mountaintop location of the transfiguration narrative also fits into an Adamic framework. A further connection between Adam traditions and the Markan transfiguration narrative is that in the former the clothing of Adam is connected with his status as "the firstborn of the world" (*Num. Rab.* 4.8; *Tanḥuma [Buber]* Toledot 6.12 [Townsend, 1.157]), while in the latter Jesus is garbed in splendor and proclaimed by a heavenly voice to be God's Son. Peter's allusion in 9:5 to the three *tents* could also be taken as an Adamic reference, since rabbinic traditions speak of the "canopies of glory" inhabited by Adam in paradise (e.g., *b. Baba Bathra* 75a; *Pes. Rab. Kah.* 26.3; *Pesik. Rab.* 14.10).

Moses. But the Old Testament/Jewish figure who is most strikingly similar to the transfigured Jesus of Mark is neither Adam nor the Messiah but Moses. Mark's readers would have been immediately alerted to this Mosaic typology by the first four words of his account, "and after six days," which correspond to the six days mentioned in Exod 24:16; the similarity is particularly impressive because time indications outside the passion narrative are rare and tend to be vague (see the NOTE on "after six days" in 9:2). There are several other parallels between the Markan transfiguration account and the descriptions of Moses' ascension of Sinai in Exodus 24 and 34, ascents that were sometimes conflated with each other in Jewish traditions (see, e.g., *L.A.B.* 11:5–12:1; *Deut. Rab.* 3.12; Jacobson, *Commentary*, 1.483):

Mark		Exodus
9:2a	after six days	24:16
9:2a	three named companions	24:1, 9
9:2b	ascent of mountain	24:9, 12–13, 15, 18; 34:4
9:2b–3	shining body/garments	34:29
9:7a	God reveals self in veiled form through cloud	24:15–16, 18
9:7b	voice out of cloud	24:16

The parallel with the Moses tradition becomes even more striking when it is noted that "listen to him" in Mark 9:7 is a virtual citation of Deut 18:15, where the person to be listened to is the Prophet-like-Moses.

Postbiblical developments of the Moses stories bring them even closer to the Markan transfiguration. Philo, for example, uses *metaballein* ("to change") and *metamorphousthai* ("to be transformed"), the word employed by Mark in 9:2, to describe the prophetic exaltation that gripped Moses (*Life of Moses* 1.57, 2.280; cf. Meeks, "Moses," and Zeller, "Bedeutung," 311–12). The radiance of Moses in Exod 34:29, moreover, is portrayed by later interpreters in ways similar to Mark's description of Jesus. Pseudo-Philo writes that "the light of his face surpassed the splendor of the sun and the moon" (*L.A.B.* 12:1; Jacobson trans.), and this is analogous to the way in which Mark describes Jesus' garments becoming so white that "no launderer on earth could whiten them so" (cf. also Philo, *Life of Moses* 2.70) in that each account stresses its hero's incomparable radiance.

In Mark, to be sure, it is Jesus' *clothing* that shines, whereas in Exodus and most later Jewish traditions, including Pseudo-Philo, it is Moses' *face* that is radiant. (Matthew and Luke amend Mark to speak also of Jesus' face, apparently to bring the account into closer conformity with Exodus 34.) But the Markan Jesus' shining garments are in line with some postbiblical Mosaic traditions, since Samaritan texts, *Memar Marqah* 4:6 and passages from *Defter*, describe Moses as being clothed with light or with a garment superior to any king's (for the *Defter* passages see Cowley, *Liturgy*, 1.32, 40–41, 61–62; cf. Fossum, "Ascensio," 74). One of the *Defter* texts also depicts Moses on Sinai as being covered with a cloud (Cowley, *Liturgy*, 1.40–41), and this is reminiscent of Mark 9:7 ("And there came a cloud, overshadowing them") and different from the Exodus account, in which the cloud covers the mountain rather than the person on it. The reference to Jesus' divine sonship in 9:7 may also be seen against a Mosaic background, since Philo describes Moses as having become a god on Sinai (*Life of Moses* 1.158). Ezekiel the Tragedian goes so far as to picture God abdicating his throne to Moses on Sinai, thus implying that Moses is his crown prince (*Exagōgē* 68–82; cf. Meeks, "Moses"). The Mosaic typology in the transfiguration, then, is very extensive.

Joseph. One other Old Testament character may be mentioned: Joseph. Jacob's presentation to Joseph of an ornamental *tunic* is not only an expression of his special *love* for his young *son* but also a designation of Joseph as the father's *principal beneficiary*. As Levenson (*Death*, 57–58) puts it: "Jacob's biological eleventh son becomes his legal first-born." Similarly, the Markan Jesus is the *beloved Son* (9:7) whose special position as the legal heir of God is shown by the glorious *garment* that his Father bestows upon him (9:3). The pseudepigraphical *Joseph and Aseneth* develops the biblical portrait in an epiphany scene that is in some ways even closer to the Markan transfiguration story: Joseph is dressed in an exquisite *white tunic* (5:5), associated with *light* (6:4, 6), and called a *"son of God"* (5:5); like the Markan Jesus, moreover, he is a *royal* figure (cf. 7:1 and *OTP*, 2.208 n. k).

A JEWISH HOLIDAY: TABERNACLES

Besides these traditions about specific Old Testament/Jewish figures, there may also be background to the Markan transfiguration narrative in aspects of a particular Jewish holiday, namely, Tabernacles, or Booths (Sûkkôt). Riesenfeld (*Jésus transfiguré*) was the first to argue this case in detail, taking his point of departure from the suggestion of Peter in 9:5 that the disciples should build three tents, or booths, on the mountain to commemorate the experience.

The fact that two of the booths in the transfiguration are for worthies of a bygone age, Moses and Elijah, and that the third is for Jesus, who links the transfiguration experience with his own resurrection (9:9), suggests that they may have something to do with postmortem existence, and this association coheres with Jewish and NT traditions according to which the righteous dead reside in tents, booths, or canopies (see, e.g., Luke 16:9; *b. B. Bat.* 75a; *Lev. Rab.* 25.2; cf. 2 Cor 5:1–5). This connection with postmortem and eschatological existence, however, is also suggestive of the Feast of Tabernacles, since that holiday not only looks *back* to the booths in which the Israelites lived during their forty years' wandering through the wilderness but also looks *forward* to the age to come, when Israel will dwell "under the cloud of the Shekhinah" (see *Cant. Rab.* 2:6).

This passage from a late midrash illustrates the connection between the booths of Sûkkôt and the motif of the cloud, and this suggests that the cloud in the Markan transfiguration may be another motif that has background in the Tabernacles festival. Indeed, the booths in which the Israelites lived during the exodus period are often equated with the radiant, protective "clouds of glory" that accompanied them in their wilderness wanderings and will reappear at the eschaton (see, e.g., *Mekilta* Pisha 14 [Lauterbach 1.108] and *Sipra* 'Emor 17 [Neusner, 3.270]). The Markan transfiguration, similarly, portrays an unearthly radiance (9:2–3) and a cloud that is filled with the divine presence (9:7). In addition, this cloud is described as *overshadowing* Jesus, Moses, and Elijah, perhaps in a protective way (see the NOTE on "overshadowing them" in 9:7), and this motif is similar to that of the protective shade provided by the *sukkāh* and the associated clouds of glory (see, e.g., *Gen. Rab.* 48.10; *Exod. Rab.* 34:3; *t. Sot. 11:1*; and the *haškibēnu* ["cause us to lie down"] blessing in the Jewish liturgy, on which see Elbogen, *Liturgy*, 770). There may even be a connection between these glorious clouds of the exodus and the whiteness of Jesus' clothing in the Markan transfiguration, since according to *Deut. Rab.* 7.11 the clothes of the exodus generation did not grow old (cf. Deut 8:4), because the pillar of *cloud* rubbed against them and *whitened* them (on all of these points see Rubenstein, "Symbolism," and *Sûkkôt*, 253, 301–2). In addition, Sûkkôt is associated with the *enthronement* of God (see, e.g., Zech 14:9, 16) and thus points forward to the *eschaton*, as the Markan transfiguration narrative discloses Jesus' royal status (9:7) and is set in an eschatological context (9:1, 9–13).

Many of these eschatological dimensions of Sûkkôt are summed up in Isa 4:5–6, a passage that is frequently cited in later descriptions of the holiday and that presents several parallels to the transfiguration narrative:

> Then the LORD will create over the whole site of *Mount* Zion and over its places of assembly a *cloud* by day and smoke and the *shining of a flaming fire* by night. Indeed over all the *glory* there will be a *canopy* (*huppāh*). It will serve as a *pavilion* (*sukkāh*), a *shade* by day from the heat, and *a refuge and a shelter* from the storm and rain.

Here, as in Mark 9:2–8, the setting is a mountain, and the depiction includes a miraculous illumination, a canopy or booth, a cloud of glory filled with divine presence, and shade/shelter/protection. In *Pes. Rab.* 37:1, moreover, this same Isaian passage is referred to the Messiah:

> And the Holy One, blessed be He, will embrace the Messiah in the sight of the righteous and bring him within the canopy where all the righteous ones, the

pious ones, the holy ones, the mighty men of Torah of every generation, will gaze upon him. (Braude trans.)

Here we see the Messiah not only dwelling under a canopy, as Peter suggests that Jesus should do, but also enjoying a special intimacy with God and being gazed at by the righteous, features that are also implied in our passage.

EVALUATION

What is one to make of this bewildering array of history-of-religions parallels to the transfiguration? First of all, the backgrounds do not have to be mutually exclusive. Already in the Qumran scrolls, for example, the glory of Adam is conflated with that of Moses (see 4QDibHam[a] [4Q504]); the idea seems to be that Moses' shining face restores the glory that Adam lost at the fall (see Orlov, "Vested"). Conceptions about the exaltation and enthronement of Moses and the Messiah, moreover, were probably influenced by the public appearances of earthly kings, and it would not be surprising if those appearances were also connected with the motif of deification, given conceptions of divine kingship in Egypt and Israel (cf. Horbury, *Messianism*). The images of Adam and of the eschatological Redeemer, similarly, affected each other. And passages such as Ezekiel the Tragedian, *Exagōgē* 68–82 and Philo, *Life of Moses* 1.155–58 show that by NT times the Moses story had been influenced by non-Jewish narratives of ascent to heaven. Since elsewhere Mark displays no phobia about conflating traditions (compare the fused biblical backgrounds in 1:2–3, 11; 12:36; 14:24, 27, 62) or merging biblical images (in 6:30–44, e.g., his Jesus is like Moses, like Elisha, and like the shepherd in Psalm 23), it is possible that he and/or his source had several different backgrounds in mind when they compiled the transfiguration narrative.

Not all parallels, however, are equally illuminating. The Moses typology has the strongest verbal echoes in the Markan transfiguration narrative ("after six days," "listen to him"); although the parallel details function in different ways, their sheer number is impressive, and even Fossum, who emphasizes the differences, is forced to admit that the Moses narratives have influenced the transfiguration story ("Ascensio"). There are also numerous parallels between the transfiguration on the one hand and traditions about Sûkkôt and royal epiphanies on the other. The relevance to the transfiguration of the traditions about the Messiah is supported by the fact that within the Markan narrative itself the divine voice calls Jesus God's Son, which is a messianic title.

The other backgrounds have a more distant sort of relationship to the Markan transfiguration narrative. There is no indication within the Markan story, for example, that Jesus is merely masquerading as a human being, as gods and angels do in Greco-Roman epiphany stories; the Markan Jesus' total participation in the human condition, culminating in his painful and even despairing death, seem to exclude such a possibility. Similarly, it is unlikely that 9:2–8 is the moment at which Jesus is divinized within the Gospel, as in Apuleius' description of Lucius' initiation; in the transfiguration Jesus is showing what he already *is* (cf. 1:11) rather than *becoming* something he was not before (see Zeller, Métamorphose," 185). "Transfigurations" such as those of Iamblichus, moreover, are recurrent rather than one-time events, and they reflect a theology in which divinity is a quality achieved by a person rather than a status granted by a god (ibid., 184). The relevance of stories of translation to heaven is attenuated by the circumstance that Mark does not specifically describe Jesus' ascent of the mountain as an ascent to the other world; nor does the other Markan mountain narrative, the calling of the Twelve (3:13-19), provide strong support for such an idea. Öhler ("Verklärung," 215-16) proposes that the transfiguration narrative has transposed the genre of a trip to heaven into a description of the coming of the kingdom of heaven on earth. This may be, but the suggestion that the Markan narrative has covered over the traces of an earlier genre is impossible to substantiate.

It also outstrips the evidence to say that the transfiguration narrative is a transposed resurrection appearance, though it is possible that certain features of the story would have reminded some Christian readers of Jesus' resurrection. Most of the characteristic features of resurrection appearances, however, are lacking here, and the common features are often either trivial or details of setting. Some of the differences, moreover, are striking. As Stein ("Transfiguration Account") points out, for example, Jesus is silent in the transfiguration, whereas he always addresses the disciples in resurrection appearances; and a voice comes from heaven in the transfiguration, whereas that never happens in the surviving accounts of resurrection appearances. Furthermore, resurrection appearance stories always begin with the disciples bereft of Jesus' presence, whereas in the transfiguration narrative he is with them throughout. Some of the alleged parallels between the two types of stories, moreover, are inexact; in the transfiguration, for example, it is not *Jesus* who "appears" but Elijah and Moses.

In conclusion, the most important backgrounds for the Markan transfiguration are traditions about Moses, the Feast of Tabernacles, and royal epiphanies; it may be that Mark has one or more of these backgrounds consciously in mind as he writes his transfiguration narrative. The other backgrounds we have explored are more distant. As David Adams points out in a private communication, however, they are still part of the "treasury—or treasuries—of stories, concepts, reports, etc. that fund(s) the imagination in any given culture, and these, even when 'distant,' may allow early readers to engage the material—engage it as immediate and plausible—in ways that would not be possible or ready-to-hand if such imagination-funding did not exist."

THE "SON OF DAVID" TITLE

◆

The designation of Jesus as "Son of David" occurs three times in Mark's Gospel, twice on the lips of Bartimaeus, a blind man whom Jesus subsequently heals (10:47–48), once on Jesus' own lips (12:35). The other explicit reference to Jesus in a Davidic role comes at the triumphal entry (11:9–10), where the crowd juxtaposes a cry acclaiming Jesus as "he who comes in the name of the Lord" with one hailing "the coming dominion of our father David" (see also 2:25–26, where Jesus invokes the example of David to justify his own behavior).

Despite these attestations, scholars have debated how positively Mark feels about the "Son of David" title because of an ambiguity in the Gospel: on the one hand, 10:47–48 and 11:9–10 (along with 2:25–26) seem to affirm the Davidic image, while on the other hand, 12:35–37 seems to question it. Those who have searched for consistency in the Markan attitude have argued two opposite viewpoints. Some have asserted that the acclamations by Bartimaeus and the crowd are mistaken; Bartimaeus is, after all, blind, and the Markan crowds end up turning against Jesus. Others have argued that 12:35–37 does not amount to a denigration of the Davidic image; the point of the pericope is that Jesus is *both* a son of David *and* a son of God. Since, however, neither of these arguments is exegetically convincing (see the COMMENTS on the respective pericopes), we are left with the impression that Mark has a genuinely ambivalent attitude toward the Davidic image. This ambivalence may reflect the usurpation of the Davidic image by the leaders of the Jewish revolts against the Romans (see Marcus, *Way*, 137–52).

In terms of its history-of-religions background, the Markan title "Son of David" has two interrelated aspects:

(1) It identifies Jesus as the coming king from the line of David, the Messiah (see the APPENDIX "The Meaning of Christ = Messiah"). On the basis of biblical passages speaking of a coming ruler from the line of David (e.g., Isa 11:1–16; Jer 23:5–6; 33:15; Ezek 34:23–24; 37:24; Mic 5:2–4; Zech 3:8; 6:12), the author of the first-century B.C.E. Jewish pseudepigrahon the *Psalms of Solomon* prays for God to send the Israelites "their king, the son of David" (*Pss. Sol.* 17:21), a military and political leader who will overthrow pagan sovereignty, purge Jerusalem of unclean Gentiles, and rule his people with wisdom and righteousness. Later in the passage the same figure is referred to as the Lord (or the Lord's) Messiah (17:32). Similarly, the fourteenth and fifteenth benedictions of the central Jewish prayer, the Eighteen Benedictions, mention the house and "shoot" of David when speaking of the Messiah, though the Palestinian and Babylonian recensions of this prayer differ in details and the date of its formulation is disputed (see Kimelman, "Messiah"). The Qumran scrolls also associate messianic hopes with a Davidic figure (see, e.g.,

4QFlor; 4QpIsa[a] [4Q161] 8–10 3:11–25 [3:15–29]; 4Q285 5[7]:2–5; 4QCommGenA [4Q252] 5:1–5; cf. Collins, *Scepter*, index under "David"), and rabbinic traditions frequently refer to the more important of two "anointed ones" as "the-Messiah-the-son-of-David" (see Chilton, "Jesus," 100; Marcus, "Mark 14:61").

(2) In the OT, however, the only person who is explicitly called "the son of David" is David's successor, Solomon (1 Chron 29:22; Prov 1:1; Eccl 1:1; cf. 1 Kgs 1:13; 2:1; 1 Chron 23:1; etc.). In later Jewish literature, partly because of his biblical reputation for wisdom (see 1 Kgs 4:29–34), Solomon becomes known as a great magician, with powers that include miraculous healing and especially exorcism (see, e.g., Josephus, *Ant.* 8.42–49; *L.A.B.* 60:3 [cf. *OTP* 2.373 note e]; *b. Git.* 68a). In *Testament of Solomon*, a second-century work that may have been influenced by Christianity, an old man pleads with Solomon to protect him from his son, who turns out to be demon possessed, by saying, "King Solomon, son of David, have mercy on me!" (20:1; cf. 1:7)—words identical with those of Bartimaeus in Mark 10:47–48. "Son of David" is also found in passages dealing with Solomon the magician in Aramaic incantation texts (see Duling, "Solomon," 246–47). The NT itself, moreover, supports an exorcistic, Solomonic nuance to "Son of David," since the Gospel of Matthew links the title especially with exorcism (12:22–23; 15:22) and other miraculous healings (9:27; 20:30–31; 21:9, 14–15; cf. Duling, "Solomon," and Chilton, "Jesus").

It would be a mistake, however, to play an exorcistic, Solomonic interpretation of "Son of David" off against a messianic, Davidic one (as I did in *Way*, 151–52). David himself is an exorcist in the Bible (1 Sam 16:23), and Solomon is a royal figure. The "shoot of Jesse," the ideal king descended from David in Isa 11:1–16, is not only a military conqueror but also a righteous judge filled with wisdom and understanding—qualities more usually associated with Solomon than with David. Moreover, 2 Samuel 7, a classic OT text that was understood as messianic by some ancient Jewish writers (see Juel, *Messianic Exegesis*, 59–88), is in its original context a prophecy of God's faithfulness to Solomon, and 4QFlor cites it to acclaim a "branch" of David who will be established on the throne of his kingship and in whose reign the Temple will be built (as it was under Solomon) and Belial = Satan will be defeated. This passage, then, combines messianic imagery with features associated with Solomon, including defeat of the devil. Similarly, as R. B. Wright (*OTP*, 2.641) points out, there are numerous similarities between the biblical portrait of Solomon and that of the Messiah in *Pss. Sol.* 17:

> Each is called the son of David, and both were extenders of boundaries, restorers and beautifiers of Jerusalem, and defenders of the worship of Yahweh. They received tribute from foreign monarchs, who came to see their glory, and stood above all other regents in wisdom and justice.

In pre-Christian Judaism, therefore, the image of the Davidic warrior-Messiah may have already begun to merge with that of the wise, even wonder-working Solomonic ruler (cf. 4Q521, in which God's Messiah may use his supernatural knowledge to perform miracles of healing, including curing the blind).

THE SADDUCEES

◆

The Sadducees were an influential Jewish sect from the second century B.C.E. until the destruction of the Temple in 70 C.E. The NT is one of the main sources for reconstructing their beliefs. They are mentioned only once, however, in Mark and Luke (Mark 12:18//Luke 20:27; cf. Matt 22:23). They are more frequently alluded to in Matthew, but most of these references portray them in an unhistorical manner as constituting a united front with the Pharisees against Jesus (Matt 3:7; 16:1, 6, 11–12; cf. also 22:34). In Acts, Luke more realistically presents the Sadducees as the opponents and rivals of the Pharisees; three of the five references are in Paul's defense speech before the Sanhedrin, where he identifies himself as a Pharisee on trial for his belief in the resurrection of the dead and thus as an opponent of Sadducean skepticism (Acts 23:6–8). In Acts 4:1 and 5:17 the Sadducees are identified as the high-priestly party and linked with the Temple.

Most of these points are confirmed by our other main source, Josephus. Neither Josephus nor any other reliable ancient authority, however, explains the name "Sadducees." It probably derives from Zadok, a descendant of Aaron who flourished in the time of David and Solomon (2 Sam 8:17; 15:24; 1 Kgs 1:34; 1 Chron 12:28) and whose posterity constituted the legitimate high-priestly line in later biblical times (Ezek 40:46; 43:19; etc.). Although the high priesthood was usurped by the Hasmonean rulers in the second and first centuries B.C.E., some of the Zadokites and their aristocratic supporters, who eventually became known as Sadducees, remained a powerful influence in the running of the Temple and of the country in general. Josephus (*Ant.* 20.197–99) specifically mentions that Ananus (= Annas) II, who was high priest in 62 C.E., was a Sadducee, and Meier argues that Ananus II's father Ananus I, the latter's five other sons, and his son-in-law Caiaphas (the high priest when Jesus was executed) were probably so also; if so, the high priest was a Sadducee for thirty-four of the sixty years of direct Roman rule (6–66 C.E.; see Meier, *Marginal Jew*, 3.396–99).

The Sadducees were thus a wealthy, elite group associated with the high priesthood (cf. Josephus, *Ant.* 13.298; 18.17). According to Josephus (*War* 2.165), they disbelieved in rewards and punishments in the afterlife; their doctrine "makes the souls [of human beings] perish along with their bodies, and they insist on observance of nothing else than the laws" (*Ant.* 18.16; my trans.). Rahmani (*Catalogue*, 53–54) challenges this report, pointing to the prevalence of individual burial and secondary interment in ossuaries in Jerusalem from about the middle of the Herodian period (20–15 C.E.) until 70 C.E. and asserting that this manner of burial implies belief in resurrection and that some of those so buried must have been Sadducees. The latter conjecture may now be supported by the discovery of an ossuary inscribed with the name *Qyp'* or *Qwp'*, which could be a reference to Caiaphas, the high priest during Jesus' time and, as noted above, a probable Sadducee (see Reich, "Caiaphas Name," but cf. the skepticism of Evans, *Ossuaries*, 106–8).

Rahmani's conclusions, however, have not met with general approval. Some scholars assert that individual and ossuary burial implies belief in postmortem existence but not necessarily a literal resurrection of dead bodies (see Meyers, *Ossuaries*, passim; McCane, *Jews, Christians, and Burial*, 72–78). Others dispute that ossuary burial necessarily suggests belief in an afterlife at all, pointing to the absence of any positive evidence confirming the linkage and suggesting other possible reasons for the spread of this mode of interment, such as economic factors and the influence of Roman customs (see Fine, "Note"; Magness, "Ossuaries," 129–40). Mark 12:26–27 and Acts 23:8, moreover, join with Josephus in implying that the Sadducees disbelieved in any sort of postmortem existence, and it is unsafe to overthrow the unambiguous testimony of three independent literary sources in favor of speculative inferences from a change in burial customs.

Josephus' statement that the Sadducees "insist on observance of nothing else than the laws" is usually taken as a reference to their rejection of the oral traditions of the Pharisees and their belief in the written Torah as the only source of legal authority (cf. *Ant.* 13.297). It is also possible, however, to interpret it in line with the claim of church fathers such as Origen (*Against Celsus* 1.49) and Jerome (*Commentary on Matthew* 22:31–32) that the Sadducees, like the Samaritans, accepted only the Pentateuch. This theory might help explain the Sadducees' rejection of the idea of resurrection, since the latter is found most clearly in the Prophets (Isa 26:19; Ezekiel 37) and the Writings (Dan 12:2, 13). It might also account for the fact that Jesus answers the Sadducees' skeptical question about the resurrection by citing a text from the Torah (Mark 12:26 pars.) and that a later rabbinic tradition, *m. Sanh.* 10:1, anathematizes people who deny that the Torah teaches the resurrection of the dead. It would make sociological sense, moreover, for an elite group such as the Sadducees to be suspicious of the Prophets, with their searing denunciations of the rich. At the same time, neither Josephus nor the NT explicitly mentions the Sadducees' rejection of the Prophets and the Writings. It is possible that the church fathers misconstrued a *preference* for the Torah—a favoritism probably shared by the Pharisees, as it was by the later rabbis—for an exclusive concentration on it, or that they confused the Sadducees with the Samaritans (cf. Schürer, 2.408–9; Meier, *Marginal Jew*, 3.400). In Mark 12:26, Jesus may respond with a text from the Pentateuch not because he knows that the Sadducees reject the other portions of the Hebrew Bible but because the Sadducees have cited a pentateuchal text, so he is answering them in kind. And the references to resurrection in the Prophets and Writings are not necessarily a refutation of the idea that the Sadducees accepted those portions of the Bible, since the Sadducees may have interpreted those references in a nonliteral manner, as allusions to continuing life through one's children, as the church father Hippolytus says they did (*Refutation* 9.29.2; cf. Van Eijk, "Marriage," 213). It is unsafe, therefore, to conclude that the Sadducees accepted only the Pentateuch (see Beckwith, *Canon*, 86–91).

Some scholars (e.g., Gundry, 705) think that Jesus' assertion that the risen dead are "like the angels who are in heaven" in Mark 12:25 combats not only Sadducean disbelief in the resurrection but also a skepticism about angels. The main evidence for such skepticism is Acts 23:8: "The Sadducees say that there is no resurrection, or angel, or spirit; but the Pharisees acknowledge all three." Davies and Allison (3.227) and Meier (*Marginal Jew*, 3.408), among others, however, argue that since the Sadducees accepted the Pentateuch as authoritative, they must have believed in angels (see the angels in Gen 19:1; 28:12; etc. and the frequent appearances of "the angel of the LORD" in the Pentateuch). Daube ("Acts 23") resolves the difficulty by interpreting "angel, or spirit" in Acts 23:8 as a reference to a component of the human being that survives death. As Meier (*Marginal Jew*, 3.408–9) points out, however, the phrasing of Acts 23:8–9 suggests that "angel" and "spirit" are separate both from each other and from the human beings to whom they relate. Meier's own solution is to argue that Acts 23:8 may simply be a mistake on Luke's part. Another possible explanation, however, is suggested by the exact wording of *Ant.* 18.16: "They insist on observance of nothing else than *the laws*; for they count it a virtue to dispute with the teachers of the *wisdom* that they pursue" (emphasis mine). This could mean that the Sadducees, like some later rabbis (see Herr, "Aggadah"), considered only *halakah* (i.e., the legal aspects of the Bible) to be binding. One was free to argue about or even to disbelieve in matters of *haggadah* (narrative), such as angels, spirits, and the resurrection— hence the Sadducees' reputation for disputing even with their own teachers about matters of "wisdom."

For other matters of Sadducean doctrine and practice, including their legal traditions and disbelief in predestination, see the excellent treatment in Meier, *Marginal Jew*, 3.389–487.

THE YOUTH WHO RAN
AWAY NAKED

◆

The strange Markan passage about the youth who runs away stripped of his linen cloth at Jesus' arrest (Mark 14:51–52) has spawned both interest and puzzlement among Christian commentators; the latter reaction probably helps explain why neither Matthew nor Luke retell it when they recast the Markan narrative, and it has no Johannine counterpart. In the COMMENT on 14:50–52 it is argued that the passage may enshrine a historical memory but that it also has a symbolic resonance, derived partly from the contrast to portraits of ideal disciples elsewhere in the Gospel, partly from the eschatological prophecy in Amos 2:16. Some commentators, however, have made more of the passage, and a review of a few of their interpretations provides a fascinating case study in the exercise of exegetical imagination (cf. Neirynck, "Fuite," and Brown, *Death*, 1.295–304).

One popular form of exegesis has been to link the youth with a known disciple. In the patristic period, the most common identification was with John the son of Zebedee—the "other disciple," according to the traditional interpretation, who, with Peter, followed Jesus after his arrest (John 18:15–16; see e.g., Ambrose, *Exposition of Psalm Thirty-Six* 60; Peter Chrysologus, *Sermon* 78, who links the two men by saying that John ran away naked but Peter became morally naked when he denied Jesus). The medieval commentator Theophylact (*Explanation of Mark* 14:50–54) mentions another theory: the young man was James the brother of the Lord, who, according to a patristic tradition, dressed in a linen garment all his life (cf. Eusebius, *Ecclesiastical History* 2.23.6).

But Theophylact also mentions another opinion, which he traces back to Victor of Antioch: the young man was a resident of the house in which the Last Supper was eaten. In the nineteenth and twentieth centuries, this hypothesis developed into the popular suggestion that the youth was none other than John Mark, the author of our Gospel, who lived in Jerusalem at the home of his mother, Mary (Acts 12:12; on the question whether the evangelist actually was John Mark, see the INTRODUCTION in vol. 1, pp. 17–21). The anonymity of the youth, then, arises not from the evangelist's ignorance of his name but from his own modesty; our short scene is like an artist's self-portrait in an inconspicuous corner of a busy painting (see Zahn, *Einleitung*, 2.245) or an Alfred Hitchcock cameo appearance (a popular comparison on today's World Wide Web). Besides explaining the young man's anonymity, this theory, which also surfaced in antiquity (see the catena cited by Neirynck, "Fuite," 57 n. 246), offers an ingenious way of accounting for his scanty apparel (see especially Zahn, *Einleitung*, 2.243–45): Mark had gone to bed when the Last Supper, which was taking place in his house, broke up; suddenly awakened by the sounds of the departing guests, and seized with curiosity as to what would happen to Jesus, he rushed out after him clad only in his underwear. Ingenious as this theory is, it relies on a tissue of questionable assumptions, the most doubtful of which is that an evangelist who had been present at Jesus' arrest, and had observed his courageous response to it, would forgo mentioning his eyewitness status and hence an opportunity to authenticate his testimony (contrast John 19:35; 21:24).

As a consequence of increasing skepticism about such reconstructions, this sort of novelistic exegesis of Mark 14:51–52 has given way in recent years to more symbolic, theological interpretations—which sometimes are no less speculative than their novelistic predecessors. The most popular of these symbolic interpretations is the baptismal theory, which links or identifies our young man with the youth clad in a white robe who appears to the women on Easter morning to announce the gospel message (16:5; see, e.g., Vanhoye, "Fuite"; Scroggs and Groff, "Baptism"; Crossan, "Empty Tomb," 147–48). The point of departure for this theory, aside from the term *neaniskos*, is sartorial: like a baptizand, the young man loses his garment and becomes naked, only to be clad in white when Easter dawns (on the Easter baptismal vigil in the early church, see Yarnold, *Awe-Inspiring Rites*, 15–36). Sometimes the young man is identified with Christ himself (partly on the basis of 15:46, where the dead Jesus, like the youth in our story, is wrapped in a *sindōn*, partly on the basis of John 20:5–7, where the risen Jesus has left his grave clothes behind); sometimes with the Markan community; sometimes with both. Aside from the fact that Mark provides no explicit indication that the two *neaniskoi* are to be identified, the main problem with this theory is the disjunction between the youth's panicked behavior and the courage that was demonstrated by Christ and expected of Christians: the youth runs away from Jesus to save his life, whereas Christians were expected to remain faithful to Jesus even under threat of death (cf. 8:34–38 and Brown, *Death*, 1.303–4). As Smith ("Score," 457 n. 19) puts it: "This interpretation neglects only the main facts: this young man deserted Christ and saved himself."

To be sure, the document that Smith himself published, *The Secret Gospel of Mark*, does connect the youth of Mark 14:51–52 with baptism, since it mentions a youth (*neaniskos*) whom Jesus raises from the dead, who subsequently comes to him by night "clothed with a linen cloth over his nakedness," and who is taught by Jesus "the mystery of the dominion of God" (cf. Mark 4:11). The description of this youth's attire is identical with that of the youth in our passage, and Smith (*Clement*, 167–88) ascribes baptismal symbolism to his resurrection from the dead and entry into the dominion of God. But since there are increasing suspicions that Smith himself forged the *Secret Gospel* (see Ehrman, *Lost Christianities*; Carlson, *Gospel Hoax*), the evidence provided by this "Gospel" may be irrelevant to the question at hand.

HISTORICAL PROBLEMS IN THE MARKAN SANHEDRIN TRIAL

◆

The historical difficulties with the Markan portrayal of Jesus' trial by the Jewish ruling body, the Sanhedrin, are very complicated; for a full treatment of the issues and history of interpretation see Brown, *Death*, 1.328–97. Some of the problems, such as the degree of Jewish self-government and the authority of the Sanhedrin to condemn to death in Jesus' time, are too involved to explore here in detail, but Brown is probably correct to assert that the Romans permitted the Jews to execute Temple trespassers, adulterers, and other clear transgressors of certain grave religious matters but required other offenders to be turned over to the imperial authorities, who had the final say on whether capital punishment should be meted out. Three other issues, however, can be discussed more tersely: conflicts with Jewish law, discrepancies with John, and doublets with the trial before Pilate.

Conflicts with Jewish law. The conflicts with Jewish law have to do with the difference between what happens in the Markan account of Jesus' Sanhedrin trial and the guidelines in the Mishnah, a compendium of legal principles and discussions edited around 200 C.E. Some of the more striking differences are summed up by Juel (*Messiah and Temple*, 59–60; for others, see Brown, *Death*, 1.358–59):

(1) [Mishnah] *Sanhedrin* 4:1 states that "in capital cases they hold the trial during the daytime and the verdict also must be reached during the daytime." According to Mark, the trial is conducted and the verdict pronounced at night.

(2) *Sanhedrin* 4:1 also states: "Therefore trials may not be held on the eve of a Sabbath or on the eve of a Festival-day." According to Mark, the trial was held on the eve of the Passover. [Juel errs here; according to the usual Jewish way of reckoning, the Markan Sanhedrin trial is conducted not on the eve of Passover but on Passover day (see the NOTE on "on the first day of the Feast of Unleavened Bread" in 14:12). Even so, such a trial would clearly have been prohibited, since Passover day was the eve of a Sabbath, and in any case all "work" was forbidden on holidays.]

(3) *Sanhedrin* 4:1 also states that "in capital cases a verdict of acquittal may be reached on the same day, but a verdict of conviction not until the following day." According to Mark, Jesus is convicted on the same day.

(4) *Sanhedrin* 7:5: "The 'blasphemer' is not culpable unless he pronounces the Name itself" [i.e., YHWH, the four-letter name of God]. Measured by this rule, nothing Jesus said at the trial could have been construed as blasphemy.

(5) According to *Sanhedrin* 11:2, the regular meeting place of the high court was the "Chamber of Hewn Stone." According to Mark, the trial was held at the home of the high priest.

(6) *Sanhedrin* 4:1 states that "capital cases must begin with reasons for acquittal and may not begin with reasons for conviction." According to Mark, the trial begins with (false) testimony against Jesus; there are no witnesses for the defense.

(7) *Sanhedrin* 4:5 states that witnesses are to be solemnly warned and carefully examined regarding their testimony. Mark reports no such procedure, nor does he suggest that the false witnesses were in any way held accountable for their false testimony.

As Juel, Brown, and others have pointed out, however, it is problematic to use the Mishnah to establish the Sanhedrin's judicial practice in Jesus' time, over one hundred fifty years earlier. In the first century, for example, "sanhedrin" may not have designated a legislative/judicial body with a fixed membership and meeting place, as it does in the Mishnah, but an *ad hoc* assemblage of the high priest and his advisors (see the APPENDIX "The Jewish Leaders in Mark"). The ruling clique in the sanhedrins of Jesus' time, moreover, was probably the Sadducean one, and the Sadducees' interpretation of the Law was generally harsher than that of the Pharisees, the spiritual ancestors of the rabbis whose opinions are collected in the Mishnah. It is possible, then, that the procedures of an early-first-century sanhedrin would have violated the (later) Mishnaic guidelines.

That being said, it remains a question whether *any* properly constituted, official Jewish court of the early first century would have proceeded in the blatantly prejudicial way that is depicted in Mark 14:53–65. Would there not have been some protest or demurral from one or more of the body's members (cf. John 7:50–52 and, on the impropriety of night trials, *Leucippe and Clitophon* 8:9)? Any answer is speculative, but portrayal of a kangaroo court does fit into later Christian stereotypes about Jewish malice against Jesus and his followers (see, e.g., 1 Thess 2:15–16; Acts 2:23; 10:39; 13:28).

This line of reasoning, however, leads to another question: *was* the Jewish body that interrogated Jesus on the night before his death a "properly constituted court," or was it something else? Although the assemblage is called a *synedrion* in 14:55 and 15:1, and both passages even use the phrase "the *whole* Sanhedrin," we have just noted that this term is often employed for *ad hoc* assemblies of the elite who function as the high priest's "brain trust." Jesus' appearance before the Sanhedrin, then, may not have been a real trial, as Mark depicts it, but something more like an informal grand jury hearing—an interrogation led by the high priest to determine whether Jesus' transgressions were sufficiently grave to justify delivery to the Romans for punishment. This hypothesis, as a matter of fact, is supported by the Johannine parallel to our story, in which Jesus is not formally charged with or convicted of anything but simply questioned by the high priest and then turned over to the Romans (John 18:13–14, 19–24; cf. Luke 22:54, 66–71, which also lacks a formal condemnation).

Discrepancies with John. This brings us to the second category of difficulty posed by the Markan portrait of Jesus' Sanhedrin trial—discrepancies with John. Although there are some basic similarities in structure, especially at the beginning and the end, the actual content of the hearings is quite different in the two Gospels, as can be seen by studying figure 48. In Mark the whole debate hinges on the question of who Jesus is, and 14:61–62 offers a compendium of the Gospel's main Christological titles (Christ, Son of God, Son of Man), to all of which Jesus lays claim. In John, by contrast, the high priest simply asks Jesus about his disciples and teaching, and Jesus answers that he has always spoken openly about them—a bold but uninformative response that earns him a slap. The Markan narrative, then, is more developed theologically than the Johannine one, which in this instance seems more plausible (see the introduction to the COMMENT on 14:53–56).

Doublets with the trial before Pilate. How, then, did the Markan story of the Sanhedrin trial develop? A clue may be found in the third category of evidence, the doublets with the Roman trial in 15:1–20. As can be seen by studying figure 52, several features of the two trial narratives are analogous to or even identical with each other. Both begin with Jesus being "led away" to the authority figure who will interrogate him, and in both that figure asks him why he makes no reply to the charges leveled against him; Jesus, however, does not "answer anything" in response. In both, moreover, the authority figure asks Jesus about his identity as Christ or the king of the Jews, which are synonymous titles, and in both this question is an unwitting double entendre, since it could be read as a statement ("You are the Christ/the king of the Jews"). In both cases Jesus answers the question by asserting that the authority figure himself has testified to his messiahship/ kingship, and in both he ends up being condemned to death, mocked, spat upon, and beaten. While it is possible that Jesus experienced similar things at two different trials, the quantity of similitude, even in matters of phrasing, makes another interpretation more likely: the narrative of the Jewish trial has been elaborated on the basis of the Roman one. This sort of doubling continued in the further development of the Gospel tradition; Matt 26:64, for example, drops "that I am" from Mark 14:62, thus making the Matthean Jesus' response to the high priest even closer to his response to Pilate (Matt 27:11//Mark 15:2).

This conclusion about the partly fictional character of the Markan Sanhedrin trial makes sense: despite the apologetic Luke 23:51, it is improbable that any adherent or subsequent follower of Jesus was present at his interrogation by the high priest (Joseph of Arimathea was at most a sympathizer, and it is doubtful that he subsequently identified with the Christians, or he would have made more of an impact on early Christian traditions; cf. the COMMENT on 15:42–45 and

Brown, *Death*, 2.1228 n. 59). Christian knowledge of that event, therefore, was necessarily sketchy, and early Christians probably filled in the picture, as they did the portrayal of the Gethsemane scene, on the basis of their theological convictions and what they took to be OT prophecies of Jesus' life (cf. the NOTE on "going forward a bit" in 14:35). This hypothesis of literary elaboration on the basis of the trial before Pilate is rendered more likely by the circumstance that if taken literally, one aspect of the double narrative creates a logical conundrum: if the whole Sanhedrin has already condemned Jesus to death (14:64), why do they meet again at the crack of dawn to decide what to do with him (15:1; cf. Nineham, 401)?

Figure 52: Doublets in the Markan Trial Scenes

Sanhedrin Trial: Mark 14:53–65	*Trial before Pilate: Mark 15:1–20*
14:53: And they led Jesus away (*apēgagon*) to the high priest, and all the chief priests and the elders and the scribes (cf. 14:55: the chief priests and the whole Sanhedrin) gathered together.	15:1: And immediately, early in the morning, the chief priests, having taken counsel with the elders and the scribes and the whole Sanhedrin, bound Jesus and led him away (*apēnenkan*) and turned him over to Pilate.
14:60: And the high priest rose up into the middle and asked Jesus, saying, "You make no reply (*ouk apokrinē ouden*)? Why are these people testifying against you?"	15:4: And Pilate asked him again, saying, "You make no reply (*ouk apokrinē ouden*)? See what great things they are charging you with!"
14:61: But he was silent, and he did not answer anything (*ouk apekrinato ouden*).	15:5: But Jesus did not answer anything anymore (*ouketi ouden apekrithē*).
14:61: And again the high priest asked him and said to him, "You are the Christ (*sy ei ho Christos*) the Son of the Blessed One!?"	15:2: And Pilate asked him, "You are the king of the Jews (*sy ei ho basileus tōn Ioudaiōn*)?"
14:62: And Jesus said, "*You* have said that I am . . ."	15:2: But he answered him, saying, "*You* are saying it."
14:64: And they all condemned him as deserving death.	15:15abd: And Pilate . . . turned Jesus over . . . in order that he might be crucified.
14:65: And some began to spit on him and to cover his face and to hit him and to say to him, "Prophesy!" And the attendants received him with slaps.	15:15c, 16–20: Pilate flogs Jesus; soldiers mock him as king, beat his head with a cane, and spit on him.

All of this is not to argue that the Markan portrayal of Jesus' Sanhedrin trial is completely unhistorical. Rather, the historical memory of a nighttime interrogation by the high priest, perhaps assisted by some advisors (a "sanhedrin"), has been elaborated in line with early Christian convictions—including those of Mark himself (cf. the introduction to the COMMENT on 14:53–65).

CRUCIFIXION

◆

Crucifixion was a gruesome mode of execution employed by the Persians, Seleucids, Carthaginians, and Romans from about the sixth century B.C.E. to the fourth century C.E. (for an accessible survey, see Hengel, *Crucifixion*). It was generally avoided in Israel during periods of self-government, partly perhaps because of the belief expressed in Deut 21:23 that "anyone hung on a tree is under God's curse," although the reference here is to suspending a dead victim rather than hanging a live one. Josephus does note that a Jewish king, Alexander Jannaeus, crucified eight hundred of this enemies (*War* 1.97; *Ant.* 13.380), and this report seems to be confirmed by the denunciation in a Qumran passage, 4QpNah 3–4 1:6–8, of the "angry lion" who "hanged living men" from a tree, an abomination that had never before been known in Israel. Not all members of the Qumran community, however, were averse to employing crucifixion as a penalty; the author of 11QTemple 64:10–11 reverses the order of words in Deut 21:22 to speak of a person whom "you shall hang on a tree, and he will die." Still, crucifixion was generally avoided by Israelite and Jewish courts in favor of quicker and supposedly more humane methods of execution such as stoning.

For the Romans, the inhumanity of crucifixion was exactly what recommended it: they believed that the torture it inflicted on criminals served as a deterrent against those who might otherwise be inclined to similar criminal behavior. As a general rule, the penalty was not imposed on Roman citizens or other persons of rank but was restricted to slaves, foreign rebels, brigands, and others who stood outside the boundary of normal legal protection (see Hengel, *Crucifixion*, 33–63). The abhorrence with which it was viewed, and the shame with which it was associated, are palpable in Cicero's description of the execution of Gavius of Messana:

> He hung there [to] suffer the worst extremes of the tortures inflicted upon slaves. To bind a Roman citizen is a crime, to flog him is an abomination, to slay him is almost an act of murder: to crucify him is—what? There is no fitting word that can possibly describe so horrible a deed. (*Against Verres* 2.5.66.170)

The horror of the punishment is probably part of the reason that we have no detailed ancient description of it; the passion narratives of the Gospels are our most elaborate accounts. As Hengel (*Crucifixion*, 25) puts it: "No ancient writer wanted to dwell too long on this cruel procedure." And these sparse traces in the literary records are supplemented by only one major archaeological find, the skeleton of a crucified man discovered in Giv'at ha-Mivtar near Jerusalem (see Kuhn, "Gekreuzigte"; Zias and Sekeles, "Crucified Man"; Zias, "Crucifixion").

From the available sources it is nevertheless possible to reconstruct some common elements in Roman crucifixions (see Fulda, *Kreuz*, 46–189, for sources and detailed discussion). Before the crucifixion itself, the victim was often painfully scourged (see the NOTE on "wishing to satisfy the crowd, released Barabbas to them and turned Jesus over, after flogging him" in 15:15). He was then forced to carry the *patibulum*, or crossbeam, which could weigh seventy-five to one hundred twenty-five pounds, to the place of execution. There he was thrown to the ground and his wrists either tied or nailed to the beam (the Romans preferred the latter). The *patibulum* was lifted onto the *stipes*, a heavy upright post of rough wood permanently anchored in the ground, and the prisoner's feet tied or nailed to it. Death could take several days (cf. Pilate's surprise in 15:44 at Jesus' quick demise), and during this slow process insects, birds of prey, and dogs might attack the flesh of the helplessly transfixed victim.

The usual cause of death in crucifixion is a matter of controversy; the two most commonly mentioned factors are shock and hampered respiration. The latter is emphasized in an article published in the *Journal of the American Medical Association* in 1986:

> The weight of the body, pulling down on the outstretched arms and shoulders, would tend to fix the intercostal muscles [the muscles between the ribs] in an inhalation state and thereby hinder passive exhalation. . . . Adequate exhalation required lifting the body by pushing up on the feet and by flexing the elbows and adducting the shoulders. However, this maneuver would place the entire weight of the body on the tarsals [the bones in the feet near the ankle] and produce searing pain. Furthermore, flexion of the elbows would cause rotation of the wrists about the iron nails and cause fiery pain along the damaged median nerves. Lifting of the body would also painfully scrape the scourged back against the rough wooden stipes. Muscle cramps and paresthesias [sensations of pricking or tingling] of the outstretched and uplifted arms would add to the discomfort. As a result, each respiratory effort would become agonizing and tiring and lead eventually to asphyxia. (Edwards et al., "Physical Death," 1461)

Death, then, would ensue when the victim became too exhausted to raise himself and exhale. This theory would explain why many crosses were equipped with a *sedile* ("seat"), a small peg or bench on which the buttocks of the crucified victim rested: the seat would enable the victim to keep breathing longer and thus prolong his agony. It would also clarify why breaking the legs, as in John 19:31–33, would be a *coup de grace*: it would make it impossible for the victim to raise himself and catch a breath.

Zugibe (*Crucifixion*) has argued against the asphyxiation theory on the basis of experiments he has conducted, simulating certain aspects of crucifixion with volunteers and monitoring their physical reactions; none of them, he reports, experienced difficulty breathing. As Maslen and Mitchell ("Medical Theories") point out, however, Zugibe's simulations omit important aspects of the crucifixion process (e.g., whipping, being nailed to the cross, and dehydration); as they drily put it: "The fact that none of the re-enactment research has actually crucified people means that these studies have only limited relevance to genuine cases." Since, moreover, Zugibe situated his volunteers on their replica crosses in positions that corresponded to Christian iconography but not to the historical and archaeological evidence, and since he removed them as soon as they began to experience discomfort, his refutation of the asphyxiation theory is flawed. Nevertheless, asphyxiation was certainly not the only factor inducing death in ancient crucifixions, and different victims probably died from different causes.

Whatever the exact cause of death, crucifixion was, from the point of view of the executioners, an appropriately agonizing form of execution for heinous offenders. It is likely that it was also considered appropriate because the raising of the victim mimicked the self-exaltation for which he or she was being punished. The Gospel of John four times employs for Jesus' crucifixion the verb "to be raised up" (*hypsōthēnai*: John 3:14; 8:28; 12:32, 34), a term that was also used to describe royal enthronement and other forms of conspicuous societal advancement (cf. Pss 68:18 [67:19 LXX]; 89:19 [88:18 LXX]; 110:7 [109:7 LXX]; 1 Sam 2:10). John 12:32, moreover, suggests that "to be raised up" = "to be crucified" was a commonly understood equation (see Hirsch, *Vierte Evangelium*, 71). This overlap in language is probably not accidental but an illustration of the principle that the punishment should fit the crime, since the persons executed by crucifixion were often people who had tried to "rise" above their station. The retaliation was to raise them up on high, sometimes in a sitting posture that mimicked royal enthronement (cf. Seneca's expression "to sit on the cross" [*Epistle* 101]). This interpretation of crucifixion as parodic enthronement is supported by the description of the Persians' Sacian feast in Dio Chrysostom, *Discourses* 4.67–70; here, in a passage with numerous parallels to Mark 15:16–32 (clothing with royal apparel, stripping, scourging, and crucifixion), Dio concludes that the crucifixion of the Persian king pro tem was meant to show "foolish and wicked people" that they would come to "a most shameful and wretched end" if they insolently attempted to acquire royal power. The mockery of Jesus as "the king of the Jews," then, may not have been anomalous but an illustration of the parodic element inherent in crucifixion (see Marcus, "Crucifixion").

THE EMPTY TOMB

♦

As Strauss (*Life*, 735–36) points out, the contrast between life and death is a basic dichotomy of existence, and so the assertion that a dead person has come to life is normally considered to be incredible. Those unable to accept that Jesus was an exception to this law of nature have customarily challenged one of two aspects of the Gospel narrative: either that he was dead when taken down from the cross or that he was afterward seen alive. In the former case, doubts about the Gospel story of the empty tomb often play a role.

Crossan (*Who Killed*, 160–77), for example, dismisses the empty tomb story as an apologetic invention of the early church. In his opinion Jesus' body was probably never entombed at all; it was either left on the cross to be devoured by scavengers, which was the usual fate of the crucified (cf. Horace, *Epistles* 1.16.48; Artemidorus, *Oneirocritica* 2.53), or dumped into a common grave for executed criminals. In either case, the early Christians did not know where his body was, and they invented the story of Joseph of Arimathaea out of embarrassment. This view is based partly on statements in Jewish and Roman sources about the withholding of honorable burial from executed criminals (see the COMMENT on 15:42–45), partly on references in Palestinian Jewish sources to collective graves for those who died shamefully, including executed criminals (see, e.g., *m. Sanh.* 6:5; and *t. Sanh.* 9:8, and cf. Matt 27:5–8), and partly on the recognition that the burial and empty tomb stories in the Gospels contain apologetic features. The confirmation of Jesus' death in Mark 15:44–45, for example, counters the rumor that he was still alive when taken down from the cross. The witnesses to the place of burial in Mark 15:47 pars. show that the women did not go to the wrong tomb on Easter morning. The guard story in Matt 27:62–66 and 28:11–15 refutes the charge that the disciples stole Jesus' body. And the tomb's emptiness establishes the facticity of his resurrection.

One can recognize apologetic features in the tomb narratives, however, without concluding that those accounts are completely fictional. As McCane (*Stone*, 100) puts it, Crossan's argument "reads like an exercise in throwing the baby out with the bath water," and the Joseph of Arimathaea tradition is not so easily dismissed. Allison (*Resurrecting Jesus*, Excursus II) cites in favor of its historicity, among other points, its conflict with the overall tendency of the Gospels to depict the Sanhedrin negatively; its linkage of Joseph with Arimathaea, an obscure and unimportant place; the pre-Pauline reference to Jesus' burial in 1 Cor 15:4; the evidence that the Roman authorities sometimes released the bodies of executed criminals, including the crucified, to their families and friends (see the COM-

MENT on 15:42–45); and the likelihood that the earliest Christians knew where Jesus had been buried, since his death had occurred in public and had generated enormous interest. In Allison's opinion, moreover, if Jesus' corpse had been dumped by his enemies into a mass grave for criminals, early Christian authors would probably have interpreted this action as a fulfillment of Isa 53:9 ("They made his grave with the wicked").

If, however, contrary to Crossan, Jesus' body was deposited in a particular tomb by Joseph of Arimathaea, it may still be questioned whether that tomb was emptied by a miracle. The body, for example, may have been stolen by the disciples. The implausible and almost certainly fictional story of the guard at the tomb, which is only in Matthew among the canonical Gospels, was probably designed to counter this theory, which must therefore have been circulating in Matthew's day; and where there is smoke (the denial that the body was stolen) there may be fire (the body *was* stolen). This is the line of attack taken by Reimarus (*Fragments*, 153–65) in his groundbreaking work on the historical Jesus. The chief problem with it is that it makes the disciples amazingly persistent in perpetrating a hoax, while at least three of them, Peter and the sons of Zebedee, were willing to die for the belief that God had raised Jesus supernaturally from the dead.

But someone else may have stolen the body of Jesus. Suspicion has often focused on Joseph of Arimathaea, and various motivations from hostility to Jesus to belief in him have been used to explain his theft of Jesus' corpse. Other candidates, such as the anonymous gardener of John 20:15, have been mentioned as well; it is also possible, as Allison (*Resurrecting Jesus*, 202–3, 334) suggests, that the Jewish authorities moved Jesus' body to prevent veneration of it or that necromancers stole it because of the supposed magical properties of the corpse of an executed holy man. Such speculations cannot, in the nature of things, be proven, but neither can they be disproved, and their seeming unlikelihood must be weighed against the even greater improbability of a dead person returning to life (see Allison, *Resurrecting Jesus*, 334–35). Here one's presuppositions will dictate what is deemed plausible or implausible.

If Jesus' corpse was not stolen, another possibility is that it was not really a corpse when deposited in the tomb. It may have been, rather, a living body in a state of suspended animation, from which it revived after being interred. Either on his own or with the help of confederates, Jesus could subsequently have exited the tomb, which would explain why the latter was found empty on the third day. As with the theory of the stolen body, there is evidence that the theory of the resuscitated body was circulating in the early years of Christianity, since Mark 15:44–45, as well as Origen's polemic against the opinion that Jesus only appeared to die (*Against Celsus* 2.56), seem designed to counter it. This theory has itself been resuscitated in modern times and was popularized by Bahrdt in the eighteenth century, Venturini in the nineteenth, and Schonfield in the twentieth (see Strauss, *Life*, 737–39; Schonfield, *Passover Plot*, 151–62). The plausibility of a postcrucifixion revival of Jesus is often supported by the parallel in Josephus' *Life* (420–21), which speaks of three friends of Josephus who were removed from the cross alive upon Josephus' appeal to Titus; two of them subsequently died, but the third came to life again (*ezēsen*).

There are some difficulties, however, with the resuscitation scenario. Although Josephus speaks of the revival of his crucified friend, he does not say explicitly that the latter appeared to be dead, much less that his death was confirmed by the officer in charge of his execution. At a crucial point, therefore, the analogy with Jesus breaks down. As Strauss (*Life*, 734) points out, moreover, if Jesus survived the cross, he did not survive for very long, because otherwise the sightings of him probably would have continued for months or years and would have terminated with his natural death, which would have been noted by someone. Jesus must therefore have died soon after the crucifixion, presumably as a result of the wounds and mistreatment he had suffered there. But as Strauss (*New Life*, 1.412) points out elsewhere, it is hard to see how the sight of a barely resuscitated, half-dead Jesus could have engendered the fiercely held resurrection belief of the early church:

> It is impossible that a being who had stolen half-dead out of the sepulchre, who crept about weak and ill, wanting medical treatment, who required bandaging, strengthening, and indulgence, and who still at last yielded to his sufferings, could have given to the disciples the impression that he was a Conqueror over death and the grave, the Prince of life, an impression which lay at the bottom of their future ministry.

To be sure, it is possible that Jesus did *not* convince his disciples that he had arisen from the dead; they may, rather, have been his confederates in a plot to simulate his death, perhaps with the help of drugs, and then to proclaim his resurrection after he revived (cf. Schweitzer, *Quest* [2001], 37–46). This sort of conspiracy theory, however, faces further challenges: why, for example, should the revived Jesus appear only to his followers, whereas an appearance to the general public would have been more effective in perpetrating the desired fraud? And, as with the stolen body theory, the question arises why some disciples would have been willing to suffer martyrdom for a proclamation that they knew to be fraudulent (cf. Origen, *Against Celsus*, 2.56; Strauss, *Life*, 737–39). Schonfield (*Passover Plot*, 151–75) attempts to meet the latter objection by including the disciples in the group that was hoodwinked by Jesus' sham death; his only confederates were Joseph of Arimathaea and perhaps Nicodemus. Schonfield, however, does not make credible this scenario in which men in the upper echelon of the Palestinian Jewish leadership were so committed to Jesus that they were willing to help him fake his death. If they were sincere religious seekers, would they not have been troubled by the subterfuge in which they were engaged? And if they were not, why would they have bothered to throw their lot in with a dangerously marginal figure from Galilee rather than sticking to more conventional forms of piety?

This survey, then, has shown that some of the theories about the empty tomb tradition are more likely than others. It is improbable that that tradition is a total invention of the early Christian community, or that Joseph of Arimathaea is an entirely fictional character, or that Jesus was still alive when placed in the tomb, or that his disciples or Joseph of Arimathaea stole his body. It remains possible that the body was stolen by someone else. But it is also possible that it was missing on the third day for the reason implied by the Gospels themselves—because Jesus had risen bodily from the dead.

MARKAN REDACTIONAL VOCABULARY

◆

This compilation reflects the redactional analysis in the body of the commentary, usually in the introduction to each COMMENT section.

ἀγανακτέω 10:41
ἀγνοέω 9:32
ἀγορά 7:4
ἀγοράζω 6:37
ἀγρυπνέω 13:33
ἀδελφός 5:37
ἀδύνατος 10:27
ἄζυμος 14:1
αἴρω 2:9 8:19 8:20
αἰτέω 10:38
ἀκάθαρτος 3:11 3:30 6:7
  7:25
ἀκοή 1:28
ἀκολουθέω 2:15 6:1?
  10:28 10:32 10:52 14:54
  15:41
ἀκούω 2:17 3:8 4:3 4:24
  6:11 6:16 6:20 7:14 7:25
  8:18 10:41 11:14 11:18
  12:28 12:37 14:11
ἅλας 9:50
ἀλείφω 6:13
ἀλεκτοροφωνία 13:35
ἀλέκτωρ 14:72
ἀλήθεια 12:14
ἀληθής 12:14
ἀλλά 3:26 9:13 14:28
  16:7
ἀλλήλος 8:16 9:50
ἄλλος 6:15 (2x) 7:4 12:5
  12:9 15:41
ἀμήν 10:15 14:9
ἄμφοδον 11:4

ἀναβαίνω 10:33
ἀναβλέπω 10:52
ἀναγινώσκω 13:14
ἀναθεματίζω 14:71
ἀνάκειμαι 14:18
ἀνὰ μέσον 7:31
ἀναμιμνήσκω 11:21
  14:72
ἀναπαύω 6:31
Ἀνδρέας 13:3
ἄνθρωπος 10:27
ἄνιπτος 7:2
ἀνίστημι 7:24 9:10
ἀπαίρω 2:20?
ἁμαρτία 2:7 2:9 2:1
ἀμπελών 12:9
ἀναβαίνω 4:8 10:33
ἀναγκάζω 6:45
ἄνεμος 6:51
ἄνθρωπος 8:2 12:14
  14:21
ἀνίστημι 9:9 9:27 10:1
  10:34
ἅπας 11:32
ἀπαγγέλλω 5:19 6:30
ἀπαρνέομαι 14:72
ἀπέρχομαι 5:17 5:20 6:32
  6:46 7:24 8:13 12:12
  14:10
ἀπιστία 6:6 9:24
ἀποθνήσκω 15:44 (2x)
ἀποκαθιστάνω 9:12
ἀποκεφαλίζω 6:16

ἀποκρίνομαι 8:29 9:6
  10:24 11:22 12:28
  12:34 12:35 14:40
  14:48
ἀποκτείνω 10:34 14:1
ἀπολύω 6:45 8:9
ἀπόλλυμι 3:6 11:18
ἀποστέλλω 3:14 6:7
  12:13
ἀπόστολος 6:30
ἀποτάσσομαι 6:46
ἀργύριον 14:11
ἄρρωστος 6:13
ἄρτος 6:52 8:14 (2x) 8:16
  8:17 8:19
ἀρχή 1:1
ἀρχιερεύς 10:33 11:18
  14:1 14:10 14:43 14:53
  15:10
ἄρχομαι 1:45 4:1 5:17
  5:20 6:2 6:7 6:34 6:56
  8:11 8:31 8:32 10:28
  10:32 10:41 11:15 12:1
  14:19 14:33
ἀσκός 2:22 end
ἀσπάζομαι 9:15
ἀσύνετος 7:18
αὐλή 14:66
αὐξάνομαι 4:8
ἀχειροποιητός 14:57
ἀφίημι 1:34 2:7 2:9 2:10
  5:19 5:37 7:27 8:13
  10:28 11:6 12:12

βάλλω 12:41
βαπτίζω 7:4 10:38 (2x)
  10:39 (2x)
βάπτισμα 10:38 10:39
βαπτισμός 7:4
βασανίζω 6:48
βασιλεία 10:23 10:24
Βηθανία 11:1 11:12
βίος 12:44
βλασφημέω 2:7
βλέπω 4:24 8:18 12:14
  13:2 13:5 13:9 13:33
βοάω 15:34
βοηθέω 9:24
βούλομαι 15:15
βρῶμα 7:19

Γαλιλαία 1:9 1:14 1:16
  1:28 1:39 7:31 9:30
  14:28 15:41 16:7
γάρ 1:16 1:22 2:15 3:10
  5:42 10:22 11:13 11:18
  12:23 14:2 14:40 15:10
  16:8
γαστήρ 13:17
γένος 9:29
γῆ 2:10 4:1 4:31 15:33
γίνομαι 1:4 1:32 4:22
  4:35 6:2 6:14 6:35
  9:6 9:33 11:19 11:23
  13:18 14:17 15:33 (2x)
  15:42
γινώσκω (οἶδα) 1:34 2:10
  4:13 7:24 8:17 9:6 9:30
  10:38 12:12 12:14 12:15
  13:33 13:35 14:40 15:10
  15:45
γραμματεύς 1:22 2:6
  3:22 7:1 8:31 9:11 9:14
  10:33 11:18 11:27 14:1
  14:43 14:53 15:31
γράφω 1:2 9:12 9:13
  14:21
γρηγορέω 13:35 13:37
γυνή 12:23 15:40

δαιμόνιον 1:34 (2x) 1:39
  3:15 6:13
δαιμονίζω 1:32 5:18
δεῖ 13:10
δέκα 10:41
Δεκάπολις 5:20 7:31
δεξιός 14:62
δεῦτε 6:31
δέω 11:2 11:4
διάγομαι 9:9
διακονέω 15:41
διακρίνω 11:23
διαλογίζομαι 2:6 2:8
  (2x) 8:16 8:17
διαστέλλομαι 5:43 7:36
  8:14 9:9
διδάσκαλος 4:38 13:1
διδάσκω 1:21 1:22 2:13
  4:1 4:2 6:2 6:6 6:30
  6:34 8:31 9:31 10:1
  11:17 12:14 12:35
  14:49
διδαχή 1:22 1:27 4:2
  11:18 12:38
δίδωμι 3:6 6:2 6:7 6:37
  6:41 12:9 12:14 (2x)
  14:11
διέρχομαι 4:35
διωγμός 10:30
δίς 14:72
δόλος 14:1
δύναμαι 1:40 1:45 2:7
  3:23 3:24 3:25 3:26
  3:27 4:32 7:15 7:18
  7:24 9:22 9:23 9:28
  9:29 9:39 10:26 10:38
  10:39
δύναμις 6:2 6:14 14:62
δυνατός 9:23 10:27 13:22
δύο 6:7 14:1
δυσκόλως 10:23 10:24
δύω 1:32
δώδεκα 3:16 5:42 6:7
  8:19 10:32 14:10 14:17
  14:20

ἑαυτός 8:14 9:10 10:26
  13:9
ἐγείρω 2:9 6:16 9:27
  14:28
ἔθνος 10:33 11:17 13:10
εἶδεν 1:10? 1:16 1:19
  2:14 4:3 6:33 6:34 6:48
  6:50 8:15 8:33 9:9 9:14
  9:15 10:28 10:33 11:20
  11:21 12:15 12:28 12:34
  13:1 14:62 14:67 14:69
  15:32 16:7
εἰ μή 2:7 5:37 6:5 10:18
  14:1
εἰμί 9:41 13:4 14:2 14:66
  15:40 15:41 15:42
εἰρηνεύω 9:50
εἰς 1:10
εἷς 2:7 6:15 10:18 12:28
  13:1 14:10 14:20
εἰσέρχομαι 1:45 2:1 3:1
  7:17 7:24 8:26 9:28
  10:23 10:24
εἰσπορεύομαι 6:56?
  11:2
εἴωθα 10:1
ἐκβάλλω 1:34 1:39 1:43
  3:15 3:23 9:28
ἑκατόν 6:40
ἐκεῖ 1:38 2:6 6:33 14:15
  16:7
ἐκεῖθεν 6:1? 7:24 [9:30
  κἀκεῖθεν] 10:1
ἐκεῖνος 1:9 2:20? 4:35
  13:17 13:24 14:21
ἐκθαμβέομαι 9:15
ἐκθαυμάζω 12:17
ἐκπλήσσομαι 1:22 6:2
  10:26 11:18
ἐκπορεύομαι 1:5 10:17
  11:19 12:1
ἕκτος 15:33
ἔκφοβος 9:6
ἔλαιον 6:13 11:1 13:3'
ἐλεέω 5:19

ἐμβαίνω 4:1 5:18 8:10
  8:13
ἐμβάπτομαι 14:20
ἐμβλέπω 10:21 10:27
  14:67
ἐμβριμάομαι 1:43
ἐμπαίζω 10:34
ἐμπτύω 10:34
ἐνάντιος 6:48
ἔνατος 15:33 15:34
ἕνεκεν 10:29 (second)
ἐνεργέω 6:14
ἐξέρχομαι 1:28 1:45 2:13
  3:1 6:1? 6:12 6:34 6:54
  7:31 8:11 8:27 9:29 9:30
  11:12 14:48
ἐξίστημι 6:51
ἐξουδενέω 9:12
ἐξουσία 1:22 1:27 2:10
  3:15 6:7 13:34
ἔξω 1:45 3:32 11:15
ἔξωθεν 7:15 7:18
ἐπαγγέλλομαι 14:11
ἐπάνω 14:5
ἐπαύριον 11:12
ἐπερωτάω 7:17 9:16 9:28
  9:32 10:10 12:34 13:3
  15:44
ἐπιβάλλω 14:72
ἐπιγινώσκω 2:8 6:33
ἐπιλανθάνομαι 8:14
ἐπιλύω 4:34
ἐπίσταμαι 14:68
ἐπιτίθημι 3:16 3:17
ἐπιτιμάω 3:12 3:30
ἑπτά 8:20 12:23
ἔρημος 1:4 1:13 1:45 6:31
  6:32 6:35
ἔρχομαι 1:7 1:9 1:14 1:39
  1:45 2:13 2:20? 3:8 4:21
  4:22 6:31 7:1 7:31 8:22
  9:12 10:1 10:46 11:15
  11:27 13:35 14:17 14:62
ἐσθίω 7:3 7:4 14:18 (2x)
  14:22

ἔσω 14:54
ἔτι 14:53
ἔτος 5:42
εὐαγγέλιον 1:1 1:14 8:35
  10:29 13:10 14:9
εὐθύς 1:10 1:12 1:18 1:20
  1:21 1:23? 1:28 1:29 2:8
  3:6 6:45 6:50 6:54 7:25
  8:10 9:15 10:52 11:2
  11:3 14:43 15:1
εὐκαίρω 6:31
εὐκαίρως 14:11
εὐλογητός 14:61
εὑρίσκω 11:2 11:4
ἔχω 1:22 3:15 3:26 3:30
  8:14 8:16 8:17 (2x) 8:18
  9:50 10:22 10:23 11:22
  11:32 12:23 13:17
ἕως 13:19 15:33

ζητέω 11:18 12:12 14:1
  14:11

ἡδέως 6:20 12:37
ἤδη 6:35 15:42 15:44
ἥκω 8:3
Ἠλίας 9:12
ἥλιος 1:32
ἡμέρα 1:9 2:1 2:20? 4:35
  8:1 10:34 13:17 13:24
  14:1 14:49
Ἡρῳδιανός 3:6 12:13

θάλασσα 2:13 4:1 (2x)
  7:31
θαμβέω 10:24
θάνατος 10:33
θαρσέω 6:50
θαυμάζω 5:20 6:6 15:44
θέλω 6:48 7:24 8:34 8:35
  9:30
θεός 2:7 10:18 10:23
  10:24 10:27 (2x) 12:14
θεραπεύω 1:34 3:10
  6:13

θεωρέω 3:11 15:40
θηλάζω 13:17

Ἰάκωβος 10:41 13:3
  14:33 15:40
ἴδιος 4:34 (2x) 6:31 6:32
  9:2 9:28 13:3
ἰδού (see εἶδεν)
Ἰδουμία 3:8
Ἰεριχώ 10:46
ἱερός 12:35 13:1 13:3
  14:49
Ἱεροσολυμίτης 1:5
Ἱεροσολύμων 3:8 3:22
  7:1 10:33 11:1 11:11
  11:15 11:27 15:41
Ἰησοῦς 10:24 10:27 10:38
  10:39 10:42 12:35 14:48
  14:67 14:72 15:34
ἵνα 4:21 (2x) 4:22 (2x)
  7:36 15:32
Ἰορδάνης 3:8 10:1
Ἰουδαία 1:5 3:7 10:1
Ἰουδαῖος 1:5 7:3
Ἰούδας 14:10
Ἰσκαριώθ 14:10
ἵστημι 11:5
ἰσχύω 9:18
Ἰωάννης 10:41 11:32
  13:3 14:33
Ἰωσῆς 15:40

καθαρίζω 7:19
καθίζω 11:2
κάθημαι 2:6 4:1 13:2
  14:62
καθώς 1:2 9:13 11:6
  14:21
καὶ ἔλεγεν αὐτοῖς 4:2
  4:11 6:10 7:14 8:21 9:1
  9:31
καινός 1:27 2:21 2:22
  end
καιρός 10:30 11:13 12:2
  13:33

κἀκεῖθεν 9:30
κακῶς ἔχων 1:32 1:34
  6:55
καλέω 11:17
καλῶς 12:28
καρδία 2:6 2:8 3:5 6:52
  8:17 11:23
καταβαίνω 3:22 9:9
καταβαρύνω 14:40
κατακρίνω 10:33
καταράω 11:21
κατέναντι 11:2 13:3
κάτω 14:66
κεντυρίων 15:44 15:45
κηρύσσω 1:4 1:14 1:39
  1:45 3:14 5:20 6:12 7:36
  13:10 14:9
κλαίω 14:72
κλάσμα 8:19 8:20
κλάω 8:19
κλίνη 7:4
κοδράντης 12:42
κοπάζω 6:51
κόσμος 14:9
κοφινός 8:19
κράβαττος 2:9 6:55
κράζω 3:11 9:24
κρατέω 7:3 7:4 9:9 12:12
  14:1 14:49
κτῆμα 10:22
κύκλος 6:6
κύριος 5:19 13:35
κώμη 6:6 6:56 8:26 11:2

λαλέω 1:34 2:2 6:50
  11:23 12:1 14:9 14:53
λαμβάνω 8:14
λανθάνω 7:24
λέγω (εἶπεν) 3:11 3:23
  3:30 6:15 (2x) 6:16 8:14
  8:19 8:20 8:30 9:13 9:24
  10:15 10:23 10:24 10:26
  10:32 10:38 10:39 (2x)
  10:42 11:3 (2x) 11:21
  12:12 12:38 13:1 13:4

13:37 (2x) 14:2 14:9
  14:20 14:31 14:48 14:72
  16:7 (2x) 16:8
ληστής 11:17 14:48
λίαν 6:51 16:2
λόγος 1:45 2:2 9:9 10:24
λυπέομαι 14:19

Μαγδαληνός 15:40
μαθητής 2:15 2:16 2:18a
  4:34 6:1? 6:41 7:17 8:10
  8:27 8:33 8:34 9:28
  9:31 10:10 10:23 10:24
  10:46 11:14 12:43 13:1
  14:14 16:7
μακρόθεν 8:3 14:54
  15:40
μᾶλλον 7:36
μανθάνω 13:28
Μαρία 15:40 (2x)
μαρτύριον 1:44? 6:11
μαστίζω 10:34
μάχαιρα 14:48
μεγαλός 13:2 15:34
μέλω 12:14
μέλλω 10:32 13:4
μέν 9:12
μέσος 7:31
μετά 1:14 3:6 5:37 8:10
  10:30 10:34 14:1 14:17
  14:18 14:20 14:28 14:33
  14:48 14:67 15:31
μετανοέω 6:12
μηδέ 8:26
μηδείς/οὐδείς 5:37 5:43
  7:15 7:24 8:30 9:9 9:29
  12:14 12:34 15:5 16:8
  (2x)
μήκετι/οὐκέτι 1:45 9:8
  12:34 15:5
μήποτε 14:2
μήτηρ 15:40
μήτι 4:21
μικρός 4:31 15:40
μνημονεύω 8:18

μνημόσυνον 14:9
μόνος 6:47

Ναζαρηνός 14:67
νεκρός 9:9
νεκρῶν 9:10
νέος 2:22 end
νεφελή 14:62
νηστεύω 2:18a 2:20?
νίπτω 7:3
νοέω 7:18 8:17 13:14
νόσος 1:34
νουνεχῶς 12:34
νυμφίος 2:20?
νῦν 10:30 13:19
νύξ 6:48

ξεστός 7:4
ξηραίνω 11:21
ξύλον 14:48

ὁδός 6:8 8:27 9:33 9:34
  10:17 10:32 10:52 12:14
οἶδα 14:68 14:71
οἰκία 6:4 7:24 9:33 10:10
  13:35
οἰκοδομή 13:1 13:2
οἶκος 5:19 7:18 9:28 11:17
  (2x)
οἶνος 2:22 end
ὀλίγος 6:31
ὅλος 1:28 12:44 14:9 15:33
ὀμνύω 14:71
ὄνομα 3:16 3:17 6:1 13:6
ὄντως 11:32
ὅπου 14:9
ὅπως 3:6
ὁράω (see εἶδεν)
ὀργίζομαι 1:41
ὅριος 5:17 7:24 7:31 (2x)
  10:1
ὄρος 6:46 9:9 11:1 13:3
ὅσος 3:8 5:19 5:20 7:36
ὅταν 13:4
οὐαί 13:17

οὐδείς (see μηδείς)
οὐκέτι (see μήκετι)
οὔπω 4:40 8:17 8:21 11:2
οὐρανός 14:62
οὖς 8:18
οὗτος 13:2 13:4 (2x)
οὕτως 2:7 2:8 7:18
οὐχ 4:21
ὀφθαλμός 8:18 14:40
ὄχλος 4:1 (2x) 6:34F 6:45
    7:14 7:17 8:1 8:34 9:14
    9:15 10:1 10:46 11:18
    11:32 12:12 12:37 15:10
ὀψέ 11:19 13:35
ὀψία 1:32 4:35 14:17
    15:42

παιδίον 9:24
πάλαι 15:44
παλαιός 2:21
πάλιν 2:1 2:13 3:1 4:1
    7:14 7:31 8:1 8:13 10:1
    (2x) 10:12 10:24 10:32
    11:27
πανταχοῦ 1:28
πάντοθεν 1:45
παραβολή 3:23 4:2 4:13
    4:30 7:17 12:1 12:12
    13:28
παράδοσις 7:3
παράγω 2:14
παραδίδωμι 1:14 3:19
    10:33 (2x) 14:10 14:11
    15:10
παρακαλέω 5:17 5:18
    6:56
παραλαμβάνω 7:4 10:32
    14:33
παραπορεύομαι 9:30
    11:20
παρατίθημι 6:41
παρέρχομαι 6:48
παρρησία 8:32
πᾶς 1:5 (2x) 1:32 2:13
    4:1 4:13 4:31 4:32 4:34

5:20 6:30 6:33 6:50 7:3
    7:14 7:18 7:19 9:12 9:15
    10:27 10:28 11:17 11:18
    11:24 13:4 13:10 13:23
    13:37 14:31
πάσχα 14:1 14:16
πάσχω 9:12
πατήρ 9:24
πεζῇ 6:33
πειράζω 8:11
πεντακισχίλιοι 8:19
πέντε 8:19
πεντήκοντα 6:40
πέραν 3:8 4:35 8:13 10:1
περιάγω 6:6
περὶ αὐτόν (αὐτούς)
    3:34 4:10 9:14
περὶ αὐτοῦ 14:21
περὶ τούτου 10:10
περιβλέπω 3:5 3:34
    10:23
περιπατέω 2:9
περισσότερον 7:36
περισσῶς 10:26
περίχωρος 1:28
Πέτρος 10:28 11:21 13:3
    14:33 14:66 14:72 16:7
πίνω 10:38 (2x) 10:39 (2x)
πιστεύω 9:23 9:24 9:42
    11:23 15:32
πίστις 11:22
πλανάω 12:27 13:5
πλεῖστος 4:1
πλῆθος 3:8
πλήρης 8:19
πληρόω 14:49
πλήρωμα 6:43 8:20
πλοῖον 4:1 5:18 6:32 8:10
    8:14
πλούσιος 12:41
πνεῦμα 2:8 3:11 3:30 6:7
    7:25
ποιέω 3:8 3:12 3:16 5:19
    5:20 6:30 11:17 14:9
    15:15

ποικίλος 1:34
ποιμήν 6:34
πόλις 1:45 6:33 6:56
    11:19
πολλά (adv.) 1:45 3:12 4:2
    5:43 6:34 8:31
πολύς 1:34 2:15 3:8 3:10
    6:2 6:13 (2x) 6:31 6:33
    6:34 6:35 7:4 8:1 9:12
    9:14 10:22 10:31 12:5
    12:27 12:37 12:41 (2x)
    15:41
πόσος 8:19 8:20
ποταπός 13:1 (2x)
πότε 13:4 13:33 13:35
ποτήριον 7:4 10:38
    10:39
πρασιά 6:40
πρεσβύτερος 7:3 11:27
    14:43 14:53
πρίν 14:72
προάγω 6:45 14:28 16:7
πρόβατον 6:34
προεῖπον 13:21
προσάββατον 15:42
προσέρχομαι 6:33 12:28
προσευχή 9:29 11:17
προσεύχομαι 6:46 13:18
προσκαλέομαι 3:23 6:7
    7:14 8:1 8:34 10:42
    12:43 15:44
προσλαμβάνομαι 8:32
προσπίπτω 3:11
προστίθημι 4:24
προστρέχω 9:15
πρόσωπος 12:14
προφήτης 1:2 6:15 (2x)
    11:32
πρωΐ 11:20 13:35 16:2
πρῶτον 7:27 9:12 13:10
πυγμή 7:3
πωρόω 6:52 8:17
πώρωσις 3:5
πῶς 3:23 4:13 9:12 10:23
    10:24 11:18 14:1 14:11

ῥαββί 11:21
ῥῆμα 9:32 14:72

Σαλωμή 15:40
σημεῖον 13:4
Σίδων 3:8 7:31
σκότος 15:33
σός 5:19
σοφία 6:2
σπείρω 4:32
σπέρμα 4:31
σπήλαιον 11:17
σπλαχνίζω 6:34
σπυρίς 8:20
σταυρόω 15:25
συγγενεύς 6:4
συζητέω 8:11 9:9 9:14
    9:16 12:28
συκῆ 11:13 11:21 13:28
συλλαμβάνω 14:48
συμβαίνω 10:32
συμβούλιον 3:6
συμπόσια 6:39
συμπορεύομαι 10:1
συνάγω 4:1 6:30 7:1
συναγωγή 1:39
συνακολουθέομαι 5:37
συναναβαίνω 15:41
συνδράμω 6:33
σύνεσις 12:33
συνίημι 6:52 7:14 8:17
    8:21

συντελέω 13:4
σχίζω 1:10?
σῴζω 10:26 13:13?

ταράσσω 6:50
τέκνον 7:27 10:24
τέλος 3:26 13:13?
τεταρτός 6:48
τετρακισχίλιοι 8:20
τίθημι 4:30; 10:16
τις 2:6 7:1 7:2 8:3 12:13
    13:4 13:5
τολμάω 12:34
τόπος 1:45 6:31 6:32
    6:35
τότε 2:20?
τοῦτ᾽ ἔστιν 7:2
τρεῖς 10:34
τρίς 14:72
τρίτος 15:25
τρύβλιον 14:20
Τύρος 3:8 7:31

ὑγιής 7:34
υἱὸς θεοῦ 3:11
υἱὸς τοῦ ἀνθρώπου
    9:9 9:12 10:33 14:21
    14:62
ὑπάγω 5:19 6:31 6:33 11:2
    16:7
ὑπόκρισις 12:15
ὑπομένω 13:13?

φάγω 6:31 6:37
φανερός/φανερῶς 1:45
    3:12 4:22 6:14
Φαρισαῖος 2:18a (2x) 3:6
    7:1 7:3 8:11 8:14
φέρω 1:32 11:2
φθόνος 15:10
φοβέομαι 9:32 10:32
    11:18 11:32 12:12
    16:8
φυλακή 6:48
φύλλον 11:13
φωνέω 14:72
φωνή 15:34
φῶς 14:54

χαίρω 14:11
χαλκίον 7:4
χειμών 13:18
χείρ 7:3 10:16
χειροποιητός 14:57
χορτάζω 7:27
χρῆμα 10:23
χρεία 11:3
Χριστός 9:41 14:61
χώρα 1:5 6:55

ὥρα 6:35 15:25 15:33 (2x)
    15:34
ὡσαύτως 14:31
ὥστε 1:45 4:1

GLOSSARY

◆

Anacoluthon An unfinished sentence in which the original thought or syntactical structure is not carried through to the end.

Anaphoric Referring back to a previous reference to a word or phrase, e.g., the definite article with "Jesus" throughout Mark after 1:9 or with "rising from among the dead" in 9:10 (cf. 9:9).

Apocalyptic Having to do with the revelation of God's plan to bring his purposes to completion and establish his dominion "on earth as it is in heaven"; often roughly synonymous with "eschatological."

Apodosis The "then" clause of a conditional sentence.

Aporia From the Greek for "difficulty"; a narrative awkwardness in a text that points to its development over time.

Asyndeton In Greek rhetoric, the absence of the normal joining particles or conjunctions. In classical Greek, asyndeton is sometimes used for emphasis, but its frequency in the NT has often been taken as an indication of the primitive level of NT Greek.

Baraitha An "extraneous" rabbinic tradition, i.e., one not found in the Mishnah but supposed to be Tannaitic and quoted anonymously in the Talmud.

B.C.E. "Before the Common (or Christian) Era"; corresponds to old-style B.C. ("Before Christ").

Blank An inadvertent disparity or failure to provide information within a narrative; contrast "gap."

Casuistic law Case law, in which a case or condition is stated in an "if" or "when" clause and the penalty in a "then" clause, as opposed to apodictic, or absolute, law. A common form for OT statutes; see, e.g., most of the statutes in Exodus 21–22.

Catechetical Having to do with oral instruction in matters of faith.

C.E. "Common (or Christian) Era"; corresponds to old-style A.D. (*Anno Domini* = "in the year of the Lord").

Chiasm, chiastic Having a structure of ABA′, ABCB′A′, etc., so that a > pattern is formed. From the Greek letter *chi*, which is written X, since the pattern is one-half of an X.

Decalogue The Ten Commandments (lit. "Ten Words") from the OT (Exod 20:1–17; Deut 5:6–21).

Deutero-Isaiah The latter half of the OT book of Isaiah (chapters 40–66), which probably comes from the Persian period (sixth–fifth centuries B.C.E.) and extends the thought of the prophet Isaiah, who lived in the eighth century B.C.E. and whose oracles form the core of First Isaiah (chapters 1–39). Some scholars think that chapter 35 originally belonged to Deutero-Isaiah, and many identify chapters 56–66 as a still later Trito-Isaiah.

Dittography A scribal error in which a letter, word, or line is mistakenly repeated.

Divine passive The use of a passive-voice verb (e.g., "it has been given") as a circumlocution for God's action (e.g., instead of saying "God has given").

Dominical Coming from Jesus; from Latin Dominus = Lord. Often used by scholars to distinguish sayings of the historical Jesus from words ascribed to him by the church.

Ellipsis Grammatical construction in which one or more words are deliberately omitted but understood from the context.

End-stress A rhetorical principle according to which what comes at the end receives the greatest emphasis.

Eschaton The end of the ages expected in Jewish and Christian theology; from the Greek word for "last."

Gap An intentional discontinuity within a narrative such as the disparity between a parable and its explanation, unexplained motives, improbable or excessive actions, and discontinuities in plot (e.g., unnarrated endings); contrast "blank."

Gematria A numerological technique in which the numerical values of the letters in a word are added up and the result is linked with other words whose letters add up to the same sum. The most famous biblical example is 666 in Rev 13:18.

Gĕzērāh šāwāh Lit. "equal category"; the rabbinic hermeneutical rule by which two passages that contain identical or similar expressions are regarded as treating the same topic.

Hapax legomenon A word that occurs only once in a given corpus of literature, e.g., the OT or the NT.

Haplography The inadvertent omission of letters, words, or lines in textual transmission.

Hendiadys Lit. "one for two"; a rhetorical form in which a second term combines with a first one, which it may simply repeat or to which it may add something.

Hermeneutical Having to do with interpretation, especially of scripture.

Homoeoarcton In textual criticism, a situation in which two words have the same beginning; a cause of scribal omissions.

Homoeoteleuton In textual criticism, a situation in which two words have the same ending; a frequent cause of scribal omissions.

Hypostasis The objectification or personification of a quality or aspect of God (e.g., his Name or Wisdom) or of human existence (e.g., Fortune) whereby this entity assumes an identity of its own.

Hypotaxis An elaborate system of grammatical subordination, as opposed to parataxis.

Inclusion The framing of a literary unit by the usage of the same or similar words at its beginning and end.

Kerygma "Preaching" or "proclamation"; the content of the primitive Christian message about Jesus.

Koine The "common" Greek of the Hellenistic period; the language in which most of the NT, including Mark, is written.

Lex talionis "The law of retaliation in kind," e.g., the "eye for eye, tooth for tooth" statute in Exod 21:23–25.

Logion Saying of Jesus.

LXX The Septuagint, the Greek translation of the OT.

Mishnah Authoritative compilation of Jewish law, promulgated under the authority of R. Judah the Prince at the beginning of the third century c.e.

MT Masoretic Text, the traditional form of the original Hebrew and Aramaic text of the OT.

Paraenetic Having to do with exhortation.

Parataxis Simple coordination of words, clauses, sentences, and paragraphs with "and." Mark's style is overwhelmingly paratactic, as are the narrative portions of the OT.

Paronomasia A pun that plays on the use of the same or similar-sounding words in two different senses.

Parousia The expected "Second Coming" of Jesus at the end of time; from the Greek word for "arrival" or "presence."

Patronymic A name that identifies someone by his or her father's name, e.g., "Simon Bar-Jona" ("Simon son of Jonah") in Matt 16:17. In the days before surnames became common, this was the standard way of differentiating between people who shared the same first name, and it is still preserved in surnames such as Johnson, MacDonald, and O'Keefe.

Pericope A self-contained unit within the scripture; from the Greek for "cut around."

Peshitta The standard Syriac translation of the Christian Bible, which was completed by the early decades of the fifth century C.E.

Pleonasm Use of more words than are necessary for mere sense; redundancy.

Protasis The "if" clause of a conditional sentence.

Q Hypothetical source for the material shared by Matthew and Luke, but not present in Mark.

Qumran Site in the Judaean Desert, near the Dead Sea, where the Dead Sea Scrolls were found; home of a dualistic Jewish sect identical to or related to the Essenes.

Redaction Editing; often used to describe an individual evangelist's adaptation of the traditions that have come down to him.

Sapiential Having to do with wisdom.

Scholion A short interpretative comment placed beside a text by an ancient or medieval commentator.

Supersessionism, -ist The belief that the church has replaced (superseded) Israel as the people of God, and one who holds that belief.

Synecdoche A figure of speech in which the part stands for the whole or vice versa, e.g., "thirty head of cattle" or "the city was sleeping."

Synoptic Gospels Matthew, Mark, and Luke, the first three Gospels in the NT; so called because they can be laid out easily in parallel columns and read synoptically ("with one eye").

Talmud Lit. "learning"; commentary on the Mishnah that appeared in two forms, the Palestinian (or Jerusalem) Talmud (fifth century C.E.) and the Babylonian (major redaction in the eighth century C.E.).

Tanna, Tannaitic "Repeater" of traditions; a rabbinic teacher from the time of Hillel and Shammai to R. Judah the Prince and his contemporaries at the beginning of the third century C.E. The opinions of the Tannaim (plural of Tanna) are compiled in the Mishnah.

Targum Jewish translation of the Hebrew Bible into Aramaic (from Aramaic term for "translation"). Extant Targumim (plural of Targum) were produced in the early centuries of the Christian era.

Torah The Hebrew word for "teaching" or "law"; often refers to the first five books of the OT, especially the legal portions of those books.

INDEX OF COMMENTATORS AND MODERN AUTHORS

INDEX OF SUBJECTS

Disciples, discipleship (*cont.*)
  linked with Jesus, mediators of his power, sharers in
    his suffering, etc. 592, 610, 613–14, 622, 623, 640,
    650, 658, 660, 745, 751, 752, 754, 758, 790, 836,
    880, 909, 919, 941, 947–48
  private instruction to 635, 656, 665–66, 671, 673,
    707, 711, 782, 866, 870, 873
  restoration of 972–73, 1025
Divine passive 696, 748, 877, 880, 902, 981, 1003
Divine sonship. *See* Son of God
Divine warrior 591, 746, 757
Dominion of God 589–91, 620–21, 630, 676, 680–81,
    686–87, 695, 715–16, 718–19, 723–25, 729, 731,
    733–35, 739, 746–47, 755, 772, 776, 787, 795,
    797, 822, 836, 841, 844–45, 850, 854, 919, 945,
    963, 967–69, 998, 1015–16, 1051–52, 1063, 1068,
    1071, 1075–76
  entering the 715, 719, 736
  mystery of 589, 669, 687, 709, 730, 734, 764, 1023,
    1067, 1087, 1125
Donkey 772, 778–80
Door 911, 917, 919–21
Double
  expressions 631, 654, 716, 777, 818, 899, 973, 996,
    1005, 1013, 1023, 1073, 1083
  negatives 635, 772, 816, 818, 841, 1083
Doublets 656, 682, 716, 982, 1005, 1019, 1026, 1045,
    1056, 1128–29

Earthquakes 876–77, 880–81, 906–7, 969
Eden, Garden of 638–39, 710
Elders 605, 784, 981, 1010, 1099, 1103
Elect, the. *See* Chosen one(s)
Elijah 611, 632–34, 637–44, 646–50, 797, 1064–65
Elisha 797, 1117
Emperor, Roman 610, 816–818, 822–26, 1034
Empty Tomb narrative 1134–37
Enemies of Jesus, human and demonic 657–58 , 669,
    708, 763, 793, 813, 815, 824, 854, 879
Enthronement 747, 752, 754
Eschatological timeline 880–81, 883
Eschatology
  imminent 878, 881, 918
  realized 622, 681, 686–87, 740, 835
  and secular wisdom 628, 674
Eternal life. *See* Life: eternal
Euthys ("immediately") 772, 1032
Eve. *See* Adam (and Eve)
Exhortation. *See* Paraenesis
Exodus traditions 598, 615, 658–59, 958
Exorcism 594, 607, 609, 614, 652–55, 657–60, 664–65,
    669, 671, 684–87, 696, 763, 782, 793, 851, 1068,
    1120. *See also* Demons, demonic powers
Expiation. *See* Atonement
Eye, eyes 593, 597, 600, 691–92, 696–97

Faith, faithfulness 657, 661–65, 694, 765–66, 785,
    788–89, 794–96, 1052, 1093, 1096
False prophet. *See* Prophet(s): false
Family 627, 727, 735–36, 738–40, 795, 870, 887–88
Farewell discourse 866
Father, Jesus and God as 716–17, 727, 739
Fear 741, 743–44, 1081–82, 1084–87, 1093, 1096
Fig tree 774, 781–82, 784, 789, 906–7, 910, 915–16

Following Jesus 657, 761, 764
Forcing the end 886, 893
Forgiveness 788, 795–96
Framing devices 672, 767–68, 798, 822, 900, 903
Future, imperatival use of 674

Galilee, Galileans 602, 776, 1019, 1024, 1069, 1081,
    1086, 1094–95
Gaps, narrative 602, 1023
Garments. *See* Clothing
Gehenna 690–91, 696, 1072
Generation, "this" or "that," etc. 619, 630, 653,
    659–60, 663–64, 911–912
Gentiles 780, 783–84, 792–93, 810, 850, 866, 891, 907,
    909, 981, 1067–68
Gĕzērāh šāwāh (scriptural reasoning by analogy) 784
Glory 751–52, 755, 908
God, Jesus comparable to. *See* Jesus (of Nazareth):
    comparable to God
Goodness of God and Jesus 720–21, 724–28

Hallel 774, 968, 971
Hand 667, 689, 696–97
Hands, laying on of. *See* Laying on of hands
Hanukkah 774, 968
Harmonization 720, 841, 905, 1041, 1044
Harvest 910–11, 916
Hastening the end. *See* Forcing the end
Hearing 762
Heaven 776, 796–97
Hebrew, Hebraisms 808, 816, 882, 910, 1054–55
Herod, Herodian family, Herodians 593, 603, 610,
    784, 815–16, 822–24
Hierarchy in the dominion of God 747, 754–55
High priest 614, 852, 856, 1001–2, 1008, 1013, 1016,
    1066, 1102, 1121, 1127–28, 1130
Hillel 633, 700, 707
Historical Jesus. *See* Jesus (of Nazareth): historical
Holy
  Spirit. *See* Spirit, Holy
  war 591, 610, 664, 744, 746, 765, 772, 780, 967
  week 932, 947

Hosanna 774, 779–80
Hospitality 682–83
Hour 886, 977, 985, 986, 988
House, household 596, 671, 677, 711, 891–92
Household codes 715–16, 723, 847
Human beings, humanity (in opposition to
    God) 609–10, 614, 667, 669, 686, 711, 726,
    799, 1068
Hypotaxis 810, 831–32

Identity of Jesus 611
Idolatry 817, 823, 825–26, 1003, 1014
Ignatius of Antioch 675
Immediately. *See Euthys* ("immediately")
Imperfect tense 596, 970, 1055
Impersonal use of third person plural 593, 713, 1013
Impotence, human 659–61, 663
Impressment 773
Inclusion. *See* Framing devices
"Inclusive language" 616–17
Incognito deities, heroes, etc. 676, 683

INDEX OF SCRIPTURE AND OTHER ANCIENT SOURCES

SCRIPTURE SOURCES

OTHER ANCIENT SOURCES